D1229855

A CONCISE HEBREW AND ARAMAIC LEXICON OF THE OLD TESTAMENT

A CONCISE HEBREW AND ARAMAIC LEXICON OF THE OLD TESTAMENT

BASED UPON THE LEXICAL WORK OF

LUDWIG KOEHLER AND WALTER BAUMGARTNER

BY

WILLIAM L. HOLLADAY

Lowry Professor of Old Testament
Andover Newton Theological School

WILLIAM B. EERDMANS PUBLISHING COMPANY
GRAND RAPIDS, MICHIGAN

E. J. BRILL
LEIDEN

First published 1971 by E. J. Brill and Wm. B. Eerdmans Publishing Co.
255 Jefferson Ave. S.E., Grand Rapids, Michigan 49503

Printed in the United States of America

00 99 98 97 96 95 94 20 19 18 17 16 15 14

Eerdmans ISBN 0-8028-3413-2

Brill ISBN 90 04 02613 4

INTRODUCTION

The advent of the first edition of the *Lexicon in Veteris Testamenti Libros* of Ludwig KOEHLER and Walter BAUMGARTNER (1953) was a major event in recent Old Testament studies, gathering together as it did a vast treasure of lexicographical material which had become available up to the time of publication, with renderings into both German and English; and the *Supplementum ad Lexicon in Veteris Testamenti Libros* (1958)—which, together with the first edition, was then called the second edition—included both corrections and more recent material from the five intervening years. This lexicon broke with the classic lexicographical tradition of GESENIUS, represented in English by *A Hebrew and English Lexicon of the Old Testament* of BROWN, DRIVER, and BRIGGS (1907, corrected impression 1952), and took a fresh look at all the lexical evidence. One advantage of the KOEHLER-BAUMGARTNER *Lexicon* was immediately evident to everyone who used it: it offered a strictly alphabetical order of entries rather than an arrangement by verbal roots, an innovation (along with the provision of generous cross-references) which saved the user much time. More fundamentally, the lexicon took full advantage of the colossal increase in our knowledge of Semitic linguistics (exemplified by the discovery of Ugaritic). But the increase of our knowledge has continued unabated in the years since, and the need to remedy the apparent defects in the first/second edition and to take account of that steady increase in our knowledge has rendered a revision more and more desirable.

Regrettably, Professor KOEHLER died in 1956, but Professor BAUMGARTNER then undertook himself the awesome task of a total revision of their joint work, a task in which Professors Benedikt HARTMANN and E. Y. KUTSCHER have been collaborating. This revision, called the third edition, is now appearing in print (first fascicle 1967). Up to the present moment approximately two-thirds of the third edition has been completed in manuscript form; but now comes word of the death of Professor BAUMGARTNER, in January of this year, at the age of 82. It is lamentable that he could not live to see the completion of this crown of his life-work, upon which he expended so much energy and acuity. We are assured that his collaborators will complete the task, though there will be inevitable delays.

In the planning of this third edition the decision was made, in the interest of saving space, to dispense with renderings in English—thus making the

90

new material unavailable to the student who does not handle German; and since the English renderings of the first edition were in some instances inadequate or misleading,[1] there has seemed to be a real need for an English edition, in abridged format, of the KOEHLER-BAUMGARTNER lexical material. The present work is a response to that need.

With some reluctance the decision was reached to prepare the English edition in hybrid fashion, using the German third edition to the extent that the material would become available, and the German first/second edition for the balance of the alphabet and for the Aramaic section. This decision was reached because of the time-span anticipated for the appearance of the total German third edition, and because of the wish expressed by many that the English edition appear as soon as possible. The first fascicle of the German third edition was of course available to me already set in type, and beyond this I have been able to make use of the manuscript of the German third edition through the letter ס; for ע and beyond I have then resorted to the German first/second edition. It is to be hoped that the nature of the present work (namely, an abridgment for school use) will minimize the disadvantages of hybridization; certainly I have made every effort to produce a work which is internally consistent. But it must be stressed that the present work *is* an abridgment and therefore in no sense a substitute for the German parent work (hereafter called simply "the German work," by which is meant the source material for this English edition, whether it be the German first/second edition, the third edition, or both); this will become clear in the detailed notices which follow.

In order to keep the English edition to moderate size, the following categories of material in the German work have been omitted.

(1) All etymological material in cognate languages. The parallels in such languages as Ugaritic and Arabic are of prime importance, but it seems plain that a student able to handle these certainly should be prepared to handle German also, and should refer to the German work. (But Hebrew cognates are cited in the Aramaic section; see the remarks on the Aramaic section below.)

(2) All bibliographical entries, and all citations of the names of specific scholars who put forth this or that suggestion on the meaning of a word. The greater number of the bibliographical citations in the German work are themselves to works in German, and all of them are the province of the

---

[1] Completely solecistic English expressions were fortunately rare, but they did exist, e.g. in the English definitions of דִּבְרוֹת, צֶבֶת, רוח *hif.*; still, the English needed thorough review and revision.

specialist. When it is felt necessary in certain instances to cite opinions other than those of KOEHLER and/or BAUMGARTNER, they are simply labelled "oth."; see, for example, III בול.

(3) All citations to, and semantic specifications of, occurrences of given words in the Hebrew text of Sirach and in the Qumrān material. Such material is obviously of great importance in its own right, but it has been felt necessary to confine an abridged lexicon to the compass of the Masoretic Text. Again, the student ready for post-biblical literature might well be expected to have learned German.

(4) All citations to manuscript variations in the Hebrew text such as those cited in KITTEL, *Biblia Hebraica*, third edition, as "Or." The spelling and vocalization of the third edition of KITTEL is taken as standard.

(5) Almost all conjectural emendations, both the newly suggested lexical entries which have been entered in the German work, and the details at the end of the standard entries of the German work which suggest conjectural additions or subtractions from the "standard" corpus of occurrences in the concordances to the MT. I have passed most of these conjectural emendations by with great regret, because the completeness of the treatment by KOEHLER and BAUMGARTNER of doubtful, difficult, or impossible readings of the MT is one of the great strengths of their work, and many of these conjectures are to me altogether convincing. But, as everyone will recognize, in the field of conjectural emendations one person's certainty is another person's doubt; and later generations inevitably dispute with earlier. Since to keep to the spirit of an abridgment would have necessitated my picking and choosing which conjectures to include or omit, and since I have been able to find no valid standard for inclusion or omission, I have passed them by except in rare instances. A handful *have* been included (more often among newly suggested entries than among the detailed notices at the end of standard entries) where there seems virtual unanimity of scholarly opinion, particularly in instances where a current translation (like the Revised Standard Version or the Jerusalem Bible—or both) adopts such a conjecture, or where a note in the critical apparatus of the third edition of KITTEL cites such a conjecture, and to omit it would confuse a student more than to include it.[1] In this connection it is essential for the reader to understand the use of the dagger (†) in the present

---

[1] Thus for example I have included entries for *בְּצִקְלֹן, 2K 4_{42} (cf. GRAY in the "Old Testament Library" to *Kings*, 1970, pp. 501-502); for *זוֹן, Jb 36_{31} (cf. DRIVER and GRAY in the "International Critical Commentary" to *Job*, Part II, p. 284, and POPE in "The Anchor Bible" to *Job*, pp. 236-37); for *צבע *hitp.*, Jb 38_{14} (cf. the Revised Standard Version and the Jerusalem Bible translations), and for קְוֵה 1K 10_{28} = קְוֵא 2C 1_{16} 'Cilicia' with all recent commentators and translations.

work, inasmuch as its use here is somewhat different from that in the German work. In the German work the dagger indicates that ***all*** the passages subsumed under a given entry have been cited, including passages with disputed or doubtful readings, some of which KOEHLER and BAUMGARTNER emend (including both the "plusses" and the "minuses" in the entry). In the present work, in which the conjectural emendations are almost always omitted, the dagger means that all ***undisputed*** passages are cited; for example, II חֵרֶם has a dagger, though Ju 14_{18} is omitted, since the text there is in doubt. Therefore if, in dealing with a given word, the student looks up the lexicon entry to which the word has traditionally been referred, and does not find a citation to the verse but does find a dagger, it is best to consult a commentary. The German work may suggest that the text needs emending; some other authority may have a second emendation, or again a suggestion as to how the MT may be preserved. The "loose ends" resulting from this problem of conjectural emendations, and the incompleteness of so many entries offering a dagger, are the occasion of real chagrin to me in the preparation of the present work. But there is simply no other way in an abridged lexicon to deal with such a body of material as the MT: it would be difficult to find a chapter of the MT free of textual and grammatical difficulties, and the student will have to have recourse to teachers and to the commentaries to gain help in unraveling such problems and will have to develop critical acumen by means of the German work.

(6) Reconstructed triliteral roots and cross-references to these roots. These roots are often hypothetical, and hypothetical roots are of no direct use to the student when translating. Roots that exist as verbs are of course entered as verbs; if the *qal* pf. 3. sg. m. is extant, then (in contrast to the practice of the German work) the entry is vocalized; but if that *qal* form is not extant, then the entry remains unvocalized. (If two homonymous verbs exist, one with the extant *qal* form and one without, only one is vocalized, but the Roman numeration of the roots is maintained; thus I זָרַק, II זרק.) *'Ayin waw*, *'ayin yod* and *'ayin 'ayin* verbs are listed, as is normal in a lexicon, by root rather than by *qal* pf. 3. sg. m.; thus שׁוב, *qal* pf. 3. sg. m. שָׁב; דקק, *qal* pf. 3. sg. m. דַּק.

(7) All letters of the alphabet; these are not lexical items. The German work offers important linguistic information under entries of the isolated consonants, but this has been dispensed with in the present work.

(8) Theoretical components of proper names, e.g. *דָּד. Again these are not lexical items needing translation

But if much is omitted, much is retained; specifically, the following categories of material.

(1) All entries of the German work when they exist as semantic items in the MT. All entries of the German work (except for the greater number of conjectural emendations, as already noted) have been retained, including the useful cross-reference entries of difficult forms, of Qere-Kethib variations, and of *scriptio plena-scriptio defectiva* variations; indeed, I have added a few more cross-references in the last-named category which are not in the German work but which would seem to be an aid to the student. But if an entry is only a theoretical root, it is omitted, with consequent renumbering of homonymous entries when necessary; for example, II באר is only a theoretical root in the German third edition, so it is omitted in the present work, the I באר of the German edition becoming simply באר here. By the same token, the entry III בער of the German third edition is omitted, so that the entry IV בער of the German edition becomes the English III בער; and again the entry I חמר of the German third edition is a theoretical root, and the entry IV חמר of the German edition only a conjectural verb, omitted in the English edition, so that the German II, III, and V חמר have had to be renumbered.

(2) The arrangement and numbering of the definitional subdivisions in the German work in almost every instance. Again, the scheme of definitions is one of the great strengths of the German work and has been carried over whenever possible intact. In rare cases, admittedly, this has not been possible. For example, there are occasional instances in which the German work offers distinctions which are trivial or non-existent in English: the directional prefixes *hin-* and *her-* sometimes seem non-significant to the Hebrew semantic problem, and I could find no graceful way to bring over "בוא *hof.*: — 1. *gebracht werden*; — 2. *herbeigebracht werden*" to English in this format, nor did I consider it necessary, so both have been combined into "1. *be brought*" in the present work, with consequent renumbering of the subsequent items. Again, once in awhile a given subsection in the German work cites only a passage from Sirach, material not within the compass of the present work; such a subsection must then be omitted, with consequent renumbering; for example, the third subsection in the German treatment of חֲלִיפָה is here omitted. But in only a handful of instances have I felt constrained to rearrange completely the German scheme of renderings.[1] (There are an even smaller number of instances where I have departed from the actual definitions of the German work and have in some way replaced them with my own; these will be discussed below.)

(3) A skeleton of chapter-and-verse citations. At least one, but usually only one, citation is given for every distinction of definition. When possible,

[1] Examples of such rearrangements are I מַצָּה, שָׁמַיִם, שָׁקַל.

these have been chosen from Genesis, Kings, or Samuel (in this order of preference), since it is recognized that the student often begins the reading of Hebrew prose from these books. It is regrettable that the complete offering of citations so often given in the German work could not be reproduced here; it would be a reassurance to the student to find "the passage" mentioned, and it would also be an indication of the frequency of occurrences of a word in a given definition, contrasting "normal" from "unusual" or "unique" occurrences; but such completeness has had to be sacrificed to considerations of space. If a given word is extant in only a few passages (the maximum is usually five) in the MT, then all citations are given and the dagger is used; note also that the dagger is used within a given "conjugation" (*qal, nifal*) of a verb when all passages are cited—and the dagger is used occasionally for a subsection within an article as well. An effort has also been made to give complete citations for rare homonyms of common words, e.g. I דבר.

(4) The various inflectional forms of the word. These are given almost exactly as in the German work. Not every extant form of every verb or noun is of course given: it is assumed that the student knows the basic patterns of verbs and nouns and is able, for example, to distinguish between an infinitive construct and an infinitive absolute. It has not been thought necessary to indicate every occurrence of a change of accent in waw-consecutive perfects, but most pausal forms are given (with *sillûq*) as in the German work. It has been felt that BAUMGARTNER's use in the third German edition of the diagonal slash to conserve space in citing inflexional forms may prove a hindrance to easy use by beginning students (e.g. אָבִיהָ/נוּ = אָבִינוּ and אָבִיהָ) and it is abandoned in the present work, full words being cited instead. But parentheses, used by BAUMGARTNER for optional wāw or yôd in *scriptio plena* have been retained (with duplicated vocalization in the case of wāw); thus אָבֹ(וֹ)ת = אָבוֹת or אָבֹת.

Information not strictly necessary for the translation of a passage, and information which is essentially non-semantic, have had to be sacrificed in the present work; for example, most information about parallelisms and contrasts (כֹּחַ :: חַיִל). Thus it is not really essential to know (entry חֲלוֹם) that God appears in dreams, nor (entry חֲמוֹר) that the donkey is used for both riding and burden-bearing; nor are various verb-noun combinations listed if the verb and the noun carry a meaning in their combination which is self-explanatory from each alone. On the other hand, theological or cultural terms which are without an exact equivalent in English receive full treatment; e.g. II חֶסֶד, שָׁלוֹם. The constant question in the preparation of the present work has been: what will be useful for adequate translation of a given passage into English?

A special word must be said about the treatment here of proper names.

The details of the occurrence of proper names, the various persons or locations designated, and the presumed original meaning of these names, take up much space in the German work. But from both a linguistic and a practical point of view a name is not a semantic problem. Thus the name זְכַרְיָה does not *mean* "Yahweh has remembered": it simply means "Zechariah," and is so translated by the student. (A student is always pleased upon coming to a verse with many proper names, because then the translation is "easy"!) The derivation of the name, and the application of the name to which person(s) or location(s), are often both controversial and better left to the detailed commentaries and dictionaries of the Bible. (But true homonyms are distinguished, thus I גֹּמֶר, II גֹּמֶר.) So masculine names of persons are simply so identified, "n.pers.," without further ado, and feminines are "n.pers.f."; similarly with names of places, tribes, and gentilics. A chapter-and-verse citation is offered only to distinguish a proper noun from a homonymous common noun, or a form which might be referred to a common noun, e.g. עִירִי, עִירָם. By the same token, an English rendering is rarely given for a name, except for names requiring extended treatment (e.g. Babylon); traditional Roman Catholic renderings have often differed from Protestant and Jewish renderings, and the reproduction of a name in English dress is usually gratuitous anyway. Compound names of places such as those with בֵּית־ are given compromise treatment, i.e. simply a bare listing.

But if the treatment of proper names is reduced to the vanishing point, the treatment of particles and quasi-particles is almost as full as in the German work; see, for example, גַּם, *דַּי. Especial care has been taken with particles to locate idiomatic English equivalents.

Material which is fully treated in the standard grammars is reduced accordingly, for example the cardinal and ordinal numbers; here the variations in form and word-order are difficult to master, but it is usually not difficult for a student to translate a phrase containing numbers from Hebrew into English.

As in the German work, each entry is in two parts, inflectional and semantic. Hebrew characters have been used in the inflectional section,[1] but for economy of typesetting any Hebrew forms and phrases cited in the semantic section have been transliterated. This transliteration is a simplified one: the presence or absence of dāgēš lene is not noted, except in the case of p/f—*nefeš* seemed preferable to *nepeš* [2] (but initial pê without dāgēš lene is simply *p*); both

[1] I have accepted for the whole of the present work the innovation in the third edition of the German, whereby *ōš* in Hebrew characters offers a doubling of the dot (מֹשֶׁה); but I have not been altogether consistent in my using the double dot for *śō* (שֹׂנֵא).

[2] At least it seemed so at the beginning, but now that we have the *Genesis* and *Psalms*

simple vocal šewâ and ḥāṭēf-segôl are rendered as ^{e} (*'elōhîm*); segôl followed by yôd is rendered by *é* (*bānékā*) (but occasionally, by carelessness, *bāneykā*); qāmeṣ followed by final silent hê is *â* (*tôrâ*), and qāmeṣ followed by yôd wāw is *āyw* (*bānāyw*); the Tetragrammaton is *yhwh* (and with a proclitic preposition is *leyhwh*, etc.); and the Qerê perpetuum הִוא is simply *hî*, like הִיא. None of this should cause anyone any trouble.

Abbreviations of English and Hebrew grammatical terms, and of other frequently used words, are listed in the table of abbreviations which follows. Occasionally the English translation of a transliterated Hebrew phrase will abbreviate a proper name (e.g. "A." for "Aaron" when *'aharôn* stands in the cited Hebrew transliteration), or an English common noun within an entry (e.g. "h." for "holiness" under קֹדֶשׁ), but there are a minimum of such instances and they are always self-evident.

There is not complete consistency in the order of adjoining entries which share a common set of consonants but offer contrasting vocalization; but in every case the verb comes first, followed by other parts of speech.

A few special features should be noted in regard to the Aramaic section. Immediately after the listing of the Aramaic word in question, at the head of the entry, any Hebrew cognate is cited: here the policy of "no citations from cognate languages" was broken; it was felt that since the student normally deals with the texts of biblical Aramaic after having gained a certain familiarity with biblical Hebrew, this addition of the Hebrew cognate was justifiable. (But note that in the case of verbs, the entry "Heb. = " merely means that the triliteral consonantal root is identical; a vocalized entry of the Aramaic verb, where the *peal* pf. 3. sg. m. is extant, will of course have a different vocalization than that of the corresponding Hebrew *qal* form.) In contrast to the practice in the Hebrew section of the lexicon, the identification of the number, person, and gender of verb forms is frequently given, as in the German work, since the student may well have more difficulty identifying the Aramaic forms than Hebrew ones. Alternation of final 'ālef and hê is sometimes indicated by the use of the diagonal slash (הַדְרָה/א). In the interests of completeness, citations to *all* passages in which a given word appears are given whenever practical, even when the number of such citations exceeds five or six (in contrast to the practice in the Hebrew section); but when completeness is impractical, at least one citation from Daniel, and one from

---

volumes of "The Anchor Bible," and such works as the English translations of RINGGREN'S *Israelite Religion* (Philadelphia, 1966) and EICHRODT'S *Theology of the Old Testament* (Philadelphia, 1961, 1967) with *nepeš*, perhaps it would have been better to be altogether consistent after all!

Ezra, when present, are given for each distinction of definition. The designations of verbal "conjugations" are given everywhere in full.

Since the needs of students in the United States of America have been foremost in the mind of the publisher, and since I could not trust myself to consistency in British spelling, American spelling has been adopted in the present work; British users will have to be tolerant of *splendor*, *recognize*, and the like.

Every effort has been made to give smooth, natural, idiomatic English equivalents to the German renderings of the German work. It is trite to say that no translation is completely successful, but it may be emphatically affirmed that when a translation involves three languages at a time, the translator faces a much more complex set of problems. I can only say that I have kept my eye as little as possible on the English renderings of the first two editions of the German work (not because they are always wrong—far from it—but because a fresh start is necessary in a work like this), that I have constantly made my own check of the MT, recent translations,[1] commentaries and other reference works,[2] all in an effort simply to rendei into English what KOEHLER and BAUMGARTNER have rendered into German, and to keep my own views as far as possible out of sight.[3] But the reader should be reminded of what has already been said about the use of the abbreviation "oth." to offer alternative renderings when this seemed necessary; I have resorted to the use of "oth." in a good many instances of debatable identifications of flora and fauna, or in instances of seemingly idiosyncratic views offered in the first/second

---

[1] Especially the Revised Standard Version, the Torah of the Jewish Publication Society of America, the various "Anchor Bible" volumes, the Zürcher Bibel in German, and the Jerusalem Bible in both English and French; unfortunately the OT of the New English Bible appeared too late to be used.

[2] The various volumes of "The International Critical Commentary," of the "Biblischer Kommentar, Altes Testament," and of *The Interpreter's Dictionary of the Bible* most particularly.

[3] I should admit to a very few instances where I have inserted my own views. Thus in the entry חֹדֶשׁ, 3., BAUMGARTNER (third edition) gives "heat (of she-camel) Je 2_{24}". That the heat in question is that of the she-camel is a hypothesis gained only by excising the reference to the female wild ass (so most commentaries); but a recent study in which I shared (*Vetus Testamentum*, XVIII, pp. 256-60) indicates otherwise, so that perhaps there is justification in my offering here "heat (of female animal)" and letting the reader choose the appropriate animal. I have further employed the semantic analysis of I שׁוב of my own published study of the root (*The Root Šûbh in the Old Testament*, Leiden, 1958) instead of the analysis in the German first edition, since BAUMGARTNER lists my study in his bibliography for the third edition, evidently with the intention of making use of it there. Small modifications of my own are also to be found in אֲנָךְ, רֶגֶל 3. b. (euphem.), and in II רדה Je 5_{31}. But in almost every case where I have disagreed with the German rendering I have been able to take refuge in my mandate to prepare an *abridgment*, so that my opposition has not been imposed upon the reader; in this way I trust I have stayed within my role as editor.

edition of the German work when more recent discussions have offered other solutions.[1] It should also be noted that I have made an effort to check the original English source if the rendering in the German work is itself a translation from English, to avoid any possible errors arising from double translation. I have furthermore attempted to check various current "standard" works for the rendering of key Hebrew words into English; for example, I have checked the translations of מָשָׁל in the English translation of EISSFELDT's *The Old Testament, An Introduction* (Oxford, 1965), the translations of various sociological terms in DE VAUX's *Ancient Israel, Its Life and Institutions* (London, 1961), and the translations of various pottery shapes in the article "Pottery" by J. L. KELSO in *The Interpreter's Dictionary of the Bible* (New York, 1962, Vol. III, pp. 846-53). I have made particular effort to locate accurate English renderings of flora and fauna where the German work has given a specific Latin identification;[2] but in many cases there is no agreed-upon common English term for the Latin identification, and in any event, as has already been indicated, many identifications remain problematical. In the case of weights and measures I have inserted a modern equivalent in both metric and English units;[3] these equivalents are of course approximations with a wide range of possible error, but it did seem helpful to offer some idea of the size of the unit in question.

Two contrary classroom purposes have impelled this work, one humble, practical, and rather less than scholarly, the other idealistic and more scientific. The first, already alluded to, is to meet the needs of the beginning student, uncertain of the way, anxious to "get the assignment done," whose overriding question is simply, "What does this word, this verse, this passage mean?" For such a student a working tool has, I trust, been provided that offers some of the riches of present-day scholarship in modest and usable compass. But the other purpose is to lead the student to ask the prior question, "How and to what extent *can* we know what this word or verse or passage means?" Too rarely is the student led to ask who compiles a dictionary, and what evidence the compiler has used in drawing his conclusions. This is the central problem in defining words in a language or dialect no longer spoken; and unfortunately, in the interests of saving space, the steps by which the German work has arrived at its conclusions have in the present work been largely suppressed: namely, the evidence offered by parallel passages, cognate

[1] See, for example, the treatment of תּוֹשָׁב (cf. the discussion in DE VAUX, *Ancient Israel*) and תַּחַשׁ (cf. ZIMMERLI, *Ezechiel* (BKAT) on Ez 16_{10}).

[2] Here George E. POST's *Flora of Syria, Palestine, and Sinai* (Beirut, 1932-33) has been very useful.

[3] These have been taken from G. A. BARROIS' article "Chronology, Metrology, etc." in *The Interpreter's Bible*, Vol. I, pp. 142 ff.

languages, and the consequent discussions of scholars. But it is my hope that, even truncated as the present work is, it still offers the student enough significant variations from the Revised Standard Version or from whatever other modern translation might be at hand, to prompt the student to raise the tolerance for uncertainty, and to begin to "test everything, holding fast to what is good." And for this purpose the German work, with all its scholarly apparatus, stands ready, urging the student to master its German and to invest in its resources.

I should like to express my appreciation to Professor BAUMGARTNER of Basel (though he cannot know it now) and to Professor Benedikt HARTMANN in Leiden, for their confidence in my undertaking an English edition of their work; to Mr. F. C. WIEDER, Jr., Director of E. J. Brill, Publishers in Leiden, whose steady encouragement and guidance have urged the edition on to completion; to my mentor Professor P. A. H. DE BOER, of the University of Leiden, who has served as a gracious mediator from the beginning to the end of the enterprise; to my neighbor the Rev. Mr. Rudolf WECKERLING, pastor of the Evangelical Church of German Language in Beirut, and to my colleagues Professor Paul LÖFFLER and Professor Dietrich MEYER in the Near East School of Theology, Beirut, for all their patient help to me in clarifying their mother-tongue; and above all to my wife and children, who have wondered for five years now when the lexicon would be done.

William L. HOLLADAY
Beirut, Lebanon
May, 1970.

NOTE TO THE SECOND IMPRESSION

This present second impression is identical with the first printing, except that some minor corrections have been made which could be incorporated into the sheets without re-setting (about 100 in number). I should like to express my appreciation here to several colleagues who have kindly called my attention to some of these errors. I reiterate my eagerness to receive notice of any further blemishes which may emerge in the course of use.

There are also a few omissions which could not be inserted in this printing; a list appears below for the convenience of users who may wish to correct their own copies. I particularly regret the duplication of the entries II **חוה eštafal** and **שחה hitp.** — they are, of course, the same word, and the oversight resulted from duplicate entries in the third and first editions of KB, which in my carelessness I did not remedy. (I thank the sharp-eyed reviewer in *ZAW* [84, 1, p. 122] for bringing this oversight to my attention.)

W.L.H.
Newton Centre, Mass.
January 1974.

NOTE TO THE THIRTEENTH IMPRESSION

The present thirteenth impression of the lexicon has continued incorporating corrections into the text or into the list of Addenda: each successive impression has taken advantage of further corrections. I continue to urge those who use the work to send me errors which they spot.

W.L.H.
Newton Centre, Mass.
June, 1993

ADDENDA

(See also page 426)

p. 2a: after entry אֲבִיטוּב insert:

אֲבִיטָל: n. pers.

p. 10a: after entry אֵחִי insert:

אֲחִי: n. pers.

p. 21b: before entry II אִמֵּר insert:

I *אִמֵּר: cs. pl. אִמְּרֵי: **lamb,** *'imrê šefer* **lovely young** (pl., animals) possible mng. of Gn 49_{21}. †

p. 46b: entry II בֹּקֶר: after line 8 (thus after Ex 14_{27}), insert:

mēhabbōqer toward morn. 2S 2_{27};

p. 59b: after entry גְּ(י)לֹנִי insert:

cj. גִּינָה: Ez 42_{12} rd הַגִּינָה, **defense wall.**†

p. 72a: entry II דמה qal: after תִּדְמֶינָה;—read:

I. **be quiet** *(nefeš)*, w. l^{e} Ps $62_{2.6}$ 65_{2} (cj. pt. דֹּמִיָּה);—2.

p. 88b: after entry *זְכוּר: insert:

זָכוּר: **mindful** Ps 103_{14}. †

p. 90a: entry II זמר qal: after line 2, insert:

nif.: impf. יִזָּמֵר: **be pruned** Is 5_{6}. †

p. 93a: under חבא nif.: after pf. נֶחְבָּא, insert: נֶחְבָּה,

under חבה: add:

nif.: pf. נֶחְבָּה Je 49_{10} נַחְבֵּתֶם Jos 2_{16}; inf. הֵחָבֵה; ↗ חבא nif.

p. 118a: after entry II חֶרֶשׁ insert:

III חֶרֶשׁ: n. pers. 1C 9_{15}. †

p. 120a: entry חָשַׁק qal: line 3, read:

91_{14}, subj. God Dt 7_{7};—2.

p. 120b: entry חֹתֵן: after entry-word חֹתֵן insert:

inflected as pt. of חתן qal, e.g. sf. חֹתְנוֹ:

p. 227a: entry נָגַע: lines 6-7 should read:

touch (to do harm), w. acc. Gn 26_{29}; obj. woman, w. acc. Ru 2_{9}, w. *'el* Gn 20_{6}; c) touch = **hurt,** w. *b^e*

p. 236b: entry נטר: lines 3-5 should read:

watch, guard (vineyard) SS 1_{6} 8_{11}f;—2. *nāṭar 'appô* **preserve one's anger, hold a grudge** cj. Am 1_{11}; w/o *'appô*: of God, w. *l^e* Na 1_{2}, w. neg. Je $3_{5\cdot12}$ Ps 103_{9}; of man, w. *'ēt* Lv 19_{18}. †

p. 237a: before entry נִין: insert:

נין: Ps 72_{17} Qr יִנּוֹן, **nif.** & Kt יָנִין ? **hif.: sprout.** †

p. 255a: after entry סחב: insert:

סְחָבוֹת: **ragged clothes** Je $38_{11\cdot12}$. †

p. 263a: entry I עָבַר qal: line 10 from end of qal entry should read:

Jos 2_{23}; w. acc. go over to Je 2_{10}; **transgress, overstep** (a command, law) 2K 18_{12}; —6. w.

p. 275a: under עִם: line 2; after עִמָּם, insert: עִמָּהֶם,

p. 295b: after entry פצע: insert:

פֶּצַע: פֶּצַע, sf. פִּצְעִי; pl. פְּצָעִים, cs. פִּצְעֵי, sf. פְּצָעָיו: **bruise** Gn 4_{23}

p. 307b: entry צמת: between **nif.** and **pilpel** entries insert:

piel: pf. צִמְּתַתְנִי: **silence** Ps 119_{139}. †

p. 323b: after II קרא: **qal** section, add 2 more sections:

nif.: pf. נִקְרָא, נִקְרֵיתִי; impf. נִקָּרֵא; inf. נִקְרֹא:—1. **arrange to meet** (of God), w. *'al* Ex 5_{3};—2. **happen to be** (at a place) 2S 1_{6};—3. **be (present)** Dt 22_{6} 2S 18_{9} 20_{1}. †

hif.: impf. וַתַּקְרֵא: w. 2 acc. **make** s.thng. **happen to** s.one Je 32_{23}. †

p. 336a: entry רוע: after **hif.** entry insert:

polal: impf. יְרֹעָע: **a shout is raised** Is 16_{10}.† **hitpolel:** cj. pf. הִתְרֹעַעְתִּי; impf. אֶתְרֹעָע, יִתְרֹעֲעוּ; impv. תִּתְרוֹעָעִי: **shout in triumph** Ps 60_{10} 65_{14} 108_{10}, cj. Jb 31_{29}.†

p. 356a: entry שֶׁ: line 7, end of line, delete semicolon and insert:

& *b^ešell^emî* for whose sake Jon 1_{7};

p. 358a: entry II שׁבח: **piel:** should read:

impf. תְּשַׁבְּחֵם, יְשַׁבְּחֶנָּה: **hush** Ps 89_{10} Pr 29_{11}.†

p. 359a: after entry שְׁבַנְיָהוּ: insert:

*שׁבס: **levy rent** Am 5_{11}: ⸗ בשׁס.

p. 365b: entry שׁחה: before the word **qal,** insert:

cf. II חוה hištafal:

entry **hitp.** should read:

hitp.: ⸗ II חוה hištafal. (Omit all Hebrew forms and definitions.)

p. 387a: after entry [תַּהֲלֻכֹת] insert:

תַּהְפֻּכ(וֹ)ת: **perversity, s.thg perverse:** *dôr tahpukōt* perverse generation Dt 32_{20}; *'îš t.* perverse, scheming man Pr 16_{28}; *ḥāšab t.* devise plots Pr 16_{30}.

entry תּוֹדָה: line 1, before **song** insert:

(song of) praise Jos 7_{19}, >

ABBREVIATIONS

BIBLICAL BOOKS

Gn	2K	Na	SS
Ex	Is	Hb	Ec
Lv	Je	Zp	La
Nu	Ez	Hg	Est
Dt	Ho	Zc	Dn
Jos	Jl	Ma	Ezr
Ju	Am	Ps	Ne
1S	Ob	Jb	1C
2S	Jon	Pr	2C
1K	Mi	Ru	

PROPER NAMES

n.pers.	name of person (masculine)	n.loc.	name of locality
n.pers.f.	name of person (feminine)	n.peop.	name of people
n.gent.	name of tribe, gentilic	n.terr.	name of territory

OTHER ABBREVIATIONS

abs.	absolute (state)
abt.	about
acc.	accusative, according
adj.	adjective
adv.	adverb(ial)
alw.	always
appos.	apposition, appositive
Aram.	Aramaic
archit.	architectural
art.	article
artif.	artificial(ly)
betw.	between
BH	Biblia Hebraica
bibl.	biblical
bk(s).	book(s)
ca.	*circa*
Can.	Canaanite
caus.	causative
cf.	*confer* = compare
ch(s).	chapter(s)
cj.	conjecture
cogn.	cognate
coh.	cohortative
coll.	collective
comb(s).	combination(s)
comm.	common gender; commentary, -ies
conj.	conjunction
cons.	consonant
consec.	consecutive
constr.	construction
contam.	contamination
corr.	corrupt(ion)
cs.	construct (state)
ctxt.	context
dat.	dative
def.	definite
del.	delete
denom.	denominative
demonstr.	demonstrative
dep.	dependent
det.	determinate
dict.	dictionary, -ies
dimin.	diminutive
dir.	direct
dittgr.	dittography, -graphic
du.	dual
dub.	dubious
e.g.	*exempli gratia* = for example
Egyp.	Egyptian
ellipt.	elliptical
elsewh.	elsewhere
emph.	emphasis, emphatic
Eng.	English
esp.	especially
euphem.	euphemism, euphemistic(ally)
evid.	evidently

exc.	except
expr.	expression
exten.	extension
f.	feminine
fig.	figurative(ly)
fin.	finite
fm.	from
foll.	followed
gen.	genitive
genl.	general
gent.	gentilic
gram.	grammar(s), grammatical(ly)
Heb.	Hebrew
hif.	hifil
hitp.	hitpael
hitpal.	hitpalel
hitpalp.	hitpalpel
hitpol.	hitpolel
hof.	hofal
hon.	honorary
idiom.	idiomatic(ally)
impf.	imperfect
impv.	imperative
incl.	including
ind.	indicative
indef.	indefinite
indep.	independent
indic.	indicative
indir.	indirect
inexplic.	inexplicable
inf.	infinitive
insep.	inseparable
interj.	interjection
interr.	interrogative
intrans.	intransitive
Isr.	Israel
Jerus.	Jerusalem
juss.	jussive
KBH_3	KITTEL, ***Biblia Hebraica***, 3rd edition
Kt	Kethib
lit.	literal(ly)
loc.	locative
LXX	Septuagint
m.	masculine
metaph.	metaphorical(ly)
misc.	miscellaneous
mng.	meaning
mod.	modern
ms(s).	manuscript(s)
MT	Masoretic Text
mus.	musical
n.	name
N.ern	Northern
neg.	negative
nif.	nifal
nitp.	nitpael
nom.	nominal
obj(s).	object(s)
oft.	often
onesf.	oneself
opp.	opposed to
ord.	ordinal
orig.	original(ly)
OT	Old Testament
oth.	other(s)
otherw.	otherwise
part.	partitive
pass.	passive
paus.	pausal
perh.	perhaps
pers.	person(al)
Pers.	Persian
pf.	perfect
phr.	phrase(s)
pilp.	pilpel
pl.	plural
pleon.	pleonastic(ally)
poet.	poetic(ally)
pol.	polel
prec.	preceding
pred.	predicate
pref.	prefix
prep.	preposition
prob.	probably
pron.	pronoun
prp.	propose(s), proposed
pt.	participle
pul.	pulal
qn.	question
Qr	Qere
rd.	read
ref.	refer(ence)
rel.	relative
S.	South
sbst.	substantive
sc.	*scilicet* (= namely)
sep.	separate
S.ern	Southern
sf.	suffix
sg.	singular
sim.	similar(ly)
s.one	someone
spec.	specific(ally), specific expression(s)

s.thg	something
styl.	stylistic(ally)
subj.	subject
sugg.	suggest(s), suggestion(s)
syl.	syllable
symb.	symbolic(ally)
tech.	technical
theol.	theological(ly)
thg.	thing
trad.	traditional(ly)
trans.	transitive
transl.	translate(d), translation
txt.	text
uncert.	uncertain
unexpl.	unexplained
usu.	usually
v.	verse
var.	various(ly), variation
vb(s).	verb(s)
Vers(s).	Version(s)
voc.	vocative
vocal.	vocalized, vocalization
w.	with
W.ern	Western
wh.	which
w/o	without
Y.	Yahweh

SIGNS

&	and
&c.	*et cetera*
†	all undisputed instances have been cited (see Introduction)
F	see, refer to; note its use in compounds or in phrases, where the reader is referred to a unit of the compound or phrase, e.g. F גֵּי־הַצְּבֹעִים refer to צְבֹעִים
×	number (of occurrences)
>	becomes
<	is derived from
√	verbal root
::	in contrast, opposition to
||	parallel to
+	plus
ʼ	(with Hebrew abbreviations)
*	theoretical form

א

אָב: cs. אֲב Gn 17_4 †, elsewh. אֲבִי; sf. אָבִי, אָבִיךָ, אָבִיהוּ > אָבִיו, אָבִינוּ, אֲבִיכֶם; pl. אָבֹ(ו)ת, cs. אֲבוֹת; sf. אֲבֹ(ו)תַי: — 1. (physical) **father** Gn 2_{24}, = **grandfather** 28_{13}, **ancestor** of tribe, nation 10_{21}; pl. = **forefathers** Gn 15_{15}; metaph. **begetter** (of rain) Jb 38_{28}; — 2. **originator, founder** of group, trade Gn 4_{20f}; — 3. fatherly **protector** Ps 68_6; — 4. hon. title: of one's elder 1S 24_{12}, prophet 2K 6_{21}, husband Je 3_4; — 5. *bêt ʾāb(ôt)* **family** Jos 22_{14}, > (ellipt.) *ʾābôt* 1K 8_1; — 6. of God: **father** (of Isr.) Dt 32_6; of the king 2S 7_{14}; title of a (tree-)god Je 2_{27}.

***אֵב** (*אֵב): sf. אִבּוֹ; pl. cs. אִבֵּי: — **shoot** of a plant growing close to the earth Jb 8_{12} SS 6_{11}. †

אֹב: ↗ אוֹב.

אֲבַגְתָא: n. pers. Est 1_{10}.

אבד: qal: pf. א׳; impf. יֹאבֵד, יֹאבַד; inf. אֲבֹד, אֲבָדְךָ, אָבְדְךָ; אָבֹד; pt. אֹבֵד, אֹבֶדֶת: — 1. **become lost** of property (*bᵉ*: among) Lv 26_{38}, of hope Ez 19_5; (*min*: to s. one) Dt 22_3; — 2. **go astray**: of cattle 1S 9_3, **lose** one's way (*derek*) Ps 2_{12}; *ʾarammî ʾōbēd* Dt 26_5 (oth.: **fugitive** ↗ Gn 31_2; oth.: 3: **near to ruin**); — 3. **perish**, of men Nu 17_{27}; — 4. **be ruined**, of nation Ex 10_7; — 5. **be carried off** (*min*: from) Nu 16_{33}, (*mēʿal*) Dt 11_{17}, (*mippᵉnê*: before) Ps 9_4; — 6. *ʾābad lēb* **courage fails** Je 4_9; *kᵉlî ʾōbēd* **ruined, broken utensil** Ps 31_{13}.

piel: pf. אִבַּד; impf. יְאַבֵּד, יְאַבְּדֵם, 1 sg. + sf. וָאַבֶּדְךָ; inf. אַבֵּד, לְאַבְּדֵנִי; pt. מְאַבְּדִים: — 1. **give up** as lost Ec 3_6; — 2. **let perish** Je 23_1; — 3. **destroy** (30×) 2K 11_1, **exterminate** (*min*: from) Je 51_{55}; — 4. **dissipate** (wealth) Pr 29_3; *ʾibbad lēb* **deprive of understanding** Ec 7_7.

hif.: pf. וְהַאֲבַדְתִּי, הֶאֱבִיד; impf. אֹבִידָה Je 46_8; inf. הַאֲבִידוֹ, לְהַאֲבִיד; pt. מַאֲבִיד: — **exterminate** 2K 10_{19}, (*min*: from) Dt 7_{24}.

אֹבֵד: (trad.: **destruction**) **duration**, *ʿadê ʾōbēd* **forever** Nu $24_{20.24}$. †

אֲבֵדָה cs. אֲבֵדַת: s.thg **lost** Ex 22_8.

אֲבַדֹּה Kt, Qr אֲבַדּוֹ(ן) Pr 27_{20} ↗ אֲבַדּוֹן.

אֲבַדּוֹן; > אֲבַדֹּה: (place of destruction), **realm of the dead** Ps 88_{12}.

אַבְדָן: **destruction** Est 9_5. †

***אָבְדַן** cs. אָבְדַן: **destruction** Est 8_6. †

אבה: **qal**: pf. א׳, אָבִיתִי, אָבוּ; impf. יֹאבֶה, יֹאבוּ; pt. אֹבִים: — alw. w. neg.: exc. Jb 39_9 (& Is 1_{19}) — 1. **accede** to s.one Dt 13_9, **accept** s.thg Pr $1_{25.30}$; — 2. **want** s.thg (ca. 35×), w. inf. 2K 13_{23}, w. *lᵉ* + inf. Gn 24_5; — 3. abs. **be willing**, a) **consent** 1K 22_{50}, b) **want to** Is 1_{19}.

אֵבֶה: **reed, papyrus**; *ʾoniyyôt ʾēbeh* Jb 9_{26} = *kᵉlê gōmeʾ* Is 18_2, Egyp. **reed skiffs**. †

אֲבוֹי: **desire** > **uneasiness**; or interj. **woe** Pr 23_{29}. †

אֵבוּס: cs. =, sf. אֲבוּסֶךָ: **feed-trough** Is 1_3.

[**אִבְחָה***: cs. אִבְחַת Ez 21_{20}: ?, rd. *טִבְחַת. †]

אֲבַטִּיחַ*: pl. אֲבַטִּחִים: **watermelon,** ***Citrullus vulgaris*** Nu 11_5. †

I **אָבִי**: interj. **O that!** Jb 34_{36} (some cj. אֲלַב, oth. = אֲבוֹי); > **if** 2K 5_{13}; 1S 24_{12} rd otherw.

II **אָבִי**: n. pers.: הוּרָם אָבִי 2C 2_{12}, better: hon. title, *ʾāb* (4); ↗ 2C $4_{11.16}$. †

III **אָבִי** 1K 21_{29} & oft., = אָבִיא (↗ בוא hif.).

אֲבִי: n. pers. f. 2K 18_2; for אֲבִיָּה 2C 29_1. †
אֲבִיאֵל: n. pers. 1S 9_1.
אֲבִיאָסָף: n. pers. Ex 6_{24}.
אָבִיב: — 1. **ears** (of grain), ripe but still soft, the grains of which are eaten either rubbed or roasted Lv 2_{14}; — 2. (month of ears), Mar/Apr; later *nîsān*, Ex 13_4.
אֲבִיגַיִל: n. pers. f.
אֲבִידָן: n. pers.
אֲבִידָע: n. pers.
אֲבִיָּה: n. pers.
אֲבִיָּהוּ: n. pers.
אֲבִיהוּא: n. pers.
אֲבִיהוּד: n. pers.
אֲבִיהַיִל: n. pers.
אֶבְיוֹן: sf. אֶבְיֹנְךָ; pl. אֶבְיֹ(וֹ)נִים; sf. אֶבְיוֹנֶיהָ: needy, **poor** Dt $15_{4\cdot7\cdot11}$, = oppressed Am 4_1, in religious sense Ps 40_{18} & oft.
אֲבִיּוֹנָה: **caper-berry**, *Capparis spinosa*, an aphrodisiac Ec 12_5. †
אֲבִיחַיִל: n. pers.
אֲבִיטוּב: n. pers.
אֲבִיָּם: n. pers.
אֲבִימָאֵל: n. pers.
אֲבִימֶלֶךְ: n. pers.
אֲבִינָדָב: n. pers.
אֲבִינֹעַם: n. pers.
אֲבִינֵר: n. pers.
אֶבְיָסָף: n. pers.
אֲבִיעֶזֶר: n. pers.
אֲבִי־עַלְבוֹן: perh. = *אֲבִיבַעַל; n. pers.
*אָבִיר: cs. אֲבִיר, artif. distinguished from אַבִּיר: **strong, powerful**: *ʾabîr yaʿaqōb* Gn 49_{24}, *ʾabîr yiśrāʾēl* Is 1_{24}, designation of Father-God (oft.: **bull** of J., of I.).
אַבִּיר: pl. אַבִּירִים; cs. אַבִּירֵי; sf. אַבִּירָיו: **strong, powerful**: of a chief 1S 21_8, stallion Ju 5_{22}; valiant Ps 76_6.
אֲבִירָם: n. pers.
אֲבִישַׁג: n. pers. f.
אֲבִישׁוּעַ: n. pers.
אֲבִישׁוּר: n. pers.
אֲבִישַׁי: n. pers.
אֲבִישָׁלוֹם: n. pers.; F אַבְשָׁלוֹם.
אֶבְיָתָר: n. pers.
אבך: **hitp.**.: impf. יִתְאַבְּכוּ: **whirl up** (of burning twigs) Is 9_{17}. †
I אָבַל: **qal**: pf. 'א; impf. תֶּאֱבַל: **mourn** Is 19_8.
hif.: pf. הֶאֱבַלְתִּי; impf. וַיַּאֲבֶל־: **move** (s.one) **to mourning** Ez 31_{15}.
hitp.: impf. וַיִּתְאַבֵּל; impv. הִתְאַבְּלִי; pt. מִתְאַבֵּל, מִתְאַבֶּלֶת: **observe mourning rites** (ca. 20×) Ex 33_4.
II אָבַל: **qal**: pf. 'א; impf. תֶּאֱבַל: **dry up** Is 24_4.
I אָבֵל: cs. כַּאֲבֶל־; pl. אֲבֵלִים; cs. אֲבֵלֵי; f. אֲבֵלוֹת: observing mourning rites, **in mourning** Gn 37_{35}.
II אָבֵל: loc. אָבֵלָה: watercourse, **brook**, only in n. loc.
אֵבֶל: **rites, ceremony of mourning; mourning**: *ʿāśâ ʾēbel le* **perform mourning-rites for** Gn 50_{10}; *yemê ʾēbel* **time of mourning** Gn 27_{41}.
אֲבָל: — 1. **truly** Gn 42_{21}, **ah** 2S 14_5; — 2. **but, however** (in later bks.) Dn 10_7; **on the contrary, no** Gn 17_{19}.
אֻבָל: cs. אוּבַל: water-course, **canal** Dn $8_{2\cdot3\cdot6}$. †
אֶבֶן: n.f.: sf. אַבְנוֹ; pl. אֲבָנִים; cs. אַבְנֵי; sf. אֲבָנָיו: **stone**, variety of contexts: I. secular: — 1. single **stone** Gn 28_{11}; — 2. coll. **stones** Jb 28_3; — 3. **precious stone** Ex 25_7; — 4. applied to a) closing (as of a cave) Jos 10_{18}; b) building material 2S 5_{11}; c) weapon: *ʾeben yād* **stone in the hand** Nu 35_{17}; d) w. var. vbs., stone **with stones** Dt 13_{11}; — 5. **plummet** Is 34_{11}; — 6. **weight**: *ʾeben hammelek* **king's weight** 2S 14_{26}; — 7. meteorological: *ʾabnê habbārād* **hailstones** Jos 10_{11}; — 8. equipment, e.g. *lûḥôt ʾeben* **stone tablets** = tables

of the law Ex 24$_{12}$; — 9. misc.: *lēb ʾeben* **stony heart** Ez 11$_{19}$.

II. sacral: — 1. *mizbaḥ ʾabānîm* **stone altar** Dt 27$_5$; — 2. *gal ʾabānîm* **heap of stones** (marking grave, frontier) Jos 7$_{26}$, Gn 31$_{46}$; — 3. (upright) stone (as marker) Gn 31$_{45}$; — 4. (sculptured) stone (idol, &c.) Je 2$_{27}$; — 5. polemically, gods of wood and stone Dt 4$_{28}$.

אֲבָנָה: n. river, 2K 5$_{12}$ Kt. †

אַבְנֵט: sf. אַבְנֵטְךָ; pl. אַבְנֵטִים: **sash**, esp. of a priest Ex 28$_4$.

אָבְנַיִם: du., sg. *אֹבֶן: — 1. **potter's wheel** (of 2 disks), Je 18$_3$; — 2. Ex 1$_{16}$?: stones of birth stool? (female) genitalia? †

אַבְנֵר: n. pers.

אבס: **qal** only pt. pass. אָבוּס **fattened** 1K 5$_3$ Pr 15$_{17}$. †

אֲבַעְבֻּעֹת: **blisters, boils** Ex 9$_{9f}$. †

אֶבֶץ: n. loc.

אִבְצָן: n. pers.

אבק: **nif.**: impf. וַיֵּאָבֵק; inf. הֵאָבְקוֹ: **wrestle** (ʿ*im*: with) Gn 32$_{25f}$. †

אָבָק: cs. אֲבַק, sf. אֲבָקָם: — 1. **dust** Is 29$_5$; — 2. **soot** Ex 9$_9$.

***אֲבָקָה**: cs. אַבְקַת: **aromatic powders** SS 3$_6$. †

אבר: **hif.**: impf. יַאֲבֶר־: **soar up** Jb 39$_{26}$. †

אֵבֶר: **wing** Is 40$_{31}$.

אֶבְרָה: f. fm. אֵבֶר: sf. אֶבְרָתוֹ; pl. sf. אֶבְרוֹתֶיהָ: **wing** Ps 68$_{14}$.

אַבְרָהָם: n. pers. **Abraham**, ↗ אַבְרָם.

אַבְרֵךְ: shout before Joseph's chariot Gn 41$_{43}$; ? Egyptian? explained as Hebr. I ברך impv. 'make obeisance'.

אַבְרָם: n. pers., = אַבְרָהָם Gn 17$_5$.

אַבְשַׁי: n. pers.

אַבְשָׁל(וֹ)ם: n. pers.

אֹבֹת: n. loc. ↗ II. אוֹב.

אָגֵא: n. pers.

אֲגַג (4×), **אֲגָג** (3×): n. pers. 1S 15$_{8ff}$.

אֲגָגִי: n. gent.

אֲגֻדָּה: cs. אֲגֻדַּת; sf. אֲגֻדָּתוֹ; pl. אֲגֻדּוֹת: bundle: — 1. **sprinkling brush** Ex 12$_{22}$; — 2. **troop** (of people) 2S 2$_{25}$; — 3. **harness cords** (of yoke) Is 58$_6$; — 4. **firmament** Am 9$_6$. †

אֱגוֹז: **walnut-tree**, *Juglans regia* SS 6$_{11}$. †

אָגוּר: n. pers.

***אֲגוֹרָה**: cs. אֲגוֹרַת: **payment** 1S 2$_{36}$ (oth.: small coin). †

***אֵגֶל**: pl. cs. אֶגְלֵי: **drop** Jb 38$_{28}$. †

אֶגְלַיִם: n. loc.

cj. **אגם**: **qal**: Jb 41$_{12}$ for אַגְמֹן cj. אֹגֵם pt. **glow(ing)**. †

I **אֲגַם**: pl. אֲגַמִּים, cs. אַגְמֵי; **reed pool** Ex 7$_{19}$.

II ***אֲגַם**: pl. אֲגַמִּים: **outwork** (of fort) Je 51$_{32}$. †

***אָגֵם**: pl. cs. אַגְמֵי: *ʾa. nefeš* **distressed** Is 19$_{10}$. †

אַגְמוֹן: **reed** Is 9$_{13}$; Jb 41$_{12}$ rd אֹגֵם.

אַגָּן: cs. אַגַּן; pl. אַגָּנוֹת: **(ritual- or banquet-) bowl** Ex 24$_6$ Is 22$_{24}$ SS 7$_3$. †

***אֲגַף**: pl. sf. אֲגַפָּיו: **troop** Ez 12$_{14}$.

אגר: **qal**: pf. אָגְרָה; impf. תֶּאֱגֹר; pt. אֹגֵר: **gather in** (harvest) Dt 28$_{39}$.

***אֲגַרְטָל**: pl.cs. אֲגַרְטְלֵי: trad. **basket**, oth.: **leather bag, metal bowl** ('gold' and 'silver' can be contents or material) Ezr 1$_9$. †

אֶגְרֹף: **fist** Ex 21$_{18}$ Is 58$_4$. †

אִגֶּרֶת; pl. אִגְּר(וֹ)ת: (official, commercial) **letter** Est 9$_{26}$.

אֵד: sf. אֵדוֹ: Gn 2$_6$ the subterranean **fresh-water stream**, surface water (?); Jb 36$_{27}$ the **heavenly stream**. †

[**אדב**: **hif.**: inf. לַאֲדִיב, rd לְהָדִיב (↗ דוב): 1S 2$_{33}$. †]

אַדְבְּאֵל: n. pers.

אֲדַד: n. pers.

אֶדַּדֵּם: Ps 42$_5$, ↗ דדה.

אִדּוֹ: n. pers.

אֱדוֹם: **Edom**: — 1. n. loc. Gn 32$_4$; — 2. n. people Nu 20$_{18}$; — 3. **the Edomites** Gn 36$_9$; — 4. n. pers. = Esau Gn 25$_{30}$.

*אֱדוֹמִי, אֲדֹמִי; pl. אֲדֹמִיִּים, אֲדֹ(ו)מִים, אֲדֹמִיֹּת: — 1. adj. **Edomite** 1K 11_{17}; — 2. sg. (an) **Edomite** 1K 11_{14}; pl. 2K 16_{6}; — 3. **the Edomites** sg. coll. Dt 23_{8} (?).

אָדוֹן: cs. אֲדוֹן, sf. of sg. only for אֲדֹנִי (& אֲדֹנוֹ Pr 30_{10} Kt, 1S 16_{16} †); otherw. pl. אֲדֹנִים, cs. אֲדֹנֵי, sf. אֲדֹנָיו, &c; 1 sg. אֲדֹנַי Gn 19_{2} †, otherw. אֲדֹנָי; w. pref. לַאד׳, בַּאד׳, וַאד׳, exc, sf. w. *e* (לַאֲדֹנֵינוּ) & לַאֲדֹן Mi 4_{13} †; of God, always אֲדֹנָי:

I. (earthly) **lord, master** (more than 300×): — 1. :: *ʿebed* Is 24_{2}; in gent., over land Gn 42_{30}, household 45_{8}, &c; pl. **lords** Is 26_{13}; — 2. polite vocative, *ʾadōnî* = **you** (sg.): wife to husb. 1K 1_{17}, dau. to father Gn 31_{35}, &c.; w. addition: my lord Moses Nu 11_{28}; — 3. in polite style, *ʾadōnî* for **you** (sg.) or **he**, **your** or **his**: Gn 24_{27}.

II. *ʾādôn* = **God** (more than 400×): — 1. God is *ʾādōn* Ps 114_{7}, *hāʾādōn* Is 1_{24}, *ʾadôn kol-hāʾāreṣ* Jos 3_{11}, *ʾadōnê hāʾadōnîm* Dt 10_{17}; — 2. *ʾadōnāy*: a) voc., Gn 18_{3}; b) in statement Gn 18_{27}; c) *ʾadōnāy yhwh* **my Lord Y.** (280×) Gn 15_{2}; — 3. *yhwh ʾadōnênû*: voc., Ps 8_{2}; statement, Ps 135_{5}.

אַדּוֹן: n. loc.

אֲדוֹרַיִם: n. loc.

אֲדוֹרָם: n. pers.

אָדֹשׁ: Is 28_{28}: ↗ דושׁ.

אֹדוֹת (8×), אוֹדוֹת (2×): sf. אוֹדֹתֶיךָ; — 1. prep. *ʿal-ʾōdôt* **on account of** Gn 21_{11}; — 2. conj. *ʿal-kol-ʾōdôt ʾašer* **precisely because** Je 3_{8}.

אַדִּיר: sf. אַדִּירוֹ, f. ↗ אַדֶּרֶת; pl. אַדִּ(י)רִ(י)ם, cs. אַדִּירֵי, sf. אַדִּירֵיהֶם: **mighty, splendid**: — 1. adj.: ship Is 33_{21b}, Isr. Je 30_{21}, Y.'s name Ps 8_{2}; — 2. noun: pl., people of rank Ju 5_{13}.

אֲדַלְיָה: n. pers.

אדם: **qal**: אָדְמוּ: **be red** La 4_{7}. †

pu.: pt. מְאָדָּם: **rubbed with ruddle** (dyed red): ram's skins Ex 25_{5}, shield Na 2_{4}.

hif.: impf. יַאְדִּימוּ: **come to be red** Is 1_{18}. †

hitp.: impf.: יִתְאַדָּם: **have a reddish sparkle** Pr 23_{31}. †

I אָדָם (only abs.; ca. 540×): — 1. coll. **people**, a) w. pl.: Je 47_{2}; but b) mostly w. sg. 1S 25_{1}; c) *bᵉnê ʾādām* (38×) Dt 8_{3}, *bᵉnê hāʾādām* Gn 11_{5}, **(single) men**; *ben-ʾādām* single man, esp. in Ez, ↗ *bēn* 4; d) in cs.-constr.: *lēb ʾādām* Gn 8_{21} &c; e) appositional: *ʾādām bᵉliyyaʿal* **men that are ruiners = ruinous** Pr 6_{12}; f) w.negation: *lōʾ . . . ʾādām* Ps 105_{14}, *ʾādām lōʾ* Lv 16_{7} **no one**; — 2. **single person** (late; coll. meaning usually possible): *bᵉʾādām* **(in) someone** Lv 22_{5}; — 3. Gn 1-5: 1_{26-31} coll. **people, men**; coll. also in chh. 2f, 5_{1b-2} :: 4_{25} $5_{1a.3.5}$, ↗ III אָדָם.

II אָדָם: **leather** Ho 11_{4}. †

III אָדָם: n. pers., ↗ I 2: **Adam**, first in Gn 4_{25}, $5_{1a.3.5}$, 1C 1_{1}. †

IV אָדָם: = I אֲדָמָה **ground**; *ʿên ʾādām* **surface of the earth** Zc 9_{1}.

V אָדָם: n. loc. Jos 3_{16} (rd: *bᵉʾādām*) & Ho 6_{7} (rd: *bᵉʾādām*). †

אָדֹם (4×), אָדוֹם (1×): f. אֲדֻמָּה, pl. אֲדֻמִּים: color of blood, **red(-brown)** Gn 25_{30}.

אֹדֶם: precious stone in priest's and king's robes, ruby or carnelian Ex 28_{17}.

אֲדַמְדָּם: f. אֲדַמְדֶּמֶת; pl. אֲדַמְדַּמֹּת: **bright red, reddish** Lv 13_{49}; *lābān ʾa.* **reddish white** Lv 13_{19}.

I אֲדָמָה: cs. אַדְמַת, sf. אַדְמָתִי; pl. אֲדָמוֹת: — 1. **ground, soil** producing plants Dt 7_{13}; — 2. misc.: *ʾadmat miṣrayim* property (of land) in E. Gn 47_{20} &c; *ʾîš hāʾadāmâ* **farmer** 9_{20}; — 3. **realm of the dead**, opens its mouth Gn 4_{11}; *ʾadmat ʿāfār* 'land of dust' Dn 12_{2}.

II אֲדָמָה: n. loc., = I; — 1. in Naphtali Jos 19_{36}; — 2. in Jordan valley 1K 7_{46}, 2C 4_{17}; also Ps 83_{11} (?).

III *אֲדָמָה: cs. w. וֹ: אַדְמָתוֹ: (red) **blood** Dt 32_{43}. †

אַדְמָה: n. loc.; Aram., = Heb. (II) אֲדָמָה.

אַדְמֹנִי (2×), אַדְמוֹנִי (1×): **reddish** Gn 25_{25}.

אֲדֹמִי: ↗ אֱדוֹמִי.

אֲדָמִי הַנֶּקֶב: n. loc.

אַדְמֹנִי (2×), **אַדְמוֹנִי** (1×): **reddish** Gn 25_{25}.

אֲדֻמִּים: n. loc.

אַדְמָתָא: n. pers.

***אֶדֶן**: pl. אֲדָנִים, cs. אַדְנֵי, sf. אֲדָנָיו: **pedestal, socket** Ex 26_{19}.

אַדָּן: n. loc.

אֲדֹנִי: ↗ אָדוֹן.

אֲדֹנִי(־)בֶזֶק: n. pers.

אֲדֹנִיָּה: n. pers.

אֲדֹנִיָּהוּ: n. pers.

אֲדֹנִי־צֶדֶק: n. pers.

אֲדֹנִיקָם: n. pers.

אֲדֹנִירָם: n. pers.

אדר: **nif.**: pt. נֶאְדָּר, cs. נֶאְדָּרִי: **glorious** Ex $15_{6 \cdot 11}$. †

hif.: impf. יַאְדִּיר **render glorious** Is 42_{21}. †

אֶדֶר: **splendor**, *ʾeder hayqār* **noble price** Zc 11_{13}; Mi 2_8 rd אַדֶּרֶת. †

אֲדָר: 12th month of year, **Adar**, = Feb./March, Est 3_7.

I **אַדָּר**: n. pers. 1C 8_3 = אַרְדְּ Gn 46_{21} Nu 26_{40}. †

II **אַדָּר**: n. loc. Jos 15_3.

אֲדַרְכֹנִים: Ezr 8_{27}, אֲדַרְכֹּנִים 1C 29_7 trad.: **daric**; :: corr. < ↗ דַּרְכְּמֹנִים **drachmas**.

אֲדֹרָם: n. pers.

I **אַדְרַמֶּלֶךְ**: name of a god, 2K 17_{31}. †

II **אַדְרַמֶּלֶךְ**: n. pers. 2K 19_{37} = Is 37_{38}. †

אֶדְרֶעִי: n. loc.

אַדֶּרֶת: sf. אַדַּרְתּוֹ: — 1. **splendor**: vine Ez 17_8; — 2. **robe** a) of state (king of Nineveh) Jon 3_6; b) *ʾadderet śēʿār* **fur garment** Gn 25_{25}.

[**אדשׁ**: inf. אָדוֹשׁ Is 28_{28}: rd דּוּשׁ (√דושׁ) or del. †]

אָהַב: **qal**: pf. אָהֵב ,א׳, sf. אֲהֵבוֹ; impf. יֶאֱהַב, 1 sg. אֹהַב Mal 1_2, אֵהָב Pr 8_{17}; impv. אֱהַב, אֶהֱבוּ; inf. אֱהוֹב, אַהֲבָם, אַהֲבַת; pt. אֹהֵב, אֹהַבְךָ, ↗ אֹהֶבֶת, pass. אָהוּב, אֲהוּבָה, אֹהֲבִים: — **like, love**: — 1. acc. **person**: father/son Gn 22_2, man/wife 24_{67}, wife/husb. 1S 18_{20}; — 2. acc. **thing**: justice Ps 37_{28}, bribe Is 1_{23}, Jerus. 66_{10}; — 3. **love God** Ex 20_6, his salvation Ps 40_{17}; — 4. **God loves**: Isr. Hos 3_1, his faithful Dt 7_{13}; — 5. *ʾāhab le* **love to** + vb. Je 14_{10}; — 6. *ʾōhēb* **friend** Je 20_4; — 7. misc.: cogn. acc. 1S 20_{17b}; — Hos 4_{18} ↗ pealal.

nif.: pt. נֶאֱהָבִים **worthy of love** 2S 1_{23}. †

piel: pt. sf. מְאַהֲבֶיהָ **lover** of woman Je 22_{20}, of man Zc 13_6.

cj. **pealal**: pf. אֲהַבְהֲבוּ **dally, caress** Ho 4_{18}. †

***אֹהַב**: or ***אֹהֶב**: אֲהָבִים: **joys of love** Pr 7_{18}. †

***אֹהַב**: pl. אֲהָבִים: — 1. **gifts of love** Hos 8_9; — 2. **charm** Pr 5_{19}. †

I **אַהֲבָה**: cs. אַהֲבַת, sf. אַהֲבָתִי: — 1. **loving** (really inf.) w. acc. Gn 29_{20}; — 2. **love**: a) betw. man and wife SS 2_{4f}; b) betw. friends and persons in general 1S 18_3; c) spec.: gods 1K 11_2, self-love 1S 20_{17b}; d) God's love for his people 1K 10_9; — Hos 11_4 & SS 3_{10} ↗ II.

II **אַהֲבָה**: ? **leather** Hos 11_4 & SS 3_{10}. †

cj. **אֲהַבְהָבֵי** for הַבְהָבַי Hos 8_{13}: **ardor of love.** †

אֹהַד: n. pers.

אֲהָהּ: interj.: cry of alarm **ah!** 2K 3_{10}; against God or his *malʾāk* Jos 7_7.

אַהֲוָא: n. loc. & river.

אֵהוּד: n. pers.

אֱהִי: Hos $13_{10 \cdot 14 \cdot 14}$: rd אַיֵּה (LXX). †

אֶהְיֶה: 'I am, shall be,' הָיָה, veiled self-designation of Y. Ex 3_{14b}. †

I **אהל**: **qal**: impf. וַיֶּאֱהַל: trad. **camp**, but oth.: **obtain pasturing rights** Gn $13_{12 \cdot 18}$. †

piel: impf. יַהֵל > *יְאַהֵל: same Is 13_{20}. †

II **אהל**: **hif.**: impf. יַאֲהִיל: be bright, **shine** (moon) Jb 25_5. †

I **אֹהֶל** (340×): loc. הָאֹהֱלָה, sf. אָהֳלוֹ, אָהָלְךָ; pl. אֹהָלִים, but בָּאֳהָלִים (*bo*-), cs. אָהֳלֵי, sf. אֹהָלָיו: — 1. **tent**: *yōšēb ʾōhel* Gn 4_{20}, and var. vbs; — 2. **tent-dwellers,** families Ju 6_5; — 3. *'ōhel yhwh* **tent of Y.** 1K 2_{28}, ↗ *'ōhel mō'ēd* Ex 28_{43} > *(hā)'ōhel* 1K 1_{39}, *bēt hā'ōhel* 1C 9_{23}.

II אֹהֶל: n. pers. 1C 3_{20}. †

אֹהֶל: 1K 7_{45} הָאֹהֶל: Qr הָאֵלֶּה; Kt ?; ? dl. †

אָהֳלָה: symb. name of Samaria, Ez 23.

אֲהָלוֹת: Ps 45_9 SS 4_{14}, & אֲהָלִים Pr 7_{17}, **aloes** (aromatic wood), *Aloexyllon Agallochum & Aquilaria Agallocha.* †

אָהֳלִיאָב: n. pers.

אָהֳלִיבָה: (↗ אָהֳלָה) symb. name of Jerusalem Ez 23.

אָהֳלִיבָמָה: n. pers. (wife of Esau) Gn 36_{2-25}, n. of Edomite tribe Gn 36_{41} 1C 1_{52}.

I אֲהָלִים: Pr 7_{17}: ↗ אֲהָלוֹת.

II אֲהָלִים: **ice-plant**, forming a luxuriant growth, *Mesembrianthemum nodiflorum* Nu 24_6. †

אַהֲרוֹן: n. pers. **Aaron.**

אוֹ: particle of choice, **or**: betw. nouns Gn 44_{19}; *'ô . . . 'ô . . .*, **either . . . or . . .** Ex 21_{31}; introducing clause, *'ô (kî)* Ex $21_{33,36}$, *'ô . . . 'ô . . .* **whether . . . or . . .** Lv 5_1; *hᵃ . . . 'ô . . .* **whether . . . or . . .** Ec 2_{19}.

אוֹ: Pr 31_4: Qr אֵי, rd Kt אוֹ; var. oth. cj. †

אוּאֵל: n. pers.

I *אוֹב: pl. אֹבוֹת: **wine-skin** (skin whose hairy side is turned out) Jb 32_{19}. †

II אוֹב = I ?: pl. אֹב(וֹ)ת: prophesying **spirit of the dead** 1S 28_3.

אוֹבִיל: n. pers.

*אוּבָל, cs. אוּבַל: ↗ אֻבָל.

אוּד: **log** Is 7_4.

אוֹדֹת: ↗ אדות.

אוה: **nif.** (oth.: ↗ נאה, ↗ יאה): pf. נַאֲוָה, נָאווּ: **be beautiful, lovely** Is 52_7, SS 1_{10}; with *lᵉ* **be fitting** Ps 93_5. †

piel: pf. אִוְּתָה, אִוָּה, אִוְּ(י)תִיךָ; impf. תְּאַוֶּה: **want, crave,** usu. w. *nefeš* subj. 1K 11_{37}.

hitp.: pf. הִתְאַוָּה, הִתְאַוּוּ; impf. יִתְאָו, יִתְאַוֶּה; pt. מִתְאַוִּים, מִתְאַוָּה: — 1. **crave** (mostly in bad sense) Nu 11_{34}, **feel a craving** 2S 23_{15}; — 2. **long for** (a day) Je 17_{16} Am 5_{18}.

*אַוָּה: cs. אַוַּת: **craving, longing** *bᵉkol-'awwat hannefeš* Dt 12_{15}.

אוּזַי: n. pers.

אוּזָל: n. loc.

אוֹי: interj.: — 1. **woe!** (threatening): *'ôy lᵉkā* **woe to you** Nu 21_{29}; (anxious) *'ôy-nā' lî* **woe is me** Je 4_{31}; w. *'al* **because of** Je 10_{19}, *kî* **because** 1S 4_7; — 2. > noun **woe** Pr 23_{29}.

אֱוִי: n. pers.

אוֹיֵב: ↗ אֹיֵב.

אוֹיָה: interj.: < אוֹי: **woe!** Ps 120_5. †

I אֱוִיל: pl. אֱוִ(י)לִים: — 1. **foolish** Je 4_{22}; — 2. **fool, simpleton** Is 19_{11}, Pr 13 ×.

II אֱוִיל: 2K 24_{15} Kt אולי, rd אֱלֵי (Qr אֵילֵי, I אַיִל): **citizenry** (of the land).

אֱוִיל מְרֹדַךְ: n. pers., son and successor of נְבוּכַדְנֶאצַּר 2K 25_{27}.

אוֹכִיל Ho 11_4: ↗ אכל hif.

*אוּל: sf. אוּלָם: body, **belly** Ps 73_4. †

אֱוִלִי: 2K 24_{15}: ↗ II אֱוִיל.

I אוּלַי: n. river Da 8_2.

II אוּלַי (43×), אֻלַי Gn 24_{39} †: adv.: **perhaps** (expr. of hope, entreaty, fear), mostly w. impf. Gn 18_{29}.

I אוּלָם: adv.: **on the other hand, however,** oft. *wᵉ'ûlām* Gn 28_{19}.

II אוּלָם: n. pers.

III אוּלָם: ↗ אֵילָם.

אִוֶּלֶת: sf. אִוַּלְתִּי: (impious) **foolishness,** Ps 38_6, Pr 5-27 22 ×.

אוֹמָר: n. pers.

אָוֶן (80×), intentionally distinguished from I אוֹן: sf. אוֹנָם: — 1. **harm, trouble** (still magical?), Is 58_9; — 2. (coming) **harm, trouble** Ps 41_7; — 3. **misdeed, injustice** Ps 66_{18}: *'îš 'āwen* Is 55_7; — 4. **deceit, nothing** Ho 12_{12} (|| *šāw'*); — 5. **false, idolatrous cult** 1S 15_{23}.

I **און**: ↗ אָוֶן: אֹ(ו)נָם: — 1. **generative power** Gn 49_3; — 2. **physical strength** Ho 12_4; — 3. **riches** Ho 12_9.

II **און**: n. pers., = I.

III **און**: n. loc., **On, Heliopolis,** in Egypt.

אונו, אנו: n. loc.

***אוני**: pl. אֹ(ו)נִים: lamentation for the dead, **mourning** Gn 35_{18}.

אוניות: 2C 8_{18} Kt: ↗ אֳנִיָּה.

אונים: ↗ אָוֶן, I און & אֹנֶה.

אונם: n. pers.

אונן: n. pers. Gn $38_{4\cdot8f}$.

אופז: n. unknown land.

I **אופיר, אפיר** 1K 10_{11}, **אופר** Gn 10_{29}: n. land; loc. **אוֹפִירָה**: — 1. **Ophir,** land of gold 1K $9_{26\cdot28}$; — 2. > **gold of Ophir** Jb 22_{24}.

II **אופיר**: n. pers., = I; 1C 1_{23}. †

אופן, cs. = ; pl. אוֹפַנִּים, cs. אוֹפַנֵּי; m. (f. in Ez 1_{16ff}); — **wheel** (of vehicle) Ex 14_{25}.

אוץ: **qal**: pf. אָץ, אַצְתִּי, pt. אָץ, אָצִים: — 1. **urge** (intrans.) Ex 5_{13}; — 2. **be in a hurry** to Jos 10_{13}; — 3. with *le* **be too narrow** for Jos 17_{15}.

hif.: impf. יָאִיצוּ: w. *be* **urge** (trans.) upon s. one Gn 19_{15}; w. *le* **insist** upon s.thg Is 22_4.

אוצר (80×): cs. אוֹצַר, sf. אוֹצָרוֹ; pl. **אוֹצָרוֹת**: — 1. a) pl. **supplies** Ne 12_{44}; **storehouses** Ne 13_{12f}; b) **treasure**, esp. of palace or temple Je 15_{13}, 1K 7_{51}; — 2. cosmic: treasure of Y. in heaven Dt 28_{12}, storehouses of wind Je 10_{13}.

אור: **qal**: pf. א׳, אֹרוּ; impf. וַיֵּאֹר, וַתָּאֹרְנָה Qr 1S 14_{27}; impv. אוֹרִי; inf. אוֹר; pt. אוֹר: — 1. **become day** Gn 44_3; — 2. **be(come) bright**, eyes 1S 14_{27}, Zion Is 60_1.

nif.: impf. וַיֵּאֹר ↗ qal; inf. לֵאוֹר < *לְהֵאוֹר Jb 33_{30} be illumined (?, cj. otherw.); pt. נָאוֹר Ps 76_5 rd נוֹרָא. †

hif.: pf. הֵאִיר; impf. יָאִיר, יָאֵר, וַיָּאֶר; impv. הָאֵר, הָאִירָה; inf. הָאִיר; pt. מֵאִיר, מְאִירַת, מְאִירֵי, מְאִירוֹת: — 1. give light, **shine** Gn 1_{15}; — 2. illumine, **brighten** Ps 77_{19}; — 3. **let be bright** (subj. God, obj. his face) Nu 6_{25}; — 4. **make bright**: eyes Ps 13_4; — 5. **kindle** Is 27_{11}.

אור (ca. 120×): sf. אוֹרוֹ; pl. אוֹרִים: — 1. brightness, **light of day** Gn 1_{3f}; — 2. **light** (from a body: sun, lightning, fire) Ps 78_{14}; — 3. **daybreak** (in statements of time): *ʿad-hāʾôr* Ju 19_{26}; — 4. metaph.: *rāʾâ ʾôr* = **live**; God is the *ʾôr* of the faithful Mi 7_8.

I **אור**: pl. אֻרִים: — 1. **light** (of fire) Is 50_{11}, > **fire** Is 31_9; — 2. region of light, **east** Is 24_{15}.

(II *אור) **אורים**: *šāʾal hāʾûrîm* Nu 27_{21}, *ʿānâ bāʾûrîm* 1S 28_6; **Urim**, usu. w. Thummim Ex 28_{30} means of gaining oracle by lot.

III **אור**: n. loc.: אוּר כַּשְׂדִּים Gn $11_{28\cdot31}$ Ur.

IV **אור**: n. pers. 1C 11_{35}. †

I **אורה**: f. of אוֹר: pl. אוֹרֹת: — 1. **light** Ps 139_{12}; — 2. metaph. **radiant joy** Est 8_{16}.

II ***אורה**: I אוֹרָה: pl. אֹרֹת: **mallow** (Malva rotundifolia), 'light-plant', very sensitive to light 2K 4_{39}. †

אֻורוֹת: 2C 32_{28}, rd אֻרָוֹת, ↗ אֻרְוָה **stall**.

אורי: n. pers.

אוריאל: n. pers.

אוריה: n. pers., husband of בַּת־שֶׁבַע 2S 11_{3ff}.

אוריהו: n. pers., prophet Je 26_{20ff}.

אֲוַרְנָא: n. pers; הָא׳ 2S 24_{16} Kt, ↗ אֲרַוְנָא.

אות: **nif.**: impf. יֵאוֹתוּ, נֵאוֹת(ה) consent, **agree to** Gn $34_{15\cdot22f}$ 2K 12_9. †

I **אות** (80×), אֹת; pl. אֹתֹ(ו)ת, sf. אֹתֹ(ו)תָיו; masc., rarely fem. (e.g. Gn $9_{12\cdot17}$): **sign**: a) (distinguishing) **mark** Gn 4_{15}; b) (battle) **banner** ? Nu 2_2; c) sign to bring to mind (covenant) obligation Gn 9_{12}; d) memorial Ex 13_9; e) sign guaranteeing afterwards the dependability of assertion Ex 3_{12}; f) miraculous sign, showing s.one's power Ex 4_8; g) omen, announcing s.thg to come Gn 1_{14}; h) warning, deterring example Nu 17_3.

II אוֹת־ & אֹת־ w. suffixes, ↗ I אֵת.

אָז (130×) — 1. **then** (in past) :: *'attâ* Jos 14_{11}; w. impf. Ex 15_1; w. pf. Gn 4_{26}; — 2. styl. device for emphasized portion of sentence (to be carefully distinguished from 1.) Jos 22_{31}; — 3. **then** (in fut.): a) after protasis: *'im...'āz* **if...then** Is 58_{13f}, after inf.-construction Ex 12_{44}, *lûlê...kî 'āz* **if not...then** 2S 2_{27}; b) the condition to be restored 2K 13_{19}; — 4. w. *min* (↗ *min*), mostly *mē'āz*: a) adv. before now, **earlier** 2S 15_{34}, long since Is 44_8; b) prep. **since** Ru 2_7; c) conj. **since** Gn 39_5.

אֶזְבָּי: n. pers.

אֵזוֹב & אֵזֹב: trad. **hyssop**, but not *Hyssopus officinalis*, which is foreign to Palestine; probably *Origanum Maru*: growing on walls, used as sprinkling brush Ex 12_{22}.

אֵזוֹר: the innermost piece of clothing, **waistcloth** 2K 1_8.

אֲזַי: *lûlê... 'ᵃzay* **if not ... then** (↗ אָז 3) Ps 124_{3-5}. †

אַזְכָּרָה: the portion of the meal-offering which is burned Lv 2_2; suggested meanings: reminiscence; summons; invocation; sign-offering.

אָזַל: **qal**: pf. א׳, אָזְלַת Dt 32_{36}; pt. אֹזֵל: **go away, disappear** 1S 9_7.

[**pual**: pt. מְאֻזָּל Ez 27_{19} rd מֵאוּזָל ↗ אוּזָל.]

*אֶזֶל: הָאֶבֶן הָאָזֶל 1S 20_{19} rd הַלָּ(א)ז, ↗ אַרְגָּב. †

I אזן: **hif.**: הֶאֱזִין, וְהַאֲזִין Ps 77_2; impf. יַאֲזִין, 1 sg. אָזִין (< אַאֲזִין) Jb 32_{11}; impv. הַאֲזִינָה; pt. מֵזִין (< מַאֲזִין) Pr 17_4: — 1. abs. use the ear, **listen** Dt 32_1; — 2. **listen to** s. one: *'el* Dt 1_{45}, also *le*, *'ad*; — 3. **listen to** s. thg, w. acc. Gn 4_{23}, also *le*, *'el*, *'al*.

II אזן: **piel**: pf. אִזֵּן: **weigh, consider carefully** Ec 12_9. †

אֹזֶן (188×): cs. = ; sf. אָזְנְךָ; du. אָזְנַיִם; cs. אָזְנֵי; f.: **ear**: of man Gn 35_4, of dog Pr 26_{17}, of God Ps 10_{17}; = understanding: *gālâ 'ozen* **uncover ear** = **reveal** 1S 9_{15}.

*אָזֵן: pl. sf. אֲזֵנֶךָ, some mss. אֲזֵנֶיךָ: 'a tent-peg at/in your 'א': uncertain; **equipment**(?) Dt 23_{14}.

אֹזֶן שֶׁאֱרָה: n. loc.

אַזְנוֹת תָּבוֹר: n. loc.

אָזְנִי: n. pers.

אֲזַנְיָה: n. pers.

אֲזִקִּים: pl. tech. term, sg. *אָזֵק; Qr הָאזִקִּים, בָּא׳; Kt *הָאֲזִקִּים, בָּאָ׳: **handcuffs** Je $40_{1.4}$. †

אזר: **qal**: pf. אָזְרוּ; impf. תֶּאְזוֹר, יַאַזְרֵנִי; impv. אֱזָר־; pt. pass. אָזוּר; — 1. **put on the** *'ēzôr* (wh. see), **gird**: for battle Je 1_{17}, pt. pass. of Elijah's costume 2K 1_8; — 2. metaph. with strength 1S 2_4; — 3. **bind up** Jb 30_{18}.

nif.: pt. נֶאְזָר: **girded** Ps 65_7. †

piel: impf. וַתְּאַזְּרֵנִי Ps 30_{12} > וַתַּזְרֵנִי 2S 22_{40}, אֲאַזֶּרְךָ; pt. הַמְאַזְּרֵנִי Ps 18_{33}: w. acc.: **clasp s. one fast, close** Is 45_5, w. 2 acc. clasp s.one w. s.thg Ps 18_{33}; metaph. Ps 30_{12}.

hitp.: pf. הִתְאַזָּר; impv. הִתְאַזְּרוּ: **gird onesf. w. the** *'ēzôr* Is 8_9; be attired with Ps 93_1. †

אֶזְרוֹעַ: = זְרוֹעַ; sf. אֶזְרֹעִי; poet.?: **arm** Je 32_{21} Jb 31_{22}. †

אֶזְרָח: cs. אֶזְרַח: one born in the land, orig. opp. to *gēr* (wh. see), later coinciding?, Ex 12_{19}; > *hā'ezrāḥ*, **native, citizen** with full rights Ex 12_{49}.

אֶזְרָחִי: n. gent.

I אָח: interj. of pain or grief: **ah!** Ez 21_{20}.

II אָח (630×): cs. אֲחִי, sf. אָחִי, אָחִיהוּ (6×) > אָחִיו (c. 80×), אָחִיהָ, אָחִינוּ, אֲחִיהֶם; pl. אַחִים; cs. אֲחֵי; sf. אַחַי, אֶחָי, אָחָיו, אַחֶיךָ, אֲחֵיכֶם, אַחֵינוּ: **brother**: — 1. full brother (same father & mother) Gn 4_8; — 2. half-brother (different mothers) Gn 37_4; — 3. **blood relative** Gn 9_{25}, = cousin (male) 29_{15}; — 4. (without blood relationship) **fellow** 2S 1_{26}; — 5. **fellow-tribesman** Gn 31_{32};

— 6. **fellow-countryman** Ex 2_{11}; — 7. in general, of belonging Jb 30_{29}; in reciprocal expr.: *'îš le'āḥîw* **each to the other** Gn 26_{31} & the like; — 8. term of politeness to stranger Gn 29_{4}; — 9. in public, official dealings 1K 9_{13}; — 10. in song of mourning, *hôy 'āḥî* Je 22_{18}.

***אַח**: הָאָח; f.: metal or clay **brazier** Je $36_{22,23}$. †

***אֹחַ**: pl. **אֹחִים**: **howling wild creature,** usually: eagle-owl, **Bubo bubo**; but oth. prp.: laughing hyena; Is 13_{21}. †

אַחְאָב: n. pers., **Ahab**, King of N. Isr. 1K 16_{28ff}.

אֶחָב: n. pers., ↗ אַחְאָב.

אַחְבָּן: n. pers.

[**אחד**: **hitp.** impv. f. הִתְאַחֲדִי: rd. (חדד) הִתְחַדִּי Ez 21_{21}. †]

אֶחָד (960×): abs. **אֶחָד** & **אַחַד** (Gn 48_{22} + 5×), cs. **אַחַד, חַד** Ez 33_{30}; pl. **אֲחָדִים**; f. **אַחַת** abs. & cs., **אֶחָת** Gn 11_{1}, 2S 23_{8} Qr: — 1. number, **one**: a) *māqôm 'eḥād* **one** (single) **place** Gn 1_{9}, *nefeš 'aḥat* **one soul** = a single person Lv 4_{27}, *mišpāṭ 'eḥād* Nu 15_{16} **one** (sort of) **justice,** *yhwh 'eḥād* Dt 6_{4} **is one Y.,** oth.: the one Y., Y. as one, Y. alone; b) part.: *'aḥad hā'ām* **one of the people** 1S 26_{15}, *'aḥîkem 'eḥād* **one of your brothers** Gn 42_{19}, *'aḥad mimmennû* **one of us** Gn 3_{22}; c) negating: *lō'...'eḥād* **no one** Ex 8_{27}, *'ên gam 'eḥād* **not even one** Ps 14_{3}; d) *qôl 'eḥād* **unanimously** Ex 24_{3}, *šekem 'eḥād* **shoulder to sh.** Zp 3_{9}, *'aḥat* (sc. *pa'am 'aḥat*) **once**: *'aḥat baššānâ* **once a year** Ex 30_{10}; *wayehî... 'eḥād* **became one, a unity** Ex 36_{13}; e) pl.: *yāmîm 'aḥādîm*, **a few days, awhile** Gn 27_{44}, *debārîm 'aḥādîm*, **the same** (one sort of) **words** Gn 11_{1}; — 2. *'eḥād* in series (one > first) *mizzeh 'eḥād ûmizzeh 'eḥād* **one here and one there** Ex 17_{12}, *'eḥād...we'eḥād... we'eḥād* **one ... another ... a third** 1S 10_{3}; — 3. indef. article, **a(n)**: *'îš 'eḥād* 1S 1_{1}, *nābî' 'eḥād* 1K 13_{11}; — 4. ordinal **first**: *yôm 'eḥād* Gn 1_{5} (:: *yôm šēnî* 1_{8}); in dates *be'eḥād laḥōdeš* **on the first (day) of the month** Gn 8_{5}; — 5. distributive: *'eḥād laššēbeṭ* **one for each tribe** Dt 1_{23}.

אָחוּ: **reeds**, marsh-plant Jb 8_{11}, reed-land Gn $41_{2\cdot18}$. †

אֵחוּד: n. pers.

I **אַחֲוָה**: **brotherhood** Zc 11_{14}. †

II ***אַחֲוָה**: sf. אַחֲוָתִי: **declaration** Jb 13_{17}. †

***אָחוּז**: sbst. & pt.: אֲחוּזִים: architectural term, **built in** :: oth.: sbst. **support, springer** Ez $41_{a.b}$. †

אֲחוֹחַ: n. pers.

אֲחוֹחִי & **אֲחֹחִי**: n. gent.

אֲחוּמַי: n. pers.

אָחוֹר: pl. cs. אֲחֹרֵי, sf. אֲחֹרַי, אֲחֹרֵיהֶן: — 1. pl. **back**, of dwelling Ex 26_{12}, of God Ex 33_{23}; — 2. sg. directional, **behind** adv. *pānîm we'āḥôr* **before and behind** Ez 2_{10}, *nāfal 'āḥôr* **fall backward** Gn 49_{17}; — 3. metaph. adv. *hēšîb...āḥôr* **turn** (wise men) **back** Is 44_{25}; — 4. sg. **west**: *mē'āḥôr* **from the west** Is 9_{11}; — 5. temporal: *le'āḥôr* **for the future** Is 42_{23}, *be'āḥôr* **at last** Pr 29_{11}.

אָחוֹת: f. of אָח: cs. אֲח(וֹ)ת, sf. אֲח(וֹ)תוֹ, אֲחֹתוֹ Nu 6_{7}; pl. *אָחוֹת & *אֲחָיוֹת, sf. אֲחוֹתַי, אֲחוֹתֵךְ :: אַחְיֹתָיו Jb 42_{11} אַחְיֹתֵיהֶם; — 1. **sister** (same father & mother) Gn 4_{22}; half-sister (common father) Gn 20_{12}, (common father or mother) Lv 18_{9}; — 2. physical relative Gn 24_{60}; metaph., Isr., sister of Judah Je 3_{7}; — 3. אֲחֹתִי to **beloved** SS 4_{9}, in dirge, of man Je 22_{18}; — 4. for spatial opposites, w. *'el*, **to each other** Ex 26_{3}.

I **אָחַז**: **qal**: pf. א׳, אֲחָזַנִי; impf. a) יֶאֱחֹז, b) יֹאחֵז, וַיֹּאחֶז > וַתֹּחֶז 2S 20_{9}, וָאֹחֶז, sf. יֹאחֲזֵמוֹ; impv. אֱחֹז, אֶחֱזִי, אֶחֱזוּ, אֶחֱזוּ Ne 7_{3}; inf. אֲחֹז, לֶאֱחֹז; pt. אֹחֵז, אֹחֶזֶת, pass. אָחוּז, אָחֻז, pl. אֲחֻזִים, אֲחֻזֵי, אֲחֻזוֹת: **lay hold of, seize, hold fast,** w. *be* (s.one, s.thg) Gn 25_{26}; w. acc. (s.one, s.thg) Ex 15_{14f};

'āḥūz min grasped out = **drawn out** (by lot) Nu 31$_{30}$.

nif.: pf. נֶאֱחַז, נֹאחֲזוּ Nu 32$_{30}$ Jos 22$_{9}$; impf. וַיֵּאָחֲזוּ; impv. הֵאָחֲזוּ; pt. נֶאֱחָז, נֶאֱחָזִים: **be seized, held fast** Gn 22$_{13}$; *ne'ᵉḥaz bā'āreṣ* **be settled in the land** Gn 34$_{10}$, *ne'ᵉḥaz* alone Jos 22$_{19}$.

[**hof.**: pt. מָאֳחָזִים 2C 9$_{18}$: ↗ II pu.]

II **אחז**: **qal**: impf. וַיֶּאֱחֹז: **cover** 1K 6$_{10}$. †

piel: pt. מְאַחֵז: **cover** Jb 26$_{9}$. †

pual: pt. מְאֻחָזִים: 2C 9$_{18}$ (Oriental ms.) (MT ↗ I hof.): **covered** (otherw.: 1K 10$_{19}$). †

אָחָז: n. pers.

אֲחֻזָּה: cs. אֲחֻזַּת, sf. אֲחֻזָּתְךָ: — 1. **landed property** Gn 47$_{11}$, *'ᵃḥuzzat qeber* **property for a grave-site** Gn 23$_{20}$, *'îr 'ᵃḥuzzātô* **city where he owns land** Lv 25$_{33}$; — 2. **property** esp. (since Ez) slaves Lv 25$_{45f}$, Y. the possession of the priests Ez 44$_{28b}$.

אַחְזַי: n. pers.

אֲחַזְיָה: n. pers.

אֲחַזְיָהוּ: n. pers., > אֲחַזְיָה, King of N. Isr. 1K 22$_{40ff}$, of Judah 2K 8$_{24ff}$.

אֲחֻזָּם: n. pers.

אֲחֻזַּת: n. pers.

אֲחֹחִי, ↗ אֲחוֹחִי.

אֵחִי: n. pers.

אֲחִיאָם: n. pers.

אֲחִיָּה: n. pers.

אֲחִיָּהוּ: n. pers., > אֲחִיָּה.

אֲחִיהוּד: n. pers.

אַחְיוֹ: n. pers.

אֲחִיחֻד: n. pers.

אֲחִיטוּב: n. pers.

אֲחִילוּד: n. pers.

אֲחִימוֹת: n. pers.

אֲחִימֶלֶךְ: n. pers.

אֲחִימַן, אֲחִימָן: n. pers.

אֲחִימַעַץ, אֲחִימָּעַץ: n. pers.

אַחְיָן: n. pers.

אֲחִינָדָב: n. pers.

אֲחִינֹעַם: n. pers.

אֲחִיסָמָךְ: n. pers.

אֲחִיעֶזֶר: n. pers.

אֲחִיקָם: n. pers.

אֲחִירָם: n. pers.

אֲחִירָמִי: n. gent.

אֲחִירַע: n. pers.

אֲחִישָׁחַר: n. pers.

אֲחִישָׁר: n. pers.

אֲחִיתֹפֶל: n. pers.

אַחְלָב: n. loc.

אַחֲלַי: Ps 119$_{5}$ & אַחֲלֵי 2K 5$_{3}$: interj. (↗ I אָח) **O that!** †

אַחְלַי: n. pers.

אַחְלָמָה: red or brown **jasper**, but trad. amethyst; on high-priest's breastplate Ex 28$_{19}$ 39$_{12}$. †

אֲחַסְבַּי: n. pers.

אחר: **qal**: impf. 1 sg. וָאֵחַר (< *וָאֶאֱחַר) Gn 32$_{5}$, וַיֵּיחַר (= *ויאחר) 2S 20$_{5}$ Kt, Qr ↗ hif.: **delay**. †

piel: pf. אֵחַר, אֵחֲרוּ; impf. תְּאַחֵר, תְּאַחַר; pt. מְאַחֲרִים: — 1. **delay** s.one Gn 24$_{56}$; — 2. hold (s.thg) back, **prove hesitant** Ex 22$_{28}$ (oth.: give to other gods); — 3. w. *'al* **delay (long)** in Pr 23$_{30}$; — 4. **defer, hesitate** (*lᵉ*: concerning) Ju 5$_{28}$.

hif.: וַיֵּיחֶר, Qr וַיּוֹחֶר (Aramaism; oth.: qal or Kt piel): w. *min*, **come too late** 2S 20$_{5}$ Qr. †

I **אַחֵר**: f. אַחֶרֶת, pl. אֲחֵרִים, אֲחֵרִין, אֲחֵרוֹת: — 1. **other** Ne 7$_{34}$; — 2. **following**, *zera' 'aḥēr* **further offspring** Gn 4$_{25}$, *yāmîm 'ᵃḥērîm* **further days** Gn 8$_{10.12}$, *baššānâ hā'aḥeret* **in the following year**; — 3. **different**: *lᵉ'îš 'aḥēr* **be transformed** 1S 10$_{9}$, *lāšôn 'aḥeret* **a foreign language** Is 28$_{11}$; — 4. *'ēl 'āḥer* **another god** Ex 34$_{14}$, pl. *'ᵉlōhîm 'ᵃḥērîm* **other gods** (esp. Dt 19×, Je 18×) Dt 5$_{7}$.

II **אַחֵר**: n. pers.

אַחַר: accent אַחַר כֵּן Lv 14$_{36}$ Dt 21$_{13}$ 1S 10$_{5}$ †, אַחַר זֶה 2C 32$_{9}$, cs. pl. אַחֲרֵי, sf. אַחֲרָיו &c.:

I. sg.: — 1. adv. a) **behind him/it** &c. Gn 22_{13}; b) **afterwards** Gn 18_5; — 2. prep. a) local: α) **behind** Gn 37_{17}, *dāraš 'aḥar* **pursue a thing** Jb 39_8; β) behind > **with** *he'ābîm 'aḥar haggešem* Ec 12_2, ↗ II 2g; b) temporal **after** α) prep. w. inf. *'aḥar šallaḥ* Je 40_1; β) conj. w. finite vb. *'aḥar dibber* Jb 42_7.

II. אַחֲרֵי: — 1. subst.: (rear) **end** *be'aḥarê haḥanît* 2S 2_{23} (?); **back**: of God Gn 16_{13}; — 2. prep. **behind**: a) *pānâ 'aḥarāyw* **turn around** 2S 2_{20}; b) *mē'aḥarêkā* (from) behind you Is 30_{21}; c) behind > **to the west** (↗ אָחוֹר 4) *mē'aḥarêhā* to the west of it (= city) Jos 8_2; d) *hālak 'aḥarê* **walk (together) with** (image: one behind the other) Ho 2_7; e) with *nā'al* (&c.) *delet* **lock the door** after her 2S 13_{17}; *hāyâ 'aḥerê* **attach oneself to** Ex 23_2; f) *sûr aḥarê* **leave off from** 2S 2_{21}; g) behind > **with, at** 1K 20_{15}; — 3. temporal, **after** *zera'*: *'aḥarê* **descendant(s) after** Gn 17_8, *'aḥarāyw* **after his death** Jb 21_{21}; *'aḥarê-zō't* afterwards Jb 42_{16}, *'aḥarê-kēn* Gn 6_4; — 4. conj. **after**, a) w. inf. 2S 17_{21}, b) w. finite vb. 1S 5_9; c) *'aḥarê-'ašer* Dt 24_4.

אַחֲרוֹן (50 ×): אַחֲרֹ(וֹ)נָה, אַחֲרֹ(וֹ)נִים: adj. **(existing) behind**: 1. local: a) in 2nd place Gn 33_2; b) **western**, *hayyām hā'aḥarôn* Dt 11_{24}; — 2. temporal: a) **later** Ex 4_8; b) **future** Dt 29_{21} (generation), Ru 3_{10} (kindness); c) **last** 2S 19_{12}f; (words) 2S 23_1 (God, first & l.) Is 44_6; d) adv. *lā'aḥarōnâ* **last** Nu 2_{31}, *bā'aḥarōnâ* **finally** 2S 2_{26}, **later** 1K 17_{13}.

[**אַחְרַח**: n. pers. 1C 8_1: rd. אֲחִירָם Nu 26_{38}. †]

אֲחַרְחֵל: n. pers.

אַחֲרַי: ?, usu. **afterward**, ? rd. אַחֲרָיו & transp. after לָשׁוֹן.

אַחֲרֵיכֵן Esr 3_5 & 1C 20_4 ↗ אחר II 3.

אַחֲרִית: **end, outcome**: — 1. spatial: **hind-part** (cows), Am 4_2, *'aḥarît yām* **farthest sea** Ps 139_9; — 2. temporal: a) *'aḥarît šānâ* **end of the year** Dt 11_{12}, *be'aḥarît hayyāmîm* Gn 49_1; b) end (= death) of s.one Nu 23_{10}; **outcome** of a matter Is 41_{22}; c) **posterity** α) **remnant** Am 9_1; β) **future** (↗ 2a) Is 46_{10}; γ) adv. **at last, finally** (w. or w/o prep.) Dt 8_{16}; — 3. **descendants** (no temporal indication) Ps 37_{37}f; — 4. last = **least** (people) Je 50_{12}.

אֲחֹרַנִּית: (go/fall/turn) **backwards** Gn 9_{23}.

*__אֲחַשְׁדַּרְפַּן__: אֲחַשְׁדַּרְפְּנִים/פְּנֵי: **satrap**, governor in Persian empire Est 3_{12}.

אֲחַשְׁוֵרוֹשׁ, Est 10_1 Kt אחשרש, Qr ־וֵרֹשׁ: n. pers., **Xerxes I.**

אֲחַשְׁתָּרִי: n. pers.

*__אֲחַשְׁתְּרָן__: רֹכְבֵי הָרֶכֶשׁ הָאֲחַשְׁתְּרָנִים Est $8_{10.14}$: sovereign, **royal**. †

I **אַט**: אִטִּי: **depressed mood, mildness**: — 1. *le'ittî* **slowly** Gn 33_{14} (↗ *le* 15); — 2. *le'at* **gently**: (treat s.one) 2S 18_5; — 3. **depressed** (go about) 1K 21_{27}.

II **אַט**, אַט: ↗ נטה hif.

אָטָד: **boxthorn** (*Lycium europaeum*) Ju 9_{14}f.

אֵטוּן: cs. = : **linen** (of Egypt) Pr 7_{16}. †

אִטִּים: (taken as pl.): **ghost** (of a dead person) Is 19_3. †

אטם: **qal**: impf. יַאְטֵם Ps 58_5 (falsely vocal. as hif.); pt. אֹטֵם, pass. אֲטֻמִים, אֲטֻמוֹת: — 1. **stop** (one's ear) Is 33_{15}, **close** (one's lips) Pr 17_{28}; — 2. unknown tech. architectural term, **closed, latticed** (?) (windows), oth.: **framed** 1K 6_4.

אטר: **qal**: impf. תֶּאְטַר: (following the context) **close** (mouth) Ps 69_{16}. †

אָטֵר: n. pers.

אִטֵּר: אִטֵּר יַד(־)יְמִינוֹ hindered on the right = **left-handed** Ju 3_{15} 20_{16}. †

אֵי: interr. word: sf. (oth. refer to אַיֵּה) אַיּוֹ, אַיָּם, Je 37_{19} אַיֵּו = Qr אַיֵּה, Kt אַיּוֹ & אַיֵּ; אַיֶּכָּה: — 1. **where?** *'ayyekkâ* **where are you?** Gn 3_9; — 2. strengthened w. demonstr. pron.: a) *'ēy(-)zeh* **where (here)?** 1K 13_{12}, more specific: *'ēy zeh hadderek* **which way**

then? 2C 18_{23}; b) *'ēy(-)mizzeh* **from where?** Gn 16_8; c) *'ēy lāzō't* **to what purpose? why?** Je 5_7; d) in indir. qn.: *'ēy mizzeh* Ju 13_6, *'ēy zeh* Ec 11_6.

I **אִי**: pl. אִיִּים, Ez 26_{18} אִיִּן, cs. אִיֵּי: — 1. **coast, island** Is 20_6, *yōšᵉbê 'î* = **Phoenicians** Is $23_{2.6}$; in var. cs. phrases, *'iyyê haggôyim* Gn 10_5; — 2. **(far) islands, shores** Is 40_{15}: the islands & coasts of the Mediterranean are for the OT the extremes of the western world.

II ***אִי**: pl. אִיִּים: trad. **jackal**; oth.: **goblin**, sg. *אִיִּי, fm. I אִי, as inhabitant of the אִיִּים Is 13_{22} 34_{14} Je 50_{39}. †

III **אִי**: — 1. **not**, *'î-nāqî* **not guiltless** Jb 22_{30}; — 2. **where?** (?) in n. pers.

IV **אִי**: **woe**: *'î-lāk* Ec 10_{16}.

איב: **qal**: pf. וְאָיַבְתִּי: **be an enemy to** Ex 23_{22}. †

אֹ(וֹ)יֵב: pt. subst. fm. prec.: sf. אֹיִבְךָ, אֹיְבִי (3× אֹיְבֶיךָ Qr, Kt pl.), אֹיִבֶךָ; pl. אֹ(וֹ)יְבִים, cs. אֹיְבֵי, sf. אֹ(וֹ)יְבַי, &c.; f. w. sf. אֹיַבְתִּי Mi $7_{8.10}$; governing acc. אֹיֵב אֶת־ 1S 18_{29}: **enemy**; personal Ex 23_4, national Gn 22_{17}, of God Ps 8_3; God as enemy of the people Is 63_{10}.

אֵיבָה: enmity Gn 3_{15}, hostile intention Nu 35_{21f}.

אֵיד: sf. אֵידִי, אֵידְךָ: (final) **disaster** Jb 18_{12}; *yôm 'ēd* Dt 32_{35}, *'ēd mô'āb* Je 48_{16}.

I **אַיָּה**: **black kite**, *Milvus migrans*; oth.: **falcon**: Dt 14_{13}.

II **אַיָּה**: n. pers.

אַיֵּה (45×): interr. wd.: Je 37_{19} Qr אַיֵּה, Kt אַיּוֹ & אַיֵּו; sf.-forms, F אַי: **where?** (never before vb., alw. in dir. qn.) Gn 18_9; *'ayyēh 'ēfô(')* **where then?** Ju 9_{38}; qn. about God 2K 2_{14}, about God's word Je 17_{15}.

אִיּוֹב: n. pers.

אִיזֶבֶל, אִיזָבֶל: n. pers.

אֵיךְ (57×): interr. wd.: **how?** — 1. dir. qn. 1K 12_6; — 2. indir. qn. Ru 3_{18}; — 3. expr. of doubt: how should we? Gn 44_8; — 4. expr. of reproach, how can you? Ju 16_{15}; — 5. expr. of mourning (F אֵיכָה 1e) 2S 1_{19}; — 6. expr. of assertion Je 3_{19}.

אִיכָבוֹד, אִי־כָבוֹד: n. pers.

אֵיכָה: interr. wd.: — 1. **how? in what way?** a) Dt 12_{30}, indir. Ju 20_3; b) = **what?** 2K 6_{15}; c) rhetorical Dt 1_{12}; d) expr. of reproach Je 8_8; e) **mourning**, standard opening word of dirge Is 1_{21}; — 2. **where?**, F אֵיכֹה Na 3_{17}.

אֵיכֹה: interr. wd.: **where** 2K 6_{13}. †

אֵיכָכָה SS 5_3 & אֵיכָכָה Est 8_6: interr. wd.: **how?**. †

I **אַיִל, אֵיל**; cs. אֵיל, Ez 31_{11} (some mss.) & 40_{48} אֵל; pl. אֵילִים, אֵלִים Jb 41_{17}, אֵלִים (oth.: gods; cf. Ps 29_1 89_7 אֵילִים for 'gods'), cs. אֵילֵי, אֵלֵי Ez 32_{21}: — 1. **ram** Gn 32_{15}; — 2. metaph. **man of power**, *'ēlê mô'āb* Ex 15_{15}.

II ***אַיִל**: pl. אֵילִים Is 1_{29} אֵלִים 57_5, cs. אֵלֵי/אֵילֵי 61_3: **mighty tree** (not a specific kind of tree), cf. I אֵלָה, Is 1_{29}; — metaph. *'ēlê haṣṣedeq* Is 61_3.

III **אַיִל**: = II ?: cs. אֵיל, אֵל Ez 40_{48}; pl. אֵלִים, sf. אֵילָיו Qr, Kt א(י)לו Ez 40_{9-37}, ? אֵלֵיהֶמָּה: archit. tech. term, **gate-post, door-post** 1K 6_{31} (oth. otherw.).

אֱיָל: **strength** Ps 88_5. †

אַיָּל: pl. אַיָּלִים: **fallow deer**, *Cervus capreolus* 1K 5_3.

אַיָּלָה & **אַיֶּלֶת** (1× abs., 2× cs.): f. of אַיָּל: pl. אַיָּלוֹת, cs. אַיְלוֹת: **doe of a fallow deer** Gn 49_{21}.

אִילוֹ, many mss. אִי לוֹ: F IV אִי: **woe to him** (oth.: אִלּוּ **if**) Ec 4_{10}. †

אַיָּלוֹן: n. loc.

I **אֵילוֹן**: n. pers.

II **אֵילוֹן**: n. loc.

אֵילוֹת: 2K 16_6 &c. F אֵילַת.

***אֱיָלוּת**: sf. אֱיָלוּתִי: **strength** Ps 22_{20}. †

***אֵילָם**: spelling varies, אוּלָם 1K 6_3 (20×, also cs.), אֻלָם 1K 7_7 (12×, mostly cs.,

Jb 17_{10} some mss. אֻלָּם), Qr אֵ(י)לַמָּו, Kt אֵ(י)לַמּוֹ Ez 40_{21} (+ 14 ×); pl. אֵלַמּוֹת & Qr אֵלַמָּו & אֵלַמֵּי Ez 41_{15}: tech. archit. term, **vestibule**: 1. of the palace, 1K 7_{6-8}; — 2. of the temple 1K $7_{12\cdot21}$.

אֵילִם: n. loc., pl. of II אַיִל; loc. אֵילִמָה.

אֵיל פָּארָן: n. loc.

אֵילַת: n. loc.

אֵילֶת: *F* אַיָּלָה.

אָיֹם: f. אֲיֻמָּה: **fear-inspiring** Hb 1_7; SS $6_{4\cdot10}$. †

אֵימָה: cs. אֵימַת, strengthened אֵימָתָה Ex 15_{16}, sf. אֵ(י)מָתִי; pl. אֵימוֹת, אֵ(י)מִים, sf. אֵמֶיךָ: **terror** Gn 15_{12}; *'ēmātî* **terror of me** &c. Ex 23_{27}; pl. **horrors** Ps 88_{16}.

אֵ(י)מִים: n. gent.

I **אַיִן**: 1) אָיִן, cs. אֵין, sf. אֵינְךָ, אֵינֵךְ, אֵינְכֶם, אֵינָם; 2) *'ên* + *an* (?): אֵינֶנִּי, אֵינֶנּוּ, אֵינֶנָּה; 3) sf. 3. pl. אֵינֵמוֹ; 4) late, w. pron. abs. אֵין אֲנַחְנוּ, אֵין אֲנִי Ne 4_{17} †; — A. abs. אַיִן: **absence** (:: יֵשׁ), 1. a) *wā'ayin* **and they were not there** 1S 9_4, *'im 'ayin* **or is he not there?** Ex 17_7, *'ayin* l^e (w. inf.) **is not there to** Gn 2_5; b) absence > **nothing**: k^e*'ayin* **like nothing** Is 40_{17}; — B. cs. *'ên* not > nothing, no, &c.: 1) simple gen. relation; a) *'ên 'îš 'immānû* **no man (= no one) is with us** Gn 31_{50}; *'ên* + l^e **not have** Gn 11_{30}, *'ên melek lānû* **we have no king** Ho 10_3; b) dependent gen. precedes: *ḥēmâ 'ên lî* **I have no hatred** Is 27_4; c) l^e lacking: w^e*'ên kōl* **and (he) has nothing** Pr 13_7; d) gen. lacking: w^e*'ên lô* Dn 9_{26} **has nothing** = has no successor; e) gen. relation broken: *'ên bāhem kōaḥ* 1S 30_4; — 2. a) (w^e)*'ên* before gen. = **-less, without**: *'ên 'ônîm* **the powerless** Is 40_{29}; b) *mē'ên*: *mē'ên yôšēb* **without inhabitant** Is 5_9; l^e*'ên*: l^e*'ên* $š^e$*'ērît* **so that no remnant remains** Ezr 9_{14}; — 3. *'ên* becomes a simple neg., = *lō'* & *'al*: *'ên-yeš-* **it is not there** Ps 135_{17}; — 4. *'ên* + inf.: *'ên hābên* **without understanding** Ps 32_9; — 5. *'ên* + l^e + inf.: *'ên lābô'* **it was not permitted to enter** Est 4_2.

II **אַיִן**: alw. w. מִן: **from where?**: *mē'ayin 'attem* **where are you from** Gn 29_4; indir. qn. Jos 2_4; rhetorical 2K 6_{27}.

אִין: 1S 21_9: rd. אִי; oth.: אִין interr. †

אִיעֶזֶר: n. pers.

אִיעֶזְרִי: n. gent.

אֵיפָה, Lv 5_{11} 6_{13} **אֵפָה**: **ephah**, 1. **a grain measure**, = 1 fluid **bath** Ez 45_{11a}; = 1/10 *ḥōmer* Ez 45_{11b} = 10 *'ōmer* Ex 16_{36}, ca. 40 liters, Nu 5_{15}; *'êfâ* w^e*'êfâ* **two sorts of ephah** Dt 25_{14}; — 2. suitable receptacle, Zc 5_{6-10}.

אֵיפֹה: interr. wd., *'ê* + *pōh* **where... there**, therefore: **where?** 1. dir. qn. 1S 19_{22}; — 2. indir. qn. Gn 37_{16}.

I **אִישׁ** (2160×): cs. =, sf. אִישִׁי; later pl. אִישִׁים Is 53_3 Ps 141_4 Pr 8_4 †, otherw. אֲנָשִׁים, cs. אַנְשֵׁי, sf. אֲנָשָׁיו, אַנְשֵׁיכֶם: — 1. **man** (:: woman) Gn 2_{24}, also male of animals Gn 7_2, man as opp. to animals Ex 11_7; as opp. to God Gn 32_{29}; male child Gn 4_1; man as valiant 1S 4_9; — 2. **husband** Gn 3_6, metaph. as God of people Ho 2_{18}; — 3. to denote position: a) b^e*nê 'îš* **those of high rank** Ps 49_3; b) **ruler of lower rank,** *'îš ṭôb* 2S $10_{6\cdot8}$; — 4. **man** (as a human being), **person**: *'ammat 'îš* ordinary cubit Dt 3_{11}, b^e*nê 'îš* children of men (// b^e*nê 'ādām*) Ps 62_{10}, *'ereṣ lō'-'îš* land empty of men Jb 38_{26}; — 5. in expr. of station, work: a) appos.: *'îš nābî'* Ju 6_8; b) w. gen. *'îš hā'adāmâ* **farmer** Gn 9_{20}; *'îš* $'^e$*lōhîm* **man of God**: *'îš hā'*^{e}*lōhîm* only when the whole phrase is def., 1S 9_{7f} :: 9_1, no specific function, orig. possessor of a spirit; a) in context of prophets: Samuel 1S 9_{6-10}; b) in wider sense, Moses Dt 33_1, David Neh 12_{24}; — 6. pl.: people belonging to s.one, s.thg.: *'anšê habbayit* **servants**

Gn 39_{11}, *'anšê dāwîd* **men of D.** 1S 23_{3}; — 7. sg. or pl. denoting nationality &c., *'anšê nîn^{e}wēh* **men of N.** Jon 3_{5}, *'îš miṣrî* Ex 2_{11}; coll. *'îš y^{e}hûdâ* Is 5_{3}; — 8. *'îš* **someone, one** Gn 13_{16}, *'îš...lō'* Gn 23_{6}, *'îš... 'al* Ex 16_{19} **no one**; — 9. **each (one),** *'îš ḥ^{a}lōmô* Gn 40_{5}; — 10. in expr. of reciprocity: **each other,** *'îš 'āḥîw, 'îš rē'ēhû* Ex 32_{27}; — 11. **each one** (in his turn): *l^{e}'îš* Je 23_{36} (oth.: 9); *'îš 'îš* Lv 17_{13} & *'îš w^{e}'îš* Ps 87_{5} & *'îš wā'îš* Est 1_{8} every one (no matter who).

II אִישׁ Pr 18_{24}: ⇒ אִשׁ. †

אִישׁ־בֹּשֶׁת: n. pers., tendentious for אֶשְׁבַּעַל or cj. *יִשְׁבַּעַל.

אִישְׁהוֹד: n. pers.

אִישׁוֹן: **pupil** (of the eye): *'îšôn 'ayin* Dt 32_{10}.

אִישׁ(־)טוֹב: 2S $10_{6.8}$; trad. n. pers., but ⇒ III טוֹב: the people (אִישׁ 7) or the ruler (⇒ אִישׁ 3b) of *ṭôb*. †

אִישַׁי: n. pers.

אִיתוֹן: Qr Ez 40_{15}; unexplained. †

אִיתַי: n. pers.

אִיתִיאֵל: n. pers.

אִיתָמָר: n. pers.

I אֵיתָן: sf. אֵיתָנוֹ; pl. אֵתָנִים: — 1. **ever-flowing**, of a *naḥal* (**wady**) Dt 21_{4}; as subst. *nah^{a}rôt 'êtān* **ever-flowing streams** Ps 74_{15}; *yeraḥ hā'ētānîm*, 7th month, Sept./Oct., when only the permanent streams are still flowing, 1K 8_{2}; — 2. (metaph.) **constant, permanent**: *'êtānô* **normal position** (of sea) Ex 14_{27}, *gôy 'êtān* **enduring** (ancient) **nation** Je 5_{15}.

II אֵיתָן: n. pers.

אַךְ (150×): particle of assurance or emphasis, variously translated according to context; 1. emphatic, **surely, indeed,** *'ak melek yiśrā'ēl hû'* **it is surely the king of I., it can only be the k. of I.** 1K 22_{32}; *'ak hinnēh 'išt^{e}kā hî'* **so she is your wife!** Gn 26_{9}; — 2. restrictive, **only**: *'ak nô^{a}ḥ* **only Noah** Gn 7_{23}, *'ak š^{e}ma'* **only obey = just do as I say** Gn 27_{13}; — 3. contrastive, **however,** *'ak š^{e}ma'* **however, hear** = nevertheless, hear Je 34_{4}.

אַכַּד: n. loc.

אַכְזָב: **deceitful**, of a spring or brook dried up in summer Je 15_{18}; in wordplay w. n. loc. *'akzîb* Mi 1_{14}.

אַכְזִיב: n. loc.

אַכְזָר: **cruel** Dt 32_{33}.

אַכְזָרִי: **cruel** Je 6_{23}.

אַכְזְרִיּוּת: **cruelty** Pr 27_{4}. †

אֲכִילָה: **food** 1K 19_{8}. †

אָכִישׁ: n. pers.

אָכַל: **qal**: pf. א׳ sf. אֲכָלַתְּם, אֲכָלַנִי, אֲכָלוֹ, אֲכָלָהוּ; impf. וָאֹכַל, וַיֹּאכַל, יֹאכֵל, יֹאכַל, וְאֹכֵל, יוֹכְלוּ Ez 42_{5}, יֹאכְלוּ(ן), sf. תֹּאכְלֶנּוּ, Jb 20_{26} תְּאָכְלֵהוּ rd. תֹּאכְלֵהוּ, אֹכְלֵם; impv. אֱכָל־, אֱכוֹל, אִכְלָה, אִכְלוּ, אֶכְלוּ, sf. אִכְלֻהוּ; inf. אֲכָל־, בַּאֲכֹל, בֶּ/לֶאֱכֹל, מֵאֲכֹל, sf. אֲכָלְךָ, אָכְלוֹ (אָכְלָה 1S 1_{9} rd. אָכְלָם); pt. אֹ(ו)כֵל, אֹכֶלֶת, אֹכְלָת, אֹכְלָה, אֹכְלָיו, אֹכְלִים, אֹכֵלָה: — 1. **eat**, of man Gn 3_{6}, of animal Gn 40_{17}; *'ōkelet 'ādām* devourer of men Ez 36_{13}; *l^{e}* La 4_{5}; *b^{e}* Ex 12_{43}; *min* Gn 3_{3}; *'ākal leḥem* **eat a meal** Gn 37_{25}; — 2. **cultic**: *'ākal lifnê yhwh* = **offer sacrifice** Dt 12_{7}; *'ākal 'al-haddām* Lv 19_{26}, ⇒ *dām* 1; — 3. **metaph. consume,** of sword Dt 32_{42}, of fire Nu 16_{35}; 2 acc.: fire consumes the *'ōlâ* to ashes Lv 6_{3}; consume money Gn 31_{15}, people Ps 14_{4}; 'eat up space' = lay claim to space Ez 42_{5}; abs.: **have sensation of taste** Dt 4_{28}, **enjoy love** Pr 30_{20}.

nif.: pf. נֶאֱכַל; impf. יֵאָכֵל, יֵאָכְלוּ, יֵאָכֵלוּ, תֵּאָכַלְנָה; inf. הֵאָכֵל; pt. נֶאֱכֶלֶת: **be eaten** Gn 6_{21}; abs. **be edible** (permitted) Lv 11_{47}; *yē'ākēl l^{e}* **serves s.one as food** Ex 12_{16}; metaph. **be consumed** Je 30_{16}.

pual (qal pass.): pf. אֻכְּלוּ; impf. תְּאֻכְּלוּ;

pt. אֻכָּל: **be consumed, devoured** (by fire) Ex 3_{2}, (by sword) Is 1_{20}.

hif.: pf. וְהַאֲכַלְתִּי, הֶאֱכַלְתִּי, sf. הֶאֱכַלְתָּם, וְהַאֲכַלְתִּיךָ; impf. תַּאֲכִל, אוֹכִיל Ho 11_{4}, sf. יַאֲכִלְךָ, יַאֲכִלֵנוּ, וַיַּאֲכִילֵהוּ; impv. sf. הַאֲכִ(י)לֵהוּ, הַאֲכִ(י)לֵהוּ; pt. מַאֲכִיל, הַמַּאֲכִלְךָ Dt 8_{16}, מַאֲכֶלֶת: **feed** s.one 2C 28_{15}; 2 acc. feed s.one s.thg 1K 22_{27}; *min* (of s.thg) Ps 81_{17}.

אֹכֶל: sf. אָכְלְךָ, אָכְלוֹ, אָכְלְכֶם: **food**, for men Gn 14_{11}, for animals Ps 104_{21}; *ʿāśâ ʾokel* **produce food** Hb 3_{17}, *ʿēt ʾokel* **meal-time** Ru 2_{14}.

אָכֵל, some mss. אָכֻל: Pr 30_{1}; uncertain; trad. n. pers. or impf. of יָכֹל; prp. וָאֵכֶל (כלה) or וָאֻכַל (כול hif.). †

אָכְלָה: f. of אֹכֶל or inf.: **food**, only in JeEzP: *hāyâ leʾoklâ* **serve as food** Gn 1_{29f}.

I אָכֵן: exclamation to emphasize the unexpected: — 1. **truly** Gn 28_{16}; — 2. strongly contrastive, **nevertheless** Ps 66_{19}; 6× after *ʾāmartî*, Is 49_{4}.

II אָכֵן: **so that** 1K 11_{2}. †

אכף: **qal**: pf. 'א: **press hard** Pr 16_{26}. †

*אֶכֶף: sf. אַכְפִּי: Jb 33_{7}: **hand** (so LXX); oth.: **pressure, urgency.** †

אִכָּר: pl. אִכָּרִים, sf. אִכָּרֵיהֶם: **serf**: peasant, not owning land, belonging to landlord Is 61_{5}.

אַכְשָׁף: n. loc.

I אַל: neg. for request, prohibition: — 1. emphatic neg. w/o vb.: a) **certainly not** 2K 3_{13}, *ʾal-nāʾ* Gn 19_{18}; b) w/o expressed verb: *ʾal-ṭal* **(let) no dew (fall)** 2S 1_{21}; c) *weʾal*, vb. supplied fm. previous impv.: Jl 2_{13}; after inf. abs. = impv. Pr 17_{12}, after juss. Pr 27_{2}; — 2. w. vb. **not**: a) prohibition, w. impf. = juss., *ʾal tîrāʾ* **do not fear** Gn 15_{1}, *ʾal-yēṣēʾ ʾîš* **let no one go out**; b) request, *ʾal-naʾ taʿabōr* **please do not go on** Gn 18_{3}; c) w. coh., *weʾal naqšîbâ* **and let us not listen** Je 18_{18}; d) w. ind. α) for emphatic statement, *ʾal-yānûm* **he does not slumber** Ps 121_{3}; β) for neg. wish & prohibition, *ʾal-tabbîṭ* **do not look back** Gn 19_{17}; e) after impv. to express purpose, *weʾal-nāmût* **that we may not die** 1S 12_{19}; — 3. subst. **nothing**, *śîm leʾal* **destroy** Jb 24_{25}; — 4. ? **surely** Ps 59_{12}.

II *־אַל: Arabic article *ʾal*, in ⊳ אַלְקוּם & אַלְמוֹדָד ?.

I אֵל: ⊳ I אַיִל ram, man of power.

II אֵל: ⊳ II אַיִל mighty tree.

III אֵל: ⊳ III אַיִל door-post.

IV אֵל: **strength, power**: *yeš-leʾēl yādî* (*le*) **it is in my power to** Gn 31_{29}; *ʾên leʾēl yādekā* **you are powerless** Dt 28_{32}.

V אֵל: sf. אֵלִי (11×); pl. אֵלִים Ex 15_{11} אֵלִם: very old Semitic term for deity, often appearing in compounds with proper names (אֱלֹהִים does not make compounds) and liturgal phrases; uneven distribution in OT, most frequent in Ps, Jb, Is, Gn, lacking in many books: — 1. distinct from Y.: a) **the high god El** Ez 28_{2}, *kôkebê ʾēl* Is 14_{13}, *ʾēl ʿelyôn* Gn $14_{18\text{-}22}$; b) pl. **gods** (subordinate to Y.) Ex 15_{11}, *benê ʾēlîm* Ps 29_{1}; — 2. **title of Y.**, claimed by himself: *ʾanî ʾēl* Is 40_{18}, *ʾēl ʾelōhê yiśrāʾēl* Gn 33_{20}; — 3. appellation in general phrases, **God/god** (no sep. f. form), *mî ʾēl* **who is a God** Mi 7_{18}, *ʾēl ʾaḥēr* **another god** Ex 34_{14}, *lōʾ-ʾēl* **non-god** Dt 32_{21}; — 4. God in contrast to man (*ʾādām* or *ʾîš*) Ho 11_{9}; — 5. (the) **God** (of Israel), // *yhwh* Nu 23_{8}, // *ʾelōhîm* Jb 5_{8}; a) w/o attribute: *ʾēl yhwh* **Y. is God** Ps 118_{27}; alone 2S 23_{5} & oft.; b) *hāʾēl* w/o attribute 2S 22_{31}; c) *ʾēl* w. attribute: α) w. gen., in var. phrases: *ʾēl ʾelōhîm* Ps 50_{1}; ⊳ the various attributes, e.g. *ʾēl bêt-ʾēl* Gn 35_{7}, *ʾēl berît* Ju 9_{46}; β) w. adj. or pt.: *gādôl* Dt 7_{21}, *nōśēʾ* forgiving Ps 99_{8}; d) *hāʾēl* w. attribute, *hāggādôl* Dt 10_{17}; e) w. pers. ref.: α) w. sf. *ʾēlî* Ex 15_{2}; *ʿimmānû ʾēl* Is 7_{14};

β) appos., *hāʿōneh ʾōtî* Gn 35_3; γ) w. gen. *ʾēl yešûʿātî* Is 12_2; f) w. gen. of worshipper, *ʾēl yiśrāʾēl* Ps 68_{36}; g) cs. phrase of his possession, *yad ʾēl* **hand of God** Jb 27_{11}; h) 'superlative'? *harᵉrê ʾēl* **mighty mountains** Ps 36_7.

VI **אֵל**: demonstr. pron.: **these** Gn $19_{8\cdot25}$ 26_{3f} + 5× OT.

אֶל: prep.; exc. Ex 32_{34} Jos 7_{23} Is 36_{12} alw. ־אֶל; long form ־אֱלֵי Jb 3_{22} &c.; alternates oft. w. עַל; sf. אֵלַי, אֵלֶי, אֵלֶיךָ, אֵלַיִךְ, אֵלָיו (Kt אֵלָו 1S 22_{13} Ez 9_4), אֵלֵינוּ, אֲלֵיכֶם/הֶם, rarely *yod* omitted, 3 pl. אֵלֵימוֹ Ps 2_5: basic mng. **toward**: — 1. with all activities & occurrences implying direction to: go, come, throw Lv 1_{16}, bring Gn 2_{19}, listen Gn 16_{11}; *nātan ʾel* **give to** Gn 18_7, *dibber ʾel* **speak to** Gn 8_{15}, *bôʾ ʾel* **go in** (to a woman), have sexual relations Gn 16_2, *zānâ ʾel* **turn harlotrously toward** Nu 25_1; :: *min*, Nu 30_{15}; — 2. of direction **toward** s.thg: *peh ʾel peh* Nu 12_8; — 3. *ʾel* (esp. in Je Ez) often represents *ʿal* (& vice versa), but may also be interpreted as motion toward, e.g. Gn 4_8, & in the formula *hinᵉnî ʾel* (↗ *hinnēh* 9); — 4. **as far as** Je 51_9; — 5. **into**, *ʾel-hayyām* **into the sea** Jon 1_5; — 6. pregnant, of rest at arrival, *yāšab ʾel* (go back to the house and) **sit at** 1K 13_{20}, so Gn 24_{11}; — 7. w. vbs. of adding and uniting, **to** Lv 18_{18}; — 8. **with regard to**, *bākâ ʾel* **weep for** 2S 1_{24}, *ʾel-nafšô* **for his life** 1K 19_3; — 9. combined with oth. prep.: *ʾel-ʾaḥarê* **(to) behind** 2K 9_{18}, *ʾel-taḥat* **(to) under** 1K 8_6.

אֵלָא: n. pers.

אֶלְגָּבִישׁ: אַבְנֵי א׳ Ez $13_{11\cdot13}$ 38_{22}, meteorological punishment, // *gešem*: **hail** or **ice-crystals**. †

אַלְגּוּמִּים 2C 9_{10f}: ↗ אַלְמֻגִּים 2C 2_7.

אֶלְדָּד: n. pers.

אֶלְדָּעָה: n. pers.

I **אלה**: **qal**: pf. אָלִית; inf. אָלֹה & אָלוֹת: **hurl a curse, imprecation** Ju 17_2 Ho 4_2 10_4.

hif.: impf. וַיֹּאֶל; inf. הַאֲלֹתוֹ: **place under a curse, imprecation** 1S 14_{24} 1K 8_{31} 2C 6_{22}. †

II **אלה**: **qal**: impv. f. אֱלִי: **lament** Jl 1_8. †

III **אלה**: **qal**: impf. וַיֹּאֶל: **be unfit to** (*lᵉ* + inf.) 1S 17_{39}. †

אָלָה: sf. אָלָתוֹ; pl. אָלֹ(וֹ)ת: — 1. **curse** (evil result) under wh. s.one places himself or is placed Gn 24_{41}; — 2. (words of a) **curse** pronounced over s.one Ez 16_{59}; *qôl ʾālâ* **public curse** Lv 5_1, *nātan ʾālâ ʿal* **put a curse on s.one** Dt 30_7; — 3. (obligation by oath which puts a) **curse** (on the transgressor) Gn 26_{28}; > **stipulation** Dt $29_{11\cdot13}$; — 4. **curse-formula** Jb 31_{30}.

I **אֵלָה**: unspecified, like II **אַיִל**, **mighty tree**, often w. cultic significance Gn 35_4.

II **אֵלָה**: n. pers.

אַלָּה: stately **tree** Jos 24_{26}. †

אֵלֶּה: demonstr. pron., pl. of זֶה & זֹאת, ↗ VI אֵל: **these** (m. & f.); — 1. referring to preceding item 2S 23_{22}; — 2. referring to following: *ʾēlleh tôlᵉdôt*... Gn 6_9; — 3. attributive, *šᵉlōšâ ʾēlleh* **these three** Gn 9_{19}, *haddᵉbārîm hāʾēlleh* Gn 15_1; — 4. misc.: *ʾēlleh hēm* **(it is) they (who are)** 1S 4_8; *ʾēlleh... ʾēlleh* **these ... those** Dt 27_{12f}.

אֱלֹהַּ, אֱלֹהִים ↗ אֱלוֹהַּ.

אִלּוּ: **if** (contrary to fact) Ec 6_6 Est 7_4. †

אֱלוֹהַּ & **אֱלֹהִים**: I. אֱלוֹהַּ (ca. 60×), אֱלֹהַּ Dt 32_{17}, 2K 17_{31} Kt, Hb 1_{11f}, Dn 11_{38} †; most oft. in Jb (41×): — 1. **a God/god** Ps 18_{32}, *kōl-ʾᵉlōah* **any god** Dn 11_{37}, *lōʾ ʾᵉlōah* **non-god(s)** Dt 32_{17}; — 2. the true **God** Jb 3_4.

II. אֱלֹהִים (2250×), with *waw* Ps 18_{47} 143_{10} 145_1 †; cs. אֱלֹהֵי, sf. אֱלֹהַי אֱלֹהָיו, אֱלֹהֵימוֹ, אֱלֹהֵיהֶם; w. pref. בֵּאלֹהִים, וֵא׳, לֵא׳, כֵּא׳; but מֵאֱ׳ Ps 8_6 (↗ מִן): — 1. **gods**, *kōl-ʾᵉlōhê miṣrayim* Ex 12_{12}, *ʾᵉlōhê hāʾᵉlōhîm*

God of gods Dt 10_{17}, *ʾᵉlōhîm ʾᵃḥērîm* (64×, F *ʾaḥēr*), *bᵉnê (hā)ʾᵉlōhîm* Gn 6_2 **sons of the gods** (oth.: sons of God) Jb 1_6 2_1 38_7 †, cf. *bᵉnê ʾēlîm*; — 2. as a sg.: **God, Deity**; a) fm. the form, occasionally construed as pl., *hitʿû ʾᵉlōhîm* Gn 20_{13}, *ʾᵉlōhîm ḥayyîm* **living God** Dt 5_{23}; b) construed as sg., *yhwh hûʾ hāʾᵉlōhîm* **it is Y. who is God** Dt 4_{35}; occurs both w. & w/o def. art. w/o difference of mng.; euphony & free choice?; c) **God/god or goddess** of a people, land, *ʾᵉlōhê yiśrāʾēl* Ex 5_1, *ʿaštoret ʾᵉlōhê ṣidōnîm* 1K 11_5; d) God/god of a specific domain: *ʾᵉlōhê haššāmayim & ʾel. hāʾāreṣ* Gn 24_3, *ʾel. kōl-bāśār* Je 32_{27}; w. qualifying gen.: *ʾᵉlōhê ʿôlām* Is 40_{28}; e) God/god of individual: of David 2K 20_5, *ʾᵉlōhê ʾābî* Gn 31_{42}; — 3. misc. a) *hēbîʾ ʾet-haddᵉbārîm ʾel-hāʾᵉlōhîm* **bring cases before God** (for judgment) Ex 18_{19}; b) Moses is *lēʾlōhîm* for Aaron **(has the place of God)** Ex 4_{16}; c) a **spirit of the dead** 1S 28_{13}; d) w. or w/o art., like a proper noun, equivalent to & interchanging w. *yhwh*, difficult to distinguish from appellative use; in Ps 42-83 *ʾᵉlōhîm* is mostly a substitute for *yhwh*; e) *ʾᵉlōhîm* superlative? *rûᵃḥ ʾᵉlōhîm* **mighty wind** Gn 1_2, *nᵉśîʾ ʾᵉlōhîm* **mighty prince** Gn 23_6.

אֱלוּל: the month **Elul**, Aug./Sept., Ne 6_{15}. †

I **אֵלוֹן**: cs. =, pl. cs. אֵלֹ(וֹ)נֵי, only in cultic n. loc., like אֵלָה **great tree**, 'tree of God'; *ʾēlôn môreh* Gn 12_6, *ʾēlōnê mamrēʾ* 13_{18} 14_{13} 18_1.

II **אֵלוֹן**: n. pers.

I **אַלּוֹן**: cs. =, pl. אַלּוֹנִים, cs. אַלּוֹנֵי: like I אֵלָה & I אֵלוֹן orig. any stately tree, then specialized: *ʾallôn bākût* Gn 35_8.

II **אַלּוֹן**: n. pers. 1C 4_{37}. †

I **אַלּוּף**: sf. אַלּוּפִי; pl. אַלֻּפִים/אַלּוּפִים, sf. אַלּוּפֵינוּ: — 1. **familiar**: a) **trusting** (lamb) Je 11_{19}; b) **confidant** Je 3_4; — 2. **cattle** (pl.) Ps 144_{14}.

II **אַלּוּף**, Zc 9_7 אַלֻּף: pl. אַלֻּפִים, cs. אַלֻּ(וּ)פֵי, sf. אַלֻּפֵיהֶם: **tribal chief** Gn $36_{15\text{-}43}$ (42×).

אָלוּשׁ: n. loc.

אָלוֹת: n. loc., F אֵילַת.

אֶלְזָבָד: n. pers.

אלח: **nif.** pf. נֶאֱלָחוּ; pt. נֶאֱלָח: **be corrupt** (morally) Ps 14_3.

אֶלְחָנָן: n. pers.

אֱלִיאָב: n. pers.

אֱלִיאֵל: n. pers.

אֱלִיאָתָה: n. pers.

אֱלִידָד: n. pers.

אֶלְיָדָע: n. pers.

אַלְיָה: **fat tail** (of sheep) Ex 29_{22}.

אֵלִיָּה: n. pers. < אֵלִיָּהוּ.

אֵלִיָּהוּ: n. pers.

אֱלִיהוּ: n. pers.

אֱלִיהוּא: n. pers.

אֶלְיְהוֹעֵינַי: n. pers.

אֶלְיוֹעֵינַי: n. pers.

אֶלְיַחְבָּא: n. pers.

אֱלִיחֹרֶף: n. pers.

אֱלִיל: pl. אֱלִיל(י)ם, cs. אֱלִילֵי: — 1. insignificant, **worthless**, Je 14_{14}; — 2. **pagan gods**, always contemptuously as nonentities, idols Lv 19_4.

אֱלִימֶלֶךְ: n. pers.

אֶלְיָסָף: n. pers.

אֱלִיעֶזֶר: n. pers.

אֱלִיעֵנַי: n. pers. < אֶלְיְהוֹעֵינַי: 1C 8_{20}. †

אֱלִיעָם: n. pers.

אֱלִיפַז, אֱלִיפָז: n. pers.

אֱלִיפַל: n. pers.

אֱלִיפְלֵהוּ: n. pers.

אֱלִיפֶלֶט: n. pers.

אֱלִיצוּר: n. pers.

אֱלִיצָפָן: n. pers.

אֱלִיקָא: n. pers.

אֶלְיָקִים: n. pers.

אֱלִישֶׁבַע: n. pers.

אֱלִישָׁה: *ʾiyyê ʾᵉlîšâ*, exports purple Ez 27_7; eponym reckoned to *Yāwān* Gn 10_4; Greek-speaking island or coastal territory, disputed identification; suggestions: Italy, Aeolia, Peloponnesus, Carthage, Canary Isl.; prob. Cyprus.

אֱלִישׁוּעַ: n. pers.

אֶלְיָשִׁיב: n. pers.

אֱלִישָׁמָע: n. pers.

אֱלִישָׁע: n. pers.

אֱלִישָׁפָט: n. pers.

אֱלִיָּתָה: n. pers.

אֱלִל: ↗ אֱלִיל.

אַלְלַי Jb 10_{15} & אַלְלַי Mi 7_1: interj.: **woe,** with *lî*. †

I אלם: **nif.**: pf. נֶאֱלַמְתִּי, נֶאֱלַמְתָּ, נֶאֱלָמָה; impf. תֵּאָלֵם, תֵּאָלַמְנָה: **be** bound, **speechless** Is 53_7, grow silent Dn 10_{15}.

II אלם: **piel**: pt. מְאַלְּמִים: **bind** (sheaves) Gn 37_7. †

אֵלֶם: Ps 58_2, trad. 'silence' I אלם, but rd אֵלִים (↗ 82_1); 56_1 cj. אֵלִים or אֵילִים (II אַיִל) or אִיִּים. †

אִלֵּם: pl. אִלְּמִים: **dumb** Ex 4_{11}.

אֻלָם: ↗ אֵילָם.

אַלְמֻגִּים: *ʿaṣê ʾalmuggîm* 1K 10_{11f} & *ʿaṣê ʾalgûmmîm* from Ophir & Lebanon 2C 2_7 &c.: **almug wood,** costly, variety not ascertainable, for building & other purposes; trad. sandalwood, but this does not occur in Leb.; oth.: **Juniperus phoenicea.**

*אֲלֻמָּה: sf. אֲלֻמָּתִי; pl. אֲלֻמִּים, sf. אֲלֻמֹּתָיו, אֲלֻמֹּתֵיכֶם: **sheaf** Gn 37_7, Ps 126_6. †

אַלְמוֹדָד: n. pers.

אַלַּמֶּלֶךְ: n. loc.

I אַלְמָן: **widower** Je 51_5. †

II *אַלְמָן: pl. sf. אַלְמְנוֹתָיו: **palace** Is 13_{22}.

אַלְמֹן: **widowhood** Is 47_9. †

אַלְמָנָה: pl. אַלְמָנוֹת, sf. אַלְמְנוֹתָיו: **widow**; *ʾiššâ ʾalmānâ* 1K 7_{14}; oft. linked w. *gēr* & *yātôm* Dt 10_{18}.

*אַלְמָנוּת: cs. אַלְמְנוּת, sf. אַלְמְנוּתָהּ, אַלְמְנוּתֵךְ: **widowhood** Gn $38_{14.19}$.

אַלְמֹנִי, 1× אַלְמוֹנִי: *pᵉlōnî ʾalmōnî*, a **certain** place 2K 6_8, man Rt 4_1.

אֵלֹנִי: gent. of II אֵילוֹן: Nu 26_{26}. †

אֶלְנַעַם: n. pers.

אֶלְנָתָן: n. pers.

אֶלָּסָר: n. loc. Gn $14_{1.9}$. †

אֶלְעָד: n. pers.

אֶלְעָדָה: n. pers.

אֶלְעוּזַי: n. pers.

אֶלְעָזָר: n. pers.

אֶלְעָלֵא: n. loc.

אֶלְעָשָׂה: n. pers.

I אלף: **qal**: impf. תֶּאֱלַף: **learn** (oth.: get accustomed to) Pr 22_{25}. †
piel: impf. יְאַלֵּף, אֲאַלֶּפְךָ; מַלְּפֵנוּ (< מְאַלְּ׳): **teach** Jb 15_5.

II אלף: **hif.**: pt. מַאֲלִיפוֹת: **produce a thousandfold** Ps 144_{13}. †

I *אֶלֶף: pl. אֲלָפִים, sf. אֲלָפֶיךָ: **cattle** Ps 8_8.

II אֶלֶף: אֶלֶף; dual אַלְפַּיִם, אַלְפָּיִם; pl. אֲלָפִים, cs. אַלְפֵי, sf. אֲלָפָו (Kt), אַלְפֵיכֶם: **thousand**; *mēʾâ lāʾelef* **100 out of 1000** Ju 20_{10}; nouns of frequent occurrence stand after the number, in sg.: *ʾelef kesef* **1000 (pieces of) silver** Gn 20_{16}; but *ʾelef pᵉʿāmîm* **1000 times** Dt 1_{11}; multiples: 603,550 Ex 38_{26}; *ʾalfê rᵉbābâ* 1000 × 10,000 = 10 million Gn 24_{60}.

III אֶלֶף: sf. אַלְפִּי; pl. cs. אַלְפֵי, sf. אַלְפֵיכֶם: — 1. **thousand,** military unit, subdivision of tribe, > **clan** 1S 10_{19}; — 2. regionally, > **district,** *ʾalfê yᵉhûdâ* 1S 23_{23}; — 3. later, oft. = **tribe,** *ʾalfê yiśrāʾēl* Nu 10_{36}.

*אֶלְפֶּלֶט, אֶלְפֶלֶט: n. pers.

*אֶלְפַּעַל, אֶלְפָּעַל: n. pers.

אלץ: **piel**: impf. וַתְּאַלְצֵהוּ: **press hard** (w. words) Ju 16_{16}. †

אֶלְצָפָן: n. pers.

אַלְקוּם: *melek ʾalqûm* Pr 30_{31}, uncertain; suggestions: military levy; irresistible; *ʾēl-qôs* = Edomite god.

אֶלְקָנָה: n. pers.

אֶלְקֹשִׁי: gent. of n. loc. **ʾelqōš*.

אֶלְתּוֹלַד: n. loc.

אֶלְתְּקֵא: n. loc.
אֶלְתְּקוֹן: n. loc.
אִם: — 1. **if** (condition capable of fulfillment): w. impf. Ex 22_1, w. pf. Gn 18_3, mixed 1S 12_{14f}, w. *yēš* & pt. Gn 43_4; **whenever**, w. pf. Gn 38_9; — 2. **if** (condition incapable of fulfillment): w. impf. Nu 22_{18}; — 3. in wishes, apodosis suppressed, w. impf.: **if only** Ps 81_9; — 4. in oaths, as a conditional (self-)imprecation: a) w. apodosis giving the consequence of the oath, Nu 14_8; often only in periphrasis, *kōh ya‘aśeh *elōhîm* 1S 3_{17}; b) apodosis suppressed (so usu.), so that *'im* now means **not**, Ps 89_{36}, & *'im lō'* = **surely**, Is 5_9; — 5. in qns.: a) rarely, introducing a simple qn., 1K 1_{27}; b) oft., in double qn., *hᵃ . . . 'im* **do you ... or do you ...?** Jos 5_{13}; *hᵃ...wᵉ'im* Gn 17_{17}; — 6. in indir. qn., **whether**: *'im lō'* Ex 22_{7b}, *hᵃ...wᵉ 'im-lō'* **whether ... or if not** Gn 18_{21}; — 7. concessive, **even if** Je 15_1; — 8. combinations: a) *kî 'im* **unless, rather**, ↗ *kî*; b) *'im lō'* **if not** (elliptic after negation) > **but rather** Gn 24_{38}; — 9. w. impf. in prohibition SS $2_{7\cdot7}$.
אֵם (220×): cs. =, sf. אִמּוֹ, 3 sg. אִמָּהּ Ez 16_{44}; pl. אִמּוֹת, sf. אִמֹּתָם: **mother**; — 1. physical, Gn 2_{24}; of animals Ex 22_{29}, birds Dt 22_6; **cousins**: *bat 'immî* Gn 20_{12}, *ben-'immî* 43_{29}; *'ēm* = father's wife, **stepmother** Gn 37_{10}; **grandmother** 1K 15_{10}, Eve = *'ēm kol-ḥay* Gn 3_{20}, mother of tribe Ez 16_3, near female relative Jb 17_{14}; — 2. metaph.: nation as mother of members Is 50_1; honorary title, Ju 5_7; *'ēm hadderek* **fork in road** Ez 21_{26}.
אָמָה: sf. אֲמָתְךָ, אֲמָתֶךָ; pl. expands ה: אֲמָה(ו)ת, cs. אַמְהוֹת, sf. אַמְהֹתָיו: **female slave**, maidservant & concubine, orig.: unfree woman, ↗ *šifḥâ* & *pilegeš*; Gn 20_{17}; *mākar lᵉ'āmâ* **sell into slavery** Ex 21_7; submissive self-designation 1S 1_{11} & oft.

I **אַמָּה** (245×): cs. אַמַּת; du. אַמָּתַיִם; pl. אַמּוֹת, אַמֹּת Ex 36_{21} †; 2K $25_{17a\beta}$ Kt אַמָּה, rd Qr אַמּוֹת: — 1. **forearm** (basic meaning, cj. in Ps 91_4); — 2. portion of door, *'ammôt hassippîm*, **pivot** of doors set into the threshold Is 6_4 †; — 3. **cubit**, basic measure taken from part of the body, ca. 50 cm., varying by locality & period; *'ammat 'îš* **ordinary cubit** Dt 3_{11}; *'el-'ammâ* **to the cubit** = precisely (?) Gn 6_{16}.
II **אַמָּה**: in גִּבְעַת אַמָּה n. loc. 2S 2_{24}, **canal**.
***אֵמָה**: ↗ אֵימָה: אֵמוֹת Ez 42_{16} rd מֵאוֹת אַמּוֹת.
אֻמָּה: pl. אֻמּוֹת, sf. אֻמּוֹתָם, & אֻמִּים Ps 117_1: **tribe, nation** Gn 25_{16}.
I **אָמוֹן**: **artisan** Je 52_{15}; Pr 8_{30} ↗ comm. †
II **אָמוֹן**: n. pers.
III **אָמוֹן**: n. of god of Thebes Je 46_{25}, ↗ *nō' 'āmôn* Na 3_8. †
I ***אֵמוּן** or ***אָמוּן**: pl. cs. אֱמוּנֵי: **true, reliable** 2S 20_{19}.
II ***אֵמוּן**, אֵמֻן Dt 32_{20}; pl. אֱמֻנִים, אֱמוּנִים: **reliability** Dt 32_{20}; pl.: *ṣîr 'ᵉmûnîm* **faithful messenger** Pr 13_{17}.
אֱמוּנָה & **אֱמֻנָה** 2K 12_{16} †; f. of I אָמוּן: cs. אֱמוּנַת, sf. אֱמוּנָתְךָ, אֱמוּנָתֶךָ; pl. אֱמוּנוֹת: — 1. **steadiness**, *wayhî yādāyw 'ᵉmûnâ* Ex 17_{12}; — 2. **reliability** a) of men 1S 26_{23}, b) of God Dt 32_4; c) of commandments Ps 119_{86}; — 3. **honesty** Je $5_{1\cdot3}$; — 4. permanent **duty** (of an office) 1C 9_{22}; — 5. adv. a) *be'ᵉmûnâ* **conscientiously** 2C 31_{12}; b) *'ᵉmûnâ* adv. acc. **in faithfulness** Ps 119_{75}; — 6. **security** Ps 37_3.
אָמוֹץ: n. pers.
אֵמוֹת Ez 42_{16}: rd מֵאוֹת. †
אָמִי: n. pers.
אֲמִילַם Ps $118_{10\text{-}12}$ ↗ II מול hif.
אֵמִים Dt 2_{10f}, ↗ אֵימִים.
אֲמִינוֹן: n. pers.; 2S 13_{20} = *אַמְנוֹן $13_{1\text{-}39}$, ? corr. (oth.: dimin.).
אַמִּיץ (4×) & **אַמִּץ** (2×): **strong** 2S 15_{12}; *'ammiṣ libbô* **stout-hearted** Am 2_{16}.

אָמִיר: branch, bough Is 17_6.

I **אמל**: [qal: pt. f. אֻמְלָלָה Ez 16_{30}, ↗ II.]

pul.: pf. אֻמְלַל, אֻמְלָל, אֻמְלְלָה, אֻמְלָלָה; אֻמְלְלוּ, אֻמְלָלוּ: — 1. wither, **dry up** Is 16_8; — 2. **waste away**, languish: men 1S 2_5, gates Je 14_2.

II **אמל**: **qal** אֲמֻלָה pt. pass. or adj.: hot, **feverish** Ez 16_{30}. †

אֻמְלָל: **ready to fall, frail** Ps 6_3.

***אֲמֵלָל**: pl. אֲמֵלָלִים: frail, **miserable** Ne 3_{34}. †

אֲמָם: n. loc.

I **אמן**: **qal**: only pt. pass. *אָמוּן (II אמן?), pl. אֱמוּנִים (:: I *אָמוּן): sustained, **supported** La 4_5. †

nif.: pf. נֶאֱמַן, נֶאֱמָן, נֶאֶמְנָה, נֶאֱמָנָה, נֶאֶמְנוּ, נֶאֱמָנוּ; impf. יֵאָמֵן, יֵאָמֵן 1K 8_{26}, יֵאָמְנוּ; pt. נֶאֱמָן, cs. נֶאֱמַן־, f. נֶאֱמֶנֶת, נֶאֱמָנָה, pl. נֶאֱמָנִים, נֶאֱמְנֵי, נֶאֱמָנוֹת: — 1. **prove oneself** steady, **reliable**, Gn 42_{20}, **stay faithful to** (*ʿim*) Ho 12_1; pt. **reliable** 1S 2_{35}; — 2. **have stability, remain, continue**: men Is 7_9, God's name 1C 17_{23f}, sickness Dt 28_{59}; *ne'ᵉmānâ* **what is reliable** Ho 5_9, *ne'ᵉman-rûᵃḥ* **faithfully inclined** Pr 11_{13}; — 3. *ne'ᵉmān bᵉ* **entrusted with** (oth.: **approved in**) Nu 12_7.

hif.: pf. הֶאֱמִין, הֶאֱמַנְתִּי, הֶאֱמִינוּ, הֶאֱמַנְתֶּם; impf. יַאֲמִין, יַאֲמֵן־, יַאֲמִן־; impv. הַאֲמִינוּ; pt. מַאֲמִין: — 1. believe = **think** (:: 3!) that, w. inf. Jb 15_{22}, w. *kî* Ps 116_{10}; **be convinced that** w. *lᵉ* + inf. Ps 27_{13}; — 2. view s.thg as reliable, **believe**: word Ex 4_{8f}; **put trust in** (person), confide in, w. *bᵉ* 1S 27_{12}, w. *lᵉ* Gn 45_{26}, abs. Ex 4_5; — 3. **rely upon** (God), **believe in**: w. *bᵉ* Gn 15_6, w. *lᵉ* Dt 9_{23}; abs. **have faith** Ex 4_{31}.

II **אמן**: **qal**: pt. אֹמֵן, אֹמְנִים; f. אֹמֶנֶת, אֹמַנְתּוֹ; pass. אֱמוּנִים: — 1. **keeper** (w. acc.) of children Nu 11_{12}; **guardian** 2K $10_{1.5}$; — 2. f. *'ōmenet* **nurse** 2S 4_4; — 3. *'ᵉmûnîm* kept, **supported** La 4_5.

nif.: impf. 3 pl. f. תֵּאָמַנָה (? rd. תִּנָּשֶׂאנָה?) **be kept, attended to** Is 60_4. †

אָמָּן: **artisan** SS 7_2. †

אָמֵן: **surely!**, solemn formula by wh. the hearer a) accepts the validity of a curse or oath, Dt 27_{15-26} (12×), b) accepts a salutary message Je 28_6, or c) joins himself to a doxology Ps 106_{48}.

אֹמֶן: **reliability**, *'ᵉmûnâ 'ōmen* **full reliability**, or *'ōmen* adv. **really reliable** Is 25_1. †

אֱמֻן, **אֱמֻנָה**: ↗ II אֵמוּן & אֱמוּנָה.

I **אֲמָנָה**: — 1. **agreement** Ne 10_1; — 2. **royal prescription** Ne 11_{23}. †

II **אֲמָנָה**: — 1. the **Antilebanon** range SS 4_8; — 2. the **Chrysorrhoas** river, flowing through Damascus 2K 5_{12}.

I **אָמְנָה**: adv. acc., in truth, **truly** Gn 20_{12} Jos 7_{20}. †

II **אָמְנָה**: attendance, **protection** Est 2_{20}.

***אֹמְנָה**: pl. אֹמְנוֹת: doorposts, or rather their (gold) **overlay**? 2K 18_{16}. †

אַמְנוֹן: n. pers.

אָמְנָם: **surely** 2K 19_{17}, **truly** Jb 36_4.

אֻמְנָם: = אָמְנָם, alw. w. הֲ interr.: **really?** Gn 18_{13}.

אֲמִנֹן = אַמְנוֹן n. pers. 1C 3_1. †

אמץ: **qal**: pf. אָמְצוּ; impf. יֶאֱמַץ, יֶאֶמְצוּ; impv. אֱמָץ, אֱמַץ; אִמְצוּ: — **be strong** 2C 13_{18}, *ḥᵃzaq weʾᵉmaṣ* **be brave and strong** Dt 31_7, w. *min* **be stronger than** Gn 25_{23}.

piel: pf. אִמֵּץ, אִמַּצְתָּ(ה), אִמַּצְתִּיךָ; impf. יְאַמֵּץ, וַיְאַמֶּץ־, וַיְאַמְּצֵהוּ, תְּאַמְּצֵנוּ, אֲאַמִּצְכֶם; impv. אַמֵּץ, אַמְּצֵהוּ, אַמְּצוּ: — 1a) **strengthen** s.one, s.thg Dt 3_{28}, b) **let** s.one, s.thg **grow strong** Is 44_{14} (tree), c) **make strong** Pr 8_{28} (clouds); — 2. metaph. w. *lēbāb* **harden s.one's heart** Dt 2_{30}; — 3. **repair** 2C 24_{13} (house).

hif.: juss. יַאֲמֵץ: w. *lēb*: **show strength, prove oneself strong** Ps 27_{14} 31_{25}. †

hitp.: pf. הִתְאַמֵּץ; impf. יִתְאַמְּצוּ; pt. מִתְאַמֶּצֶת: **prove oneself strong**; w. *lᵉ* & inf.

persist in s.thg Ru 1_{18}, *hit'ammēṣ la'alôt* **he succeeded in** mounting (oth.: **hurried** to mount) 1K 12_{18}; w. *'al* **be superior over** 2C 13_7.

אָמֹץ: pl. אֲמֻצִּים: flesh-colored, **piebald** (horses) Zc $6_{3\cdot7}$. †

אַמִּץ: ↗ אַמִּיץ.

אֹמֶץ: **strength** Jb 17_9. †

אַמְצָה: **strength** Zc 12_5. †

אַמְצִי: n. pers.

אֲמַצְיָה: n. pers., < אֲמַצְיָהוּ.

אֲמַצְיָהוּ: n. pers.

I **אמר** (5280×): **qal**: pf. אָמַרְתִּי ,אָמַרְתִּי ,א׳; impf. וַיֹּאמֶר ,תֹּאמֶר ,תֹּאמַר ,יֹאמֶר ,יֹאמַר, וַיֹּאמֶר ,אֹמַר ,אֹמֶר ,וָא(ו)מַר ,וְ/וָאוֹמְרָה, יֹאמְרוּ ,יֹאמֵרוּ ,תֹּאמַרְנָה ,תֹּאמַרְךָ ,תֹּמְרוּ 2S 19_{14}, וַנֹּאמֶר ,נֹאמַר ,תֹּאמְרָן; impv. (וֶ)אֱמֹר, אֱמֹר ,אֱמָר־ ,(כֶּ/בֶּ)אֱמֹר; inf. אֱמָר־ ,אִמְרִי, Ez 25_8, alw. לֵאמֹר (3× לֵאמוֹר), אִמְרִי, אָ(ו)מֵר, אֲמָרְךָ, אָמְרָם, abs. אָמֹ(ו)ר; pt. אֹמֵר, אֹמֶרֶת ,אֹמְרָה ,אֹמְרִים ,אֹמְרֵי ,אֹמֶר(ו)ת, הֶאָמוּר Mi 2_7 (txt ?): — 1. **say**, the simple rendering of speech (:: דִּבֶּר speak Lv 1_2), of men Gn 2_{23}, God 1_3, animal 3_1; speech follows in dir. Gn 3_2 or indir. 12_{13} discourse; prophetic oracle oft. introduced by *kōh 'āmar yhwh*; *'āmar* never appears w/o words of speech, so that Gn 4_8 &c. lack s.thg; **say** s.thg **to s.one**, w. *'el* Gn 3_{16}, *le* 3_{17}; **say** s.thg **about s.one** *'el* (for *'al*) 2K 19_{32}; — 2. *lē'mōr*, 'in order to say' usually means 'as he/she said,' 'with these words,' Gn 1_{22}; often no more than our quotation marks, pause before dir. discourse Ex 6_{10}, even after *dabbēr* 2S 19_{12}, & in cases like Am 8_5 1K 1_5; — 3. w. acc.: a) **mention**: α) s.one Gn 43_{27}, β) s.thg Gn 22_2, mention with praise, **praise** Ps 40_{11}, γ) **name, call**, w. *le* Is 5_{20}, w. 2 acc. La 2_{15}; **say s.thg** of s.one (*le*) Ps 41_6; **promise** 2K 8_{19}, w. *le* w. inf. Ne 9_{15}; — 4. say to oneself = **think**, *'āmar belibbô* Gn 17_{17}, *'a. 'el-libbô* 8_{21}, *lelibbô* Ho 7_2, *'āmar* alone, oft. for a false assumption Gn 44_{28}; — 5. *'āmar* w. *le* & inf. **intend** Ex 2_{14}; — 6. **order** Est 1_{17}; contents of order in its fulfillment Ps $105_{31\cdot34}$.

nif.: pf. נֶאֱמַר; impf. יֵאָמֵר ,יֵאָמֶר ,יֵאָמֵר, Is 4_3: — 1. **be said** Nu 21_{14}; — 2. = **one says** (current saying), Gn 10_9; — 3. **be named, called** (↗ qal 3) Gn 32_{29}.

hif.: pf. הֶאֱמַרְתָּ ,הֶאֱמִירְךָ: **cause to say, proclaim** (covenant formulation), Dt 26_{17f}. †

II **אמר**: **hitp.**: impf. יִתְאַמְּרוּ, > תִּתְיַמָּרוּ Is 61_6: **pride oneself** (*be*) Is 61_6 (oth.: hitp. *ymr* = *mwr*, 'exchange, enter [into]'); abs. **boast** Ps 94_4. †

אֹמֶר: אוֹמֶר 1×: — 1. opinion, **information**, Ps 19_{3f}; — 2. thing > **something** (cf. *dābār*) Jb 22_{28}.

I ***אֵמֶר**: sf. אִמְרוֹ; pl. אֲמָרִים, sf. אֲמָרַי, אִמְרֵיכֶם ,אֲמָרֶי: **word**: *'āmar 'amārîm* **say words** Pr 1_{21}, *'imrê 'ēl* Nu $24_{4\cdot16}$; in genl. Dt 32_1.

II **אֵמֶר**: cs. pl. אִמְרֵי: **branch**, ↗ *'imrê šefer* **branched antlers** Gn 49_{21}; oth.: *אִמֵּר **lamb.**

II **אִמֵּר**: n. pers.

III **אִמֵּר**: n. loc. Ezr 2_{59} Ne 7_{61}. †

***אִמְרָה**, ***אֶמְרָה**: cs. אִמְרַת, sf. אִמְרָתִי, אִמְרָתְךָ ,אֶמְרָתוֹ La 2_{17}; pl. אֲמָרוֹת ,אִמְרוֹת, sf. אִמְרֹתֶיךָ: word, **opinion**: 1. of men Ps 17_6, esp. poetic word Gn 4_{23}; — 2. **(God's) word** Dt 33_9.

אֱמֹרִי: name of a people, w. geographical & political, not ethnic significance: — 1. *'emōrî* **an Amorite**, ancestor of Jerusalem Ez 16_{45}; — 2. *hā'emōrî* **the Amorite** (sg.), Gn 14_{13}; — 3. *hā'emōrî* coll. **the Amorites**, construed as pl. 2K 21_{11}.

אִמְרִי: n. pers.

אֲמַרְיָה: n. pers.

אֲמַרְיָהוּ: n. pers.

אַמְרָפֶל: n. pers.

אֶמֶשׁ: paus. אָמֶשׁ: **yesterday evening** Gn 19_{34}; **yesterday** 2K 9_{26}.

אֱמֶת: sf. אֲמִתֶּךָ, אֲמִתְּךָ: — 1. **steadiness, reliability**: *ʾanšê ʾᵉmet* **reliable people** Ex 18_{21}, *šālôm weʾᵉmet* **peace and security** 2K 20_{19}; — 2. **permanence, continuance**: *beʾᵉmet* **continually** Is 16_5, *ḥesed weʾᵉmet* **lasting kindness** Gn 24_{49}; a) of God 24_{27}, b) of men 24_{49}; — 3. **fidelity** (oft. difficult to distinguish from 2 & 4): a) of God Is 38_{18f}, b) of men Ps 85_{12}; *beʾᵉmet* **faithfully** 1K 2_4 & oft.; — 4) **truth** 1K 17_{24}; w. *dibber* 1K 22_{16}; — 5. a) in cs.-phrases, = **true**: *ʾᵉlōhê ʾᵉmet* **the true God** 2C 15_3; b) *hāyâ ʾᵉmet* **be true** 1K 10_6; — 6. in adv. acc. **truly** 1K 17_{24}.

***אַמְתַּחַת**: cs. =, sf. אַמְתַּחְתּוֹ; pl. cs. אַמְתְּחֹת, sf. אַמְתְּחֹתֵיכֶם: **sack** (oth.: **load**) Gn 42_{27f} (+ 43, 44).

אֲמִתַּי: n. pers.

אָן: 1S 10_{14}, 2K 5_{25a} Kt, Jb 8_2; אָ֫נָה oft.; אָ֫נָה Dt 1_{28} Ps 139_7; אָ֫נָה וָאָ֫נָה 1K $2_{36.42}$ 2K 5_{25b}: — 1. *ʾānâ* **where?** Rt 2_{19}; *mēʾān* **from where?** 2K 5_{25a} Kt; — 2. *ʾānâ* **(to) where?** Gn 16_8; *ʾāneh weʾānâ* **(to) here and there** 1K 2_{42}, w. *lōʾ* **(to) nowhere** 1K 2_{36} 5_{25b}; — 3. *ʿad-ʾān(â)* **till when? how long?** Ex 16_{28}.

אֹן: ☞ I & III אוֹן.

אָנָּא & **אָ֫נָּא**, accentuation varies; **oh, please, I pray** before impv. Gn 50_{17}; before request Ne $1_{5.11}$; as a sigh before statement Ex 32_{31}, before wish Jon 1_{14}.

I **אנה**: **qal**: pf. אָנוּ: **lament** Is 3_{26} 19_8. †

II **אנה**: **piel**: pf. אִנָּה: w. *le* **let** (s.one) **happen, fall into** Ex 21_{13}. †

pual: impf. יְאֻנֶּה: **happen, fall** Ps 91_{10} Pr 12_{21}. †

hitp.: pt. מִתְאַנֶּה: **seek opportunity** (for quarrel) w. *le* 2K 5_7. †

אָנָה: ☞ אָן.

אָנָּה: ☞ אָנָּא.

***אֳנָה**: ☞ *אוֹנִי.

אנו: Je 42_6 Kt אֲנוּ, analogy אֲנִי: **we**. †

אָנוּשׁ & **אָנֻשׁ** Je 17_9: f. **אֲנוּשָׁה**: — 1. **incurable** Is 17_{11}; — 2. **calamitous** Je 17_{16}.

I **אֱנוֹשׁ**: mostly poetic: — 1. **men** Dt 32_{26}; — 2. **(particular) men**, people Is 24_6; — 3. **single man** a) *ben-ʾᵉnôš* Ps 144_3, b) *ʾᵉnôš* Ps 8_5; — 4. misc.: *ʾᵉnôš šᵉlômî* **my trusted friends** Je 20_{10}; *lᵉbāb ʾᵉnôš* **heart of man** Is 13_7.

II **אֱנוֹשׁ**: n. pers. Gn 4_{26} $5_{6f.9-11}$ 1C 1_1. †

אנח: **nif.**: pf. נֶאֶנְחָה, 2 sg. f. נֶחַנְתְּ < *נֶחַנְתְּ < נֶאֱנַחְתְּ Je 22_{23}, נֶאֱנָחוּ; impf. יֵאָנַח, וַיֵּאָנְחוּ; impv. הֵאָנַח; pt. נֶאֱנָח, נֶאֱנָחָה, נֶאֱנָחִים; **sigh, groan** Ex 2_{23}.

אֲנָחָה: sf. אַנְחָתִי, אַנְחָתָה (= ־הּ) Is 21_2; pl. sf. אַנְחֹתַי: **sigh, groan** Is 35_{10}; Is 21_2 her sighing? sighing over her?

אֲנַחְנוּ, **אֲנָ֫חְנוּ**: **we** Gn 13_8; *ʾittānû ʾᵃnaḥnû* **with ourselves** (emph.) Dt 5_3.

אֲנָחֲרַת: n. loc.

אֲנִי, **אָ֫נִי**: **I** (☞ *ʾānōkî*): w. pt. *ʿōśeh ʾᵃnî* **I do** Ju 15_3; esp. for emph. *ʾemšōl ʾᵃnî* **it is I who rule** Ju 8_{23}; later oft. w/o this emph. Ec 2_{11} &c.; *ʾānî* as answer to qn.: **I am, yes** Gn 27_{24}; *haʾᵃnî* Is 66_9; formula of introduction *ʾᵃnî parʿōh* Gn 41_{44}.

אֳנִי: cs. =; m. (f. Is 33_{21}): coll. **ships, fleet** 1K 9_{26f}.

אֳנִיָּה: pl. אֳנִיּ(וֹ)ת, אוֹנִיּוֹת 2C 8_{18} Kt, sf. אֳנִיּוֹתֵיהֶם: **ship**, *ʾᵒniyyôt hayyām* Ez 27_9.

אֲנִיָּה: **lamentation**, *taʾᵃniyyâ waʾᵃniyyâ* (reinforcement) Is 29_2 La 2_5. †

אֲנִיעָם: n. pers.

אֲנָךְ: **lead, plumb-line** Am $7_{7.8}$; oth.: **tin**. †

אָנֹכִי: אָנֹ֫כִי, אָנֹכִי Jb 33_9 †: **I**: a) formula of introduction, *ʾānōkî yhwh* **I am Y.** Ex 20_2; b) in contrasts, *ʾattem… weʾānōkî* Ho 1_9; c) emph. of subj., *ʾānōkî nātattî* **I myself gave** Ho 2_{10}; for pattern of usage in comparison to *ʾᵃnî*, see the larger lexicons.

אנן: **hitpol.**: impf. יִתְאוֹנֵן; pt. מִתְאוֹנְנִים: **complain** Nu 11_1 La 3_{39}. †

אנס: **qal**: pt. אֹנֵס: **compel** Est 1_8. †

אנף: **qal**: pf. אָנַפְתָּ; impf. יֶאֱנַף: **be angry** (of God) w. *bᵉ* with s.one 1K 8_{46}.

hitp.: pf. הִתְאַנַּף; impf. וַיִּתְאַנַּף: **feel angry** (of God) w. *bᵉ* with s.one 1K 11_9.

***אֲנַף**: du. cs. אַנְפֵּי Ec 8_2: **face**: ↗ II אַף 3b. †

אֲנָפָה: a kind of bird forbidden for food, plover or cormorant Lv 11_{19} Dt 14_{18}. †

אנק: **qal**: impf. יֶאֱנֹק; inf. אֱנֹק: **groan** (of wounded) Je 51_{52} Ez 26_{15}. †

nif.: impv. הֵאָנֵק; pt. נֶאֱנָקִים: **groan** Ez 9_4 24_{17}. †

I **אֲנָקָה**: cs. אֶנְקַת: **groan** Ps 12_6.

II **אֲנָקָה**: unclean animal: **gecko**, *Hemidactylus turcicus*, Lv 11_{30}. †

אנשׁ: **nif.**: וַיֵּאָנַשׁ: **be in poor health** 2S 12_{15}. †

אָסָא: n. pers.

אָסוּךְ: small **jar** (for oil) 2K 4_2. †

אָסוֹן: **mortal accident** Gn $42_{4.38}$.

אֵסוּר: **fetters** Ju 15_{14}; *bêt hāʼēsûr* **prison** Je 37_{15}.

אָסִיף, אָסִף Ex 23_{16}: **ingathering** from threshing-floor & winepress before beginning of rainy season, Ex 23_{16} 34_{22}. †

אָסִיר: pl. אֲסִירִים, Gn 39_{22} ־רם, cs. אֲסִירֵי, sf. אֲסִירָיו: **prisoner** employed for various kinds of work Is 14_{17}.

I **אַסִּיר**, 1C 3_{17} אַסִּר: **prisoner** Is 24_{22}.

II **אַסִּיר**: n. pers. Ex 6_{24} 1C $6_{7.8.22}$. †

***אָסָם**: pl. sf. אֲסָמֶיךָ: **stores** Dt 28_8 Pr 3_{10}. †

אַסְנָה: n. pers.

אָסְנַת: n. pers.

אָסַף (200×): **qal**: pf. א׳, וְאָסַפְתָּ(ה), אֲסַפְתּוֹ; impf. יֶאֱסֹף, וַיֹּסֶף (< *וַיֶּאסֹף) 2S 6_1, תֹּסֵף (< *תֶּאסֵף) Ps 104_{29}, תַּאַסְפִי, אֶאֱסֹף, sf. יַאַסְפֵהוּ, אֹסִפְךָ 1S 15_6; impv. אֱסֹף, אֶסְפָה Nu 11_{16}, אִסְפִי Je 10_{17}, אִסְפוּ; inf. לֶאֱסֹף, כֶּאֱסֹף, אָסְפְּךָ, אָסְפְּכֶם, אָסֹף; pt. אֹסֵף, אֹסְפָם, אֹסִפְךָ 2K 22_{20}, אֹסְפֵי; pass. אֲסֻפֵי: — 1. **gather**: food Gn 6_{21}, money 2K 22_4; men Gn 29_{22}; — 2. **gather in** (from threshing-floor and winepress) Dt 16_{13}; abs. **harvest** 28_{38}; — 3. **take in**: wife into a house 2S 11_{27}, orphan Ps 27_{10}; — 4. remove: a) **take away** peace from s.one Je 16_5, breath Ps 104_{29}; **exterminate** 1S 15_6; b) **draw back** feet Gn 49_{33}, hand, impv. = **stop!** 1S 14_{19}; of God, fury Ps 85_4.

nif.: pf. נֶאֱסַף, נֶאֶסְפָה, נֶאֱסַפְתָּ, נֶאֶסְפוּ, נֶאֱסָפוּ; impf. וַיֵּאָסֵף, וַיֵּאָסֶף, יֵאָסְפוּ, יֵאָסֵפוּ, יֵאָסְפוּן; impv. הֵאָסְפִי, הֵאָסְפוּ; inf. הֵאָסֵף, הֵאָסֹף; pt. נֶאֱסָף: — 1. **be gathered**, **gather** (intrans.): a) flocks Gn $29_{3.7}$, soldiers Ju 10_{17}; b) w. *ʿal* **unite against**, **conspire against** Gn 34_{30}; c) *neʼᵉsaf ʼel-ʿammāyw* **be gathered to his family** = die Gn $25_{8.17}$ & oft.; d) **withdraw to** 2S 17_{13}; — 2. **be taken away** (↗ qal 4) Is 16_{10}.

piel: pt. מְאַסֵּף, מְאַסִּפְכֶם, מְאַסְפָיו: — 1. **glean** Je 9_{21}; — 2. **shelter** in house (↗ qal 3) Ju $19_{15.18}$; — 3. **form a rear-guard** Nu 10_{25}.

pual: pf. אֻסַּף, אֻסְּפוּ; pt. מְאֻסָּף: **be gathered**: booty Is 33_4, peoples Ez 38_{12}.

hitp.: inf. הִתְאַסֵּף: **gather** (intrans.) Dt 33_5.

אָסָף: n. pers.

אָסִף: ↗ אָסִיף.

***אֹסֶף**: pl. אֲסֻפִּים, אֲסֻפֵּי: **stores**, *bêt hāʼᵃsuppîm* 1C 26_{15}.

אֹסֶף: **harvest**, fruit Is 32_{10}.

אֲסֵפָה: **imprisonment** Is 24_{22}. †

***אֲסֻפָּה**: pl. אֲסֻפּוֹת: **collection** Ec 12_{11}. †

***אֲסַפְסֻף**: הָאֲסַ׳ < הָאסַ׳: **rabble** Nu 11_4. †

אַסְפָּתָא: n. pers.

אֶסַּק Ps 139_8: ↗ סלק. †

אסר: **qal**: pf. אֲסָרָם, אֲסַרְתֶּם, אֲסָרָה, אֲסַרְנֻהוּ; impf. יַאַסְרֵהוּ, יֶאֱסֹר, יֶאְסֹר, נֶאֱסָרְךָ, יַאַסְרֻהוּ; impv. אֱסֹר, אִסְרוּ; inf. אָסֹ(וֹ)ר, לֶאֱסָרְךָ, לֶאֱסֹ(וֹ)ר, לֶאְסֹ(וֹ)ר; pt. אֹסְרִי Gn 49_{11}, pass. אָסוּר, הָסוּרִים Ec 4_{14}

< *אֱסָרוֹת, הָאֲסוּרִים: — 1. **fetter** Gn 42_{24}; *'āsûr* **imprisoned** Gn 39_{20} $40_{3.5}$; **hold prisoner** 2K 23_{33}; — 2. **tie up**: animals 2K 7_{10}, **harness** horses Je 46_{4}, **yoke** 1S $6_{7.10}$; — 3. tech. term, *'āsar 'issār* **bind oneself to a vow of abstention** Nu 30_{3ff}.

nif.: impf. יֵאָסֵר; impv. הֵאָסְרוּ: **be fettered** Gn $42_{16.19}$.

pual (pass. qal?): pf. אֻסְּרוּ, אֻסָּרוּ: **be imprisoned** Is 22_{3}; ₣ qal 3. †

אִסָּר (7×); & **אֱסָר** (4×): cs. אִסַּר, sf. אֱסָרָהּ; pl. sf. אֱסָרֶיהָ: (binding), **vow of abstention** Nu 30_{3ff}.

אַסִּר: ₣ אַסִּיר.

אֵסַר(־)חַדֹּן: n. pers.

אֶסְתֵּר: n. pers.

I **אַף**: (ca. 120×): **also, even**: — 1. expr. of addition, *'af 'anî* Gn 40_{16}; — 2. expr. of emphasis, *'af 'anî* **I for my part** Ps 89_{28}; — 3. expr. of ascending importance, *'af qodqōd* **and even the crown of the head** Dt 33_{20}; — 4. expr. of contrast, *'af-zānaḥtā* **yet thou hast cast...** Ps 44_{10}; — 5. var. combinations: *'af-'omnām* **yes, indeed** Jb 34_{12}, *'af-'ên* **there was no one at all who** Is 41_{26}; — 6. *'af kî*: a) oft. *kî* simply introduces a conditional clause: *'af kî... šillaḥtî* **yes, if I...** Ez 14_{21}; or *'af* introduces elliptically a qn. whose content follows *kî*: *'af kî 'āmar* **has God really said** Gn 3_{1}; or *'af* stresses a temporal clause, *'af kî* **even when** Ne 9_{18}; b) *'af kî* has become a unit: **how much more when** 2S 4_{11}; after neg., **how much less can I** Jb 9_{14}.

II **אַף**: אָף; sf. אַפּוֹ, אַפְּךָ; du. אַפַּיִם, אַפָּיִם, sf. אַפָּיו: — 1. sg. **nose**: Gn 24_{47}; — 2. area of nose = **face**, *śîm 'af* **be resolute** Jb 36_{13}; — 3. sg. **anger**, *wayyiḥar 'appô* (₣ *ḥrh*) his nose became hot = **his anger became inflamed** Gn 30_{2}, (ca. 80×); *ḥarôn 'appô* Dt 13_{18} & *ḥarôn 'af yhwh* Nu 25_{4}, lit. burning of the nose = **anger**; so *'af* generally has the meaning **anger**: *šāb 'appô min* **his anger subsides from** Gn 27_{45}, *hēšîb 'af* **appease anger** Pr 29_{8}; *ba'al af* **bad-tempered** person Pr 22_{24}; — 4. *'appayim* du. a) **nostrils** Gn 2_{7}; b) area of nose = **face**, *'appayim 'arṣâ* **with face to the ground** Gn 19_{1}; c) **anger** (like 3) Pr 30_{33}; — 5. *'appayim* **face** w. preps.: *le'appê* **before**, in front of 1S 25_{23}.

אפד: **qal**: pf. אָפַדְתָּ; impf. וַיֶּאְפֹּד: **put on tightly** Ex 29_{5} Lv 8_{7}. †

I **אֵפֹד** & **אֵפוֹד**: — 1. in P-Code: **ephod**, a priestly garment Ex 28_{4} & oft.; — 2. **cult object** (image?) along w. teraphim Ju 8_{27}, 17_{5}, used to obtain oracle 1S 23_{9}; — 3. *'ēfôd bad*, **linen ephod** as cultic dress 1S 2_{18}; note: Ju 8_{24ff} does not imply an image covered w. precious metal; linguistic & archeological evidence indicates a metallic sacral robe, like a cuirass, first on an image of a god, later on cultic leader, high-priest.

II **אֵפֹד**: n. pers. Nu 34_{23}. †

אֲפֻדָּה: cs. אֲפֻדַּת, sf. אֲפֻדָּתוֹ: — 1. = inf. **to fasten** Ex 28_{8} 39_{5}; — 2. **closely-fitting cover**, plate Is 30_{22}. †

***אַפֶּדֶן**: **palace**: *'ohᵒlê 'appadnô* Dn 11_{45}. †

אָפָה: **qal**: pf. 'א, אָפִיתָ, אָפוּ; impf. יֹאפוּ, תֹּאפֵהוּ; impv. אֵפוּ; pt. אֹפֶה, אֹ(ו)פִים: **bake** Gn 19_{3}.

nif.: impf. תֵּאָפֶה, תֵּאָפֶינָה: w. *ḥāmēṣ* **be baked** (w. leaven) Lv 6_{10}.

אֹפֶה: **baker** Gn 40_{5}, *śar hā'ōfîm* **chief baker** 40_{2}, *ōfôt* (women) **bakers** 1S 8_{13}.

אֵפָה: ₣ אֵיפָה.

אֵפוֹא & (4× Jb) **אֵפוֹ**: unaccented **then, so**: — 1. after interr. word, *mî 'ēfô'* **who then** Gn 27_{33}; separated fm. interr. word, *bammeh yiwwāda' 'ēfô'* **how then shall it be known** Ex 33_{16}; — 2. before interr. word, *'ēfô' mâ* **what then** Gn 27_{37}; — 3. in wishes: after *mî yittēn* (₣ *ntn*), **would that** Jb 19_{23}; after *'im* & *'im lō'*, **if then (... not)** Jb 9_{24} 24_{25}; separated fm. *'im* Gn 43_{11}; — 4. in exhortations, *d^e'û 'ēfô'* **know then** 2K 10_{10}; separated fm. impv., Pr 6_3.

אֵפוֹד, ↗ אֵפֹד.

אֲפוּנָה Ps 88_{16}: uncertain; פּוּן ??; prp. אָפוּגָה (*pwg*). †

אֲפִיחַ: n. pers.

***אָפִיל**: pl. אֲפִילוֹת: **late**(-ripening) Ex 9_{32}. †

I **אַפַּיִם**: ↗ II אַף 4.

II **אַפַּיִם**: n. pers. 1C 2_{30f}. †

I ***אָפִיק**: cs. אֲפִיק; pl. אֲפִ(י)קִים, cs. אֲפִ(י)קֵי, sf. אֲפִיקָיו: — 1. the deepest water-channel of a valley, **stream-channel** Ez 6_3 (+ 14×); — 2. **tube** (of bone) Jb 40_{18}, grooves (betw. scales of crocodile) 41_7.

II ***אָפִיק**: אֲפִיקִים: **strong** Jb 12_{21}. †

אֹפִיר: ↗ אוֹפִיר.

אֹפֶל: **darkness** Is 29_{18}.

אָפֵל: **dark** (oth.: **darkness**) Am 5_{20}. †

אֲפֵלָה: sf. אֲפֵלָתְךָ; pl. abs. אֲפֵלוֹת: **darkness** Ex 10_{22}.

אֶפְלָל: n. pers.

***אֹפֶן**: pl. sf. אָפְנָיו: — **(right) time**, a word spoken at... Pr 25_{11}. †

אָפֵס: **qal**: pf. 'א: **be gone, be at an end** Gn 47_{15f}.

אֶפֶס: אָפֶס; cs. אַפְסֵי (see 2 below) Is $47_{8\cdot10}$ Zp 2_{15}; pl. cs. אַפְסֵי: **extremity, end**: — 1. *'afsê 'ereṣ* **ends of the earth** Dt 33_{17}; — 2. **end, nothing(ness)** *hāyâ (k^e)'efes* **be at an end** Is 34_{12} 41_{12}; *'efes* **it is all over with** 2K 14_{26}; *w^e'afsî 'ôd* **and no one else** (oth.: sf.: **except**) Is $47_{8\cdot10}$ Zp 2_{15}; — 3. **only** Nu 22_{35} 23_{13}; — 4. *'efes kî*: limiting, **only that** Nu 13_{28}.

אֶפֶס דַּמִּים: n. loc.

***אֹפֶס**: du. אָפְסַיִם, אָפְסָיִם: **ankle**; *mê 'ofsayim*, **shallow ankle-deep water** Ez 47_3. †

***אֶפַע**: אֶפַע: **worthless** Is 41_{24}. †

אֶפְעֶה: a **snake** (some say: carpet viper, Echis colorata, poisonous) Is 30_6 59_5 Jb 20_{16}. †

אפף: **qal**: pf. אֲפָפוּ, אֲפָפוּנִי, אֲפָפֻנִי: **encompass** 2S 22_5 (billows).

אפק: **hitp.**: pf. הִתְאַפַּק; impf. יִתְאַפַּק, אֶתְאַפַּק; inf. הִתְאַפֵּק: — 1. **pull oneself together, risk s.thg** 1S 13_{12}; — 2. collect oneself, **restrain oneself** Gn 43_{31} (+ 5×).

אֲפֵק: n. loc.

אֲפֵקָה: n. loc., = אֲפֵק.

אֵפֶר: — 1. loose **soil**, crumbling to **dust**: a) on the head, sign of mourning 2S 13_{19}; *śaq wā'ēfer* Is 58_5; b) *'ēfer* under foot Ma 3_{21}; *'āfār wā'ēfer* Gn 18_{27}; — 2. **ashes** Nu 19_{9f}, also Ez 28_{18}?.

אֲפֵר: **bandage** 1K $20_{38\cdot41}$. †

***אֶפְרֹחַ**: pl. אֶפְרֹחִים, sf. אֶפְרֹחָיו: **young bird** Dt 22_6.

אַפִּרְיוֹן: **sedan-chair** SS 3_9. †

אֶפְרַיִם: **Ephraim**: — 1. son of Joseph, Gn 41_{52}; — 2. name of tribe Nu 1_{10}; — 3. Northern Kingdom, Is 7_2; — 4. name of territory, mountain area of Ephraim 1S 1_1; — 5. **Ephraimites**, members of 2, 3, or 4, Ju 7_{24}; — 6. n. loc. ? near Jerusalem 2S 13_{23}; — 7. *ša'ar 'efrayim*, north gate of Jerusalem 2K 14_{13}.

אֶפְרָת: n. pers.

אֶפְרָתָה: n. loc.

אֶפְרָתִי: n. gent.; pl. אֶפְרָתִים: — 1. **Ephrathite** 1S 17_{12}; — 2. **Ephraimite** Ju 12_5.

אֶצְבֹּ(וֹ)ן: n. pers.

אֶצְבַּע: cs. =; sf. אֶצְבָּעוֹ; pl. אֶצְבָּע(וֹ)ת, cs. אֶצְבְּעוֹת, sf. אֶצְבְּעוֹתָיו: — 1. **finger**, also **toe** 2S 21_{20}; *šālaḥ 'eṣba'*, **extend a finger** Is 58_9; — 2. *'eṣba' 'elōhîm*, works Ex 8_{15}, writes 31_{18}.

I ***אָצִיל**: pl. sf. אֲצִילֶיהָ: **most distant parts** (of the earth) Is 41_9. †

II **אָצִיל**: pl. cs. אֲצִילֵי: **eminent** Ex 24_{11}. †

***אַצִּיל** & **אַצִּילָה**: pl. cs. אַצִּלֵי & אַצִּילוֹת: — 1. **joint**, *'aṣṣîlôt yādayim* **armpits** Je 38_{12}, *'aṣṣîlê yādayim* **wrists** Ez 13_{18}; — 2. architectural tech. term, uncertain Ez 41_8: in side measure? in height of terrace?

אצל: **qal**: pf. אָצַלְתָּ, וְאָצַלְתִּי; impf. וַיָּאצֶל Nu 11_{25}: **take away** Nu $11_{17 \cdot 25}$; **lay aside** Gn 27_{36}; w. *min* **refuse** Ec 2_{10}. †

nif.: pf. נֶאֱצַל: **be taken away**: architectural tech. term, **be shortened, taken in** Ez 42_{6}.

אֵצֶל: sf. אֶצְלִי: ***side**, only w. gen. or sf. as prep., at the side of, **beside** Ne 4_{12}; hostility **over against** Dn 10_{13}; *mē'ēṣel* **from beside** 1S 20_{41}.

אָצַל: n. pers.

אֲצַלְיָהוּ: n. pers.

אֹצֶם: n. pers.

אֶצְעָדָה: **'pace-chain'**: chain between 2 ankles Nu 31_{50}; — 2. **armlet** 2S 1_{10}. †

אצר: **qal**: pf. אָצְרוּ; pt. אוֹצְרִים: **store up** 2K 20_{17}.

nif.: impf. יֵאָצֵר: **be stored up** Is 23_{18}. †

[**hif.**: impf. וָאוֹצְרָה Ne 13_{13} rd וָאֲצַוֶּה. †]

אֵצֶר: n. pers.

אֶקְדָּח: precious stone, **beryl** in genl. sense, *'abnê 'eqdāḥ* Is 54_{12}. †

אַקּוֹ: (edible) **wild goat**, *Capra aegagrus*, Dt 14_{5}. †

אֹר: כָּאֹר Am 8_{8} rd כַּיְאֹר, ᶠ יְאֹר.

אֲרָא: n. pers.

אֲרִאֵיל Ez $43_{15b \cdot 16}$: ᶠ I אֲרִיאֵל.

אַרְאֵל: 2S 23_{20} rd אראֵלִי (vocal.?) **warrior**. †

אַרְאֵלִי: — 1. n. pers. Gn 46_{16} Nu 26_{17}; — 2. n. gent. of 1. Nu 26_{17}. †

אֶרְאֶלָּם Is 33_{7}: ??, corr.; prp. אַרְאֵלִים **heroes** or אֲרִאֵלִים **priests** or **inhabitants of Jerusalem**; ᶠ comm.

אָרַב: **qal**: pf. אֲרַבְתֶּם, אָרְבוּ, אָרַבְתִּי, א׳; impf. נֶאֶרְבָה, יֶאֱרֹבוּ, יֶאֶרְבוּ, יֶאֱרֹב; impv. אֱרֹב; inf. אֱרָב־; pt. אֹרְבִים, א(וֹ)רֵב: — **lie in ambush** Ps 10_{9}, w. *le* **lie in wait** for s.one Dt 19_{11}, w. *'al* Ju 9_{34}; pt. coll. *'ōrēb* (an army in) **ambush** Jos 8_{2ff}.

piel: pt. מְאָרְבִים: pt. w. *śûm*, **put** (people) **in ambush** Ju 9_{25}.

hif.: impf. וַיָּרֶב (< *וַיַּאֲרֵב), **lay an ambush** 1S 15_{5}. †

אֲרַב: n. loc.

***אֶרֶב**: אֶרֶב: **hiding-place** Jb 37_{8} 38_{40}. †

אֹרֵב: pt. **qal** אָרַב, ᶠ above.

***אֹרֶב**: sf. אָרְבּוֹ: **ambush** Je 9_{7}.

אַרְבֵּאל, Ho 10_{14}: ᶠ בֵּית־אַרְבֵּאל.

אַרְבֶּה: **locust**, spec. migratory or desert **locust**, *Schistocera gregaria*, in winging stage: Ex 10_{4ff}.

***אָרְבָּה**: pl. cs. אָרְבּוֹת: *'im 'orbôt yādāyw* ? in spite of (suitable) movements of his hands Is 25_{11}. †

אֲרֻבָּה: pl. אֲרֻבּוֹת, sf. אֲרֻבֹּתֵיהֶם: — 1. **window** in the wall through which smoke escapes, **chimney** Ho 13_{3}; in dovecotes Is 60_{8}; metaph. of eyesockets Ec 12_{3}; — 2. windows in ᶠ *rāqîaʿ*, through which rain falls Gn 7_{11} 8_{2}.

אֲרֻבּוֹת: n. loc. 1K 4_{10}. †

אַרְבִּי: gent. of אֲרַב.

I **אַרְבַּע**: אַרְבָּע; f. אַרְבָּעָה, cs. אַרְבַּעַת, sf. אַרְבַּעְתָּם; du. אַרְבַּעְתָּיִם; pl. אַרְבָּעִים: — sg. **four**, du. **fourfold**, pl. **forty**; for details of use, see gramm.; a) *'arbaʿ 'ammôt* Dt 3_{11}, *ʿārîm 'arbaʿ* Jos 19_{7}; b) *'arbāʿâ rā'šîm* Gn 2_{10}; *be'arbāʿâ laḥōdeš*, on the 4th day of the month Zc 7_{1}; c) *'arbaʿat yāmîm* Ju 11_{40}; d) *'arbaʿ ʿeśrēh* & *'arbāʿâ ʿāśār* 14; *'arbaʿ mē'ôt* 400, *'arbaʿat 'alāfîm* 4000.

II **אַרְבַּע**: n. pers. Jos 14_{15} 15_{13} 21_{11}. †

ארג: **qal**: impf. תַּאַרְגִי, יֶאֱרֹג; pt. אֹרֵג, אֹרְגִים, אֹרְגוֹת: **weave** 2K 23_{7}; pt. weaver Ex 28_{32}.

אֶרֶג: אֶרֶג: **shuttle** Jb 7_{6}. †

אַרְגֹּב: n. terr.

אַרְגְּוָן 2C 2_{6} = ᶠ אַרְגָּמָן. †

אַרְגַּז: **saddlebag** 1S $6_{8 \cdot 11 \cdot 15}$. †

אַרְגָּמָן: **wool dyed w. red purple** Ex 25_{4}; *beged 'argāmān* Nu 4_{13}.

אַרְדְּ, **אֶרֶד**: n. pers.

אַרְדּוֹן: n. pers.

אַרְדִּי: gent. of אַרְדְּ.

אֲרַדִּי: n. pers.

ארה: **qal**: pf. אָרִיתִי, אָרוּהָ: **pluck** Ps 80$_{13}$ SS 5$_{1}$. †

אֲרוֹד: n. pers.

אַרְוָד: n. loc.

אֲרוֹדִי: — 1. n. pers. Gn 46$_{16}$; — 2. n. gent. Nu 26$_{17}$. †

אַרְוָדִי: n. gent.

***אֻרְוָה**: pl. אֻרָוֹת, cs. אֻרְוֹת > אֻרְיוֹת: **stable** 1K 5$_{6}$.

***אָרוּז**: pl. אֲרֻזִים: **tightly twisted** (rope) Ez 27$_{24}$. †

אֲרוּכָה & אֲרֻכָה; cs. אֲרֻכַת, sf. אֲרֻכָתְךָ, new flesh in a healing wound: — 1. **healing** Je 8$_{22}$; — 2. metaph. of masonry, **repair, mending** Ne 4$_{1}$.

אֲרוּמָה: n. loc.

אֲרוֹן (ca. 200×): w. art. הָאָר(וֹ)ן, cs. אֲר(וֹ)ן; m., f. Nu 1S 4$_{17}$ 2C 8$_{11}$ Ps 132$_{6}$ (?) †
I secular: — 1. **coffin** Gn 50$_{26}$ †; — 2. **money-chest** 2K 12$_{10f}$.
II cultic: **ark of the covenant**: in various combinations: *ʾarôn hāʾelōhîm* 1S 3$_{3}$, *ʾarôn yhwh* Jos 4$_{5}$, *hāʾārôn* Ex 25$_{14}$, *ʾarôn berît yhwh*, Nu 10$_{33}$, *ʾarôn habberît* Jos 3$_{6}$; meaning: a) trad.: container for tables of the law, Dt 10$_{1ff}$, P; b) older critical opinion: chest in which God was thought to be present 1S 4-6; c) more recently: throne for the invisible God; d) recent combinations, e.g.: sacred object of nomadic wandering or Canaanite processions.

אֲרַוְנָה: n. pers.

אֶרֶז: אָרֶז; pl. אֲרָזִים, cs. אַרְזֵי: 1K 5$_{13}$ & oft.; kind of tree, and its wood, from Lebanon, used for beams, paneling, pillars; trad. **cedar**, *Cedrus Libani Barrel* does not have long enough trunks for building, so that it is more likely the **fir**, *Abies Cilicica* or another evergreen with long trunk.

אַרְזָה: paneling of *ʾerez*-wood Zp 2$_{14}$, corr ? †

אָרַח: **qal**: pf. א׳; inf. sf. אָרְחִי; pt. אֹרֵחַ, אֹרְחִים: — 1. **be on the way** (*le* to) Jb 34$_{8}$; — 2. abs. **wander** Ps 139$_{3}$; pt. **wanderer** 2S 12$_{4}$.

אָרַח: n. pers.

אֹרַח: sf. אָרְחֲךָ, אָרְחוֹ, אָרְחָךְ; pl. אֳרָחוֹת, cs. אָרְחוֹת, sf. אָרְחֹתָם, אֹרְחֹתָיו; f.: — 1. **stretch** (of path) (distinction w. 2ff oft. questionable) Gn 49$_{17}$; — 2. **ground** Is 41$_{3}$; — 3. **dam** (their barriers of disaster) Jb 30$_{12}$; — 4. **manner** (of women) = menstruation Gn 18$_{11}$; — 5. way (one must go), **behavior** Ps 119$_{9}$: *ʾōraḥ ḥayyîm* leading to life Ps 16$_{11}$; — 6. **way** set forth by Y. Ps 44$_{19}$; other phrases: *ʾōraḥ mišpāṭ* Is 40$_{14}$, *ʾōraḥ ṣedāqâ* Pr 8$_{20}$.

***אֹרְחָה**: pt. f.: cs. אֹרְחַת; pl. cs. אֹרְחוֹת: nomadic host, **caravan** Gn 37$_{25}$.

אֲרֻחָה: cs. אֲרֻחַת, sf. אֲרֻחָתוֹ: **provisions** Je 40$_{5}$, **allowance** 52$_{34}$, **portion** Pr 15$_{17}$.

אֲרִי: pl. אֲרָיוֹת, 1K 10$_{20}$ אֲרָיִים: (African) **lion** Nu 23$_{24}$.

אֲרִי: n. pers.

I **אֲרִיאֵל** Ez 43$_{15b}$ & $_{16}$ Qr, אראיל $_{16}$ Kt, הַרְאֵל $_{15a}$: **altar hearth** of sanctuary whose constant fire consumes the sacrifice; oth.: **altar of burnt offering** as cosmic mountain. †

II **אֲרִיאֵל**: n. loc.: ? = I, Jerusalem or part of it, Is 29$_{1f.7}$. †

III **אֲרִיאֵל**: n. pers. Ezr 8$_{16}$. †

אֲרִידָתָא: n. pers.

I **אַרְיֵה**: pl., ↗ אֲרִי: (African) **lion** Gn 49$_{9}$.

[II **אַרְיֵה**: הָאַרְיֵה 2K 15$_{25}$ corr., ↗ comm. †]

***אֻרְיָה**: ↗ אֻרְוָה.

אַרְיוֹךְ: n. pers.

אֲרִים: ↗ I אוּר.

אֲרִיסַי: n. pers.

ארך: **qal**: pf. אָרְכוּ; impf. יַאַרְכוּ, וַתֶּאֱרַכְנָה: **be, become long**: branches Ez 31$_{5}$, days Gn 26$_{8}$ Ez 12$_{22}$ = last long. †
hif.: pf. הֶאֱרִיךְ, הֶאֱרִיכוּ, וְהַאֲרַכְתָּ; impf. יַאֲרִיךְ, יַאֲרִיכוּ, תַּאֲרִיכוּן, יַאֲר(י)כוּן; impv. הַאֲרִיכוּ; inf.: הַאֲרִיךְ; pt. מַאֲרִיךְ: — 1.

make long, **lengthen**: a) in space: cords Is 54_2; **extend** tongue 57_4; b) in time: s.one's days = **let** s.one **live long** 1K 3_{14}, one's own days = **live long** Nu 9_{19}; **hold in anger** Is 48_9; — 2. **be long** 1K 8_8.

*אָרֵךְ or = אָרֹךְ: cs. אֶרֶךְ: — 1. *'erek 'appayim* **slow** in regard **to anger**, patient Ex 34_6; — 2. *'erek hā'ēber* with long wings Ez 17_3.

*אָרֹךְ: f. אֲרֻכָּה: — 1. **extended** (in space) Jb 11_9; — 2. **long-lasting** (battle) 2S 3_1. †

אֹרֶךְ (100×): sf. אָרְכּוֹ: **length** — 1. (in space) Gn 6_{15}; — 2. (in time) *'ōrek yāmîm* **long life** Dt 30_{20}.

I אֶרֶךְ: cs. ↗ *אָרֵךְ.

II אֶרֶךְ: n. loc. Gn 10_{10}. †

אַרְכִּי: n. gent.

אֲרָם: cs. אֲרַם: **Aram(eans)**: 1. n. pers. Gn 10_{22}; — 2. n. terr. *'aram naharayim* (↗ *naharayim*) Gn 24_{10}; — 3. n. terr. *paddan-'aram* (↗ *paddan*) Gn 31_{18}; — 4. *'aram dammeśeq* Aramean kingdom (w. capital in Damascus) 2S 8_6; — 5. misc. phrases: *'aram ṣôbâ* 2S 10_6 ↗ *ṣôbâ*; *'elōhê 'aram* Ju 10_6.

אַרְמוֹן: pl. cs. אַרְמְנוֹת, sf. אַרְמְנוֹתָיו: (fortified) **palace** Am 1_4-2_5.

*אֲרָמִי: f. אֲרָמִית: f. adv. **in** (the) **Aramaic** (language) 2K 18_{26}.

אֲרַמִּי: gent., f. אֲרַמִּיָּה: **Aramean** Gn 25_{20}.

אַרְמֹנִי: n. pers.

אֲרָן: n. pers.

I אֹרֶן: (bay or sweet) **laurel**, *Laurus nobilis* Is 44_{14}. †

II אֹרֶן: n. pers. 1C 2_{25}. †

אַרְנֶבֶת: **hare** Lv 11_6 Dt 14_7. †

אַרְנוֹן & אַרְנֹן: name of river, **Arnon** Nu 21_{31ff}.

אֲרַנְיָה 2S 24_{18} Kt: n. pers., ↗ אֲרַוְנָה, אָרְנָן.

אַרְנָן: n. pers.

אָרְנָן: n. pers.

אַרְפָּד, Is 10_9 אַרְפַּד: n. loc.

אַרְפַּכְשַׁד, אַרְפַּכְשָׁד: n. pers.

אֶרֶץ (ca. 2400×): אֶרֶץ, הָאָרֶץ, loc. אַרְצָה & אָ֫רְצָה (also in cs.); sf. אַרְצְךָ, אַרְצֶךָ; pl. אֲרָצ(וֹ)ת, cs. אַרְצוֹת, sf. אַרְצֹתָם; f.: — 1. **ground**: esp. loc. *'árṣâ*, Gn 18_2 did obeisance to the ground, 38_9 spilled it on the ground; *'ereṣ*, Ju 6_{37ff}; — 2. **piece of land** Gn 23_{15}; — 3. **territory, land**: *'ereṣ miṣrayim, 'ereṣ kena'an* Gn 47_{13}, pl. Is 37_{18}; 4. — totality of land, **earth**: *haššāmayim wehā'āreṣ* Gn $2_{1 \cdot 4a}$; — 5. *taḥtiyyôt 'ereṣ* **depths of the earth** Is 44_{23}, > *'ereṣ* **underworld** Ex 15_{12}.

אַרְצָה: n. pers. 1K 16_9. †

ארר: **qal**: pf. וְאָרוֹתִי & אֲרוֹתִיהָ; impf. תָּאוֹר; impv. אָרָה־, אֹ(וֹ)רוּ; inf. אָרוֹר; pt. אֹרְרֵי, אֹרְרֶיךָ, pass. אָרוּר, אֲרוּרָה: — **curse**, spec.: **inflict with a curse** (:: *qillēl* = characterise as cursed): — 1. God subj.: Gn 3_{14}; — 2. man subj. 9_{25}; w. *min*, away from Gn 3_{14} 4_{11}; w. *lifnê*: under God's call, that he follow through on contents of curse Jos 6_{26} 1S 26_{19}.

nif.: pt. נֵאָרִים: **inflicted with a curse** Mal 3_9. †

piel: pf. אֵרְרָהּ; pt. מְאָרְרִים (1× מְאָֽרְרִים): **inflict with a curse** Gn 5_{29}; **bring about a curse** Nu 5_{18ff}.

hof. (or **qal pass.**): impf. יוּאַר: **be inflicted with a curse** Nu 22_6. †

אֲרָרַט, אֲרָרָט: n. terr., **Ararat**.

*אֲרָרִי: n. pers.: 2S 23_{33} Kt האררי, Qr ↗ הֲרָרִי. †

ארשׂ: **piel**: pf. אֵרַשׂ, אֵרַשְׂתִּי, אֵרַשְׂתִּיךְ; impf. תְּאָרֵשׂ: w. acc., **become engaged to** (a woman) Dt 20_7; w. *be* + bride-price 2S 3_{14}.

pual: pf. אֹרָשָׂה; pt. מְאֹרָשָׂה: **be, become engaged** (subj. woman) Ex 22_{15}.

אֲרֶשֶׁת: **desire** Ps 21_3.†

אֹרַת 2K 4_{39}: ↗ אוֹרָה.

אַרְתַּחְשַׁסְתְּא, אַרְתַּחְשַׁשְׂתָּא ,־שַׁשְׂתְּא־: n. pers. **Artaxerxes**.

אֲשַׂרְאֵל: n. pers.

אֲשַׂרְאֵלָה: n. pers.

אַשְׂרִיאֵל: n. pers.

אַשְׂרִיאֵלִי: gent. of prec.

I אֵשׁ (380×), mostly f.: sf. אִשּׁוֹ, אֶשְׁכֶם: **fire**, in variety of idioms, e.g.: w. *yāṣâ'*, breaks out Ex 22_5; *nātan bᵉ*, light, put fire in Lv 10_1; oft. *śāraf bā'ēš* Ex 29_{14}; ↗ accompanying word.

II אֵשׁ: little, **trifle**, *bᵉdê-'ēš* Je 51_{58} Hb 2_{13}. †

אֶשׁ, אִישׁ: **there is/are (on hand)** 2S 14_{19} Pr 18_{24} Mi 6_{10}. †

אַשְׁבֵּל: n. pers.

אַשְׁבֵּלִי: gent. of prec.

אֶשְׁבָּן: n. pers.

אַשְׁבֵּעַ: n. loc., unknown.

אֶשְׁבָּעַל, אֶשְׁבַּעַל: n. pers.

*אֶשֶׁד: cs. אֶשֶׁד; pl. אֲשֵׁדוֹת, cs. אַשְׁד(וֹ)ת: **slope** Jos 10_{40}.

אַשְׁדּוֹד: n. loc. **Ashdod**.

אַשְׁדּוֹדִי: gent. of prec.

אֵשְׁדָּת: Dt 33_2, obscure, prp. אֵשׁ דֹּלֶקֶת/יֹקֶדֶת — ?. †

אִשָּׁה (775×): sg. cs. אֵשֶׁת, ? as abs. Dt 21_{11} 1S 28_7 Ps 58_9 †; sf. אִשְׁתִּי &c., אֶשְׁתְּךָ Ps 128_3 †; pl. נָשִׁים, אִשֹּׁת Ez 23_{44}, cs. נְשֵׁי, sf. נְשֵׁיהֶם, נָשֵׁינוּ, נָשַׁי: — 1. **woman** (:: *'îš*) Gn 2_{23}, *bêt hannāšîm* **harem** Est 2_3; oft. in appos., *'iššâ 'almānâ* 1K 7_{14}, *'iššâ zônâ* Jos 2_1; — 2. **wife**, *nātan lᵉ'iššâ*, give s.one as a wife Gn 34_8, *'ēšet 'āb* **stepmother** Lv 18_{11}; also for concubine Gn 30_4, widow 1S 30_5; — 3. **female** (animal) Gn 7_2; — 4. **each** (woman) Ex 3_{22}.

אִשֶּׁה: cs. אִשֵּׁה, sf. אִשּׁוֹ; pl. cs. אִשֵּׁי, sf. אִשַּׁי, אִשָּׁיו: **offering by fire**, ref. to *'ôlâ* & to other types of sacrifice, mostly P, oft. in phrase *'iššeh lᵉyhwh* & the like, Ex 29_{18}.

*אשויה Je 50_{15}: ↗ *אָשְׁיָה.

אֱשׁוּן Qr, Kt אִישׁוֹן: time, **approach** (of darkness) Pr 20_{20}.

אַשּׁוּר: name of people & terr.: loc. אַשּׁוּרָה Gn 25_{18}: — 1. n. pers. **Asshur** Gn 10_{22}; — 2. name of territory, from name of city Asshur: **Assyria** Gn 2_{14}; — 3. name of people & empire, **Assyria**, m. (f. Nu 24_{22} Ez 32_{22}) Is 10_5; — 4. *melek 'aššûr* = king of Persia Ezr 6_{22}.

הָאֲ׳ אֲשׁוּרִי: n. terr. 2S 2_9: corrupt?

אַשּׁוּרִם: n. pers. Gn 25_3.

אַשְׁחוּר: n. pers.

*אָשְׁיָה: pl. Qr אָשְׁיוֹתֶיהָ Kt uncertain; **tower** Je 50_{15}. †

אֲשִׁימָה: deity of Hamath 2K 17_{30}. †

אֲשֵׁרָה 2K 17_{19}: ↗ אֲשֵׁרָה.

*אָשִׁישׁ: pl. cs. אֲשִׁישֵׁי: **man** Is 16_7. †

אֲשִׁישָׁה: **raisin-cakes**, as luxury food 2S 6_{19}, cultic Ho 3_1.

*אֶשֶׁךְ: אֶשֶׁךְ: **testicle** Lv 21_{20}. †

I אֶשְׁכּוֹל (4×) & אֶשְׁכֹּל (1×): pl. abs. אַשְׁכֹּלוֹת, cs. אַשְׁכְּלוֹת, אֶשְׁ־, sf. אַשְׁכְּלֹתֶיהָ: — 1. strictly, the empty **vine-stalk** Gn 40_{10}, then the whole **cluster** of grapes Nu 13_{23}; — 2. cluster (of henna-blossoms) SS 1_{14}.

II אֶשְׁכֹּ(וֹ)ל: n. loc.; = I; Nu 13_{23f} 32_9 Dt 1_{24}. †

III אֶשְׁכֹּל: n. pers.; = I; Gn $14_{13.24}$. †

אַשְׁכְּנַז, אַשְׁכְּנָז: n. pers. Gn 10_3 1C 1_6; tribe Je 51_{27}; **Scythians**. †

אֶשְׁכָּר: sf. אֶשְׁכָּרֵךְ: **tribute** Ez 27_{15} Ps 72_{10}. †

אֵשֶׁל: **tamarisk**, *Tamarix syriaca* Gn 21_{33}.

אָשַׁם: **qal**: pf. א׳, אָשֵׁם, אָשְׁמָה, אָשַׁמְתָּ, אָשֵׁמוּ; impf. יֶאְשַׁם, יֶאְשְׁמוּ, יֶאְשָׁמוּ, נֶאְשָׁם; inf. אָשׁ(וֹ)ם, cs. אַשְׁמָה Lv 5_{26}: — 1. **incur guilt, become guilty** Lv 5_2; w. *lᵉ*, in regard to (*Yhwh*) Lv 5_{19}; — 2. **accept** (consequences of) **guilt**, a) by sufferings of punishment, Is 24_6; b) confess guilt by act of expiation Lv 5_{23}.

nif.: pf. נֶאְשָׁמוּ: **suffer punishment** Jl 1_{18}, but rd *nāšammû*, ↗ *šmm*. †

hif.: impv. הַאֲשִׁימֵם: **hold guilty** Ps 5_{11}. †

אָשָׁם: sf. אֲשָׁמוֹ; pl. sf. אֲשָׁמָיו: — 1. **guilt** Gn 26_{10}; — 2. (equivalent amount of) **wrong** (in case of property damage) Nu 5_{7f}; — 3. **guilt**

offering 2K 12_{17}; — 4. **compensating gift** 1S 6_{3ff}.

אָשֵׁם: pl. אֲשֵׁמִים: **bearing** (consequence of) **guilt** Gn 42_{21} 2S 14_{13}. †

אַשְׁמָה: cs. אַשְׁמַת, sf. אַשְׁמָתוֹ, אַשְׁמָתֵינוּ Ezr 9_{15}; pl. אֲשָׁמוֹת, sf. אַשְׁמוֹתַי: (act of) **guilt**, consequence of guilt, acceptance of guilt: Lv 4_{3}, 5_{24}, pl. Ps 69_{6}.

אַשְׁמוּרָה Ps 90_{4} & **אַשְׁמֹרֶת** Ju 7_{19}, cs. אַשְׁמֹרֶת Ex 14_{24} 1S 11_{11}: **night-watch** Ps 90_{4}; *ʾašmōret habbōqer*, evidently last watch of night Ex 14_{24} 1S 11_{11}.

***אַשְׁמָן**: pl. אַשְׁמַנִּים: Is 59_{10}: ??; prp.: 'among the stout'; 'in health'; 'uninhabited places' = cemetery; 'in dusk'. †

אַשְׁמֹרֶת: ℱ אַשְׁמוּרָה.

אֶשְׁנָב: sf. אֶשְׁנַבִּי: airhole in the wall, (latticed) **window** Ju 5_{28} Pr 7_{6}. †

אַשְׁנָה: n. loc.

אֶשְׁעָן: n. loc.

אַשָּׁף: pl. אַשָּׁפִים: **conjurer** Da 1_{20} 2_{2}. †

אַשְׁפָּה: sf. אַשְׁפָּתוֹ: **quiver** Is 22_{6}, *b^{e}nê ʾašpātô* = his arrows La 3_{13}.

אַשְׁפְּנַז: n. pers.

אֶשְׁפָּר: **date-cake** 2S 6_{19} 1C 16_{3}. †

אַשְׁפֹּת, **אַשְׁפּוֹת** 1×: pl. אַשְׁפַּתּוֹת; הָשֲׁפוֹת Ne 3_{13}: — 1. **ash-pit** 1S 2_{8} Ps 113_{7}; **dungheap, dump** La 4_{5}; — 2. n. loc. *šaʿar hāʾašpôt* Ne 2_{13}.

אַשְׁקְלוֹן: n. loc.

אַשְׁקְלוֹנִי: gent. of prec.

I **אשר**: **qal**: impv. אִשְׁרוּ: **step** Pr 9_{6}. †

piel: impf. תְּאַשֵּׁר; impv. אַשֵּׁר, אַשְּׁרוּ; pt. pl. מְאַשְּׁרֵי, מְאַשְּׁרֶיךָ: — 1. intr. **step** (cj. qal) Pr 4_{14}; — 2. **lead** Is 3_{12} 9_{15}; Is 1_{17} trad. **restrain, reprove** (?).

pual: pt. pl. מְאֻשָּׁרָיו: **be led** Is 9_{15}. †

II **אשר**: **piel**: pf. אִשְּׁרוּ, אִשְּׁרוּנִי; impf. וַיְאַשְּׁרוּהָ, וַתְּאַשְּׁרֵנִי: **call** s.one **fortunate** Gn 30_{13}.

pual: impf. יְאֻשַּׁר; pt. מְאֻשָּׁר: **be called fortunate** Ps 41_{3}.

אָשֵׁר: n. pers. Gn 30_{13} &c.; n. tribe Gn 49_{20} &c.

אֲשֶׁר: I. as relative particle: — 1. sporadically in old or poetic texts, originally the relative clause was joined to the noun w/o *ʾ^{a}šer*, Is 40_{20}; — 2. *ʾ^{a}šer* can be added to connect the noun to the clause, Ho 2_{1}; — 3. *ʾ^{a}šer* adds to the explicitness of the expression, the relation being more precisely expressed by deferred prep. & sf. or acc. sign, Gn 21_{2}, Dt 1_{22}; — 4. later, prep. & sf. or other explanatory word occurs directly after *ʾ^{a}šer*, Is 5_{28}; — 5. later still, any explanatory word is omitted altogether, Gn 2_{8}, *hāʾādām ʾ^{a}šer yāṣar*, **the man whom he formed** (:: 1.); — 6. prep. may be prefixed to *ʾ^{a}šer*: *baʾ^{a}šer* Gn 21_{17}, *mēʾ^{a}šer* Ex 5_{11}, *ʾet-ʾ^{a}šer* **whom** Ex 33_{12}; — 7. nouns in cs. before *ʾ^{a}šer*: *m^{e}qôm ʾ^{a}šer* Gn 39_{20}.

II. as conj.: *rāʿātām ʾ^{a}šer ʿ^{a}zābûnî* Je 1_{16} their wickedness (in) which they left me = wickedness that they...: thus *ʾ^{a}šer* comes to = older *kî*: a) in object clause, **that**: *šāmaʿnû ʾēt ʾ^{a}šer*, we have heard that (or, how) Jos 2_{10}; b) introducing dir. discourse 1S 15_{20}; c) giving cause, **because** (< in that) Gn 30_{18}; d) giving consequence, **so that** Gn 11_{7}; e) comparison, **as** Ex 10_{6}; f) final, **so that** Ru 3_{1}; g) conditional, **if** Lv 4_{22}.

***אֶשֶׁר**: sf. אַשְׁרֵהוּ Pr 29_{18}; pl. ℱ אַשְׁרֵי: **fortune**: = fortunate is he Pr 29_{18}. †

***אֹשֶׁר**: sf. אָשְׁרִי: **fortune** Gn 30_{13}. †

***אָשֻׁר** & Jb 31_{7} *אַשֻּׁר: sf. אֲשֻׁרוֹ, אַשֻּׁרַי; f.: — 1. **step** Ps 17_{5}; — 2. **track** Jb 23_{11}.

I **אַשֻּׁר**: ℱ *אָשֻׁר; II **אַשֻּׁר**, ℱ אַשּׁוּר.

אֲשֵׁרָה & 2K 17_{16} אֲשֵׁירָה: — 1. name of goddess **Asherah**, in Ugarit the wife of El and mother of the gods 1K 18_{19}; mostly *hāʾ^{a}šērâ*, pl. *(hā)ʾ^{a}šērôt*, but 2C 24_{18} *hāʾ^{a}šērîm*; — 2. cultic post, **Asherah**, Dt 16_{21}; pl. *ʾ^{a}šērîm*, sf. *ʾ^{a}šērêkā* &c.; much confusion in OT between 1 and 2.

אַשְׁרִי: gent. of אָשֵׁר.
אַשְׁרֵי: pl. cs. of *אֶשֶׁר fortune; sf. אַשְׁרָיו, אַשְׁרֵיךְ Ec 10_{17}; introduction to word of blessing; **fortunate, blessed is (he who), are (they who)**: — 1. followed by noun, 1K 10_8; — 2. followed by suffix, Dt 33_{29}; — 3. *'ašrê še* Ps 137_{8f} 146_5; — 4. followed by relative clause w/o relative particle Pr 8_{32}.
אשש: **hitpo.**: impv. הִתְאֹשָׁשׁוּ: **take courage** Is 46_8. †
אֵשֶׁת: — 1. ↗ אִשָּׁה cs.; — 2. Ps 58_9 corr.
אֶשְׁתָּאֹל (4×) & אֶשְׁתָּאוֹל (3×): n. loc.; אֶשְׁתָּאֻלִי gent.
אֶשְׁתּוֹן: n. pers.
מֵאֶשְׁתֵּם Je 6_{29}: rd Qr מֵאֵשׁ תַּם & ↗ comm.
אֶשְׁתְּמֹה Jos 15_{50}: ↗ אֶשְׁתְּמֹעַ.
אֶשְׁתְּמֹעַ: n. loc.
אַתְּ: ↗ אַתָּה.
אַתְּ: **you** f. sg. Gn $12_{11\cdot 13}$; Kt w. אתי preserves earlier form *'attî*.
I אֵת: acc.-particle in prosaic & later material: אֶת־, אֵת־ Jb 41_{26}; sf. א(ו)תִי, אֹתָךְ, אֹתָכָה Ex 29_{35}, א(ו)תְךָ, א(ו)תָנוּ, א(ו)תָם, אֶתְהֶן/הֶם, אוֹתְכֶם, אֶתְכֶם Jos 23_{15}, אוֹתְהֶן, א(ו)תְהֶם, א(ו)תָנָה, אֹתָן Ez 23_{45} & 23_{47}: — 1. bearing pers. sf., esp. if stressed, *'ōtî* 1S 8_7; — 2. indicating acc. of noun when definite, either by def. art. Gn 1_1, w. proper name 2S 3_{11}, by def. gen. Gn 1_{25}, or w. noun w. sf. Ru 2_{15}; rarely w. indef. acc., but: *'et-'îš* Ex 21_{28}; omission does not affect mng.; — 3. before non-pers. pron.: *'et-mî*, **whom** Is 6_8, cf. *'ēt 'ašer* Nu 22_6; — 4. remarks: a) *'et-* can mark any sort of acc., esp. that of limitation: **diseased** *'et-raglāyw* **as to his feet** 1K 15_{23}; b) after a pass. vb. it is construed impersonally: one told Esau's words (acc.!) to Rebekah Gn 27_{42}; c) at times *'et-* seems to stand before a stressed nominative, felt psychologically as acc., Ne 9_{19}; d) oft. *'ōtô* &c. stands for *'ittô*, ↗ II *'ēt*: Gn $34_{2\cdot 9}$.

II אֵת: prep. **with**: אֶת־; sf. אִתִּי, אִתְּךָ (אִתָּךְ Is 54_{10}), אִתָּנוּ, אִתְּכֶם, אִתָּם; sf.-forms oft. mistakenly for I אֵת: — 1. **(together) with**: w. *hālak* 2S 16_{17b}; — 2. **with (help of)**, 1C 2_{18}; *'et-mî* **with whose help?** Jb 26_4; — 3. **by, at the side of**: **in their presence** Is 30_8; **beside me, besides me** Ex 20_{23}; *'ittô ḥ^alôm* **he had a dream** Je 23_{28}; — 4. w. *min*: *mē'et, mē'ittô* &c., **away from** w. vbs. of removing, Gn 17_{27} acquisition (away) from a foreigner.
III אֵת: 1.: sf. אִתּוֹ; pl. אִתִּים, 1S 13_{21} אֵתִים, sf. אִתֵּיכֶם: iron farm-tool, **plowshare** or **mattock** 1S 13_{20f}; — 2. *'et-habbarzel* 2K 6_5, ? **axe-blade**, ? del., ? better I *'ēt* 4c.
אֹת: ↗ אוֹת.
אֶתְבַּעַל: n. pers.
אתה: **qal**: pf. אָתָנוּ, א׳; impf. יֶאֱתֶה, תֵּאתֶה, וַיֵּתֵא, וַיֵּאת Qr, וַיֶּאֱתָיֵנִי, יֶאֱתָיוּ, יֶאֱתָיוּן; impv. אֵתָיוּ; pt. אֹתִיּוֹת: **come** (in var. contexts) Je 3_{22}.
hif.: הֵתָיוּ (< *הַאֲתָיוּ): **bring** Is 21_{14}.
אַתָּה: אַתָּה, also אַתָּה 2C 14_{10}; in Nu 11_{15} Dt 5_{27} Ez 28_{14} אַתְּ is error for אַתָּה; in some cases Kt את is corrected by Qr to אַתָּה: **you** m. sg.; emphasizes previous sf., *'alêkā 'attâ* 2C 35_{21}.
אָתוֹן: sf. אֲתֹנוֹ; pl. אֲתֹ(ו)נ(ו)ת: **she-ass** Gn 12_{16}.
*אַתּוּק: אתוקיהא Ez 41_{15} Kt: ↗ אַתִּיק.
*אַתַּי: ↗ אַתְּ.
אַתַּי: n. pers.
אַתִּיק; Ez 41_{15} Kt *אַתּוּק; pl. אַתִּיקִים, sf. אַתִּיקֶהָא 41_{15} Qr: unknown architectural term; prp: passage, street; Ez 41_{15f} $42_{3\cdot 5}$. †
אַתֶּם: **you** m. pl.; emphasizing previous sf., *lākem 'attem* Hg 1_4.
אֵתָם: n. loc.
אֶתְמוֹל & אֶתְמוֹל Is 30_{33}, אִתְמוֹל 1S 10_{11}: **yesterday**, *yôm 'etmôl* Ps 90_4; *'etmôl šilšōm* **yesterday and the day before (yesterday)** 1S 4_7.

אֵתָן: ☞ אֵיתָן.

אַתֵּן Ez 34_{31} & אַתֵּנָה Gn 31_{6} Ez $31_{11 \cdot 20a}$ 34_{17}: **you** f. pl. †

אֶתְנָה: **gift** (to harlot), **harlot's pay** Ho 2_{14}. †

אֶתְנִי: n. pers.

אֶתְנַן: אֶתְנַן: sf. אֶתְנַנָּהּ & Is 23_{17} אֶתְנַנָּה; pl. sf. אֶתְנַנֶּיהָ: **gift**, spec. **harlot's pay** Dt 23_{19}.

אֶתְנָן: n. pers. 1C 4_{7}. †

אֲתָרִים: n. loc.

ב

בְּ: alw. proclitic, vowel varies: בְּדָם, בַּדָּם, בִּדְמוּת, בַּאֲרוֹן, בֶּאֱדוֹם, בָּחֳרִי (bŏ), בֵּאלֹהִים; sf. בִּי; בְּךָ, בְּכָה 4× & בָּךְ; f. בָּךְ; בּוֹ & בֹּה Je 17_{24} †; בָּהּ; pl. בָּנוּ; בָּכֶם, בָּכֶן; בָּהֶם, בָּהֵמָּה 3×, בָּם; f. בָּהֶן, בָּהֵן, 3× בָּהֵנָּה: basic mng. local & instrumental, **in, at**: — 1. (remain) **in**: *babbayit, bā'āreṣ*; abstract: *be'ênê* **in the eyes of** = in the judgment of, Gn 16_{4}; spatial mng. reinforced, *beqereb, betôk*; — 2. (be) **among** (a group), *baggôyîm* La 1_{3}; — 3. before sg., expressing type or character ('beth essentiae'), **as**: *be'ēl šadday*, **as El Sh.** Ex 6_{3}; — 4. (area) **within** (which): *biš'ārêkā* **within your gates** Ex 20_{10}; — 5. with a high object, **on**: *beḥōrēb* **on Horeb** 1K 8_{9}; — 6. temporal: *bayyôm* **on the (7th) day** Gn 2_{2}, *baššānâ hāhî'* **(in) that year** Ju 10_{8}; — 7. characteristic, circumstantial: *bešālôm* **in peace** 1S 29_{7}; Is 9_{11} *bekol-zō't* **in all this > in spite of all this**; — 8. **according to**: *bederek* **according to the way of** Is $10_{24 \cdot 26}$; — 9. after vbs. of motion, **into**: Gn 19_{8}; — 10. fm. idea of remaining come exprs. like *yôm beyôm* **day by day** Ne 8_{18}; — 11. w. vbs. such as 'grasp', 'persist', 'trust'; expr. of pleasure & aversion w. vbs. of perception: 'look into' > 'look w. pleasure at,' Ob $_{12}$; — 12. sharing: a) **(together) with,** (build) Zc 6_{15}; *belō', be'ên, biblî, be'efes* **without**; hostility, **against**: *nilḥam be* **fight against** Ex 1_{10}; — 13. oft., coupled w. *'ad, le*, or *hê* local, **(away) from**: *beśē'îr 'ad* **from S. to** Dt 1_{44}; — 14. **more than,** *bāhem* Ps 89_{3}; — 15. means, tool: a) *bešôr* (plow) **with an ox** Dt 22_{10}; b) God speaks **through (by)** a prophet 1K 22_{28}; c) swear **by** God Gn 21_{23}; — 16. price, value: *bekesef* **for silver** Gn 23_{9}; — 17. material: *bemar'ōt* **from mirrors** Ex 38_{8}; — 18. cause: **because of, for the sake of** (five men) Gn 18_{28}; — 19. in later material, a substitute for *'et* acc., *pēraś beyādayim* **spread out hands** La 1_{17}; — 20. w. inf. cs., **when,** *behibbāre'ām* **when they were created** Gn 2_{4}; — 21. oft. missing before *bayit, petaḥ*: *šebî bêt'ābîk* **stay in your father's house** Gn 38_{11}.

בִּאָה: **entrance** Ez 8_{5}. †

באר: **piel**: pf. בֵּאֵר; impv. בָּאֵר; inf. בַּאֵר: **make plain, explain** (law) Dt 1_{5}; *wekātabtâ ...ba'ēr* **record carefully** Dt 27_{8} Hb 2_{2}. †

I בְּאֵר: f.; בְּאֵרָה, sf. paus. בְּאֵרֶךָ; pl. cs. בְּאֵרֹת & בְּאֶרֹת: **watering place, well** (of underground water): *ḥāfar be'ēr* **dig a well** Gn 21_{30}, var. vbs.; *be'ēr* in Ps 55_{24} 69_{16} = **underworld,** ☞ *bôr* 3; *be'erōt ḥēmār* **bitumen pits** Gn 14_{10}.

II בְּאֵר: n. loc., Nu 21_{16} Ju 9_{21}. †

III בְּאֵר in many n. loc.; בְּאֵר שֶׁבַע **Beersheba** & oth.

בֹּאר: ☞ בּוֹר.

בְּאֵרָא: n. pers.

בְּאֵרוֹת: n. loc.

בְּאֵרִי: n. pers.

בְּאֵרֹת בְּנֵי־יַעֲקָן: n. loc.

בְּאֵרֹתִי: gent. of בְּאֵרוֹת.

בָּאַשׁ: **qal**: pf. 'בּ; impf. יִבְאַשׁ: **stink** Ex $7_{18.21}$.

nif.: pf. נִבְאַשׁ, נִבְאַשְׁתָּ, נִבְאֲשׁוּ: **become odious**, w. *b^e* **to** 1S 13_{4};

hif.: pf. הִבְאִישׁ, הִבְאַשְׁתֶּם; impf. יַבְאִישׁ; inf. הַבְאִישׁ, הַבְאִישֵׁנִי: — 1. **make stinking, rank** Ec 10_{1}; **make odious** Gn 34_{30}; — 2. **become stinking** Ex 16_{24}, **become odious** 1S 27_{12}.

hitp.: pf. הִתְבָּאֲשׁוּ: **bring oneself into bad odor** 1C 19_{6}. †

בְּאֹשׁ: sf. בָּאְשׁוֹ: **stench** Is 34_{3}.

*בְּאֻשׁ: pl. בְּאֻשִׁים: **sour, unripe grapes** (oth.: wild grapes) Is $5_{2.4}$. †

בָּאְשָׁה: **darnel**, *Lolium tenulentum* Jb 31_{40}. †

בַּאֲשֶׁר: **because** Gn $39_{9.23}$ Ec 7_{2} 8_{4}; otherwise *b^e* + relative particle, ↗ *ᵓašer* I 6.

*בָּבָה: *bābat ʿayin* **eyeball** Zc 2_{12}. †

בֵּבַי, בֵּבָי: n. pers.

בָּבֶל: loc. בָּבֶלָה: n. loc., n. people: — 1. city, **Babylon**, *ᵓanšê bābel* 2K 17_{30}; — territory & empire of **Babylon**, *ᵓereṣ bābel* Je 50_{28}; Ne 13_{6} *melek bābel* = king of Persia.

בַּג: — 1. Ez 25_{7} Kt, rd Qr *baz*; — 2. ↗ פַּת־בַּג.

בגד: **qal**: pf. בָּגְדָה, בָּגַדְתָּה, בָּגַדְתִּי, בָּגְדוּ, נִבְגַּד; impf. יִבְגֹּ(וֹ)ד, יִבְגְּדוּ, תִּבְגְּדוּ, בָּגֵדוּ Mal 2_{10}; inf. לִבְגּוֹד, sf. בִּגְדוֹ, abs. בָּגוֹד; pt. בּוֹ(ו)גֵד, f. בּוֹגֵדָה, pl. בֹּגְדִים, בֹּגְדֵי: — 1. **treat faithlessly**, a) w. *b^e*, woman Ex 21_{8}; b) w. acc. Ps 73_{15}; — 2. *bāgad min*, **leave** s.one **faithlessly** Je 3_{20}; — 3. absolute: **deal faithlessly** 1S 14_{33}; *bōgēdâ y^ehûdâ* **faithless J.** Je 3_{8}; — 4. *bāgad beged* **commit faithlessness** Is 24_{16}.

I בֶּגֶד: **faithlessness, fraud** (alw. w. vb. *bāgad*) Is 24_{16} Je 12_{1}. †

II בֶּגֶד (200×): בֶּגֶד; sf. בִּגְדִי; pl. בְּגָדִים, cs. בִּגְדֵי, sf. בְּגָדַי, בִּגְדֵיכֶם, בִּגְדֹתֶיךָ Ps 45_{9} †; m.: — (any kind of) **clothes, garment**: *bigdê ᵓalmānût* **widow's garments**, *bigdê qōdeš* **cultic** garments Ex 28_{2}; *m^elōᵓ beged*, **fullness of garment** = **his lap full** 2K 4_{39}.

בֹּגְדוֹת: **faithlessness**, *ᵓanšê bōg^edôt* Zp 3_{4}. †

*בָּגוֹד: f. בָּגוֹדָה: **faithless** Je $3_{7.10}$. †

בִּגְוַי, בִּגְוָי: n. pers.

בִּגְלַל: ↗ II *גָּלָל.

בִּגְתָא: n. pers.

בִּגְתָן Est 2_{21}, בִּגְתָנָא 6_{2}: n. pers. = בִּגְתָא.

I בַּד: בַּד; sf. בַּדּוֹ, בַּדָּם, בַּדְּהֶן, בַּדֵּנָה; pl. בַּדִּים: — 1. **part, piece**, *bad b^ebad* **in equal parts** Ex 30_{34}; **limbs** Jb 18_{13}; — 2. **solitude**, *l^ebad* Ec 7_{29} †; a) adv. w. sf., *l^ebaddî*, in my **solitude** = **I alone** &c. 1K 19_{10}; *hāyâ l^ebaddô* **be alone** Gn 2_{18}; b) *l^ebad min* **besides, without regard to** Ex 12_{37}; *mill^ebad* **besides** Gn 26_{1}.

II *בַּד: pl. בַּדִּים, בַּדֵּי, sf. בַּדָּיו: — 1. (carrying) **poles** (of ark &c.) Ex 25_{14}*t*; — 2. **shoots** (on vine) Ez 19_{14}.

III בַּד: בַּד; pl. בַּדִּים: piece of fabric, prob. **linen**, as garment of priest: *ᵓēfōd bad* 1S 2_{18}, *bigdê bad* Lv 16_{23}.

IV *בַּד: pl. sf. בַּדָּיו, בַּדֶּיךָ: **empty talk, bragging** Is 16_{6}.

V *בַּד: pl. בַּדִּים, sf. בַּדָּיו: **diviner** Is 44_{25}.

בָּדָא: **qal**: pf. 'בּ; pt. sf. בּוֹדָאם (< Kt בּוֹדָאָם, Qr בּוֹדָם): **devise** 1K 12_{33} Ne 6_{8}. †

בדד: **qal**: pt. בּוֹדֵד: separate, **alone** Is 14_{31}.

בָּדָד: orig. **solitude**: *l^ebādād* **alone** Ps 4_{9}, *bādād* adv. **alone** Is 27_{10}.

בְּדַד: n. pers.

בְּדֵי: ↗ דַּי.

בֵּדְיָה: n. pers.

בְּדִיל: **tin** Nu 31_{22}; *hāᵓeben habb^edîl* Zc 4_{10} uncertain, **plumbline**?

*בְּדִיל: pl. בְּדִילָיִךְ: separations, **dross** (in smelting) Is 1_{25}.†

בדל: **nif.**: pf. נִבְדְּלוּ; impf. יִבָּדֵל, יִבָּדְלוּ; impv. pl. הִבָּדְלוּ; pt. נִבְדָּל: — 1. **separate oneself**, w. *min* **from** Ezr 9_{1}, & w. *ᵓel* **to** 6_{21}; — 2. **go over to** 1C 12_{9}; — 3. **be excluded from** Ezr 10_{8}; — 4. **be singled out** 1C 23_{13}.

hif.: pf. הִבְדִּיל, הִבְדַּלְתָּ, הִבְדִּילוּ, הִבְדִּילוֹ; impf. יַבְדִּיל, וַיַּבְדֵּל, וָאַבְדִּל, וַיַּבְדִּילֵם, יַבְדִּילֵנִי; inf. לְהַבְדִּיל, הַבְדֵּל; pt. מַבְדִּיל, מַבְדִּלִים: **separate, distinguish between**: w. *bên...ûbên*, Gn 1_{4ff}, *bên...lebên* Is 59_{2}, *bên...le* Gn 1_{6}; **make a distinction** between ... and, Ez 22_{26}; — 2. **separate, segregate** s.one, s.thg, **from** (*min*) Lv 20_{24}; — 3. **separate, detach** Lv 1_{17}.

*בָּדָל: cs. בְּדַל: **earlobe** Am 3_{12}. †

בְּדֹלַח: 'bdellium,' the fragrant, transparent, yellowish gum-resin of a South Arabian tree, Gn 2_{12} Nu 11_{7}. †

בְּדָן: n. pers.

בדק: **qal**: inf. לִבְדּוֹק: **repair** 1C 34_{10}. †

בֶּדֶק: בֶּדֶק; sf. בִּדְקֵךְ: **chink, crack** (in temple) 2K 12_{6ff}, **leak** (in ship) Ez 27_{9}.

בִּדְקַר: n. pers.

בֹּהוּ: alw. w. תֹּהוּ: **void, waste** Gn 1_{2}.

*בֹּהוֹן: pl. cs. בְּהֹנוֹת (oth.: < *בֹּהֶן): **thumb, big toe** Ju 1_{6f}. †

בַּהַט: a precious stone, uncertain: Est 1_{6}. †

בָּהִיר: **darkened**; oth.: brilliant Jb 37_{21}. †

בהל: **nif.**: pf. נִבְהַל, נִבְהֲלָה, נִבְהַלְתִּי, נִבְהֲלוּ, נִבְהָלוּ, נִבְהָלְנוּ; impf. יִבָּהֵל, אֶבָּהֵל, נִבְהָל; pt. תִּבָּהַלְנָה, יִבָּהֵלוּן, יִבָּהֲלוּ, נִבְהָל, Pr 28_{22}, נִבְהָלָה: — 1. **be terrified, out of one's senses** Ex 15_{15}; of hands Ez 7_{27}; — 2. **be hasty** Ec 8_{3}.

piel: impf. יְבַהֵל, תְּבַהֲלֵם, יְבַהֲלֻמוֹ, וִיבַהֶלְךָ, יְבַהֲלֻהוּ; inf. בַּהֲלֵנִי, בַּהֲלָם; pt. Ezr 4_{4} מְבַלְּהִים Kt = Qr מְבַהֲלִים: — 1. **terrify** Ps 2_{5}; — 2. **be hasty** Ec 5_{1} 7_{9}.

pual: pt. f. מְבֹהֶלֶת Pr 20_{21} Qr, pl. מְבֹהָלִים: **in haste** Est 8_{14}; hastily won Pr 20_{21} Qr.

hif.: pf. הִבְהִילָנִי; impf. וַיַּבְהִלוּהוּ, וַיַּבְהִלוּ: — 1. **terrify** Jb 23_{16}; — 2. **get rid of quickly** 2C 26_{20}; — 3. w. *le* & inf. **hurry** Est 6_{14}. †

בֶּהָלָה: **terror** Je 15_{8}.

בְּהֵמָה: cs. בֶּהֱמַת, sf. בְּהֶמְתּוֹ; pl. בְּהֵמוֹת, cs. בַּהֲמוֹת: usu. coll., exc. Ne $2_{12\cdot14}$: — 1. **animals** in genl.: a) :: man Ex 9_{9}; b) four-footed animals :: birds, fish, reptiles 1K 5_{13}; — 2. **wild animals,** *behemat hā’āreṣ* Dt 28_{26}, *behemat haśśādeh* 1S 17_{44}, oft. pl. Dt 32_{24}; — 3. domestic animals, **cattle** :: *ḥayyâ* Gn 8_{1}, :: *šôr* & *ḥamôr* Dt 5_{14}; = *bāqār* & *ṣō’n* Lv 1_{2} (thus also sheep); included under *ḥayyâ* Lv 11_{2}; beasts of burden Gn 34_{23}.

בְּהֵמוֹת: Jb 40_{15}, pl. of extension of *behēmâ*: trad. **hippopotamus**; oth.: **crocodile**. †

*בֹּהֶן: cs. =: **thumb, big toe** Ex 29_{20}.

בֹּהַן: n. pers.

בֹּהַק: *leucoderma, vitiligo alba*, harmless skin condition relevant to ↗ *ṣāraʿat*, Lv 13_{39}. †

בַּהֶרֶת: pl. בֶּהָרֹת: **white patch of skin**, possible sign of *ṣāraʿat* Lv 13_{2ff}.

בוא (2550×): **qal**: pf. בָּא, בָּאָה, וּבָאָה consecutive Mi 4_{8}, בָּאתָ(ה), וּבָאתָ Ex 3_{18}, f. בָּאת, בָּאתִי, בָּאוּ, וָבָאוּ, בָּאתֶם, בָּאנוּ & 1S 25_{8} בָּנוּ; sf. וּבָאָה Je 43_{11} Kt, בָּאַתְנוּ; impf. יָבֹ(ו)א, וַיָּבֹ(ו)א & 1K 12_{12} וַיָּבוֹ, תָּבוֹאָה Is 5_{19}, תָּבוֹאִי, אָבֹ(ו)אָה, יָבֹ(ו)אוּ & יְבֹאוּן, תָּבֹ(ו)אנָה & תְּבֹ(ו)אֶינָה & תָּבֹאןָ Gn 30_{38}; sf. יְבֹ(ו)אֶנּוּ, תְּבוֹאֵנִי; יַתָּבֹאתִי 1S 25_{34} Kt, תָּבוֹאתָה Dt 33_{16} & תְּבוֹאָתְךָ Jb 22_{21} seem to be mixed forms; impv.: בֹּ(ו)א, בֹּאָה, בֹּ(ו)אִי, בֹּאוּ; inf. בֹּ(ו)א, לָבֹ(ו)א, sf. בֹּ(ו)אוֹ, בֹּאֲנוּ, בֹּאֲכֶם, בֹּאִי, בֹּ(ו)אֲךָ, בֹּאֲכָה, בֹּאֵךְ, בֹּאָנָה; pt. בָּא, בָּאָה, בָּאִים, בָּאֵי, בָּאוֹת: — 1. **go in**: a) :: *yṣ’* Jos 6_{1}; w. loc. Gn 12_{11}, w. acc. *bêt* Ju 18_{18}; b) to an audience, *’el-melek* Est 2_{12}; w. *be*, **penetrate** (hand) 2K 18_{21}; abs. of bride on wedding day Jos 15_{18}; c) *bô’ ’el ’iššâ* **cohabit with** Gn 16_{2}; — 2. **come, arrive**: a) in genl., Pr 18_{3}; b) geographical Gn 19_{22}; c) temporal, days Je 7_{32}; d) **come in**, of harvest Lv 25_{22}; e) *bô’ be*, come with s.thg = **bring** s.thg 1K 13_{1}; f) **come up to, match** 2S $23_{19\cdot23}$; g) **come upon** s.one (hostility), w. *ʿal*, *’el*, *le*:

Gn 34_{27}; h) come = **happen, be fulfilled** 1S 9_6; — 3. **come back, come home**: a) 1K 22_{27} (= *šûb*); (guard) go off (duty) 2K 11_5; b) *ṣē't wābô'* (↗ *yṣ'* 5c), & the like, **march out and in** 1S 29_6; similarly of work, go out & in Dt 28_6; — 4. of God's epiphany, Dt 33_2; — 5. misc.: a) *bô' b*^{e}, **have dealings with** Jos 23_7, w. other preps.: *'ēt* Pr 22_{24}, *'im* Ps 26_4; idiomatic usages, *b*^{e}*dāmîm* **be involved w. bloodguilt** 1S 25_{26}; b) w. *'aḥ*^{a}*rê* **be in pursuit of** s.one or s.thg Ex 14_{17}; c) **be descended from** (*min*) 1C 2_{55}.

hif.: pf.: הֵבִיא, הֵבִ֫יאָה, הֵבֵ(י)אתִי & Je 25_{13} Kt הֲבִאוֹתִי, הֵבִ֫יאוּ, הֲבֵאתֶם & הֲבֵ(י)אתִיהָ, הֱבִיאֲךָ, הֱבִיאוֹ, sf. הֲבִיאוֹתָם, הֲבִיאוֹתִים, הֲבִיאֹתִיו, הֲבִיאוֹתָיו (Ne 1_9 Qr) & הֲבִיאֹתָם, הֱבִיאוּם, הֱבִיאָהוּ, הֲבֵאתִים; impf. יָבִיאוּ, יָבִ(י)א, אָבִי 1K 21_{29} & Mi 1_{15}, וַיָּבִיא & וַיָּבֵא, נָבִ(י)א, תְּבִיאֶינָה, יְבִיאוּן Ne 8_2 & וַיָּבֵיא Ez 40_3, וָאָבִ(י)א, וָאָבִאָה Jos 24_8 Kt, וַיָּבִ(י)אוּ, sf. יְבִ(י)אֵהוּ, יְבִיאֶנּוּ, אֲבִיאֶנּוּ, יְבִיאוּם, יְבִאֶהוּ, אֲבִיאֵם, יְבִיאֲךָ; impv. הָבֵ(י)א, הָבִ֫יאָה; inf. cs. הָבִיא, לְהָבִיא > לָבִיא Je 39_7 2C 31_{10}, הֲבִיאִי, abs. הָבֵא; pt. מֵבִיא (4× מֵבִי before א), מְבִיאֲךָ, מְבִ(י)אִים, מְבִ(י)אֵי, מְבִיאֶיהָ: — 1. **bring, carry (in)** Gn 6_{19} & oft., w. var. preps. (*'el, l*^{e}*, b*^{e}, loc., *lifnê*); — 2. **let** (s.one) **come** Est 5_{12}; — 3. **obtain** bride (*l*^{e}, for), Ju 12_9; — 4. **conduct** (water) 2K 20_{20}; — 5. **bring home** (army from the field) (:: *hôṣê'*, ↗ qal 3b) 2S 5_2; — 6. **gather in** (harvest) 2S 9_{10}; — 7. **earn** SS 8_{11}; — 8. *hēbî' b*^{e}*'ālâ* **put under oath, make** s.one **swear**, Ez 17_{13}; — 9. *hēbî' bammišpāṭ* **bring to justice** Ec 11_9, *hēbî' d*^{e}*bārîm 'el* **bring legal cases before** Ex 18_{19}; — 10. *hēbî' mē'aḥar* **take** s.one **away from** (s.thg) Ps 78_{71}; — 11. **present, sacrifice** Gn 4_3; — 12. *hēbî' 'āšām 'al* **bring guilt upon** Gn 26_{10}; — 13. **bring about** (s.thg promised) Is 37_{26}; — 14. *hēbî' libbô l*^{e} **apply one's mind to** Pr 23_{12}; — 15. *hēbî' 'al y*^{e}*dê* **hand over to** 2K 10_{24}.

hof.: pf. הָבָאתָה, הֻבָאת, הוּבָא; impf. יוּבָאוּ, יוּבָא; pt. מוּבָאִים, מוּבָא; — 1. **be brought** (gift) Gn 33_{11}, (people) 43_{18}; — 2. **be offered** (sacrifice) Lv 6_{23}; — 3. **be put into**, *bammayim*, Lv 11_{32}.

בוז: **qal**: pf. בַּז, בָּ֫זָה, בָּ֫זוּ; impf. יָבוּז, יָבוּזוּ; inf. abs. בּוֹז; pt. בָּז, בָּז־ Pr 11_{12} 14_{21}: — 1. w. *l*^{e}, **show contempt for** 2K 19_{21}; — 2. w. acc., **despise** Pr 1_7.

I **בּוּז**: **contempt** Ps 31_{19}; *hāyâ lābûz* **become a laughingstock** Gn 38_{23}.

II **בּוּז**: 1. name of terr. Je 25_{23}; — 2. n. pers. Gn 22_{21}; another, 1C 5_{14}. †

בּוּזָה: **contempt** Ne 3_{36}. †

I **בּוּזִי**: gent. of בּוּז n. terr.

II **בּוּזִי**: n. pers.

בַּוַּי: n. pers.

בוך: **nif.**: pf. נָבֹ֫כוּ, נָבֹ֫כָה; pt. נְבֻכִים: — 1. **be agitated** Est 3_{15}; — 2. **wander in agitation** Ex 14_3 Jl 1_{18}. †

I **בּוּל**: name of 8th month (in Canaanite calendar), Oct.-Nov., 1K 6_{38}. †

II **בּוּל**: *bûl 'ēṣ*, **block of wood** Is 44_{19}. †

III **בּוּל**: Jb 40_{20}, uncertain: trad. 'yield'; oth.: 'tribute'; 'animals'. †

בּוּנָה: n. pers.

בּוּנִּי: n. pers.

בוס: **qal**: impf. יָבוּס, אֲבוּסֶנּוּ; pt. בּוֹסִים: — **trample under foot** Is 14_{25}.

pol.: pf. בּוֹסְסוּ: trample under foot > **desecrate** Je 12_{10}.

hof.: pt. מוּבָס: **trampled** Is 14_{19}. †

hitpol.: pt. מִתְבּוֹסֶסֶת: **kicking about, floundering** Ez $16_{6.22}$. †

בּוּץ: a fine, costly white fabric (only in Ez & later), **byssus**, prob. a fine linen Ez 27_{16}.

בּוֹצֵץ: n. loc. (?) 1S 14_4. †

בּוּקָה: void, **waste** Na 2_{11}. †

בּוֹקֵר: **herdsman** Am 7_{14}. †

בור: **qal**: inf. לָבוּר: examine Ec 9_1; *l*^{e}*bārām* Ec 3_{18} ↗ *brr*. †

בּוֹר Je 6_7: ↗ Qr בַּיִר.

בּוֹר, בֹּר Ex 21_{33}; **בּאר** Qr **בֹּר** 2S $23_{15\cdot16\cdot20}$: loc. **בֹּרָה**; sf. **בּוֹרוֹ**, **בּוֹרְךָ**; pl. **בֹּ(ו)רוֹת**, Je 2_{13} **בֹּארוֹת**, Qr **בֹּרוֹת** †; m.:

I. — 1. **cistern**, artificial excavation in rocky soil, pear-shaped, oft. some meters deep, for collecting & storing winter rain; also for grain-storage; walls cemented; *pātaḥ bôr* **dig a cistern** Ex 21_{33}; used as prison, Gn 37_{20ff}; *bêt habbôr* **prison** Ex 12_{29}; — 2. **pitfall** Ps 7_{16}; — 3. cistern as entrance to Sheol; a) **abode of the dead** Is 14_{15}; therefore *yôrᵉdê bôr* **the dying** Is 38_{18} & oft.; b) single **grave** Pr 28_{17} (or 3a?); — 4. erotic metaphor for wife, Pr 5_{15}.

II. *bôr* in proper names: 1. *bôr hassirâ*: n. loc.; — 2. *bôr-ʿāšān*: n. loc.; ↗ 2nd element.

I **בּוֹשׁ** (105×): **qal**: pf. **בֹּשְׁתִּי**, **בֹּושָׁה**, **בֹּ(ו)שׁ**, **בֹּ(ו)שׁוּ**; impf. **אֵבוֹשָׁה**, **אֵבוֹשׁ**, **תֵּבוֹשִׁי**, **יֵבוֹשׁ**, **יֵבֹ(ו)שׁוּ**; impv. **בֹּושִׁי**, **בֹּושׁוּ**; inf. **בֹּ(ו)שׁ**; pt. **בּוֹשִׁים**: — 1. **be ashamed of** (*min*) Is 1_{29}, (*bᵉ*) Ps 69_{7}, abs. Is 19_{9}; cogn. acc., *bôš bōšet* **be thoroughly ashamed** Is 42_{17}; *ʿad-bôš* until shame = immoderately Ju 3_{25}; inf. abs. adv. Je 48_{39}; — 2. in appos. w. 2nd vb. Jb 19_{3} **be ashamed to . . .**; w. *lᵉ* w. inf., Ezr 8_{22}.

hif.: **I**: **forms**: pf. **הֱבִישׁ(ו)תָ(ה)**; impf. **תְּבִישֵׁנִי**, **תָּבִישׁוּ**; pt. **מֵבִישׁ**, **מְבִישָׁה**: — 1. **put to shame** Ps 44_{8}; **let** s.one **be ashamed** Ps $119_{31\cdot116}$; — 2. **מֵבִישׁ**, **acting shamefully** Pr 10_{5};

hif.: **II**: **forms**: pf. **הֹ(ו)בִישָׁה**, **הֹ(ו)בִישׁ**, **הֹבִישׁוּ**, **הֹבַשְׁתָּ**; impv. **הֹבִישׁוּ**: — 1. **shame** 2S 19_{6}; — 2. **behave shamefully** Ho 2_{7}; — 3. a) **stand ashamed** (of men) Je 2_{26}; b) **come to ruin** (of hope) Zc 9_{5}.

hitpol.: impf. **יִתְבּוֹשָׁשׁוּ**: **be ashamed before one another** Gn 2_{25}. †

II **בּוֹשׁ**: **qal**: pf. **בֹּשְׁתִּי**; inf. **בֹּ(ו)שׁ**: **delay**, w. *lᵉ* w. inf. Ezr 8_{22}. †

pol.: pf. **בֹּשֵׁשׁ**: w. *lᵉ* w. inf. **be delayed, be long** Ex 32_{1} Ju 5_{28}. †

בּוֹשָׁה: **shame** (covers s.one) Ez 7_{18}.

בַּז: **בַּז** & **בָּז**; sf. **בִּזָּה**: (act of) **plundering**, (objs. of) **plunder**: *bāzaz baz* Is 10_{6}, *hāyâ lᵉbaz* 2K 21_{14}.

בזא: **qal**: pf. **בָּזְאוּ**: **wash away** Is $18_{2\cdot7}$. †

בָּזָה: **qal**: pf. **בָּזִיתָ**, **בּ׳**, **בְּזִתָנִי**; impf. **תִּבְזֶה**, **וַיִּבֶז**, **יִבְזֵהוּ**, **יִבְזָהוּ**; pt. **בּוֹזֶה**, cs. **בּוֹזֵה**, **בּוֹזֵהוּ**, **בּוֹזִים**, **בּוֹזַי**, pass. **בָּזוּי**, cs. **בְּזוּי**, f. **בְּזוּיָה**: — **despise**, w. acc. Gn 25_{34}, w. *lᵉ* **think lightly of** 2S 6_{16}; *bᵉzûy ʿam* contemptible to the people Ps 22_{7}.

nif.: pt. **נִבְזֶה**, **נִבְזִים**: pt. **despised, contemptible** Is 53_{3a}.

hif.: inf. **הַבְזוֹת** **make** (s.one) **contemptuous of** Est 1_{17}. †

בִּזָּה: (act of) **plundering**, (objs. of) **plunder** Est $9_{10\cdot15f}$.

בָּזַז: **qal**: pf. **בּ׳**, **בָּזַזְוּ**, **בְּזַזְנוּ** & **בַּזּוֹנוּ**, **בְּזָזוּם**; impf. **תָּבֹז**, **יָבֹזּוּ**, **יְבָזּוּם**; impv. **בֹּזּוּ**; inf. **לָבֹ(ו)ז**; pt. **בֹּזְזִים**, **בֹּזְזֵינוּ**, pass. **בָּזוּז**: — **plunder**, city Gn 34_{27}, men & cattle Nu 31_{9}; cogn. acc. Is 10_{6}.

nif.: pf. **נָבֹזּוּ**; impf. **תִּבּוֹז**; inf. **הִבּוֹז**: **be plundered** Is 24_{3} Am 3_{11}. †

pual (or qal pass.): pf. **בֻּזָּזוּ**: **be plundered** Je 50_{37}. †

בִּזָּיוֹן: **contempt** Est 1_{18}. †

[**בִּזְיוֹתְיָה** Jos 15_{28}: rd w. LXX* & Ne 11_{27} **בְּנוֹתֶיהָ**. †]

בָּזָק: **lightning** Ez 1_{14}. †

בֶּזֶק: n. loc.

בזר: **qal**: impf. **יִבְזוֹר**: **scatter** (money &c.) Dn 11_{24}. †

piel: pf. **בִּזַּר**: **disperse** Ps 68_{31}. †

בִּזְּתָא: n. pers.

בָּחוֹן: **assayer** Je 6_{27}. †

***בַּחוּן** Qr, Kt ***בַּחִין**?: Is 23_{13}: pl. sf. **בַּחוּנָיו**: ? **siege tower**. †

I **בָּחוּר**: pl. **בַּחוּרִים**, **בַּחוּרֵי**, **בַּחוּרָיו**, 3× **בַּחֻר׳**: **young man** (fully grown, vigorous, still unmarried) 2K 8_{12}; opp. *bᵉtûlâ* Dt 32_{25}, opp. *zᵉqēnîm* Je 31_{13}.

II **בָּחוּר**: pt. pass. qal of I בָּחַר.

***בְּחוּרוֹת**: sf. בְּחוּרֹתֶיךָ: **age, situation of young man** Ec 11_9 12_1. †

***בְּחוּרִים**: sf. בְּחֻרָיו: **age, situation of young man** Nu 11_{28}. †

I **בַּחוּרִים**: F I בָּחוּר.

II **בַּחוּרִים**: n. loc.

***בַּחִין**: Is 23_{13} Kt: F *בַּחוּן Qr.

***בָּחִיר**: cs. בְּחִיר; sf. בְּחִירוֹ, בְּחִירִי: **chosen** (by God): Moses Ps 106_{23}, David 89_4, *ʿebed yhwh* Is 42_1.

בחל: **qal**: pf. בָּחֲלָה: w. *b^e^* **become tired** of s.one, **disdain** Zc 11_8.

pual: pt. מְבֹחֶלֶת Pr 20_{21} Kt: ?; rd w. mss. Qr מְבֹהֶלֶת. †

בחן: **qal**: pf. בָּחַנְתָּ, בָּחֲנוּ, בְּחָנַנִי, בְּחַנְתָּנוּ, בְּחָנוּנִי; impf. יִבְחָן, יִבְחֲנוּ, אֶבְחָנְךָ, תִּבְחָנֶנּוּ; impv. sf. בְּחָנֵנִי, בְּחָנוּנִי; inf. בְּחֹן; pt. בֹּחֵן: — 1. **test** precious metal by smelting Zc 13_9; — 2. metaph. **put to the test**: heart = mind Je 12_3, words Jb 12_{11}; God usu. subj., but obj. Ma 3_{10} Ps 95_9.

nif.: impf. יִבָּחֵן, יִבָּחֲנוּ, תִּבָּחֲנוּ: **be put to the test** Gn 42_{15f} Jb 34_{36}. †

pual (or pass. qal): cj. pf. בֹּחַן Ez 21_{18} **be tested** ?. †

בַּחַן: **watchtower** Is 32_{14}. †

I **בֹּחַן**: Ez 21_{18}: ?? txt. uncert.; בחן pual pf. ?, F comm. †

II **בֹּחַן**: *ʾeben bōḥan* Is 28_{16}: trad. w. verss., a **tested** stone; a **touchstone** for testing gold; oth.: fine-grained **schist gneiss** used for statues &c. †

I **בָּחַר**: **qal**: pf. בָּחַרְתָּ, בָּחַרְתָּ, בָּחֲרוּ, בָּחַרְתָּ, בָּחֲרוּ, בְּחַרְתִּיךָ, בְּחַרְתֶּם; impf. יִבְחַר, יִבְחָר, אֶבְחָרֵהוּ, וַיִּבְחָרְךָ, יִבְחֲרוּ, אֶבְחֲרָה; impv. בַּחֲרוּ, בְּחַר־; inf. בָּח(וֹ)ר, sf. בָּחֳרִי; pt. בֹּחֵר, pass. בָּחוּר, בְּחוּרֵי: — take a keen look at > 1. **test** Is 48_{10}; — 2. **select** (w. acc. or *b^e^*) wife Gn 6_2, words Jb 9_{14}; w. *min* **give preference to** 2S 6_{21}; — 3. **elect** a) God obj. Ju 5_8 (txt. ?); b) God subj. (w. acc. or *b^e^*), Jacob Ps 135_4, a city 1K 8_{16}.

nif.: pf. נִבְחַר; pt. נִבְחָר: — 1. pt. **tested** = purified in fire (silver) Pr 10_{20}; — 2. pt. to be chosen, w. *min* **more desirable than** Je 8_3.

?II **בחר**: **qal**: pt. בֹּחֵר: **enter into covenant** 1S 20_{30}. †

pual: impf. יְבֻחַר: **be joined** Ec 9_4. †

בַּחֻרִים: n. loc., F II בַּחוּרִים.

cj. **בַּחֻרְמִי** 2S 23_{31} for בַּרְחֻמִי, & בַּחוּרְמִי 1C 11_{33} for בַּחֲרוּמִי: n. gent. of II בַּחוּרִים. †

בטא/ה: **qal**: pt. בּוֹטֶה: **chatter** Pr 12_{18}. †

piel: impf. יְבַטֵּא; inf. בַּטֵּא: **chatter** Lv 5_4 Ps 106_{33}. †

בָּטֻחַ & **בָּטוּחַ**: **confident** Is 26_3 Ps 112_7. †

I **בָּטַח**: **qal**: pf. בָּטַחְתִּי, בָּטַחְתִּי, בִּ׳, בָּטְחוּ, בָּטָחְנוּ; impf. יִבְטַח, יִבְטָח, אֶבְטַח, תִּבְטְחִי, תִּבְטְחוּ, תִּבְטָחוּ; impv. בְּטַח, בִּטְחוּ; inf. sf. בִּטְחֵךְ, abs. בָּטוּחַ; pt. בּ(וֹ)טֵחַ, בֹּטְחָה, בֹּטְחִים, pass. F בָּטוּחַ: — **feel safe, trust**: — 1. w. *b^e^* Dt 28_{52}; w. *ʿal* 2K 18_{20}; — 2. abs. **be full of confidence** Is 12_2; — 3. *bōṭēaḥ* careless, **unsuspecting** Ju 18_{10}.

hif.: pf. הִבְטַחְתָּ; impf. יַבְטַח, וַיַּבְטַח; pt. sf. מַבְטִיחִי: — 1. **direct** (s.one's) **trust** (to s.one, s.thg) w. *ʾel* 2K 18_{30}; — 2. **inspire trust** Ps 22_{10}.

II **בטח**: **qal**: pt. בּוֹטֵחַ: **fall to the ground** Je 12_5 Pr 14_{16}. †

I **בֶּטַח**: בָּטַח: trust > **safety** Is 32_{17}; mostly w. vbs. of going, dwelling, &c.: a) *lābeṭaḥ* in safety, w/o worry 1K 5_5; b) *beṭaḥ* (adv. acc.) 1S 12_{11}; c) peacefully Gn 34_{25}.

II **בֶּטַח**: n. loc. 2S 8_8.

בָּטֻחַ: F בָּטוּחַ.

בִּטְחָה: **trust** Is 30_{15}. †

בִּטָּחוֹן: **trust** 2K 18_{19} Is 36_4 Ec 9_4. †

***בַּטֻּחָה**: בַּטֻּחוֹת: idiom. pl. ? (in) **security** Jb 12_6. †

בטל: **qal**: pf. בָּטְלוּ: **be idle, inactive** Ec 12_3. †

I **בֶּטֶן**: בָּטֶן; sf. בִּטְנוֹ; f.: **belly**, a) of a **man**

Ju 3$_{21f}$; *p^{e}rî biṭn^{e}kā* = **sons** Ps 132$_{11}$; b) of a **woman** SS 7$_3$; *beṭen hā'ēm* **womb** Ju 16$_{17}$; > *beṭen* alone Gn 25$_{23f}$; *p^{e}rî-beṭen* **offspring**, embryo Gn 30$_2$; *ben-beṭen* (physical) **son**; c) of a **animal** Jb 40$_{16}$; — 2. **inner self**, as seat of perception Pr 22$_{18}$; — 3. *habbeṭen* architec. term, 1K 7$_{20}$, **bulge** (?) in the capital of a pillar.

II בֶּטֶן: n. loc. Jos 19$_{25}$. †

*בָּטְנָה: pl. בָּטְנִים: **pistachio nuts**, of *Pistacia terebinthus L.* Gn 43$_{11}$. †

בְּטֹנִים: n. loc.

בִּי אֲדֹנָי & בִּי אֲדֹנִי: formula to open conversation w. a superior, = **with your permission**; ellipt. < 'on me, my lord (let there come whatever unwelcome or hurtful thing our conversation might bring)': to man Gn 43$_{20}$, to God Ex 4$_{10.13}$.

בין: **qal**: pf. בִּינֹתִי, בַּנְתָּה, בִּין; impf. (or hif.!) יָבִינוּ, (וְ)אָבִינָה, וַיָּבֶן, יָבֶן, יָבִין; impv. בִּין, בִּינָה; inf. abs. בִּין; pt. pl. בָּנִים Je 49$_7$: — 1. w. acc. **understand, perceive** Je 9$_{11}$, abs. Is 6$_{9f}$; w. *l^e* w. inf. be capable, able Is 32$_4$; — 2. **pay attention to, consider** w. acc. Dt 32$_7$, w. *'al*, **give heed to** Dn 11$_{30}$; w. oth. preps., **consider, notice**.

nif.: pf. נְבוּנֹתִי; pt. נָבוֹן, cs. נְבוֹן, pl. נְבֹנָיו, נְבֹ(וֹ)נִים: **be perceptive** Is 10$_{13}$; *n^{e}bôn dābār* skillful in speech 1S 16$_{18}$.

pol.: impf. יְבוֹנְנֵהוּ: **take care of** Dt 32$_{10}$. †

hif.: pf. הֲבִינֹתֶם, הֵבִינוּ, הֵבִין; impf. (↗ qal!) תְּבִינֵם, וַיְבִינֵהוּ, יָבִין; impv. הָבֵן, הֲבִינֵנִי, הָבִינוּ; inf. הָבִין, הֲבִינְךָ; pt. מֵבִין, מְבִינֵי, מְבִינִים: — 1. like qal: a) **be able to discern** 1K 3$_9$ w. *bên ... l^e*; b) **have, gain insight** Is 29$_{16}$; *mēbîn* perceptive Pr 8$_9$; c) **comprehend, understand** w. acc. Is 28$_{19}$; d) w. *b^e* **understand well**, be expert in Dn 1$_{17}$; e) **pay attention to** Ps 33$_{15}$; f) (subj. God) **be acquainted w.** Jb 28$_{23}$; — 2. **bring to insight** a) w. 2 acc. have s.one understand s.thg Is 28$_{9.19}$; b) w. acc. give s.one insight Is 40$_{14}$; c) w. acc. make s.one perceptive Ps 119$_{34}$; d) **explain** s.thg to s.one Dn 8$_{16}$; e) **instruct** Jb 6$_{24}$.

hitpol.: pf. הִתְבּוֹנָנוּ, הִתְבֹּ(וֹ)נַנְתָּ, הִתְבּוֹנָן; impf. אֶתְבּוֹנָן, אֶתְבּוֹנֵן; וַתִּתְבֹּנֵן כִּי, יִתְבּוֹנָן, יִתְבּוֹנָנוּ, יִתְבּוֹנְנוּ; impv. הִתְבּוֹנְנוּ, הִתְבּוֹנֵן: — 1. **behave perceptively** Is 1$_3$; — 2. **give** (one's) **attention**, abs. Jb 11$_{11}$, w. acc. to s.thg Is 43$_{18}$, w. *b^e* Je 23$_{20}$; — 3. w. *'el* **look at, consider closely** 1K 3$_{21}$; w. *'al* **look out for** Ps 37$_{10}$.

*בַּיִן: cs. בֵּין: — I. **interval**, *bên yāmîm 'aśeret* (at an) interval of 10 days Ne 5$_{18}$. II. cs. as prep. בֵּין, & w. sg. sf. בֵּינִי &c.; w. pl. sf. בֵּינֵיהֶם, בֵּינֵיכֶם, בֵּינֵינוּ, but בֵּינֵנוּ Jos 22$_{25}$ & בֵּינֵכֶם Is 59$_2$; בֵּינוֹת (= בֵּין) Ez 10$_{2.2.6f}$; בֵּינ(וֹ)תָם, בֵּינ(וֹ)תֵינוּ Gn 26$_{28}$ & elsewh.; ↗ II בַּיִת: **between**, mostly w. vbs. of distinguishing: — 1. alone, a) once, *bên hagg^{e}zārîm* Gn 15$_{17}$; b) **between ... and,** mostly *bên ... ûbên* Gn 1$_4$, also *bên ... l^{e}bên* Is 59$_2$, *bên ... l^e* Gn 1$_6$; c) *bênôt*, alw. betw. 2 parties, Gn 26$_{28}$; d) **within** Pr 26$_{13}$; — 2. w. oth. preps.: a) *'el-bên* **(to) between** Ez 31$_{10.14}$; *'el-bênôt l^e* **in among** Ez 10$_2$; b) *b^{e}bên* Is 44$_4$; c) *'al-bên* Ez 19$_{11}$; d) *mibbên* **from between** Gn 49$_{10}$.

בִּינָה; cs. בִּינַת; sf. בִּינָתִי, בִּינָתְךָ, בִּינַתְכֶם; pl. בִּינוֹת: — **insight** Dt 4$_6$; *yāda' bînâ* **gain insight** Is 29$_{24}$; *'imrê bînâ* **perceptive words** Pr 1$_2$.

*בֵּ(י)צָה: pl. (f.!) בֵּיצִים, בֵּיצֵי, sf. בֵּיצֶיהָ, בֵּיצֵיהֶם: **egg** Dt 22$_6$; of snake Is 59$_5$.

בִּיר: Je 6$_7$ Qr = *בֵּיר = בְּאֵר f.; Kt בּוֹר m.! †

בִּירָה: pl. (!) בִּירָנִיּוֹת 2C 17$_{12}$ 27$_4$: — 1. **citadel, acropolis** Est 1$_2$ Ne 2$_8$; — 2. **temple** 1C 29$_{1.19}$.

בִּירָנִיּוֹת 2C 17$_{12}$ 27$_4$: pl. of ↗ בִּירָה. †

I בַּיִת (2000×): cs. בֵּית; sf. בֵּיתִי, בֵּיתְךָ, בֵּיתָם; pl. בָּתִּים (*bātîm*), בָּתֵּי, sf. בָּתֶּיךָ, בָּתֵּימוֹ; loc. בַּיְתָה, בֵּיתָה, cs. בֵּיתָה Gn 28$_2$ (6×), m.:

A. **house** (of mud, brick, stone): — 1. **dwelling**, oft. a single room for man & animals Ju 11_{31}; — a) *bêt hammelek* **palace** & *bātê hā'ām* Je 39_8; *'ašer 'al habbayit* **steward** Gn 39_4, **majordomo** $43_{16 \cdot 19}$; — b) god's house, **temple**: of Dagon 1S 5_2; of God at Shiloh Ju 18_{31}, in Jerus. 1K 6_5; > *habbayit* (in Jerus.) Ez. 41_{7ff}; *bêt hammamlākâ* royal temple (at Bethel) Am 7_{13}; Y.'s heavenly palace Ps 36_9; — c) portion of a house of more than one room: *bātê haqq^edēšîm*, cubicles of male prostitutes, 2K 23_7; — 2. **place to stay**: Sheol Jb 17_{13}, halo of a fire Ez 1_{27}, spiderweb Jb 8_{14}; *bêt 'ôlām* = grave Ec 12_5; **container**: *bātê nefeš* perfume-bottles Is 3_{20}; *bātê l^ebādîm* rings for the poles Ex 25_{27}; — 3. **the interior**: *báytâ* inwards 1K 7_{25}; *mibbayit* Gn 6_{14}; — 4. **household, family**: a) *bêt^ekâ* = wife/wives, children, servants Gn 7_1; subdivision of *mišpāḥâ* Jos 7_{14}; *y^elîd bayit* homeborn slave Gn 17_{27}; — b) *bêt par'ōh* Ph.'s court Gn 50_4; *bêt dāwîd* dynasty of D. 1K 12_{26}; — c) *bānâ bayit* start a household Pr 24_{27}; *'āśâ bātîm* give blessing of children Ex 1_{21}; — 5. *bêt 'āb*, pl. *bêt 'ābôt*, **paternal family** Gn 24_{38}; ell. > *'ābôt* Ex 6_{25}.

B. In place-names; for details, ↗ comm. & dict. of the Bible: — 1. בֵּית אָוֶן, defamation of בֵּית־אֵל; — 2. בֵּית(־)אֵל, gentilic בֵּית הָאֱלִי; — 3. בֵּית הָאֵצֶל; — 4. בֵּית אַרְבֵּאל; — 5. בֵּית אַשְׁבֵּעַ; — 6. בֵּית בַּעַל מְעוֹן, > בַּעַל מְעוֹן; > בֵּית מְעוֹן; > בְּעֹן; — 7. בֵּית בִּרְאִי; — 8. בֵּית בָּרָה; — 9. בֵּית גָּדֵר; — 10. בֵּית הַגִּלְגָּל; — 11. בֵּית גָּמוּל; — 12. בֵּית הַגָּן; — 13. בֵּית דִּבְלָתַיִם; — 14. בֵּית דָּגוֹן; — 15. בֵּית הָרָם; — 16. בֵּית הָרָן; — 17. בֵּית חָגְלָה; — 18. בֵּית חָנָן; — 19. בֵּית(־)חֹ(ו)רֹ(ו)ן; — 20. בֵּית יוֹאָב; — 21. בֵּית הַיְשִׁימֹ(ו)ת; — 22. בֵּית כָּר; — 23. בֵּית הַכֶּרֶם; — 24. בֵּית לְבָאוֹת; — 25. בֵּית לֶחֶם, בֵּית לָחֶם, gentilic בֵּית הַלַּחְמִי; — 26. בֵּית עַפְרָה; — 27. בֵּית מִלּוֹא; — 28. בֵּית מְעוֹן = בֵּית בַּעַל מְעוֹן & בַּעַל מְעוֹן = בְּעֹן; — 29. בֵּית מַעֲכָה; — 30. בֵּית הַמֶּרְחָק; — 31. בֵּית הַמַּרְכָּבוֹת; — 32. בֵּית נִמְרָה; — 33. בֵּית עֶדֶן; — 34. בֵּית עַזְמָוֶת; — 35. בֵּית הָעֵמֶק; — 36. בֵּית עֲנוֹת; — 37. בֵּית עֲנָת; — 38. בֵּית הָרֹעִים; — 39. בֵּית הָעֲרָבָה; — 40. בֵּית פְּעוֹר, = בַּעַל פְּעוֹר > בֵּית בַּעַל פְּעוֹר*; — 41. בֵּית פֶּלֶט; — 42. בֵּית פַּצֵּץ; — 43. בֵּית צוּר; — 44. בֵּית רְחוֹב; —45. בֵּית רָכָב; — 46. בֵּית הָרָן = בֵּית הָרָם, — 47. בֵּית רָפָא; — 48. בֵּית שְׁאָן > בֵּית שָׁן & בֵּית שַׁן; — 49. בֵּית הַשִּׁטָּה; — 50. בֵּית שֶׁמֶשׁ, שֶׁמֶשׁ; — 51. בֵּית תּוֹגַרְמָה; — 52. בֵּית תַּפּוּחַ.

II **בַּיִת***: f. of **בַּיִן***; cs. בֵּית: **between** Ez 41_9 Jb 8_{17}; *bêt n^etîbôt* **crossroads** Pr 8_2.

בִּיתָן: cs. בִּיתַן: **palace** Est 1_5 7_{7f}. †

בָּכָא: pl. בְּכָאִים: **baka-shrubs** 2S 5_{23f} 1C 14_{14f}; *'ēmeq habbākâ* Ps 84_7, a specific valley, or in general a valley w. rich vegetation? †

בָּכָה: **qal**: pf.: בָּכוּ, בָּכִיתִי, בָּכְתָה, ב׳, בְּכִיתֶם; impf. אֶבְכֶּה, תִּבְכִּי, תִּבְכֶּה, וַיֵּבְךְּ, בְּכֶינָה; תִּבְכֶּינָה, יִבְכָּיוּן, יִבְכּוּ; impv. בְּכוּ, בְּכֶינָה; inf. לִבְכּוֹת, לִבְכֹּתָהּ, בָּכֹה & בָּכוֹ; pt. בֹּ(ו)כִים, בּוֹכִיָּה, בֹּ(ו)כֶה: — 1. **weep**, abs. Gn 33_4 & oft.; observe mourning rites Zc 7_3; *'al-pānāyw* before him 2K 13_{14}, *l^e* for s.one Je 22_{10}; as greeting Gn 29_{11}; — 2. w. acc. **bewail** Gn 23_2; cogn. acc. 2K 20_3.

piel: pt. f. מְבַכָּה, מְבַכּוֹת: **bewail**, w. acc. Ez 8_{14}, w. *'al* Je 31_{15}. †

בֶּכֶה: **weeping** Est 10_1. †

בְּכוֹר: ↗ בְּכֹר.

בִּכּוּרָה & **בִּכֻּרָה***; pl. בִּכֻּרוֹת: **early figs** (from June on) Is 28_4.

בִּכּוּרִים: cs. בִּכּוּרֵי: **first-fruits**: grapes Nu 13_{20}, seed Ex 23_{16}, in genl. Nu 18_{13}.

בְּכוֹרַת: n. pers.

בָּכוּת: **weeping**, in name of oak Gn 35_8. †

בְּכִי : בֶּכִי ; sf. בִּכְיִי : **weeping** Gn 42_5; w. cogn. vb. Ju 21_2; *bᵉkî ʾēbel mōšeh* **weeping in mourning for** M. Dt 34_8.
בֹּכִים: n. loc.
*בָּכִיר: f. בְּכִירָה: first-born, **elder** Gn $19_{31 \cdot 33f \cdot 37}$.
*בְּכִית: sf. בְּכִיתוֹ: **bewailing** Gn 50_4. †
בְּכֵן: ↗ II כֵּן 8.
בכר: **piel**: impf. יְבַכֵּר; inf. בַּכֵּר: — 1. **bear early fruit** Ez 47_{12}; — 2. **treat as first-born** Dt 21_{16}. †
pual: impf. יְבֻכַּר: **belong** (to Y.) **as first-born** Lv 27_{26}. †
hif.: pt. f. מַבְכִּירָה: one **bearing her first child** Je 4_{31}. †
*בֵּכֶר: pl. cs. בִּכְרֵי: **young bull camel** Is 60_6. †
בֶּכֶר: n. pers.
בְּכֹר & בְּכוֹר: sf. בְּכֹ(ו)רִי, בְּכֹרְךָ, בְּכֹרֶךָ; pl. cs. בְּכוֹרֵי, sf. בְּכוֹרֵיהֶם, f. בְּכֹר(ו)ת, f. sg. ↗ בְּכִירָה: — 1. **firstborn**: of cattle Gn 4_4; of persons: first counted on mother's side, later on father's Gn 25_{13}; — 2. metaph.: Isr. is first born of Y. Ex 4_{22}; *bᵉkōr māwet* = pestilence Jb 18_{13}.
בְּכֹרָה: sf. בְּכֹרָתוֹ: **rank** and **rights as first-born** Gn 25_{31ff}.
בִּכְרָה: f. of *בֵּכֶר: **young cow-camel** which has calved once Je 2_{23}. †
בֹּכְרוּ: trad. n. pers.; emend w. LXX &c. to בְּכֹרוֹ ? 1C 8_{38} 9_{44}. †
בַּכְרִי: n. gent. of בֶּכֶר.
בִּכְרִי: n. pers.
I בַּל (ca. 50×): < ↗ בְּלִי; sbst. > neg., ↗ אֲבָל: — **not**: mostly in poet. texts, oft. repetitively (e.g. Is $26_{10 \cdot 18}$ 7×); — a) w. pf. *bal pārᵉšû* Is 33_{23}; — b) w. impf. (52×) *bal ʾemmôṭ* Ps 30_7 (w. *môṭ* 16×); w. modal overtones: *bal yāqûmû* they dare not rise Is 14_{21}, lest Ps 78_{44}; *ʾal … ûbal* Ps 141_4; — c) in nominal clause Pr 23_7; — d) not yet, **scarcely** Is 40_{24}.
II בַּל: **surely** ? Ps 16_2, Pr 19_{23}; perh. = I בַּל after all. †

בֵּל: Babylonian god, Is 46_1.
בַּלְאֲדָן: n. pers.
בֵּלְאשַׁצַּר: ↗ בֵּלְשַׁאצַּר.
בלג: **hif.**: impf. אַבְלִיגָה; pt. מַבְלִיג: — 1. **let** (s.thg) **flare up, flash** Am 5_9; — 2. **be cheerful, happy** Ps 39_{14}.
בִּלְגָּה: n. pers.
בִּלְגַּי: n. pers.
בִּלְדַּד: n. pers.
בלה: **qal**: pf. בָּלְתָה, בָּלוּ; impf. יִבְלֶה, יִבְלוּ; inf. sf. בְּלֹתִי: **be used up, worn out, exhausted**: clothes Jos 9_{13}, old woman Gn 18_{12}.
piel: pf. בִּלָּה; impf. יְבַלּוּ; inf. בַּלּוֹת, בַּלֹּתוֹ: **let** (s.one, s.thg) **waste away** La 3_4, **wipe out** (people) 1C 17_9; — 2. **enjoy fully** Is 65_{22} Jb 21_{13}. †
*בָּלֶה: f. בָּלָה; pl. בָּלִים, בָּלוֹת: worn out, **old** Jos 9_{4f}. †
בָּלָה: n. loc.
בלה: **piel**: pt. pl. מְבַלְהִים (Qr מְבַהֲלִים) **frighten, deter** from Ezr 4_4, w. *lᵉ* w. inf. †
בַּלָּהָה: pl. בַּלָּהוֹת, cs. בַּלְהוֹת: **sudden terror** Is 17_{14}; *melek ballāhôt*, a sovereign of the underworld Jb 18_{14}.
I בִּלְהָה: n. pers.
II בִּלְהָה: n. loc. 1C 4_{29}. †
בִּלְהָן: n. pers.
*בְּלוֹא: ↗ *בְּלוֹי.
*בְּלוֹי: pl. cs. בְּלוֹיֵ Je 38_{11} > בְּלוֹאֵי 38_{12}: **rags**. †
בֵּלְטְשַׁאצַּר, or טֶ, Dn 10_1 בֵּלְטְאשַׁצַּר: n. pers.
בְּלִי (ca. 50×); ↗ בַּל: — 1. subst. a) wearing out, **destruction** Is 38_{17}; b) **cessation**, *ʿad-bᵉlî yārēaḥ* until there is no more moon Ps 72_7; — 2. **negation**, = **un-, -less, without**: a) w. sbst. *bᵉlî-šēm* nameless Jb 30_8, *bᵉlî-māqôm* so that there is no more place = to the last place Is 28_8; — b) w. pass. m. pt. or adj.: *bᵉlî-nišmāʿ* unheard Ps 19_4; — 3. *biblî* w. sbst. **without**: *biblî daʿat* unintentionally Dt 4_{42}; — 4. *mibbᵉlî* **with-**

out Je 2_{15}; — 5. *liblî* w. sbst. **without** Is 5_{14}; — 6. neg. w. fin. vb.: a) w. impf. (↗ *bal*) Is 32_{40}; b) w. pf. > conj. because not: *mibbelî hiš'îr* Dt 28_{55}.

בְּלִיל: mixed fodder, **mash**, for horned cattle Jb 6_5 Is 30_{24}. †

בְּלִימָה: var. of בְּלִי־מָה Jb 26_7: ↗ בְּלִי 2a. †

בְּלִיַּעַל: בְּלִיַּעַל; הַבְּלִיַּעַל: — 1. **worthlessness, wickedness**, w. gen. = adj.: *debar beliyya'al* = illness Ps 41_9; *ben-b.* scoundrel 1S 25_{17};—2. > adj. **worthless**, *rā' ûbeliyya'al* 1S 30_{22}.

בָּלַל: **qal**: pf. בַּלֹּתִי, ב׳; impf. וַיָּבָל (Kt וַיָּבוֹל) Ju 19_{21}, נָבְלָה Gn 11_7; pt. pass. בָּלוּל, בְּלוּלָה, בְּלוּלֹת: — 1. **moisten** (w. oil): *maṣṣôt* Ex 29_2, *sōlet* Ex 29_{40}; **pour** (oil on s.one) Ps 92_{11}; — 2. mix, **confuse** (languages) Gn $11_{7\cdot9}$; — 3. denom. of *belîl*: **throw down** (mash) Ju 19_{21}.

hitpol.: impf. יִתְבּוֹלָל: **be shaken back & forth** Ho 7_8. †

בלם: **qal**: inf. בְּלוֹם: check, **curb** Ps 32_9. †

בלס: **qal** (denom.): pt. בּוֹלֵס: *bôlēs šiqmîm* Am 7_{14} **scratch open** (sycamore fruit, to promote ripening). †

I **בָּלַע**: **qal**: pf. ב׳, בָּלְעָה, Je 51_{34} Kt בְּלָעַנִי Qr בְּלָעָנוּ; impf. יִבְלָע, יִבְלַע, תִּבְלָעֵנָה = תִּבְלָעֵמוֹ, תִּבְלָעֵם, תִּבְלָעֵנִי, יִבְלָעֶנָּה, תִּבְלָעֵן, יִבְלָעֵהוּ; inf. בְּלֹעַ, sf. בִּלְעִי: **swallow, gulp down**: a) subj. men Is 28_4, fish Jon 2_1, earth Ex 15_{12}; b) obj. ears (of grain) Gn 41_7, rod Ex 7_{12}; metaph. riches Jb $20_{15\cdot18}$.

nif.: pf. נִבְלַע: **be swallowed up** Ho 8_8. †

piel: pf. בִּלַּע, בִּלַּע, בִּלְּעָנוּ, בִּלְּעָנוּהוּ; impf. יְבַלַּע, אֲבַלַּע, אֲבַלֵּעַ, יְבַלְּעֶנּוּ, יְבַלְּעֵם, תְּבַלְּעֵנִי; inf. בַּלַּע, abs. בַּלֵּעַ, sf. בַּלְּעוֹ; pt. sf. מְבַלְּעֵךְ: — 1. **swallow up**: obj. land 2S 20_{19f}, people Is 49_{19}; wipe out, destroy Ps 21_{10}.

II **בלע**: **piel**: impf. יְבַלַּע: communicate, **spread abroad** Pr 19_{28}. †

pual: impf. יְבֻלַּע, יְבֻלָּע: **be communicated** 2S 17_{16} Jb 37_{20}. †

III **בלע**: **nif.**: pf. נִבְלְעוּ: **be confused** Is 28_7. †

piel: pf. בִּלֵּעוּ; impf. אֲבַלֵּעַ: **confuse** Is 3_{12} 19_3. †

pual: pt. pl. מְבֻלָּעִים: **confused** Is 9_{15}. †

hitp.: impf. תִּתְבַּלָּע: **prove** (onesf.) **confused** Ps 107_{27}. †

I ***בֶּלַע**: sf. בִּלְעוֹ: **what is swallowed** Je 51_{44}. †

II ***בֶּלַע**: בֶּלַע: **confusion** Ps 52_6. †

III **בֶּלַע**, בֶּלַע: n. pers.

IV **בֶּלַע**: n. loc. Gn $14_{2\cdot8}$. †

***בִּלְעֲדֵי** & **בַּלְעֲדֵי**: בַּל + עֲדֵי ↗ עַד; sf. בִּלְעָדַי, בִּלְעָדֶיךָ, בִּלְעָדֵי: prep. **apart from, except for**; — 1. w. sf. Gn 41_{44}; by exten., I am not involved Gn 14_{24} 41_{16}; — 2. pleon. w. *min*: **except for** Nu 5_{20} **against the will of** 2K 18_{25}; — 3. w. fin. vb. *bil'adê 'eḥezeh* except for what I see Jb 34_{32} (txt.?). †

בַּלְעִי: gent. of III בֶּלַע Nu 26_{38}. †

I **בִּלְעָם**: n. pers.

II **בִּלְעָם**: n. loc. 1C 6_{55}. †

בלק: **qal**: pt. sf. בּוֹלְקָהּ: **devastate** (the land) Is 24_1. †

pual: pt. f. מְבֻלָּקָה, sbst. **devastation** Na 2_{11}. †

בָּלָק: n. pers.

בֵּלְשַׁאצַּר: n. pers.

בִּלְשָׁן: n. pers.

בִּלְתִּי: sf. בִּלְתִּי, בִּלְתֶּךָ: — 1. sbst. abs. & cs. **non-existence, existence no more**: *'ad-biltî šāmayim* Jb 14_{12}; > neg. — 2. **not** w. adj. 1S 20_{26}; — 3. **except for**: a) *biltî hayyôm* except for today Gn 21_{26}; w. nom. clause, **unless** Gn $43_{3\cdot5}$; b) *biltî 'im* **unless** Am 3_{3f}, **except** Gn 47_{18}; c) w. *kāra'* ? unless > only Is 10_4; — 4. **without** Is 14_6; — 5. *lebiltî* (86×): w. inf. a) **not to** Gn 3_{11}; b) after *šb'* nif. 'swear', **that ... not** Dt 4_{21}; c) w. inf. of purpose, **so that ... not** Gn 4_{15}; — 6. w. impf. **so that ... not, lest** Ex 20_{20}; — 7. *lebiltî le* w. inf. **so that ... not, lest** 2K 23_{10};

— 8. *'ad-biltî* w. pf., **until, so that ... not** 2K 10_{11}.

בָּמָה (ca. 100×): loc. הַבָּמָתָה 1S 9_{13}; pl. בָּמוֹת, cs. בָּמוֹת (10×), בָּמוֹתֵי Kt Dt 32_{13} Is 58_{14} Mi 1_3 †, & בָּמֳתֵי (*bomotê* < sg. *בֹּמֶת) Is 14_{14} Am 4_{13} Jb 9_8 & Qr Dt 32_{13} Is 58_{14} Mi 1_3; sf. בָּמֹ(ו)תָיו, בָּמוֹתַי, בָּמוֹתֵימוֹ: — 1. **back** a) Dt 33_{29}; b) metaph. Is 14_{14}, Jb 9_8 (backs of the sea); — 2. (not easily distinguishable from 1b & 3!) mountain ridge, **height**, a) of land 2S $1_{19\cdot25}$, b) God treads on Am 4_{13}; — 3. Can. **burial ground** Ez 43_7; — 4. (cultic) **high place** (ca. 80×, esp. in 1 & 2K, 2C) 1K 11_7 associated w. pagan worship & cultic prostitution.

בִּמְהָל: n. pers.

בְּמוֹ: prep. = בְּ: **by, in** Is 43_2.

בָּמוֹת: n. loc. Nu $21_{19f.}$ †

I **בֵּן** (4850×): abs. בֵּן, בֶּן־ 1S 22_{20} Ez 18_{10} †; cs. בֶּן־ (בֶּן Ne 6_{18} 1C 9_{21} †, מִבֶּן before number Nu 8_{25} & oft., בֵּן Gn 49_{22}) & בִּן־ (בִּן Dt 25_2 †), בְּנִי Gn 49_{11} & בְּנוֹ Nu 23_{18} $24_{3\cdot15}$; sf. בְּנוֹ, בְּנִי, בִּנְךָ, בִּנְךְ; pl. בָּנִים, cs. בְּנֵי (note: Ju 20_{13} Qr w/o Kt), sf. בָּנָיו, בָּנַיִכִי Kt & בָּנַיִךְ Qr, בְּנֵיהֶם; var. Kt/Qr problems, e.g. Dn 11_{10} בְּנוֹ Kt & בָּנָיו Qr; f. ↗ בַּת: — 1. a) **son** Gn 5_4; *ben-zequnîm* son conceived in old age Gn 37_3; *bēn zākār* male child Je 20_{15}, *bānîm* **children** (incl. daughters) Gn 3_{16}, *ben-bêtî* born in my house Gn 15_3; *benî 'attâ* formula of adoption Ps 2_7; *benê 'elōhîm* ↗ *'elôah* II 1; — b) **young** (of an animal): *ben-bāqār* calf Gn 18_7, *benê ṣō'n* lambs Ps 114_4; *bānîm* young (birds) Dt 22_6; — 2. **grandson** Gn 32_1; — 3. intimate address to younger comrade, disciple: *benî* 1S $26_{17\cdot21\cdot25}$; *binkā*, formula of servility, = 'I' 2K 8_9; — 4. w. coll. to indicate an individual: *ben-'ādām*, human being Ez 2_1 (93× in Ez), Dn 8_{17}; *benê 'ādām* individual men Dt 32_8, *benê 'ebyôn* individual poor Ps 72_4; — 5. **member of a people**, tribe: *benê 'edôm* Ps 137_7; — 6. **member of a group**, class, guild, *ben-nābî'* member of a group of prophets Am 7_{14}, pl. *benê hann.* 1K 20_{35}; — 7. one **belonging to a category**, manner, destiny: *benê merî* sons of rebellion = rebels Nu 17_{25}; *bin hakkôt* one deserving to be beaten Dt 25_2; *ben-māwet* one who deserves death 1S 20_{31}; — 8. in stating s.one's age, *ben-šemōnat yāmîm* 8 days old Gn 17_{12}; — 9. used in contempt instead of s.one's own name: son of Jesse 1S 20_{30f}; — 10. metaph.: *ben-qešet* = arrow Jb 41_{20}; — 11. **son to God**: Solomon becomes 2S 7_{14}, pl. of Isr. Dt 14_1.

II **בֵּן**: n. pers. 1C 15_{18}, but corr. †

בֶּן־אוֹנִי: n. pers.

בֶּן־הֲדַד: n. pers.

בֶּן־זוֹחֵת: n. pers.

בֶּן־חוּר: n. pers.

בֶּן־חַיִל: n. pers.

בֶּן־חָנָן: n. pers.

בָּנָה (370×): **qal**: pf. בּ׳, בָּנְתָה, בָּנִ(י)תָ(ה), בָּנִיתִי (1K 8_{48} Kt ־תִ) בָּנוּ (בָּנוּ לָךְ Ez 27_5), בְּנִיתֶם, בָּנִינוּ, בְּנִיתִיהָ; impf. יִבְנֶה, אֶבְנֶה, וַיִּבֶן, וַיִּבֶן, תִּבְנִי, יִבְנוּ, יִבְנֵהוּ, יִבְנֶנִּי, יִבְנֵם, אֶבְנֶנָּה, אֶבְנֵךְ; impv. בְּנוּ; inf. בְּנ(וֹ)ת, בְּנוֹתַיִךְ (Ez 16_{31}), בָּנֹה; pt. בֹּ(ו)נֶה, cs. בֹּנֵה, בֹּ(ו)נִים, pass. בָּנוּי, בְּנוּיָה: — 1. **build**: city Gn 4_{17}, house 33_{17}; — 2. w. acc. of material Is 9_9; w. acc. of obj. & acc. of material 1K 18_{32}; — 3. w. *le*, **build up** *lemāṣôr* cities for fortification 2C 11_5, > **fortify** 1K 15_{22} 16_{24}; rib to a woman Gn 2_{22}; — 4. **rebuild** Jos 6_{26}; — 5. w. *be* **built at, work on** Zc 6_{15} Ne $4_{4\cdot11}$; — 6. metaph. (or a II *bānâ*, denom. of *bēn*?) *bānâ bayit le* build a family for, provide offspring for s.one Dt 25_9, let one live on in his children Je 24_6.

nif.: pf. נִבְנָה, נִבְנְתָה, נִבְנֵית, נִבְנוּ; impf. יִבָּנֶה, אִבָּנֶה, תִּבָּנֶינָה; inf. הִבָּנוֹת, הִבָּנֹתוֹ; pt. נִבְנֶה: — 1. **be built**, city Nu 13_{22}, temple 1K 3_2; — 2. men are built = live on in their children Je 12_{16}; of a woman, be built = **get a child** from (*min*) Gn 16_2; — 3. metaph. of God's *ḥesed* Ps 89_3.

בְּנוּי: n. pers.

[**בְּנָי**: n. pers. 1C 24_{23}, but txt. corr.]

בָּנִי: n. pers.

בֻּנִּי: n. pers.

בְּנֵי בְרַק: n. loc.

בְּנֵי יַעֲקָן: n. loc.

בִּנְיָה: **building** Ez 41_{13}. †

בְּנָיָה: n. pers.

בְּנָיָהוּ: n. pers.

בֵּנַיִם: אִישׁ הַבֵּנַיִם, **champion, single fighter** 1S $17_{4 \cdot 23}$. †

בִּנְיָמִין, בִּנְיָמִן, בן־ימין 1S 9_1 Kt: n. pers., n. tribe.

בֶּן־יְמִינִי: gent. of בִּנְיָמִן; note בֶּן־הַיְמִינִי 1K 2_8 + 3×; pl. בְּנֵי יְמִינִי Ju 19_{16} 1S 22_7.

[**בָּנִימִן**: 1C 9_4: Kt בִּנְיָמִן, rd w. Qr ⸢ בְּנֵי מִן. †]

בִּנְיָן: **building** Ez 40_5.

בְּנִינוּ: n. pers.

בִּנְעָא: n. pers.

בְּסוֹדְיָה: n. pers.

בֵּסַי: בֵּסָי: n. pers.

בסס: ⸢ בוס.

בֹּסֶר: sf. בִּסְרוֹ: **unripe fruit** Is 18_5.

I **בַּ֫עַד** (100×): abs. in *mibbaʿad lᵉ*, cs. בְּעַד; sf. בַּעֲדִי, בַּעֲדֵנִי & Ps 139_{11} בַּעֲדֵנִי, בַּעַדְךָ, בַּעֲדֵךְ, בַּעֲדוֹ, בַּעֲדֵנוּ & Am 9_{10} בַּעֲדֵינוּ, בַּעַדְכֶם: — sbst. > prep.: 1. at a distance from > **behind**; with vbs. of shutting: shut (doors) behind (s.one, onesf.), shutting one in (not out), Gn 7_{16} Jon 2_7; shut *bᵉʿad-reḥem* the womb Gn 20_{18}; *mibbaʿad lᵉ* (from) behind SS $4_{1 \cdot 3}$ 6_7 †; — 2. at a distance from > **through** (esp. a window) Gn 26_8, (motion) **over** (a wall) 2S 20_{21}; — 3. behind > **around** Ps 3_4 139_{11}; — 4. in protection around > **for** (the benefit of); w. *hitpallēl* pray for Gn 20_7 (12×), *heʿtîr*, & similar vbs.; *hitḥazzēq bᵉʿad* stand up valiantly for 2S 10_{12}; — 5. *ʿôr bᵉʿad ʿôr* skin for skin Jb 2_4, but ⸢ comm.

II ***בַּ֫עַד** (or ***בָּעָד**): cs. בְּעַד: exchange, **price** Pr 6_{26}. †

I **בעה**: **qal**: impf. תִּבְעָיוּן; impv. בְּעָיוּ: **ask** Is 21_{12}. †

nif.: pf. נִבְעוּ: **be ransacked** Ob $_6$. †

II **בעה**: **qal**: impf. תִּבְעֶה: **bring to a boil** Is 64_1. †

nif.: pt. נִבְעֶה: **protrude** Is 30_{13}. †

בְּעוֹר: בְּעֹר Nu $24_{3 \cdot 15}$: n. pers.

***בִּעוּת**: pl. בִּעוּתֵי, בִּעוּתֶיךָ: **horror** Ps 88_{17} Jb 6_4. †

I **בֹּ֫עַז**: n. pers.

II **בֹּ֫עַז**: name of the left pillar in front of Temple 1K 7_{21} 2C 3_{17}. †

בעט: **qal**: impf. וַיִּבְעַט, תִּבְעֲטוּ: **kick** Dt 32_{15}; w. *bᵉ*, fig., **disdain** 1S 2_{29}. †

בְּעִי: Jb 30_{24}: ??, ? *bᵉ* + *ʿî* among ruins; but txt. corr. †

[**בְּעָיִם**: Is 11_{15}: ⸢ עָיִם. †]

***בְּעִיר**: sf. בְּעִירֹה, בְּעִירָם: coll. **cattle, beasts** Gn 45_{17}.

I **בָּעַל**: **qal**: pf. בָּעַלְתִּי ,בְּ׳, בְּעָלוּ, בְּעָלָהּ, בְּעָלְתַּנִי, בְּעַלְתָּהּ; impf. יִבְעַל, יִבְעָלוּךְ; pt. בֹּעֲלַיִךְ, pass. בְּעֻלַת, בְּעוּלָה: — 1. possess, **rule over** (subj. God., obj. people) Is 26_{13}; w. *bᵉ*, **prove onesf. to be Lord** Je 3_{14} 31_{32}; — 2. take s.one into possession as betrothed, wife, **marry** Dt 21_{13}; *bᵉʿulat baʿal* one belonging to a man as betrothed or wife Gn 20_3.

nif.: impf. תִּבָּעֵל: **be embraced** (in marriage relation) Pr 30_{23}, of land Is 62_4. †

II **בעל**: **qal** pt. בֹּעֲלַיִךְ Is 54_5: **make.**

I **בַּ֫עַל**: בַּעַל, *בַּעַל־ in n. pers.; sf. בַּעְלִי, בַּעְלָהּ, בַּעְלָיו, בַּעֲלֵיהֶן; pl. בְּעָלִים, בַּעֲלֵי, בְּעָלָיו, sf. בְּעָלֶיהָ: I. **possessor**: — 1. **husband, lord** (in marriage) Gn 20_3, Ex 21_3; — 2. **owner of land, citizen,** *baʿalê yᵉrîḥô* Jos 24_{11}; — 3. *baʿalê gôyîm* lords over the nations Is 16_8; — 4. **partner in a community**: *baʿalê bᵉrît* allies Gn 14_{13}; — 5. **owner,** of ox Ex 21_{28}, of pit 21_{34}; — 6. **fig.**: master of s.thg characterizing one's manner, occupation, profession: *ba'al ḥ^alômôt* dreamer Gn 37_{19}; *ba'al d^ebārîm* s.one w. a legal case Ex 24_{14}; *ba'al mišpāṭî* my (legal) adversary Is 50_{8}; w. *ṭôb*, s.one who has title to (good) Pr 3_{27}; *ba'al 'af* bad-tempered man Pr 22_{24}; *ba'al nefeš* greedy Pr 23_{2}; *ba'al lāšôn* charmer Ec 10_{11}; II. — 1. designates the anonymous numinous beings that manifest themselves at wells, trees, rocks &c. as possessors of the spot, having, to begin with, a purely local significance & oft. mentioned in the pl.: a) *habba'al* the (individual) **Baal** Ju 6_{31f}; — b) *habb^e'ālîm* **the Baals** 1K 18_{18}; — 2. (the individual god) **Baal** as a higher god (oft. not distinguishable from 1a w. certainty) w. developed cult, > proper name; *šēm habba'al* 1K 18_{26}, *'ōb^edê habba'al* 2K 10_{19}; — spec., a) *ba'al p^e'ôr*, the B. honored in P. Nu 25_{3}; — b) *ba'al b^erît* the B. of Shechem who watches over agreements Ju 8_{33}; — c) *ba'al z^ebûb 'elōhê 'eqrôn* 2K 1_{2f} ⟶ *z^ebûb*; — d) n. loc. ⟶ III; — e) *habba'al*, city god of Tyre 1K 16_{31}; — 3. designation of Y.! Ho 2_{18};

III. in place-names: — 1. בַּעַל 1C 4_{33}; — 2. בַּעַל־גָּד; — 3. בַּעַל־הָמוֹן; — 4. בַּעַל־חָצוֹר; — 5. בַּעַל־חֶרְמוֹן; — 6. בַּעֲלֵי־יְהוּדָה; — 7. בַּעַל־מְעוֹן; — 8. בַּעַל־פְּעוֹר; — 9. בַּעַל־פְּרָצִים; — 10. בַּעַל־צְפֹן; — 11. בַּעַל־שָׁלִשָׁה; — 12. בַּעַל־תָּמָר.

II **בַּעַל**: n. pers: — 1. 1C 5_{5}; — 2. 1C 8_{30} 9_{36}. †

I **בַּעֲלָה**: f. of I בַּעַל; cs. בַּעֲלַת: — 1. female possessor, *ba'^alat bayit* 1K 17_{17}; *ba'^alat 'ôb* necromancer 1S 28_{7}, *ba'^alat k^ešāfîm* enchantress Na 3_{4}; — 2. name of goddess, in OT only in names of localities.

II **בַּעֲלָה**: n. loc.

בְּעָלוֹת: n. loc.

בַּעַל חָנָן: n. pers.

בְּעֶלְיָדָע: n. pers.

בְּעַלְיָה: n. pers.

בַּעֲלִיס: n. pers.

בַּעֲלַת: n. loc. Jos 19_{44}. †

בַּעֲלָת: n. loc.

בַּעֲלַת בְּאֵר: n. loc.

בְּעֹן: n. loc.

בַּעֲנָא: n. pers.

I **בער**: **qal**: pf. בָּעֲרָה, בָּעֲרוּ; impf. יִבְעַר, יִבְעָר; pt. בֹּעֵר, בֹּעֲרָה, בֹּעֶ֫רֶת, בֹּעֲרָה, בֹּעֲרוֹת: — 1. **burn**: of bush Ex 3_{2}, fire Je 20_{9}; metaph., of wickedness Is 9_{17}, Y.'s anger Is 30_{27}; — 2. **blaze up**, w. *b^e*, of fire Ps 106_{18}; fig., anger Je 44_{6}; — 3. **burn up** (trans.: subj. fire, obj. wood) Ps 83_{15}; **singe** (w. *b^e*) Is 42_{25}.

piel: pf. בִּעֵר, בִּעַרְתֶּם, בִּעֲרוּ, sf. בִּעַרְתִּיהָ; impf. יְבַעֲרוּ; inf. בָּעֵר 5×, בַּעֵר 1×, sf. לְבַעֲרָם; pt. מְבַעֲרִים: — 1. **kindle**, w. acc. fire Ex 35_{3}, wood Lv 6_{5}; — 2. abs. **maintain a fire** Ne 10_{35}; — 3. **burn down**: *hāyâ l^ebā'ēr* for burning up, serve as fuel Is 6_{13} 44_{15}.

pual: pt. מְבֹעֶרֶת: **be kindled** Je 36_{22}.

hif.: pf. הִבְעַרְתִּי; impf. תַּבְעִיר, יַבְעֶר־, וַיַּבְעֶר־, וַיַּבְעֵר; pt. מַבְעִ(י)ר: — 1. **set on fire** (field, olive-trees, &c.) Ex 22_{5}; — 2. w. *be'āšân* **burn to ashes** Na 2_{14}; — 3. 2C 28_{3} *wayyab'ēr* burn up (people), txt. corr. ?

II **בער**: **piel**: pf. בִּעֵר, בִּעַרְתָּ; impf. יְבַעֵר, נְבַעֲרָה; inf. בָּעֵר: — 1. **graze** (a field), **allow** (a field) **to be grazed** Ex $22_{4a\beta}$; — 2. **ruin**; *hāyâ l^ebā'ēr* fall into ruin Nu 24_{22}; — 3. **sweep away** (dung) 1K $14_{10b\alpha}$; — 4. w. *min*, a) **get rid of** (the *'ōbôt*) 2K 23_{24}; b) **root out**, extirpate (evil) Dt 13_{6}.

hif.: impf. יַבְעֶר־: **let** (a field) **be grazed** Ex $22_{4a\alpha}$.

III **בער**, denom. of בְּעִיר: **qal**: impf. יִבְעֲרוּ; pt. בֹּעֲרִים: **be stupid** (like cattle) Je 10_{8}.

nif.: pf. נִבְעַר, נִבְעֲרוּ; pt. f. נִבְעָרָה: **prove to be stupid** (like cattle) Je $10_{14.21}$.

בַּעַר: בָּעַר: **stupid** (like cattle) Ps 49_{11}.

בַּעֲרָא: n. pers.
בְּעֵרָה: **fire**, conflagration Ex 22_5; oth.: **goods** damaged by fire. †
בַּעֲשֵׂיָה: n. pers.
בַּעְשָׁא: n. pers.
בְּעֶשְׁתְּרָה: n. loc.
בעת: **nif.**: pf. נִבְעַתִּי, נִבְעַת: **be overtaken by sudden terror** Dn 8_{17}.
piel: pf. sf. בִּעֲתַתּוּ, בִּעֲתָתְנִי, בִּעֲתַתְהוּ; impf. תְּבַעֵת, תְּבַעֲתֶהוּ, יְבַעֲתֻנִי; pt. מְבַעִתֶּךָ; — 1. **terrify** (of evil spirit, &c.) 1S 16_{14f}: **startle** s.one Jb 7_{14}.
בְּעָתָה: **terror** Je 8_{15} 14_{19}. †
בֹּץ: **silt** Je 38_{22}. †
בִּצָּה: pl. sf. rd Qr בִּצּוֹתָיו: **marshy place** Jb 8_{11}.
בָּצוּר: בְּצֻר(ו)ֹת, בְּצוּרָה: — 1. **inaccessible, impregnable** (city) 2K 18_{13}; — metaph. *beṣurôt* incomprehensible things Je 33_3.
בֵּצַי: בֵּצָי: n. pers.
I **בָּצִיר**: cs. בְּצִיר, sf. בְּצִירֵךְ: **vintage** Ju 8_2.
II **בָּצִיר**: **inaccessible**: *ya'ar habbāṣîr* forbidden forest Zc 11_2 Qr. †
***בָּצָל**: pl. בְּצָלִים: **onion**, *Allium cepa* Nu 11_5. †
בְּצַלְאֵל: n. pers.
בַּצְלוּת: n. pers.
בצע: **qal**: impf. יִבְצָעוּ, יִבְצַע; inf. בְּצֹעַ, בִּצְעֵךְ; pt. בּ(וֹ)צֵעַ: tech. weaver's term, **cut off** (woof); — 1. **cut off** (threads of life) (ꟻ piel 1.), *'ammat biṣēk* Je 51_{13} the cubit of your being cut off = of your end; — 2. *bāṣa' beṣa'* ('make one's cut') **make a profit** Je 6_{13}; — 3. abs. **break off** (of locust flight), **stop** Jl 2_8.
piel: pf. בִּצַּע; impf. וַתְּבַצְּעִי, יְבַצַּע, תְּבַצַּעְנָה, יְבַצְּעֵנִי: — 1. **cut off** (from the warp, i.e. the threads of life), make an end to life Is 38_{12}; — 2. **bring to an end** Is 10_{12}; — 3. **carry out** (subj. God, obj. his word) La 2_{17}; — 4. w. acc. **injure** s.one Ez 22_{12}.
בֶּצַע: בָּצַע; sf. בִּצְעָם, בִּצְעֵךְ: — 1. a **piece** (of material &c.) **cut off**, of threads of life Je 51_{13}; *beṣa' kesef* Ju 5_{19}; — 2. > (illegal) **profit** Gn 37_{26}.
[**בְּצַעֲנַנִּים**: n. loc. Ju 4_{11}: ꟻ Qr. (בְּ)צַעֲנַנִּים.]
בצק: **qal**: pf. בָּצְקוּ, בָּצֵקָה: **swell** (of feet) Dt 8_4 Ne 9_{21}. †
בָּצֵק: sf. בְּצֵקוֹ: **dough** Ex $12_{34.39}$.
cj ***בְּצִקְלוֹן**: 2K 4_{42} for בְּצִקְלֹנוֹ, ? rd בְּצִקְלֹנוֹ: **ear** (of grain). †
בָּצְקַת: n. loc.
I **בצר**: **qal**: impf. יִבְצְרוּ, תִּבְצֹר; pt. בּוֹצֵר, בֹּצְרִים: **gather** (ripe) **grapes, harvest** (vineyard) Dt 24_{21}; pt. **vintager** Je 6_9.
II **בצר**: **qal**: impf. יִבְצֹר: reduce, **humble** Ps 76_{13}. †
III **בצר**: **nif.**: impf. יִבָּצֵר: **be** inaccessible, **impossible** (*min* for) Gn 11_6 Jb 42_2. †
piel: impf. תְּבַצֵּר: **make inaccessible** (wall, height) Is 22_{10} Je 51_{53}. †
cj IV **בצר**: **piel** pt cj מְבַצֵּר Je 6_{27}: **gold-tester**, but ꟻ comm. †
I ***בֶּצֶר**: בֶּצֶר; pl. sf. בְּצָרֶיךָ: **gold ore** Jb 22_{24f}. †
II **בֶּצֶר**: n. pers. 1C 7_{37}. †
III **בֶּצֶר**: n. loc. Dt 4_{43} Jos 20_8 21_{36} 1C 6_{63}. †
בְּצַר: Jb 36_{19}: ?? ꟻ comm.
בָּצְרָה: n. loc.
בַּצָּרָה: pl. בַּצָּרוֹת: **lack of rain, drought**: — 1. sg. Ps 9_{10} 10_1; — 2. pl. (intensive) Je 14_1? †
[**בִּצָּרוֹן**: rd *לְבִצָּרוֹן 'in multitudes' Zc 9_{12}.]
בַּצֹּרֶת: pl. בַּצָּרוֹת ? Je 14_1: **lack of rain** Je 17_8.
בַּקְבּוּק: n. pers.
בַּקְבֻּק: **flask** for water, honey &c. 1K 14_3 Je $19_{1.10}$. †
בַּקְבֻּקְיָה: n. pers.
בַּקְבַּקַּר: n. pers.
בֻּקִּי: n. pers.
בֻּקִּיָּהוּ: n. pers.
***בָּקִיעַ**: pl. בְּקִיעִים, בְּקִעֵי: **breach** (in wall) Is 22_9, **ruins** Am 6_{11}. †

בָּקַע: qal: ב׳, בְּקָעָה, בָּקַעְתָּ; impf. וַיִּבְקַע, וַיִּבְקְעוּ, וַיִּבְקָעוּהָ; impv. בְּקָעֵהוּ; inf. בְּקָעָם; pt. בּ(וֹ)קֵעַ: — 1. trans. **split**: wood Ec 10_{9}, sea Ex 14_{16}; break open (spring) Ps 74_{15}, rip open (bodies of pregnant women) Am 1_{13}; — 2. **hatch out** (eggs) Is 34_{15}; — 3. **force breach** into, w. acc. 2C 21_{17}, w. *bᵉ* 2S 23_{16}.

nif.: pf. נִבְקַע, נִבְקְעוּ; impf. יִבָּקַע, יִבָּקֵעַ, וַיִּבָּקְעוּ; inf. הִבָּקַע: — 1. intrans. **split**: mountain Zc 14_{4}, water Ex 14_{21}; burst, of wineskin Jb 32_{19}; be smashed, of bodies 2C 25_{12}; be breached and conquered 2K 25_{4}; — 2. **break forth**, of light Is 58_{8}; — 3. be hatched (↗ qal 2) Is 59_{5}; — 4. be stormed (↗ qal 3) Ez 30_{16}.

piel: pf. בִּקַּע, בִּקְּעוּ, בִּקַּעְתִּי; impf. תְּבַקַּע, תְּבַקֵּעַ, תְּבַקְּעֵם, וַיְבַקְּעוּ, וַתְּבַקַּעְנָה: — 1. trans. **split** Gn 22_{3}; w. 2 acc. split into Hb 3_{9}; **rip open** 2K 8_{12}; — 2. **make** (wind) **break out** Ez 13_{13}; — 3. **pull to pieces** 2K 2_{24}; — 4. **hatch** Is 59_{5}; — 5. tech. *biqqēaᵃʿ yᵉʾōrîm* hew out tunnels Jb 28_{10}.

pual: impf. יְבֻקָּעוּ; pt. מְבֻקָּעָה: — 1. pt. **burst** (wineskins) Jos 9_{4}; — 2. **be ripped open** Ho 14_{1}; — 3. **be stormed** (of city) Ez 26_{10}. †

hif.: impf. sf. נַבְקִעֶנָּה; inf. הַבְקִיעַ: — 1. **take possession** (of a city) **by storm** (↗ qal 3) Is 7_{6}; — 2. **cut** (one's way) **through**, w. *ʾel* 2K 3_{26}. †

hof.: pf. הָבְקְעָה: **be stormed** Je 39_{2}. †

hitp.: pf. הִתְבַּקָּעוּ; impf. יִתְבַּקָּעוּ: **be burst** (wineskins) Jos 9_{13}, **be split** (valleys) Mi 1_{4}. †

בֶּקַע: **half-shekel** Gn 24_{22} Ex 38_{26}. †

בִּקְעָה: cs. בִּקְעַת; pl. בְּקָעוֹת.

I. **valley-plain**, broad, w. shallow walls Gn 11_{2};

II. names of places compounded w. *biqʿâ*: — 1. בִּקְעַת אָוֶן; — 2. בִּקְעַת אוֹנוֹ; — 3. בִּקְעַת יְרֵחוֹ; — 4. בִּקְעַת הַלְּבָנוֹן; — 5. בִּקְעַת מְגִדּוֹ(ן); — 6. בִּקְעַת מִצְפֶּה.

I **בקק**: **qal**: pf. בַּקֹּתִי, בְּקָקוּם; pt. בּוֹקֵק, בֹּקְקִים: **lay waste**, land Is 24_{1}, plan Je 19_{7}.

nif.: pf. נָבְקָה; impf. תִּבּוֹק; inf. הִבּוֹק: **be laid waste** (land) Is 24_{3}, **be agitated** (spirit) Is 19_{3}. †

polel: impf. יְבֹקְקוּ: **lay waste** Je 51_{2}. †

II **בקק**: **qal**: pt. בּוֹקֵק: be luxuriant, **grow luxuriantly** Ho 10_{1}. †

בקר: **piel**: pf. בִּקַּרְתִּים; impf. יְבַקֵּר; inf. בַּקֵּר: — 1. cultic tech. term: **undertake inspection of sacrifice** ? 2K 16_{15}; — 2. a) **investigate** carefully, w. *lᵉ* Lv 13_{36}, w. *lᵉ … bên* 27_{33}; b) **grieve over** w. acc. Ez 34_{11f}; c) abs. **consider** Pr 20_{25}.

בָּקָר (180×): cs. בְּקַר; sf. בְּקָרְךָ, בְּקָרוֹ; pl. בְּקָרֵינוּ Ne 10_{37}; otherw. coll.; m. & f.: — 1. **cows** f., thus *habbāqār ʿālôt* Gn 33_{13}; — 2. **(herd of) cattle** (both sexes) Ex 21_{37}; single animal, = *šôr* Ex 21_{37}; *ben-bāqār* calf Gn 18_{7}; — 3. *bāqār* as draught-animal 2S 6_{6}, beast of burden 1C 12_{41}; — 4. artificial 1K $7_{25\cdot29}$.

I **בֹּקֶר**: cultic tech. term, **sacrifice for omens** Ps 5_{4b}. †

II **בֹּקֶר** (ca. 200×): pl. בְּקָרִים: — **morning**: — 1. *ʾôr habbōqer* light of **daybreak** Ju 16_{2}; *habbōqer ʾôr* when the day became light Gn 44_{3}; — 2. *babbōqer* in the morning Gn 19_{27}; *babbōqer babbōqer* every morning Ex 30_{7}; sim. *labbōqer* Ex 34_{2}, *labbōqer labbōqer* 1C 9_{27}; *hāyâ bōqer* it became morning Gn 1_{5ff}; *lifnôt bōqer* toward morn. Ex 14_{27}; *bᵉṭerem bōqer* before dawn Is 17_{14}; — 3. *bōqer* :: *ʿereb*: *ʿereb bōqer* = one day Dn $8_{14\cdot26}$; many phrases, e.g. *min-habbōqer ʿad-hāʿāreb* Ex 18_{13}; — 4. the next morning: *ʿad-bōqer* Ex 12_{10} & sim. phrases; — 5. var. phrases: *babbōqer kizrōᵃḥ haššemeš* in the morning as the sun rises Ju 9_{33}.

בַּקָּרָה*: בַּקָּרַת (w. acc.): **care** Ez 34_{12}. †

בִּקֹּרֶת: **reprimanding** Lv 19_{20}. †

בקש: **piel**: pf.: בִּקֵּשׁ, בִּקֶּשׁ־, בִּקְשָׁה, בִּקַּשְׁתִּי,

בִּקְשׁוּ, sf. בִּקְשָׁתָם, בִּקַּשְׁתִּיהוּ, בִּקַּשְׁתִּיו,
בִּקְשֻׁהוּ; impf. יְבַקֵּשׁ, יְבַקֶּשׁ־, תְּבַקְּשִׁי,
אֲבַקֵּשׁ, אֲבַקְשָׁה, יְבַקְשׁוּ, יְבַקְשׁוּ, וַיְבַקְשׁוּ,
וַיבַקְשׁוּ, תְּבַקְשׁוּ, תְּבַקְּשׁוּ, sf. וַיְבַקְשֵׁהוּ,
תְּבַקְשֵׁם, תְּבַקְשֶׁנּוּ, וַיְבַקְשֵׁהוּ; impv. בַּקֵּשׁ,
בַּקְשׁוּ, בַּקְשׁוּנִי; inf. בַּקֵּשׁ, בַּקְשׁוֹ, בַּקֶּשְׁךָ,
בַּקְשֵׁנִי; pt. מְבַקֵּשׁ, מְבַקֶּשׁ־, מְבַקְשִׁים,
מְבַקְשֶׁיךָ: — 1. **seek** (to find), **look for** (an object) Gn 31_{39}; w. *le* Jb 10_6; *biqqēš nefeš* seek s.one's life Ex 4_{19}, sim. *raʿâ* 1S 25_{26}, *ṭôbâ* Ne 2_{10}; — 2. **seek to, try to** w. inf. Ex 4_{24}, w. *le* & inf. Ex 2_{15}; — 3. **seek to obtain, try to get**, priesthood 16_{10}; **require** Is 1_{12}; — 4. **seek**, *pe nê*, s.one's presence, esp. of Y., 1K 10_{24}; *debar yhwh* Am 8_{12}; — 5. var.: a) *biqqēš tefillâ* **seek prayer** Dn 9_3; w. acc. **plead for** Ps 122_9; c) *biqqēš* w. inf. **be near to** Gn 43_{30}.

pual: impf. וּתְבֻקְשִׁי, יְבֻקַּשׁ: **be sought** (for) Je 50_{20} Ez 26_{21}, be examined Est 2_{23}. †

בַּקָּשָׁה: sf. בַּקָּשָׁתֵךְ, בַּקָּשָׁתוֹ: **request, desire** Est 5_3.

I **בַּר**: sf. בְּרִי: **son** Pr 31_2.

II **בַּר**: בָּר; f. בָּרָה, pl. cs. בָּרֵי: — 1. **pure**, commandment Ps 19_9, heart Ps 24_4, beloved SS 6_{10}; — 2. empty Pr 14_4.

III **בַּר**: בָּר: cleaned, threshed **grain** Gn 41_{35}.

IV ***בַּר**: בָּר: **open country** Jb 39_4. †

I **בֹּר**: **purity** Ps $18_{21\cdot25}$.

II **בֹּר**: **potash, lye** (potassium carbonate, made from wood- & plant-ashes) Is 1_{25}.

I **בָּרָא**: **qal**: pf. בְּרָאנוּ, בְּרָאָהּ, בָּרָאתִי, ב׳, בְּרָאתִיו, בְּרָאתָם, בְּרָאָם; impf. יִבְרָא; impv. בְּרָא; pt. בּ(וֹ)רֵא, בֹּרַאֲךָ, Ec 12_1 rd בּוֹרְאֶךָ: **create** (only of God), heaven & earth Gn 1_1, Jacob Is 43_1, pure heart Ps 51_{12}.

nif.: pf. נִבְרָאוּ, נִבְרָאוּ, נִבְרֵאת; impf. יִבָּרֵאוּן; inf. הִבָּרְאָם, הִבָּרְאֲךָ, הִבָּרַאֲךָ; pt. נִבְרָא: — **be created**, heaven & earth Gn 2_4, king of Tyre Ez $28_{13\cdot15}$.

II **ברא**: **hif.**: inf. sf. הַבְרִיאֲכֶם: **fatten onesf.** 1S 2_{29}. †

III **ברא**: **piel**: בֵּרֵאתָ, בֵּרֵאתוֹ: cut down timber, **clear ground**, abs. Jos 17_{15}, obj. woods $_{18}$. †

IV **ברא**: 2S 12_{17}, ↗ I בָּרָה.

בָּרָא: ↗ בָּרִיא.

בְּרֹאדַךְ: 2K 20_{12}, ↗ מְרֹדַךְ.

בִּרְאִי: ↗ בֵּית בִּרְאִי.

בְּרָאיָה: n. pers.

***בַּרְבֻּר**: pl. בַּרְבֻּרִים: a bird fattened for Solomon's table 1K 5_3; unidentifiable; some: **cuckoo**; oth.: **goose**; oth.: **young chicken**. †

בָּרַד: **qal**: pf. ב׳: **hail** Is 32_{19}. †

בָּרָד: **hail** Ex $9_{18\cdot34}$; *ʾeben bārād* Is 30_{30}.

בָּרֹד: pl. בְּרֻדִּים, בְּרֻדֹּת: **speckled, dappled** Gn $31_{10\cdot12}$. †

I **בֶּרֶד**: n. loc. Gn 16_{14}. †

II **בֶּרֶד**: n. pers. 1C 7_{20}. †

I **בָּרָה**: **qal**: pf.: בָּרָא (!); impf. אֶבְרֶה: — 1. *bārâ leḥem ʾēt* **eat** together w. s.one 2S 12_{17}; — 2. *bārâ miyyad* **receive a diet** from 2S $13_{6\cdot10}$. †

piel: inf. לְבָרוֹת La 4_{10}: trad. **eat**, but ↗ comm. †

hif.: impf. תַּבְרֵנִי; inf. הַבְרוֹת: — 1. w. *leḥem* & acc. pers. **give food for comfort** (in misfortune) 2S 3_{35}; — 2. w. *leḥem* & acc. pers. **give diet** 2S 13_5. †

II **ברה**: **qal**: impv. בְּרוּ: enter into a *berît* w. s.one: give s.one task as representative 1S 17_8. †

בָּרוּךְ: n. pers.

בָּרוּר: f. בְּרוּרָה: — 1. *śāfâ berûrâ* Zp 3_9 **pure** (lips) or **clear** (speech); — 2. *bārûr millēl* Jb 33_3 **s.thg pure** or adv. purely; — 3. **selected**, ↗ I בָּרַר 2. †

בְּרוֹשׁ: pl. בְּרֹשָׁיו, בְּרוֹשִׁים: — 1. Phoenician **juniper**, *Juniperus phoenicea* (tree & wood) 1K $5_{22\cdot24}$; — 2. **spear shafts** (?) are brandished Na 2_4, but oth.: **text corr.**

*בְּרוֹת: pl. בְּרוֹתִים: **juniper** SS 1_{17}. †

*בָּרוּת: sf. בְּרוּתִי: **food** (for the sick or unfortunate) Ps 69_{22}. †

בֵּרוֹתָה: n. loc.

בִּרְזָוִת: n. loc.; Qr בִּרְזָיִת; Kt ?.

בַּרְזֶל: **iron**: — 1. in lists of metals: Nu 31_{22}; — 2. preparation Gn 4_{22}; — 3. objs. from iron: *kelî* tool 1K 6_7, *qeren* horn 1K 22_{11} &c.; — 4. sinews like iron Is 48_4; iron in the earth Dt 8_9.

בַּרְזִלַּי: n. pers.

I בָּרַח: **qal**: pf. בָּ׳, בָּרְחוּ, בָּרָחוּ; impf. יִבְרַח, נִבְרְחָה, יִבְרְחוּ, אֶבְרַח, יִבְרָח; impv. בְּרַח, בִּרְחוּ; inf. בְּרֹחַ, בָּרְחִי, בָּרְחֲךָ, בָּרוֹחַ; pt. בֹּרֵחַ, בֹּרַחַת: — 1. **run away, flee**: w. *mē'ēt* 1K 11_{23}, w. *mippenê* Gn $16_{6\cdot8}$, w. *min* 1S 20_1; w. *'aḥarê* 1S 22_{20}, w. *'el* Gn 27_{43}, w. *le* Ne 13_{10}; abs. Gn 31_{20}; — 2. pass away, **disappear**: days Jb 9_{25}, shadow Jb 14_2; — 3. pass through, **slide**, of bars Ex 36_{33}.

hif.: pf. הִבְרִיחוּ; impf. יַבְרִיחֶנּוּ, וָאַבְרִיחֵהוּ; pt. מַבְרִחַ: — 1. **drive out** Jb 41_{20}; — 2. pt. **sliding** (bar, ↗ qal 3) Ex 26_{28}.

II ברח: **hif.**: impf. יַבְרִיחַ: **injure** Pr 19_{26}. †

III ברח: **hif.**: impf. וַיַּבְרִיחוּ: bar (a door), **make impassable** 1C 12_{16}. †

בָּרִחַ, בָּרִיחַ: pl. בָּרִיחִים: — 1. **fugitive**, cj Is 15_5 בָּרִיחָה; — 2. *nāḥāš* Is 27_1 Jb 26_{13} fugitive = quick; oth.: twisted; or hairless, slippery; oth.: evil; Is 43_{14} text corr. †

בַּרְחֻמִי 2S 23_{31}: ↗ *בַּחֲרֻמִי.

בֵּרִי n. pers.

בְּרִי: Jb 37_{11}: ↗ רִי.

בָּרִיא: pl. בְּרִיאִים, בְּרִיא(וֹ)ת: **fat**: cattle Gn 41_4, man Ju 3_{17}; *berî'ê bāśār* Gn 41_2.

בְּרִיאָה: **something new** Nu 16_{30}.

בִּרְיָה: **diet** (for sick) 2S $13_{5\cdot7\cdot10}$. †

בָּרִיחַ: n. pers.

בְּרִיחַ: pl. בְּרִיחִ(י)ם, בְּרִיחֵי, בְּרִיחָ(י)ו: **bar**: — 1. on doors 1S 23_7, gates Ju 16_3; crosspieces joining wooden frames Ex 26_{26-29}; — 2. cosmic: of underworld Jon 2_7, of sea Jb 38_{10}, of heavens Jb 26_{13}.

בֵּרִים: *kol-habbērîm* 2S 20_{14}; inexplic., ↗ comm. †

בְּרִיעָה: n. pers.

בְּרִיעִי: gent. of בְּרִיעָה.

בְּרִית: cs. =; sf. בְּרִיתִי, בְּרִיתֶךָ, בְּרִיתֵךְ: — **agreement, alliance, covenant**:

I. **between men**: — 1. *kārat berît* (↗ *kārat*) **reach an agreement, make a pact, covenant** Gn $21_{27\cdot32}$; w. *'ēt* 2S 3_{13}, w. *'im* Gn 26_{28}, abs. Ho 10_4; *lifnê yhwh* before Y. Je $34_{15\cdot18}$; — 2. *kārat berît le* **grant, extend an agreement to** s.one Ex 23_{32}, w. *lifnê yhwh* 2S 5_3; — 3. *bô' babberît* enter **into an agreement** Je 34_{10}; — 4. *lāqaḥ 'et-... 'immô babberît* **admit** s.one **into the agreement** 2C 23_1; — 5. *berît bên...ûbên* **agreement betw. ... and** 1K 15_{19}; — 6. *ba'alê berît* Gn 14_{13}, *'anšê berit* Ob $_7$ partners of an agreement, **allies**; — 7. *berît 'aḥîm* **obligation against brothers** Am 1_9; — 8. ↗ III 1-5; *šāmar berît* **keep** Ez 17_{14}; w. *zākar* **keep in mind** Am 1_9; w. *hēfēr* **break** 1K 15_{19}; — 9. **matrimony** Ma 2_{14};

II. **misc. covenants**: — 1. God's *berît* w. animals Ho 2_{20}; — 2. man's *berît* w. stones of field Jb 5_{23}; w. death Is $28_{15\cdot18}$.

III. **covenant betw. God & men**: (a) the covenant is established: — 1. *kārat berît 'et-* God concludes a covenant w. Gn 15_{18}; w. *'im* 1K 8_{21}; — 2. *kārat berît le* concludes a cov't for the benefit of Is 55_3; — 3. God *hēqîm berîtô 'et-* establishes his cov't w. Gn 6_{18}; w. *bên ... ûbên* betw. ... and Gn 9_{17}; w. *le* on behalf of Ez 16_{60}; — 4. God *nātan berîtô* Gn 17_2; w. *higgîd* Dt 4_{13}; *nišba' berît le* Dt 4_{31}; *bā' bibrît 'et-* enters into a cov't w. Ez 16_8; *ṣiwwâ berîtô* Dt 4_{13}; — 5. God gives an unbreakable promise *śām berît 'ôlām* 2S 23_5; — 6. a person concludes a cov't w. God for the community ***kārat*** *berît* 2K 11_{17}; *lifnê yhwh* 2K 23_3, *leyhwh* (!) 2C 29_{10}; — 7. enter into the cov't w. God *bō' babberît* (F I 3) 2C 15_{12}; *'ābar babberît* Dt 29_{11}, *'āmad babberît* 2K 23_3; — (b) expressions associated w. *berît*: — 1. *'ôt (hab)berît* Gn 9_{12f}; — 2. *dibrê habberît* 2K 23_3; — 3. *sēfer habberît* 2K 23_2; — 4. *'arôn berît yhwh* 1K 6_{19}; — 5. *dam habberît* Ex 24_8; — 6. *neqam berît* Lv 26_{25}; — 7. *berît 'ôlām* Gn 9_{16}; — 8. *berît 'elōhîm* 2C 34_{32}; — 9. *berît rî'šōnîm* Lv 26_{45}; *berît 'abôtêkā* Dt 4_{31}; — 10. *mal'ak habberît* Ma 3_1 guardian angel of the congregation; *negîd berît* head of the cov't, the high priest Dn 11_{22}; *benê 'ereṣ habberît* those belonging to the land of the cov't Ez 30_5 = Jewish soldiers in Egyp. army; — 11. *berîtô* w. Abr., Isaac, Jacob 2K 13_{23}; *berîtî šālôm* my cov't of peace Nu 25_{12}; — 12. *berît melaḥ* cov't of salt Nu 18_{19}; — 13. *ba'al berît* Ju 8_{33} 9_4 & *'ēl berît* 9_{46} Canaanite deity; — 14. *berît kehunnat 'ôlām* claim to lasting priesthood Nu 25_{13}; — (c) the maintenance of the cov't: — 1. God *zākar berîtô* Gn 9_{15f}; — 2. *šāmar berît*: subj. God 1K 8_{23}, men Gn 17_{9f}; — 3. *'āśâ kibrît* 2C 34_{32}; — 4. *heḥezîq bibrît* Is $56_{4.6}$; — 5. *hēqîm* maintain Dt 8_{18}; *ne'emān bibrît* faithful to Ps 78_{37}; —(d) neglect, dissolution of the cov't: — 1. *hēfēr* 1K 15_{19}; — 2. *šākaḥ* Dt 4_{23}, subj. God 4_{31}; — 3. *'āzab* 1K $19_{10.14}$; — 4. *'ābar* 2K 18_{12}; — 5. *mā'as* 2K 17_{15}, *šiḥēt* Ma 2_8, *ḥillēl* Ma 2_{10}, *šiqqēr* Ps 44_{18}; *nē'ar*, subj. God Ps 89_{40}; — (e) var.: *mibberîtēk* because of the cov't w. you Ez 16_{61}; *kārat berît 'al-zebaḥ* make a cov't at a common sacrifice Ps 50_5; *nāśā' berît 'al-peh* continue the cov't (only) on the lips Ps 50_{16}; *berît 'am* blood-brotherhood Is 42_6 49_8.

בֹּרִית: **alkali**, obtained from soap-bearing plants, *Mesembrianthemum cristallinum* (iceplant): Je 2_{22} Ma 3_2. †

I **ברך**: **qal**: impf. וַיִּבְרַךְ, נִבְרְכָה: **kneel** Ps 95_6 2C 6_{13}. †

hif.: impf. וַיַּבְרֵךְ: **make** (camels) **kneel** Gn 24_{11}. †

II **ברך**: **qal**: only pt. pass. בָּרוּךְ, cs. בְּרוּךְ, f. בְּרוּכָה, pl. בְּרוּכִים, בְּרוּכֵי: — 1. **blessed**, filled w. power, filled w. *berākâ*: a) he is (may he be) blessed Gn 27_{29}, you are (may you be) blessed Dt 7_{14}; b) w. names of God: *bārûk le'ēl, leyhwh* he is (may be he) blessed by God/Y. Gn 14_{19}; *berûk yhwh* Gn 24_{31}, *berûkê yhwh* Is 65_{23}; c) other subjs.: e.g. fruit of your womb Dt 28_{4f}; — 2. (God) **be praised**: a) *bārûk yhwh* 1K 10_9; b) *bārûk yhwh* w. pt. Ps 72_{18}; *bārûk yhwh 'ašer* Gn 24_{27}.

nif.: pf. נִבְרְכוּ: **wish for onesf. blessing like**, w. *be* & person compared: Gn 12_3 18_{18} (like Abr.), 28_{14} (Jacob); F hitp. †

piel (235×): pf. בֵּרַךְ, בֵּרַךְ, וּבֵרַכְתִּי, בֵּרְכוּ, sf. בֵּרְכוֹ, בֵּרַכְךָ, בֵּרְכַנִי, בֵּרַכְתָּנִי, בֵּרַכְתִּיךָ, בֵּרְכוּנִי, בֵּרַכְנוּךָ; impf. וַיְבָרֵךְ, תְּבָרֵךְ, תְּבָרְכוּ, יְבָרְכוּ, וַיְבָרֶךְ, וַאֲבָרֵךְ, אֲבָרֲכָה, sf. יְבָרֲכֵהוּ, יְבָרְכֶנְהוּ, תְּבָרֲכֵנִי, אֲבָרֶכְךָ, אֲבָרְכֵם, אֲבָרֶכְךָ, תְּבָרְכֶנּוּ, יְבָרֶכְכָה; inf. בָּרֵךְ (also abs. Nu 23_{11}), בָּרוּךְ, בָּרְכוֹ; impv. בָּרֲכִי, בָּרְכוּ, בָּרֲכֵנִי; pt. מְבָרֲכֶיךָ: — 1. subj. God: **bless** = bestow power for success, prosperity, fertility: animals Gn 1_{22}, men 1_{28}, 7th day 2_3, field 27_{27}; — 2. **bless** = declare a person endowed w. power for success, prosperity, fertility: God — Abraham Gn 12_2; men — Jacob 27_{29}; Melchizedek — Abraham 14_{19}; father — his son 27_4; Israel — Pharaoh Ex 12_{32}; — 3. **bless** = wish s.one power for success, prosperity, fertility Gn 24_{60}; (greeting on arrival) 1S 13_{10}, (on leave-taking) 2S 13_{25}; — 4. bless God = declare God the origin of power for success, prosperity, fertility = **praise God** Gn 24_{48}; obj. *šemô* Ps 96_2; — 5. **formulas & phrases**: *bērak lifnê yhwh* Gn

27_{7}; *bērak b*^{e} by name of s.one Gn 48_{20} (cf. nif.), *b*^{e}*šēm yhwh* Dt 21_{5}; *bērak l*^{e} speak the blessing over Ne 11_{2}; — 6. euphem. for *'ārar* curse 1K $21_{10\cdot13}$.

pual: impf. יְבֹרַךְ, יְבֹרָךְ; pt. מְבֹרָךְ, מְבֹרָכָיו, מְבֹרֶכֶת; — 1. **be blessed** (action or condition) 2S 7_{29}; *m*^{e}*bōreket yhwh* blessed by Y. Dt 33_{13}; *t*^{e}*bōrak min* blessed among (or: more than) Ju 5_{24}; — 2. **be praised** (God's name) Ps 113_{2}.

hitp.: pf. הִתְבָּרֵךְ, הִתְבָּרְכוּ; impf. יִתְבָּרֵךְ; pt. מִתְבָּרֵךְ: — 1. **wish a blessing to onesf.** (to one another?), w. *b*^{e} Gn 22_{18} (Abr.) 26_{4} (Isaac); — 2. **bless onesf.** Is 65_{16}; **call onesf. happy** Dt 29_{18}.

בֶּרֶךְ: du. בִּרְכַּיִם, בִּרְכֵּי, sf. בִּרְכָּיו, בִּרְכֶּיהָ, בִּרְכֵיהֶם, בִּרְכַּי (pl. !); f.: — **knee**: w. vb. *kāraʿ* bend Is 45_{23}, *ʿal-birkāyw* 1K 8_{54}; *tēlaknâ birkayim mayim* drip w. water (urine) Ez 7_{17} 21_{12} (here euphem. = penis?); *ʿal-birkéhā* on knees = lap of mother 2K 4_{20}.

בַּרַכְאֵל: n. pers.

I **בְּרָכָה**: cs. בִּרְכַּת, sf. בִּרְכָתִי, בִּרְכָתְךָ, בִּרְכָתֶךָ; pl. בְּרָכ(וֹ)ת, cs. בִּרְכ(וֹ)ת, sf. בִּרְכוֹתֵיכֶם: — 1. **blessing** (in operation) Gn 28_{4}; — 2. (words of) **blessing** Gn 27_{12}; — 3. (formula of) **blessing** Gn 49_{28}; — 4. **gift** w. associated blessing Gn 33_{11}; — 5. **capitulation**, w. *ʿāśâ* & *'ēt*: only 2K 18_{31} = Is 36_{16}.

II **בְּרָכָה**: n. pers. 1C 12_{3}. †

בְּרֵכָה: cs. בְּרֵכַת; cs. pl. בְּרֵכוֹת: **pond, pool** 2K 18_{17}.

בֶּרֶכְיָה: n. pers.

בֶּרֶכְיָהוּ: n. pers.

בְּרֹמִים: *ginzê b*^{e}*rōmîm*: **fabric of two colors** Ez 27_{24}. †

בַּרְנֵעַ: n. loc.; F קָדֵשׁ בַּרְנֵעַ.

בֶּרַע: n. pers.

בְּרִעָה: n. pers., F בְּרִיעָה.

ברק: **qal**: impv. בְּרוֹק: **flash lightning** Ps 144_{6}. †

I **בָּרָק**: cs. בְּרַק; pl. בְּרָקִים, sf. בְּרָקָיו: **lightning** Ex 19_{16}; metaph. of sword Dt 32_{41}.

II **בָּרָק**: n. pers. Ju 4-5.

בְּרַק: n. pers. or tribe; F n. loc. בְּנֵי בְרַק Jos 19_{45}.

בַּרְקוֹס: n. pers.

***בַּרְקָן**: pl. בַּרְקֳנִים: Ju $8_{7\cdot16}$: **thorny growth**. †

בָּרֶקֶת: **emerald**, dark-green **beryl** Ex 28_{17} 39_{10}. †

בָּרְקַת: dark-green **beryl** Ez 28_{13}. †

I **ברר**: **qal**: pf. בָּרוֹתִי: inf. sf. לְבָרָם Ec 3_{18}; pt. pass. בְּרֻרוֹת, בְּרוּרִים: — 1. **purge out** Ez 20_{38}; — 2. **sort** Ec 3_{18}; pt. selected Ne 5_{18}.

nif.: impv. הִבָּרוּ: **keep onesf. pure** Is 52_{11}. †

piel: inf. בָּרֵר: **sift** Dn 11_{35}. †

hif.: inf. הָבַר: **sift, purify** Je 4_{11}. †

hitp.: impf. יִתְבָּרְרוּ: **be sifted** Dn 12_{10}. †

II **ברר**: **qal**: pt. pass. בָּרוּר: **sharpen**: sharpened arrow Is 49_{2}. †

hif.: impv. הָבֵרוּ: **sharpen** (arrow) Je 51_{11}. †

בִּרְשַׁע: n. pers.

בֵּרֹתִי: 1C 11_{39}: F בְּאֵרֹתִי.

בֵּרֹתַי: n. loc.

בְּשׂוֹר: name of river.

בְּשׂוֹרָה: F בְּשֹׂרָה.

בֹּשֶׂם (8×), **בֶּשֶׂם** Ex 30_{23}, ***בָּשָׂם** SS 5_{1}; sf. בְּשָׂמִי; pl. בְּשָׂמִים, בְּשָׂמָיו: — 1. **balsam shrub**, *Balsamodendrium Opolbalsamum*: SS $5_{1\cdot13}$; — 2. **balsam oil**, which easily congeals, sg. Ex 35_{28}, pl. 1K 10_{2}; — 3. **perfume** (in general): *qinn*^{e}*mon-beśem* sweet-smelling cinnamon Ex 30_{23}; — 4. *q*^{e}*nēh bōśem* (sweet) **cane**, *Cymbopogon* Ex 30_{23}.

בָּשְׂמַת: n. pers. f.

בשׂר: **piel**: pf. בִּשַּׂר, בִּשַּׂרְתִּי; impf. אֲבַשְּׂרָה, יְבַשְּׂרוּ, תְּבַשְּׂרוּ; impv. בַּשְּׂרוּ; inf. בַּשֵּׂר; pt. מְבַשֵּׂר, מְבַשֶּׂרֶת, מְבַשְּׂרוֹת: — 1. **bring** (good or bad) **news**: a) neutral 2S 18_{20}; pt. sbst. 1S 4_{17}; b) *biśśar ṭôb* bring good news 1K 1_{42}, *m^e^baśśēr* messenger (of good news) Na 2_1, f. Is 40_9; — 2. **make known** 2S 1_{20}.

hitp.: impf. יִתְבַּשֵּׂר: **receive** (good) **news** 2S 18_{31}. †

בָּשָׂר (266×): cs. בְּשַׂר, sf. בְּשָׂרִי, בְּשָׂרְךָ, בְּשַׂרְכֶם, בְּשָׂרֶךָ; pl. בְּשָׂרִים: — 1. **skin** Ps 102_6; — 2. **flesh** of living men Gn 2_{21}, of dead men 1S 17_{44}, of cows Gn 41_2; — 3. **meat** as food 1S $2_{13\cdot15}$; — 4. **sacrificial meat**: *b^e^śar qōdeš* Je 11_{15}, *b^e^śar mizbēaḥ* Lv 7_{20}; — 5. **flesh** as a part of the body: a) *ʿeṣem & bāśār* Gn 2_{23}; b) euphem. for pubic region, *b^e^śar ʿorlâ* Gn 17_{11}, *b^e^śar ʿerwâ* Ex 28_{42}; penis Lv $15_{2f\cdot7}$; genitals of woman Lv 15_{19}; — 6. **body** Ps 63_2; — 7. **relationship**: *bāśār mibb^e^śārî* Gn 2_{23}; *bāśār ʾeḥād* 2_{24}; *ʾāḥînû b^e^śārēnû* our own brother Gn 37_{27}; — 8. a) **living**: *lēb bāśār* :: *lēb ʾeben* Ez 11_{19}; b) perishable, **transitory**: *minnefeš we^e^ʿad bāśār* Is 10_{18}; — 9. *kol-bāśār*: a) men and beasts Gn $6_{12\cdot17}$; b) world of men Nu 16_{22}; c) world of beasts Gn 6_{19}; d) any man Dt 5_{23}; e) every man Is 40_6.

בְּשֹׂרָה & 2S 18_{25} בְּשׂוֹרָה: — 1. **message** 2S 18_{20}, good news 2K 7_9; — 2. **messenger's reward** 2S 4_{10}.

בְּשַׁגַּם Gn 6_3: ↗ גַּם.

בָּשַׁל: **qal**: pf. בָּשְׁלוּ ,בּ׳: — 1. **ripen** Jl 4_{13}; — 2. **cook** (intrans.) Ez 24_5. †

piel: pf. בִּשְּׁלָם ,בִּשְּׁלוּ ,בִּשַּׁלְתָּ; impf. וַנְּבַשֵּׁל ,יְבַשְּׁלוּ ,תְּבַשֵּׁל; impv. בַּשְּׁלוּ ,בַּשֵּׁלוּ; inf. בַּשֵּׁל; pt. מְבַשְּׁלִים: — **cook, boil, roast** Dt 16_7, *biššēl bāśār* 1K 19_{21}; bake (cakes) 2S 13_8.

pual: pf. בֻּשָּׁלָה; impf. יְבֻשַּׁל; pt. מְבֻשָּׁל: **be boiled, cooked** Ex 12_9.

hif.: pf. הִבְשִׁילוּ: **ripen** Gn 40_{10}. †

בָּשֵׁל: f. בְּשֵׁלָה: **boiled**, cooked Ex 12_9.

בִּשְׁלָם: Ezr 4_7 uncert.: trad. n. pers.; oth.: 'on good terms w.' or txt. emended; ↗ comm. †

I **בָּשָׁן**: n. territory.

II (?) **בָּשָׁן**: **serpent** Dt 33_{22} Ps 68_{23}. †

בָּשְׁנָה: rd. בֹּשֶׁת or בּוּשָׁה ?: **shame** Ho 10_6. †

בשס: בּוֹשַׁסְכֶם Am 5_{11}: בשס (??) inf. poel; text. corr.; rd. שַׁבְסְכֶם **levy rent**. †

בֹּשֶׁת: sf. בָּשְׁתִּי, בָּשְׁתְּכֶם: — 1. (feeling of) **shame** 1S 20_{30}; *bōšet pānîm* face full of shame Je 7_{19}; *bôš bōšet* feel deeply ashamed Is 42_{17}; *lābēš bōšet* dress onesf. in shame Ps 35_{26}; — 2. **shamefulness**: substitute for *baʿal* Je 3_{24} 11_{13} Ho 9_{10}, and in n. pers., e.g. 2S 2_8.

I **בַּת** (585×): f. of ↗ בֵּן: cs. בַּת, sf. בִּתִּי; pl. בָּנוֹת, cs. בְּנוֹת, sf. בְּנֹתַי: — 1. **daughter** (natural) Gn 11_{29}; *bat ʾābî* half-sister (different mother) & *bat ʾimmî* full sister (same mother) Gn 20_{12}; combinations, e.g. *b^e^nôt bānîm* granddaughters Gn 46_7; *bat ʿomrî* granddau. of O. 2K 8_{26}; *bānôt* daughters-in-law Ju 12_9; — 2. daughter in the sense of **membership**: *b^e^nôt ḥēt* Hittite women Gn 27_{46}; *ḥešbôn wekol-b^e^nôtêhā* H. & all its daughter-villages Nu 21_{25}; *bat ʾēl nēkār* woman worshipping a foreign god Mal 2_{11}; *bat b^e^liyyaʿal* useless woman 1S 1_{16}; *b^e^nôt haššîr* tones or songs? Ec 12_4; *bat ʿayin* eyeball Ps 17_8; — 3. **personification** of city, land, *bat ṣiyyôn* Is 1_8, *bat ʿammî* Is 22_4; — 4. in **statement of age** (↗ *bēn* 8): *bat tišʿîm šānâ* Gn 17_{17}; — 5. young girls or women Gn 30_{13}; *b^e^nôt hāʾādām* Gn $6_{2\cdot4}$.

II **בַּת**: pl. בַּתִּים: **bath**, liquid measure, = 1 *ʾēfâ* = 40-45 liters: 1K $7_{26\cdot38}$.

cj III **בַּת**: pl. *בַּתִּים, rd. בַּתֵּי for בָּתֵּי 2K 23_7: **woven garment**. †

בָּתָה: fm. ctxt. **devastation, desert**: Is 5_6. †

[**בַּתָּה***: בְּחַר בַּתֵּיהֶם 2C 34_6: txt. corr., rd. בִּרְחֹבוֹתֵיהֶם. †]

***בַּתָּה**: pl. בַּתּוֹת: **precipice, cliff face** Is 7_{19}. †

I **בְּתוּאֵל**: n. pers.

II **בְּתוּאֵל**: n. loc. 1C 4_{30}. †

בְּתוּל: n. loc.

בְּתוּלָה: cs. בְּתוּלַת; pl. בְּתֻל(וֹ)ת, בְּתוּל(וֹ)ת: **virgin**: — 1. mature girl 'whom no man has known,' Gn 24_{16}; :: widow & divorcee, Lv 21_{14}, :: *bāḥûr* Dt 32_{25}; — 2. **personified** (↗ *bat* 3): *betûlat yiśrāʾēl* virgin Israel (not: of Isr.!) Je 18_{13}; *betûlat bat ṣiyyôn* 2K 19_{21}.

בְּתוּלִים: cs. בְּתוּלֵי, sf. בְּתוּלֶיהָ: — 1. state of **virginity** Lv 21_{13}; — 2. **evidence of virginity** Dt 22_{14f}.

בִּתְיָה: n. pers. f.

בָּתִּים: ↗ בַּיִת, III בַּת.

בתק: **piel**: pf. בִּתְּקוּךְ: **slaughter** Ez 16_{40}. †

בתר: **qal**: pf. בָּתַר: **cut in pieces**, cut in two Gn 15_{10}. †

I **בֶּתֶר**: **piece** (of sacrificial meat) Gn 15_{10} Je 34_{18f}. †

II ***בֶּתֶר**: הָרֵי בָתֶר SS 2_{17}, uncert.; some, n. loc.; oth.: w. many ravines, or, of fragrances; ↗ comm. †

בִּתְרוֹן: trad. **ravine**; oth. **forenoon**: 2S 2_{29}. †

בַּת־שֶׁבַע, ־שָׁבַע: n. pers. f.

בַּת־שׁוּעַ: n. pers. f.

ג

גֵּא: **haughty** Is 16_{6}. †

גָּאָה: **qal**: pf. גָּאוּ, גּ׳; impf. יִגְאֶה; inf. גָּאֹה: **be, become high**: of plants Jb 8_{11}, waves Ez 47_{5}, God Ex $15_{1.21}$.

גֵּאָה: **haughtiness** Pr 8_{13}. †

גֵּאֶה: pl. גֵּאִים: **haughty** Ps 94_{2}.

גְּאוּאֵל: n. pers.

גַּאֲוָה: cs. גַּאֲוַת, sf. גַּאֲוָתוֹ: — 1. **raging** (of sea) Ps 46_{4}; — 2. **loftiness** (of God) Ps 68_{35}; — 3. **haughtiness** Is 9_{8}; *ʿāśâ gaʾawâ* act haughtily Ps 31_{24}.

גְּאוּלָּה Ru 4_{7}: ↗ גְּאֻלָּה.

גְּאוּלִים: sf. גְּאוּלַי: time, **condition of the** *gōʾēl*, **avenger of bloodshed**: *šenat geʾûlay* year of my blood-revenge Is 63_{4}. †

גָּאוֹן: cs. גְּאוֹן, sf. גְּאוֹנְךָ, גְּאוֹנֵךְ, pl. sf. גְּאוֹנָיִךְ Ez 16_{56}: — 1. **height** (of waves) Jb 38_{11}; *geʾôn hayyardēn* thicket of the J. Je 12_{5}; — 2. **loftiness** Ex 15_{7}; — 3. a) **pride**, of Jacob Am 6_{8}, *hāyâ legāʾôn* redound to the pride Is 4_{2}; b) > **arrogance**: of city or land Je 13_{9}.

גֵּאוּת: cs. =: — 1. **ascent**: of smoke Is 9_{17}, sea Ps 89_{10}; — 2. **majesty** (of God) Is 26_{10}; *ʿāśâ gēʾût* do sublime things Is 12_{5}; — 3. **arrogance** Ps 17_{10}.

***גַּאֲיוֹן**: גַּאֲיוֹנִים Kt: **haughty** Ps 123_{4} (Qr לְגְאֵי יוֹנִים). †

גֵּאָי(וֹ)ת: ↗ גַּיְא.

I **גָּאַל**: **qal**: pf. גְּאַלְתִּיךָ, גְּאָלוֹ, גָּאַלְתָּ, גּ׳; impf. יִגְאָלֵהוּ, יִגְאָלֶנּוּ, יִגְאָל, יִגְאַל; impv. גְּאָלָה, גְּאָל, גְּאַל; inf. לִגְאוֹל (Ru 4_{6} Kt, Qr לִגְאָל־), לְגָאֳלֵךְ, גָּאוֹל; pt. גֹּ(וֹ)אֵל, גֹּאֲלוֹ, גֹּאַלְךָ, גֹּאַלְכֶם, גֹּאֲלֵךְ, גֹּאֲלֵנוּ, pass. גְּאוּלִים (:: sbst. ↗ גְּאוּלִים): make a claim for a person or thing > reclaim him/it, **redeem**; — 1. property law: buy back a house (which has been sold) Lv 25_{33}, buy freedom of person (who has fallen into slavery for debt) Lv 25_{48f}; — 2. duty of the male relative of s.one who has died leaving a childless widow to **deliver** her from childlessness by marriage Ru $4_{4.6}$, the man in question being called *gōʾēl* **deliverer** Ru 2_{20}; one who receives the restitution-payment at the relief of a wrong Nu 5_{8}; — 3. *gōʾēl haddām* avenger of bloodshed (who, by killing the murderer of one's relative, clears away the crime) 1K 16_{11}; — 4. **lay claim to**: a) subj. darkness Jb 3_{5}; b) subj. God, **redeem, ransom** Ex 6_{6} Israel, Pr 23_{11} widows & orphans.

nif.: pf. נִגְאַל; impf. יִגָּאֵל, תִּגָּאֲלוּ: **be bought back, redeemed** Lv 25_{30}.

II **גאל**: **nif.**: pt. f. נִגְאָלָה; נְגֹאֲלוּ Is 59_3 La 4_{14} is combination of nif. נִגְאֲלוּ w. pual גֹּאֲלוּ: **become impure** Zp 3_1.

piel: pf. גֵּאַלְנוּךָ: defile, **make** (cultically) **impure** Ma 1_7. †

pual: pf. ↗ nif.; impf. וַיְגֹאֲלוּ; pt. מְגֹאָל: **become** (cultically) **impure** Ma $1_{7.12}$; Is 59_3 & La 4_{14} ↗ nif.

hif.: אֶגְאָלְתִּי Is 63_3: *'af'el*; or rd. piel pf. גֵּאַלְתִּי or impf. אֲגָאֵל: **stain.** †

hitp.: impf. יִתְגָּאֵל, יִתְגָּאַל: **make onesf.** (cultically) **impure** Dn 1_8. †

***גֹּאַל**: pl. cs. גָּאֳלֵי: (cultic) **pollution** Ne 13_{29}. †

גְּאֻלָּה: cs. גְּאֻלַּת, sf. גְּאֻלָּתִי, גְּאֻלָּתְךָ: — 1. **right & duty of redemption** Lv 25_{24}; *'anšê ge'ullātekā* those to whom your claim for ransoming extends = your blood relatives Ez 11_{15}; — 2. **redemption** Lv 25_{26}.

I **גַּב**: גֶּב; sf. גַּבִּי; pl. גַּבֵּי, גַּבֵּיהֶם, & גַּבֹּ(ו)ת, גַּבֹּתָם: s.thg arched: — 1. **back** Ez 10_{12} Ps 129_3; — 2. *gabbōt 'ênayim* **eyebrows** Lv 14_9; — 3. **torus** (rounded molding) of altar-base Ez $16_{24.31.39}$; — 4. **boss** (i.e. protuberant knob of a shield) Jb 15_{26}.

*II **גַּב**: pl. גַּבֵּי, גַּבֵּיכֶם: **answer, rejoinder,** *gabbê ḥōmer* Jb 13_{12}. †

I ***גֵּב**: pl. גֵּבִים: **cistern** 2K 3_{16} Je 14_3. †

II ***גֵּב**: pl. גֵּבִים: tech. archit. term 1K 6_9, unexplained, Verss.: paneled ceiling. †

III **גֵּב**: ↗ *גֵּבֶה.

גֶּבֶא: **cistern** Is 30_{14} Ez 47_{11}. †

***גֵּבֶה**: pl. גֵּבִים: **swarm** (of locusts) Is 33_4. †

גָּבַהּ: **qal**: pf. ג׳, גָּבְהָא Ez 31_5 (א Aram.) גָּבַהְתָּ, גָּבְהוּ; impf. יִגְבַּהּ, יִגְבְּהוּ, תִּגְבְּהוּ, תִּגְבְּהֶ(י)נָה Ez 16_{50}; inf. גְּבֹהַּ, גָּבְהָה: — 1. **be high** Ez 19_{11}; *gābah min* be higher than Is 55_9; — 2. **be exalted** Is 5_{16}; — 3. **be haughty** Is 3_{16}; *gābah lēb* have high aims Ez $28_{2.5.17}$; **be courageous** 2C 17_6.

hif.: pf. הִגְבַּהְתִּי; impf. יַגְבִּיהַּ, יַגְבִּיהוּ, וַיַּגְבִּיהֶהָ; מַגְבִּיהִי, מַגְבִּהִי; inf. הַגְבֵּהַּ: — **make high**; wall 2C 33_{14}; let (tree) grow high Ez 17_{24}; *higbî'ah 'ûf* fly high Jb 5_7; let (request) reach high Is 7_{11}.

***גְּבַהּ**: cs. גְּבַהּ: **high**: *gebah qômâ* grown high Ez 31_3; *gebah 'ênayim, gebah rû'ah, gebah lēb* haughty Ps 101_5 Ec 7_8 courageous Pr 16_5. †

גָּבֹהַּ: cs. גְּבֹהַּ, f. גְּבֹהָה; pl. גְּבֹהִים, גְּבֹה(ו)ת: **high**: mountain Gn 7_{19}, trees Is 10_{33}; *gebō'ah qōmātô* his tall figure 1S 16_7; what is high Ez 21_{31}; *dibber gebōhâ* speak haughtily 1S 2_3; *gebōhîm* haughty ones Is 5_{15}; Ec 5_7 ↗ comm.

גֹּבַהּ: sf. גָּבְהוֹ, גָּבְהָם: **height**: — 1. of a man 1S 17_4, tree Ez 19_{11}, table Ez 40_{42}; — 2. metaph. majesty Jb 40_{10}; *gōbah 'af* superciliousness Ps 10_4, *gōbah lēb* haughtiness 2C 32_{26}.

גַּבְהוּת: **haughtiness** Is $2_{11.17}$. †

[**גְּבוֹל** Jos 15_{47}: rd Qr הַגָּדוֹל. †]

גְּבוּל & (rare) גְּבֻל (240×): cs. =, sf. גְּבוּלוֹ, גְּבֻלוֹ; pl. גְּבוּלֶיךָ, גְּבוּלַיִךְ: — 1. **mountain** 1S 13_{18} Ps 78_{54}; — 2. **boundary** Ps 104_9, *gebûl rē'akā* boundary-stone of your neighbor Dt 19_{14}, *gebûl 'ôlām* ancient boundary-stone Pr 22_{28}; — 3. tech. archit. term: a) barrier, lattice Ez 40_{12}, b) enclosure, molding Ez $43_{13.17.20}$; — 4. **territory** Dt 19_3.

***גְּבוּלָה**: sf. גְּבֻלָתוֹ; pl. גְּבֻלֹת, גְּבוּל(ו)ת, sf. גְּבוּל(ו)תֶיהָ, גְּבֻל(ו)תֶיהָ: — 1. **boundary** Is 10_{13}; — 2. enclosure, **border-strips** (of a field) Is 28_{25}; — 3. **territory** Nu 32_{33}; *ligbulōtêhā* according to its portions of territory Nu 34_2, *gebûlôt 'ereṣ* zones of the earth Ps 74_{17}.

גִּבֹּר & **גִּבּוֹר** (ca. 160×): sf. גִּבֹּרָם; pl. גִּבֹּ(ו)רִים, גִּבֹּ(ו)רֵי, גִּבּוֹרֵי, גִּבּוֹרֶיהוּ (Na 2_4): — 1. **manly, vigorous**: *'îš gibbôr* 1S 14_{52}; of lion Pr 30_{30}; Nimrod was a **despot** Gn 10_8; — 2. **hero** (in battle): champion 1S 17_{51}; *gibbôrîm* warriors Is 21_{17}, *gibbôrîm 'ōšê* *milḥāmâ* seasoned warriors 2K 24_{16}; David's *gibbôrîm* = bodyguard, elite troops 2S 20_7; *bêt haggibbôrîm* barracks Ne 3_{16}; metaph. influential, respected Ps 112_2; ironic: in drinking wine Is 5_{22}; — 3. ref. to king Ps 45_4, Messiah *'ēl gibbôr* Is 9_5 trad. God a mighty hero, oth.: God, hero; — 4. ref. to God, *'ēl gibbôr* Is 10_{21}, *hā'ēl haggibbôr* Je 32_{18}, other var. Ps 24_8, Dt 10_{17} Zp 3_{17}; **angel** *gibbôrê kōᵃḥ* Ps 103_{20}.

גְּבוּרָה: cs. גְּבוּרַת, sf. גְּבוּרָתִי, גְּבֻרָתִי, גְּבוּרָתְךָ, גְּבוּרָתֶךָ, גְּבוּרַתְכֶם, גְּבֻרָתְךָ; pl. גְּבוּר(וֹ)ת, גְּבֻר(וֹ)ת, גְּבוּרֹתֶךָ: — 1. **strength**: a) of animal: horse Ps 147_{10}, crocodile Jb 41_4; b) of man Ju 8_{21} *malkûtô ûgᵉbûrātô* his mighty reign 1C 29_{30}; *bigbûrōt* Ps 90_{10} w. strength = at the most; c) of God Ps 21_{14} & oft.; d) var.: mighty appearance (of sun) Ju 5_{31}; *'ēṣâ ûgᵉbûrâ* powerful resolution 2K 18_{20}; — 2. **God's powerful deeds** Ps 20_7.

גִּבֵּחַ: w. **bald forehead** Lv 13_{41}. †

גַּבַּחַת: sf. גַּבַּחְתּוֹ — 1. **baldness of forehead** Lv 13_{42f}; — 2. **bare place** on the front of a garment Lv 13_{55}. †

גֹּבַי, גֵּבִי: **swarm of locusts** Am 7_1 Na 3_{17}. †

גַּבַּי: n. pers. Ne 11_8, but dub.; F comm. †

גֵּבִים: n. loc.

גָּבִיעַ: cs. גְּבִיעַ, sf. גְּבִיעִי; pl. גְּבִיעִים, גְּבִיעֶיהָ: — 1. (drinking-)**bowl** Gn 44_2 Je 35_5; — 2. (golden) **cup** on the lampstand Ex 25_{31-34}.

גְּבִיר: **lord, master** Gn $27_{29\cdot37}$. †

גְּבִירָה: cs. F גְּבֶרֶת, sf. גְּבִרְתִּי: — 1. **lady, mistress** Gn $16_{4\cdot8f}$ 2K 5_3; — 2. 'lady,' title of **queen mother** 2K 10_{13}, metaph. of Babylon Is 47_5; *hēsîr miggᵉbîrâ* take s.one from the position of 'lady' 1K 15_{13}; *bᵉnê haggᵉbîrâ* full brothers of the king 2K 10_{13}; — 3. title of the **queen**, chief consort of the Pharaoh 1K 11_{19}.

גָּבִישׁ: **rock-crystal** Jb 28_{18}. †

גבל: **qal**: pf. גָּבְלוּ; impf. תִּגְבֹּל, תִּגְבָּל־: — 1. **establish a boundary** Dt 19_{14}; — 2. **bound** (an area) Jos 18_{20}; — 3. *gābal bᵉ* **border on** Zc 9_2. †

hif.: pf. הִגְבַּלְתָּ; impv. הַגְבֵּל: — **set bounds around** Ex $19_{12\cdot23}$. †

גְּבַל: n. loc. **Byblos** Ez 27_9. †

גְּבָל: n. terr. Ps 83_8. †

גִּבְלִי: gent. of גְּבַל Jos 13_5.

גַּבְלֻת: **welding together** Ex 28_{22}. †

גִּבֵּן: **hunchbacked** Lv 21_{20}. †

גְּבִנָה: **cheese** Jb 10_{10}. †

*גַּבְנֹן: pl. גַּבְנֻנִּים: **high-arched**, *hārîm gabnunnîm* Ps 68_{17}; $_{16}$ F comm. †

גֶּבַע: גֶּבַע: n. loc.

*גָּבִעַ: F גָּבִיעַ.

גִּבְעָא: n. pers.

I גִּבְעָה (60×): גִּבְעַת, sf. גִּבְעָתָהּ; pl. גְּבָעוֹת, cs. גִּבְעוֹ(ו)ת, sf. גִּבְעוֹתֶיךָ: — A. **hill** 1K 14_{23}, oft. cultic place; oft. difficult to distinguish from II; — B. combinations: — 1. גִּבְעַת הָאֱלֹהִים; — 2. גִּבְעַת אַמָּה; — 3. גִּבְעַת בִּנְיָמִן & גִּבְעַת בְּנֵי בִנְיָמִן, F II; — 4. גִּבְעַת גָּרֵב; — 5. גִּבְעַת הַחֲכִילָה; — 6. גִּבְעַת הַמּוֹרֶה; — 7. גִּבְעַת הָעֲרָלוֹת; — 8. גִּבְעַת פִּינְחָס.

II (הַ)גִּבְעָה, גִּבְעַת, loc. (הַ)גִּבְעָתָה: n. loc., = I; **Gibeah**; several places by this name.

גִּבְעֹל: **bud** Ex 9_{31}; oth.: name of a month. †

גִּבְעֹן, גִּבְעוֹן: n. loc.

גִּבְעֹ(ו)נִי: gent. of גִּבְעֹן.

גָּבַר: **qal**: pf. גָּ׳, גָּבְרוּ, גָּבֵרוּ; impf. יִגְבַּר, יִגְבְּרוּ: — 1. **excel** Ex 17_{11}, w. *min* prevail over 2S 1_{23}; metaph. *šeqer* Je 9_2 (rd *gābᵉrâ*); — 2. **accomplish** s.thg 1S 2_9; — 3. *mayim*: **swell, rise** Gn $7_{18\cdot20\cdot24}$.

piel: pf. גִּבַּרְתִּי; impf. יְגַבֵּר: — 1. **make superior** Zc 10_6; — 2. w. *ḥᵃyālîm* **exert** all one's strength Ec 10_{10}.

hif.: pf. הִגְבִּיר; impf. נַגְבִּיר: **be strong** Ps 12_5; ? Dn 9_{27} w. *bᵉrît*: Verss.: make a firm covenant; oth.: make heavy = let become faithless (in cov't), or become heavy, oppressive. †

hitp.: impf. יִתְגַּבָּר, יִתְגַּבְּרוּ: — **show onesf. superior** Is 42_{13}, be overbearing Jb 15_{25} 36_{9}. †

I גֶּ֫בֶר: גֶּבֶר; pl. גְּבָרִים: — 1. **young**, strong **man** Pr 30_{19}, new-born male Jb 3_{3}; :: both women & children; oft. in counts: *ligbārîm* in men 1C 23_{3}, *lerōʾš geber* to each man Ju 5_{30}, so *gebārîm* individual men Jos $7_{14 \cdot 17f}$; *geber* > everyone Mi 2_{2}, > one who Hb 2_{5}, > he who La 3_{1}, > (some)one Pr 28_{21}; — 2. *geber* in wisdom sayings: *ʾārûr haggeber* Je 17_{5}, *bārûk haggeber* 17_{7}, *ʾašrê haggeber* Ps 34_{9}; — 3. spec.: *geber ʿamîtî* **my fellow** Zc 13_{7}.

II גֶּ֫בֶר: n. pers. 1K $4_{13 \cdot 19}$. †

גִּבָּר: n. loc.

גִּבֹּר: F גִּבּוֹר.

גַּבְרִיאֵל: n. pers.: the angel **Gabriel** Dn 8_{16} 9_{12}. †

גְּבֶ֫רֶת: cs. of F גְּבִירָה Is 47_{5}. †

גִּבְּתוֹן: n. loc.

גָּג: cs. גַּג, sf. גַּגֶּ֫ךָ, loc. הַגָּ֫גָה; pl. גַּגּוֹת, sf. גַּגּוֹתֶיהָ, גַּגּ(וֹ)תֵיהֶם: — 1. (flat) **roof** (upon wh. one may walk): 1S 9_{25f}; of palace 2S 11_{2}, of tower Ju 9_{51}; place for cult 2K 23_{12}, for lament Is 15_{3}; *pinnat gāg* F Pr 21_{9}; — 2. **top slab** of altar of incense Ex 30_{3} 37_{26}.

I גַּד: **coriander**, *Coriandrum sativum* Ex 16_{31} Nu 11_{7}. †

II גַּד, גָּד: — 1. **luck**: *begād* Gn 30_{11} Kt; — 2. name of a deity **Gad** || *menî* Is 65_{11}; — 3. n. loc. in ־גָּד F בַּעַל (בֵּית).

גָּד: — 1. n. pers., son of Jacob Gn 30_{11}; — 2. name of tribe Gn 49_{19}.

גִּדְגָּד: in n. loc. *haggidgād*, F חֹר Nu 33_{32f}.

גֻּדְגֹּ֫דָה: n. loc. Dt 10_{7}, F חֹר הַגִּדְגָּד. †

I גדד: **hitpol.**: impf. תִּתְגֹּדְדִי, תִּתְגּוֹדְדִי, יִתְגֹּדָד, יִתְגֹּדָ֫דוּ; pt. מִתְגֹּדְדִים: **inflict cuts on onesf.** 1K 18_{28}.

II גדד: **qal**: impf. יָגוֹדּוּ: w. *ʿal* **band together against** Ps 94_{21}. †

גַּדָּה: F n. loc. חֲצַר גַּדָּה.

I גְּדוּד: pl. sf. גְּדוּדֶ֫יהָ: — 1. **wall** 2S 22_{30} = Ps 18_{30}; — 2. **edge of furrow** Ps 65_{11}. †

II גְּדוּד: pl. גְּדוּדִים, cs. גְּדוּדֵי, sf. גְּדוּדָיו: — 1. **raiding party** 2K 6_{23}; *ʾîš gedûdîm* **robber** Ho 6_{9}; *yāṣeʾû gedûdîm* set out to plunder 2K 5_{2}; — 2. **military troops** Jb 29_{25} 2C 25_{9ff}; *ligdûdîm* in divisions 2C 26_{11}; God's hosts (= angels) Jb 19_{12} 25_{3}.

*גְּדוּדָה: pl. גְּדֻדֹת Je 48_{37}: **incision**. †

גָּדוֹל & גָּדֹל (ca. 520×): cs. גְּדָל־, גְּד(וֹ)ל Na 1_{3} Qr (Kt גְּדוֹל) & Pr 19_{19} Qr; f. גְּד(וֹ)לָה, pl. גְּד(וֹ)לִים, גְּדֹלֵי, גְּדֹלָיו; f. גְּד(וֹ)ל(וֹ)ת: **great**: — 1. shape, size: men Jos 14_{15}, animals Gn 1_{21}, things Is 8_{1}; — 2. height: mountain Zc 4_{7}, tower Ne 3_{27}; — 3. extent: city Gn 10_{12}, river Dt 1_{7}, fire Dt 4_{36}; — 4. number: people Gn 12_{2}, kingdom Je 28_{8}, assembly Ne 5_{7}; — 5. intensity: power Dt 4_{37}, vengeance Ez 25_{17}, fear Dt 26_{8}, rain 1K 18_{45}, hunger 2K 6_{25}; — 6. significance: guilt Gn 4_{13}, sight (phenomenon) Ex 3_{3}, feast Gn 21_{8}; — 7. level: loud voice Gn 39_{14}, cry Gn 27_{34}; — 8. age: old(er) Gn 27_{1} 29_{16}; — 9. station: *gādôl babbayit* (be) master Gn 39_{9}, *gedōlê hāʿîr* the leading people in the city 2K 10_{6}, *hammelek haggādôl* the great king (= k. of Assyria) 2K $18_{19 \cdot 28}$; — 10. combs.: *gedōl ʿēṣâ* great in counsel Je 32_{19}; *gedōl kenāfayim* w. great wings Ez $17_{3 \cdot 7}$, &c.; — 11. fixed expr.: *hammelek haggādôl*, F 9.; *hakkōhēn haggādôl* high priest Lv 21_{10}; *hayyām haggādôl* = Mediterranean S. Nu 34_{6}; *hannāhār haggādôl* = Euphrates Dt 1_{7}; — 12. misc.: *hayyôm gādôl* broad daylight Gn 29_{7}; *qāṭōn wegādôl* Jb 3_{19}; — 13. *gādôl* as sbst.: *gedōlôt* great things Ps 131_{1}, great deeds 2K 8_{4}; *dibber gedōlôt* be boastful Ps 12_{4} &c.; — 14. God is great: *ʾēl* Dt 7_{21}, *hāʾēl* Dt 10_{17}, *hāʾelōhîm* Ne 8_6, *yhwh* Je 10_6 &c.

גְּדוּלָּה (4×), גְּדוּלָה (2×), גְּדֻלָּה (1×): cs. גְּדֻלַּת, sf. גְּדוּלָּתוֹ, גְּדֻלָּתִי; pl. גְּדֻלּוֹת, גְּדֻלֹּתֶיךָ Kt (Qr sg) Ps 145_6; — 1. **greatness, majesty** Est 1_4; — 2. **greatness** (in deeds) 2S $7_{21\cdot23}$; pl. **great deeds** (of God) 1C $17_{19\cdot21}$.

*גִּדּוּף: pl. גִּדּוּפִים, גִּדּוּפֵי: **reviling** Is 43_{28} Zp 2_8. †

*גִּדּוּפָה: pl. sf. גִּדֻּפֹתָם: **reviling** Is 51_7. †

גְּדוֹר: n. pers.

*גְּדוֹת Is 8_7: ↗ גִּדְיָה.

גְּדִי: pl. גְּדָיִים, גְּדָיֵי: **kid**, by implication, young of oth. animals Gn $27_{9\cdot16}$.

גָּדִי: — 1. gent. of גָּד; — 2. n. pers. 2K $15_{14\cdot17}$.

גַּדִּי: n. pers.

גַּדִּיאֵל: n. pers.

*גִּדְיָה: pl. sf. גְּדוֹתָיו, 1C 12_{16} Kt גִּדְיֹתָיו: (river-)**bank** Jos 3_{15}.

*גְּדִיָּה: pl. sf. גְּדִיֹּתַיִךְ: female **kid** SS 1_8. †

I גָּדִישׁ: **stack of grain** Ex 22_5 Jud 15_5 Jb 5_{26}. †

II גָּדִישׁ: **grave-mound** Jb 21_{32}. †

גָּדַל: **qal**: pf. ג׳, גָּדְלָה, גָּדַלְתָּ, גָּדְלוּ; impf. יִגְדַּל, יִגְדַּל, יִגְדְּלוּ, יִגְדָּלוּ; inf. גָּדוֹל: — 1. **grow up, become great** Gn $21_{8\cdot20}$; *wayyēlek ...hālôk wegādôl* 2S 5_{10} ↗ *hālak* 4, cf. *gādēl*; — 2. **be great** 2S 7_{26}, of God 2S 7_{22}; — 3. **become wealthy** Gn 24_{35}; — 4. **become important** Gn 41_{40}; *gādôl beʿênê* is valuable for 1S 26_{24}.

piel: pf. גִּדֵּל, גִּדַּל, גִּדְּלָה, גִּדַּלְתִּי, גִּדְּלוֹ, גִּדְּלוּהוּ; impf. יְגַדֵּל, אֲגַדְּלָה, יְגַדְּלוּ, תְּגַדְּלֵנוּ, וַיְגַדְּלֵהוּ; impv. גַּדֵּל, גַּדְּלוּ; inf. גַּדֵּל, גַּדֶּלְךָ, גַּדְּלָם; pt. מְגַדְּלִים: — 1. **bring up** (a child), **save** (from infant mortality) Is 1_2; educate Dn 1_5; raise (a plant) Jon 4_{10}; — 2. **let grow** (hair) Nu 6_5, (tree) Is 44_{14}; — 3. w. *min*, **make greater** than 1K $1_{37\cdot47}$; — 4. w. words: extol, **praise** Gn 12_2; treat w. distinction Est 3_1.

pual: pt. מְגֻדָּלִים: **grown** (tall) (plants) Ps 144_{12}. †

hif.: pf. הִגְדִּ(י)ל, הִגְדַּלְתָּ, הִגְדִּילוּ; impf. יַגְדִּיל, תַּגְדֵּל, וַתַּגְדֵּל, וַיַּגְדִּ(י)לוּ; inf. לְהַגְדִּיל; pt. מַגְדִּילִים, מַגְדִּל: — 1. **make** s.thg **great**: *ḥesed* Gn 19_{19}, *šeqel* Am 8_5, *šēm* Ps 138_2; abs. w. *ʿim* do a great thing for 1S 12_{24}; *higdîl laʿaśôt* (God) accomplishes great things Jl 2_{21}; — 2. **make onesf. great**: a) boast La 1_9, w. *ʿal* over against Je $48_{26\cdot42}$; b) ? take courage 1S 20_{41}.

hitp.: pf. הִתְגַּדִּלְתִּי Ez 38_{23}; impf. יִתְגַּדֵּל, יִתְגַּדַּל: — 1. **boast** Is 10_{15}; w. *ʿal* against Dn 11_{36f}; — 2. **show onesf. great** (God) Ez 38_{23}. †

גָּדֵל: cs. pl. גִּדְלֵי: **great**: *gidlê bāśār* (↗ *bāśār*) w. great (male) member Ez 16_{26}; *hālak hālōk wegādēl* became greater & greater = increase in riches Gn 26_{13}; in age & favor 1S 2_{26}, in power 2C 17_{12}. †

גֹּדֶל: cs. = (4×), גֹּדֶל Ex 15_{16}; sf. גָּדְלוֹ, גָּדְלְךָ, גֻּדְלוֹ Ps 150_2: **greatness**: tree Ez 31_7, man Ez 31_2, God Dt 3_{24}, God's grace Nu 14_{19}; *gōdel lēbāb* **bravado** Is 9_8 10_{12}.

גִּדֵּל: n. pers.

*גְּדִל: pl. גְּדִלִים: — 1. **tassel** on garment Dt 22_{12}; — 2. **chain-like decoration** on the capitals (of pillars) 1K 7_{17}. †

גְּדֻלָּה: ↗ גְּדוּלָּה.

גְּדַלְיָה: n. pers.

גְּדַלְיָהוּ: n. pers.

גִּדַּלְתִּי: trad. n. pers.: 1C $25_{4\cdot29}$. †

גָּדַע: **qal**: pf. ג׳, גָּדַעְתִּי; impf. וָאֶגְדַּע; pt. pass. גְּדוּעִים: — 1. **cut off**: arm 1S 2_{31}, horn La 2_3; — 2. **break in pieces**: staff Zc $11_{10\cdot14}$.

nif.: pf. נִגְדַּע, נִגְדְּעָה, נִגְדַּעְתָּ, נִגְדְּעוּ: — 1. **be cut off**: peg Is 22_{25}, tribe Ju 21_6; — 2. **be broken in pieces**: incense altars Ez 6_6, star Is 14_{12}.

piel: pf. גִּדַּע, גִּדֵּעַ; impf. וַיְגַדַּע, אֲגַדֵּעַ, תְּגַדֵּעוּן: — 1. **cut down**: bolt Is 45_2, horns Ps 75_{11}; — 2. **break in pieces**: *ʾašērîm* Dt 7_5.

pual: pf. גֻּדְּעוּ: **be cut down** (trees) Is 9_9. †

גִּדְעוֹן: n. pers.

גִּדְעֹם: n. loc.

גִּדְעֹנִי: gent.

גדף: **piel**: pf. גִּדַּפְתָּ, גִּדְּפוּ; pt. מְגַדֵּף: **revile** Ps 44_{17}, **blaspheme** (God) 2K $19_{6\cdot22}$.

גָּדַר: **qal**: pf. גָּדַרְתִּי ,גָּדְרוּ ,גּ׳; pt. גֹּדֵר, גֹּדְרִים: — 1. **erect a wall** of stones Ez 13_5; wall up a breach Am 9_{11}; *gōdēr* mason 2K 12_{13}; — 2. **block up a way** through a stone wall Ho 2_8, w. *be'ad* La 3_7.

גֶּדֶר: n. loc.

גָּדֵר: cs. גֶּדֶר; sf. גְּדֵרוֹ; pl. sf. גְּדֵרֶיךָ; f. Ps 62_4 txt. corr.: **stone wall** made of loose field-stones piled up without mortar Nu 22_{24}; city wall Mi 7_{11}.

גְּדֹר (3×), גְּדוֹר (1×): n. loc.

I **גְּדֵרָה**: cs. ⸗ גֶּדֶרֶת; pl. גְּדֵר(ו)ת, cs. גִּדְר(ו)ת, sf. גְּדֵרֹתָיו: — 1. **stone pen**: *gidrôt ṣō'n* sheepfold Nu $32_{16\cdot36}$; — 2. (city-)**wall** Ps 89_{41}.

II **גְּדֵרָה**: n. loc. Jos 15_{36} 1C 4_{23}. †

גְּדֵרוֹת: n. loc. Jos 15_{41} 2C 28_{18}. †

גְּדֵרִי: gent. of בֵּית גָּדֵר or גֶּדֶר.

גְּדֶרֶת: abs., or cs. of גְּדֵרָה: **wall** Ez 42_{12}. †

גְּדֵרָתִי: gent. of II גְּדֵרָה.

גְּדֵרֹתַיִם: n. loc.

[**גֵּה**: Ez 47_{13} rd זֶה (mss., Verss.). †]

גהה: **qal**: impf. יִגְהֶה: **heal** Ho 5_{13}. †

גֵּהָה: **healing** Pr 17_{22}. †

גהר: **qal**: impf. וַיִּגְהַר: **bow down** 1K 18_{42} 2K 4_{34f}. †

גֵּו: sf. גֵּוְּךָ ,גַּוְּךָ: **back**; *hišlîk 'aḥarê gawwô* throw behind onesf., not consider 1K 14_9.

I ***גֵּו**: cs. גֵּו, sf. גֵּוִי, גֵּוְּךָ ,גַּוְּךָ: **back** Is 50_6; w. *hišlîk 'aḥarê* (⸗ *gaw*) Is 38_{17}.

II **גֵּו**: **community** Jb 30_5. †

I **גּוֹב**: n. loc.

[II **גּוֹב** Na 3_{17}: dittgr rd. כְּגֹבָי.]

גּוֹג: n. pers.

גוד: **qal**: impf. יָגֻד, sf. 1. pl. יְגוּדֶנּוּ: **raid, attack** Gn $49_{19\cdot19}$. †

I **גֵּוָה**: **arrogance, pride** Je 13_{17}.

[II **גֵּוָה** Jb 20_{25} txt. corr., ⸗ comm. †]

גוז: **qal**: pf. גָּז; impf. וַיָּגָז Nu 11_{31} but perh. to be revocalized as hif., ⸗ comm.: **pass by** Ps 90_{10}.

גוֹזָל: pl. sf. גוֹזָלָיו: young bird: **turtledove** Gn 15_9, young eagle Dt 32_{11}. †

גּוֹזָן: n. terr.

גוח: ⸗ גיח.

גּוֹי (555×): sf. גּוֹי Zp 2_9, גּוֹיֵךְ ,גּוֹיֶךָ (Ez $36_{13\text{-}15}$ Kt); pl. גּוֹיִם, Kt גֹּיִים Gn 25_{23} Ps 79_{10}, cs. גּוֹיֵי ,גּוֹיֵ Esr 6_{21} 2C 32_{13}, sf. גּוֹיַיִךְ Ez $36_{13\text{-}15}$ Qr, גּוֹיֵהֶם Gn 10_{31}; — 1. (a specific) **people**: a) **nation**: α) *'āśâ legôy* make (an individual) (into) a nation Gn 12_2, *nātan legôyîm* Gn $17_{6\cdot16}$; β) *kol-gôyê hā'āreṣ* all the nations of the earth Gn 18_{18}, *'elōhê haggôyîm* gods of the n. 2K 18_{33}; many *gôyîm* become *le'ām* for *Yhwh* Zc 2_{15}; γ) Isr. a *gôy* Gn 18_{18}; b) oft. the **pagan peoples** in distinction & contrast to Isr. Ex 34_{24}; the **'heathen'** Ez $5_{6\text{-}8}$; c) mankind Is 42_6; d) **people** (in genl.) 2K 6_{18}, *gôy ṣaddîq* Is 26_2; — 2. of animals, **swarm** (locusts) Jl 1_6.

גְּוִיָּה: cs. גְּוִיַּת, sf. גְּוִיָּתוֹ, pl. גְּוִי(ו)ת, sf. גְּוִיֹּתֵיהֶם, גְּוִיֹּתֵיהֶנָה Ez 1_{11}: — 1. **body** Ez $1_{11\cdot23}$; — 2. **corpse** 1S $31_{10\cdot12}$; — 3. *gewiyyātēnû* our body = **we ourselves** Gn 47_{18}.

גּוֹיִם: proper name, referring to various peoples, Gn $14_{1\cdot9}$, Jos 12_{23} Ju $4_{2\cdot13\cdot16}$ Is 8_{23}; ⸗ comm. on each passage. †

גּוֹלָה, גֹּלָה Na 3_{10} Est 2_6 1C 5_{22} †; pt. f. of **גָּלָה**: — 1. those deported into exile, the **exiles** 2K 24_{15f}; *ziqnê haggôlâ* Je 29_1; *haggôlâ* the Jewish congregation found to be in existence by Ezra Ezr 9_4 10_6; — 2. **deportation, exile** *yāṣâ begôlâ* Je 29_{16}, *kelê gôlâ* exiles' baggage Je 46_{19}; *'ad-haggôlâ* until the (time of the) exile 1C 5_{22}.

גּוֹלָן: n. loc.

גּוּמָּץ: **pit** Ec 10_8. †

גּוּנִי: n. pers. & gent.

גָּוַע: qal: pf. 'גּ, גָּוְעוּ, גָּוַעְנוּ; impf. יִגְוַע, יִגְוָע, אֶגְוַע, יִגְוְעוּ, יִגְוָעוּ, יִגְוָעוּן; inf. לִגְוֹעַ, בִּגְוַע; pt. גֹּוֵעַ: — 1. **expire**, breathe one's last Gn $25_{8\cdot17}$; — 2. **die** Gn 6_{17} 7_{21}.

גוף: **hif.**: impf. יָגִיפוּ: shut (door) Ne 7_3. †

***גּוּפָה**: cs. גּוּפַת, pl. גּוּפֹת: **corpse** 1C $10_{12\cdot12}$. †

I **גור**: **qal**: pf. גָּר (גָּר־ Gn 35_{27}), גַּרְתָּה, גָּרוּ; impf. יָגוּר, וַיָּגָר, תָּגוּרִי, אָגוּרָה, יְגָרְךָ; impv. גּוּרִי; inf. לָגוּר; pt. גָּר, גָּרָה, גָּרִים, גָּרֵי: **stay as foreigner and sojourner** (F *gēr*) Gn $21_{23\cdot34}$; w. acc. *'oniyyôt* as rowers Ju 5_{17}; *lō' yegūrekā rā'* nothing evil dares to stay with you Ps 5_5; oft. w. *šām* Gn 12_{10} &c.; w. *'im* Gn 32_5, w. *'ēt* Ex 12_{48}, w. *betôk* Ex 12_{48}, w. *be* among a people Lv 20_2, in sanctuary Ps 15_1; abs. Gn 19_9; *gārat bêtāh* her protected lodger Ex 3_{22}.

hitpol.: impf. יִתְגּוֹרָרוּ; pt. מִתְגּוֹרֵר: **stay around as a** *gēr* 1K 17_{20}.

II **גור**: **qal**: impf. יָגוּר; inf. abs. גּוֹר; pt. גָּר: show enmity, **attack**: abs. Is 54_{15a}, w. *'ēt* $_{15b}$, w. *'al* Ps 59_4.

III **גור**: **qal**: impf. יָגוּרוּ, וַיָּגָר, תָּגוּר, אָגוּר; impv. גּוּרוּ: **be afraid**, w. *min* of Dt 18_{22}, w. *mippenê* 1S 18_{15}, abs. Dt 32_{27}.

***גּוּר**: pl. גּוּרֵי, sf. גּוּרֹתָיו: **lion cub** Je 51_{38} Na 2_{13}. †

I **גּוֹר**: pl. sf. גּוֹרֶיהָ, גּוֹרֵיהֶן: **cub** (still unweaned): lion Gn 49_9, jackal La 4_3.

II **גּוּר**: n. loc. (?); 2K 9_{27}. †

גּוּר־בַּעַל: n. loc.

גּוֹרָל (ca. 75×): cs. גּוֹרַל; pl. גּ(וֹ)רָלוֹת; m.: — 1. **lot** (stone thrown to determine a decision): at division of land Nu 26_{55}, of clothing Ps 22_{19}, & in many other decisions; vbs.: *'ālâ* Lv 16_9, *yāṣâ* Nu 33_{54}, *wayhî le* fall to Jos 15_1, *nāfal 'al* Jon 1_7; *nātan gôrāl le* throw the lot over Lv 16_8, &c.; — 2. **that which falls to one by lot**: a) *gôral naḥalātēnû* our allotted inheritance Nu 36_3, *'ārê gôrālām* their allotted cities Jos 21_{20}, *gebûl gôrālām* their allotted territory Jos 18_{11}; b) *gôrāl* **allotted portion** Jos 15_1; c) lot = **fate** Ps 16_5.

גּוּשׁ Qr, גִּישׁ Kt Jb 7_5, **crust** (of dirt in the grave, or of wounds). †

גֵּז: pl. cs. גִּזֵּי: — 1. **fleece** of sheep Dt 18_4 Jb 31_{20}; — 2. **mown grass** Ps 72_6, *gizzê hammelek* Am 7_1. †

גִּזְבָּר: **treasurer** Ezr 1_8. †

גזה: **qal**: pt. sf. גּוֹזִי: **cut off** (the umbilical cord) Ps 71_6, but txt. perh. corr.; F comm. †

גִּזָּה: cs. גִּזַּת: **fleece, wool** Ju $6_{37\text{-}40}$; *gizzat ṣemer* freshly shorn fleece 6_{37}. †

גִּזוֹנִי: gent., 1C 11_{34}, but txt. perh. corr.; F comm. †

גזז: **qal**: impf. וַיָּגָז, תָּגֹז; impv. גֹּזִּי, וָגֹזִּי; inf. לָגֹז, לִגְזֹז, בִּגְזֹז; pt. גֹּזֵז, גֹּזְזִים, גֹּזְזֵי, גֹּזְזֶיךָ: **shear** (sheep) Gn 31_{19}; **cut** (hair) Je 7_{29}.

nif.: pf. נָגֹזּוּ: **be cut off** Na 1_{12}. †

גָּזֵז: n. pers.

גָּזִית: hewing; *'abnê gāzît* **hewn stones, ashlar** 1K 5_{31}; > *gāzît* hewn stones 1K 6_{36}.

גָּזַל: **qal**: pf. 'גּ, גָּזַל, גָּזַלְתִּי, גָּזָלוּ, גְּזָלוּ; impf. יִגְזֹל, תִּגְזָל־, יִגְזְלוּ; inf. לִגְזֹל; pt. גֹּזֵל, גֹּזְלוֹ, pl. cs. גֹּזְלֵי, pass. גָּזוּל: — 1. **tear off, pull off**: skin Mi 3_2; — 2. tear away, **take away by force**: wells Gn 21_{25}, women Gn 31_{31}; *gāzal mišpaṭ* … deprive s.one of his rights Is 10_2; — 3. **rob** Ju 9_{25}.

nif.: pf. נִגְזְלָה: **be taken away** (sleep) Pr 4_{16}. †

גֵּזֶל: **robbery**: *gēzel mišpāṭ* deprivation of justice Ec 5_7. †

גָּזֵל: **robbery** Lv 5_{21}.

גְּזֵלָה: cs. גְּזֵלַת: — 1. **robbery** Lv 5_{23}; *gāzal gezēlâ* commit robbery Ez 18_7; — 2. **stolen goods** Ez 33_{15}, *gezēlat he'ānî* goods stolen from the poor Is 3_{14}.

גָּזָם: trad. **locust** (just become mature, ready for flight); better **caterpillar** ?: Am 4_9 Jl 1_4 2_{25}. †

גַּזָּם: n. pers.

גֶּזַע: sf. גִּזְעוֹ, גִּזְעָם: — 1. **stump** (of tree),

rootstock Jb 14_8, metaph. Is 11_1; — 2. the **shoot** sprouting from a stump Is 40_{24}. †

I **גזר**: **qal**: impf. תִּגְזֹר; impv. גִּזְרוּ; pt. גֹּזֵר: — 1. **cut** 1K 3_{26}, *gāzar ligzārîm* cut in pieces Ps 136_{13}, cut down 2K 6_4; — 2. **decide** Jb 22_{28}.

nif.: pf. נִגְזַר, נִגְזַרְתִּי, נִגְזְרוּ: — 1. **be cut off** from life Is 53_8, from God Ps 31_{23}; be lost La 3_{54}; — 2. **be decided** Est 2_1.

II **גזר**: **qal**: impf. וַיִּגְזֹר: **devour** Is 9_{19}. †

I ***גֶּזֶר**: pl. גְּזָרִים: cuts, **pieces** Gn 15_{17} Ps 136_{13}. †

II **גֶּזֶר**: n. loc.: גָּזֶר, loc. גֶּזְרָה.

***גְּזָר**, f. גְּזֵרָה: *ʾereṣ gezērâ* **unfertile land** Lv 16_{22}. †

גִּזְרָה: sf. גִּזְרָתָם: — 1. separated space, **yard** Ez $41_{12\cdot15}$ $42_{1\cdot10\cdot13}$; — 2. ? La 4_7: cut, form of the body?; oth.: veins; ↗ comm. †

גִּזְרִי: gent. of II גֶּזֶר.

גחה: **qal**: pt. sf. גֹּחִי: **draw out** (from womb) Ps 22_{10}. †

גָּחוֹן: sf. גְּחֹנְךָ: **belly** (of reptiles) Gn 3_{14} Lv 11_{42}. †

גִּחוֹן: ↗ גִּיחוֹן.

גֵּחֲזִי: ↗ גֵּיחֲזִי.

***גַּחַל** or *גֶּחֶל or sg. גַּחֶלֶה ?: pl. גֶּחָלִים, גַּחֲלֵי, גֶּחָלָיו: glowing **charcoal** 2S 22_9; *gaḥalê ʾēš* 2S 22_{13}; *gaḥalê retāmîm* charcoal from ↗ *retem*-wood (in the fire of which arrow-heads are hammered out) Ps 120_4; metaph. Pr 25_{22}.

גַּחֶלֶת: sf. גַּחַלְתִּי: **live coals** 2S 14_7 Is 47_{14}. †

גַּחַם: n. pers.

גַּחַר: גֹּחַר: n. pers.

גַּיְא: גַּיְ, גֵּי (Qr גֵּיא) Dt 34_6, גֵּי Jos 8_{11} Mi 1_6 (50×): — I: גָּיְא, גֵּיא Is 40_4, גֵּיא Zc 14_4; f. 2K 2_{16} Zc 14_4; cs. גֵּיא & Is 22_5 גֵּי; pl. גֵּאָי(וֹ)ת, 2K 2_{16} Kt גֵּיְאוֹת?, sf. גֵּאוֹתֶיךָ: **valley**, either wide or narrow 2K 2_{16}; mostly in ref. to spec. valley, e.g. Nu 21_{20}; *gêʾ šemānîm* rich valley Is $28_{1\cdot4}$; — II. גַּיְא in names of loc.: a) גֵּי(א) בֶן־הִנֹּם, ↗ הִנֹּם; < גֵּי בְנֵי הִנֹּם 2K 23_{10} Kt & גֵּי הִנֹּם (3×); — b) ↗ גֵּיא הֲמוֹן גּוֹג; — c) גֵּיא הַהֲרֵגָה 'murder valley' Je 7_{32} 19_6 = † גֵּי בֶן הִנֹּם; — d) גֵּיא־הָרִים & גֵּי־הָרִים Zc 14_5; — e) ↗ גֵּיא חִזָּיוֹן 'valley of vision' Is $22_{1\cdot5}$: n. loc.? ↗ comm.; — f) גֵּיא חֲרָשִׁים; — g) גֵּי יִפְתַּח־אֵל; — h) גֵּיא (הַ)מֶּלַח; — i) גֵּי הָעֹבְרִים 'valley of travelers' Ez 39_{11}: n. loc.? ↗ comm.; — j) גֵּי הַצְּבֹעִים; — k) גֵּיא צְפָתָה 2C 14_9 txt. corr.?; — l) גֵּיא שְׁמָנִים, rd גְּאֵי שׁ׳ (↗ גֵּאֶה); — m) שַׁעַר הַגַּיְא.

גִּיד: pl. גִּידִים, גִּ(י)דֵי: **sinew** Gn $32_{33\cdot33}$.

גיח, **גוח**: **qal**: impf. יָגִיחַ; impv. גֹּחִי; inf. גִּיחוֹ: **burst forth** Jb 38_8 (sea); Mi 4_{10} **bawl** (?), txt. corr.?

hif.: impf. וַתָּגַח; pt. מֵגִיחַ: **break loose** (army in ambush) Ju 20_{33}, sputter Ez 32_2. †

גִּיחַ: n. loc. 2S 2_{24}; txt. corr.? †

גִּיחוֹן, **גִּחוֹן**: — 1. n. loc. 1K 1_{33ff} 2C 30 33_{14}; — 2. n. of river Gn 2_{13}. †

גֵּ(י)חֲזִי: n. pers.

גיל: **qal**: pf. גַּלְתִּי; impf. יָגִיל (Pr 23_{24} Qr, Kt יָגוֹל), יָגֵל (Ps 21_2 Qr, Kt יָגִיל), וַיָּגֶל, יְגִילוּן, תָּגֵלְנָה; impv. גִּילִי (Zc 9_9 גִּילִי); inf. cs. ↗ II גִּיל below, inf. abs. Pr 23_{24} Qr גִּיל:, Kt גּוֹל tech. term of Canaanite fertility cult language, **shriek ecstatically, shout with joy**: — 1. cultic: abs. Is 9_2; w. *be* Is 25_9, w. *ʿal* Ho 10_5; — 2. secular: abs. Is $35_{1\cdot2}$; w. *be* Is 65_{19}.

I ***גִּיל**: sf. גִּילְכֶם: **age, stage of life** Dn 1_{10}. †

II **גִּיל**: **rejoicing** Is 16_{10}.

גִּילָה: **rejoicing** Is 65_{18}.

גִּ(י)לֹנִי: gent. of גִּלֹה.

גִּינַת: n. pers. or loc.; 1K 16_{21f}. †

גִּיר: ↗ גִּר.

***גֵּיר**: ↗ גֵּר.

גִּישׁ: ↗ גּוּשׁ.

גֵּישָׁן: n. pers.; ?; 1C 2_{47}. †

I **גַּל**: גָּל; pl. גַּלִּים: **heap**, *gal ʾabānîm* **heap of stones** Gn 31_{46}; pl. 2K 19_{25}.

II ***גַּל**: pl. גַּלִּים, גַּלֵּי, sf. גַּלָּיו, גַּלֵּיהֶם: **wave** Is 48_{18}.

*גֵּל: sf. גֶּלְלוֹ; pl. cs. גֶּלְלֵי: **dung cakes** Ez $4_{12\cdot15}$ Jb 20_7. †
*גֹּל: sf. גֻּלָּה Zc 4_2: F גֻּלָּה.
*גַּלָּב: pl. גַּלָּבִים: **barber** Ez 5_1. †
גִּלְבֹּעַ: n. terr.
I גַּלְגַּל: pl. sf. גַּלְגַּלָּיו: — 1. **wheel** (of war chariot) Is 5_{28}, on Y.'s chariot Ps 77_{19}; coll. wheelwork ? Ez $10_{2\cdot6\cdot13}$; — 2. **well-wheel** Ec 12_6.
II גַּלְגַּל: = I metaph.: '**wheel**(-plant),' w. wheel-shaped stem & thistles, *Gundelia Tournefortii*, a sort of tumbleweed, Is 17_{13} Ps 83_{14}. †
I *גִּלְגָּל: cs. גִּלְגַּל: **cartwheel** Is 28_{28}. †
II גִּלְגָּל: הַגִּלְגָּל: לְגִלְגָּל Jos 12_{23} †, loc. הַגִּלְגָּלָה: n. loc. **Gilgal**.
גֻּלְגֹּלֶת: sf. גֻּלְגָּלְתּוֹ; pl. sf. גֻּלְגְּלֹתָם: **skull** 2K 9_{35}; *laggulgōlet* per head = per person Ex 16_{16}; *laggulg^{e}lōtām* according to their head-count, head by head Nu 1_2.
*גֶּלֶד: sf. גִּלְדִּי: **skin** Jb 16_{15}. †
גָּלָה: qal: pf. גָּ׳, גָּלְתָה, גָּלִיתָ(ה), גָּלוּ; impf. יִגְלֶה, יִגֶל, וַיִּגֶל, אֶגְלֶה; impv. גְּלֵה; inf. גְּלוֹת, גָּלֹה; pt. גֹּלֶה, גֹּלָה, גֹּלִים, גֹּ(וֹ)לָה, pass. גָּלוּי, cs. גְּלוּי: — 1. **uncover**, reveal: secret Am 3_7, disclose secret Pr 20_{19}, publish Est 3_{14}; *sēfer gālûy* open copy of bill of sale Je $32_{11\cdot14}$; *gālâ ʾoznô* open s.one's ear = announce to s.one: subj. men 1S 20_2, subj. God 1S 9_{15}; *gālûy ʿênayim* w. open eyes Nu 24_4; — 2. a) (have to) **go away**, disappear: of joy Is 24_{11}, of grass Pr 27_{25}; w. *min* 1S 4_{21f}, w. *mēʿal* 2K 17_{23}; abs. Ez 12_3; w. *l^e* 2S 15_{19}; b) **go into exile** Is 5_{13}; *g^{e}lôt hāʾāreṣ* exile of the (people of the) land Ju 18_{30}, of Jerus. Je 1_3.

nif.: pf. נִגְלָה, נִגְלְתָה, נִגְלֵיתִי, נִגְלִינוּ; impf. יִגָּלֶה, תִּגָּל, יִגָּלוּ; impv. הִגָּלוּ; inf. cs. הִגָּלוֹת, abs. נִגְלֹה & 2S 6_{20} נִגְלוֹת; pt. pl. f. נִגְלֹת Dt 29_{28}: — 1. **expose onesf.** 2S 6_{20}; **be** uncovered, **exposed**: foundation 2S 22_{16}; private parts Ex 20_{26}, transgression Ez 21_{29}; — 2. **appear** Is 49_9; make onesf. known 1S $14_{8\cdot11}$ (w. *ʾel*); (God) **reveal onesf.** Gn 35_7, his *kābôd* Is 40_5; — 3. **be announced** Is 23_1, **be revealed** 1S 3_7; *hanniglōt* what is revealed Dt 29_{28}.

piel: pf. גִּלָּה, גִּלְּתָה, גִּלִּית, גִּלֵּיתִי (4×) & גִּלִּיתִי (1×), גִּלּוּ; impf. יְגַלֶּה, וַיְגַל, תְּגַלֶּה (8×), תְּגַל, תְּגַלִּי, תְּגַל; impv. גַּל, גַּלִּי; inf. גַּלּוֹת; pt. מְגַלֶּה: — 1. **uncover, reveal**: hiding places Je 49_{10}, private parts Ho 2_{12}, foundation Mi 1_6; *gillâ ʿênê* open s.one's eyes Nu 22_{31}; *gillâ ʾēt* betray s.one Is 16_3, *watt^{e}gal taznûtêhā* she practiced her harlotry openly Ez 23_{18}; — 2. spec.: *gillâ ʿerwat āb* uncover the nakedness of one's father = lie with father's wife Lv 18_7; likewise *gillâ k^{e}naf āb* uncover the skirt of one's father Dt 23_1; > lie with s.one (i.e. not his/her spouse) Lv 18_6.

pual: pt. f. מְגֻלָּה: uncovered, **open** (reprimand) Pr 27_5. †

hif.: pf. הִגְלָה (1×) & הֶגְלָה (10×), הִגְלִית, הִגְלֵיתִי, הִגְלוּ, הִגְלִיתֶם, sf. הִגְלָם & הֶגְלָם; impf. וַיֶּגֶל, וַיַּגְלֶהָ, וַיַּגְלוּם; inf. הַגְלוֹת, הַגְלוֹתִי, בַּגְלוֹתוֹ < בְּהַגְלוֹתוֹ Je 27_{20}; **take into exile, deport** 2K 15_{29}.

hof.: pf. הָגְלָה, הָגְלַת, הָגְלוּ; pt. מָגְלִים: **be taken into exile, deported** Je $40_{1\cdot7}$.

hitp.: impf. וַיִּתְגַּל; inf. הִתְגַּלּוֹת: — 1. **expose onesf.** Gn 9_{21}; — 2. **become known, manifest** (F *lēb*, thought or mind?) Pr 18_2. †
גִּלֹה: n. loc.
גֻּלָּה: cs. גֻּלַּת; pl. גֻּלֹּ(וֹ)ת: — 1. a) **basin for** oil Zc 4_3, of gold Ec 12_6; b) 'bowls,' horizontal projections on pillars 1K 7_{41f}; — 2. **waterbasin**: *gullōt mayim* (F *gullōt*) n. terr. Jos 15_{19} Ju 1_{15}. †
גִּלּוּלִים & גִּלֻּלִים 1K 15_{12} † (48×): **idols**, alw. contemptuous 1K 15_{12}; ca. 40× Ez.
*גְּלוֹם: pl. cs. גְּלוֹמֵי: mantle, **wrap** Ez 27_{24}. †
גֹּלָן: Jos 20_8 21_{27}: F גּוֹלָן. †
גָּלוּת: cs. =, גָּלֻת, sf. גָּלוּתִי, גָּלוּתֵנוּ: — 1.

exile, **deportation** 2K 25_{27}; *gālût šᵉlēmâ* comprehensive exile Am $1_{6.9}$; — 2. **exiles, those deported** Is 20_4.

גלח: **piel**: pf. גִּלַּח, גִּלְּחָה, sf. גִּלְּחוֹ; impf. יְגַלְּחֶנּוּ, יְגַלְּחֵם, יְגַלֵּחוּ, יְגַלֵּחַ, יְגַלַּח; inf. גַּלְּחוֹ: **shave**: head 2S 14_{26}, head, beard, eyebrows Lv 14_9, head & pubic hair Is 7_{20}.

pual: pf. גֻּלַּחְתִּי, גֻּלָּח; pt. pl. cs. מְגֻלְּחֵי: **be shaved** Ju $16_{17.22}$ Je 41_5. †

hitp.: pf. הִתְגַּלָּח; impf. יִתְגַּלָּח; inf. הִתְגַּלְּחוֹ: **have onesf. shaved** Lv 13_{33} Nu 6_{19}. †

גִּלָּיוֹן: — 1. Is 3_{23}: **papyrus garments**, but trad.: 'mirrors'; — 2. Is 8_1 *gillāyôn gādôl* **tablet** of metal, wood, or leather; oth.: **papyrus**. †

I ***גָּלִיל**: pl. גְּלִילִים: — 1. **turnable** (door) (so LXX) 1K 6_{34}; oth.: pivot (of door-hinges); **rollers** (metaph.: the arms) SS 5_{14}; — 2. round **rod** or **ring** Est 1_6. †

II **גָּלִיל**: הַגָּלִיל, cs. גְּלִיל, loc. (?) הַגָּלִ֫ילָה: n. terr., later Galilee.

גְּלִילָה: f. of גָּלִיל: pl. גְּלִילוֹת: **district** Ez 47_8, of the Philistines Jos 13_2, ↗ n. loc. *gᵉlîlôt*; *gᵉlîlôt hayyardēn* the fertile district east of the upper Jordan Jos 22_{10f}.

גְּלִילוֹת, pl. of גְּלִילָה: n. loc. in Benj., Jos 18_{17}. †

גַּלִּים: n. loc.

גָּלְיָת: n. pers., **Goliath**.

I **גלל**: **qal**: pf. גַּ֫לּוֹתִי, גָּלְלוּ; impf. וַיָּ֫גֶל Gn 29_{10}; impv. גֹּ(ו)ל, גַּל Ps 119_{22}, גֹּלּוּ; pt. גֹּלֵל: — 1. **roll**: stone Gn 29_3; — 2. metaph. a) **roll away** (reproach) *mēʿal* from Jos 5_9; b) **roll off** onto (*ʾel*) God (a concern &c.) Ps 22_9.

nif.: pf. נָגֹלּוּ; impf. יִגַּל: — 1. **be rolled up** Is 34_4; — 2. roll, **flow down** (flood) Am 5_{24}. †

polal: pt. מְגוֹלָלָה: rolled, (robes) **dragged** (in blood) Is 9_4 (oth.: II). †

hitpol.: inf. הִתְגֹּלֵל; pt. מִתְגֹּלֵל: — 1. **fall upon** Gn 43_{18}; — 2. **wallow** in (blood) 2S 20_{12}. †

pilp.: pf. גִּלְגַּלְתִּיךָ: w. *min*, **roll down** Je 51_{25}. †

hitpalp.: pf. הִתְגַּלְגָּלוּ: **roll on** (of enemy) Jb 30_{14}. †

II **גלל**: **polal**: pt. מְגוֹלָלָה: **befouled** Is 9_4 (↗ I). †

hitpol.: pt. מִתְגֹּלֵל: **befouled** 2S 20_{12} (oth.: I). †

I **גָּלָל**: pl. גְּלָלִים: **dung-pellets** 1K 14_{10} Zp 1_{17}. †

II ***גָּלָל**: cs. גְּלַל only w. *bᵉ* as prep.: בִּגְלַל, בִּגְלַלְכֶם, בִּגְלָלֵךְ, בִּגְלָלֶךָ: **on account of** Gn 12_{13}.

III **גָּלָל**: n. pers. Neh 11_{17} 1C 9_{15f}. †

גֶּלֶלוֹ & גֶּלְלֵי Ez $4_{12.15}$ Jb 20_7: ↗ גֵּל.

גִּלֲלַי: n. pers.

גלם: **qal**: impf. יִגְלֹם: **roll up** (mantle) 2K 2_8. †

***גֹּלֶם**: גָּלְמִי: formless thing, **embryo** Ps 139_{16}. †

גַּלְמוּד, f. גַּלְמוּדָה: **barren**: woman Is 49_{21}, night Jb 3_7.

גלע: **hitp.**: pf. הִתְגַּלָּע; impf. יִתְגַּלָּע: **break out** (of dispute) Pr 17_{14} 18_1 20_3. †

גִּלְעָד: n. terr.: often הַגִּלְעָד, loc. (הַ)גִּלְעָ֫דָה: — 1. n. terr., **Gilead** Gn 31_{21} & oft.; — 2. n. pers., *bᵉnê gilʿād* Nu 36_1.

גַּלְעֵד: n. terr. Gn 31_{47f}; cf. I *gal*. †

גִּלְעָדִי: gent. of גִּלְעָד.

גלשׁ: **qal**: pf. גָּֽלְשׁוּ: **frisk**, **leap** (oth.: move down) SS 4_1 6_5. †

גִּלֹת: n. terr.

גַּם (ca. 700×): — 1. associating: *ḥᵃdāšîm gam yᵉšānîm* new as well as old SS 7_{14}, *gam šᵉnêkem* both of you together Gn 27_{45}; — 2. adding: *gam lᵉʾîšāh* to her husband too Gn 3_6; — 3. emphasizing: *gam laddābār hazzeh* in this matter also Gn 19_{21}; — 4. emphasizing rather than associating: *gam hûʾ* he himself Gn 32_{19}; — 5. intensifying: *gam* *ṣaddîq* even an innocent one Gn 20_4; — 6. in (actual or implied) repetition as a figure of speech: *wehî'-gam-hî'* and even she herself Gn 20_5, *wayyō'kal gam-'ākōl* but he has even used up Gn 31_{15}; — 7. *gam* w. negation: *gam ... lō'* not ... either 1S 28_{20}, *gam ... 'ên* there is not even Ec 8_4, *gam 'ad-hā'ēt hahî' lō'* it is true that up to that time ... not Ne 6_1; — 8. uniting clauses, intensifying, = **even**: *wegam bārûk yihyeh* and he must stay blessed Gn 27_{33}, *gam yakōltî* I have even won Gn 30_8; adversative **yet**: *gam lō' yākelû lî* and yet they have not ... Ps 129_2; — 9. in combinations: *kî gam* even if Ec 4_{14}, *gam 'ašer* what ... too Ne 3_{35}, *gam kî* even though Is 1_{15}; *gam 'attâ* formula of continuation: so now Gn 44_{10}; — 10. *gam* often stands at the beginning of a clause instead of where it logically belongs: *kî-gam-'ôy lāhem* woe also to them from whom... Ho 9_{12}; — 11. *wegam* is used like *gam*: a) adding: *wegam 'aḥarê kēn* and also afterward Gn 6_4; b) emphasizing: *wegam 'attâ* yet even now Jl 2_{12}; emphasizing w/o adding: *wegam 'anî* I for my part Am 4_6; — 12. when *wegam* connects two clauses, the stressed element is put first: *wegam 'et-lôṭ hēšîb* and Lot too Gn 14_{16}; *wegam* w. negation: *wegam lō'* and yet...not Ez 16_{28}; — 13. *gam...gam*: *gam teben gam maspô'* both straw and feed Gn 24_{25}; *gam...wegam* both...and 1S 2_{26}; *gam hēmmâ...gam 'anî* (contrasting) these...but I Is 66_{3f}; *gam... (we) gam...lō'* neither...nor 1S 21_9; *gam 'attâ lō' ... wegam 'ānōkî* neither did you ... nor have I ... Gn 21_{26}; *gam ... gam ... gam ... lō'* neither ... nor ... nor Ex 4_{10}; — 14. *bešaggam* Gn 6_3: ?; F comm.

גמא: **piel**: impf. יְגַמֶּא: metaph. **swallow up** (the ground, said of a horse) Jb 39_{24}. †

hif.: impv. sf. הַגְמִיאִינִי: **let sip** Gn 24_{17}. †

גֹּמֶא: **papyrus**, *Cyperus Papyrus* Is 35_7; *tēbat gōmeh* (small) case of pap. Ex 2_3; *kelê gōmeh* pap. skiffs Is 18_2.

גֹּמֶד: a measure of length (of a sword); a short cubit, oth.: ? span Ju 3_{16}. †

גַּמָּדִים: Ez 27_{11}, name of unknown people, F comm. †

גָּמוּל: n. pers.

גְּמוּל: sf. גְּמֻלוֹ, גְּמֻלְךָ; pl. sf. גְּמוּלָיו: — 1. **doings**, what one's hands have done Ju 9_{16} Is 3_{11}; — 2. **reprisal, reward**: of God Is 35_4; *šillēm gemûl* offer retaliation (w. *le*) Is 66_6; *hēšîb gemûl* (w. *le*) Ps 28_4; *šāb gemûl berō'šô* Ob $_{15}$.

גְּמוּלָה: pl. גְּמֻלוֹת, גְּמוּלוֹת: — 1. pl. **deeds** Is 59_{18} (txt.?); — 2. **reprisal, reward** 2S 19_{37}; *'ēl gemûlôt* a God who requites Je 51_{56}. †

גִּמְזוֹ: n. loc.

גָּמַל: **qal**: pf. 'ג, גָּמַלְתָּ, גְּמָלָנוּ, גְּמָלַתְהוּ, גְּמָלַתּוּ, גְּמָלוּךָ; impf. יִגְמֹל, תִּגְמְלֵנִי; impv. גְּמֹל; pt. גֹּמֵל, pass. גָּמוּל, גָּמֻל; — 1. a) **finish**: *gāmal šeqēdîm* produce ripe almonds Nu 17_{23}, *bōser gōmēl* ripened (soft & sweet) Is 18_5; b) **wean** 1S 1_{23f}, *gemûlê mēḥālāb* Is 28_9, *gāmûl* Is 11_8; — 2. **render, do** (good, evil to s.one) Gn $50_{15.17}$; w. *'ēt* often; w. *le* Dt 32_6, *'al* Ps 13_6; *gāmal ke* treat according to 2S 22_{21}.

nif.: impf. יִגָּמֵל, יִגָּמַל; inf. הִגָּמֵל: **be weaned** Gn 21_8.

גָּמָל: pl. גְּמַלִּים, גְּמַלֵּי, sf. גְּמַלָּיו: common gender, f. Gn 32_{16}: one-humped **camel**, *Camelus Dromedarius* Gn 12_{16}.

גְּמַלִּי: n. pers.

גַּמְלִיאֵל: n. pers.

גָּמַר: **qal**: pf. 'ג; impf. יִגְמֹר; pt. גֹּמֵר: — 1. **be at an end** Ps 12_2 77_9; — 2. **revenge, requite**, w. acc. Ps 7_{10}, w. *'al* for the benefit of Ps 57_3, w. *ba'ad* as protection for Ps 138_8. †

I **גֹּמֶר**: name of a people, Gomer = **Cimmerians** Gn 10_{2f} 1C 1_{5f} Ez 38_6. †

II **גֹּמֶר**: n. pers., wife of Hosea Ho 1_3. †

גְּמַרְיָה: n. pers.

גְּמַרְיָהוּ: n. pers.

גַּן: גַּן, הַגָּן, sf. גַּנִּי; pl. גַּנִּים; m., f. Gn 2_{15}; — 1. **garden**: *gan yārāq* vegetable garden 1K 21_2; — 2. *gan ʾelōhîm* **garden of God** Ez 28_{13}, *gan yhwh* Gn 13_{10}, *gan beʿēden* garden (= oasis) in (the country of) Eden Gn 2_8 > *gan ʿēden* garden of (!) Eden 2_{15}.

גנב: qal: pf. גְּנַבְתִּי, גָּנְבוּ, גְּנַבְתּוֹ, גְּנַבְתֶּם, גְּנָבוּךָ; impf. יִגְנֹ(וֹ)ב, יִגְנְבוּ, תִּגְנְבוּ; inf. גְּנֹב; pt. גֹּנֵב, pass. גָּנוּב, גְּנוּבִים, f. cs. גְּנֻבְתִי: — 1. **steal, rob** Gn 44_8; manstealing Ex 21_{16}; 2K 11_2 steal (s.one away for safety); cattle Gn 30_{33}, objects Gn 31_{19}; take away secretly 2S 21_{12}; *genubtî laylâ/yôm* what was stolen by day or by night Gn 31_{39}; carry off (of storm) Jb 21_{18} 27_{20}; — 2. *gānab lēb* **deceive** Gn $31_{20\cdot 26}$, w/o *lēb* 31_{27}.

nif.: impf. יִגָּנֵב: **be stolen** Ex 22_{11}. †

piel: impf. וַיְגַנֵּב; pt. מְגַנְּבֵי: **steal away** (loyalty) 2S 15_6, (words of God) Je 23_{30}. †

pual: pf. גֻּנַּב, גֻּנַּבְתִּי; impf. יְגֻנַּב: — 1. **be stolen away** Gn 40_{15} Ex 22_6; metaph. **steal in secretly** Jb 4_{12}. †

hitp.: impf. וַיִּתְגַּנֵּב: **steal** (into a place) 2S 19_4. †

גַּנָּב: pl. גַּנָּבִים: **thief** Ex $22_{1\cdot 6f}$.

גְּנֵבָה: **stolen object** Ex 22_{2f}. †

גְּנֻבַת: n. pers.

גַּנָּה: cs. גַּנַּת, sf. גַּנָּתוֹ; pl. גַּנּ(וֹ)ת, sf. גַּנּוֹתֵיכֶם: **garden** Nu 24_6; as cult place Is 1_{29}.

I *גֶּנֶז: pl. cs. גִּנְזֵי: *ginzê hammelek* royal **treasury** Est 3_9 4_7. †

II *גֶּנֶז: = I ?: pl. גְּנָזִים: woolen cover, rug, or chest Ez 27_{24}. †

*גַּנְזַךְ: pl. sf. גַּנְזַכָּיו: **treasury** 1C 28_{11}. †

גנן: qal: pf. גַּנּוֹתִי; impf. יָגֵן: **enclose, fence in, hedge in, protect**: w. *ʿal* 2K 20_6; w. *ʾel* (rd *ʿal*?) 2K 19_{34}, w. *baʿad* Zc 12_8.

[גִּנְּתוֹי: Ne 12_4: rd. גִּנְּתוֹן.]

גִּנְּתוֹן: n. pers.

געה: qal: impf. יִגְעֶה; inf. abs. גָּעוֹ: **low, bellow** 1S 6_{12} Jb 6_5. †

*גֹּעָה or *גֹּעַת: loc. גֹּעָתָה: n. loc.

געל: qal: pf. גָּעֲלָה, גָּעֲלוּ, גְּעַלְתִּים; impf. תִּגְעַל: **abhor**, grow tired of, w. acc. Lv 26_{11}, w. b^e Je 14_{19}.

nif.: pf. נִגְעַל: **be defiled** 2S 1_{21}. †

hif.: impf. יַגְעִל: soil = **fail**, miss (in impregnation) Jb 21_{10}. †

*גֹּעַל: cs. גֹּעַל: aversion, **neglect** Ez 16_5. †

גַּעַל: n. pers.

גָּעַר: qal: pf. גָּעַרְתָּ, 'ג; impf. יִגְעַר, תִּגְעֲרוּ; inf. גְּעָר־; pt. גּ(וֹ)עֵר: **reproach, rebuke**; w. b^e Gn 37_{10}; w. acc. Ps 9_6.

גְּעָרָה: cs. גַּעֲרַת, sf. גַּעֲרָתִי: — 1. **rebuke** Pr $13_{1\cdot 8}$; — 2. **threat**: a) of enemy in battle Is 30_{17}; b) of God against enemy powers 2S 22_{16}.

געשׁ: qal: impf. תִּגְעַשׁ: **rise and fall noisily** (of earth) Ps 18_8. †

[**pual**: יְגֹעֲשׁוּ (עָם) Jb 34_{20}: rd. יִגְוְעוּ שׁוֹעִים.]

hitp.: impf. וַתִּתְגָּעַשׁ, יִתְגָּעֲשׁוּ: **rise and fall noisily** 2S 22_8/Ps 18_8 (of earth), Je 5_{22} (of waves).

hitpoel: pf. הִתְגֹּעֲשׁוּ; impf. יִתְגֹּעֲשׁוּ: **vomit** (of drunken nations) Je 25_{16}, **send up a roar** (of waters) Je 46_8. †

*גַּעַשׁ, גָּעַשׁ: n. terr.: *har-gāʿaš* Jos 24_{30} Ju 2_9, *naḥalê gāʿaš* 2S 23_{30} 1C 11_{32}. †

גַּעְתָּם: n. pers.

I *גַּף: *ʿal-gappê*: **at the top of** (?) Pr 9_3. †

II *גַּף: **body**: *begappô* he **alone** Ex 21_{3f}. †

גֶּפֶן (55×): גֶּפֶן, sf. גַּפְנִי, pl. גְּפָנִים: f., m. 2K 4_{39} Ho 10_1: **creeping plant**: *gefen haśśādeh* wild vine 2K 4_{39}; >(grape-)**vine**, *vitis vinifera* Gn 40_{9f}, oft. mentioned with fig tree 1K 5_5 & other fruits; symbol for Isr. Ez $17_{6\text{-}10}$ Ho 10_1 Ps $80_{9\text{-}17}$.

גֹּפֶר: *ʿaṣê-gōfer* Gn 6_{14}, unknown wood used in building ark. †

גָּפְרִית: **sulphur** Gn 19_{24}.

גֵּר (92×): sf. גֵּרְךָ, גֵּרוֹ; pl. גֵּרִים (גֵּירִים 2C

2_{16} †): *gēr* is a man who, either alone or w. his family, leaves his village & tribe, because of war (2S 4_3), famine (Ru 1_1), pestilence, blood-guilt &c., & seeks shelter & sojourn elsewhere, where his right to own land, to marry, & to participate in the administration of justice, in the cult, & in war is curtailed: **sojourner, alien** Gn 15_{13}; *nefeš haggēr* as it feels to a *gēr* Ex 23_9.

גִּר: **chalk**, *'abnê gir* Is 27_9. †

גָּרָא: n. pers.

גָּרָב: **festering eruption** Lv 21_{20} 22_{22} Dt 28_{27}. †

גָּרֵב: n. pers.

*גַּרְגַּר: pl. גַּרְגְּרִים: **ripe olives** Is 17_6. †

*גַּרְגָּרוֹת: sf. גַּרְגְּר(וֹ)תֶיךָ: **neck** Pr 1_9 $3_{3.22}$ 6_{21}. †

גִּרְגָּשִׁי: n. people.

גרד: **hitp.**: inf. הִתְגָּרֵד: **scrape onesf.** Jb 2_8. †

גרה: **piel**: impf. יְגָרֶה: **begin a dispute, go to law**, w. *mādôn* Pr 15_{18} 28_{25} 29_{22}. †
hitp.: pf. הִתְגָּרִית; impf. יִתְגָּרֶה, תִּתְגָּר, תִּתְגָּרוּ; impv. הִתְגָּר: — 1. stir onesf. up (against), **oppose**, w. *bᵉ* Pr 28_4; — 2. **venture into struggle** (*bᵉ* with) Dt $2_{5.24}$; *bᵉrā'â* plunge into misfortune 2K 14_{10}; — 3. abs. **get ready** Dn 11_{10}, w. *lammilḥāmâ* 11_{25}.

I גֵּרָה: **cud** Dt 14_8; *gārar gērâ* Lv 11_7.

II גֵּרָה: smallest weight, 1/20 of a *šeqel* Ex 30_{13}.

גָּרוֹן: sf. גְּרוֹנִי: — 1. **throat**, windpipe, seat of thirst Je 2_{25}, of voice Is 58_1, of ornament Ez 16_{11}; — 2. **neck**, *nᵉṭuyyôt gārôn* w. outstretched neck Is 3_{16}.

גֵּרוּת: **hospitality**, n. loc. *gērût kimhām* Je 41_{17} Qr. †

גרז: **nif.**: pf. נִגְרַזְתִּי: 2 mss. נִגְזַרְתִּי & נִגְרַשְׁתִּי: **be cut off** Ps 31_{23}. †

גִּרְזִי 1S 27_8: rd Qr הַגִּזְרִי.

גְּרִזִים: mount **Gerizim** Dt 11_{29}.

גַּרְזֶן: **axe** Is 10_{15}; **(quarrying-) axe** 1K 6_7.

גֹּרָל, ↗ גּוֹרָל; — גְּרָל־ Pr 19_{19}: rd גְּדָל־ (גָּדוֹל, ↗ BH).

גרם: **qal**: pf. גָּרְמוּ: Zp 3_3 ??, trad. (denom.) gnaw or break bones, but text corr.? †
piel: impf. יְגָרֵם: **gnaw** (bones) Nu 24_8.

גֶּרֶם: pl. sf. גְּרָמָיו: **bones** Pr 17_{22}; *ḥᵃmôr gārem* bony ass Gn 49_{14} (oth.: castrated); uncert. *gerem hammaᶜᵃlôt* 2K 9_{13}: the steps themselves = the bare steps? unknown archit. term?

גַּרְמִי: n. gent. 1C 4_{19}. †

גֹּרֶן: loc. גֹּרְנָה, sf. גָּרְנִי; pl. גֳּרָנוֹת, cs. גָּרְנוֹת; f.:
I. **threshing-floor** 1K 22_{10}; *ben-gornî* my threshed one Is 21_{10}.
II. *gōren* in names of loc.: a) *gōren hā'āṭād* 'bramble threshing-floor' Gn 50_{10}; — b) *gōren kîdôn* 1C 13_9; = c) *gōren nākôn* 2S 6_6; ↗ *kîdôn* & *nākôn*.

גרס: **qal**: pf. גָּרְסָה: w. *nafšî* metaph., wear onesf. down, **waste away** Ps 119_{20}. †
hif.: impf. וַיַּגְרֵס: **make** (s.one's teeth) **grind** La 3_{16}. †

I גרע: **qal**: impf. יִגְרַע, יִגְרָע, תִּגְרְעוּ; inf. לִגְרֹעַ; pt. pass. גְּרוּעָה, גְּרֻעָה: — 1. **shave, trim** (beard) Je 48_{37}; abs. Ez 5_{11}; — 2. **diminish** Ex 21_{10}; make a reduction Ex $5_{8.19}$; — 3. **take away** Dt 4_2.
nif.: pf. נִגְרַע, נִגְרְעָה; impf. יִגָּרַע, יִגָּרֵעַ, נִגָּרַע; pt. נִגְרָע: — 1. **be reduced** Ex 5_{11}; — 2. **be taken away** Nu 36_{3f}; *niggāraᶜ mibbiltî* we are abridged so that we do not ... Nu 9_7.

II גרע: **piel**: impf. יְגָרַע: **draw up** (drops of water) Jb 36_{27}. †

גרף: **qal**: pf. גְּרָפָם: **wash away** (of a current) Ju 5_{21}. †

גרר: **qal**: I. impf. יְגֹרֵם, יְגֹרֵהוּ: **drag out** Hb 1_{15}, carry off Pr 21_7; — II. impf. יָגֹר: w. *gērâ* **ruminate** Lv 11_7. †
polal: pt. מְגֹרָרוֹת: **sawn up** (stones) 1K 7_9. †

גְּרָר: loc. גְּרָרָה: n. loc.

גֶּרֶשׂ: sf. גִּרְשָׂהּ: crushed grains of wheat, **grits** Lv $2_{14.16}$. †

I גֹּרשׁ: **qal**: pt. גֹּרֵשׁ, pass. גְּרוּשָׁה: I. **banish** (people) Ex 34_{11}; — 2. **divorce** (wife) Lv 21_{7}.

nif.: pf. נִגְרַשְׁתִּי: — **be cast off** Jon 2_{5}. †

piel: pf. גֵּרְשָׁה, גֵּרַשְׁתָּ, גֵּרַשְׁתָּמוֹ, גֵּרַשְׁתִּיהוּ, גֵּרַשְׁתִּין, גֵּרְשׁוּנִי; impf. יְגָרֵשׁ, וַיְגָרֶשׁ, תְּגָרְשׁוּן, וַיְגָרְשֵׁהוּ, יְגָרְשׁוּהָ, וַתְּגָרְשׁוּנִי, אֲגָרְשֶׁנּוּ; impv. גָּרֵשׁ; inf. abs. גָּרֵשׁ, cs. לְגָרְשֵׁנוּ: — **drive out**, banish Gn 3_{24}; w. *mē'al* Gn 4_{14}, w. *min* Ex 6_{1}, w. *mē'ēt* Ex 10_{11}, &c.

pual: pf. גֹּרְשׁוּ; impf. יְגֹרָשׁוּ: — **be driven out** Ex 12_{39} Jb 30_{5}. †

II גרשׁ: **qal**: impf. וַיִּגְרְשׁוּ: throw out, **toss up** (of the sea, mud) Is 57_{20b}, ⸗ nif. †

nif.: pf. נִגְרַשׁ (oth.: pt.), נִגְרְשָׁה: **be stirred up** Is 57_{20a} Am 8_{8}. †

גֶּרֶשׁ: *gereš yᵉrāḥîm* what the months yield, **produce** Dt 33_{14}. †

*גְּרֻשָּׁה: pl. גְּרֻשֹׁתֵיכֶם: **expropriation** Ez 45_{9}. †

גֵּרְשׁוֹן: n. pers.

גֵּרְשֹׁם: n. pers.

גֵּרְשֻׁנִּי: gent. of גֵּרְשׁוֹן.

גְּשׁוּר: loc. גְּשׁוּרָה: n. terr. & peop.: small Aramean state betw. Bashan & Hermon.

גְּשׁוּרִי: gent. of גְּשׁוּר.

גשׁם: **hif.**: pt. מַגְשִׁמִים: **make rain fall** Je 14_{22}. †

I גֶּשֶׁם: גֶּשֶׁם; pl. גְּשָׁמִים, גִּשְׁמֵי, גִּשְׁמֵיכֶם: **rain-shower > rain**: — I. sg.: *hāyâ gešem* rain falls, it rains Gn 7_{12}; *bô' gešem* Ho 6_{3}, *yārad gešem* Is 55_{10}; many comb.: *mᵉṭar gešem* heavy shower Zc 10_{1}; *hᵃmôn haggešem* roar of rain 1K 18_{41}; — 2. pl. *gᵉšāmîm* rain showers Ezr 10_{9}, *hā'ēt gᵉšāmîm* the season was rainshowers = rainy season 10_{13}; *gišmê bᵉrākâ* rich in blessing Ez 34_{26}.

II גֶּשֶׁם: n. pers. Ne 2_{19} 6_{1f}. †

גֹּשֶׁם: sf. גֻּשְׁמָהּ Ez 22_{24}: text corr.? cj. rd. גֻּשְׁמָה (גשׁם pual **be rained on**). †

גַּשְׁמוּ: n. pers.

גֹּשֶׁן: name of two territories, in Canaan & in Egypt.

גִּשְׁפָּא: n. pers.

גשׁשׁ: **piel**: impf. נְגַשְׁשָׁה, נְגַשְׁשָׁה: **grope** (of blind) Is 59_{10}. †

I גַּת: pl. גִּתּוֹת: **wine-press**, upper basin where the grapes were trodden out: *dārak gat* Ne 13_{15}, *dārak bᵉgat* Is 63_{2}; metaph. bring on a bloodbath La 1_{15}, cf. Jl 4_{13}, as secret threshing floor Ju 6_{11}. †

II גַּת: n. loc.: גַּת, loc. גִּתָּה 1K 2_{40}, גִּתָּה Jos 19_{13}: Philistine city; also 1C 7_{21} in Ephraim.

III גַּת in comb., n. loc.: — 1. גַּת־הַחֵפֶר; — 2. גַּת־רִמּוֹן.

גִּתִּי: gent. of גַּת Philistine city.

*גִּתַּיִם: n. loc.: גִּתָּיִם, loc. גִּתַּיְמָה.

גִּתִּית: עַל־הַגִּתִּית Ps 8_{1} 81_{1} 84_{1}, unknown musical term: a) Gathite instrument; b) 'by the wine-presses,' of feast of tabernacles; c) of New Year's festival ?

גֶּתֶר: n. pers.

ד

דאב: **qal**: pf. דָּאֲבָה; inf. דַּאֲבָה: **languish**, waste away Je $31_{12 \cdot 25}$ Ps 88_{10}. †

דְּאָבָה: trad. languor, despair Jb 41_{14}; but prob. rd. ⸗ דְּבָאָה **violence**. †

*דְּאָבוֹן: cs. דַּאֲבוֹן: languor (of the *nefeš*), **despair** Dt 28_{65}. †

דָּאַג: **qal**: pf. ד׳, דָּאַגְתִּי; impf. יִדְאָג, אֶדְאַג; pt. דֹּאֵג, דֹּאֲגִים: — 1. **be** anxious, **worried**, abs. Je 17_{8}, w. *lᵉ* 1S 9_{5}, w. *min* because of Je 42_{16}; — 2. **fear**, dread w. acc. Is 57_{11}.

דָּאג: Ne 13_{16} **fish**, ⸗ דָּג. †

דֹּאֵג: 1S 21_{8} 22_{9}, דּוֹאֵג Ps 52_{2} 1S $22_{18 \cdot 22}$ Qr: n. pers.

דְּאָגָה: **anxiety** Ez 4_{16}.
דאה: **qal**: impf. יִדְאֶה, וַיֵּדֶא: **fly** (= swoop for booty) Dt 28_{49}; **soar** (of God) Ps 18_{11}.
דָּאָה: unclean bird of prey, **kite**, *Milvus milvus* Lv 11_{14}.
דֹּאר: Jos 17_{11} 1K 4_{11}, דּוֹר Jos 11_2 12_{23} Ju 1_{27} 1C 7_{29}: n. loc.
דֹּב (8×) & דּוֹב (2×): pl. דֻּבִּים: (he- or she-) **bear**, *Ursus syriacus* 2K 2_{24}.
*דֹּבֶא: sf. דָּבְאֶךָ: **strength** Dt 33_{25}. †
cj. דְּבָאָה **strength** Jb 41_{14}. †
דבב: **qal**: pt. דּוֹבֵב: drop ? glide ? SS 7_{10}. †
דִּבָּה: cs. דִּבַּת, sf. דִּבָּתְךָ, דִּבָּתָם: **rumor, calumny** Nu 13_{32} Je 20_{10}; *dibbâ rāʿâ* Gn 37_2.
I דְּבוֹרָה: pl. דְּבוֹרִים: (wild) **honey-bee**, *Apis mellifica* Dt 1_{44} Is 7_{18}; *ʿadat debôrîm* swarm of bees Ju 14_8.
II דְּבוֹרָה: n. pers. f.: Gn 35_8; Ju 4_{4-14} 5_{1-15}. †
דִּבְיֹנִים: pl. tech. term 2K 6_{25} Qr, Kt חֲרֵי יוֹנִים (↗ חֲרָאִים): **doves' dung** (emergency substitute for salt); oth.: a plant, ↗ *ḥarāʾîm*. †
I דְּבִיר: rear room, the cubical **holy of holies** of a Syrian type of temple, the later *qōdeš haqqodāšîm* 1K 6_5.
II דְּבִיר: n. pers. Jos 10_3. †
III דְּבִיר: n. loc., ↗ דְּבִר.
דְּבֵלָה: cs. דְּבֶלֶת; pl. דְּבֵלִים: **fig cakes**: figs pressed in form of cake; *debēlîm ʿiggûlîm* round, & *debēlîm malbenîm* brick-shaped; 2K 20_7.
דִּבְלַיִם, דִּבְלָיִם: n. pers.; or n. loc. ↗ *diblātayim*; or appellative, the price of harlotry: Ho 1_3. †
דִּבְלָתָה Ez 6_{14}: rd. רִבְלָתָה.
דִּבְלָתַיִם: n. loc., ↗ בַּיִת B 13.
דָּבַק: **qal**: pf. ד׳, דָּבֵק, דָּבְקָה, דָּבֵקָה, דָּבַקְתִּי, דָּבְקוּ, דָּבֵקוּ; impf. יִדְבַּק, תִּדְבַּק, תִּדְבָּקְנִי, תִּדְבָּקוּן, תִּדְבָּקוּ, יִדְבְּקוּ, תִּדְבָּקִין; inf. לְדָבְקָה: — 1. w. *be*: a) **stick, cling to** Ez 29_4 Jb 19_{20}; b) abstract: **cling, cleave to**: man to woman Gn 2_{24}, disease to s.one 2K 5_{27}, evil works to s.one Ps 101_3; c) allegiance: **join** Jos 23_{12}, **follow** (king) 2S 20_2, esp. Y. 2K 18_6; d) **hold onto** (inheritance) Nu 36_7, (sin) 2K 3_3; — 2. w. *le*: **stick, cling** to Ps 102_6; — 3. w. *ʾel*: **stick, cling** to 2S 23_{10}; — 4. w. *ʿim* **join** Rt $2_{8.21}$; — 5. w. *ʾaḥarê* **pursue** Je 42_{16}; — 6. w. acc. **fasten onesf. on** Gn 19_{19}.

pual: impf. יְדֻבָּקוּ: be stuck to each other (clods, from rain) Jb 38_{38}; be tightly joined together (scales of crocodile) Jb 41_9. †

hif.: pf. הִדְבַּקְתִּי, הִדְבִּיקָתְהוּ, הִדְבִּקָהוּ; impf. אַדְבִּיק, יַדְבֵּק, וַיַּדְבִּיקוּ, וַיַּדְבְּקוּ 1S 14_{22} 31_2 1C 10_2: — 1. **catch up with** Gn 31_{23}; — w. *be* **make** s.thg **stick** to Ez 29_4, **make** (pestilence) **cling** to Dt 28_{21}, w. *ʾel* Je 13_{11}; — 3. **follow hard** after, w. *ʾaḥarê* 1S 14_{22}.

hof.: pt. מֻדְבָּק: **stuck** Ps 22_{16}. †
דָּבֵק: f. דְּבֵקָה; pl. דְּבֵקִים: — 1. w. *le* **in contact w.** 2C 3_{12}; **faithful to** w. *be* Dt 4_4, w. *min* Pr 18_{24}. †
דֶּבֶק: pl. דְּבָקִים: — 1. **soldering**, welding Is 41_7; — 2. 'appendage,' i.e. **scales** of coat of mail 1K 22_{34}/2C 18_{33}. †
I דבר: **piel**: impf. וַתְּדַבֵּר, וַיְדַבְּרוּ; inf. דַּבֵּר, בְּדַבְּרוֹ: — 1. turn the back, **turn away** SS 5_6 Ps 75_6, w. *be* from (↗ *be* 13 !) Jb 19_{18}; — 2. **drive away** Is 32_7 Ps 127_5; **exterminate** 2C 22_{10}. †

cj. **pual**: Ps 116_{10} rd. אֲדֻבַּר: **be persecuted.** †

hif.: impf. יַדְבֵּר, וַיַּדְבֵּר: **subjugate** Ps 18_{48} 47_4. †
II דבר: **qal** (40×): inf. דָּבְרְךָ Ps 51_6 †, otherw. pt. דֹּבֵר, pl. דֹּבְרִים, דֹּבְרֵי, ד(ו)בְרוֹת, pass. דָּבֻר Pr 25_{11} †: **speak**, ↗ piel: — 1. abs., w. *ʾel* to Gn 16_{13}, w. *be* with Zc 1_9 (+ 10×, ↗ *be* 15f), *beʾoznê* before Dt 5_1; — 2. speak s.thg: *ʾemet* Ps 15_2, *ṭôbâ* Je 32_{42}, *šālôm* Ps 28_3.

nif.: pf. נִדְבְּרוּ, נִדְבָּרוּ, נִדְבַּרְנוּ; pt.

נִדְבָּרִים: **speak together** Ma 3_{16}, about *ʿal* 3_{13}, *b^e* Ez 33_{30} Ps 119_{23}. †

piel (1100×): pf. דִּבֶּר, דִּבֵּר, דִּבַּרְתִּי (Kt Je 3_5 2.f.), דִּבְּרוּ, דִּבֵּרוּ, דִּבַּרְנוּ, דִּבְּרוֹ (sf.); impf. יְדַבֵּר, תְּדַבֶּר־, אֲדַבֶּר־, אֲדַבְּרָה, אֲדַבֵּרָה, יְדַבְּרוּ, יְדַבֵּרוּ, תְּדַבֵּרְנָה, תְּדַבְּרוּן, תְּדַבֵּרוּן, וַיְדַבְּרֵם; impv. דַּבֵּר, דַּבְּרִי, דַּבֵּרִי; inf. cs., abs. דַּבֵּר, דַּבֶּר־, דַּבְּרוֹ, דַּבֶּרְךָ, pt. מְדַבֵּר, מְדַבֶּרֶת, מְדַבְּרוֹת: **speak, talk** (:: *ʾāmar* say) Gn 21_1: — 1. abs. **speak** Ex 4_{14}; — 2. **speak to, with** s.one: w. *ʾel* Gn 8_{15}, w. *l^e* 1K 2_{19}, w. *ʾēt* Gn 23_8, w. *ʿim* 31_{29}, w. *b^e* Nu 12_2; w. sf. Gn 37_4; w. *ʿal* Je 6_{10}; — 3. **speak s.thg** Ex 6_{29}; *šeqer* Is 59_3, *ʾ^emet* Je 9_4; *dibber d^ebārîm* speak (mere) words 2S 19_{30}, make plans Is 8_{10}; *dibber šîr* sing a song Ju 5_{12}, *dibber māšāl* compose proverbs 1K 5_{12}; *dibber qāšôt ʾēt* speak sharply with Gn 42_{30}; — 4. **speak about** s.one, s.thg: w. *ʿal* Gn 18_{19}, w. *b^e* Ps 119_{46}; in *ʾ^ašer*-clauses *ʿal* is omitted Gn 19_{21}; — 5. a) *dibber ʿal*, speak against Ho 7_{13}, w. *rāʿâ* **threaten** Je 18_8; b) *dibber l^e* **promise** Dt 6_3; — 6. **command** Gn 12_4; — 7. *dibber b^e* speak against Nu 12_1, speak through 1K 22_{28}, *dibber b^eʾiššâ* court 1S 25_{39}; — 8. spec.: a) *dibber ś^efat (k^enaʿan)* speak a language Ne 13_{24}; b) *dibber batt^efillâ* offer prayer Dn 9_{21}; c) *dibber b^elibbô* Ec 2_{15}, *ʿal-l.* 1S 1_{13}, *ʿim-l.* Ec 1_{16}, *ʾel-l.* Gn 24_{45} speak to onesf., think; d) *dibber ʿal lēb* (try to) persuade graciously Gn 34_3, show recognition 2C 30_{22}; *dabb^erô l^ešālôm* speak kindly with Gn 37_4; *dibber ṭôb ʿal* put in a good word for Est 7_9.

pual: impf. יְדֻבַּר; pt. מְדֻבָּר: **be spoken** Ps 87_3; SS 8_8 w. *b^e* one courts her (ꟳ piel 7) = she is marriageable. †

hitp.: pt. מִדַּבֵּר: w. *ʾel* **converse with** Nu 7_{89} Ez 2_2 43_6. †

III דבר: **piel**: impf. יְדַבֵּר: **have descendants** Pr 21_{28}. †

דָּבָר (1430×): cs. דְּבַר; sf. דְּבָרוֹ, דְּבָרְךָ, דְּבָרֶךָ; pl. דְּבָרִים, cs. דִּבְרֵי, sf. דְּבָרֶיךָ, דְּבָרַי, דְּבָרֶי, דִּבְרֵיהֶם: — 1. **word**: *d^ebārîm ʾ^aḥādîm* the same words Gn 11_1, *dibrê hassēfer* words = contents of the letter 2K 22_{13}; *hēqîm d^ebārô* carry out his word 1K 2_4, *hēšîb dābār* answer 1K 12_6; *d^ebar bilʿām* advice of B. Nu 31_{16}; *dābār hûʾ* it is merely a word 1S 17_{29}, *d^ebar ś^efātayim* a mere word 2K 18_{20}; *ʿāśâ d^ebārô* follow his advice 2S 17_6; *wayyihyû d^ebārāyw ʿim* conduct negotiations with 1K 1_7; *d^ebar hammelek* royal command Est 1_{12}; *d^ebārîm* sayings 1K 10_6 Je 1_1, command Pr 13_{13}, refusal Est 1_{17}; — 2. **affair, thing**: a) sg.: *d^ebar ʾûriyyāhû* the case of U. 1K 15_5, *d^ebar hamm^elûkâ* the matter of kingship 1S 10_{16}; *haddābār hazzeh* this thing Gn 20_{10}; *laddābār hazzeh* for this purpose Ne 8_4; *kaddābār hārîʾšôn* as before 1S 17_{30}; *kol-d^ebar* every case of Ex 22_8; *ʿal-d^ebār* because of Gn 12_{17}; *haddābār ʾ^ašer* the reason why 1K 11_{27}; *dābār ʾên lāhem ʿim* had no dealings with Ju 18_7; *d^ebar yôm b^eyômô* day's task Ex 5_{13}; — b) pl.: *d^ebārênu* our business Jos 2_{14}, *l^ekol-d^ebārāyw* in all its parts 1K 6_{38}; *dibrê š^elōmōh* history of S. 1K 11_{41}; *dibber d^ebārāyw* accomplish one's mission Gn 24_{33}; *baʿal d^ebārîm* who has a legal case Ex 24_{14}; — 3) thing > **something**: a) sg.: *ʿāśâ dābār* do s.thg Am 3_7, *yēš dābār* there is s.thg Ec 1_{10}, *dābār gādôl* s.thg great 1S 20_2, *d^ebar-mah* whatever Nu 23_3; *lōʾ…dābār* nothing at all Ex 9_4; *kaddābār hazzeh* so (= thus) Gn 18_{25}; *kol-dābār ṭāmēʾ* anything unclean Lv 5_2; *kōl-dābār ʾ^ašer bāʾāreṣ* everything on earth Ju 18_{10}, *ʾên dābār* there is nothing the matter 1S 20_{21}; *ʿerwat dābār* anything shameful Dt 23_{15}; *śîm dābār b^e* impute s.thg to 1S 22_{15}; — b) pl.: *kol-hadd^ebārîm* everything Gn 24_{66}, *kadd^ebārîm hāʾēlleh* such things 1S 2_{23}; *ʾaḥar hadd^ebārîm hāʾēlleh* afterwards Gn 15_1; — 4. **word of**

God: a) *d*^{e}*bar* ʾ^{e}*lōhîm* 1S 9_{27} (+ 2×); b) *d*^{e}*bar hā*ʾ^{e}*lōhîm* 2S 16_{23} (+ 1×), N.B. 1C 26_{32} † affairs of God; c) *d*^{e}*bar* ʾ^{e}*lōhênû* Is 40_{8}; d) *d*^{e}*bar yhwh* Gn 15_{1} & oft.; e) *dibrê yhwh* Ex 4_{28} (+ 16×); f) *dibrê hā*ʾ^{e}*lōhîm* 1C 25_{5}.

I **דֶּבֶר**, דָּ֫בֶר: **(bubonic) plague** 1K 8_{37}; oft. in series Je 14_{12}.

II **דֶּבֶר**: pl. sf. דְּבָרֶיךָ: **thorn** Ho 13_{14} Ps 91_{3}. †

* **דֹּ֫בֶר**: sf. דָּבְרָם: **pasture** Is 5_{17} Mi 2_{12}. †

דְּבִר: Ju 1_{11} & III דְּבִיר 1C 6_{43}: n. loc. = I דְּבִיר, loc. דְּבִרָה.

דַּבֵּר: pl. ☞ דַּבֶּ֫רֶת: **word of God** Je 5_{13}. †

***דִּבְרָה** or *דְּבָרָה: cs. דִּבְרַת & דִּבְרָתִי Ps 110_{4}; sf. דִּבְרָתִי Jb 5_{8}: — 1. (legal) case Jb 5_{8}; — 2. manner, way Ps 110_{4}; — 3. *ʿal-dibrat* on account of Ec 3_{18} 8_{2}; w. *šellō*ʾ (☞ *še*) so that...not 7_{14}. †

דֹּבְרוֹת: sg. *דֹּבְרָה or *דֹּבֶ֫רֶת: raft: collection of logs towed behind a ship 1K 5_{23}. †

דִּבְרִי: n. pers. Lv 24_{11}. †

דָּֽבְרַת & הַדָּֽבְרַת Jos 19_{12}: n. loc.

***דַּבֶּ֫רֶת**: pl. sf. דַּבְּרֹתֶיךָ: Dt 33_{3} uncert.; usu. 'pronouncement,' = דִּבְּרָה; :: oth.: 'from behind.' †

דְּבַשׁ: (ca. 50×): דְּבָשׁ; sf. דִּבְשִׁי: **honey** 1S 14_{25}; also used for date- and grape syrup, thickened by boiling; oft. w. *ḥālāb* Ex 3_{8}.

I **דַּבֶּ֫שֶׁת**: **(camel's) hump** Is 30_{6}. †

II **דַּבָּ֫שֶׁת, דַּבֶּ֫שֶׁת**: n. loc. Jos 19_{11}. †

דָּג & דָּאג Ne 13_{16}: pl. דָּגִים, cs. דְּגֵי: **fish** Jon $2_{1.11}$, coll. Ne 3_{16}; pl. 1K 5_{13}.

דגה: **qal**: impf. יִדְגּוּ: **multiply** Gn 48_{16}. †

דָּגָה: f. of דָּג: cs. דְּגַת, sf. דְּגָתָם: **fish** (coll. pl.) Ex $7_{18.21}$.

דָּגוֹן: name of deity: **Dagon** 1S $5_{1\text{-}7}$.

I **דגל**: **qal**: pt. pass. דָּגוּל: visible, **distinguished** SS 5_{10}. †

II **דגל**: [**qal**: impf. נִדְגֹּל: lift the banner (?) Ps 20_{6}; but txt. dub.].

nif.: organized in sections; noun, **"troop"** (?) SS $6_{4.10}$. †

דֶּ֫גֶל: sf. דִּגְלוֹ; pl. sf. דִּגְלֵיהֶם: — 1. **banner, signal** Nu 1_{52} 2_{2}; — 2. **tribal division** Nu 2_{3ff} 10_{14ff}; — 3. **sign**(-board) (of an inn) (?), SS 2_{4}.

דָּגָן (40×): cs. דְּגַן, sf. דְּגָנְךָ, דְּגָנָם: (cereal) **grain** Dt 7_{13}.

דגר: **qal**: pf. דָּגַר, דָּֽגְרָה: **hatch** (eggs) Is 34_{15} Je 17_{11}; oth.: gather. †

***דַּד**: du. cs. דַּדֵּי, sf. דַּדֶּיהָ, דַּדַּיִךְ: **breast** Ez $23_{3.8.21}$.

דדה: **hitp.**: impf. אֶדַּדֶּה Is 38_{15} walk, but txt. dub.; אֶדַּדֵּם Ps 42_{5} ?, prp. I walk, but txt. dub. †

דֹּדָוָהוּ: n. pers.

דֹּדִי: n. pers.

דְּדָן: n. pers. & terr.: loc. דְּדָנֶה; pl. (gent. ?) דְּדָנִים Is 21_{13}.

דֹּדָנִים: n. pers. Gn 10_{4}, but = רֹדָנִים 1C 1_{7}. †

דהם: **nif.**: pt. נִדְהָם: surprised, **bewildered** Je 14_{9}. †

דהר: **qal**: pt. דֹּהֵר: **gallop** (horse) Na 3_{2}. †

***דַּהֲרָה**: pl. abs. & cs. דַּהֲרוֹת: **galloping** Ju 5_{22}. †

דּוֹאֵג, ☞ דֹּאֵג: n. pers.

דוב: **hif.**: pt. pl. f. מְדִיבֹת: what consumes, wears away the *nefeš* (☞ *nefeš* 7) Lv 26_{16}. †

***דַּוָּג**: pl. דַּוָּגִים: **fisherman** Je 16_{16} Kt, Ez 47_{10}. †

דּוּגָה: **fishing**, *sîrôt dûgâ* fishhooks Am 4_{2}. †

דּוֹד, Lv 10_{4} Est 2_{15} דֹּד: sf. דֹּ(וֹ)דוֹ, דֹּדְךָ; pl. דֹּ(וֹ)דִים, sf. דֹּדֶיךָ, דֹּדֵיהֶן: — 1. **beloved, lover** (son of father's brother as usual husband) Is 5_{1}, SS 1_{13f} & oft.; — 2. a) **father's brother** 2K 24_{17}; b) *ben-dôd* son of father's br. Je 32_{8f}; *bat-dôd* dau. of father's br. Est 2_{7}; — 3. *dōdîm* **love**(-making) Ez 16_{8} SS $1_{2.4}$.

דּוּד: pl. דּוּדִים & דְּוָדִים 2C 35_{13}, cs. דּוּדָאֵי Je 24_{1}: — 1. deep, two-handled **cooking pot** 1S 2_{14}; — 2. **basket** 2K 10_{7}.

דָּוִד, later דָּוִיד: n. pers., **David**.

דּוּדָאִים: cs. דּוּדָאֵי: **mandrake**, *Atropa*

Mandragora or *A.M. officinarum*, trad. aphrodisiac, Gn 30_{14-16} SS 7_{14}; *dûdā'ê* Je 24_1 ꟻ *dûd*. †

***דּוֹדָה**: f. of דּוֹד; sf. דֹּדָתוֹ, דֹּדָתְךָ: — 1. **father's sister** Ex 6_{20}; — 2. **wife of father's brother** Lv 18_{14} 20_{20}. †

דּוֹדוֹ & דֹּדוֹ: n. pers.

דּוֹדַי: n. pers.

דוה: **qal**: inf. דְּוֹתָהּ: **menstruate** Lv 12_2. †

דָּוֶה: f. דָּוָה: — 1. **sick** La 1_{13} 5_{17}; — 2. f. **menstruating** Lv 15_{33} 20_{18} Is 30_{22}. †

דוח: **hif.**: impf. יָדִיחַ, יְדִיחוּ: **wash off, away** Is 4_4 Ez 40_{38} 2C 4_6.

***דְּוַי**: דְּוָי: (menstrual) **indisposition** Ps 41_4; Jb 6_7 ꟻ comm. †

דַּוָּי: **sick** Is 1_5 Je 8_{18} La 1_{22}. †

דּוֹיֵג 1S 22_{18} Kt: ꟻ דּוֹאֵג. †

דָּוִיד: ꟻ דָּוִד.

דוך: **qal**: pf. דָּכוּ: **pound** (in mortars) Nu 11_8. †

דּוּכִיפַת: **hoopoe**, *Upupa epops*, Lv 11_{19} Dt 14_{18}. †

I **דּוּמָה**: **silence** Ps 94_{17} 115_{17}. †

II **דּוּמָה**: n. loc. Jos 15_{52}. †

III **דּוּמָה**: n. terr. & peop.: — 1. Arab tribe Gn 25_{14} 1C 1_{30}; — 2. n. terr., **Idumea** Is 21_{11}. †

דּוּמִיָּה, דֻּמִיָּה Is 65_2: **silence**, rest Ps 22_3; 39_3 adv. acc. in silence.

דּוּמָם: **stillness, silence**, — 1. *'eben dûmām* silent stone Hb 2_{19}; — 2. adv. acc. **silent** Is 47_5 La 3_{26}. †

דּוּמֶשֶׂק, = ꟻ דַּמֶּשֶׂק: 2K 16_{10}. †

? **דון**: **qal**: impf. יָדוֹן: Gn 6_3, unexpl., ctxt. sugg. 'remain,' ꟻ comm. †

דּוּן: Jb 19_{29} Qr שַׁדּוּן, Kt ?; ? rd יֵשׁ דַּיָּן.

דּוֹנַג, דּוֹנָג: **wax**, alw. metaph. of melting Mi 1_4 Ps 22_{15} 68_3 97_5. †

דוץ: **qal**: impf. תָּדוּץ **leap** Jb 41_{14}. †

דוק: **qal**: impf. יְדוּקֶנּוּ Is 28_{28}, ꟻ דקק. †

I **דור**: **qal**: impv. or inf. abs. דּוּר: **pile up** (logs around) Ez 24_5. †

II **דור**: **qal**: inf. דּוּר: stay, **dwell** Ps 84_{11}. †

דּוּר: Is 22_{18} כַּדּוּר, ctxt. sugg. **ball** ?; uncert. †

I **דּוּר**: sf. דּוּרִי: circular (tent-)camp, **dwelling-place** Is 38_{12}. †

II **דּוֹר** (160×), also דֹּר: sf. דּוֹרִי; pl. דּוֹרִים, דֹּרֹת, דֹּ(וֹ)רֹ(וֹ)ת Is 51_8 Ps 72_5 102_5 †, sf. דֹּרֹתָיו, דֹּרֹתָם, דּוֹרֹ(וֹ)תֵינוּ: — 1. sg. circuit, lifetime, **generation** (from a man's birth to the birth of his first son; the totality of (adult) contemporaries; a time with its noteworthy events & people): *haddôr hazzeh* Gn 7_1; *le'elef dôr* to the 1000th gener. Dt 7_9; *dôr dôr* Ex 3_{15}, *dôr wādôr* Dt 32_7, & *dôr ledôr* Ps 145_4 gener. to gener.; — 2. pl. **generations**: *dōrôtênû 'aḥarênû* the generations coming after us Jos 22_{27}; *bedōrōtāyw* among his contemporaries Gn 6_7.

III **דּוֹר**: n. loc.; ꟻ דּאֹר, נָפַת דּוֹר.

דוש & **דיש**: **qal**: pf. דַּשְׁתִּי; impf. תָּדוּשׁ, תְּדוּשֶׁהָ, יְדוּשֶׁנּוּ; impv. דּוֹשִׁי; inf. דּוּשׁ, דִּשׁ, דִּישׁוֹ, abs. אָדוֹשׁ Is 28_{28}; pt. דָּשׁ: — 1. **trample** Is 41_{15}; — 2. trample out (grain), **thresh** Dt 25_4 Ho 10_{11}; — 3. (metaph.) **trample** (men, nations) = **exterminate** 2K 13_7.

nif.: pf. נָדוֹשׁ; inf. הִדּוּשׁ: **be trampled** (ꟻ qal 3) Is 25_{10}. †

hof. (or qal pass.): impf. יוּדַשׁ: **be threshed** Is 28_{27}. †

דחה: **qal**: pf. דְּחִיתַנִי; inf. cs. דְּחוֹת, abs. דָּחֹה; pt. דֹּחֶה, pass. דְּחוּיָה: **push** (down) Ps 35_5 118_{13} 140_5, push in(stone wall)62_4. †

nif.: impf. יִדַּחוּ, יִדָּחֶה Je 23_{12}: **be pushed** Je 23_{12}, **be overturned** Pr 14_{32}. †

pual (or qal pass.): pf. דֹּחוּ: **be overturned** Ps 36_{13}. †

דחח = דחה.

nif.: impf. יִדַּח, יִדַּחוּ; pt. נִדָּח: **be pushed** Je 23_{12}; be dispossessed 2S 14_{14}. †

דְּחִי, דֶּחִי: **stumbling** Ps 56_{14} 116_8. †

דֹּחַן: **sorghum**, *Sorghum vulgare* Ez 4_9. †

דחף: **qal**: pt. pass. דְּחוּפִים **hurrying** (F nif.) Est 3_{15} 8_{14}. †

nif.: pf. נִדְחַף: **hurry** Est 6_{12} 2C 26_{20}. †

דחק: **qal**: impf. יִדְחָקוּן; pt. sf. דֹּחֲקֵיהֶם: — **afflict** Jl 2_8, pt. **oppressor** Ju 2_{18}. †

*דַּי: דֵּי, cs. דֵּי, sf. דַּיָּם, דַּיֶּךָ: **sufficiency, necessary supply, enough**: — 1. full mng. of noun: a) *dayyām* their necessities, enough for them Ex 36_7; *dayyekkā* as much as suits you Pr 25_{16}; *dê śeh* expenditure for a sheep Lv 5_7; *ʾên dê bāʿēr* does not suffice for Is 40_{16}; *dê hāšîb lô* necessities for restitution Lv 25_{28}; b) neg. mng.: *bᵉdê rîq* for nothing Je 51_{58} Hb 2_{13}, *ʿad bᵉlî dāy* until there is no more necessity, sufficient Ma 3_{10}; c) *middê* more than necessary Ex 36_5; — 2. idiom. mng. w. prep.: a) *bᵉdê šôfār* as often as the trumpet sounds Jb 39_{25}; b) *kᵉdê* corresponding to Dt 25_2, *kᵉdê...lārōb* as numerous as Ju 6_5; c) *middê* (:: 1c) according to the need: esp. in an idiom like: *middê šānâ bᵉšānâ* year by year 1S 7_{16}; d) *middê* as often as, α) w. inf. 1K 14_{28}; β) w. impf. *middê ʾᵃdabbēr* Je 20_8; e) *lᵉmadday* (= *lᵉ* + *mâ* + *day*) in sufficient number 2C 30_3.

דִּיבוֹן & דִּיבֹן: n. loc., mostly in Moab Nu 21_{30} &c., but also in Judah Ne 11_{25}.

דיג: **qal**: pf. וְדִיגוּם: **catch** (fish) Je 16_{16}. †

*דַּיָּג: pl. דַּיָּגִים: **fisherman** Is 19_8, Je 16_{16} Qr. †

דַּיָּה: pl. דַּיּוֹת: unclean **bird of prey** in ruins & waste places, uncert., Dt 14_{13} Is 34_{15}. †

דְּיוֹ: **ink** (from gall-nuts & soot) Je 36_{18}. †

דִּי זָהָב: n. loc. Dt 1_1. †

דִּימוֹן: n. loc.

דִּימוֹנָה: n. loc.

דין: **qal**: pf. דָּן, דָּנוּ, דָּנַנִּי; impf. יָדִין, תְּדִינֵנִי; impv. דִּין, דִּינוּ; inf. דִּין; pt. דָּן; — 1. **bring justice** (= redress a wrong) to s.one, w. acc. Ps 72_2; subj. God Gn 30_6; *dān dîn* help s.one obtain justice Je 5_{28}, *dān mišpāṭ* Je 21_{12}; — 2. *dān ʿim* **go to law w.** Ec 6_{10}; — 3. **pass sentence, execute justice**: w. acc., call s.one to account, subj. God Gn 15_{14}.

nif.: pt. נָדוֹן: **quarrel** 2S 19_{10}. †

דִּין: sf. דִּינִי, דִּינֵךְ: — 1. **legal claim** Dt 17_8; — 2. **lawsuit** Jb 35_{14}; — 3. **verdict**, sentence Ps 76_9; *kissēʾ dîn* judgment-seat Pr 20_8; — 4. **dispute** Pr 22_{10}.

דַּיָּן: cs. דַּיַּן **judge** 1S 24_{16} Ps 68_6. †

דִּינָה: n. pers. f.

דִּיפַת: n. pers.

דָּיֵק: **siege-mound**, w. *bānâ* or *sābîb*, 2K 25_1.

דִּישׁ, F דושׁ.

דַּיִשׁ: **threshing(-time)** Lv 26_5. †

I דִּישׁוֹן: **bison** ? Dt 14_5. †

II דִּשׁ(וֹ)ן & דִּישׁ(וֹ)ן: n. pers.

דִּישָׁן: n. pers.

דַּךְ: דָּךְ: **oppressed, miserable** Ps 9_{10} 10_{18} 74_{21}. †

דכא: **nif.**: pt. נִדְכָּאִים: **oppressed** Is 57_{15}. †

piel: pf. דִּכָּא, דִּכְּאתָ (!); impf. יְדַכֵּא, תְּדַכְּאוּ, יְדַכְּאֻנִי, תְּדַכְּאוּנַּנִי; inf. דַּכֵּא, דַּכְּאוֹ: **beat to pieces, crush** Is 3_{15}.

pual: pf. דֻּכְּאוּ; pt. מְדֻכָּא, מְדֻכָּאִים: **be beaten to pieces, crushed** Is 19_{10}.

hitp.: יִדַּכְּאוּ, יִדַּכָּאוּ (< *yitd-*): **lie crushed** Jb 5_4 34_{25}. †

I דַּכָּא: pl. cs. דַּכְּאֵי: — 1. **crushed** = humble Is 57_{15} Ps 34_{19}; — 2. what is crushed = **dust** = abode of the dead ? Ps 90_3. †

II דַּכָּא: **crushing**, *pᵉṣûaʿ-dakkāʾ* **emasculated** by crushing (of testicles) Dt 23_2. †

דכה: [**qal**: impf. יִדְכֶּה Ps 10_{10} Qr, but txt. uncert; rd. nif. pf. or impf.]

nif.: pf. נִדְכֵּיתִי; pt. נִדְכֶּה: **be crushed** Ps 38_9 51_{19}, cj. 10_{10} (F qal). †

piel: pf. דִּכִּיתָ, דִּכִּיתָנוּ: **crush** Ps 44_{20} 51_{10}. †

דֳּכִי: sf. דָּכְיָם: **pounding** (of waves) Ps 93_3. †

I *דַּל or *דֶּל: cs. דַּל: **door**, metaph.: *dal śᵉfātay* Ps 141_3. †

II דַּל: — 1. **mean, scanty**: Gn 41_{19} (scrawny

cows), Ju 6_{15} (unimportant clan); — 2. **helpless** (oft.) Ex 30_{15} 1S 2_8; — 3. **powerless** Ex 23_3, **insignificant**, small Je 5_4; — 4. **poor** Lv 14_{21} Je 39_{10}; — 5. oppressed, **dejected** 2S 13_4.

דלג: **qal**: pt. דּוֹלֵג: w. *ʿal* **jump** over Zp 1_9. †
piel: impf. יְדַלֵּג, אֲדַלֶּג־; pt. מְדַלֵּג: **jump** Is 35_6; over w. acc. Ps 18_{30} = 2S 22_{30}, w. *ʿal* SS 2_8. †

I **דָּלָה**: **qal**: pf. ד׳; impf. יִדְלֶנָּה, וַתִּדְלֶנָה; inf. abs. דָּלֹה: **draw** (water) Ex $2_{16\cdot19}$ Pr 20_5. †
piel: pf. דִּלִּיתָנִי: draw out, **save** (from the deep) Ps 30_2. †

II **דלה**: **qal**: pf. דַּלְיוּ: **dangle** Pr 26_7. †

I **דַּלָּה**: cs. דַּלַּת: — 1. **thrum** (warp-threads remaining on the loom after woven material is removed) Is 38_{12}; — 2. **unbound hair** SS 7_6. †

II **דַּלָּה**: cs. דַּלַּת, pl. דַּלּוֹת: coll. **the unimportant** (people), the poor population: w. *hāʾāreṣ* 2K 25_{12}, w. *hāʿām* Je 52_{15}.

דלח: **qal**: impf. תִּדְלַח, תִּדְלָחֵם: **trouble** (acc. waters) Ez $32_{2\cdot13}$. †

דְּלִי: du. sf. דָּלְיָו: **bucket** (for scooping, of leather, mouth kept open by two wooden crosspieces) Nu 24_7 Is 40_{15}. †

דְּלָיָה: n. pers.

דְּלָיָהוּ: n. pers.

דְּלִילָה: n. pers. f.

***דָּלִית**: pl. sf. דָּלִיּוֹתָיו: (leafy) **branch**, pl. **foliage** Je 11_{16}.

I **דלל**: **qal**: pf. דַּלּוֹתִי, דַּלּוֹתִי Ps 116_6, דָּלְלוּ, דַּלּוּנוּ; impf. יִדַּל: **be(come) small, unimportant** Ju 6_6 Ps 79_8.

II **דלל**: **qal**: pf. דַּלּוּ **dangle** (of miners, by a rope) Jb 28_4. †

דִּלְעָן: n. loc.

I **דלף**: **qal**: pf. דָּלְפָה; impf. יִדְלֹף: — 1. **leak** Ec 10_{18}; — 2. fill with tears, **weep** Jb 16_{20} Ps 119_{28}; oth.: refer to II. †

II **דלף**: **qal**: pf. דָּלְפָה: **be sleepless** Ps 119_{28}; ↗ I. †

דֶּלֶף: **leaky roof** Pr 19_{13} 27_{15}. †

דַּלְפוֹן: n. pers.

דלק: **qal**: pf. דְּלָקְנוּ, דָּלְקוּ, דָּלַקְתָּ; impf. יִדְלָק; inf. דְּלֹק; pt. דֹּלְקִים: — 1. **set on fire** Ob $_{18}$; — 2. **burn** (intrans.) Ps 7_{14}; metaph. of lips Pr 26_{23}; — 3. **hotly pursue** Ps 10_2 La 4_{19}, w. *ʾaḥarê* Gn 31_{36} 1S 17_{53}. †
hif.: impf. יַדְלִיקֵם; impv. הַדְלֵק: — 1. **kindle** (fire) Ez 24_{10}; — 2. metaph. **inflame** (of wine) Is 5_{11}. †

דַּלֶּקֶת: (heat of) **fever** Dt 28_{22}. †

דֶּלֶת (85×): דֶּלֶת, sf. דַּלְתּוֹ, דְּלָתֶךָ Is 26_{20} Qr; du. דְּלָתַיִם, דְּלָתָיִם, cs. דַּלְתֵי, sf. דְּלָתֶיךָ; pl. דְּלָתוֹת, cs. דַּלְתוֹת, sf. דַּלְתוֹתָיו; f.: I. sg.: — 1. **door**: of house Gn 19_6, room 2S 13_{17}; — 2. **leaf** (of a door) 1K 6_{34} Ez 41_{24}; — 3. **lid** (of chest) 2K 12_{10}; — 4. metaph. beloved as door SS 8_9; — 5. verbs: close *sāgar* 2K 4_4, *nāʿal* 2S 13_{17}; open *pātaḥ* 2K 4_4. II. pl. & du.: 6. a) **door, gate** of city Dt 3_5; b) *daltê* of a house Jos 2_{19}; c) doors variously defined (inner, upper) Ju 3_{23} 2C 4_{22}; d) of wood 1K 6_{31ff}, bronze Is 45_2; e) w. var. vbs.: *hiṣṣîb* set up Jos 6_{26}, *sāgar* close Ma 1_{10}; — 7. cosmic: *daltê šāmayim* Ps 78_{23}, *deˡlātayim* of the sea Jb 38_8; — 8. metaph. doors of my belly Jb 3_{10}, of his face (animal) Jb 41_6, of wisdom Pr 8_{34}; — 9. column of writing in a scroll Je 36_{23}.

דָּם (360×): cs. דַּם, sf. דָּמִי &c., דִּמְכֶם; pl. דָּמִים, cs. דְּמֵי, sf. דָּמָיו, דָּמֶיהָ, דְּמֵיהֶם: — 1. **blood** of man & animal Gn 9_6 1K 21_{19}; of new-born Ez 16_{22}, of menstruation Lv 15_{19}; as the seat of life Gn 9_4; *ʾākal ʿal-haddām* eat together w. the blood 1S 14_{32}, red as blood 2K 3_{22}; — 2. metaph. blood of grapes Gn 49_{11}; — 3. sacrifice of blood: *dam zebaḥ* Ex 23_{18}; so w. *ʿôlâ*, *ḥaṭṭāʾt* &c.; *nesek middām* drink-offering of blood Ps 16_4; phrases: *ṭābal baddām* dip in the blood Ex 12_{22} &c.; — 4. **blood shed by violence** Nu 35_{33}: a) w. *šāfak* shed, spill Gn 9_6;

b) *dām* (↗) *nāqî* innocent bloodshed Dt 19_{10}, *dām yēḥāšēb* be reckoned as bloodshed Lv 17_4; *ʿāmad ʿal dam*: come forward against s.one's life Lv 19_{16}; *bên dām ledām* (legal case) because of bloodshed (↗ *bayin* 1b) Dt 17_8; *haddām* blood-guilt Dt 21_8; *dāmô berōʾšô* let his blood come on his head Jos 2_{19}; *biqqēš dām miyyad* execute blood-vengeance on 2S 4_{11}; c) *bedām* bloodstained 1K 2_9; — 5. pl. *dāmîm*: (shed) **blood** Gn 4_{10}: a) *demê ṭohŏrâ* blood of purification (after childbirth) Lv 12_{4t}; *ḥatan dāmîm* Ex 4_{25t} ↗ *ḥātān* 2; b) **cruel deed, blood-guilt** 2S 21_1; *dāmāyw bô* Lv 20_9 *ʿālêkā dāmîm* Dt 19_{10}; *bāʾ bedāmîm* enter into blood-guilt 2S 25_{26}; *ʾîš dāmîm* murderer 2S 16_7; c) *demê milḥāmâ* blood shed in war 1K 2_5; *demê ḥinnām* blood shed unnecessarily 2_{31}.

I דָּמָה: **qal**: pf. דָּמוּ, דָּמִיתִי, דָּמְתָה, ד׳; impf. נִדְמֶה, יִדְמֶה; impv. דְּמֵה; pt. דֹּמֶה: — **be (a)like**: a) abs. Is 46_5; b) be like s.one, w. *le* Is 1_9, w. *ʾel* Ez 31_2; *demēh lekā le* do like SS 2_9 7_8; c) spec.: w. *ʾel* with regard to Ez 31_8.

nif.: pf. נִדְמֵיתָ: **become like** Ez 32_2 (oth.: III). †

piel: pf. דִּמִּיתִיךָ, דִּמִּינוּ, דִּמִּית, דִּמָּה; impf. תְּדַמְּיוּנִי, אֲדַמֶּה, תְּדַמִּי, יְדַמֶּה: — 1. a) **compare** Is 46_5, w. *ʾel* Is $40_{18.25}$; b) speak in parables Ho 12_{11} (:: oth.: III); — 2. a) think proper, plan, w. *le* against 2S 21_5, w. *le* & inf. Nu 33_{56}; b) w. *kēn* & *kaʾašer* **intend** Is 10_7 14_{24}; — 3. a) w. acc. **ponder** Ps 48_{10}; b) **imagine**, w. *le* & inf. Est 4_{13}.

hitp.: impf. אֶדַּמֶּה: w. *le* feel equal to s.one, **put onesf. on a par** w. Is 14_{14}. †

II דמה: **qal**: impf. תִּדְמֶינָה, תִּדְמֶה: — **come to rest, end** (of tears) Je 14_{17} La 3_{49}. †

nif.: pf. נִדְמֵיתִי, נִדְמֵיתָה, נִדְמְתָה, נִדְמָה, נִדְמוּ; inf. נִדְמֹה; pt. נִדְמֶה: — 1. **be dumb** Ps $49_{13.21}$ (cattle); — 2. **be silent** Je 47_5 (oth.: III); — 3. ? (pass. of caus.) be brought to silence, **have to be silent** Is 6_5 &c., ? ↗ III. †

III דמה: **qal**: pf. דָּמִיתִי: Ho 4_5 ?, destroy, or be destroyed, but txt. corr. †

nif.: pf. נִדְמֵיתִי, נִדְמֵיתָ(ה), נִדְמְתָה, נִדְמָה, נִדְמוּ; inf. נִדְמֹה: **be destroyed** (↗ II nif. 3. !) Is 6_5; cities, lands Is 15_1, king Ez 32_2.

[דֻּמָה: Ez 27_{32} כְּד׳ txt. corr.]

דְּמוּת: sf. דְּמוּתֵנוּ, דְּמוּתוֹ: — 1. **pattern** 2K 16_{10}; — 2. **form, shape** Gn 1_{26}; *demût* **something like** Ez 1_{26}; — 3. **image** (of God) Is 40_{18}, (of man) Ez 23_{15}.

דֳּמִי: **half** Is 38_{10}. †

דֳּמִי: **rest**, w. *nātan* & *le* Is 62_7; w. *ʾal*, no rest for you Is 62_6 Ps 83_2. †

דֻּמִיָּה Ps 22_3 39_3; ↗ דּוּמִיָּה.

דַּמִּים: אֶפֶס דַּ׳ 1S 17_1: ↗ פַּס דַּ׳.

*דִּמְיוֹן or *דִּמָּיוֹן: sf. דִּמְינוֹ: **similarity**, w. sf. he is like Ps 17_{12}. †

I דמם: **qal**: pf. דַּמּוּ; impf. תִּדְּמִי, וַיִּדֹּם, וְאֶדֹּם; יִדְּמוּ & נִדְּמָה; impv. דֹּמִּי, דֹּ(וֹ)ם, דֹּמּוּ: — 1. be motionless, **stand still** Jos 10_{12t} (sun); have rest Jb 30_{27}; — 2. **keep still** Lv 10_3 Am 5_{13}; — 3. **be motionless, rigid** Ex 15_{16} (like a stone), Je 48_2 (oth.: III).

II דמם: **qal**: pf. דַּמּוּ; impf. יִדְּמוּ (↗ I); impv. דֹּם, דֹּמּוּ: **wail, lament** Is 23_2, Ps 4_5 La 2_{10} (oth.: I 2). †

III דמם: **qal**: impf. תִּדְּמִי, נִדְּמָה (↗ I qal): be destroyed, **perish** Je 8_{14} 48_2 (oth.: II). †

nif.: pf. נָדַמּוּ; impf. יִדַּמּוּ, יִדֹּמוּ: **be devastated** (meadows) Je 25_{37}, **perish** 1S 2_9.

hif.: pf. הֲדִמָּנוּ: **let perish** Je 8_{14}. †

דְּמָמָה: **calm** (of wind), cessation of any strong air movement, Ps 107_{29}, Jb 4_{16}; *qôl demāmâ* humming stillness 1K 19_{12}. †

דֹּמֶן: **dung**, simile for bodies 2K 9_{37} Je 8_2.

[דִּמְנָה: n. loc. Jos 21_{35}, rd. ↗ III רִמּוֹן or *רִמּוֹנָה.]

דמע: **qal**: impf. תִּדְמַע; inf. דָּמֹעַ: **shed tears** Je 13_{17}. †

דֶּמַע: sf. דִּמְעֲךָ: **juice** (from your winevat) Ex 22_{28}; oth.: **best.** †

דִּמְעָה: cs. דִּמְעַת, sf. דִּמְעָתִי; pl. דְּמָעוֹת: sg. coll. **tears** 2K 20_{5}.

דַּמֶּשֶׂק: n. loc.: דַּמֶּשֶׂק; ƒ דּוּמֶּשֶׂק 2K 16_{10} & ƒ דַּרְמֶשֶׂק 1C 18_{5f} (5×): **Damascus.**

דְּמֶשֶׁק: וּבִדְ׳ עָרֶשׂ Am 3_{12}: trad. damask, but ƒ comm. †

דָּן: n. pers., terr.: loc. דָּנָה: **Dan**: — 1. n. pers., son of Jacob Gn 30_{6}; — 2. of tribe: Nu 1_{12}; gent. דָּנִי; — 3. n. loc. Ju 18_{29}.

דָּנִאֵל Ez $14_{14 \cdot 20}$ 28_{3}: ƒ דָּנִיֵּאל.

דַּנָּה: n. loc.

דִּנְהָבָה: n. loc.

דָּנִי: gntl. of דָּן 2.

דָּנִיֵּאל: n. pers. **Daniel.**

***דֵּעַ**: sf. דֵּעִי; pl. דֵּעִים: **knowledge** Jb 32_{6}.

דעה: **qal**: (forms cf. I יָדַע); impv. דְּעֵה Pr 24_{14}; inf. ƒ II דַּעַת: **seek, ask about** Ho 6_{3} Pr 10_{32} 29_{7}. †

דֵּעָה: pl. דֵּעוֹת: **wisdom** Is 28_{9}.

דְּעוּאֵל: n. pers.

דעך: **qal**: pf. דָּעֲכוּ; impf. יִדְעַךְ, יִדְעָךְ: **be extinguished** Is 43_{17}.

nif.: pf. נִדְעֲכוּ: be obliterated, **disappear** (watercourses) Jb 6_{17}. †

I **דַּעַת** (ca. 90×, Pr 40×): inf. of יָדַע: sf. דַּעְתּוֹ, דַּעְתְּךָ, דַּעְתָּם; verbal use Gn 2_{9} Je 22_{16}; — 1. a) general **knowledge** Pr 24_{4}, b) technical knowledge, **ability** Ex 31_{3}; — 2. **knowledge** about a thing: *biblî daʿat* unwittingly Dt 4_{42}; *daʿat rûaḥ* 'windy,' idle knowledge Jb 15_{2}; — 3. **knowledge** (of) (= acquaintance with): a) of God Nu 24_{16}; b) of good & evil Gn $2_{9 \cdot 17}$; c) in gen'l Is 11_{2}; — 4. **insight**: *mibbelî daʿat* w/o insight Is 5_{13}.

II ***דַּעַת**: דָּעַת: **claim** Pr 29_{7}. †

III ***דַּעַת**: sf. דַּעְתּוֹ: **sweat** Is 53_{11}. †

***דֳּפִי**: דָּפִי: **stain,** fault Ps 50_{20}. †

דפק **qal**: pf. דְּפָקוּם; pt. דּוֹפֵק: — 1. **drive** (small cattle) **hard** Gn 33_{13}; — 2. abs. **knock** (at door) SS 5_{2}. †

hitp.: pt. מִתְדַּפְּקִים: **push each other** Ju 19_{22}. †

דָּפְקָה: n. loc.

דַּק: דַּק, דַּק; f. דַּקָּה, pl. דַּקּוֹת: **thin**: — 1. **scanty**: hair Lv 13_{30}, beard of grain Gn 41_{6f}; — 2. **fine**: hoarfrost Ex 16_{14}, dust Is 29_{5}; — 3. **lean**: cows Gn 41_{3f}; Lv 21_{20}: some trad. with cataract, oth. consumptive or dwarfed; — 4. **soft** (quiet) *demāmâ* 1K 9_{12}.

דֹּק: s.thg thin, **veil? gauze?** Is 40_{22}. †

דִּקְלָה: n. pers.

דקק: **qal**: pf. דַּק, דָּק; impf. תָּדֹק, יְדוּקֶנּוּ: — 1. **crush**: grain Is 28_{28}, mountains 41_{15}; — 2. abs., **be ground fine** Ex 32_{20} Dt 9_{21}. †

hif.: pf. הֵדַק, הֵדַקּוֹת; impf. וַיָּדֶק, אֲדִקֵּם; inf. הָדֵק: — 1. **crush fine** 2K 23_{6}; reinforcing: Ex 30_{36} (*hādēq*); — 2. metaph. peoples 2S 22_{43}.

hof.: impf. יוּדַק: **be crushed fine** Is 28_{28}. †

דקר: **qal**: pf. דְּקָרוּ, דְּקָרֻהוּ, דְּקָרֻנִי; impf. יִדְקֹר, יִדְקְרֵהוּ; impv. דָּקְרֵנִי: **pierce** 1S 31_{4}.

nif.: impf. יִדָּקֵר: **be pierced** Is 13_{15}. †

pual: pt. מְדֻקָּרִים: **pierced** Je 37_{10} 51_{4}. †

דֶּקֶר: n. pers.

דַּר: trad. mother-of-pearl: a costly flooring in Pers. king's palace Est 1_{6}. †

דֹּר: ƒ דּוֹר, דֹּאר.

דֵּרָאוֹן: cs. דִּרְאוֹן: **abhorrence** Is 66_{24} Dn 12_{2}. †

דָּרְבָן: pl. דָּרְבֹנוֹת: — **ox-goad,** iron-tip of a pole w. which one drives cattle fm. behind, 1S 13_{21}; metaph. Ec 12_{11}. †

דַּרְדַּע: n. pers.

דַּרְדַּר: subspecies of *Centaurea pallescens*: a sort of **thistle** Gn 3_{18} Ho 10_{8}. †

דָּרוֹם: alw. הַדּ׳ exc. for Dt 33_{23}: — 1. **south** Dt 33_{23}; — 2. **south wind** Ez 42_{18}.

I **דְּרוֹר**: **kind of bird,** trad. swallow or dove Ps 84_{4} Pr 26_{2}. †

II **דְּרוֹר**: מָר־דְּ׳ lumps of myrrh, **myrrh-oil,** granulated stiff drops of myrrh, viscid oil for anointing Ex 30_{23}. †

III דְּרוֹר: **emancipation** of slaves in sabbath-year Lv 25_{10} Je 34_{8ff}; of prisoners Is 61_1.

דָּרְיָוֶשׁ: n. pers.: **Darius.**

דָּרַךְ: **qal**: pf. ד׳, דָּרְכָה, דָּרַכְתָּ; impf. יִדְרֹךְ, יִדְרְכוּן, תִּדְרְכִי; pt. דֹּרְכִים, דֹּרְכֵי, pass. דְּרֻכוֹת, דְּרוּכָה: — 1. **tread**, w. b^e on Dt 1_{36}, w. *ʿal* 1S 5_5; w. *ʾōraḥ* tread a path Jb 22_{15}; abs. come forth Nu 24_{17}; — 2. *dārak qešet* **draw** the bow Is 5_{28}, metaph. *dārak hallāšôn* Je 9_2 = lie; — 3. **tread** (wine, oil), **press**: w. *ʿanābîm* Am 9_{13}, *yayin* Is 16_{10}, *zayit* Mi 6_{15}; w. *gat* La 1_{15}; abs. Ju 9_{27}.

hif.: pf. הִדְרִיךְ, הִדְרִיכָה, הִדְרַכְתִּיךְ; impf. יַדְרֵךְ, וַיַּדְרִיכֵם, יַדְרְכֵנִי; impv. הַדְרִיכֵנִי; pt. מַדְרִיכֲךָ Is 48_{17}: — 1. **stamp firm** (threshing floor) Je 51_{33}, (path) Jb 28_8; — 2. w. acc. & b^e **let** s.one **tread** on s.thg Is 42_{16}, **let walk** Hb 3_{19}, let walk through Is 11_{15}; metaph. in fidelity Ps 25_5; — 3. **overtake** Ju 20_{43}.

דֶּרֶךְ (710×): דֶּרֶךְ, sf. דַּרְכּוֹ; dual דְּרָכַיִם Pr $28_{6.18}$; pl. דְּרָכִים, דַּרְכֵי, sf. דְּרָכָיו (דְּרָכָו 1S 8_3 + 3×), דְּרָכֶךָ, דַּרְכֵיהֶם; בְּהַדֶּרֶךְ Ne 9_{19}; sg. f., also m. (1S 21_6), pl. alw. m.: stretch of land which has become a path (*ʾōraḥ*) by being frequented, :: *m^e sillâ* 'highway': — 1. **way, path**: to tree Gn 3_{24}; *b^e derek* underway 2K 10_{12}; *badderek badderek* only on the road Dt 2_{27}, *ʿal-hadderek* on the way Gn 38_{21}; *hālak derek* walk a path Gn 28_{20}, *ʿāśâ darkô* go one's way Ju 17_8, *hēkîn derek* prepare/maintain road (oth.: measure off) Dt 19_3; *derek hāʿîr* in the direction of the city 1K 8_{44}, *derek hayyām* toward the sea, westward 18_{43}; *derek hammelek* the old commercial road betw. Damascus & Aqaba Nu 20_{17} 21_{22}, *derek hayyām* Is 8_{23} the Damascus-Gaza road; — 2. stretch of road: *derek š^e lōšet yāmîm* distance of 3 days' journey Gn 30_{36}; — 3. **journey**: a) *derek r^e ḥōqâ* long journey, *ladderek* for the journey; b) **undertaking, business** 2C 13_{22}, errand Gn 24_{21}, campaign 1S 15_{18}, pilgrimage Am 8_{14}; — 4. way = **manner, custom, conduct**: *derek kol-hāʾāreṣ* as is the custom in the whole world Gn 19_{31}, *derek nāšîm lî* way of women is upon me (= menstrual period) 31_{35}; *derek yārobʿām* Jerob.'s conduct 1K 16_{26}; *derek šālôm* way of peace Is 59_8; — 5. pl. theol.: a) God's **way of behavior** Dt 32_4, **activity** Pr 8_{22}; b) the **behavior demanded** by God: sg. *derek yhwh* Gn 18_{19}, pl. *darkê yhwh* 1K 2_3; c) *derek haḥayyîm* Je 21_8, *derek ʿôlām* Ps 139_{24}; — 6. **situation**: *darkî* Is 40_{27}; *lāʾādām darkô* men have their ultimate situation in their hands Je 10_{23}; — 7. ? **strength, might**: ? Je 3_{13}, Ho 10_{13}, Ps 138_{5b} Pr 31_3.

דַּרְכְּמ(וֹ)נִים: pl.; sg. not *דַּרְכְּמוֹן but *דַּרְכָּם or דַּרְכְּמָה: **drachma** Ezr 2_{69} Ne 7_{69-71}. †

דַּרְמֶשֶׂק, דַּרְמֶשֶׂק: n. loc. **Damascus.**

[דָּרַע: n. pers.; 1C 2_6: rd. ⟹ דַּרְדַּע. †]

דַּרְקוֹן: n. pers.

דָּרַשׁ: **qal**: pf. ד׳, דָּרַשְׁתִּי, דָּרְשׁוּ, דְּרָשָׁהוּ, דְּרַשְׁנֻהוּ, דְּרָשׁוּם; impf. יִדְרֹשׁ, אֶדְרְשָׁה, יִדְרְשֵׁהוּ, נִדְרְשָׁה, נִדְרוֹשׁ, יִדְרְשׁוּן, יִדְרְשֵׁהוּ, תִּדְרְשֶׁנּוּ, תִּדְרְשֵׁנִי; impv. דְּרָשׁ־נָא, דִּרְשׁוּ(נִי); inf. דָּרוֹשׁ, דְּרֹשׁ, לִדְרוֹשׁ, לִדְרָשׁ־; pt. דֹּ(וֹ)רֵשׁ, דֹּרְשֵׁי, דֹּרְשָׁיו, pass. דְּרוּשָׁה, דְּרוּשִׁים: — 1. w. acc. inquire about, **care about** (s.one or s.thg): person Je 30_{14}, strayed animal Dt 22_2, land Dt 11_{12}; study & expound Ezr 7_{10}; *d^e rûšîm* worth investigating (oth.: investigated, God's works) Ps 111_2; — 2. w. l^e, **inquire about** s.one: 2S 11_3, *l^e nefeš* Ps 142_5; *lēʾlōhîm* **worship** Ezr 4_2, *l^e yhwh* 6_{21}, *labb^e ʿālîm* 2C 17_3; — 3. **examine, inquire** (into s.thg) Dt 13_{15}; — 4. w. acc. **demand** (s.one's blood, life) Gn 9_5; call to account Ps $10_{4.13}$ 2C 24_{22}, w. *mēʿim* Dt 18_{19}, *rešaʿ* for misdeed Ps 10_{15}; w. *ʿal* punish 2C 24_6; — 5. **seek** Ju 6_{29} Am 5_{14};

— 6. w. acc. **be intent on s.thg**, consider: *(hā)rā‘â* Ps 38_{13}, *šālôm* Dt 23_{7}, *mišpāṭ* Is 1_{17}; — 7. **turn** (in petition) **to Y.** (45 ×): w. acc. Gn 25_{22}; *dōrᵉšê yhwh* Ps 34_{11}, w. *’el yhwh* Dt 12_{5}; — 8. **question**: w. *mē’ēt* 1K 22_{7}, w. *mē‘im* 1K 14_{5}, w. *bᵉ* Ez 14_{7}; — 9. **seek a word from Y.**: *dāraš dᵉbar yhwh* 1K 22_{5}, *bidbar y.* (w. *mē’ēt* fm. the prophet) 2K 3_{11}.

nif.: pf. נִדְרַשְׁתִּי, נִדְרְשׁוּ; impf. אִדָּרֵשׁ; inf. אִדָּרֹשׁ: — 1. **be sought** (blood, ꟻ qal 4) Gn 42_{22}; — 2. **let onesf. be sought** (God) Is 65_{1}.

דשא: **qal**: pf. דָּשְׁאוּ: **be green** (pastures) Jl 2_{22}. †

hif.: impf. juss. תַּדְשֵׁא: **let sprout** Gn 1_{11}. †

דֶּשֶׁא: **new fresh grass** after rain 2S 23_{4}; some say distinguished fm. both *‘ēśeb* & *‘ēṣ*, i.e. vegetation of which only the upper side is visible, Gn 1_{11f}; oth.: larger category, incl. *‘ēśeb* & *‘ēṣ* greenness, vegetation.

דָּשֵׁן: **qal**: pf. ’דּ: **become fat** Dt 31_{20}. †

piel: pf. דִּשַּׁנְתָּ, דִּשְּׁנוּ; impf. יְדַשְּׁנֶה Ps 20_{4}, תְּדַשֶּׁן־; inf. וּלְדַשְּׁנוֹ Ex 27_{3}: — 1. **revive** Ps 23_{5}; — 2. **clean** (s.thg) **of fatty ashes** Ex 27_{3}; — 3. consider the *‘ôlâ* as ‘fat,’ **accept**.

pual: impf. יְדֻשָּׁן: **be made fat** Is 34_{7}.

hotpa‘al: pf. הֻדַּשְּׁנָה: **drip** (w. fat) Is 34_{6}. †

דֶּשֶׁן: דֶּשֶׁן, sf. דִּשְׁנִי: — 1. **fat**: of olive Ju 9_{9}, = food & drink Is 55_{2}; — 2. **fatty ashes** (wood ashes & fat fm. the altar) 1K $13_{3.5}$.

דָּשֵׁן: דְּשֵׁנִים: **fat, juicy** Is 30_{23} Ps 92_{15}. †

דָּת: sf. דָּתוֹ; pl. דָּתֵי, דָּתֵיהֶם: — 1. **regulation** w. *kᵉ* Est 1_{8}; *dāt hannāšîm* regulation in force for the women 2_{12}; — 2. **law** Est 1_{19} Ezr 8_{36}.

דָּתָן: n. pers.

דֹּתָן & *דֹּתַיִן, loc. דֹּתַיְנָה: n. loc.

ה

הַ: w. *dageš forte* &c. ꟻ gramm., def. art., **the**: I: — 1. in older & poet. Heb., oft. omitted, *šāmayim* & *’ereṣ* Is 1_{2}; art. then had **demonstr.** mng.: *hayyôm*, the day there, today Gn 4_{14}, *happa‘am* this time; — 2. rarely,, before fin. vb., introducing **rel. clause** *hehālᵉkû* who went Jos 10_{24}; — 3. before pt., as **appos.**: *hannōtēn* who gives Gn 49_{21}.

II. **def. art.**: — 1. individually, w. **known** noun: *hā‘îr* the (already mentioned) city Gn 11_{5}; — 2. w. **voc.**: *hammelek* (O) king! 1S 24_{9}; — 3. w. proper nouns, spec. *hayyardēn, hakkarmel, hallᵉbānôn, haśśāṭān*; — 4. indicates the spec. **category**: *kābēd bammiqneh* rich in cattle Gn 13_{2}; spec. category of men: *haṣṣādîq* the righteous (coll.) Ec 3_{17}; *hārō‘eh* the shepherd(s) (coll.) > a shepherd; — 5. in comparison: *kammōṣ* like chaff Ps 1_{4}; lacking when comparison is more spec. described: *kᵉqēn mᵉšullaḥ* Is 16_{2}; — 6. w. **abstracts**: *baṣṣāmā’* w. thirst Is 41_{17}.

הֲ, הַ, הֶ: interr. word, wh. may, however, be omitted; alw. proclitic (exc. Dt 32_{6}), before first word of qn.; forms: הֲרָצַחְתָּ, הֲנֵלֵךְ :: הַלְבֶן, הַאֵל :: הַמְכַסֶּה, הַיְדַעְתֶּם, הַאֵלֵךְ, הֶאָנֹכִי, הֶחֳדַלְתִּי, הֶהָמֵת :: הַרְאִיתֶם: — 1. simple qn.: a) w. **answer ‘no’**: *hᵃšōmēr ’āḥî ’ānōkî* am I ... ? Gn 4_{9}, repeated *hᵃ* ... *hᵃlō’* Ps 94_{9f}; b) w. **answer ‘yes’**: *hamṣā’tanî* 1K 21_{20}; c) **rhetorical** *hᵃkî ’āḥî ’attâ* you are of course ... Gn 29_{15}; — 2. **double qn.**: a) *ha‘ôlâ* ... *hayōredet* is he the one who (cj)

Ec 3_{21}; b) *hᵃ* … *ʾim* Je 2_{14}; *hᵃ* … *ʾô* Ec 2_{19}; — 3. dependent qn., = **whether**: w. *rāʾâ* Gn 8_8.

הֵא: interj.: **there! see!** Gn 47_{23}.

הֶאָח: interj.: **aha!** — 1. expr. of joy Is 44_{16}; — 2. of malicious joy Ez 25_3; — 3. cry of horse eager for battle Jb 39_{25}.

I **הַב**: impv. הָבָה, Gn 29_{21} הָבָה before א, הָבָה־לִּי & הָבָה־נָּא, הָבִי, הָבוּ w. uncertain stress; — 1. impv. **give** Gn 29_{21}; *hab hab* Pr 30_{15}; f. Ru 3_{15}; pl. Gn 47_{16}; *hābû lākem* provide Dt 1_{13}; — 2. interj. *hābâ* **come on!** w. 1 sg. Gn 38_{16}, w. coh. pl. Gn $11_{3f.7}$.

II *__הַב__ elephant (?), ⟶ שֶׁנְהַבִּים.

*__הַבְהַב__: זִבְחֵי הַבְהָבַי Ho 8_{13} uncert., cj. זְבָחִים אָהֵבוּ.

[**הֵבוּ** Ho 4_{18}: uncert., cj. אָהוֹב אָהֲבוּ.]

הבל: qal: impf. תֶּהְבָּלוּ, יֶהְבָּלוּ: — 1. **become** *hebel* (i.e. empty, void) 2K 17_{15} Je 2_5; — 2. **speak, carry on what is empty, void** Jb 27_{12}, trust in what is empty Ps 62_{11}.

hif.: pt. מַהְבִּלִים: make void, **delude** Je 23_{16}. †

I **הֶבֶל** (70×, 35× Ec): הֲבֵל, cs. only in הֲבֵל הֲבָלִים, sf. הֶבְלוֹ, הֶבְלֶךָ; pl. הֲבָלִים, הַבְלֵי, הַבְלֵיהֶם: — 1. (transitory) **breath** Is 57_{13}; — 2. > **nothingness, perishableness**: Ec 1_2; **void** Je $10_{3.15}$; *hᵃbēl hᵃbālîm* complete nothingness Ec 1_2; *ḥayyê heblô* his empty life 6_{12}; *hābal hebel* speak, carry on what is empty Jb 27_{12}; adv. *hebel* for what is empty Jb 35_{16}; — 3. *hebel, hᵃbālîm* nothings, **idols**: *hālak ʾaḥᵃrê hebel* 2K 17_{15}.

II **הֶבֶל**: n. pers. **Abel** Gn 4_{2ff}.

הָבְנִים: **ebony**, *Diospyros mespiliformis* Ez 27_{15}. †

הבר: **qal**: pt. הֹבְרֵי Is 47_{13} Qr (Kt הָבְרוּ): those who classify (the heavens, for astrology), **astrologer**. †

הֵגֶא: n. pers.

I **הגה**: **qal**: pf. הָגִיתָ; impf. תֶּהְגֶּה, יֶהְגּוּ; inf. הָגֹה: mutter; — 1. animals: a) **coo** (of dove) Is 38_{14}; b) **growl** (of lion) Is 31_4; — 2. men: a) emit a sound Ps 115_7; b) moan, w. *lᵉ* for Is 16_7, w. *ʾel* Je 48_{31}; c) **read in an undertone** Ps 1_2; d) **ponder (by talking to onesf.)** w. acc. Is 33_{18}, w. *bᵉ* Ps 63_7; e) **plan** w. acc. Ps 2_1; f) **speak**, proclaim Is 59_3.

hif.: pt. מַהְגִּים: **mutter** Is 8_{19}. †

II **הָגָה**: **qal**: pf. ה׳; inf. הָגוֹ: **separate** (impurities fm. silver) Pr 25_4; metaph. **remove** 25_5; drive away Is 27_8.

הֶגֶה: **groan** (oth.: thought) Ps 90_9, groaning Ez 2_{10}, rumbling (of thunder) Jb 37_2. †

הָגוּת: **thinking, planning** Ps 49_4.

הֵגַי: n. pers.

*__הָגִיג__: sf. הֲגִיגִי: **groaning** (in prayer) Ps 5_2 39_4. †

הִגָּיוֹן: cs. הֶגְיוֹן, sf. הֶגְיוֹנָם: — 1. **talk** (or mockery) La 3_{62}; — 2. **thinking, planning** Ps 19_{15}; — 3. sounding, **playing** (of zither) Ps 92_4; unexpl. tech. mus. term Ps 9_{17}. †

[**הֲגִינָה** Ez 42_{12}: ⟶ גִּינָה.]

הָגָר: n. pers. f.: **Hagar**.

הַגְרִי: n. peop., gntl. of הָגָר.

הֵד: Ez 7_7; (usual cj. הֵ(י)דָד): **thunderclap** (?). †

הֲדַד: n. pers.: **Hadad**.

הֲדַדְעֶזֶר: n. pers.: **Hadadezer**.

הֲדַד־רִמּוֹן: n. loc.

הָדָה: **qal**: pf. ה׳, w. *yād* stretch out hand Is 11_8. †

הֹדּוּ: Pers. satrapy of **India**: Est 1_1 8_9. †

הֲדוּרִים Is 45_2: cj. *הֲרָרִים (so now 1Q Isᵃ): mountainous land. †

I **הֲדוֹרָם**: n. peop. Gn 10_{27} 1C 1_{21}.

II **הֲדוֹרָם**: n. pers.

הִדַּי: n. pers.

הֹדַוְיָהוּ 1C 3_{24}: ⟶ הוֹדַוְיָהוּ.

הדך: **qal**: impv. הֲדֹךְ: **tread down** Jb 40_{12}. †

*__הֲדֹם__: cs. =: **footstool**, alw. w. *raglayim*: — 1. of God: earth Is 66_1, ark Ps 99_5, **Zion**

La 2_1; — 2. of king Ps 110_1 (i.e. enemy).

הֲדַס: הֲדַס; pl. הֲדַסִּים: **myrtle**, *Myrtus communis* Is 41_{19}.

הֲדַסָּה: n. pers. f., alternate name of Esther: Est 2_7. †

הדף: **qal**: pf. הֲדָפוֹ, הֲדַפְתִּיךָ; impf. יֶהְדֹּף, יֶהְדָּפֶנּוּ, יֶהְדָּפֵם, תֶּהְדְּפוּ; impv. הֲדֹף, הָדְפָה: **shove**, w. acc.: Nu $35_{20.22}$, shove away Ez 34_{21}, drive away 2K 4_{27}.

הדר: **qal**: pf. הָדַרְתָּ; impf. תֶּהְדַּר; pt. pass. הָדוּר: **treat w. distinction** Lv $19_{15.32}$; favor (?) Ex 23_3; pt. pass. w. b^e Is 63_1.

nif.: pf. נֶהְדָּרוּ: **be honored** La 5_{12}. †

hitp.: impf. תִּתְהַדַּר: **give onesf. airs** Pr 25_6.

הֲדַר: n. pers.

הָדָר: cs. הֲדַר, הֶדֶר Da 11_{20}, sf. הֲדָרְךָ, הֲדָרֵךְ; pl. cs. הַדְרֵי: the soul in its highest manifestation of power: — 1. **ornament, attire, splendor**, a) in nature: of Carmel Is 35_2, *p^erî ʿēṣ hādār* Lv 23_{40}; b) in man: Ps 8_6; — 2. **God's glory, grandeur**: *hôd w^ehādār* Ps 96_6; Y. is *hādār* Ps 149_9, has *hādār* Ps 29_4; — 3. *hādār* **of king** Ps 21_6; *hadrê qōdeš* royal robes Ps 110_3; of tribe of Joseph Dt 33_{17}, of a city Is 5_{14}.

***הֲדָרָה**: cs. הַדְרַת: — 1. **attire**, *hadrat qōdeš* Ps 29_2; — 2. **grandeur** of king Pr 14_{28}.

הָהּ: interj.: **alas!** Ez 30_2. †

הוֹ: interj.: **alas!**, doubling for emphasis Am 5_{16}. †

הוּא: f. הִיא; pl. m. הֵם, הֵמָּה, f. הֵנָּה; for sf. forms, Qr-Kt problem, ↗ gramm.: — 1. pron. 3rd sg. **he, she, it, they**, *hû' w^e'ištô* he & his wife Gn 13_1; — 2. demonstr. pron. **that**: a) *hû' yām hammelaḥ* that is ... Gn 14_3; introduces glosses Gn $2_{11\text{-}13}$; b) *hû' 'ašer dibber* that is what Y. said Lv 10_3; — 3. summarizing: *hû' ḥayyéka* that constitutes life Dt 30_{20}; — 4. *hû'* emphasizes the subj. *hû' hahōlēk* it is he who goes Gn 2_{14}; oft. w. numbers, *š^etayim hēnnâ* the two Is 51_{19}; — 5. as subj. w. interr.: *mâ hî'* what is that? Gn 23_{15}, *mî hû' zeh* who is it? Ps 24_{10}; — 6. in appos., restrictive: *hallēwî hû'* only the Levite Nu 18_{23}; — 7. preceding the noun, **precisely**, or the like: *hû' hallaylâ hazzeh* this very night Ex 12_{42}; — 8. w. pron., expresses identity: *'anî hû'* it is I Is 52_6; — 9. **the same**: *šām hû'* there it is the same Jb 3_{19}; — 10. *hahû'*, *hahî'* w. nouns, **that** (adj.), *hā'îš hahû'* Jb 1_1; — 11. as 'copula,' *ṣaddîq hû' yhwh* Y. is righteous La 1_{18}; — 12. in n. pers. as confession, ↗ *'abîhû'*, *'elîhû(')*.

הֱוֵא Jb 37_6: ↗ I הוה.

I **הוֹד**: sf. הוֹדוֹ: weight, power, splendor, **height**, majesty; possessed by: — 1. in nature: thunder Is 30_{30}, snorting horse Jb 39_{20}, olive-tree Ho 14_7; — 2. God Ps 8_2; — 3. men: king Ps 21_6, Messiah Zc 6_{13}, Moses Nu 27_{20}; complexion Dn 10_8; metaph., bloom Pr 5_9.

II **הוֹד**: n. pers. 1C 7_{37}. †

הוֹדְוָה: n. pers.

הוֹדַוְיָה: n. pers.

הוֹדַוְיָהוּ: n. pers.

הוֹדִיָּה: n. pers.

הוֹדִיָּה: n. pers.

I **הוה**: **qal**: impv. הֱוֵא (= הֱוֵה): — **fall** (of snow) Jb 37_6. †

II **הוה**: **qal**: impf. יְהוּא Ec 11_3 = יְהוּ **juss.**; impv. הֱוֵה, f. הֱוִי; pt. הֹוֶה: — 1. **become** Gn 27_{29} Is 16_4, w. l^e Ne 6_6; fall to s.one's share Ec 2_{22}; — 2. **lie** (stay) Ec 11_3. †

I **הַוָּה**: cs. הַוַּת: — 1. (arbitrary) **choice** Mi 7_3; — 2. **greed** Pr 10_3. †

II **הַוָּה**: sf. הַוָּתִי Jb 6_2 Qr, 30_{13} Qr; pl. הַוּ(ו)ֹת: — 1. sg. **ruin** Jb 30_{13}, misery 6_2; — 2. pl. a) **ruin** Ps 5_{10}; b) **threats** Ps 38_{13}.

הֹוָה: **disaster** Is 47_{11} Ez 7_{26}. †

הוֹהָם: n. pers.

הוֹי: interj.: **alas! woe!**: — 1. in lament 1K 13_{30}; — 2. in prophetic threat a) w. pt. or adj. Am 5_{18}, b) w. voc. Is 1_4, c) w. *ʿal* Je 48_1, w. *le* Ex 13_{18}; d) abs. Is 1_{24}; — 3. encouraging, inciting, **ho!** Is 18_1, doubled Zc 2_{10}.

הוֹלֵלוֹת: **folly, delusion** Ec 1_{17}.

הוֹלֵלוּת: **folly, delusion** Ec 10_{13}. †

הוֹלֵם: Is 41_7, ↗ הלם pt. †

הום: **qal**: pf. sf. הָמָם: **throw into confusion** Dt 7_{23}. †

nif.: impf. וַתֵּהֹם: **be in an uproar** 1S 4_5 1K 1_{45} Rt 1_{19}. †

[**hif.**: תְּהִימֶנָה Mi 2_{12}, אָהִימָה Ps 55_3 txts. corr., ↗ comm.]

הוֹמָם: n. pers.

הון: **hif.**: impf. וַתָּהִינוּ: consider easy, risk Dt 1_{41}. †

הוֹן: sf. הוֹנוֹ, pl. sf. הוֹנַיִךְ: — 1. **wealth**, possessions Ps 44_{13}; — 2. sufficiency, adv. **enough!** Pr 30_{15f}.

הוֹשָׁמָע: n. pers.

הוֹשֵׁעַ: n. pers.: **Hosea**.

הוֹשַׁעְיָה: n. pers.

***הות**: **pol.**: impf. תְּהוֹתְתוּ: w. *ʿal*: **attack** (violently), assail Ps 62_4. †

הוֹתִיר: n. pers.

הזה: **qal**: pt. הֹזִים: **pant** in sleep (dogs) Is 56_{10}. †

הִי: interj.: **woe!** Ez 2_{10}. †

הִיא: pron. 3 f. sg., ↗ הוּא.

הֵידָד: — 1. **shout** Is 16_{10}; — 2. metaph. **war-cry** of enemy Is 16_9.

הֻיְּדוֹת: most rd. הוֹדוֹת, hif. inf. ידה, or הוּדָיוֹת, pl. of הוּדָיָה **song of thanksgiving, of praise**: Ne 12_8. †

הָיָה (ca. 3750×): ↗ II הָוָה: **qal**: pf. הָיְתָה, ה׳, הָיָתָה, 2K 9_{37} Kt הָיַת, הָיִ(י)תָ(ה), הָיִיתִי 2 f. Ez 16_{31} Kt, 1 sg., וְהָיָה Jos 15_4 + 3× = Qr וְהָיוּ, Kt וְהָיָה (3 pl. f. ?), הֱיִיתֶם, וִהְיִ(י)תֶם, הָיִינוּ; impf. יִהְיֶה, תִּהְיֶה Je 17_{17}, יְהִי, יֶהִי, יִהְיוּ, וָאֱהִי, וָאֶהְיֶה, אֶהְיֶה; יֶהִי, וַיְהִי, וַיִּהְיוּ, וַנִּהְיֶה; תִּהְיֶין, תִּהְיֶ(י)ןָ, תִּהְיֶ(י)נָה, תִּהְיוּ, impv. הֱיֵה, וֶהְיֵה, הֲיִי, הֱיוּ; inf. הֱיוֹת (הֱיֵה Ez 21_{15} ↗ comm.), הֱיוֹתִי, מִהְיוֹת, בִּ/לִהְיוֹ(ו)ת, לִהְיֹתְךָ, מִהְיוֹתָם, abs. הָיֹה, הָיוֹ; pt. הוֹיָה: — 1. **become, take place**: *hāyâ ʿereb* it became evening Gn 1_5, *hāyâ gešem* rain fell Je 14_4, *tihyeh rāʿâ* disaster happens Am 3_6, *hāyâ môrāʾ ʿal* fear comes over Gn 9_2, *hāyâ/wayhî debar-yhwh ʾel* came to Je 1_{11} & oft.; — 2. esp. **happen**: a) *wayhî kēn* and so it happened Gn 1_7 (cf. c)), *lōʾ tihyeh* it will not happen Is 7_7; b) *wehāyâ* and it will happen = 'and then': *wehāyâ … weʾāmartî* and then I shall say Gn 24_{43}; pers. of vb. *hāyâ* same as following vb.: *hāyîtî … ʾakālanî* Gn 31_{40}; c) *wayhî* and it happened = 'and then': *wayhî … wayyābōʾ* Gn 39_{11}; *wayhî haššemeš lābōʾ* when the sun was about to set Gn 15_{12} :: *wayhî … bāʾâ* when … had set 15_{17}; *wayhî kebōʾ* as he came Gn 12_{14}; so *wayhî* becomes the formal sign of consecutive narration: *wayhî kî* and when Gn 27_1, and because Ex 1_{21}; *wayhî* (at the very beginning) Ez 1_1 Ru 1_1 Est 1_1; — 3. **be, become**: a) be, exist 1S 14_{25}; *ʾîš hāyâ* there was a man Jb 1_1; b) stay, live Je 1_3; c) introducing pred. noun or adj.: *hāyâ ʿārûm* was clever Gn 3_1, *heyîtem gērîm* Ex 23_9, *meh-hāyâ haddābār* how has the thing gone? 2S 1_4; *ʾehyeh ʾašer ʾehyeh* I shall be who I shall turn out to be Ex 3_{14}; d) w. pt. esp. for continued or repeated action: *hāyâ maʿaleh* he was offering 1S 7_{10}; w. inf. for continued action: *hāyû hālôk wehāsôr* went on diminishing Gn 8_5 (↗ *hlk* 4); — 4. from 3 c) & d) develops the usage as **copula**: *hāʾāreṣ hāyetâ tōhû wābōhû* Gn 1_2; — 5. follow s.one: *hāyâ* w. *ʾaḥarê* 2S 2_{10}, w. *le* be for s.one = on s.one's side Ps 124_1; — 6. *hāyâ be* be (present) in Ex 1_5, stay 24_{18}, come against 1S 5_9; — 7. *hāyâ le* a) **serve as** Gn 1_{29}; b) **have**: *yihyeh lekā* you shall have Ex 20_3, w. *ʾet* before subj. Nu 5_{10}, *hāyâ leʾîš* belong to s.one (as a wife) Je 3_1; **become**:

lᵉnefeš ḥayyâ Gn 2$_{7}$; amount to 1S 13$_{21}$; d) **fall to s.one's share**, i.e. that s.one receives s.thg Jos 11$_{20}$, happen (to s.one) Ex 32$_{1}$; *wayhî dᵉbar* ... *lᵉ* the word went forth, came, to 1S 4$_{1}$; — 8. *hāyâ ʿim* be with s.one, at s.one's house Dt 22$_{2}$, sexually Gn 39$_{10}$; *hāyâ ʿim lᵉbābô* he had in mind 1K 8$_{17}$; — 9. *hāyâ ʿal* be (found) on Gn 9$_{2}$; (in hostility) push back 2S 11$_{23}$; — 10. var.: *hāyâ min* excel Ez 15$_{2}$ :: appertain to Ex 12$_{4}$; *hāyā* w. number, amount to Ex 1$_{5}$; w. *ʿad* (territory) reach to Jos 19$_{10}$.

nif.: pf. נִהְיֵיתָ, נִהְיְתָה, נִהְיָתָה, נִהְיָה; pt. נִהְיָה: — 1. **be** Zc 8$_{10}$; — 2. a) **happen, occur** Ex 11$_{6}$; *nihyâ mē'ēt* went out from 1K 12$_{24}$; b) have taken place Ez 21$_{12}$; *ta'ᵃwâ nihwâ* fulfilled desire Pr 13$_{19}$; — 3. wear out, **be gone**: *nihyêtî* I am done for Dn 8$_{27}$, flee 2$_{1}$.

***הַיָּה**: הַיָּתִי Jb 6$_{2}$: ƒ II הַוָּה.

הֵיךְ: **how** Dn 10$_{17}$ 1C 13$_{12}$. †

הֵיכָל (78×), הַהֵיכָל, cs. הֵיכַל, sf. הֵיכָלֶךָ; pl. הֵיכָלוֹת, הֵיכְלֵי, הֵיכְלֵיכֶם; — 1. **palace**, a) earthly: of Ahab 1K 21$_{1}$, of king of Babylon 2K 20$_{18}$; b) Y's heavenly palace Mi 1$_{2}$; — 2. **temple**: *hêkal yhwh* in Shiloh 1S 1$_{9}$, in Jerusalem 2K 18$_{16}$, w/o art. = temple in Jerus. Is 44$_{28}$; — 3. the **main room** of the temple :: *'ûlām & dᵉbîr* 1K 6$_{5}$ = *hêkal habbayit* 6$_{3}$.

הֵילֵל: the **morning star** (or the crescent moon) Is 14$_{12}$. †

הֵימָם: n. pers.

הֵימָן: n. pers.

הִין: liquid measure, **hin**: of oil Ex 29$_{40}$, wine Lv 23$_{13}$, water Ez 4$_{11}$; c. 3.8 liters, 1 gal.

[**הכר**: תַּהְכְּרוּ Jb 19$_{3}$: ƒ *חכר.†]

***הַכָּרָה**: cs. הַכָּרַת: *hakkārat *pānîm* **bias** Is 3$_{9}$. †

הָלָא: ƒ לא.

הלא: **nif.**: pt. הַנַּהֲלָאָה coll. those who have **strayed far** ? Mi 4$_{7}$, but perh. txt. corr. †

הָלְאָה: adv. of place & time: — 1. place, **to there, farther**: a) *zᵉrēh-hālᵉ'â* scatter elsewhere Nu 17$_{2}$, *geš-hālᵉ'â* be gone Gn 19$_{9}$; b) *mēhālᵉ'â lᵉ* beyond Gn 35$_{21}$; c) *wāhālᵉ'â* and beyond Nu 32$_{19}$; d) *miššām wāhālᵉ'â* further from there 1S 10$_{3}$, *min-hû' wāhālᵉ'â* far & wide Is 18$_{2\cdot7}$; — 2. time, **from then on** 1S 18$_{9}$.

הִלּוּלִים: **joyous celebration** Ju 9$_{27}$ *qōdeš hillûlîm* joyous votive offering Lv 19$_{24}$. †

הַלָּז: **this** (m. & f.) 1S 17$_{26}$; *mēʿēber hallāz* over there 1S 14$_{1}$.

הַלָּזֶה: **this** (m.) Gn 24$_{65}$ 37$_{19}$; f. הַלֵּזוּ Ez 36$_{35}$. †

***הָלִיךְ**: pl. הֲלִיכַי: **step** Jb 29$_{6}$. †

***הֲלִיכָה**: sf. הֲלִכָתָם Na 2$_{6}$ Qr (Kt pl. sf.); pl. הֲלִיכ(וֹ)ת, sf. הֲלִיכוֹתֶיךָ: — 1a) walking, **way** Na 2$_{6}$ (oth.: tech. military term: column); b) pl. *hᵃlîkôt ʿôlām* (eternal) **paths** (of stars) Hb 3$_{6}$; — 2a) **caravan** Jb 6$_{19}$; b) **procession** Ps 68$_{25}$; — 3. pl. *hᵃlîkôt bêtāh* **doings** Pr 31$_{27}$. †

הָלַךְ: **qal**: pf. הָלְכָה, הָלַךְ, ה׳, 2 f. הָלַכְתִּי Je 31$_{21}$ Kt, הָלְכוּא (before א) Jos 10$_{24}$, הֲלַכְתֶּם; impf., &c.: I. (rare & late): תִּהֲלַךְ Ps 73$_{9}$, אֶהֱלֹךְ, יַהֲלֹכוּ; impv. הֲלֹךְ Pr 13$_{20}$ Kt, הִלְכוּ, inf. הֲלֹךְ, הֲלָךְ־. II. impf. וַיֵּלַךְ, וַיֵּלֶךְ, יֵלֶךְ־, יֵלֵךְ, תֵּלְכִי, (וָ)אֵלֵךְ, וָאֵלְכָה, אֵלְכָה (אֵילְכָה Mi 1$_{8}$), נֵלֵךְ, תֵּלַכְנָה, תֵּלְכוּן, יֵלֵכוּן, וַיֵּלְכוּ, וַיֵּלֵכוּ, לֶךְ־, לֵךְ; impv. נֵלְכָה (3× נֵלֲכָה), וַנֵּלֶךְ, לֵכְנָה, לְכוּ, לֵכָה (לֵךְ Nu 23$_{13}$ 2C 25$_{17}$), לְכָה (לֵכְןָ Ru 1$_{12}$); inf. (לָ)לֶכֶת, לֶכֶת, בְּלֶכְתּוֹ, הָלוֹךְ; pt. הֹ(וֹ)לֵךְ, הֹלְכָה, הֹלֶכֶת, הֹלַכְתִּי 2K 4$_{23}$ Kt, הֹלְכִים, הֹלְכוֹת: — 1. **go**: men Dt 11$_{19}$, animals 1S 6$_{12}$, snakes (creep) Gn 3$_{14}$, water (flow) 1K 18$_{35}$, fire (come down) Ex 9$_{23}$, letters Ne 6$_{17}$; — 2. forms of impv.: *lek-lᵉkā* Gn 12$_{1}$, *qaḥ wᵉlēk* 12$_{19}$; *lᵉkû wᵉnēlᵉkâ* come on, let's go 1S 9$_{9}$; — 3. makes the action vivid: *wayyēlek wayyiqaḥ* he went and took Gn 27$_{14}$; — 4. *hālôk* expresses the continuation & progress of the action: *wayyissa‘ hālôk wenāsôa‘* he journeyed further & further Gn 12_{9}; — 5. *hōlēk* expresses the progress of the action: *wayyēlek hōlēk weqārēb* went nearer & nearer 1S 17_{41}, *hōlēk wā’ôr* brighter & brighter Pr 4_{18}; — 6. metaph. **walk** = conduct onesf. w. adv. acc.: *hālak ṣedāqôt* act w. integrity Is 33_{15}; *hēṭîb leket* move out proudly Pr 30_{29}; — 7. spec. go away Gn 18_{33}; **die** Gn 15_{2}; be gone (rain) SS 2_{11}; run (boundary) Jos 16_{8}; spread out (of shoots) Ho 14_{7}; go down (wine) SS 7_{10}; — 8. in combs.: a) *hālak ‘arîrî* die childless Gn 15_{2}, *hālak derek* make a journey Gn 28_{20}, *hālak ledarkô* go on one's way 19_{2}; *hālak bederek hā’āreṣ* go the way of the earth = have to die 1K 2_{2}; — b) **flow with**: *hālak ḥālāb* flow w. milk Jl 4_{18}; *birkayim tēlaknâ mayim* = urinate Ez 7_{17} 21_{12}; metaph. *hōlēk rûaḥ wāšeqer* overflowing w. ... Mi 2_{11}; — 9. *hālak ’aḥarê* a) secular: **go behind** s.one Gn 32_{20}; b) theol. **follow, adhere to** a god/God 1K 18_{21}, mostly neg., of Baal Dt 4_{3}; — 10. *hālak ’el* go to Gn 12_{1}; (sexually) seek out Am 2_{7}; — 11. *hālak ’ēt* go with Gn 12_{4}, *‘im* accompany Ju 4_{8}, consort w. Jb 34_{8}; — 12. *hālak be* go with Ex 10_{9} &c.; — 13. *hālak le*: *hālak le’oholô* Dt 16_{7}; *hālak lifnê* go before Gn 32_{21} > stand in s.one's service 1K 3_{6}; — 14. *hālak min* Gn 12_{1}, *mē‘im* 1S 10_{2}; — 15. *hālak ‘ad* go as far as Ju 19_{18}; — 16. *hālak ‘al* crawl on Gn 3_{14}, *‘al ’arba‘* on all fours Lv 11_{20}; *hālak ‘al-hadderek* go in a direction 2S 15_{20}, *hālak ‘al* take the field against 1K 22_{6}.

nif.: pf. נֶהֱלָכְתִּי: (have to) **die** (ꟻ qal 7) Ps 109_{23}. †

piel: pf. הִלַּכְתִּי, הִלְּכְתִּי, הִלְּכוּ; impf. יְהַלֵּךְ, יְהַלְּכוּ, יְהַלֵּכוּן; pt. מְהַלֵּךְ, מְהַלְּכִים: — 1. **go** a) gods Ps 115_{7}, animals La 5_{18}, flow (brooks) Ps 104_{10}; b) **walk around** Ec 4_{15}; w. adj., e.g. *’aṭ* 1K 21_{27}; c) walk (*bedarkê*) Ps 81_{14}, w. *lifnê* Ps 85_{14}; — 2. **go away**: sun & moonlight Hb 3_{11}, godless Ps 55_{15}; — 3. spec.: *hillēk be* be occupied w. s.thg Ps 131_{1}; *mehallēk* tramp Ps 6_{11}.

hif.: pf. הוֹלִיךְ, הוֹלִיכוּ, הוֹלִיכְךָ; impf. אוֹלִיךְ, וַיּוֹלֵךְ, וַיּוֹלֶךְ, יוֹ(ו)לֵךְ, יוֹלִ(י)ךְ, וַיּוֹלִכֵנִי, אוֹלִיכָה; impv. הוֹלֵךְ, f. הֵילִיכִי (Ex 2_{9}), הוֹלִיכוּ; inf. הֹלִיכוֹ; pt. מוֹלִיךְ, מוֹלִכוֹת, מוֹלִיכָם, מוֹלִיכֵךְ, מוֹלִיכֵךְ: — 1. **bring** a) s.thg 2S 13_{13}; b) s.one 1K 1_{38}; — 2. **take** w. onesf. s.thg Ec 5_{14}, s.one Ex 2_{9}; — 3. **make, let** s.thg **go**: of God, his arm Is 63_{12}; make rivers run Ez 32_{14}; let ... go into exile 2K 24_{15}; — 4. **lead** Dt 8_{2}.

hitp.: pf. הִתְהַלַּכְתָּ, הִתְהַלֶּךְ־, הִתְהַלֵּךְ, הִתְהַלַּכְתִּי; impf. אֶתְהַלְּכָה, יִתְהַלָּךְ, יִתְהַלֵּךְ, תִּתְהַלַּכְנָה, יִתְהַלָּכוּן, יִתְהַלָּכוּ, יִתְהַלְּכוּ; impv. הִתְהַלֵּךְ, הִתְהַלְּכוּ; inf. הִתְהַלֵּךְ, הִתְהַלֶּכְךָ; pt. מִתְהַלְּכִים, מִתְהַלֶּכֶת, מִתְהַלֵּךְ: — 1. walk back & forth, **walk around**: *began* Gn 3_{8}; *mithallekîm beraglê* those who are followers 1S 25_{27}; — 2. **wander** Gn 13_{17}; — 3. **move back & forth** Ez 1_{13}; — 4. **go away** (from e/o) Ju 21_{24}, flow away (water) Ps 58_{8}; — 5. **walk** (constantly) (of God) Dt 23_{15}, (of man) *’ēt* w. God Gn $5_{22\cdot24}$; — 6. spec. go down, taste well (wine) Pr 23_{31}.

הֵלֶךְ: — 1. **visitor** 2S 12_{4}; — 2. **flowing**, *hēlek debaš* flowing honey 1S 14_{26}. †

I הלל: **hif.**: impf. יָהֵל, תָּהֵל, יָהֵלּוּ; inf. בְּהִלּוֹ Jb 29_{3}: — 1. **let shine** Is 13_{10} Jb 41_{10}; — 2. **shine** Jb 29_{3} 31_{26}. †

II הלל: **piel**: pf. הִלַּלְתִּיךָ, הִלַּלְנוּ, הִלְלוּ, הִלְלוּךָ; impf. אֲהַלֵּל, תְּהַלֵּל, יְהַלֶּל־, (וַ)יְהַלְלוּ, אֲהַלְלֶנּוּ, יְהַלְלֶךָּ, יְהַלְלוּךָ, אֲהַלְלָה, וִיהַלְלוּהָ; impv. הַלְלִי, הַלְלוּ(הוּ); inf. הַלֵּל; pt. מְהַלְלִים: — 1. **praise**: a beautiful woman Gn 12_{15}, a beaut. man 2S 14_{25}; — 2. **praise** God: a) the Philistines their god Ju 16_{24}; b) Yahweh Ps 22_{23f}; c) Y's name Ps 69_{31}; — 3. *hillēl* + *yāh*: a) verbal form in genl.: Ps 102_{19}; b) spec. *F* *halᵉlû-yāh* Ps 104_{35}-150_{6}; — 4. *hillēl lᵉyhwh* Ezr 3_{11}; — 5. *hillēl lᵉšēm* 1C 19_{13}; — 6. **sing 'Hallelujah'** Ezr 3_{11}; — 7. abs. praise Je 31_{7}.

pual: pf. הֻלְּלוּ, הֻלָּלָה; impf. יְהֻלַּל; pt. מְהֻלָּל: — 1. **be praised, feted**: maidens Ps 78_{63}, city Ez 26_{17}; — 2. pt. **praiseworthy**: Y. Ps 48_{2}, his name 113_{3}.

hitp.: impf. יִתְהַלֵּל, תִּתְהַלֵּל, תִּתְהַלְלִי, יִתְהַלְלוּ, יִתְהַלָּלוּ; impv. הִתְהַלְלוּ; inf. הִתְהַלֵּל; pt. מִתְהַלֵּל, מִתְהַלְלִים: — 1. **boast** a) in genl. 1K 20_{11}; w. *bᵉ* about Je 9_{22f}; b) w. *bᵉšēm yhwh* glory in the name of Y. Ps 105_{3}; abs. Ps 106_{5}; w. *bᵉ* & God Is 41_{16}; — 2. **be praised** Pr 31_{30}.

III הלל: **qal**: impf. תָּהֹלּוּ; pt. הֹלְלִים: **be** confused, **deluded** Ps 5_{6} 73_{3} 75_{5}. †

poel: impf. יְהוֹלֵל: — 1. **make** (s.one) **a fool** Jb 12_{17} Ec 7_{7}; — 2. treat as a fool, **make mock of** Is 44_{25} Ps 102_{9}. †

poal: pt. מְהוֹלָל: foolish, **senseless** Ec 2_{2}. †

hitpoel: pf. הִתְהוֹלָלוּ; impf. יִתְהוֹלֵל, יִתְהוֹלָלוּ, יִתְהוֹלְלוּ, impv. הִתְהֹלְלוּ: — 1. **pretend to be mad** 1S 21_{14}; — 2. **behave as if mad** Je 25_{16}; **run as if mad** (of chariot) Je 46_{9}.

הִלֵּל: n. pers.

הַלְלוּ־יָהּ, הַלְלוּיָהּ: **Hallelujah**, at beginning or end of Pss. 104-150.

הלם: **qal**: pf. הָלְמוּנִי, הָלְמָה; impf. יֶהֶלְמוּן, יֶהֶלְמֵנִי; pt. הֹלֵם Is 41_{7}, pass. הֲלוּמֵי: **strike**: obj. men Ju 5_{26}, anvil Is 41_{7}; beat to pieces Ps 74_{6}; *hᵃlûmê yayin* overcome by wine Is 28_{1}.

הֲלֹם: adv. of place: — 1. **to here** Ex 3_{5} 1S 10_{22}; *'ad-hᵃlōm* as far as this 2S 7_{18}; — 2. **here** Gn 16_{13} Ju 20_{7}.

הֶלֶם: n. pers.

הַלְמוּת: **hammer** Ju 5_{26}.

הָם n. loc.

הֵם, הֵמָּה: pl. of הוּא; both forms used alike, though הָהֵם is more frequent than הָהֵמָּה; לָהֶם 1×, כָּהֶם 3×, כָּהֵם, בָּהֶם, הֶם־ Ec 3_{18}, מֵהֶם, מִנְהֶם 1×; הֵמָּה rare w. insep. preps.: **they**: f. הֵנָּה 3×; *F* הוּא.

הַמְּדָתָא: n. pers.

המה: **qal**: pf. הָמוּ; impf. יֶהֱמֶה, תֶּהֱמִי, נֶהֱמֶה, יֶהֱמָיוּן, יֶהֱמוּ Ps 77_{4}, אֶהֱמָיָה; inf. הֲמוֹת; pt. הֹמֶה, הֹמָה & הֹמִיָּה: — 1. **make noise, uproar**: city 1K 1_{41}, enemies Ps 83_{3}, beer Pr 20_{1}; — 2. **roar** (sea, waves) Is 17_{12}; — 3. **give a sound**: growl (bear) Is 59_{11}, bark (dog) Ps $59_{7.15}$, sound (musical instruments) Is 16_{11}; — 4. **be unsteady, restless**: inward parts Is 16_{11}, heart Je 4_{19}; man Ps 77_{4}; — 5. **groan** Ps 55_{18}.

הֵמָּה: *F* הֵם; בָּהֵמָּה Ex 30_{4} 36_{1} Hb 1_{16} = בָּהֶם. †

הֲמוּלָּה Je 11_{16}: *F* הֲמֻלָּה. †

הָמוֹן: cs. הֲמוֹן, sf. הֲמוֹנוֹ, הֲמוֹנֹה, הֲמֹ(ו)נָהּ, הֲמוֹנֵךְ; pl. הֲמוֹנִים, sf. הֲמוֹנֶיהָ; m., ? f. Jb 31_{34}: — 1. **agitation** (of *mē'ayim*) Is 63_{15}; — 2. **bustle, turmoil** 1K 20_{13}; — 3. (acoustic) **din, uproar** 1K 18_{41} (rain); — 4. **procession, pomp** Ez 7_{11}; — 5. **crowd** Gn 17_{4f} > **army** Ju 4_{7}; — 6. (4. >) **display, riches** Ez 29_{19}.

הֲמוֹנָה: n. loc.

*הֶמְיָה: cs. הֶמְיַת: **sound, tone** (of harp) Is 14_{11}. †

הֲמֻלָּה Ez 1_{24} & הֲמוּלָּה Je 11_{16} (noisy) **crowd of people**: *qôl hᵃmullâ*. †

I המם: **qal**: pf. הָמַם, וְהַמֹּתִי, ה׳; impf. וַיָּהָם, וַיָּהֹם, 2S 22_{15} Qr, Kt וַיְהֻמֵּם like Ps 18_{15}, וּתְהֻמֵּם; inf. הָמֹם: — 1. **bring into movement & confusion** (army camp) Ex 14_{24}, (people) Ex 23_{27}; — 2. w. *min* **rouse up** from Dt 2_{15}, drive (cart w. shouts) Is 28_{28}.

nif.: impf. וַתֵּהֹם: **be in a uproar** 1K 1_{45}.

II המם: **qal**: pf. הֲמָמוּ Kt, Qr הֲמָמֻנִי **drain, suck out** Je 51_{34}. †

הָמָן: n. pers. **Haman**.

[הֲמָנְכֶם Ez 5_7: הָמוֹן ? ↗ comm.]
הֲמָסִים: **brushwood** Is 64_1. †
הַמְשֵׁל Jb 25_2, ↗ II משל hif. †
I הֵן, הֵן־ & הֶן־, 100× (Jb 30×, Is 40-66 22×): demonstr. interj. & conj.: — 1. **behold**, emphasizes the following word, phrase, or clause: *hēn lî lōʾ* Gn 15_3, *hēn hāʾādām hāyâ* Gn 3_{22}, followed by impv. Is 64_8; (agreeing) 'Good!' Gn 30_{34}; — 2. **if** (Aram. ?) Ex 4_1.
II *הֵן: f. of הֵם, ↗ II הֵנָּה; only w. pref.: בָּהֵן Gn 19_{29}; לָהֵן Ru 1_{13} 2× †; כָּהֵן Ez 18_{14}; מֵהֵן more than they Ez 16_{47}.
I הֵנָּה: adv. of place & time: — 1. **here** Gn 21_{23}; — 2. **(to) here** Gn 42_{15}; — 3. *ʿad-hēnnâ* (as far as to) here 2K 8_7, thus far Je 48_{47}; — 4. *hēnnâ* ... *hēnnâ* **here ... there** = on this side ... on that side Dn 12_5; w. *ʾaḥat* back & forth 2K 4_{35}; *hēnnâ wāhēnnâ* to one side & to the other 2K $2_{8.14}$; *mimmᵉkā wāhēnnâ* on this side of you 1S 20_{21}; — 5. temporal: **until now** Gn 15_{16}.
II הֵ֫נָּה: f. of הֵם, הֵ֫מָּה: **they** (f. pl.): *mâ hēnnâ* what do these mean? Gn 21_{29}; neuter: *hēnna wāhēnnâ* this & that 1K 20_{40}.
הִנֵּה (436×, וְהִנֵּה 343×): demonstr. interj.; הִנֶּה נָּא Gn 19_2; הִנְּךָ, הִנְּכָה, הִנְּךְ, הִנֵּנִי, הִנְנִי, *הִנֵּהוּ Je 18_3 Kt (Qr הִנֵּה־הוּא) הִנּוֹ Nu 23_{17} Jb 2_6 1C 11_{25} †, הִנֵּנוּ, הִנְנוּ, הִנְּכֶם, הִנָּם; w. '*nûn* energic' הִנֶּ֫נּוּ, הִנֶּךָ, הִנֶּנִּי; also הִנֵּה אָנֹכִי &c.; **behold**: — 1. stresses the following word *wᵉhinnēh tannûr* Gn 15_{17}; — 2. *hinᵉnî* answer of a person called: here I am Gn 22_1; — 3. after the noun stressed *wᵉhāʾāreṣ hinnēh* Gn 34_{21}; — 4. after stressed pron.: a) subj. of following vb. *waʾᵃnî hinnēh lāqaḥtî* but I myself Nu 13_2, b) referring to the following noun: *ʾᵃnî hinnēh bᵉrîtî* the covenant wh. I have made Gn 17_4; — 5. emphasizes the entire clause wh. follows *hinnēh nātattî* see, I give Gn 1_{29}; causes inversion of subj. & pred. *hinnēh rûᵃḥ bāʾâ* Jb 1_{19}; — 6. introduces an unexpected new development: *wᵉhinnēh rāḥēl* Gn 29_6; — 7. introduces an emphatic apodosis: *hinᵉnî* Ex 8_{17} then I will; — 8. after vbs. of perception: *wayyarʾ wᵉhinnēh* Gn 19_{28}, *wayyaḥᵃlōm wᵉhinnēh* 28_{12}; introducing announcement *lēʾmōr hinnēh* Gn 38_{13}; — 9. *hinᵉnî* a) w. pt. *hinᵉnî mēbîʾ* Gn 6_{17}; b) *hinᵉnî ʾēlékā/ʿālékā* formula of challenge, behold I am against you Je 21_{13}; c) w. 3 sg. impf. *hinᵉnî yôsîf* Is 29_{14} 38_5, ? rel. or rd. *yôsēf*; — 10. before a conditional clause = **if** *wᵉhinnēh nēlēk* 1S 9_7.
הֲנָחָה: **remission of taxes**; oth.: holiday or amnesty Est 2_{18}. †
*הִנֹּם: n. pers.; only in גֵּי(א) בֶן־ה׳; ↗ גַּיְא. †
הֵנַע: n. loc.
הֲנָפָה: **'waving'** of the offering, Is 30_{28}. †
הַס: interj.; הָס, pl. (as if piel impv.) הַסּוּ Ne 8_{11}: **hush! quiet!** Ju 3_{19}.
הסה: **hif.**: impf. וַיַּ֫הַס: **hush** (people) Nu 13_{30}. †
הָסוּרִים Ec 4_{14}: = הָאֲסוּרִים mss., ↗ אסר.
*הֲפָגָה: הֲפֻגוֹת: **stopping** La 3_{49}. †
הָפַךְ: **qal**: pf. ה׳, הָפְכָה, הָפַכְתָּ, הֲפַכְתֶּם, הֲפָכָם; impf. וַיַּהֲפֹךְ, וַיַּהֲפָךְ־, אֶהְפֹּךְ, וַיַּהַפְכֵהוּ; impv. הֲפֹךְ; inf. הֲפֹךְ, הָפְכִּי, הָפְכָהּ; pt. הֹפֵךְ, הַהֹפְכִי Ps 114_8, pass. הֲפוּכָה: — 1. **turn** (over on the other side): dish 2K 21_{13}, hand (back & forth) La 3_3; — 2. (upside down): **overturn**: throne Hg 2_{22}; overthrow, **destroy**: city Gn 19_{21}, men Jb 34_{25}; — 3. **turn around** (in another direction): *hāfak ʿōref lifnê* turn one's back on Ju 7_8; *hāfak yād(ayim)* turn (chariot) around (by reining about) 1K 22_{34}; — 4. a) **transform**: w. acc. & *lᵉ* curse to blessing Dt 23_6, sorrow to joy Je 31_{13}; w. acc. & *bᵉ* Ps 41_4, w. 2 accs. Ps 114_8; b) **change** (characteristics): skin Je 13_{23}; — 5. intrans. **turn** (around) 2K 5_{26}.
nif.: pf. נֶהְפַּךְ, נֶהְפָּךְ, נֶהֶפְכָה, נֶהְפַּכְתְּ,

נֶהֶפְכוּ, נֶהְפְּכוּ; impf. יֵהָפְכוּ, יֵהָפֵךְ; inf. abs. נַהֲפוֹךְ; pt. נֶהְפָּךְ, נֶהְפֶּכֶת: — 1. a) **turn against**, w. *ʼel* Jos 8_{20}, w. *bᵉ* Jb 19_{19}; b) (of property) **pass to**, w. *ʻal* Is 60_{5}, w. *lᵉ* La 5_{2}; c) **turn around** Ez 4_{8}; — 2. **be** turned upside down, **destroyed**: city Jon 3_{4}; — 3. turn into, **be turned** into (of heart) Ex 14_{5}; abs. Ps 32_{4}; w. *lᵉ* Ex 7_{15}; — 4. var.: *nehfᵉkû haṣṣîrîm* pains came over 1S 4_{19}; *wᵉnahᵃfôk hûʼ ʼᵃšer* and it happened on the contrary that Est 9_{1}.

hof.: pf. הָהְפַּךְ: w. *ʻal* be turned against Jb 30_{15}, but ℱ comm. †

hitp.: impf. תִּתְהַפֵּךְ; pt. מִתְהַפֵּךְ, מִתְהַפֶּכֶת: — 1. **turn this way & that** Jb 37_{12}; roll (of loaf of bread) Ju 7_{13}; flash, quiver (sword) Gn 3_{24}; — 2. **change** Jb 38_{14}. †

הֵפֶךְ: sf. הַפְכְּכֶם: — 1. **opposite** Ez 16_{34}; — 2. **perversity** Is 29_{16}. †

הֲפֵכָה: **destruction** Gn 19_{29}. †

הֲפַכְפַּךְ: **winding** (path) Pr 21_{8}. †

הַצָּלָה: **deliverance** Est 4_{14}. †

הַצְלֶלְפּוֹנִי: n. pers. f.

הֹצֶן Ez 23_{24} unexpl., ℱ comm. †

הַקּוֹץ: n. pers.

הַר (c. 520×): הָהָר; loc. הָרָה 13×, Gn 14_{10} הֶרָה; sf. הַרְרִי, הַרְרִי Ps 30_{8}, הֲרָרִי Je 17_{3}, הַרְכֶם Gn 14_{6}; pl. הָרִים, cs. הַרְרֵי & הָרֵי, הַרְרָם, sf. הָרַי, הָרָיו, הֲרָרֶיהָ; m.: — 1. sg. **mountains, mountain range**, *har haggilʻād* Gn 31_{21}; — 2. (individual) **mountain**, e.g. *har sînay* & oft.; — 3. pl. *ʼaḥad hehārîm* (in the land of Moriah) Gn 22_{2}; — 4. Mountain of God: *ʼᵉlōhê hārîm* 1K 20_{23}, *har ʼᵉlōhîm* Ps 68_{16}; — 5. as place of forbidden cults: Dt 12_{2}.

הֹר, alw. הֹר הָהָר: n. terr.

הָרָא: n. terr.

הַרְאֵל: הַהַרְאֵל Ez 43_{15a}, the altar of burnt offering, = ℱ הָאֲרִיאֵל mss. & $43_{15b.16}$. †

***הַרְבָּה**: cs. הַרְבַּת Qr (Kt הַרְבִּית) 2S 14_{11}; ℱ I רבה hif. †

הַרְבֵּה: — 1. **great number, many, much**: a) as subj.: *harbēh nāfal min hāʻām* many fell 2S 1_{4}, *harbēh miššᵉtēm-ʻeśrēh* more than … Jon 4_{11}; b) as obj.: *zᵉraʻtem harbēh* Hg 1_{6}; c) as appos.: *nᵉḥōšet harbēh mᵉʼōd* a very great quantity of bronze 2S 8_{8}; d) as pred. *śᵉkārᵉkā harbēh mᵉʼōd* shall be very great Gn 15_{1}; — 2. adv. **much, very**: *wāʼîrāʼ harbēh mᵉʼōd* I was very much afraid Ne 2_{2}; *lōʼ harbēh yizkōr* not often remember Ec 5_{19}; — 3. w. prep.: *lᵉharbēh mᵉʼōd* very much 2C 11_{12}.

הָרַג: **qal**: pf. ה׳, הָרַג, הָרַגְתְּ, הָרְגוּ, הֲרַגְתֶּם, הֲרַגְתִּים; impf. יַהֲרֹג, יַהֲרָג־, אֶהֱרֹג, אַהַרְגָה, יַהַרְגוּ, יַהַרְגֻהוּ, יַהַרְגֵנוּ, וָאֶהֶרְגֵהוּ; impv. הֲרֹג, הִרְגוּ, הַרְגוּ; inf. הֲרוֹג, הָרְגוֹ, הָרְגְךָ, לַהֲרָגְךָ 1S 24_{11}, לְהָרְגֵךְ, הַלְהָרְגֵנִי, abs. הָרֹג; pt. הֹ(ו)רֵג, הֹרְגִים, הֹרְגֵךְ pl. Ez 28_{9}; pass. הֲרוּגִים, הֲרֻגִים, הֲרֻגֵי, הֲרֻגָיו, הֲרֻגֶיהָ: — 1. **kill**: a) = slay, murder Gn 4_{8} 27_{42}; b) = legally execute Lv 20_{16}; *hōrēg* executioner Ho 9_{13}; in war, 1K 9_{16}; w. *lᵉ* (prepare death for) 2S 3_{30}; *ḥereb* subj. Am 9_{4}; c) slaughter (animal) Is 22_{13}; — 2. metaph. viper's tongue Jb 20_{16}, hail Ps 78_{47}; — 3. spec.: God subj.: Gn 20_{4} & oft.

nif.: impf. יֵהָרֵג, תֵּהָרַגְנָה; inf. בֵּהָרֵג Ez 26_{15} < *בְּהֵהָרֵג: **be killed** Ez 26_{6}.

pual (or pass. **qal**): pf. הֹרַג: **be killed** Is 27_{7} Ps 44_{23}. †

הֶרֶג: **killing, murder** Is 27_{7}.

הֲרֵגָה: — 1. **killing** Je 12_{3}; — 2. **slaughter** Zc $11_{4.7}$.

הָרָה: **qal**: pf. ה׳, הָרְתָה, הָרִית, הָרִינוּ; impf. וַתַּהַר, תַּהֲרִין, תַּהֲרוּ; inf. abs. הָרֹה, הָרוֹ; pt. הוֹרָתָם, הוֹרָתִי: **conceive, be pregnant** Gn 16_{4f}; w. *lᵉ* by Gn 38_{18}, w. *min* by 19_{36}.

pual (or pass. **qal**): הֹרָה **be conceived** Jb 3_{3}. †

***הָרֶה**: f. הָרָה; cs. הָרַת, pl. cs. הָרוֹת, sf. הָרוֹתֶיהָ, הָרוֹתֵיהֶם & הָרִיּוֹתָיו: **pregnant**

Gn 16_{11}, *lᵉʾîš* by a man 38_{25}, *liznûnîm* by prostitution 38_{24}.

הָרוּם: n. pers.

הֵרוֹן: Gn 3_{16}: trad. **pregnancy**; oth.: **sensory pleasure.**

[**הֲרוֹרִי**: gent. 1C 11_{27}: but rd. הַחֲרוֹדִי 2S 23_{25}. †]

הֵרָיוֹן: **conception** Ho 9_{11} Rt 4_{13}. †

***הֲרִיסָה**: pl. sf. הֲרִסֹתָיו: **ruins** Am 9_{11}. †

***הֲרִיסוּת**: pl. sf. הֲרִסֻתֵיִךְ (Kt ־תַיִךְ ?) **ruins** Is 49_{19}. †

הָרִ(י)פוֹת 2S 17_{19} Pr 27_{22}; ⸗ חֲרִיפוֹת.

הָרָם Jos 13_{27}: ⸗ בֵּית הָרָם n. loc., I בַּיִת B 45.

הֹרָם: n. pers.

***הַרְמוֹן**: loc. הַהַרְמוֹנָה Am 4_3: uncert.; n. loc. ?

הָרָן: n. pers.

הרס: **qal**: pf. הָרַסְתָּ ,ה׳, הָרָסוּ; impf. יֶהֱרוֹס, יֶהֶרְסֵךְ, יֶהֶרְסֶנָּה, יַהַרְסוּ, יֶהֶרְסוּ, אֶהֱרֹס, יֶהֶרְסֵם, יֶהֶרְסֶהָ; impv. הֲרָס־, הָרְסָה; inf. הֲרֹ(ו)ס; pt. הֹרֵס, pass. הָרֻס: — 1. **demolish** Je 1_{10}, **altar** 1K 18_{30}, **city** 2S 11_{25}; — 2. metaph. **pull down** (a person from his station) Is 22_{19}; subj. God, **destroy** (a people) Je 24_6, **throw down** (enemy) Ex 15_7; — 3. **break through** (intrans.) Ex $19_{21 \cdot 24}$; — 4. **knock out** (teeth) Ps 58_7.

nif.: pf. נֶהֶרְסוּ, נֶהֶרְסָה; impf. יֵהָרֵס, יֵהָרֵסוּן; pt. נֶהֱרָסוֹת: **be laid in ruins** Je 31_{40}.

piel: impf. תְּהָרְסֵם; inf. abs. הָרֵס; pt. sf. מְהָרְסַיִךְ: **lay in ruins, destroy**: Ex 23_{24} (gods), Is 49_{17} (city). †

הֶרֶס: n. loc. in Egypt, עִיר הַהֶרֶס Is 19_{18}, deliberate change from הַחֶרֶס = **Heliopolis.** †

הֲרָרִי: gent. of *הָרָר (? הָר), unknown terr. or loc.

הָשֵׁם: n. pers.

הַשְׁמָעוּת: *lᵉhašmāʿût ʾoznayim* for personal **communication** Ez 24_{26}. †

[**הָשֲׁפוֹת**: Ne 3_{13}, rd. הָאַשְׁפּוֹת as 2_{13} &c. †]

הִתּוּךְ: **melting** Ez 22_{22}. †

הִתְחַבְּרוּת: alliance, **union** w. *ʾel* Dn 11_{23}. †

הִתְיַחֵשׂ: sf. הִתְיַחְשָׂם: **registration** 1C 4_{33}; genealogy Ezr 8_1.

הֲתָךְ: n. pers.

התל: **piel**: impf. וַיְהַתֵּל: **mock** 1K 18_{27}. †

הֲתֻלִים: **mockery** Jb 17_2. †

התת: **poel**: impf. תְּהוֹתְתוּ: **overwhelm w. reproaches** Ps 62_4. †

ו

וְ: form: mostly וְ, but a) וּ before ב, מ, & פ, & before cons. w. simple *shewa*; b) וָ immediately before tone-syl.: וָבָ֫יְתָה; c) וַ, וֶ, וָ (*wŏ*) before cons. w. corresponding *ḥatef*: וַאֲנִי; d) וִ before יְ: וִיהִי; e) וַ w. *dageš* forte & וָ before א in impf. consec.; — 1. **and,** connecting 2 words or phrases: *ʾereṣ wᵉšāmayim*; oft. in hendiadys: *šālôm wāšeqet* complete peace 1C 22_9; — 2. connecting 3 or more words, standing either a) before every word but the first: *yayin wᵉqayiṣ wᵉšemen* Je 40_{10}, or b) only before the last: *bammiqneh bakkesef ûbazzāhāb* Gn 13_2; the 3rd-5th words have *wᵉ* 2K 23_5; — 3. intensifying: **also, even**: *ûbᵉmôtām* and in ... too 2S 1_{23}; — 4. inclusive: **with, and in addition**: *ûmaṣṣôt* Ex 12_8; — 5. explanatory: **and indeed**: *ûbᵉʾappᵉkem* Am 4_{10}; **namely** *wᵉdeber* 1C 21_{12}; — 6. *wᵉ* > **or** in conditional & interr. clauses: *ûbᵉʾištô* or his wife Gn 26_{11}; — 7. in repetition of a word, *wᵉ* expresses variety: *ʾeben wāʾeben* various weights Pr 20_{10}; — 8. after *kᵉ* 'as,' *wᵉ* = **so**: *ûšᵉmûʿâ ṭôbâ* so is good news Pr 25_{25}; — 9.

we ... *we* both ... and Nu 9_{14}; — 10. connecting 2 or more clauses: *wehû' gār* Ju 19_{16}; — 11. a circumstantial clause introduced by *we* becomes like a relative clause: *wehēm* and they = who Gn 14_{13}, *ûšemāh* and her name = whose name Gn 16_1; — 12. in older Heb. a 2nd clause introduced by *we* adds accompanying circumstances, supplementary comments, &c.: *wenāʿal* and in doing so closed ... Ju 3_{23}; — 13. connecting impvs. & jussives: Ju 19_6; — 14. connecting comparisons & parallelisms: Jb 5_7; — 15. w. antitheses, *we* = **but**: *we'et-berîtî* but my covenant Gn 17_{21}; — 16. a series of clauses w. *we* may express alternatives: **whether ... or** Ex 21_{16}; — 17. introducing clauses of conditions or circumstances: *wehî' yōšebet* while she sat Ju 13_9; — 18. taking up the subj. of a main clause preceded by a clause of circumstance: *wehî' šāleḥâ* then she sent Gn 38_{25}; — 19. similarly *we* can be translated by a great variety of conjunctions: *we'ānōkî* since I Gn 15_2, *wešāw'* because Ps 60_{13} &c.; — 20. introducing an asseveration: *we'attem ʿēday* Is 43_{12}; — 21. after a command, question, or denial, *we* before a juss. or coh. expresses subordination: *we'ēdeʿâ* so that I may know Gn 42_{34}; — 22. likewise, following an impv. or juss., w. *we* + impv.: *wehyēh* so that you are Gn 12_2; — 23. introducing an apodosis after a conditional clause: *weyāledû* then ... Gn 31_8; — 24. similarly when the conditional clause is a 'casus pendens': *wenikretâ* Gn 17_{14}; — **25. introducing the verb after word of time: *bayyôm haššelîšî wayyiššā'*** Gn 22_4; — **26. introducing deductions & qns. (oral style): *wehāšîbû*** so repent! Ez 18_{32}; ***we'ayyô* and** where is he? Ex 2_{20}; — 27. **as impf. consec.,** vocalized *wa* in expressing the **progression** of the action: ***wayyifgaʿ* ... *wayyālen* ...** *wayyaḥalōm* Gn 28_{11}, oft. = **(and) then,** also after word of time (*F* 25). **Even at** beginning of books (Ez Ru Est); **as expr.** of deduction: *wattesîtēnî* **so that you ... Jb** 2_3; — 28. in the **'pf. consec.' *we* +** pf. **after** impf. or impv., juss.: ***'aḥappēś ûleqaḥtîm*** Am 9_3; *lēk we'āmartā* 2S 7_5; — 29. **other** usages before pf.: a) iterative ***'ēd yaʿaleh*** *wehišqâ* Gn 2_6; b) **Aram.** for **impf. consec.** Ec 9_{14-16}; c) archival 2K 18_{3ff} 23_{4-15}; — 30. *we* includes the negation of ***lō'*** (Ps 121_6) and *'al* (38_2).

[**וְאוּצָאה** Ezr 8_{17}; rd w. Qr **וָאֲצַוֶּה**, Kt וָאוֹצִאָה. †]

וְדָן Ez 27_{19}: trad. n. loc.; ??; corr., del. †

וָהֵב: n. loc.

***וָו**: pl. **וָוִים**, **וָוֵי**, sf. **וָוֵיהֶם**: **nail from wh. the** curtains hang in tent of meeting **Ex** 26_{32}.

וָזָר: **אִישׁ וָזָר** Pr 21_8; uncert.; laden w. guilt, or wrong, or dishonest; or dittgr. †

וַיְזָתָא: n. pers.

וָלָד: Gn 11_{30}: **child.** †

וַנְיָה: n. pers.; txt. ?: Ezr 10_{36}. †

וָפְסִי: n. pers.

וַשְׁנִי: 1C 6_{13}, trad. n. pers., **but txt.** ? †

וַשְׁתִּי: n. pers. f.

ז

I **זְאֵב**: pl. **זְאֵבִים**, **זְאֵבֵי**: **wolf** (*Canis lupus, C. pallipes*) Gn 49_{27}.

II **זְאֵב**: n. pers. Jud 7_{25} 8_3 Ps 83_{12}. †

זֹאת: f. of *F* **זֶה**.

זבד: **qal**: pf. **זְבָדַנִי**: w. 2 acc. **make s.one a gift of** s.thg Gn 30_{20}. †

זֶבֶד: **gift** Gn 30_{20}. †

זָבָד: n. pers.

זַבְדִּי: n. pers.

זַבְדִּיאֵל: n. pers.

זְבַדְיָה: n. pers.

זְבַדְיָהוּ: n. pers.

זְבוּב: pl. cs. זְבוּבֵי (see below): coll. **flies**: Is 7_{18}, *z^e^bûbê māwet* Ec 10_1 dead (or poisonous) flies; בַּעַל זְבוּב 2K $1_{2f.6.16}$ 'Lord of the flies,' god of Ekron, distorted fm. *ba'al z^e^bûl* (title of Baal).

זָבוּד: n. pers.

זְבוּדָּה: n. pers. f. 2K 23_{36} Qr. †

זְבוּל: ꜰ I זְבֻל.

זְבוּלוּן & זְבוּלֻן, זְבֻלוּן, זְבֻלֻן: n. pers. & tribe.

זְבוּלֹנִי: gent. of זְבוּלוּן.

זָבַח: **qal**: pf. ז׳, זְבַחְתֶּם, זָבַחְתִּי; impf. יִזְבַּח, יִזְבְּחוּ, יִזְבָּחוּ, נִזְבְּחָה, וַיִּזְבָּחֵהוּ, תִּזְבָּחֻנּוּ, וַתִּזְבָּחִים, תִּזְבָּחֻהוּ; impv. זְבַח, זִבְחוּ; inf. זְבֹחַ, לִזְבֹּחַ, זָבְחוֹ; pt. זֹ(ו)בֵחַ, זֹבְחִים, זֹבְחֵי: — 1. **slaughter**: large & small cattle 1K 1_9, calf 1S 28_{24}, sheep Ez 34_3; — 2. *zābaḥ zebaḥ* **slaughter for a (communion) sacrifice** Gn 31_{54}, ꜰ *zebaḥ*; = *zābaḥ z^e^bāḥîm* Gn 46_1; — 3. w. *l^e^* + God/god to whom sacrifice is made: *lē'lōhē 'ābîw* Gn 46_1 &c.; — 4. w. other objs. than *zebaḥ*: *tô'^a^bat miṣrayim* Ex 8_{22} & other nouns referring to sacrifice; — 5. spec.: *zābaḥ 'al-ḥāmēṣ* w. s.thg leavened Ex 23_{18}; sacrifice priests 1K 13_2 2K 23_{20}.

piel: pf. זִבַּח, זִבְּחוּ, זִבֵּחוּ; impf. יְזַבֵּחַ, אֲזַבֵּחַ, יְזַבֵּחוּ; inf. לְזַבֵּחַ; pt. מְזַבֵּחַ, מְזַבְּחִים: — 1. **offer** (the regular communion sacrifice) 1K 3_3; w. obj. *ṣō'n ûbāqār* 1K 8_5; — 2. *l^e^* + God/god to whom sacrifice is made: *lē'lōhîm* 1K 11_8; — 3. *zibbaḥ babbāmôt* 1K 3_{2f}; — 4. *zibbaḥ* in company w. *q^e^dēšôt* Ho 4_{14}.

I **זֶבַח**: זֶבַח, sf. זִבְחִי; pl. זְבָחִים, זִבְחֵי: — **(communion) sacrifice** = of sheep, goat, cattle, the purpose of which is communion between those sacrificing and the deity to whom the sacrifice is offered, who is himself a partner in the act; — 1. w. var. vbs.: a) *zābaḥ* Gn 31_{54}; b) *'āśâ* 1K 12_{27}; c) others, e.g. *bô' b^e^* 1S 16_5; — 2. noun combinations: *zebaḥ pesaḥ* Ex 12_{27}; *zebaḥ tôdâ* Lv 7_{12}, &c.; — 3. relations w. oth. types of sacrifice: a) *zebaḥ* : :*'ōlâ* 2K 10_{24}; b) *zebaḥ & minḥâ* 1S 2_{19}; c) *zebaḥ (haš)š^e^lāmîm* 1K 8_{63}; — 4. var. spec. phrases, e.g. *zebaḥ gādôl labba'al* 2K 10_{19}.

II **זֶבַח**: n. pers. Ju 8_{5-21} Ps 83_{12}. †

זַבַּי: n. pers.

זְבִידָה: n. pers. f.

זְבִינָא: n. pers.

זבל: **qal**: impf. יִזְבְּלֵנִי: **exalt**, make s.one a lawful wife Gn 30_{20}. †

I **זְבֻל**: n. pers. Ju 9_{28-41}. †

II **זְבֻל**: **exalted dwelling** of God; place of moon Hb 3_{11}, temple for Y. 1K 8_{13} Is 63_{15} 2C 6_2. †

זְבֻלוּן: ꜰ זְבוּלוּן.

זָג: **seed** or **peel** (of grape) Nu 6_4. †

זֵד: pl. זֵדִים: **presumptuous, arrogant** Ps 19_{14}.

זָדוֹן: cs. זְדוֹן, sf. זְדוֹנְךָ: **presumption, arrogance** 1S 17_{28}; *'ebrat zādôn* boundless arrogance Pr 21_{24}.

זֶה: demonstr. & rel. pron.; f. זֹאת, 11 × זוֹ, 2 × זֹה; comm. ꜰ זוּ; pl. אֵלֶּה & אֵל: — **this**, (these): — 1. emphatic: this (is the one that) Gn 38_{28}; — 2. **such** (a one) *zeh dōr dōr^e^šāw* such is the generation ... Ps 24_6; — 3. neuter: *w^e^zeh '^a^šer* and this is what ... Gn 6_{15}; *'ên zeh kî-'im* this is nothing else but Gn 28_{17}; — 4. *zō't* neuter: *zō't '^a^śû* Gn 42_{18}; — 5. referring to what follows: *'ēlleh* these are Ex 35_1; — 6. referring to what precedes: *'ēlleh* these are Gn 2_4; — 7. *zeh ... zeh* this one ... that one Ps 75_8, so *zō't ... zō't* Gn 29_{27}; — 8. preceding a noun: *zeh mōšeh* this Moses Ex 32_1, *zō't hārā'â* this trouble 2K 6_{33}; — 9. following a suffixed noun: *d^e^bārēnû zeh* Jos 2_{20} = this (word) of ours; — 10. attributively, w. art. & noun w. art.: *haddōr hazzeh* Gn 7_{1}; — 11. w. gen., **he of**: *zeh sînay* the one from Sinai Ju 5_{5}; — 12. like *ʾašer*, introduces rel. clause: *zeh šākantā bô* upon which you ... Ps 74_{2}; — 13. adv. of place: *bāzeh* here Gn 38_{21}; *mizzeh* from here Gn 37_{17}; *mizzeh...mizzeh* on either side Nu 22_{24}; — 14. adv. of place, pointing: *zeh laḥmēnû* our bread here Jos 9_{12}; w. adv. of time *ʿattâ zeh* now (then) 1K 17_{24}; — 15. strengthens interr. words: *mah-zzeh* how then? Ju 18_{24}, *lāmmā zzeh* Gn 18_{13}; — 16. w. preps.: a) *bāzeh* under the following circumstances Est 2_{13}; *bezōʾt* under the following condition Gn 34_{15}; *bezōʾt* in spite of this Lv 26_{27}; b) *kāzeh* such a one Gn 41_{38}; *kāzōʾt wekāzōʾt* thus & so 2S 17_{15}; c) min ↗ 13; d) *ʿal-zōʾt* on this account Am 8_{8}.

זֹה: f., ↗ זוֹ, זֹאת: — 1. **this** Ec 2_{2}; — 2. neuter **this** 2K 6_{19}.

זָהָב (385×): cs. זְהַב, זֲהַב Gn 2_{12} †, sf. זְהָבִי, זְהָבָם, וּזְהָבְךָ: — **gold** Gn 2_{12}; *lešôn zāhāb* bar of gold Jos 7_{21}; *ʿaśārâ zāhāb* 10 (shekels of) gold Gn 24_{22}.

זהם: **piel**: pf. זִהֲמַתּוּ: w. 2 acc. **make** s.thg **loathsome** to s.one Jb 33_{20}. †

***זַהַם**, זֶהַם: n. pers.

I **זהר**: **hif.**: impf. יַזְהִרוּ: **shine** Dn 12_{3}. †

II **זהר**: **nif.**: pf. נִזְהָר; inf. הִזָּהֵר; pt. נִזְהָר: — 1. **take warning** Ps 19_{12}; — **be warned** Ez 33_{6}.

hif.: pf. הִזְהִיר, הִזְהַרְתָּ(ה), הִזְהִירָה Kt (Qr ־רוּ), הִזְהַרְתּוֹ; inf. הַזְהִיר: **warn** 2K 6_{10}; w. *min* **warn of** Ez 3_{18b}.

זֹהַר: **shining, splendor** Ez 8_{2} Dn 12_{3}. †

זִו: name of 2d month (in Canaanite calendar) Apr.-May, **Ziv** 1K $6_{1.37}$. †

זוֹ: ↗ זֹה & זֶה: f. sg. — 1. **this** Ps 132_{12}; — 2. neuter **this** Ho 7_{16}. †

זוּ: demonstr. & rel. pron., ↗ זֶה, comm.: — 1. demonstr., f. & neuter **this** Ps 62_{12}; — 2. rel. = *ʾašer* Ex 15_{13}.

זוב: **qal**: impf. יָזוּב, יָזֻבוּ, וַיָּזוּבוּ; pt. זָב, f. זָבַת, זָבָה: — 1. **flow**, of water Ps 78_{20}; — 2. w. acc. **trickle** w. s.thg: *ʾereṣ zābat ḥālāb ûdebāš* Ex 3_{8} & oft.; — 3. **suffer from a discharge**: of a man (gonorrhea) *zāb mibbeśārô* Lv 15_{2}, *hazzāb ʾet-zôbô* 15_{33}; of a woman (menstruation) Lv 15_{19}; — 4. ? **flow away**, die Je 49_{4}.

זוֹב: — 1. **mucous discharge** of a man (*gonorrhea benigna*) Lv 15_{2f}; — 2. **discharge of blood** of a woman (within & outside the menstrual period) Lv 15_{19}.

זוד: ↗ זיד.

זוּזִים: n. peop. Gn 14_{5}. †

זוח: **nif.**: impf. יִזַּח: **come loose, get out of place** Ex 28_{28} 39_{21}. †

זוֹחֵת: n. pers.

***זָוִית**: pl. (also cs.) זָוִיּ(וֹ)ת: **corner**, of altar Zc 9_{15}, corner-posts of house Ps 144_{12}. †

זול: **qal**: pt. זָלִים: **pour out, weigh out** Is 46_{6}. †

***זוּלָה**: cs. זוּלַת & זוּלָתִי Ps 18_{32}; sf. זוּלָתִי, זוּלָתֶךָ, זוּלָתְךָ: removal, cessation > 1. prep. **except, besides** (after neg. or qn. implying neg.) 1K 3_{18}; — 2. conj. **except that** Jos 11_{13}.

cj. **זון**: **qal**: impf. יָזוּן: **feed** Jb 36_{31}. †

זוֹנָה: ↗ זנה.

זוע: **qal**: impf. יָזֻעוּ; pt. זָע: **tremble** Ec 12_{3}, w. *min* before Est 5_{9}. †

pilp.: pt. מְזַעְזְעֶיךָ: make tremble, **oppress** Hb 2_{7}. †

זַוָעֲה: Je 15_{4} 2C 29_{8} & **זַעֲוָה** Je 24_{9} 28_{18} 34_{17} = Kt זְוָעָה & Qr זַעֲוָה: ↗ זְעָוָה: **trembling, fright** Is 28_{19}, *nātan lez.* Je 15_{4}.

I **זור**: **qal**: impf. תְּזוּרֶהָ, וַיָּזַר; pt. זוּרֶה Is 59_{5}, a blend of זוֹרָה & pt. pass. הַזּוּרָה: — 1. **press**: on eggs Is 59_{5}, wring out (wet fleece) Ju 6_{38}; — 2. **crush** Jb 39_{15}. †

II **זור**: **qal**: pf. זָרוּ, זֹרוּ Ps 78_{30}: **turn away** from, w. *min* Ps 78_{30} Jb 19_{13}. †

nif.: pf. נָזֹרוּ: **turn away** from, w. *mēʿal*

Ez 14_{5}, w. *ʾāḥôr* alienate onesf. Is 1_{4}. †
hof.: pt. מוּזָר: **alienated** Ps 69_{9}. †

III זור: **qal**: pf. זָרָה: stink, **be offensive** (breath) Jb 19_{17}. †

זָזָא: n. pers.

I זחל: **qal**: pt. זֹחֲלֵי: **crawl** (of snake) Dt 32_{24} Mi 7_{17}. †

II זחל: **qal**: pf. זָחַלְתִּי: **be afraid** Jb 32_{6}. †

זֹחֶלֶת: n. loc.

זיד: **qal**: pf. זָדוּ, זָדָה: **treat insolently**, w. *ʿal* Ex 18_{11}, w. *ʾel* Je 50_{29}. †
hif.: pf. הֵזִידוּ; impf. יְזִידוּן, וַיָּזֶד, יָז(י)ד, וַתָּזִדוּ: — 1. **boil** s.thg Gn 25_{29}; — 2. **become heated** (of passion) Ex 21_{14}; — 3. **treat arrogantly**: a) w. *ʿal* Ne 9_{10}; b) abs. Dt 17_{13}; c) followed by fin. vb. Dt 1_{43}, by inf. Dt 18_{20}.

*זֵידוֹן: pl. זֵידוֹנִים: **raging** (water) Ps 124_{5}. †

I זִיז: cs. =: small creatures that ravage fields Ps 50_{11} 80_{14}. †

II זִיז: **nipple,** metaph. *zîz kābôd* full breast Is 66_{11}. †

זִיזָא: n. pers.

זִיזָה: n. pers.

[זִינָא: n. pers. 1C 23_{10}, rd. זִיזָא.]

זִיעַ: n. pers.

I זִיף: n. loc.

II זִיף: n. pers.; ? = I: 1C 4_{16}. †

זִיפָה: n. pers.

*זִיפִי: gent. of I זִיף: pl. זִיפִים: 1S 23_{19}.

זִיקוֹת: sg. *זִיקָה or II *זֵק, F II זֵק, זִקִּים: **flaming arrow** Is 50_{11}. †

זַיִת: cs. זֵית, sf. זֵיתְךָ, זֵיתֶךָ; pl. זֵיתִים, זֵיתֵיכֶם: — 1. **olive** (tree or fruit), *Olea europaea*: *zayit* = (one) o.-tree Ju 9_{8}, *zêtîm* o.-trees 2K 5_{26}, *zayit* olive orchard Ex 23_{11}; *šemen zayit* o.-oil Ex 27_{20}; *zêt šemen* (oil-rich) olive-trees Dt 8_{8}; — 2. metaph. *zayit raʿanān* Je 11_{16}; n. terr. *har* (*maʿalēh*) *hazzêtîm* Mt. of Olives Zc 14_{4} 2S 15_{30}.

זֵיתָן: n. pers.

זַךְ: זָךְ, f. זַכָּה: **clear, pure**: — 1. of oil Ex 27_{20}, frankincense 30_{34}; — 2. metaph. a) man Pr 16_{2}; b) works Pr 20_{11}, prayer Jb 16_{7}.

זכה: **qal**: impf. יִזְכֶּה, אֶזְכֶּה: **be** (morally) **pure**, stand blameless Ps 51_{6}.
piel: pf. זִכִּיתִי; impf. יְזַכֶּה: **keep** s.thg **pure** Ps 73_{13}.
hitp.: impv. הִזַּכּוּ: **clean onesf.** Is 1_{16}. †

זְכוֹכִית: transparent **glass** as ornament Jb 28_{17}. †

*זָכוּר: sf. זְכוּרְךָ, זְכוּרָהּ: coll. **what is male** Ex 23_{17}.

זַכּוּר: n. pers.

זַכַּי, זַכָּי: n. pers.

זכך: **qal**: pf. זַכּוּ: — 1. **be clear, bright** La 4_{7}; — 2. **be pure, guiltless** Jb 15_{15} 25_{5}. †
hif.: pf. הֲזִכּוֹתִי: **clean** Jb 9_{30}. †

זכר: **qal** (165×, 43×Ps): pf. זָכַרְתָּ, ז׳, 2. f. זָכַרְתִּי Ez 16_{22} Kt, זְכַרְתֻּנִי, זְכַרְתֶּם, זְכַרְתִּיךְ; impf. וַיִּזְכֹּר, יִזְכָּר־, וַיִּזְכְּרֶהָ, תִּזְכֹּר, אֶזְכֹּר, אֶזְכְּרֵכִי Ps 137_{6}, אֶזְכְּרֶנּוּ, יִזְכְּרוּנִי; inf. לִזְכֹּר, כִּזְכֹּר Je 17_{2}, abs. זָכוֹר; impv. זְכֹר, זְכָר־, זָכְרָה, זִכְרוּ, זָכְרוּ, זָכְרֵנִי; pt. pl. זֹכְרֵי, pass. F זָכוּר: — 1. **mention** Je 23_{36}; — 2. **remember**: a) w. acc., subj. God: Gn 8_{1}; subj. Isr., obj. God Ju 8_{34}; b) w. l^{e} for the sake of Je 2_{2}, against Ps 137_{7}; c) think of: w. l^{e} Dt 9_{27}, w. b^{e} Je 3_{16}; d) abs. be mindful Je 14_{21}; e) remember that, w. *ʾet-ʾašer* 2S 19_{20}; — f) F זָכוּר mindful, w. *kî* Dt 5_{15}, w. interr. clause Jb 4_{7}.
nif.: pf. נִזְכַּרְתֶּם; impf. יִזָּכֵר, תִּזָּכֵרִי, תִּזָּכַרְןָ, תִּנָּכַרְנָה; inf. הִזָּכֶרְכֶם; pt. נִזְכָּרִים: — 1. *nizkar*: **it is mentioned, named** Ez 25_{10}, esp. one's name Je 11_{19}; — 2. *nizkar*: **he is remembered, thought of** Is 23_{16}; — 3. **be reckoned, imputed**, w. l^{e}, *lifnê* Nu 10_{9}.
hif.: pf. הִזְכִּיר, הִזְכַּרְתֻּנִי; impf. אַזְכִּיר, יַזְכִּירוּ; impv. הַזְכִּירֵנִי, הַזְכִּירוּ; inf. הַזְכִּיר, הַזְכִּרְכֶם, הַזְכִּירוֹ Ez 21_{29}; pt. מַזְכִּיר, מַזְכִּירִים, מַזְכֶּרֶת: — 1. w. acc. **summon** (to court) Is 43_{26} †; — 2. **have** (one's name)

mentioned 2S 18_{18}; **mention** Gn 41_{9}; — 3. **make known**: *ʿāwôn* 1K 17_{18}, *šēm* Is 49_{1}; **announce**, w. *ʾel* Gn 40_{14}, abs. Je 4_{16} †; — 4. (in hymn) **acknowledge, praise**, *šēm ʾelōhîm* Ex 23_{13}, *bešēm* swear by Is 48_{1} Am 6_{10}; — 5. denom. of ↗ *ʾazkārâ*: bring as an *ʾazkārâ* Is 66_{3}; *lehazkîr* Ps 38_{1} to sing while bringing to *ʾazkārâ*.

זָכָר: pl. זְכָרִים: — 1. **man** (as a male, opp. to woman) Gn 1_{27}; *kol-zākār* everything male Gn 17_{10}; *bēn zākār* male child Je 20_{15}; *zekārîm* men Ex 13_{12}; *šākab ʾēt zākār* homosexuality Lv 18_{22}, *miškab zākār* intercourse of woman w. man Nu 31_{17}; — 2. **male animal**, esp. **ram** Ex 12_{5}.

זֵכֶר: cs. =; sf. זִכְרִי, זִכְרְךָ: — 1. **mention** (of a name) Dt 32_{26}; — 2. **solemn naming or address of God** Ex 3_{15}.

***זֶכֶר**: זָכֶר: n. pers.

זִכָּרוֹן, 3 × זִכְרֹן: cs. זִכְרוֹן; sf. זִכְרוֹנֵךְ; pl. זִכְרֹנֹת, זִכְרֹנֵיכֶם: mention, **reminder**: — 1. a) *lezikkārôn* Ex 28_{12}; b) *ʾabnê zikkārôn le* Ex 28_{12}; *zikkārôn bên ʿênêkā* memorial sign Ex 13_{9}; *hāyâ lāhem zikkārôn* remembers them Ec 1_{11}; memorial Ne 2_{20}; — 2. *zikrōnêkem* what you put forward Jb 13_{12}; *minḥâ zikkārôn* cereal offering of confession of sin Nu 5_{15}; — 3. a) *sēfer zikrōnôt* **official record** Est 6_{1}; b) *sēfer zikkārôn* heavenly book before Y. Ma 3_{16}; — 4. *zikrônēk* erotic symbol, phallus?, on door & posts Is 57_{8}.

זִכְרִי: n. pers.

זְכַרְיָה: n. pers.

זְכַרְיָהוּ: n. pers.

זֻלּוּת: **vileness** ? Ps 12_{9}. †

***זַלְזַל**: pl. זַלְזַלִּים: **shoot** (of vine before onset of fruit)? Is 18_{5}. †

I **זלל**: **qal**: pt. זוֹלֵל, זוֹלֵלָה, זוֹלְלִים, זוֹלֲלֵי: — 1. **be frivolous** Dt 21_{20}, Pr 23_{21}; *zōlalê bāśār* gluttons at eating meat Pr 23_{20}; neuter *zôlēl* what is frivolous Je 15_{19}; — 2. **be despised** La 1_{11}. †

hif.: pf. הִזִּילוּהָ: **despise** La 1_{8}. †

II **זלל**: **nif.**: pf. נָזֹלּוּ > נָזֹלּוּ: **quake** (of mountains) Ju 5_{5} Is 63_{19} 64_{2}. †

זַלְעָפָה: pl. זַלְעָפוֹת, cs. זַלְעֲפוֹת: — 1. **rage** Ps 119_{53}, *rûaḥ zilʿāfôt* whirlwind Ps 11_{6}; — 2. metaph. *zalʿafôt rāʿāb* **hunger-pangs** La 5_{10}. †

זִלְפָּה: n. pers. f.

זֻלֻּת: ↗ זֻלּוּת.

I **זִמָּה**: cs. זִמַּת, sf. זִמָּתֵךְ, זִמָּתְכֶנָה; pl. זִמּוֹת, זִמֹּתַי: — 1. **plan**: a) intention Jb 17_{11}; b) evil plan, plot Is 32_{7}, adv. acc. cunningly Ps 119_{150}; — 2. tech. term in cultic law, **infamy**, infamous treatment; a) spec. prostitution & incest Ju 20_{6}; b) otherw. Ho 6_{9} Ps 26_{10}.

II **זִמָּה**: n. pers. 1C $6_{5.27}$ 2C 29_{12}. †

זְמוֹרָה: cs. זְמֹרַת; pl. sf. זְמֹרֵיהֶם: — 1. **branch** (of vine) Nu 13_{23}; — 2. *šōleḥîm ʾet-hazzemôrâ ʾel ʾappām* Ez 8_{17}: ?; some: harass, irritate; oth.: pagan cultic practice; ↗ comm.

זַמְזֻמִּים: n. peop.

I **זָמִיר**: **song** 2S 23_{1}.

II **זָמִיר**: SS 2_{12}: usu.: **pruning** (of vines), or **vintage**; oth.: = I *zāmîr*. †

זְמִירָה: n. pers.

זמם: **qal**: pf. זַמֹּתִי, זַמֹּתִי, זַמּוֹתָ, זָמְמָה, זָמַם, ז׳ Ps 17_{3} & זָמְמוּ, זָמָמְתִּי; impf. יָזֹמּוּ; pt. זֹמֵם: murmur > **think, plan**: — 1. a) acc. have one's eye on s.thg Pr 31_{16}; purpose Je 4_{28}; b) plan (of God) Je 51_{12}; c) consider Pr 30_{32}; — 2. **plan evil** Ps 31_{14}.

זמן: **pual**: pt. מְזֻמָּנִים, מְזֻמָּנוֹת: **be appointed** (time &c.) Ezr 10_{14}.

זְמָן: זְמַן; pl. זְמַנִּים, זְמַנֵּיהֶם: **specific time, hour** Ec 3_{1}.

I **זמר**: **piel**: impf. אֲזַמְּרָה, אֲזַמְּרָה, אֲזַמֵּר, נְזַמְּרָה, יְזַמֶּרְךָ, אֲזַמֶּרְךָ; impv. זַמְּרוּ, זַמְּרוּ; inf. זַמֵּר, זַמְּרָה Ps 147_{1}: — 1. play an instrument, **sing** *leyhwh* Ju 5_{3}, *lemalkēnû* Ps 47_{7} &c.; — 2. **praise**: Y. Ps 30_{13}, *kebôd šemô* 66_{2}; — 3. abs. **sing, praise** Ps 47_{7}; —

4. w. *bᵉ* **play an instrument**: *bᵉkinnôr* Ps 71_{22}.

II **זמר**: **qal**: impf. תִּזְמֹר: **prune** (vines) Lv 25_{3f}. †

***זֶמֶר**: זֶמֶר: **kind of gazelle** Dt 14_5. †

I **זִמְרָה**: **playing, sound** (of an instrument) Is 51_3.

II ***זִמְרָה**: זִמְרָת Ex 15_2 Is 12_2 Ps 118_{14} = זִמְרָתִי: **strength** Ex 15_2; *zimrat hā'āreṣ* best produce of the land Gn 43_{11}. †

I **זִמְרִי**: n. pers.

II **זִמְרִי**: n. peop. Je 25_{25}. †

זִמְרָן: n. peop.

זִמְרָת: Ex 15_2 Is 12_2 Ps 118_{14}: ↗ II *זִמְרָה.

זַן: pl. זְנִים: **kind, sort** 2C 16_{14}; *mizzan 'el-zan* Ps 144_{13} of every sort (?), txt. corr. ?. †

זנב: **piel**: pf. זִנַּבְתֶּם; impf. יְזַנֵּב: **seize** & **destroy** the tail, i.e. the **rear-guard** Dt 25_{18} Jos 10_{19}. †

זָנָב: sf. זְנָבוֹ; pl. זְנָבוֹת, cs. זַנְבוֹת: — **tail**, of snake Ex 4_4, fox Ju 15_4; — 2. metaph. end, **stump** Is 7_4.

I **זָנָה**: **qal**: pf. ז׳, זָנְתָה, זָנִית, זָנוּ; impf. 3. f. sg. וַתִּזְנֶה & וַתִּזֶן Je 3_8 & וַתִּזְנִי 3_6, 2. f. sg. Ez 16_{28a}, יִזְנֶה, וַיִּזְנוּ Ez 23_{43} (Kt יִזְנֶה, Qr יִזְנוּ), תִּזְנֶינָה; inf. זְנ(וֹ)ת, זְנוּתֵךְ, abs. זָנֹה; pt. זֹ(וֹ)נֶה, זֹ(וֹ)נָה, זוֹנִים, זוֹנוֹת: — 1. (of wife, bride) be involved w. another man, **have illicit intercourse** Gn 38_{24}; *'iššâ zônâ* ↗ *zōnâ*; w. *'ēt* Is 23_{17}, w. *'el* Ez 16_{24}, w. *bᵉ* Ez 16_{17}; cult prostitution Ho 4_{13f}; of a man, w. pagan women Nu 25_1; — 2. in relation to God, **be faithless**: a) *libbām hazzōneh* & *'ênêkem hazzōnôt* Ex 6_9, *zôneh yiśrā'ēl* Ho 4_{15}; *zānâ 'aḥᵃrê* run wantonly after **Ex** 34_{15}; b) **wantonly turn from** *zānâ mittaḥat* Ho 4_{12}, oth. comb. of *min*: *mē'aḥᵃrê* Ho 1_2 &c.

pual: (pass. qal?): pf. זוּנָּה: w. *'aḥᵃrê* s.one is solicited for prostitution Ez 16_{34}. †

hif.: pf. הִזְנֵיתָ, הִזְנוּ; impf. וַיֶּזֶן, וַתַּזְנֶה; inf. הַזְנוֹת, הַזְנוֹתָהּ, abs. הַזְנֵה: — 1. **urge into** (cultic) **prostitution** Lv 19_{29}; metaph. seduce into idol-worship Ex 34_{16}; — 2. **practice prostitution** Ho 4_{10} (oth.: teach harlotry).

II **זנה**: **qal**: impf. וַתִּזְנֶה: w. *'al* **feel a dislike** for Ju 19_2. †

זֹנָה, זוֹנָה: s.one practicing prostitution either occasionally or professionally: **prostitute**: *'iššâ zōnâ* 1K 3_{16}; > *zōnâ* Gn 34_{31}.

I **זָנוֹחַ**: n. loc.

II **זָנוֹחַ**: n. pers. 1C 4_{18}. †

זְנוּנִים: cs. זְנוּנֵי, sf. זְנוּנֶיהָ, זְנוּנַיִךְ: circumstance & practice of the *zōnâ*, **prostitution** Gn 38_{24}; *'ēšet zᵉnûnîm* Ho 1_2: some: a woman endowed w. the tendency to pr., but other comms. differ.

זְנוּת: sf. זְנוּתֵךְ, זְנוּתָהּ; pl. sf. זְנוּתַיִךְ, זְנוּתֵיכֶם: — 1. **prostitution** Je 3_2; — 2. **unfaithfulness** to God Nu 14_{33}.

I **זנח**: **hif.**: pf. וְהֶאֶזְנִיחוּ: **become foul-smelling** (waters) Is 19_6. †

II **זָנַח**: **qal**: pf. ז׳, זָנַחְתָּ, זְנַחְתָּנוּ, זְנַחְתַּנִי, זְנַחְתִּים; impf. יִזְנַח: **reject** Ho 8_3 Ps 43_2; w. *min* **exclude from** La 3_{17}.

hif.: pf. הִזְנִיחַ, הִזְנִיחָם; impf. יַזְנִיחֲךָ: **declare** s.one **rejected** 1C 28_9; **remove** (vessels) **from use** 2C 29_{19}; w. *mikkāhēn* exclude fm. priestly office 2C 11_{14}. †

זנק: **piel**: impf. יְזַנֵּק: **jump forth** Dt 33_{22}. †

***זעה**: **pilp.**: pt. מְזַעְזְעֶיךָ: w. word-play, who bark at you Hb 2_7.

***זֵעָה**: cs. זֵעַת: **sweat** Gn 3_{19}. †

זַעֲוָה: < ↗ זְוָעָה: trembling, **terror**; *hāyâ lᵉza'ᵃwâ* Dt 28_{25}, *nātan lᵉza'ᵃwâ* Ez 23_{46}.

זַעֲוָן: n. pers.

זעזע: ↗ זוע.

זְעֵיר: **a little** Is $28_{10.13}$; a short time Jb 36_2. †

זעך: **nif.**: pf. נִזְעָכוּ: **be extinguished** Jb 17_1. †

זָעַם: **qal**: pf. ז׳, זְעַמְתָּה; impf. אֶזְעֹם, יִזְעָמוּהוּ; impv. זֹעֲמָה; pt. זֹעֵם, pass. cs. זְעוּם, זְעוּמָה: **curse, scold** Nu 23_{7f}; *zᵉ'ûm* *yhwh* cursed by Y. Pr 22_{14}; *'ēl zō'ēm* a God who passes sentence Ps 7_{12}.

nif.: pt. נִזְעָמִים: **struck w. the curse** Pr 25_{23} (oth.: peevish). †

זַעַם: זָעַם, sf. זַעְמִי, זַעְמוֹ: — 1. **curse (from God)** Is 10_5; — 2. **curse** (w. *lešônām* **against God** or his prophets) Ho 7_{16} (oth.: stuttering).

I **זעף**: **qal**: impf. יִזְעַף; inf. זַעְפּוֹ: **rage** against Jon 1_{15}, w. *'al* Pr 19_3, w. *'im* 2C 26_{19b}.

II **זעף**: **qal**: pt. זֹעֲפִים: **look wretched, pitiful** Gn 40_6 Dn 1_{10}. †

זַעַף: **rage**: of king Pr 19_{12}, of Y. Mi 7_9.

זָעֵף: **raging**: 1K 20_{43} 21_4. †

זעק: **qal**: pf. זָעֲקָה, זָעַקְתִּי, זָעֲקוּ; impf. יִזְעַק, אֶזְעַק, יִזְעֲקוּ, וַיִּזְעָקוּךָ; impv. זְעַק, זַעֲקִי, זַעֲקוּ, זְעָקוּ; inf. זְעֹק, זַעֲקָךְ, זַעֲקֵךְ: **cry out**: — 1. **call for help** 2S 19_{29} (w. *'el*), Ho 8_2 (w. *le*); — 2. **send out a call to arms** Ju 12_2; — 3. **call out the password** 1K 22_{32}.

nif.: pf. נִזְעֲקוּ, נִזְעַקְתָּ; impf. וַיִּזָּעֵק, וַיִּזָּעֲקוּ: — 1. **be called up** (to arms) Jos 8_{16}; — 2. **be assembled** (after a call to arms) 1S 14_{20}.

hif.: impf. וַיַּזְעֵק, וַיַּזְעִיקוּ; impv. הַזְעֶק־; inf. הַזְעִיק: — 1. **utter a plaintive cry** Jb 35_9; — 2. **send out a call to arms** 2S 20_{4f}; — 3. have s.thg **be proclaimed** Jon 3_7; — 4. w. acc. **call loudly** to s.one Zc 6_8.

זְעָקָה: cs. זַעֲקַת, sf. זַעֲקָתִי, זַעֲקָתָם: — 1. **plaintive cry, call for help** Gn 18_{20}; — 2. **shouting** Ez 27_{28}.

***זִפְרֹון**: loc. זִפְרֹנָה: n. loc.

זֶפֶת: זֶפֶת: **pitch** Ex 2_3 Is 34_9. †

I ***זֵק**: pl. זִקִּים: **chains, fetters** Is 45_{14}.

II ***זֵק**: pl. זִקִּים: **flaming arrows** Pr 26_{18}. †

זָקֵן: **qal**: pf. ז׳, זָקְנָה, זָקַנְתָּ(ה); impf. יִזְקַן: — 1. **be an old man, woman** Gn 27_2 18_{13}; — 2. age, **become old** Gn 18_{12}.

hif.: impf. יַזְקִין: **become older** Pr 22_6 Jb 14_8. †

זָקָן: cs. זְקַן, sf. זְקָנְךָ, זְקָנוֹ, זְקַנְכֶם: **beard** (on cheeks & chin, :: *śāfām*), of men 1S 21_{14}, lion 1S 17_{35}.

זָקֵן (174×): cs. זְקַן; pl. זְקֵנִים, cs. זִקְנֵי, sf. זְקֵנָיו, זְקֵנֵינוּ, זִקְנֵיכֶם, f. זְקֵנוֹת: **old**: — 1. *'îš zāqēn* 1S 28_{14}; *zeqēnîm ûbā'îm bayyāmîm* Gn 18_{11}, *zāqên ûśeba' yāmîm* Gn 25_8; — 2. *zeqan bêtô* his oldest (slave) in the house Gn 24_2; — 3. *hā'anāšîm hazzeqēnîm* the old men Ez 9_6; — 4. *hazzeqēnîm* a particular social class, **'the elders'**: *ziqnê hā'ām* Ex 19_7; — 5. *hazzeqēnîm* the totality of men (w. full beard) of mature years w. legal competence in a community: *ziqnê hā'îr* 1S 16_4.

זֹקֶן: **old age** Gn 48_{10}. †

זִקְנָה: cs. זִקְנַת, sf. זִקְנָתוֹ: growing old, **old age** Gn 24_{36}.

זְקֻנִים: sf. זְקֻנָיו: time & circumstance of the aged, **old age** Gn 21_2.

זקף: **qal**: pt. זֹ(ו)קֵף: **raise up** (those bowed down) Ps 145_{14} 146_8. †

זקק: **qal**: impf. יָזֹקּוּ: **strain** (water) Jb 36_{27}, wash (gold) 28_1. †

piel: pf. זִקַּק: filter, **refine** Mal 3_3. †

pual: pt. מְזֻקָּק, מְזֻקָּקִים: **filtered, refined** Is 25_6.

זָר: < pt. זור; f. זָרָה; pl. זָרִים, זָרוֹת: **strange, foreign, completely different, unlawful**: — 1. (one who is) **unauthorized**: non-Aaronite Lv 22_{10}, non-Levite Nu 1_{51}, one who does not share in the cult, i.e. layman Ex 30_{33}; — 2. **non-Israelite** Ex 29_{33} & oft.; — 3. strange = **forbidden**: *'ēš zārâ* illegitimate, forbidden fire Lv 10_1; *zārîm* foreigners w. whom marriage is forbidden Je 2_{25}, *bānîm zārîm* illegitimate children Ho 5_7; — 4. *('ēl) zār* foreign, forbidden god Ps 44_{21} Is 17_{10}; — 5. *'iššâ zārâ* **foreign**, unchaste **woman** Pr 2_{16}; — 6. *'îš zār* man from foreign family Dt 25_5; — 7. **other**: *'ên zār* no one else 1K 3_{18}; Jb 19_{27} *welō'-zār*: some: 'no one else,' oth.: 'I as enemy,' or 'God as enemy,' ꟻ comm.; — 8. **strange, surprising** Is 28_{21} Pr 23_{33}, loathsome Jb 19_{17}.

***זֵר**: cs. =, sf. זֵרוֹ: (only in P) **molding** (of gold) around the ark &c. Ex 25_{11}.

זָרָא: **sickness, nausea** Nu 11_{20}. †

זרב: **pual**: impf. יְזֹרְבוּ: (cease, be submerged) **dry up** Jb 6_{17}. †

זְרֻבָּבֶל: n. pers., **Zerubbabel**.

***זֶרֶד**: זֶרֶד: name of a river.

I **זרה**: **qal**: impf. תִּזְרֶה, וַיִּזֶר, וַתִּזְרֵם, וָאֶזְרֵם; impv. זְרֵה; inf. זְרוֹת; pt. זֹרֶה: — 1. **scatter** (powder) Ex 32_{20}; sow Is 30_{22}; — 2. **winnow** Is 30_{24}.

nif.: impf. וַיִּזָּרוּ; inf. הִזָּרוֹתֵיכֶם: **be scattered** (of Isr.) Ez 6_8 36_{19}. †

piel: pf. זֵרִיתִי, זֵרוּ, זֵרָם, זֵר(י)תִים, זֵרוּהָ; impf. אֱזָרֶה יְזָרוּ Pr 15_7; inf. זָרוֹת, זָרוֹתָם; pt. מְזָרֶה, cs. מְזָרֵה: — 1. **scatter**, bones Ez 6_5, people 1K 14_{15}; — 2. **spread** (dung) Mal 2_3; — 3. metaph. **spread** (knowledge) Pr 15_7.

pual: impf. יְזֹרֶה; pt. f. מְזֹרָה: — 1. **be scattered** (brimstone) Jb 18_{15}; — 2. **be sprinkled** (a net w. grain) Pr 1_{17}. †

II **זרה**: **piel**: pf. זֵרִיתָ: **measure off** Ps 139_3. †

זְרוֹעַ & **זְרֹעַ**: sf. זְרֹעוֹ, זְרֹעֲךָ, זְרֹעֶךָ; pl. זְרֹעִים, cs. זְרֹעֵי, sf. זְרֹעָיו & זְרֹ(ו)עֹ(ו)ת, זְרֹעֹתֵיכֶם, זְרֹעֹתָי: — 1. **arm, forearm**: of men Ju 15_{19}, of animal (shoulder) Nu 6_{19}; *bên zᵉrōʿāyw* between his shoulders 2K 9_{24}; — 2. metaph.: a) **(activity of) power**, violence: *ʾîš zᵉrôaʿ* Jb 22_8; b) **help**: *hāyā zᵉrôaʿ lᵉ* lend help to Ps 83_9; — 3. **God's arm** (esp. in leading people in Exodus or eschatological) 1K 8_{42} & oft.; — 4. **military forces** *zᵉrōʿōt* Ez 30_{22}.

זֵרוּעַ: pl. sf. זֵרוּעֶיהָ: any plant growing from seeds Lv 11_{37} Is 61_{11}. †

זַרְזִיף, Ps 72_6: ꟻ זרף pilpel.

***זַרְזִיר**, cs. =: *zarzîr motnayim*: **cock** (?) Pr 30_{31}. †

זָרַח: **qal**: pf. ז׳, זָרַח, זָרְחָה; impf. יִזְרַח; inf. **זְרֹחַ**: — 1. **go forth, shine**: sun Gn 32_{32}, light Is 58_{10}, Y. Dt 33_2; — 2. **break out** (leprosy) 2C 26_{19}.

I ***זֶרַח**: sf. זַרְחֵךְ: the shining forth of light, sunrise Is 60_3. †

II **זֶרַח**: n. pers.

זַרְחִי: gent. of II זֶרַח.

זְרַחְיָה: n. pers.

I **זרם**: **qal**: pf. זְרַמְתָּם: stop, **put an end to life** Ps 90_5. †

II **זרם**: **poel**: pf. זֹרְמוּ: **relieve** (clouds, water) **of thunder** Ps 77_{18}. †

זֶרֶם: **heavy rain**, cloudburst (w. thunder) Is 4_6.

***זִרְמָה**: cs. זִרְמַת: **phallus** Ez 23_{20}. †

זָרַע: **qal**: pf. ז׳, זָרְעוּ, זְרַעְתֶּם; impf. יִזְרַע, יִזְרֶע, אֶזְרְעָא, יִזְרְעוּ, נִזְרַע, יִזְרָעֶהָ, אֶזְרָעֵם; impv. זְרַע, זִרְעוּ; inf. זְרֹעַ; pt. זֹרֵעַ, pl. cs. זֹרְעֵי, pass. f. זְרוּעָה: **sow**: — 1. abs. **sow** Gn 26_{12}; — 2. a) w. acc. **sow** (the ground, a field) Gn 47_{23}; b) w. acc. of the seed: cogn. acc. Dt 22_9, wheat Je 12_{13}; metaph. *rûᵃḥ* Ho 8_7; c) w. 2 acc. **sow** (field &c.) w. s.thg Ju 9_{45} (city w. salt); d) w. preps. & place, *bᵉ* Ex 23_{16}, *ʿal* Is 32_{20}, *ʾel* Je 4_3; — 3. spec.: *zōrēᵃʿ zeraʿ* yielding seed Gn 1_{29}.

nif.: pf. נִזְרַעְתֶּם, נִזְרָעָה; impf. יִזָּרַע, תִּזָּרַע: — 1. **be sown** (seed) Lv 11_{37}; — 2. **be sown** (place): valley Dt 21_4, land 29_{22}; — 3. (of a woman) capable of impregnation Nu 5_{28}.

pual (pass. qal?): pf. זֹרָעוּ: **be sown** (metaph.) Is 40_{24}. †

hif.: impf. תַּזְרִיעַ; pt. מַזְרִיעַ: — 1. **form seed** Gn 1_{11f}; — 2. **conceive** (child) Lv 12_2. †

זֶרַע: זָרַע; cs. זֶרַע & זְרַע, sf. זַרְעוֹ; pl. sf. זַרְעֵיכֶם: **seed**: — 1. in genl. *zeraʿ haśśādeh* seed of the field Gn 47_{22}; *zeraʿ* = seedtime Gn 8_{22}; a) specific kinds of seed: of tree Gn 1_{11}, shrub 1_{29}, coriander Ex 16_{31}; *zeraʿ ʾᵉmet* (vine) of good sort Je 2_{21}; b) seed (for sowing) Gn 47_{19}; *mᵉqôm zeraʿ* place fit for sowing; *bêt zeraʿ* a portion of sown land 1K 18_{32}; — 2. of men & animals: *zeraʿ ʾādām* & *zeraʿ behēmâ* seed Je 31_{27}, *zeraʿ ʾanāšîm* = son 1S 1_{11}; *zeraʿ* = descendants of *ʾiššâ* & *nāḥāš* Gn 3_{15}, *ʿôf* 7_3; *šikbat zeraʿ* ejaculation of semen Lv 15_{16}; — 3. **offspring, descendants**: a) sg. coll. 1S 2_{20}; oft. of patriarchs, Gn 12_7 &c., & David 2S 7_{12}; *rāʾâ zeraʿ* see offspring = have offspr. Is 53_{10}; many phrases, e.g. *zeraʿ ʾên lāh* she has no children Lv 22_{13}, *hēqîm zeraʿ le* supply offspring for him Gn 38_8; b) single offspring, *zeraʿ ʾaḥēr* Gn 4_{25}; — 4. **origin, descent** Ezr 2_{59} Ne 7_{61}.

זֵרֹעִים: Dn 1_{12} rd. ⟶ זֵרְעֹנִים. †

זֵרְעֹנִים: seeds, **vegetables** Dn 1_{16}. †

***זרף**: cj. **pilpel**: pf. זִרְזְפוּ: **sprinkle richly** Ps 72_6. †

I **זרק**: **qal**: pf. זָרַק, זָרְקוּ, זָרְקוּ, ז׳; impf. יִזְרֹק, יִזְרְקֵהוּ; inf. זְרֹק; pt. זֹרֵק: — 1. **scatter**, ashes Ex $9_{8.10}$, dust Jb 2_{12}; — 2. **sprinkle**: a) blood on the altar 2K $16_{13.15}$; b) pure water Ez 36_{25}.

pual (pass. qal): pf. זֹרַק: **be sprinkled** Nu $19_{13.20}$. †

II **זרק**: **qal**: pf. זָרְקָה: **creep in** Ho 7_9. †

I **זרר**: **qal** (pass.): pf. זֹרוּ: **be pressed out** (wounds) Is 1_6. †

II **זרר**: **poel**: impf. וַיְזוֹרֵר: **sneeze** 2K 4_{35}. †

זֶרֶשׁ: n. pers. f.

זֶרֶת: זֶרֶת: **span** (of hand, as a measure), 1/2 *ʾammâ* = ca. 25 cm. Ex 28_{16}.

זַתּוּא: n. pers.

זֵתָם: n. pers.

זֵתַר: n. pers.

ח

***חֹב**: sf. חֻבִּי: **pocket of shirt** (as place of safe-keeping) Jb 31_{33}. †

חבא: **nif.**: pf. נַחְבֵּתֶם, נֶחְבְּאוּ, נַחְבֵּאתָ, נֶחְבָּא; impf. וַיֵּחָבְאוּ, אֵחָבֵא, תֵּחָבֵא; inf. הֵחָבֵא, הֵחָבֵה; pt. נֶחְבָּאִים, נֶחְבָּא: — 1. **hide** (onesf.) Gn 3_{10}; — 2. **be** hidden, **safe** Jb 5_{21}.

pual: pf. חֻבְּאוּ: **have to go into hiding** Jb 24_4. †

hif.: pf. הֶחְבִּיאָה, הֶחְבִּיאָנִי; impf. וַיַּחְבִּיאֵנִי, וַתַּחְבִּיא, וָאַחְבִּא: **hide** (s.one, s.thg), **keep hidden** 1K $18_{4.13}$.

hof.: pf. הָחְבָּאוּ: **be kept hidden** Is 42_{22}. †

hitp.: pf. הִתְחַבְּאוּ; impf. יִתְחַבֵּא, יִתְחַבְּאוּ, יִתְחַבָּאוּ; pt. מִתְחַבֵּא: **keep onesf. hidden** Gn 3_8.

חבב: **qal**: pt. חֹבֵב: **love** Dt 33_3. †

חֹבָב: n. pers.

חבה: **qal**: impv. f. חֲבִי: **hide** (onesf.) Is 26_{20}. †

חֳבָה: n. pers.

חָבוֹר: n. river, left tributary of middle Euphrates, Habor, 2K 17_6.

חַבּוּרָה & ***חֲבוּרָה**: sf. חַבּוּרָתִי, חֲבֻרָתוֹ Is 53_5; pl. חַבֻּרֹת, sf. חַבֻּרֹתָי: **wound, stripe** Gn 4_{23}.

חבט: **qal**: impf. יַחְבֹּט; pt. חֹבֵט: — 1. **beat** (olive trees) Dt 24_{20}; — 2. **beat out** (grain, accomplishing what threshing does) Ju 6_{11}; metaph., subj. Y., obj. people Is 27_{12}.

nif.: impf. יֵחָבֵט: **be beaten out** (cummin) Is 28_{27}. †

חֲבַיָּה: n. pers.

***חֶבְיוֹן** or ***חֶבְיוֹן**: cs. חֶבְיוֹן: **covering**, veil, w. *ʿuzzô* 'his strong covering' (? ⟶ comm.) Hb 3_4. †

I **חבל**: **qal**: pf. חָבַל; impf. יַחְבֹּל, תַּחְבֹּל, תַּחְבֹּל, יַחְבְּלוּ, יַחְבֹּלוּ; impv. חֲבְלֵהוּ; inf.

חֲבֹל; pt. חֹבֵל, חֹבְלִים, pass. חֲבֻלִים: — 1. **take** s.thg **in pledge** Ex 22_{25}; — 2. **exact a pledge of** s.one (w. acc.) Jb 22_{6}.

nif.: impf. יֵחָבֵל: he **is forced to give a pledge** Pr 13_{13} (oth.: II *ḥābal*). †

II חבל: **qal**: pf. חָבַלְנוּ; impf. אֶחְבֹּל; inf. חֲבֹל Ne 1_{7}: offend, **treat badly** Jb 34_{31}, Ne 1_{7} (w. *le*). †

nif.: impf. יֵחָבֶל: w. *le* **it will go badly for** him Pr 13_{13} (oth.: I *ḥābal*). †

piel: pf. חִבֵּל; inf. חַבֵּל; pt. מְחַבְּלִים: **destroy** Is 13_{5}.

pual: pf. חֻבְּלָה, וְחֻבַּל: — 1. **be troubled** (spirit) Jb 17_{1}; — 2. **be torn away** w. *mēʿal* Is 10_{27}. †

III חבל: **piel**: pf. חִבְּלָה, חִבְּלַתְךָ; impf. יְחַבֶּל־: **be pregnant** w. (metaph.) Ps 7_{15}, **come into travail** w. SS $8_{5\cdot 5}$. †

I חֶבֶל: band, **troop** (of prophets) 1S $10_{5\cdot 10}$; ? Jb 39_{3} flock of goats & hinds (⟹ *hēbel*). †

II חֶבֶל: sf. חַבְלוֹ; pl. חֲבָלִים, cs. חַבְלֵי (6×) & חֶבְלֵי (4×), sf. חֲבָלָיו, חֲבָלַיִךְ: — 1. **rope**: a) to demolish a city 2S 17_{13}, on head as sign of submission 1K 20_{31f}, on tent Is 33_{20}; (linen) **cord** Est 1_{6}; b) *ḥᵃbālîm*: cords (binding prisoner) Jb 36_{8}; **snares**, mostly metaph. Ps 119_{61}; — 2. length of rope, **line** as a unit of measure: 2S 8_{2}; — > 3. **plot of ground** (for allotment) Dt 32_{9}; — 4. tract, **district** 1K 4_{13}.

III חֶבֶל: pl. חֲבָלִים: **destruction, annihilation** Mi 2_{10} Jb 21_{17}. †

חֵבֶל: pl. חֲבָלִים, cs. חֶבְלֵי, sf. חֲבָלֶיהָ: — 1. pangs of childbirth, **travail**: exc. Is 66_{7}, alw. pl. Is 26_{17}; metaph. Is 13_{8}; — 2. **fetus** Jb 39_{3} (oth.: *hebel* I). †

חֲבֹל: **pledge**, taken over on non-repayment of debt, but remaining the property of debtor Ez $18_{12\cdot 16}$ 33_{15}. †

חִבֵּל: בְּרֹאשׁ חִבֵּל Pr 23_{34}, cj IV חֶבֶל **mountain**. †

חֹבֵל: pl. cs. חֹבְלֵי, sf. חֹבְלַיִךְ: **sailor** Ez $27_{8\cdot 27\cdot 29}$; coll. in *rab haḥōbēl* Jon 1_{6}. †

*חֲבֹלָה: sf. חֲבֹלָתוֹ: **pledge** Ez 18_{7}. †

חֹבְלִים: **union** Zc $11_{7\cdot 14}$. †

חֲבַצֶּלֶת: חֲבַצֶּלֶת: **asphodel**, *Asphodelos* Is 35_{1} SS 2_{1}. †

חֲבַצִּנְיָה: חֲבַצִּנְיָה: n. pers.

חבק: **qal**: inf. חֲבֹק; pt. חֹבֵק, חֹבֶקֶת: — 1. **embrace** 2K 4_{16} Ec 3_{5}; — 2. **fold** (hands) (in idleness) Ec 4_{5}. †

piel: pf. חִבְּקוּ; impf. וַיְחַבֵּק, וַיְחַבֶּק־, תְּחַבְּקֶנָּה, תְּחַבְּקֵנִי; inf. חַבֵּק: **embrace**: s.one Gn 33_{4}, w. *le* Gn 29_{13}, abs. Ec 3_{5}; obj. rock Jb 24_{8}, ash-heaps La 4_{5}, metaph. wisdom Pr 4_{8}.

חִבֻּק: **folding** (of hands) Pr 6_{10} 24_{33}. †

חֲבַקּוּק: n. pers. **Habakkuk** Hb 1_{1} 3_{1}. †

I חבר: **hif.**: impf. אַחְבִּירָה: **utter many loud words** Jb 16_{4} (oth.: II *ḥbr* join together). †

II חבר: **qal**: pf. חָבְרוּ; impf. יְחָבְרְךָ Ps 94_{20}; pt. חֹבֵר, חֹ(וֹ)בֶרֶת, חֹבֶרֶת, חֹבְרֹ(וֹ)ת, pass. cs. חֲבוּר: — 1. **ally onesf.** w., be allied w. Ho 4_{17}; **join forces** Gn 14_{3}; — 2. **be joined, touch** (curtains, &c.) Ex $26_{3\cdot 3}$; — 3. **charm, conjure**: pt. Dt 18_{11} Ps 58_{6}.

piel: pf. חִבֵּר, וְחִבַּרְתָּ; impf. יְחַבֵּר, יְחַבְּרֵהוּ; inf. חַבֵּר: — 1. **join** (pieces of construction) Ex 26_{6}; — 2. **join** (w. s.one in doing s.thg) 2C 20_{36}.

pual: pf. חֻבַּר, חֻבְּרָה; impf. יְחֻבַּר: **be joined** Ex 28_{7}.

hitp.: pf. אֶתְחַבַּר (2C 20_{35}); impf. יִתְחַבַּר; inf. הִתְחַבֶּרְךָ, הִתְחַבְּרוּת: — 1. **ally onesf.** w. Dn 11_{6}; — 2. **share business** w. 2C $20_{35\cdot 37}$.

I חֶבֶר: חֶבֶר; sf. חֶבְרָה; pl. חֲבָרִים, sf. חֲבָרַיִךְ: — 1. **company**: a) *ḥeber kōhᵃnîm* band (!) of priests Ho 6_{9}; b) *bêt ḥeber* common house Pr 21_{9} 25_{24}; — 2. **exorcism, spell** Is $47_{9\cdot 12}$.

II חֶבֶר: חֶבֶר: n. pers.

חָבֵר: sf. חֲבֵרוֹ; pl. חֲבֵרִים, cs. חַבְרֵי, sf. חֲבֵרָיו: **comrade, companion** Ju 20_{11} Is 1_{23}.

חַבָּר: pl. חַבָּרִים: (fellow-)**member of the same trade** Jb 40_{30}. †

***חֲבַרְבֻּרוֹת**: sf. חֲבַרְבֻּרֹתָיו: **spots** (on skin of leopard) Je 13_{23}. †

חֶבְרָה: **company** Jb 34_{8}. †

I **חֶבְרוֹן** n. loc. **Hebron**.

II **חֶבְרוֹן**: n. pers. Ex 6_{18} & oft.

חֶבְר(וֹ)נִי: gent. of II חֶבְרוֹן.

חֶבְרִי: gent. of II חֶבֶר.

***חֲבֶרֶת** or ***חֲבֵרָה**: sf. חֲבֶרְתְּךָ: **(marriage-)companion** (f.) Ma 2_{14}. †

חֹבֶרֶת: חֹבֶרֶת: set of **draperies** Ex 26_{4}.

חבשׁ: **qal**: pf. חָבַשְׁתָּ, וְחָבַשְׁתֶּם; impf. יַחֲב(וֹ)שׁ, יַחֲבָשׁ־, יֶחְבָּשׁ, אֶחֱבֹשׁ, אֶחְבְּשָׁה, וַיַּחְבְּשׁוּ, אֶחְבָּשֵׁךְ, יַחְבְּשֵׁנוּ; impv. חִבְשׁוּ; inf. חֲב(וֹ)שׁ, לַחֲבֹשָׁה; pt. חֹבֵשׁ, pass. חָבוּשׁ, חֲבֻשִׁים, חֲבוּשִׁים: — 1. **saddle** Gn 22_{3}; — 2. **tie around** (cap, turban) Ex 29_{9}; — 3. bind, **tie up** (wound) Is 30_{26}; *ḥōbēš* dresser (of a wound) Is 3_{7} (ᚠ 6); — 4. **twist** (rope) Ez 27_{24}; — 5. fetter, **imprison** Jb 40_{13}; — 6. hold the reins, **rule** (?) Jb 34_{17} Is 3_{7} (word-play w. 3 ?).

piel: pf. חִבֵּשׁ; pt. מְחַבֵּשׁ: — 1. bind, **tie up** (wound) Ps 147_{3}; — 2. **dam up** (trickling water in mines) Jb 28_{11}. †

pual (qal pass.): pf. חֻבָּשׁוּ, חֻבְּשָׁה: **be bound up** (wound) Is 1_{6} Ez 30_{21}. †

חֲבִתִּים: flat **cakes** baked in a pan 1C 9_{31}. †

חַג & חָג 1K 12_{32f} Ez 45_{21} (txt. ?) Ne 8_{18}: sf. חַגִּי, חַגֶּךָ, חַגָּהּ, חַגֵּנוּ; pl. sf. חַגֵּיכֶם: — 1. **procession, round dance, festival** (oft. connected w. pilgrimage); cogn. acc. w. ᚠ *ḥāgag*; *ʿāśâ ḥag* **hold a festival** 1K 12_{32f}; — 2. comb. for spec. festivals, ᚠ *(hā)ʾāsîf*, *(ham)maṣṣôt*, *(has)sukkôt*, *(hap)pesaḥ*, *(haq)qāṣîr*, *(haš)šābuʿôt*; *heḥag* &c. oft. = spec. festivals: = *hammaṣṣôt* Nu 28_{17}, *hassukkôt* Ez 45_{24}, *happesaḥ* Ez 45_{23}.

חָגָּא: **confusion** Is 19_{17}. †

I **חָגָב**: pl. חֲגָבִים: — 1. a **type of locust** permitted for eating, not more spec. identifiable Is 40_{22}; — 2. ? metaph. (for hip, or penis, or knuckles) Ec 12_{5} (oth.: early summer, ᚠ comm.).

II **חָגָב**: n. pers. Ezr 2_{46}. †

חֲגָבָה: n. pers.

חגג: **qal**: pf. חַגֹּתֶם; impf. תָּחֹג, יָח(וֹ)גּוּ, תְּחָגֻּהוּ, תְּחָגֶּינָה; impv. חָגִּי; inf. חֹג; pt. חוֹגֵג, חֹגְגִים: — 1. **make leaps** (like a drunk) Ps 107_{27} †; — 2. denom. hold a procession, **celebrate a pilgrimage festival**, w. *le* to the honor of God Ex 5_{1}, w. cogn. acc. Lv 23_{39}; *ḥāgag yôm* celebrate a day festively Ex 12_{14}; 1S 30_{16} practice prostitution.

***חָגוּ** or ***חֲגֶוֶה**: pl. cs. חַגְוֵי: **hiding place**, *ḥagwê hasselaʿ* **clefts in the rock** Je 49_{16}.

***חֲגוֹר** or ***חָגוֹר**: sf. חֲגֹרוֹ: **belt, sash** 1S 18_{4} Pr 31_{24}. †

***חָגוֹר**: pl. cs. חֲגוֹרֵי: **girded** Ez 23_{15}. †

חֲגוֹרָה & חֲגֹרָה: sf. חֲגֹרָתוֹ; pl. חֲגֹרֹת: — 1. **belt, sash** 1K 2_{5}; — 2. **loincloth** Gn 3_{7}.

חַגִּי: n. pers. Gn 46_{16} Nu 26_{15}; gent. Nu 26_{15}. †

חַגַּי: n. pers. **Haggai**.

חַגִּיָּה: n. pers.

חַגִּית: n. pers. f.

חָגְלָה: n. pers. f.

חגר: **qal**: pf. חָגְרוּ, וְחָגַרְתָּ; impf. יַחְגֹּר, יַחְגְּרוּ, יַחְגְּרָה, תַּחְגֹּרְנָה; impv. חֲגֹר, חִגְרִי, חִגְרוּ, pl. f. חֲגֹרָה & חֲגֹרְנָה Is 32_{11}; inf. חֲגֹר; pt. חֹגֵר, pass. חָגוּר, f. חֲגֻרַת־, pl. חֲגוּרִים, חֲגֻרִים: **put on a belt, make ready** for activity: — 1. for war: a) gird onesf. w., **buckle on** a weapon 1S 17_{39}; *kol ḥōgēr ḥagôrâ* everyone fit for military service 2K 3_{21}; b) w. 2 acc. **gird s.one** w. Ex 29_{9}; pt. pass. & acc. **girded w.** 1K 20_{11}; — 2. ceremonially: a) king, w. sword Ps 45_{4}, metaph. w. *ṣedeq* Is 11_{5}; angel w. gold Dn 10_{5}; b) priest w. var. articles, e.g. ephod 1S 2_{18}; c) *ḥāgar saq*, in mourning 1K 20_{32}; *saq* omitted Is 32_{11}; — 3. *ḥāgar motnayim*, prepare onesf., **get ready**: for journey 2K 4_{29}, other activity Pr 31_{17}; — 4. metaph.: gird w. sweat Ez 44_{18}, w. joy Ps 65_{13}.

I ***חַד**: f. חַדָּה: **sharp** (sword) Is 49_{2}.

II חַד: Aram. one; *ḥad ʼet-ʼaḥad* **each other** Ez 33_{30}. †

חדד: **qal**: pf. חַדּוּ: **be quick** Hb 1_8. †
hof.: pf. הוּחַדָּה: **be sharpened** (sword) Ez $21_{14\cdot16}$. †

חֲדַד: n. pers.

I חדה: **qal**: impf. וַיִּחַדְּ: **rejoice** Ex 18_9. †
piel: impf. תְּחַדֵּהוּ: w. *b^e* gladden, **make happy** Ps 21_7. †

II חדה: cj **qal**: impf. יַחַד Ps 33_{15} & יַחַד 49_{11} &יַחַד Jb 34_{29} ? rd. (ה)יֶחֱדֶ see, w. *ʻal* **gaze on**.†
? **nif.**: let onesf. be seen, **appear**: Gn 49_6 תֵּחַד, Jb 3_6 rd יַחַד for יִחַדְּ; so Ps 139_{16} for אֶחָד rd (ה)אֵחָדֶ. †

*חַדּוּד: pl. cs. חַדּוּדֵי: **point, spike**, w. *ḥereś*, sharp scales on the belly of the crocodile Jb 41_{22}. †

חֶדְוָה: cs. חֶדְוַת: **joy** Ne 8_{10}.

חָדִי: n. loc.

I חָדַל: **qal**: pf. ח׳, חָדַלְתָּ, הֶחֳדַלְתִּי Ju $9_{9\cdot11\cdot13}$, אֶחְדַּל, יֶחְדַּל, impf. חָדְלוּ, חָדָלוּ, חָדֵלוּ; יֶחְדְּלוּן, יֶחְדָּלוּ, וַיֶּחְדְּלוּ, אֶחְדְּלָה, נֶחְדָּל; impv. חֲדַל, חִדְלוּ, חֲדָל, חֲדָלוּ, חֲדַל; inf. חֲדֹל: — 1. **end, stop** a) make an end: storm Ex 9_{29}, merriment Is 24_8; b) no longer be in existence: the poor Dt 15_{11}, caravans Ju 5_{6t}; c) stay away: shoots of tree Jb 14_7, friends 19_{14}; — 2. **stop** doing s.thg: a) w. inf. Is 1_{16}; b) w. *min* & inf. 1K 15_{21}; c) w. *l^e* & inf. Gn 11_8; d) abs. Ju 15_7; — 3. **let s.thg stay, not do** s.thg Je 40_4; w. *l^e* & inf. Dt 23_{23}; leave off, **discontinue** 1S 23_{13}; 'shall I, or shall I not?' 1K 22_6; — 4. w. acc. **give up** s.thg Ju 9_9; — 5. w. *min*: a) **leave** s.one **alone** Ex 14_{12}, b) **leave** s.thg **alone** (understanding) Pr 23_4; c) not trouble onesf. about 1S 9_5.

II חדל: **qal**: pf. חָדָלוּ; impf. יֶחְדַּל; impv. חֲדַל, חֲדָל: **become fat** 1S 2_5 Jb 14_6; metaph. **have success** Pr 19_{27} 23_4. †

חָדֵל: cs. חֲדַל: — 1. **he who lets s.thg stay** Ez 3_{27}; — 2. **fleeting, passing** Ps 39_5; — 3. pass. **forsaken**, *ḥ^adal ʼîšîm* Is 53_3; oth.: keeping onesf. far from, the last, the least, F comm.). †

*חֶדֶל: חָדֶל: *yôš^ebê ḥādel* Is 38_{11}; trad.: ending = realm of dead; txt. ?. †

חַדְלָי: n. pers.

חֵדֶק: חֵדֶק: **brier**, *Solanum coagulans*, nightshade of Jordan valley, as well as other briers Mi 7_4 Pr 15_{19}. †

חִדֶּקֶל: חִדֶּקֶל: n. river, **Tigris** Gn 2_{14} Dn 10_4. †

חדר: **qal**: pt. חֹדֶרֶת: **penetrate deeply** (sword) Ez 21_{19}. †

חֶדֶר: (בְּ)חֶדֶר, loc. הַחַדְרָה & הֶחָדְרָה, cs. חֶדֶר & חֲדַר, sf. חֶדְרוֹ; pl. חֲדָרִים, חַדְרֵי, sf. חֲדָרָיו: dark (inner) room, space: — 1. **dark room**: *ḥ^adar miškāb* sleeping chamber 2K 6_{12}; in gen'l, inner room Gn 43_{30}; *ḥ^adar hammiṭṭôt* bedroom 2K 11_2; *ḥ^adar hamm^eqērâ* cool room (privy) Ju 3_{24}; *ḥeder b^eḥeder* (flee) fm. one room to another 1K 20_{30}; *mēhaḥ^adārîm* indoors Dt 32_{25}; — 2. *ḥadrê beṭen* dark chambers of the body Pr 18_8; — 3. cosmic: *ḥadrê māwet* Pr 7_{27} = chambers of Sheol; *ḥadrê têmān* constellations of southern heavens Jb 9_9.

חַדְרָךְ: n. city in N. Syria Zc 9_1. †

חדשׁ: **piel**: pf. חִדְּשׁוּ, impf. וַיְחַדֵּשׁ; inf. חַדֵּשׁ: **make new, restore**: altar 1S 11_{14}, surface of ground Ps 104_{30}; *ḥiddēš rûªḥ* give a new (firm) spirit Ps 51_{12}.
hitp.: impf. תִּתְחַדֵּשׁ: **renew onesf.** (youth) Ps 103_5. †

חָדָשׁ: f. חֲדָשָׁה; pl. חֲדָשִׁים, חֲדָשׁוֹת: **new, fresh**: king Ex 1_8, house Dt 20_5, covenant Je 31_{31}, heaven & earth Is 65_{17}; abs. m. sg., or f. sg., or f. pl., s.thg new Ec 1_{9t}; *ʼiššâ ḥ^adāšâ* bride Dt 24_5; *minḥâ ḥ^adāšâ* cereal offering of new grain Lv 23_{16}.

I חֹדֶשׁ (280×): sf. חָדְשׁוֹ; pl. חֳדָשִׁים, חָדְשֵׁי, sf. חָדְשֵׁיכֶם, חֳדָשָׁיו; art. הֶחֳדָשִׁים, -בֶּ, -לֶ, w/o art. בָּחֳדָשִׁים, -לְ (*bo-, lo-*); m. Gn 7_{11}, f. Gn 38_{24}: — 1. **new moon**, the day on wh.

the crescent moon is again visible 2K 4_{23}; *mimmoḥ^{o}rat haḥōdeš* on the day after the new moon 1S 20_{27}; *yôm haḥōdeš haššēnî* on the 2nd day after the new moon 1S 20_{34}; — 2. **month** 1K 6_1; *ḥōdeš yāmîm* a full month Gn 29_{14}; oth. idioms, e.g. *ḥōdeš b^{e}ḥodšô* a whole month long Nu 28_{14}; *'îš ḥodšô* each one during his month 1K 5_7; dating: *šib'â 'āśār yōm laḥōdeš* 17th day of month Gn 7_{11}; *ben-ḥōdeš* a month old Lv 27_6; *šib'â ḥ^{o}dāšîm* for 7 months 1S 6_1; — 3. **heat** (of female animal) Je 2_{24}.

II חֹדֶשׁ: n. pers. f. 1C 8_9. †

חֳדָשָׁה: n. loc.

[חָדְשִׁי 2S 24_6: rd הַחִתִּים קָדֵשָׁה.]

חֲדַתָּה: in n. loc. חָצוֹר חֲדַתָּה.

חוב: cj. qal: 1S 22_{22} rd חַבְתִּי for סַבֹּתִי: w. *b^{e}* **be guilty** of. †
piel: pf. חִיַּבְתֶּם: make guilty, w. *rō'š*: **forfeit** one's head Dn 1_{10}. †

חוֹב: **debt** (dittgr. ?) Ez 18_7. †

חוֹבָה: n. loc.

חוג: **qal**: pf. חָג: w. *ḥōq*, **describe** a circle Jb 26_{10}. †

חוּג: **circle**; *ḥûg hā'āreṣ*, the earth conceived as a disk Is 40_{22}; *ḥûg 'al-p^{e}nê t^{e}hôm* horizon on the sea Pr 8_{27}; *ḥûg šāmayim* vault of the heavens Jb 22_{14}. †

חוד: **qal**: pf. חַדְתָּ; impf. אָחוּדָה; impv. חוּד, חוּדָה: **ask (a riddle)** Ju 14_{12-16} Ez 17_2. †

I חוה: **piel**: impf. אֲחַוְּךָ, אֲחַוֶּךָּ, אֲחַוֶּה, יְחַוֶּה; inf. חַוֹּת: — 1. give notice of, **announce** s.thg Ps 19_3; — 2. **inform** s.one Jb 36_2.

II חוה: **hištafal** (170×): pf. הִשְׁתַּחֲוָה, הִשְׁתַּחֲוֵיתָ, הִשְׁתַּחֲוֵיתִי, הִשְׁתַּחֲווּ; impf. וַיִּשְׁתַּחוּ, וַיִּשְׁתַּחֲוֶה, אֶשְׁתַּחֲוֶה, יִשְׁתַּחֲוֶה, וַיִּשְׁתַּחוּ, pl. יִשְׁתַּחֲווּ, וַיִּשְׁתַּחֲוּ Gn 43_{28} (Qr ־חֲווּ, Kt ־חוּ), וַתִּשְׁתַּחֲוֶיןָ; impv. הִשְׁתַּחֲוִי, הִשְׁתַּחֲווּ; inf. הִשְׁתַּחֲוֹת, בְּהִשְׁתַּחֲוָיָתִי 2K 5_{18}; pt. מִשְׁתַּחֲוֶה, מִשְׁתַּחֲוִים, מִשְׁתַּחֲוִיתֶם Ez 8_{16} contam. of pt. & pf., rd מִשְׁתַּחֲוִים): **bow down deeply, do obeisance**: w. *'arṣâ* to the ground Gn 18_2; w. *l^{e}* Ps 99_5, w. *'al* Lv 26_1 (both = 'before'); w. *'el* toward Ps 5_8: — 1. profane usage, before a superior: beggar 1S 2_{36}, suppliant Gn 33_7; metaph. peoples before Isr. Gn 27_{29}; — 2. cultic usage: before constellations Dt 4_{19}, holy mountain Ps 99_9.

I חַוָּה: pl. חַוֹּת, sf. חַוֹּתֵיהֶם: — 1. **(tent-)camp, tent-village** Nu 32_{41a}; — 2. חַוֹּת יָאִיר (Ϝ יָאִיר): n. loc.

II חַוָּה: n. pers. f. **Eve**.

[חוֹזָי 2C 33_{19}: trad. n. pers.; rd. חֹזָיו pt. pl. sf. חזה. †]

I חוֹחַ: pl. חוֹחִים: — 1. a **thornbush** 2K 14_9; — 2. **thorn** inserted in gills of fish to carry it back Jb 40_{26}; for men 2C 33_{11}.

II *חוֹחַ: pl. חֲוָחִים, חוֹחִים: **hollow, cleft in rock** 1S 13_6.

חוּט: **thread, string, cord** Ju 16_{12} 1K 7_{15}; *miḥûṭ w^{e}'ad ś^{e}rôk na'al* neither thread nor sandal-thong Gn 14_{23}.

חִוִּי: n. peop. **Hivite**.

חֲוִילָה: n. terr.

חול: **qal**: pf. חָלוּ, חָלָה; impf. יָחוּל, אָחוּלָה Je 4_{19} Kt (Qr אוֹחִילָה & אָחִילָה), יָחִלוּ; inf. חִיל: — 1. **go around in succession** Ho 11_6; — 2. **turn toward**, light on, w. *'al* 2S 3_{29}; — 3. w. cogn. acc. **dance (round-)dances** Ju 21_{21}, whirl Je 23_{19} 30_{23}. †
polel: pt. מְחֹלְלוֹת, shortened חֹלְלִים: **dancing (round-)dances** Ju 21_{23} Ps 87_7.
hitpolel: pt. מִתְחוֹלֵל: **whirl** Je 23_{19}. †

חוּל: (n. pers.), n. terr. Gn 10_{23} 1C 1_{17}. †

I חוֹל: **mud, sand** Gn 22_{17}; *ḥôl hayyām* Gn 32_{13}; numerous as sand 1K 4_{20}.

II חוֹל: Jb 29_{18}: trad. palm-tree, or **phoenix-bird**; Ϝ comm. †

חוּם: **undefined color** betw. white & black Gn 30_{32-40}. †

חוֹמָה, 8× חֹמָה (ca. 120×): cs. חוֹמַת, sf. חוֹמָתָהּ; pl. ח(ו)מ(ו)ת, sf. ח(ו)מ(ו)תָיו; dual חוֹמֹתַיִם: — 1. **city-wall** 2K 3_{27}; *'îr ḥômâ* walled city Lv 25_{29}; — 2. **wall** around building or portion of city: around Temple Ez 40_5; — 3. metaph.: water as a wall 1S 25_{16}, bronze wall Je 1_{18}, body of girl SS 8_{9f}.

חוס: **qal**: pf. חַסְתָּ, חָסָה; impf. יָחוּס, יָח(ו)ס, תָּח(ו)ס (both indic.), וַתָּחָס; impv. חוּסָה: — 1. **be troubled** about: a) *tāḥôs ʿayin ʿal* (lit.: the eye begrudges) Gn 45_{20}; b) abs. *tāḥôs ʿayin* Dt 19_{21}; c) pers.: *ḥās ʿal* Jon 4_{10f}; — 2. **look compassionately** (on): a) *ḥāsâ ʿayin ʿal* Ez 16_5; b) pers. *ḥās ʿal* Ps 72_{13}, abs. Jer 13_{14}; — 3. **spare** s.one; w. *ʿal* 1S 24_{11}, abs. Ez 24_{14}.

חוֹף: **shore**: *ḥôf hayyām* Dt 1_7, *ḥôf yammîm* Gn 49_{13}; *ḥôf ʾoniyyôt* harbor for ships ? Gn 49_{13b}.

חוּפָּם: n. pers. or tribe.

חוּפָמִי: gent. of חוּפָם.

חוּץ: loc. חוּצָה(הַ), חֻצָה; pl. חוּצ(וֹ)ת, חֻצ(וֹ)ת, sf. חוּצֹתָיו, חוּצוֹתֵינוּ: space outside the house, the **outside** Pr 24_{27}.

I. sg.: — 1. *(ha)ḥûṣ*: a) **outside**: *hôṣîʾ haḥûṣ* bring outside Ju 19_{25}, *derek ḥûṣ* out around Ez 47_2, *šaʿar haḥûṣ* outer gate Ez 47_2; b) **lane, street**: *ḥûṣ hāʾōfîm* Street of the Bakers Je 37_{21}; metaph. Is 51_{23}; — 2. *(ha)ḥûṣâ*: (to the) outside 2S 13_{17} (= *haḥûṣ* $_{18}$), *miqqîr haḥûṣâ* from the wall outward Nu 35_4; (on the) outside 1K 6_6 = in the street Is 33_7; *tihyeh ... ḥûṣâ* marry outside (the family) Dt 25_5, cf. Ju 12_9; — 3. w. prep.: a) *baḥûṣ* outside Gn 9_{22}; *laḥûṣ* (*le*) outside (of) 2C 32_5, Ez 42_7; c) *ʾel-haḥûṣ* toward the outside Ez 41_9; d) *min haḥûṣ*: from outside = from the neighbors 2K 4_3, from other families Ju 12_9; outside Gn 6_{14}; *miḥûṣ le* outside (of) Gn 19_{16}; — 4. *ḥûṣ min* except for Ec 2_{25}.

II. pl. חוּצוֹת: — 1. **open fields** Ps 144_{13}; — 2. **lanes, streets**: *ḥûṣôt ʾašqelôn* 2S 1_{20}; *rōʾš ḥûṣôt* street-corner Ne 3_{10}, street w. shops 1K 20_{34}.

***חוק**: חוּקוֹ Pr $8_{27\cdot29}$ ↗ חקק.

***חוֹק**: ↗ חֹק; Ps 74_{11} חוֹקְךָ Kt rd Qr חֵיקְךָ.

***חוּקֹק**: n. loc.: loc. חוּקֹקָה.

I **חור**: **qal**: impf. יֶחֱוָרוּ: **grow pale** Is 29_{22}. †

II **חור**: **qal**: pf. חָרוּ Is 24_6, ms. var. of חָרוּ: **become less**. †

I **חוּר**: **linen cloths** as awning Est 1_6 8_{15}. †

II **חוּר**: n. pers.

III **חוֹר, חוּר**: ↗ חֹר, חָר.

חוֹרֵב: ↗ חֹרֵב.

חוֹרִי: ↗ חֹרִי.

חוּרָי: Is 19_9: rd חָוָרוּ (I חור).

חוּרַי: n. pers. 1C 11_{32}. †

חוּרִי: n. pers.

חוּרָם: n. pers.

חַוְרָן: n. terr. **Hauran**.

חוֹרֹנַיִם: Is 15_5 Je 48_5, חֹרוֹנַיִם 48_3 & חֹרֹנַיִם 48_{34}: n. loc.

I **חוש, חיש**: **qal**: pf. חָשׁ, חַשְׁתִּי; impv. חוּשָׁה: **hurry** 1S 20_{38}; w. *le* & inf. Hb 1_8.

hif.: pf. הֶחִישׁוּ; impf. וַתָּחַשׁ, יָחִישָׁה, אָחִישָׁה, אֲחִישֶׁנָּה: — 1. **hurry** (intrans.) Ju 20_{37}; — 2. **hasten** s.thg Is 60_{22}; look for s.thg in a hurry Ps 55_9; — 3. (qal?, oth. II hif.) hurry away, **yield** Is 28_{16}.

II **חוש**: **qal**: impf. יָחוּשׁ; impv. חוּשָׁה: — 1. be painful Jb 20_2 (rd. *yāḥûšû*); Ec 2_{25} be happy, **rejoice**; — 2. **attend to** (*le*) Ps 141_1. †

חוּשָׁה: n. pers.

חוּשַׁי, חוּשִׁי: n. pers.

חוּשִׁים: n. pers. f. 1C 8_8; = חֻשִׁים v. $_{11}$. †

חוּשָׁם: n. pers.

חוּת: ↗ I חַוָּה 2.

I **חוֹתָם** & 3× חֹתָם: cs. חוֹתַם, sf. חוֹתָמוֹ, חוֹתָמְךָ: — 1. **seal** (for identification) Gn 38_{18}; *ḥōmer ḥôtām* clay for seal (oth.: earthen mold) Jb 38_{14}; — 2. metaph. person as a seal (closely bound) Je 22_{24}.

II **חוֹתָם**: n. pers. 1C 7_{32} 11_{44}. †

חֲזָאֵל & 2K $8_{8\cdot29}$ 2C 22_6 חֲזָהאֵל: n. pers. **Hazael**.

חָזָה: **qal**: pf. חָזָה, חָזוּ, חָזִית, ח׳, חֲזִיתֶם, חֲזִיתִיךָ;

impf. תֶּחֱזֶה ,יֶחֱזֶה ,(וְ)אֶחֱזֶה > אָחַז Jb 23$_9$, תֶּחֱזֶה > נֶחֱזֶה, תֶּחֱזֶינָה, יֶחֱזְיוּן, יֶחֱזוּ, תַּחַז; impv. חֲזֵה, חֲזוּ; inf. חֲזוֹת; pt. חֹזֶה, pl. חֹזִים: — 1. **see, perceive** Is 26$_{11}$; God sees Ps 11$_7$; man sees God Ex 24$_{11}$; obj. *šāw'* Ez 13$_6$, *šeqer* Zc 10$_2$; — 2. *ḥāzâ maḥ^azeh* see a vision Nu 24$_4$, *ḥāzâ ḥāzôn* Is 1$_1$; *ḥāzâ dābār* perceive word (of Y.) Is 2$_1$, *ḥāzâ maśśā'* Is 13$_1$; see as a seer Am 1$_1$; — 3. *ḥāzâ lô* select Ex 18$_{21}$; *ḥāzâ b^e* look w. desire, gratification Mi 4$_{11}$ Ps 27$_4$.

חָזֶה: cs. חֲזֵה; pl. חָזוֹת: **chest, brisket** of sacrificial animal (P only) Ex 29$_{26f}$.

I **חֹזֶה**: חָזָה pt.; cs. חֹזֵה; pl. חֹזִים: **seer,** orig. distinguished fm. *nābî'*, then identical: *ḥōzēh dāwîd* 2S 24$_{11}$; used w. contempt Am 7$_{12}$.

II **חֹזֶה**: Is 28$_{15}$: trad. vision > **agreement** (?); txt. corr. ?. †

חֲזָהאֵל: ↗ חֲזָאֵל.

חֲזוֹ: n. pers.

חָזוֹן: cs. חֲזוֹן: — 1. **vision**: *rā'â ḥāzôn* Dn 8$_{15}$; *ḥ^azôn laylâ* night-vision Is 29$_7$; *ḥ^azôn šeqer* lying vision Je 14$_{14}$; — 2. **revelatory word**: in superscriptions Is 1$_1$ &c.; sought fm. prophet Ez 7$_{26}$.

חָזוּת: cs. =: — 1. **revelation** Is 21$_2$; — 2. **consequence**: *qeren ḥāzût* conspicuous horn Dn 8$_5$.

חֲזוֹת: **vision** 2C 9$_{29}$. †

חֲזִיאֵל: n. pers.

חֲזָיָה: n. pers.

חֶזְיוֹן: n. pers.

חִזָּיוֹן: cs. חֶזְיוֹן, sf. חֶזְיֹנוֹ; pl. חֶזְיֹנוֹת: — 1. **vision** Jl 3$_1$; — 2. **revelation** 2S 7$_{17}$; — 3. *gê' ḥizzāyôn*, 'Valley of Vision,' Is 22$_{1.5}$: n. loc. in or around Jerus.

***חָזִיז**: cs. חֲזִיז; pl. חֲזִיזִים: **strong** (gust of) **wind** Zc 10$_1$; — 2. *ḥ^azîz qôlôt* **thunderclap** Jb 28$_{26}$ 38$_{25}$. †

חֲזִיר: **wild boar,** *Sus scrofa* Dt 14$_8$ Ps 80$_{14}$.

חֵזִיר: n. pers.

חָזַק: **qal**: pf. ח׳, חָזַק, חָזְקָה, חָזַקְתָּ, חֲזַקְתֶּם, חָזְקוּ, יֶחֱזַק, impf. חֲזַקְתַּנִי; & יֶחֶזְקוּ, יֶחֶזְקוּ, תֶּחֱזַקְנָה; impv. חֲזַק, חֲזַק, חִזְקוּ; inf. sf. לְחָזְקָה Ez 30$_{21}$, inf. cs. חֶזְקַת: — 1. **be(come) strong**: a) so usually 1K 2$_2$; (kingdom) lies secure (in his hand) 2K 14$_5$; (famine) becomes severe Gn 41$_{56f}$; (hand) lies heavy on Gn 47$_{20}$; b) *ḥāzaq min* be stronger than, **overpower** 1K 20$_{23.25}$; so *ḥāzaq 'al*: king's word constrains him 2S 24$_4$; c) recover, get well Is 39$_1$; d) abs. *ḥāz^eqû dibrêkem* you use shameless words Ma 3$_{13}$; — 2. **have courage**: a) *ḥāz^eqû yādêkā* find courage 2S 2$_7$; *ḥāzaq* w. *l^e* & inf. stand firm to Jos 23$_6$, w. *l^ebiltî* not to Dt 12$_{23}$; b) impv. be brave Is 41$_6$; var. comb., e.g. *h^azaq we'^emaṣ* be brave & strong Jos 1$_{6f}$; — 3. *ḥāzaq lēb* mind, heart is hardened, stubborn Ex 7$_{13}$; — 4. var.: a) *ḥāzaq 'al*, w. *l^e* & inf. be urgent w. s.one to Ex 12$_{33}$; b) *ḥāzaq b^e* remain hanging on 2S 18$_9$, hold tight to 2C 31$_4$.

piel: pf. חִזַּק, חִזַּקְתִּי, חִזְּקוּ, חִזַּקְתַּנִי; impf. וַיְחַזֵּק, יְחַזְּקוּ, וַיְחַזְּקֵנִי, אֲחַזְּקֶנּוּ, וַיְחַזְּקוּם; impv. חַזֵּק, חַזְּקִי, חַזְּקֵהוּ, חַזֵּק; inf. חַזֵּק; pt. מְחַזֵּק: — 1. caus.: a) **make strong, firm** (bar of gate) Ps 147$_{13}$; b) **strengthen** (arms) Ez 30$_{24}$, bring (back sick sheep) to strength Ez 34$_4$; c) *ḥizzaq y^edê* strengthen s.one's hands = arouse, encourage 1S 23$_{16}$; d) *ḥizzaq yādayim* take in hand, set about Ne 2$_{18}$; e) encourage, w. acc. 2S 11$_{25}$, w. *l^e* 1C 29$_{12}$; f) harden, make stubborn (heart, ↗ qal 3.) Ex 4$_{21}$; *ḥizzaq pānîm* offer a hard brow Je 5$_3$; — 2. tech.: a) w. 2 acc., **tie** s.thg **tight** on s.one, **gird** w. Is 22$_{21}$, *ḥizzaq motnayim* gird onesf. Na 2$_2$; b) **repair** (building) 2K 12$_6$; c) hold (a mast) firm Is 33$_{23}$; — 3. **support**: person 2C 29$_{34}$, benefit (temple) 1C 26$_{27}$ (oth.: repair 2b.).

hif.: pf. הֶחֱזִיק, הֶחֱזִיקָה, הֶחֱזַקְתִּי 1S 17$_{35}$, וְהַחֲזַקְתִּי Ez 30$_{25}$, הֶחֱזִיקַתְנוּ, הֶחֱזִיקַתְנִי;

impf. אֶחֱזַק, וַיֶּחֱזַק־, וַיַּחֲזֵק, יַחֲזֵק, יַחֲזִיק, יַחֲזִ(י)קוּ; impv. הַחֲזֵק, הַחֲזִיקִי; inf. הַחֲזִיק, הַחֲזִיקִי; pt. מַחֲזִיק, מַחֲזִקָה, מַחֲזֶקֶת: — 1. w. b^e: **take hold of, seize** 1K 1_{50}; *heḥ^e^zîq b^e^yad* take by the hand Gn 19_{16}; *heḥ^e^zîq b^e^* hold on Ex 9_2; *heḥ^e^zîq bē'lōhîm* cling to God 1K 9_9; — 2. w. acc. **take hold of** Is 41_{13}; *heḥ^e^zîq yādô b^e^* hold one's hand (in protection) over Gn 21_{18}; — 3. caus. *heḥ^e^zîq milḥāmâ* wage war w. determination 2S 11_{25}; *mamlākâ* strengthen control 2K 15_{19}; — 4. var.: w. *'al*: join with Ne 10_{30}; abs.: be, stay strong Dn $11_{7.32}$ 2C 26_8.

hitp.: pf. הִתְחַזֵּק; impf. יִתְחַזֵּק, יִתְחַזְּקוּ, נִתְחַזֵּק; impv. הִתְחַזֵּק; pt. מִתְחַזֵּק: — 1. a) abs. **show onesf. courageous** 1K 20_{22}; take courage Gn 48_2; feel onesf. strengthened 1S 30_6; b) keep faithful to, w. b^e 2S 3_6, w. *'im* Dn 10_{21}; — 2. a) **show onesf. strong** 2C 1_1 17_1, w. *lifnê* make one's way against 2C 13_{7f}; b) become powerful 2C 12_{13}.

חָזָק: f. חֲזָקָה; pl. חֲזָקִים, חִזְקֵי: — 1. **firm, hard**: rock Ez 3_9, face 3_8, heart 2_4; — 2. **strong**: a) of God: *b^e^yād ḥ^a^zāqâ* Ex 3_{19}; God comes *b^e^ḥāzāq* as the strong one Is 40_{10} (↗ b^e 3.); b) of man: people Nu 13_{18}, man Jos 14_{11}, animal Ez 34_{16}; c) of things: wind Ez 10_{19}, sound of trumpet Ex 19_{16}; — 3. **violent, severe**: battle 1S 14_{52}, illness 1K 17_{17}, famine 18_2.

חָזֵק: **strong**: trumpet-blast *hōlēk w^e^ḥāzēq* became stronger & stronger (↗ *hālak* qal 5.) Ex 19_{19}; 2S 3_1 David. †

*חֵזֶק: sf. חִזְקִי: **strength** Ps 18_2. †

חֹזֶק: sf. חָזְקֵנוּ: **strength**, power Am 6_{13}; *b^e^ḥōzeq yād* vigorously Ex 13_3.

*חֶזְקָה: sf. חֶזְקָתוֹ: **growing strong**: *k^e^hezqātô* as he became strong Dn 11_2.

חָזְקָה: **strength, power**: *b^e^ḥozqâ* w. power 1S 2_{16}, violently Ju 4_3.

חִזְקִי: n. pers.

חִזְקִיָּה: n. pers. **Hezekiah.**

חִזְקִיָּהוּ: n. pers. **Hezekiah.**

חָח: sf. חַחִי; pl. חַחִים Ez 29_4 Qr: — 1. **thorn, hook** through nose or cheek to lead animals & prisoners 2K 19_{28}; — 2. **fibula** Ex 35_{22}.

חָטָא: **qal**: pf. ח׳, חָטָאָה, חָטָאתִי, חֲטָאתֶם, חָטָאנוּ; impf. יֶחֱטָא, יֶחֱטָא, תֶּחֶטְאוּ, תֶּחֶטְאוּ; inf. חֲ(וֹ)טֹא, חֲטוֹ, חֲטֹאתוֹ; pt. חֹ(וֹ)טֵא & חֹ(וֹ)טֶא Is 65_{20} Ec 2_{28} 8_{12} $9_{2.18}$, חֹטֵאת, חֹטְאִי, חֹטְאִים (Qr חֹטִים): — 1. **miss** (a goal) Pr 8_{36}; miss (= feel the lack) Jb 5_{24} > be displeasing, pt. Ec 2_{26} 7_{26} †; — 2. **be at fault, offend** (in manners or morals) 2K 18_{14}, w. l^e against Gn 20_9; — 3. **be blameworthy, guilty** Gn 43_9 44_{32}; — 4. **sin**; *ḥāṭā'tî/nû* is formula of confession: w. prep. or acc.: a) l^e against God Gn 20_6 &c. (50×); b) b^e against a man Gn 42_{22} 1S 19_{4f}, likewise w. *'al* Nu 6_{11}, *min* Lv 4_2; c) b^e sin by means of an act Lv 5_{22}; d) w. acc. *nafšô* against onesf. Pr 20_2; — 5. abs.: **sin** Ex 9_{27} &c. (72×): — 6. w. cogn. acc. *ḥ^a^ṭā'â* or *ḥaṭṭā't* **commit a sin** Ex 32_{30f} &c. (23×); — 7. *ḥāṭā' ballāšôn* Ps 39_2; *ḥāṭā' l^e'ašmat hā'ām* so that guilt comes on the people Lv 4_3.

piel: pf. חִטֵּא, חִטֵּאתָ, חִטְּאוּ; impf. יְחַטֵּא, אֲחַטֶּנָּה, יְחַטְּאֶהוּ; inf. חַטֵּא; pt. מְחַטֵּא: — 1. make amends for, **have to compensate** Gn 31_{39} †; — 2. w. acc. **free from sin**: a) s.one Nu 19_{19}, b) s.thg: altar Lv 8_{15}, house Lv 14_{49}; — 3. bring as a sin-offering Lv 6_{19}.

hif.: pf. הֶחֱטִיא, הֶחֱטִי 2K 13_6 Kt, הֶחֱטִיאָם; impf. וַיַּחֲטִא, תַּחֲטִ(י)א, יַחֲטִ(י)א, יַחֲטִיאוּ, וַתַּחֲטִא; inf. הַחֲטִיא & הַחֲטִי Je 32_{35}, לַחֲטִיא Ec 5_5: — 1. **miss** (a goal) Ju 20_{16} †; — 2. **lead off into sin** (obj. Isr.) 1K 14_{16}; c. *ḥ^a^ṭā'â g^e^dôlâ* 2K 17_{21}; w. l^e against Ex 23_{33}.

hitp.: impf. יִתְחַטָּא, יִתְחַטְּאוּ, תִּתְחַטְּאוּ: — 1. **free onesf. from sin** Nu 8_{21}, w. b^e by 19_{12}; — 2. **withdraw** Jb 41_{17}.

חֵטְא: sf. חֶטְאוֹ, חֶטְאָם; בְּחֶטְאָה Nu 15_{28} = ־אָהּ; pl. חֲטָאִים, cs. חֲטָאֵי, sf. חֲטָאֵיכֶם,

חֲטָאָיו, חֲטָאָו La 3_{39} Qr (Kt חֶטְאוֹ): — 1. **fault** (against men) Gn 41_9 Ec 10_4 †; — 2. **sin** (against God) 2K 10_{29}; *ḥāṭā' ḥēṭ'* commit sin La 1_8; *ḥeṭ' mišpaṭ māwet* deserve the death penalty Dt 21_{22}, > *ḥeṭ' māwet* 22_{26}; — 3. *nāśā' ḥēṭ'* take guilt on onesf. Lv 19_{17}, = *nāśā' ḥeṭ'ô* Lv 20_{20}; *hāyâ ḥēṭ' bᵉ* guilt falls on Dt 15_9; *nāśā' ḥēṭ'* w. gen., bear guilt for Is 53_{12}; *ḥᵃṭā'ê gillûlêken* the guilt you have incurred w. your idols Ez 23_{49}.

חַטָּא: f. חַטָּאָה; pl. חַטָּאֶיהָ, חַטָּאֵי, חַטָּאִים: — 1. fallible, **sinful** (inclined to sin) Nu 32_{14}, burdened w. guilt 1K 1_{21}; — 2. **sinner** Gn 13_{13} (*lᵉ* against) 1S 15_{18}.

חֶטְאָה: **lapse, fault** Nu 15_{28}. †

חֲטָאָה: — 1. **sin** Ps 32_1; as cogn. acc. Ex 32_{30} commit sin; *hēbî' ḥᵃṭā'â ‘al* bring guilt on Gn 20_9; — 2. **sin-offering** Ps 40_7.

חַטָּאָה: **sin** Ex 34_7 Is 5_{18}. †

חַטָּאת, חַטַּאת Zc 13_1 & חַטָּת Nu 15_{24}: cs. חַטַּאת, sf. חַטָּאתוֹ, חַטָּאתְךָ, חַטַּאתְכֶם; pl. abs. חַטָּאוֹת, cs. חַטֹּאת Nu 5_6 (6×), חַטֹּאות 1K 14_{16} (18×), abs. Dn 9_{24} Qr חַטָּאת Kt חַטָּאוֹת; sf. חַטֹּאתַי, חַטֹּא(ו)תֵיכֶם: 288× (mostly Lv & Nu): — 1. **sin** (155×): *kābᵉdâ* Gn 18_{20}; *nāśā' ḥaṭṭā't* Gn 50_{17}, *nāśā' lᵉḥaṭṭā't* Jos 24_{19}; many other vbs., e.g. *sālaḥ ḥaṭṭā't* forgive sin Ex 34_9, *he‘ᵉbîr ḥaṭṭā't* let sin go 2S 12_{13}; — 2. **pardon, sin-offering** (135×): *par ḥaṭṭā't* Ex 29_{36}, *dam ḥaṭṭā't* Lv 4_{25} &c.

חטב: **qal**: impf. יַחְטְבוּ; inf. לַחְטֹב; pt. חֹטֵב, חֹטְבֵי, חֹטְבִים: w. *‘ēṣîm* **gather** firewood Dt 19_5; abs. Ez 39_{10}.

pual: pt. מְחֻטָּבוֹת: **cut** (corner-pillars) Ps 144_{12}. †

חֲטֻבוֹת: **colored, embroidered fabric** Pr 7_{16}. †

חִטָּה: pl. חִטִּים & Ez 4_9 חִטִּין: **wheat**, *Triticum savitum*: — 1. (the plant) Ex 9_{32} †; — 2. (the grain) Dt 8_8; ears, Ju 6_{11}, grains 1K 5_{25}; *qᵉṣîr ḥiṭṭîm* wheat harvest Gn 30_{14}.

חַטּוּשׁ: n. pers.

חֲטִיטָא: n. pers.

חַטִּיל: n. pers.

חֲטִיפָא: n. pers.

חטם: **qal**: impf. ־אֶחֱטָם: **restrain onesf.**, w. *lᵉ* for the sake of Is 48_9. †

חטף: **qal**: pf. חֲטַפְתֶּם; impf. יַחְטֹף; inf. לַחְטֹף: **ravish**, seize & take away (woman) Ju 21_{21}; seize Ps 10_9. †

חֹטֶר: **rod**, switch Pr 14_3; shoot Is 11_1. †

חַטָּת Nu 15_{24}: ↗ חַטָּאת.

I חַי: A. sg., cs. חֵי: — in oath, **life**: — 1. *ḥê-nafšᵉkā*, as you live = 'I swear' 1S 1_{26}, *ḥê-par‘ōh* Gn 42_{15f}; — 2. *ḥay* before Y. & sim. designations: a) *ḥay hā'ᵉlōhîm* 2S 2_{27}, b) *ḥay-yhwh* 1K 1_{29}; c) *ḥay 'ānî* (spoken by God) Nu 14_{21}.

B. pl. חַיִּים: cs. חַיֵּי, sf. חַיַּי, חַיַּי, חַיֶּיךָ & חַיֶּךָ 2S 11_{11}, חַיָּיְכִי Ps 103_4, חַיָּו 2S 18_{18} Je 52_{33} Ec 5_{17}, חַיֵּיכֶם: — 1. **lifetime, duration of life**: *ḥayyê nōᵃḥ* Gn 7_{11}; *nišmat ḥayyîm* breath of life Gn 2_7; *bᵉḥayyêkā* as long as you live Dt 28_{66}; *ḥayyê ‘ôlām* endless life Dn 12_2; — 2. **state of life** (:: death) 2S 15_{21}; *ḥayyay* the fact that I live Gn 27_{46}; — 3. (possessions, joy of) **life**; *ḥayyîm* = health, entirety: *'ôr haḥayyîm* Ps 56_{14}, *derek haḥayyîm* Je 21_8; — 4. **livelihood** Pr 27_{27}.

II חַי: חָי, הַחַי & Gn 6_{19} הָחַי, הֶחָי, לֶחָי, cs. חֵי; f. חַיָּה; pl. חַיִּים, חַיּוֹת: — 1. **living** (:: dead): dog Ec 9_4; *bāśār ḥay* raw meat 1S 2_{15}, raw flesh Lv $13_{10\text{-}16}$; *mayim ḥayyîm* running water Gn 26_{19}; *kol-ḥay* everything that lives Gn 3_{20}, *nefeš ḥayyâ* living being Gn 1_{20}; — 2. **alive** (of men): *bihyôt … ḥay* when it was alive 2S 12_{18}, *ha‘ôd ḥay* is he still alive? Gn 43_7; *'ereṣ haḥayyîm* land of the living Is 38_{11}; — 3. **living** (God): *'ᵉlōhîm ḥayyîm* 1S 17_{26}, *'ᵉlōhîm ḥay* 2K $19_{4\cdot16}$; — 4. var.: *kā‘ēt ḥayyâ* Gn $18_{10\cdot14}$ 2K 4_{16} a year from now.

III חַי: **kinsmen** 1S 18_{18}. †

חִיאֵל: n. pers.

חִידָה: sf. חִידָתִי, חִידָתְךָ, חִידֹתְךָ; pl. חִ(י)ד(ו)ת, sf. חִידֹתָם: designation for a thing by sly hints: — 1. **riddle, enigmatic question** Ju 14_{12-19} 1K 10_1; *pātaḥ ḥîdâ* answer a riddle Ps 49_5; — 2. **ambiguous saying,** *mēbîn ḥîdôt* skilled at intrigue Dn 8_{23}.

חָיָה: **qal**: pf. a) following ע״ו vbs.: חַי, חָי, חַי Lv 25_{36}, f. וָחָיָה Ex 1_{16}; b) following ל״ה vbs.: חָיָה, חָיְתָה, חָיִית, חָיוּ, וִחְיִיתֶם; impf. יִחְיֶה, יְחִי, וַיְחִי, וַיֶּחִי, (וַ)יֶּחִי, תְּחִי, אֶחְיֶה, נִחְיֶה, תִּחְיוּ(ן), תִּחְיֶינָה; impv. חֲיִי, וֶחְיֵה, וִחְיוּ; inf. חֲיוֹתָם, לִחְיוֹת, חָיֹה, חָיוֹ; Je 21_9 יְחָיָה = Kt יִחְיֶה, Qr וְחָיָה: — 1. **be, stay alive** (ca. 120×) Gn 5_3, *ḥāyâ le'ôlām* Gn 3_{22}; *yeḥî hammelek* 1K 1_{25}; — 2. *ḥāyâ be* **live by** (means of) s.thg Lv 18_5, w. *'al* support onesf. by Gn 27_{40}; — 3. **be revived, get well** Gn 20_7 1K 17_{22}f; — 4. **come back to life again** 2K 13_{21}.

piel: pf. חִיָּה, חִיּוּ, חִיִּיתֶם, חִיִּתַנִי, חִיִּתָנִי; impf. יְחַיֶּה, יְחַיּוּ, תְּחַיֶּינָה, תְּחַיֶּין, תְּחַיּוּן, תְּחַיֵּנוּ, תְּחַיֵּנִי, וַיְחַיֵּהוּ Ps 71_{20} (Qr ־נִי, Kt ־נוּ), וַיְחַיֶּה, וַיְחַיֵּנוּ; impv. חַיֵּנִי, חַיֵּיהוּ; inf. חַיּוֹת, חַיּוֹתוֹ; pt. מְחַיֶּה: — 1. **preserve, keep alive** Gn 12_{12}; *ḥiyyâ zera'* Gn 7_3; **let live** (in prosperity) Jos 9_{15}; — 2. **bring (back) to life**: the ill Ps 30_4, stones fm. rubbish-heaps Ne 3_{34}; realize (a work) Hb 3_2; — 3. *ḥiyyâ dāgān* grow grain Ho 14_8.

hif.: pf. הֶחֱיָה, הֶחֱיֵיתִי, הַחֲיִתֶם, הֶחֱיִתַנִי; impv. הַחֲיוּ, הַחֲיֵנִי; inf. הַחֲי(ו)ת, הַחֲיֵה אוֹתָם Jos 9_{20}: — 1. **preserve, keep alive** Gn 6_{19}f 2K 5_7; **leave alive** Jos 6_{25}; — 2. **restore** Is 57_{15}.

*חָיֶה: pl. חָיוֹת: **vigorous** Ex 1_{19}. †

I חַיָּה: cs. חַיַּת & חַיְתוֹ (7×), sf. חַיָּתוֹ; pl. חַיּוֹת: **animals,** חַיּוֹת or coll. sg., rarely a single animal Gn 37_{20}: — 1. **animals of all kinds, mostly untamed**: *ḥayyat hā'āreṣ* Gn 1_{25}, *ḥaytô 'ereṣ* 1_{24}; = land animals Gn 1_{28}, **beasts of burden** Is 46_1, **water animals** Ps 104_{25}; — 2. **wild, predatory animals** (:: *behēmâ* 3.) Ez 14_{15}; *ḥayyâ rā'â* Gn $37_{20 \cdot 33}$; — 3. **beings like animals** Ez $1_{5 \cdot 13 \cdot 22}$.

II חַיָּה: — 1. that wh. lives > **life** Ez 7_{13a} (F comm.), Jb 33_{18}; — 2. > **desire, greed** Jb 33_{20}.

III *חַיָּה: cs. חַיַּת, sf. חַיָּתְךָ: = I חַוָּה: — 1. **army** 2S 23_{13}; — 2. **home** Ps 68_{11}. †

חַיּוּת: **lifetime**: *'almenût ḥayyût* as widows **in** the lifetime (of husband) 2S 20_3. †

I חיל: **qal**: pf. חָלָה, חַלְתִּי, חָלוּ & Dt 2_{25} חָלוּ, חַלְנוּ; impf. a) יָחִילוּן, יָחִילוּ, יָחִיל, וְתָחֵל, נַתָּחֵל, וַיָּחֶל (Ps 97_4), impv. חִילִי, חִילוּ; b) תָּחוּל, וַתָּחֹל, אָחוּלָה Je 4_{19} Kt (Qr אֹחִילָה), impv. חוּלִי; inf. חוּל (Ez 30_{16} inf. abs.): — 1. **be in labor** (childbirth) Is 13_8; — 2. a) **writhe** Je 4_{19}; b) **tremble** Ps 55_5.

polel: impf. יְחוֹלֵל, תְּחוֹלֵלְכֶם; inf. חֹלֵל; pt. מְחֹלֶלְךָ: — 1. **bring** (female) **into labor** (birth-pangs) Ps 29_9 †; — 2. **bring** (young) **to birth** Dt 32_{18} Is 51_2 Ps 90_2. †

polal: pf. חוֹלָלְתָּ, חוֹלָלְתִּי: — 1. **be brought to birth** (of young) Ps 51_7; — 2. **be brought to trembling** Jb 26_5.

hif.: impf. יָחִיל: **make tremble** Ps 29_8. †

hof.: impf. יוּחַל: **be brought to birth** (of young) Is 66_8. †

hitpolel: pt. מִתְחוֹלֵל: **writhe in fear** Jb 15_{20}. †

hitpalpal: impf. וַתִּתְחַלְחַל: **be overtaken by terror** Est 4_4. †

II חיל: **qal** (hif. ?): impf. יָחִיל: **endure** Jb 20_{21}. †

חַיִל (245×): חָיִל, cs. חֵיל, sf. חֵילְךָ, חֵילָם; pl. חֲיָלִים, sf. חֵילֵהֶם Is 30_6: — 1. **capacity, power**: sexual Pr 31_3, of horse Ps 33_{17}; *'āzar ḥayil* gird onesf. w. strength 1S 2_4; never of God's power; — 2. **property, wealth**: a) in genl. Gn 34_{29}; *'āśâ ḥayil* gain wealth Dt 8_{18}; *ḥêl temûrâ* business profit Jb 20_{18}; > b) *'îš ḥayil* wealthy landowner, **qualified, fit for military service** (F below), brave 1K 1_{42}, *'anšê ḥayil* Gn 47_6; *ben-ḥayil* of good family, valiant 1S 14_{52}, pl. *b^{e}nê-ḥayil* Dt 3_{18}; *'ēšet-ḥayil* worthy wife Pr 12_4; c) *gibbôr ḥayil* brave man Ju 11_1; as a designation of class: (large) **landowner**, obligated to military service & the furnishing of a certain number of men; then valiant man w/o regard to property; — 3. **army** Ex 14_4 &c.; *ḥayil gādôl* Ez 17_{17}, *ḥayil kābēd* 2K 6_{14}: *kol-ḥêl 'am ûm^{e}dînâ* all the armed host of a people & a satrapy Est 8_{11}; — 4. (foreign) **upper classes** of a city (important by virtue of property & military value) Ne 3_{34}.

חֵיל (6×), חֵל (4×): sf. חֵילָהּ: **bulwark, outer wall** 2S 20_{15}.

חִיל: **fear & pain** Ex 15_{14} Je 6_{24}.

חִילָה: birthpangs, metaph. **pain** Jb 6_{10}. †

חֵילָה Ps 48_{14}: rd. חֵילָהּ, F חֵיל.

חִילֵז: n. loc.

חֵילֵךְ: n. terr. or peop. = **Cilicia** Ez 27_{11}. †

חֵילָם: n. loc.; loc. חֵלָאמָה 2S 10_{17}: 2S 10_{16f}. †

חִילֵן: some mss. for. n. loc. חָלֵיז 1C 6_{43}. †

[חִין: Jb 41_4, ? rd. אֵין. †]

חַיִץ: **inner wall** Ez 13_{10}. †

חִיצוֹן: f. חִיצֹ(וֹ)נָה: lying outside, **outer**: ref. to *mābô'* 2K 16_{18}, *ḥāṣēr* Ez 10_5; *baḥîṣôn* outside Ez 41_7, *laḥîṣôn* (to the) outside 1K 6_{29f}.

חֵיק, 2× חֵק: cs. =, sf. חֵיקִי, 1× חֵקִי, חֵיקְךָ Ps 74_{11} Qr, חֵיקָךְ: f. (Ex 43_{13}): — 1. **lap, bosom**, lower part of body where one clasps one's beloved, children, animals 1K 3_{20}; of a man Gn 16_5, of woman Dt 28_{56}; — 2. **bosom** = fold of garment above the belt where one hides hands or objects Ex 4_{6f}; — 3. metaph. a) hollow of chariot 1K 22_{35}; b) archit. tech. term, channel around altar Ex 43_{13}.

חִירָה: n. pers.

חִירוֹם: 1K $5_{24.32}$ 7_{40}, & חִירָם (14×) & F חוּרָם: n. pers. **Hiram**.

חִירֹת Nu 33_8: F פִּי הַחִירֹת.

חִישׁ: speed, > adv. **in haste** Ps 90_{10}. †

חֵךְ: sf. חִכּוֹ, חִכֵּךְ: **palate** Ps 137_6, seat of taste Ps 119_{103}, of speech Jb 6_{30}.

חכה: **qal**: pt. pl. cs. חוֹכֵי: w. l^e **wait for** Is 30_{18}. †

piel: pf. חִכָּה, חִכְּתָה, חִכִּיתִי; impf. יְחַכֶּה; impv. חַכֵּה, חַכּוּ; pt. מְחַכֶּה, cs. מְחַכֵּה, pl. מְחַכִּים: — 1. **wait for** w. l^e Is 8_{17}, w. *'al* until 2K 7_9; — 2. abs. **be patient** Dn 12_{12}, **delay** 2K 9_3; lie in wait for Ho 6_9.

חַכָּה: **fishhook** Is 19_8 Hb 1_{15} Jb 40_{25}. †

חֲכִילָה: n. loc.

חֲכַלְיָה: n. pers.

*חַכְלִיל: cs. חַכְלִילִי: **sparkling** Gn 49_{12}; oth.: dark. †

חַכְלִלוּת: **sparkling** Pr 23_{29}. †

חכם: **qal**: pf. חָכַמְתָּ, ח׳, חָכְמוּ; impf. יֶחְכַּם, יֶחְכָּם, אֶחְכָּמָה, יֶחְכָּמוּ; impv. חֲכַם, חֲכָם, חֲכָמוּ; וַחֲכָם Pr 13_{20} = Kt וַחֲכָם, Qr יֶחְכָּם: — 1. **be wise** 1K 5_{11}; — 2. **become wise** Pr 6_6; — 3. **act wisely** Ec 2_{19}.

piel: impf. יְחַכֵּם, יְחַכְּמֵנִי, יְחַכְּמֵנוּ, תְּחַכְּמֵנוּ, תְּחַכְּמֵנִי: — 1. **instruct** Ps 105_{22}; — 2. **make wise** Ps 119_{98} Jb 35_{11}. †

pual: pt. מְחֻכָּם: **instructed, expert** Ps 58_6. †

hif.: pt. מַחְכִּימַת: **make wise** Ps 19_8. †

hitp.: impf. תִּתְחַכַּם, נִתְחַכְּמָה: — 1. **show onesf. wise** (l^e to) Ex 1_{10}; — 2. **show one's wisdom** Ec 7_{16}. †

חָכָם (ca. 130×, Pr 46×): cs. חֲכַם; f. חֲכָמָה, cs. חַכְמַת; pl. חֲכָמִים, cs. חַכְמֵי, sf. חֲכָמָיו; f. חֲכָמוֹת, cs. חַכְמוֹת: — 1. **fit, skilled**: *ḥārāš ḥākām* Is 40_{20}; *ḥ^{a}kamôt* mourning women Je 9_{16}; technically skilled 1C 22_{15}; (later) *ḥ^{a}kam lēb* skilled in cultic matters Ex 28_3; — 2. **able, experienced**: *'îš ḥākām* 1K 2_9, *'iššâ ḥ^{a}kāmâ* 2S 14_2; — > 3. *ḥ^{a}kāmîm* **the wise (men)**: of Egypt Gn 41_8; *ben-ḥ^{a}kāmîm* one who belongs to the wise men Is 19_{11}; *nābôn w^{e}ḥākām* sensible

& experienced Gn $41_{33.39}$; — 4. *ḥākām* :: *ʾewîl* Pr 12_{15}, :: *nābāl* Dt 32_6, &c.; — 5. *ḥākām* **the God-fearing wise man**, who knows & keeps the law Ps 107_{43}.

חָכְמָה (140×, Pr 32×, Ec 28×, Jb 18×): cs. חָכְמַת (Is 33_6 abs.), sf. חָכְמָתוֹ, חָכְמַתְכֶם; — 1. **technical skill, aptitude** 1K 7_{14}; — 2. **experience, good sense**: wise woman 2S 20_{22}, political 1K 2_6; — 3. **worldly wisdom** of the *bᵉnê qedem* & of Egypt 1K 5_{10}; — 4. **wisdom of godly Isr.** Ps 90_{12}; — 5. **God's wisdom** 1K 3_{28}; *ḥokmat malʾak ʾᵉlōhîm* 2S 14_{20}; *rûᵃḥ ḥokmâ* Dt 34_9; — 6. **personified Wisdom** Jb 28_{12ff} Pr 8_{1-36}.

חָכְמוֹת: **wisdom** Pr 1_{20}.

חַכְמֹנִי: n. pers.

***חכר**: **qal**: impf. תַּחְכְּרוּ Jb 19_3, so read for תַּהְכְּרוּ: w. *lᵉ* **attack** s.one **vigorously**. †

חֹל: **profane**, approachable & usable w/o ceremony, :: *qōdeš*; bread 1S 21_5, area of city Ez 48_{15}.

חֵל: ↗ חֵיל.

חלא: **qal**: impf. וַיֶּחֱלֶא: **fall ill** 2C 16_{12}. †

hif.: pf. הֶחֱלִי, Is 53_{10}, ↗ חָלָה. †

I ***חֶלְאָה**: sf. חֶלְאָתָהּ & Ez 24_6 חֶלְאָתָה: **rust** Ez $24_{6.11f}$. †

II **חֶלְאָה**: n. pers. f. 1C $4_{5.7}$. †

חֲלָאִים: ↗ I חֳלִי.

חֵלָאמָה 2S 10_{17}: n. loc., ↗ חֵילָם.

חָלָב: cs. חֲלֵב, sf. חֲלָבִי: **milk**: *ḥᵃlēb ṣōʾn* Dt 32_{14}, *ḥᵃlēb ʿizzîm* Pr 27_{27}, *ḥᵃlēb ʾimmô* Ex 23_{19}; *ṭᵉlēʾ ḥālāb* sucking lamb 1S 7_9.

I **חֵלֶב**: sf. חֶלְבּוֹ, חֶלְבְּהֶן Lv $8_{16.25}$; pl. חֲלָבִים, cs. חֶלְבֵי, sf. חֶלְבֵהֶן Gn 4_4: — 1. **fat**, covering the interior of the body Ex 29_{13}; of belly Ju 3_{22}, of man's face Jb 15_{27}; — 2. fat of offerings: *ḥᵃlābîm* pieces of fat Gn 4_4; *ḥēleb zebaḥ* Lv 4_{26}; — 3. metaph. **the best, select**: *ḥēleb hāʾāreṣ* Gn 45_{18}; — 4. fat burned on altar as God's portion 1S 2_{15f}.

II **חֵלֶב**: n. pers. 2S 23_{29}. †

חֶלְבָּה: n. loc.

חֶלְבּוֹן: n. terr.

חֶלְבְּנָה: **galbanum**, unpleasant-smelling resin of 3 types of ferula, used in incense Ex 30_{34}. †

חֶלֶד: חֶלֶד, sf. חֶלְדִּי: — 1. **(duration of) life, lifetime** Ps 39_6; — 2. **world** Ps 17_{14}.

חֶלֶד: n. pers.

חֹלֶד: **mole**, *Spalax ehrenbergi* Lv 11_{29}. †

חֻלְדָּה: n. pers. f.

חֶלְדַּי: n. pers.

חָלָה: **qal**: pf. חָלִיתִי, ח׳; impf. וַיֶּחַל; inf. חֲלֹתוֹ; pt. חֹ(ו)לֶה, חוֹלָה, חוֹלַת: — 1. **become weak, tired** Gn 48_1; — 2. **be(come) ill** 1K $14_{1.5}$, through accident 2K 1_2; of animal Ez 34_4; w. *ʾet-raglāyw* in the feet 1K 15_{23}; w. *lāmût* mortally 2K 20_1; *ḥālâ ʾet-ḥolyô* w. his particular illness 2K 13_{14}; *ḥôlat ʾahᵃbâ* lovesick SS 2_5; *rāʿâ ḥôlâ* great evil Ec 5_{12}; — 3. **feel pain, regret** 1S 22_8 Je 5_3.

nif.: pf. נֶחֱלֵיתִי, נֶחְלוּ; pt. f. נַחְלָה & נַחֲלָה, pl. נַחְלוֹת: — 1. **be exhausted** Je 12_{13}, pt. Ez 34_4; — 2. **be taken ill** Dn 8_{27}; w. neg. grieve for (w. *ʿal*) Am 6_6 (↗ qal 3.); *yôm naḥᵃlâ* day of chronic illness Is 17_{11}; *makkâ naḥᵃlâ* incurable blow Je 10_{19}.

piel: pf. חִלָּה, חִלִּיתִי; impf. וַיְחַל, יְחַלּוּ; impv. חַל, חַלּוּ; inf. חַלּוֹת: — 1. **appease, flatter** a) men Ps 45_{13}; b) put (God) in gentle mood 1K 13_6; — 2. *ḥillâ taḥᵃluʾîm bᵉ* let sicknesses break out in the land = strike the land w. chronic illness Dt 29_{21}.

pual: pf. חֻלֵּיתָ: **be made weak** Is 14_{10}. †

hif.: pf. הֶחֱלִי Is 53_{10} ↗ חָלָא; pt. f. מַחֲלָה: **make ill** Pr 13_{12}. †

hof.: pf. הָחֳלֵיתִי: **be severely wounded** 1K 22_{34}.

hitp.: impf. וַיִּתְחַל; impv. הִתְחַל; inf. הִתְחַלּוֹת: — 1. **become ill** (w. pangs of love) 2S 13_2; — 2. **pretend to be ill** 2S 13_{5f}. †

חַלָּה: cs. חַלַּת; pl. חַלּ(וֹ)ת: **(ring-shaped)**

bread, used in offerings: *ḥillat leḥem* 2S 6$_{19}$, *ḥillat maṣṣôt* Ex 29$_{2}$.

חֲלוֹם: cs. =, sf. חֲלֹמוֹ, חֲלוֹמִי; pl. חֲלֹמוֹת, sf. חֲלֹמֹתָיו: **dream**: *ḥᵃlôm hallaylâ* Gn 20$_{3}$ 31$_{11}$ 1K 3$_{5}$; cogn. acc. *ḥālam ḥᵃlôm* Gn 37$_{5f}$ & oft.; *baʿal haḥᵃlōmôt* dreamer & dream-interpreter Gn 37$_{19}$.

חַלּוֹן: pl. חַלּוֹנִים, sf. חַלּוֹנֵינוּ & חַלֹּ(וֹ)נוֹת: hole in the wall for air & light, **window**(-opening) Gn 8$_{6}$ 1K 6$_{4}$.

חֹלוֹן Je 48$_{21}$ & חֹלֹן Jos 15$_{51}$ 21$_{15}$: n. loc. †

[חַלּוֹנָי Je 22$_{14}$: rd. חַלּוֹנָיו.]

חָלוּץ: ↗ חלץ.

חֲלוּשָׁה: **defeat** Ex 32$_{18}$. †

חֲלַח: n. terr.

חַלְחוּל: n. loc.

חַלְחָלָה: **shaking**, trembling Is 21$_{3}$.

חלט: **qal**: impf. וַיַּחְלְטוּ: **take** s.thg **as a valid pronouncement**, w. *min* 1K 20$_{33}$. †

חֳלִי: חֳלִי; sf. חָלְיוֹ; pl. בָּ/וָחֳלָיִ(י)ם, חֳלָיֵנוּ: — 1. **illness** 2K 1$_{2}$; *ḥᵒlî ḥāzāq* violent illness 1K 17$_{17}$, *ḥᵒlî neʾᵉmān* persistent illness Dt 28$_{59}$; — 2. general **suffering**: *ḥᵒlî rāʿ* Ec 6$_{2}$, torments Je 6$_{7}$ 10$_{19}$.

I חֲלִי: pl. חֲלָאִים: **ornament** Pr 25$_{12}$ SS 7$_{2}$. †

II חֲלִי: n. loc. Jos 19$_{25}$. †

*חֶלְיָה: sf. חֶלְיָתָהּ: **ornament** Ho 2$_{15}$. †

I חָלִיל: pl. חֲלִ(י)לִים: **flute**: — 1. instrument for joy 1S 10$_{5}$ 1K 1$_{40}$ Is 5$_{12}$; *hālak beḥālil* go out to the sound of flute Is 30$_{29}$; — 2. instrument for lament Je 48$_{36}$. †

II חָלִיל: alw. aversive, negative interj. חָלִ(י)לָה, orig. 'to the profane': **be it far from**: — 1. a) w. *lᵉ*: Gn 18$_{25}$; b) w. *min* & inf., that I/he should … Gn 18$_{25}$; c) w. *lᵉ* & inf., to do Jos 22$_{29}$; — 2. strengthened by *min* + *yhwh* before Y.: a) 1S 24$_{7}$; b) w. *min* & inf., that I/he should … 1S 26$_{11}$; — 3. abs. be it far 1S 14$_{45}$.

חֲלִיפָה: sf. חֲלִיפָתִי; pl. חֲלִ(י)פ(וֹ)ת: **substitute**: — 1. **change, relief**: *ḥᵃlîfôt ḥodeš* in turns for a month 1K 5$_{28}$; *ḥᵃlîfātî* (sg. only here) relief for me Jb 14$_{14}$; — 2. *ḥᵃlîfôt* **settlement** Ps 55$_{20}$ †; — 3. substitute clothing > special, **gala garments**: w. *śᵉmālôt* Gn 45$_{22}$, w. *bᵉgadîm* 2K 5$_{5}$; abs. (festal) clothes Ju 14$_{19}$.

*חֲלִיצָה: sf. חֲלִצָתוֹ; pl. sf. חֲלִצוֹתָם: **equipment** (or clothes) **stripped off** a slain enemy Ju 14$_{19}$ 2S 2$_{21}$. †

חֵלְכָה Ps 10$_{8}$ & חֵלֶכָה 10$_{14}$, pl. חֵלְכָּאִים 10$_{10}$: **unfortunate** person Ps 10$_{8.14}$, ? scoundrel 10$_{10}$. †

I חלל: **nif.**: pf. נִחֲלוּ, נִחַלְתְּ, נִחָל; impf. יֵחָל, תֵּחַל, וָאֵחַל; inf. הֵחֵל, הֵחַלּוֹ: **be taken into** common use, **profaned**: name of God Ez 20$_{9}$, priest Lv 21$_{4}$; profane onesf. (dau. of priest, by harlotry) Lv 21$_{9}$.

piel: pf. חִלֵּל, חִלַּלְתָּ, חִלְּלוּ, חִלַּלְתֶּם, חִלְּלֻנוּ, חִלְלוּהָ, חִלְלוֹ; impf. יְחַלֵּל, יְחַלְּלוּ, יְחַלְּלֻנוּ, יְחַלְּלֻהוּ, וַתְּחַלֶּלְנָה, וַתְּחַלְּלֶהָ Ex 20$_{25}$; inf. חַלֵּל, חַלְּלוֹ; pt. מְחַלֶּלֶת, pl. sf. מְחַלְלֶיהָ: — 1. **profane**: a) altar, by (iron) tool Ex 20$_{25}$; sabbath Ex 31$_{14}$, name of God Lv 18$_{21}$, God himself Ez 13$_{19}$; a bed Gn 49$_{4}$; dau. of priest profanes her father Lv 21$_{9}$; land Je 16$_{18}$; b) God himself profanes his inheritance Is 47$_{6}$, his covenant Ps 89$_{35}$; c) *ḥillēl min* expel from (mountain of God) Ez 28$_{16}$; — 2. **make** (profane) **use of** Dt 20$_{6}$.

pual: pt. מְחֻלָּל: **profaned** (name of Y.) Ez 36$_{23}$. †

hif.: pf. הֵחֵל, הֵחֵלָּה, הֵחֵלּוּ, הַחִלֹּ(וֹ)תָ; impf. יָחֵל, אָחֵל & יַחֵל, אַחֵל, וַיָּחֶל, תָּחֵלּוּ, תְּחִלֶּינָה; inf. הָחֵל, הַחִלָּם; pt. מֵחֵל: — 1. **let** s.thg **be profaned** Ez 39$_{7}$ †; — 2. (untie >) **begin** Gn 9$_{20}$; w. inf. 1S 3$_{2}$; w. *lᵉ* & inf. Gn 6$_{1}$; *hāḥēl wᵉkallēh* beginning & end, totality 1S 3$_{12}$; — 3. **make invalid**: *yaḥēl dᵉbārô* break one's word Nu 30$_{3}$.

hof.: pf. הוּחַל: **be begun** Gn 4$_{26}$. †

II חלל: [qal חָלַל Ps 109$_{22}$, חַלּוֹתִי Ps 77$_{11}$: txt.? ↗ comm.]

[**pual**: pt. pl. cs. מְחֻלְלֵי Ez 32$_{26}$ rd. חַלְלֵי.]

polel: pf. חֹלְלָה; pt. מְחוֹלֵל, מְחוֹלֶלֶת: **pierce** Is 51_9 Jb 26_{13}; **wound** Ps 26_{10}. †

polal: pt. מְחֹלָל: **wounded** Is 53_5. †

III חלל: **piel**: pt. מְחַלְּלִים: **play the flute** 1K 1_{40}. †

חָלָל (90×, 34× Ez): cs. חֲלַל, f. חֲלָלָה; pl. חֲלָלִים, cs. חַלְלֵי, sf. חֲלָלָיו, חַלְלֵיהֶם: **pierced**: — 1. a) *ḥalal ḥereb* Nu 19_{16} pierced w. a sword; **struck dead** 1S 17_{52} &c.; *ḥalᵉlê yhwh* struck by Y. Je 25_{33}; b) metaph., killed: *ḥalᵉlê rāʿāb* by hunger La 4_9; *ḥalᵉlê rᵉšāʿîm* foul transgressors Ez 21_{34}; — 2. **deflowered**, deprived of virginity Lv $21_{7.14}$.

חָלַם: **qal**: pf. ח׳, חָלַמְתִּי, חָלָמְתִּי, חָלַמְנוּ; impf. יַחֲלֹם, וַיַּחֲלֹמוּ, יַחְלְמוּ, יַחֲלֹמוּן, וַנַּחַלְמָה; pt. חֹלְמִים, ח(ו)לֵם: — 1. **become powerful** (animals) Jb 39_4 †; — 2. **dream** (sexual, then general) a) Gn 28_{12}; cogn. acc. *ḥālam ḥᵃlôm* ≠ *ḥᵃlôm*; b) **dreamer** as a class (alongside *nābîʾ* &c.) Dt 13_2.

hif.: impf. תַּחֲלִימֵנִי; pt. מַחְלְמִים: — 1. **let** s.one **grow strong** Is 38_{16}; — 2. **dream** Je 29_8. †

[חֵלֶם: n. pers. Zc 6_{14}: rd. חֶלְדַּי.]

חַלָּמוּת: **bugloss**, 'ox-tongue,' *Anchusa officinalis* Jb 6_6. †

חַלָּמִישׁ: cs. חַלְּמִישׁ: **flint** Dt 8_{15}.

חֵלֹן: n. pers.

I חָלַף: **qal**: pf. ח׳, חָלַף; impf. יַחֲלְפוּ; inf. חֲלֹף: — 1. succeed each other, **follow each other** Is 21_1; — 2. *ḥālaf min* **go on from** 1S 10_3; — 3. **pass by**: a) of God Jb 9_{11}; b) **pass away, vanish**: water Is 8_8, heavens Ps 102_{27}.

piel: impf. וַיְחַלֵּף: **change** (clothes) Gn 41_{14} 2S 12_{20}. †

hif.: pf. הֶחֱלִיף; impf. יַחֲלִיף, וַתַּחֲלֵף, יַחֲלִיפוּ, נַחֲלִיף, יַחֲלִיפֶנּוּ, תַּחֲלִיפֵם; impv. הַחֲלִיפוּ: — 1. **replace** s.thg w. s.thg else Is 9_9, **substitute** Lv 27_{10}; — 2. **change** (wages) Gn $31_{7.41}$, (garment) 35_2; — 3. **let** s.thg **follow, succeed**: newly gain (strength) Is 40_{31}; (of a tree) sprout again Jb 14_7; metaph. (of a bow) sprout Jb 29_{20}.

II חלף: **qal**: pf. חָלְפָה; impf. תַּחְלְפֵהוּ: **cut through** Ju 5_{26} Jb 20_{24}. †

I חֵלֶף: n. loc. Jos 19_{33}. †

II חֵלֶף: **as compensation for, instead of** Nu $18_{21.31}$. †

חָלַץ: **qal**: pf. ח׳, חָלְצָה; impf. תַּחֲלֹץ; pt. pass. חָלוּץ, cs. חֲלוּץ, pl. חֲלוּצִים, חֲלוּצֵי: — 1. **take off** (sandal) Dt 25_9; *ḥᵃluṣ hannaʿal* one who is barefoot Dt 25_{10}; expose & extend (the breast) La 4_3; — 2. *ḥālûṣ* girt, **ready for battle** Nu 32_{21}; *ḥᵃlûṣê (haṣ)ṣābāʾ* Jos 4_{13}; — 3. *ḥālas min* **withdraw** Ho 5_6.

nif.: impf. יֵחָלֵצוּ, יֵחָלְצוּן, תֵּחָלְצוּ, נֵחָלֵץ; impv. הֵחָלְצוּ; pt. נֶחֱלָץ: — 1. **be saved** Ps 60_7; — 2. **prepare** (onesf.) Nu $32_{17.20}$.

piel: pf. חִלַּצְתָּ, חִלְּצוּ; impf. יְחַלֵּץ, יְחַלְּצֵנִי, אֲחַלֶּצְךָ; impv. חַלְּצָה, חַלְּצֵנִי; inf. חַלֵּץ Lv 14_{43}: — 1. **plunder** Ps 7_5; — 2. **pull out** (stones from wall) Lv $14_{40.43}$; — 3. deliver, **save** 2S 22_{20} Ps 6_5.

hif.: impf. יַחֲלִיץ: **make strong** (bones) Is 58_{11}. †

חֶלֶץ: n. pers.

חֲלָצַיִם: dual; חֲלָצָיִם, sf. חֲלָצָ(י)ו: **loins** (body betw. ribs & hipbones) Je 30_6; *yāṣāʾ mēḥᵃlāṣāyw* = is one's physical descendant Gn 35_{11} 1K 8_{19}.

I חָלַק: **qal**: pf. ח׳: **be smooth, slippery, false**: *lēb* Ho 10_2, *peh* Ps 55_{22}. †

hif.: pf. הֶחֱלִיק, הֶחֱלִיקָה; impf. יַחֲלִיקוּן; pt. מַחֲלִיק: — 1. **beat smooth** (metal, w. hammer) Is 41_7; — 2. w. *lāšôn*, use a smooth tongue, **flatter** Ps 5_{10}; w. *ʾᵃmārîm* speak smooth words, flatteries Pr 2_{16} 7_5; ellipt. w. *ʿal* 29_5.

II חָלַק: **qal**: pf. ח׳, חָלְקוּ; impf. יַחֲלֹק, יַחְלְקוּ, יַחְלְקֻם, וַתַּחְלְקוּ, 1C 23_6 24_3, וַיַּחְלְקוּם; impv. חִלְקוּ; inf. חַלֵּק; pt. חוֹלֵק: — 1. **divide** (w. one another), **obtain one's share** (land, booty) 1S 30_{24}; — 2. **allot** Dt

4_{19}; — 3. **give share to,** w. *bᵉ* Jb 39_{17}; — 4. **divide** (into groups) 1C 23_6; — 5. **be partner with,** w. *ʿim* Pr 29_{24}.

nif.: impf. יֵחָלֵק, יֵחָ֫לֶק: — 1. **be divided** Nu $26_{53\cdot55f}$; — 2. **divide onesf.**, split up Gn 14_{15} 1K 16_{21} Jb 38_{24}. †

piel: pf. חִלְּקוּ, חִלְּקָהּ, חִלְּקָם, חִלַּקְתָּם; impf. יְחַלֵּק, וַיְחַלֶּק־, אֲחַלְּקָה, אֲחַלְּקֵם; impv. חַלֵּק; inf. חַלֵּק, חַלְּקָם: — 1. **divide, allot** 1K 18_6; w. *šālāl* divide booty Gn 49_{27}; — 2. **divide in pieces** Ez 5_1, **scatter** Gn 49_7.

pual: pf. חֻלָּק; impf. תְּחֻלָּק: **be divided** (land, booty) Am 7_{17} Zc 14_1. †

hif.: inf. לַחֲלֹק: **participate in the distribution** Je 37_{12}. †

hitp.: pf. הִתְחַלְּקוּ: **divide w. one another** Jos 18_5. †

III **חלק**: **piel**: pf. חִלְּקָם: **destroy** La 4_{16} (trad. II!). †

חָלָק: f. pl. חֲלָקוֹת & חֲלַקְלַקּוֹת: — 1. **smooth**: *ʾîš ḥālāq* Gn 27_{11}; stones in river-bed Is 57_6; — 2. smooth, **flattering**: mouth Ps 26_{28}; pl. f. *ḥᵃlāqôt*: **smoothness, falsehood**: *śᵉfat* (*śiftê*) *ḥᵃlāqôt* Ps 12_{3f}; — 3. smooth, **slippery**: *ḥᵃlāqôt*, slippery footing Ps 73_{18}; — 4. n. terr *hāhār heḥālāq* Jos 11_{17} 12_7.

I **חֵלֶק**: **smoothness** (of lips) Pr 7_{21}. †

II **חֵלֶק**: sf. חֶלְקוֹ; pl. חֲלָקִים, sf. חֶלְקֵיהֶם: share distributed by lot: — 1. **share of booty** Gn 14_{24}; — 2. **share of property**: a) Jos 14_4; commercial Ec 11_2; b) *ḥēleq wᵉnaḥᵃlâ* Gn 31_{14}; *ḥᵃlāqîm* lots of property Jos $18_{5f\cdot9}$; c) share (of offering) Lv 6_{10}; plot of ground, territory 2K 9_{10}; d) title, claim 2S 20_1 1K 12_{16}; *ḥēleq ʿim* company w. Ps 50_{18}; profit Ec $2_{10\cdot21}$; e) what belongs to s.one Is 61_7; answer one's part Jb 32_{17}; f) fate Is 57_6; — 3. metaph. of relation betw. God & man: God is *ḥēleq* Dt 32_9, *ḥelqî* Ps 16_5; *ḥēleq mēʾᵉlōhîm* what is alloted **by God** Jb 20_{29}.

III **חֵלֶק**: n. pers. Nu 26_{30} Jos 17_2. †

***חַלָּק** (or *חַלּוּק): pl. cs. חַלֻּקֵי: **smooth** (stones) 1S 17_{40}. †

I ***חֶלְקָה**: cs. חֶלְקַת: **smoothness**: — 1. *ḥelqat ṣawwāʾrāyw* hairless portions of the neck Gn 27_{16}; *ḥelqat lāšôn* smooth tongue Pr 6_{24}. †

II **חֶלְקָה**: cs. חֶלְקַת, sf. חֶלְקָתָם: portion of common field of a locality distributed to an individual by lot, **piece of land, plot of ground**: *ḥelqat haśśādeh* Gn 33_{19}, *ḥelqâ ṭôbâ* 2K 3_{19}.

***חֲלֻקָּה**: cs. חֲלֻקַּת: **division,** section 2C 35_5. †

חֲלַקּוֹת: ↗ חָלָק.

חֶלְקִי: gent. of III חֵלֶק.

חֶלְקַי: var. of חֶלְקִי.

חִלְקִיָּה: n. pers.

חִלְקִיָּהוּ: n. pers.

***חֲלַקְלַק**: pl. חֲלַקְלַקּוֹת: **smooth,** pl. f. sbst.: — 1. **smooth portions** (of road) Je 23_{12}; — 2. smoothness, **intrigue** Dn 11_{21}, hypocrisy 11_{34}.

חֶלְקַת: n. loc.

I **חלש**: **qal**: impf. יֶחֱלַשׁ: **be enfeebled, disappear** Jb 14_{10}. †

II **חלש**: **qal**: impf. יַחֲלֹשׁ; pt. חוֹלֵשׁ: **defeat** Ex 17_{13} Is 14_{12}. †

חַלָּשׁ: **weakling** Jl 4_{10}. †

I ***חָם**: sf. חָמִיךְ: husband's father, **father-in-law** Gn $38_{13\cdot25}$ 1S $4_{19\cdot21}$. †

II **חָם**: pl. חַמִּים: **hot** Jos 9_{12} (bread), Jb 37_{17} (clothes, fm. south-wind). †

III **חָם**: n. pers. **Ham.**

חֹם: — 1. **warmth**: *leḥem ḥōm* 1S 21_7 = fresh bread; — 2. (temperature) **heat**: of the summer Gn 8_{22} Je 17_8 Jb 24_{19}, cf. *ḥmm* qal inf.

חֵמָא Dn 11_{44}: ↗ II חֵמָה.

חֶמְאָה: cs. חֶמְאַת: a type of **curdled milk,** similar to yoghurt Gn 18_8 2S 17_{29}.

חָמַד: **qal**: pf. ח׳, חֲמַדְתֶּם; impf. יַחְמֹד,

וָאֶחְמְדֵם; pt. pass. חֲמוּדוֹ, חֲמוּדֵיהֶם, חֲמֻדוֹת: — 1. **desire and try to acquire, crave, covet** Ex 20_{17}; — 2. **find pleasure in** Is 1_{29} 53_{2} †; — 3. חָמוּד a) **beloved** Is 44_{9}; b) treasure Jb 20_{20}.

nif.: pt. נֶחְמָדִים, נֶחְמָד: **desirable** Gn 2_{9} 3_{6}.

piel: pf. חִמַּדְתִּי: **desire passionately** SS 2_{3}. †

חֶמֶד: **charm, beauty**: *śᵉdê-ḥemed* Is 32_{12}, *karmê-ḥemed* Am 5_{11}.

חֶמְדָּה: cs. חֶמְדַּת, sf. חֶמְדָּתוֹ: **s.thg desirable, precious**: *ḥemdat yiśrā'ēl* 1S 9_{20}; = **excellent**: ships Is 2_{16}, houses Ez 26_{12}; *ḥemdat nāšîm* beloved of women = Tammuz-Adonis Dn 11_{37}.

חֲמֻדוֹת, חֲמֻדֹת 2×, חֲמוּד(וֹ)ת (2×): — 1. **valuables, treasure** Gn 27_{15}; — 2. adj: *leḥem ḥᵃmudôt* dainty Dn 10_{3}, *'îš ḥᵃmudôt* beloved Dn $10_{11.19}$.

חֶמְדָּן: n. pers.

cj **חמה**: **qal**: pf. 3 f. חָמְתָ (אֲדָמָה) for חֲמַת & חֵמֹת Ps $76_{11a.b}$ (?); impv. חֲמֵה 'watch out' Jb 36_{18}; inf. sf. חַמָּתוֹ Ps 19_{7}: see. †

nif.: pf. נֶחֱמוּ: **become visible** Je 13_{22}. †

חֵמָה (120×): cs. חֲמַת, sf. חֲמָתִי; pl. חֵמ(וֹ)ת: — 1. **heat**: *ḥᵃmat rûḥî* Ez 3_{14} †; — 2. **poison**: of animals Dt 32_{24}, of arrows Jb 6_{4}, of men Ps 58_{5}; — 3. excitement, **anger** (26×): Gn 27_{44}; — 3. **God's anger** (ca. 80×; Je 14× Ez 29×): 2K 22_{13}; w. *'af* Dt 9_{19}.

חַמָּה: sf. חַמָּתוֹ: — 1. **glow** (of sun) Ps 19_{7}; — 2. **sun** Is 24_{23} 30_{26} SS 6_{10}. †

חֲמוּאֵל: n. pers.

חֲמוּטַל, 2× Kt חֲמִיטַל: n. pers. f.

חָמוּל: n. pers.

חַמּוֹן: n. loc.

***חָמוּץ**: cs. חֲמוּץ: *ḥᵃmûṣ bᵉgādîm* dressed in vivid colors Is 63_{1}. †

***חָמוֹץ**: **oppressor**: so Is 1_{17}, but Verss. rd. *ḥāmûṣ*; cj in Is 16_{4} (so Qumran text).

***חַמּוּק**: *ḥammûqê yᵉrēkayim* **curve** (of the hips) SS 7_{2}. †

I **חֲמוֹר**, חֲמֹר Gn 49_{14} (97×): sf. חֲמֹרְךָ, חֲמֹרֶךָ; pl. חֲמ(וֹ)רִים, sf. חֲמ(וֹ)רֵינוּ, חֲמ(וֹ)רֵיהֶם: male **ass, donkey**, *Equus asinus* Gn 12_{16}.

II **חֲמוֹר**: dual חֲמֹרָתַיִם (as if fm. *חֲמוֹרָה): **heap** 1S 16_{20}; *ḥᵃmôr ḥᵃmōrātāyim* Ju 15_{16}, trad.: in heaps. †

III **חֲמוֹר**: n. pers.

***חָמוֹת**: sf. חֲמוֹתָהּ: husband's mother, **mother-in-law** Mi 7_{6} Ru 1_{14}.

חֹמֶט: unclean **reptile**, not precisely specified, perh. a type of skink, Lv 11_{30}. †

חֻמְטָה: n. loc.

חֲמִיטַל: 2K 24_{18} Je 52_{1}: n. pers. f., ↑ חֲמוּטַל.

חָמִיץ: **sorrel**, *Rumex*, ↑ *bᵉlîl*: *bᵉlîl ḥāmîṣ*, fodder of sorrel prepared by soaking Is 30_{24}. †

חֲמִישִׁי & **חֲמִשִּׁי**: f. חֲמִ(י)שִׁית, sf. חֲמִ(י)שִׁ(י)תוֹ: ord. **fifth**: day Gn 1_{23}, son 30_{17}; *ḥᵃmîšît* fraction **one-fifth**; *ḥᵃmišitô* a fifth part of it Lv 5_{16}, *pa'am ḥᵃmîšît* a fifth time Ne 6_{5}; *ḥᵃmîšît* pentagon 1K 6_{31}.

חָמַל: **qal**: pf. חָמַל, ח׳, חָמַלְתָּ, חֲמַלְתֶּם; impf. יַחְמֹ(וֹ)ל, אֶחְמ(וֹ)ל, יַחְמְלוּ, תַּחְמְלוּ, תַּחְמֹלוּ; inf. ↑ חֶמְלָה & חֶמְלָה: — 1. **feel compassion, pity for, take compassion, pity on**, a) w. *'al* Ex 2_{6} 1S 15_{3}; b) abs. 2S 12_{6}; *lō' ḥāmal/yaḥmōl* without pity Is 30_{14} La 2_{2}; — 2. **spare, keep back** Je 50_{14} Jb 20_{13}; w. *lᵉ* & inf. could not bear to ... 2S 12_{4}.

***חֶמְלָה**: inf. f. of חָמַל: cs. חֶמְלַת, sf. חֶמְלָתוֹ: **sparing**, forbearance Gn 19_{16}, compassion Is 63_{9}. †

חֶמְלָה: inf. f. of חָמַל: **compassion** Ez 16_{5}. †

חמם: **qal**: pf. חַם, חַמּוֹתִי; impf. וַיָּחָם, יֵחַם & יֵחַם, יֵחָם, יֵחַמּוּ; inf. חֹם, חַמּוֹ: — 1. *ḥam lô* **feels warm** 1K 1_{1f}; — 2. *ḥam* **be(come) warm, hot**: *bāśār* 2K 4_{34}, *lēb* Dt 19_{6}; **warm onesf.** Is 44_{15f}; — 3. **become warm, hot** (weather) Jb 6_{17}, sun 1S 11_{9}; *ḥōm hayyôm* when the day is hottest Gn 18_1 1S 11_{11}; — 4. **become** hot, **provoked** (lions) Je 51_{39}.

nif.: pt. נֶחָמִים: hot, **lustful** Is 57_5 (cult prostitution). †

piel: impf. תְּחַמֵּם: **let** s.thg **get warm** Jb 39_{14}. †

hitp.: impf. יִתְחַמָּם: **let** s.one **get warm**, ... **warm himsf.** Jb 31_{20}. †

*חַמָּן: pl. חַמָּנִים, חַמָּנֵיכֶם: (portable) **incense-altar** Lv 26_{30} Is 17_8.

I חמס: **qal**: pf. חָמְסוּ; impf. יַחְמֹס, תַּחְמְסוּ; pt. חֹמֵס: — 1. **treat violently** Je 22_3; — 2. (of vine): **knock off** (part of plant) Jb 15_{33}; spec., strip Pr 26_6.

nif.: pf. נֶחְמְסוּ: **suffer violence, be stripped** Je 13_{22}. †

II חמס: **qal**: impf. תַּחְמֹסוּ: **think up, devise** (w. *mᵉzimmôt*) Jb 21_{27}. †

חָמָס: cs. חֲמַס, sf. חֲמָסִי; pl. חֲמָסִים: **violence, wrong,** oft. a cry for help; *ḥᵃmāsî* the violence wh. I suffer, w. *ʿal* expressing responsibility for the violence, as a curse Gn 16_5; *ḥᵃmāsô* the violence wh. he practices Ps 7_{17}; *ʾîš ḥāmās* violent man Ps 18_{49}; *ʿēd ḥāmās* witness who practices violence, false witness Ex 23_1.

I חָמֵץ: **qal**: pf. חָמֵץ; impf. יֶחְמַץ; inf. sf. חֻמְצָתוֹ: **be** (thoroughly) **leavened** (dough) Ex $12_{34 \cdot 39}$ Ho 7_4. †

hif.: pt. מַחְמֶצֶת: **taste leavened** Ex 12_{19f}. †

hitp.: impf. יִתְחַמֵּץ: **turn sharp, bitter** Ps 73_{21}. †

II חמץ: **qal**: pt. חוֹמֵץ: **oppress** Ps 71_4. †

חָמֵץ: s.thg **leavened** (bread & other food): Ex 12_{15} Am 4_5.

חֹמֶץ: **vinegar** Nu 6_3 Ps 69_{22}.

חָמַק: **qal**: pf. ח׳: **turn aside**, go away; *ḥāmaq ʿābār* was up & away SS 5_6. †

hitp.: impf. תִּתְחַמָּקִין: **turn this way & that, waver** Je 31_{22}. †

I חָמַר: **qal**: pf. ח׳; impf. יֶחְמְרוּ: **foam** Ps 46_4 (water). †

poalal: pf. חֳמַרְמָרוּ: usu.: **ferment** La 1_{20} 2_{11}, but ↗ II. †

II חמר: **poalal**: pf. חֳמַרְמְרָה Kt Jb 16_{16}, ־רָה Qr; חֳמַרְמָרוּ: **glow, burn** (*mēʿîm*) La 1_{20} 2_{11}; (*pānîm*) Jb 16_{16}. †

III חמר: **qal**: impf. sf. תַּחְמְרָה: w. *ḥēmār*: **stop** (w. pitch) Ex 2_3. †

חֶמֶר: חֶמֶר: **wine** (wh. is still fermenting) Dt 32_{14}. †

I חֹמֶר: **storming, raging** Hb 3_{15}. †

II חֹמֶר: **clay**: — 1. raw material, (clayey) **mud**, to be trodden Is 10_6; — 2. building material, **mortar**; (w. brick) Ex 1_{14}; bitumen as mortar Gn 11_3; — 3. material for pottery: a) *ḥomer bᵉyad hayyāṣēr* Je $18_{4 \cdot 6}$; b) metaph. of men in contrast to God Is 45_9; — 4. spec. Jb 38_{14} ↗ *ḥôtām*, Jb 13_{12} ↗ II *gab*.

III חֹמֶר: pl. חֳמָר(י)ם: — 1. **homer**, a dry measure, = 394 liters Ho 3_2 Nu 11_{32}; — 2. **heaps** *ḥomārîm ḥomārîm* in heaps Ex 8_{10}.

חֵמָר: **bitumen, asphalt** Gn 11_3 14_{10} Ex 2_3. †

חַמְרָן: n. pers.

*חֲמוֹרָה: ↗ II חֲמוֹר.

חמשׁ: **qal**: pt. pass. חֲמֻשִׁים: arranged in companies of 50, **organized for war** Ex 13_{18} Jos 1_{14}.

piel: pf. חִמֵּשׁ: w. acc. as tax, **levy a fifth part** Gn 41_{34}. †

חָמֵשׁ: cs. חֲמֵשׁ, f. חֲמִשָּׁה (Ez 45_3 Qr; Kt חָמֵשׁ), חֲמֵשֶׁת: **five**: *ḥāmēs šānîm* 5 years Gn 5_6, *ḥāmēš yādôt* 5 times 43_{34}; *ḥᵃmiššâ ʿāśār* **fifteen** Ho 3_2; — pl. *ḥᵃmiššîm* **fifty**: *ḥᵃmiššîm ʾîš rāṣîm* 50 men as runners 2S 15_1; ↗ gram.

I חֹמֶשׁ: **fifth** Gn 47_{26}, but perh. rd. חִמֵּשׁ. †

II חֹמֶשׁ: **belly** 2S 2_{23} 3_{27} 20_{10}. †

חֲמִשִׁית, חֲמִשִׁי: ↗ חֲמִישִׁי.

חֵמֶת: cs. חֵמַת; f. ?: (goat-)**skin**, stopped at both ends w. pitch, for water, wine, oil &c. Gn $21_{14f \cdot 19}$. †

חֲמָת: n. loc. **Hamath**.

I חַמַּת: n. loc.

II חַמַּת: n. pers. 1C 2_{55}. †

חֲמָתִי: gent. of חֲמָת.

חֵן: הַחֵן Pr 31_{30} †; sf. חִנּוֹ Gn 39_{21} †: — 1. **agreeableness, charm** (attractive, pleasing quality): *'ēšet ḥēn* pleasant, gracious wife Pr 11_{16}; God bestows *ḥēn w^ekābôd* favor & honor Ps 84_{12}; — 2. **favor** (approval or affection of s.one): a wife w. her husband Dt 24_1; *nātan ḥinnô b^e'ênê* got him favor with Gn 39_{21}, cf Ex 3_{21}; *māṣā' ḥēn b^e'ênê* find pleasure, satisfaction Gn 6_8 & oft.; — 3. *rûaḥ ḥēn* spirit of compassion Zc 12_{10}.

חֵנָדָד: n. pers.

I חָנָה (140×): qal: pf. חָנוּ, חָנִיתִי, ח׳; impf. נַחֲנֶה, יַחֲנוּ, תַּחֲנֶה, וַיִּחַן; impv. חֲנוּ, חֲנֵה; inf. חֲנֹ(וֹ)ת, חֲנֹתְכֶם; pt. חֹנֶה, f. חֹנָה, pl. ח(ֹו)נִים: — 1. **decline** (draw toward evening): *ḥanôt hayyôm* Ju 19_9; — 2. **encamp** Gn 26_{17}; **camp** (for the night) Ex 14_9; — 3. **pitch a** (military) **camp** against, w. *'al* 1S 11_1, w. *b^e* Ju 9_{50}, abs. Is 29_1; — 4. **encamp in protection** Zc 9_8.

II חנה: piel: inf. חַנּוֹת Ps 77_{10} ⸗ I חָנַן. †

חַנָּה: n. pers. f. **Hannah**.

I חֲנוֹךְ & חֲנֹךְ Gn 25_4: n. pers. **Enoch**.

II חֲנוֹךְ: n. loc. Gn 4_{17}. †

חָנוּן: n. pers.

חַנּוּן: — 1. (of God) **gracious** Ex 22_{26}; — 2. (of men) **friendly**, gracious Ps 112_4.

*חָנוּת: pl. חֲנֻיוֹת: **vault, cellar** Je 37_{16}. †

I חנט: qal: pf. חָנְטָה: **ripen** SS 2_{13} (oth.: get red). †

II חנט: qal: impf. וַיַּחַנְטוּ; inf. חֲנֹט: **embalm** Gn $50_{2\cdot26}$. †

חֲנֻטִים: **embalming** Gn 50_3. †

חַנִּיאֵל: n. pers.

חֲנֻיוֹת: ⸗ *חָנוּת.

*חָנִיךְ: pl. sf. חֲנִיכָיו: **follower, vassal** Gn 14_{14}. †

חֲנִינָא: **pity** Je 16_{13}. †

חֲנִית: sf. חֲנִיתוֹ, חֲנִיתֶךָ; pl. חֲנִיתִים, sf. חֲנִית(וֹ)תֵיהֶם; f.: **spear** 1S 13_{19}; *'ēṣ ḥanît* spear-shaft 1S 17_7, *lahebet ḥanît* spear-head 1S 17_7; *hērîq ḥanît* take from the sheath, prepare for throwing Ps 35_3.

חנך: qal: pf. חֲנָכוֹ; impf. יַחְנְכֶנּוּ, וַיַּחְנְכוּ; inf. חֲנֹךְ: — 1. **train** (w. *l^e*) Pr 22_6; — 2. **dedicate** (a house) Dt 20_5 1K 8_{63} 2C 7_5. †

חֲנֻכָּה: **dedication**, of altar Nu 7_{10ff}, temple Ps 30_1.

חֲנֹכִי: gent. of I חֲנוֹךְ.

חִנָּם: adv.: — 1. **without compensation** Gn 29_{15}, without paying for it 2S 24_{24}; — 2. **for nothing** = **in vain** Ez 6_{10}; — 3. **without cause, undeservedly** 1S 19_5; *d^emê ḥinnām* guiltless blood 1K 2_{31}, *qillat ḥinnām* undeserved curse Pr 26_2.

חֲנַמְאֵל: n. pers.

חֲנָמַל: devastating **flood** Ps 78_{47}. †

I חָנַן: qal: pf. ח׳, וְחַנֹּתִי, חֲנָנוּ, חַנַּנִי; impf. יָחֹן, יְחָנְּךָ, וַיְחָנֶּךָּ, יְחָנְנוּ, תְּחַנֵּם, Am 5_{15}, יֶחֱנַן, וַיָּחַן, יָחְנְךָ Gn 43_{29}, יְחַנַּנִי (Qr וְחַנַּנִי, Kt יְחָנַנִי) 2S 12_{22}; impv. חָנֵּנִי, Ps 9_{14} חָנְנֵנִי (polel?), חָנֵּנִי, חָנֵּנוּ; inf. חָנוֹן, לַחֲנַנְכֶם Is 30_{18}, לְחֶנְנָהּ Ps 102_{14}, חַנּוֹת Ps 77_{10}; pt. חוֹנֵן: — 1. w. acc. **be gracious to** s.one (of God) Gn 33_{11} 2K 13_{23}; (of men) Dt 7_2; — 2. w. 2 acc. **graciously provide** s.one w. s.thg Gn 33_5; — 3. *ḥônēn* **generous** Ps $37_{21\cdot26}$.

[nif.: pf. נֵחַנְתְּ Je 22_{23} < נֶאֱנַחְתְּ ⸗ אנח.]

pilel: impf. יְחַנֵּן: **make charming** (voice) Pr 26_{25}. †

polel: impf. יְחֹנֵנוּ; pt. מְחוֹנֵן: w. acc. **take pity on** Pr 14_{21}, be sorry for Ps 102_{15}. †

hof. (pass. qal): impf. יֻחַן: **be shown compassion** Is 26_{10} Pr 21_{10}. †

hitp.: pf. הִתְחַנַּנְתָּה; impf. וַיִּתְחַנֵּן, יִתְחַנֶּן־, אֶתְחַנֵּן, אֶתְחַנֶּן־; inf. לְהִתְחַנֶּן־, הִתְחַנְנוּ: **plead for grace, pity**, w. *'el* to Gn 42_{21} 1K $8_{33\cdot47}$; w. *l^e* Ho 12_5; w. *lifnê* before 1K 8_{59}.

II חנן: qal: pf. וְחַנֹּתִי: **be stinking, loathsome** Jb 19_{17}. †

חָנָן: n. pers.

חֲנַנְאֵל: n. loc. (tower in Jerus.); n. pers.

חֲנָנִי: n. pers.

חֲנַנְיָה: n. pers.

חֲנַנְיָהוּ: n. pers.

חָנֵס: n. loc.

I **חנף**: **qal**: pf. חָנְפָה, חָנְפוּ; impf. תֶּחֱנַף; inf. חָנוֹף: — 1. **be godless** (priest, prophet) Je 23_{11}; — 2. **be defiled** (land) Is 24_5 Je 3_1 Ps 106_{38}. †

hif.: impf. יַחֲנִיף, תַּחֲנִיפוּ: — 1. **defile** (land) Nu 35_{33} Je 3_2; — 2. Dn 11_{32}? **bring to apostasy** (oth.: flatter; ꟻ comm.). †

cj II **חנף**: **qal**: cj inf. בְּחַנְפִי: **limp** Ps 35_{16}. †

חָנֵף: pl. חֲנֵפִים, חַנְפֵי: estranged fm. God, **godless** Is 10_6.

חֹנֶף: **godlessness**, w. *ʿāśâ* Is 32_6. †

חֲנֻפָּה: **godlessness** Je 23_{15}. †

חנק: **nif.**: impf. וַיֵּחָנַק: **hang onesf.** 2S 17_{23}. †

piel: pf. מְחַנֵּק: **strangle** (prey, of a lion) Na 2_{13}. †

חַנָּתֹן: n. loc.

I **חסד**: **piel**: impf. יְחַסֶּדְךָ: **insult** Pr 25_{10}. †

II **חסד**: **hitp.**: impf. תִּתְחַסָּד: **conduct onesf. as** *ḥāsîd* (loyal, faithful) 2S 22_{26}/Ps 18_{26}. †

I **חֶסֶד**: **disgrace**, shameful thing Lv 20_{17} Pr 14_{34}. †

II **חֶסֶד** (ca. 250×; sg. 234×, 125× Ps): חָסֶד, sf. חַסְדּוֹ, חַסְדְּךָ; pl. חֲסָדִים, cs. חַסְדֵי, sf. חֲסָדָיו, חֲסָדָו (Ps 106_{45} & La 3_{22}, Kt חַסְדּוֹ), Ps 119_{41} חֲסָדֶךָ: — 1. **obligation to the community** in relation to relatives, friends, guests, master & servants, &c.; unity, solidarity, **loyalty**: a) *ḥesed & beʳît*: a *beʳît* is initiated by ceremony, *ḥesed* results fm. closer relation betw. parties, but the obligations are largely the same; *ḥesed weʾemet* Gn $24_{27\cdot49}$ lasting loyalty, **faithfulness**; *ʿāśâ ḥesed* show loyalty Gn 21_{23}; b) *ḥesed* exists betw. son & dying father Gn 47_{29}, wife & husband Gn 20_{13}, relatives Ru 2_{20}, guests Gn 19_{19}, friends 1S 20_8, people who do favors for each other Ju 1_{24}, king & people 2S 3_8; c) spec.: *ʾîš ḥesed* **confidant** Pr 11_{17}, *ʾanšê ḥesed* **devout men** Is 57_1; *malkê ḥesed* **loyal kings** 1K 20_{31}; *ʾîš ḥasdô* everyone his faithfulness Ps 20_6; d) community > protection Ps 144_2 > **favor** Est $2_{9\cdot17}$, *ḥesed lifnê hammelek* Ezr 7_{28}; *tôrat ḥesed* friendly instruction Pr 31_{26}; charm (of flowers) Is 40_6; — 2. *ḥesed* in relation of God to people or individuals, **faithfulness, kindness, grace**: a) *ḥesed yhwh* Ps 33_5; *leʿôlām ḥasdô* Je 33_{11}; b) *ʿāśâ ḥesed* show faithfulness, w. *le* Ex 20_6; *šāmar ḥesed* Dt 7_9, oth. vbs.; c) God is *rab ḥesed* rich in faithfulness Ex 34_6; — 3. pl. *ḥasādîm*, *ḥasdê* &c. individual acts flowing fm. solidarity: a) (of men) **godly deeds** Ne 13_{14}; b) (of God) **evidences of grace** Is 55_3.

III **חֶסֶד**: n. pers. 1K 4_{10}. †

חֲסַדְיָה: n. pers.

חָסָה: **qal**: pf. חָסָיוּ & חָסוּ, חָסִיתִי, ח׳; impf. יֶחֱסֶה, אֶחֱסֶה, יֶחֱסוּ, יֶחֱסָיוּן; impv. חֲסוּ; inf. לַחֲסוֹת, לַחְסוֹת; pt. חוֹסֶה, ח(ו)סִים, ח(ו)סֵי: **seek refuge**, w. *be*: a) w. men Ju 9_{15}; b) w. God 2S $22_{3\cdot31}$.

I **חֹסָה**: n. pers.

II **חֹסָה**: n. loc. Jos 19_{29}. †

חָסוּת: **refuge** Is 30_3. †

חָסִיד: pl. חֲסִידִים, sf. חֲסִידָ(י)ו: one is *ḥāsîd* if he practices *ḥesed*: **one who is faithful, devout**: 1S 2_9 & oft.; of God Je 3_{12}.

חֲסִידָה: unclean bird Lv 11_{19} Dt 14_{18}, trad. **stork**, more recently **heron**, perh. both: Je 8_7 Zc 5_9 Ps 104_{17}. †

חָסִיל: specific stage of the **locust** or **cockroach** ?: 1K 8_{37}.

חֲסִין: Ps 89_9, trad. 'strong'; but txt.? ꟻ comm. †

חסל: **hif.** (or *qal*): impf. יַחְסְלֶנּוּ: **consume** (locusts) Dt 28_{38}. †

חסם: **qal**: impf. תַחְסֹם; pt. חֹסֶמֶת: — 1. **muzzle** (ox when threshing) Dt 25_4; — 2. **block** (road of travellers) Ez 39_{11} (? ꟻ comm.). †

חסן: nif.: impf. יֵחָסֵן: **be stored up** Is 23_{18}. †

חֹסֶן: **treasure, stores** Is 33_6.

חָסֹן: **strong** Is 1_{31} Am 2_9. †

חספס: **pualal**: pt. מְחֻסְפָּס: crackling, **crisp** (manna) Ex 16_{14}. †

חָסֵר: **qal**: pf. ח׳, חָסֵרוּ, חָסַרְנוּ; impf. יֶחְסַר, תֶּחְסַר, יַחְסְרוּן(ן); inf. חֲסֹר; ꜰ adj. חָסֵר: — 1. **diminish**, become less: water Gn $8_{3\cdot5}$; lack (be less by) Gn 18_{28}; be empty 1K $17_{14\cdot16}$; — 2. **do without**, lack Dt 2_7 Ps 23_1.

piel: impf. וַתְּחַסְּרֵהוּ; pt. מְחַסֵּר: w. acc. & *min*, **make** s.one **lack, deprive** s.one of s.thg Ec 4_8; Ps 8_6 (*min* = in comparison w.). †

hif.: pf. הֶחְסִיר; impf. יַחְסִיר: — 1. abs. **have a deficiency**, lack Ex 16_{18}; — 2. w. acc. **make** s.one **lack, deprive** Is 32_6. †

חָסֵר: cs. חֲסַר: w. gen. **one who lacks** 1S 21_{16} 1K 11_{22}; *ḥ^a^sar lēb* one who has no sense Pr 6_{32} & oft.; *ḥāsēr l^e^nafšô* Ec 6_2.

חֶסֶר: **lack** Pr 28_{22} Jb 30_3. †

חֹסֶר: **lack** Dt $28_{48\cdot57}$ Am 4_6. †

חַסְרָה: n. pers.

חֶסְרוֹן: **deficit, what is missing** Ec 1_{15}. †

I **חַף**: **clean** Jb 33_9. †

cj II **חַף**: n. deity, **Apis**, Je 46_{15}: for *nisḥaf*, rd. *nās ḥaf*. †

חפא: **piel**: impf. וַיְחַפְּאוּ: **attribute** s.thg. (*ʿal* to s.one) 2K 17_9. †

חפה: **qal**: pf. חָפוּ; pt. pass. חָפוּי, cs. חֲפוּי: **cover, veil**: head (in affliction) 2S 15_{30}, of condemned man Est 7_8.

nif.: pf. נֶחְפָּה: **be covered** w. *b^e^* Ps 68_{14}. †

piel: pf. חִפָּה; impf. וַיְחַף, וַיְחַפֵּהוּ: w. 2 acc. **cover** s.thg w. 2C $3_{5\cdot7\cdot9}$. †

I **חֻפָּה**: sf. חֻפָּתוֹ: — 1. **shelter(ing roof)** Is 4_5; — 2. **bridal chamber** Jl 2_{16} Ps 19_6. †

II **חֻפָּה**: n. pers. (tribe) 1C 24_{13}. †

חפז: **qal**: impf. יַחְפֹּז, תַּחְפְּזוּ; inf. בְּחָפְזִי, בְּחָפְזָם, חָפְזָה 2K 7_{15} Qr (Kt nif.): **hurry away** (in fear) 2S 4_4.

nif.: pf. נֶחְפְּזוּ; impf. יֵחָפֵזוּן; inf. בְּהֵחָפְזָם Kt 2K 7_{15} (Qr qal); pt. נֶחְפָּז: *neḥpāz lāleket* run away hurriedly 1S 23_{26}.

חִפָּזוֹן: **hurried flight**: *b^e^ḥippāzôn* **in haste** Ex 12_{11} Dt 16_3 Is 52_{12}. †

חֻפִּים, חֻפָּם: n. pers.

***חֹפֶן**: du. חָפְנַיִם, חָפְנֵי, sf. חָפְנָיו, חָפְנֵיכֶם: mostly w. √ *mlʾ* (fill): (fill) **the 2 hollow hands**, Ex 9_8 handfuls.

חָפְנִי: n. pers.

חפף: **qal**: pt. חֹפֵף: w. *ʿal*, **screen, shelter** Dt 33_{12}. †

I **חָפֵץ**: **qal**: pf. ח׳, חָפֵצָה, חָפַצְתִּי, חֲפֵצְנוּ; impf. יַחְפֹּץ, יֶחְפַּץ, תַּחְפֹּץ, אֶחְפֹּץ, אֶחְפָּץ, יַחְפְּצוּ, יֶחְפָּצוּ, יֶחְפָּצוּן; inf. חֲפֹץ: — 1. **want, desire** Is 1_{11}; — 2. w. *b^e^* **take pleasure** in Gn 34_{19} 1K 10_9; — 3. **wish to**: a) w. inf. Jb 13_3, b) w. *l^e^* & inf. 1K 9_1; — 4. abs. **be willing** Is 42_{21}; **be inclined** SS 2_7.

II **חפץ**: **qal**: impf. יַחְפֹּץ: **let** (tail) **hang** (oth.: hold stiff, so Verss.) Jb 40_{17}. †

חָפֵץ: f. חֲפֵצָה; pl. חֲפֵצִים, חֲפֵצֵי, sf. חֶפְצֵיהֶם: — 1. a) **one who takes pleasure in** s.thg: abs. 1K 13_{33}; w. obj. Ps 5_5; b) **one who has a desire** for s.thg Ps 34_{13}; — 2. **willing** 1C 28_9, w. *l^e^* & inf. Ne 1_{11}.

חֵפֶץ: sf. חֶפְצוֹ; pl. חֲפָצִים, sf. חֲפָצֶיךָ: — 1. **joy, pleasure**, w. *l^e^* in 1S 15_{22}; w. *b^e^* in Je 22_{28}; *dibrê ḥēfeṣ* words that give pleasure Ec 12_{10}, *b^e^ḥēfeṣ kappéhā* w. her eager hands Pr 31_{13}; — 2. **wish** 1K 5_{24}; — 3. *ʾabnê ḥēfeṣ* **costly jewels** Is 54_{12} > *ḥēfeṣ* **treasure, jewel** Pr 3_{15} & 8_{11}; — 4. **affair, business** Ec $3_{1\cdot17}$, pl. Is 58_{13}; *ʿal-haḥēfeṣ* about it Ec 5_7.

חֶפְצִי־בָהּ: n. pers. f.

I **חָפַר**: **qal**: pf. ח׳, חָפַרְתָּ(ה), וְחָפְרוּ, חָפְרוּ, חֲפָרוּהָ; impf. וַיַּחְפֹּר, וָאֶחְפֹּר, וַיַּחְפְּרֵהוּ, וַיַּחְפְּרוּהוּ, וַיַּחְפְּרֻהוּ; inf. לַחְפֹּר; pt. חֹפֵר: — 1. **paw** (of horse) Jb 39_{21} †; — 2. **dig**: wells Gn 21_{30}, hole Dt 23_{14}; — 3. metaph. dig for > a) **track, seek food** Jb 39_{29}, death 3_{21}; b) > **scout out** (land) Dt 1_2 Jos 2_{2f}.

II **חפר**: **qal**: חָפְרָה, חָפֵרָה, חָפְרוּ; impf. יֶחְפְּרוּ, יַחְפְּרוּ: **be ashamed** Is 1_{29} Ps 34_6.

hif.: pf. הֶחְפִּיר; impf. יַחְפִּיר, תַּחְפִּירִי; pt. מַחְפִּיר: **feel ashamed** Is 33_9 55_4; — 2. **behave shamefully** Pr 13_5 19_{26}. †

I חֵפֶר: n. pers.

II חֵפֶר: n. loc. Jos 12_{17} 1K 4_{10}. †

חֶפְרִי: gent. of I חֵפֶר.

חֲפָרַיִם: n. loc.

חָפְרַע: n. pers. **Hophra** Je 44_{30}. †

*חֲפַרְפָּרָה: pl. rd. לַחֲפַרְפָּרוֹת for לַחְפֹּר פֵּרוֹת Is 2_{20}: **shrew**. †

חפש: **qal**: impf. יַחְפְּשׂוּ, נַחְפְּשָׂה, תַּחְפְּשֶׂנָּה; pt. חֹפֵשׂ: **search out, check** Ps 64_7.

nif.: pf. נֶחְפְּשׂוּ: **be searched out** Ob $_6$. †

piel: pf. חִפְּשׂוּ, וְחִפַּשְׂתִּי; impf. יְחַפֵּשׂ; impv. חַפְּשׂוּ: — 1. **look** (thoroughly) **for** s.thg Gn 31_{35} 1K 20_6; — 2. **trace out, track** Am 9_3.

[pual: impf. יְחֻפַּשׂ Pr 28_{12}; pt. מְחֻפָּשׂ Ps 64_7: txt. corr.? ↗ comm.]

hitp.: impf. יִתְחַפֵּשׂ; impv. & inf. הִתְחַפֵּשׂ: let onesf. be searched for > **disguise onesf.** 1K 20_{38}.

חֵפֶשׂ: **plot** Ps 64_7. †

חפשׁ: **pual**: pf. חֻפְּשָׁה: **be given one's freedom** Lv 19_{20}. †

חֹפֶשׁ: **material for saddlecloths** Ez 27_{20}. †

חֻפְשָׁה: **emancipation** (fm. slavery) Lv 19_{20}. †

חָפְשׁוּת 2C 26_{21} Kt: ↗ Qr חָפְשִׁית. †

חָפְשִׁי: pl. חָפְשִׁים: — 1. **freed** (fm. slavery) Ex 21_5 & oft.; — 2. **free fm. taxes** 1S 17_{25} †; — 3. **free**: fm. violence Is 58_6; wild ass Jb 39_5.

חָפְשִׁית: (בְּ)בֵית הַחָפְשִׁית 2K 15_5 2C 26_{21} Qr: domicile of leprous King Azariah; ? house of separation, exemption fm. state affairs.

חֵץ: sf. חִצִּי; pl. חִצִּים, חִצֵּי, sf. חִצֶּיךָ & Ps 77_{18} חֲצָצֶיךָ: — 1. **arrow** 2K 13_{15}; *baʿalê ḥiṣṣîm* archers Gn 49_{23}; — 2. **Y.'s arrows** Dt 32_{23}; *ʾôr ḥiṣṣèkā* (lightning) Hb 3_{11}; — 3. metaph.: Je 9_7 (of tongue), Ps 127_4 (of sons).

I חָצַב: **qal**: pf. חָצַבְתָּ, ח׳; impf. תַּחְצֹב; inf. לַחְצֹב; pt. חֹצֵב, cs. חֹצְבֵי Is 22_{16}, חֹצְבִים, חֹצְבֵי, pass. חֲצוּבִים: — 1. **quarry** (stones) 2C $2_{1.17}$; — 2. **hew out** (of the rock): cisterns Dt 6_{11}, wine-vat Is 5_2, grave Is 22_{16}; — 3. **hew, dress** (stones) 1C 22_2; — 4. **dig, mine** (copper) Dt 8_9; — 5. **strike down, hew down** Ho 6_5.

nif.: impf. יֵחָצְבוּן: **be hewn out** Jb 19_{24}. †

pual: pf. חֻצַּבְתֶּם: **be hewn out** Is 51_1. †

hif.: pt. מַחְצֶבֶת: **cut in pieces** Is 51_9. †

II חצב: **qal**: pt. חֹצֵב: **stir, poke** (fire) Ps 29_7. †

חֹצֵב: pt. qal: **quarryman, stone-cutter** 1K 5_{29} 2K 12_{13}.

חָצָה: **qal**: pf. ח׳, חָצִיתָ, חָצוּ; impf. יֶחֱצֶה, יֶחֱצוּהוּ, יֶחֱצֵם, יֶחֱצוּ(ן), וַיַּחַץ: — 1. **divide** (trans.) Gn 32_8; w. *ʿal* among Gn 33_1, w. *bên* Nu 31_{27}; — 2. **divide** s.thg into, w. 2 acc. Ju 7_{16}, w. acc. & *le* 9_{43}; w. *ʿad* **reach to** Is 30_{28}.

nif.: impf. יֵחָצוּ, וַתֵּחָץ: — 1. **be divided** (water) 2K $2_{8.14}$, w. *le* Ez 37_{22}; — 2. **be divided up**, dispersed, w. *le* Dn 11_4. †

I חָצוֹר: n. loc. **Hazor**.

II חָצוֹר: Je 49_{33} = מַמְלְכוֹת חָצוֹר 49_{28} & יֹשְׁבֵי חָצוֹר 49_{30} **sedentary Arabs**, :: *qēdār*. †

חֲצוֹת, חֲצֹת: **middle**: *ḥaṣôt (hal)laylâ* midnight Ex 11_4 Ps 119_{62} Jb 34_{20}. †

חֲצִי (ca. 120×): חֲצִי; sf. חֶצְיוֹ, חֶצְיֵנוּ: — 1. **half** (as a noun) *ḥaṣî zeqānām* 2S 10_4; *ḥeṣyēnû* half of us 2S 18_3; — 2. half of the height, **middle**: spatial Ex 27_5, temporal Je 17_{11}; *ḥaṣî hallaylâ* midnight Ex 12_{29}.

I חֵצִי: **arrow** 1S $20_{36b.37.38}$ Kt 2K 9_{24}. †

II חֵצִי: ↗ חֲצִי.

I חָצִיר: cs. חֲצִיר: **grass** 1K 18_5, 2K 19_{26}.

II חָצִיר: **leek**, *Allium porrum* Nu 11_5. †

III חָצִיר: **reeds**, spec. **cattails**, *Typha* Is 35_7 44_4 Jb 8_{12}. †

חֹצֶן: sf. חִצְנוֹ, חָצְנִי: **bosom** (of garment) Is 49_{22}.

חצץ: **qal**: pt. חֹצֵץ: **keeping distance, order** Pr 30_{27}. †

piel: pt. מְחַצְּצִים: **divide, share** (water) Ju 5_{11}. †

pual: pf. חֻצָּצוּ: **be at an end** Jb 21_{21}. †

חָצָץ: **gravel** Pr 20_{17} La 3_{16}. †

*חֲצָצוֹן: חַצְצ(וֹ)ן תָּמָר: n. loc. Gn 14_7. †

חצצר: **piel**: pt. מַחְצְצְרִים 1C 15_{24} 2C 5_{12} 29_{28}; plus other var. of vocal. in Qr-Kt comb., but w. cons. as given: **blow the** *ḥaṣōṣerâ* (see below).

חֲצֹצְרָה: cs. =; f.: **trumpet**, long, straight instrument of metal for signalling, 2K 11_4.

חָצֵר: cs. חֲצַר; loc. חָצֵ֫רָה; sf. חֲצֵרוֹ; pl. I חֲצֵרִים, חַצְרֵי, sf. חַצְרֵיהֶם, חֲצֵרֶיךָ, & pl. II חֲצֵרוֹת, cs. חַצְרוֹת, sf. חֲצֵרוֹתַי, חֲצֵרוֹתָיו: mostly f.

A. 1. permanent **settlement** without wall, **farm** (premises) Gn 25_{16}; — 2. **court(yard), enclosed space** (i.e. by buildings) 2S 17_{18}, palace court Je 36_{20}, temple courts 2K 21_5; many comb. for designated courts, e.g. *heḥāṣēr happenîmît* 1K 6_{36}.

B. *ḥāṣēr* in names of loc.: — 1. חֲצַר־אַדָּר; — 2. חֲצַר גַּדָּה; — 3. חֲצַר סוּסָה; — 4. חֲצַר עֵינוֹן; — 5. חֲצַר שׁוּעָל.

חֶצְרוֹ: n. pers. 2S 23_{35} Kt 1C 11_{37}: ← חֶצְרַי. †

I חֶצְרוֹן & חֶצְרֹן: n. pers.

II חֶצְרוֹן: n. loc. Jos $15_{3.25}$. †

חֶצְרוֹנִי: gent. of I חֶצְרוֹן.

חֲצֵרוֹת & חֲצֵרֹת: n. loc.

חֶצְרַי: n. pers.

חֲצַרְמָוֶת: n. terr. **Hadhramaut.**

חֲצֹת Ex 11_4: ← חָצוֹת. †

חֵק: ← חֵיק.

חֹק: חָק־; sf. חֻקִּי, חָקְךָ & חָקְכֶם; pl. חֻקִּים, cs. חֻקֵּי, חוּקֵּי & חִקְקֵי Is 10_1, sf. חֻקָּיו: something prescribed: — 1. **portion, limit** (of life): *leḥem ḥuqqî* my proper portion of food Pr 30_8; limit Jb $14_{5.13}$; — 2. **work** imposed, **task** Ex 5_{14}; — 3. (what is) **due** (e.g. to the priests) Lv 6_{15}; income (of priests) Gn 47_{22}; — 4. **obligation** Ex 30_{21}; — 5. **claim** Lv 6_{11}; — 6. **specific time** Mi 7_{11}, moment Zp 2_2; — 7. **boundary, limit** (for the sea) Je 5_{22}, *lebiltî ḥōq* boundlessly Is 5_{14}; — 8. **law, order**: for stars Ps 148_6, rain Jb 28_{26}; — 9. **definition, rule, prescription**: a) secular: Gn 47_{26}; b) given by God 1K 8_{58} & oft.

חקה: **pual**: pt. מְחֻקֶּה: **scratched** Ez 8_{10}; *hammeḥuqqeh* incised work 1K 6_{35}; *'anšê hammeḥuqqeh*, men in wall-carvings Ez 23_{14}. †

hitp.: impf. תִּתְחַקֶּה: **scratch** (names on the soles of feet of slaves) Jb 13_{27}. †

חֻקָּה: cs. חֻקַּת; pl. חֻקּ(וֹ)ת, sf. חֻקֹּתַי, חֻקֹּתָיו: — 1. **due**: *ḥuqqat 'ôlām* perpetual due Lv 7_{36}; *ḥuqqôt qāṣîr* the fixed times for harvest Je 5_{24}; — 2. (human) **statutes**: of nations 2K 17_8, of David 1K 3_3; — 3. divine statute Ex 12_{14} & oft.

חֲקוּפָא: n. pers.

חקק: **qal**: pf. חַקּוֹתִיךָ, וְחַקּוֹתָ֫; impv. חֻקָּהּ; inf. חוּקוֹ Pr 8_{27}; pt. חֹקְקִי Is 22_{16}, ח(וֹ)קְקִים, ח(וֹ)קְקֵי, pass. חֲקֻקִים: — 1. **hew out** (grave) Is 22_{16}; — 2. scratch, mark (in tablet, &c.) Is 30_8; — 3. specify, **decree**, w. cogn. acc. Is 10_1.

pual: pt. מְחֻקָּק: **what has been prescribed** Pr 31_5. †

poal: impf. יְחוֹקְקוּ; pt. מְחֹקֵק, מְחֹקְקֵי, מְחֹקְקִים, מְחֹקְקֵנוּ: — 1. **decree** Pr 8_{15}; — 2. pt. *meḥōqēq*: a) director, **leader** Ju 5_{14}, Is 33_{22} (Y.); b) **scepter** Gn 49_{10}.

hof. (pass. qal): impf. יֻחָקוּ: **be inscribed** Jb 19_{23}. †

חִקְקֵי Is 10_1: ← חֹק. †

חקר: **qal**: pf. חֲקַרְתַּ֫נִי, חֲקָרָהּ, חֲקָרוֹ, חֲקַרְתָּ, חֲקַרְנוּהָ; impf. יַחְקֹר, יַחֲקָר־, אֶחְקֹר, אֶחְקְרֵהוּ, יַחְקְרֶנּוּ, נַחְקְרָה, תַּחְקְרוּן, יַחְקְרוּ; impv. חִקְרוּ, חָקְרֵנִי; inf. חֲק(וֹ)ר, לַחְקֹר, חָקְרָהּ; pt. ח(וֹ)קֵר: investigate, **spy out**: city 2S 10_3, land Ju 18_2; taste (wine) Pr 23_{30}, try (a legal case) Jb 29_{16}; Y. is *ḥōqēr lēb* Je 17_{10}; sound out (s.one about his opinion) 1S 20_{12}; in cross-examination Pr 18_{17}.

nif.: pf. נֶחְקַר; impf. יֵחָקֵר, יֵחָקְרוּ: **be explored**, foundations of the earth Je 31_{37}; w. neg. impenetrable (forest) Je 46_{23}, unascertainable (weight) 1K 7_{47} 2C 4_{18}. †

piel: pf. חִקֵּר: **think up**, invent *mᵉšālîm* Ec 12_9. †

חֵקֶר: pl. cs. חִקְרֵי: — 1. **searching**: *ḥiqrê lēb* (ironic) prudent deliberations Ju 5_{16}; *ḥēqer ʾᵃbôtām* what their fathers have discovered Jb 8_8; *ʾên ḥēqer* unsearchable Is 40_{28}; — 2. **the object of searching**: *ḥēqer tᵉhôm* basis of searching Jb 38_{16}, *ḥēqer ʾᵉlôᵃh* the depths of God Jb 11_7.

I *חֹר: pl. חֹ(וֹ)רִים, חֹרֵי, חֹרֶיהָ: **freeborn, nobles** 1K $21_{8\cdot 11}$.

II חֹר: pl. חֹרִים, חֹרֵי, חֹרָיו, חֹרֵיהֶן: **hole, cave**: for men 1S 14_{11} animals Na 2_{13}; eye-socket Zc 14_{12}; ? erotic SS 5_4 key-hole ? (oth.: vagina).

חֻר: pl. חוּרִים: **hole, cave**, for snake Is 11_8, hiding-place for men 42_{22}. †

חֹר הַגִּדְגָּד: n. loc.

*חֲרָאִים: *חֲרָאֵיהֶם Is 36_{12} Kt > חֲרֵיהֶם 2K 18_{27} Kt; חִרְיוֹנִים 2K 6_{25} = Kt חֲרֵי יוֹנִים doves' dung; 2K 18_{27} חֹרֵיהֶם & Is 36_{12} חֹרָאֵיהֶם = Qr צֹאָתָם, Kt *חֲרָאֵי > *חֲרֵי: content of bowels, **dung**, replaced by צֹאָה. †

I חרב: **qal**: pf. חָרְבוּ; impf. יֶחֱרַב, יֶחֱרַב, תֶּחֱרַבְנָה, יֶחֶרְבוּ; impv. חֲרַב, חֲרְבִי, חָרְבוּ & חִרְבוּ; inf. חֲרֹב: — 1. **drain off** (intrans.), of water Gn 8_{13}, **dry up** (intrans.), of land Gn 8_{13}; — 2. **lie in ruins**, wrecked: land Is 34_{10}, city Je 26_9.

nif.: pt. נֶחֱרֶבֶת, pl. נֶחֱרָבוֹת: **be laid in ruins**, city Ez 26_1 30_7. †

pual: pf. חֹרָבוּ: **be dried** (bowstrings) Ju 16_{7f}. †

hif.: pf. הֶחֱרִיב, הֶחֱרַבְתִּי, וְהַחֲרַבְתִּי; impf. אַחֲרִיב; pt. מַחֲרִיב, מַחֲרֶבֶת, מַחֲרִבַיִךְ: — 1. **dry up** (trans.), make s.thg dry up: water 2K 19_{24}, land Is 42_{15}; — 2. **lay in ruins**, make desolate: land 2K 19_{17}.

hof.: pf. הָחֳרָבָה; **be devastated, made desolate** Ez 26_2. †

II חרב: **qal**: impv. חֲרֹב, חִרְבוּ: **slay** Je $50_{21\cdot 27}$. †

nif.: pf. נֶחֶרְבוּ: **fight each other** 2K 3_{23}. †

חָרֵב: f. חֲרֵבָה; pl. הֶחֳרָבוֹת: — 1. **dry** Lv 7_{10}; — 2. **waste, desolate** Je $33_{10\cdot 12}$.

חֶרֶב (410×): חָרֶב; sf. חַרְבּוֹ; pl. חֲרָבוֹת, cs. חַרְבוֹת, sf. חַרְבֹתָיו, חַרְבֹתָם: **dagger** & (short-)**sword**: — 1. *ḥarbôt ṣurîm* **flint knives** Jos 5_{2f}; — 2. **dagger** Ju 3_{16}; — 3. **chisel** (of stone-dresser) Ex 20_{25}, crowbar Ez 26_9; — 4. **sword** Gn 3_{24} & oft.; many phrases, e.g. *šᵉbuyôt ḥereb* led away w. the sword, prisoners of war Gn 31_{26}.

חֹרֶב: — 1. **dryness, drought**: of the ground Ju $6_{37\cdot 39f}$, of the skin Jb 30_{30}; > **heat** Gn 31_{40}; — 2. **devastation** Is 61_4.

חֹרֵב: loc. חֹרֵבָה: n. mountain, **Horeb**.

חָרְבָּה: pl. חֳרָבוֹת, cs. חָרְבוֹת, sf. חָרְבוֹתֶיהָ: place of ruin & rubble, **waste** Lv 26_{33} Is 5_{17}.

חָרָבָה: **dry land** Gn 7_{22} 2K 2_8.

*חֲרָבוֹן: pl. cs. חַרְבֹנֵי: **dry heat** Ps 32_4. †

חַרְבוֹנָא Est 1_{10} & חַרְבוֹנָה 7_9: n. pers.

חרג: **qal**: impf. יַחְרְגוּ: **come out trembling** Ps 18_{46}. †

חַרְגֹּל: **a kind of grasshopper**, *Tettigoniidae* Lv 11_{22}. †

חרד: **qal**: pf. חָרַד, ח׳, חָרְדוּ; impf. יֶחֱרַד, יֶחֶרְדוּ & יֶחֶרְדוּ, יֶחֶרְדוּ; impv. חִרְדוּ: — 1. **tremble, shudder** Gn 27_{33} 1K 1_{49}; — 2. w. *ʾel* look w. trembling to Gn 42_{28}; w. *liqraʾt* go w. trembling to meet 1S 16_4; w. *min* come w. trembling fm. Ho 11_{10f}; w. *ʾaḥᵃrê* hurry after 1S 13_7; — 3. w. *ḥᵃrādâ ʾel* go to the trouble for 2K 4_{13}.

hif.: pf. הֶחֱרִיד, וְהַחֲרַדְתִּי; inf. הַחֲרִיד; pt. מַחֲרִיד: **startle** s.one 2S 17_2; *wᵉʾên maḥᵃrîd* without anyone's frightening (you) Lv 26_6 & oft.

חָרֵד: pl. חֲרֵדִים: — 1. **fearful** Ju 7_3 1S 4_{13}; — 2. **frightened of,** w. *ʿal* Is 66_2, w. *ʾel* 66_5, w. *bᵉ* Ezr 9_4 10_3. †
I חֲרֹד: in n. loc. עֵין חֲרֹד.
II *חֲרֹד: ғ חֲרֹדִי.
I חֲרָדָה: cs. חֶרְדַּת: **trembling, fear** Is 21_4; w. *hāyâ bᵉ* 1S 14_{15}; *ḥārad ḥarādâ gᵉdōlâ* be full of fear Gn 27_{33}.
II חֲרָדָה: n. loc. Nu 33_{24f}. †
חֲרֹדִי: n. loc.
I חָרָה: qal: pf. ח׳; impf. וַיִּחַר, יִחַר, יֶחֱרֶה; inf. חֲרוֹת, חָרֹה: **be(come) hot**: — 1. *ḥārâ ʾappô* his nose became hot = **his anger broke out** Gn 30_2 (*bᵉ*, against) & oft., esp. of Y.'s anger Ex 4_{14}; — 2. *ḥārâ lô* without *ʾappô*, w. *bᵉ* or *ʿal* **become angry** Gn 45_{5f} & oft.; **become indignant** (at Y.) 1S 15_{11} 2S 6_8; — 3. *ḥārâ bᵉʿênāyw* **be angry** Gn 31_{35} 45_5.
nif.: pt. נֶחֱרִים: w. *bᵉ* **be angry** w. s.one Is 41_{11} 45_{24}.
hif.: impf. וַיִּחַר: **make** s.one **become inflamed** Jb 19_{11}; but rd. qal?. †
hitp.: impf. תִּתְחַר: **fly into a passion** Ps $37_{1.7f}$ Pr 24_{19}. †
tifʿel: impf. תְּתַחֲרֶה; pt. מְתַחֲרֶה: **compete** w., **try to outdo** Je 22_{15}, w. *ʾēt* run a race w. Je 12_5. †
II חרה: qal: pf. חָרוּ: disappear, **become few in number** Is 24_6. †
חַרְהֲיָה: n. pers.
חֲרוּזִים: **necklace of shells** SS 1_{10}. †
חָרוּל: pl. חֲרֻלִים: **weeds in field & orchard** Zp 2_9 Pr 24_{31}; shade for desert vagabonds Jb 30_7: some say **wild artichoke**; oth.: **vetchling**, *Lathyrus ochrus*. †
חָרוּם: ғ II חרם.
חֲרוּמַף: n. pers.
חָרוֹן: cs. חֲרוֹן; sf. חֲרֹנוֹ; pl. sf. חֲרוֹנֶיךָ: **glow, anger** (only of God): *ḥarôn ʾaf* glow of the nose = glow of Y.'s anger 2K 23_{26} & oft., esp. in prophets.
חֹרוֹן, ח(ו)ר(ו)ן: n. deity, ғ בֵּית חוֹרוֹן.
חֹרֹנַיִם, ғ חוֹרֹנַיִם.
חָרוּפִי: gent., ғ חֲרִיפִי.
I חָרוּץ: **gold** (poetic & late) Zc 9_3 Ps 68_{14}.
II חָרוּץ: **moat** Dn 9_{25}. †
III חָרוּץ: pl. f. חֲרֻצוֹת: — 1. **sharp-cutting** (threshing sledge) Is 41_{15}; — 2. **threshing-sledge, threshing-cart** Is 28_{27}, Am 1_3 Jb 41_{22}. †
IV חָרוּץ: cut, **mutilation** (harelip?); oth.: adj. mutilated Lv 22_{22}. †
V חָרוּץ: **decision,** *ʿēmeq heḥārûṣ* Jl 4_{14}. †
VI חָרוּץ: pl. חֲרוּצִים, חֲרֻצִים: **industrious, diligent** Pr 10_4 $12_{24.27}$ 13_4 21_5. †
VII חָרוּץ: n. pers. 2K 21_{19}. †
חַרְחוּר: n. pers.
חַרְחֲיָה: n. pers.
חַרְחַס: n. pers.
חַרְחֻר: **heat of fever** Dt 28_{22}. †
חֶרֶט: **stylus** Is 8_1. †
*חָרֶט: ғ חָרִיט.
חַרְטֹם: pl. חַרְטֻמִּים, חַרְטֻמֵּי: **soothsayer-priest,** of Egypt Gn $41_{8.24}$, of Babylon Dn 1_{20}.
*חֳרִי: cs. =: **heat** (of anger), alw. w. *ʾaf*: 1S 20_{34}.
I חֹרִי: **cake of fine flour** Gn 40_{16}. †
II חֹרִי: n. pers. Gn 36_{22} 1C 1_{39}; Nu 13_5. †
III חֹרִי: pl. חֹרִים: remnants of the **Horite** (Hurrian) people Gn 14_6.
חָרִיט, *חָרֶט: pl. חֲרִטִים: **bag, purse** 2K 5_{23} Is 3_{22}. †
חִרְייוֹנִים 2K 6_{25}: ғ *חֲרָאִים.
חָרִיף: n. pers.
cj חֲרִיפוֹת: **grains of sand,** added at the time of pounding grain 2S 17_{19}. †
חֲרִיפִי: 1C 12_6, gent. of n. loc. *חָרוּף/חָרִיף. †
I *חָרִיץ: pl. cs. חֲרִצֵי: **slice, piece** (of cheese) 1S 17_{18}. †
II *חָרִיץ: pl. cs. חֲרִ(י)צֵי: w. ***habbarzel,*** (iron) **hoe** 2S 12_{31} 1C 20_3. †
*חָרִישׁ: sf. חֲרִישׁוֹ: — 1. **plowing** 1S 8_{12}; — 2. **time of plowing** Gn 45_6 Ex 34_{21}. †

*חֲרִישִׁי: Jon 4_{8} רוּחַ קָדִים חֲרִישִׁית; ?; Verss. scorching, or silent; cj *חֲרִיפִית: **sharp, scorching**; oth. *חֲרִירִית hot. †

חרך: **qal**: Pr 12_{27} יַחֲרֹךְ צֵידוֹ: trad. roast, or scare away; rd. יַדְרִךְ get, or יַחֲרֹף. †

*חֲרַךְ: pl. חֲרַכִּים: **lattice window** SS 2_{9}. †

I חרם: **hif.**: pf. הֶחֱרַמְתִּי, וְהַחֲרַמְתָּה, הֶחֱרִים, וְהַחֲרַמְתִּי (Mi 4_{13} 2f.), הֶחֱרִימָם, וְהַחֲרַמְתִּים; impf. נַחֲרִם, תַּחֲרִים, תַּחֲרִימוּ, וַיַּחֲרֵם, יַחֲרִם, וַיַּחֲרִימֵהּ, תַּחֲרִימֵם; impv. הַחֲרֵם, הַחֲרִימוּ, הַחֲרִימוּהָ; inf. הַחֲרֵם, הַחֲרִימָם: — 1. **devote to the ban** (↗ *ḥērem*), dedicate to destruction, esp. war booty, men, cattle 1K 9_{21} & oft.; destroy Dn 11_{44}; Y. bans Is 34_{2} Je 25_{9}; — 2. *heḥerîm leyhwh* **dedicate** s.thg to Y. **by the ban** & thus exclude redemption (↗ *g'l*) Lv 27_{28} Mi 4_{13}.

hof.: impf. יָחֳרַם: **be devoted** to destruction **by the ban** Ex 22_{19} & Lv 27_{29} (men), Ezr 10_{8} (goods). †

II חרם: **qal**: pt. pass. (or adj.) חָרֻם: **w. a split nose** Lv 21_{18}. †

hif.: pf. הֶחֱרִים: **split** (portion of sea) Is 11_{15}. †

I חֵרֶם: sf. חֶרְמִי: — 1. dedication to exclusion from profane use, to destruction, or to solely cultic use, **ban**, what is **banned**: Jos 22_{20}; *'îš ḥermî* one who has fallen under my (Y.'s) ban 1K 20_{42}; *hāyâ (le)ḥērem* fall under the ban Jos 6_{17} 7_{12}; — 2. what has been dedicated by the ban, **banned goods** (actually Y.'s share of booty) 1S 15_{21}.

II חֵרֶם: sf. חֶרְמוֹ; pl. חֲרָמִים: **dragnet** Ez $26_{5.14}$; metaph. (of woman's heart) Ec 7_{26}.

חָרִם: n. pers.

חֳרֵם: n. loc.

חָרְמָה: n. loc.

חֶרְמוֹן: n. of mountain, **Hermon**.

חֶרְמֵשׁ: **sickle** Dt 16_{9} 23_{26}. †

I חָרָן: n. loc. **Haran**.

II חָרָן: n. pers. 1C 2_{46}. †

חֹרֹנִי: gent. of בֵּית־חֹרֹן, or חֹרוֹנַיִם.

חֹרֹנַיִם: n. loc., ↗ ח(ו)ר(ו)נַיִם.

חַרְנֶפֶר: n. pers.

I *חֶרֶס, חֶרֶס: חֶרֶס: **itch** Dt 28_{27}. †

II חֶרֶס: **sun** Jb 9_{7}. †

III *חֶרֶס: n. loc. Ju 8_{13}. †

חַרְסוּת, Qr חַרְסִית Kt חַרְסוּת: *ša'ar haharsît (-ût)* Je 19_{2} 'Potsherd Gate' or 'Clay-pit Gate'. †

I חרף: **qal**: impf. תֶּחֱרַף: spend the time of *ḥōref*, **winter** Is 18_{6}. †

II חרף: **qal**: impf. יֶחֱרַף; pt. חֹרְפִי, חוֹרְפֶיךָ: **taunt, reproach**: *ḥōrefî* who taunts me Ps 119_{42}.

piel: pf. חֵרֵף, חֵרַפְתָּ, חֵרְפוּ, חֵרַפְתֶּם, חֵרְפוּנִי; impf. וַיְחָרֵף, יְחָרֵף, יְחָרְפֵנִי, יְחָרְפוּנִי; inf. חָרֵף, חָרְפָם; pt. מְחָרֵף: **reproach, revile**, w. acc. 2K 19_{4}; obj. God Ne 6_{13}; w. *nafšô lāmût* stake one's life Ju 5_{18}.

III חרף: **piel**: pf. חֵרֵף: confuse, **disillusion** Ps 57_{4}. †

IV חרף: **nif.**: pt. נֶחֱרֶפֶת: w. *le'îš*, intended for a(nother) man, **engaged** Lv 19_{20}. †

חָרֵף: n. pers.

חֹרֶף: sf. חָרְפִּי: — 1. (time of) **youth**, *yemê ḥorfî* Jb 29_{4}; — 2. **winter** as time of sowing and early growth Gn 8_{22}.

חֶרְפָּה (70×): cs. חֶרְפַּת, sf. חֶרְפָּתוֹ; pl. חֲרָפוֹת, cs. חֶרְפוֹת: — 1. **abuse, scorn** Ez 21_{33}; — 2. **disgrace**: *ḥerpātî* disgrace done to me 1S 25_{39}.

*חֲרֻפוֹת, ↗ cj חֲרִיפוֹת.

I חָרַץ: **qal**: pf. חָרַצְתָּ, חָ׳; impf. יֶחֱרַץ; pt. pass. חָרוּץ, חֲרוּצִים: — 1. *ḥāraṣ lāšôn le* point the tongue = **threaten** s.one Ex 11_{7}; — 2. **settle, determine** 1K 20_{40} (judgment).

nif.: pt. נֶחֱרֶצֶת, נֶחֱרָצָה: what is **determined**, a **determined end** Is 10_{23}.

II חרץ: **qal**: impf. תֶּחֱרַץ: be eager for s.thg, **pay attention** 2S 5_{24}. †

*חָרִץ: ↗ I, II *חָרִיץ.

*חַרְצֹב: pl. חַרְצֻבּוֹת: — 1. *ḥarṣubbôt reša'*

illegal fetters Is 58_{6}; — 2. metaph. **torments** Ps 73_{4}. †

*חַרְצָן: pl. חַרְצַנִּים: **unripe grapes** Nu 6_{4}. †

חָרַק: qal: pf. ח׳; impf. וַיַּחַרְקוּ, יַחֲרֹק; inf. חָרֹק; pt. חֹרֵק: **gnash** (one's teeth) Ps 35_{16}.

I חרר: **qal**: pf. חָרָה: **glow, burn** Ez 24_{11} Jb 30_{30}; חָרוּ Is 24_{6} ↗ II חור. †

nif.: pf. נָחַר, נִחָרוּ; impf. יֵחָרוּ, וַיֵּחַר: **be set aglow** Ez 15_{4f}.

pilpel: inf. חַרְחַר: **make s.thg glow** Pr 26_{21}. †

II חרר: **nif.**: pf. נִחַר: **be hoarse** Ps 69_{4}. †

חֲרֵרִים: **lava-field, stony desert** Je 17_{6}. †

חֶרֶשׂ: חֶרֶשׂ; pl. cs. חַרְשֵׂי: **fired clay**: — a) **pottery** Pr 26_{23}; *kelî ḥereś* Lv 11_{33}; b) **potsherd** Is 30_{14}.

I חרשׁ: **qal**: pf. חָרְשׁוּ, חֲרַשְׁתֶּם; impf. יַחֲרֹ(וֹ)שׁ; inf. חֲרֹשׁ; pt. חֹרֵשׁ, חֹרְשִׁים, חֹרְשֵׁי, חֹרְשׁוֹת, pass. חֲרוּשָׁה: — 1. **plow** 1K 19_{19}; w. *be* with an animal Dt 22_{10}; w. acc. Ho 10_{13}; — 2. w. *ʿal* **engrave** in Je 17_{1}; — 3. **work, prepare** (good, evil) Pr 3_{29}; — 4. *ḥōrēš* craftsman Gn 4_{22} 1K 7_{14}.

nif.: impf. תֵּחָרֵשׁ: **be plowed** Je 26_{18} Mi 3_{12}. †

hif.: pt. מַחֲרִישׁ: w. *rāʿâ ʿal* **plan evil against** 1S 23_{9}. †

II חרשׁ: **qal**: impf. יֶחֱרַשׁ, תֶּחֱרַשְׁנָה: **be deaf** Mi 7_{16} Ps 35_{22}; w. *min* to Ps 28_{1}.

hif.: pf. הֶחֱרִ(י)שׁ, הֶחֱרַשְׁתִּי; impf. יַחֲרִישׁ, אַחֲרִישׁ, יַחֲרִישׁוּ, תַּחֲרִישׁוּן; impv. הַחֲרֵשׁ; pt. מַחֲרִישׁ, מַחֲרִישִׁים: — 1. **keep still, be silent** Gn 24_{21} 2K 18_{36}; — 2. **let s.one do s.thg without objection** Nu 30_{5}; — 3. **keep inactive** 2S 19_{11}; *wayhî kemaḥarîš* acted dumb 1S 10_{27}; — 4. **become silent** Je 38_{27}; — 5. **silence s.one** Jb 11_{3}.

hitp.: impf. וַיִּתְחָרְשׁוּ: **keep still** Ju 16_{2}. †

I *חֶרֶשׁ: pl. חֲרָשִׁים: **magic, sorcery**: *ḥakam ḥarāšîm* magician Is 3_{3}. †

II חֶרֶשׁ: > adv. **in quiet, secretly** Jos 2_{1}. †

חֹרֶשׁ: pl. חֳרָשִׁים: **wood(land)** Ez 31_{3} 2C 27_{4}. †

חָרָשׁ: cs. חָרַשׁ; pl. חָרָשִׁים & Ne 11_{35} 1C 4_{14} חֲרָשִׁים, cs. חָרָשֵׁי: **craftsman** of any sort: stoneworker Ex 28_{11}; carpenter 2K 12_{12}; metalworker, armorer 1S 13_{19}.

חֵרֵשׁ: pl. חֵרְשִׁים: **deaf** Ex 4_{11}; metaph. Is 29_{18}.

חַרְשָׁא: n. pers.

(הַ)חֹרְשָׁה: n. loc., = חֹרֶשׁ, frozen loc.

I חֲרֹשֶׁת: **working** (in stone & wood) Ex 31_{5} 35_{33}. †

II חֲרֹשֶׁת: 'woodland,' in n. loc. חֲרֹשֶׁת הַגּוֹיִם Ju $4_{2.13.16}$. †

חרת: **qal**: pt. pass. חָרוּת: **engraved** (writing) Ex 32_{16}. †

*חֶרֶת: חֲרֶת: n. terr.

חֲשׂוּפָה: n. pers.

חֲשׂוּפַי Is 20_{4}: rd. חֲשׂוּפֵי, ↗ I חָשַׂף. †

חָשַׂךְ: **qal**: pf. ח׳, חָשַׂכְתָּ, חָשְׂכוּ, חָשָׂכוּ; impf. אֶחְשָׂךְ, תַּחְשְׂכִי, תַּחְשׂוֹךְ, יַחְשֹׂךְ (ŏ!) Jb 7_{11}; impv. חֲשׂךְ; pt. חֹ(וֹ)שֵׂךְ: — 1. **restrain, hold back,** a) w. acc. 2S 18_{16}, w. *min* from Gn 20_{6}; b) abs. Is 14_{6}; — 2. w. *min* **withhold** Gn $22_{12.16}$; — 3. **take good care of, spare**: abs. Is 54_{2}; obj. feet Je 14_{10}; — 4. intrans. restrain onesf., **fail to appear** Ez 30_{18}.

nif.: impf. יֵחָשֵׂךְ: — 1. **restrain onesf.** Jb 16_{6}; — 2. **be spared** Jb 21_{30}. †

I חָשַׂף: **qal**: pf. ח׳, חָשְׂפָה; impv. חֶשְׂפִּי; inf. לַחְשֹׂף; pt. pass. חֲשׂוּפָה, חֲשׂוּפֵי Is 20_{4} rd חֲשׂוּפֵי: — 1. **strip the bark from** Jl 1_{7}; — 2. **bare** (one's arm) Is 52_{10}; — 3. **scoop, skim**: water Is 30_{14}, wine Hg 2_{16}.

II חשׂף: **qal**: impf. וַיֶּחֱשֹׂף: rd **piel** וַיְחַשֵּׂף: **bring to premature birth** Ps 29_{9}. †

*חָשִׂף: pl. cs. חֲשִׂפֵי: חֲשִׂפֵי עִזִּים 1K 20_{27}: usu. small flock; oth. prematurely dropped kid. †

חָשַׁב: **qal**: pf. ח׳, חָשַׁבְתָּה, חָשָׁבוּ, חֲשָׁבָהּ, חֲשַׁבְנֻהוּ; impf. יַחְשֹׁב, יַחֲשָׁב־, יַחְשְׁבוּ, תַּחְשְׁבֵנִי, יַחְשְׁבֵנִי, וַיַּחְשְׁבֶהָ, יַחְשְׁבוּן, יַחְשֹׁבוּ 3. f. pl.; inf. לַחְשֹׁב; pt. חֹ(וֹ)שֵׁב: — 1. **weave** (↗ *ḥōšēb*); — 2. **value, esteem s.thg**

Is 13_{17}; — 3. **consider, think** s.one **to be s.thg, take** s.one **for**: a) w. acc. & *l^e* Gn 38_{15}; b) w. 2 acc. Is 53_4; c) w. acc. & *k^e* consider as Jb 19_{11}; — 4. **reckon**: a) *ḥāšab ʿāwōn l^e* as guilt 2S 19_{20}; b) *ḥāšab l^eṭôbâ* for good Gn 50_{20b}; — 5. **plan** a) w. *ʿal* against Gn 50_{20a}; b) w. *l^e* for Ps 41_8; c) *ḥāšab rāʿat ʾîš* s.one's misfortune Zc 7_{10}; d) cogn. acc. *maḥ^ašābôt* 2S 14_{14}; e) *ḥāšab ʾāwen* Ez 11_2; — 6. w. *l^e* & inf. **intend** 1S 18_{25}; — 7. **think out, invent**: *k^elê šîr* Am 6_5, devise artistic designs Ex 31_4.

nif.: pf. נֶחְשַׁב, נֶחְשַׁבְתִּי, נֶחְשָׁבוּ, נֶחְשָׁבוּ; impf. יֵחָשֵׁב; pt. נֶחְשָׁב: — 1. **be reckoned, accounted** 1K 10_{21}; w. *ʾēt* accounts will be settled with 2K 22_7; — 2. **be considered as** Dt 2_{11}; w. *l^e* Gn 31_{15}.

piel: pf. חִשַּׁב, חִשַּׁבְתִּי; impf. יְחַשֵּׁב, וַאֲחַשְּׁבָה, וַתְּחַשְּׁבֵהוּ; pt. מְחַשֵּׁב: — 1. **calculate** Lv 25_{27}; w. *ʾēt* settle accounts w. 2K 12_{16}; w. *l^e* put down to s.one's account Lv 25_{52}; — 2. **consider** Ps 77_6; — 3. **plan, think out** Pr 16_9; *raʿ* + *ʾel* Ho 7_{15}; — 4. w. inf. nif. **be near to**, almost Jon 1_4.

hitp.: impf. יִתְחַשָּׁב: **count onesf. among** w. *b^e* Nu 23_9. †

חֵשֶׁב: **band, girdle** on ephod Ex 28_{27f}, on *ʾ^afuddâ* Ex 28_8.

חֹשֵׁב: — 1. worker w. cloth, **weaver** Ex 38_{23}; — 2. **technician** 2C 26_{15}.

חֲשַׁבְדָּנָה: n. pers.

חֲשֻׁבָה: n. pers.

I חֶשְׁבּוֹן: **account**; (systematic) **result** Ec $7_{25 \cdot 27}$ 9_{10}. †

II חֶשְׁבּוֹן: n. loc. **Heshbon.**

*חִשָּׁבוֹן: pl. abs. חִשְּׁבֹנוֹת: — 1. **plan, invention** Ec 7_{29}; — 2. (skillfully contrived) **war-machines**, spec. catapults 2C 26_{15}. †

חֲשַׁבְיָה: n. pers.

חֲשַׁבְיָהוּ: n. pers.

חֲשַׁבְנָה: n. pers.

חֲשַׁבְנְיָה: n. pers.

חשה: **qal**: impf. יֶחֱשׁוּ, אֶחֱשֶׁה, תֶּחֱשֶׁה; inf. לַחֲשׁוֹת: **be silent** Is 61_2.

hif.: pf. הֶחֱשֵׁיתִי; impv. הֶחֱשׁוּ; pt. מַחְשֶׁה, מַחְשִׁים: — 1. w. *l^e* **command** s.one **to be silent** Ne 8_{11}; — 2. **be silent** 2K $2_{3 \cdot 5}$; — 3. **delay**, postpone 2K 7_9; w. *min* & inf. 1K 22_3.

חָשׁוּב: n. pers.

*חָשׁוּק: pl. sf. חֲשֻׁקֵיהֶם, חֲשׁוּקֵיהֶם: (silver) 'bands' of the pillars of the tabernacle, bindings on pillars or cross-bars; F comm. Ex 27_{10f}.

חֲשֵׁיכָה Ps 139_{12}: F חֲשֵׁכָה.

חֻשִׁים: n. pers. (peop.?).

חָשַׁךְ: **qal**: pf. ח׳, חָשְׁכוּ; impf. יֶחְשְׁכוּ, תֶּחְשַׁךְ, תֶּחְשַׁכְנָה: — 1. **be(come) dim, dark**: sun Is 13_{10}, *ʾôr* Jb 18_6, earth Ex 10_{15}; — 2. **become dark** (eyes) Ps 69_{24}.

hif.: pf. הֶחְשִׁיךְ, וְהַחֲשַׁכְתִּי; impf. יַחְשִׁיךְ, וַיַּחְשִׁךְ Ps 105_{28}; pt. מַחְשִׁיךְ: — 1. **darken** Am 5_8, bring darkness 8_9; — 2. **become dark** Ps 139_{12}.

חֹשֶׁךְ: sf. חָשְׁכִּי: — 1. **darkness**: cosmic Gn 1_2; = night $1_{4f \cdot 18}$, within the earth Jb 28_3; — 2. **darkening** Ex 10_{21}; — 3. (metaph.) **darkness**: way of guilty Ps 35_6, sad situation 2S 22_{29} &c.

*חָשֹׁךְ: pl. חֲשֻׁכִּים: dark, unknown, **unimportant** Pr 22_{29}. †

חֲשֵׁכָה, חֲשֵׁיכָה Ps 139_{12}: cs. חֶשְׁכַת; pl. חֲשֵׁכִים: **darkness** Gn 15_{12}; metaph. Is 8_{22}.

חשל: **nif.**: pt. נֶחֱשָׁלִים: unfit to march, **straggler** Dt 25_{18}. †

חָשֻׁם: n. pers.

חֻשָׁם: n. pers.

חֻשִׁם: n. pers. (peop.?).

חֶשְׁמוֹן: n. loc.

חַשְׁמַל, Ez 8_2 חַשְׁמַלָה; *k^eʿên hahašmal* Ez $1_{4 \cdot 27}$ like the gleaming of *ḥašmal*, uncert.; sugg.: 1. bluish stone; — 2. electrum (alloy of gold & silver); — 3. a precious stone resembling gold; also brass; — 4. inlay-work. †

*חַשְׁמַן: pl. חַשְׁמַנִּים: **bronze objects** or **red cloth**, Egyp. gifts for Y. Ps. 68_{32}. †

חַשְׁמֹנָה: n. loc.

חֹשֶׁן: **breast-piece, -pouch** of high priest Ex 25_7.

חָשַׁק: **qal**: pf. ח׳, חָשְׁקָה, חָשַׁקְתָּ: — 1. w. b^e **cling to, love**: obj. woman Gn 34_8, God Ps 91_{14}; — 2. w. l^e & inf. **desire to** 1K 9_{19}.

piel: pf. חִשֵּׁק: **bind** Ex 38_{28}. †

pual: pt. מְחֻשָּׁק: **bound** Ex 27_{17} 38_{17}. †

חֵשֶׁק: sf. חִשְׁקִי: **desire** 1K $9_{1 \cdot 19}$; *nešef ḥišqî* the twilight I love Is 21_4.

*חִשֻּׁק: pl. sf. חִשֻּׁקֵיהֶם: **spoke** (of wheel) 1K 7_{33}. †

*חִשֻּׁר: pl. sf. חִשֻּׁרֵיהֶם: **hub** (of wheel) 1K 7_{33}. †

*חַשְׁרָה: cs. חַשְׁרַת: **sieve, strainer**: *ḥašrat mayim* (heavenly) strainer 2S 22_{12}. †

חֲשַׁשׁ: **dry grass, leaves** Is 5_{24} 33_{11}. †

חֻשָׁתִי: gent. of חוּשָׁה.

I חַת: חָת; sf. חִתְּכֶם: **terror** (of you) Gn 9_2; *lᵉbiltî-ḥāt* without fear, dauntless Jb 41_{25}. †

II *חַת: pl. חַתִּים: **filled with terror** 1S 2_4 Je 46_5. †

חֵת: n. pers. **Heth**.

cj חתא: **nif.**: impf. לְ־תֵּחָתֶאנָה for לוֹ תַחַת אָוֶן: **be destroyed** Hb 3_{6-7}. †

חתה: **qal**: impf. יַחְתֶּה, יַחְתְּךָ; inf. לַחְתּוֹת; pt. חֹתֶה: — 1. **take away** w. *min* Is 30_{14} (obj. fire), Ps 52_7 (obj. men); — 2. **fetch**, go and get Pr 6_{27} (obj. fire). †

*חִתָּה: cs. חִתַּת: **terror** Gn 35_5. †

חִתּוּל: **bandage, splint** for broken arm Ez 30_{21}. †

חַתְחַת: **horror** Ec 12_5. †

חִתִּי: f. חִתִּית; pl. חִתִּים, f. חִתִּיֹּת: **Hittite** Gn 15_{20}.

חִתִּית: sf. חִתִּיתוֹ, חִתִּיתָם: **terror** of, w. gen. Ez 32_{27} or sf. 32_{30}, w. *nātan* & sf. 26_{17}.

חתך: **nif.**: pf. נֶחְתַּךְ: c. *ʿal* **is decreed, ordained** Dn 9_{24}. †

חתל: **pual**: pf. חֻתַּלְתְּ: **be swaddled** Ez 16_4. †

hof.: inf. abs. הָחְתֵּל: **be swaddled** Ez 16_4. †

*חֲתֻלָּה: sf. חֲתֻלָּתוֹ: **swaddling** Jb 38_9. †

חֶתְלוֹן: n. loc.

חתם: **qal**: impf. וָאֶחְתֹּם, יַחְתֹּ(וֹ)ם; impv. חִתְמוּ, חֲתֹ(וֹ)ם; inf. לַחְתֹּם, חָתֹם; pt. חוֹתֵם, pass. חֲתֻמִים, חָתוּם: — 1. **affix a seal, seal up**: letter 1K 21_8, bill of sale Je 32_{10}; — 2. metaph. Is 8_{16}; SS 4_{12} (fountain); **confirm** (a vision) Dn 9_{24b}.

nif.: pt. נֶחְתָּם: **sealed** Est 3_{12}. †

piel: pf. חִתְּמוּ: **keep** (a house) **sealed, shut up** Jb 24_{16}. †

hif.: pf. הֶחְתִּים: w. *bᵉśārô mizzôbô* **keep** (one's member) **stopped up** (retention of urine?) Lv 15_3. †

חֹתֶמֶת: **signet-ring** Gn 38_{25}. †

חתן: **qal**: only pt. F חֹתֵן, חֹתֶנֶת.

hitp.: pf. הִתְחַתַּנְתֶּם; impf. תִּתְחַתֵּן; impv. הִתְחַתְּנוּ, הִתְחַתֵּן; inf. הִתְחַתֵּן: — 1. **become related by marriage** to (w. *ʾēt*) Gn 34_9, (w. b^e) Dt 7_3; — 2. **become son-in-law** of (w. *ʾēt*) 1K 3_1, (w. b^e) 1S $18_{21 \cdot 23 \cdot 26f}$, (w. l^e) 2C 18_1.

חֹתֵן: he who has a son-in-law, i.e. **father-in-law** Ex 3_1.

חָתָן: cs. חֲתַן, sf. חֲתָנוֹ; pl. sf. חֲתָנָיו: one who becomes related to another family by marriage (as son-in-law or brother-in-law) and who enjoys its protection; connection w. circumcision as originally a puberty-rite: — 1. **son-in-law** Gn 19_{14} 1S 18_{18}; — 2. **bridegroom** Is 61_{10}; *ḥᵃtan dammîm* Ex 4_{25f}; — 3. *ḥᵃtan bêt ʾaḥāb* **related** to the house of A. **by marriage** 2K 8_{27}.

*חֲתֻנָּה: sf. חֲתֻנָּתוֹ: **wedding** SS 3_{11}. †

*חֹתֶנֶת: sf. חֹתַנְתּוֹ: she who has a son-in-law, i.e. **mother-in-law** Dt 27_{23}. †

חתף: **qal**: impf. יַחְתֹּף: **carry off** (s.one by disease) Jb 9_{12}. †

חֶתֶף: **robber** Pr 23_{28}. †

חָתַר: **qal**: pf. ח׳, חָתַרְתִּי; impf. וָאֶחְתֹּר,

יַחְתְּרוּ; impv. חֲתָר־: — 1. **break through, dig through**: a) w. b^e (through) Ez 8_8; b) w. b^e (through to) Am 9_2; — 2. **make one's way by rowing** Jon 1_{13}.

חתת: qal: pf. חַת, חַתָּ, חַתָּה, חַתּוּ, וָחַתּוּ; impv. חֹתּוּ: **be shattered, filled with terror** 2K 19_{26}.

nif.: pf. נִחַת; impf. יֵחַת, יֵחָת, תֵּחַתּוּ, אֵחַתָּה: — 1. **be dashed to pieces** Is 7_8, metaph. 51_6; — 2. **be struck down** 1S 2_{10}; — 3. **be terrified** Is 31_4.

piel: pf. חִתְּתַנִי: **discourage** Jb 7_{14}. †

hif.: pf. הַחִתֹּתָ, וְהַחְתַּתִּי Je 49_{37}; impf. יְחִתֵּנִי, אֲחִתְּךָ: **shatter**: physically Is 9_3, psych. Je 1_{17}.

I **חֲתַת**: **horror** Jb 6_{21}. †

II **חֲתַת**: n. pers. 1C 4_{13}. †

ט

טאטא: pilpel: pf. וְטֵאטֵאתִיהָ: **sweep away** Is 14_{23}. †

טָבְאַל Is 7_6 = טָבְאֵל.

טָבְאֵל: n. pers.

טבב: qal: inf. טוֹב: **speak**, *heḥešētî miṭṭôb* Ps 39_3. †

cj **טָבָה**: cj pl. sf. טִבּוֹתָיו Ne 6_{19}: **rumor**. †

טְבוּלִים: **turban** Ez 23_{15}. †

טַבּוּר: **navel**, only metaph. of center of land Ju 9_{37} Ez 38_{12}. †

טבח: qal: pf. טָבְחָה, טָבַחְתָּ, טָבְחוּ; impv. טְבֹחַ; inf. לִטְבוֹחַ; pt. pass. טָבוּחַ: — 1. **slaughter** (:: *zbḥ* slaughter for sacrifice) Gn 43_{16}; — 2. metaph. **slaughter** (men) Je 25_{24}, (animals) Ex 21_{37}.

I **טֶבַח**: טָבַח; sf. טִבְחָהּ: — 1. **slaughtering** (of animals) Is 53_7; — 2. metaph. **slaughtering** (of men) Is $34_{2\cdot6}$; — 3. as cogn. acc. prepare a slaughtering Gn 43_{16}.

II **טֶבַח**: n. pers. Gn 22_{24}. †

cj III **טֶבַח** for בֶּטַח 2S 8_8: n. loc. †

טַבָּח: pl. טַבָּחִים: — 1. **butcher & cook for meat** (who also serves) 1S 9_{23f}; — 2. pl. **bodyguards & executioners**: *śar tabbāḥîm* Gn 37_{36}, *rab tabbāḥîm* 2K 25_{8-20} provost-marshal.

***טַבָּחָה**: pl. טַבָּחוֹת: (female) **cook** (for meat) 1S 8_{13}. †

טִבְחָה: sf. טִבְחָתִי: — 1. **slaughtering** Je 12_3; *ṣō'n tibḥâ* beasts to be slaughtered Ps 44_{23}; — 2. **meat** (which has been slaughtered) 1S 25_{11}. †

טִבְחַת: n. loc.

טָבַל: qal: pf. טָבַלְתָּ, ט׳; impf. יִטְבֹּל, תִּטְבְּלֵנִי: — 1. **dip** s.thg into (b^e) Gn 37_{31} 2K 8_{15}; (*min*) Lv 4_{17}; — 2. **dip into** (intrans.) (b^e) 2K 5_{14}.

nif.: pf. נִטְבְּלוּ: **be dipped** Jos 3_{15}. †

טְבַלְיָהוּ: n. pers.

טבע: qal: pf. טָבְעוּ, טָבַעְתִּי; impf. יִטְבַּע: — 1. **sink in** (b^e) Je 38_6; metaph. sink into (the earth: of destroyed gates) La 2_9; — 2. **pierce into** (of stone into forehead) 1S 17_{49}

pual: pf. טֻבְּעוּ: **be sunk** Ex 15_4. †

hof.: pf. הָטְבָּעוּ, הָטְבְּעוּ: **be sunk** (action or state): mountains Pr 8_{25}; feet in mud Je 38_{22}.

טַבָּעוֹת: n. pers.

טַבַּעַת: sf. טַבַּעְתּוֹ; pl. טַבָּע(וֹ)ת, cs. טַבְּע(וֹ)ת, sf. טַבְּעֹתֵיהֶם, טַבְּעֹתָיו: — 1. **ring**: a) **signet-ring** Gn 41_{12}; b) as woman's ornament Ex 35_{22}; — 2. **ring for poles of ark**, curtains &c. Ex 25_{12}.

טַבְרִמֹּן: n. pers.

טֵבֵת: **Tebeth**, name of 10th month, Dec.-Jan. Est 2_{16}. †

טַבַּת: n. loc.

טָהוֹר, rarely טָהֹר (90×): cs. טְהוֹר & טְהָר־

Pr 22_{11} Qr & וּטֲהָר־ Jb 17_{9}; f. טְהֹ(ו)רָה, pl. טְהוֹרִים, טְהוֹרוֹת: — 1. **clean, pure, genuine**: gold Ex 25_{11ff}, incense 30_{35}; — 2. **(cultically) clean** (:: *ṭāmēʼ*): man Lv 7_{19}, animal Gn 7_{2}, bird Gn 8_{20}, water Ez 36_{25}; *haṭṭāhôr* he who is clean Dt 12_{15}; *beyôm haṭṭāhôr* when s.thg is clean Lv 14_{57}; — 3. **(morally) pure**: eyes Hb 1_{3}, words Ps 12_{7}.

טָהֵר: **qal**: pf. טָהַרְתִּי, טָהֵרָה, טָהֳרָה, ט׳; impf. אֶטְהָר, תִּטְהֲרִי, תִּטְהָר, יִטְהַר; impv. טְהָר 2K 5_{10}: **be clean, pure** (w. *min* of cultic impurity) Lv 11_{32}; of illness 2K 5_{10}; moral Je 13_{27}.

piel: pf. טִהַרְתִּים, טִהֲרוּ, וְטִהַרְתָּ, טִהַר; impf. תְּטַהֲרֵם, וַיְטַהֲרוּ, אֲטַהֵר; impv. טַהֲרֵנִי; inf. טַהֲרָם, טַהֲרוֹ, טַהֵר; pt. מְטַהֵר: — 1. **sweep clean, scour**: silver Ma 3_{3}, heavens Jb 37_{21}; — 2. (*min* from cultic impurity) **declare clean**: the sick Lv 13_{6}, house Lv 14_{48}.

pual: cj pf. טֹהָר **be declared clean** 1S $20_{26b\beta}$.

hitp.: pf. הִטַּהַרְנוּ, הִטֶּהָרוּ, הִטַּהֲרוּ; impf. וַיִּטַּהֲרוּ (Ne 12_{30} ־טָּ־); impv. הִטַּהֲרוּ; pt. מִטַּהֲרִים, מִטַּהֵר: **purify onesf.** (cultically) Gn 35_{2}.

טֹהַר: sf. טָהֳרָהּ: — 1. purity, **brightness** (of heavens) Ex 24_{10}; — 2. (cultic) **purity** Lv $12_{4.6}$. †

[**טְהָר***: sf. מִטְּהָרוֹ Ps 89_{45}: w. 17 mss. rd. מִטְהָרוֹ, *F* cj *מִטְהָר.]

טָהֳרָה: cs. טָהֳרַת, sf. טָהֳרָתוֹ: — 1. **(cultic) purity**, *ṭohorat qōdeš* 2C 30_{19}; — 2. **determination of cultic purity** Lv 13_{7}; — 3. **purification** 1C 23_{28}.

טוב (vb): **qal**: pf. טוֹב (not easily distinguished fm. adj., *F* 5.), טֹבוּ; impf. יִיטַב; inf. טוֹב (= adj. also) & טוּב Pr 11_{10}, abs. טוֹב Ju 11_{25}: 'good' in every variety: — 1. **be joyous**, glad, happy 1S 25_{36}; *keṭôb lēb ʼamnôn* when A. is in good spirits 2S 13_{28}; — 2. **be in favor**, pleasing 1S 2_{26}; be sweet (love) SS 4_{10}, lovely (tents) Nu 24_{5}; — 3. *ṭôb beʻênê* **it seems good, advisable** 2S 3_{19}, w. *le* & inf. Nu 24_{1}; — 4. **be tolerable, comfortable**: *ṭôb lānû* Nu 11_{18}; *ṭôb lô ʻimmāk* he is happy with you Dt 15_{16}; — 5. **be valuable**: *haṭôb ʼattâ min* are you better than Ju 11_{25}.

hif.: pf. הֵטִיבוֹתָ: **do right, act rightly, do well**; you have done right, w. *kî* 1K 8_{18}, w. *le* & inf. 2K 10_{30}.

I **טוֹב**: adj.: f. טוֹבָה, cs. טוֹבַת; pl. טֹ(ו)בִים, טֹ(ו)בֵי, f. טֹ(ו)בֹ(ו)ת: **good** in every variety of mng.; — 1. **joyous**, glad: *ṭôb lēb* in good spirits Ju 16_{25} Qr; *hāyâ beṭôb* in good spirits Ec 7_{14}; — 2. **pleasing, desirable**: resting-place Gn 49_{15}; good to eat Gn 2_{9} 3_{6}; *ṭôb beʻênay* I should like ... 1S 29_{6}; — 3. **in order, usable**: soldering Is 41_{7}; prosperous (years) Gn 41_{35}; *ṭôb haddābār*: fine! agreed! 1K 2_{38} 18_{24}; — 4. qualitatively good, **suitable**: *ṭôb debārekā* you are right 1S 9_{10}; *haṭôb lekā* do you gain anything by ... Jb 10_{3}; — 5. **lovely**: new-born child Ex 2_{2}, girl Ju 15_{2}, cities Dt 6_{10}; — 6. **friendly, kind**: a) *ṭôbîm lānû* 1S 25_{15}; *dibber ṭôb ʻim* speak kindly w. Gn $31_{24.29}$; b) fm. Y.: Je 30_{18}; — 7. **good** (in character & value): land Ex 3_{8}, gold Gn 2_{12}; *ṭôbat śekel* shrewd 1S 25_{3}; precious (wine) SS 1_{2}; *yôm ṭôb* feast-day 1S 25_{8}; *ʼîš ṭôb* valiant 2S 18_{27}, pl. 1K 2_{32}; God's *rûaḥ* Ps 143_{10}; — 8. (morally) **good**: a) *mâ ṭôb* what is good Mi 6_{8}, *haṭṭôb beʻênê* what is right in s.one's judgment Gn 16_{6}; *hadderek haṭṭôbâ* the right path 1K 8_{36} (:: *derek haṭṭôb* the path to success Je 6_{16}); b) *haṭṭôb* :: *hārāʻ* 2S 14_{17}, *ṭôb ʼô raʻ* Gn 24_{50}; c) *ṭôb wārāʻ* Gn 2_{17} (w. *yādaʻ*); *ṭôb weraʻ* = everything possible 2S 14_{17}; — 9. var.: a) *baṭṭôb lô* where it pleases him Dt 23_{17}; b) *ʻāśâ ṭôb* enjoy onesf. Ec 3_{12}; c) happiness, success: *ʼê-zeh ṭôb* how it is with success Ec 2_{3}.

II **טוֹב**: **perfume**: *qāneh haṭṭôb* Je 6_{20} variety of **oil-grass**, *Cymbopogon*; *šemen haṭṭôb* perfumed oil 2K 20_{13}; *yayin haṭṭôb* spiced wine SS 7_{10}. †

III **טוֹב**: n. terr. Ju $11_{3.5}$ 2S $10_{6.8}$. †

IV **טוֹב**: Ps 39_3, cj. טְבָה ↗ טבב; Ho 14_3 ? rd טוּבֵנוּ. †

טוּב: sf. טוּבְךָ: — 1. a) **the best** of what a place or person has Gn 24_{10}; b) **well-being** Pr 11_{10}; c) **beauty** Ho 10_{11}; d) **happiness**: *ṭûb lēb(āb)* Dt 28_{47}; — 2. **success,** happiness **sent by Y.**: possessions, blessing, salvation: produce of the land Is 63_7, forgiveness of sins Ps 25_7.

טוֹבָה & **טֹבָה**: sf. טוֹבָתִי, ט(ו)ב(ו); pl. sf. טוֹבֹתָיו: good: — 1. **good (done by s.one)**: a) *derek haṭṭôbâ* the right path 1S 12_{23}; w. *ʿāśâ* 1S 24_{19} & oth. vbs.; w. *šillēm* repay w. good 1S 24_{20}, *hēšîb* Gn 44_4; b) **kindness, goodwill**: of God Ps 65_{12}; *dibber ṭôbôt ʾēt* speak friendly words 2K 25_{28}; intercession (w. *ʿal*) Je 18_{20}; — 2. **good (which happens to s.one), success, salvation** Ps 106_5; *yôm ṭôbâ* Ec 7_{14}; w. *rāʾâ* experience Jb 9_{25}; good end Gn 50_{20}.

טוֹבִיָּה: n. pers.

טוֹבִיָּהוּ: n. pers.

טוה: **qal**: pf. טָווּ: **spin** Ex 35_{25f}. †

טוח: **qal**: pf. טָח, טָחוּ, טַחְתֶּם; inf. טוֹחַ; pt. טָחֵי, טָחִים: — 1. **plaster, coat** wall of house w. *ʿāfār* Lv 14_{42}, *tāfāl* Ex 13_{10ff}; **overlay** w. gold, silver 1C 29_4; — 2. spread, **paint** s.one w. s.thg Ez 22_{28}. †

nif.: inf. הִטּ(ו)חַ: **be plastered** Lv $14_{43.48}$. †

ט(ו)טָפֹת: **signs on forehead & arm, phylacteries** Ex 13_{16} Dt 6_8 11_{18}. †

טול: **hif.**: pf. הֵטִיל, וְהֵטַלְתִּי; impf. וַיָּטֶל, וַיְטִילֵהוּ, אֲטִילְךָ, וַיָּטִלוּ; impv. הֲטִילֻנִי: **throw**: a spear 1S 18_{11}, men into sea Jon $1_{12.15}$; subj. God, obj. wind Jon 1_{4f}.

hof.: pf. הוּטָלוּ; impf. יוּטַל, יֻטַל: **be thrown** Je 22_{28}.

pilpel: pt. מְטַלְטֶלְךָ: **throw far away** Is 22_{17}. †

טוּר: pl. טוּרִים, טֻרִים: **row,** course: of building-stones 1K 6_{36}; of jewels Ex 28_{17ff}.

טוּשׂ: **qal**: impf. יָטוּשׂ: **flutter** above the ground Jb 9_{26}. †

טחה: **pilel**: pt. כִּמְטַחֲוֵי קֶשֶׁת: as far as an archer shoots = **distance of a bowshot** Gn 21_{16}. †

טְחוֹן: **hand-mill** La 5_{13}, but ↗ comm. †

טֻחוֹת: — 1. *battuḥôt* Ps 51_8 **in secret, within** (entrails), **in the dark**; — 2. *battuḥôt* Jb 38_{36}: most follow 1.; but better the **ibis,** bird of **Thoth**. †

טחח: **qal**: pf. טַח: **be covered** over, **stuck shut** (eyes) Is 44_{18}, w. *min* so that ... not. †

טחן: **qal**: pf. טָחֲנוּ; impf. תִּטְחַן; impv. טַחֲנוּ; inf. ↗ טְחוֹן, טָחוֹן; pt. טֹחֵן, טֹחֲנָה: — 1. **grind, mill** Ju 16_{21}; — 2. **crush** Ex 32_{20}, metaph. oppress Is 3_{15}.

cj. **nif.**: impf. תִּטָּחֵן for תִּטְחַן: **be lain with** Jb 31_{10}. †

טַחֲנָה: **mill** Ec 12_4 ? metaph.; ↗ comm. †

***טֹחֲנָה**: pl. טֹחֲנוֹת: (female) miller, metaph. **molar** Ec 12_3. †

טְחֹרִים: cs. טְחֹרֵי, sf. טְחֹרֵיהֶם: **tumors** at anus, **hemorrhoids** 1S $6_{11.17}$; elsewhere Qr for עפלים (↗ I *ʿōfel*). †

טֹטָפֹת: ↗ ט(ו)טָפֹת.

טִיחַ: **daubing** (of clay) Ez 13_{12}. †

טִיט: — 1. **wet clay, mud** Je 38_6 (at bottom of cistern); *ṭîṭ ḥûṣôt* 2S 22_{43}; — 2. **potter's clay** Is 41_{25}.

***טִירָה**: cs. טִירַת, sf. טִירָתָם; pl. טִירוֹת, sf. טִרֹתָם: — 1. **(tent-)camp** protected by stone wall Gn 25_{16}; — 2. a) **row of stones** (along the walls) Ez 46_{23b}; b) **battlement** SS 8_9.

טַל: sf. טַלְּךָ, טַלָּם: **dew, light rain** Gn 27_{28}.

טלא: **qal**: pt. pass.: טָלוּא, טְלֻאִים, טְלֻאוֹת: — 1. **spotted** (sheep) Gn 30_{32-39}; — 2. *bāmôt ṭᵉluʾôt* **colored padding,** made of

quilting, for sacred prostitution Ez 16_{16}. †
pual: pt. מְטֻלָּאוֹת: **patched** (sandals) Jos 9_5. †

טְלָאִים: n. loc.

טָלֶה: cs. טְלֵה; pl. טְלָאִים Is 40_{11}: **lamb** Is 40_{11} 65_{25}; *ṭelēh ḥālāb* 1S 7_9. †

טַלְטֵלָה: cogn. acc. **throwing** (to) **a great** distance Is 22_{17}. †

טלל: **piel**: impf. וַיְטַלְלֻהוּ: **supply w. a roof** Ne 3_{15}. †

I טֶלֶם: n. loc. Jos 15_{24}. †

II טֶלֶם: n. pers. Ezr 10_{24}. †

טַלְמוֹן: n. pers.

טָמֵא: qal: pf. טָמְאוּ, טָמֵאת, טָמְאָה, ט׳; impf. יִטְמָא, יִטְמְאוּ; inf. טָמְאָה: **become (cultically) unclean**: a) men Lv 11_{24-39}; (w. *be* from) Lv 5_3; b) things Lv 11_{32-38}; *leṭom'â* so that uncleanness arises Ez 22_3.
nif.: pf. נִטְמָא, נִטְמְאָה, נִטְמָאָה, נִטְמֵאת; נִטְמֵתֶם > נִטְמֵאתֶם; pt. נִטְמָאִים: **defile, pollute onesf.** Ho 5_3, w. *be* by Lv 11_{43}.
piel: pf. טִמֵּא, טִמֵּאת, טִמֵּאתֶם, טִמְּאוֹ, טִמְּאוּהָ; impf. יְטַמְּאוּ, תְּטַמְּאוּ, תְּטַמֵּא, וַיְטַמְּאֵהוּ; inf. טַמֵּא, abs. Lv 13_{44}: — 1. **dishonor**: ravish (a girl) Gn 34_5; profane (Y.'s name) Ez 43_{7f}; — 2. **defile, profane**: tabernacle Lv 15_{31}, land 18_{28}; — 3. (cultically) **defile**: onesf. Lv 11_{44}, a *nāzîr* Nu 6_9, altar 2K 23_{16}, house of Y. Je 7_{30}; — 4. **declare unclean** Lv 13_{8-59}.
pual: pt. מְטֻמָּאָה **be defiled** Ez 4_{14}. †
hitp.: impf. יִטַּמָּא, יִטַּמְּאוּ, יִטַּמָּאוּ: incur uncleanness, **become unclean** (*le* from) Lv 11_{24}, (*be* with) 11_{43}.
hotpaal: pf. הֻטַּמָּאָה: **be touched by uncleanness** Dt 24_4. †

טָמֵא: cs. טְמֵא; f. טְמֵאָה, cs. טְמֵאַת; pl. טְמֵאִים: — 1. **unclean**: cry of leper Lv 13_{45}; — 2. **(cultically) unclean**: animals Lv 5_{2a}; from corpse 22_4; *ṭāmē'* s.one who is unclean Is 35_8, s.thg unclean 52_{11}; *ṭemē' śefātayim* w. unclean lips Is 6_5.

טֻמְאָה: cs. טֻמְאַת, sf. טֻמְאָתוֹ; pl. cs. טֻמְאֹת: **state of cultic uncleanness**: men Lv 5_3, women 15_{25f}, food Ju 13_{7-14}, things Ez 24_{11}; *rûaḥ haṭṭum'â* spirit of uncleanness Zc 13_2.

[טָמְאָה Mi 2_{10}: rd לִמְעַט מְלוּמָה. †]

[*טמה: נִטְמִינוּ Jb 18_3; ? trad. טמא nif. **are taken as unclean**; ? rd נִטְמֹנוּ 3 mss **are stopped up, 'nailed down,'** ↗ *טמם nif. †]

*טמם: cj nif. Jb 18_3 **be stopped up, 'nailed down.'** †

טָמַן: **qal**: pf. ט׳, טָמַנְתִּי, טָמְנוּ, טָמָנוּ, טְמַנְתִּיו, טְמַנְתֶּם; impf. וַיִּטְמְנֵהוּ, וַיִּטְמֹן, וַתִּטְמְנֵם, וָאֶטְמְנֵהוּ; impv. טָמְנֵהוּ; inf. טָמוֹן, טָמְנוֹ; pt. pass. טָמוּן, טְמוּנָה, טְמֻנִים, טְמֻנֵי: — 1. **hide** (trans.) Je 13_4ff; *baṭṭāmûn* in secret Jb 40_{13} (oth.: hiding, or prison); — 2. **set up secretly**: net Ps 9_{16}, trap 64_6.
nif.: impv. הִטָּמֵן: **keep (onesf.) hidden** Is 2_{10}. †
hif.: impf. וַיַּטְמִנוּ (impf. qal ?): **keep (s.thg) hidden** 2K $7_{8a.b}$. †

טֶנֶא: sf. טַנְאֲךָ: **basket** Dt $26_{2.4}$ $28_{5.17}$. †

טנף: **piel**: impf. אֲטַנְּפֵם: **dirty** (feet just washed) SS 5_3. †

טעה: cj. **qal**: pt. f. טֹעִיָּה (for עֹטְיָה) **roam around** SS 1_7. †
hif.: pf. הִטְעוּ: **lead astray** Ez 13_{10}. †

טָעַם: **qal**: pf. ט׳, טָעֲמָה; impf. יִטְעַם, יִטְעֲמוּ; impv. טַעֲמוּ; inf. טְעֹם: — 1. **taste** foods 2S 19_{36}; — 2. **eat food** 1S 14_{24}; — 3. **discover** by experience, notice, learn Ps 34_9.

טַעַם: טָעֶם; sf. טַעְמוֹ, טַעֲמֵךְ: — 1. **taste** (of food) Ex 16_{31}; — 2. **perception**, (good) **sense** 1S 25_{33}; *hēšîb ṭaʿam* answer sensibly Pr 26_{16}; *šinnâ ṭaʿamô* pretend to be insane 1S 21_{14}; — 3. **order, decree** Jon 3_7.

I טען: **pual**: pt. pl. cs. מְטֹעֲנֵי: **pierced** Is 14_{19}. †

II טען: qal: impv. טַעֲנוּ: **load** (beast of burden) Gn 45_{17}. †

I טַף: טָף: sf. טַפְּכֶם, טַפֵּנוּ: — 1. small children Dt 1_{39}; — 2. those of a wandering tribe who are not (or hardly) fit to march: a) incl. women & elderly Gn 43_{8}; b) incl. children & elderly Gn 34_{29}.

II טַף: (trad. to I): **drops** Gn 47_{12}. †

I טפח: piel: pf. טִפַּחְתָּה: **spread out** (heavens) Is 48_{13}. †

II טפח: piel: pf. טִפַּחְתִּי: **bear healthy children** (trad.: carry on palms, dandle) La 2_{22}. †

טֶפַח: **handbreadth** (4 fingers = 7.5 cm.): 1K 7_{26} 2C 4_{5}. †

טֹפַח: **handbreadth** Ex 25_{25}.

I *טְפָחָה: pl. טְפָחוֹת: **handbreadth** ? as brief measure of time Ps 39_{6}. †

II *טְפָחָה: unknown archit. term: 1K 7_{9}: pl. טְפָחוֹת: corbel?, covering. †

טִפֻּחִים: **health & loveliness of new-born child**: *ʿōlᵉlê tippuḥîm* children of such quality, or fm. II *ṭpḥ*, children tenderly cared for La 2_{20}. †

טפל: qal: pf. טָפְלוּ; impf. וַתִּטְפֹּל; pt. טֹפְלֵי: **smear on**: metaph. a) *šeqer (ʿal)* **besmear** s.one (w. *lie*) Ps 119_{69} Jb 13_{4}; b) **plaster over** (s.one's sin) Jb 14_{17}. †

טִפְסָר Je 51_{27} & *טַפְסָר Na 3_{17}: pl. sf. טַפְסְרַיִךְ: 'clerk,' i.e. **official**: Je 51_{27} military, Na 3_{17} governmental. †

טפף: qal: inf. טָפֹף: **trip, skip along** Is 3_{16}. †

טָפַשׁ: qal: pf. טָ׳: **be insensible, unfeeling** Ps 119_{70}; cj. impf. *yiṭpaš* Jb 33_{25}.†

טָפַת: n. pers. f.

טרד: qal: pt. ט(ו)רֵד: **drip steadily**: *delef ṭōrēd* steadily dripping, leaky roof Pr 19_{13} 27_{15}. †

טְרוֹם: conj. **before** Rt 3_{14} Kt (Qr *ṭerem*). †

טרח: hif.: impf. יַטְרִיחַ: **load** (*bᵉ* with) Jb 37_{11}. †

טֹרַח: sf. טָרְחֲכֶם: **load** Dt 1_{12} Is 1_{14}. †

*טָרִי: f. טְרִיָּה: **fresh**: bone Ju 15_{15}, wound Is 1_{6}. †

טֶרֶם: neg. not yet > conj. before > prep.: — 1. *ṭerem* **not yet**: a) w. pf. Gn 24_{15}, b) w. impf. Gn 2_{5}; — 2. *ṭerem* **before**: Ex 12_{34}; — 3. *bᵉṭerem* a) prep. **before** Is 17_{14}; b) conj. **before**: w. pf. (alw. pass.) Ps 90_{2}; w. impf. Gn 27_{4}; w. pleon. *lōʾ* Zp 2_{2b}; — 4. *miṭṭerem* w. inf. **before** Hg 2_{15}.

טָרַף: qal: pf., טָ׳, טָרַף; impf. יִטְרָף, יִטְרֹף Gn 49_{27}, אֶטְרוֹף; inf. טְרֹף, לִטְרָף־, טָרֹף; pt. טֹרֵף, טֹרְפֵי: **tear in pieces** (of wild animals) Gn 37_{33}; of God in wrath Jb 16_{9}.

nif.: impf. יִטָּרֵף: **be torn in pieces** (by wild animals) Ex 22_{15} Je 5_{6}. †

pual (qal pass.): pf. טֹרַף, טֹרָף: **be torn in pieces** Gn 37_{33} 44_{28}. †

hif.: impv. הַטְרִיפֵנִי: (softened mng.) **let s.one enjoy, provide with** Pr 30_{8}. †

טֶרֶף: טָרֶף; sf. טַרְפּוֹ, טַרְפֵּךְ: — 1. **prey** (of wild animals) Nu 23_{24}; cogn. acc. Ez 19_{3}; — 2. what the prey provides, **nourishment** Ma 3_{10}.

טָרָף: pl. cs. טַרְפֵּי: **freshly plucked** Gn 8_{11} Ez 17_{9}. †

טְרֵפָה: **animal torn in pieces by wild animal** Gn 31_{39} Lv 7_{24}.

י

יאב: qal: pf. יָאַבְתִּי: w. *lᵉ* **long for** Ps 119_{131}. †

יֹאָב: ↗ יוֹאָב.

יאה: qal: pf. יָאָתָה: **be fitting, proper** Je 10_{7}. †

יְאוֹר: ↗ יְאֹר.

יַאֲזַנְיָה: n. pers.

יַאֲזַנְיָהוּ: n. pers.

יָאִיר: n. pers.
I יאל: nif.: pf. נוֹאַלְנוּ, נוֹאֲ־לוּ, נוֹאֲלוּ: **prove** (onesf.) **foolish** Nu 12_{11} Is 19_{13} Je 5_4 50_{36}. †
II יאל: hif.: pf. הוֹאַלְנוּ, הוֹאַלְתָּ, הוֹאִיל; impf. וַיּוֹאֶל, יֹאֵל; impv. הוֹאֶל־, הוֹאֵל, הוֹאִילוּ: **make a beginning** (usu. expression of politeness or modesty): — 1. **be intent on** s.thg: *hô'îl hālak* was intent on going Ho 5_{11}; — 2. **resolve** (w. self-mastery) **to, agree to**: a) w. impf. *hô'alnû wannēšeb* if we had only agreed to live ... Jos 7_7; w. 2 impf. Jb 6_9; b) impv. w. impv. *hô'ēl qaḥ* go on, take (or, please take) 2K 5_{23}; c) w. *le* & inf. Gn 18_{27}; — 3. **begin to** Dt 1_5.
יְאֹר & יְאוֹר (6×): כִּיא(וֹ)ר; כַּי׳, בַּי׳, הַיְאֹר; sf. יְאֹרִי; loc. הַיְאֹרָה; pl. יְאֹרִים, cs. יְאֹרֵי, sf. יְאֹרָיו, יְאֹרֵיהֶם: — 1. the river **Nile** Gn $41_{1\text{-}3}$; — 2. (great) **river**: spec. Tigris Dn $12_{5\text{-}7}$; in genl. Is 33_{21b}; — 3. pl. **branches & canals of Nile** Ex 7_{19}; = **the Nile** 2K 19_{24}; — 4. water-filled **galleries** (of mine) Jb 28_{10}.
יָאִרִי: gent. of יָאִיר: 2S 20_{26}. †
יאשׁ: nif.: pf. נוֹאָשׁ; pt. נ(וֹ)אָשׁ: — 1. w. *min*, **despair of, desist fm.** 1S 27_1; pt. **one who despairs** Jb 6_{26}; — 2. pt. > interj. of hopelessness, like Eng. 'to hell with it' Is 57_{10} Je 2_{25} 18_{12}. †
piel: inf. יַאֵשׁ: **let** (one's heart) **despair** Ec 2_{20}. †
יֹאָשׁ: n. pers.: ⊦ יוֹאָשׁ.
יֹאשִׁיָּה: n. pers.
יֹאשִׁיָּהוּ: יאוֹשִׁיָּהוּ Je 27_1: n. pers.
יָאֲתָה Je 10_7: ⊦ יאה.
(הָ)יאתוֹן Ez 40_{15}: ⊦ Qr (הָ)אִיתוֹן.
יְאָתְרַי: n. pers.
יבב: piel: impf. וַתְּיַבֵּב: **lament** Ju 5_{28}. †
יְבוּל, *יְבָל: sf. יְבוּלָהּ, וִיבֻלָהּ: **produce** (of the soil) Lv 26_4; of man's work Ps 78_{46}.
יְבוּס: n. loc., identified w. Jerus.
יְבוּסִי & יְבֻסִי (5×): gent. of יְבוּס: **Jebusite.**
יִבְחָר: n. pers.
יָבִין: n. pers.
יָבֵישׁ: — 1. 1S 11_3 &c. n. loc., ⊦ III יָבֵשׁ; — 2. 2K 15_{13f} n. pers. (?), ⊦ II יָבֵשׁ.
יבל: hif.: impf. יוֹבִלוּהָ, יוֹבִילוּן, י(וֹ)בִילוּ, יוֹבִלְנִי, אוֹבִלֵם: **bring**: as gift Is 23_7, as tribute Zp 3_{10}, as booty Ho 10_6.
hof.: impf. יוּבָלוּ, יוּבַל, יוּבָל, אוּבָל: **be brought**: as gift Is 18_7, as sacrifice Is 53_7; **be led** Is 55_{12}, as a bride Ps 45_{15}.
I *יָבָל: pl. cs. יִבְלֵי: **watercourse** Is 30_{25} 44_4. †
II יָבָל: n. pers. Gn 4_{20}. †
יְבֻל: ⊦ יוּבַל.
יִבְלְעָם: n. loc.
יַבֶּלֶת: **wart** Lv 22_{22}. †
יבם: piel: pf. יִבְּמָהּ; impv. יַבֵּם; inf. יַבְּמִי: **consummate the marriage of a brother-in-law, in which the obligation is fulfilled of marrying one's brother's widow to produce offspring** Gn 38_8 Dt $25_{5\text{-}7}$. †
*יָבָם: sf. יְבָמָהּ, יְבָמִי: **brother of deceased husband** Dt $25_{5\text{-}7}$.
*יְבָמָה or *יְבֶמֶת: sf. יְבִמְתּוֹ, יְבִמְתֵּךְ: — 1. (ref. to a man): **brother's widow** Dt $25_{7\text{-}9}$; — 2. (ref. to a woman): **husband's brother's widow** Ru 1_{15}. †
יַבְנְאֵל: n. loc.
יַבְנֵה: n. loc.
יִבְנְיָה & יִבְנִיָּה: n. pers.
יְבֻסִי: ⊦ יְבוּסִי.
יַבֹּק: n. river.
יְבֶרֶכְיָהוּ: n. pers.
יִבְשָׂם: n. pers.
יָבֵשׁ: qal: pf. יָבֵשׁוּ, יָבְשׁוּ, יָבְשָׁה, י׳; impf. יִיבַשׁ, יִיבָשׁ, וַתִּיבַשׁ, יָבֵשׁוּ; inf. בִּיבֹשׁ & יְבֹשֶׁת, abs. יָב(וֹ)שׁ: — 1. **dry up** (of water) Gn 8_7; — 2. **become dry** (of land) Gn 8_{14}; — 3. **dry up**: of bread Jos $9_{5.12}$, of hand 1K 13_4; — 4. **dry up, wither**: of grass Is 15_6, of plants Is 40_{24}.
piel: impf. תְּיַבֵּשׁ, תְּיַבֶּשׁ־, וַיְבַשְׁהוּ: — 1. **dry up** (trans., obj. sea) Na 1_4; — 2. **dry out** (trans., obj. shoots) Jb 15_{30}, (bones) Pr 17_{22}. †

hif.: pf. הֹ(וֹ)בַשְׁתִּי, הוֹבִישָׁה, הֹ(וֹ)בִ(י)שׁ, הֹבִשׁוּ; impf. אוֹבִישׁ: — 1. make (water) dry up Jos 2_{10}; — 2. make (plants) dry up, wither Is 42_{15}; — 3. intrans. dry up: of plants Jl 1_{10}, metaph. of joy Jl 1_{12b}.

I יָבֵשׁ: adj.: f. יְבֵשָׁה; pl. יְבֵשִׁים, יְבֵשׁוֹת: dry, withered: tree Ez 17_{24}, bones Ez $37_{2.4}$; *nafšēnû yebēšâ* we are wasting away Nu 11_6.

II יָבֵשׁ (1×) & יָבֵישׁ (2×): n. pers. 2K $15_{10.13f.}$ †

III יָבֵשׁ 1S 11 (4×), otherw. יָבֵישׁ: n. loc.; loc. יָבֵשָׁה & בְּיָבֵשָׁה 1S 31_{13}.

יַבָּשָׁה: — 1. dry ground Ex 4_9 (near water); — 2. dry land (opp. 'sea', the 2 parts of earth's surface) Gn $1_{9f.}$

יַבֶּשֶׁת: — 1. dry ground Ex 4_9 Ps 95_5. †

יִגְאָל: n. pers.

יגב: qal: pt. יֹגְבִים: ? farmer 2K 25_{12} Je 52_{16}. †

*יָגֵב: pl. יְגֵבִים: field Je 39_{10}. †

יָגְבְּהָה: n. loc.

יְגַדַּלְיָהוּ: n. pers.

I יגה: nif.: pt. pl. נוּגוֹת: afflicted La 1_4. †
piel: impf. וַיַּגֶּה: grieve (trans.) La 3_{33}. †
hif.: pf. הוֹגָה, הֹגָה; impf. תּוֹגְיוּן; pt. מוֹגַיִךְ: torment Is 51_{23}.

II יגה: hif.: pf. הֹגָה (w/o expressed obj.): carry off 2S 20_{13}. †

יָגוֹן: sf. יְגוֹנָם: torment, trouble Gn 42_{38}.

יָגוּר: n. loc.

יָגוֹר: filled with fear Je 22_{25} 39_{17}. †

*יָגִיעַ: pl. cs. יְגִיעֵי: exhausted Jb 3_{17}. †

*יְגִיעַ or *יָגִיעַ: cs. יְגִיעַ, sf. יְגִיעוֹ, יְגִיעֲךָ, יְגִיעֶךָ; w. *min*: מִיגִיעוֹ; pl. sf. יְגִיעֵי: — 1. labor, work Gn 31_{42}; — 2. a) produce of labor, gain Dt 28_{33}; b) property Ne 5_{13}.

*יְגִיעָה: cs. יְגִיעַת: weariness Ec 12_{12}. †

יָגְלִי: n. pers.

יגע: qal: pf. יָגְעָה, יָגַעְתָּ, יָגַעַתְּ (*יָגַעְתְּ + יָגַעַת) Is 47_{12}, יָגַעְנוּ; impf. יִיגַע, תִּיגַע, אִיגָא, יִ(י)גְעוּ, יִ(י)גָעוּ: — 1. grow tired, weary 2S 23_{10}; — 2. exert onesf. Is 49_4; — 3. take pains for, about (s.one, s.thg): w. acc. Is 47_{15}, w. *be* Jos 24_{13}.
piel: impf. תְּיַגַּע: — 1. tire, weary (s.one) Ec 10_{15}; — 2. trouble (s.one) Jos 7_3.
hif.: pf. הוֹגַעְתַּנִי, הוֹגַעְנוּ, הוֹגַעְתֶּם, הוֹגַעְתִּיךָ: weary Is 43_{23f} Ma 2_{17}. †

יְגָע: produce of labor Jb 20_{18}. †

יָגֵעַ: pl. יְגֵעִים: — 1. tired, weary Dt 25_{18} 2S 17_2; — 2. wearisome Ec 1_8. †

יגר: qal: pf. יָגֹרְתִּי, יָגֹרְתָּ: be afraid (of what is to come) Dt 9_{19}.

יְגַר Gn 31_{47}: יְגַר שָׂהֲדוּתָא: ↗ Aram.

יָד (1600×): cs. יַד; sf. יָדוֹ, יָדְךָ, יָדֵךְ, יֶדְכֶם, יֶדְהֶם, יֶדְכֶן; du. יָדַיִם, cs. יְדֵי (יַד 2K 12_{12} Qr, Kt יַד), בִּידֵי, כִּ׳, לִ׳, also מִידֵי, sf. יָדָיו (יָדָו Lv 16_{21} + 3×, usu. Kt יָדוֹ) & יָדֵיהוּ Hb 3_{10}, יָדֶיךָ & יָדֶךָ 2S 3_{34} Je 40_4, יְדֵיכֶם (יְדֵכֶם Ps 134_2), יְדֵיהֶם; pl. יָדוֹת, cs. יְדוֹת, sf. יְדוֹתָם, יְדוֹתֶיהָ, יְדוֹתָיו: f. (m. Ex 17_{12}): forearm, hand: — 1. literal, bodily: a) (fore-)arm Ex 17_{11}; b) hand Gn 3_{22}; *kelî ʿēṣ-yād* wooden hand-tool Nu 35_{18}; c) of animal: forepaw (of dog) Ps 22_{21} (or is this metaph., ↗ 5 c ?); of seraph Is 6_6; d) du. hands Gn 27_{22}; *bên yādêkā* on the shoulders, back Zc 13_6; c) penis † Is $57_{8.10}$; — 2. verbal comb.: a) w. *nātan*, offer hand, shake hands 2K 10_{15}, in promise Ezr 10_{19}, in submission 1C 29_{24}; b) w. *šālaḥ*, extend Gn 3_{22}; c) *hērîm & nāśāʾ*, raise hand (in oath) Gn 14_{22}, (in prayer) Ps 28_2; d) *sāmak & šît*, lay one's hand on Gn 48_{14}; e) *qābaṣ ʿal-yād* gather handful by handful Pr 13_{11}; f) *nātan yādô be* Ex 7_4 lay (violent) hands on s.one (cf. *hāyetā yādô be* Gn 37_{27}); g) *šît yād ʿim* make common cause w. Ex 23_1; h) *higgîaʿ yādô* Lv 5_7 defray expenses (cf. *hiśśîg yādô* 5_{11}); i) *nātan ʿal yād* entrust s.thg to s.one Gn 24_{37}; j) *hôṣîʾ ʿal yād* bring out in the care of s.one Ezr 1_8; k) *miyyad* w. *qānâ* buy Gn 33_{19}; — 3. nominal comb.: *yād ʿal-peh* hand on mouth (as gesture of silence &

astonishment) Jb 21_5; *yādô bakkol* one's hand against everyone Gn 16_{12}; *yād leyād* (my) hand upon it = assuredly Pr 11_{21}; *yad* … *'ittekā* be implicated 2S 14_{19}; — 4. **hand of God**: a) *yad yhwh* Ex 9_3; b) *yad yhwh* (&c.) *hāyetâ 'el/'al* **came over** (of inspiration) 1K 18_{46} 2K 3_{15}; & sim. phrases; — 5. sg. & du. metaph.: a) **side**: of land: *raḥabat yādayim* spacious Gn 32_{21}; α) *'al-yad/yedê* **near, next to** 2C 17_{15}; *'îš 'al-yādô* each in his place Nu 2_{17}, *leyad 'ābî* at the side of my f. 1S 19_3; β) **bank** (of stream, river) Dt 2_{37}; b) **portion, range**: α) *'îš yādô* each his portion Je 6_3, *'ên beyādî* I have nothing in mind 1S 24_{12}; β) **possession**: *beyādî* 1S 9_8; γ) **strength** Dt 32_{36}; *yādayim lānûs* strength to flee Jos 8_{20}; *beyad* as reinforced *be*: **by, through** Ex 9_{35} (w. *dibber*), 8_{36} (w. *ṣiwwâ*); c) **power**: *beyad lāšôn* Pr 18_{21}, *mittaḥat yad 'arām* (escaped) from the power of Syria 2K 13_5; *lō' beyād* not by human assistance 2S 23_6; *keyad hammelek* according to royal generosity 1K 10_{13}; — 6. var.: a) *yād* **monument** 1S 15_{12}, road-marker Ez 21_{24}; b) *yādayim* = the 2 flaps or nets of a trap Ps 141_9; c) **place** (for latrine outside the camp) Dt 23_{13}; — 7. pl. *yādôt*: a) **axles** (of wheels) 1K 7_{32f}; **handles** (?) 7_{35}; **arm-rests** 10_{19}; **tenons** of a frame Ex 26_{17} 36_{22}; b) **part**: α) multiplicative: *ḥāmēš yādôt* five times (as much) Gn 43_{34}; β) military division (of palace- & temple-guard) 2K 11_7.

יִדְאֲלָה: n. loc.

יִדְבָּשׁ: n. pers.

ידד: **qal**: pf. יַדּוּ: w. *gôrāl 'al*, **throw** Jl 4_3 Ob$_{11}$ Na 3_{10}. †

יְדִדוּת: **beloved** Je 12_7. †

I **ידה**: **qal**: impv. יְדוּ: w. *'el* **shoot at** Je 50_{14}. †

piel: impf. וַיַּדּוּ; inf. יַדּוֹת: — 1. **throw** (stones at) La 3_{53}; — 2. ? **throw down** Zc 2_4. †

II **ידה**: **hif.**: pf. הוֹדוּ, הוֹדִינוּ; impf. יוֹדֶה, אוֹדֶה, יוֹדוּ, נוֹדֶה, יוֹדְךָ, יוֹדֶךָ, אוֹדֶךָּ, אוֹדֶנּוּ, יוֹדֻךָ, יוֹדוּךָ, אֲהוֹדֶה & אֲהוֹדֶנּוּ; impv. הוֹדוּ; inf. הוֹדוֹת 2C 7_3: — 1. **praise** (obj. men) Gn 49_8; — 2. **praise** (obj. God): a) w. acc. Gn 29_{35}; w. *šēm* 1K 8_{33}; b) w. *le* Ps 6_6; — 3. **confess** (sin) Pr 28_{13}; — 4. **give voice to** (praise & thanksgiving): *lattefillâ* Ne 11_{17}.

hitp.: pf. הִתְוַדָּה, הִתְוַדּוּ; impf. וָאֶתְוַדֶּה, יִתְוַדּוּ; pt. מִתְוַדֶּה, מִתְוַדִּים: **confess**: sins Lv 5_5; w. *'al* in regard to Ne 1_6.

יִדּוֹ: n. pers.

יָדוֹן: n. pers.

יַדּוּעַ: n. pers.

יְדוּתוּן, 2× יְדֻתוּן, יְדִיתוּן 1C 16_{38}, Kt Ps 39_1 77_1 Ne 11_{17}: n. pers.

יַדַּי: n. pers.

***יָדִיד**: cs. יְדִיד, sf. יְדִידוֹ; pl. sf. יְדִידֶיךָ; pl. יְדִידוֹת: — 1. noun: **beloved** Is 5_1 (= friend?), Ps 127_2; *yedîd yhwh* Dt 33_{12}; *yedîdêkā* the godly Ps 60_7 108_7; — 2. adj. **lovely** Ps 84_2. †

יְדִידָה: n. pers. f.

יְדִידֹת: **love** Ps 45_1. †

יְדִידְיָה: n. pers.

יְדָיָה: n. pers.

יְדִיעֲאֵל: n. pers.

יְדִיתוּן: 1C 16_{38} &c. ↗ יְדוּתוּן.

יִדְלָף: n. pers.

יָדַע: qal (ca. 810×): pf. י׳, יָדַעְתָּ(ה), יָדַ֫עַתְּ, יָדַעְתְּ, יָדַעַתְּ Ps 140_{13} & Jb 42_2 Kt, יָדְעוּ, יָדְעוּ, יְדַעְתֶּם, יָדַעְנוּ, יְדָעוּן Dt $8_{3.16}$, יְדָעוּ, יְדַעְתּוֹ, יְדַעְתַּנִי, יְדַעְתִּיו, יְדַעְתִּין, יְדַעֲנוּךָ, יְדַעֲנוּם; impf. יֵדַע, יֵדַע, יֵדַע Ps 138_6, אַל־יֵ֫דַע 1S 21_3, אֵדְעָה, אֵדְעָה, וְאֵדַע Ru 4_4 (Kt אֵדַע), תֵּדְעִי, תֵּדְעִין, תֵּדְעוּן, יֵדָעֻנוּ, אֵדָעֲךָ, תֵּדָעוּהָ; impv. דַּע, דַּע, דָּעֵהוּ; inf. דַּ֫עַת, דֵּ֫עַת (& ↗ דֵּעָה), לְדַעְתּוֹ; pt. יוֹ(ו)דֵעַ, יֹ֫דַעַת, יוֹ(ו)דְעִים, יֹדְעֵי Ps 119_{79} (rd Qr יֹדְעֵי; Kt יָדְעוּ), pass. יָדוּעַ, יְדֻעִים: in genl., **notice, observe**: — 1. **observe, realize** Gn 3_7 Ex 2_4; *yāda' šelôm* … find out how it is with ... Est 2_{11}; — 2. **find out** (fm. information, communication) 2S 24_{2}; = **experience** Is 47_{8}; — 3. **recognize, perceive** (fm. observation, deliberation) Gn 15_{8}; know (= perceive) that I am Y. Ex 6_{7}; *daʿ ûreʾēh kî* 1K 20_{7}; — 4. **care about, be concerned about** Gn 39_{6}; — 5. **(get to) know, be(come) acquainted w.** (French connaître): a) obj. person Gn 29_{5} (personally), Ex 1_{8} (historically); obj. thing (path) Jb 28_{7}; b) pt.: act. *yōdeʿîm* acquaintances, confidants Jb 19_{13}; pass. *yedûʿîm* experienced Dt $1_{13 \cdot 15}$, *yedûaʿ ḥŏlî* familiar w. illness Is 53_{3}; — 6. sexual relations: **have intercourse** w. Gn 4_{1} 1K 1_{4}; homosexually Gn 19_{5}; subj. woman Gn 19_{8}; — 7. theologically: **care about, be concerned about** s.one: a) God subj., take care of, take up the cause of 2S 7_{20}; **select, choose** Gn 18_{19}; b) God obj. Je 2_{8}, *lōʾ yādaʿ* 1S 2_{12}; — 8. **understand** s.thg: a) w. acc. Pr 30_{18}; *yōdēaʿ ṣayid* skilled in hunting Gn 25_{27}, *yōdeʿê hayyām* 1K 9_{27}; b) w. inf., understand how to do s.thg 1S 16_{18}, w. *le* & inf. Je 4_{22}; c) w. impf. Jb 32_{22}, w. *we* & impf. Jb 23_{3}, w. pt. 1S 16_{16}; — 9. **know, come to understand** Is 40_{21}; w. acc. of thing 1S 20_{39}, w. *kî* Gn 12_{11}, w. *ʾet-ʾašer* Dt 29_{15}; w. inf. know how to ... Is 7_{15}; *yādaʿ ... bên ... le* be able to distinguish between ... 2S 19_{36}; *mî yōdēaʿ* who knows = perhaps 2S 12_{22}, w. *ha* ... *ʾô* = no one knows whether ... or Ec 2_{19}; — 10. **know, have insight, judgment**: *lōʾ yādaʿ* be w/o judgment Is 1_{3}.

nif.: pf. נוֹדַע, נוֹדְעָה, נוֹדַעְנוּ; impf. יִוָּדַע, יִוָּדֵעַ, תִּוָּדְעִי, וְאִוָּדַע; inf. הִוָּדְעִי; pt. נוֹדָע: **make onesf. known, reveal onesf.** Ex 6_{3}; — 2. **let onesf. be seen** Ru 3_{3}; — 3. **be noticed, observed, known** Gn 41_{31}; **be detected** Pr 10_{9}; — 4. **be(come) known** (subj. a fact &c.) 1K 18_{36} & oft.; — 5. **know onesf., gain insight** Je 31_{19}.

piel: pf. יִדַּעְתָּה (rd. Qr תָּ־): **cause** s.thg **to know** ... Jb 38_{12}. †

pual: pt. מְיֻדָּע Ru 2_{1} Kt (Qr מוֹדָע), מְיֻדַּעַת, מְיֻדָּעָיו, מְיֻדָּעַי, מְיֻדָּעֵי, מְיֻדָּעִי Is 12_{5} Kt (Qr hof.): — 1. **acquaintance, confidant** 2K 10_{11}; — 2. f. (= neuter) **s.thg known** Is 12_{5}.

[**polel**: pf. יוֹדַעְתִּי 1S 21_{3} txt.? prp. נוֹדַעְתִּי.] †

hif. (ca. 70×): pf. הוֹדַעְתָּ, הוֹדִיעַ, הוֹדַעְתָּם, הוֹדִיעַנִי, הוֹדַעְתֶּם, הוֹדַעְתָּ, הוֹדַעְתַּנִי; impf. יוֹדִיעַ, וְיֹדַע, אוֹדִיעַ, יֹדִעוּ, אוֹדִיעֲךָ, יֹדִיעֵם, תּוֹדִיעֵנִי, יוֹדְעֶנּוּ, נוֹדִיעָה; impv. הוֹדַע, הוֹדִיעוּ, הֹ(וֹ)דִיעֵנִי, הוֹדִעֵנִי; inf. הֹ(וֹ)דִיעַ, לְהוֹדִיעֵנִי; pt. מוֹדִיעֲךָ, מוֹדִיעָם, מוֹדִ(י)עִ(י)ם: — 1. w. 2 acc. **let** s.one **know** s.thg, **make known** s.thg to s.one Gn 41_{39}; — 2. w. acc. of thing: **inform, announce, make known** 1S 10_{8}; — 3. a) w. acc. **apprise** s.one of s.thg, **inform** s.one: *kî* that Dt 8_{3}, *lēʾmōr* Jos 4_{22}, *mâ* 1K 1_{27}; b) w. *le*/*ʾel* make an announcement to s.one Is 38_{19}; — 4. w. *le* & inf.: a) **teach** (s.one to do s.thg) Ps 90_{12}; *hôdîaʿ bên ... le* teach to distinguish between ... Ez 22_{26}; b) **give the signal to** 2C 23_{13}.

hof.: pf. הוֹדַע; pt. מוּדַעַת Is 12_{5} Qr: — 1. **be made known, set forth** Is 12_{5}; — 2. **be brought to s.one's awareness, consciousness** Lv $4_{23 \cdot 28}$. †

hitp.: impf. אֶתְוַדַּע; inf. הִתְוַדַּע: **make onesf. known** Gn 45_{1} Nu 12_{6}. †

יָדָע: n. pers.

יְדַעְיָה: n. pers.

יִדְּעֹנִי: pl. יִדְּעֹנִים: — 1. **spirit of the dead** Lv 20_{27}; — 2. one who possesses such a spirit, **soothsayer** 2K 21_{6}.

יָהּ & **יָה**: alternate form of יהוה Ps 68_{19} & oft.

***יְהָב**: sf. יְהָבְךָ: **burden** Ps 55_{23}. †

יהד: **hitp.**: pt. מִתְיַהֲדִים: **pretend to be a Jew** Est 8_{17}. †

יְהֻד Jos 19_{45}: ↗ יְהוּד.

יָהְדַּי n. pers.

יֵהוּא: n. pers.

יְהוּא Ec 11_3: ↗ II הוה.

יְהוֹאָחָז: n. pers.

יְהוֹאָשׁ: n. pers.

יְהוּד, וִיהֻד Jos 19_{45}: n. loc.

יְהוּדָה (820×): **Judah**: n. terr., n. pers.

I יְהוּדִי: gent. of יְהוּדָה: — 1. adj. **belonging to Judah, Jewish** Je 43_9; — 2. noun **Judahite, Judean, Jew** 2K 16_6.

II יְהוּדִי: n. pers. Je $36_{14\cdot21\cdot23}$. †

יְהוּדִית: n. pers. f. Gn 26_{34}.

יהוה: the name of God, first in Gn 2_4; Qr אֲדֹנָי, hence printed texts יְהוָה; for pronunciation (almost certainly *yahweh*), etymology, occurrence &c. see comm. & theologies; w. prep. בַּיהוה, כַּ׳, לַ׳; וַיהוה.

יְהוֹזָבָד: n. pers.

יְהוֹחָנָן: n. pers.

יְהוֹיָדָע: n. pers.

יְהוֹיָכִ(י)ן: n. pers.

יְהוֹיָקִים: n. pers.

יְהוֹיָרִיב: n. pers.

יְהוּכַל: n. pers.

יְהוֹנָדָב: n. pers.

יְהוֹנָתָן: n. pers.

יְהוֹסֵף: n. pers.

יְהוֹעַדָּה: n. pers.

יְהוֹעַדָּן; 2K 14_2 Qr ־עַדָּן, Kt ־עָדִין or ־עַדִּין: n. pers. f.

יְהוֹצָדָק: n. pers.

יְהוֹרָם: n. pers.

יְהוֹשֶׁבַע: n. pers. f.

יְהוֹשַׁבְעַת: n. pers. f. = יְהוֹשֶׁבַע.

יְהוֹשׁוּעַ Dt 3_{21} Ju 2_7, elsewh. יְהוֹשֻׁעַ: n. pers.

I יְהוֹשָׁפָט: n. pers.

II יְהוֹשָׁפָט: n. terr. Jl $4_{2\cdot12}$. †

יָהִיר: **arrogant, proud** Hb 2_{15} Pr 21_{24}. †

יַהֵל: Is 13_{20}; < יַאֲהֵל, ↗ I אהל. †

יְהַלֶּלְאֵל: n. pers.

יַהֲלֹם & יָהֲלֹם: a precious stone, mng. uncert. Ex 28_{18} 39_{11} Ez 28_{13}. †

יַהַץ: n. loc.

יוֹאָב, 1× יֹאָב: n. pers.

יוֹאָח: n. pers.

יוֹאָחָז: n. pers.

יוֹאֵל: n. pers.

יוֹאָשׁ, יֹאָשׁ 2C 24_1: n. pers.

יוֹב: n. pers. Gn 46_{13} rd I יָשׁוּב. †

I יוֹבָב: n. peop. Gn 10_{29} 1C 1_{23}. †

II יוֹבָב: n. pers.

יוֹבֵל & יֹבֵל: pl. יוֹבְלִים: — 1. **ram**: *qeren yôbēl* ram's horn (as wind instrument) Jos 6_5, so *šôfᵉrôt hayyôbᵉlîm* 6_4; — 2. *šᵉnat hayyōbēl* **year of release, jubilee year**, inaugurated by blowing the ram's horn Lv 25_{13}; *hayyōbēl* alone Lv 25_{15}; *yōbēl* alone Lv $25_{10\text{-}12}$.

I יוּבַל: **watercourse, canal** Je 17_8. †

II יוּבַל: n. pers. Gn 4_{21}. †

יוֹזָבָד: n. pers.

יוֹזָכָר: n. pers.

יוֹחָא & יֹחָא: n. pers.

יוֹחָנָן: n. pers. < יְהוֹחָנָן.

יוּטָּה Jos 15_{55} & יֻטָּה Jos 21_{16}: n. loc.

יוֹיָדָע: n. pers. < יְהוֹיָדָע.

יוֹיָכִין: n. pers. < יְהוֹיָכִין.

יוֹיָקִים: n. pers. < יְהוֹיָקִים.

יוֹיָרִיב: n. pers. < יְהוֹיָרִיב.

יוֹכֶבֶד: n. pers. f.

יוּכַל: n. pers. = ↗ יְהוּכַל.

I יוֹם (2225×): cs. =, sf. יוֹמְךָ, יוֹמָם; du. יוֹמַיִם, יוֹמָיִם; pl. יָמִים, cs. יְמֵי, בִּימֵי, וִ׳, כִּ׳, מִ׳; sf. יָמָיו (יָמָו Je 17_{11}: Qr יָמָיו, Kt יָמוֹ); pl. Dn 12_{13} יָמִין; pl. cs. יְמוֹת Dt 32_7 Ps 90_{15}; loc. יָמִימָה; m.: — 1. **day** (daylight hours, :: night) Gn 8_{22}; *rûªḥ hayyôm* (late afternoon breeze) Gn 3_8; — 2. **day of 24 hours**: Gn 1_5; *yôm tāmîm* a full day Jos 10_{13}; *yôm yôm* day by day, every day Gn 39_{10}; var.: *yôm wāyôm* Est 3_4 &c.; *kᵉyôm bᵉyôm* as (he did) every day 1S 18_{10}; *lišlōšet yāmîm* on the 3rd day Am 4_{4}; *d^ebar yôm b^eyômô* what is necessary for each day Ex 5_{13}; *kol-hayyôm* the whole day Is 62_{6}, every day Ps 140_{3}; — 3. special days: *yôm haššeleg* 2S 23_{20}; *yôm ṭôb* holiday Est 8_{17}, *yôm rā'â* fatal day La 1_{21} &c.; — 4. day of Y. (eschatological) Am 5_{18}; *bayyôm hahû'* prophetic introductory formula Am 2_{16}, ↗ 5d.; — 5. pl.: a) in genl. *šib'at yāmîm* 7 days Gn 8_{10}; b) acc. of time: *yāmîm* some time Gn 40_{4}, *šib'at yāmîm* for 7 days Ex 13_{6}, *šib'at hayyāmîm* these 7 days Ex 13_{7}; *kol-hayyāmîm* for ever Dt 4_{40}, w. *lō'* never 1S 2_{32}; c) *miyyāmîm* after a time Ju 11_{4}; d) eschatological *hinnēh yāmîm bā'îm* 2K 20_{17}; — 6. pl. w. more spec. mng.: a) w. gen., *y^emê 'ôlām* Am 9_{11}; b) w. vb.: *y^emê h^eyôt* (all) the time that he was ... 1S 22_{4}; c) **lifetime**: *y^emê š^enê ḥayyêka* Gn 47_{8}, *miyyāmêkā* as long as you live 1S 25_{28}; time of government *y^emê dawîd* 2S 21_{1}; d) *layyāmîm* spec. (end-)time Dn 10_{14}; — 7. pl.: extent of time: **a year**: a) *zebaḥ hayyāmîm* yearly offering 1S 1_{21} 2_{19} 20_{6}; season of 4 months 1S 27_{7}, presumably also 1K 17_{15}, cf. Gn 24_{55} 40_{4}; b) *miyyāmîm yāmîmâ* from year to year, yearly 1S 1_{3} 2_{19}; c) *yāmîm* as appos. after expr. of time: *miqqēs š^enātayim yāmîm* after 2 full years Gn 41_{1}; *ḥōdeš yāmîm* Gn 29_{14}, *y^eraḥ yāmîm* 2K 15_{13} a (full) month; — 8. du. *yôm 'ô yômayim* Ex 21_{21} &c.; — 9. *hayyôm*: a) on the specific day 1S 1_{4}; one day 2K 4_{8}; b) this day, **today** Gn 4_{14}; *hayyôm hazzeh* (just) today 2S 18_{20}; — 10. w. prep.: a) *b^eyôm*: α) w. noun clause: (in the day) when ... Ps 102_{3}, when (he spoke) Ex 6_{28}; β) w. inf.: *b^eyôm 'a^śôt* on the day when (Y.) made Gn 2_{4}; w. inf. nif. *b^eyôm hibbār^e'ām* Gn 5_{2}; γ) *b^eyôm haṭṭāmē'/haṭṭāhôr* when s.thg is (un)clean Lv 14_{57}; b) *bayyôm*: α) during the day Gn 31_{40}; β) at once Pr 12_{16}; γ) *bayyôm hahû'* then Gn 15_{18}; δ) at the same time Ezr 8_{34}; ε) *bayyôm hazzeh* this day Gn 7_{11}, *b^e'eṣem hayyôm hazzeh* (just) today 1S 11_{13}; ζ) *bayyôm hahû'* eschatological Am 9_{11} ↗ 4. above; c) w. *k^e*: α) *k^eyôm b^eyôm* ↗ 2. above; β) *kayyôm* today, now Is 58_{4}; first Gn 25_{31}; *kayyôm hazzeh* today, now Gn 50_{20}; *kayyôm hahû'*, w. *lō'* was not a day like it Jos 10_{14}; *k^ehayyôm* just now 1S 9_{13}; d) *l^eyôm* w. gen.: on the day of Is 10_{3}; e) *miyyôm* from the day when, since: α) w. inf. Ex 10_{6}; β) w. finite vb.: *miyyôm dibbartî* since I ... Je 36_{2}; γ) *l^emîmê* 2K 19_{25} since; f) w. *'ad*: *'ad-hayyôm* Gn 19_{37f}, *'ad-hayyôm hazzeh* Gn 26_{33} until today; *'ad 'eṣem hayyôm hazzeh* until this very day Lv 23_{14}.

II יוֹם: — 1. **wind, storm** SS 2_{17}, ? Zp 2_{2} (↗ comm.); — 2. **breath**, *q^ešeh hayyôm* Jb 30_{25}. †

יוֹמָם (50×): — **during the day, by day** Ex 13_{21}.

יָוָן: pl. יְוָנִים: **Javan**: (= **Ionia[ns]**) — 1. n. pers. Gn 10_{2}; — 2. n. peop. Is 66_{19}.

יָוֵן: cs. יְוַן: **mud** Ps 40_{3} 69_{3}. †

יוֹנָדָב: n. pers. < יְהוֹנָדָב.

I יוֹנָה: cs. יוֹנַת, sf. יוֹנָתִי; pl. יוֹנִים, cs. יוֹנֵי: — 1. **dove**, *Columba* Gn 8_{8-12}; cooing, symbol of the moaning of those who suffer Is 38_{14}; item of booty, plated w. precious metal Ps 68_{14}; — 2. term of endearment for beloved SS 2_{14}; — 3. ? in Ps.-superscription 56_{1}.

II יוֹנָה: n. pers. **Jonah** 2K 14_{25} Jon 1-4. †

III יוֹנָה: *ḥereb hayyônâ* Je 46_{16} 50_{16}, ↗ ינה.

*יְוָנִי: gent. of יָוָן: pl. יְוָנִים: **Greek** Jl 4_{6}.

יוֹנֵק & יֹנֵק (4×): pl. יוֹנְקִים, cs. יוֹנְקֵי: — 1. (nursing) **infant, child** 1S 15_{3}; spec. *yôn^eqê šādayim* nursing infants Jl 2_{16}; — 2. **shoot, stripling** Is 53_{2}.

*יוֹנֶקֶת: f. of יוֹנֵק: sf. י(וֹ)נַקְתּוֹ; pl. sf. י(וֹ)נְקוֹתֶיהָ: **shoot, stripling** Ez 17_{22}.

יוֹנָתָן: n. pers. < יְהוֹנָתָן.

יוֹסֵף: **Joseph**: — 1. n. pers. Gn 30_{24}; — 2. n.

peop. & tribe Gn 49_{22-26}, = N.ern kingdom Am 6_6.

יוֹסִפְיָה: n. pers.

יוֹעֵאלָה: n. pers.

יוֹעֵד: n. pers.

יוֹעֶזֶר: n. pers.

יוֹעֵץ & f. *יוֹעֶצֶת, sf. יוֹעַצְתּוֹ: pt. יעץ: **counsellor** 2S 15_{12}; f. 2C 22_3.

יוֹעָשׁ: n. pers.

יוֹצֵאת: pt. f. יצא: departure > **miscarriage** (of cattle) Ps 144_{14}. †

יוֹצָדָק: n. pers. < יְהוֹצָדָק.

יוֹצֵר, 1× יֹצֵר: pt. יצר: pl. יוֹצְרִים, cs. יֹצְרֵי Is 44_9: — 1. **potter** Is 41_{25}; *ḥōmer hayyôṣᵉrîm* potter's clay Is 29_{16}; — 2. **founder** (of metal-casting) *hišlîk ʾel-hayyôṣēr* remit to the office for deposits (= treasury) of the temple Zc 11_{13}.

יוֹקִים: n. pers.

יוֹרֶא Pr 11_{25}: ⸗ II ירה hof. **be given to drink to one's fill.** †

I *יוֹרֶה: pl. יֹ(וֹ)רִים: **archer** 1C 10_{3b} 2C 35_{23}. †

II **יוֹרֶה**: **early rain** (end Oct.-beginning Dec.) Dt 11_{14} Je 5_{24}. †

יוֹרָה: n. pers.

יוֹרַי: n. pers.

יוֹרָם, 1× יֹרָם: n. pers. < יְהוֹרָם.

יוּשַׁב חֶסֶד: n. pers.

יוֹשִׁבְיָה: n. pers.

יוֹשָׁה: n. pers.

יוֹשַׁוְיָה: n. pers.

יוֹשָׁפָט: n. pers. < יְהוֹשָׁפָט

יוֹתָם: n. pers.

יוֹתֵר & יֹתֵר: pt. יתר: — 1. **what remains, is left over** 1S 15_{15}; — 2. what is too much, in excess > adv. **so very, extremely** Ec 2_{15}; — 3. w. prep.: a) *yôtēr lᵉ* **preference, advantage**: *mah yôtēr leḥākām* how does the wise man excel Ec 6_8; b) *yôtēr min*, more than Est 6_6; c) w. *še*, not to mention that Ec 12_9.

יוֹתֶרֶת: ⸗ יֹתֶרֶת.

יְזִוֹאֵל 1C 12_3 Kt: ⸗ יְזִיאֵל.

יְזִיאֵל 1C 12_3 Qr, Kt יְזוּאֵם: n. pers.

יְזִיָּה: n. pers.

יָזִיז: n. pers.

יִזְלִיאָה: n. pers.

יזן: Je 5_8 Qr מְיֻזָּנִים **pual**, Kt מוּזָנִים **hof.**: **be lustful, on rut.** †

יְזַנְיָה: n. pers.

יְזַנְיָהוּ: n. pers.

***יֶזַע**: יֶזַע: **sweat**; Ez 44_{18} garment causing sweat. †

יִזְרָח (w. art.) 1C 27_8, rd. הַזַּרְחִי. †

יִזְרַחְיָה: n. pers.

I **יִזְרְעֶאל**: n. pers. Hos 1_4 2_{24}, 1C 4_3. †

II **יִזְרְעֶאל**: n. loc., = I.

יִזְרְעֵאלִי: gent. of II יִזְרְעֶאל.

יֹחָא: ⸗ יוֹחָא.

יְחֻבָּה 1C 7_{34}: Kt (& 1 ms. Qr) יַחְבָּה, rd Qr וְחֻבָּה. †

יחד: **qal**: impf. תֵּחַד: **join** (onesf. w.), w. *bᵉ* Gn 49_6, w. *ʾēt* Is 14_{20}. †

piel: impv. יַחֵד: **determine exclusively, concentrate** Ps 86_{11}. †

יַחַד: יָחַד; Je 48_7 יַחְדָּ = Kt יַחַד, Qr יַחְדָּו: — 1. **noun**: union, association, **community** 1C 12_{18}; totality Dt 33_5 (oth. = **2**); — **2.** > adv.: a) placed first: **with each other, all together** Mi 2_{12}; b) placed last: *šᵉnayim yaḥad* 2 together 1S 11_{11}; **all together** Is 27_4; (fight) **with each other** 1S 17_{10}; w. other vbs., e.g. *neʾᵉsaf* (gather) together 2S 10_{15} &c.; **at the same time** Is 42_{14}; **completely** Ps 33_{15}.

יַחְדָּו (90×), יַחְדָּיו Je $46_{12.21}$; invariable for gender & number; adv. = *yaḥad* 2: — 1. placed first: **together, with each other** Is 11_7; **all together** 1S 30_{24}; **equally** Ex 26_{24}; — 2. placed last: **together** Gn 13_6 22_6; **all together** Ps 19_{10}; at the same time Is 40_5.

יַחְדּוֹ: n. pers.

יַחְדִּיאֵל: n. pers.

יֶחְדְּיָהוּ: n. pers.

יְחוּאֵל: Qr ↗ יְחִיאֵל, Kt יחואל ?: n. pers.
יַחֲזִיאֵל: n. pers.
יַחְזְיָה: n. pers.
יְחֶזְקֵאל: n. pers. **Ezekiel.**
יְחִזְקִיָּה: n. pers. **Hezekiah.**
יְחִזְקִיָּהוּ: n. pers. **Hezekiah.**
יַחְזֵרָה: n. pers.
יְחִיאֵל: n. pers.
יָחִיד: f. יְחִידָה, sf. יְחִידָתִי; pl. יְחִידִים: — 1. **only**; one's only son Gn 22_{2}, *'ēbel (hay)yāḥîd* mourning for an only (son) Je 6_{26}; f. only daughter Ju 11_{34}; — 2. **lonely, abandoned** Ps 25_{16}; *y^e^ḥîdātî* my soul (suffering & complaining) Ps 22_{21}.
יְחִיָּה: n. pers.
יָחִיל La 3_{26}: rd יחיל (יחל hif.). †
יחל: [**nif.**: pf. נוֹחֲלָה Ez 19_{5} rd נוֹאֲלָה (יאל nif.); impf. וַיִּיָּחֶל Gn 8_{12} rd וַיְיַחֵל.]
piel: pf. יִחַלְנוּ, יִחֵלוּ, יִחֲלוּ, יִחַלְתִּי, יִחַלְתָּנִי; impf. יְיַחֵל, אֲיַחֵלָה, יְיַחֲלוּ, יְיַחֵלוּן; impv. יַחֵל; pt. מְיַחֲלִים: — 1. **wait**: a) abs. Gn $8_{10 \cdot 12}$ (rd. וַיְיַחֵל), endure Jb 6_{11}; b) w. *l^e^* wait for 1S 13_{8} Kt, Is 42_{4}; w. *'el* Is 51_{5}; — 2. **make** s.one **hope** Ps 119_{49}.
hif.: pf. הוֹחַלְתִּי, הוֹחָלְתִּי; impf. תּוֹחֵל, אוֹחִיל, אוֹחִילָה; impv. הוֹחִילִי: stand waiting, **wait** 1S 10_{8}; w. *l^e^* stand waiting before 2K 6_{33}.
יַחְלְאֵל: n. pers.
יחם: **qal**: impf. וַיֵּחֱמוּ, וַתֵּחַמְנָה: **be on rut, in heat** Gn 30_{38f}. †
piel: pf. יֶחֱמַתְנִי; inf. יַחֵם, sf. 3 pl. f. יַחְמֵנָּה Gn 30_{41b}: — 1. **be on rut, in heat** Gn 30_{41a} 31_{10}; w. acc. **conceive in (sexual) ardor** Ps 51_{7}; — 2. **make** (flocks) **be on rut, in heat** Gn 30_{41b}. †
יַחְמוּר: **roebuck** Dt 14_{5} 1K 5_{3}. †
יַחְמַי: n. pers.
יָחֵף: **barefoot** 2S 15_{30} Is 20_{2-4}, *miyyāḥēf* so that he does not become barefoot Je 2_{25}. †
יַחְצְאֵל: n. pers.
יַחְצִיאֵל: n. pers.

[**יחר**: ? וַיִּיַחֵר 2S 20_{5} Kt; ↗ אחר hif.)
יחשׂ: **hitp.**: pf. הִתְיַחֲשׂוּ; inf. הִתְיַחֵשׂ, הִתְיַחֲשָׂם; pt. מִתְיַחְשִׂים: **have onesf. registered in a genealogical table** by the establishment of one's descent Ezr 2_{62}; inf. *hityaḥēś* > noun **registration, pedigree** Ezr 8_{1}.
יַחַשׂ: **pedigree**, (genealogical) **register**: *sēfer hayyaḥaś* Ne 7_{5}. †
יַחַת: n. pers.
יַחַת: — 1. ↗ חתת nif.; — 2. ↗ נחת qal.
יטב: **qal**: impf. (also represents the vb. טוב) יִ(י)טַב, תֵּיטְבִי Na 3_{8}; וַיִּיטְבוּ: — 1. *yîṭab lô/lāh* it **is going well** w. him/her Gn 12_{13}; *yîṭab min* he is (fares) better than Na 3_{8}; — 2. a) *yîṭab b^e^'ênê* (word, plan) **suits, pleases** s.one Gn 34_{18}; w. *min*, pleases s.one more than Ps 69_{32}; b) *yîṭab lifnê* it is **acceptable, popular** Ne 2_{5}; — 3. *yîṭab lēb* is (becomes) **happy** 1K 21_{7}.
hif.: pf. הֵיטִיב, הֵיטַבְתָּ, הֵיטַבֹתִי, וְהֵיטִבֹתִי, הֵיטִיבוּ, הֵיטַבְנוּ, וְהֵיטִבְךָ; impf. יֵיטִיב (יֵיטִיב Jb 24_{21} is mistake), יֵיטֵב, וַיֵּיטֶב, תֵּיטִיבִי, וַיֵּטִיבוּ, הֵיטִיבִי; impv. הֵיטִיבָה, הֵי(י)טִיב; inf. הֵי(י)טִיב, הֵיטֵ(י)ב, לְהֵיטִיבִי, הֵיטִבְךָ; pt. מֵ(י)טִ(י)ב, מֵיטִ(י)בֵי, מֵיטִבִים: — 1. *hêṭîb l^e^* **treat kindly, graciously** Gn 12_{16}; — 2. w. acc. **do good to** s.one 1S 23_{2}; w. *'im* **make things go well for** Gn $32_{10 \cdot 13}$; — 3. **make** s.thg **good**: a) words Dt 5_{28} 8_{17} = speak well; b) put in order: dress (lamps) Ex 30_{7}, adorn (one's head) 2K 9_{30}; c) w. *maṣṣēbôt* erect handsome pillars Ho 10_{1}, w. *leket* walk in stately fashion Pr 30_{29}, w. *ḥesed* & *min* do a finer act of kindness than Ru 3_{10}, &c.; w. *šēm* & *min* make s.one more glorious 1K 1_{47}; d) w. inf. or fin. vb. = adv.: w. *naggēn* play beautifully Is 23_{16}, *l^e^naggēn* 1S 16_{17}; *lir'ôt* see rightly Je 1_{12}; — 4. **behave well** Gn 4_{7}; — 5. adv. *hêṭēb* **well, thoroughly** 2K 11_{18}.
יָטְבָה: n. loc.
יָטְבָתָה: n. loc.
יֻטָּה: n. loc. ↗ יוּטָּה.

יְטוּר: n. pers.

יַיִן (ca. 140×): יַיִן, cs. יֵין, sf. יֵינוֹ, יֵינְךָ: **wine**; occurs in all expected contexts: bread & wine Gn 14_{18}, wine of Lebanon Ho 14_{8}; = drunkenness Gn 9_{24}; in cult 1S 10_{3}; *ḥōmeṣ yayin* wine vinegar Nu 6_{3}.

יַךְ: 1. ↗ נכה hif.; — 2. 1S 4_{13} rd w. Qr יַד. †

יְכָנְיָה Je 27_{20}, Qr יְכָנְ׳, Kt ?; n. pers. = יְהוֹיָכִין. †

יכח: nif.: impf. נִוָּכְחָה; pt. נוֹכָח, נֹכַחַת: — 1. **argue out together** (in legal dispute) Is 1_{18}, w. *ʿim* with Jb 23_{7}; — 2. **turn out to be in the right, be vindicated** Gn 20_{16}. †

hif.: pf. הוֹכַחְתִּיו, הוֹכַחְתָּ, הֹ(וֹ)כִ(י)חַ; impf. יוֹכִחֵנוּ, אוֹכִיחַ, וַיּוֹכַח, יוֹכַח, יוֹכִיחַ, תּוֹכִחֵךְ, אוֹכִחֲךָ, אוֹכִיחֲךָ, יוֹכִחֶךָ, יוֹכִחֵנִי; impv. הוֹכַח; inf. הוֹכֵחַ & הוֹכִיחַ & הוֹכַח; pt. מוֹכִיחַ, מוֹכִיחִים: — 1. **set s.one right, reprove**: a) abs. Jb 32_{12}; b) w. acc. Is 11_{3}; w. *le* Is 11_{4}; c) w. *ʿal* (+ person) **reproach** s.one for s.thg Jb 19_{5}, w. *ʾel* go to law with Jb 13_{3}; w. *be* **requite** s.thg 2K 19_{4}; — 2. **give judgment** Gn 31_{42}, w. *bên* 31_{37}; **settle quarrels** Is 2_{4}; w. *le* & *ʿim* against Jb 16_{21}; ***môkîaḥ*** **arbitrator** Is 29_{21}, preacher of punishment Ez 3_{26}, admonisher Pr 25_{12}; — 3. **determine, assign** Gn $24_{14\cdot44}$.

hof.: pf. הוּכַח: **be admonished** Jb 33_{19}. †

hitp.: impf. יִתְוַכָּח: **argue out together** w. *ʿim* Mi 6_{2}. †

יְכִילְיָה 2C 26_{3}: n. pers. f. rd w. ↗ Qr יְכָלְיָה.

יָכִין: n. pers.

יָכִינִי: gent. of יָכִין.

יכל (ca. 200×): **qal**: pf. יָכֹ(וֹ)ל, יָכֹלָה, יְכָלְתִּיו, יָכֹלוּ, יָכֹלְתִּי, וְיָכֹלְתָּ; impf. אוּכַל, אוּכַל, וַתּוּכַל, תּוּכַל, יוּכַל, יוּכַל, נוּכְלָה, נוּכַל, תּוּכְלוּ, יוּכְלוּ, יוּכְלוּן, יָכְלוּ; inf. יְכֹלֶת, abs. יָכוֹל: — 1. **hold on to, endure**: a) s.thg Is 1_{13}, s.one Ps 101_{5}; b) **be capable of**, w. acc. Ho 8_{5}; — 2. **be able to, have power to**: a) w. fin. vb. ***ʾûkal nakkeh*** Nu 22_{6}, ***ʾûkal werāʾîtî*** (how) am I capable of seeing Est 8_{6}; b) w. inf.: α) w/o *le*: ***ʾûkal dabbēr*** able to speak Gn 24_{50}; β) w. *le* & inf. ***ʾûkal lāqûm*** Gn 31_{35}; esp. w. neg. Nu 9_{6}; γ) w. inf. first: *hašqēṭ lōʾ yûkal* Is 57_{20}; δ) abs. **can, dare** Gn 29_{8}; ε) ***lōʾ tûkal leʾekōl*** **you** may not, dare not eat Dt 12_{17}; ***lōʾ yākelû dabberô*** could not bear to speak to him Gn 37_{4}; — 3. **be superior, be victorious, win**: a) abs. Gn 30_{8}; w. *lōʾ* achieve nothing Is 16_{12}; b) w. acc. **conquer** Ps 13_{5}; c) w. *le* Gn 32_{26}; d) **grasp, understand** w. *le* Ps 139_{6}.

יְכָלְיָהוּ: n. pers. f.

יְכָנְיָהוּ Je 24_{1}, יְכָנְיָה otherw.: n. pers.

ילד (ca. 600×): **qal**: pf. יָלְדָה, יָלָדָה, יָ׳, יָלַדְתְּ, יָלָדוּ, יָלְדוּ, יְלִדְתִּי, 2 sg. f. יְלִדְתִּנִי Je 15_{10}, 1 sg. יְלִדְתִּיךָ, יְלִדְתִּיךְ, יְלִדְתִּיךָ; impf. יֵלֵד, יֵלְדוּ, וָאֵלֵד, וַתֵּלֶד, תֵּלֵד, יֵלֵד Pr 27_{1}, לָלֶדֶת, תֵּלַדְןָ, תֵּלַדְנָה, יֵלְדוּן, וַיֵּלְדוּ; inf. לָלֶדֶת, לְלֵדָה, לָלַת 1S 4_{19}, לְדָתִּי, לְדָתְּנָה Jb 39_{2}, abs. יָלוֹד; pt. יֹלֵד, יֹלֶדֶת, וְיֹלַדְתְּ Gn 16_{11} Ju $13_{5\cdot7}$ (mixed form w. וְיָלַדְתְּ), יוֹלֵדָה, הַיֹּלְדוֹת, יוֹלַדְתְּכֶם, יוֹלַדְתֶּךָ, יוֹלַדְתּוֹ, pass. יָלוּד, cs. יְלוּד, הַיִּלּוֹדִים: — 1. (subj. woman) **bear** (children) Gn 3_{16}; (of animals) **bring forth** (young) Gn 30_{39}; lay (eggs) Je 17_{11}; *yālûd* new-born (baby) 1K 3_{26f}, pl. 1C 14_{4}; — 2. (subj. man) beget, procreate, **become the father of** Gn 4_{18}; — 3. metaph. *yālōd ʾāwen* Jb 15_{35}; Moses 'conceives' the people Nu 11_{12}; God the Rock that begets Isr. Dt 32_{18}; ***ma-yyēled yôm*** what a/the day brings forth Pr 27_{1}.

nif.: pf. נוֹלַד, נוֹלְדוּ; impf. אִוָּלֵד־, יִוָּלֵד, יִוָּלְדוּ, יִוָּלֵדוּ; inf. הִוָּלֵד, הִוָּלְדוֹ; pt. נוֹלָד, הַנּוֹלַד־לוֹ Gn 31_{3}, נוֹלָדִים: **be born** Gn 10_{1}; of animals Lv 22_{27}; ***wayyiwwālēd laḥanôk ʾet-(!)ʿîrād*** I. was born to E. Gn 4_{18}; ***yôm hiwwāledāh*** day of her birth Ho 2_{5}; metaph. of people Is 66_{8} who are to be born in the future.

piel: inf. יַלֶּדְכֶם; pt. מְיַלֶּדֶת, מְיַלְּדוֹת: **help at birth, serve as midwife** Ex 1_{16}; **pt. f. midwife** Ex $1_{15\cdot17\cdot21}$. †

pual (or pass. *qal?*): יוּלַּד, יֻלַּד, יוּלָּד, יֻלַּד, יֻלָּדָה, יֻלַּדְתִּי, יֻלְּדוּ, יֻלְּדוּ, יֻלַּדְתֶּם; pt. יֻלָּד, הַיּוּלָּד Ju 13_{8}: **be born** Gn 4_{26}; metaph. of mountains Ps 90_{2}.

hif.: pf. הוֹלִיד, הוֹלַדְתָּ, הוֹלִידוּ, הוֹלִידָה; impf. יוֹלִיד, וַיּוֹלֶד; impv. הוֹלִידוּ; inf. הוֹלִידוֹ, הוֹלֵד; pt. מוֹלִיד, מוֹלְדִים: — 1. beget, procreate, **become the father of** (☞ qal 2) Gn 5_{3}; w. *min*, by 1C 8_{9}; — 2. **make** (s.thg, s.one) **bring forth** Is $66_{9a.b}$; (rain, earth) Is 55_{10}; metaph. *'āwen* Is 59_{4}.

hof.: inf. הֻלֶּדֶת & הוּלֶּדֶת: **be born** (only w. *yôm*) Gn 40_{2} Ez 16_{4f}. †

hitp.: impf. וַיִּתְיַלְדוּ (not לְ): denom. **have onesf. entered in a family register** and so have one's descent acknowledged Nu 1_{18}. †

יֶלֶד: יֶלֶד; pl. יְלָדִים, cs. יַלְדֵי (4×) & יִלְדֵי (Is 57_{4}), sf. יְלָדָיו, יַלְדֵיהֶם: — 1. **boy**, male child: a) Gn 4_{23}; b) pl. boys, children Gn 30_{26}; = fetus (in a miscarriage) Ex 21_{22}; c) *yeled zequnîm* child of one's old age Gn 44_{20}; — 2. *haylādîm* 'the young men,' advising group (:: elders) 1K 12_{8}; — 3. young of animals: cow & bear Is 11_{7}, raven Jb 38_{41}, hinds, mountain goats 39_{3}.

יַלְדָּה: pl. יְלָדוֹת: — 1. **girl**, female child, pl. Zc 8_{5}; — 2. girl ready for marriage Gn 34_{4} Jl 4_{3}. †

יַלְדוּת sf. יַלְדוּתֶךָ, יַלְדֻתֶךָ: — 1. **childhood** Ec 11_{9f}; — 2. **young manhood** (?) Ps 110_{3}. †

ילה: **qal**: impf. וַתֵּלַהּ: **be anxious** Gn 47_{13}. †

יִלּוֹד: **born** Ex 1_{22}, w. *le* to s.one 2S 12_{14}, at a given place Jos 5_{5} 2S 5_{14} Je 16_{3}. †

יָלוֹן: n. pers.

***יָלִיד**: cs. יְלִיד; pl. cs. יְלִידֵי: — 1. **son**: of *'anaq* Nu 13_{22}, of *rāfâ* 2S $21_{16.18}$; — 2. **slave** born in the household Gn 14_{14} $17_{12f.23.27}$.

ילל: **hif.**: pf. הֵילִיל; impf. יְיֵלִיל, אֲיֵלִיל, אֵילִילָה, יְיֵלִילוּ, יְהֵילִילוּ Is 52_{5}, תְּיֵלִילוּ, תְּהֵילִילוּ; impv. הֵילֵל, הֵילִילִי, הֵילִ(י)לוּ: **howl, wail** Is 14_{31}.

יְלֵל: **howling, wailing-cry**, *yelēl yešîmôn* auditory hallucinations of the desert Dt 32_{10}. †

יְלָלָה: cs. יִלְלַת, sf. יִלְלָתָהּ: **howling, cry of wailing** Is 15_{8}.

יָלַע Pr 20_{25}: ☞ I לעע.

יַלֶּפֶת: skin disease w. scabs, prob. **ringworm** Lv 21_{20} 22_{22}. †

ילק: יֶלֶק: creeping, unwinged stage of **locust** Je $51_{14.27}$.

יַלְקוּט: **shepherd's pouch** (for sling-stones &c.) 1S 17_{40}. †

יָם (390×): cs. usu. יָם(־), but alw. יַם־סוּף Ex 13_{8} & oft.; loc. יָמָּה, sf. יַמָּהּ; pl. יַמִּים, m.: — **sea**, i.e. the great inland waters & larger rivers: — 1. genl.: sg. Gn 1_{26}; :: land Ex 20_{11}; — 2. pl. **sea** Dn 11_{45} = totality of waters (cf. Gn 1_{10}); pl. **seas** Dt 33_{19}; — 3. spec. seas: a) the Mediterranean & its portions: *yām haggādôl* Jos 1_{4}, *yām pelištîm* Ex 23_{31}, *hayyām hā'aḥarôn* Dt 11_{24}; b) the Dead Sea: *yām hammelaḥ* Gn 14_{3}, *yām ha'arābâ* 2K 14_{25}, *hayyām haqqadmônî* Ez 47_{18}; c) the Sea of Galilee: *yām kinneret* Nu 34_{11}, *yām kinrôt* Jos 12_{3}; d) *yam-sûf* Sea of Reeds, loc. *yāmmâ sûf* Ex 10_{19}, ☞ I *sûf*; e) *yām-miṣrayim* Is 11_{15} the Sea of Reeds (but oth.: the Medit. Sea, or the Nile); — 3. *miyyām 'ad yām* Am 8_{12}: geogr.: fm. the Dead Sea to the Medit. Sea, or fm. the Euphrates to the Medit., or mythological; — 4. *yām* oft. = Medit. Sea, thus *yām* = **west**: *yāmmâ* to the west Gn 13_{14}, *miyyām* from the west Gn 12_{8}, *pe'at yām* the west side Ex 27_{12}, *rûaḥ yām* west wind Ez 10_{19} > west side Ez 42_{19}; *miyyām le* westward fm. Jos 8_{9}; — 5. of large rivers: Nile Is 18_{1}, branches of N. Ez 32_{2}; Euphrates Je 51_{36}; — 6. cosmological: *qarqa' hayyām* Am 9_{3}; — 7. name of Ugaritic god of sea Ps 74_{13}; — 8. cultic, **the bronze 'sea'** 1K $7_{24f.44}$.

יְמוּאֵל: n. pers.

יְמִימָה: n. pers. f.

I **יָמִין** (ca. 140×): cs. יְמִין, בִּימִין, מִימִין, sf. יְמִינוֹ; f.: — 1. **right (side)**: *yad yemînô* his right hand Gn 48_{17}, *šôq hayyāmîn* right hind leg Ex 29_{22}, *ʿên yāmîn* right eye; > *yemînô* his right hand Gn 48_{13}; — 2. adv. *hayyāmîn* to the right Gn 13_9, = *ʿal-yāmîn* 24_{49}, *mîmîn* to the right of 48_{13}, *lîmînekā* on your right Ps 45_{10}; — 3. particularly valued: God swears by his right hand Is 62_8, thus *yāmîn* > **oath**, *yemîn šeqer* Ps $144_{8.11}$; honored person at right hand Ps 110_1, king's mother 1K 2_{19}; — 4. right side = **south**: *yāmîn* Jb 23_9 & *ʾel-hayyāmîn* to the south Jos 17_7; *ʾel-yemîn* 1S 23_{24}, *mîmîn* 23_{19}, *mîmîn le* 2K 23_{13} south from; *miyyamîn* on the south side 1K 7_{39}.

II **יָמִין**: n. pers.: son of Simeon Gn 46_{10} Ex 6_{15} Nu 26_{12} 1C 4_{24}; descendant of Jerahmeel 1C 2_{27}; Levite Ne 8_7. †

יְמִינִי Ez 4_6 & 2C 3_{17}: Qr הַיְמָנִי, Kt הַיְמִינִי: adj. **right**. †

יְמִינִי: as part of compound as gent. of בִּנְיָמִין: — 1. בֶּן־יְמִינִי 1S 9_{21} &c.; בֶּן־הַיְמִינִי 1K 2_8 &c., pl. בְּנֵי־יְמִינִי Ju 19_{16} 1S 22_7; — 2. אִישׁ־יְמִינִי 2S 20_1 Est 2_5; — 3. בֶּן־אִישׁ יְמִינִי 1S 9_1, אֶרֶץ־יְמִינִי 1S 9_4.

יִמְלָא 2C 18_{7f} & **יִמְלָה** 1K 22_{8f}: n. pers.

יַמְלֵךְ: n. pers.

יֵמִם: trad. **mules**; Vulgate hot springs; oth. vipers; Gn 36_{24}. †

ימן: **hif.**: impf. אֵימִינָה, תֵּאָמִינוּ; impv. הֵימִינוּ; inf. לְהֵמִין; pt. מַיְמִינִים 1C 12_2: — 1. **stay to the right, go to the right** Gn 13_9; *hēmîn min* to the the right from 2S 14_{19}; — 2. pt. **right-handed** 1C 12_2.

יִמְנָה: n. pers.

יְמָנִי: Kt Ez 4_6 & 2C 3_{17} יְמִינִי; f. יְמָנִית, adj.: — 1. **right** Ex 29_{20}; standing on the right (pillar) 1K 7_{21}; — 2. **southern** 1K 6_8 7_{39}.

יִמְנָע: n. pers.

ימר: **hif.**: pf. הֵימִיר: Je $2_{11a.b}$ **exchange**. †

hitp.: impf. תִּתְיַמָּרוּ Is 61_6: ↗ II אמר. †

יִמְרָה: n. pers.

ימשׁ: **hif.**: impv. הֲיְמִשֵׁנִי: Kt יְהֵימִשֵׁנִי, rd Qr וַהֲמִישֵׁנִי, ↗ I מושׁ. †

ינה: **qal**: pt. f. יוֹנָה־, pl. יוֹנִים: **be violent, oppress**: *ḥereb* Je 46_{16} 50_{16}, *ʿîr* Zp 3_1. †

hif.: pf. הוֹנָה, הוֹנוּ; impf. יוֹנֶה, תּ(וֹ)נוּ, תּוֹנוּ; inf. הוֹנֹתָם; pt. מוֹנַיִךְ: **oppress** Ex 22_{20}.

יָנוֹחַ: n. loc.; loc. יָנוֹחָה.

יָנוּם, Kt יָנִים: n. loc.

***יְנִיקָה**: pl. sf. יְנִיקוֹתָיו: **shoot** of a plant Ez 17_4. †

ינק: **qal**: pf. יָנָקְתְּ; impf. יִינַק, תִּינְקִי, אִינַק, יִינָקוּ, תִּינְקוּ; pt. ↗ יוֹנֵק & יוֹנֶקֶת: **suck** Is 60_{16}; metaph. **suck in** (obj. abundance of the seas) Dt 33_{19}.

hif.: pf. הֵינִיקָה, הֵינִיקוּ; impf. תֵּינִיק, וַתֵּינֶק, וַתְּנִיקֵהוּ, וַיֵּנִקֵהוּ Ex 2_9; impv. הֵינִקֵהוּ; inf. הֵינִיק; pt. ↗ מֵינֶקֶת, מֵינִקְתָּהּ, pl. מֵינִיקוֹת, sf. מֵינִיקֹתַיִךְ: — 1. **suckle, nurse** Gn 21_7 1K 3_{21}; of animals Gn 32_{16}; — 2. **make** s.one **suck** Dt 32_{13}.

יֹנֵק: ↗ יוֹנֵק.

יַנְשׁוּף & Is 34_{11} יַנְשׁוֹף: an unclean bird: some, **ibis**; oth., **eared owl**, *Asia otus*, or **bee-eater** *Merops apiaster* Lv 11_{17} Dt 14_{16} Is 34_{11}. †

I **יָסַד**: **qal**: pf. יְסַדְתּוֹ, יָסְדָה, יָסַדְתִּי, י׳; inf. לְיִסּוֹד, 2C 31_7 לִיסוֹד, וִיסוֹד, וִיסַדְתִּיךָ; pt. יֹסֵד, יֹסְדֵי: — 1. found firmly, **lay the foundations of**: a) *ʾereṣ* Is 48_{13}; b) lay the foundation-wall of the temple Is 54_{11}; c) lay the foundation stone Is 28_{16}; — 2. **destine, assign** Is 23_{13}.

nif.: impf. תִּוָּסֵד; inf. sf. הִוָּסְדָהּ: **be founded** Ex 9_{18} Is 44_{28}. †

piel: pf. יִסַּד, יִסְּדוּ; impf. יְיַסְּדֶנָּה; inf. יַסֵּד: — 1. **found, lay the foundation-wall of**: obj. house 1K 5_{31}, city 1K 16_{34}; — 2. **determine** Est 1_8; — 3. **appoint, install** s.one 1C 9_{22}.

pual: pf. יֻסַּד; pt. מְיֻסָּד, pl. מְיֻסָּדִים, f. cs.

מְיֻסָּדוֹת Ez 41_{8} Kt: be founded: i.e. **foundation** of s.thg **is laid** 1K 6_{37}; *מְיֻסָּדוֹת **foundation (-layer)** Ez 41_{8} Kt.

hof.: inf. הוּסַד; pt. מוּסָד: be founded: i.e. **foundation** of s.thg **is laid** Is 28_{16} Ezr 3_{11}. †

II יסד: **nif.**: pf. נוֹסְדוּ; inf. הִוָּסְדָם: **associate, conspire (together)** Ps 2_{2} 31_{14}. †

יְסֻד Ezr 7_{9}: rd יְסַּד. †

יְסוֹד: sf. יְסֹדוֹ, pl. sf. יְסוֹדֶיהָ, יְסוֹדֹתֶיהָ: **foundation (-wall), base** Ex 29_{12} Ez 13_{14}; *bîsōdô* in its permanence Ezr 3_{12}; metaph. *yesôd ʿôlām* Pr 10_{25}.

יְסוֹד 2C 31_{7}: ↗ I יָסַד qal.

*יְסוּדָה: sf. יְסוּדָתוֹ: **foundation, establishment** Ps 87_{1}. †

יִסּוֹר: **faultfinder** (?) Jb 40_{2}; or rd יָסוּר (סור, ↗ comm.). †

יְסוּרַי Je 17_{13}: rd. וְסוּרֶיךָ (סור). †

יִסְכָּה: n. pers. f.

יִסְמַכְיָהוּ: n. pers.

יָסַף: **qal** (30×): pf. יָסַף, 'י, יָסְפוּ, יָסַפְנוּ; impv. סְפוּ; inf. (לְ)סְפוֹת; pt. יוֹסֵף 1S 27_{4} Kt (Qr pf.), יֹסְפִים: — 1. **add** 2K 19_{30}; w. *ʿal* to 1S 12_{19}; *yāsaf śimḥâ* had more joy, increased joy Is 29_{19}; — 2. **continue** (to do), (do) **more, again** (↗ hif. 3): a) w. inf. Gn 8_{12}; b) w. *le* & inf. Gn 38_{26}; *welōʾ yāsefû* but they did so no more Nu 11_{25}.

nif.: pf. נוֹסַף, נוֹסְפָה; pt. נוֹסָף, נוֹסָפוֹת: w. *ʿal* **be added** (to) Ex 1_{10}; *nôsāfôt* further (disaster) Is 15_{9}.

hif. (170×): pf. הוֹסִיף, ה(וֹ)סַפְתִּי; impf. וַתּוֹסֶף, תּ(וֹ)סִיף, וַיּ(וֹ)סֶף, יוֹסֵף, יֹ(וֹ)סִ(י)ף, תּוֹסֵף, תּוֹסְףְּ, תּוֹסֵף Pr 30_{6}, אֹ(וֹ)סִ(י)ף, תֹּ(וֹ)סִ(י)ף (juss.), אֹסְפָה, יֹ(וֹ)סִ(י)פוּן, אֹ(וֹ)סֵף (וַיֹּאסֶף 1S 18_{29} & תֹּאסִיפוּן Ex 5_{7} contaminated w. אסף); inf. ה(וֹ)סִיף; pt. מוֹסִיפִים: — 1. **add** Gn 30_{24}; w. *ʿal* to 2K 20_{6}, w. *ʾel* 2S 24_{3}; — 2. **enhance, increase** Is 1_{5}, *ʿal ʿōl* make it heavy 1K $12_{11 \cdot 14}$; — 3. (do) again, **go on** (doing) (↗ qal 2): a) w. fin. vb. *wayyôsef wayyiqqaḥ* and once more he took Gn 25_{1}; b) w. inf. continue to Gn 8_{10}; w. *le* & inf. *wattôsef lāledet*, again Gn 4_{2}; c) w. neg. (do s.thg) **no more, no longer**: w. inf. Ho 9_{15}, w. *le* & inf. Gn 4_{12}; abs. Ex 11_{6}; — 4. (do s.thg) still more, all the more: w. inf. Gn $37_{5 \cdot 8}$; — 5. oath-formula: *kōh yaʿaśeh-llî wekōh yôsîf* may God do this to me and more 1K 2_{23}.

I יסר: **qal**: pt. יֹסֵר: **teach** Ps 94_{10} Pr 9_{7}. †

nif.: impf. יִוָּסֵר, תִּוָּסְרוּ; impv. הִוָּסְרִי, הִוָּסְרוּ: **teach onesf., take advice, listen to reason** Je 6_{8}.

piel: pf. יִסַּר, יִסַּרְתִּי, יִסְּרוּ, יִסְּרוֹ, יִסְּרַנִי, יִסַּרְתַּנִי, יִסַּרְתּוּ, יִסְּרוּנִי; impf. יְיַסֵּר, אֲיַסֵּר, תְּיַסְּרֵנִי, תְּיַסְּרֵנוּ, תְּיַסְּרֶךָּ; impv. יַסֵּר, יַסְּרֵנִי; inf. יַסְּרָה Lv 26_{18}, יַסְּרוֹ, יַסֶּרְךָ; pt. מְיַסֶּרְךָ: — 1. **chastise, discipline, rebuke** 1K $12_{11 \cdot 14}$; — 2. **teach, train** Dt 4_{36}; — 3. **guide** (s.one in doing s.thg) Is 28_{26}.

[**hif.**: impf. אַיְסִרֵם Ho 7_{12}: cj אֲיַסְּרֵם, oth.: אֲסִירֵם (סיר hif.). †]

nitp.: pf. נִוַּסְּרוּ: **take warning** Ez 23_{48}. †

II יסר: **piel**: pf. יִסַּרְתִּי, יִסַּרְתָּ: **strengthen** Ho 7_{15} Jb 4_{3} (or I 3 ?). †

יָסֹר 1C 15_{22}: (trad. inf. abs.): noun, **inspector, instructor**. †

*יָע (or *יָעֶה ?): pl. יָעִים, sf. יָעָיו: (fire-) **shovel** (for cleaning the altar) 1K $7_{40 \cdot 45}$.

יַעְבֵּץ: — 1. n. loc. 1C 2_{55}; — 2. n. pers. 1C 4_{9f}. †

יעד: **qal**: pf. יְעָדָהּ, יְעָדוֹ; impf. יִיעָדֶנָּה: **designate**: — 1. assign a woman Ex 21_{8}; — 2. a) w. *môʿēd* arrange a meeting, appointment 2S 20_{5}; b) appoint s.one to a place Je 47_{7}. †

nif.: pf. נוֹעֲדוּ, נוֹעֲדוּ, נ(וֹ)עַדְתִּי; impf. וַיִּוָּעֲדוּ; pt. נוֹעָדִים: — 1. **appear, come**: w. *ʾel* Nu 10_{3f}, w. *ʿal* 1K 8_{5}; — 2. **gather** (onesf.) against (w. *ʿal*) Nu 14_{35}; — 3. **agree, have an appointment** Am 3_{3}; — 4.

(of God) **let** (onesf.) **appear, reveal onesf.**, w. l^e Ex 25_{22}.

hif.: impf. יוֹעִידֵנִי, יְעִדֵנִי: **summon** Je 49_{19} 50_{44} Jb 9_{19}. †

hof.: pt. מֻעָדוֹת: **ordered, directed** Ez 21_{21}. †

cj יַעְדָּה for יַעְרָה 1C 9_{42} (w. some mss. & Vers.): n. pers.

יֶעְדּוֹ Qr, Kt יעדי: n. pers. 2C 9_{29}. †

יָעָה: **qal**: pf. יָ׳: **sweep away** Is 28_{17}. †

יְעוּאֵל, oft Qr יְעִיאֵל: n. pers.

יְעוּץ: n. pers. (or tribe).

יָעוּר: n. pers. 1C 20_5 Kt, → Qr יָעִיר. †

יעוֹרִים Ez 34_{25}: → I יַעַר. †

יְעוּשׁ: Gn $36_{5.14}$ & 1C 7_{10} Qr, Kt יעישׁ: n. pers.

יעז: **nif.**: pt. נוֹעָז: **insolent** Is 33_{19}. †

יַעֲזִיאֵל: n. pers.

יַעֲזִיָּהוּ: n. pers.

יַעְזֵיר 1C 6_{66} 26_{31}, otherw. יַעְזֵר: n. loc.

*יעט: Is 61_{10}: → עטה. †

יְעִיאֵל: n. pers., Kt → יְעוּאֵל.

יָעִיר Qr, Kt יָעוּר: n. pers. 1C 20_5. †

יְעִישׁ: n. pers. 1C 7_{10} Kt; → יְעוּשׁ. †

יַעְכָּן: n. pers.

יעל: **hif.**: pf. הוֹעִיל; impf. יוֹעִיל, אוֹעִיל, יוֹעִילוּךְ, יוֹ(וֹ)עִ(י)לוּ; inf. הוֹעִיל, abs. הוֹעֵל; pt. מוֹעִיל: — 1. **help, be of use**: esp.: gods cannot ... 1S 12_{21}; — 2. **get profit, advantage** Je 12_{13}.

I יָעֵל: pl. יְעֵלִים, cs. יַעֲלֵי: **ibex**, *Capra nubiana*, or **mountain goat**, *Capra sinaitica* Ps 104_{18}; *ṣûrê hayy^{e}ʿēlîm* n. loc. 1S 24_3.

II יָעֵל: n. pers. f. Ju $4_{17f.21f}$ $5_{6.24}$. †

יַעְלָא Ne 7_{58} & יַעְלָה Ezr 2_{56}: n. pers.

I *יַעֲלָה: **female ibex** Pr 5_{19}. †

II *יַעֲלָה Ezr 2_{56}: n. pers.; → יַעְלָא. †

יַעְלָם: n. pers.

יַעַן (ca. 90×): — 1. prep. **because of**: a) w. noun Ez 5_9; b) w. inf. 2K 19_{28}; c) *yaʿan meh*, why? Hg 1_{9a}; — 2. conj. **because**: a) *yaʿan* w. pf. 1S 15_{13}; b) *yaʿan ʾašer* (ca. 30×): Gn 22_{16}; c) *yaʿan kî* (6×) Nu 11_{20}; d) *yaʿan (û)b^{e}yaʿan* therefore because: w. inf. Ez 36_3, w. pf. Ez 13_{10}.

*יָעֵן: La 4_3 כִּי עֵנִים, rd Qr כַּיְעֵנִים (Kt ?), ostrich, → יַעֲנָה. †

יַעֲנָה: sg. בַּת הַיַּעֲנָה Dt 14_{15}, pl. בְּנוֹת יַעֲנָה Is 13_{21} trad.: **ostrich**, *Struthio camelus*, but more prob. a kind of owl.

יַעְנַי: n. pers.

I יעף: **qal**: pf. יָעֵפוּ; impf. יִיעַף, וַיִּיעָף, יִיעֲפוּ, יִעָפוּ: **become tired** Is 40_{30f}.

II יעף: **hof.**: pt. מֻעָף Dn 9_{21}: Vrsns. & rabbis: in swift flight; trad. = I *yʿf*, deeply weary. †

יָעֵף: pl. יְעֵפִים: **fatigued, tired out** 2S 16_2.

*יְעָף: **flight** (trad.: fatigue) Dn 9_{21}, → comm. †

יעץ: **qal**: pf. יָ׳, יָעַץ, יָעֲצוּ, יְעָצָהּ, יְעָצַנִי, יְעָצָהוּ; impf. אִיעָצֵךְ, אִיעָצְךָ, אִיעָצָה; pt. יוֹ(וֹ)עֵץ, יֹעֲצֵךְ, f. sf. יוֹעַצְתּוֹ, pl. יוֹעֲצִים, cs. יֹעֲצֵי, sf. יֹעֲצַיִךְ, pass. יְעוּצָה: — 1. **advise, counsel**: a) w. acc. pers. Ex 18_{19}; b) cogn. acc. *ʿēṣâ* give advice 1K 1_{12}; c) dir. quotation 2S 17_{11}; d) pt. → *yôʿēṣ*; — 2. **plan, decide**: abs. Is 14_{24}; acc. of thing (oft. w. *ʿal* against): *ʿēṣâ* Is 14_{26}, *rāʿâ* Is 7_5.

nif.: pf. נוֹעָצוּ, נוֹעָץ; impf. וַיִּוָּעַץ, יִוָּעֲצוּ, נִוָּעֲצָה; pt. נוֹעָצִים: — 1. **(allow onesf. to) be advised** Pr 13_{10}; — 2. **take counsel together, deliberate**: w. *yaḥdāw* Is 45_{21}, w. *ʾēt* with 1K 12_{6a}, w. *ʾel* 2K 6_8; — 3. **advise (after consultation)** 1K 12_{6b}; — 3. **decide**, w. inf. 2C 30_2, w. fin. vb. 1K 12_{28}.

hitp.: impf. יִתְיָעֲצוּ: w. *ʿal* **take counsel** Ps 83_4. †

יַעֲקֹב, יַעֲקוֹב 4×: n. pers. & peop. **Jacob**.

יַעֲקֹבָה: n. pers.

יַעֲקָן: n. loc.

I יַעַר: יַעַר, sf. יַעְרוֹ, יַעְרָה, loc. הַיַּעְרָה; pl. יְעָרִים: — 1. **thicket, wood, forest** 2S 18_8 1K 7_2; — 2. **park** (wh. has been laid out) Ec 2_{6f}; — 3. in proper names, as → קִרְיַת יְעָרִים &c.

II יַעַר: pl. cs. יַעֲרֵי: **honeycomb** 1S 14$_{26}$ SS 5$_{1}$. †

I *יַעֲרָה: cs. יַעֲרַת: **honeycomb** 1S 14$_{27}$. †

cj II *יַעֲרָה: pl. יְעָרוֹת: **kid** Ps 29$_{9}$. †

יַעְרָה: n. pers. 1C 9$_{42}$. †

יַעְרֵי: n. pers. 2S 21$_{19}$. †

יַעֲרֶשְׁיָה: n. pers.

יַעֲשָׂו: n. pers.

יַעֲשִׂיאֵל: n. pers.

יִפְדְיָה: n. pers.

יפה: **qal**: pf. יָפִית; impf. וַיִּיף (mixed form qal & piel Ez 31$_{7}$), וַתִּיפִי; **become beautiful** Ez 16$_{13}$ 31$_{7}$ SS 4$_{10}$ 7$_{2\cdot7}$. †

piel: impf. וַיְיַפֵּהוּ: **decorate, adorn** Je 10$_{4}$. †

hitp.: impf. תִּתְיַפִּי: **make onesf. beautiful** Je 4$_{30}$. †

יָפֶה: cs. יְפֵה, f. יָפָה, cs. יְפַת, sf. יָפָתִי; pl. f. יָפוֹת, cs. יְפוֹת: — 1. **handsome, beautiful**: *'îš* Gn 39$_{6}$, *'iššâ* Gn 12$_{11}$; *yāfātî* (term of endearment) SS 2$_{10\cdot13}$; cows Gn 41$_{2}$, eyes 1S 16$_{12}$, trees Je 11$_{16}$, voice Ez 33$_{32}$; — 2. = *ṭôb*: **right, appropriate** Ec 3$_{11}$, pleasing Ex 5$_{17}$.

יָפוֹ (3×) & יָפוֹא (1×): n. loc. **Joppa** = **Jaffa.**

יפח: **hitp.**: impf. תִּתְיַפֵּחַ: **gasp for breath, groan** Je 4$_{31}$. †

יָפֵחַ: cs. וִיפֵחַ: **witness** Ps 27$_{12}$; but txt. corr. ? †

*יֳפִי: יוֹפִי, cs. יְפִי, sf. יָפְיוֹ, יָפְיֵךְ: **beauty**: of *'iššâ* Is 3$_{24}$, of king Is 33$_{17}$, of Zion Ps 50$_{2}$, of tree Ez 31$_{8}$.

cj יְפֵיפִיָּה: m. *יְפֵפֶה: **very handsome** (cow) Je 46$_{20}$. †

I יָפִיעַ: n. loc. Jos 19$_{12}$. †

II יָפִיעַ: n. pers.

יַפְלֵט: n. pers.

יַפְלֵטִי: gent. of יַפְלֵט, > n. loc. *g^{e}bûl yafleṭî* Jos 16$_{3}$. †

יְפֻנֶּה: n. pers.

יפע: **hif.**: pf. הוֹפִיעַ, הוֹפַעְתָּ; impf. תּוֹפַע, וַתּוֹפַע; impv. הוֹפִיעָה: — 1. **let shine** Jb 10$_{3}$ (oth.: shine); — 2. **rise** (as of sun), **appear in radiance** Dt 33$_{2}$; ? be bright, shine Jb 10$_{22}$ (*F* comm.).

*יִפְעָה: יִפְעָתֵךְ: **radiant brightness, splendor** Ez 28$_{7\cdot17}$. †

יֶפֶת: n. pers.

I יִפְתָּח: n. loc. Jos 15$_{43}$. †

II יִפְתָּח: n. pers.

יִפְתַּח־אֵל: n. loc.

יצא: **qal** (ca. 750×): pf. י״, יָצְאָה, יָצָאת, יָצָאתִי & יָצָתִי (Jb 1$_{21}$), יָצְאוּ, יָצָאוּ; impf. יֵצֵא, וַיֵּצֵא, יֵצְאוּ, יָצְאוּ, וַתֵּצֶאנָ(ה); impv. צֵא, צְאָה, צְאִי, צְאוּ, צְאֶינָה SS 3$_{11}$; inf. צֵאת, לָצֵאת, cs. לְצֵאת 1K 6$_{1}$, צֵאתְךָ, בְּצֵאתוֹ, abs. יָצ(וֹ)א; pt. י(וֹ)צֵא, יוֹצְאָה (> יֹצְאָה Ec 10$_{5}$) & יֹצֵאת (> יוֹצֵת Dt 28$_{57}$), יֹצְאִים, יֹצְאֵי: — 1. **come out, come forth**: of rising of sun Gn 19$_{23}$, of stars Ne 4$_{15}$, of birth of child Gn 25$_{26}$, of plants 1K 5$_{13}$; river arises Gn 2$_{10}$; of command Est 1$_{17}$; — 2. **go out, go forth** Gn 19$_{6}$; — 3. **come forward** (to fight &c.), **step forth** 1S 17$_{4}$ 2S 16$_{5}$; — 4. **march out, set forth**: a) abs. set out Ex 17$_{9}$; impv. *ṣē'* 'out (with you)' Is 30$_{22}$; b) w. *millifnê* went away (fm. the presence of s.one) Gn 4$_{16}$, w. *mē'ēt* 44$_{28}$, w. *mē'im* Ex 8$_{26}$, w. *liqra't* Gn 14$_{17}$; c) military: **march out** Dt 20$_{1}$, (locusts) Pr 30$_{29}$, *yāṣā' lifnê*, of king at head of army 1S 8$_{20}$, *yōṣ^{e}'ê ṣābā'* those fit for military service 1C 5$_{18}$; α) *ṣē't wābô'* march out & come back (victorious) 1S 29$_{6}$, 1K 3$_{7}$ (= take care of daily affairs); cultic, in temple Ex 28$_{35}$; *yāṣô' wāšôb* fly here & there Gn 8$_{7}$; — 5. comb.: a) *yāṣā' min* be descended from Gn 10$_{14}$; b) *yāṣ^{e}'â nafšô* lose one's wits SS 5$_{6}$, *b^{e}ṣē't nafšāh* as her life slipped away Gn 35$_{18}$, *wayyēṣē' libbām* courage failed them 42$_{28}$, *yāṣ^{e}'û y^{e}lādéhā* her fetus died Ex 21$_{22}$; c) *ṣē't haššānâ* beginning of the year Ex 23$_{16}$; d) *b^{e}ṣē't hayyayin*, when his drunkenness had worn off 1S 25_{37}; *ʿad-ʾᵃšer yēṣēʾ mēʾappᵉkem* until you are heartily sick, fed up, with it Nu 11_{20}; succeed Pr 25_4; project (of a tower) Ne 3_{25}; stretch (of border) Jos 15_3; be spent (of money) 2K 12_{13}; *wattaʿᵃleh wattēṣēʾ* cost for export 1K 10_{29a}; — 6. var.: a) get out = escape 1S 14_{41}; be through, finished with Dn 10_{20}; stop Pr 22_{10}; end disastrously Ez 26_{18}; become free Lv $25_{28.30}$; b) w. *ʿal-ereṣ* travel through (on inspection) Gn 41_{45}; c) w. *ḥofšî* go free Ex $21_{2.5}$; w. *ʾaḥᵃrê* pursue 1S 17_{35}; w. acc. escape Ec 7_{18}.

hif. (ca. 280×): pf. הוֹצִיא, הוֹצֵאתָ, הוֹצִיאוֹ, הוֹצֵאתֶם, הוֹצִיאַנִי, הוֹצִיאָנִי, הוֹצִיאֲךָ, הוֹצֵתַנִי, הֵצֵתָנִי, הוֹצֵאתִיךָ; impf. יוֹ(וֹ)צִ(י)א, וַיּוֹצֵא, וַיֵּצֵא, וַיּוֹצִאָה, תּוֹצִיא, תּוֹצֵא, וַתּוֹצֵא, אוֹצִ(י)אָה, וָאוֹצִיאֵם, וַיֹּצִאֵהוּ, וַיּוֹצִ(י)אוּם; impv. הוֹצֵא, Gn 8_{17} הַוְצֵא (Qr הַיְצֵא), הוֹצִיא Is 43_8, הוֹצִיאִי, הוֹצִיאֻם, הוֹצִאֵהוּ; inf. הוֹצִיא, הוֹצִיאֲךָ, הוֹצִיאָם, לְהוֹצִיאֵהוּ; pt. מוֹצִיא, מוֹצֵא, מוֹצֵאת (SS 8_{10}), מוֹצִיאִים, מוֹצִיאֵי: — 1. **make ... come out, ... go out, lead out**: a) persons, fm. house Gn 15_5; hand over Jos 2_3, send away Ezr 10_3, free fm. net Ps 31_5, lead out to execution Gn 38_{24}, take (children) fm. s.one's bosom Gn 48_{12}; lead troops in the field 2S 5_2; *hôṣîʾ wᵉhēbîʾ* (F qal 5c) rule a land 1C 11_2; b) animals & things: animals Gn 8_{17}, stars Is 40_{26}, let (fire) break out Ez 28_{18}, let (water) burst forth Nu 28_8; force out (blood) Pr 30_{33}; bring out (gifts fm. container) Gn 24_{53}, w. *ʿal-yad* entrust (items to s.one) Ezr 1_8; (food) Gn 14_8; let (curse) go forth Zc 5_4; c) God subj. (125×): saving deed fm. Egypt Dt 1_{27}; — 2. **bring forth, produce**: (subj. earth, obj. plants) Gn 1_{12}, (subj. smith, obj. weapon) Is 54_{16}; — 3. var.: *hôṣîʾ rûḥô* give vent to one's displeasure Pr 29_{11}; *hôṣîʾ dibbâ* bring bad news of, bring into discredit Nu 13_{32}; *hôṣîʾ dᵉbārāyw* report (one's words) Ne 6_{19}; *hôṣîʾ mišpāṭ* bring forth justice (truth?) Is $42_{1.3}$; *hôṣîʾ kesef ʿal* exact tribute by apportionment 2K 15_{20}.

hof.: pf. הוּצָאָה; pt. מוּצֵאת Gn 38_{25}, מוּצָאִים, מוּצָאוֹת: — 1. **be led out**, to execution Gn 38_5, to exile Ez 14_{22}; pt. מוּצָאִים those who are to be excluded (fm. sanctuary) Ez 44_5; be handed over Ez 38_{22}; — 2. **be paid out** 2S 18_{22} (rd. *mûṣēʾt*).

יצב: **hitp.**: pf. הִתְיַצְּבוּ; impf. יִתְיַצֵּב, יִתְיַצֵּב, יִתְיַצָּב, אֶתְיַצְּבָה, for וַתֵּתַצַּב Ex 2_4 rd. וַתִּתְיַצֵּב; impv. הִתְיַצֵּב, הִתְיַצְּבָה, הִתְיַצְּבוּ; inf. הִתְיַצֵּב: — 1. **take one's stand, position; stand (firm)** 1S 3_{10} 10_{19}; — 2. **appear, arrive** Dt 31_{14}; w. *minneged* stand aside 2K 18_{13}; — 3. **resist** Jos 1_5.

יצג: **hif.**: pf. הִצִּיגַנִי, הִצַּגְתִּיו; impf. וַיַּצֵּג, תַּצִּיג, אַצִּיגָה, וַיַּצִּגוּ; impv. הַצִּיגוּ; inf. הַצֵּג; pt. מַצִּיג: — 1. **set (down), place** Gn 30_{38} 1S 5_2, provide a place for Ju 8_{27}; leave (s.one w. s.one) Gn 33_{15}; — 2. var.: a) w. *lifnê* **bring** s.one **forward, produce** s.one Gn 43_9; b) w. *limšōl* expose (to mockery) Jb 17_6; c) w. *mišpāṭ* make (justice) valid Am 5_{15}; d) w. *ʾōtô lᵉbād* set s.one by himself Ju 7_5.

hof.: impf. יֻצַּג: **be left behind** Ex 10_{24}. †

I **יִצְהָר**: sf. יִצְהָרְךָ: **olive-oil** 2K 18_{32}; *bᵉnê yiṣhār* those anointed Zc 4_{14}.

II **יִצְהָר**: n. pers. Ex $6_{18.21}$ Nu 3_{19} 16_1 1C 5_{28} $6_{3.23}$ $23_{12.18}$. †

יִצְהָרִי: gent. of II יִצְהָר.

I ***יָצוּעַ**: pl. יְצוּעֵי, יְצוּעַי: **couch, bed** Gn 49_4.

II **יָצוּעַ**: 1K $6_{5.10}$ Kt: F יָצִיעַ Qr. †

יִצְחָק: n. pers. **Isaac.**

יִצְחַר 1C 4_7: n. pers.; rd. Qr F וְצֹחַר, Kt ? יִצְחַר. †

***יָצִיא**: 2C 32_{21} Qr מִיצִיאֵי (*min* & cs. pl.), Kt ?: **coming forth**: *mîṣîʾê mēʿāyw* some of his beloved sons. †

***יָצִיעַ**: 1K $6_{5.10}$ Qr, Kt II יָצוּעַ: unknown

archit. term; usu.: **wing** (of building), oth.: layer. †

יצע: **hif.**: impf. אַצִּיעָה, יַצִּיעַ: **spread out a couch** Is 58_5 Ps 139_8. †

hof.: impf. יֻצַּע: **be spread out for a couch** Is 14_{11} Est 4_3. †

יָצַק: **qal**: pf. יָצַקְתָּ, יְצָקָם, 'י; impf. וַיִּצֹק, וַתִּצֹק, וַיִּצֶק, אֶצָק־; impv. יְצֹק & צַק, inf. צֶקֶת; pt. pass. יָצוּק, יְצוּקִים, יְצֻקִים: — 1. **dish up** (food) 2S 13_9 2K 4_{40f}; — 2. **pour out** (liquid): oil Gn 28_{18}, water 1K 18_{34}, metaph. *dābār* Ps 41_9, *rûᵃḥ* Is 44_{3b}; — 3. **cast** (metal) 1K 7_{24}; metaph. *yāṣûq* = firm Jb 41_{15f}; — 4. intrans. **spread**: dust Jb 38_{38}, blood 1K 22_{35}.

hif.: impf. וַיַּצִּקוּ, וַיַּצִּקֻם; pt. מוֹצֶקֶת 2K 4_5 Qr (Kt מְיַצֶּקֶת or מֵיצֶקֶת): — 1. **empty out** Jos 7_{23}; — 2. **fill up** 2K 4_5. †

hof.: pf. הוּצַק; impf. יוּצַק; pt. מוּצָק, מֻצָּק, cs. מוּצַק: **be emptied out, poured out**: oil Lv 21_{10}, river Jb 22_{16}; metaph. *ḥēn* Ps 45_3; — 2. **be cast** 1K $7_{23\cdot33}$; pt. metaph. (ℱ qal 3) **firmly founded** Jb 11_{15}.

***יְצֻקָה**: sf. יְצֻקָתוֹ: **casting** (of metal) 1K 7_{24}. †

יָצַר: **qal**: pf. יְצַרְתִּיו, יְצַרְתָּם, יָצַר, יָצְרוּ, 'י; impf. אֶצָּרְךָ, יִצְּרֵהוּ, וַיִּ(י)צֶר (Qr אֶצּוֹרְךָ, Kt plene) Je 1_5; pt. יֹ(וֹ)צֵר, יֹצְרוֹ, יֹצְרֵנוּ, יֹצֶרְךָ, pl. יֹצְרִים, יֹצְרֵי: **form, shape** (as a potter): — 1. subj. men: **form, fashion**: a) obj. *pesel* (idol) Is 44_9; b) metaph., prepare (obj. misfortune) Ps 94_{20}; — 2. subj. God: **create, form** (older, concrete synonym of *bārā'*): obj. man Gn 2_{7f}, animals Gn 2_{19}, light Is 45_7, &c.; destiny 2K 19_{25}.

nif.: pf. נוֹצַר: **be formed** Is 43_{10}. †

pual (or qal pass.): pf. יֻצָּרוּ: **be formed** Ps 139_{16}. †

hof. (or qal pass.): impf. יוּצַר: **be formed** (by God) Is 54_{17}. †

יֹצֵר: ℱ יוֹצֵר: pt. of יָצַר.

I **יֵצֶר**: **what is shaped or made**, esp. a **pot** Is 29_{16}; idol Is 45_{16}; — 2. **thought, impulse, tendency** Gn 6_5 8_{21}.

II **יֵצֶר**: n. pers. Gn 46_{24} Nu 6_{49} 1C 7_{13}. †

***יְצֻרִים**: sf. יְצֻרַי: ?, limbs or inner organs?, Syriac: thoughts: Jb 17_7. †

יצת: **qal**: impf. תִּצַּתְנָה, יִצַּתּוּ, וַתִּצַּת: — 1. w. *bᵉ* **kindle** Is 9_{17}; — 2. w. *bā'ēš* **burn up** s.thg Is 33_{12} Je 49_2 51_{58}. †

nif.: pf. נִצְּתָה, נִצְּתוּ: — 1. metaph., of God's anger, **become inflamed, break out** 2K $22_{13\cdot17}$; — 2. **be burned up** Ne 1_3 2_{17} Je 2_{15} Qr (Kt 3 pl. f., or root *nṣh*). †

hif.: pf. הִצִּית, הִצַּתִּי, הִצִּיתוּהָ; impf. וַיַּצֶּת־, וַיַּצִּ(י)תוּ, תַּצִּיתוּ; impv. הַצִּיתוּהָ 2S 14_{30} Qr (Kt הוציתיה); pt. מַצִּית: — 1. w. *bā'ēš* **set on fire** 2S 14_{30f}; — 2. *hiṣṣît 'ēš* **set fire to**, w. *'al* Je 11_{16}, w. *bᵉ* Je 17_{27}.

יֶקֶב: יֶקֶב, sf. יִקְבֶךָ; pl. יְקָבִים, cs. יִקְבֵי: arrangement for wine-press, usually w. 2 rock-cavities, one above the other, connected by a channel, the upper for pressing, the lower for collecting: — 1. the lower cavity of wine-press, **wine-vat** Is 5_2; — 2. both cavities together, or upper-cavity, wine-press (usu. Hebr. *gat*): pl. Is 16_{10}, sg. 2K 6_{27}; — 3. in names of localities: a) יֶקֶב זְאֵב; b) יִקְבֵי הַמֶּלֶךְ.

יְקַבְצְאֵל: n. loc. Ne 11_{25}; ℱ קַבְצְאֵל. †

יקד: **qal**: impf. יֵקַד, וַתִּיקַד; pt. יֹקֶדֶת: **burn** Dt 32_{22} Is 10_{16} 65_5. †

hof.: (qal pass. ?): impf. תּוּקַד: **be kindled** Lv $6_{2\cdot5f}$ Je 15_{14} 17_4. †

יְקֹד: **fire, conflagration** Is 10_{16}. †

יָקְדְעָם: n. loc.

יָקֶה: n. pers.

***יְקָהָה**: cs. יִקְּהַת, לִיקְּהַת: **obedience** Gn 49_{10}; Pr 30_{17} txt. ? †

יָקוּד: **hearth** Is 30_{14}. †

[**יָקוּט** Jb 8_{14}: txt. corr.; sugg. rd. *qiššurê qayiṭ* 'gossamer'; ℱ comm.]

יְקוּם: הַיְקוּם: **what subsists, what is living** Gn $7_{4\cdot23}$ Dt 11_6. †

יָקוּשׁ Ps 91_3 Pr 6_5, **יָקֹשׁ** Ho 9_8: pl. **יְקֹשִׁים**: **bird-catcher, fowler** Je 5_{26} Ho 9_8 Ps 91_3 Pr 6_5. †

יְקוּתִיאֵל: n. pers.

cj **יקח**: **hif.**: impf. rd. **וַיִּקַּח** for **וַיִּקַּח**: **behave shamelessly, have the audacity to** ... Nu 16_1. †

יָקְטָן: n. pers. (peop.).

יָקִים: n. pers. 1C 8_9 24_{12}. †

יַקִּיר: **precious, dear** Je 31_{20}. †

יְקַמְיָה: n. pers.

יְקַמְעָם: n. pers.

יָקְמְעָם 1C 6_{53} & **יָקְמֳעָם** 1K 4_{12}: n. loc.

יָקְנְעָם: n. loc.

יקע: **qal**: impf. **(וַ)תֵּקַע**: — 1. **turn away with a jerk**, be suddenly alienated Je 6_8 Ez 23_{17f}; — 2. **dislocate, sprain** (hip-joint) Gn 32_{26}. †

hif.: pf. **הוֹקַעֲנוּם**; impf. **וַיֹּקִיעוּם**; impv. **הוֹקַע**: **expose** (the dead?) **with broken limbs** (oth.: impale, or break on a wheel) Nu 25_4 2S $21_{6\cdot 9}$. †

hof.: pt. **מוּקָעִים**: (of the dead) **be exposed with broken limbs** 2S 21_{13}. †

[**יִקְפָּאוֹן** Zc 14_6: rd. **וְקִפָּאוֹן**. †)

יקץ: **qal**: impf. (**קיץ** hif.) **וַיִּ(י)קַץ**, **וַיִּיקַץ**, **יִקְצוּ**, **וָאִיקָץ** Hb 2_7: **awake, wake up** (intrans.) Gn 28_{16}; from drunkenness Gn 9_{24}; of enemies or God, = become active Hb 2_7 Ps 78_{65}.

יקר: **qal**: pf. **יָקְרָה**, **יָקַרְתִּי**; impf. **יֵ(י)קַר**, **וַיֵּקַר**, **תֵּיקַר**: — 1. **be difficult** Ps 139_{17}; — 2. **be valued** Zc 11_{13}; — 3. **be precious, rare** (*be'ênê*) 2K 1_{13f}; — 4. **be honored** 1S 18_{30}.

hif.: impf. **אוֹקִיר**; impv. **הֹקַר**: **make precious, rare** (obj. man) Is 13_{12}; w. *regel* visit rarely Pr 25_{17}. †

יָקָר: f. **יְקָרָה**, cs. **יְקַרַת**; pl. **יְקָרִים**, f. **יְקָר(וֹ)ת**: — 1. **rare** 1S 3_1; *'eben yeqārâ* **precious stone** 2S 12_{30}, coll. 1K $10_{2\cdot 10f}$, cf. *'abānîm yeqārôt* precious (building-)stones 1K 5_{31}; — 2. a) **costly, valuable** Ps 36_8, w. *min*, more valuable than Pr 3_{15}; b) adv. (?) magnificently (w. *hālak*) Jb 31_{26}; — 3. **noble** Je 15_{19}.

יְקָר: cs. **יְקָר** (*ŏ*), sf. **יְקָרוֹ**: — 1. **preciousness**: a) *kelî yeqār* precious vessel(s), article(s) Pr 20_{15}; *'eder yeqār* splendid price Zc 11_{13}; *yeqor tif'eret gedullātô* Est 1_4 costly luxury of his greatness; b) coll. precious things Je 20_5; — 2. **honoring, esteeming** Est 6_{6ff}, w. *'āśâ* 6_3, w. *nātan* 1_{20}.

יקשׁ: **qal**: pf. **יָקֹשׁוּ**, **יָקֹשְׁתִּי**; pt. **יֹקְשִׁים**: **catch** (birds) **with a snare** Je 50_{24} Ps 124_7 141_9. †

nif.: pf. **נוֹקַשְׁתְּ**, **נוֹקְשׁוּ**; impf. **תִּוָּקֵשׁ**: **be caught**; **let onesf. get entangled** Dt 7_{25} Is 8_{15} 28_{13} Pr 6_2.

pual: pt. **יוּקָשִׁים** (w/o **מְ**, ? pass. qal): **caught** Ec 9_{12}. †

יָקְשָׁן: n. (pers.,) peop.

יָקְתְאֵל: n. loc.

I **יָרֵא** (ca. 320×): **qal**: pf. **יָרֵאתִי**, **יָרְאָה**, **׳י**, **יְרֵאתֶם**, **יְרֵאנוּ**, **יְרֵאוּהוּ**, **יְרֵאוּנִי**; impf. **יִירָא**, **וַיִּירָאוּ**, **יִרְאוּ**, **וָאִירָא**, **תִּירָאִי**, **תִּירְאִי**, **וַיִּירָא**, **נִירָא**, **וַתִּירֶאנָה**, **תִּירְאוּן**, **וְיִרְאוּן**, **וַיִּירָאוּ**, **תִּירָאוּם**, **יִ(י)רָאוּךָ**, **אִירָאֶנּוּ**, **וַיִּירָאֵנִי**, **יִרָאֲךָ**, **תִּירָאֻם**; impv. **יְרָא**, **יִירְאוּ** & **יְראוּ** Jos 24_{14}; inf. **יְרֹא**, **לְרֹא** (1S 18_{29}), usu. **יִרְאָה**; pt. *F* **יָרֵא**: — 1. **fear**: w. acc. Gn 32_{12}, w. *mippenê* 1K 1_{50}; — 2. **fear**, obj. God, i.e. shudder at, **be in awe of, hold in deference**: a) specifically God of Isr. Gn 22_{12}; b) gods 2K 17_7; c) sanctuary Lv 19_{30}; d) father & mother Lv 19_3; — 3. **be afraid**: a) abs. Gn 3_{10}; b) spec. *'al-tîrā'* don't be afraid (during theophany) Gn 15_1; b) w. inf.: α) *le* & inf. Gn 19_{30}; β) *min* & inf. 1S 3_{15}.

nif.: impf. **תִּוָּרֵא**; pt. **נוֹרָא**, **נוֹרָאָה**, **נוֹרָאוֹת**, **נוֹרְאֹתֶיךָ**: — 1. **be feared, reverenced, held in honor** (of God) Ps 130_4; — 2. pt. a) **feared**: *'am* Is $18_{2\cdot 7}$, *gôy* Hb 1_7; — b) **fearful, to be feared**: Y. Ex 15_{11}; other designations of God Ps 47_3, name of God Dt 28_{58}, place Gn 28_{17}; c) *nôrātôt* God's fearful deeds 2S 7_{23}; king's Ps 45_5; d) evoking fear, awe: *midbār* Dt 1_{19}, *ʼereṣ* Is 21_1; e) adv. in fearful way Ps 139_{14}.

piel: pf. יִרְאֻנִי; inf. יְרָאֵנִי, יָרְאָם; pt. מְיָרְאִים: **overawe, alarm** 2S 14_{15} Ne $6_{9\cdot14\cdot19}$ 2C 32_{18}. †

II **ירא**: ↗ I ירה qal, hif.; — III ירא: ↗ II ירה hof.

יָרֵא: cs. יְרֵא, f. cs. יִרְאַת; pl. יְרֵאִים, יִרְאֵי: — 1. **afraid of**: a) w. *ʼēt* & acc. α) obj. men Gn 32_{12}; β) obj. God Gn 22_{12}; b) w. gen.: *yerēʼ yhwh* Is 50_{10}, pl. Ps 15_4, f. *ʼiššâ yirʼat yhwh* Pr 31_{20}; w. sf. Ps 22_{26}; c) w. *min* Dt 7_{19}; — 2. **fearful** 1S 23_3.

יִרְאָה: cs. יִרְאַת, sf. יִרְאָתוֹ: — 1. **fear**: of thorns Is 7_{25}, *yirāt^ekā* fear of you Dt 2_{25}, cogn. acc. Jon 1_{10}, takes *ʼēt* & acc. Jos 4_{24}; — 2. **fear of God** (objective gen.) Gn 20_{11}, w. sf. fear of him Ex 20_{20}.

יִרְאוֹן: n. loc.

יִרְאִיָּה: n. pers.

יָרֵב: designation of Assyrian king Ho 5_{13} 10_6; = 'great king'; or word-play connected with *rîb* 'quarrel'?

יְרֻבַּעַל: n. pers., = Gideon; cf. יְרֻבֶּשֶׁת.

יָרָבְעָם: n. pers., **Jeroboam**.

יְרֻבֶּשֶׁת: n. pers., deformation of יְרֻבַּעַל.

יָרַד (ca. 360×): **qal**: pf. ״, יָרֵד, 2 f. יָרַדְתִּי Rt 3_3 Kt; impf. יֵרֵד, יֵּרֶד, וַיֵּרֶד, תֵּרֵד, אֵרְדָה, אֵרְדָה, וָאֵרֵד, (וַ)תֵּרֶד, תֵּרֶד, תֵּרֵד (Gn 18_{21}), יֵרְדוּ, תֵּרַדְנָה, נֵרֵד, נֵרְדָה; impv. רֵד, רְדָה, רֵדָה, רְדִי, רְדוּ; inf. (מִ/לְ/בְּ)רֶדֶת, בְּרִדְתִּי, מִיָּרְדִי Ps 30_4 Qr, abs. יָרֹד; pt. יֹ(ו)רֵד, יֹרְדָה, יֹ(ו)רְדִים, יֹ(ו)רְדֵי, יֹ(ו)רְדוֹת: — 1. mostly **go down**, but occasionally **go up**: Ju 11_{37}; so also Ju 1_9 15_8 2S 5_{17} 2K 2_2 6_{18} 1C 11_{15}; *yārad babbekî* Is 15_3 go up & down weeping (?), oth.: melting into tears †; — 2. motion downward: a) **come down**, of rain & snow Is 55_{10}, fire 2K 1_{10}; b) **go down**: to spring Gn 24_{16}; to Egypt Gn 12_{10}, from mountain Ex 19_{14}; sink down (of stone in water) Ex 15_5, (to slaughter) Je 48_{15}; c) go on board (a ship) Jon 1_3, come off (ship) Ez 27_{29}; *yôr^edê hayyām* who sail the sea Is 42_{10}; get out of bed 2K 1_4; — 3. Y. comes down in theophany Gn 11_5; — 4. of the dead, go down to Sheol Gn 37_{35}, to dust Ps 22_{30}; *yôr^edê bôr* Is 38_{18}; — 5. var.: disaster comes down from Y. Mi 1_{12}; come humbly Ex 11_8; *hayyōrēd bammilḥāmâ* he who participates in the battle 1S 30_{24} Qr (Kt ↗ hof); boundary reaches down as far as Nu 34_{11f}; besieged city gives up Dt 20_{20}; walls collapse Dt 28_{52}; sink to the ground Is 32_{19}; shadow sinks 2K 20_{11}; day draws to a close Ju 19_{11}; *tērēd ʻênî dimʻa* my eye dissolves in tears Je 13_{17}, pl. 9_{17}.

hif.: pf. הוֹרִד, הוֹרִידוּ, הוֹרַדְתֶּם, הוֹרַדְנוּ, הוֹרִדְהוּ, הוֹרַדְתִּיךָ; impf. וַיּ(וֹ)רֶד, וַיֹּרִדֵהוּ, תּוֹרֵד, וַתּוֹרִדֵם, יוֹרִידוּ, וַיּוֹרִידוּם; impv. הוֹרֵד, הוֹרִדֵמוֹ, הוֹרִידִי, הוֹרִידוּ; inf. הוֹרִיד, הוֹרִדִי; pt. מוֹרִיד: — 1. **bring down** Gn 37_{25}, lead down (animal) Dt 21_4, take down (jar) Gn 24_{18}, let s.one down 1S 19_{12}; let s.one go down (to Sheol) (↗ qal 4) Gn 42_{38}; — 2. **throw down** Ps 56_8; take down (the tabernacle) Nu 1_{51}; — 3. **make** (rain) **fall** Ez 34_{26}, let (spittle) run down 1S 21_{14}, let (tears) flow La 2_{18}, let (head) hang La 2_{10}, subjugate (peoples) 2S 22_{48}.

hof.: pf. הוּרַד, הוּרַדְתְּ; impf. תּוּרַד: — 1. **be brought down** Gn 39_1, be taken down (tabernacle) Nu 10_{17}; — 2. metaph. **be overturned** Zc 10_{11}.

יֶרֶד: n. pers.

יַרְדֵּן: Ps 42_7 Jb 40_{23}, otherw. הַיַּרְדֵּן & הַיַּרְדֵּנָה: n. river, **Jordan**.

I **יָרָה**: **qal**: pf. ״, יָרִיתִי; impf. וַנִּירָם Nu 21_{30}; impv. יְרֵה; inf. לִירוֹת, לִירוֹא 2C 26_{15}, abs. יָרֹה; pt. יֹרֶה, יֹ(ו)רִים: — 1. **throw**: lot Jos 18_6, chariot into sea Ex 15_4; — 2. **shoot**: a) w. acc. arrows 1S 20_{36f}, w. *b^e* stones 2C 26_{15}; b) w. *b^e* on s.one Nu 21_{30} Ps 11_2; c) raise (a heap of stones) Gn 31_{51}, lay (a cornerstone) Jb 38_{6}.

nif.: impf. יִיָּרֶה: **be shot** Ex 19_{13}. †

hif.: pf. הוֹרָנִי; impf. יוֹרֶה, וַיּוֹר, אוֹרֶה, וַיֹּרְאוּ, יֹרוּ, וַיֹּרֶם, יֹרְהוּ; pt. מוֹרֶה, מוֹרִים, הַמּוֹרְאִים 2S 11_{24} (Qr w/o א's): — 1. **throw** (ꟳ qal 1), obj. men Jb 30_{19}; — 2. **shoot**: abs. 2K 13_{7}; w. acc., at s.one Ps $64_{5 \cdot 8}$; w. *le* 2C 35_{23}, w. *'el* Je 50_{14}; obj. arrows 2K 19_{32}.

II ירה: **hif.**: impf. יוֹרֶה: **give to drink** Ho 6_{3}; metaph. w. *ṣedeq* let it rain Ho 10_{12}. †

hof.: Pr 11_{25} יוֹרֶא: rd. יוּרֶה: **be given to drink to one's fill.** †

III ירה: **hif.**: pf. הוֹרְתָנִי, הוֹרָהוּ, הוֹרֵיתִי, ה(ו)רֵיתִיךָ; impf. יוֹרֶה, וַיֹּרֵנִי, יֹ(ו)רֵם, תֹּרְךָ, יוֹרוּ(ךָ), אוֹרְךָ, תֹּרֶךָ, (?); impv. ה(ו)רֵנִי, הוֹרוּנִי; pt. מוֹרֶה (Is 9_{14} & Hb 2_{18} מוֹרֶה שֶׁקֶר cs ? oth.: acc.), pl. מוֹרַי, מוֹרֶיךָ: — 1. **instruct, teach**: subj. priest 2K 12_{3}, God Ex 24_{12}; — 2. **teach** s.one s.thg: a) w. 2 acc. 1K 8_{36}; b) w. acc. of pers., *be* + thing 1S 12_{23}; c) w. acc. of pers., *bên* ... *le* the difference between ... † Ez 44_{23}; d) w. fingers Pr 6_{13}; e) *min* + thing Is 2_{3}; — 3. var. objs.: *hattôrâ* Dt 17_{11}, *lemišpāṭîm* Dt 33_{10}; *môreh šāqer* Is 9_{14} Hb 2_{18}; — 4. abs., on cultic or tech. matters Ex 35_{34}; — 5. followed by clause, *'et-'ašer* Ex $4_{12 \cdot 15}$, *mâ* Ju 13_{8}, *'êk* 2K 17_{28}.

ירה: **qal**: impf. תִּרְהוּ (rd. תִּ'!): **be paralyzed with fright** Is 44_{8}. †

יְרוּאֵל: n. loc.

יָרוֹחַ: n. pers.

?? יָרוּם: usu. as impf. of רום, but sugg.: pt. pass. of ירם, **be exalted** Is 52_{13} Ps 18_{47} 61_{3}.

יָרוֹק: **verdant plants** Jb 39_{8}. †

יְרוּשָׁא: n. pers. f. 2K 15_{33} < יְרוּשָׁה 2C 27_{1}.

יְרוּשָׁלַםִ, יְרוּשָׁלֵם, so alw. exc. Je 26_{18} Est 2_{6} 1C 3_{5} 2C 25_{1} יְרוּשָׁלָיִם, & 2C 32_{9} יְרוּשָׁלַיְמָה, Qr perpetuum, Kt יְרוּשָׁלֵם: n. of city, f.: **Jerusalem.**

I יֶרַח: pl. יְרָחִים, cs. יַרְחֵי: **month** 1K 6_{37f} (earlier word than *ḥōdeš*).

II יֶרַח: n. pers. Gn 10_{26} 1C 1_{20}. †

יָרֵחַ: sf. וְיָרֵחַ: **moon** Gn 37_{9}.

יְרִיחוֹ, יְרֵחוֹ Jos, 2S, 2K, Je; יְרִיחֹה 1K 16_{34} & יְרֵחוֹ Nu, Dt, Ezr, Ne, 1C, 2C: **Jericho.**

יְרֹחָם: n. pers.

יְרַחְמְאֵל: n. pers.

יְרַחְמְאֵלִי: gent. of יְרַחְמְאֵל.

יַרְחָע: n. pers.

ירט: **qal**: pf. ״; impf. יִרְטֵנִי: — 1. **push, shove, into s.one's hands** Jb 16_{11}; — 2. ? intrans. **be steep** (of path) Nu 22_{32} (txt.?). †

יְרִיאֵל: n. pers.

I *יָרִיב: sf. יְרִיבֶךָ; pl. sf. יְרִיבָי: **adversary** (in legal case) Is 49_{25} Ps 35_{1}. †

II יָרִיב: n. pers.

יְרִיבַי: n. pers.

יְרִיָּה: n. pers.

יְרִיָּהוּ: n. pers.

יְרִיחֹה 1K 16_{34}, יְרִיחוֹ: ꟳ יְרֵחוֹ.

יְרִימוֹת: n. pers.

יְרִיעָה: pl. יְרִיע(ו)ת, sf. יְרִיעֹתַי, יְרִיעוֹתֵיהֶם: — 1. **tent-fabric**, of goat-hair Ex 26_{7}, other material for tabernacle Ex 26_{1ff}; — 2. **tent**: a) for the ark 2S 7_{2}; b) as a dwelling Je 4_{20}.

יְרִיעוֹת: n. pers. f.

יָרֵךְ: cs. יֶרֶךְ, sf. יְרֵכִי; du. יְרֵכַיִם, sf. יְרֵכֶיךָ: — 1. the fleshy portion of the **upper thigh**: posterior Ex 28_{42}, seat of limping Gn 32_{32}; seat of procreation Gn 46_{26}; *taḥat yārēk* area of sexual organs (hand placed there in oaths) Gn $24_{2 \cdot 9}$; *kaf yārēk* hip-socket Gn $32_{26 \cdot 33}$; — 2. metaph. **side**: a) of altar 2K 16_{14}; b) foot of lampstand Ex 25_{31}.

*יְרֵכָה: sf. יַרְכָתוֹ; יַרְכָתָם Ez 46_{19} Kt; du. יַרְכָתַיִם, יַרְכְּתַיִם, cs. יַרְכְּתֵי 1K 6_{16} Qr: — 1. **rear** (oth.: flank) Gn 49_{13}; narrow rear side of building (:: *sēlaʿ*, long side) Ex 26_{22f}; — 2. **rear (portion)**: a) most distant part of mountain 2K 19_{23}, of earth Je 6_{22}, of north Is 14_{13}; b) farthest to the rear, inmost part:

yark^etê bôr Is 14_{15} = Sheol; of house 1K 6_{16}, of ship Jon 1_5.

***ירם**: **qal**: pt. pass ꟳ ? יָרוּם.

יָרָם: ꟳ יוֹרָם.

יַרְמוּת: n. loc.

יְרֵמוֹת Ezr 10_{29}, ꟳ יְרֵמוֹת.

יְרֵמוֹת: n. pers.

יְרֵמַי: n. pers.

יִרְמְיָה: n. pers., **Jeremiah**.

יִרְמְיָהוּ: n. pers., **Jeremiah**.

ירע: **qal**: pf. יָרְעָה: **tremble, be faint-hearted** Is 15_4. †

יִרְפְּאֵל: n. loc.

יָרַק: **qal**: pf. יָרְקָה, י׳; inf. abs. יָרֹק: **spit** (in s.one's face) as a gesture of curse & rejection Nu 12_{14} Dt 25_9. †

יָרָק: **greens, vegetables** Dt 11_{10} 1K 21_2 Pr 15_{17}. †

יֶרֶק: cs. יֶרֶק: **green plant**, verdure Gn 1_{30}.

יַרְקוֹן: name of wadi or river.

יֵרָקוֹן: disease of grain, **rust or mildew**, alw. ‖ *šiddāfôn* 1K 8_{37}; — 2. **pallor** (of face) Je 30_6.

יָרְקְעָם: n. loc.

יְרַקְרַק: — 1. morbid coloration of skin & leather (mildew?): a mark of *ṣara'at* Lv 13_{49}, on houses (fungus? dry-rot?) 14_{37}; — 2. attribute of gold w. strong admixture of silver: yellow gold Ps 68_{14}. †

I **יָרַשׁ** (ca. 230×): **qal**: pf. י׳, יְרַשְׁנוּ, וִירִשְׁתֶּם & וִירִשְׁתָּם, וִירַשׁוּהָ, וִירַשׁוּךָ; impf. יִ(י)רַשׁ, נִירֲשָׁה, נִירַשׁ, תִּירָשׁוּן, יִירְשׁוּ, תִּירַשׁ, וַיִּירַשׁ, יִירָשׁוּם, אִירָשֶׁנָּה, תִּירָשֶׁנָּה, יִירָשֶׁךָ, יִירָשְׁךָ, יְרֵשָׁה, וַיִּירָשׁוּהָ; impv. רֵשׁ, רַשׁ, יִירָשָׁם, רְשׁוּ; inf. רֶשֶׁת, רִשְׁתּוֹ, רִשְׁתּוֹ, רָשֵׁנוּ Ju 14_{15} ꟳ piel; pt. יֹ(וֹ)רֵשׁ, יֹרֶשֶׁת: — 1. **take possession of, get**: land Gn 15_8, a territory Ju 11_{22}, city Ju 3_{13}, house Ez 7_{24}; — 2. w. acc.: **inherit from** s.one, **be the/an heir of** s.one Gn 15_{3f}, w. *'im* together with Gn 21_{10}; *yôrēš* heir 2S 14_7; — 3. **displace s.one from his property**, dispossess Dt 2_{12}, drive out Nu 21_{32}; *yōr^ešîm* conquerors Je 8_{10}.

nif.: impf. יִוָּרֵשׁ: **be deprived of property, become poor** Gn 45_{11}.

piel: impf. יְיָרֵשׁ; inf. לְיָרְשֵׁנִי Ju 14_{15}: **take possession of** Dt 28_{42}.

hif.: pf. הוֹרִישׁ, הוֹרַשְׁתֶּם, הוֹרִישׁוּ, הוֹרַשְׁתָּם, הוֹרַשְׁתִּים; impf. יוֹרִישׁ, וַיֹּ(וֹ)רֶשׁ, תּוֹרִשֵׁמוֹ, וַיֹּרִשֵׁם, יוֹרִישְׁךָ, יֹ(וֹ)רִשֶׁנָּה, תּוֹרִישׁוּ, אוֹרִשֶׁנּוּ; inf. לְהוֹרִישָׁם; pt. מוֹרִשָׁם: — 1. **take possession of** Nu 14_{24}; — 2. **drive out, dispossess** (ꟳ qal 3) Ex 15_9; — 3. metaph. make inherit = **make** s.one **suffer** Jb 13_{26}.

II **ירשׁ**: **qal**: impf. תִּירוֹשׁ: tread, **press** (grapes) Mi 6_{15}. †

יְרֵשָׁה: **property** (= conquered, occupied land) Nu 24_{18}. †

יְרֻשָּׁה: cs. יְרֻשַּׁת, sf. יְרֻשָּׁתוֹ, יְרֻשַּׁתְכֶם: **property** (= conquered land) Dt 2_5; *'ereṣ y^eruššātô* land which is its possession Dt 2_{12}; *mišpaṭ hayruššâ* right of possession Je 32_8.

יִשְׂחָק: n. pers. = ꟳ יִצְחָק. †

יִשִׁימָאֵל: n. pers.

יִשְׂרָאֵל: n. pers. & peop. **Israel**.

יִשְׂרְאֵלִי: gent. of יִשְׂרָאֵל; f. יִשְׂרְאֵלִית.

יִשָּׂשכָר: Qr perpetuum יִשָּׂכָר; Kt?; n. pers. & peop. **Issachar**.

יֵשׁ (ca. 130×), יֶשׁ־, יֵשׁ־ Ezr 10_2, הֲיֵשׁ־ & וְיֵשׁ־; sf. יֶשְׁךָ, יֶשְׁכֶם, יֶשְׁנוֹ Dt 29_4 + 3×: — 1. noun: existence: **property** Pr 8_{21}; — 2. **it exists, there is** (French il y a) Gn 24_{23}; *yēš ḥ^amiššîm* there are 50 Gn 18_{24}; *yēš yhwh* Y. is present Gn 28_{16}; w. proleptic suffix: *yešnô 'am-'eḥād* Est 3_8; as answer to *h^ayēš*: *yēš* = yes 2K 10_{15}; — 3. after a noun: a) abs.: *leḥem yēš* 1S 21_5; b) w. *'ēt* with Gn 44_{26}, w. *'im* 2K 10_{23}; c) *yēš 'et-nafš^ekem* you are willing Gn 23_8; — 4. *yēš* w. pt.: there are those who = many: *yēš m^efazzēr* Pr 11_{24} many scatter; — 5. *yēš* w. sf. + pt.: *yeškā maṣli^aḥ* you give success Gn 24_{42}; — 6. *yeš-l^e* = dat. of possession: a) *yēš-lô* he possesses Gn 33_9; b) *l^e* & inf., (I) have to, should 2K 4_{13}; c) w. neg.: *'ên yēš* 1S 21_9; — 7. *yēš* w. adv. of place: a) w. *pōh* here is 1S 21_9; b) w. *b^e* in, at 1S 9_{11}; c) w. *taḥat* 1S 21_4.

יָשַׁב (1090×): **qal**: pf. יָ״, יָשַׁב, יָשַׁבְתָּ, יָשְׁבוּ, יָשָׁבוּ; impf. יֵשֵׁב, יֵשֵׁב, יֵשֶׁב, וַיֵּשֶׁב, וַיֵּשֶׁב, וָאֵשְׁבָה, תֵּשַׁבְנָה*, יֵשְׁבוּ, יֵשֵׁבוּ, וָאֵשְׁבָה Ez 35_9 Kt (Qr √ *šwb*); impv. שֵׁב, שֵׁב־, שְׁבָה, שְׁבוּ, שְׁבִי; inf. (לָ)שֶׁבֶת, cs. לָשֶׁבֶת Gn 16_3, שִׁבְתִּי, abs. יָשֹׁב־ 1S 20_5; pt. יֹ(וֹ)שֵׁב, הַיֹּשְׁבִי Ps 123_1, f. יֹשְׁבָה, cs. *יוֹשַׁבְתִּי Kt, Qr יוֹשֶׁבֶת Je 10_{17} La 4_{21}, pl. יֹשְׁבִים, יֹ(וֹ)שְׁבֵי, יֹשְׁב(וֹ)ת: — 1. **sit down** Gn 27_{19}, 1K 2_{19}; — 2. **sit** Dt 6_7; = hold a meeting Je 39_3; w. loc. Gn 18_1, w. *b^e* in Gn 19_1, w. *'al* on 1K 22_{10}; Y. subj.: *yōšēb hakk^erubîm* who sits (enthroned) on the ch. 1S 4_4; *yāšab 'al-hammišpāṭ* preside at a trial Is 28_6; — 3. var.: a) *yāšab 'al kissē' m^elûkâ* ascend the royal throne 1K 1_{46}, *hayyōš^ebîm* those who are enthroned Is 10_{13}; b) (of lion) **crouch** Ps 17_{12}; w. *'ōrēb* lie concealed Ju 16_9; c) sit ready Je 3_2; w. *lifnê* be a disciple 2K 4_{38}; w. *b^e* & n. loc. **keep** (a place) besieged 1K 11_{16}; d) abs. **sit** (here/there) Je 8_{14}; — 4. **remain sitting** 2K 14_{10}, stay Gn 24_{55}; w. *l^e* wait for Ex 24_{14}; — 5. **dwell, live** (somewhere) Gn 13_6; *yōšēb* inhabitant(s): coll. Gn 4_{20}, pl. 36_{20}; *yōšebet* population Je 46_9, *yōš^ebôt* 1S 27_8; — 6. **be inhabited**: a) city Is 13_{20}; b) countryside Je 17_6; c) house Jb 15_{28}.

nif.: pf. נוֹשָׁבָה, נֹשְׁבוּ, נוֹשָׁבוּ; pt. נוֹשֶׁבֶת, נוֹשָׁבוֹת: **be inhabited**: land Ex 16_{35}, city Je 22_6, ruins Ez 38_{12}.

piel: pf. יִשְּׁבוּ: **set up, pitch** (obj. camp) Ez 25_4. †

hif.: pf. הֹשִׁיב, הוֹשַׁבְתִּי, הוֹשִׁיבַנִי, הוֹשַׁבְתִּים, הוֹשַׁבְתִּיךְ; impf. וַיּוֹשִׁבֵנִי 1K 2_{24} Qr, אוֹשִׁיבְךָ, וַנּוֹשֵׁב, וַיֹּשִׁבוּם; impv. הוֹשֵׁב; inf. הוֹשִׁיב; pt. מוֹשִׁיב, cs. מוֹשִׁיבִי Ps 113_9: — 1. **make** (s.one) **sit, set**: a) 1K $21_{9f.12}$; b) obj. king on throne 1K 2_{24}; — 2. **settle**, populate (**a** city) Is 54_3; — 3. **let** (s.one) **dwell, live** (somewhere) Gn $47_{6.11}$; — 4. **leave behind** 1S 30_{21}; — 5. a) **let** (unmarried, barren ones &c.) **establish** (a household, *bayit*) Ps 68_7; b) make (a foreign woman) a resident, **marry** Ezr 10_2.

hof.: pf. הוּשַׁבְתֶּם Is 5_8; impf. תּוּשַׁב: — 1. **be inhabited** Is 44_{26}; — 2. denom. of *yōšēb*: be settled, **be a landowner** Is 5_8. †

יֹשֵׁב בַּשֶּׁבֶת: n. pers. (deformed from *יִשְׁבֹּשֶׁת < יִשְׁבַּעַל).

יֶשֶׁבְאָב: n. pers.

יִשְׁבָּח: n. pers.

cj **יִשְׁבַּעַל**: n. pers. 2S 23_8 & 1C 11_{11} 27_2.

יָשָׁבְעָם: n. pers.

יִשְׁבָּק: n. pers.

יָשְׁבְּקָשָׁה: n. pers. (?).

I **יָשׁוּב**: n. pers. Nu 26_{24} 1C 7_1 Qr; Ezr 10_{29}. †

cj II **יָשׁוּב**: n. loc.? Jos 17_7. †

יָשׁוּבִי: gent. of I יָשׁוּב.

יִשְׁוָה: n. pers.

יְשׁוֹחָיָה: n. pers.

יִשְׁוִי: n. pers., gent.

I **יֵשׁוּעַ**: n. pers.

II **יֵשׁוּעַ**: n. loc. Ne 11_{26}. †

יְשׁוּעָה: cs. יְשׁוּעַת, sf. יְשֻׁעָתִי, יְשׁוּעָתִי, יְשׁוּעָתֵנוּ, יְשׁוּעָתָהּ, יְשׁוּעָתֶךָ, יְשׁוּעָתְךָ; pl. יְשֻׁעוֹת, יְשׁוּע(וֹ)ת: **help, prosperity, salvation**: I. sg.: 1. a) God's help, Gn 49_{18}; b) God's salvation Is $49_{6.8}$; — 2. human help 1S 14_{48}; — 3. help gained fm. things Is 26_1 (walls); — II. pl.: 1. **help** Is 26_{18}; — 2. a) helping deeds Ps 74_{12}; b) salvation 2S 22_{51}.

***יֶשַׁח**: sf. יֶשְׁחֲךָ: **dung** Mi 6_{14}. †

ישט: **hif.**: impf. יוֹשִׁיט, וַיּוֹשֶׁט: **hold out, extend** Est 4_{11} 5_2 8_4. †

יִשַׁי: n. pers. **Jesse**.

יָשִׁיב: n. pers.

יִשִּׁיָּה: n. pers.

יִשִּׁיָּהוּ: n. pers.

יְשִׁימוֹן, יְשִׁמוֹן Dt 32_{10}: **desert, wilderness**: — 1. common noun, never w. art. Dt 32_{10}; —† 2. n. loc. or terr. 1S $23_{19.24}$ $26_{1.3}$; Nu 21_{20} 23_{18}.

יְשִׁימוֹת, F בֵּית יְשִׁימוֹת (בַּיִת I B 21) & יְשִׁמֹת.

יַשִּׁימָוֶת Ps 55_{16}: usu. Qr יַשִּׁיא מָוֶת, hif. II **נשא** exchange, or hif. **שוא** use (s.one) ill, but sugg.: **devastation**. †

יָשִׁישׁ: pl. יְשִׁישִׁים: **elderly, very aged** Jb 12_{12} 15_{10} 29_{8} 32_{6}. †

יְשִׁישַׁי: n. pers.

יִשְׁמָא: n. pers.

יִשְׁמָעֵאל: (n. pers.), n. tribe, **Ishmael**.

יִשְׁמְעֵאלִי: gent. of יִשְׁמָעֵאל; > יִשְׁמְעֵלִי 1C 27_{30}; pl. יִשְׁמְעֵאלִים.

יִשְׁמַעְיָה: n. pers.

יִשְׁמַעְיָהוּ: n. pers.

יִשְׁמְרַי: n. pers.

I **ישׁן**: **qal**: pf. יָשַׁנְתִּי, יָשְׁנוּ; impf. וַיִּישַׁן, וַיִּשָׁן, אִישַׁן, אִישָׁן, וְאִישָׁנָה Ps 3_{6}, יִשְׁנוּ; inf. לִישׁוֹן: — 1. **go to sleep** Gn 2_{21}; — 2. **sleep** Ez 34_{25}; — 3. of sleep of the dead Jb 3_{13}; — 4. of God Ps 44_{24}, neg. Ps 121_{4}.

piel: impf. תְּיַשְּׁנֵהוּ: **make** (s.one) **go to sleep** Ju 16_{19}. †

II **ישׁן**: **nif.**: נוֹשַׁנְתֶּם; pt. נוֹשָׁן, נוֹשֶׁנֶת: — 1. **become old** = become familiar (w. the land) Dt 4_{25}; — 2. chronic skin disease Lv 13_{11}; of grain, old & stored up Lv 26_{10}. †

יָשָׁן: f. יְשָׁנָה; pl. יְשָׁנִים: **old**: of architecture: gate Ne 3_{6}, reservoir Is 22_{11}; old = last year's Lv 25_{22} 26_{10}.

I **יָשֵׁן**: f. יְשֵׁנָה, pl. יְשֵׁנִים, יְשֵׁנֵי: — 1. **sleeping** 1K 3_{20}; of God Ps 78_{65}, of Baal 1K 18_{27}; — 2. pl. = **the dead** Ps 22_{30}.

II **יָשֵׁן**: n. pers. 2S 23_{32}. †

יְשָׁנָה: n. loc. 2C 13_{19}. †

ישׁע: **nif.**: pf. נוֹשַׁע, נוֹשַׁעְתֶּם, נוֹשָׁעְנוּ; impf. תִּוָּשֵׁעוּן, אִוָּשֵׁעָה, אִוָּשֵׁעַ, תִּוָּשַׁע, תִּוָּשְׁעִי, יִוָּשֵׁעַ, נִוָּשֵׁעָה, נִוָּשֵׁעַ; impv. הִוָּשְׁעוּ; pt. נוֹשָׁע: — 1. **receive help** 2S 22_{4}; — 2. **be victorious** Is 33_{16}; pt. victorious Dt 33_{29}; — 3. **let onesf. be helped** Is 45_{22}.

hif.: pf. הוֹשִׁיעַ, הוֹשַׁעְתָּ, הוֹשִׁיעוּ, הוֹשִׁיעוֹ, יְהוֹשִׁיעַ, הוֹשַׁעְתִּים, הוֹשַׁעְתָּנוּ; impf. יוֹשִׁיעַ (יְהוֹשִׁיעַ 1S 17_{47} Ps 116_{6}), וַיּ(וֹ)שַׁע, יוֹשַׁע, יוֹשִׁעוּ, תּוֹשִׁיעוּן, יוֹשִׁיעֵךְ, וַיּוֹשִׁיעָן, יוֹשִׁעוּ, יוֹשַׁעֲכֶם Is 35_{4}, יוֹשִׁיעֵנוּ, אוֹשִׁיעַ, אוֹשִׁיעָה, אוֹשִׁיעֵם, וַיּ(וֹ)שִׁיעוּם, יוֹשִׁיעוּךְ; impv. הוֹשַׁע, הוֹשִׁיעָה, הוֹשִׁיעֵנִי; inf. הוֹשַׁע, הוֹשִׁיעַ, לְהוֹשִׁיעַ, הוֹשִׁיעָה, הוֹשִׁיעֲךָ; pt. מוֹשִׁיעַ, מוֹשִׁיעוֹ, מוֹשִׁיעֵךְ, מ(וֹ)שִׁיעִי, pl. מוֹשִׁיעִים: — 1. **help** (s.one at work) Ex 2_{17}; — 2. **help, save, rescue** (s.one in trouble): a) subj. men Dt 22_{27} (42×); b) subj. God Ex 14_{30} (100×); *hôšî'â* = the call 'help' 2S 14_{4} (10×); — 3. **come to (the) aid**, w. *le* of 2S 10_{11}; subj. *yād* hand 1S 25_{26}; — 4. var.: a) *'ēl lō' yôšî'a'* a god who does not help Is 45_{20}; b) pt. F *môšî'a'* helper.

יֵשַׁע: cs. =, sf. יִשְׁעִי, יִשְׁעֲךָ, יֶשְׁעֵךְ: **help, liberation, salvation**: a) *'elōhê yiš'î* Ps 18_{47}; *'emet yiš'akā* your true help Ps 69_{14}; b) of the salvation fm. God 2S 22_{36}; which man finds (w. God) 2S 23_{5}; > favor, fortune Jb $5_{4\cdot11}$.

***ישׁע**: יֹשַׁעֲכֶם Is 35_{4}: **help**. †

יִשְׁעִי: n. pers.

יְשַׁעְיָה: n. pers.

יְשַׁעְיָהוּ: n. pers., **Isaiah**.

יְשֻׁעָתָה Ps 80_{3}: F יְשׁוּעָה.

יִשְׁפָּה: n. pers.

יָשְׁפֵה: **jasper** Ex 28_{20} 39_{13} Ez 28_{13}. †

יִשְׁפָּן: n. pers.

ישׁר: **qal**: pf. 'י, יָשְׁרָה; impf. יִישַׁר, וַתִּישַׁר, יִישְׁרוּ, וַיִּשַּׁרְנָה: **be straight, upright, level, right**: — 1. **go straight ahead** (subj. cows) 1S 6_{12}; — 2. be right, **please**: a) w. *be'ênê* 1K 9_{12}; b) w. *le* & inf. = it pleases s.one to = he wants to Je 18_{4}.

piel: pf. יִשַּׁרְתִּי; impf. יְיַשֵּׁר, יְיַשֶּׁר־, אֲיַשֵּׁר, אֲוַשֵּׁר Is 45_{2} Qr 'אֲיַ (Kt *אושר); 2C 32_{30} Qr וַיְּשְּׁרֵם < Kt וַיְיַשְּׁרֵם; impv. יַשְּׁרוּ; pt. מְיַשְּׁרִים: — 1. **level** (obj. path) Is 40_{3}, (mountains) Is 45_{2}; — 2. **direct** (water) **straight** 2C 32_{30}; — 3. a) **go straight ahead** Pr 9_{15}; b) metaph. **keep** (testimonies) **precisely** Ps 119_{128}.

pual: pt. מְיֻשָּׁר: **evenly hammered** (gold-plate) 1K 6_{35}. †

hif.: impf. יַיְשִׁרוּ; impv. הַיְשַׁר Ps 5_9 Qr: — 1. **level** (obj. mountains) Ps 5_9 Qr; — 2. **look straight ahead** (of eyes) Pr 4_{25}. †

יָשָׁר (115×): cs. יְשַׁר, f. יְשָׁרָה; pl. יְשָׁרִים, יִשְׁרֵי, f. יְשָׁרוֹת: — 1. **straight, stretched out** (opp. crooked, bent) Ez 1_7; — 2. **level** (path) Je 31_9; — 3-6. in ethical context: — 3. **right, correct** (thing): a) (path) 1S 12_{23}; b) right in one's own eyes 2S 19_7; c) in God's eyes 1K 11_{33} (28×); — 4. **right, fitting** (person): a) able, qualified 2K 10_3, hard-working Pr 15_{19}; b) righteous, upright Mi 7_2; c) sincere, honest: *yišrê lēb* Ps 7_{11}; d) *hayyešārîm*, the honest, godly Ps 33_1; — 5. **just, righteous**: a) of God Dt 32_4; b) of *debar-yhwh* Ps 33_4 &c.; — 6. **what is right** Jb 33_{27}; *kol-hayyešārâ* everything straight Mi 3_9.

יֵשֶׁר: n. pers.

יֹשֶׁר: sf. יָשְׁרוֹ, יָשְׁרֵהוּ Jb 37_3; pl. יְשָׁרִים (:: יָשָׁר!): — 1. **straightness, uprightness, honesty**: a) *hālak beyōšer* 1K 9_4; b) w. *ᵓamārîm* (words) Jb 6_{25}; — 2. **integrity** a) w. *lēb(āb)* Dt 9_5; b) *miyyōšer* immoderately Pr 11_{24}, *ʿal-yōšer* against justice Pr 17_{26}; c) adv. rightly Ec 12_{10}; — 3. pl. **agreement** Dn 11_{17}.

***יְשְׁרָה**: cs. יִשְׁרַת: **sincerity** 1K 3_6. †

יְשֻׁרוּן: n. peop. (?): **Jeshurun**, honorary name for Isr. Dt 32_{15} $33_{5.26}$ Is 44_2. †

יָשֵׁשׁ: **decrepit** 2C 36_{17}. †

יָתֵד: cs. יְתַד, יְתֶד; pl. יְתֵדוֹת, cs. יִתְדוֹת, sf. יְתֵדֹתָיו: **peg,** (large) **pin, nail**: — 1. a) (wooden tent-) **peg** Ju 4_{21f}; peg in plaster wall, for hanging cloak &c. Is 22_{23}; digging-stick Dt 23_{14}; peg for beating up the weft on a loom Ju 16_{14}; b) (metal) tent-pin Ex 27_{19}; genl. **hold(ing)** Ezr 9_8; — 2. metaph. 'support', = leader of people Zc 10_4.

יָתוֹם: pl. יְתוֹמִים, sf. יְתוֹמָיו: **orphan**: a boy who has become fatherless Ex 22_{21}.

יְתוּר Jb 39_8: rd. יָתוּר (√ תור).

יַתִּיר (1×) & **יַתִּר** (3×): n. loc.

יִתְלָה: n. loc.

יִתְמָה: n. pers. m. (!)

cj I ***יתן**: **qal**: impf. cj יָתַן (= יִיתַן) Pr 12_{12}, & ? Is 33_{16}: **be constant, durable.** †

cj II ***יתן**: **qal**: pt cj יֹתֵן: **give** 2S 22_{41} Ps 18_{33}. †

יַתְנִיאֵל: n. pers.

יִתְנָן: n. loc.

יתר: **qal**: pt. → יוֹתֵר, יֹתֶרֶת.

nif.: pf. נוֹתַר, נוֹתְרָה, נוֹתַרְתִּי; impf. יִוָּתֵר, יִוָּתֶר, וָאִוָּתֵר, יִוָּתְרוּ; pt. נוֹתָר, נוֹתֶרֶת, נוֹתָרִים, נוֹתָרוֹת: **be left over, remain over** Ex 10_{15}; *lōᵓ nôtar ʿanāqîm* there were no A. left Jos 11_{22}.

hif.: pf. הוֹתִיר, הוֹתַרְתִּי, הוֹתִרָה, הוֹתִירְךָ; impf. יוֹתֵר, וַיּוֹתֵר, (וַ)תּוֹתַר, וַיּוֹתִרוּ, נוֹתַר 2S 17_{12} (oth.: nif. pf.); impv. הוֹתֵר; inf. הוֹתֵר: — 1. **leave (over)** Ex 10_{15} (which the hail had left); leave behind Dn 10_{13}; — 2. **have** (s.thg) **remaining, have** (s.thg) **left** 2K 4_{44}; *wehôtēr* enough and to spare Ex 36_7; — 3. w. acc. **pour out an abundance on** (s.one) Dt 28_{11}; — 4. **have precedence, be first** Gn 49_4.

I **יֶתֶר**: sf. יִתְרוֹ: — 1. **remainder**, what s.one leaves (over) Jl 1_4; — 2. **remainder**, what is left over Ex 10_5; *yeter dibrê* what there still is to say 1K 11_{41} (34×); — 3. adv. excessively: *gādôl yeter meᵓōd* very grand indeed Is 56_{12}; *ʿal-yeter* beyond measure Ps 31_{24}.

II **יֶתֶר**: sf. יִתְרָם, pl. יְתָרִים: — 1. the (moist) **sinews** of a newly killed animal Ju 16_{7-9}; — 2. **bow-string** Ps 11_2 Jb 30_{11}; — 3. **tent-ropes** Jb 4_{21} (?; oth.: threads of life). †

III **יֶתֶר**: n. pers.

יֹתֶר: n. pers., → יוֹתֵר.

יַתִּר: n. loc., → יַתִּיר.

יִתְרָא: n. pers.

יִתְרָה Is 15_7 & יִתְרַת (cs.?) Je 48_{36}: **savings.** †

יִתְרוֹ: n. pers., **Jethro**.

יִתְרוֹן: — 1. what comes out, **outcome** Ec 1_3; — 2. **profit, benefit** Ec 2_{13} (w. *min*, over).

יִתְרִי: gent. of III יֶתֶר.

יִתְרָן: n. pers.

יִתְרְעָם: n. pers.

יֹתֶרֶת & יוֹתֶרֶת: הַיּוֹתֶרֶת עַל־הַכָּבֵד: appendage, the extra **lobes of the liver** in cattle, sheep, & goats but not in man Ex 29_{13}.

יְתֵת: n. pers.

כ

כְּ: ≠ כְּמוֹ, כַּאֲשֶׁר; alw. proclitic, vowel varies: כַּאֲבוֹתָם, כַּמָּה; כְּמָה, כְּהַיּוֹם & כַּיּוֹם, כַּאדֹנָיו, כַּיהוה 1S 2_2, כַּאַבִּיר Is 10_{13} (Qr כַּבִּיר, rd Kt כְּאַבִּיר), כֵּאלֹהִים, כֶּאֱמוֹר, כָּהֶם, כָּכֶם Is 24_2; sf. כַּגְּבִירְתָּהּ, כִּבְרִיתִי, כָּהֵנָּה, כָּהֵן, כָּהֵמָּה, otherw. ≠ כְּמוֹ: particle of comparison, **like**: — 1. expresses identity: a) *kullô keʾaddeVet śēʿār* altogether like a hairy mantle Gn 25_{25}, *weʾāhabtā lereʿakā kāmôka* like yourself Lv 19_{18}; *ʾên qādôš keyhwh* = except ? 1S 2_2; *kelōʾ hāyû* like those who had not been = as if they had not been Ob $_{10}$; b) w. *ke* 2× : α) the designated subj. first: *kāʿām kakkōhēn* the people like the pr. Is 24_2, *kāmônî kāmôkā* I, like you Gn 44_{18}; β) the term of comparison first: *kaṣṣaddîq kārāšāʿ* the godless like the righteous Gn 18_{25}; *ke* … *kēn* Ps 127_4; — 2. agreement in measure: a) **as much as**: *kākem ʾelef peʿāmîm* 1000 times as many as you are Dt 1_{11}; b) > **about** (= approximately): *kepeśaʿ* only (about) a pace 1S 20_3, *kemišlōš ḥodāšîm* about 3 months later Gn 38_{24}; — 3. agreement in kind: in the same way as, of the same sort as: *kēʾlōhîm* Gn 3_5, *ʾîš kāmônî* Gn 44_{15}; *kāzōʾt* (something) like this, such a thing Is 66_8; > **suitable to, according to**: *kidmûtēnû* Gn 1_{26}, *kešēm* after the name of Gn 4_{17}; — 4. preps. a) are included in *ke*: *kehar* as on the mountain Is 28_{21}, *kaḥalôm* as in a dream Is 29_7; b) otherwise, in fixed expressions: *kebāriʾšōnâ* Ju 20_{32}; — 5. seemingly superfluous, accentuating: *ʾattâ keʾaḥad mēhem*, just like Ob $_{11}$; — 6. as stylistic device to describe a vision, 'something like': *kemarʾēh gāber* one who looked like a man Dn 8_{15}; — 7. *ke* & inf.: a) comparison: *keʾekōl* as … devours Is 5_{24}; b) temporal: *kebôʾ* when he came Gn 12_{14}, *kirʾōtô* as soon as he sees Gn 44_{31}; before a noun in verbal sense: *ketom-* when it is finished Is 18_5.

כאב: qal: impf. יִכְאַב, יִכְאָב; pt. כֹּאֵב, כֹּאֲבִים: **be in pain** Gn 34_{25} (wound-fever) Ps 69_{30} Pr 14_{13}, w. *ʿal* Jb 14_{22}. †

hif.: pf. הִכְאַבְתִּיו; impf. יַכְאִיב, תַּכְאִיב; pt. מַכְאִיב: — 1. **cause pain, anguish** (w. acc. of pers.) Ez $13_{22aβ}$ 28_{24} Jb 5_{18}; — 2. metaph. **ruin** (a field w. stones) 2K 3_{19}. †

כְּאֵב: sf. כְּאֵבִי: **pain, anguish** Jb 2_{13}.

כאה: nif.: pf. נִכְאָה: **jump back startled** Dn 11_{30}. †

[hif.: inf. הַכְאוֹת Ez 13_{22} rd. הַכְאִיב.]

כָּאֲרִי Ps 22_{17}: ??: ≠ I כרה, or cj IV כרה; ≠ comm.

כַּאֲשֶׁר (ca. 550×): כְּ + אֲשֶׁר: conj.: — 1. as (in the sense of 'in the way that'): *kaʾašer ṣiwwâ* Gn 7_9, *kaʾašer ʾāmar* Gn 34_{12} (note: strengthened form: *kekol-ʾašer ṣiwwâ* just as he … Gn 7_5); b) elliptic, w/o repetition of verb: *kaʾašer [killîtem] bihyôt* … Ex 5_{13}; c) in expression of submission: *kaʾašer šākōltî šakāltî* Gn 43_{14}; d) *kaʾašer* … *kēn*, as … so Nu 2_{17}, the more … the more Ex 1_{12};

— 2. causal: accordingly that = **because** 2K 17_{26}; — 3. hypothetical: **as though** Zc 10_{6}; — 4. temporal: a) as = **when** w. pf. Gn $32_{3.32}$; b) **after** Ju 16_{22}, pleonastic *'aḥªrê ka'ªšer* Jos 2_{7}; c) w. impf. **when** Ec 4_{17}.

כָּבֵד: **qal**: pf. כ׳ (↗ adj. כָּבֵד), כָּבֵד Is 24_{20}, כָּבְדוּ, כָּבְדָה, כָּבֵדָה; impf. יִכְבַּד, יִכְבַּד, נִכְבַּד, יִכְבְּדוּ, וַתִּכְבְּדִי: — 1. **weigh heavily** (on s.one): subj. hand = power 1S 5_{6}; sin is grave Gn 18_{20}; of guests, be a burden (to s.one) 2S 13_{25}; w. *min*, be too heavy for Ps 38_{5}; — 2. **be heavy = dull**: of eyes Gn 48_{10}, ear Is 59_{1}, heart Ex 9_{7}; — 3. **be weighty, honored** Jb 14_{21}.

nif.: pf. נִכְבַּד, נִכְבַּדְתָּ, נִכְבַּדְתִּי; impf. אֶכָּבֵד Hg 1_{8} Kt (Qr אֶכָּבְדָה), אִכָּבְדָה, אִכָּבֵדָה; impv. הִכָּבֵד; inf. הִכָּבְדִי; pt. נִכְבָּד, נִכְבַּדֵּי, נִכְבָּדִים, נִכְבַּדֶּיהָ & (!), נִכְבָּדוֹת, נִכְבְּדֵיהֶם: — 1. be recognized as weighty, **be honored** Gn 34_{19}; *nikbād mē'eḥāyw* esteemed as 1C 4_{9}; — 2. let onesf. be honored, **enjoy respect** 2K 14_{10}; — 3. **behave with dignity** 2S 6_{20}; — 4. (of God) **appear in one's glory** Ex 14_{4}; — 5. what is splendid, glorious Ps 87_{3}.

piel: pf. כִּבְּדוּ, כִּבַּדְתּוֹ, כִּבַּדְתָּנִי, כִּבְּדוּנִי, כִּבַּדְנוּךָ; impf. אֲכַבֵּדֵהוּ, תְּכַבְּדוּ, יְכַבֵּד, תְּכַבֵּדְךָ Pr 4_{8}, יְכַבְּדָנְנִי Ps 50_{23}; impv. כַּבֵּד, כַּבְּדוּהוּ; inf. כַּבֵּד, כַּבֶּדְךָ; pt. מְכַבֵּד, מְכַבְּדַי, מְכַבְּדֶיךָ, מְכַבְּדוֹ: — 1. **make dull, insensitive** (↗ qal 2), obj. heart 1S 6_{6}; — 2. **honor**: a) obj. men 1S 15_{30}, father & mother Ex 20_{12}, metaph. city La 1_{8}; = reward richly Nu 22_{17}; b) obj. God 1S 2_{30}; w. 2 acc. honor with Is 43_{23}; c) God honors men 1S 2_{30}; — 3. **honor** s.thg: Sabbath Is 58_{13}, place 60_{13}.

pual: impf. יְכֻבָּד; pt. מְכֻבָּד: — 1. **be honored** Pr 13_{18}, 27_{18} (= become rich?, ↗ piel 2. a)); — 2. pt. **honorable** Is 58_{13}. †

hif.: pf. הִכְבִּיד, הִכְבַּדְתָּ, הִכְבַּדְתִּים; impf. וַיַּכְבֵּד; inf. הַכְבֵּד; pt. מַכְבִּיד: — 1. make heavy, **let** s.thg **weigh heavily**: yoke 1K $12_{10.14}$, pledges Hb 2_{6}; — 2. make dull, **harden**: heart Ex 8_{11}, ear Is 6_{10}; — 3. **bring to honor** Is 8_{23}; — 4. **make numerous** Je 30_{19}.

hitp.: impv. הִתְכַּבֵּד, הִתְכַּבְּדִי; pt. מִתְכַּבֵּד: — 1. **multiply, increase** (intrans.) Na 3_{15}; — 2. **swagger, put on airs** Pr 12_{9}. †

I **כָּבֵד** adj.: cs. כְּבַד & Is 1_{4} כֶּבֶד; pl. כְּבֵדִים, כִּבְדֵי: — 1. **heavy, weighty**: hair 2S 14_{26}, yoke 1K 12_{4}, hands (= weary) Ex 17_{12}; — 2. **heavy, oppressive, grievous**: famine Gn 12_{10}, hail Ex 9_{18}, baggage 1K 10_{2}; — 3. **weighty, impressive**: a) rich Gn 13_{2}; b) numerous Gn 50_{9}; — 4. difficult 1K 3_{9}; — 5. **dull, hard** (heart) Ex 7_{14}; — 6. **clumsy, slow**: tongue Ez 3_{5f}, mouth Ex 4_{10}; — 7. var.: *kebed 'āwōn* encumbered w. guilt Is 1_{4}; *kābēd min* heavier than Pr 27_{3}.

II **כָּבֵד**: sf. כְּבֵדִי, כְּבֵדוֹ: — 1. **liver** Ex 29_{13}; — 2. **inspection of the liver** (for divination) Ez 21_{26}.

כֹּבֶד: — 1. **heaviness, weight, burden**: of battle Is 21_{15}, of heavy clouds 30_{27}; — 2. **heavy mass**: of corpses Na 3_{3}, of stone Pr 27_{3}. †

כָּבֹד: ↗ כָּבוֹד.

כְּבֵדֻת: **difficulty, awkwardness**: *bikbēdut* labouriously Ex 14_{25}. †

כבה: **qal**: pf. כָּבוּ: impf. יִכְבֶּה, תִּכְבֶּה: **be extinguished, go out**: fire Lv 6_{5f}; lamp 1S 3_{3}; metaph. anger of God 2K 22_{17}; = die Is 43_{17}.

piel: pf. כִּבּוּ; impf. תְּכַבֶּה, וַיְכַבּוּ, יְכַבֶּנָּה; inf. כַּבּוֹת, כַּבּוֹתְךָ; pt. מְכַבֶּה: — 1. **extinguish, put out**, obj. lamp (metaph. of king) 2S 21_{17}; — 2. **quench** (metaph., obj. love) SS 8_{7}; *we'ên mekabbeh* without anyone to quench (them) Is 1_{31}.

כָּבוֹד & 2× כָּבֹד (ca. 200×): cs. כְּבוֹד, sf. כְּבוֹדוֹ.

I. non-theological: — 1. **weight, burden** Is 22_{24}; — 2. a) **possessions** Gn 31_1; b) **(impressive) appearance**, weightiness Gn 45_3; *kᵉbôdô* coll. his nobles Is 5_{13}; c) great **number** Ho 9_{11}; — 3. **splendor, magnificence**: of woods Is 10_{18}, Lebanon Is 35_2, temple Hg 2_3; — 4. **distinction, respect, mark of honor**: a) gift of honor 1S 6_5, seat of honor 1S 2_8; b) || riches &c. 1K 3_{13}; c) honor: abs. Pr 15_{33}, of Isr. Is 10_3; d) *nātan kābôd* show honor to Pr 26_8.

II. theological: — 1. give honor to Y. (↗ I 4. c): a) w. *śîm* Jos 7_{19}, w. *nātan* Je 13_{16} &c.; b) Y. is the *kābôd* of the godly &c. Ps 3_4; Y. is *likbôd* for Jerus. Zc 2_9; Y. is Isr.'s *kābôd* Je 2_{11}; — 2. *kᵉbôd yhwh*: a) fixed phrase, 1K 8_{11}, 10× Ez; power, authority, honor of God, but also connected with manifestations of light; b) oth. expr. for God: *kᵉbôd ʾēl* Ps 19_2; *melek hakkābôd* Ps 24_{7-10} &c.; c) as the outward appearance of Y.: appears to elders Dt 5_{24}; Moses sees Ex 33_{13}; seen in sanctuary Ps 26_8, clouds Ex 16_{10}; d) appears at sacrifice Lv 9_6 & elsewh.; e) manifestations in wider sense: fills the whole earth Is 6_3, will be set among the nations Ez 39_{21}.

כְּבוּדָּה: **valuable property** Ju 18_{21}. †

כָּבוּל: n. loc.

כַּבּוֹן: n. loc.

כַּבִּיר: pl. כַּבִּרִים; only in Is & Jb: **strong, powerful**: person Jb 34_{17}, waters Is 17_{12}, God Jb 36_{5a}; neut. much Jb 31_{25}; *kabbîr* … *yāmîm* aged Jb 15_{10}.

***כָּבִיר**: cs. כְּבִיר: something **braided**: *kᵉbîr ʿizzîm* fm. goats' hair, evid. a cushion or the like 1S $19_{13.16}$. †

כֶּבֶל: pl. cs. כַּבְלֵי: **fetters** Ps 105_{18} 149_8. †

כבס: **qal**: pt. כּוֹבֵס: **full**, i.e. clean cloth by treading, kneading & beating (no soap was available in ancient times); *śᵉdēh kôbēs* Fuller's Field 2K 18_{17} = Is 36_2, Is 7_3. †

piel: pf. כִּבְּסָתֶם, כִּבְּסוּ, כִּבֵּס, כִּבֶּס, כִּבֵּס; impf. יְכַבֵּס, תְּכַבְּסִי, תְּכַבְּסֵנִי; impv. כַּבְּסִי, כַּבְּסֵנִי; pt. מְכַבְּסִים: — 1. **full** (a garment), clean Gn 49_{11}; — 2. metaph. **clean**, obj. *lēb* Je 4_{14}, wash away guilt Je 2_{27}.

pual: pf. כֻּבַּס: **be washed** Lv 13_{58} 15_{17}. †

hotpael: pf. הֻכַּבֵּס (< *hutk-*); w. acc. **be washed off** Lv $13_{55f.}$ †

כבר: **hif.**: impf. יַכְבִּר: **make many** (words) Jb 35_{16}; *lᵉmakbîr*, in abundance Jb 36_{31}. †

I **כְּבָר**: **already, long ago** Ec 1_{10}.

II **כְּבָר**: n. river (canal) Ez 1_1.

I **כְּבָרָה**: **sieve** Am 9_9. †

II ***כְּבָרָה** or ***כִּבְרָה**: cs. כִּבְרַת: (a given) **distance**; *kibrat ʾereṣ* a little way Gn 48_7 2K 5_{19}, *kibrat hāʾāreṣ* Gn 35_{16}. †

כֶּבֶשׂ (108×): pl. כְּבָשִׂים, sf. כְּבָשַׂי: **young ram**, usu. sacrificial animal Ex 12_5.

כִּבְשָׂה: pl. כְּבָשׂוֹת, cs. כִּבְשׂוֹת: **young ewe-lamb** Gn 21_{28-30} Lv 14_{10} Nu 6_{14} 2S $12_{3f.}$ †

כבשׁ: **qal**: pf. כָּבְשׁוּ; impf. תִּכְבְּשׁוּ, וַיִּכְבְּשׁוּם Je 34_{11} Qr (Kt hif.); impv. כִּבְשֻׁהָ; inf. לִכְבּ(וֹ)שׁ; pt. כֹּבְשִׁים: — 1. w. acc. **subject** s.one, **make subservient**: earth Gn 1_{28}, people Je 34_{16}, as slaves Je 34_{11}; — 2. **violate, rape** (a woman) Est 7_8.

nif.: pf. נִכְבְּשָׁה; pt. נִכְבָּשׁוֹת: — 1. **be subjugated** (of land) Nu 32_{22}; — 2. **be degraded** (sexually?) Ne 5_5.

piel: pf. כִּבֵּשׁ: **subdue, subjugate** (peoples) 2S 8_{11}. †

hif.: impf. וַיַּכְבִּישׁוּם: **subdue, subjugate** (peoples) Je 34_{11} Kt. †

כֶּבֶשׁ: **footstool** 2C 9_{18}. †

כִּבְשָׁן: **furnace, forge** Gn 19_{28} Ex $9_{8.10}$ 19_{18}. †

כַּד: sf. כַּדֵּךְ, כַּדָּהּ; pl. כַּדִּים: **large** (pottery) **jar**, for water Gn 24_{14} 1K 18_{34}, flour 1K 17_{12}.

כַּדּוּר: skein (of yarn), **ball** Is 22_{18}?, or ↗ דּוּר. †

כְּדֵי: ↗ דַּי.

כַּדְכֹּד & **כַּדְכֹּד**: **a precious stone, ruby** (?) Is 54_{12} Ez 27_{16}. †

כְּדֻמָה Ez 27_{32} (?); like a silence? like s.thg destroyed? ꟻ comm.

כְּדָרְלָעֹמֶר, כְּדָר־לָ׳ Gn 14_{17}: n. of king of Elam Gn 14_{1}.

כֹּה: — 1. loc. **here** Nu 23_{15}; *kōh wākōh* this way & that Ex 2_{12}, *ʿad-kōh* to that place, (to) there Gn 22_{5}; — 2. temporal, **now**: *ʿad-kōh* until now Ex 7_{16}, *ʿad-kōh weʿad kōh* meanwhile 1K 18_{45}; — 3. **so, thus**: a) just so (= in the same way) (20×) Gn 15_{5}; b) so, thus (= as follows) (50×) Gn 24_{30}; c) *kōh ʾāmar* thus says (introducing an oral message): α) profane (26×) Gn 32_{5}; β) *kōh ʾāmar yhwh* (435×) Ex 4_{22}; *kōh neʾum yhwh* Je 9_{21}; — 4. repeated *kōh yaʿaśeh wekōh yôsîf* (12×) 1S 3_{17}; *zeh bekōh wezeh bekōh* one (said) one thing, another another 1K 22_{20}.

I כהה: **qal**: pf. כָּהֲתָה; impf. יִכְהֶה, וַתִּכְהֶ, תִּכְהֶיךָ; inf. abs. כָּהֹה: (of eyes) **become expressionless** Gn 27_{1} Dt 34_{7} Is 42_{4} Zc 11_{17} Jb 17_{7}. †

piel: pf. כִּהֲתָה, כֵּהָה: — 1. (of spot on the skin) **become colorless** Lv $13_{6\cdot 56}$; — 2. (of spirit) **be disheartened** Ez 21_{12}. †

II כהה: **piel**: pf. כִּהָה: w. *be* set s.one **right, rebuke** 1S 3_{13}. †

כֵּהֶה: f. כֵּהָה; pl. כֵּהוֹת: — 1. a) (of a place on the skin) **colorless** Lv 13_{21}; b) (of eyes) **clouded, dull** 1S 3_{2}; c) metaph. (of spirit) **fearful** Is 61_{3}; — 2. **without light**, (dimly) **glowing** (of a wick) Is 42_{3}.

כֵּהָה: quenching (?) Na 3_{19} (? or rd. גֵּהָה healing). †

כהן: **piel**: pf. כִּהֵן, כִּהֲנָה; impf. יְכַהֵן, וַיְכַהֲנוּ; inf. כַּהֵן, כַּהֲנוֹ: **perform the duties of a priest** (w. *le* & God) Ex 28_{1}.

כֹּהֵן (740×): pl. כֹּהֲנִים, cs. כֹּהֲנֵי, sf. כֹּהֲנַי: **priest**, both pagan & of Y.: — 1. *kōhēn ʾôn* (in Egypt) Gn 41_{45}, *kōhanê dāgôn* 1S 5_{5}; — 2. *ʾadmat hakkōhanîm* land of the priests Gn 47_{22}; *ʿîr hakkōhanîm* 1S 22_{19}; *benê hakkōhanîm* Ezr 10_{18}, *naʿar hakkōhēn* 1S 2_{13}; — 3. *ʾîš kōhēn* a priest Lv 21_{9}, *bāḥar lekōhēn* 1S 2_{28}, *ʿāśâ/nātan kōhēn* appoint a priest 1K 12_{31} Je 29_{26}; — 4. *hakkōhanîm hanniggāšîm ʾel-yhwh* Ex 19_{22} & oth. phrases; — 5. **the high priest**: a) *hakkōhēn hārōʾš* Ezr 7_{5}, > *kōhēn hārōʾš* 2K 25_{18}, > *hārōʾš* 2C 24_{6}; *kōhēn hammišneh* his deputy 2K 25_{18}; b) *hakkōhēn haggādôl* 2K 12_{11}; c) *hakkōhēn hammāšîaḥ* Lv 4_{3}; d) **Levitical priests**: *hakkōhanîm halwiyyîm* Dt 17_{9}, *hal. hak.* Je 33_{21}, *hak. wehal.* 1K 8_{4} ! (47×), *hal. wehak.* 2C 19_{8}; e) Aaron the priest (22×) Ex 31_{10}; *benê ʾaharōn halwiyyîm* Lv 1_{5} (10×); — 6. *kōhēn* + *tôrâ* Mi 3_{11}.

כְּהֻנָּה: cs. כְּהֻנַּת, sf. כְּהֻנָּתְכֶם; pl. כְּהֻנּוֹת: — 1. **priesthood** (i.e. group of priests at a sanctuary) 1S 2_{36}; — 2. **priesthood** (i.e. office or order of priest) Ex 29_{29}; *kehunnat ʿôlām* perpetual priesthood Ex 40_{15}.

כּוּב Ez 30_{5}: n. peop.; but most rd לוּב.

כּוֹבַע: = ꟻ קוֹבַע; כּוֹבַע; cs. כּוֹבַע; pl. כּוֹבָעִים: **helmet** 1S 17_{5}.

כוה: cj. **qal**: pt. כֹּוֶה for כֹּה: **burn, scorch** Je 23_{29}. †

nif.: impf. תִּכָּוֶה, תִּכָּוֶינָה: **be burned, scorched** Is 43_{2} Pr 6_{28}. †

כּוֹחַ Dn 11_{6}: ꟻ כֹּחַ.

כְּוִיָּה: **scar** Ex 21_{25}. †

כּוֹכָב: cs. כּוֹכַב; pl. כּוֹכָבִים, כּוֹכְבֵי, sf. כּוֹכְבֵיהֶם: **star** Gn 1_{16}, *kôkebê haššāmayim* Gn 22_{17}; *rōʾš kôkābîm* pole of the heavens Jb 22_{12}; w. *yāṣâ* come out Ne 4_{15}.

כול: **qal**: pf. כָּל: **lay hold of, seize** Is 40_{12}. †

pilpel: pf. כִּלְכֵּל, כִּלְכַּלְתִּי, כִּלְכְּלוּ, כִּלְכְּלָם; impf. יְכַלְכֵּל, אֲכַלְכֵּל, וַיְכַלְכְּלֵם, יְכַלְכְּלֶךָּ, יְכַלְכְּלֵהוּ; inf. כַּלְכֵּל (כַּלְכֵּל Je 20_{7}); pt. מְכַלְכֵּל: — 1. **clasp, hold in, contain**: obj. fire Je 20_{9}, God 1K 8_{27}; — 2. **provide** (food) Gn 45_{11}; — 3. **manage** (one's business) Ps 112_{5}.

polpal: pf. כָּלְכְּלוּ: **be provided** (w. food) 1K 20_{27}. †

hif.: impf. יְכִילֶנָּה, יָכִילוּ, יָכִיל; inf. הָכִיל: — 1. **hold, contain** (a given amount) 1K 7_{26}; hold, not let run out (subj. cisterns, obj. water) Je 2_{13}; — 2. **endure**, bear Je 6_{11}.

כּוּמָז: feminine ornament for neck & breast Ex 35_{22} Nu 31_{50}.

כּוּן: [**qal**: impf. וַיְכֻנֶנּוּ Jb 31_{15}, rd. w. oth. mss. וַיְכוֹנְנֵנוּ. †]

nif.: pf. נָכֹ(ו)נוּ, נָכוֹנָה; impf. יִכּוֹן, וַתִּכּוֹן, יִכֹּנוּ; impv. הִכֹּ(ו)ן, הִכּוֹנוּ 2C 35_4 Kt (Qr hif.); pt. נָכוֹן, cs. נְכוֹן, f. נְכוֹנָה, pl. נְכוֹנִים: — 1. **stand firm, fast**: moon Ps 89_{38}, house Ju $16_{26\cdot29}$; *'ad-nᵉkôn hayyôm* until high noon Pr 4_{18}; stand firm, taut (of breasts) Ez 16_7; — 2. **be stable, secure**: a) *dᵉrākîm* Ps 119_5; *lᵉ'ên nākôn lô*, to one who possesses nothing Ne 8_{10}; b) *rûᵃḥ nākôn* steady spirit Ps 51_{12}, *lēb nākôn* Ps 57_8; c) *hāyâ nākôn 'im* be reliable in relation to Ps 78_{37}; — 3. **be re-established** (of worship service) 2C 29_{35}; — 4. **be lasting, durable**: a) fin. vb.: subj. *zera'* Ps 102_{29}; kingship 1K 2_{12}; congregation Je 30_{20}; b) pt. 1K 2_{45}; — 5. **be ready** Ez 38_7, w. *lᵉ* Ex 19_{11}; — 6. a) *nākôn haddābār*: a thing is decided, agreed upon Gn 41_{32}; it is pertinent Dt 13_{15}; *nᵉkônâ* reliable, true Ps 5_{10}; b) *'el-nākôn* 1S 23_{23} adv. safely, certainly (?); c) *nākôn* & inf. **it is legitimate to** Ex 8_{22}.

polel: pf. כּוֹנֵן, כּוֹנַנְתָּ, כּוֹנְנָתָה, כּוֹנְנוּ, וַיְכוֹנְנֶךָ, וַיְכוֹנְנֶהָ, יְכוֹנֵן; impf. כּוֹנַנְתָּה, כּוֹנְנָה, וַיְכוֹנְנוּנִי; impv. כּוֹנֵן, כּוֹנְנָה, כּוֹנְנֵהוּ: — 1. **set up, prepare**: a) sanctuary Ex 15_{17}, throne 2S 7_{13}; b) **establish, found**: city Is 62_7, earth Is 45_{18}, put in its place: heavens Pr 3_{19}; c) **appoint** s.one as (a people) 2S 7_{24}; d) **beget, fashion** (men) cj. Jb 31_{15} (→ qal); — 2. **set up firmly, give permanence to**: men Dt 32_6, city Ps 87_5; *ma'ᵃśeh* give firmness, solidity to, promote Ps 90_{17}; — 3. tech. term for holding the arrow firmly on the bow > **take aim** Ps 11_2, w/o *ḥēṣ* 21_{13}, prepare (bow) to shoot Ps 7_{13}; — 4. metaph. **establish** = find out Jb 8_8.

polal: pf. כּוֹנָנוּ: **be prepared** Ez 28_{13}. †

hif. (ca. 100×): pf. הֵכִין, הֲכִינֹ(ו)תָ(ה), הֲכִינֹתִי, הֱכִינוּ, הֵכִינוּ, הֲכִינֹנוּ, הֵכַנּוּ 2C 29_{19}, הֱכִינוּ, הֱכִינַנִי; impf. יָכִין, וַיָּכֶן, אָכִין, אָכִינָה, וַיָּכִינוּ, תְּכִינֶהָ; impv. הָכֵן, הָכִינוּ; inf. הָכִין (cs. & abs.); pt. מֵכִין: — 1. **prepare** (rain for earth) Ps 147_8, (meat) Gn 43_{16}, (gift) 43_{25}; set up, establish (throne) Ps 103_{19}, (altar) Ezr 3_3; other objects 1K 5_{32}; *hākēn lāk* keep yourself ready Je 46_{14}; — 2. **determine**: a) fix (a day) Na 2_4, (a place) Ex 23_{20}; direct Pr 16_9; b) appoint, **install** (persons) 1K 2_{24}, w. *lᵉmelek* 2S 5_{12}; — 3. prepare = create (subj. God) Je 10_{12}; — 4. fasten, consolidate: a) **make firm**: steps Ps 119_{133}, heart 78_8; b) put/keep in good repair: temple 2C 33_{16} Kt; c) inf. as adv.: *'āmēd hākēn* (stand) firm, immovable Jos 3_{17}; — 5. metaph. a) w. *lēb* & *'el*, direct one's thoughts, **consider**, make up one's mind 1S 7_3; w. *pānāyw* Ez $43_{\cdot7}$ direct one's face (w. *'el* against); — 6. var.: w. *'ᵉmûnātô bᵉ* keep unshaken one's faithfulness towards Ps 89_3; w. *darkô* go one's way w. perseverance Pr 21_{29}.

hof.: pf. הוּכַן, הוּכָן, הֻכַן; pt. מוּכָן, מוּכָנִים: — 1. **be established, set up firmly** Is 16_5 30_{33} Ez 40_{43} Na 2_6; — 2. **be made ready, trained** (?) Pr 21_{31}. †

hitpolel: impf. יִתְכּוֹנֵן Pr 24_3 & תִּכּוֹנֵן, יִכּוֹנָנוּ, תִּכּוֹנָנִי (<* *titk-*, *yitk-*): — 1. **draw** onesf. **up** (in battle array), **form up** Ps 59_5; — 2. **be firmly founded**: city Nu 21_{27}, Is 54_{14}, house Pr 24_{31}. †

כּוּן: n. loc. 1C 18_8. †

***כַּוָּן**: pl. כַּוָּנִים: (sacrificial) **cakes** Je 7_{18} 44_{19}. †

כָּנְיָהוּ: n. pers.; Kt כּוֹ׳, Qr כָּ׳.

I כּוֹס: sf. כּוֹסִי; pl. כֹּסוֹת; f.: **(drinking-)cup**: — 1. in genl.: Gn 40_{21} 1K 7_{26}; — 2. in Y.'s hand Hb 2_{16}, cup of salvation Ps 116_{13}; other phrases, cup of drunkenness Is 51_{22} & of poison Is 51_{17}; — 3. *menāt kôsām* portion of their cup Ps 11_{6} = their fate.

II כּוֹס: small owl, unclean bird living in ruins: **screech-owl** or **little owl** Lv 11_{17} Dt 14_{16} Ps 102_{7}. †

כּוּר: **small furnace** or **forge** 1K 8_{51}.

כּוֹר עָשָׁן: n. loc.

כּוֹרֶשׁ: n. pers. **Cyrus.**

I כּוּשׁ: n. terr. in south, variously located: Nubia & S. Sudan, or astride the Red Sea, or land of Kassites, to the east.

II כּוּשׁ: n. pers. Ps 7_{1}. †

I כּוּשִׁי, כֻּשִׁי 1×: gent. of I כּוּשׁ; n. peop.; f. כֻּשִׁית; pl. כּוּשִׁים, כֻּשִׁים, כֻּשִׁיִּים: **Cushite.**

II כּוּשִׁי: n. pers.; = I: Je 36_{14} Zp 1_{1}. †

כּוּשָׁן: n. peop. Hb 3_{7}. †

כּוּשַׁן רִשְׁעָתַיִם: n. of king, prob. deformed name Ju $3_{8\cdot10}$. †

*כּוֹשָׁרָה; pl. כּוֹשָׁרוֹת: **prosperity, fortune** Ps 68_{7}. †

כּוּת 2K 17_{30}, כּוּתָה 17_{24}: name of Mesopotamian city.

כּוּתָה 2K 17_{24}: ↗ כּוּת.

כּוֹתֶרֶת: ↗ כֹּתֶרֶת.

כזב: **qal**: pt. כֹּזֵב: **lie** (tell a falsehood) Ps 116_{11}. †

nif.: pf. נִכְזַבָה, נִכְזַבְתָּ: **turn out, prove to be a liar** Pr 30_{6}, subj. hope Jb 41_{1}. †

piel: pf. כִּזֵּב; impf. אֲכַזֵּב, תְּכַזְּבִי, יְכַזֵּב; inf. כַּזֶּבְכֶם: — 1. **lie** (tell a falsehood) Nu 23_{19}, w. *be* lie to s.one's face 2K 4_{16}, w. *le* tell a person lies Ez 13_{19}; — 2. **deceive, cheat** Is 58_{11}.

hif.: impf. יַכְזִיבֵנִי: **brand** s.one **a liar** Jb 24_{25}. †

כָּזָב: pl. כְּזָבִים, sf. כִּזְבֵיהֶם: **lie** (falsehood) Ju $16_{10\cdot13}$; *leḥem kezābîm* deceptive food Pr 23_{3}; *kezābîm* false gods Am 2_{4}.

כֹּזֵבָא: n. loc.

כָּזְבִּי: n. pers. f.

כְּזִיב: n. loc.

I כֹּחַ (ca. 120×) & כּוֹחַ Dn 11_{6}: sf. כֹּחוֹ, כֹּחֵךְ, כֹּחֲךָ, כֹּחֲכֶם; no pl.: — 1. **strength, power**: a) of man Ju 16_{5}, of people Jos 17_{17}, of prophet Mi 3_{8}, of bull Pr 14_{4}, of field = yield Gn 4_{12}; *kōḥî* my manly vigor = my first-born son Gn 49_{3}, strength for work Lv 26_{20}; *ma'amaṣṣê kōaḥ* efforts Jb 36_{19}; fasting takes away *kōaḥ* 1S 28_{20}, strength of (= from) food 1K 19_{8}; *mikkōaḥ* powerless Je 48_{45}; b) **(deed of) violence** Ec 4_{1}; — 2. **capacity, ability**: a) physical & intellectual, Ec 9_{10}; b) **possession, means** Pr 5_{10}; — 3. God's power 2K 17_{36}.

II כֹּחַ: a kind of **lizard** Lv 11_{30}. †

כחד: **nif.**: pf. נִכְחַד, נִכְחָד; impf. יִכָּחֵד; pt. נִכְחֶדֶת, נִכְחָדוֹת: — 1. **be hidden** 2S 18_{13}; — 2. **be destroyed, effaced** Ex 9_{15}; scatter, go to ruin (of sheep) Zc $11_{9\cdot16}$.

piel: pf. כִּחֵד, כִּחַדְתִּי, כִּחֲדוּ, כִּחֵדוּ; impf. תְּכַחֵד, אֲכַחֵד, תְּכַחֲדִי, תְּכַחֲדוּ: **keep hidden, cover up** (trans.) Gn 47_{18} 1S 3_{17f}.

hif.: pf. הִכְחַדְתִּיו; impf. וַיַּכְחֵד, יַכְחִידֶנָּה, וְאַכְחִיד, נַכְחִידֵם; inf. הַכְחִיד: **make** s.thg **disappear**: — 1. **destroy, efface** 1K 13_{34}; — 2. **hide** Jb 20_{12}.

כחל: **qal**: pf. כָּחַלְתְּ: **paint** (the eyes) Ez 23_{40}. †

כָּחַשׁ: **qal**: pf. כ׳: **become lean** Ps 109_{24}. †

nif.: impf. וַיִּכָּחֲשׁוּ: **feign submission** Dt 33_{29}. †

piel: pf. כִּחֵשׁ, כִּחֶשׁ Lv 5_{22} Jb 8_{18}, כִּחֲשׁוּ; impf. יְכַחֵשׁ, יְכַחֶשׁ Ho 9_{2}, וַתְּכַחֵשׁ, יְכַחֲשׁוּ, תְּכַחֲשׁוּן; inf. כַּחֵשׁ Zc 13_{4}: — 1. **deny** Gn 18_{15}: w. *be* of thing Lv 5_{22}, w. *be* of person to whom denial is made Lv 5_{21}; — 2. **conceal** Jos 7_{11}; — 3. a) **lie, deceive** (by false show) Zc 13_{4}; b) w. *le* tell (s.one) lies 1K 13_{18}; — 4. **leave in the lurch, fail to appear** (out of deceit) Ho 9_{2}; — 5. **deny,**

disown, w. *b*ᵉ: a) obj. of *b*ᵉ men Jb 8_{14}; b) obj. of *b*ᵉ God Jos 24_{27}, w. *l*ᵉ Jb 31_{28}; — 6. **feign submission** Ps 18_{45}.

hitp.: impf. יִתְכַּחֲשׁוּ: w. *l*ᵉ **feign submission** to 2S 22_{45}.

כַּחַשׁ: כַּחַשׁ; sf. כַּחֲשִׁי; pl. sf. כַּחֲשֵׁיהֶם: — 1. **emaciation**, (chronic) **sickliness** Jb 16_{8}; — 2. **lie, deception** Ho 10_{13}.

***כֶּחָשׁ**: pl. כֶּחָשִׁים: **untruthful** Is 30_{9}. †

I **כִּי**: **scar** (from burning) Is 3_{24}. †

II **כִּי**: — I. demonstr. particle: — 1. 'emphatic,' corroborative, strengthening: a) oft. = **yes, indeed**: *kî rabbâ* is certainly great Gn 18_{20}, *kî môt tāmût*, yes, you shall surely die 1S 14_{44}; b) introducing positive clauses in an oath (⸢ *kî-'im* II 1. b), **truly** Gn 42_{16}; — 2. a) introduces conclusion after condition-clause introduced by *'im lō'*: *'im lō' ta'ᵃmînû kî lō' tē'āmēnû* if you are not ..., then you will not ... Is 7_{9}; b) *kî 'āz* introduces conclusion after a condition introduced by *lûlē'/lûlê*: if ... had not ..., then you would have ... Gn 31_{42}; introduced by *lu'/lû* 2S 19_{7}; introduced by *'im* Jb 11_{14}; c) *kî 'attâ* introduces a conclusion when the condition is only implied: for then I would have ... Jb 3_{13}; — 3. *kî* after a neg. clause: a) **rather** Gn 3_{5} 17_{5} 24_{4}; b) in a contradicting reply: α) *lō' kî* **no**, on the contrary, (you did laugh) Gn 18_{15b} 19_{2} 42_{12b}; β) *lō' kî* (w/o dagesh lene) **no!** 1K 3_{22}; c) preceding negation only implied Gn 31_{16}; — 4. (nothing ...) **but, except** 1S 18_{25}; — 5. in an objection raised by the speaker: but would he really ...? 1K 8_{27}.

II. true conj.: — 1. causal (causal clause before main clause): **because** Gn 3_{14}; — 2. causal clause after main clause: **for** Ps 6_{3}; introducing an interpretation Is 5_{7}; two reasons, *kî* ... *kî* for ... and Gn 3_{19}, *kî* ... *wᵉkî* Gn 33_{11}; — 3. a reason, long in existence, is finally recognized, *kî 'al-kēn* for that is the reason that Gn 19_{8}; as a polite formula Gn 18_{5}; — 4. comb. a) *kî* may be separated from its clause by an *'im*-clause: *kî 'im* for if 2S 18_{3}; b) *hᵃkî* is it true that ...? 2S 9_{1}; *hᵃkî* implies a positive answer Gn 27_{36} 2S 23_{19}; *hᵃlō' kî* implying a positive answer 1S 10_{1}; c) *wᵉkî* introducing a rhetorical qn.: it is true, is it not, that ...? 1S 24_{20}; d) *'af kî*, ⸢ *'af*; e) *'ak kî* only 1S 8_{9}; — 5. introduces an obj.-clause after vb. of seeing, hearing, saying, knowing, believing, remembering, forgetting, rejoicing, regretting &c.: **that** Gn 1_{10} 1K 21_{15}; — 6. obj. of the main clause is identical w. the subj. of the subordinate clause: Gn 1_{4} that it was good (oth.: how good it was); reinforced by *hû'*, *hî'* Gn 12_{14}; same anticipation w. time-phrase: I know after my death that = I know that after my death ... Dt 31_{29}; *kî* separated fm. governing vb. Jb 20_{4-5}; — 7. introducing direct discourse: *wattō'mer kî šāma'* and she said, 'he has heard ...' Gn 29_{33}; — 8. comb. *'efes kî, ya'an kî, 'ad-kî, 'al-kî, 'ēqeb kî, taḥat kî*, ⸢ *'efes, ya'an* &c.; ⸢ *kî 'im*; — 9. after a main clause which is neg. or interr. (asking information), *kî* introduces a subordinate clause of definition & amplification: *mᵉ'ûmâ kî* (I have not done) anything (which could give cause) that (they should put me ...) Gn 40_{15}, ⸢ Gn 20_{10} 31_{36}; — 10. temporal, **when** (almost = **if**) Gn 4_{12}; *wayhî kî* and it happened that = when Gn 6_{1}, *wᵉhāyâ kî* and it will happen that = when Gn 12_{12}; subj. placed before *kî* (⸢ 6): the daughter of any priest, if = if the dau... Lv 21_{9}; — 11. conditional: **if, in case**: *kî 'āmartî* assuming that I say = when, if I say Jb 7_{13}; approaches the true 'if,' *'im*; in casuistic laws, *kî* introduces the basic case (when), and *'im* the subsidiary cases (if) Ex 21_{2-5}; later there seems to be no distinction Nu

5_{19f}; — 12. concessive: **even when, even though** Is 16_{12}; *kî gam* Ec 4_{14}; — 13. modal: **as** Is 55_9; — 14. final: *kî yaʿaleh* let him go up 1C 21_{18}.

כִּי־אִם Gn 15_4 Nu 35_{33} Ne 2_2, otherw. כִּי אִם־.

I. *kî* & *ʾim* introduce 2 separate clauses: **for if** Ex 8_{17}, **that when** Gn 47_{18}, **indeed if** 1S 20_9, on the contrary if La 3_{32} & oft.

II. as a logical unity (ca. 140 ×): — 1. as an affirmative particle: a) **nevertheless, yet** Gn 40_{14}, **actually** 1S 21_6; b) to introduce a positive oath-clause: **truly** 2K 5_{20}; — 2. particle expressing exception after a negative: a) **but (rather)** (German sondern) (ca. 70 ×) Gn 15_4 1K 8_{19}; b) **unless, except**: α) before a clause: **unless, except if** Gn 32_{27} 2K 4_{24}; β) before a noun: **except, but** Gn 28_{17} 2K 4_2; γ) *mî* … *kî ʾim* who is … if not/except Is 42_{19} & *mâ* … *kî ʾim* what … except = nothing but Mi 6_8.

***כִּיד**: כִּידוֹ Jb 21_{20}, fm. context, ruin, destruction, but txt.? ꟳ comm. †

***כִּידוֹד**: pl. cs. כִּידוֹדֵי: **son**, *kîdôdê ʾēš* = sparks Jb 41_{11}. †

כִּידוֹן: trad. **javelin**; but Qumran material sugg. short sword for cutting & thrusting, and for hunting, or curved (crescent-shaped) sword: 1S $17_{6.45}$.

כִּידוֹר: **attack, battle**: *melek ʿātîd lakkîdôr* Jb 15_{24}. †

כִּידֹן: n. pers.

כִּיּוּן: (portable) **pedestal** or **carrier** (for images); but usu. vocalized *kêwān*, name of astral god Saturn: Am 5_{26}. †

כִּיּוֹר & **כִּיֹּר**: pl. כִּיֹּר(וֹ)ת & כִּיֹּרִים: — 1. (bronze) **(wash-)basin** Ex 30_{18}; — 2. **caldron** 1S 2_{14}; *kiyyôr ʾēš* movable hearth, brazier Zc 12_6; — 3. transportable **basin** (for washing) 1K 7_{30}; — 4. **platform** for the king in court of temple 2C 6_{13}.

כִּילַי Is 32_5 & כֵּלַי 32_7: ? **scoundrel.** †

***כֵּילַף** (?): pl. כֵּילַפּוֹת: **crowbar** Ps 74_6. †

כִּימָה: **Pleiades** Am 5_8 Jb 9_9 38_{31}. †

כִּיס: **bag**: for weight-stones Pr 16_{11}, for gold Is 46_6; = lot, destiny Pr 1_{14}.

***כִּיר**: du. כִּירַיִם: **small** (cook-)**stove** for 2 pots Lv 11_{35}. †

כִּיֹּר: ꟳ כִּיּוֹר.

כִּישׁוֹר: **spindle-whorl** (small disk at the bottom of the spindle to give momentum to the spin): Pr 31_{19}. †

כָּכָה: — 1. **so, thus** = **as follows** 1K 1_{48}; — 2. **so** = in the way just stated 1K 1_6; — 3. **so** = to this degree: w. adj., *kākâ dal*, so dejected 2S 13_4; in genl., *šekkākâ llô* who is in such a condition Ps 144_{15}; *kaʾašer* … *kākâ* as … so Ec 11_5; *zeh* … *kākâ wezeh* … *kākâ* one (said) one thing, another another 2C 18_{19}; *ʿal-kākâ* for this reason Est 9_{26}.

כִּכָּר: cs. כִּכַּר (Ex 37_{24} rd. *-kăr*); pl. כִּכָּרִים, cs. כִּכְּרֵי & כִּכְּרוֹת; du. כִּכָּרַיִם, כִּכְּרַיִם: — 1. (disk-shaped, round, thin) **loaf of bread** 1S 2_{36}, pl. *kikkerôt leḥem* 1S 10_3; — 2. *kikkar ʿōferet* **lead disk, cover** Zc 5_7; — 3. disk of gold or silver as unit of weight or value, **talent** (normally abt. 35 kilograms = 75 lbs.): *kikkar zāhāb* (weight) 1K 10_{10}, (value) 1K 9_{14}; *kikkar kesef* 1K 20_{39}; — 4. **circuit, environs**: *kikkar hayyardēn* the broad southern portion of the Ghor Gn 13_{10f}; > *hakkikkar* Gn $19_{17\text{-}25}$; > *ʾereṣ hak.* Gn 19_{28}, *ʿārê hak.* Gn 13_{12} 19_{29} (= Sodom, Gomorrah &c.).

***כֵּלִי**: ꟳ כְּלִי.

כֹּל, כּוֹל Je 33_8 Kt †: cs. כֹּל Gn 2_5, usu. כָּל־; כָּל Ps 35_{10} & Pr 19_7; sf. כֻּלּוֹ, כֻּלֹּה, f. כֻּלָּהּ & כֻּלָּא Ez 36_5; 2. m. כֻּלְּךָ Mi 2_{12}, 2. f. כֻּלֵּךְ, כֻּלָּךְ Is 22_1 SS 4_7; כּוּלָּם, כֻּלָּם Je 31_{34} & 2S 23_6, כֻּלְּהֶם, f. כֻּלָּנָה Gn 42_{36} Pr 31_{29} & כֻּלְּהֶנָּה 1K 7_{37}, כֻּלְּכֶם, כֻּלָּנוּ: **totality**: — 1. abs.: a) *hakkōl*: α) **everything** (there is) Ec 11_5; *ḥāzût hakkōl* the vision of all this Is 29_{11}; β) **everyone**: *yādô bakkōl* his hand against everyone Gn 16_{12}; b) *kōl*: α) **everything**: *ʿōśeh kōl* maker of all things Is 44_{24}; *kol-ʾašer* everything that Gn 39_{5} (:: *kekol-ʾašer* 'just as,' Gn 6_{22}, strengthened *kaʾašer*); β) **everyone**: *wetammû kōl* and everyone will perish Je 44_{12}; — 2. *kōl* before a determinate noun (i.e. w. art. or possessive suffix) expresses unity: *kol-hāʾāreṣ* the **whole** earth Gn 9_{19}, *kol-ʿammî* my whole people Gn 41_{10}, *kullāh* its entirety = it all (was watered) Gn 13_{10}; — 3. as appositive, having a sf., placed after the noun: *yiśrāʾēl kullōh* Isr. its entirety = all Isr. 2S 2_{9}; *hāʿām kullô* Is 9_{8}; *kōl* repeated: *kol-bêt-yiśrāʾēl kullô* Ez 11_{15}; — 4. before an indeterminate noun: *kol-peh* the whole mouth Is 9_{11} (:: every mouth 9_{16}); *bekol-lēb* w. all one's heart, wholeheartedly 2K 23_{3}; *kol-ʿôd* the whole duration = as long as Jb 27_{3}, = still, yet 2S 1_{9}; — 5. w. an enumeration: **total, all together**: *kol-ʿārîm ʿeśer* the total of cities, the cities in all were 10 Jos 21_{26}; — 6. before a pl.: **all**: *kol-haggôyim* Is 2_{2}, *kullām* all of them Ps 102_{27}; w. *kōl* repeated: *kol-malkê gôyim kullām* Is 14_{18}; — 7. before a collective: **all, every**: *kol-hāʾādām* all men Gn 7_{21}, *kol-habbehēmâ* Gn 2_{20}; — 8. before a noun indicating single members: *kol-habbēn* everyone who was a son = every son Ex 1_{22}; *bekol-hammāqôm* at every place Ex 20_{24}; *kol-hāʾîš* everyone 2S 15_{2} = *kullô* Is 1_{23}; w. inf.: *bekol-yaḥēm* at every (instance of) being in heat = whenever they were in heat Gn 30_{41}; — 9. before sg. w/o art.: **every**: a) *kol-ʿam* every people Est 3_{8}; b) w. inf.: *lekol-hēʿîr hāʾelōhîm* to everyone (whose spirit) God had raised Ezr 1_{5}; c) *kol-ʾîš ḥayil* every = none but valiant men Ju 3_{29}; — 10. qualitative: a) of whatever sort, **any**: *kol-behēmâ* any animal Lv 18_{23}; b) of every sort, **of all sorts**: *kol-ṭûb* every sort of valuable Gn 24_{10}; — 11. w. a neg. (usu. separated fm. *kol-*), **no ... at all**: *lōʾ ... mikkol-* from no tree ... at all Gn 3_{1}, *ʾên-kōl* nothing at all 2S 12_{3}; — 12. w. dependent pt.: *kol-ʾîš zōbēaḥ* everyone who, any time anyone offered sacrifice 1S 2_{13}; — 13. *kōl* in adv. acc.: ? **totally**: *kol-tiśśāʾ ʿāwōn* Ho 14_{3}.

I **כלא**: **qal**: pf. כָּלְאָה, כָּלְאוּ; impf. תִּכְלָא, תִּכְלְאִי, אֶכְלָא; impv. כְּלָאֵם; inf. כְּלוֹא; pt. pass. כָּלֻא; transitional forms to I כלה: pf. כְּלִתִינִי, כָּלוּ, כָּלָאתִי; impf. יִכְלֶה: — 1. **keep (back)** 1S 6_{10} (calves at home), keep in detention Je 32_{3}; *kālāʾ śefātayim* shut one's lips Ps 40_{10}; abs. Is 43_{6}; — 2. w. acc. of thg. & *min* + pers., **withhold** s.thg fm. s.one Gn 23_{6}; w. inf. **keep** s.one fm. 1S 25_{33}; — 3. *kālu'* (be) **kept imprisoned** Je 32_{2}.

nif.: impf. וַיִּכָּלֵא, וַיִּכָּלְאוּ: — 1. **be kept back** (of water) Gn 8_{2} Ez 31_{15}; — 2. **be restrained** Ex 36_{6}. †

II **כלא**: inf. piel כַּלֵּא Dn 9_{24}; back-formation fm. ↗ I כָּלָה.

כֶּלֶא: sf. כִּלְאוֹ; pl. כְּלָאִים: **confinement, imprisonment**: — 1. *bêt (hak)keleʾ* **prison** 1K 22_{27}; *bêt hakkelîʾ/-lûʾ* Je 37_{4} & 52_{31} (= ?); pl. *bāttê kelāʾîm* Is 42_{22}; — 2. *bigdê kilʾô* his convict's garb 2K 25_{29}.

כְּלָא Ez 36_{5}: rd. כְּלָה. †

כִּלְאָב: n. pers.

כִּלְאַיִם: כִּלְאָיִם: **two kinds**; mixing forbidden among cattle, seeds, vines Lv 19_{19a} Dt 22_{9}, garment of two kinds of cloth Lv 19_{19b}. †

כֶּלֶב: כָּלֶב; pl. כְּלָבִים, כַּלְבֵי, sf. כְּלָבֶיךָ: **dog**: — 1. the animal: a) manner of drinking Ju 7_{5-7}; b) watchdog for herds Is 56_{10f}; c) hunting dog Ps 22_{17}; d) stray (and unclean) dog 1K 14_{11}; — 2. metaph.: a) term of contempt 1S 17_{43}; b) of self-abasement, *keleb mēt* 1S 24_{15}, *rōʾš keleb* 2S 3_{8}; c) faithful servant of a superior or a deity 2S 7_{21}; d) male cult prostitute (pederast) Dt 23_{19}; — 3. sacrifice of dog Is 66_{3}.

כָּלֵב: n. pers. & tribe.

כָּלִבּוֹ 1S 25_3 Qr כָּלִבִּי gent. of כָּלֵב; Kt כְּלִבּוֹ ?. †

I **כָּלָה** (210×): **qal**: pf. כ׳, כָּלְתָה, כָּלָתָה, כָּלִיתִי, כָּלוּ & כָּלוּ Ps 37_{20}, כְּלִיתֶם, כָּלִינוּ; impf. יִכְלֶה, יִכֶל, תִּכְלָה 1K 17_{14}, וַתֵּכֶל, יִכְלוּ, יִכְלְיוּן, וַתִּכְלֶינָה (־לֶנָה Jb 17_5); inf. כְּלוֹת, כְּלֹתוֹ, כְּלוֹתָם; pt. F *כָּלֶה: — 1. **come to an end**: water in waterskin Gn 21_{15}, period of time Gn 41_{53}; Ma 3_6 do not come to an end = remain the same; — 2. **become finished, complete**: (construction of) house 1K 6_{38}, sacrifice 2C 29_{28}; be fulfilled, accomplished: *debar-yhwh* Ezr 1_1; — 3. **disappear, perish**: grass Is 15_6, men Ps 39_{11}; — 4. **be destroyed, ruined** Is 1_{28}; — 5. **be determined, resolved** 1S $20_{7.9}$; — 6. **become weak**: eyes Je 14_6; kidneys (= emotions) languish Jb 19_{27}; — 7. **be consumed, waste away**: *rûaḥ* Ps 143_7.

piel (140×): pf. כִּלָּה, כִּלְּתָה, כִּלִּיתָ, כִּלֵּיתִי, כִּלּוּ, כִּלִּיתֶם, sf. כִּלָּם, כִּלַּתּוּ, כִּלִּיתָם, כִּלִּיתִים, כִּלּוּנִי; impf. וַיְכַל, תְּכַלֶּה, תְּכַלֶּנָּה, וַיְכַלֵּהוּ, וַיְכַלּוּ, וָאֲכַל, אֲכַלֶּה, אֲכַלֵּם, אֲכֶלְךָ Ex 33_3; impv. כַּלּוּ; inf. כַּלּ(ו)ֹת, כַּלּ(ו)ֹתוֹ, abs. לְכַלֵּא (Dn 9_{24} F 4 c) & 6× כַּלֵּה; pt. מְכַלֶּה, מְכַלּוֹת: — 1. **complete, finish**: a) building Gn 6_{16}, *maʿaśeh* Ex 5_{13}; b) period of time: days Ez 4_6, years Ps 90_9; c) idiom.: *hāḥēl wekallēh* from beginning to end 1S 3_{12}; *ʿad-kallēh* until destruction 2K $13_{17.19}$; — 2. become finished, complete, **end with**: a) w. *be* with Gn 44_{12}; b) followed by inf.: α) *le* & inf.: *waykal ledabber* finish speaking Gn 17_{22} (50×); β) *min* & inf.: *middabbēr* Ex 34_{33}; — 3. a) **use up** Dt 32_{23} (obj. arrows); b) bring to an end, **exhaust**: obj. land Gn 41_{30}; let (eyes) go dead 1S 2_{33}; c) **destroy, exterminate** (32×) Ex 32_{10}.

pual: pf. כֻּלּוּ; impf. וַיְכֻלּוּ: **be completed, finished** Gn 2_1 Ps 72_{20}. †

II ***כלה**: F כלא.

***כָּלֶה**: pl. f. כָּלוֹת: serves as pt. of I כָּלָה: longing for, yearning for (w. *ʾel*) Dt 28_{32}. †

כָּלָה: **destruction, annihilation** 1S 20_{33}; *kālâ weneḥerāṣâ* destruction as resolved (by God) Is 10_{23}.

כַּלָּה: sf. כַּלָּתוֹ, כַּלָּתֵךְ, כַּלָּתְךָ; pl. sf. כַּלֹּתֶיךָ: woman who is first under control of her father, then of her husband and her father-in-law (as his representative): — 1. **bride** Is 49_{18}; — 2. **(young) daughter-in-law** Gn 11_{31}; — 3. **young married woman** cj. 2S 17_3.

כְּלֻהַי: n. pers.

כְּלוּא Je 37_4 & 52_{31} Qr: F כֶּלֶא.

I **כְּלוּב**: — 1. **basket** for fruit Am 8_{1f}; — 2. **bird-cage** Je 5_{27}. †

II **כְּלוּב**: n. pers.

כְּלוּבָי: n. pers.

***כְּלוּלֹת**: sf. כְּלוּלֹתָיִךְ: **time** or **state of betrothal**, engagement Je 2_2. †

I **כֶּלַח**, **כֶּלַח**: **maturity** Jb 5_{26}, **full vigor** 30_2. †

II **כֶּלַח**, **כֶּלַח**: n. loc. in Assyria Gn 10_{11f}. †

כָּל־חֹזֶה: n. pers.

כְּלִי (320×): כְּלִי; sf. כֶּלְיְךָ; pl. כֵּלִים, cs. כְּלֵי, sf. כֵּלַי, כֵּלֶיהָ, כְּלֵיהֶם: useful object in the widest sense: — 1. **vessel, receptacle, gear**: in genl. Gn 31_{37}; wooden object Lv 11_{32}; vessel of pottery 2S 17_{28}, of bronze Lv 6_{21b}; to store documents Je 32_{14}, wine, oil, fruit Je 40_{10}; for eating Ez 4_9, drinking 1K 10_{21}; grain-sacks Gn 42_{25}; shepherd's pouch 1S 17_{40}; — 2. **equipment, gear** of all sorts: a) profane: household furnishings Gn 45_{20}; implements for the oxen = yokes & goads 2S 24_{22}; implements of war & of riding & chariotry 1S 8_{12}; ship's gear Jon 1_5; baggage (of army) 1S 17_{22}, (of exiles) Je 46_{19}; b) cultic: for slaughtering Ez 40_{42}, cultic objects & utensils 2K 23_4; musical instruments Ps 71_{22}; — 3. **implement** Gn 49_5; for hunting Gn 27_3; — 4. other objects: a) **ornaments**: *kelê kesef ûkelê zāhāb* Gn

24_{53}; b) **clothes**: *kᵉlî beged* Dt 22_5; — 5. **weapons** 2K 7_{15}; — 6. vessel = **ship** Is 18_2.

כֵּלַי Is 32_7: F כִּילַי.

כְּלִיא Je 37_4 52_{31}: Kt כְּלִיא, Qr כְּלוּא; F כֶּלֶא.

***כִּלְיָה**: pl. כְּלָי(וֹ)ת, cs. כִּלְיוֹת, sf. כִּלְיוֹתַי, כִּלְיוֹתֵיהֶם: **kidneys**: — 1. as organ of sacrificial animals Ex 29_{13}; — 2. as the inmost & most secret part of man Je 11_{20}; — 3. metaph. *kilyôt ḥiṭṭâ* choicest wheat Dt 32_{14}.

כִּלָּיוֹן: — 1. **destruction, annihilation** Is 10_{22}; — 2. **failure** (of eyes) Dt 28_{65}. †

כִּלְיוֹן: n. pers.

כָּלִיל: cs. כְּלִיל, f. cs. כְּלִילַת: — 1. **entirety,** > **entire, complete, perfect**: a) entire: *kᵉlîl hāʿîr* the whole city Ju 20_{40}; b) adj. complete, perfect Ez 16_4; c) adv. completely, utterly Is 2_{18}; — 2. a kind of sacrifice, 'whole-offering,' nothing of which is eaten, a term replaced at early date by *ʿôlâ* Lv 6_{15}.

כַּלְכֹּל: n. pers.

כלל: qal: pf. כָּלְלוּ: **make complete** Ez $27_{4.11}$. †

כְּלָל: n. pers.

כלם: nif.: pf. נִכְלַמְתָּ, נִכְלָמְנוּ; impf. תִּכָּלֵם, תִּכָּלְמִי; impv. הִכָּלְמוּ; inf. הִכָּלֵם; pt. נִכְלָם, נִכְלָמִים: — 1. **be shamed, disgraced** (by action of another) 2S 10_5; — 2. **be ashamed, feel ashamed** (by one's own action) 2S 19_4 & oft.; — 3. **be confounded** Is 50_7.

hif.: pf. הִכְלִימוּ, הֶכְלַמְנוּם; impf. יַכְלִים, תַּכְלִימוּנִי, וַתַּכְלִימֵנוּ; inf. הַכְלִים; pt. מַכְלִים: — 1. **disgrace, hurt** 1S 20_{34} 25_7; — 2. **abuse** (w. words) Jb 11_3; — 3. **put to shame** Pr 28_7.

hof.: pf. הָכְלַמְנוּ: — 1. **suffer harm** 1S 25_{15}; — 2. **be abashed, ashamed** Je 14_3. †

כִּלְמַד: n. terr.

כְּלִמָּה: sf. כְּלִמָּתוֹ, כְּלִמָּתָם; pl. כְּלִמּוֹת: **disgrace** Is 30_3.

כְּלִמּוּת: **disgrace** Je 23_{40}. †

כַּלְנֵה: n. loc.

כָּמַהּ: **qal**: pf. 'כ: **long for, yearn for** (*lᵉ*) Ps 63_2. †

כַּמָּה & **כַּמֶּה**: F מָה.

כִּמְהָם 2S 19_{38f}, כִּמְהָן 19_{41}, כְּמוֹהָם Je 41_{17} rd. Qr כִּמְהָם (Kt ?): n. pers.

כְּמוֹ (ca. 120×): F כְּ; sf. כָּמוֹהוּ (Ez 5_9 כָּמֹהוּ), כָּמוֹךָ, כָּמֹהָ, כָּמֹכָה Ex 15_{11}, כָּמוֹנִי & 1× כָּמֹנִי, כְּמוֹהֶם, כְּמוֹכֶם, כָּמֹנוּ: — 1. **just like** (= כְּ) Ex 15_5; — 2. *kᵉmô* ... *kᵉ*: *kāmôkā kᵉfarʿôh* you (are) like Ph. Gn 44_{18}; *kāmônî kāmôkā* I am like you 1K 22_4; — 3. *kᵉmô* w. fin. vb.: a) *wᵉrābû kᵉmô rābû* they shall be as many as they used to be Zc 10_8; b) **when** Gn 19_{15} 38_{29}.

כְּמוֹהָם Je 41_{17} rd. Qr כִּמְהָם n. pers. †

כְּמוֹשׁ: n. of chief god of Moab.

כְּמִישׁ Je 48_7: F Qr כְּמוֹשׁ.

כַּמֹּן: **cummin,** *Cuminum cyminum* Is $28_{25.27}$. †

כמס: **qal**: pt. pass. כָּמֻס: **stored up** Dt 32_{34}. †

כמר: **nif.**: pf. נִכְמְרוּ, נִכְמָרוּ: — 1. **be agitated** Gn 43_{30} 1K 3_{26} Ho 11_8; — 2. subj. skin La 5_{10}: usu. become hot, burn; oth.: shrivel up. †

כֹּמֶר: pl. כְּמָרִים, sf. כְּמָרָיו: **priest** (of pagan gods) 2K 23_5 Ho 10_5 Zp 1_4. †

cj ***כַּמְרִיר**: **darkening** Jb 3_5. †

I **כֵּן**: pl. כֵּנִים: — 1. **rightly, justly, aptly** 1S 23_{17}; — 2. morally: a) **upright, honest** Gn 42_{11}; b) w. *ʿāśâ* do right Ec 8_{10}, w. *dibber* be **right** Ex 10_{29}; c) *lōʾ-kēn* = **wrong** Is 23_{10}; w. *ʿāśâ* 2K 7_9; untrue (words) 2K 17_4; — 3. confirming: **of course** Jos 4_4.

II **כֵּן** (ca. 340×), כֶּן־ Gn 44_{10} Jb 5_{27}; < I; adv.: — 1. **so, thus** (= as has just been said) (120×) Gn 1_7; *lōʾ kēn* Ex 10_{14}; — 2. **so, thus** (= as is now to be said) Gn 29_{26}; — 3. **just so, (just) the same way** Ex 7_{11}; — 4. so in var. extended mngs.: = **therefore, that is why** Ps 63_5; = **so much** 1K 10_{12}; = **something like it** 1K 10_{20}; — 5. **as ... so**: a) *kᵉ* ... *kēn* Dt 8_{20} (60×); b) *kaʾᵃšer* ... *kēn* Gn 41_{13} (66×); c) *kᵉmô* ... *kēn* Is 26_{17}; — 6. **just as ... so**: *kᵉkōl* ... *kēn* 2S 7_{17}, *kᵉkōl ʾᵃšer* ... *kēn* Gn 6_{22} (10×); — 7. **so ... as**: a) *kēn* ... *ke* Ex 10_{14}; b) *kēn* ... *ka'ašer* Gn 18_5; — 8. temporal: **then**: a) unaccented: Ps 61_9; b) *'aḥarê-kēn* (ꟳ *'aḥar* II 3) **afterwards** Gn 6_5 & oft.; c) *bekēn* **so then** Ec 8_{10}; d) *'ad-kēn* until then Ne 2_{16}; — 9. var.: a) ꟳ *lākēn* & *'al-kēn*; b) *lākēn* = *lō' kēn* ? Gn 4_{15}; c) as continuation, *kēn* ... *wekēn* Nu 2_{34}.

III **כֵּן**: for periphrastic pluperfect: *hammizbēaḥ kēn 'āśâ* the altar (which) he had made 1K 12_{32}, *bā'îr 'ašer kēn 'āśû* Ec 8_{10}.

IV **כֵּן**: כֵּן־ Is 33_{23}, sf. כַּנּוֹ: **stand** (for basin) Ex 30_{18} 1K 7_{31}; **housing** (for the base of mast) Is 33_{23}.

V **כֵּן**: sf. כַּנּוֹ, כַּנֶּךָ: — 1. **place** Dn 11_7; — 2. **position, office** Gn 40_{13} 41_{13}. †

VI **כֵּן**: pl. כִּנִּים: **gnat**; sg. coll. Nu 13_{33}, pl. Ex 8_{12}.

כנה: **piel**: impf. אֲכַנֶּה, אֲכַנְּךָ: **give s.one an honorary name** Is 45_4 Jb 32_{21f}. †

cj **pual**: Is 44_5 rd. יְכֻנֶּה: **be named**. †

כַּנֵּה: n. loc.

כַּנָּה Ps 80_{16}: rd כַּנָּהּ, ꟳ IV כֵּן.

כִּנּוֹר: sf. כִּנֹּרִי; pl. כִּנֹּרוֹת, כִּנּ(וֹ)רוֹת, כִּנֹּרֶיךָ, כִּנֹּרֹתֵינוּ: **lyre** (stringed instrument w. sounding-board or -chest) Gn 4_{21}.

כָּנְיָהוּ: n. pers.

כִּנְלֹתְךָ Is 33_1: ꟳ נלה.

כִּנָּם: **gnats** Ex 8_{12-14}. †

כְּנָנִי: n. pers.

כְּנַנְיָה: n. pers.

כְּנַנְיָהוּ: n. pers.

כנס: **qal**: pf. כָּנַסְתִּי; inf. כְּנוֹס; pt. כֹּנֵס: **gather, collect**: silver & gold Ec 2_8, levies Ne 12_{44}, people Est 4_{16}.

piel: pf. כִּנַּסְתִּי, כִּנַּסְתִּים; impf. יְכַנֵּס: **gather, assemble** (exiles) Ez 22_{21} 39_{28} Ps 147_2. †

hitp.: inf. הִתְכַּנֵּס: **wrap onesf. (up tight)** (in a blanket) Is 28_{20}. †

כנע: **nif.**: pf. נִכְנַע, נִכְנְעוּ; impf. יִכָּנַע, יִכָּנְעוּ; inf. הִכָּנְעוֹ: — 1. **be subdued** 1S 7_{13}; — 2. **be humbled** Lv 26_{41}; — 3. **humble onesf.** 1K 21_{29}.

hif.: pf. הִכְנִיעַ, הִכְנַעְתִּי; impf. תַּכְנִיעַ, וַתַּכְנַע, אַכְנִיעַ, יַכְנִיעֵם; impv. הַכְנִיעֵהוּ: **humble** s.one 2S 8_1.

***כִּנְעָה** (*כְּנָעָה ?): sf. כִּנְעָתֵךְ: **bundle, (hand-)luggage** (w. *'āsaf* pick up fm. ground; oth.: tie up) Je 10_{17}. †

כְּנַעַן, כְּנָעַן: n. pers., peop., terr.: **Canaan**.

***כְּנַעַן** (or *כְּנַעַן ?) or *כְּנַעֲנִי: pl. sf. כִּנְעָנֶיהָ: **tradesman** Is 23_8. †

כְּנַעֲנָה: n. pers.

כְּנַעֲנִי: gent. of כְּנַעַן: — 1. **Canaanite** Gn 12_6; — 2. **tradesman** † Zc 14_{21} Pr 31_{24}.

כנף: **nif.**: impf. יִכָּנֵף: **hide** (onesf.) Is 30_{20}. †

כָּנָף: cs. כְּנַף, sf. כְּנָפִי, כְּנָפֶךָ; pl. cs. כַּנְפוֹת, du. כְּנָפַיִם, כְּנָפַיִם, cs. כַּנְפֵי, sf. כְּנָפֶיךָ, כְּנָפָיו, כְּנָפָו, כְּנָפֶךְ Jb 39_{26}, כַּנְפֵיהֶם; f.: — 1. **wing** of var. birds Ex 19_4; *'ôf kānāf* winged creature Gn 1_{21}; *kol-kānāf* everything that has wings Gn 7_{14}; — 2. **wing of other beings**: a) of *kerûb* 1K 6_{24}; b) others: *śārāf* Is 6_2; women in vision Zc 5_9; *rûaḥ* 2S 22_{11}; c) *yhwh* Ps 17_8; d) *muṭṭôt kenāfāyw* of overflowing river, or outstretched wings of eagle Is 8_8; — 3. **skirt of garment**: *kenaf me'îlô* 1S 15_{27}; *pāraś kānāf 'al* = take to wife Ez 16_8; — 4. **outermost (edge)**: a) *kenāfôt hā'āreṣ* the (4) corners or ends of the world Is 11_{12}, *kenaf hā'āreṣ* end of the w. Is 24_{16}; b) *'al-kenaf šiqquṣîm* Dn 9_{27}, tech. archit. term, pinnacle of the Temple (?).

כִּנֶּרֶת, כִּנֶּרֶת: n. loc.

כִּנְּרוֹת, כִּנְרוֹת: = ꟳ כִּנֶּרֶת.

***כְּנָת**: Ezr 4_7: Qr כְּנָוֹתָיו, Kt כְּנָוְתָו: **(travelling) companion**. †

כֶּסֶא Pr 7_{20} & כֶּסֶה Ps 81_4 **full moon**. †

כִּסֵּא (130×), 1K 10_{19} כִּסֵּה: cs. כִּסֵּא, sf. כִּסְאִי, כִּסְאֶךָ, כִּסְאֲךָ; pl. כִּסְאוֹת, sf. כִּסְאוֹתָם, m.: — 1. **chair** (w. or w/o arms): for visitor 1K 2_{19}, old man 1S 1_9, judge Ps 9_5; — 2. **seat of honor, throne**: for king Gn

41_{40} 2S 3_{10}; for prince before besieged city Je 1_{15}; *yāšab ʿal-kisʾô* = succeed s.one as ruler 1K 1_{13} &c.; hif. 1K 2_{24}, oth. vbs. 2K 10_{3} &c.; — 3. throne of Y.: 1K 22_{19}.

כסה: **qal**: pt. כֹּסֶה, pass. cs. כְּסוּי: **cover**: — 1. **forgive** (sin): *kᵉsûy ḥaṭāʾâ* whose sin is forgiven Ps 32_{1}; — 2. **keep** s.thg **hidden** Pr $12_{16 \cdot 23}$. †

nif.: pf. נִכְסְתָה; inf. הִכָּסוֹת: **be covered** Je 51_{42} Ez 24_{8}. †

piel: pf. כִּסָּה, כִּסְּתָה, כִּסִּית, כִּסֵּ(י)תִי, כִּסִּיתִי, כִּסּוּ, כִּסִּינוּ, כִּסָּהוּ, כִּסָּמוֹ Ex 15_{10}, כִּסַּתְנִי, כִּסִּיתִיךְ, כִּסּוּךְ; impf. וַיְכַס, יְכַסֶּה, וַיְכַסֵּהוּ, וַיְכַסּוּ, אֲכַסֶּה, תְּכַסִּי, וַתְּכַס, תְּכַסֶּה, יְכַסֵּימוֹ Ps 140_{10} Qr (Kt ־סּוּמוֹ), יְכַסֶּנּוּ, יְכַסֶּנָּה, תְּכַסֵּנוּ, תְּכַסֶּךָּ, תְּכַסְּךְ, יְכַסֵּךְ, יְכַסֶּךָּ, יְכַסְיֻמוּ Ex 15_{5}; impv. וַיְכַסֵּהוּ, וַתְּכַסִּים, כַּסֻּנוּ; inf. כַּסֹּתוֹ, כַּסּ(וֹ)ת; pt. מְכַסֶּה, מְכַסִּים, מְכַסּוֹת: **cover** (trans.): — 1. subj. the covering: a) w. acc.: subj. water Ex 15_{5}, cloud Ex 24_{15f}, darkness Is 60_{2}, metaph. dishonor Je 3_{25}; b) w. *ʿal*: subj. water Hb 2_{14} &c.; — 2. covering in pred.: a) 2 acc. Mal 2_{13}, = clothe with Ez 16_{10}; b) acc. & *bᵉ* with 1K 1_{1}; c) acc. of covering & *ʿal* Ez 24_{7}; — 3. covering named in earlier clause: w. acc. 1K 7_{18}; — 4. covering unexpressed: a) w. acc. Gn 9_{33}; b) w. *ʿal* Dt 13_{9}; — 5. **cover up, conceal**: a) acc. blood Gn 37_{26}; b) conceal one's sin Ps 32_{5}, other wrong Pr 10_{11}; keep s.thg secret fm. (*min*) Gn 18_{17}; — 6. intrans. **clothe onesf. w., put on**, w. acc. clothes Ez 16_{18}, sackcloth Jon 3_{6}.

pual: pf. כֻּסּוּ; impf. יְכֻסֶּה, וַיְכֻסּוּ; pt. מְכֻסּוֹת, מְכֻסִּים: **be covered**: mountains (w. water) Gn 7_{19f}; covering in acc. Ps 80_{11}; w. *bᵉ* Ec 6_{4}.

hitp.: impf. יִתְכַּסּוּ, וַתִּתְכַּס, וַיִּתְכַּס; pt. מִתְכַּסִּים, מִתְכַּסֶּה: **cover onesf.**: w/o obj. Gn 24_{65}; obj. in acc. Jon 3_{8}, w. *bᵉ* 1K 11_{29}.

כֶּסֶה Ps 81_{4}: ↗ כֶּסֶא.

כִּסֵּה 1K 10_{19}: ↗ כִּסֵּא.

***כָּסוּי**: cs. כְּסוּי: **covering** Nu $4_{6 \cdot 14}$. †

כְּסוּלוֹת: n. loc.

כְּסוּת: cs. = Gn 20_{16}, sf. כְּסוּתָהּ, כְּסוּתוֹ: — 1. covering, **clothing** Ex 21_{10}; = outer garment Ex 22_{26a}; = sackcloth Is 50_{3}; genl. covering Jb 26_{6}; — 2. metaph. *kᵉsût ʿênayim* covering for the eyes: declaration of unbesmirched honor of a woman (oth.: veil) Gn 20_{16}.

כסח: **qal**: pt. pass. f. כְּסוּחָה, pl. כְּסוּחִים: **cut down** (vines, thorns) Is 33_{12} Ps 80_{17}. †

cj. **piel**: impf. יְכַסֵּחַ: **destroy, cancel** Jb 33_{17}. †

כֵּסְיָהּ Ex 17_{16}: rd נֵס יָהּ ↗ נֵס; oth.: כִּסֵּא יָהּ. †

I **כְּסִיל**: pl. כְּסִילִים: **foolish** (in practical affairs), **shameless** (in religious affairs) Pr 1_{1}.

II **כְּסִיל**: pl. sf. כְּסִילֵיהֶם: **Orion** Am 5_{8} Jb 9_{9} 38_{31}; pl. Orion & its adjoining constellations Is 13_{10}. †

III **כְּסִיל**: n. loc. Jos 15_{30}. †

כְּסִילוּת: **shamelessness, foolishness**: *ʾēšet kᵉsîlût* a foolish woman Pr 9_{13}, or 'Lady Foolishness' (cf. 9_{1}). †

כסל: **qal**: impf. יִכְסָלוּ: **be foolish** Je 10_{8}. †

I **כֶּסֶל**: כֶּסֶל; sf. כִּסְלֶךָ; pl. כְּסָלִים, sf. כְּסָלַי: — 1. **loins**, the fatty muscles around the kidney area Lv 3_{4}; — 2. **flank, side** (as protection) Pr 3_{26}.

II **כֶּסֶל**: — 1. a) **confidence** Ps 78_{7} Jb 8_{14} 31_{24}; b) (false) **self-confidence** Ps 49_{14}; — 2. **stupidity** Ec 7_{25}. †

כִּסְלָה: sf. כִּסְלָתֶךָ: **confidence** Ps 85_{9} Jb 4_{6}. †

כִּסְלֵו: name of 9th month, Nov./Dec. Zc 7_{1} Ne 1_{1}. †

כְּסָלוֹן: n. loc.

כִּסְלוֹן: n. pers.

כַּסְלֻחִים: n. of unknown peop.

כִּסְלֹת תָּבוֹר: n. loc.

כסם: **qal**: impf. יִכְסְמוּ; inf. כָּסוֹם: **clip** (hair of head) Ez 44_{20}. †

כֻּסְּמִים Ez 4_{9}: ↗ כֻּסֶּמֶת.

כֻּסֶּמֶת: pl. כֻּסְּמִים: **emmer-wheat**, *Triticum*

sativum, grain w. split kernels Ex 9_{32} Is 28_{25}, pl. Ez 4_{9}. †

כסס: **qal**: impf. תָּכֹסּוּ: w. *'al*: **reckon** (for) Ex 12_{4}. †

כסף: **qal**: impf. יִכְס(וֹ)ף: w. *le*: **long** (for) Ps 17_{12} Jb 14_{5}. †

nif.: pf. נִכְסְפָה, נִכְסַפְתָּה; inf. נִכְסוֹף; pt. נִכְסָף: — 1. **deeply long for** (*le*) Gn 31_{30} Ps 84_{3}; — 2. *gôy lō' niksāf* Zp 2_{1}: shameless, not broken (by punishment); oth.: without force. †

כֶּסֶף (ca. 400×): כֶּסֶף, sf. כַּסְפִּי, כַּסְפָּם, כַּסְפֵּנוּ; pl. sf. כַּסְפֵּיהֶם: — 1. **silver** as metal Zc 13_{9}; — 2. as material Ez 27_{12}, *kelê kesef* silver ornaments Gn 24_{53}; — 3. in genl., **money** (not coinage in early period but as medium of exchange) Gn 31_{15}; *bekesef mālē'* in full weight, in full value Gn 23_{9}; — 4. var.: pl. silver pieces Gn 44_{25}; *kesef kippurîm* money to atone for misdeed Ex 30_{16}.

כָּסִפְיָא: n. loc.

***כֶּסֶת**: pl. כְּסָתוֹת, sf. כִּסְּתוֹתֵיכֶנָה; **bands** for magic purposes Ez $13_{18.20}$. †

כָּעַס: **qal**: pf. כָּעַס, כ׳; impf. יִכְעַס, אֶכְעַס, inf. כְּעוֹס: **be irritated, angry** Ps 112_{10}.

piel: pf. כִּעֲסַתָּה (3. f. w. sf.), כִּעֲסוּנִי: **provoke to irritation, anger** Dt 32_{21}, w. cogn. acc. provoke deeply 1S 1_{6}. †

hif.: pf. הִכְעִיס, הִכְעַסְתָּ, וְהִכְעַסְתִּי, הִכְעִיסוּ, הִכְעִסוּנִי; impf. וַיַּכְעֵס, תַּכְעִיסוּ, תַּכְעִסֶנָּה, יַכְעִיסֻהוּ; inf. הַכְעִיס, הַכְעִ(י)סֵנִי (Je 25_{7} Qr); pt. מַכְעִ(י)סִים: — 1. **provoke** (subj. men) 1S 1_{7} (ƒ piel); **disturb** (subj. God, obj. nations) Ez 32_{9}; — 2. **offend, insult, provoke to rage** (obj. God) 1K 14_{9} & oft.; w. *ka'as* 1K 21_{22} & *tamrûrîm* Ho 12_{15} provoke bitterly.

כַּעַס: כַּעַס, sf. כַּעְסוֹ, כַּעַסְךָ, כַּעְסִי, כַּעֲסוֹ; pl. כְּעָסִים: — 1. of man: a) **irritation, anger** 1S 1_{16}; b) **provocation** 1S 1_{6}; — 2. of God: a) **irritation, anger** 1K 5_{30}, *ka'as qorbānām* offerings offensive to me Ez 20_{28}; b) **provocation** 2K 23_{26}.

כַּעַשׂ: ƒ כַּעַס: כַּעַשׂ; sf. כַּעַשְׂךָ, כַּעְשִׂי: **trouble** Jb 5_{2} 6_{2} 17_{7}; (God's) **irritation, anger** (toward man) 10_{17}. †

כַּף (ca. 200×): כַּף; sf. כַּפִּי, כַּפְּךָ, כַּפֶּךָ, כַּפֶּכָה (Ps 139_{5}); du. כַּפַּיִם, cs. כַּפֵּי, sf. כַּפַּי, כַּפֵּיהֶם, כַּפֵּימוֹ (Jb 27_{23}); pl. כַּפּוֹת, sf. כַּפֹּתָיו, f.: — 1. **palm** (= the hollow, outspread hand) (:: hand as part of body, but oft. ||) Lv 14_{15}; *kappôt yād* 2K 9_{35}; *pāraš kappayim 'el* spread out open hand to = pray to Ex 9_{29}; *melō' kaf* handful 1K 17_{12}; *śîm nafšô bekappô* take one's life into one's hands = be in danger, risk one's life Ju 12_{3}, *nafšî bekappî* = I am in danger Ps 119_{109}; — 2. = *yād*, the **whole hand** Dt 25_{12}, of God Jb 13_{21}; — 3. transferred mng.: *bô' bekaf* fall into s.one's power Pr 6_{3}; (save) *mikkaf* 1S 4_{3}; *hikkâ kaf*, clap hands 2K 11_{12}; *taqa' kaf*, Pr 6_{1} shake hands = strike a bargain, but Ps 47_{2} clap hands (in joy), Na 3_{19} clap hands (in malignity); *sāfaq/śāfaq kappayim*, strike hands together (to avert evil) Nu 24_{10}; — 4. *kaf regel* **sole** (of foot) Jos 3_{13}; foot (of dove) Gn 8_{9}; *mikkaf regel we'ad-rō'š* Is 1_{6}; pl. *kappôt raglayim* Is 60_{14}; w/o *regel*: *hōlēk 'al-kappayim*, who walks on soles = paws Lv 11_{27}; *kaf pe'āmay* my footsteps 2K 19_{24}; — 5. metaph., of obj. sim. to palm of hand: a) *kappôt hamman'ûl* handle of door-bolt SS 5_{5}; *kaf hayyārēk* hip-socket Gn 32_{26}; *kaf qela'* hollow of a sling 1S 25_{29}; b) metal **basin** 1K 7_{50}.

***כֵּף**: pl. כֵּפִים: **rock** Je 4_{29} Jb 30_{6}. †

כפה: **qal**: impf. יִכְפֶּה: **soothe**, avert (anger) Pr 21_{14}. †

כִּפָּה & *כַּפָּה: pl. כַּפּוֹת: **shoot, sprout** of reeds Is 9_{13} 19_{15} Jb 15_{32}, pl. **palm-branches** Lv 23_{40}. †

I **כְּפוֹר**: small **bowl** of gold or silver Ezr 1_{10} 8_{27} 1C 28_{17}. †

II כְּפוֹר: **hoar-frost** Ex 16_{14} Ps 147_{16} Jb 36_{29}. †

כָּפִיס: **rafter** Hb 2_{11}. †

כְּפִיר: pl. כְּפִירִים, sf. כְּפִירַיִךְ: **young lion** Ju 14_{5}; metaph. *kᵉfîr gôyîm* Ez 32_{2}.

הַכְּפִירָה, כְּפִירָה: n. loc.

כְּפִירִים: Ne 6_{2} בַּכְּ׳: usu. rd. w. Verss. *bakkᵉfārîm* = in one of the villages; but better unknown n. loc. †

כפל: **qal**: pf. כָּפַלְתָּ; pt. pass. כָּפוּל: **fold double** Ex 26_{9} 28_{16} 39_{19}. †

nif.: impf. תִּכָּפֵל: **be doubled** Ez 21_{19}. †

כֶּפֶל: du. כִּפְלַיִם: — 1. double (coat of mail) Jb 41_{5}; — 2. du. **double amount** Is 40_{2}. †

כפן: **qal**: pf. כָּפְנָה: **twist, turn** Ez 17_{7}. †

כָּפָן: **hunger** Jb 5_{22} 30_{3}. †

כפף: **qal**: inf. כֹּף; pt. pass. כְּפוּפִים: **bow** (one's head) Is 58_{5}, w. *nefeš* oppress Ps 57_{7}; pt. bowed down Ps 145_{14} 146_{8}. †

nif.: impf. אִכַּף: **bow down** before (*lᵉ*) Mi 6_{6}. †

כפר: **qal**: pf. וְכָפַרְתָּ: w. *kōfer*, spread over = cover w. pitch Gn 6_{14}. †

piel: pf. כִּפֶּר, כִּפַּרְתֶּם, כִּפַּרְתָּה; impf. תְּכַפְּרֵם, יְכַפְּרֶנָּה, אֲכַפְּרָה, אֲכַפֵּר, יְכַפֵּר; impv. כַּפֵּר; inf. כַּפֵּר, כַּפְּרִי, כַּפְּרָה, כַּפֶּרְךָ: — 1. older idiom: a) *kipper pānāyw bᵉ* cover s.one's face (w. a gift) = **appease** Gn 32_{21}; b) *kipper bᵉ* cover w. s.thg = **make amends** 2S 21_{3}; c) w. acc. cover up (trouble) = ward off Is 47_{11}; d) *kipper bᵉʿad ḥaṭṭāʾt* provide reconciliation, atonement Ex 32_{30}; e) w. *ʿal* effect reconcil., atonement for s.one Ez 45_{15}; f) w. acc. (subj. priest) expiate, purge (altar, temple) Ez 43_{20}; g) w. *lᵉ* (subj. God) cover for the benefit of, not charge s.one, reckon to s.one Dt 21_{8}; h) (subj. God) cover up (sin), so that no punishment is necessary Je 18_{23}; — 2. idiom in P: a) fully: *kipper ʿālāyw hakkōhēn* the priest provides reconcil., atonement for s.one *bᵉ*... *lifnê yhwh ʿal* ... by [an offering] before Y. because of a sin Lv 19_{22}; b) abbreviated: *kipper ʿal* provide reconcil., atonement for s.one Lv 4_{20}, *ʿālāyw* for onesf. Lv 1_{4}, for s.thg Lv 14_{53}; c) *ʿal-hammizbēaḥ* at the altar Ex 29_{36f}; d) abs. provide reconcil., atonement Lv 6_{23}; e) *kipper bᵉnefeš* (blood) makes atonement through soul = life Lv 17_{11}; — 3. later idiom: a) subj. man: cover up = ward off (wrath) Pr 16_{14}; obj. *ʿāwōn* **atone** by punishment Dn 9_{24}; b) God covers up sin = forgives: w. acc. of sin Ps 65_{4}, w. *ʿal* 79_{9}, w. *bᵉʿad* 2C 30_{18}.

pual: pf. כֻּפַּר; impf. יְכֻפַּר, תְּכֻפַּר: — 1. subj. sin: **be removed, atoned for** Is 6_{7}, w. *bᵉ* by means of Ex 29_{33}, w. *lᵉ* with regard to Nu 35_{33}; — 2. subj. covenant: **be** covered over, **lifted** Is 28_{18}.

hitp.: impf. יִתְכַּפֵּר: **allow for atonement** 1S 3_{14}. †

nitp.: pf. וְנִכַּפֵּר (< * *nitk-*) **be atoned for** Dt 21_{8}. †

*כָּפָר: cs. כְּפַר, pl. כְּפָרִים: (unwalled) **village** 1C 27_{25}, F *kᵉfîrîm* Ne 6_{2}. †

כְּפַר הָעַמֹּנִי, Qr ־נָה: n. loc. Jos 18_{24}. †

I כֹּפֶר: = כָּפָר: (unwalled) **village** 1S 6_{18}. †

II כֹּפֶר: **bitumen, asphalt** for the ark Gn 6_{14}. †

III כֹּפֶר: pl. כְּפָרִים: **henna**: flowering shrub used for orange dye for hair, nails, fingers, toes SS 1_{14}; pl. henna-shrubs 4_{13} 7_{12}. †

IV כֹּפֶר: — 1. **bribe** (to keep silent) 1S 12_{3}; — 2. **ransom** Ex 21_{30}.

כִּפֻּרִים: — 1. act of reconciliation/atonement Ex 29_{36} Nu 5_{8} 29_{11}; — 2. *yôm kippurîm* day of atonement Lv 23_{27f} 25_{9}. †

כַּפֹּרֶת: lit. performance of reconciliation/atonement; trad.: 'mercy-seat': the gold covering-slab of the ark as base for 2 cherubim, Ex 25_{17}, functioning in the ritual of atonement Lv 16_{13f}; *bêt hakkappōret* = holy of holies 1C 28_{11}.

כפשׁ: **hif.**: pf. הִכְפִּישַׁנִי: **trample down** La 3_{16}. †

I **כַּפְתּוֹר**: n. terr.; = *Cilicia Tracheia* (= mod. Turkish coast N. of Cyprus); oth.: = Crete: Am 9_7.

II **כַּפְתּוֹר** Am 9_1, otherw. כַּפְתֹּר: pl. sf. כַּפְתֹּרֶיהָ, כַּפְתֹּרֵיהֶם: knobby fruit of tree & correspondingly shaped decoration: — 1. knob of lampstand Ex 25_{31}; — 2. capital of pillar Am 9_1.

***כַּפְתֹּרִי**: pl. כַּפְתֹּרִים: gent. of I כַּפְתּוֹר Gn 10_{14} Dt 2_{23} 1C 1_{12}. †

I **כַּר**: — 1. (young) **ram** 2K 3_4; — 2. **battering ram** Ez 4_2.

II **כַּר**: pl. כָּרִים: **pasture** Is 30_{23} Ps 37_{20} 65_{14}. †

III **כַּר**: **saddle-bag** (on camel) Gn 31_{34}. †

כֹּר: **kor**, measure of capacity, 350-400 liters, about 100 gallons: — 1. dry measure 1K 5_2; — 2. liquid measure 1K 5_{25}.

כרבל: **pual**: pt. מְכֻרְבָּל: **wrapped** 1C 15_{27}. †

I **כָּרָה**: **qal**: pf. כָּרוּהָ, כָּרִיתָ, כ׳; impf. וַיִּכְרוּ, יִכְרֶה; pt. כֹּרֶה: **excavate, dig** (well, cistern, pit) Gn 26_{25}.

nif.: impf. יִכָּרֶה: **be dug** Ps 94_{13}. †

II **כרה**: **qal**: impf. וָאֶכְּרֶהָ, יִכְרוּ Ho 3_2: — 1. **purchase, buy** Dt 2_6 Ho 3_2; — 2. **haggle, bargain** (over s.thg, *ʿal*) Jb 6_{27} 40_{30}. †

III **כרה**: **qal**: impf. וַיִּכְרֶה: w. *kērâ*, **give a banquet** 2K 6_{23}, feast Jb 40_{30}. †

cj. **hif.**: inf. הַכְרוֹת (so some mss.): **invite to dinner** 2S 3_{35}. †

cj. IV **כרה**: **qal**: pf. rd. כָּרוּ for כָּאֲרִי: **tie together** Ps 22_{17}.†

כֵּרָה: **banquet** 2K 6_{23}. †

I **כְּרוּב** (90×): pl. כְּרוּבִים, כְּרֻבִים: **cherub**: — 1. at Garden of Eden Gn 3_{24}; Y. sitting on *kᵉrûbîm* 2K 19_{15} &c.; — 2. representation of such: of gold Ex 25_{18}, wood 1K 6_{23}.

II **כְּרוּב**: n. loc. in Babylon Ezr 2_{59} Ne 7_{61}. †

כָּרִי: n. peop. הַכָּרִי, coll.: **Carites** 2S 20_{23} Kt 2K $11_{4.19}$. †

כְּרִית: n. of river flowing into Jordan 1K $17_{3.5}$. †

כְּרִיתוּת, כְּרִיתֻת: pl. sf. כְּרִיתֻתֶיהָ: **dismissal, divorce** Dt $24_{1.3}$ Is 50_1 Je 3_8. †

כַּרְכֹּב: **edge, rim** (of altar) Ex 27_5 28_4. †

כַּרְכֹּם: **saffron**, *Curcuma longa* or *Crocus sativus* SS 4_{14}. †

כַּרְכְּמִישׁ: n. loc. **Carchemish**.

כַּרְכַּס: n. pers.

***כִּרְכָּרָה** or *כִּרְכֶּרֶת: pl. כִּרְכָּרוֹת: **fast-running female camel** Is 66_{20}. †

I **כֶּרֶם** (ca. 90×): כָּרֶם, sf. כַּרְמוֹ; pl. כְּרָמִים, cs. כַּרְמֵי, sf. כְּרָמֶיהָ, כַּרְמֵיכֶם; m. (f. Lv 25_3 Is 27_2): **vineyard** Gn 9_{20}; *maṭṭāʿê kerem*, land suitable for planting a vineyard Mi 1_6; *kerem zayit*, olive orchard Ju 15_5 (but txt. ?); erotic metaphor SS 1_6.

II **כֶּרֶם**: n. loc. Jos 15_{59}. †

כֹּרֵם: denom. pt. of כֶּרֶם: pl. כֹּרְמִים, sf. כֹּרְמֵיכֶם: **vinedresser, wine-grower** 2K 25_{12}.

כַּרְמִי: — I. n. pers. Gn 46_9 &c.; — II gent. of I † Nu 26_6.

כַּרְמִיל: **crimson**: a dye extracted fm. cochineal insects (i.e. shield-lice), & material dyed with it 2C $2_{6.13}$ 3_{14}. †

I **כַּרְמֶל**: sf. כַּרְמִלּוֹ: — 1. **orchard** (w. fruit trees & vines) Is 10_{18}; — 2. **plantation** of trees in genl.: *yaʿar karmillô* dense forest 2K 19_{23}.

II **כַּרְמֶל**: n. loc. in Judah; loc. הַכַּרְמֶ֫לָה: 1S 25_2.

III **כַּרְמֶל**: **(Mt.) Carmel**: *har hakkarmel* 1K 18_{19}, > *hakkarmel* 1K 18_{42}, > *karmel* Jos 19_{26}.

IV **כַּרְמֶל**: **fresh, newly ripe grain** Lv 2_{14} 23_{14} 2K 4_{42}. †

כַּרְמְלִי: gent. of II כַּרְמֶל: f. כַּרְמְלִית: 1S 27_3.

כְּרָן: n. pers.

כרסם: **piel**: impf. יְכַרְסְמֶנָּה: **ravage, gobble up** Ps 80_{14}. †

כָּרַע: **qal**: pf. כ׳, כָּרְעוּ; impf. יִכְרַע, תִּכְרַעְנָה, תִּכְרְעוּ, יִכְרְעוּן, וָאֶכְרְעָה, נִכְרְעָה; inf. כְּרֹעַ; pt. כֹּרֵעַ, כֹּרְעִים, כֹּרְעוֹת: — 1. **bend the knee** (deliberately & voluntarily): a) (of lions) **crouch** (to rest) Gn 49_{9}; b) (of men) **kneel**: in prayer 1K 8_{54}, in loyal supplication 2K 1_{13}; subj. knee(s), **bend** 1K 19_{18}; (sexually) **crouch** over (a woman) Jb 31_{10}; — 2. **fall to one's knees** (involuntarily) 2K 9_{24}; **collapse** Is 10_{4}, of woman in labor 1S 4_{19}.

hif.: pf. הִכְרִיעַ, הִכְרַעְתִּנִי (2. f.); impf. תַּכְרִיעַ; impv. הַכְרִיעֵנִי; inf. הַכְרֵעַ: — 1. **force to one's knees** 2S 22_{40}; — 2. metaph. depress greatly, **plunge into misery** Ju 11_{35}.

***כֶּרַע**: pl. sf. כְּרָעָיו: **lower leg, fibula-bone** Ex 12_{9}; jumping-legs of locust Lv 11_{21}.

כַּרְפַּס: finely woven material, **linen** Est 1_{6}. †

כרר: **pilpel**: pt. מְכַרְכֵּר: **dance** 2S $6_{14 \cdot 16}$. †

***כָּרֵשׂ**: sf. כְּרֵשׂוֹ: **belly** Je 51_{34}. †

כַּרְשְׁנָא: n. pers.

כָּרַת: **qal** (130×): pf. כ׳, כָּרַתָּ, כָּרַתִּי, כָּרְתוּ, כְּרָתוֹ; impf. אֶכְרֹת, וַיִּכְרָת־, וַיִּכְרֹת, תִּכְרֹתוּן, תִּכְרְתוּ, יִכְרְתוּ, Jos 9_{7}, אֶכְרָות־, נִכְרְתֶנּוּ, וַיִּכְרְתֻהוּ, נִכְרְתָה, נִכְרָת־, נִכְרֹת; impv. כְּרֹת, כְּרָת־, כִּרְתָה, כִּרְתוּ; inf. כְּרֹת, כְּרָת־, לִכְרוֹת, כָּרְתִי, abs. כָּרוֹת; pt. כֹּרֵת, pass. כָּרוּת, cs. כְּרוּת, pl. f. כְּרֻתֹת: — 1. **cut off**: foreskin Ex 4_{25}, head, hand 1S 5 ; *kᵉrût šofkâ* one whose urinary canal is cut (= whose male organ is cut off) Dt 23_{4}, > *kārût* Lv 22_{24}; — 2. **cut down**: idolatrous image 1K 15_{13}; — 3. **cut down, fell**: trees 1K 5_{20}; *kōrēt* woodcutter Is 14_{8}; — 4. cut out > **root out**, eliminate Je 11_{19}; — 5. *kārat bᵉrît*: trad.: make a covenant by cutting up a sacrificial animal, but oth.: cut > resolve, settle, or: cut up animal in intervening space (between parties): a) **make** an agreement Dt 29_{11}; b) ellipt.: *kārat lᵉ* establish an agreement w. s.one 1S 11_{2}, *kārat ʿim* conclude a covenant w. 1K 8_{9}; c) w. *dābār* instead of *bᵉrît* Hg 2_{5}, *ʾamānâ* Ne 10_{1}.

nif.: (70×, never in Dt): pf. נִכְרַת, נִכְרְתוּ, נִכְרַתָּ, נִכְרְתָה, נִכְרֶתָה, נִכְרַת, נִכְרָתוּ; impf. יִכָּרֵת, יִכָּרֶת־, יִכָּרְתוּ, יִכָּרֵתוּן; inf. הִכָּרֵת: — 1. a) **be cut down, felled** (tree) Jb 14_{7}; b) **be cut off** (waters) Jos 3_{13}; — 2. (pass. of qal 4.): a) **be rooted out, eliminated** Gn 9_{11}; b) **be extinguished, blotted out, removed**: name Is 48_{19}, light 55_{13}, weapons Zc 9_{10}; c) **be excluded from cultic community** Ex 12_{15}; — 3. var.: **be ruined**, of land by famine Gn 41_{36}; **be chewed up** Nu 11_{33}.

pual: pf. כֹּרַת, כֹּרְתָה: — 1. **be cut down** (*asherah*) Ju 6_{28}; — 2. **be cut** (umbilical cord) Ez 16_{4}. †

hif.: pf. הִכְרִית, הִכְרִיתָה, הִכְרַתִּי, הִכְרַתִּיו, הִכְרַתִּיךְ, הִכְרִיתוּ; impf. יַכְרִית, יַכְרֵת, וַיַּכְרֵת, וָאַכְרִית, תַּכְרִיתֵךְ, נַכְרִיתֶנָּה; inf. הַכְרִית, הַכְרִיתֶךָ: — 1. **root out, eliminate** 1S 28_{9} (w. *min, mēʿim, mēʿal, mippᵉnê*); — 2. subj. God: a) **root out, eliminate, destroy** (by early death): people Ez 25_{7}, descendants 1S 14_{22}; b) **destroy**: objects Lv 26_{30}; remove (his steadfast love) 1S 20_{15}; — 3. var.: *hikrît* w. acc. & *lᵉ* root out, eliminate s.thg/s.one from 1K 14_{10}; work one's own ruin Je 44_{8}; b) *min-habbᵉhēmâ* have to kill a portion of the cattle 1K 18_{5}, let perish Nu 4_{18}; c) *hāyâ lᵉhakrît* fall to destruction Ps 109_{13}.

hof.: pf. הָכְרַת: **be rooted out, eliminated; be lacking** Jl 1_{9}. †

כְּרֹת Zp 2_{6}: dittgr. of נוֹת or pl. cs. of II כַּר. †

כְּרֻת(וֹ)ת: **beams**, hewn and cut short 1K 6_{36} $7_{2 \cdot 12}$. †

כְּרֵתִי: coll.; pl. כְּרֵתִים: **Cretans** 1K 1_{38}.

כֶּשֶׂב: pl. כְּשָׂבִים: **young ram** Gn 30_{32f}.

כִּשְׂבָּה: f. of כֶּשֶׂב: **young lamb** Lv 5_{6}. †

כֶּשֶׂד: n. pers.

כַּשְׂדִּים; כַּשְׂדִּיים Ez 23_{14} 2C 36_{17}; loc,

כַּשְׂדִּימָה: n. peop. & terr.: — 1. **Chaldeans** 2K 24_{2}; — 2. **Chaldea** Is 43_{14}, loc. Ez 11_{24}; *'ûr kaśdîm* ↗ III *'ûr*; — 3. *hakkaśdîm*: Babyl. **wise men**, astrologers, soothsayers, Magi Dn 2_{24}.

כשה: **qal**: pf. כָּשִׂיתָ: **become stubborn, headstrong** Dt 32_{15}. †

cj. כשח: **qal**: impf. תִּכְשַׁח: **become lame, crippled** (for תִּשְׁכַּח) Ps 137_{5}. †

*כְּשִׁי: כֻּשִׁים & כֻּשִׁית: ↗ כּוּשִׁי.

כַּשִּׁיל: **ax** Ps 74_{6}. †

כָּשַׁל: **qal**: pf. כ׳, כָּשַׁלְתָּ, כָּשְׁלוּ, כָּשָׁלוּ; impf. יִכְשְׁלוּ; inf. abs. כָּשׁוֹל; pt. כּוֹשֵׁל, כּוֹשְׁלוֹת: **stumble, totter** Is 3_{8}.

nif.: pf. נִכְשַׁל, נִכְשְׁלוּ, נִכְשָׁלוּ; impf. יִכָּשֶׁל־, תִּכָּשֵׁל, יִכָּשְׁלוּ, יִכָּשֵׁלוּ; inf. הִכָּשְׁלָם, בִּכָּשְׁלוֹ Pr 24_{17} (< *b^{e}hikk-*); pt. נִכְשָׁל, נִכְשָׁלִים: be led to stumble = **stumble, totter** 1S 2_{4}; be ruined Dn 11_{14}.

[**piel**: impf. תְּכַשְּׁלִי Ez 36_{14} rd תְּשַׁכְּלִי w. some mss.]

hif.: pf. הִכְשַׁלְתֶּם, הִכְשִׁיל; impf. יַכְשִׁילוּ, יַכְשִׁילֻךָ; inf. הַכְשִׁילוֹ, הַכְשִׁיל: **lead** s.one **to stumble, totter** Ma 2_{8}; make (s.one's strength) unsteady La 1_{14}.

hof.: pt. מֻכְשָׁלִים: **be brought to ruin** Je 18_{23}. †

כִּשָּׁלוֹן: **stumbling, fall** Pr 16_{18}. †

כשף: **piel**: pf. כִּשֵּׁף; pt. מְכַשֵּׁף, מְכַשֵּׁפָה, מְכַשְּׁפִים: **practice sorcery** 2C 33_{6}, pt. sorcerer Ex 7_{11}, f. sorceress Ex 22_{17}.

*כֶּשֶׁף: pl. כְּשָׁפִים, sf. כְּשָׁפַיִךְ, כְּשָׁפֶיהָ: **sorcery** 2K 9_{22}; *ba'^{a}lat k^{e}šāfîm* sorceress Na 3_{4}.

*כַּשָּׁף: pl. sf. כַּשָּׁפֵיכֶם: **sorcerer** Je 27_{9}. †

כָּשֵׁר: **qal**: pf. כ׳; impf. יִכְשַׁר: w. *lifnê* it **pleases him, he likes ...** Est 8_{5}; abs. **succeeds** Ec 11_{6}. †

hif.: inf. הַכְשֵׁיר: make a right application (?; txt. ?) Ec 10_{10}. †

כִּשְׁרוֹן: usefulness: — 1. **success** Ec 2_{21} 4_{4}; — 2. **profit** 5_{10}. †

כָּתַב (ca. 200×): **qal**: pf. כ׳, כָּתַבְתָּ, כָּתְבוּ, כְּתַבְתֶּם; impf. וַיִּכְתֹּב, וַיִּכְתָּב־, וָאֶכְתֹּב, אֶכְתָּוב־ Ho 8_{12} (Qr אֶכְתָּב־), יִכְתְּבוּ, יִכְתְּבֵם, וַיִּכְתְּבוּהָ, אֶכְתֳּבֶנָּה Je 31_{33}; impv. כְּתֹב, כְּתָב־, כְּתוֹב־ Ez 24_{2}, כִּתְבוּ, כָּתְבָה, כָּתְבֵם; inf. כְּתוֹב, לִכְתֹּב, abs. כָּתוֹב; pt. כֹּתֵב, כֹּתְבִים, pass. כָּתוּב, כְּתוּבָה, כְּתוּבִים, כְּתוּבוֹת: — 1. **write on** (*'al*) s.thg: stones Dt 27_{3}, book 2K 23_{3}; *k^{e}tûbîm 'al-sēfer dibrê* ... 1K 11_{41} &c. oft.; — 2. *kātab bassēfer* write in a book Ex 17_{14}; — 3. *kātab* cover w. writing Ex 32_{15}; — 4. *kātab sēfer* write a book, letters 1K 21_{8}; — 5. *kātab* w. acc. of message &c., **write** s.thg **down** Ex 24_{4}; w. acc. of person, **register, record** Ju 8_{14}, acc. trees Is 10_{19}; w. 2 acc. write down, record s.one as Je 22_{30}; — 6. var.: a) *kātab 'ereṣ* make a written survey of country Jos 18_{4}; *kātab laḥayyîm* record (= destine) s.one for life Is 4_{3}; *k^{e}tûbâ pānîm w^{e}'āḥôr* written on front & back Ez 2_{10}; *kātûb* s.thg written Est 6_{2}; b) *kātab mippî* write at dictation Je 36_{4}; *kātab* **sign** Je 32_{12}; c) **engrave** † Ex 39_{30}.

nif.: pf. נִכְתָּב; impf. וַיִּכָּתֵב, תִּכָּתֵב, תִּכָּתֵב, יִכָּתֵבוּ, יִכָּתְבוּן; pt. נִכְתָּב: — 1. (of book or words in a book) **be written** Ma 3_{16} Jb 19_{23}; — 2. (of a matter) **be written down, recorded** Est 2_{23}; (of persons) **be recorded, registered** Ez 13_{9}; — 3. **be noted down in writing** Ezr 8_{34}, *bā'āreṣ* = destined for Sheol (?) Je 17_{13}; — 4. **be commanded in writing** Est 3_{9}.

piel: pf. כִּתֵּבוּ; pt. מְכַתְּבִים: **keep writing** Is 10_{1}. †

כְּתָב: sf. כְּתָבָם: — 1. **document** Est 3_{14}; *biktāb* in writing 1C 28_{19}, as prescribed 2C 35_{4}; — 2. **register, list** Ez 13_{9}; — 3. **script** Est 1_{22}.

כְּתֹבֶת: inscription: *k^{e}tōbet qa'qa'* **tattooing** Lv 19_{28}. †

כִּתִּיִּים, כִּתִּים Is 23_{12} (Qr כִּתִּים), כִּתִּים Ez

27_6 & כִּתִּים Gn 10_4 Nu 24_{24} Is $23_{1.12}$ Qr Dn 11_{30} 1C 1_7: n. peop. **Kittim,** for var. peoples in Medit. area: — 1. sons of *yāwān* (= Greeks) Gn 10_4; — 2. people of S.ern Cyprus Is 23_1; — 3. *'iyyê kittiyyîm* = Greek island regions Je 2_{10}; — 4. adj. *ṣiyyîm kittîm* Dn 11_{30} = Roman.

כָּתִית: *šemen kātît*, (the first) oil (produced) from **beaten** (but not yet pressed) olives, **pure** 1K 5_{25}.

***כֹּתֶל**: sf. כָּתְלֵנוּ: **wall** SS 2_9. †

כִּתְלִישׁ: n. loc.

כתם: **nif.**: pt. נִכְתָּם: **remain stained** Je 2_{22}. †

כֶּתֶם, כָּתֶם: **gold**, poet. synonym for *zāhāb* Jb 31_{24}, modified: *'ôfîr* fm. the east Is 13_{12}, *ṭāhôr* pure Jb 28_{19}.

כֻּתֹּנֶת: cs. כְּתֹנֶת, sf. כֻּתָּנְתּוֹ, כֻּתָּנְתֶּךָ; pl. abs. כֻּתֳּנֹת & כָּתְנֹת Ex 39_{27}, cs. כָּתְנוֹת, sf. כָּתְנֹתָם: long **shirt-like (under-)garment** Gn 37_3 (ℱ *passîm*); not nec. of linen; of skin Gn 3_{21}; for women 2S 13_{18f}; for priests Ex 28_4.

כָּתֵף: cs. כֶּתֶף, sf. כְּתֵפִי; pl. כְּתֵפ(וֹ)ת, cs. = & כִּתְפוֹת, sf. כְּתֵפֶיהָ, כְּתֵ(י)פָיו; f.: — 1. **shoulder(-blade)**; (whole) arm (including shoulder-area), **upper arm** (including chest): *bên keṯēfāyw* (javelin slung) between his shoulders 1S 17_6; a) of man Ex 28_{12}, of beast of burden = back Is 30_6; b) for carrying Nu 7_9, pushing Ez 34_{21}; *nātan kātēf sōreret* display a stubborn shoulder Zc 7_{11}; metaph. *bên keṯêfāyw* = behind, in the shelter of Dt 33_{12}; — 2. metaph.: a) shoulder-pieces of ephod Ex 28_7; b) side-pieces, supports (on stand for laver) 1K 7_{30}; c) tech. archit. term, **side**: *'al-/'el-ketef* on the side of 1K 6_8; — 3. shoulder = (mountain-)**slope**: *ketef haybûsî*, 'Jebusite slope,' S. side of W.ern hill of Jerus. Jos 15_8; so also oth. phr. for spec. slopes.

כתף Jb 21_{12}: sugg. ℱ תֹּף, בְּתֹף to the accompaniment of tambourine; oth. sugg. rd. *כָּתִיף sword-dance. †

I **כתר**: **piel**: impv. כַּתַּר: w. *le* wait for, **have patience** w. Jb 36_2. †

II **כתר**: **piel**: pf. כִּתְּרוּנִי, כִּתְּרוּ: **surround** Ps 22_{13}; Ju 20_{43} (txt. ?). †

hif.: impf. יַכְתִּרוּ; pt. מַכְתִּיר: — 1. **surround** s.one Hb 1_4; — 2. **congregate around** Ps 142_8. †

III **כתר**: **hif.**: impf. יַכְתִּרוּ: **wear s.thg as a ornament on the head** Pr 14_{18}. †

כֶּתֶר: — 1. **high turban** (of Pers. king) Est 1_{11} 2_{17} (queen); — 2. **decoration on head** of horse Est 6_8. †

כֹּתֶרֶת: — 1. tech. archit. term: **capital of column** 1K 7_{16}; — 2. (round?) crown-piece on stand for laver † 1K 7_{31}.

כתשׁ: **qal**: impf. תִּכְתּוֹשׁ: **pound** (in a mortar) Pr 27_{22}. †

כתת: **qal**: pf. כַּתּוֹתִי; impf. וָאֶכּוֹת; impv. כֹּתּוּ; pt. pass. כָּתוּת: **beat fine, pound up** Dt 9_{21}; *kātût* w. crushed testicles Lv 22_{24}.

piel: pf. כִּתַּת, כִּתְּתוּ: **beat, hammer into pieces** 2K 18_4.

pual: pf. כֻּתְּתוּ: **be shoved** *be* against, better reflexive **hurt onesf. by striking** (against) 2C 15_6. †

hif.: impf. וַיַּכְּתוּ, וַיַּכְּתוּם: **disperse** (enemies) Nu 14_{45} Dt 1_{44}. †

hof. (pass. qal?): impf. יֻכַּת, יֻכַּתּוּ: — 1. **be beaten, hammered to pieces** Is 24_{12} Mi 1_7 Jb 4_{20}; — 2. (of enemies) **be dispersed** Je 46_5. †

ל

I **לְ**: exc. w. sf., alw. proclitic; before consonant w. shewa, *li-*; otherw. follows next vowel: *la'amōd, le'ehōb, loḥolî*; before accented syl., *lā-*: *lābéṭaḥ, lāzeh*, w. monosyl.

inf., *lātēt* (but *letēt* before gen. Gn 16_3, also *leḥōm lô* Hg 1_6) & *lắtet*, but *letittî*; special cases: לֵאמֹר, לַיהוה; syncope of ה betw. 2 vowels w. art.: *lehammelek* > *lammelek*, *lehārō'š* > *lārō'š*, occasionally w. inf. nif. *lehērā'ôt* > *lērā'ôt* & hif. *lehamrôt* > *lamrôt*; w. sf.: לוֹ (15×, acc. to M.T., written לֹא, also לֹא), לָהּ (לָה Nu 32_4 Zc 5_{11} Rt 1_{14}), לְךָ (לְכָה Gn 27_{37} 2S 18_{22} Is 3_6), לָךְ, f. לָךְ & לָכִי 2K 4_2 & SS 2_{13} (Qr לָךְ), לִי, לָהֶם, לָהֵמָּה & F לָמוֹ, לָהֶן, לָהֵנָּה (לָהֵן Rt 1_{13}), לָכֶם, f. לָכֵנָה Ez 13_{18} (לָכֶן never appears), לָנוּ; alw. prep., expressing existence or action towards, over against, or for s.thg or s.one: — 1. spatial: **to, towards**: movement in a given direction (arrival at a destination not at issue): *lammizraḥ* to the east Ne 3_{26}, *lefānîm* forward Je 7_{24}; *pānâ ledarkô* turn to his own way Is 53_6; — 2. **to** (expressing arrival at destination): *lā'āreṣ* to the ground Ps 44_{26}, *qārab laššaḥat* comes near to the Pit Jb 33_{22}; — 3. temporal: a) **until**: *labbōqer* Dt 16_4, *lammō'ēd* 1S 13_8, *le'ôlām* forever Gn 3_{22}; b) **at, in**: *le'ēt 'ereb* at the time of evening, in the eve. Gn 8_{11}, *lerûaḥ hayyôm* in the cool of the evening Gn 3_8; *leyôm pequddâ* on the day of ... Is 10_3, *lammāṭār* during rain Je 10_{13}; w. inf. *leda'tô* when he knows Is 7_{15}; c) for a time > for a duration: *leyāmîm 'ôd šib'â* after 7 more days Gn 7_4, *lišnātayim* after 2 years 2S 13_{23}; — 4. direction (no physical movement): *niksaftâ lebêt* you long for the house of Gn 31_{30}; *he'emîn lāhem* feel secure toward them = believe them Je 40_{14}; — 5. therefore w. vbs. of saying, **of, about**: *'imrî lî* say of me Gn 20_{13}; *le'ittîm ... nibbā'* prophesy of times ... Ez 12_{27}; therefore in superscriptions: *lannebî'îm* concerning the prophets Je 23_9; — 6. intention, purpose of an action: office or station to which s.one is appointed (in Eng. **into**, ... **to be** ..., or 2 acc.): *'āśâ le* Gn 12_2, *nātan le* 17_6, *śām le* Is 5_{20} all: make s.one s.thg; *bānâ le* build out into Gn 2_{22}; material or obj. into which s.thg is made: *śāraf le* burn to (lime) Am 2_1; so sim. *lelō'-lāh* as if they were not hers Jb 39_{16}; *le'akzār* (have become) s.thg cruel La 4_3; — 7. 'dat. of advantage, disadvantage,' indicating the pers. for whose (dis)advantage an action is performed: a) *ṭôb lô* good w. regard to = good for him, an advantage to him Jb 10_3; *hēnîaḥ lākem* grant safety for you Dt 12_{10}; so w. vbs. of giving, inflicting, sending, &c.; b) *mar lāh*, bitter for her La 1_4; (means of salvation) for = against: *leḥaṭṭā't ûleniddâ* against sin & uncleanness Zc 13_1; c) in the interest of, in favor of: *hāyâ lānû* was for us Ps 124_1; — 8. 'ethical dat.': pers. ref. same as subj. of vb., emphasizing the interest or share the subj. has in the action; oft. omitted in Eng. transl.: *wayyēlek lô* he went (for himsf.) Ex 18_{27}, *wattēšeb lāh* Gn 21_{16}; oft. w. impv. *lek-lekā*, go Gn 12_1, *beraḥ lekā*, flee 27_{43}; — 9. expresses belonging (to a given party, group, leader): *hēmmâ leyārob'ām* are of (the people of) Jeroboam 1K 14_{11}, *lō' 'ehyeh lākem* I am not concerned w. you Ho 1_9; — 10. > 'dat. of possession': *yēš lî* & *'ên lî* I (do not) have > (elliptical) *lî* 'belongs to me': *lô hayyām* the sea is his Ps 95_5; — 11. preparation, disposition, fitness: *yôm leyhwh*, a day (prepared) for Y. Is 2_{12}, *lākem leda'at* it is your affair to know Mi 3_1, *lō' lākem* it is not your affair Ezr 4_3, *leyhwh hayšû'â* help lies w. Y. Ps 3_9, *lā'ādām* (does not) lie w. man = in the power, disposition of man Je 10_{23}; *'al lammelākîm* it is not for kings = kings are not to (drink wine) Pr 31_4; *'ên lî kesef*, it is not a matter of (silver) 2S 21_4; — 12. expresses result, product of an action: *wayhî hā'ādam lenefeš ḥayyâ* changed into a living being Gn 2_7, *wayyiben yhwh ʾet-haṣṣēlāʿ leʾiššâ* into a woman 2_{22}; *wayyēṣēʾ leḥofšî* go out as a free man Ex 21_2; — 13. genitive-relationship for indef. nouns: *bēn leyišay* a son of Jesse 1S 16_{18}, *ʾōhēb ledāwid* a friend of D. 1K 5_{15}, *mizmôr ledāwid* Ps 3_1 & oft.; — 14. thus *le* replaces gen. a) after a noun or noun-substitute wh. cannot be (specifically) in the cs.: *ʾaḥat lāhem* one of them Ez 1_6, *šenat šetayim ledāreyāweš* = in the 2nd year of D. Hg 1_1, *dimkem lenafšōtêkem* your own blood Gn 9_5; b) instead of 2 gens.: *dibrê hayyāmîm lemalkê* of the kings of 1K 15_{31}; — 15. reinforces a prep.: *mittaḥat le* Gn 1_7, *sābîb le* Ex 16_{13}; — 16. expressing w. a noun an adverbial phrase of situation, manner: *lārōb* in abundance Gn 48_{16}, *lāṭōhar* in clearness Ex 24_{10}; w. sf. *leʾittî* I comfortably Gn 33_{14}, *lebaddô* he alone 44_{20}; — 17. distributive: a) w. sg. repeated: *labbōqer labbōqer*, every morning 1C 9_{27}; b) w. pl.: *lirgāʿîm* every moment Is 27_3; — 18. specification: expresses that in respect to wh. s.thg is affirmed: **in (regard to), concerning**: *leʿōšer* (excelled everyone) in riches 1K 10_{23}, *lemātôq* (like honey) in sweetness Ez 3_3; *lô* with *ṣiwwâ* concerning him Est 3_2; ? > *le* of comparison: *ṣāʿir lihyôt* too little to be Mi 5_1, *ṭôbîm… lerêaḥ* sweeter than… SS 1_3; — 19. indicates the composition of the whole by sections: **according to, by**: *lemînô* according to its kind Gn 1_{11}, *ûleʾalfêkem* and by your 1000's 1S 10_{19}, *hāʾāreṣ leʾarkāh ûleroḥbāh* the land by (= in) its length & breadth Gn 13_{17}; — 20. in the later period, like Aram., *le* **(in relation to, in the direction of)** may introduce the logical dir. obj., usu. pers.: w. *qārāʾ* Gn 1_5, *lāqaḥ* Je 40_2, *ʿāzab* 1C 16_{37} &c.; — 21. in mng. **namely**, logical apposition: *lemalkê* namely the kings of Je 1_{18}; *lekol-kelê* specifically all the utensils of Ex 27_{19}; — 22. introduces cause or reason: **for, because of**: *lifṣeʿî* for wounding me Gn 4_{23}, *lerekeb* Is 36_9; — 23. w. pass. vbs. introduces the originator of the action (subj. of corresponding active vb.): *bārûk ʾabrām leʾēl* blessed be A. by God Gn 14_{19}, *nibḥar lekōl* is preferred by all Je 8_3; — 24. used w. labels, inscriptions, but best omitted in transl.: *lemahēr š-* Is 8_1, *lîhûdâ* Ez 37_{16}; — 25. *le* w. inf., expressing: a) purpose: *lirʾôt* (in order) to see Gn 11_5, *lihyôt ʾalmānôt šelālām* (different subj.) in order that widows might be their spoil Is 10_2; b) completion of incomplete verbal ideas: after *yākōl* be able to Gn 45_1, *ʾābâ* want to Ex 10_{27}, *ḥāfēṣ* delight to Ju 13_{23}, *ḥādal* cease Ps 36_4; c) a more precise determination of the governing vb., translated adverbially: *hêṭîb lirʾôt* see rightly Je 1_{12}, *hirbâ laʿaśôt* do much 2K 21_6, *higdîl laʿaśôt* do s.thg great Jl 2_{21}; d) accompanying circumstance: *lišʾôl* (know that your wickedness is great) in that you asked 1S 12_{17}; *lelēdâ* (no strength) that one might bring forth (children) Is 37_3; *lēʾmôr* **namely** (↗ I *ʾāmar* 2.); e) *hāyâ* w. *le* & inf.: *wayhî lidrôš* he aimed to seek 2C 26_5, *wayhî lisgōr* was to be closed Jos 2_5, *wehāyâ lebāʿēr* is to be grazed off Is 5_5; f) after *yēš*: *yēš ledabbēr* it is necessary to speak 2K 4_{13}; *yēš leyhwh lātet lekā* Y. can give you 2C 25_9; g) after *lōʾ*, *le* & inf.: *lōʾ lehityaḥēš* was not to be registered 1C 5_1, *lōʾ lāśēʾt* no one may (= is to) carry 1C 15_2; h) *le* & inf. as the vb. of an indep. clause, equivalent to saying that s.thg will, must, is to happen: *meh laʿaśôt* what can one do? 2K 4_{13}, *ma llaʿaśôt* what was there (= would there have been) to do? Is 5_4; *wayhî haššemeš lābôʾ* was setting Gn 15_{12}; *lehakkôt* you should have struck 2K 13_{19}; — i) time: *lifnôt ʿereb* toward evening Gn 24_{63}, *lifnôt bōqer* Ex 14_{27}.

II לְ: emphatic, vocative: is evident e.g. before impv.: *lᵉhôšîʿēnî* do save me! Is 38_{20}; before subj., for emphasis: *lᵉyhwh maginnēnû* yes, Y. is our shield Ps 89_{19}, *kî lᵉkeleb ḥay hûʾ ṭôb* for certainly a living dog is better ... Ec 9_4; before pred.: *bat-ʿammî lᵉʾakzār* is certainly cruel La 4_3; for reinforcement: *lᵉkol-nādîb* everyone who is willing 1C 28_{21}; to sum up at the end of a narrative: *lᵉsîḥôn* ... *lᵉʿôg* namely S. & Og Ps 135_{10f}; this *lᵉ* is oft. debatable, or identified w. I *lᵉ* 20.; written לֹא 1S 20_9 2K 5_{26}.

לֹא, 35× לוֹא, 6× בְּלוֹא, 140× הֲלוֹא, הֲלֹה Dt 3_{11}, לוֹ 1S 2_{16} 20_2: — 1. ordinary, declarative negation (:: *ʾal, ʾayin*): **not**: *lōʾ môt tᵉmutûn* you will certainly not die Gn 3_4, *lōʾ šālawtî* I am not at ease Jb 3_{26}; occasionally **not only**: not (only) w. our fathers did Y. make this cov't, but w. us Dt 5_3; — 2. a) w. impf. (2nd pers.) may express unconditional prohibition: *lōʾ tirṣaḥ* you shall not (= are not [ever] to) kill Ex 20_{13}; b) rarely w. juss.: *lōʾ tōsēf* you must not add Dt 13_1, Ho 9_{15} (but perh. scriptio defectiva for *tōsîf* &c.); — 3. negates a single word in sentence: *lōʾ yaʿaqōb* (your name shall be called) not Jacob (but) Gn 32_{29}; *lōʾ ʾōtᵉkā* (they have rejected) not you (but) 1S 8_7; w. emphasis: *lōʾ* ... *mikkōl* from none at all Gn 3_1, *lōʾ* ... *kōl* nothing at all 11_6; — 4. negates a nominal clause: *lōʾ śōnēʾ* he does not hate Dt 4_{42}; *lōʾ bî hîʾ* it is not in me Jb 28_{14}; — 5. *lōʾ* & following word make up the whole clause: *lōʾ ʿēt hēʾāsēf* it is not the time for (the animals) to be gathered Gn 29_7; *lōʾ hûʾ* he is nothing (= of no consequence) Je 5_{12}; — 6. negates 2 successive vbs.: *lōʾ taḥmōd* ... *wᵉlāqaḥtā* you shall not covet ... or take Dt 7_{25}; — 7. introduces a subordinate clause: *lōʾ yiqqārēaʿ* so that it may not be torn Ex 28_{32}; so frequently w. *wᵉlōʾ* (so formally coordinate, but logically subordinate): *wᵉnišmaʿ qôlô* ... *wᵉlōʾ yāmût* that he may not die Ex 28_{35}; — 8. before a noun, really a circumstantial clause: a) adv. = **without**: *lōʾ pišʿî* without guilt on my part Ps 59_4; b) appositionally in a negative description, **without, -less**: *bōqer lōʾ ʿābôt* cloudless morning 2S 23_4, *ʾereṣ lōʾ ʾîš* empty of people Jb 38_6; litotes for greater emphasis: *lōʾ kabbîr* = feeble Is 16_{14}; — 9. *lōʾ* & *wᵉlōʾ* = *hᵃlōʾ wahᵃlōʾ* if the context of a qn. is already clear: *wᵉlōʾ ʾōtāh ʾaggîd lāk* (if I knew...) would I not tell it to you? 1S 20_9; — 10. *lōʾ* = **no** (in answer to qn.): Gn 42_{10}; *lōʾ kî* **no, rather** Gn 18_{15} 19_2; — 11. *wᵉʾim lōʾ* continues a dependent (indirect) qn. introduced by *hᵃ*, **(whether) ... or if not** Gn 18_{21} 42_{16}; — 12. *wālōʾ* **and if not, (then)** 2S 13_{26} 2K 5_{17}; — 13. negates a noun or adj. into the opposite: **without, un-, -less, &c.**: *lōʾ ṭᵉhōrâ* unclean Gn 7_2; *lᵉlōʾ kōaḥ* to (one who is) powerless Jb 26_2; *lōʾ ʿēṣ* (him who) is not wood Is 10_{15}; *lōʾ ʿām* & *lōʾ ʾēl* non-people, non-god Dt 32_{21}; — 14. as a noun: **a nothing** Jb 6_{21} Kt; — 15. comb.: a) w. *bᵉ*: *bᵉlōʾ* **without**: *bᵉlōʾ kesef* without money Is 55_1; *bᵉlōʾ ʿet-niddātāh* outside the time of her menstrual flow Lv 15_{25}; = **not with**: *bᵉlōʾ śiftê mirmâ* without lips of deceit = lips free of d. Ps 17_1; *bᵉlōʾ kakkātûb* not as written 2C 30_{18}; *bᵉlōʾ leḥem* for what is not bread Is 55_2; b) w. *kᵉ*: *kᵉlōʾ hāyû* like those who had never been = as if they had ... Ob $_{16}$; c) w. *lᵉ*: **without**: *lᵉlōʾ ʾᵉlōhê ʾᵉmet ûlᵉlōʾ kōhēn môreh* without the true God & without a teaching priest 2C 15_3 (:: dat., *lᵉ* 7, to such as Is 65_1); d) w. *hᵃ*: *hᵃlōʾ*, often *hᵃlôʾ*, *wahᵃlôʾ*: Gn 20_5; *hᵃlôʾ ʾim-* is it not if = (is it not true that) when Gn 4_7; e) *ṭerem lōʾ* ꟳ *ṭerem*; *šellōʾ* ꟳ *šel*.

לֹא 2S 18_{12}: ꟳ לוֹ.

לֹא דְבָר 2S 17_{27}: ꟳ לוֹ דְבָר.

לאה: **qal**: impf. תִּלְאֶה, וַתֵּלֶא, וַיִּלְאוּ: — 1.

become tired Jb $4_{2\cdot5}$; — 2. w. *le* & inf., become tired of (doing s.thg), **give up** Gn 19_{11}.

nif.: pf. נִלְאָה, נִלְאֵית, נִלְאֵיתִי, נִלְאוּ; pt. f. נִלְאָה: — 1. **tire onesf. out**: w. *ʿal* Is 16_{12a}, w. *be* 47_{13}, w. inf. Je 6_{11} 20_{9}; *naḥalāteka wenilʾâ* your impoverished inheritance Ps 68_{10}; — 2. **be tired** of a thing: w. inf. Is 1_{14}; **be too lazy** (to) Pr 26_{15}; — 3. **no longer** be in a position (to) Ex 7_{18}. †

hif.: pf. הֶלְאֵתִיךָ, הֶלְאָנִי; impf. תַּלְאוּ, וַיִּלְאוּךָ; inf. הַלְאוֹת: **make** s.one **tired, weary** Is 7_{13}; **think** s.one **powerless, incapable** Je 12_{5} Mi 6_{3} Jb 16_{7}. †

לֵאָה: n. pers. f. **Leah**.

לְאוֹם Pr 11_{26}: F לְאֹם.

cj. **לָאז**: 1S 20_{19} cj. הַלָּאז (for הָאָזֶל) = הַלָּז: **yonder, that.** †

לאט: — לְאַט־ 2S 19_{5} rd לָאט = לָט, לוט pf. **cover**; — 2. בַּלָּאט Ju 4_{21} = בַּלָּט **quietly** F לָט. †

לְאַט 2S 18_{5} Is 8_{6} & לְאַט Jb 15_{11} F אַט. †

לְאִיתִיאֵל Pr 30_{1}: F אִיתִיאֵל.

לָאֵל: n. pers.

לְאֹם: sf. לְאוּמִּי Is 51_{4} (? rd pl); pl. לְאוּמִּים, לְאֻמִּים: — 1. **people** (ethnic community) (archaic word) Gn 25_{23} & oft.; — 2. **people** (in genl., French *on*) † Pr 11_{26}.

לְאֻמִּים: n. peop. Gn 25_{3}. †

לֹא עַמִּי: symbolic name, 'Not-my-people,' Ho 1_{9}. †

לֹא רֻחָמָה: symbolic name, 'Not-pitied,' Ho $1_{6\cdot8}$ 2_{25}. †

לֵב, F לֵבָב: (ca. 600×) (:: לֵבָב ca. 250×): cs. לֵב Ex 7_{13}, לֶב־ 1S 17_{32}, לֶב־ Pr 12_{25}, sf. לִבִּי, לִבְּךָ, לִבְּכֶם, לִבְּהֶם; pl. (rare, sg. oft. for many 2S $15_{6\cdot13}$) לִבּוֹת, sf. לִבּ(וֹ)תָם: **heart**: — 1. physical organ: 2K 9_{24}, of crocodile Jb 41_{16}; *ʿal-lēb* = on the chest Ex 28_{29}; — 2. seat of vitality: Ps 22_{27}; of illness Is 1_{5}; *nāgaʿ ʿad-libbēk* reaches to your very life Je 4_{18}; — 3. inner self, seat of feelings & impulses: *hitʿaṣṣēb ʾel-libbô* (God) took it to heart, felt deeply grieved Gn 6_{6}, so also *śām ʾel-libbô* 2S 19_{20}; *ṭôb libbām* in good spirits Ju 16_{25}, *yiṭab lēb* be satisfied, happy 1K 21_{7}, *nisʿar lēb* became uneasy 2K 6_{11} & many vbs. of emotion; seat of secrets in one's life Ju 16_{15ff}, of 'second sight' 2K 5_{26f}; — 4. **mind, character, disposition, inclination, loyalty, concern**: *maḥšebôt libbô* thoughts or schemes of one's mind Gn 6_{5}; *nāgaʿ belibbô* stir s.one's mind, inclination 1S 10_{26}; *hāyâ lēb ʾaḥarê* one's loyalty has turned toward 2S 15_{13}; *hiṭṭâ libbô* corrupt s.one's character 1K 11_{3}; *śām libbô le* worry about 1S 9_{20}; *bekol-lēb* 1K 8_{23} & oft.; — 5. **determination, courage,** (high) **morale**: *yāṣāʾ libbô* one's heart sinks, one's courage fails Gn 42_{28}, so *yippōl (nāfal) lēb* 1S 17_{32}, *yōʾbad lēb* Je 4_{9}; *mālēʾ libbô le* & inf. become bold enough to Ec 8_{11}; — 6. **intention, purpose**: *nātan belibbô le* & inf. give s.one the idea of, inspire s.one to Ex 35_{34}, *millibbî* according to my wishes Nu 16_{28}, *millibbô* willingly La 3_{33}; *māṣāʾ libbô le* & inf. venture to 2S 7_{27}; *ʿālâ ʿal-libbô le* & inf. volunteer to 2K 12_{5}; *mānaʿ libbô min*, refuse, desist from Ec 2_{10}; — 7. **mind, attention, consideration, understanding**: *gānab libbô* outwit Gn 31_{20}; *šālaḥ ʾel-libbô* let (Pharaoh) perceive (plagues) Ex 9_{14}, *ḥakam-lēb* sensitive, gifted w. taste Ex 31_{6}, wise Pr 10_{8}; *lēb ledaʿat* mind which would be understanding Dt 29_{3}; *šāt libbô* 1S 4_{20} = *śām lēb ʾel* 2S 18_{3} = *śām ʿal-leb* Is 42_{25} pay attention to; *lēb šōmēaʿ* understanding mind 1K 3_{9}; *ʾên lēb* without understanding Je 5_{21}; — 8. mind & mood in its totality, the self: *ʾāmar ʾel-libbô* to oneself Gn 8_{21} = *belibbô* 17_{17}; *dibber ʿal-lēb-* speak pleasantly to s.one Gn 34_{3}, *dibber ʿal-libbô* to oneself 1S 1_{13}, *śām ʾel-libbô* assume, jump to the conclusion that 2S 13_{33}; *hēšîb ʾel-libbô* come to one's senses 1K 8_{47}; *neśāʾekā libbekā* your heart has lifted you up = you are haughty, stuck-up 2K 14_{10}; *belēb wālēb* w. divided, false heart Ps 12_3, so 1C 12_{34} *belō' lēb wālēb* w. undivided heart; — 9. **conscience** 1S 24_6 2S 24_{10}; *mikšôl lēb* scruples (of conscience) 1S 25_{31}; — 10. metaph. **interior, middle**: *beleb-yām* Ex 15_8, *'ad-lēb haššāmayim* into heaven itself Dt 4_{11}; — 11. organizing power of the ↗ *nefeš*: a) **life**: *'ārab libbô* give one's life in pledge Je 30_{21}; b) **person** *'im libbî* to myself Ec 1_{16}; — 12. God's heart: Ex $28_{2\cdot6}$; God gives a heart 1K 3_9, another heart 1S 10_9 &c.; — 13. var.: *yōšebê lēb qāmāy* Je 51_1: inhab. of 'heart of my adversaries,' a cipher for *kaśdîm*.

***לָבָא**, *לָבוֹא; cs. לְבוֹ(ו)א: *lebô' ḥamāt* = Isr.'s N.ern border Nu 13_{21}; trad. **entrance**; oth. n. loc. = modern Lebweh; but *lebô'* appears otherw.: *'ad lebô' midbārâ* 1C 5_9, *'ad lebô' miṣrayim* 2C 26_8.

***לָבֶא**: pl. לְבָאִים: **lion** Ps 57_5. †

***לְבָאָה**: f. of לָבֶא: pl. sf. לְבְאֹתָיו: **lioness** Na 2_{13}. †

לְבָאוֹת: n. loc. Jos 19_6. †

I **לבב**: **nif.**: impf. יִלָּבֵב: **become intelligent** Jb 11_{12}. †
piel: pf. 2. f. sf. לִבַּבְתִּנִי: **take away the heart, bewitch** SS 4_9. †

II **לבב**: **piel**: impf. וַתְּלַבֵּב: **bake cakes** 2S $13_{6\cdot8}$. †

לֵבָב: ↗ לֵב: cs. לְבַב, sf. לְבָבְךָ, לְבָבֵךְ, לְבַבְכֶם, לְבָבֵנוּ (4×); pl. לִבְבֹהֶן (sf.) & לְבָבוֹת: **heart**; semantically like ↗ *lēb*; sg. also use for many Ex 14_5; spec.: **chest** Ne 2_8; *hāyâ 'im lebābî* am quite determined 1C 22_7; *yihyeh-llî 'alêkem lēb leyaḥad* am ready for an alliance with you 1C 12_{18}; in genl. the idioms follow *lēb*.

***לְבִבָה**: pl. לְבִבוֹת: **(heart-shaped) cake** 2S $13_{6\cdot8\cdot10}$. †

לְבַד: ↗ I בַּד.

***לַבָּה**: cs. לַבַּת: **flame** Ex 3_2. †

***לַבָּה**: sf. לַבָּתֵךְ: **rage** (against you) Ez 16_{30}. †

I **לְבוֹנָה**: **frankincense**, ↗ לְבֹנָה.

II **לְבוֹנָה**: n. loc. Ju 21_{19}. †

לָבוּשׁ (6×), לָבֻשׁ (8×): cs. לְבוּשׁ, לְבֻשׁ; pl. cs. לְבֻשֵׁי: **clothed, dressed** w. acc. **in** 1S 17_5; covered with Is 14_{19}.

לְבוּשׁ, 3× לְבֻשׁ: **garment**: a) of a man Gn 49_{11}, of a woman Ps 49_{14}; coll. **clothes**, of men Is 14_{19}, of women 2K 10_{22}; b) of wool Pr 27_{26}; sackcloth Ps 35_{13}; = skin Jb 30_{18}; metaph. of clouds over sea Jb 38_9; of idols Je 10_9; of Pers. king's robes Est 6_8.

לבט: **nif.**: impf. יִלָּבֵט: **be ruined** Ho 4_{14} Pr 10_8. †

לָבִיא: **lioness** (only poet.) Gn 49_9.

לְבִיָּא: **lioness** Ez 19_2. †

לֻבִים Dn 11_{43}: ↗ לוּבִים.

I **לבן**: **hif.**: pf. הִלְבִּינוּ; impf. אַלְבִּין, יַלְבִּינוּ; inf. וְלַלְבֵּן Dn 11_{35} (< *ûlehalbēn*): — 1. **become white** Is 1_{18} Jl 1_7 Ps 51_9; — 2. **make white, whiten, clean** Dn 11_{35}. †
hitp.: impf. יִתְלַבְּנוּ: **be cleansed** Dn 12_{10}.†

II **לבן**: **qal**: impf. נִלְבְּנָה; inf. לִלְבֹּן: **mold bricks** Gn 11_3 Ex $5_{7\cdot14}$. †

I **לָבָן**: cs. לְבֶן־, f. לְבָנָה; pl. לְבָנִים, לְבָנוֹת: **white**: milk, teeth Gn 49_{12}, sheep 30_{35}, hair of skin Lv 13_3; *lābān 'adamdām* reddish white Lv 13_{42f}, *kēheh lābān* dull white 13_{39}.

II **לָבָן**: n. pers. **Laban**.

III **לָבָן**: n. loc. Dt 1_1. †

לִבְנֶה: **storax-tree**, *Styrax officinalis* Gn 30_{37} Ho 4_{13}. †

לִבְנָה: n. loc.

I **לְבָנָה**: **full moon** Is 24_{23} 30_{26} SS 6_{10}. †

II **לְבָנָה**: n. pers. Ezr 2_{45} Ne 7_{48}. †

לְבֵנָה: cs. לִבְנַת; pl. לְבֵנִים, sf. לִבְנֵיכֶם: — 1. (unfired, dried) **brick** Gn 11_3; — 2. **stone slab, paving-stone** (of sapphire) Ex 24_{10}; — 3. *meqaṭṭerîm 'al-hallebēnîm* Is 65_3, ? pavement or incense-altar of offering place; txt. ?

לְבֹנָה & לְבוֹנָה: sf. לְבֹנָתָהּ: **frankincense, a** white resin (yellow at breakage-points) from the tree *Boswellia Carteri & Frereana*, brought from Hadramaut & Somaliland: Ex 30_{34}.

לְבָנוֹן, Dt 3_{25} לְבָנֹן: n. mountain: **Lebanon** 1K 5_{13}, both as source of cedar &c. & in geogr. phrases.

לִבְנִי: n. pers. (Nu 3_{18}) & gent. of same name (3_{21}).

לִבְנָת Jos 19_{26}: ↗ שִׁיחוֹר לִבְנָת.

לֵב קָמָי Je 51_1: ↗ לֵב 13.

לָבַשׁ: qal: pf. ל׳, לָבֵשׁ Ps 93_1, לָבְשָׁה, לָבַשְׁתְּ, לָבַשְׁתִּי, לָבְשׁוּ, לְבֵשָׁם Lv 16_4; impf. וַיִּלְבַּשׁ, תִּלְבָּשׁוּ, יִלְבְּשׁוּ, תִּלְבָּשִׁי, תִּלְבְּשִׁי, יִלְבָּשׁ, תִּלְבַּשְׁךְ, יִלְבָּשֵׁנִי, יִלְבָּשֵׁם & ־שָׁם Ex 29_{30}, אֶלְבָּשֶׁנָּה; impv. לְבַשׁ, לִבְשִׁי; inf. לִלְבֹּשׁ, abs. לָבֹשׁ; pt. לְבֻשִׁים: — 1. w. acc. a) **put on** (a garment) Gn 28_{20}, (armor) Is 59_{17}; b) metaph. (men of Zion like a garment) Is 49_{18}; be clothed w.: righteousness Is 59_{17} &c.; — 2. metaph. material of garment (*rûᵃh yhwh*) subj., pers. obj.: **clothe** = take possession of Ju 6_{34}; — † 3. w. *bᵉ*: **wear** Est 6_8, abs. **be clothed** 2S 13_{18} Hg 1_6.

pual: pt. מְלֻבָּשִׁים: w. acc. **clothed with** 1K 22_{10} 2C 5_{12} 18_9; abs. Ezr 3_{10} in official attire. †

hif.: pf. הִלְבִּישָׁה, הִלְבַּשְׁתָּ, הִלְבִּ(י)שׁוּ, הִלְבַּשְׁתִּיו, הִלְבַּשְׁתָּם, הִלְבִּישֵׁנִי; impf. וַיַּלְבִּישׁוּם, אַלְבִּישֵׁךְ, וַיַּלְבִּשֵׁם, אַלְבִּישׁ, וַיַּלְבֵּשׁ, וַיַּלְבִּשֵׁהוּ; inf. הַלְבִּישׁ, הַלְבֵּשׁ; pt. מַלְבִּישִׁים: — 1. **clothe**: a) w. acc. pers. Gn 3_{21}; b) w. acc. thing, clothe with Pr 23_{21}; c) 2 acc., pers. & thing Gn 41_{42}; — 2. w. *ʿal* + pers., acc. of thing: **put s.thg on s.one** Gn 27_{16}.

לְבֻשׁ & לְבֻשׁ: ↗ לְבוּשׁ, לְבוּשׁ.

לֹג: **log** = a liquid measure: less than 1/3 liter, abt. 2/3 pint Lv 14_{10}.

לֹד: n. loc.

לִדְבִר Jos 13_{26}: n. loc.: rd לֹא דְבָר.

לֵדָה: (time or process of) **childbirth** 2K 19_3 Is 37_3 Ho 9_{11}; *ʾēšet lēdâ* woman in labor Je 13_{21}. †

לֹה: הֲלֹה Dt 3_{11} rd הֲלֹא. †

לַהַב: pl. לְהָבִים, cs. לַהֲבֵי: — 1. **flame** Ju 13_{20}, *lahab ʾēš* Is 29_6; *pᵉnê lᵉhābîm* flaming, hot faces Is 13_8; — 2. > **blade** (of sword) Ju 3_{22}.

לֶהָבָה: cs. לַהֶבֶת; pl. לֶהָבוֹת, cs. לַהֲבוֹת: — 1. **flame** Nu 21_{28}; reinforced: *lahebet šalhebet* Ez 21_3; *ʾēš lehābâ* Is 4_5; — 2. > **blade** (of *ḥᵃnît*) 1S 17_7.

לְהָבִים: n. of unknown peop. Gn 10_{13} 1C 1_{11}. †

לַהַג: usu.: **studying** (oth.: II *lᵉ* + *hege(h)* studying, reckoning) Ec 12_{12}. †

לַהַד: n. pers.

להה: **hitpalpel**: pt. מִתְלַהְלֵהַּ: **behave like a madman** Pr 26_{18}. †

להה: **qal**: impf. וַתֵּלַהּ: **languish** (of the land, from hunger) Gn 47_{13}. †

I **להט**: **qal**: pt. לוֹהֵט: **glow, burn** Ps 104_4. †

piel: pf. לִהַט, לִהֲטָה; impf. תְּלַהֵט, וַתְּלַהֲטֵהוּ: **devour, scorch** (of fire, flame) Dt 32_{22}, (of war) Is 42_{25}; kindle (coals) Jb 41_{13}.

II **להט**: **qal**: pt. לֹהֲטִים: **swallow down** Ps 57_5. †

לַהַט: flame; metaph. **blade** (of sword) Gn 3_{24}. †

***לְהָטִים**: sf. לַהֲטֵיהֶם: **secret arts, sorcery** Ex 7_{11}. †

להם: **hitp.**: pt. מִתְלַהֲמִים: **let onesf. be swallowed greedily**; pt. pl. **delicacies** Pr 18_8 26_{22}. †

לָהֵן: w. *hᵃ* Ru 1_{13} 2× **therefore** (↗ II הֵן); oth.: rd. לָהֶם (ref. to 'sons'). †

[**לָהֶן** Jb 30_{24}: for לָהֶן שׁוּעַ rd. לֹה (= לֹא) יְשַׁוֵּעַ.]

***לַהֲקָה**: 1S 19_{20} *lahᵃqat nᵉbîʾîm*: usu. cj. *qᵉhillat* ↗ *qᵉhillâ*; but better: group of elders, dignitaries, thus: the venerable community (of the pr.). †

לוֹ 1S 2_{16} 20_{1} rd **לֹא**; Jb 6_{21} rd **לִי**.

לוּ, לֻא 2S 18_{12} 19_{7}, **לוּא** 1S 14_{30} Is 48_{18} 63_{19}: 1. w. impf. **O that … might, if only … might, let …** (as prayer, devout wish, not juss.) Gn 17_{18}; > now if, what if, suppose … Gn 50_{15}; — 2. w. impv. Gn 23_{13} *lû šᵉmāʿanî* but (please) listen to me; — 3. w. pf.: past contrary to fact: *lû matnû* O, if we only had died Nu 14_{2} 1S 14_{30} > **if** (in past contrary to fact) Ju 13_{23} if he had meant …; — 4. w. pt.: 2S 18_{12} if I were feeling …; w. *yēš* Nu 22_{29} if there were a sword …; in nominal clause: 2S 19_{11} if A. were (alive).

***לוּב**: pl. **לוּבִים**, Dn 11_{43} **לֻבִים**: n. peop. **Libyans.**

לוּד: pl. **לוּדִים**, 1C 1_{11} **לוּדִיִּים** Kt: n. peop. **Lydians.**

לֹא דְבָר לוֹ דְבָר 2S 9_{4f}, **לֹא דְבָר** 2S 17_{27}, **לֹא דָבָר** Am 6_{13}, **לִדְבִר** Jos 13_{26}: n. loc.

I **לוה**: **qal**: impf. **יִלְוֶנּוּ**: **accompany** Ec 8_{15}. †

nif.: pf. **נִלְוָה, נִלְווּ**; impf. **יִלָּוֶה, יִלָּווּ**; pt. **נִלְוִים**: w. *ʾel, ʿal, & ʿim,* **join, attach onesf. to**: obj. wife Gn 29_{34}, fellow-tribesmen Nu $18_{2.4}$, of worshipper to God Is $56_{3.6}$.

II **לוה**: **qal**: pf. **לָוִינוּ**; impf. **תִּלְוֶה**; pt. **לֹוֶה**: **borrow** s.thg for onesf. Dt 28_{12}.

hif.: pf. **הִלְוִיתָ**; impf. **יַלְוְךָ, תַּלְוֶה, תַּלְוֶנּוּ**; pt. **מַלְוֶה**, cs. **מַלְוֵה**: **lend to** w. acc. pers. Dt 28_{12}.

לוז: **qal**: impf. **יָלֻזוּ**: w. *mēʿênê,* **be lost to s.one's sight** Pr 3_{21}. †

nif.: pt. **נָלוֹז**, cs. **נְלוֹז**, pl. **נְלוֹזִים**: — 1. **go the wrong way**: *nᵉlôz dᵉrākîm* he who is on the wrong paths Pr 14_{2}; > *nālôz* Pr 3_{32}, pl. 2_{15} (oth.: wrong ways); — 2. pt. **perversity, deceit** Is 30_{12}. †

hif.: impf. **יַלִּיזוּ**: **be lost to s.one's sight** Pr 4_{21}. †

I **לוּז**: **almond-tree,** *Amygdalus communis* Gn 30_{37}. †

II **לוּז**: n. loc.

לוּחַ: du. **לוּחֹתַיִם**; pl. **לֻחֹ(וּ)ת, לוּחֹ(וּ)ת**; m.: — 1. (stone) **tablet, slab** 1K 8_{9}; phr. *luḥōt hāʿēdut* Ex 31_{18}, *lûḥōt habbᵉrît* Dt 9_{9}; metaph. *lûᵃḥ libbām* Je 17_{1}; — 2. **plank, board** (of frame of altar) Ex 27_{8}; ship Ex 27_{5}; panel 1K 7_{36} SS 8_{9}.

לוּחִית Is 15_{5}, **לֻחִית** Je 48_{5} Qr: n. loc.

לוֹחֵשׁ, הַלּוֹחֵשׁ: n. pers.

לוט: **qal**: **לָאט** 2S 19_{5} = **לָאט**; pt. pass. **לוּטָה**: **wrap up, cover** 1S 21_{10} 2S 19_{5}. †

hif.: impf. **וַיָּלֶט**: **wrap up, cover** 1K 19_{13}. †

I **לוֹט**: **covering** Is 25_{7}. †

II **לוֹט**: n. pers. **Lot.**

לוֹטָן: n. pers.

לֵוִי: pl. **לְוִיִּם, הַלְוִיִּם, הַלְ׳** Dt 17_{18}, sf. 1 pl. **לְוִיֵּנוּ** Ne 10_{1}: — 1. n. pers. **Levi** Gn 29_{34}; — 2. *bᵉnê lēwî* **Levites** 1K 12_{31}; *bᵉnê hallēwî* Ne 10_{40}, *maṭṭēh lēwî* Nu 1_{49}, *šēbeṭ hallēwî* Dt 10_{8}; *lēwî* = tribe of Levi Dt 10_{9}, so *hallēwî* Nu 18_{23}; — 3. *hallēwî* = **Levite** (sg.) Ju 17_{10ff}, so *lēwî* Ju 17_{7}; — 4. pl. **Levites** 1K 8_{4}.

***לִוְיָה**: cs. **לִוְיַת**: **wreath, garland**: *liwyat ḥēn* Pr 1_{9} 4_{9}. †

לִוְיָתָן: **Leviathan, sea-monster** Is 27_{1} Ps 104_{26} Jb 3_{8} 40_{25}; the last-named passage, esp., sugg. that the mythological creature represents the ocean encircling the earth, or the crocodile, or the whale. †

***לוּל**: pl. **לוּלִים**: tech. archit. term: (?) **trap-door** 1K 6_{8} (oth.: spiral staircase). †

לוּלֵא Gn 43_{10} Ju 14_{18} 2S 2_{27}, otherw. **לוּלֵי**: — 1. **if not** (contrary to fact): w. pf., *lûlēʾ hāyâ* if he had not been Gn 31_{42} 43_{10}; w. impf., *lûlê ʾāgûr* if I did not fear Dt 32_{27}; w. pt., *lûlê … ʾᵃnî nōśēʾ* (*pᵉnê* …) if I had no regard for … 2K 3_{14}; in nominal clause Ps 94_{17}; — 2. affirmative: **surely** (< 1. by suppression of apodosis) Ps 27_{13} (but txt. ?).

I **לון**: only in Ex 15-17 Nu 14-17 Jos 9_{18}: **nif.**: impf. **וַיִּלֹּנוּ** Ex 16_{2} Qr, Nu 14_{36} Kt,

תִּלּוֹנוּ Nu 16_{11} Kt (oth. rdgs. **hif.**): w. *ʿal* **murmur, grumble at** Ex 15_{24}.

hif.: pf. הֲלִינוֹתֶם; impf. וַיַּלִּינוּ, וַיָּלֶן Ex 16_2 Kt, Nu 14_{36} Nu 16_{11} (both Qr); pt. מַלִּינִים: w. *ʿal* **murmur, grumble at** Ex 16_7.

II **לון**: ↱ לין.

לוע: ↱ לעע.

לוץ: ↱ ליץ.

לוש: **qal**: impf. וַתָּלוֹשׁ, וַתָּלָשׁ 2S 13_8 Kt; impv. לוּשִׁי; inf. לוּשׁ; pt. לָשׁוֹת: **knead** (dough) Gn 18_6.

לָוִשׁ: n. pers.: Kt לוש, Qr לַיִשׁ, ↱ לַיִשׁ: 2S 3_{15}. †

***לָזוּת**: cs. לְזוּת: **perversity** Pr 4_{24}. †

לַח: לַח; pl. לַחִים: **still moist, still fresh**: rod Gn 30_{37}, grapes Nu 6_3, bowstring Ju 16_{7f}, wood Ez 17_{24} 21_3. †

***לֵחַ**: sf. (3. sg. m.) לֵחֹה: **sap** (of life), **vigor** Dt 34_7; Je 11_{19} (w. *mêm*-enclitic & sf.). †

***לֻחַ**: pl. לֻחֹ(ו)ת: ↱ לוּחַ.

***לְחוּם**, ***לְחֶם**: sf. לְחוּמוֹ Jb 20_{23}, לְחֻמָם Zp 1_{17}: Zp 1_{17} **flesh, bodies**; Jb 20_{23} txt. uncert. †

I **לְחִי**: לְחִי, sf. לְחֶיְהָ ,לֶחֱיָהּ ,לְחֶיוֹ; du. לְחָיַיִם, cs. לְחָיֵי, sf. לְחָיֵךְ ,לְחָיֶיךָ ,לְחָיָו ,לְחָיַי ,לְחָיֵי, לְחָיֵיהֶם; f.: a) **chin** cj. SS 5_{13} (rd. sg. לֶחֱיוֹ); b) **jawbone** Ju 15_{15}, Ho 11_4 (of draft-animal), metaph. Is 30_{28} (peoples); c) **cheek** 1K 22_{24}; d) portion of sacrifice given to priest Dt 18_3, but txt. ?.

II ***לְחִי**: n. loc.: לֶחִי, הַלֶּחִי Ju 15_9, cj. loc. לְחִיָה 2S 23_{11}.

לַחַי רֹאִי Gn 16_{14} 25_{11}: ↱ רֹאִי.

לְחִית Je 48_5 Qr: ↱ לוּחִית.

לחך: **qal**: inf. לְחֹךְ: lick up, **devour** (subj. ox, obj. grass) Nu 22_4. †

piel: pf. לִחֲכָה; impf. יְלַחֲכוּ ,יְלַחֵכוּ: — 1. **lick up** (subj. fire, obj. water) 1K 18_{38}, (subj. snake, obj. dust) Mi 7_{17}; lick off (subj. subjects, obj. dust of feet of overlord) Is 49_{23} Ps 72_9; — 2. **eat** (the land) **bare** Nu 22_4. †

I **לחם**: **qal**: impv. לְחַם; pt. לֹחֵם, pl. לֹחֲמִים, לֹחֲמָי: **do battle w.**, w. acc. Ps 35_1 56_2, w. *le* 56_3. †

nif. (ca. 165×): pf. נִלְחַם (Dn 11_{11} נִלְחַם), נִלְחַמְנוּ ,נִלְחֲמוּ ,נִלְחֲמוּ ,נִלְחַמְתִּי ,נִלְחַם; impf. תִּלָּחֲמוּן ,וַיִּלָּחֲמוּ ,וַיִּלָּחֶם ,יִלָּחֵם, נִלָּחֲמָה ,וַיִּלָּחֲמוּנִי; impv. הִלָּחֲמוּ; inf. הִלָּחֵם ,הִלָּחֶם ,הִלָּחֲמוֹ, abs. נִלְחֹם; pt. נִלְחָם ,נִלְחָמִים: **come to close quarters, do battle** w., **fight**: — 1. w. *ʾēt* Jos 10_{25} (20×), w. sf. Ps 109_3, w. *ʿim* Ex 17_8 (28×), w. *ʿal* against Dt 20_{10} (20×), w. *ʾel* Je 1_{19}, w. *be* Ex 1_{10} (60×); — 2. **fight for, on behalf of**: w. *le* Ex 14_{14} (10×), w. *ʿal* Ne 4_8, abs. Dt 1_4 (20×); — 3. var.: a) *nilḥam milḥamôt* 1S 8_{20}; *nillāḥamâ yaḥad* let us fight w. each other 1S 17_{10}; b) God subj. Ex 14_{14} & oft.

II **לחם**: **qal**: pf. לָחֲמוּ; impf. תִּלְחַם ,אֶלְחַם; impv. לַחֲמוּ; inf. לְחֹם; pt. pass. לְחֻמֵי: — 1. **dine, eat** (at s.one's house) Pr 23_1; cj Ob $_7$ *lōḥᵃmêkā* those eating w. you; — 2. w. *be* **taste** (a bite) of Ps 141_4; — 3. abs. **eat** Pr 4_{17}; — 4. pass. *leḥumê rešef* those consumed by pestilence Dt 32_{24}.

לֶחֶם (ca. 300×): לָחֶם, sf. לַחְמוֹ, לַחְמֵנוּ: — 1. **grain (for bread)** Is 28_{28} 36_{17} †; — 2. **bread** Gn 14_{18} & oft.; *ʿaśārâ leḥem* 10 loaves of bread 1S 17_{17}; — 3. bread in the cult: *leḥem (hap)pānîm* 'showbread' Ex 25_{30}, *leḥem tenûfâ* br. to be waved Lv 23_{17}, *leḥem bikkûrîm* br. of first-fruits 2K 4_{42}; — 4. in genl., = **food, nourishment** Gn 3_{19}, for cattle Ps 147_9; *leḥem ʾiššeh leyhwh* food of fire-offering to Y. Lv 3_{11}; — 5. spec.: *leḥem happeḥâ* food allowance of the governor Ne 5_{14}; *leḥem (miš)šāmayim* Ne 9_{15} Ps 105_{40} = manna; *leḥem ʿōnî* br. of affliction = unleavened br. Dt 16_3; metaph. *leḥem dimʿâ* br. of tears Ps 80_6.

***לְחֶם**: ↱ לְחוּם.

לַחְמִי: n. pers.

לַחְמָס: n. loc.

לָחַץ: qal: pf. ל׳; impf. תִּלְחַץ, תִּלְחָץ, וַיִּלְחָצוּם, תִּלְחָצֵנוּ, יִלְחָצֵנִי, יִלְחָצוּ; pt. לֹחֲצֵיהֶם, לֹחֲצִים: — 1. **crowd, press** s.one in a given direction: w. *'el* Nu 22_{25}, w. *be* with 2K 6_{32}; — 2. **oppress, torment** 2K $13_{4 \cdot 22}$.

nif.: impf. וַתִּלָּחֵץ: **push** (onesf.) against Nu 22_{25}. †

לַחַץ: לָחַץ, sf. לַחֲצֵנוּ: — 1. **oppression, affliction** 2K 13_4; — 2. *mayim laḥaṣ* (appos.) water such as is appropriate to hardship (siege), short rations of w. 1K 22_{27}, so *leḥem laḥaṣ* 22_{27}.

לחשׁ: **piel**: pt. מְלַחֲשִׁים: conjure by whispering, pt. **conjurer, enchanter** Ps 58_6. †

hitp.: impf. יִתְלַחֲשׁוּ; pt. מִתְלַחֲשִׁים: **whisper w. each other** 2S 12_{19} Ps 41_8. †

לַחַשׁ: pl. לְחָשִׁים: — 1. whispering, **charming** (of a snake) Is 3_3 Je 8_{17} Ec 10_{11}; — 2. **amulet** (? humming shells) as ornament Is 3_{20}. †

לָט: **secrecy**: — 1. *ballāṭ*, Ju 4_{21} *ballā'ṭ* secretly 1S 18_{22}; — 2. pl. **secret arts, sorcery** Ex 7_{22}.

לֹט: the resinous bark of *Pistacia mutica*, **mastic** (oth.: the gum of a kind of *Cistus* [rockrose]) Gn 37_{25} 43_{11}. †

לְטָאָה: **gecko**, *Platodactylus muralis*, or other lizard, unclean Lv 11_{30}. †

לְטוּשִׁים: n. peop. unknown Gn 25_3. †

לטשׁ: **qal**: impf. יִלְטֹשׁ; pt. לֹטֵשׁ: — 1. **sharpen**: (plowshare) 1S 13_{20}, (sword) Ps 7_{13}; pt. **smith** Gn 4_{22}; — 2. metaph.: w. *le* **whet** (the eyes against s.one) Jb 16_9. †

pual: pt. מְלֻטָּשׁ: **sharpened** Ps 52_4. †

***לֹיָה**: pl. לֹיוֹת: tech. archit. term: metal ornament, spiral?: **garlands** 1K 7_{29}. †

לַיִל, poet. Is 16_3 La 2_{19}, > לֵיל Is 21_{11}: cs. לֵיל, = F לַיְלָה **night**.

לַיְלָה (ca. 225×): לֵיל, לַיְלָה Pr 31_{18} (Kt לַיִל, Qr לַיְלָה); pl. לֵילוֹת: **night** Gn 1_5; *laylâ* = at night (:: *yômām*) Ex 13_{21}; *hallaylâ* tonight Gn 19_5, *ballaylâ* in the night Gn 19_{33}, *belaylâ* at night Ne 9_{19}; *ḥaṣōt/ḥaṣî hallaylâ* at midnight Ex 11_4 12_{29}; *mah-mmillaylâ* how late in the night? Is 21_{11}; *bin-laylâ* within a night Jon 4_{10}; *lêlôt* through the nights Ps 16_7.

לִילִית: **Lilith**, (female) demon relating to sexual life (oth.: nightmare, or wood-owl) Is 34_{14}, cj. Jb 18_{15} (for *mibbelî-lô*). †

לין: **qal**: pf. לָן, 3. f. sg. לָנָה Zc 5_4, לַנּוּ; impf. יָלִין, וַיָּלֶן, תָּלִין, תָּלֶן, תָּלִן Ju 19_{20}, תָּלִינִי, אָלִין, וַיָּל(י)נוּ, נָלִין, נָלִינָה; impv. לִין, לִינִי, לִינוּ; inf. לִין Gn 24_{23} & לוּן 24_{25}; pt. לָן, לָנִים Ne 13_{21}: — 1. **remain (over) through the night**: meat of sacrifice Ex 23_{18}, bodies on a tree Dt 21_{23}, wages of a servant (w. the master) Lv 19_{13} (oth.: hif.); — 2. **spend the night** Gn 19_2 & oft.; — 3. **remain, stay, live** (= dwell) Is 1_{21}.

hif.: impf. יָלִין, תָּלִין: — 1. **grant, permit** (army) **rest for the night** 2S 17_8 (oth.: qal); — 2. **let** (s.thg) **tarry, remain** Je 4_{14} (oth.: qal); — 3. **retain** (wages) **overnight** Lv 19_{13} (oth.: qal). †

hitpolal: impf. יִתְלוֹנָן: **stay for the night** Ps 91_1 Jb 39_{28}. †

ליץ: **qal**: pf. לַצְתָּ: **talk big, boast** Pr 9_{12}. †

polel: pt. לֹצְצִים (w/o מ) as noun: **mockers or rebels** Ho 7_5. †

hif.: pf. הֱלִיצֻנִי; impf. יָלִיץ; pt. מֵלִיץ, pl. cs. מְלִיצֵי, sf. מְלִיצַי, מְלִיצֶיךָ: — 1. **mock, ridicule**: acc. pers. Ps 119_{51}, metaph. acc. mock at (justice) Pr 19_{28}, make fun of (God subj., *le* & obj.) Pr 3_{34}; — 2. pt. *mēlîṣ* **spokesman** Is 43_{27} Jb 33_{23} 2C 32_{31}; > **interpreter** (of foreign language) Gn 42_{23}. †

hitpolal: impf. תִּתְלוֹצָצוּ: **give onesf. airs** Is 28_{22}. †

I **לַיִשׁ**: **lion** Is 30_6 Jb 4_{11} Pr 30_3. †

II **לַיִשׁ**: n. pers. 1S 25_{44}, 2S 3_{15} Qr לַיִשׁ (Kt לוּשׁ.) †

III **לַיִשׁ**: n. loc. Ju $18_{7 \cdot 27 \cdot 29}$. †

לַ֫יְשָׁה: n. loc. Is 10_{30}. †

לָכַד: **qal** (85×): pf. לָכַד, לָכֶד, ל׳, וּלְכָדָהּ; impf. יִלְכֹּד, וַיִּלְכֹּד־, יִלְכְּדוּ, וַיִּלְכְּדוּ, וַיִּלְכְּדוּהוּ, תִּלְכְּדוֹ, יִלְכְּדֶנָּה, יִלְכְּדֵנוּ, יִלְכְּדָה (־דְהוּ), יִלְכָּדְנוֹ; impv. לִכְדוּ, לָכְדָה; inf. לָכְדָה, לָכְדֵנִי, abs. לָכוֹד; pt. לֹכֵד: — 1. **catch**: animals (in trap) Am 3_{4f}, capture (obj. men) Ju 7_{25}; take (as prisoners) 2S 8_4; — 2. **take** (possession of), **capture**: city Nu 21_{32}, land Jos 10_{42}; occupy (a ford) Ju 3_{28}; seize (= cut off) (waters) Ju 7_{24}; — 3. var.: a) catch = designate (by lot) (subj. Y.) Jos 7_{14}; b) take over (the government) 1S 14_{47}.

nif.: pf. נִלְכַּד, נִלְכְּדָה, נִלְכָּדוּ; impf. יִלָּכֵד, יִלָּ֫כֶד, יִלָּכְדוּ(ן); pt. נִלְכָּד: — 1. **be caught**: a) animals (in trap) Is 8_{15}; b) men Je 6_{11}; metaph., by a woman Ec 7_{26}, by words Pr 6_2; — 2. **be captured**: city 1K 16_{18}; — 3. **be chosen** (by lot) 1S 10_{20f}.

hitp.: impf. יִתְלַכְּדוּ, יִתְלַכָּ֫דוּ: (of surface of the sea) **collect together** Jb 38_{30}; **clasp each other** 41_9. †

***לֶכֶד**, לֶ֫כֶד: **capture** (oth.: trap) Pr 3_{26}. †

לְכָה: 1. ☞ הָלַךְ impv.; 2. = לְךָ, ☞ I לְ.

לֵכָה: n. loc. (?) unknown, 1C 4_{21}; — לֵכָה 1S 23_{27}, ☞ הָלַךְ impv. †

לָכִישׁ: n. loc.; loc. לָכִ֫ישָׁה: **Lachish**.

לָכֵן (188×): I לְ + II כֵּן: — 1. **therefore** Ex 6_6 (ca. 80×); *lākēn kōh ʾāmar yhwh* 2K 19_{32} (66×, 22× Je), *welākēn* 1S 3_{14}; many similar phrases, esp. in prophetic contexts; — 2. **for this** Gn 30_{15} Is 61_7 †; — 3. **indeed, all right** (II לְ) 1S 28_2 Je 2_{33} † (oth.: 1.).

לֻלָאוֹת: cs. לֻלְאֹת: **loops** Ex $26_{4f.10f}$ $36_{11f.17}$. †

[***לַם**: Is 9_6 לְםַרְבֵּה (final ם!), Qr & mss. לְמַרְבֵּה for increase; usu. (so Qumran ms.) רַבָּה (רַב f.) & לַם dittgr.; oth.: remains of a 5th throne-name w. v. $_5$. †]

למד: **qal**: pf. לָמַדְתִּי, לָמְדוּ; impf. יִלְמַד, תִּלְמְדוּ, יִלְמְדוּן, אֶלְמְדָה; impv. לִמְדוּ; inf. לְמָדִי; pt. pass. לְמוּדֵי: **learn**: — 1. w. acc. of thg.: war Is 2_4; *lemûdê milḥāmâ* battle-trained 1C 5_{18}; obj. insight Is 29_{24}, righteousness Is 26_9, commandments Dt 5_1; — 2. w. *le* & inf., learn to: Dt 4_{10} (*lirʾôt*, :: *weyāreʾû* 31_{12}).

[cj. **nif.**: impf. *יִלָּמֵד Jb 11_{12} for יִוָּלֵד: **be tamed, docile**.]

piel (ca. 50×): pf. לִמַּד, 2. f. לִמַּדְתְּ & Je 2_{33} Kt לִמַּדְתִּי (oth.: 1 sg., subj. Y.), לִמְּדוּם, לִמַּדְתַּנִי; impf. יְלַמֵּד, יְלַמֶּד־, תְּלַמְּדֶנּוּ, יְלַמְּדָה, יְלַמְּדֵהוּ, יְלַמְּדוּן, אֲלַמְּדָה, אֲלַמֶּדְכֶם; impv. לַמְּדֵנִי, לַמֵּדְנָה; inf. לַמֵּד; pt. מְלַמֵּד, מְלַמֶּדְךָ: **teach**: — 1. syntax: a) abs.: 2C $17_{7.9}$; pt. teacher Ps 119_{99}; b) w. acc. pers. Je 31_{34}; c) 2 acc., pers. & thg.: Dt 4_1; d) acc. thg, *le* & pers. Jb 21_{22}; e) acc. pers., *le* & thg. Ps 18_{35}; f) acc. pers., *be* instruct s.one in s.thg Is 40_{14}; g) acc. pers., *min* = from Ps 94_{12}; h) acc. pers., *le* & inf. Dt 6_1; — 2. content of teaching: war Ju 3_2, bow 2S 1_{18}, song Dt 31_{19}, foreign lang. Dn 1_4, commandments Dt 4_5, s.thg bad Je 2_{33}.

pual: pf. לֻמַּד Je 31_{18}; pt. מְלֻמָּד, מְלֻמְּדֵי, מְלֻמָּדָה: **be instructed, well-versed** Is 29_{13}, *ʿēgel lōʾ lummād* unruly Je 31_{18}, *ʿeglâ melummādâ* docile (oth.: trained) Ho 10_{11}.

לִמֻּד & **לִמּוּד**: pl. לִמֻּדִים, לִמּוּדֵי, לִמֻּדַי, לִמֻּדָי: — 1. adj. **learned, practiced**: w. *hārēaʿ*: accustomed to do evil Je 13_{23}; — 2. **disciple** Is 50_4; Is 8_{16} ?, trad. 'in/through the disciples,' but txt. ? ☞ comm.

לָמָה, **לָ֫מָּה**, & **לָ֫מָה**: ☞ מָה.

לָמוֹ (50×): = לָהֶם, sometimes לוֹ: *yehî* … *ʿebed lāmô* let him be a slave to (?) him Gn 9_{26}.

לְמוֹ: fuller form of לְ: Jb 27_{14} 29_{21} 38_{40} 40_4. †

לְמוּאֵל & **לְמוֹאֵל**: n. pers. Pr $31_{1.4}$. †

לְמוֹאֵל Ne 12_{38}: rd. לִשְׂמֹאל. †

לִמּוּד: ☞ לִמֻּד.

[**לַמְחוֹת** Pr 31_3: rd. לִמְחוֹת (I מחה). †]

לֶמֶךְ, **לָ֫מֶךְ**: n. pers.

לְמַעַן: ☞ מַעַן.

*לֵן: לֵנִים Ne 13_{21}: F לין pt. †

*לֹעַ: sf. לֹעֲךָ: from ctxt. *śîm śakkîn bᵉlōʿᵃkā* **throat** = control yourself Pr 23_2. †

לעב: **hif.**: pt. מַלְעִבִים: **make a game of** s.one 2C 36_{16}. †

לעג: **qal**: pf. לָעֲגָה; impf. אֶלְעַג, יִלְעַג, יִלְעָג, יִלְעֲגוּ; pt. לֹעֵג: w. *lᵉ*, stammer in s.one's face, **ridicule** 2K 19_{21}.

nif.: pt. cs. נִלְעַג: *nilʿag lāšôn*, w. stammering tongue = in a foreign language Is 33_{19}. †

hif.: impf. יַלְעִגוּ, תַּלְעִיג, וַיַּלְעֵג; pt. מַלְעִגִים: **mock** Jb 21_3; ridicule s.one: w. *lᵉ* Ps 22_8 Ne 2_{19}, w. *ʿal* Ne 3_{33}, w. *bᵉ* 2C 30_{10}. †

לַעַג: sf. לַעְגָּם; pl. cs. לַעֲגֵי: — 1. **stammering**: *bᵉlaʿᵃgê śāfâ* with stammering of lips Is 28_{11}; — 2. **derision** Ez 23_{32}.

*לָעֵג: לַעֲגֵי Is 28_{11} F לַעַג; Ps 35_{16} F לעג qal. †

לַעְדָּה: n. pers.

לַעְדָּן: n. pers.

לעז: **qal**: pt. לֹעֵז: **speak an incomprehensible foreign language** Ps 114_1. †

לעט: cj. **qal**: Ps 57_5 cj. pt. לֹעֲטִים for לֹהֲטִים: **devour greedily**. †

hif.: impv. הַלְעִיטֵנִי: **let** s.one **gulp down** Gn 25_{30}. †

לָעִיר: *ûmelek lāʿîr sᵉfarwayim* 2K 19_{13} = Is 37_{13}: n. loc. in Elamite border area. †

לַעֲנָה: trad. **wormwood**, *Artemisia absinthium*, containing a bitter taste, alw. metaph. **bitter(ness)** Pr 5_4.

I לעע: **qal**: pf. לָעוּ; impf. יָלַע: **stammer, rave** Jb 6_3, speak rashly (hif.?) Pr 20_{25}. †

II לעע: **qal**: pf. וְלָעוּ: **slurp** (drink noisily) Ob $_{16}$, but perh. should rd. *עָלוּ (Arab. vb. of sim. mng.) †

cj. **pilpel**: impf. rd. יְלַעְלְעוּ: **lick up** (blood) **eagerly** Jb 39_{30}. †

לַפִּיד: pl. לַפִּ(י)דִ(י)ם, cs. לַפִּידֵי: — 1. **torch** Gn 15_{17}; — 2. **lightning** † Ex 20_{18}.

לַפִּידוֹת: n. pers.

לפת: **qal**: impf. יִלְפֹּת: **feel out** Ju 16_{29}. †

nif.: impf. יִלָּפְתוּ, יִלָּפֵת: **feel around** Ru 3_8; turn, wend one's way Jb 6_{18}. †

לֵץ: pl. לֵצִים: **babbler, scoffer** Ps 1_1.

לָצוֹן: **bragging, foolish talk** Pr 1_{22}; *ʾanšê lāṣôn* babbler, scoffer Is 28_{14} Pr 29_8. †

לצץ: **qal**: pt. לֹצְצִים: **rebels** or **scoffers** (F ליץ polel) Ho 7_5. †

לַקּוּם: n. loc.

לָקַח: **qal**: pf. לִ׳, לָקַח, לָקַחְתָּ, וְלָקַחְתָּ, לָקַחְתְּ (Ez 17_5 & Ho 11_3 are errors), לָקְחוּ; impf. יִקַּח, יִקַּח, אֶקְחָה, יִקְחוּ, יִקְּחוּ, (2K 20_{18} יִקָּח: Kt F pual), נִקַּח, נִקְחָה, יִקָּחֵנִי, יִקָּחֶנָּה, אֶקָּחֲךָ, אֶקָּחֵהוּ, יִקָּחוּם; impv. קַח (& 3× לְקַח), קַח, קְחָה, קְחִי (1K 17_{11} לְקְחִי), קְחוּ, קְחוּ, קְחֵנוּ, קְחֶם, קְחֶם־נָא Gn 48_9, קָחֶהוּ; inf. (לָ)קַחַת (קַחַת 2K 12_9 error?), קַחְתִּי, לְקַחְתּוֹ, abs. לָקֹ(וֹ)חַ; pt. לֹקֵחַ, לֹקְחִים, לֹקְחֵי, pass. לְקֻחִים: — 1. **take, lay hold of, seize**: *qaḥ bᵉyādᵉkā* Ex 17_5, take (s.one) by (the hair) Ez 8_3; = keep Gn 14_{21}; — 2. **take** (person or animal) w. one Gn 12_5; take words Ho 14_3; — 3. take = **receive** *miyyad-* 2K 5_{20}; **acquire,** buy Pr 31_{16}; metaph. = obey: commandments Pr 10_8; (God) receives (& accepts) (prayer) Ps 6_{10}; — 4. take up = **shelter** (subj. bird, obj. its young) Dt 32_{11}; — 5. **fetch, bring**: *qaḥ lî* Gn 27_{13}; **have** s.one **brought** 1S 17_{31}; take = take an interest in (s.one) Je 40_2; *lᵉquḥîm lammāwet* those dragged to death Pr 24_{11}; *lāqaḥ ʿal* take (& load) on Ju 19_{28}, take (& spread) on 2S 13_{19}; — 6. **take** (on as a slave) 2K 4_1, take (in as a daughter) Est 2_7; — 7. *lāqaḥ ʾiššâ* take a wife Gn 25_1, for onesf. Gn 4_{19}, for s.one else Gn 24_4, *lāqaḥ ʾōtāh lô lᵉʾiššâ* Gn 12_{19}; — 8. **take away**: s.one's garment Pr 27_{13}, blessing Gn 27_{35}; — 9. (God) carries off s.one Gn 5_{24}; — 10. var.: obj. *nāqām* Is 47_3 (*nᵉqāmâ* Je 22_{10}) vengeance, *ḥerpâ* disgrace Ez 36_{30}; obj. *dābār*, take = receive

& understand Je 9_{19}; subj. heart (sweeps away s.one) Jb 15_{12}.

nif.: pf. נִלְקָחָה, נִלְקָח, נִלְקַח 1S 4_{17}; impf. תִּלָּקַח, אֶלָּקַח; inf. הִלָּקַח, הִלָּקְחוֹ: — 1. **be taken away** 2K 2_9; — 2. **be brought** (in) Est 2_8.

pual (or qal pass.): pf. לֻקָּחָה, לֻקַּח, לֻקָּח, לֻקְּחוּ, לֻקָּחְתְּ; impf. יֻקַּח, יֻקָּח, וַתֻּקַּח; pt. לֻקָּח (!): — 1. **be taken** Gn 2_{23}, = stolen Ju 17_2, w. *mē'ēt* from (by death) 2K 2_{10}, w/o prep. Is 53_8; = taken away in slavery Is 52_5; = be accepted (of a curse-formula) Je 29_{22}; — 2. **be fetched, brought** Gn 12_{15} (into the harem).

hitp.: pt. מִתְלַקַּחַת: (of fire) **flash here & there** Ex 9_{24} Ez 1_4. †

לֶקַח: sf. לִקְחִי, לִקְחָהּ: — 1. **teaching** Dt 32_2; — 2. **gift of persuasion** † Pr 7_{21}; — 3. **insight** † Is 29_{24} Pr 1_5.

לִקְחִי: n. pers.

לקט: **qal**: pf. לָקְטוּ, לָקְטוּ; impf. יִלְקְטוּ, תִּלְקְטָהוּ, יִלְקֹטוּן; impv. לִקְטוּ; inf. לְקֹט: — 1. **gather** (up): stones Gn 31_{46}, manna Ex 16_4; — 2. spec.: **glean** † Ru 2_8.

piel: pf. לִקַּטְתָּ, לִקְּטָה, לִקֵּטָה; impf. וַיְלַקֵּט, אֲלַקֳטָה Ru $2_{2.7}$; pt. מְלַקֵּט, מְלַקְּטִים: — 1. **gather**: wood Je 7_{18}, herbs 2K 4_{39}; glean Is 17_5 Ru 2_{2ff}; — 2. **gather together**: remains of food Ju 1_7, arrows 1S 20_{38}; — 3. cogn. acc. *liqqēṭ leqeṭ* **gather gleanings** Lv 19_9, *liqqēṭ pereṭ* gather up grapes that have fallen Lv 19_{10}; — 4. **bring together** (money) Is 27_{12}.

pual: impf. תְּלֻקְּטוּ: **be gathered up** Is 27_{12}. †

hitp.: impf. וַיִּתְלַקְּטוּ: **gather around** (*'el*) Ju 11_3. †

*לֶקֶט: cs. =: **gleanings** (of harvest) Lv 19_9 23_{22}. †

לקק: **qal**: pf. לָקְקוּ; impf. יָלֹק, יָלֹקּוּ: **lick up, lap** (water, like a dog) Ju 7_5 1K 21_{19} 22_{38}. †

piel: pt. מְלַקְקִים: **lap** (like a dog) Ju 7_{6f}. †

לקשׁ: **piel**: impf. יְלַקֵּשׁוּ: **rake up** (a vineyard) Jb 24_6 (oth.: glean). †

לֶקֶשׁ: **late grass** Am 7_1. †

*לָשָׁד: cs. לְשַׁד, sf. לְשַׁדִּי: **cake**: *lešad haššāmen* cake baked w. oil Nu 11_8; Ps 32_4 ?, ꟳ comm. †

לָשׁוֹן & לָשֹׁן (115×): cs. לְשׁוֹן, sf. לְשׁוֹנוֹ; pl. לְשֹׁנוֹת, sf. לְשׁוֹנֹתָם; m. & f.: — 1. **tongue** (as a part of the body): of man La 4_4, dog Ex 11_7; of Y. Is 30_{27}; — 2. **tongue** (as a shape): *lešôn zāhāb* gold bar Jos 7_{21}, *lešôn 'ēš* tongue of fire Is 5_{24}; *lešôn hayyām* bay Jos 15_5, > *lāšôn* Jos 15_2; — 3. as instrument of speech: *'al-lešônî* 2S 23_2, *kebad lāšôn* not eloquent Ex 4_{10}; *'îš lāšôn* a hero w. words Ps 140_{12}, *ba'al hallāšôn* charmer (of snakes) Ec 10_{11}; — 4. tongue = **language**: *'îš lilšônô* each according to his lang. Gn 10_5, *kilšôn 'am wā'ām* according to the lang. of each people Ne 13_{24}; *medabbēr kilšôn 'ammô* imitation of official style ? Est 1_{22b}.

לִשְׁכָּה: cs. לִשְׁכַּת; pl. לְשָׁכוֹת, cs. לִשְׁכוֹת: **hall**, i.e. a room on 3 walls of which were benches where worshippers ate sacrificial meal, 4th open to the courtyard 1S 9_{22}; w. name of person, cell or cubicle of individual 2K 23_{11}.

I לֶשֶׁם: unknown precious stone, carnelian, jacinth, reddish-yellow amber, or bluish-white felspar Ex 28_{19} 39_{12}. †

II לֶשֶׁם: n. loc. Jos 19_{47}. †

לשׁן: **hif.**: impf. תַּלְשֵׁן: **slander** Pr 30_{10}. †

poel: pt. מְלָושְׁנִי (Qr -ō-, Kt -ō-), cs. before prep.; perhaps rd. hif. מַלְשִׁין: **slander** Ps 101_5. †

לָשֹׁן: ꟳ לָשׁוֹן.

*לֶשַׁע: לָשַׁע: n. loc.

לַשָּׁרוֹן: n. loc. (?) Jos 12_{18}. †

לַת: 1S 4_{19} לָלַת, ꟳ ילד qal inf. †

לֶתֶךְ: measure of capacity, = 115 liters or 30 gal. Ho 3_2. †

מ

מ enclitic, in MT understood & vocalized otherw., no discernible difference of mng.; rd. Ju 5_{13} אַדִּירֵי־ם, Ps 29_{6} וַיַּרְקִד־ם &c.; ⸢F⸣ e.g. Dahood *Anchor Bible Psalms passim.*

מַ־ w. daghesh ⸢F⸣ מָה; מִ־ w. daghesh ⸢F⸣ מִן.

***מַאֲבוּס**: pl. sf. מַאֲבֻסֶיהָ: **granary** Je 50_{26}. †

מְאֹד (300×): sf. מְאֹדוֹ; מְאֹדֶךָ: — 1. sbst. **power, might** Dt 6_{5} 2K 23_{25} †; — 2. adv. **very**: *ṭôb meʾōd* Gn 1_{31}, *ḥaṭṭāʾîm leyhwh meʿōd* sinners against Y. **in the highest degree** Gn 13_{13}; (placed first) Ps 47_{10}, (at a distance) 1K 11_{19}; *meʾōd meʾōd* reinforcing: very much indeed Gn 7_{19}, *bimʾōd meʾōd* Gn 17_{2}, *ʿad-meʾōd* Gn 27_{33}.

I **מֵאָה** (580×): cs. מְאַת, pl. מֵאוֹת, מֵאיוֹת 2K $11_{4 \cdot 9f \cdot 15}$ = Qr מֵאוֹת, Kt מֵאיוֹת; du. מָאתַיִם, מָאתָיִם: — 1. sg. **hundred**: *mēʾâ šānâ* Gn 17_{17}, *meʾat šānâ* 5_{3}; — 2. du. = 200, *māʾtayim ʾîš* 1S 18_{27}; — 3. pl. **hundreds**: a) military unit 1S 29_{2}; b) otherw., *šelōš meʾôt* Ju 15_{4}; — 4. in comb. 105 Gn 5_{6}.

II **מֵאָה**: *migdal hammēʾâ* Ne 3_{1} 12_{39}, n. loc. in Jerus.

***מַאֲוַיִּים**: cs. מַאֲוַיֵּי: **desires** Ps 140_{9}. †

מאום Jb 31_{7} & מְאוּם Dn 1_{4}: ⸢F⸣ מוּם. †

מְאוּמָה, מוּמָה 2K 5_{20}: **anything** (at all) 1K 10_{21}; *meʾûmâ raʿ* any harm Je 39_{20}; w. neg., may be translated 'nothing at all' Gn 30_{31} &c.

מָאוֹס: inf. as sbst. **trash** La 3_{45}. †

מָאוֹר, מָאֹר Ex 25_{6}: cs. מְאוֹר; pl. מְאוֹרִים, cs. מְאוֹרֵי, & מְאוֹרוֹת: — 1. **luminous place** Ez 32_{8}; — 2. object of light: a) **luminary**, sun & moon Gn $1_{14 \cdot 16}$; b) **lamp** Ex 25_{6}; — 3. *meʾôr ʿênayim* luminous eyes Pr 15_{30}, *m. pānîm* Ps 90_{8}.

***מְאוּרָה**: cs. מְאוּרַת Is 11_{8} fiery eyes (?), but prob. rd. מְעָרַת hole. †

מֹאזְנַיִם: מֹאזְנָיִם, cs. מֹאזְנֵי: the 2 scale-pans, **scales, balance** Is 40_{12}.

מְאָיוֹת 2K $11_{4 \cdot 15}$ Kt: ⸢F⸣ I מֵאָה.

מֵאַיִן: ⸢F⸣ II אַיִן.

מַאֲכָל: cs. מַאֲכַל, sf. מַאֲכָלוֹ: **food** for men & animals, **fodder** Gn 6_{21}; *ṭôb lemaʾakāl* good to eat Gn 2_{9}; *ʿēṣ maʾakāl* fruit tree Dt 20_{20}, *ṣōʾn maʾakāl* goat or sheep for slaughter Ps 44_{12}; *maʾakal taʾaweh* favorite dishes Jb 33_{20}.

מַאֲכֶלֶת: pausal = ; pl. מַאֲכָלוֹת: **butcher-knife** Gn $22_{6 \cdot 10}$ Ju 19_{29} Pr 30_{14}. †

מַאֲכֹלֶת: **food** (for fire) Is 9_{4}; 9_{18} ?, ⸢F⸣ comm. †

***מַאֲמָץ**: pl. cs. מַאֲמַצֵּי: w. *kōaḥ* **exertions** Jb 36_{19} (oth.: expenditures of every sort). †

***מַאֲמָר**: cs. מַאֲמַר: **command** Est 1_{15} 2_{20} 9_{32}. †

מאן: **piel**: pf. מֵאֵנוּ, מֵאַנְתְּ, מֵאֲנָה, מֵאֵן; impf. יְמָאֵן, וַיְמָאֲנוּ; inf. מָאֵן; pt. מָאֵן < *מְמָאֵן & הַמֵּאֲנִים < *הַמָּ־ < *הַמְמָ־ Je 13_{10}: — 1. abs. **refuse** 2K 5_{16}; *waymāʾēn wayyōʾmer* Gn 39_{8}; — 2. **refuse to**: a) w. inf. Nu 20_{21}, b) w. *le* & inf. Gn 37_{35}.

I **מָאַס**: **qal**: pf. מ׳, מָאֲסוּ, מְאָסוּ, מְאַסְתֶּם; impf. אֶמְאָסְךָ, תִּמְאָס, יִמְאַס, Ho 4_{6} Qr (Kt ־סאך), יִמְאָסֵם, תִּמְאָסוּנִי, יִמְאָסוּן; inf. מָאֳסֵם & מָאָסְכֶם (*-ŏʾŏ-*), abs. מָא(וֹ)ס; pt. מוֹאֵס, מֹאֶסֶת: — 1. **refuse, reject**: a) man subj.: w. *be*, obj. land Nu 14_{31}, woman Je 4_{30}, God's words Is 30_{12}; w. acc. Ps 36_{5}; b) God subj.: w. *be* 2K 17_{20}, w. acc. Isr. Je 7_{29}, Jerus. 2K 23_{27}; — 2. var.: a) disavowal (thus rejection) of earlier words Jb 42_{6}; b) inf. abs. > sbst. **trash** La 3_{45}.

nif.: impf. תִּמָּאֵס; pt. נִמְאָס: — 1. **be rejected** Is 54_{6}; — 2. pt. **scorned**, silver Je 6_{30}, man Ps 15_{4}. †

II **מאס**: **nif.**: impf. יִמָּאֵס, יִמָּאֲסוּ: **vanish** Ps 58_{8} Jb $7_{5.16}$ (?).†

מְאַסֵּף: הַמְאַסֵּף **rear-guard** Jos $6_{9.13}$. †

***מַאֲפֶה**: cs. מַאֲפֵה: *ma'ᵃpēh tannûr* **something baked** in an oven Lv 2_{4}. †

מַאֲפֵל: **darkness** Jos 24_{7}. †

מַאְפֵלְיָה: **darkness** Je 2_{31}. †

מאר: **hif.**: pt. מַמְאִיר, מַמְאֶרֶת: **sore, hurtful**: skin eruption Lv 13_{51f} 14_{44}, thorn Ez 28_{24}. †

מַאֲרָב: cs. מַאֲרַב: **ambush** Ju 9_{23} Jos 8_{9} Ps 10_{8}, (men waiting in) ambush 2C 13_{13}. †

מְאֵרָה: cs. מְאֵרַת, pl. מְאֵרוֹת: **curse, malediction** Dt $28_{20.27}$ Ma 2_{2} 3_{9} Pr 3_{33}. †

מֵאֵת: ↗ מִן + II אֵת.

מִבְדָּלוֹת: trad. enclaves, but better **singled out, selected** Jos 16_{9}. †

***מְבָא** 2S 3_{25} Qr: ↗ *מוֹבָא.

מָבוֹא: cs. מְבוֹא, sf. מְבוֹאוֹ; pl. מְבֹ(ו)אוֹת, cs. מְבוֹאֵי; ↗ also *מוֹבָא for Qr/Kt 2S 3_{25} Ez 43_{11}: — 1. **entrance**: of city Ju 1_{24f}, for horses 2K 11_{16}; — 2. **access** (to sea) Ez 27_{3}; — 3. **setting (of sun)** > **west** Dt 11_{30}; — 4. making one's appearance, **entering**: of people = in troops Ez 33_{31}, of house = access to temple Ez 44_{5}.

מְבוּכָה: sf. מְבוּכָתָם: **confusion** Is 22_{5} Mi 7_{4}. †

מַבּוּל: **heavenly ocean** Gn 7_{10} 9_{11} Ps 29_{10} † > **deluge** Gn 6_{17}.

מְבוֹנִים 2C 35_{3}: Qr מְבִי־, Kt מְבוֹ־, ↗ בין.

מְבוּסָה: **trampling** Is $18_{2.7}$ 22_{5}. †

מַבּוּעַ: **spring** (of water) Is 35_{7} 49_{10} Ec 12_{6}. †

מְבוּקָה: **desert, devastation** Na 2_{11}. †

מְבוּשִׁים: **private parts, genitals** (of a man) Dt 25_{11}. †

מִבְחוֹר: **choicest, best** 2K 3_{19} 19_{23}. †

I **מִבְחָר**: cs. מִבְחַר; pl. sf. מִבְחָרָיו: **choicest, best** Gn 23_{6}; *'am mibḥārāyw* elite troops Dn 11_{15}.

II **מִבְחָר**: n. pers. 1C 11_{38}. †

מַבָּט: sf. מַבָּטָם, מַבָּטֵנוּ; מֶבָּטָהּ Zc 9_{5}: **hope** (i.e. ground or goal of one's hoping) Is 20_{5f} Zc 9_{5}. †

מִבְטָא: **rash utterance**, w. *śiftêkem* rash vow Nu $30_{7.9}$. †

***מִבְטָח**: cs. מִבְטַח, sf. מִבְטַחוֹ, מִבְטַחֵךְ, מִבְטַחִי, מִבְטֶחָה Pr 21_{22} & מִבְטֶחָם Je 48_{13}; pl. מִבְטַחִים: **trust, confidence** (i.e. person or thing in whom/which one trusts), w. gen. or sf.: Je 17_{7}; pl. Je 2_{37}.

cj. ***מַבָּךְ**: Jb 28_{11} for מִבְּכִי rd. pl. cs. מַבְּכֵי: **source**, place fm. wh. water trickles in mine. †

[***מַבְלִיגִית**: Je 8_{18}: rd. מִבְּלִי גֵּהָה/גְהוֹת without healing. †]

מְבֻלָּקָה: = בלק **pual** pt. f. as sbst.: **destruction** Na 2_{11}. †

***מִבְנֶה**: cs. מִבְנֵה: **structure**, *mibnēh 'îr* Ez 40_{2}. †

מְבֻנַּי: n. pers.

cj. **מַבְנִית**: **structure, frame, body**: sugg. Jb 20_{3} *mabnîtî*. †

I **מִבְצָר**: cs. מִבְצַר; pl. מִבְצָרִים, Dn 11_{15} מִבְצָרוֹת, cs. מִבְצְרֵי, sf. מִבְצָרָיו, מִבְצְרֵיהֶם: fortified place (:: camp, without defenses Nu 13_{19}): — 1. *'îr mibṣār* **fortified city** 2K 3_{19}; — 2. > *mibṣār* firm city, **fortress**, sg. Is 25_{2}, pl. 2K 8_{12}; — 3. var.: *mibṣᵉrê mā'uzzîm* strong fortifications Dn 11_{29}, *'îr mibṣārôt* strongly fortified city 11_{15}.

II **מִבְצָר**: n. pers. Gn 36_{42} 1C 1_{53}. †

***מִבְרָח**: Ez 17_{21} Kt מִבְרָחוֹ, Qr ־חָיו: trad. refugee, fugitive; oth.: select(ed). †

מִבְשָׂם: n. pers.

מְבַשְּׁלוֹת: בשל **piel** pt.: **cooking-places, hearths** Ez 46_{23}. †

מָג: Je $39_{3.13}$ *rab-māg*: title of high Babylonian official. †

מַגְבִּישׁ: n. pers. (or loc. ?).

מִגְבָּלוֹת: (hammered) **chains** Ex 28_{14}. †

***מִגְבָּעָה**: pl. מִגְבָּעוֹת: **head-band** (of priest) Ex 28_{40} 29_{9} 39_{28} Lv 8_{13}. †

מֶגֶד: pl. מְגָדִים, sf. מְגָדָיו, & extended pl. מִגְדָּנ(ו)ת: **choice gift**: — 1. *meged*: **yield of fruit** Dt 33_{13ff}, *pᵉrî mᵉgādîm* excellent fruit

SS $4_{13\cdot16}$, *kol-m.* 7_{14}; — 2. *migdānôt* **precious gifts** Gn 24_{53} Ezr 1_{62} 2C 21_3 32_{23}. †
מְגִדּוֹ, Zc 12_{11} מְגִדּוֹן: n. loc. **Megiddo.**
מְגִדּוֹן Zc 12_{11}, ↗ מְגִדּוֹ. †
מַגְדִּיאֵל: n. pers.
[**מִגְדִּיל** 2S 22_{51}: Qr מִגְדּוֹל, rd Kt & Ps 18_{51} גדל מַגְדִּיל, hif.]
I **מִגְדָּל**: cs. מִגְדַּל; pl. מִגְדָּלִים, מִגְדָּלוֹת, cs. מִגְדְּלוֹת: — 1. **tower** Gn 11_4; in vineyard Is 5_2, in defense wall 2C 14_6, isolated 1C 27_{25}; towers often named, e.g. Ju 9_{52}; — 2. *migdal ʿēṣ* wooden **platform** † Ne 8_4.
II **מִגְדָּל**: = I, in var. compound proper names: — 1. מִגְדַּל־אֵל; — 2. מִגְדַּל־גָּד; — 3. מִגְדַּל־עֵדֶר; — 4. מִגְדַּל־שְׁכֶם.
מִגְדֹּל: n. loc.
מִגְדָּנ(וֹ)ת: pl. of ↗ מֶגֶד.
מָגוֹג: n. terr.
I **מָגוֹר**: — 1. **terror, horror** Is 31_9, *māgôr missābîb* Je 6_{25}; — 2. (object of) **horror, terror** † Je 20_4.
II ***מָגוֹר**: pl. cs. מְגוּרֵי, sf. מְגֻרֶיךָ, מְגוּרֵיהֶם, מְגֻרֵיהֶם: — 1. **stopover place, place of residence** (of a ↗ *gēr*, resident alien), **(protected) alien citizenship**: *ʾereṣ megurêkā* Gn 17_8; — 2. **home, place of residence** in genl. † Jb 18_{19}.
III ***מָגוֹר**: sf. מְגוּרָם: **grain-pit, storage chamber** = **heart,** mind Ps 55_{16}. †
***מְגוֹרָה**: cs. מְגֹרַת, pl. sf. מְגוּרֹתָם, מְגוּרֹתַי: **horror** Pr 10_{24}, pl. Is 66_4 Ps 34_5. †
מְגוּרָה: **grain-pit, storage chamber** Hg 2_{19}. †
***מַגְזֵרָה**: pl. cs. מַגְזְרוֹת: **axe** 2S 12_{31}. †
מַגָּל: **sickle** Je 50_{16} Jl 4_{13}. †
מְגִלָּה: cs. מְגִלַּת: (written) **scroll** Je 36_{2-32}.
***מְגַמָּה**: cs. מְגַמַּת: **totality, all of** Hb 1_9. †
מגן: **piel**: pf. מִגֵּן; impf. אֲמַגֶּנְךָ, תְּמַגְּנֶךָּ: — 1. w. acc. **deliver, hand over** Gn 14_{20} Ho 11_8; — 2. w. 2 acc. **bestow on** Pr 4_9. †
I **מָגֵן**: cs. =; pl. מָגִנִּים, cs. מָגִנֵּי, sf. מָגִנָּיו, & מָגִנּוֹת: — 1. **shield** (as a weapon) 1K 14_{27}; — 2. **shield** (as ornament, display): of gold 1K 10_{17} &c.; — 3. metaph. = **protection, refuge**: a) king Ps 84_{10}; b) God Gn 15_{1f} & oft.; c) (?) earthly rulers Ps 47_{10}; — 4. = **scales** (of crocodile) Jb 41_7.
II **מָגֵן**: **insolent**: *ʾîš māgēn* Pr 6_{11} 24_{34}. †
***מֶגֶן** or ***מָגָן**: pl. sf. מָגִנֶּיהָ: **gift, present** Ho 4_{18}: gifts made in return. †
***מְגִנָּה**: cs. מְגִנַּת: **insolence** La 3_{65}. †
מִגְעֶרֶת: **reproach, rebuke** Dt 28_{20}. †
מַגֵּפָה: cs. מַגֵּפַת; pl. sf. מַגֵּפֹתַי: **plague, torment** produced by God Ex 9_{14}; = **pestilence** 1S 6_4, causing death Nu 14_{37}.
מַגְפִּיעָשׁ: n. pers.
מגר: [**qal**: pt. pass. pl. cs. מְגוּרֵי Ez 21_{17}: rd. מְגֻרֵי (√נגר).]
piel: pf. מִגַּרְתָּה: w. *le* **throw down on** Ps 89_{45}. †
מְגֵרָה: **saw** for stone-working 1K 7_9 1C $20_{3\alpha\beta}$. †
מִגְרוֹן: n. loc.
***מִגְרָע**: pl. מִגְרָעוֹת: tech. archit. term, **ledge, rebatement** (of wall) 1K 6_6. †
***מַגְרֵף** or ***מֶגְרָפָה**: pl. sf. מֶגְרְפֹתֵיהֶם: **spade or hoe** Jl 1_{17}. †
מִגְרָשׁ: cs. מִגְרַשׁ, sf. מִגְרָשָׁהּ; pl. cs. מִגְרְשֵׁי, sf. מִגְרְשֵׁיהֶם, מִגְרָשֶׁ(י)הָ: **pasture-land** (belonging to a city), belt of land outside the walls under the jurisdiction of a city Nu 35_{3-5}.
***מַד**: sf. מַדּוֹ, pl. sf. מַדָּיו & sg. sf. מִדּוֹ, pl. sf. מִדּוֹתָיו Ps 133_2; also pl. (?) מִדִּין Ju 5_{10}: **garment** in genl. 1S 4_{12}.
I **מִדְבָּר** (270×): cs. מִדְבַּר, loc. מִדְבָּ֫רָה & Jos 18_{12} 1K 19_{15} מִדְבָּ֫רָה, sf. מִדְבָּרָהּ: **pasturage, wilderness, desert,** i.e. area not cultivated: — 1. in genl. Gn 37_{22}; — 2. often a particular area: a) *hammidbār haggādôl* = Sinai Dt 2_7; b) w. n. loc. & terr., ↗ בְּאֵר שֶׁבַע, אֱדוֹם &c.
II **מִדְבָּר**: SS 4_3 Qr מִדְבָּרֵךְ, Kt מִדְבָּרֵיךְ: instrument of speech = **mouth.** †
מָדַד: **qal**: pf. מ׳, מָדַד, מַדֹּתִי, מַדֹּתֶם, מְדָדוֹ; impf. וַיָּמָד, תָּמֹד, וַיָּמֹ֫דּוּ; inf. (לָ)מֹד: — 1.

measure off (a distance, area) Nu 35_5; — 2. **measure out** (grain) Ru 3_{15}; w. *b^e* with Is 40_{12}; **mete out** (payment) Is 65_7.

nif.: impf. יִמַּד, יִמַּדּוּ: **be measured** Je 31_{37} 33_{22} Ho 2_1. †

piel: impf. אֲמַדֵּד, וַיְמַדְּדֵם: **measure off** 2S 8_2, **measure out** Ps 60_8 108_8. †

[polel: impf. וַיְמֹדֶד Hb 3_6: ↗ מוד polel. †]

hitpolel: impf. וַיִּתְמֹדֵד: c. *ʿal* **stretch (onesf.) out** on 1K 17_{21}. †

I מִדָּה: cs. מִדַּת; pl. מִדּוֹת, sf. מִדּוֹתֶיהָ: — 1. **measure, size**: the same measure, size Ex 26_2 1K 6_{25}; spec. measure of length 1C 23_{29}; adv. by measure Ez 48_{30}; — 2. *bammiddâ hāriʾšōnâ* the old **standard** (of measurement) 2C 3_3; — 3. **measurement** (= both act of m. and measured portion): (act) Lv 19_{35}; (measured portion) Ne 3_{11}; — 4. (unusual) **size** = **stature**: *ʾîš middâ* 1C 11_{23}; *bêt middôt* spacious house Je 22_{14}.

II *מִדָּה: cs. מִדַּת: **tax**: *middat hammelek* Ne 5_4. †

מַדְהֵבָה Is 14_4: rd מַרְהֵבָה. †

*מַד or I *מַדְוֶה: pl. sf. מַדְוֵיהֶם: **garment** 2S 10_4 1C 19_4. †

II *מַדְוֶה: cs. מַדְוֵה; pl. cs. מַדְוֵי: **disease** Dt 7_{15} 28_{60}. †

מַדּוּחִים: **repudiation** La 2_{14}. †

I מָדוֹן: pl. מְדָנִים Pr 6_{19} 10_{12}; 6_{14} Kt ?; מְדוֹנִים Pr 18_{19} Kt; מִדְיָנִים Pr 18_{18} &c., cs. מִדְיְנֵי Pr 19_{13}: **quarrel, dispute, nagging** Pr 17_{14}; *ʾîš mādôn* Je 15_{10}; pl. Pr 18_{19}.

II מָדוֹן: n. loc. Jos 11_1 12_{19}. †

מַדּוּעַ (70×) & מַדֻּעַ Ez 18_{19}: **why** Gn 26_{27}.

מְדוּרָה: sf. מְדוּרָתָהּ: (circular) **pile of wood** Is 30_{33} Ez 24_9. †

מִדְחֶה: **ruin, downfall** Ps 26_{28}. †

*מַדְחֵפָה: pl. מַדְחֵפוֹת: **blow**: *l^emadhēfôt* blow after blow Ps 140_{12}. †

מָדַי מָדָי: — 1. (n. pers. as ancestor) Gn 10_2; — 2. n. terr. **Media** 2K 17_6; — 3. n. peop. **Medes** Is 13_{17}.

מָדִי: gent. of מָדַי.

(לְ)מַדַּי 2C 30_3 & מִדַּי 1S 7_{16} ↗ דַּי 2 c.d.

מִדִּין: n. loc.

I *מִדְיָן: pl. מִדְיָנִים, cs. מִדְיְנֵי: ↗ I מָדוֹן.

II מִדְיָן: — 1. (n. pers.) Gn 25_2; — 2. n. peop. Gn 36_{35}.

מְדִינָה: pl. מְדִינוֹת: **province, district** 1K 20_{14f}, esp. **satrapy** of Persian empire Est 1_1.

מִדְיָנִי: gent. of II מִדְיָן.

מְדֹכָה: **mortar** (for grinding food &c.) Nu 11_8. †

מַדְמֵן: n. loc.

I מַדְמֵנָה: **dung-heap** Is 25_{10}. †

II מַדְמֵנָה: n. loc.

מַדְמַנָּה: n. loc.

I מְדָן: n. (pers. &) peop. Gn 25_2 1C 2_{32f}. †

II *מְדָן: pl. מְדָנִים Pr 6_{19}, ↗ I מָדוֹן.

מַדָּע: sf. מַדָּעֲךָ: — 1. **knowledge** (= academic learning) Dn 1_4; — 2. *b^emaddāʿ^akā* Ec 10_{20}: trad. 'thoughts,' but sugg. rd. *b^emaṣṣāʿ^akā* 'night-lodging'.

מֹדָע Pr 7_4 & מוֹדַע Ru 2_1 Qr: kinship > (distant) **kinsman**. †

*מֹדַעַת: מוֹדַעְתָּנוּ (distant) **kinsman** Ru 3_2. †

*מַדְקֵרָה or *מַדְקָרָה: pl. cs. מַדְקְרוֹת: **thrust** (of sword) Pr 12_{18}. †

מַדְרֵגָה: pl. מַדְרֵגוֹת: **step** (cut in rocks), **mountain path** Ez 38_{20} SS 2_{14}. †

*מִדְרָךְ: cs. מִדְרַךְ: footprint, **foot-width** Dt 2_5. †

*מִדְרָשׁ: cs. מִדְרַשׁ: **study, writing** 2C 13_{22} 24_{27}. †

*מְדֻשָׁה: sf. מְדֻשָׁתִי: something (or s.one) **downtrodden**, metaph. of the people Is 21_{10}. †

מָה: מֶה־ (Gn 31_{43} + 25×); מֶה & מֶה־ (Ex 32_1 + 12×); מַה or מַה־ oft. w. dagheš; מָ in מָהֵם Ez 8_6 (Qr מָה הֵם); מַ w. dagheš Ex 4_2 Is 3_{15} Ma 1_{13} 1C 15_{13} 2C 30_3 †: — (A) pron. **what**: — 1. *mâ raʾîtî* Gn 20_{10}; *ḥokmat-meh* wisdom in what? = what kind of w. Je 8_{9}; w. *min*: *ma-mmillaylâ* how much of = how late (is it) in the night Is 21_{11}; — 2. indir. question: *lir'ôt ma-yyiqrā'* Gn 2_{19}; — 3. w. *zeh*: *mazzeh bᵉyādekā* what is that in your hand? Ex 4_{2}; — 4. ellipt. *mah-llāk* what do you have? Ju 1_{14}; w. *kî*: *mah-llā'ām kî* what is the matter with the people, that they ... 1S 11_{5}; w/o *kî* Is 3_{15}; w. *lᵉ* & inf.: *mah-llᵉkā lᵉsappēr* Ps 50_{16}, w. pt. Jon 1_{6}; *mah-llî wālāk* what do I have to do with you? Ju 11_{12}; *mah-llᵉkā ûlᵉšālôm* what do you care about whether all is well? 2K 9_{18}; w. *'ēt*: *mah-llatteben 'et-habbār* what has straw to do with wheat? Je 23_{28}; *meh hayâ še* how does it happen that Ec 7_{10}; — 5. after vb. of telling, seeing, &c., **what = that which**: *higgîd mah-ṭṭôb* Mi 6_{8}; — 6. after neg.: *lō'... mâ* does not know about what = anything Gn 39_{8}; — 7. w. *še* **whatever** Ec 1_{9}; — 8. as indef. pron.: *wᵉrā'îtî mâ* and if I learn anything 1S 19_{3}; *dᵉbar mah-yyar'ēnî* whatever he shows me Nu 23_{3}; — (B) adv. what > **how**: *mah-nnôrā'* how awesome Gn 28_{17}; **how much**: *mâ-'āhabtî* Ps 119_{97}; *mah-zzeh* how is it that ...? Gn 27_{20}; = **why** Gn 3_{13}; *mah-zzeh rûḥᵃkā sārâ* why (in the world) is your spirit so low? 1K 21_{5}; — (C) 'what,' 'how' > neg.: *mah-nništeh* what have we to drink? = we have nothing to dr. Ex 15_{24}; *mah-llānû ḥēleq* = we have no share 1K 12_{16}; — (D) w. prep.: — 1. *bammâ, bammeh* **how** (shall I know) Gn 15_{8}; **in what** (else) Ex 22_{26} &c.; — 2. *kammâ, kammeh*: **how much, how many** Gn 47_{8}, = how few 2S 19_{35}; = how often Ps 78_{40}; *'ad-kammeh pᵉ'āmîm* how many times 1K 22_{16}, *zeh kammeh šānîm* how many years now Zc 7_{3}; — 3. *lāmâ* 4× & *lấmā* Jb 7_{20}, *lấmeh* 1S 1_{8} & *lấmmâ*: a) to what = **why** Gn 12_{18} & oft.; *lāmmâ zzeh* why (in the world) Gn 18_{13}; b) > conj. = **so that ... not, lest** Ec 5_{5}; **otherwise** 1S 19_{17}; *'ᵃšer lāmmâ* Dn 1_{10} & *šallāmâ* SS 1_{7}, so that... not; — 4. *'ad-mâ* & *'ad-meh* how long (still) Nu 24_{22} Ps 4_{3}; — 5. *'al-mâ* on what basis, **why**? Is 1_{5}.

מהה: **hitpalpel**: pf. הִתְמַהְמָהְתִּי, הִתְמַהְמָהְנוּ; impf. יִתְמַהְמָהּ, יִתְמַהְמַהּ; impv. הִתְמַהְמְהוּ, inf. הִתְמַהְמְהָם, לְהִתְמַהְמֵהַּ; pt. מִתְמַהְמֵהַּ: **linger, delay** Gn 19_{16}.

מְהוּמָה: cs. מְהוּמַת; pl. מְהוּמֹת: **confusion, panic** 1S 5_{9}, pl. Am 3_{9}; *mᵉhûmat māwet* deadly panic 1S 5_{11}; *mᵉhûmat yhwh* panic produced by Y. Zc 14_{13}.

מְהוּמָן: n. pers.

מְהֵיטַבְאֵל: n. pers. f.

מָהִיר: cs. מְהִיר: **skilled, experienced** Ps 45_{2} Pr 22_{29} Ezr 7_{6}; *mᵉhîr ṣedeq* diligent in righteousness Is 16_{5}. †

מהל: **qal**: pt. pass. מָהוּל: changed (by the addition of water), **adulterated** Is 1_{22}. †

מַהֲלָךְ: sf. מַהֲלַכְךָ; pl. מַהְלְכִים Zc 3_{7}: — 1. **passageway** Ez 42_{4}; — 2. **distance**, length of way Jon 3_{3f}; — 3. **journey** Ne 2_{6}; — 4. Zc 3_{7} trad. 'access,' but vocal. or txt. perh. corr., F comm. †

*__מַהֲלָל__: sf. מַהֲלָלוֹ: praise, recognition by others, **reputation** Pr 27_{21}. †

מַהֲלַלְאֵל: n. pers.

מַהֲלֻמוֹת: **blows, thrashing** Pr 18_{6} 19_{29}. †

[**מֵהֶם** Ez 8_{6}: rd Qr מָה הֵם.]

*__מַהֲמֹר__: pl. מַהֲמֹרוֹת: **watery pits** Ps 140_{11}. †

מַהְפֵּכָה: cs. מַהְפֵּכַת: **overthrow, demolishing, destruction**, (almost?) alw. of Sodom: *kᵉmahpēkat 'ᵉlōhîm 'et-sᵉdôm* Is 13_{19} > *kᵉmahpēkat sᵉdôm* Dt 29_{22}.

מַהְפֶּכֶת: מַהְפֶּכֶת: **stocks to confine prisoners** in stooped posture Je 20_{2f} 29_{26}; *bêt hammahpeket* = prison 2C 16_{10}. †

מְהֻקְצָעוֹת Ez 46_{22}: **corner-rooms** (? — dub., F comm.). †

I **מהר**: **piel**: pf. מִהַר, מִהֲרָה, מִהַרְתָּ, מִהֲרוּ; impf. יְמַהֵר, יְמַהֲרוּ, וַתְּמַהֵרְנָה; impv. מַהֵר,

מַהֲרָה, מַהֲרִי, מַהֲרוּ; inf. מַהֵר; pt. מְמַהֵר > מַהֵר Is $8_{1.3}$ Zp 1_4, מְמַהֲרוֹת: — 1. **hurry** (to somewhere) Gn 18_{6a}; — 2. before fin. vb., oft. used adverbially, **quickly, in a hurry**: *wattᵉmahēr wattôred* and she quickly brought down Gn 24_{18} & oft.; — 3. impv. before another impv.: *mahēr himmālēṭ* **hurry** and escape, escape **quickly** Gn 19_{22}; w. *wᵉ* 1S 23_{27}; — 4. w. acc.: **bring** (s.one or s.thg) **quickly** Gn 18_{6b} 1K 22_9; — 5. **hurry** (w. activity in genl.): a) w. *laddābār* 2C 25_{4a}, abs. 25_{4b}; b) w. inf.: *maddûaᶜ mihartem bô'* why have you come so quickly? Ex 2_{18}; w. *lᵉ* & inf. Gn 18_7; — 6. inf. *mahēr* adv. **quickly, in a hurry**: *sārû mahēr* Ex 32_8; — 7. var.: a) *lᵉmahēr* in a hurry Ex 12_{33}, in swiftness 1C 12_9; b) מַהֵר־שָׁלָל־חָשׁ־בַּז Is $8_{1.3}$ ↗ independent entry below.

nif.: pf. נִמְהָרָה; pt. נִמְהָר, נִמְהָרִים, נִמְהָרֵי: **dash headlong, tumble over** Jb 5_{13}; pt. **hasty, rash** Is 32_4, **impetuous** Hb 1_6; w. *lēb* terrified, dismayed Is 35_4. †

II **מהר**: **qal**: impf. יִמְהָרֶנָּה; inf. מָהֹר: **acquire** (s.one as) **a wife** (by paying the *mōhar*) Ex 22_{15}. †

מֹהַר: **bridal money** paid to the bride's family: not purchase-money but compensation Gn 34_{12} Ex 22_{16} 1S 18_{25}. †

מְהֵרָה: — 1. **speed, hurry** † Ps 147_{15} Ec 4_{12}; — 2. > adv. **quickly, in a hurry** 2K 1_{11}; *ᶜattâ mᵉhērâ* now quickly Je 27_{16}; *qal mᵉhērâ & mᵉhērâ qal* very quickly Is 5_{26} Jl 4_4.

מַהֲרַי: n. pers.

מַהֵר־שָׁלָל־חָשׁ־בַּז: symbolic name, Is $8_{1.3}$: sugg. 2 impvs.: מַהֵר & חָשׁ, or 2 pts.: מְמַהֵר & חָשׁ. †

***מַהֲתַלָּה**: pl. מַהֲתַלּוֹת: **deception** Is 30_{10}. †

מוֹאָב: — 1. n. pers. **Moab** Gn 19_{30ff}; — 2. n. terr. & peop. **Moab** Gn 36_{35}.

מוֹאָבִי: gent. of מוֹאָב.

[**מוֹאל** (לְ) Ne 12_{38}: rd. לִשְׂמֹאל.]

***מוֹבָא**: < מָבוֹא by analogy of מוֹצָא: 2S 3_{25} מֹבָאֶךָ rd מְבוֹאֲךָ; Ez 43_{11} מוֹבָאָיו rd מְבוֹאָיו: — 1. **going in, entering** 2S 3_{25}; — 2. **entrance (way)** Ez 43_{11}. †

מוג: **qal**: impf. תָּמוֹג, וַתָּמוֹג; inf. מוֹג: subj. earth: **waver, reel, melt** Am 9_5 Ps 46_7. †

nif.: pf. נָמוֹג, נָמֹגוּ; pt. נְמֹגִים: — 1. **heave** (intrans.), **rock, move back & forth** 1S 14_{16}; — 2. **be disheartened** Ex 15_{15}.

polel: impf. תְּמֹגְגֶנָּה, תְּמֹגְגֵנִי: **soften, make** (s.thg) **dissolve** Ps 65_{11} Jb 30_{22}. †

hitpolel: pf. הִתְמֹגָגוּ; impf. תִּתְמוֹגַגְנָה: **be set moving, melt, dissolve** (intrans.) Am 9_{13} Na 1_5, of *nefeš* Ps 107_{26}. †

מוד: **polel**: וַיְמֹדֶד: **set into motion, shake, convulse** Hb 3_6. †

מוֹדַע Ru 2_1 Qr: ↗ מְדַע.

מוט: **qal**: pf. מָטָה, מָטוּ; impf. תָּמוּט, תְּמוּטֶנָה; inf. בְּמוֹט Ps 38_{17} 46_3, לָמוֹט 66_9 121_3; pt. מָט, מָטִים: — 1. **waver, reel** (of mountains &c.) Is 54_{10}, **totter** Ps 46_7, **stagger, flinch** (of foot) Dt 32_{35}; — 2. *māṭâ yādô* his hand wavers = he becomes economically weak Lv 25_{35}, ↗ *yād* 5b.

nif.: pf. נָמוֹטוּ; impf. יִמּוֹט, אֶמּוֹט, יִמּוֹטוּ: **be made to stagger, stumble, totter**: man Ps 10_6, mountain Ps 125_1; — 2. **be made to wobble** Is 40_{20}.

hitpolel: pf. הִתְמוֹטְטָה: **shake, reel** Is 24_{19} 54_{10}. †

[**hif.**: impf. יָמִיטוּ Ps 55_4 140_{11} ? txt. ? ↗ comm.]

מוֹט: — 1. **carrying frame** Nu $4_{10.12}$; — 2. **pole** (for carrying) Nu 13_{23}. †

מוֹטָה: — 1. **yoke, collar** (of harness) Is 58_6; — 2. **carrying-pole** † 1C 15_{15}.

מוך: **qal**: pf. מָךְ: **become poor** Lv $25_{25.35.39.47}$ 27_8. †

מוֹכִיחַ: ↗ יכח hif.

I **מול**: **qal**: pf. מָל, מָלוּ, וּמַלְתָּ, וּמַלְתֶּם; impf. וַיָּמָל; pt. pass. מוּל, מֻלִים: **circumcise**: obj. *bᵉśar ᶜorlâ* Gn 17_{23}, s.one 21_4; abs. Jos 5_4; metaph. Dt 10_{16}.

nif.: pf. וּנְמַלְתֶּם, נִמֹּלוּ, נִמּוֹל Gn 17_{11}; impf. יִמּוֹל, וַיִּמֹּלוּ; impv. הִמֹּלוּ; inf. הִמּ(וֹ)ל, sf. הִמֹּלוֹ; pt. נִמֹּלִים: **(let onesf.) be circumcised** Gn 17_{10ff}, w. acc. *'et-beśar 'orlatkem* 17_{11}.

II מול: **hif.**: impf. אֲמִילַם: **ward off** Ps 118_{10-12}. †

מוּל Dt 1_1: ↗ מוּל. †

מוּל (ca. 60×) & מוֹל Dt 1_1 (if true reading), sf. מֻלַי Nu 22_5: — 1. subst. **front** 1K 7_5; — 2. prep. in comb.: *mûl-penê* **the front of** 2S 11_{15}; *'el-mûl* towards the front of, **towards** 1S 17_{30}, geogr. in front of, **opposite** Ex 34_3; *mimmûl* (off) the front of Lv 5_8, = in the direction of 1K 7_{39}.

מוֹלָדָה: n. loc.

מוֹלֶדֶת: sf. מוֹלַדְתּוֹ, מוֹלַדְתִּי; pl. sf. מ(וֹ)לְד(וֹ)תַיִךְ: — 1. **descendants, offspring** Gn 48_6; — 2. **relationship, relations** Gn 12_1; *môledet bayit*, born **in** the same household Lv 18_9; — 3. **descent, parentage** Ez 16_3, **birth** 16_4; — 4. *'ereṣ môladtô* land of his origin Gn 11_{28}.

*מוּלָה: pl. מוּלֹת: **circumcision** Ex 4_{26}. †

מוֹלִיד: n. pers.

מוּם, מְאוּם Dn 1_4 & מְאוּם Jb 31_7: sf. מוּמוֹ, מוּמָם: **blemish**: — 1. (on the body) 2S 14_{25}; *nātan mûm be* cause a disfigurement to Lv 24_{19f}; — 2. (moral) Pr 9_7.

מוֹמְכָן: n. pers., Qr מְמוּכָן Est 1_{16}. †

מוּסַב־ Ez 41_7: ?? ↗ סבב hof. pt. ?. †

מוּסָד: cs. מוּסַד: **foundation, laying of the foundation-stone** Is 28_{16} 2C 8_{16}. †

מוֹסָד: pl. cs. מוֹסְדֵי: — 1. **foundation-wall**, metaph. Is 58_{12}; — 2. **foundation, base** (of earth, mountains) Dt 32_{22} Is 24_{18}.

מוּסָדָה: pl. cs. מוּסְדוֹת: **foundation-wall** Ez 41_8. †

מוֹסָדָה: pl. מוֹסָדוֹת, cs. מוֹסְדוֹת: **foundation-wall** Je 51_{26}; — 2. **foundation, base** (of world, heavens &c.) 2S $22_{8.16}$.

*מוּסָךְ 2K 16_{18}: cs. Qr מוּסַךְ, Kt מֵיסַךְ ?: tech. archit. term, unknown, ↗ comm. †

מוֹסֵר: pl. cs. מוֹסְרֵי, sf. מוֹסֵרַי, מוֹסְרֵיכֶם: **fetters, chains** Is 28_{22} 52_2 Ps 116_{16}. †

מוּסָר: cs. מוּסַר, מוּסָרְךָ: m., f. Pr 4_{13}: — 1. **correction, chastisement** Pr 13_{24}, *mûsārekā* chastisement by you (= God) Is 26_{16}; *mûsar ḥokmâ* correction that leads to wisdom Pr 15_{33}; — 2. **discipline, education, instruction** Ps 50_{17}; — 3. **warning, reminder** Ez 5_{15}.

I מוֹסֵרָה: pl. מוֹסֵרוֹת, cs. מוֹסְרוֹת, sf. מוֹסְרוֹתֵימוֹ, מוֹסְרוֹתֶיךָ: **fetters, chains** Je 2_{20}.

II מוֹסֵרָה Dt 10_6 & מֹסֵרוֹת Nu 33_{30f}: n. loc. †

מוֹעֵד (ca. 200×) & מֹעֵד Dt 31_{10}: sf. מוֹעֲדוֹ, מוֹעֲדֶךָ; pl. cs. מוֹעֲדֵי, sf. מוֹעֲדַי, מוֹעֲדֵיכֶם: — 1. **meeting-place** Jos 8_{14}; *'ōhel mô'ēd* ↗ 5; *har mô'ēd* Is 14_{13} = meeting-place of gods; *bêt mô'ēd* Jb 30_{23} = underworld; — 2. **meeting, assembly**: *yôm mô'ēd* Ho 9_5; — 3. **appointed time, fixed day**: *wayyāśem mô'ēd* Ex 9_5; *mô'adêhâ* specific time (of migratory bird) Je 8_7, (of *tîrôš* wine) Ho 2_{11}; *lammô'ēd* for, until the appointed time 1S 9_{24}, *lammô'ēd hazzeh* at this time (next year) Gn 17_{21}; **space of time** (determined) Dn 12_7; — 4. **(time of) feast**: a) sg. *yôm mô'ēd* La 2_7 > *mô'ēd* alone Ho 2_{13}; pl. *yemê mô'adîm* Ho 12_{10}, > *mô'adîm* alone Gn 1_{14}; *mô'adîm ṭôbîm* joyous assemblies Zc 8_{19}; — 5. *'ōhel mô'ēd* (ca. 140×): **tent of meeting** 1K 8_4.

*מוֹעָד: pl. sf. מוֹעָדָיו Is 14_{31}: band, host ? meeting-place ?. †

מוּעָדָה: agreement, arrangement: *'ārê mû'ādâ* cities agreed upon Jos 20_9. †

מוֹעַדְיָה: n. pers.

מוּעָף: **glimmer (of light)** Is 8_{23}. †

*מוֹעֵצָה: pl. מֹעֵצוֹת, sf. מֹעֲצוֹתָם, מ(וֹ)עֲצ(וֹ)תֵיהֶם: — 1. **advice, counsel** Pr 22_{20}; — 2. **plan** Je 7_{24}.

מוּעָקָה: **misery, hardship** Ps 66_{11}. †

מוּפַז 1K 10_{18}: ✓ פזז hof.

[**מוֹפַעַת** Je 48_{21} Kt, rd Qr מֵיפַעַת n. loc.]

מוֹפֵת: sf. מ(ו)פֶתְכֶם; pl. מוֹפְתִים, sf. מוֹפְתָיו: **sign, omen**: given by man Ex 4_{21}, oft. phenomenon in skies Jl 3_3.

I **מוֹצָא**, **מֹצָא**: cs. =, sf. מ(ו)צָאוֹ, מוֹצָאֲךָ; pl. cs. מ(ו)צָאֵי, sf. מוֹצָאָיו, מוֹצָאֵיהֶם: — 1. **outlet**: for water 2K 2_{21}; place out of which the sun comes = east Ps 19_7; — 2. **exit** (in temple) Ez 42_{11}; — 3. **what comes out** (of lips, mouth) = utterance Nu 30_{13}; — 4. (act of) **going out**: *môṣāʼ ûmābôʼ* one's actions 2S 3_{25}; *môṣāʼ sûsîm* = **import** of horses (into Palestine) 1K 10_{28}.

II **מוֹצָא**: n. pers.

***מוֹצָאָה**: pl. מוֹצָאוֹת 2K 10_{17} Qr, sf. מוֹצָאוֹתָיו: — 1. **origin** Mi 5_1; — 2. **latrine** 2K 10_{27} Qr. †

I **מוּצָק**: cs. מֻצַק: **casting** (of metal) 1K $7_{16.37}$ Jb 38_{38}. †

II **מוּצָק**: — 1. **narrowness** Jb 37_{10}; — 2. **hardship** Is 8_{23}. †

***מוּצָקָה**: sf. מֻצַקְתּוֹ; pl. מוּצָקוֹת: — 1. **casting** (of metal) 2C 4_3; — 2. pl. **lip** (of a lamp, where wick is placed) Zc 4_2. †

מוק: **hif.**: impf. יָמִיקוּ: **scoff** Ps 73_8. †

מוֹקֵד: sf. cj. מוֹקְדָהּ; pl. cs. מוֹקְדֵי: **hearth** Lv 6_2 Ps 102_4; metaph. of last judgment Is 33_{14}. †

[**מוֹקְדָה** Lv 6_2, rd. מוֹקְדָהּ.]

מוֹקֵשׁ: pl. מ(ו)קְשִׁים, cs. מ(ו)קְשֵׁי: **trigger** (?) or **sling** (?), or else **bait** (?) of bird-trap Am 3_5, then **trap** itself, mostly metaph. Ps 64_6; *hāyâ lᵉmôqēš* become a snare to s.one Ex 10_7; *môqᵉšê māwet* 2S 22_6.

I **מור**: **nif.**: pf. נָמַר: **change** (intrans.) Je 48_{11}. †

hif.: pf. הֵימִיר Je 2_{11}; impf. יָמֵר, יָמ(י)ר, אָמִיר, וַיָּמִירוּ, יְמִירֶנּוּ; inf. הָמֵר: — 1. **exchange** (w. *bᵉ*, for s.thg else) Je 2_{11}; — 2. **change** (intrans.) Ps 15_4.

II **מור**: **nif.**: cj. inf. הִמּוֹר: **shake, quake** Ps 46_3. †

מוֹר myrrh: ✓ מֹר.

מוֹרָא, 1× **מֹרָא**, Ps 9_{21} מוֹרָה: sf. מוֹרָאוֹ, מוֹרַאֲכֶם; pl. מוֹרָאִים: — 1. **fear**: a) wh. one feels (expr. for Y.) Is 8_{13}; b) w. objective gen., fear of s.thg Gn 9_2; — 2. **terror** (wh. Y. arouses) Dt 26_8, pl. terrors Dt 4_{34}; — 3. **awe** (of Y.) Ma 2_5.

מוֹרַג: pl. מ(ו)רִגִים: **threshing-sledge**, heavy wooden slab, fitted on the bottom w. projecting flint or iron knives Is 41_{15}, pl. 2S 24_{22} 1C 21_{23}. †

מוֹרָד: cs. מוֹרַד: **slope** (of mountain, hill) Jos 7_5 10_{11} Je 48_5 Mi 1_4; 1K 7_{29}, unknown tech. archit. term, ✓ comm. †

I **מוֹרֶה**: pl. מוֹרִים: **archer** 1S 31_{3b} 2S 11_{24}. †

II **מוֹרֶה**: **rain** Jl $2_{23a.b}$ Ps 84_7; but ✓ comms. †

III **מוֹרֶה**: sf. (sg. or pl.?) מוֹרֶיךָ, pl. sf. מוֹרָי: **teacher** Is $30_{20a.b}$ Jb 36_{22} Pr 5_{13}; *môreh šāqer* teacher of lies Hb 2_{18}. †

IV **מוֹרֶה** in names of loc.: a) אֵלוֹן מוֹרֶה Gn 12_6 & אֵלוֹנֵי מ׳ Dt 11_{30}; b) גִּבְעַת מוֹרֶה Ju 7_1. †

I **מוֹרָה**: m.: shaving tool, **razor** Ju 13_5 16_{17} 1S 1_{11} (alw. in Nazirite formula). †

II **מוֹרָה** Ps 9_{21}: rd מוֹרָא w. some mss.; oth. sugg. מְאֵרָה. †

I ***מוֹרָשׁ**: cs. מוֹרַשׁ: **possession, inheritance** Is 14_{23}. †

II ***מוֹרָשׁ**: מוֹרָשֵׁי לְבָבִי Jb 17_{11}: **desire**. †

מוֹרָשָׁה: **acquisition, possession** Ex 6_8.

מוֹרֶשֶׁת גַּת: n. loc.

מוֹרַשְׁתִּי Je 26_{18} & מֹרַשְׁתִּי Mi 1_1: gent. of (מוֹרֶשֶׁת גַּת). †

I **מוש**: **qal.**: impf. אֲמֻשְׁךָ: **touch, feel** Gn 27_{21}. †

hif.: impf. יְמִישׁוּן; impv. הֲמִשֵׁנִי Ju 16_{26} Qr (Kt הֵימ׳ √ ימשׁ ?): **let** (s.one) **touch, feel** Ju 16_{26}; **(be able to) touch, feel** Ps 115_7. †

II **מוש** & **מיש**: **qal**: pf. מָשׁ, מַשְׁתִּי, מָשׁוּ; impf. יָמִישׁ, יָמוּשׁ, יָמֻשׁוּ, יָמוּשׁוּ, תָּמֻשׁ, תָּמוּשׁ & יָמִישׁ, תָּמִישׁ, אָמִישׁ: — 1. **withdraw, give way, fail to be present**: a) persons Ex 33_{11}; b) things:

pillar of cloud Ex 13_{22}, mountains Is 54_{10}, my (= God's) word 59_{21}; — 2. w. *min*: **leave off, depart, stop** Jb 23_{12}, w. inf. Jer 17_{8}.

hif.: impf. תָּמִישׁוּ: **remove** Mi 2_{3}. †

מוֹשָׁב: cs. מוֹשַׁב, sf. מוֹשָׁבִי, מוֹשָׁבֵךְ; pl. cs. מוֹשְׁבֵי, sf. מוֹשְׁבֹתֵיכֶם, מֹ(וֹ)שְׁבֹתָם: — 1. place of sitting, **seat** 1S $20_{18.25}$; (order of) **seating** 1K 10_{5}; **site, position** (of a city) 2K 2_{19}; — 2. **residence, area** (or place) **of living** Gn 10_{30}; pl. residences Ez 48_{15}; — 3. (temporary) **abode** Lv 13_{46}; — 4. (extent of) **time of sojourn** Ex 12_{40}; — 5. **location** (of images) Ez 8_{3}; — 6. *bêt môšāb* **dwelling-house** Lv 25_{29}, *ʿîr môšāb* inhabited city Ps 107_{4}; *kol-môšab bayit*, all those living in the same house 2S 9_{12}.

מוּשִׁי & מֻשִׁי 1C 6_{4}: — 1. n. pers.; — 2. gent. of 1.

מוֹשִׁיעַ: sf. מוֹשִׁיעֵךְ, מוֹשִׁיעֶךָ, מוֹשִׁ(י)עֵךְ, מוֹשִׁיעוֹ, מוֹשִׁיעָם; pl. מוֹשִׁ(י)עִים: **helper, deliverer, rescuer, savior**: — 1. human: a) pl. Ob 21; b) *weʾên môšîaʿ* &c. 2S 22_{42}; c) s.one aroused by Y. to deliver the people 2K 13_{5}; — 2. Y. as *môšîaʿ*: a) 1S 10_{19}; b) w. sf. 2S 22_{3}; c) no *môšîaʿ* except Y. Is 43_{11}.

***מוֹשָׁעָה**: pl. מוֹשָׁעוֹת: **act of help** Ps 68_{21}. †

מוּת: **qal**: pf. מֵת, מֵתָה, מַתָּ, מַתִּי, מֵתוּ, מַתְנוּ, מָתְנוּ; impf. יָמוּת, יָמֻת Pr 19_{16} Qr (Kt יוּמַת), אָמוּת, וַתָּמֹת, וַתָּמָת, תָּמֹ(וּ)ת, וַיָּמָת, יָמוּת, תְּמֻתוּן, תְּמוּתוּן, יָמֻתוּ, יָמוּתוּ, אָמוּתָה, אָמֻת, תְּמוּתֶנָה; impv. מֻת; inf. לָמוּת, מוּתִי, מוּתֵנוּ, מוֹת, מֻתָן, מֻתֵנוּ; pt. מֵת, sf. מֵתִי, f. מֵתָה, pl. מֵתִים, cs. מֵתֵי, sf. מֵתֶיךָ: — 1. **die**: a) natural death Gn 5_{8}; animal Is 66_{24}, plant Jb 14_{8}, metaph. of wisdom Jb 12_{2}; b) violent death Jb 1_{19}, death penalty Dt 19_{12}; become mortal (of gods) Ps 82_{7}; c) in phr.: w. *qṣr* impatient to die Ju 16_{16}, w. *ḥlh* mortally ill 2K 20_{1}; — 2. pt. *mēt*: **dying** Gn 20_{3}, **dead** Dt 25_{5}; *mēt ʾādām* a dead man Ez 44_{25}, one who is going to die Dt 4_{22}, (anyone) subject to death Ez 18_{32}, stillborn Nu 12_{12}; *mēt* (m. form) = body of woman Gn 23_{3ff}; ***zibḥê mētîm*** sacrifices offered to the dead Ps 106_{28}.

polel: pf. מוֹתַתִּי, מוֹתְתַנִי; impf. תְּמוֹתֵת, וַאֲמֹתְתֵהוּ, אֲמֹתֵת; impv. מֹ(וֹ)תְתֵנִי; inf. לְמוֹתֵת; pt. מְמוֹתֵת: — 1. **finally kill, give the death-blow** 1S 14_{13}; — 2. **slay, kill** Je 20_{17}.

polal: pt. מְמוֹתָתִים 2K 11_{2} Kt (Qr hof): **those who were to be killed.** †

hif. (ca. 130×): pf. הֵמִית, וְהֵמַתָּה, וְהֵמַתִּי, הֱמִיתָיו, הֱמִיתֵנִי, הֱמִיתְךָ, הֲמִתֶּן, הֵמִיתוּ, הֱמִיתָהוּ, הֱמִתְתֻהוּ, וַהֲמִתִּיהָ; impf. יָמִית, נְמִיתֶךָ, נְמִיתֵם, תְּמִיתֵנִי, וַיְמִיתֵהוּ, וַיָּמֶת; impv. הָמִיתוּ, הֲמִיתֵנִי; inf. הָמִית, הֲמִיתוֹ, הָמֵת, הֲמִיתָם; pt. מֵמִית, מְמִ(י)תִים: — 1. **kill:** a) subj. animals 1K 13_{24}; b) subj. men Gn 37_{18}, carry out death penalty Ju 6_{30}; c) subj. God: Gn 18_{25} & oft.; d) subj. jealousy Jb 5_{2}; — 2. **have** (s.one) **executed, have** (s.one) **be put to death** 2K 14_{6}; **bring death** Pr 21_{25}.

hof.: pf. הוּמַת, הֻמְתוּ; impf. יוּמַת, יוּמָת, יוּמְתוּ, וַתּוּמַת, pt. מוּמָת, מוּמָתִים, מֻמָתִים: — 1. **be killed** 1K 2_{24}; *môt yûmat* **suffer death,** be punished by death Gn 26_{11}.

מָוֶת (ca. 160×): cs. מוֹת, sf. מֹ(וֹ)תוֹ, מֹ(וֹ)תָם; pl. cs. מוֹתֵי, sf. מֹתָיו: — 1. **death, dying**: a) sg. Gn 21_{16}; death & life Pr 18_{21}; *ben-māwet* 1S 20_{31}, *benê-māwet* 1S 26_{16}, *ʾîš māwet* 1K 2_{26}, *ʾanšê māwet* 2S 19_{29} = s.one who deserves to die, who is doomed to die; b) pl. intensive, **death**: *môtê ʿarēlîm* Ez 28_{10}; c) ? *māwet* = a superlative, to the utmost: *ʿad-māwet* Jon 4_{9}; — 2. mortal illness, epidemic, **pestilence** Je 15_{2}; — 3. personified, **Death** ? Je 9_{20}; — 4. realm of the dead Is 28_{15}.

מוֹתָר: cs. מוֹתַר: **profit, benefit** Pr 14_{23} 21_{25} Ec 3_{19}. †

מִזְבֵּחַ (ca. 400×): cs. מִזְבַּח, sf. מִזְבְּחִי, מִזְבַּחֲךָ, מִזְבַּחֶךָ, loc. הַמִּזְבֵּחָה; pl. abs. & cs. מִזְבְּחֹ(וֹ)ת, sf. מִזְבְּחֹ(וֹ)תֵיהֶם: **altar**: — 1. for

Y. a) of earth Ex 20_{24}, stone 20_{25}; b) phr.: *mizbēaḥ leyhwh* Gn 8_{20}, *mizbaḥ yhwh* 1K 8_{22}, *mizbaḥ 'elōhîm* Ps 43_4; — 2. non-Israelite 1K 16_{32}.

*מֶזֶג: מֶזֶג: **mixed wine**, prob. spiced, mulled wine SS 7_3. †

*מָזֶה: pl. cs. מְזֵי: **exhausted** (fm. hunger) Dt 32_{24}. †

מַזֶּה Ex 4_2: < מַה־זֶּה.

מִזֶּה Ps 75_9: < מִן־זֶה.

מִזָּה: n. pers.

*מָזוּ: pl. sf. מְזָוֵינוּ: **granary** Ps 144_{13}. †

מְזוּזָה: cs. מְזוּזַת, sf. מְזוּזָתִי; pl. מְזוּזוֹ(ו)ת: **door-post** 1K 6_{31}.

מָזוֹן: **food** Gn 45_{23} 2C 11_{23}.

I מָזוֹר: sf. מְזֹרוֹ: **boil, ulcer** Je 30_{13} Ho 5_{13}. †

II מָזוֹר: **(man-)trap** Ob $_7$. †

I מֵזַח Is 23_{10}: **wharf, dockyard** (perh. rd. מָחוֹז). †

II מֵזַח: a **girdle** worn next to bare skin Ps 109_{19}. †

*מָזִיחַ: cs. מְזִיחַ: **girdle, belt** Jb 12_{21}. †

מֵזִין Pr 17_4: < מֵאֲזִין < מַאֲזִין (I אזן hif.).

מַזְכִּיר: **clerk, secretary** 1K 4_3.

*מַזָּל: pl. מַזָּלוֹת: **zodiacal signs** 2K 23_5. †

מַזְלֵג & *מִזְלָג: pl. מִזְלָגוֹ(ו)ת, sf. מִזְלְגֹתָיו: (three-tined) **(meat-)fork** 1S 2_{13f}.

מְזִמָּה: sf. מְזִמָּתוֹ; pl. מְזִמּוֹת, sf. מְזִמּוֹתָיו: — 1. **deliberation, plan**: of God Je 23_{20}; — 2. **evil plan, plot** (of man) Je 11_{15}; pl. intrigues Jb 21_{27}; *ba'al mezimmâ* & *'îš mezimmâ* intriguing Pr 12_2 24_8; — 3. **shrewdness, prudence** Pr 1_4.

מִזְמוֹר: **psalm** Ps 3_1.

מַזְמֵרָה: **vine-knife** Is 2_4 Jl 4_{10} Mi 4_3. †

*מְזַמֶּרֶת: pl. מְזַמְּרוֹת: **snuffer** (to trim wicks?) 1K 7_{50} 2K 12_{14} 25_{14} Je 52_{18} 2C 4_{22}. †

מִזְעָר: **a small matter, a few**: *'enôš miz'ār*, a few men Is 24_6; *me'at miz'ār* a very little Is 10_{25} 16_{14} 29_{17}. †

cj. מזר: **qal**: cj. pt. pass. f. מְזֹרָה (for מְזֹרָה √זרה pual): **spread out** (a net) Pr 1_{17}. †

מִזְרֶה: **winnowing-fork** Is 30_{24}, metaph. Je 15_7. †

מַזָּרוֹת Jb 38_{32}: **constellations**; sugg.: Venus as evening & morning star; Hyades (in Taurus); boat of Arcturus; southern constellations of zodiac. †

מִזְרָח: cs. מִזְרַח, מִזְרָחָה Dt 4_{41}, loc. מִזְרָחָה: — 1. *mizraḥ (haš)šemeš* **sunrise = east** 1K 7_{25}; — 2. more oft. w/o. *šemeš*: **east** Jos 11_3; in the east Ne 12_{37}, to the east 1C 9_{24}; *lammizrāḥ* in the east Ne 3_{26}, *mizraḥ le* eastward from 2C 5_{12} &c.

מְזָרִים: **north-winds** (that scatter cold) Jb 37_9. †

*מִזְרָע: cs. מִזְרַע: **land sown** Is 19_7. †

מִזְרָק: pl. מִזְרָקִים, cs. מִזְרְקֵי, & pl. מִזְרָקוֹת, sf. מִזְרְקוֹתָן: metal **sprinkling basins** 1K 7_{40}.

*מֵחַ: pl. מֵחִים: **fatling**, sheep raised for fat Is 5_{17} Ps 66_{15}. †

מֹחַ: **marrow** Jb 21_{24}. †

I מחא: **qal**: impf. יִמְחֲאוּ; inf. מַחְאֲךָ: **strike**: w. *yād* or *kaf*, **clap the hands** Is 55_{12} Ez 26_5 Ps 98_8. †

[II מחא: מְמֻחָאִים **pual** pt. Is 25_6 Qr, rd. Kt מְמֻחִים, ↗ מחה.]

*מַחֲבֵא: cs. =: **hiding-place** (fm. the wind) Is 32_2. †

*מַחֲבֹא: pl. מַחֲבֹאִים: **hiding-place** 1S 23_{23}. †

מְחַבְּרוֹת: **binders** or **clamps**: tech. archit. term, of iron 1C 22_3, wood 2C 34_{11}. †

מַחְבֶּרֶת: מַחְבֶּרֶת, sf. מַחְבַּרְתּוֹ: — 1. **join(ing)**, connecting point on ephod Ex 28_{27} 39_{20}; — 2. **tie, loop** (on curtain) Ex $26_{4f.10}$ $36_{11f.17}$. †

מַחֲבַת: — 1. (metal) **plate, griddle** for roasting & frying Lv 2_5 6_{14} 7_9 Ez 4_3; — 2. **griddle-cake** 1C 23_{29}. †

מַחֲגֹרֶת: **girding** (of sackcloth) Is 3_{24}. †

I מָחָה: **qal**: pf. מָחִיתִי, מָחָתָה, מ׳; impf. יִמְחֶה, אֶמְחֶה, אֶמְחֶנּוּ, וַיִּמַח; impv. מְחֵה, מְחֵנִי; inf. מָחֹה, מְחוֹת: — 1. **wipe (off)** (one's mouth) Pr 30_{20}, wipe away (tears) Is 25_8, (dish) 2K 21_{13}; — 2. **wipe out, destroy** (s.one's name)

2K 14_{27}, (remembrance) Ex 17_{14}, (creatures) Gn 6_7.

nif. pf. נִמְחוּ; impf. יִמָּחוּ, תִּמָּחֶה, יִמַּח, יִמָּח: — 1. **be wiped out**: name Dt 25_6; — 2. **be destroyed**: creature Gn 7_{23}, tribe Ju 21_{17}, sin Ps 109_{14}.

hif.: impf. תֶּמַח Ne 13_{14} & תֶּמְחִי Je 18_{23}; inf. לִמְחוֹת: **let** (s.thg) **be blotted out**; but perh. rd. all these as qal. †

II מָחָה: **qal**: pf. מ׳: w. *ʿal*: **border upon** (subj. frontier) Nu 34_{11}; oth.: stretch along. †

III מחה: **pual**: pt. Kt מְמֻחִים: (fatty dishes) **garnished with marrow** Is 25_6. †

מְחוּגָה: **compass** (for making circles) Is 44_{13}. †

*מָחוֹז: cs. מְחוֹז: **harbor** Ps 107_{30}. †

מְחוּיָאֵל Gn 4_{18a} & מְחִיָּיאֵל $_{18b}$ (Qr מְחִיָּאֵל): n. pers.

מַחֲוִים: gent. 1C 11_{46}. †

I מָחוֹל: **circle-dance** Je 31_4.

II מָחוֹל: n. pers. 1K 5_{11}. †

מַחֲזֶה: **vision** (of God &c.) Gn 15_1 Nu $24_{4.16}$ Ez 13_7. †

מֶחֱזָה: **opening for light, prospect** 1K 7_{4f}. †

מַחֲזִיאוֹת: n. pers.

מְחִי: **shock, blow** (of battering rams) Ez 26_9. †

מְחִידָא: n. pers.

מִחְיָה: cs. מִחְיַת, sf. מִחְיָתְךָ: — 1. **preservation of life** Gn 45_5; — 2. **emergence** of new flesh Lv $13_{10.24}$; — 3. **subsistence, food** Ju 16_4 17_{10}; — 4. **reviving** Esr 9_{8f}; — 5. (s.thg, s.one) **living** 2C 14_{12}. †

מְחִיָּיאֵל Gn 4_{18b}: ↗ מְחוּיָאֵל.

I מְחִיר: sf. מְחִירָהּ; pl. sf. מְחִירֵיהֶם: — 1. **equivalent value** (in barter), **(market) price** 1K 10_{28}; — 2. > **money** Mi 3_{11}; — 3. metaph.: *bimḥîr* **in recompense** (for sins) Je 15_{13}.

II מְחִיר: n. pers. 1C 4_{11}. †

*מַחֲלֶה: cs. מַחֲלֵה, sf. מַחֲלֵהוּ: **sickness** Pr 18_{14} 2C 21_{15}. †

מַחֲלָה: **sickness** Ex 15_{26} 23_{25} 1K 8_{37} 2C 6_{28}. †

מַחְלָה: n. pers. m. & f.

*מְחֹלָה: cs. מְחֹלַת; pl. מְחֹל(וֹ)ת: **circle-dance** 1S 21_{12}; SS 7_1 *kimḥōlat hammaḥᵃnāyim* ? dance in double row; oth. dance of (army) camp, ↗ comm.

*מְחִלָּה: pl. מְחִלּוֹת: **hole** Is 2_{19}. †

מַחְלוֹן: n. pers.

מַחְלִי: — 1. n. pers.; — 2. gent.

מַחֲלֻיִים: **sickness**: *bᵉmaḥᵃluyîm rabbîm* seriously ill 2C 24_{25}. †

*מַחֲלָף: pl. מַחֲלָפִים Ezr 1_9: var. sugg.: knife; braid of hair; duplicate; oth. sugg. *moḥᵒlāfîm* 'to be changed,' as marginal notation, ↗ comm. †

*מַחְלָפָה: pl. מַחְלְפוֹת: **braid of hair**, exuberant lock(s) of hair Ju $16_{13.19}$. †

מַחֲלָצוֹת: extra fine, white clothing, **festival clothing** Is 3_{22} Zc 3_4. †

מַחֲלֹקֶת: sf. מַחֲלֻקְתּוֹ; pl. abs. & cs. מַחְלְקוֹת, sf. מַחְלְקוֹתֵיהֶם, מַחְלְק(וֹ)תָם: — 1. **portion, share** (of land) Ez 48_{29}; — 2. **division** a) of people Jos 11_{23}; b) of priests & Levites 1C 23_6; — 3. *selaʿ hammaḥlᵉqôt* n. terr. 1S 23_{28}.

I מָחֲלַת: *ʿal-māḥᵃlat* Ps 53_1 88_1 musical term. †

II מָחֲלַת: n. pers. f.

מְחֹלָתִי: gent. of ↗ אָבֵל מְחוֹלָה.

[מַחְמָאֹת Ps 55_{22}: trad. milk-foods, but rd. מֵחֶמְאָה more than ↗ חֶמְאָה.]

*מַחְמָד: cs. מַחְמַד; pl. מַחְמַדִּים, cs. מַחְמַדֵּי, sf. מַחְמַדֵּיהֶם, מַחֲמֹדֵּי La 1_{11} Qr: — 1. **s.thg** desirable, **precious** Is 64_{10}; — 2. metaph., *maḥdad ʿênayim*, delight of one's eyes 1K 20_6.

מַחְמֹד: pl. sf. מַחֲמוּדֶּיהָ: **s.thg precious** La 1_{11} Kt (Qr ↗ *מַחְמָד). †

*מַחְמָל: cs. מַחְמַל: w. *nefeš*, **yearning** Ez 24_{21}. †

מַחְמֶצֶת: **s.thg wh. tastes sour**, = what is leavened Ex 12_{19f}. †

מַחֲנֶה (ca. 200×): cs. מַחֲנֵה, sf. מַחֲנֶךָ Dt 23_{15}, מַחֲנֵיכֶם, מַחֲנֵהוּ sg. Am 4_{10}; pl. מַחֲנִים & מַחֲנוֹת; du. מַחֲנַיִם, מַחֲנָיִם; m. Gn 32_{9b}, f. 2K

7_7: — 1. **camp** = place of encampment Ex 29_{14}; for war Ju 7_9; of nomads Gn 32_8; — 2. men (& animals) of a **camp**: nomads 2K 5_{15}, besiegers Ez 4_2; — 3. **army outside a** camp 1S 17_1, on the march 2K 3_9, = battle-front 1K 22_{34}; — 4. *maḥ^{a}nēh ʾ^{e}lōhîm* Gn 32_3 (? is ʾ^e*lōhîm* sg. or pl.? army of spirits?), 1C 12_{23} (superlative?).

מַחֲנֵה־דָן: n. loc.

מַחֲנַיִם: n. loc.

מַחֲנָק: **suffocation** Jb 7_{15}. †

מַחְסֶה & **מַחֲסֶה** (3×): cs. מַחְסֵה; sf. מַחְסִי, מַחֲסִי, מַחְסֵהוּ, מַחְסֵנוּ: — 1. **(place of) refuge** Is 4_6; — 2. metaph. **refuge**: a) a lie Is 28_{15}, b) Y. Je 17_{17}.

מַחְסוֹם: thin metal plate over the lips as a **muzzle** Ps 39_2. †

מַחְסוֹר: sf. מַחְסֹרְךָ, מַחְסֹרוֹ: **want, lack** Dt 15_8; *ʾak l^{e}maḥsôr* (leads) only to impoverishment Pr 11_{24}.

מַחְסֵיָה: n. pers.

מחץ: **qal**: pf. מָחֲצָה ,מ׳; impf. יִמְחַץ, יִמְחָץ, אֶמְחָצֵם; impv. מְחַץ: **beat to pieces, smite** 2S 22_{39}.

***מַחַץ**: cs. =: **blow**: *maḥaṣ makkātô* wound fm. a blow, metaph. Is 30_{26}. †

מַחְצֵב: **hewing**: *ʾabnê maḥṣēb* hewn stone, quarried stone 2K 12_{13} 22_6 2C 34_{11}. †

מֶחֱצָה: cs. מֶחֱצַת: **half** Nu $31_{36 \cdot 43}$. †

***מַחֲצִית**: cs. מַחֲצִ(י)ת, sf. מַחֲצִיתִי: — 1. **half** (of the chariotry) 1K 16_9; — 2. *maḥ^{a}ṣît hayyôm* midday Ne 8_3.

מחק: **qal**: pf. מָחֲקָה: **smash, crush** (s.one's head) Ju 5_{26}. †

***מֶחְקָר**: pl. cs. מֶחְקְרֵי: **exploration**, *meḥq^{e}rê ʾereṣ* Ps 95_4 unexplored depths. †

מָחָר (ca. 50×): — 1. **(on) the next day, tomorrow** Ex 8_{25}; = *yôm māḥār* Gn 30_{33}, = *l^{e}māḥār* Ex 8_6; *kāʿēt māḥār* at this time tomorrow 1K 19_2, = *māḥār kāʿēt hazzōʾt* Jos 11_6; — 2. **in the future, in time to come** Ex 13_{14}.

***מַחֲרָאָה**: pl. מַחֲרָאוֹת 2K 10_{27} Kt (Qr מוֹצָאוֹת): **latrine.** †

***מַחֲרֵשָׁה**: sf. מַחֲרַשְׁתּוֹ & מַחֲרַשְׁתִּי; pl. מַחֲרֵשֹׁת: **plowshare** 1S 13_{20f}. †

מָחֳרָת: cs. מָחֳרַת: — 1. sbst. **the following day**, *yôm hammoḥ^{o}rāt* Nu 11_{32} = *l^{e}moḥ^{o}rat hayyôm* 1C 29_{21} = *lammoḥ^{o}rāt* Jon 4_7; — 2. adv. **on the next day**: *mimmoḥ^{o}rāt* on the following day Gn 19_{34}; *mimmoḥ^{o}rat* on the day after, w. *haššabbāt* Lv 23_{11}, *haḥōdeš* 1S 20_{27}.

מַחְשֹׂף: **peeling** (the bark), **laying bare** (the wood) Gn 30_{37}. †

מַחֲשָׁבָה (2×) & **מַחֲשֶׁבֶת** (4×, 2× cs.): מַחֲשֶׁבֶת; sf. מַחֲשַׁבְתּוֹ; pl. מַחֲשָׁב(וֹ)ת, cs. מַחְשְׁב(וֹ)ת, sf. מַחְשְׁב(וֹ)תָיו, מַחְשְׁבֹתֵיהֶם: — 1. **thought, idea, intention**: a) of man Gn 6_5, b) of God Is 55_{8f}; *maḥš^{e}bōt šālôm* intentions (of God) wh. bring well-being Je 29_{11}; — 2. (gradual transition from 1): **plan**: *maḥš^{e}bôt ʿammîm* Ps 33_{10}; — 3. **design, invention** Ex 31_4; *ḥišš^{e}bōnōt maḥ^{a}šebet ḥōšēb* cleverly designed (war-)machines 2C 26_{15}.

מַחְשָׁךְ: pl. מַחֲשַׁכִּים: — 1. **dark place, dark abode** Is 29_{15} 42_{16} Ps 88_7 143_3; — 2. **secret recess, hiding place** Ps 74_{20}. †

מַ֫חַת: n. pers.

מְחִתָּה: — 1. **terror** Is 54_{14}; — 2. **ruins** Ps 89_{41}, **destruction** Pr 10_{14f}.

מַחְתָּה: — 1. **bucket** for carrying burning coals and ashes 1K 7_{50}; — 2. **pan for coals** in incense offering, **censer** Lv 16_{12}; — 3. small **pan** as accessory of lampstand Ex 25_{38}.

מַחְתֶּרֶת: **housebreaking, trespassing** Ex 22_1 Je 2_{34}. †

מַטְאֲטֵא: **broom** Is 14_{23}. †

מַטְבֵּחַ: **slaughter-yard** Is 14_{21}. †

מַטֶּה: cs. מַטֵּה, sf. מַטֵּהוּ, מַטְּךָ; pl. מַטּ(וֹ)ת, sf. מַטֹּתָם: — 1. **staff, stock, stick**: a) as support: Gn 38_{18}; to beat out dill Is 28_{27}; b) for chastisement: *maṭṭēh ʾ^{e}lōhîm* Ex 4_{20}; Assyria as *maṭṭeh* Is 10_{5}; c) botanical: **branch** of vine Ez 19_{12}; d) **arrow** Hb $3_{9 \cdot 14}$; e) *maṭṭēh leḥem*, bread-pole, stick on wh. ring-shaped bread is stacked (to keep it away fm. mice &c.) Lv 26_{26} Ez 5_{16}; — 2. **tribe** 1K 7_{14}.

מַ֫טָּה: — 1. adv. **below, beneath** Pr 15_{24}; loc. *máṭṭâ máṭṭâ*, w. *yārad* lower & lower Dt 28_{43}; — 2. *lᵉmáṭṭâ* downward 2K 19_{30}; *lᵉmáṭṭâ mē‘āwōn* less than deserved Ezr 9_{13}; — 3. *millᵉmáṭṭâ* **below (on), beneath (on)** Ex 26_{24}.

מִטָּה: cs. מִטַּת, sf. מִטָּתוֹ; pl. מִטּוֹת: place for lying down, **bed** (of cloths, quilts &c. spread out): for sleeping 2K 4_{10}, for the sick Gn 47_{31}, for the dead 2S 3_{31}; portable **litter** 2K 4_{21}; **bedstead** decorated w. ivory Est 1_{6}; *ḥᵃdar hammiṭṭôt* room in wh. quilts &c. for *miṭṭâ* are stored 2K 11_{2}.

מֹטָה: ↗ מוֹטָה.

מֻטֶּה: bending: metaph. **warping** (of justice) Ez 9_{9}. †

***מֻטָּה**: pl. מֻטּוֹת: **stretching** (of wings) Is 8_{8}. †

cj. ***מְטֹהָר** Ps 89_{45}: sugg. מְטֹהָרוֹ for מִטְּהָרוֹ: **purity, splendor** of king. †

מַטְוֶה: **what is spun** Ex 35_{25}. †

***מְטִיל**: cs. מְטִיל בַּרְזֶל Jb 40_{18}: **iron rod**?. †

מַטְמוֹן: pl. מַטְמֹ(וֹ)נִים, cs. מַטְמֻנֵי Is 45_{3}: (hidden) **treasure** Gn 43_{23} Is 45_{3} Je 41_{8} Jb 3_{21} Pr 2_{4}. †

מַטָּע: cs. מַטַּע, sf. מַטָּעָהּ; pl. cs. מַטָּעֵי: (act of) **planting** Ez 17_{7}, (place of) **planting** Mi 1_{6}; *maṭṭa‘ yhwh*, metaph. for the community Is 61_{3}.

***מַטְעָם**: pl. מַטְעַמִּים & מַטְעַמּוֹת: **delicacy, tidbit** Gn 27_{4ff}.

מִטְפַּחַת: **wrapper, mantle** (for women) Is 3_{22} Ru 3_{15}. †

מטר: nif.: impf. תִּמָּטֵר: **be rained on** Am 4_{7}. †

hif.: pf. הִמְטַרְתִּי, הִמְטִיר; impf. יַמְטֵר, אַמְטִיר; inf. הַמְטִיר; pt. מַמְטִיר: — 1. *himṭîr māṭār ‘al*, **have/make rain fall** on Is 5_{6}; — 2. *himṭîr (‘al)* **let it rain, have it rain** Gn 2_{5}; obj. brimstone Gn 19_{24} &c.

cj. **hof.** pt. מָמְטָרָה (oth.: pual מְמֻטָּרָה) for מְטֹהָרָה Ez 22_{24}: **rained on.** †

מָטָר: cs. מְטַר; pl. מְטָרוֹת Jb 37_{6}: **rain** 1K 8_{35}; *mᵉṭar gešem* heavy shower Zc 10_{1}.

מַטָּרָא La 3_{12}: ↗ מַטָּרָה.

מַטְרֵד: n. pers. f.

מַטָּרָה & La 3_{12} מַטָּרָא: — 1. **target** 1S 20_{20}; — 2. **(men on) guard**: *ḥᵃṣar hammaṭṭārâ* court of the guard Je 32_{2}, *ša‘ar hammaṭṭārâ* Ne 12_{39}.

מַטְרִי: n. pers.

מַי: מַי־לִי Is 52_{15}: Qr מַה־לִּי, Kt מִי־לִי. †

מִי (420×): — 1. interr. **who?**: *mî hā’îš* who is the man? Gn 24_{65}; *bat-mî* whose daughter? Gn 24_{23}; *bᵉmî* through whom? 1S 14_{38}; pl. *mî ’attem* who are you? 2K 10_{13}; acc. *’et-mî* whom? 1S 12_{3}; almost neuter, *mî peša‘* who (= what) is the crime of ...? Mi 1_{5}; doubled: *mî wāmî* who individually? who (are the ones)? Ex 10_{8}; — 2. partitive: *mî bᵉkol-* who of all? 1S 22_{14}; *mî ’eḥād miššibṭê* what one is there of? Ju 21_{8}; — 3. w. dep. clause: a) *mî ’attâ qārā’tā* who are you, that you 1S 26_{14}; *mî kol-bāśār ’ᵃšer* who is (= where is there) a mortal who Dt 5_{26}; b) *mî ’ānōkî kî* who am I, that I Ex 3_{11}; c) *mî ’att wattîrᵉ’î* who are you, that you Is 51_{12}; — 4. in indir. qn.: *yāda‘nû mî*, we know who Gn 43_{22}; — 5. *mî* w. impf.: a) *mî yō’mar* who would (dare to) say? Jb 9_{12}; b) in unattainable wish: *mî yᵉśimēnî šōfēṭ* who would make me judge 2S 15_{4}; > *mî yittēn* as an expr. of wish Dt 28_{67}, w. following clause *mî yittēn yāda‘tî* if I only knew Jb 23_{3}; — 6. **whoever**: *mî lᵉyhwh*, whoever is for Y. Ex 32_{26}; — 7. condition: a) **how?**: *mî yāqûm ya‘ᵃqōb* who is J. that he should stand? = how can J. stand? Am 7_{2}; *mî ’att* = how are you? Ru 3_{16}; b) = **where?**: *mî gôy gādôl* Dt 4_{7}; — 8. var.: *mî hû’* ↗ *hû’* 5; *mî zeh*, *mî zō’t* ↗ *zeh* 15.

מֵידְבָא: n. loc.
מֵידָד: n. pers.
מֹידַע Ru 2_{1}: Kt מְיֻדָּע, rd Qr מוֹדַע.
מֵי זָהָב: trad. n. pers. Gn 36_{39} 1C 1_{50}, but perh. n. loc. †
מֵי הַיַּרְקוֹן: trad. n. loc. Jos 19_{46}, but perh. n. river. †
מֵיטָב: cs. מֵיטַב: **the best (portion)**: w. *'ereṣ* Gn $47_{6\cdot11}$, w. *śādeh & kerem* Ex 22_{4}, w. *ṣō'n & bāqār* 1S $15_{9\cdot15}$. †
מִיכָא: n. pers.
מִיכָאֵל: n. pers.
מִיכָה: n. pers.
מִיכָהוּ: n. pers.
מִיכָיָה: n. pers.
מִיכָיָהוּ: n. pers. m. & f.
מִיכָיְהוּ: n. pers.
*מִיכָל: cs. מִיכַל הַמָּיִם 2S 17_{20}: **accumulation, reservoir**; oth. rd. מִכֹּה אֶל־ from here to the water. †
מִיכַל, מִיכָל: n. pers. f.
מַיִם (ca. 580×): מָיִם, 3× מָיִם, cs. מֵי & מֵימֵי, sf. מֵימָיו, מֵימֶיךָ, מֵימֵינוּ, מֵימֵיהֶם, loc. הַמַּיְמָה, הַמָּיְמָה: **water**: — 1. as element, material Gn 1_{2}; — 2. rain-water 2S 21_{10}; in sea Am 5_{8}, in well Nu 20_{17}, in spring Is 22_{9}; *mayim ḥayyîm* ↗ I *ḥay*; — 3. other liquids: *mê rō'š* poisoned water Je 8_{14}; *mêmê raglayim* 2K 18_{27} Qr urine, > *mayim* Ez 7_{12}; = sperm? Is 48_{1}; — 4. in cult, ↗ *ḥaṭṭa't, niddâ*; — 5. as dangerous power, water of underworld: *mayim rabbîm* Ps 18_{17}; — 6. metaph.: a) = weakness: *lēbāb* becomes water Jos 7_{5}; b) copiousness Am 5_{24}; — 7. in names of loc.: מֵי דִימוֹן; מֵי יְרִיחוֹ; מֵי מְגִדּוֹ; מֵי מְרִיבָה; מֵי נִמְרִין; מֵי נֶפְתּוֹחַ; עִיר הַמַּיִם; מֵי עֵין שֶׁמֶשׁ.
מִיָּמִין Ne 12_{5}, מִיָּמִן Ezr 10_{25} Ne 10_{8} 1C 24_{9}: n. pers.
*מִין: sf. מִינוֹ & מִינֵהוּ Gn 1_{11f}, מִינָהּ, מִינֵהֶם: **kind, species** Gn 1_{11f}.
מֵינֶקֶת, מֵנֶקֶת Gn 24_{59}: sf. מְ(י)נִקְתּוֹ, מְ(י)נִקְתָּהּ; pl. מֵינִיקוֹת, sf. מֵינִיקוֹתַיִךְ: **(wet-)nurse** Gn 24_{59}.

מֵיסַךְ 2K 16_{18}: Qr מוּסַךְ, Kt מֵיסַךְ: tech. archit. term, unknown, ↗ comm. †
מֵיפַעַת, מֵפַעַת: מֵיפָעַת; Je 48_{21} מוֹפָעַת (Kt 'מוֹ, Qr 'מֵי): n. loc.
מִיץ: **pressing** Pr 30_{33}. †
מְיצִיאִים 2C 32_{21}: ↗ יָצִיא.
מִישׁ: ↗ II מוּשׁ.
מֵישָׁא: n. pers.
מִישָׁאֵל: n. pers.
מִישׁוֹר & מִישֹׁר: — 1. **level ground**, oft. metaph.: a) w. *'āmad*, stand Ps 26_{12}; b) w. gen. = level: *'ōraḥ mîšôr* Ps 27_{11}; — 2. **plain** (= level country) 1K 20_{23}; — 3. n. terr. for spec. plains, e.g. Arnon plateau Jos 13_{9}; — 4. metaph.: **straightness, fairness, righteousness** Is 11_{4}.
מֵישַׁךְ: n. pers.
מֵישַׁע: n. pers.
מֵישָׁע: n. pers.
מֵישָׁרִים, Pr 1_{3} מֵשָׁרִים: — 1. **level way** (metaph.) Is 26_{7}; *bᵉmêšārîm* ? smoothly (wine goes down) Pr 23_{31}, = *lᵉmêšārîm* SS 7_{10}; — 2. God: a) creates **order, regulation** Ps 99_{4}; b) directs *bᵉmêšārîm* **justly, rightly** Ps 9_{9}; *mêšārîm* acc. adv. **with justice** Ps 58_{2}; — 3. among men: **uprightness, straightness** Ps 17_{2}; b) speak **truth** Is 33_{15}; w. *'āśâ* come to an **agreement** Dn 11_{6}.
מֵיתָר: pl. sf. מֵיתָרָיו, מֵיתְרֵיהֶם: — 1. **bow-string** Ps 21_{13} †; — 2. **tent-cord, -rope** Ex 35_{18}.
מַכְאֹב: sf. מַכְאֹבוֹ; pl. מַכְאֹ(וֹ)בִים & מַכְאֹבוֹת, sf. מַכְאֹבָיו: — 1. **pain** Is 53_{4}, *'îš mak'ōbôt* full of pain Is 53_{3}; — 2. **suffering** Ex 3_{7}.
מַכְבִּיר Jb 36_{31}: ↗ כבר hif.
מַכְבֵּנָה: n. pers.
מַכְבַּנַּי: n. pers.
מַכְבֵּר: s.thg twisted or interlaced: **blanket** or **mat** (oth.: netting) 2K 8_{15}. †
מִכְבָּר: **grating** Ex 27_{4} 35_{16} $38_{4f\cdot30}$ 39_{39}. †
מַכָּה: cs. מַכַּת, sf. מַכָּתוֹ, מַכָּתְךָ; pl. מַכּוֹת (4×) & מַכִּים 2K 8_{29} 9_{15} 2C 22_{6}, sf. מַכּוֹתֶיהָ,

מַכּוֹתֶךָ & מַכּוֹתֶהָ Je 19_8 49_{17}, מַכּוֹתְךָ Dt 28_{59}: — 1. **blow, stroke** Dt 25_3 (*makkâ rabbâ*, many = more strokes); — 2. **wound** 1K 22_{35}; — 3. **plague, misery** Dt 28_{61}; — 4. **defeat** 1S 4_{10}; *hikkâ makkâ bᵉ* inflict a defeat on 1K 20_{21}, w. acc. Jos 10_{10}.

מִכְוָה: cs. מִכְוַת: **burn** (on the skin) Lv $13_{24\cdot28}$. †

מָכוֹן: cs. מְכוֹן, sf. מְכוֹנוֹ; pl. sf. מְכוֹנֶיהָ: — 1. **place** (to stand), **abode** 1K 8_{13}; — 2. **support** (of Y.'s throne) Ps 89_{15}; pl. foundations (of earth) Ps 104_5.

מְכוֹנָה & 3× מְכֹנָה: sf. מְכוֹנָתָהּ Zc 5_{11}; pl. מְכֹנוֹת, sf. מְכוֹנֹתָיו: — 1. (proper) **place, abode** Zc 5_{11}; *ʿal-mᵉkônōtāyw* on the (old) foundations Ezr 2_{68}; — 2. temple equipment: **undercarriage**, (wheeled) **stand** (for cauldron) 1K 7_{27ff}.

*מְכוּרָה: sf. מְכוּרֹתָם; pl. sf. מְכֹרֹתַיִךְ & מְכֻרוֹתַיִךְ: 2× w. *ʾereṣ*, (land of one's) **origin, parentage** Ez 29_{14}, = pl. 16_3 21_{35}. †

מָכִי: n. pers.

מָכִיר: n. pers. & tribe.

מָכִירִי: gent. of מָכִיר.

מכך: **qal**: impf. וַיָּמֹכּוּ: **sink, go down** Ps 106_{43}. †

nif.: impf. יִמַּךְ: — 1. **settle, sink in** (of roof) Ec 10_{18}; — 2. cj. impv. הִמַּכּוּ for hof., **give in** Jb 24_{24} F comm. †

[**hof.**: pf. הֻמְּכוּ Jb 24_{24}, rd. nif. impv.]

*מִכְלָא Ps 50_9 & מִכְלָה Hb 3_{17}: pl. cs. מִכְלְאֹת, sf. מִכְלְאֹתֶיךָ: **pen** (for sheep & goats) Hb 3_{17} Ps 50_9 78_{70}. †

מִכְלוֹל: **completeness, perfection**: *lᵉbušê miklôl*: splendidly, perfectly clothed Ez 23_{12} 38_4. †

*מַכְלוֹל: pl. מַכְלוּלִים: unspecified **splendid garment, finery** Ez 27_{24}. †

מִכְלוֹת: perfection (?): *miklôt zāhāb*, purest gold 2C 4_{21}. †

*מִכְלָל: cs. מִכְלַל: **perfection**, *miklal yōfî*, perfect beauty (Zion) Ps 50_2. †

מַכֹּלֶת 1K 5_{25}: < מַאֲכֹלֶת: **food**. †

*מִכְמָן: pl. מִכְמַנִּים: (hidden) **treasure** Dn 11_{43}. †

מִכְמָס Ezr 2_{27} Ne 7_{31}, otherw. מִכְמָשׂ: n. loc.

מִכְמָר Is 51_{20} & *מִכְמֹר (pl. sf. מִכְמֹרָיו) Ps 141_{10}: **net** (for hunting birds &c.), **fishnet**, metaph. Is 51_{20} Ps 141_{10}. †

*מִכְמֶרֶת Hb 1_{15f} & מִכְמֹרֶת Is 19_8: sf. מִכְמַרְתּוֹ: **fishnet** Is 19_8 Hb 1_{15f}. †

מִכְמָשׂ: n. loc., F מִכְמָס.

מִכְמְתָת (alw. הַמּ׳): n. loc.

מַכְנַדְבַי: n. pers.?

מְכֹנָה: n. loc.

* מִכְנָסַיִם: cs. מִכְנְסֵי: (linen) trousers of the priests, a kind of double-apron serving as garment for the hips, **breeches** Ex 28_{42}.

מֶכֶס: (cultic) **dues** Nu $31_{28\cdot37\cdot41}$. †

מִכְסָה: cs. מִכְסַת: **number** (of persons) Ex 12_4; **amount, valuation** Lv 27_{23}. †

מִכְסֶה: cs. מִכְסֵה, sf. מִכְסֵהוּ: **cover(ing)** of ark Gn 8_{13}, of tent Ex 26_{14}.

מְכַסֶּה: (prob. sg.) sf. מְכַסֶּיךָ: — 1. **cover(ing)** Is 14_{11} 23_{18}; — 2. the **fatty layer** (omentum) over the entrails Lv 9_{19}. †

מַכְפֵּלָה: alw. מְעָרַת הַמּ׳: n. loc.

מָכַר: **qal**: pf. מ׳, sf. מְכָרוֹ, מְכָרָנוּ; impf. נִמְכְּרֶנּוּ, תִּמְכְּרֵם, תִּמְכְּרוּ, יִמְכָּר־, יִמְכֹּר, תִּמְכְּרֶנָּה; impv. מִכְרָה, מִכְרִי; inf. לִמְכֹּר, מָכֹר; pt. מ(ו)כֵר, מֹכֶרֶת, מֹכְרִים, מֹכְרֵיהֶם, מֹכְרֵי: — 1. **sell**: a) things: land Gn 47_{20}, cattle Ex 21_{35}, oil 2K 4_7, right of firstborn Gn 25_{31}, metaph. wisdom Pr 23_{23}; b) persons: father sells daughter as wife Gn 31_{15}; sell into slavery Gn 37_{27f}; obj. slaves Ex 21_8, prisoners of war Dt 21_{14}; — 2. **hand over, give up, surrender**: subj. God, obj. his people 1S 12_9, a land Ez 30_{12}, an individual Ju 4_9.

nif.: pf. נִמְכַּר, נִמְכַּרְנוּ; impf. יִמָּכֵר; inf. הִמָּכְרוֹ; pt. נִמְכָּרִים: — 1. **be sold**, w. *bᵉ* & price Ex 22_2, w. *bᵉ* because of Is 50_1; w. *lᵉʿebed* as a slave Ps 105_{17}; — 2. **sell onesf.** (into slavery) Lv 25_{47f}.

hitp.: pf. הִתְמַכֵּר; impf. וַיִּתְמַכְּרוּ; inf. הִתְמַכֶּרְךָ: — 1. w. l^e let onesf. be sold Dt 28_{68}; — 2. w. $la^{\prime a}$*śôt hāra'* give onesf. up to 1K $21_{20.25}$ 2K 17_{17}. †

מֶכֶר: sf. מִכְרָהּ, מִכְרָם: — 1. purchase-money Nu 20_{19}, (buying) price Pr 31_{10}; — 2. saleable wares Ne 13_{16}. †

*מַכָּר: sf. מַכָּרוֹ; pl. sf. מַכָּרֵיכֶם: trader (perh. business assessor &c.) 2K $12_{6.8}$. †

*מִכְרֶה: cs. מִכְרֵה: *mikrēh-melaḥ* (salt-)pit Zp 2_9. †

*מְכֵרָה: pl. sf. מְכֵרֹתֵיהֶם: plan, advice Gn 49_5. †

מִכְרִי: n. pers.

מְכֵרָתִי: gent. of n. loc. or terr. *מְכֵרָה.

מִכְשׁוֹל, 1× מִכְשֹׁל: sf. מִכְשֹׁלָם; pl. מִכְשֹׁלִים: s.thg stumbled over, offense, obstacle Is 57_{14}, pl. Je 6_{21}; *mikšôl lēb* self-reproach 1S 25_{31}.

מַכְשֵׁלָה: heap of rubble or ruins Is 3_6. †

מִכְתָּב: cs. מִכְתַּב: — 1. writing (of God) Ex 32_{16}; inscription Ex 39_{30} Dt 10_4; *b^emiktāb* in writing Ezr 1_1 2C 36_{22}; — 2. document 2C 21_{12}, written order 2C 35_4. †

*מְכִתָּה: sf. מְכִתָּתוֹ: fragments Is 30_{14}. †

מִכְתָּם: inscription Ps 16_1 56_1 57_1 60_1. †

מַכְתֵּשׁ: — 1. molar (in jawbone) Ju 15_{19}; — 2. mortar (for grinding) Pr 27_{22}; — 3. n. terr. Zp 1_{11}. †

מָלֵא: qal: pf. מ׳, מָלְאָה, מָלֵאתִי > מָלֵתִי Jb 32_{18}, מָלְאוּ, מָלֵאוּ > מָלוּ Ez 28_{16}, sf. מְלָאוֹ; impf. יִמְלְאוּ, תִּמְלָאֵמוֹ Ex 15_9; impv. מִלְאוּ; inf. מְלֹ(ו)ת; pt. מָלֵא (also adj.!), מְלֵאִים: — 1. be full 2K 4_6; of days, be complete = be at an end Gn 25_{24}; — 2. w. acc. fill (of creatures, obj. waters &c.) Gn 1_{22}; — 3. w. acc. of material: be full of (violence) Gn 6_{13}; fill onesf. w. Ex 15_9; — 4. 2 acc., container & material: fill up with 1K 18_{24}; — 5. var.: *mālᵉ'â ṣᵉbā'āh* her time of service is finished Is 40_2; *mālē' 'al-gᵉdôtāyw* (river) has overflowed its banks Jos 3_{15}; *mālē' šᵉlāṭîm* (fill =) seize the shields Je 51_{11}; *mālē' yādô lᵉyhwh* = dedicate onesf. to the service of Y. Ex 32_{29}; *mālē' lēb*, w. l^e & inf., pick up the courage to Ec 8_{11} Est 7_5.

nif.: impf. תִּמָּלְאִי, וַתִּמָּלֵא, יִמָּלֵא, יִמָּלְאוּ(ן); pt. נִמְלָא: — 1. w. acc. of material: be filled with Gn 6_{11}; — 2. subj. days, go (entirely) by Ex 7_{25}; — 3. abs. be filled 2K 10_{21}.

piel: pf. מִלֵּא & Je 51_{34} מִלָּא, מִלֵּאתָ, מִלְאוּ, מִלְאוּהָ, מִלֵּאנוּ, וּמִלֵּאתֶם, וּמִלֵּאתִי, מִלֵּאתִיךָ; impf. יְמַלֵּא, יְמַלֶּה Jb 8_{21}, אֲמַלֵּא, וָאֲמַלְאֵהוּ, תְּמַלֶּאנָה, וַיְמַלְאוּם, וַיְמַלְאוּ; impv, מַלְאוּ, מַלֵּא; inf. מַלֵּא, מַלְּא(ו)ת, מַלְאָם; pt. מְמַלֵּא, מְמַלְאִים: — 1. 2 acc., fill s.thg w. s.thg 1S 16_1; — 2. a) w. acc. of container, fill s.thg; w. *'al* & material 1C 12_{16}, w. b^e Jb 40_{13}; offer in full number 1S 18_{27}; b) complete, finish a period of time Ex 23_{26}; c) w. acc. of material: fill up w., pour in Is 65_{11}; — 3. w. acc. of pers. & acc. of thg.: subj. God, fill, endow s.one w. (capacity, character-trait, emotion) Ex 28_3 Je 15_{17}; — 4. *millē' yad* (*hakkōhēn* &c.) fill s.one's hand = install s.one as priest, ordain 1K 13_{33}; fill one's own hand (w. sacrificial offerings) (not: ordain onesf.) Ex 32_{29}; consecrate (an altar), put into service Ez 43_{26}; — 5. fulfill, perform, carry out: obj. word 1K 2_{27}, request Ps 20_6; confirm, enforce (word) 1K 1_{14}; — 6. w. *kappô* + *min*: take a handful of Lv 9_{17}; — 7. w. *'aḥ^arê*, remain loyal to 1K 11_6; — 8. w. b^e & acc. of material: set (jewels) Ex 28_{17}, abs. Ex 31_5; w. *yādô baqqešet* lay the arrow on the bow 2K 9_{24}; w. acc. apply as an arrow Zc 9_{13}; — 9. var.: *qir'û mal'û* call in a loud voice Je 4_5; subj. river, w. *'al*, overflow (its banks) 1C 12_{16}; obj. *nefeš*, satisfy (hunger), fill Je 31_{25}, appease (appetite) Pr 6_{30}.

pual: pt. מְמֻלָּאִים: set with (of jewels) SS 5_{14}. †

hitp.: impf. יִתְמַלָּאוּן: **congregate together** (intrans.) Jb 16_{10}. †

מָלֵא: cs. מְלֵא, f. מְלֵאָה, הַמְלֵאָה Am 2_{13}, cs. מְלֵאַתִי; pl. מְלֵאִים, f. מְלֵא(וֹ)ת: — 1. **full** (attributive adj.): ears of grain Gn 41_7, vessel 2K 4_4, wind Je 4_{12}; of full value, *kesef* Gn 23_9; — 2. adj. > sbst.: *m^elē'â* pregnant woman Ec 11_5, woman w. husband & sons Ru 1_{21}; — 3. a) in abs., w. material following in acc.: **full of** 2K 7_{15}; b) in cs. w. material following in gen.: **full of** Je 6_{11}; — 4. *mālē'* after the material: *t^ešu'ôt m^elē'â* full of shoutings Is 22_2; — 5. **full** (pred. adj.) Ec 1_7.

מְלוֹא, מְלֹא, Ez 41_8 מְלוֹ: sf. מְלֹאוֹ, מְלֹאָהּ: — 1. **what fills, makes s.thg full**: a) *m^elō' kāf* a handful 1K 17_{12}, *m^elō' beged* a skirtful 2K 4_{39}; b) *hayyām ûm^elō'ô* the sea & everything in it Is 42_{10}, so *'ereṣ ûm^elō'āh* Dt 33_{16}; — 2. **abundance, full number, multitude, extent**: w. *haggôyim* Gn 48_{19}, w. *qōmātô* = (in) full length 1S 28_{20}.

מִלֹּא 2K 12_{21}: ↗ בֵּית מִלֹּא.

מְלֵאָה: sf. מְלֵאָתְךָ: **full yield** (of vineyard, winepress &c.) Ex 22_{28} Nu 18_{27} Dt 22_9. †

***מִלֻּאָה**: cs. מִלֻּאַת; pl. sf. מִלּוּאוֹתָם, מִלֻּאוֹתָם: **setting** (of jewels) Ex 28_{17} 39_{13}. †

מִלֻּאִים, 2× מִלּוּאִים: — 1. **consecration, ordination** (of priest) Ex 29_{22}; — 2. **setting** (of jewels) Ex 25_7.

מַלְאָךְ: cs. מַלְאַךְ, sf. מַלְאָכוֹ, מַלְאָכִי; pl. מַלְאָכִים, cs. מַלְאֲכֵי, sf. מַלְאָכָיו: — 1. (of men) **messenger**: of Jacob Gn $32_{4.7}$ & oft.; ? business agent Is 23_2; — 2. **God's messenger(s)**, viz. a) prophet(s) Is 44_{26}, b) priest(s) Ma 2_7 (so *hammal'āk* Ec 5_5); c) cosmic: the wind(s) Ps 104_4; — 3. heavenly messenger(s), **angel(s)**: a) sg. Gn 48_{16}, *mal'ākô* Gn 24_7; b) pl. Gn 19_1; c) spec. uses: *mal'ak habb^erît* Ma 3_1 ↗ *b^erît* III 10; *hammal'āk hammašḥît bā'ām* 2S 24_{16} & sim. expr., *mal'^akê māwet* Pr 16_{14}; d) oft. *mal'ak '^elōhîm* Gn 21_{17}, *mal'ak yhwh* Gn 16_7.

מְלָאכָה: cs. מְלָאכֶת, מְלֶאכֶת, sf. מְלַאכְתְּךָ, מְלַאכְתֶּךָ; pl. cs. מַלְאֲכוֹת, sf. מַלְאֲכוֹתֶיךָ: — 1. (business) **mission, business trip** Ps 107_{23}; — 2. **business, work** Pr 24_{27}, (one's) **occupation** Jon 1_8; *'āśâ m^elā'ktô* (God has) done his work Gn 2_2, (subj. man) 1K 7_{14}; *'āśâ limlā'ktô* put (people) to (one's) work 1S 8_{16}; — 3. **labor, employment**: a) (specific) **craft, job, task** Ex 31_3; *'āśâ m^elā'kâ* carry out a task Ex 35_{35}; *killâ m^elā'kâ* finish a work, job Ex 40_{33}; b) *m^ele'ket haḥômâ* work on the wall Ne 5_{16}; *'āśâ m^ele'ket '^abōdâ* do work-day labor Lv 23_{7f}; *'āśâ m^elā'kâ b^e* serve in (tent of meeting) Nu 4_3; c) *'ōśîm bamm^elā'kâ* occupied w. work 1K 5_{30}; *'ōśê hamm^elā'kâ* workers 2K 12_{12}, those employed 1C 23_{24}, officials Est 3_9; d) a work (in bronze) 1K 7_{14}; *mal'^akôt hattabnît* work according to the plan 1C 28_{19}; *m^ele'ket 'ôr* anything made of leather Lv 13_{48}; — 4. **article** (esp. of commerce), **thing** (of any sort): affair, enterprise Ezr 10_{13}; wares, items 1S 15_9; supplies 2C 17_{13}; (total) expedition (implying cattle &c.) Gn 33_{14}; goods Ex 22_6; anything Lv 11_{32}; any possible [use] Lv 7_{24}; — 5. **service** (to the king) 1C 4_{23}; — 6. **cultic service**: *m^ele'ket bêt '^elōhîm* Ne 11_{22}; cultic treasury Ne 7_{69a}.

***מַלְאֲכוּת**: cs. מַלְאֲכוּת: **message** Hg 1_{13}. †

מַלְאָכִי: n. pers. Ma 1_1, prophet Malachi, if not < 'my messenger' Ma 3_1. †

מְלֶאכֶת: ↗ מְלָאכָה.

מִלֵּאת: SS 5_{12}, uncert.: a) trad.: abundance of water, pool; b) setting (of eyes, like jewels); c) of teeth, (firm) mounting. †

מִלְבַד 1K 12_{33}: Kt מִלְּבַד (↗ I בַּד), rd Qr מִלִּבּוֹ. †

מַלְבּוּשׁ: sf. מַלְבֻּשְׁךָ; pl. sf. מַלְבּוּשַׁי, מַלְבֻּשֵׁיהֶם: (costly) **garment** 1K 10_5 Ez 16_{13}

2C 9_4; foreign Zp 1_8; (cultic) vestment 2K 10_{22}, (work-)clothes Is 63_3 Jb 27_{16}. †

מַלְבֵּן: — 1. (rectangular) **brick-mold** 2S 12_{31} Qr, Na 3_{14}; — 2. **brick-terrace, clay pavement** Je 43_9. †

[**מלה**: **qal**: מָלוּ Ez 28_{16}; **piel**: יְמַלֵּה Jb 8_{21} &c. ↗ מלא.]

מִלָּה: sf. מִלָּתוֹ; pl. מִלִּים 10× & מִלִּין 13× Jb, sf. מִלֶּיהֶם, מִלַּי, מִלֶּיךָ: **word** (utterance rather than lexical unit) 2S 23_2; in lawsuit Jb 23_5; *hāyâ lᵉmillâ ʼēt* become (the object of) talk Jb 30_9.

מִלּוֹ Ez 41_8: ↗ מְלֹא.

מְלוֹא: ↗ מְלֹא.

מִלּוֹא: "fill(ing)," **construction** built out **on an** (artificial) **terrace** for various purposes: in Jerus. 1K 9_{15}; *bêt millôʼ* 2K 12_{21}; in Shechem, *bêt millôʼ* Ju $9_{6\cdot 20}$.

מִלּוּאָה & **מִלּוּאִים**: ↗ מְלֵאָה, מִלֻּאִים.

מַלּוּחַ: Jb 30_4, a salty plant, food of the destitute; some identify as *Mesembrianthemum Forskahlei*, a species of fig-marigold; oth.: **sea orache**, *Atriplex Halimus*. †

מַלּוּךְ: n. pers.

מְלוּכָה, **מְלֻכָה** 1S 10_{25}: — 1. position or rank of king, **kingship** 1K 2_{15}; — 2. phr.: *ʻāśâ mᵉlûkâ ʻal*, rule as king over 1K 21_7; *qārāʼ mᵉlûkâ* proclaim kingship Is 34_{12}; *mišpaṭ hammᵉlûkâ* regulations of kingship 1S 10_{25}; *kissēʼ hammᵉlûkâ* 1K 1_{46}; *zeraʻ hammᵉlûkâ* 2K 25_{25}.

מְלוּכִי Ne 12_{14}, Qr מְלִיכוּ, Kt מַלּוּכִי, ↗ מַלּוּךְ. †

מָלוֹן: cs. מְלוֹן: **lodging** or **camping-ground for the night** Gn 42_{27}; *mᵉlôn qiṣṣô* its most remote night-shelter 2K 19_{23}.

מְלוּנָה: (shaky) **structure** for the night-guard in the fields Is 1_8 24_{20}. †

מַלּוֹתִי: n. pers., but artificial formation 1C $25_{4\cdot 26}$. †

I **מלח**: **nif.**: pf. נִמְלָחוּ: **be torn to pieces, flutter away** (of heavens, like smoke) Is 51_6. †

II **מלח**: **qal**: impf. תִּמְלָח: **salt, sprinkle salt on** (cereal offering) Lv 2_{13}. †

pual: pt. מְמֻלָּח: **be salted, be seasoned w. salt** Ex 30_{35}. †

hof.: pf. הָמְלַחַת; inf. הָמְלֵחַ: (of new-born infant) **be rubbed down w. salt(-water)** Ez 16_4 (oth.: be dipped in salt). †

I ***מֶלַח**: pl. מְלָחִים: **rags fm. torn clothing, clothing-scraps** Je 38_{11f}. †

II **מֶלַח**: **salt** Gn 19_{26}.

***מַלָּח**: pl. מַלָּחִים, sf. מַלָּחַיִךְ: **seaman, sailor** Ez $27_{9\cdot 27\cdot 29}$ Jon 1_5. †

מְלֵחָה: *ʼereṣ mᵉlēḥâ* salty, barren **land, saltplain** Je 17_6 > *mᵉlēḥâ* Ps 107_{34} Jb 39_6. †

מִלְחָמָה, **מִלְחֶמֶת** 1S 13_{22}: sf. מִלְחַמְתִּי; pl. מִלְחָמוֹת, cs. מִלְחֲמוֹת, sf. מִלְחֲמֹתָיו: — 1. **crowding, shoving** > **scuffle, combat, war**: a) *ʻāśâ milḥāmâ* Gn 14_2; *wattikbad milḥāmâ* was furious 1S 31_3, so *ḥăzᵉqâ* (so rd.) *milḥāmâ* 2K 3_{26}; b) *ʼîš milḥāmâ*, *ʼanšê hammilḥāmâ* **combattant, fighter** 1S 16_{18} 1K 9_{22}; *ʻōśēh milḥāmâ* those capable of field-service 2K 24_{16}; *ʼanšê milḥamtekā* your enemies, foes Is 41_{12}; *ʼîš milḥāmôt* accustomed to battle Is 42_{13}; *ʻam milḥāmâ*, *ṣᵉbāʼ milḥāmâ* Jos 8_1 Nu 31_{14}; — 2. w. Y.: *milḥāmâ lᵉyhwh* 1S 17_{17}; Y. is *ʼîš milḥāmâ* Ex 15_3, *gibbôr milḥāmâ* Ps 24_8; *milḥᵃmôt yhwh* 1S 18_{17}; — 3. a spec. **weapon**, lance or club Ps 76_4.

I **מלט**: **nif.** (60×): pf. נִמְלְטוּ, נִמְלַטְתִּי, נִמְלַט, נִמְלָטוּ; impf. יִמָּלְטוּ, אִמָּלְטָה, יִמָּלֵט; impv. הִמָּלְטִי; inf. הִמָּלֵט; pt. נִמְלָט, נִמְלֶטָה Je 48_{19}: **get onesf. to safety** Gn 19_{17}.

piel: pf. מִלֵּט, מִלַּט־ Ec 9_{15}, מִלְּטָנוּ; impf. אֲמַלֶּטְךָ, יְמַלְּטֵהוּ, יְמַלְּטוּ, אֲמַלֵּט, יְמַלֵּט; impv. מַלְּטוּנִי, מַלְּטוּ, מַלְּטָה; inf. abs. & cs. מַלֵּט; pt. מְמַלְּטִים, מְמַלֵּט: — 1. w. acc.: a) **save** s.one (fm. death &c.) 2S 19_6, abs. Is 46_4; b) **let** s.one **escape** cj. 2K 10_{24}; — 2. *millēṭ nafšô* **save onesf.** 1K 1_{12}; — 3. **leave** s.one **undisturbed, leave** s.one **alone** 2K 23_{18};

— 4. **lay and brood over** (eggs) † Is 34_{15}.

hif.: pf. הִמְלִיטָה, הִמְלִיט: — 1. **deliver** Is 31_5; — 2. **give birth to** Is 66_7. †

hitp.: impf. יִתְמַלָּטוּ: (of sparks) **fly out (in a shower)** Jb 41_{11}. †

II מלט: **hitp.**: impf. וָאֶתְמַלְּטָה: **be bald** Jb 19_{20}. †

מֶלֶט: **clay flooring** (?) Je 43_9. †

מְלַטְיָה: n. pers.

מְלִיכוּ: n. pers. Ne 12_{14} Qr: ↗ Kt מַלּוּכִי.

*מְלִילָה: pl. מְלִילֹת: **(rubbed) grains** (of wheat &c.), grains rubbed off when still milky Dt 23_{26}. †

מֵלִיץ: — 1. official, **middleman**: a) **interpreter** (of foreign language) Gn 42_{23}; b) **envoy** 2C 32_{31}; c) **intermediary, mediator** (i.e. prophet) Is 43_{27}; — 2. **subordinate heavenly being**, angel-intercessor Jb 33_{23}. †

מְלִיצָה: **allusive saying** Hb 2_6 Pr 1_6. †

I מָלַךְ: **qal** (ca. 300×): pf. מָלַכְתָּ, מָלָךְ, מ׳, מָלְכוּ; impf. אֶמְלוֹךְ, יִמְלָךְ־, יִמְלֹךְ; impv. מְלָךְ־, מָלְכָה (Ju 9_8 Kt מְלוֹכָה), מָלְכִי (Ju 9_{12} Kt מְלוֹכִי); inf. מְלָךְ־, מְלֹךְ, מָלְכוֹ; pt. מֹלֶכֶת: — 1. **be king, rule**: *ʿal* over Ju 9_8, *bᵉ* in Gn 36_{31a}, *lᵉ* among 36_{31b}; abs. **become king**, come into rule Pr 30_{22}; subj. *malkût* (kingship) is established 2C 36_{20}; subj. woman, rule, **be queen** 2K 11_3; *bᵉmolkô* when he became king 1S 13_1; *šᵉnat molkô* 2K 25_{27}: some: accession year, oth.: first full year of reign; — 2. subj. God: be king: a) 1S 8_7; b) Y. subj. Is 24_{23}, *yhwh mālak* as formula of acclamation 1K 1_{11}.

hif. (ca. 50×): pf. הִמְלַכְתִּי, הִמְלִיךְ, וְהִמְלַכְתָּ, וְהִמְלַכְתַּנִי, הִמְלִכוּ; impf. וַיַּמְלֵךְ, וַיַּמְלִכֻהוּ, נַמְלִיךְ, וַיַּמְלִ(י)כוּ, וָאַמְלִיךְ, וַיַּמְלִיכֶהָ; inf. הַמְלִיךְ, הַמְלִיכוֹ; pt. מַמְלִיךְ: **make** s.one **king, install** s.one **as king**: a) subj. Y.: w. acc., & oft. w. *lᵉmelek* 1K 3_7; subj. the people 1K 12_{20}, king of Babylon 2K 24_{17}; make kings Ho 8_4; make s.one queen Est 2_{17}.

hof.: pf. הָמְלַךְ Dn 9_1: trad.: be made king, but no indication of subordinate position: **become king.** †

II מלך: **nif.**: impf. וַיִּמָּלֵךְ: **take counsel w. onesf.** Ne 5_7. †

I מֶלֶךְ (ca. 2500×): pausal =; sf. מַלְכִּי; pl. מְלָכִים, מְלָכִין Pr 31_3, cs. מַלְכֵי, sf. מְלָכֶיהָ, מַלְכֵיהֶם: **king** in var. degrees: — 1. man: a) genl.: of Isr. 1S 15_{26}; of city Jos 10_1, of empire (Assyria) Is 36_4; pl. *malkê kᵉnaʿan* Ju 5_{19}; b) as title: *melek*, the king Ps 21_2, *ʾanōkî hammelek* 2S 3_{21}, *hammelek dāwîd* 2S 3_{31}, (esp. later) *dāwîd hammelek* 1C 24_{31}; *hammelek haggādôl* (= Assyrian king) 2K 18_{19}, *melek mᵉlākîm* (= king of Babylon) Ez 26_7; *yᵉḥî hammelek* 1K 1_{34}; *melek* = future David Ez 37_{22}; — 2. designation of God/a god: a) for Y. 1S 12_{12}; many comb., e.g. *melek yaʿᵃqōb* Is 41_{21}, *melek haggôyim* Je 10_7, *melek ʿôlām* Je 10_{10}; b) of other gods: *melek ballāhôt* Jb 18_{14}; — 3. comb. w. *melek*: *ʾeben hammelek*, king's weight 2S 14_{26} (↗ *ʾeben* I.6); *derek hammelek* King's Highway Nu 20_{17}; *kᵉyad hammelek*, w. royal liberality 1K 10_{13}; — 4. metaph.: of plants Ju 9_8, animals Jb 41_{26}.

II מֶלֶךְ: n. pers. 1C 8_{35} 9_{41}. †

מֹלֶךְ: הַמֹּלֶךְ Lv 20_5, לַמֹּלֶךְ 2K 23_{10} &c.: usu. explained as *melek*, name of a god, w. vowels of *bōšet*, 'shame'; oth.: *mōlek* = votive offering, so 2K 23_{10} &c., but certainly understood by O.T. tradition as god.

*מַלְכֹּדֶת: sf. מַלְכֻּדְתּוֹ: **snare in the path** Jb 18_{10}. †

מַלְכָּה: cs. מַלְכַּת; pl. מְלָכוֹת: — 1. **wife of king**, pl. SS 6_{8f}; — 2. **queen** (outside Isr.) 1K 10_1.

מִלְכָּה: n. pers. f.

מְלֻכָה 1S 10_{25}: ↗ מְלוּכָה.

מַלְכוּת, 3× מַלְכֻת: sf. מַלְכוּתוֹ; pl. מַלְכֻיּוֹת:

— 1. **royal power, dominion** Nu 24_7; *tikkôn malkûtô* his royal power was stabilized 1K 2_{12}; — 2. **royal dignity, kingship** 1C 11_{10}; — 3. **governmental activity** 1C 29_{30}; — 4. (period of) **reign** Je 49_{34}; — 5. **kingdom, realm** Est 1_{14}; — 6. = **royal**: *kissēh malkûtô* Est 1_2 &c.; — 7. of Y.: **dominion** Ps 103_{19}.

מַלְכִּיאֵל: n. pers.

מַלְכִּיָּה: n. pers.

מַלְכִּיָּהוּ: n. pers.

מַלְכִּי־צֶדֶק: n. pers.

מַלְכִּירָם: n. pers.

מַלְכִּי־שׁוּעַ: n. pers.

מַלְכָּם: n. pers.

מִלְכֹּם: n. of deity, **Milcom** 1K 11_5.

מַלְכֵּן 2S 12_{31} Kt: ꟻ Qr מַלְבֵּן.

***מְלֶכֶת**: מְלֶכֶת הַשָּׁמַיִם Je 7_{18} $44_{17\cdot19\cdot25}$, understood as מְלֶאכֶת 'host' (of heaven), but distortion of *מַלְכַּת 'queen' (of heaven) = ʿAstarte & oth. fertility goddesses. †

מֹלֶכֶת: n. pers. f.

מַלְכַּת: ꟻ מַלְכוּת.

I **מלל**: **qal** (or **nif.**): impf. יִמָּלוּ, יִמַּל: **dry up, wither** Ps 37_2 Jb 14_2 18_{16} 24_{24}. †

polel: impf. יְמוֹלֵל: **dry up, wither** (? rd. qal) Ps 90_6. †

hitpolel: impf. יִתְמוֹלָלוּ: **dry up, wither** Ps 58_8. †

II **מלל**: **qal**: impv. מֹל: **circumcise** Jos 5_2. †

nif.: pf. נְמַלְתֶּם: **let onesf. be circumcised** Gn 17_{11}. †

III **מלל**: **qal**: pf. ꟻ מִלּוֹתַי: **speak** 1C $25_{4\cdot6}$ as n. pers. †

piel: pf. מִלֵּל, מִלְּלוּ; impf. יְמַלֵּל, תְּמַלֶּל־: **say, declare** Gn 21_7 Ps 106_2 Jb 8_2 33_3. †

IV **מלל**: **qal**: pt. מֹלֵל: w. *beraglāyw*, **scrape** (w. the feet) = **give a sign** Pr 6_{13}. †

מִלֲלַי: n. pers.

***מַלְמָד**: cs. מַלְמַד: (ox-)**goad**, fitted w. pin or nail Ju 3_{31}. †

מלץ: **nif.**: pf. נִמְלְצוּ: **slide, slip by**, metaph. of Y.'s word, going in easily (to the mouth) Ps 119_{103}. †

מֶלְצַר: pausal =: **warden**, overseer Dn $1_{11\cdot16}$. †

מלק: **qal**: pf. מ׳: **pinch off** (head of bird) w. fingernail Lv 1_{15} 5_8. †

מַלְקוֹחַ: cs. =: **war-booty** Nu $31_{11f\cdot26f\cdot32}$ Is 49_{24f}. †

***מַלְקוֹחַיִם**: sf. מַלְקוֹחָי: **palate** Ps 22_{16}. †

מַלְקוֹשׁ: **late rain** (Mar.-Apr.) Dt 11_{14}.

מֶלְקָחַיִם: sf. מֶלְקָחֶיהָ: (pair of) **snuffers** (to cut wick) 1K 7_{49}.

מֶלְתָּחָה: **wardrobe** (storeroom) 2K 10_{22} cj. Je 38_{11}. †

***מַלְתָּעוֹת**: cs. מַלְתְּעוֹת: **jaw-bone** Ps 58_7. †

***מַמְּגוּרָה**: pl. מַמְּגֻרוֹת: **grain-pit** Jl 1_{17}. †

***מֵמַד** or ***מְמָד**: pl. sf. מְמַדֶּיהָ: **measurement** Jb 38_5. †

מְמוּכָן: n. pers.

***מָמוֹת**: pl. cs. מְמוֹתֵי: coll. pl. (a type of) **death** Je 16_4 Ez 28_8. †

מַמְזֵר: **bastard** Dt 23_3 Zc 9_6. †

מִמְכָּר: cs. מִמְכַּר, sf. מִמְכָּרוֹ; pl. sf. מִמְכָּרָיו: — 1. **s.thg wh. has been sold** Lv $25_{25\cdot28}$; — 2. **s.thg saleable** Lv 25_{14} Ne 13_{20}; — 3. **selling, sale** Lv $25_{27\cdot29\cdot33}$; *kesef mimkārô* selling price 25_{50}. †

מִמְכֶּרֶת: **selling, sale** (of slaves) Lv 25_{42}. †

מַמְלָכָה (ca. 115×): cs. מַמְלֶכֶת, sf. מַמְלַכְתּוֹ; pl. מַמְלָכוֹת, cs. מַמְלְכוֹת: — 1. **kingdom, dominion** Gn 10_{10}, pl. *mamlekôt hāʾāreṣ* Dt 28_{25}; *ʾānōkî ûmamlaktî* (i.e. of David) 2S 3_{28}; — 2. **royal power** or **dignity** 1S 28_{17}; *ʿîr hammamlākâ* royal city 1S 27_5; *bêt mamlākâ* imperial temple Am 7_{13}; — 3. **king**: *hammamlākôt hallōḥaṣîm ʾetkem* 1S 10_{18}; — 4. theol.: *lekā yhwh hammamlākâ* 1C 29_{11}.

***מַמְלָכוּת**: alw. cs. מַמְלְכוּת: — 1. **royal power, dominion** Jos $13_{12\cdot31}$ 1S 15_{28} 2S 16_3 Je 26_1; — 2. **kingdom** Ho 1_4. †

מִמְסָךְ: **mixing vessel** Is 65_{11} Pr 23_{20} (trad.: mixed wine). †

מֶמֶר: bitterness Pr 17_{25}. †

I **מַמְרֵא**: n. loc.

II **מַמְרֵא**: n. pers. Gn $14_{13 \cdot 24}$. †

מַמְרֹרִים: bitterness Jb 9_{18}. †

מִמְשַׁח: Ex 28_{14} *kᵉrûb mimšaḥ*, unexpl., *F* comm. †

מִמְשָׁל: — 1. **dominion, sovereign authority** Dn $11_{3 \cdot 5}$; — 2. *bānîm hammimšālîm* rulers, sovereigns 1C 26_6. †

מֶמְשָׁלָה: cs. מֶמְשֶׁלֶת, sf. מֶמְשַׁלְתְּךָ, מֶמְשַׁלְתֶּךָ; pl. cs. מֶמְשְׁלוֹת, sf. מַמְשְׁלוֹתָיו: — 1. (ruling power =) **dominion, authority** over, as cs. Gn 1_{16}, w. *bᵉ* Ps 136_8, abs. Is 22_{21}; — 2. (territory of one's) **dominion, authority**: *ʾereṣ memšālâ* 1K 9_{19}, > *memšālâ* 2K 20_{13}, pl. Ps 114_2; — 3. **military forces** 2C 32_9.

***מִמְשָׁק**: cs. מִמְשַׁק: *mimšaq ḥārûl* Zp 2_9, **ground** overrun w. weeds. †

מַמְתַקִּים: **sweet things** SS 5_{16}, sweet drinks Ne 8_{10}. †

I **מָן**: sf. מַנְךָ Ne 9_{20}: **manna** Ex 16_{15} &c., exudant of certain plant-lice feeding on sap of tamarisk-tree.

II **מָן** Ex $16_{15a\alpha}$ = מָה $_{15a\beta}$: **what.** †

***מֵן**: pl. מִנִּים: **string**, pl. **string-instruments** Ps 150_4; Ps 45_9 *F* comm. †

מִן: extended form מִנִּי 30×, מִנֵּי־ Is 30_{11}; usu. keeps form מִן־ before art., rarely otherw.; usu. assimilated, מִבֵּן, before gutturals & ר usu. מֵ, מֵאָדָם &c., but מִחוּץ, מִהְיוֹת; before cons. w. *shewa* כְּמִשְׁלֹשׁ Gn 38_{24}; before יְ: מִידֵי, but מִיְּשֵׁנֵי Dn 12_2; sf. מִמֶּנִּי, מִמְּךָ, מִמֶּנּוּ, מִמֶּנָּה, but מִמְּךָ, מִמֵּךְ, also מִנִּי (4×) & מֶנִּי (6×), מֶנְהוּ Jb 4_{12}, מִן־הוּא Is $18_{2 \cdot 7}$; מִכֶּם, מֵהֶם, מֵהֵמָּה (2×), מִנְהֶם (1×), מֵהֵן Ez $16_{47 \cdot 52}$: basic meaning **out of, away from**: — 1. spatial, a) indicates beginning-point of motion, **out of**, w. *yāṣāʾ* &c. Ex 12_{42}, w. 'save' 1S 17_{35}; *min-haḥōr* from (the door-hole) = through SS 5_4; *min-hûʾ wᵉhālᵉʾâ* near & far Is $18_{2 \cdot 7}$; b) direction of movement, w. *ʾel*: *mizzan ʾel-zan* Ps 144_{13}, w. (*wᵉ*)*ʿad* Ex 22_3 Lv 13_{12}, cf. *mimmᵉkā wāhinnâ* away fm. you in this direction 1S 20_{21}, *miššᵉmōʾl* (to) northward Jos 19_{27}, *mērāḥôq* (flee [to]) far away Is 22_3; c) indicates the place in whose direction (= where) s.thg is: *miqqedem* eastward, in the east Gn 2_8, *mibbayit* inside Lv 14_{41}; — 2. temporal: a) **since, from** (the time of): *minnᵉʿurîm* 1S 12_2; the beginning-point is included: *miššᵉnat hayyōbēl* from the year of jubilee (on) Lv 27_{17}; b) **just after**: *mēhāqîṣ* just after awakening Ps 73_{20}, *mimmoḥᵒrāt* on the very next day Gn 19_{34}; c) **after**: *miqqēṣ yāmîm* a few days later Gn 4_3, *miyyāmîm* some time later Ju 11_4; d) from the time when s.thg happens: *mîmê qedem* in primeval times Is 37_{26}; w. inf., *mibbôʾ* at homecoming Is 23_1; — 3. designates a) the material out of wh. s.thg is made: *min-hāʾᵃdāmâ* Gn 2_{19}, *niskêhem middām* their bloody drink-offerings Ps 16_4; b) the place of origin: *miṣṣorʿâ* from Z. Ju 13_2; — 4. designates a) cause: *mērêᵃḥ mayim* because of (= at) the scent of water Jb 14_9, *mērōb* because of (= by) the multitude of Ez 28_{18}; b) originator: *mēhammelek* (resulted) from the king = by the king's will 2S 3_{37}, *mimmennî ûmēhem* (which word,) mine or theirs Je 44_{28}; c) subj. of active verb becomes obj. of *min*- w. passive vb.: *mimmê hammabbûl* (all life shall be cut off) by the waters of a flood Gn 9_{11}; — 5. designates position or standard of an assessor: a) *qāṭōntî min* I am small, unimportant for (= I am too small for, I am unworthy of) (all the mercies) Gn 32_{11}; *rab mimmᵉkā hadderek*, journey is too far for you 1K 19_4; b) in expressions of comparison, **more than**: *ḥākām min*, wiser than 1K 5_{11}; w. vb., *gaddēl min*, make s.thg greater than 1K 1_{47}; — 6. designates the logical cause: in consequence of, **because of** (cf.

4a): *miqqōl haqqōrē'* Is 6_4, *mippî yhwh* by Y.'s command 2C 36_{12}; thus *mibbelî*, *mibbiltî*, because it is not, fm. lack of; — 7. w. vbs. of fearing, hiding, protecting, warning, **from, against**: a) *yārē' min* Ex 34_{30}, *str* (nif.) *min* Gn 4_{14} &c.; b) thus, far from > **without**: *mippaḥad* without fear Jb 21_9; — 8. part.; a) part of a whole: *mikkol-yiśrā'ēl* (men) fm. all Isr. Ex 18_{25}, *mēharbēh* (a few) of many Je 42_2; b) after adj., superlative: *haṭṭôb wehayyāšār mibbenê* the best & fittest of 2K 10_3; c) the part is omitted: *min-śārāyw* = one of his princes Dn 11_5; w. neg., *mē'abdê* (not) anyone of the servants = none of 2K 10_{23}; d) indef. part of the whole: *middām* some of the blood Lv 5_9; w. *'eḥād, 'aḥat*, any of the things Lv 4_2; — 9. *min* w. inf.: a) *mē'ahabat* from his loving = because he loves Dt 7_8; b) *mērē'ôt* (eyes) dim from seeing = too dim to see, dim so that he could not see Gn 27_1; c) temporal: *min-šilḥô 'ōtām* after he sent them away 1C 8_8; — 10. w. oth. preps.: a) *min* before oth. prep.: *mē'aḥar, mibbên* &c., ↗ respective preps.; b) *min* after oth. prep.: *lemin*: *lemērāḥôq* (I will fetch my knowledge) from afar Jb 36_3; temporal: from long ago Is 37_{26}; *lemibbêt le* on the inner side of Nu 18_7, *lemittaḥat le* underneath 1K 7_{32}; *lemiyyôm* since the days when 2S 7_{11}; — 11. Dt 33_{11} *min-yeqûmûn* conj. that … not (if true reading).

מְנָאוֹת Ne 12_{44}: ↗ מְנָת.

***מַנְגִּינָה**: sf. מַנְגִּינָתָם: **mocking song** La 3_{63}. †

מָנָה: **qal**: pf. מ', מָנִיתִי; impf. יִמְנוּ, תִּמְנֶה; impv. מְנֵה; inf. מְנוֹת; pt. מוֹנֶה: — 1. **divide in parts, count**: grains of dust Gn 13_{16}, money 2K 12_{11}; count out (for yourself) (an army) 1K 20_{25}; — 2. count (s.thg) out (for s.one), **consign, commit** Is 65_{12}.

nif.: pf. נִמְנָה; impf. יִמָּנֶה, יִמָּנוּ; inf. הִמָּנוֹת: — 1. **let onesf. be counted, be open to counting**: w. neg. be innumerable 1K 3_8 8_5 Ec 1_{15} 2C 5_6; — 2. **be counted** Gn 13_{16}, w. *'ēt* among Is 53_{12}. †

piel: pf. מִנָּה, מִנּוּ; impf. וַיְמַן: — 1. **allot, apportion** Jb 7_3, determine, appoint Ps 16_5; — 2. **supply** Jon 2_1 $4_{6\text{-}8}$ Dn $1_{5\cdot10f}$. †

pual: pt. מְמֻנִּים: appointed 1C 9_{29}. †

מָנֶה: pl. מָנִים: **mina**, unit of weight of gold & silver, a little more than 1/2 kilogram or 1 lb., 1K 10_{17} Ez 45_{12}, Ezr 2_{67} Ne 7_{70f}. †

מָנָה: pl. מָנוֹת, sf. מְנוּתֶהָ Est 2_9: **portion, share**: a) of sacrificial meat 1S 1_{4f}, b) of delicacies of feast Est 9_{19}; c) **food due** s.one Est 2_9.

***מֹנֶה**: pl. מֹנִים: **time** (= occurrence, French *fois*) Gn $31_{7\cdot41}$. †

מִנְהָג: cs. מִנְהַג: **manner of driving** (chariot) 2K 9_{20}. †

***מִנְהָרָה**: pl. מִנְהָרוֹת: **hole in rocky ground** for underground storage Ju 6_2. †

***מָנוֹד**: cs. מְנוֹד: (object of) **shaking (of head)** (as gesture of mocking) Ps 44_{15}. †

I **מָנוֹחַ**: cs. מְנוֹחַ; pl. sf. מְנוּחָיְכִי Ps 116_7: — 1. **resting place**: for animals Gn 8_9, exiles Dt 28_{65} La 1_3, those w/o kin Ru 3_1, Lilith Is 34_{14}; for *nefeš* Ps 116_7; — 2. temporal: after the resting-place of ark = after it had found its resting-place 1C 6_{16}. †

II **מָנוֹחַ**: n. pers.

מְנֻחָה, מְנוּחָה: sf. מְנוּחָתִי, מְנֻחָתְךָ, מְנֻחָתוֹ; pl. מְנֻחוֹת, מְנוּחוֹת: **rest**: — 1. spatial: a) **resting-place** Gn 49_{15}, *mê menûḥâ* beside the water Ps 23_1, *śar menûḥâ* quarter-master Je 51_{59}; b) place of quiet, tranquility Is 28_{12}, home Ru 1_9; c) Canaan as residence for Isr. 1K 8_{56}; d) God's abode Is 66_1; *bêt menûḥâ* for the ark 1C 28_2; — 2. psychological: **quieting, calming** 2S 14_{17}; *'îš menûḥâ* calm, cool man 1C 22_9.

cj. ***מָנוֹל**: Jb 15_{29}: rd. מְנֹלָם for מִנְלָם: **property, possessions**. †

מָנוֹס: sf. מְנוּסִי: **place of refuge** 2S 22_3 Je 46_5

Ps 59_{17}; subj. of *'ābad*, refuge will perish = will be lost Je 25_{35} Am 2_{14} Ps 142_5 Jb 11_{20}. †
מְנוּסָה: cs. מְנֻסַת: **place of refuge** Lv 26_{36} Is 52_{12}. †
***מָנוֹר**: cs. in phr. מְנוֹר אֹרְגִים: **weaver's beam**, beam on wh. the warp-threads are wound or tied 1S 17_7 2S 21_{19} 1C 11_{23} 20_5. †
מְנוֹרָה & מְנֹרָה: cs. מְנֹ(ו)רַת; pl. מְנֹ(ו)רוֹת: **lampstand** (not candlestick): in house 2K 4_{10}, in tabernacle & temple 1K 7_{49} &c.
***מִנְּזָר**: pl. sf. מִנְּזָרַיִךְ: **courtier** Na 3_{17}. †
מֻנָּח: Ez $41_{9.11}$: ? free, open space, fire-alley. †
מִנְחָה: cs. מִנְחַת, sf. מִנְחָתִי, מִנְחָתְךָ, מִנְחָתֵךְ; pl. sf. מִנְחֹתֵיכֶם, מִנְחֹתֶךָ: **gift**.

I. (37×) (secular) gift, **present**, to express: a) reverence or respect: people to king 1S 10_{27}, king to prophet 2K 8_8; b) thanks: Jews to king 2C 17_5; c) homage, allegiance: Jacob to Esau Gn 32_{14}; d) (political) friendship between kings & empires 1K 5_1 2K 20_{12}; e) **tribute** 2K 17_{3f}.

II. **offering, sacrifice**: a) older passages: offering or sacrifice of homage, allegiance (of either meat or cereal) Gn 4_{3ff}, so also prob. 1S 2_{29} &c.; b) in the laws (never in Dt): vegetable offering, usu. cereal, Ex 29_{41} &c.; c) so in oth. passages 1K 8_{64}; as designation of time 1K 18_{29}.

מְנֻחָה: ↗ מְנוּחָה.
מְנַחֵם: n. pers.
I **מָנַחַת**: n. pers. Gn 36_{23} 1C 1_{40}. †
II ***מָנַחַת**: מָנַחַת: n. loc. 1C 8_6. †
מָנַחְתִּי: gent. of II *מנחת.
מְנִי: name of god of fate, **Meni** Is 65_{11}. †
I **מִנִּי**: Je 51_{27}, people & region in Armenia. †
II **מִנִּי**: — 1. (30×) & מִנֵּי Is 30_{11}, ↗ מִן; — 2. מִנִּים Ps 45_9 150_4 ↗ מֵן.
מְנָיוֹת: pl. of ↗ מְנָת.
מִנְיָמִין: n. pers.
I **מִנִּית**: n. loc. Ju 11_{33}. †
II **מִנִּית**: חִטֵּי מִנִּית Ez 27_{17} ?, "wheat of minnith," sugg. rice. †

[מִנְלָם Jb 15_{29}: ↗ cj. *מָנוֹל.]
מָנַע: qal: pf. מָנַעְתִּי, מ׳, מָנָעֲךָ; impf. יִמְנַע, יִמְנְעוּ, יִמְנָעֵנִי, יִמְנָעֶנָּה, אֶמְנַע; impv. מְנַע, מִנְעִי; pt. מֹנֵעַ: — 1. **retain, hold back** Ez 31_{15}, grain fm. market Pr 11_{26}; — 2. **withhold, deny** s.thg fm. s.one Gn 30_2; — 3. **restrain** s.one fm. s.thg 1S 25_{26}, **keep** s.one **away** fm. s.thg Nu 24_{11}.

nif.: pf. נִמְנַע; impf. יִמָּנַע: — 1. **be withheld** Jl 1_{13} Jb 38_{15}, subj. rain Je 3_3; — 2. **let onesf. be kept back** Nu 22_{16}. †

מַנְעוּל: pl. sf. מַנְעוּלָיו: **lock, bolt** (for gate) Ne $3_{3.6.13.15}$. †
***מִנְעָל**: pl. sf. מִנְעָלֶיךָ: **bolt** Dt 33_{25}. †
מַנְעַמִּים: **delicacies** (to eat) Ps 141_4. †
מְנַעַנְעִים: **sistrum**, small percussion instrument wh. is rattled 2S 6_5. †
***מְנַקִּית**: pl. מְנַקִּיּוֹת, sf. מְנַקִּיֹּתָיו: **offering-bowl** Ex 25_{29} 37_{16} Nu 4_7 Je 52_{19}. †
מֵנֶקֶת Gn 24_{59}: ↗ מֵינֶקֶת.
מְנֹרָה: ↗ מְנוֹרָה.
מְנַשֶּׁה: n. pers. & tribe: **Manasseh**: I. n. pers. Gn 41_{51} 2K 20_{21} Ezr 10_{30}; — II. n. tribe Nu 26_{28}.
מְנַשִּׁי: gent. of מְנַשֶּׁה.
***מְנָת**: cs. =; pl. cs. מְנָיוֹת Ne 12_{47} 13_{10}, מְנָאוֹת Ne 12_{44}: **portion** Je 13_{25}, pl. Ne 12_{44}; *m^{e}nāt kôs* portion of one's cup Ps 11_6.
מָס: Jb 6_{14}: לַמָּס: presumably 'despondent,' but difficult, ↗ comm. †
מַס: מַס Jos 17_{13} Pr 12_{24}; pl. מִסִּים: **compulsory labor, obligatory service**: — 1. exceptionally heavy output of work (compulsory labor or assessment) imposed on subjugated people: Canaanites Dt 20_{11}, Assyrians Is 31_8; — 2. compulsory labor in Isr. 1K 5_{28}; *śar 'al-hammas* overseer of forced labor 1K 4_6; in Egypt, *śārê missîm* Ex 1_{11}, metaph. of Jerus., *hay^{e}tâ l^{e}mas* La 1_1; — 3. *mas 'ōbēd*, esp. low form of 2., complete enslavement Gn 49_{15}; *he'^{e}lâ l^{e}mas 'ōbēd* levy slaves 1K 9_{21}.

*מֵסַב or *מֵסֵב: sf. מְסִבּוֹ; pl. cs. מְסִבֵּי, sf. מְסִבָּי: — 1. a) **circle of feasters** SS 1_{12}; b) pl. **neighborhood, surroundings** 2K 23_5, territory of city-state of Jerus.; — 2. adv. **round about** 1K 6_{29}, pl. sf. all around me Ps 140_{10}, but F comm. †

*מְסִבָּה: pl. מְסִבּוֹת: — 1. adv. **round about** Jb 37_{12}; — 2. cj. Ez 41_7 **circular passage** (?). †

I מַסְגֵּר: **dungeon** Is 24_{22} 42_7 Ps 142_8. †

II מַסְגֵּר: **metal-worker, fitter,** coll. 2K $24_{14 \cdot 16}$ Je 24_1 29_2. †

מִסְגֶּרֶת: sf. מִסְגַּרְתּוֹ; (pl. abs.!) מִסְגְּרוֹת, sf. מִסְגְּרוֹתֵיהֶם, מִסְגְּרֹתֶיהָ: — 1. **dungeon** 2S 22_{46}; — 2. **rim** (of table or base) 1K 7_{28f}.

מַסַּד: **foundation** 1K 7_9. †

*מִסְדְּרוֹן: loc. מִסְדְּרוֹנָה: uncert.: vestibule, ? latrine, sugg. air-hole: Ju 3_{23}. †

מסה: **hif.**: pf. sf. הִמְסִיו; impf. אַמְסֶה, וַתֶּמֶס, יַמְסֵם: — 1. **make** (ice) **melt** Ps 147_{18}; metaph. let s.thg disappear: heart (= morale) Jos 14_8, charm Ps 39_{12}; — 2. **drench** (w. tears) Ps 6_7. †

I *מַסָּה: pl. מַסּוֹת: **trial, temptation** Dt 4_{34} 7_{19} 29_2. †

II *מַסָּה: cs. מַסַּת: **despair** Jb 9_{23}. †

III מַסָּה: n. loc. Ex 17_7 Dt 9_{22} 33_8 Ps 95_8, *hammassâ* Dt 6_{16}. †

*מִסָּה: cs. מִסַּת: **measure,** Dt 16_{10} *missat nidbat yādᵉkā* = as many as. †

מַסְוֶה: **covering** Ex 34_{33-35}; sugg. veil, or priest's mask. †

מְסוּכָה: **thorn-hedge** Mi 7_4. †

מַסָּח: **replacement** > adv. **alternately** 2K 11_6. †

[מִסְחַר 1K 10_{15}: rd. וּמִסְחַר.]

מָסַךְ: **qal**: pf. מָסַכְתִּי, מ׳; inf. מְסֹךְ: **mix** (honey or spices) (to wine &c.) Is 5_{22} 19_{14} Ps 102_{10} Pr $9_{2 \cdot 5}$. †

מֶסֶךְ: **admixture of spices** (to a drink) Ps 75_9. †

מָסָךְ: cs. מָסַךְ: — 1. **covering** (temporary, over mouth of well) 2S 17_{19}; metaph., of clouds Ps 105_{39}; Is 22_8; — 2. **curtain,** at entrance to tabernacle Ex 26_{36f}, court-gate 27_{16}; *pārōket hammāsāk* the covering curtain Ex 35_{12}.

*מְסֻכָה: sf. מְסֻכָתֶךָ: **covering,** garment or fencing Ez 28_{13f}. †

I מַסֵּכָה: cs. מַסֵּכַת; pl. מַסֵּכוֹת, sf. מַסֵּכוֹתָם: — 1. metal-casting, **cast image** Dt 27_{15}; many comb., e.g. *ṣalmê massēkâ* cast images Nu 33_{52}, *massēkat zāhāb* image cast of gold Is 30_{22}; *ʾᵉlōhê massēkâ* cast images of gods (amulets?) Ex 34_{17}; cast idol 2K 17_{16}; — 2. **drink offering,** w. 1 *nāsak*, accompanying settlement of treaty, thus = **conclude an alliance** † Is 30_1.

II מַסֵּכָה: **covering** Is 25_7 28_{20}. †

מִסְכֵּן: **poor** Ec 4_{13} 9_{15f}. †

מְסֻכָּן: Is 40_{20} *hamᵉsukkān tᵉrûmâ*: trad. *skn* pual pt., 'who is too poor for such a gift'; but perh. rd. cj. *hammᵉsakkēn tᵉmûnâ* 'who sets up an image,' or 'has an image restored'; or sugg. *mᵉsukkān* = a kind of tree. †

מִסְכְּנוֹת: **stores, supplies, storerooms, warehouses** 2C 32_{28}, *miskᵉnôt ʿārê* 2C 16_4; *ʿārê (ham)miskᵉnôt* "warehouse-cities," military bases w. armories & supply depots Ex 1_{11} 1K 9_{19} 2C $8_{4 \cdot 6}$ 17_{12}. †

מִסְכֵּנֻת: **poverty** Dt 8_9. †

* מַסֶּכֶת, מַסֶּכֶת: **warp-threads** (of horizontal loom) Ju 16_{13f}. †

מְסִלָּה: cs. מְסִלַּת, sf. מְסִלָּתוֹ; pl. מְסִלּוֹת, sf. מְסִלּוֹתָם, מְסִלֹּתַי: (built-up) **road, highway,** orig. laid out w. layer of stone, gravel, or the like Ju 20_{31}; within Jerus. 2K 18_{17}; course of stars Ju 5_{20}; metaph. road of life: *mᵉsillat yᵉšārîm* Pr 16_{17}.

מַסְלוּל: **highway** Is 35_8. †

*מַסְמֵר & *מִסְמֵר: pl. מַסְמְרִים Is 41_7, מַסְמְרִים Je 10_4, מִסְמְרִים 1C 22_3, מִסְמְרוֹת 2C 3_9: **pin, nail.** †

מסס: **qal**: inf. מְסֹס Is 10_{18} & מְשׁוֹשׂ 8_6 & Jb 8_{19} (?): **lose courage.** †

nif.: pf. נָמַס, נָמֵס, נָמַסּוּ; impf. יִמַּס, יִמָּס, יִמַּסּוּ; inf. הִמֵּס; pt. נָמֵס: — 1. **dissolve, melt** (intrans.): subj. manna Ex 16_{21}, wax Ps 68_{3}; metaph. mountains Is 34_{3}; dwindle away, metaph., subj. *lēb* = courage Jos 2_{11}; — 2. **become weak**, subj. fetters Ju 15_{14}, warrior 2S 17_{10}.

hif.: pf. הֵמַסּוּ; cj. impf. יָמֵס: **make s.thg melt**, obj. *lēb* = courage Dt 1_{28} cj. 20_{8}. †

מַסָּע: pl. cs. מַסְּעֵי & sf. מַסְעֵיהֶם, & pl. sf. מַסָּעָיו: — 1. **breaking** (of camp), w. acc. (as if inf.) Nu 10_{2}; — 2. **(making of) departure** (of nomadic army): a) *lᵉmassaʿ lifnê hāʿām* Dt 10_{11}; b) pl. **order of departure** Nu 10_{28} 33_{1}; departures Nu 10_{6} > day's marches Gn 13_{3}, *lᵉmasʿêhem* Ex 17_{1} Nu 10_{12} 33_{2}; c) = time of wandering, *bᵉkol-masʿêhem* Ex $40_{36.38}$. †

מַסָּע: breaking out, quarrying (of stones): *ʾeben massāʿ* (unhewn) **quarry-stones** 1K 6_{7}; Jb 41_{18} evid. a kind of weapon. †

מִסְעָד: 1K 10_{12}, unknown tech. archit. term: ? **railing**; oth.: step (of stairs). †

מִסְפֵּד: cs. מִסְפַּד, sf. מִסְפְּדִי: **rites** or **customs of mourning** Zc 12_{10f}; *sāpad mispēd* Gn 50_{10}, *qārāʾ mispēd* Is 22_{12}.

מִסְפּוֹא: **fodder**: for camels Gn $24_{25.32}$, donkeys 42_{27} 43_{24} Ju 19_{19}. †

***מִסְפָּחָה**: pl. מִסְפָּחוֹת, sf. מִסְפְּחֹתֵיכֶם: **(head-)covering**, or veil? Ez $13_{18.21}$. †

מִסְפַּחַת: (harmless) **skin eruption** (such as rashes or scab) Lv 13_{6-8}. †

I **מִסְפָּר** (ca. 130×): cs. מִסְפַּר, sf. מִסְפָּרָם, מִסְפַּרְכֶם; pl. cs. מִסְפְּרֵי: — 1. **number, quantity** in genl.: *mispar haššānîm* number of years Dn 9_{2}; *mispar kol-zākār* number of all males Nu 3_{22}, *mispar ʿārêkā* as numerous as are your cities Je 2_{28}; *hᵃyēš mispār lāhem* can you be counted? Jb 25_{3}; *mispar mifqad-*, result (of census) 2S 24_{9}; — 2. a) *bᵉmispār* counted 1C 9_{28}; b) counted, countable = **(a) few**: α) *mispār* as appos. after noun: *yāmîm mispār* Nu 9_{20}; β) *mispār* after cs., *mᵉtê mispār* Gn 34_{30}; γ) *hāyâ mispār* shall be few Dt 33_{6}; c) considerable, great number: α) w. neg.: innumerable: *ʾên mispār* Gn 41_{49}; infinite: (Y.'s) understanding Ps 147_{5}, *ʿad lᵉʾên mispār* Ps 40_{13}; β) as qn. Jb 25_{3}; — 3. w. prep.: a) w. *bᵉ*: according to, corresponding to: *bᵉmispar hayyāmîm* Nu 14_{34}; *bᵉmispār* in the necessary number 1C 23_{31}; b) w. *kᵉ*: according to the number, *kᵉmispar šibṭê* 1K 18_{31}; c) = w. *lᵉ*: *lᵉmispar šibṭê* Jos 4_{5}; d) = w/o prep., in adv. or coll. pl. acc.: *mispar nafšōtêkem* according to the number of their "souls" (= individuals) Ex 16_{16}; *ʿeśrîm wᵉʾarbaʿ mispār* 24 in number 2S 21_{20}; *mispar yᵉmê ḥayyêhem* their whole (short) lifetime through = as long as they live Ec 2_{3}; — 4. w. vb.: w. *hāyâ* become a considerable number Dt 33_{6}, a limited number Is 10_{19}; w. *nātan*, make a report of 2S 24_{9}; *nāśāʾ mispār* determine the number 1C 27_{23}, *ʿālâ mispār* be recorded (in a book) 1C 27_{24}; *ʿābar bᵉmispār* be counted off 2S 2_{15}; — 5. **narration** Ju 7_{15}.

II **מִסְפָּר**: n. pers. Ezr 2_{2}. †

מִסְפֶּרֶת: n. pers. (m.!).

מסר: **qal**: inf. לִמְסָר־: *hāyû limsor-maʿal* Nu 31_{16}: Targum 'became an occasion for apostasy,' but perh. rd. לִמְעָל־. †

nif.: impf. וַיִּמָּסְרוּ: be counted = **be chosen, elevated** Nu 31_{5}. †

מֹסֵרוֹת: n. loc.

[**מֹסָרָם** Jb 33_{16}: rd יְחִתֵּם & בְּמֹרָאִים.]

מָסֹרֶת: *māsōret habbᵉrît*, w. *hēbîʾ bᵉ*: trad. 'tradition' or 'binding,' but sugg. del. *habbᵉrît* & rd. *mispar* 'in counting' = bring in counted Ez 20_{37}. †

מִסְתּוֹר: hiding-place, **shelter** (from rain) Is 4_{6}. †

מַסְתֵּר: Is 53_{3}, rd. מַסְתִּיר *str* hif. pt. as one from whom one hides his face (in abhorrence). †

מִסְתָּר: pl. מִסְתָּרִים, sf. מִסְתָּרָיו: sg. Hb 3_{14} Ps 10_9, otherw. pl.: **hiding-place** Is 45_3.

*מַעְבָּד: pl. sf. מַעְבָּדֵיהֶם: **deed** Jb 34_{25}. †

*מַעֲבֶה: cs. מַעֲבֵה: 1K 7_{46} *maʿabēh haʾadāmâ* **(ore-)foundry.** †

*מַעֲבָר: cs. מַעֲבַר: — 1. movement, **blow** (of a stick) Is 30_{32}; — 2. **ford** (of river) Gn 32_{23}; — 3. pass(age), **ravine** 1S 13_{23}. †

מַעְבָּרָה: pl. מַעְבָּרוֹת, cs. מַעְבְּרוֹת: — 1. **ford** Jos 2_7, pl. (over Euphrates) Je 51_{32}; — 2. pass(age), **ravine** 1S 14_4.

I מַעְגָּל: loc. הַמַּעְגָּלָה: **(circle of a) camp, encampment** 1S 17_{20} $26_{5.7}$. †

II מַעְגָּל: cs. מַעְגַּל; pl. cs. מַעְגְּלֵי, sf. מַעְגָּלֶיךָ & מַעְגְּלֹתֶיךָ: **track** of wagon, **rut** Ps 65_{12}; metaph. Is 26_7.

מעד: **qal**: pf. מָעֲדוּ; impf. אֶמְעַד, תִּמְעַד; pt. מוֹעֲדֵי: **wobble, shake** 2S 22_{37} Ps 18_{37} 26_1 37_{31} Jb 12_5. †

[**pual**: pt. מוּעֶדֶת Pr 25_{19}, rd. מוֹעֶדֶת qal pt. †]

hif.: impv. הַמְעַד: **make** s.thg **shake** Ps 69_{24}. †

מַעֲדַי: n. pers.

מַעַדְיָה: n. pers.

מַעֲדַנִּים: cs. מַעֲדַנֵּי: — 1. **delicacies** (to eat) Gn 49_{20} La 4_5; — 2. metaph. **refreshment, delight** Pr 29_{17}. †

מַעֲדַנּוֹת, מַעֲדַנֹּת: — 1. *maʿadannôt* ↗ *kîmâ* Jb 38_{31}, **bands** of the Pleiades; — 2. 1S 15_{32}, adv. acc. w. *hālak*: 'in fetters,' oth.: 'trembling,' or 'cheerful, calm.' †

מַעְדֵּר: **hoe** Is 7_{25}. †

*מָעָה: pl. sf. מְעֹתָיו: **grain** (of sand) Is 48_{19}. †

*מֵעֶה: du. cs. מְעֵי, sf. מֵעָיו, מֵעֶיךָ, מֵעַי, מֵעֵיהֶם (*mē-*!): — 1. **bowels, entrails, intestines** 2S 20_{10}; — 2. **(trunk of) body, belly** as seat of origin of man Gn 15_4; Jon 2_{1f} (of fish); — 3. **inner parts** (as seat of feelings & excitement) Is 16_{11}; — 4. **belly, abdomen** (fm. exterior) SS 5_{14}.

מָעוֹג: ? **supply, provision** 1K 17_{12}; — Ps 35_{16} sugg. rd. *lōʿagê meʿuwwāg* mockers of a cripple. †

מָעוֹז: cs. = (!) Is 30_2 Dn 11_7, sf. מָעֻזִּי, מָעֻזְּךָ, מָעוּזּוֹ & מָעֻזָּהּ, מָעֻזְּכֶם; pl. מָעֻזִּים, cs. מָעֻזֵּי: — 1. **mountain stronghold, place of refuge** Ju 6_{26}, more genl. **fortress** Dn 11_7, pleon. *mibṣerê māʿuzzîm* strong fortresses 11_{39}; spec.: *hammiqdāš hammāʿôz* fortress sanctuary = temple Dn 11_{31}; *ʾelōhê maʿuzzîm* god of fortresses; spec. fortresses: *māʿôz miṣrayim* Ez 30_{15} &c.; — 2. God as *māʿôz* Je 16_{19}; *māʿôz ḥayyay* defense of my life Ps 27_1.

*מָעוֹזֶן: מָעֻזְנֶיהָ Is 23_{11} pl. sf., **refuge**, but perh. contamination of *māʿôz* & *māʿôn*. †

מָעוֹךְ: n. pers.

I מָעוֹן: **help** Ps 90_1. †

II מָעוֹן: cs. מְעוֹן, sf. מְעוֹנוֹ, מְעוֹנְךָ: — 1. **hidden den, lair**, of lions Na 2_{12}, jackals Je 9_{10}; — 2. **dwelling, habitation**, spec. of God Dt 26_{15}.

III מָעוֹן: n. pers. 1C 2_{45} & n. loc. 1S 25_2 &c.

מְעוֹנָה: ↗ מְעֹנָה.

מְעוּנִים: n. of tribe.

מְעוֹנֹתַי: n. pers.

[מָעוּף Is 8_{22}: rd מֵעִיף, √ עוף.]

*מָעוֹר: pl. sf. מְעוֹרֵיהֶם: coll. pl. **sexual organs, nakedness** Hb 2_{15}. †

מַעַזְיָה: n. pers.

מַעַזְיָהוּ: n. pers.

מעט: **qal**: impf. יִמְעַט, יִמְעָט, יִמְעֲטוּ, תִּמְעָטוּ; inf. מְעֹט: — 1. **be few** Lv 25_{16} Is 21_{17}; **become few** Je 29_6 30_{19} Ps 107_{39}, **diminish** Pr 13_{11}; — 2. **be too small** w. *min* & inf. Ex 12_4, **appear trifling** Ne 9_{32}. †

piel: pf. מִעֲטוּ: **become few** (of teeth) Ec 12_3. †

hif.: pf. הִמְעִיטָה, הִמְעַטְתִּים; impf. יַמְעִיט, תַּמְעִיטוּ, תַּמְעִיטֵנִי; pt. מַמְעִיט: — 1. **gather little, few** Ex 16_{17f} Nu 11_{32}, take away (= deduct) few Nu 35_8; use few (vessels) 2K 4_3, give less Ex 30_{15}; — 2. **diminish, reduce**:

make the number few (of people) Lv 26_{22}, (of cattle) Ps 107_{38}; obj. price Lv 25_{16}, inheritance Nu 26_{54} 33_{54}; — 3. (by decrease) **destroy** (people &c.) Je 10_{24} Ez 29_{15}. †

מְעַט (100×): מְעָט Ez 11_{16} & 5× מְעָט; pl. מְעַטִּים: — 1. subst. abs. **a little** Gn 30_{30}, pred. adj. **few** Nu 13_{18}; *meʿaṭ bemispār* **a few** Ez 5_3; — 2. w. gen. **a little, a few**: *meʿaṭ ṣorî* a little balm Gn 43_{11}, *meʿaṭ haṣṣō'n* a few sheep 1S 17_{28}; — 3. placed after the noun: a) after cs., *metê meʿaṭ* a few people Dt 26_5; b) as appos.: *'anāšîm meʿaṭ* Ne 12_{12}; — 4. adj.: *hammeʿaṭ* the smallest, poorest of all peoples Dt 7_7; *debārîm meʿaṭṭîm* few words Ec 5_1; — 5. adv.: a) (serve Baal) **a little** 2K 10_{18}; *ʿôd meʿaṭ* a little more, **almost** Ex 17_4; b) temporal: for a short time Jb 24_{24}; *ʿôd meʿaṭ* soon Ho 1_4, *meʿaṭ meʿaṭ* by and by Ex 23_{30}; — 6. w. prep.: a) *kimʿaṭ* nearly, almost: *kimʿaṭ šākab 'aḥad* ... someone almost lay = might have lain Gn 26_{10}; pleon. after *lûlê* Is 1_9; easily, quickly (anger kindles) Ps 2_{12}; soon Ps 81_{15}; (when they were) first (in the land) Ps 105_{12} (oth.: few in number); *kimʿaṭ regaʿ* a short moment Is 26_{20}; *kimʿaṭ še* scarcely SS 5_4; b) *limʿaṭ* too few 2C 29_{34}; — 7. **too little** Gn 30_{15} 2S 12_8, w. *mikkem* for you Nu 16_9, *meʿaṭ lānû* not yet enough for us Jos 22_{17}, *hamʿaṭ* was it not enough? Ez 16_{20}.

מְעֻטָּה Ez 21_{20}: usu. cj. מְרֻטָּה as 21_{15}, or understand √ *ʿṭh*, 'drawn' (of sword). †

***מַעֲטֶה**: cs. מַעֲטֵה: **wrapper, mantle,** metaph. Is 61_3. †

***מַעֲטֶפֶת**: pl. מַעֲטָפוֹת: **outer garment** Is 3_{22}. †

[מְעִי Is 17_1: dittgr.? or < לְעִי ?. †]

מַעַי: n. pers.

מְעִיל: sf. מְעִ(י)לוֹ; pl. sf. מְעִילֵיהֶם; (sleeveless) **robe**: — 1. secular use 1S 15_{27}; w. *qāraʿ* tear Jb 1_{20}; — 2. cultic use 1S 2_{19}; garb of high priest Ex 28_4.

***מֵעִים**: ↗ *מֵעֶה.

מַעְיָן: cs. מַעְיַן & מַעְיְנוֹ Ps 114_8, sf. מַעְיָנוֹ; pl. מַעְיָנִים, cs. מַעְיְנֵי, sf. מַעְיָנַי, & pl. מַעְיָנוֹת, cs. מַעְיְנוֹת, sf. מַעְיְנֹתֶיךָ: (place of) **spring** (of water) 1K 18_5; *maʿyenôt tehôm* Gn 7_{11} 8_2; metaph. *maʿyenê hayšûʿâ* Is 12_3, of sexual life Pr 5_{16}.

מעך: **qal**: pt. pass. מָעוּךְ, מְעוּכָה: — 1. cj. Ez 23_{21} inf. לְמְעֹךְ **press, squeeze** (breasts); — 2. (bull, ram w.) **crushed** (testicles) Lv 22_{24}; — 3. **thrust in** (spear, in ground) 2S 26_7. †

pual: pf. מֹעֲכוּ: **be felt, pressed, squeezed** Ez 23_3.

I **מַעֲכָה**, מַעֲכָת Jos 13_{13}: n. terr. 2S $10_{6.8}$ 1C $19_{6.7}$. †

II **מַעֲכָה**: n. pers. m. & f.

מַעֲכָת Jos 13_{13b}: ↗ I מַעֲכָה.

מַעֲכָתִי: gent. of I & II מַעֲכָה.

מָעַל: **qal**: pf. מ׳, מָעֲלָה, מָעַלְתָּ, מְעַלְתֶּם, מָעָלְנוּ; impf. תִּמְעֹל, יִמְעַל Lv 5_{15} Nu 5_{27}, תִּמְעֲלוּ, תִּמְעָלוּ; inf. מְעֹל, לִמְעָל־, מַעֲלָם Ez 20_{27}, abs. מָעוֹל: **act counter to one's duty, be unfaithful**: a) against (*be*) God Lv 5_{15}; b) against husband Nu 5_{12}; **lay hold of, seize banned goods** (goods under the *ḥērem*) Jos 7_1; abs. Ez 18_{24}.

I **מַעַל**: מָעַל, sf. מַעֲלוֹ, מַעְלוֹ 2C 33_{19}, מַעֲלָם (but also inf. sf.!): — 1. **undutifulness, unfaithfulness** (alw. against God) Jos 22_{16}; w. *māʿal* Lv 5_{15}; — 2. **deceit** † Jb 21_{34}.

II **מַעַל**: מָעַל, (loc.) מַעְלָה, מָעְלָה: adv. **above**: — 1. *mimmaʿal*, from above > **above**: a) *baššāmayim mimmaʿal* Ex 20_4, *'elōah mimmaʿal* Jb 3_4; b) *mimmaʿal le* as prep., **above** (him) Is 6_2, **on the top of** Gn 22_9, = *mimmaʿal ʿal* 1K 7_3, *mimmaʿal mille-* 1K 7_{20}; — 2. *maʿlâ/māʿlâ*, **(to) above** > **above**: a) *maʿlâ māʿlâ* higher & higher Dt 28_{43}; *miššikmô wāmaʿlâ* (from his shoulder) and upward 1S 9_2; temporal, *min-hayyôm hahû' wāmāʿlâ* and afterward 1S 16_{13}; b) *lᵉmaʿlâ* (to) above Ex 25_{20}; *ʿad-lᵉmaʿlâ* (illness) was quite severe 2C 16_{12}, *lᵉmaʿlâ min* over and above 1C 29_{3}; c) *milmaʿlâ/milmāʿlâ* down from above Jos 3_{13} > above Gn 6_{16}; *ʿal* ... *milmaʿlâ* on top of Ex 25_{21}, above upon (them) 1K 7_{25}.

מֵעַל: F עַל (+ מִן).

מֹעַל: being lifted, **lifting** (of hands) Ne 8_{6}. †

*מַעֲלֶה: cs. מַעֲלֵה, sf. מַעֲלוֹ Kt, Qr ־לָיו Ez $40_{31\cdot34\cdot37}$: — 1. (path of) **ascent, way up, steep path**: a) w. sf. ascent to it Ez 40_{31}; w. gen. *maʿᵃlēh hāʿîr* 1S 9_{11}; b) in names of loc., w. gen., ascent, pass, e.g. *maʿᵃlēh ʾᵃdummîm* Jos 15_{7}; — 2. tech. archit. term: a) **platform, podium** Ne 9_{4}; b) **a level, story** 2C 32_{33}.

מַעֲלָה: pl. abs. & cs. מַעֲל(וֹ)ת, sf. מַעֲלֹתוֹ, מַעֲלֹתֵהוּ Ez 43_{17}; — 1. (event of) ascent, **return home** (from Babylon) Ezr 7_{9}; b) pl. festival caravans (to Jerus.): *šîr hammaʿᵃlôt* (*lamm-*) Ps 120_{1} 121_{1}; — 2. **step, stair**: of altar Ex 20_{26}, throne 1K 10_{19f}; *maʿᵃlôt ʾāḥāz* 2K $20_{9\text{-}11}$ Is 38_{8} a kind of sun-dial; — 3. metaph. *maʿᵃlôt rûḥᵃkem* rising thoughts Ez 11_{5}.

מַעְלָה, מָעְלָה: F II מַעַל 2.

*מַעֲלִיל Zc 1_{4} Kt: F *מַעֲלָל.

*מַעֲלָל: pl. מַעֲלָלִים, cs. מַעַלְלֵי, sf. מַעֲלָלָיו, מַעֲלָלֶיךָ, מַעַלְלֵיכֶם, מַעַלְלֵינוּ (so also Zc 1_{4} Qr): (good or bad) **deed** (of man) Dt 28_{20}.

מַעֲמָד: cs. מַעֲמַד, sf. מַעֲמָדְךָ, מַעֲמָדָם: — 1. **attendance** (of servants at table), waiting (on table) 1K 10_{5} 2C 9_{4}; — 2. **station, post** Is 22_{19} 1C 23_{28} 2C 35_{15}. †

מָעֳמָד: **firm ground** Ps 69_{3}. †

מַעֲמָסָה: lifting heavy weights (in competition): *ʾeben maʿᵃmāsâ* **heavy stone** (for competitive weight-lifting) Zc 12_{3}. †

*מַעֲמַקִּים: cs. מַעֲמַקֵּי: **depth** Is 51_{10} Ez 27_{34} Ps $69_{3\cdot15}$ 130_{1}. †

מַעַן (270×): alw. w. לְ: sf. לְמַעֲנִי, לְמַעַנְךָ, לְמַעַנְכֶם: — 1. prep.: **with regard to, for the sake of, because of**: *lᵉmaʿᵃnî* (God) 2K 19_{34}, *lᵉmaʿan zōʾt* on that account 1K 11_{39}; — 2. conj. a) w. inf., **(in order) to,** *lᵉmaʿan haṣṣîl* in order to save Gn 37_{22}; w. same subj. Ex 10_{1}, w. different subj. 11_{9}; b) w. impf., **in order that, so that**: *lᵉmaʿan ʾᵃšer* Gn 18_{19} > *lᵉmaʿan* alone Gn 12_{13}; sometimes used to express not purpose but result Je 27_{15}, oft. w. irony Ho 8_{4}.

I מַעֲנֶה: cs. מַעֲנֵה: **answer** Mi 3_{7} Pr $15_{1\cdot23}$ 16_{1} Jb $32_{3\cdot5}$. †

II *מַעֲנֶה: sf. מַעֲנֵהוּ: **purpose** Pr 16_{4}. †

מַעֲנָה: **plow-path, furrow(-length)** 1S 14_{14} (txt.?) Ps 129_{3}. †

מְעֹנָה: sf. מְעֹ(וֹ)נָתוֹ; pl. מְעוֹנוֹת, cs. מְעֹנוֹת, sf. מְעֹנֹתֶיהָ, מְעוֹנֹתֵינוּ: **hidden den, lair** (for lions) Am 3_{4}; (for oth. animals) Jb 37_{8}; (for Y.) Ps 76_{3}.

*מַעֲנִית Ps 129_{3} Qr: F מַעֲנָה.

מַעַץ: n. pers.

מַעֲצֵבָה: **place of torment** Is 50_{11}. †

מַעֲצָד: a wood-working tool, sugg. (curved) **bill-hook** (for pruning); oth.: adze Is 44_{12} Je 10_{3}. †

מַעְצוֹר 1S 14_{6} & מַעְצָר Pr 25_{28}: **hindrance** 1S 14_{6}; *lᵉrûḥô* self-control Pr 25_{28}. †

מַעֲקֶה: **parapet** Dt 22_{8}. †

מַעֲקַשִּׁים: **uneven terrain** Is 42_{16}. †

מַעַר: sf. מַעְרֵךְ: **nakedness** Na 3_{5}; 1K 7_{36} *maʿar ʾîš* unexpl., F comm. †

I *מַעֲרָב: sf. מַעֲרָבֵךְ; pl. sf. מַעֲרָבַיִךְ: **goods for exchange, for barter** Ez 27_{13}; w. cogn. vb. carry on exchange of goods, barter Ez 27_{9}.

II מַעֲרָב: cs. מַעֲרַב, loc. מַעֲרָבָה: **sunset, west** Is 43_{5}; loc. westward 1C 26_{30}, w. *lᵉ* to the west side of 2C 32_{30}.

מַעֲרָבָה Is 45_{6}: rd. מַעֲרָבָה (II מַעֲרָב).

*מַעֲרֶה: cs. in מִמַּעֲרֵה־גָבַע Ju 20_{33}: ? nakedness, clearing; ? rd מִמַּעֲרַב־הַגֶּבַע westward from G. †

I מְעָרָה: cs. מְעָרַת; pl. abs. & cs. מְעָרוֹת: **cave** Gn 19_{30}.

II מְעָרָה: pl. מְעָרוֹת: **bare field** Is 32_{14}. †

*מַעֲרָךְ: pl. cs. מַעַרְכֵי לֵב: **consideration** Pr 16_1. †

מַעֲרָכָה: pl. cs. מַעַרְכ(ו)ת: **row** (of lamps) Ex 39_{37}, Ju 6_{26} (stones) *bammaʿarākâ* in the usual order (oth.: w. the same layer of stones); — 2. tech. military term: **battle-line** 1S 4_2, of God 1S 17_{26}.

מַעֲרֶכֶת: מַעֲרֶכֶת; pl. מַעֲרָכוֹת: **layer(ing), layer-bread** (trad.: 'show-bread'): *leḥem hammaʿarākôt* Ne 10_{34}; *maʿareket leḥem* 2C 13_{11}; *maʿareket tāmîd* daily layering (of bread) 2C 2_3, *šulḥan hammaʿareket* 2C 29_{18}.

*מַעֲרֹם: pl. sf. מַעֲרֻמֵּיהֶם: nakedness > **naked person** 2C 28_{15}. †

cj. *מַעֲרָץ for *מַעֲרָץ Is 8_{13}: rd מַעֲרִצְכֶם for ־רִצ־; **terror.** †

מַעֲרָצָה: **terrifying power** Is 10_{33}, but perh. rd. F מַעֲצָד. †

מַעֲרָת: n. loc.

מַעֲשֶׂה (220×): cs. מַעֲשֵׂה (מְעָשֵׂי sg.? Ps 138_8), sf. מַעֲשֵׂהוּ, מַעֲשֶׂךָ, מַעֲשֶׂיךָ Ps 66_3, מַעֲשֵׂנוּ; pl. מַעֲשִׂים, cs. מַעֲשֵׂי, sf. מַעֲשָׂיו, מַעֲשַׂי, מַעֲשֵׂיכֶם: — 1. a) **doing, s.thg done** Gn 44_{15}; *maʿaśēh ʾiššâ zônâ* Ez 16_{30}; b) befalling, **what happens to** (righteous or wicked) Ec 8_{14}; — 2. **work** (as activity) Gn 5_{29}; pl. work (of var. people) Ex 5_4, agricultural labor Ex 23_{16}; *yemê hammaʿaśeh* working-days (:: sabbath) Ez 46_1; product or yield of one's work Is 65_{22}; of spec. workers & craftsmen, e.g. *maʿaśēh ḥōšēb* weaver's work Ex 26_1; — 3. **work** (as an object), **product** (of a technique) Is 59_6, *maʿaśēh yādayim* Hg 2_{17}; *maʿaśēh ʾōfeh* baked goods Gn 40_{17}; *maʿaśēh ṣaʿaṣuʿîm* cast-work, work of cast metal 2C 3_{10}; *kelî maʿaśeh* things wrought in metal Nu 31_{51}; *kemaʿaśēhû* of the same workmanship Ex 28_8; (manner of) construction 1K $7_{8.28}$; (*mirqaḥat*) *maʿaśeh* (mixture of ointments) according to the rule, recipe 2C 16_{14}; *maʿaśeh miqšeh* hair artificially set or curled Is 3_{24}; — 4. works & deeds of God Ex 34_{10} & oft., *maʿaśēh yādāyw* Is 5_{12}; = creation Ps 8_7, = Isr. Is 60_{21}, = Assyria 19_{25}; God does *maʿaśēnû* for us Is 26_{12}; — 5. *maʿaśēh yādayim* = idol Je 25_{6f}; *maʿaśēh taʿtuʿîm* work of giddiness = idol Je 10_{15}; — 6. var.: *ʿāśâ maʿaśeh ʿim* behave toward s.one, treat s.one (in a given way) Gn 20_9; *maʿaśēh ʿabōdat* … what there is to do for service in … 1C 23_{28}; *maʿaśēh tiqpô* demonstration of his power Est 10_2; *maʿaśēh hāʿôlâ* what pertains to the *ʿôlâ* 2C 4_6; *maʿaśēhû* his manner of dealing Ju 13_{12}, his business, occupation 1S 25_2.

מַעֲשַׂי: n. pers.

מַעֲשֵׂיָה: n. pers.

מַעֲשֵׂיָהוּ: n. pers.

מַעֲשֵׂר: cs. מַעְשַׂר, Ne 10_{39} מַעֲשַׂר, sf. מַעְשְׂרוֹ; pl. מַעְשְׂרוֹת, sf. מַעְשְׂרֹתֵיכֶם: — 1. **one-tenth** (in measures) Ez 45_{11}; — 2. **tithe** (as offering) Gn 14_{20}; *šenat hammaʿaśēr* year in which tithe is given Dt 26_{12}.

מַעֲשַׁקּוֹת: coll. **extortion** Is 33_{15} Pr 28_{16}. †

מֹף: n. loc. **Memphis** Ho 9_6. †

מְפִבֹשֶׁת: F מְפִיבֹשֶׁת.

מִפְגָּע: **target** Jb 7_{20}. †

מַפָּח: **exhaling** (of soul) = deep affliction Jb 11_{20}. †

מַפֻּחַ: **bellows** Je 6_{29}. †

מְפִ(י)בֹשֶׁת: n. pers., deformed fm. F מְרִי־בַעַל.

מֻפִּים: n. pers.

[מֵפִיץ Pr 25_{18}; F מַפֵּץ hammer.]

מַפָּל: cs. מַפַּל; pl. cs. מַפְּלֵי: — 1. **waste, sweepings** (of grain) Am 8_6; — 2. *mappelê bāśār* **fleshy belly** or dewlaps (of crocodile) Jb 41_{15}. †

*מִפְלָאוֹת: cs. מִפְלְאוֹת: **marvelous work** Jb 37_{16}. †

*מִפְלַגָּה: pl. מִפְלַגּוֹת: division, **family-grouping** (of laymen) 2C 35_{12}. †

מַפָּלָה: — 1. heap of rubble Is 17_1; — 2. ruin Is 23_{13} 25_2. †

מִפְלָט: place of refuge Ps 55_9. †

מִפְלֶצֶת: sf. מִפְלַצְתָּהּ: 1K 15_{13} 2C 15_{16} *mifleṣet laʾᵃšērâ*: horror > **disgraceful image**. †

*מִפְלָשׂ: pl. cs. מִפְלְשֵׂי: (?) **floating, hovering** (of cloud) Jb 37_{16}. †

מַפֶּלֶת: sf. מַפַּלְתּוֹ: — 1. s.thg fallen, **carcass** (of lion) Ju 14_9; — 2. **felled trunk** (of tree) Ez 31_{13}; — 3. **fall, collapse** Ez $26_{15\cdot18}$ 27_{27} 31_{16} 32_{10} Pr 29_{16}. †

*מִפְעָל: pl. cs. מִפְעֲלוֹת, sf. מִפְעָלָיו: **work, deed** (of God) Ps 46_9 66_5 Pr 8_{22}. †

מֵפַעַת: n. loc., ☞ מֵיפַעַת.

*מַפָּץ: sf. מַפָּצוֹ: **wrecking**: *kelî mappāṣô* wrecking tool Ez 9_2. †

מַפֵּץ: **war-club** Je 51_{20}. †

מִפְקָד: cs. מִפְקַד: — 1. **regulation** (by the king) 2C 31_{13}; — 2. **counting, mustering** (w. *hāʿām*) 2S 24_9 1C 21_5; — 3. n. loc.? Ne 3_{31} Ez 43_{21}. †

*מִפְרָץ: pl. sf. מִפְרָצָיו: **inlet, landing-place** (for boats) Ju 5_{17}. †

*מַפְרֶקֶת: sf. מַפְרַקְתּוֹ: **neck** 1S 4_{18}. †

*מִפְרָשׂ: sf. מִפְרָשֵׂךְ; pl. cs. מִפְרְשֵׂי: **spreading**, of sails Ez 27_7, of clouds Jb 36_{29}. †

מִפְשָׂעָה: place of covering, **posterior area** 1C 19_4. †

*מִפְתָּח: cs. מִפְתַּח: **opening** (of lips) Pr 8_6 1C 9_{27}. †

מַפְתֵּחַ: cs. = Is 22_{22}: **key** Ju 3_{25}, as badge of office, worn on shoulder Is 22_{22}. †

מִפְתָּן: cs. מִפְתַּן: **threshold** 1S 5_{4f} Ez 9_3 $10_{4\cdot18}$ 46_2 47_1 Zp 1_9. †

[מֵץ: Is 16_4 הַמֵּץ: rd. חָמוּץ]

מֹץ: **chaff** Is 17_{13}.

מָצָא: qal (320×): pf. מ׳, מָצְאָה, מָצָאתָ, מָצָאנוּ, מְצָאתֶם, מָצָתִי, מָצָאת, וּמָצָאתָ/וּמָצָאתָ, sf. מְצָאוֹ, מְצָאַתְנוּ, מְצָאֻתְנוּ, מְצָאתָהּ, מְצָאתַם, מְצָאתַנִי, מְצָאתִיהוּ, מְצָאתִים (2. f.), מְצָאֻהוּ, מְצָאנֻהוּ; impf. יִמְצָא, תִּמְצְאִי, יִמְצְאוּ, sf. תִּמְצָאֵךְ, תִּמְצָאֶךָּ, יִמְצָאֻהוּ, יִמְצָאֻנְנִי, יִמְצָאוּנְהָ; impv. מְצָא־, מִצְאוּ, מְצֶאןָ; inf. מְצ(וֹ)א, לִמְצֹא־ Pr 19_8, מֹצַאֲכֶם Gn 32_{20}; pt. מוֹצֵא, מוֹצֵא Ec 7_{26}, מ(וֹ)צֵאת, מוֹצְאֵת SS 8_{10}, מֹצְאִים, מֹצְאֵי, מֹצְאוֹת, sf. מֹצְאִי, מֹצְאֵיהֶם: — 1. **reach**: subj. s.one's hand, w. acc. pers. 1S 23_{17}, w. *le* Is 10_{10}, w. *ʿad* Jb 11_7; **suffice for** (s.one) Nu 11_{22}; — 2. **meet by chance, happen to meet** Gn 4_{14}, hit (by chance) Dt 19_5, find = come upon Gn 11_2, find (by chance), happen to find 2K 22_8, *hammôṣeʾôt ʾōtām* wh. had happened to them Jos 2_{23}; *timṣāʾ yād* what presents itself to (one) 1S 10_7; — 3. **find** (s.thg for wh. one is looking) Gn 2_{20}, seek out 1S 31_3, look & find 1S 20_{21}, catch (s.one doing s.thg) Je 2_{34}; w. *be* find (anythg. of s.one) 2K 9_{35}, find God Dt 4_{29}, solve (riddle) Ju 14_{18}, discover (guilt) Gn 44_{16}; *māṣāʾ dābār* find a word = an answer Ne 5_8; *māṣāʾ ḥāzôn* get a vision La 2_9; *māṣāʾ libbô lô* find courage to 2S 7_{27}; *māṣāʾ ḥēn* (☞ *ḥēn* 2); discover Jb 33_{10}; — 4. **obtain**: obj. harvest Gn 26_{12}, booty Nu 31_{50}; *māṣeʾû yedêhem* know how to use their hands Ps 76_6.

nif. (135×): pf. נִמְצָא, נִמְצֵאת, נִמְצֵאתִי, נִמְצְאוּ, נִמְצָאוּ; impf. יִמָּצֵא, תִּמָּצְאִי, יִמָּצְאוּ(ן), תִּמָּצֶאינָה (as if *lamed-hê*!); inf. הִמָּצֵא, הִמָּצְאוֹ; pt. נִמְצָא, נִמְצָאָה, נִמְצְאִים (12×), נִמְצָאִים (1×), נִמְצָאוֹת, נִמְצָאַיִךְ: — 1. **be found** (both full pass., and = **be**) Gn 18_{29}; = be discovered to be ... Dn 1_{19}, be discovered to be so Est 2_{23}; be established, gained Pr 16_{31}; — 2. **be caught, detected** (as a thief &c.) Ex 22_1; — 3. **be found incidentally, by chance, happen to be found** Dt 21_1; — 4. (of God) **let onesf. be found** Is 55_6; — 5. *nimṣāʾ le* **be enough** for Jos 17_{16}.

hif.: pf. הִמְצִיאוּ, הִמְצִיתִךָ; impf. וַיַּמְצִאוּ, יַמְצִאֻהוּ, יַמְצִאֶנּוּ; pt. מַמְצִיא: — 1. **present** s.thg Lv $9_{12f\cdot18}$; — 2. **make** s.thg **befall**

s.one Jb 34_{11}; — 3. make s.one **fall** (into s.one's hand) 2S 3_8 Zc 11_6. †

מַצָּב: cs. מַצַּב, sf. מַצָּבְךָ: — 1. **place (where feet stand)** Jos $4_{3.9}$; — 2. **outpost, sentry-post** 1S 13_{23} $14_{1.4.6.11.15}$; — 3. **station, office** Is 22_{19}. †

מֻצָּב: uncertain military term, trad. 'siege-wall' Is 29_3. †

מַצָּבָה: **outpost, sentry-post** 1S 14_{12}. †

מַצֵּבָה: cs. מַצֶּבֶת & מַצְּבַת, sf. מַצַּבְתָּהּ Is 6_{13}; pl. מַצֵּבוֹת, cs. מַצְּבוֹת, sf. מַצֵּבֹתֶיךָ, מַצֵּבֹתָם & מַצֵּבֹתֵיהֶם: **standing-stone**, usu. an unhewn, upright stone for cult, burial-marking, or memorial purposes: Jacob at Bethel Gn 28_{18}, Canaanite Ex 23_{24}, pl. erected by Moses at altar Ex 24_4, by Ahab for Baal 2K 3_2; in Egypt for Y. Is 19_{19}; Egyp. obelisks Is 43_{13}, forbidden in Isr. Dt 16_{22}; as memorial of covenant betw. Jacob & Laban Gn 31_{45}; at Rachel's grave Gn 35_{20}; 2S 18_{18} ⸢ *maṣṣebet*.

מְצֹבָיָה: הַמְּ' 1C 11_{47}, ? mixed form of 'from צוֹבָא' & הַצֹּבָתִי* gent. fm. צוֹבָא. †

מַצֶּבֶת: = ⸢ מַצֵּבָה: sf. מַצַּבְתָּהּ: — 1. **standing-stone**, "stone of Absalom" 2S 18_{18} as memorial to self; — 2. Is 6_{13}; earlier "root-stock" impossible; either "bare trunk" after burning of branches, or "new growth". †

מְצָד, מְצַד 1C 12_9; pl. abs. & cs. מְצָדוֹת: **stronghold**, place difficult of access (for campers, fugitives, waylayers) 1S 23_{14}.

מְצֻדָה, מְצֹדָה: ⸢ מְצָדָה, מְצוּדָה.

מצה: qal: pf. מָצִית; impf. יִמְצוּ, וַיִּמֶץ: — 1. **squeeze out** (wet hide) Ju 6_{38}; — 2. **drain** (a cup) **dry** (by drinking) Is 51_{17} Ez 23_{34} Ps 75_9. †

nif.: pf. נִמְצָה; impf. יִמָּצֵה: **be pressed out** (blood) Lv 1_{15} 5_9; Ps 73_{10} ⸢ comm. †

מֹצָה: n. loc.

I **מַצָּה**: pl. מַצּ(וֹ)ת: **unleavened bread**: flat loaves of flour & water, baked quickly: — 1. for ordinary meals Gn 19_3; — 2. in Passover ritual Ex 12_{15}; *ḥag hammaṣṣôt* 12_{17}; — 3. in P, **unleavened bread withheld for the priests at the sanctuary** fm. unburned portion of the *minḥâ* Lv 2_{4f}.

II **מַצָּה**: **quarrel, scuffle, brawl** Is 58_4 Pr 13_{10} 17_{19}. †

מֻצְהָב: *neḥōšet muṣhāb* **brass**, or **brightness of gold** Ezr 8_{27}. †

***מִצְהָלוֹת**: cs. מִצְהֲלוֹת, sf. מִצְהֲלוֹתַיִךְ: **neighing** Je 8_{16} 13_{27}. †

I ***מָצוֹד**: sf. מְצוּדוֹ (?) Jb 19_6 (oth. II, ⸢ comm.); pl. מְצוֹדִים: **snare, net** Jb 19_6 (?), Ec 7_{26}. †

II ***מָצוֹד**: cs. מְצוֹד; pl. מְצוֹדִים: **mountain stronghold**, *meṣôd rāʿîm* Pr 12_{12}, but txt.?. †

I **מְצוּדָה**: sf. מְצוּדָתִי: — 1. **hunting-net** Ez 12_{13} 17_{20}; — 2. (huntsman's) **bag** (i.e. game taken) Ez 13_{21}. †

II **מְצוּדָה** & 4× מְצָדָה: cs. מְצֻדַת, sf. מְצֻדָתִי, מְצוּדָתִי; pl. מְצוּדוֹת: **mountain stronghold** 1S 22_4; *meṣudat ṣiyyôn* stronghold of Zion 2S 5_7; metaph.: Y. is *bêt meṣûdôt* Ps 31_3.

מְצוֹדָה: **net** Ec 9_{12}. †

מִצְוָה (180×, Dt 43×): cs. מִצְוַת; pl. מִצְוֹת (מִצְוֹות Ne 9_{14}), sf. מִצְוֹתָיו: **command**, (single) **commandment**, (sum of all) **commandments**; **right or claim**: — 1. given by man: *ṣiwwâ miṣwâ* (subj. Solomon) 1K 2_{43}; *miṣwat ʾanāšîm* precept of men Is 29_{13}; *miṣwat ʾāb* Pr 6_{20}, *miṣwat dāwîd* (concerning cult) Ne 12_{24}; *heʿemîd ʿālāyw miṣwôt* accept obligations for onesf. Ne 10_{33}; — 2. given by God (so alw. Gn-Dt): a) pl. Gn 26_5; b) sg. 1K 13_{21}.

מְצֹלָה, מְצוֹלָה, מְצוּלָה: pl. מְצֹ(וּ)ל(וֹ)ת, מְצֹלֹת, מְצוּלֹת: — 1. sg.: **deep, depths** (of sea) Jon 2_4; — 2. pl.: **depth(s)** (of Nile) Ex 15_5, (of sea) Mi 7_{19}.

מָצוֹק: **hardship** Dt 28_{53}; *ʾîš māṣôq* in distressful situation 1S 22_2.

*מָצוֹק or *מָצוּק: pl. cs. מְצֻקֵי: *mᵉṣuqê ʼereṣ* 1S 2_8 **pillar**. †

מְצוּקָה: pl. sf. מְצוּקוֹתַי, מְצוּקוֹתֵיהֶם: **affliction** Zp 1_{15}.

I מָצוֹר: cs. מְצוֹר, מְצוּרֵךְ: — 1. **affliction** Dt 28_{53}; — 2. **siege**: *bôʼ bammāṣôr* be besieged 2K 24_{10}; *yāšab bᵉmāṣôr* calmly let onesf. be besieged 2C 32_{10}; *bānâ māṣôr ʻal* build siege-works against Dt 20_{20}; *nātan (śîm) māṣôr ʻal* inflict siege on Ez 4_2 Mi 4_{14}; *hāyâ bammāṣôr* be under siege Ez 4_3; *mê māṣôr* water (supply) for a siege Na 3_{14}.

II מָצוֹר: **fortification, fortified city** Ps 60_{11} (= Petra), 2C 8_5 11_5. †

III מָצוֹר: n. terr. = מִצְרַיִם **Egypt** Mi 7_{12a}; *yᵉʼōrê māṣôr* 2K 19_{24} = Is 37_{25}, Is 19_6. †

מְצוּרָה & מְצֻרָה: pl. מְצֻרֹת, מְצוּרוֹת: **fortification**; *ʻārê mᵉṣûrâ/ôt* fortified cities 2C 11_{10} 14_5; > *mᵉṣurôt* 2C 11_{11}; *mᵉṣurōt* Is 29_3 siege-mound.

*מַצּוּת: sf מַצֻּתֶךָ: **strife**, *ʼanšê-maṣṣutekā* your adversaries Is 41_{12}. †

מֵצַח: sf. מִצְחוֹ, מִצְחֵךְ, מִצְחֲךָ; pl. cs. מִצְחוֹת: **forehead** 1S 17_{49}; brow (of prostitute) Je 3_3.

*מִצְחָה: cs. מִצְחַת: front > **greaves** 1S 17_6. †

*מְצִלָּה: pl. מְצִלּוֹת: (small) **bell** (on horses) Zc 14_{20}. †

מְצִלְתַּיִם: (pair of) **cymbals** Ezr 3_{10}.

מִצְנֶפֶת: **headband** like a turban: of king Ez 21_{31}, high-priest Ex 28_4.

מַצָּע: **couch** Is 28_{20}. †

*מִצְעָד: pl. cs. מִצְעֲדֵי, sf. מִצְעָדָיו: — 1. **step** (of a man) Ps 37_{23} Pr 20_{24}; — 2. **track**: *bᵉmiṣʻādāyw* in his train Dn 11_{43}. †

מִצְעָר: cs. מִצְעַר: **small quantity**: — 1. as pred.: **modest** (in number, size) Gn 19_{20} Jb 8_7; — 2. w. gen. **few** 2C 24_{24}; — 3. in n. terr. (?) *har miṣʻār* Ps 42_7. †

I מִצְפֶּה: **watch-tower, observation-post** 2C 20_{24}. †

II מִצְפֶּה: = I: cs. מִצְפֵּה: favorite n. loc., both alone & in comb., e.g. *miṣpēh môʼāb* 1S 22_3.

מִצְפָּה: n. loc. = I מִצְפֶּה; loc. מִצְפָּתָה.

*מַצְפּוֹן: pl. sf. מַצְפֻּנָיו: hidden treasures, or hiding-places Ob $_6$. †

מצץ: **qal**: impf. תָּמֹצּוּ: **quaff** Is 66_{11}. †

מֻצָק Jb 11_{15}: ↗ יצק **hof.**; מֻצָק־ 1K 7_{16}: ↗ מוּצָק.

מֵצַר: pl. מְצָרִים: **hardship, distress** Ps 118_5, pl. La 1_3. †

מִצְרִי: gent. of מִצְרַיִם: — 1. an **Egyptian** Gn 39_5; — 2. adj. **Egyptian** Gn 39_{1f}.

מִצְרַיִם (680×): n. peop. & terr.: **Egypt**: — 1. land Gn 10_6; spec. lower Egypt Is 11_{11}; — 2. **the Egyptians** (vb. either sg. f. or pl.) Gn 45_2; — 3. perh. confusion w. Muṣri in Asia Minor † 1K 10_{28} 2K 7_6 2C 1_{16f} ↗ comm.

מַצְרֵף: **crucible** Pr 17_3 27_{21}. †

*מַצַּת: ↗ *מַצּוּת.

מַק, מֶק: **musty smell, smell of decay** Is 3_{24} 5_{24}. †

מַקֶּבֶת: pl. מַקָּבוֹת—1. **excavation**, *maqqebet bôr* mouth of cistern Is 51_1 (oth.: quarry); — 2. > instrument for driving nail or peg, (small work-) **hammer** (opp. blacksmith's hammer or war-club) 1 K 6_7.

מַקֵּדָה: n. loc.

מִקְדָּשׁ, מִקְּדָשׁ Ex 15_{17}: cs. מִקְדַּשׁ, sf. מִקְדָּשׁוֹ, מִקְדָּשֵׁנוּ; pl. מִקְדָּשִׁים, cs. מִקְדְּשֵׁי, sf. מִקְדָּשֶׁיךָ, מִקְדְּשֵׁיכֶם: — 1. holy place or abode, **sanctuary** (favorite word in Lv [P] & Ez): in Moab Is 16_{12}; *miqdaš melek*, in Bethel Am 7_{13}, *miqdᵉšê yiśrāʼēl* 7_9; *hammiqdāš* = tabernacle Ex 25_8; = temple in Jerus. Ez 45_3; confined to curtain & altar Lv 21_{23}, to most holy place 16_{33}; = holy vessels, furnishings &c. Nu 10_{21}; pl. including var. structures of temple Je 51_{51}, total holy precinct Ex 25_8; — 2. spec.: holy tribute Nu 18_{29}; ? Palestine as God's land Ex 15_{17}.

*מַקְהֵל: pl. מַקְהֵלִים & מַקְהֵלוֹת: **assembly** Ps 26_{12} 68_{27}. †

מַקְהֵלֹות: n. loc. Nu 33_{25f}. †

מִקְוֵא 2C 1_{16}: rd מִקְוֵא, ↗ cj. קְוֵא, קְוֵה.

I **מִקְוֶה**: cs. מִקְוֵה: **hope** Ezr 10_2; 1C 29_{15} confidence, security; Je 14_8 17_{13} (I, or ? to II). †

II **מִקְוֶה**: cs. מִקְוֵה: **accumulation**, of water Gn 1_{10} Ex 7_{19} Lv 11_{36}; 1K 10_{28} ↗ cj. קְוֵה, קְוֵא.

מִקְוָה: **reservoir** Is 22_{11}. †

מָקוֹם (ca. 400×): cs. מְקוֹם, sf. מְקֹ(ו)מוֹ; pl. מְקֹ(ו)מֹ(ו)ת, m. (1S 19_{13} Qr f.): — 1. **stand** (of statue) 1S 5_3, *meqôm haššebet* seat (of throne) 1K 10_{19}; source (of jewels) Jb 28_6; — 2. **place, location** (unspecified): a) in one place Gn 1_9, *bekol-hammāqôm* in every place (where ...) Ex 20_{24}, *bekol-māqôm* everywhere Am 8_3; b) w. rel. clause: *māqôm ʾašer ... (šāmmâ)* (to) where Ex 21_{13}, usu. *meqôm ʾašer* Gn 39_{20} = *bimqôm ʾašer* Lv 4_{24} = *bimqôm še* Ec 1_7; *bimqôm ʾašer* instead of (saying) Ho 2_1; *meqôm lōʾ yādaʿ ʾel* place of him who ... Jb 18_{21}; — 3. **place, location** (specified): a) *māqôm* of wicked Ps 37_{10}, *māqôm lāšebet* living-place, -space 2K 6_1, *laḥanôt* camping-place Dt 1_{33}; b) at table 1S 20_{25}, *nātan, śîm māqôm* designate a place 1S 9_{22} 1K 8_{21}; — 4. **space**: a) *laʿabōr* (for the animal) to pass Ne 2_{14}, *māqôm bên* 1S 26_{13}; b) **region, area** Ju 18_{10}; *meqôm miqneh* region for cattle-breeding Nu 32_1; — 5. inhabited area, **town, site**: Gn 18_{24}; *ʾanšê hammāqôm* 26_7, *šēm hammāqôm* 22_{14}; w. sf. Gn 18_{33}; — 6. **holy place**: *meqômî* said by God Ho 5_{15}; *hammāqôm hazzeh* = Jerus. 1K 8_{30}; *meqôm šekem* Gn 12_6; *hammāqôm* the (holy) place Gn 22_{3f}, pagan Dt 12_2; *mimmaqôm ʾaḥēr* Est 4_{14} = from God.

מָקוֹר: sf. מְקֹ(ו)רוֹ, מְקֹרָהּ: **spring, fountain, source**: — 1. lit. Ho 13_5; of Euphrates Je 51_{36}, eschatological Zc 13_1; — 2. metaph.: a) fountain of tears Je 8_{23}, of life Ps 36_{10}; Y. is fountain of living water Je 2_{13}; = wife Pr 5_{18}; b) of menstrual blood Lv 20_{18}, of blood in childbirth Lv 12_7.

***מִקָּח**: cs. מִקַּח: **accepting** (of bribes) 2C 19_7. †

מַקָּחוֹת: **wares** Ne 10_{32}. †

***מִקְטָר**: cs. מִקְטַר: *mizbēaḥ miqṭar qeṭōret*: **burning** (incense), phr. incense-altar Ex 30_1. †

מֻקְטָר: **incense** Mal 1_{11}. †

* **מְקַטֶּרֶת** or *־טְּרָה: pl. מְקַטְּרוֹת: **incense-altar** 2C 30_{14}. †

מִקְטֶרֶת: sf. מִקְטַרְתּוֹ: (metal) **incense-burner** (as censer) Ez 8_{11} 2C 29_{19}. †

מַקֵּל: cs = Ez 39_9, מַקַּל Gn 30_{37}; sf. מַקְלוֹ, מַקְלִי, מַקֶּלְכֶם; pl. מַקְלוֹת: m. Je 48_{17} (*bāhen* Gn 30_{37} neuter): — 1. **shoot, twig** Gn 30_{37ff}, switch (in hand of rider) Nu 22_{27}; — 2. **staff** (of foot-traveler) Gn 32_{11}, (of shepherd) 1S 17_{40}; symb. Zc 11_{7ff}; for oracles Ho 4_{12}.

מִקְלוֹת: n. pers.

מִקְלָט: cs. מִקְלַט, sf. מִקְלָטוֹ: **refuge, asylum** Nu 35_6.

***מִקְלַעַת**: cs. =; pl. מִקְלָעוֹת, cs. מִקְלְעוֹת: **wood-carving** 1K $6_{18\cdot29\cdot32}$ 7_{31}. †

מִקְנֶה (75×): cs. מִקְנֵה, sf. מִקְנְךָ, מִקְנֵהוּ, מִקְנֵנוּ, sg. also מִקְנֶיךָ, מִקְנַי, מִקְנֵיהֶם, מִקְנֵיכֶם: **gain, possessions**: — 1. **landed property**, *miqnēh haśśādeh* Gn 49_{32}; — 2. usu. = **livestock, cattle** (which one owns): *miqnēh ṣōʾn ûmiqnēh bāqār* Gn 26_{14}, *miqnēh behēmâ* 47_{18}, > *miqneh* 4_{20}; :: *rekûš* ('goods')31_{18}; *ʾoholê miqneh*, tents w. all herds of cattle 2C 14_{14}; *ʾanšê miqneh* cattle-breeders Gn 46_{32}, *rōʿê miqneh* herdsmen 13_7, *śārê miqneh* overseers of cattle 47_6; *miqnêkem ûbehemtekem* beasts for slaughter & beasts of burden 2K 3_{17}.

מִקְנָה: cs. מִקְנַת, sf. מִקְנָתוֹ: **acquisition** (by purchase): *śedēh miqnâ* a field wh. has been bought Lv 27_{22}, *miqnat kesef* (slave who is) bought w. your money Gn 17_{12f}; *kesef* *miqnâ* purchase-price Lv 25_{51}, > *miqnâ* 25_{16}; *sēfer miqnâ* bill/deed of sale Je 32_{11f}; *qûm l^{e}miqnâ l^e*, be made over by purchase to Gn 23_{17f}.

מִקְנֵיָהוּ: n. pers.

***מִקְסָם**: cs. מִקְסַם: **(bestowal of an) oracle** Ez 12_{24} 13_7. †

מָקָץ: n. loc.

מִקְצֹ(וֹ)עַ: pl. cs. מִקְצוֹעֵי & pl. f. מִקְצֹעוֹת, sf. מִקְצְעוֹתָם: — 1. **corner**: of altar Ex 26_{24}, of court Ez 46_{21}; — 2. n. of places in Jerus. † Ne $3_{19f.24f}$ 2C 26_9.

***מַקְצֻעָה**: pl. מַקְצֻעוֹת: (wood-)**carving-knife** Is 44_{13}. †

מִקְצָת Dn $1_{2.5.15.18}$ Ne 7_7 ↗ קְצָת.

מקק: **nif.**: pf. נָמַקּוּ, נְמַקֹּתֶם; impf. יִמַּקּוּ, יִמַּקּוּ, תִּמַּקְנָה; pt. נְמַקִּים: — 1. **putrefy, rot**: wounds Ps 38_6, eyes & tongue Zc 14_{12}; — 2. metaph. **dwindle away** (cj. hills) Is 34_4, **waste away** (men) Lv 26_{39} Ez 4_{17} 24_{23} 33_{10}. **hif.**: inf. הָמֵק: **make** (s.thg) **rot** Zc 14_{12}. †

מָקֹר: ↗ מָקוֹר.

מִקְרָא: pl. cs. מִקְרָאֵי, sf. מִקְרָאֶהָ Is 4_5: — 1. a) **convocation** † Nu 10_2; b) **assembly** Ex 12_{16}; — 2. **reading (aloud)** † Ne 8_8.

מִקְרֶה: cs. מִקְרֵה, sf. מִקְרֶהָ (sg.): what happens by itself w/o any assistance or wish of person involved, w/o any known originator: — 1. **happening, occurrence** 1S 6_9; *wayyiqer miqrehā* her chance met = she happened to come upon Ru 2_3; *miqreh hû'* it is an accident (i.e. an involuntary pollution?) 1S 20_{26}; — 2. **fate, fortune** Ec 2_{14f} 3_{19} 9_{2f}. †

מְקָרֶה: **roof-beams** Ec 10_{18}. †

מְקֵרָה: **cooling**; in gen. phr., > **cool**: *ʿ^{a}liyyat hamm^{e}qērâ* Ju 3_{20} & *ḥ^{a}dar hamm^{e}qērâ* 3_{24} cool chamber. †

מֹקֵשׁ: ↗ מוֹקֵשׁ.

מִקְשֶׁה: **well-set hair, "hair-do"** Is 3_{24}. †

I **מִקְשָׁה**: **hammered** (or **embossed**) (metal-) **work** Ex 25_{18}.

II **מִקְשָׁה**: **cucumber-field** Is 1_8 Je 10_5. †

I **מַר**: מָר, f. מָרָה & Ru 1_{20} מָרָא, cs. מָרַת; pl. מָרִים, cs. מָרֵי: — 1. **bitter** (in taste): water Ex 15_{23}; *mê hammārîm* bitter-water (mng. ?) Nu 5_{18f} (oth.: dispute-water); — 2. **bitter** (as experience): a) death 1S 15_{32}, cry Gn 27_{34} &c.; b) adv. **bitterly**: *bākâ mar* Is 33_7; — 3. **bitter** (as a feeling): a) attributive, *nefeš mārâ* w. gloomy heart Jb 21_{25}; b) w. gen.: *mārê nefeš* provoked 2S 17_8, embittered 1S 1_{10}, > *mar* Ez 3_{14}; furious (people) Hb 1_6; — 4. *mar*, noun, **bitterness**: a) *mar lî* Is 38_{17}; b) w. gen.: *mar nefeš* Ez 27_{31}, *mar nafšî* Is 38_{15}.

II **מַר**: **drop** Is 40_{15}. †

מֹר (6×) & מוֹר (4×): cs. מָר־ Ex 30_{23}: **myrrh**, resin of *Commiphora abessinica* Ex 30_{23}; note: *har hammōr* SS 4_6 erotic ref.

I **מרא**: **qal**: pt. f. מֹרְאָה Zp 3_1: trad. = √מרה 'obstinate'; oth.: hof. pt. (denom.) from (post-bibl. Heb.) *r$^{o'}$î* 'dung,' i.e. 'befouled'. †

II **מרא**: **hif.**: impf. תַּמְרִיא Jb 39_{18}, of ostrich, uncert., sugg. drive the air w. wings, spring aloft, ↗ comm. †

cj. III **מרא**: cj. **qal**: impf. יִמְרְאוּ (for וּמְרִיא) Is 11_6: **fatten** (intrans.), **graze**. †

מָרָא Ru 1_{20}: ↗ I מַר.

מַרְאֶה: cs. מַרְאֵה, sf. מַרְאֵהוּ, מַרְאֶהָ, מַרְאַיִךְ (SS 2_{14b} Qr מַרְאֵךְ), מַרְאָיו, מַרְאֵינוּ (all sg.): — 1. **seeing**: *neḥmād l^{e}mar'eh* lovely to look at Gn 2_9; *l^{e}kol-mar'ēh ʿênê hakkōhēn* to everything wh. the eyes of the priest could see Lv 13_{12}; *gādôl l^{e}mar'eh* visible from far off Jos 22_{10}; — 2. **appearance**: w. *y^{e}fēh, y^{e}fat* Gn 39_6 12_{11}, w. *ṭōbat* 24_{16}, w. *raʿ* 41_{21}; b) of s.thg: *mar'ēh hannegaʿ* appearance of the spot (on skin) Lv 13_3; of person (in health) Dn 1_{13}; c) appearance of a person (what he looks like) 1S 16_7; *lō' mar'eh* poor-looking, insignificant Is 53_2; total appearance, stature SS 5_{15}; — 3. **vision, ap-**

parition Ex 3_{8}; — 4. **shining, light**: of fire Nu 9_{15f}, of lightning Dn 10_{6}.

מַרְאָה: pl. cs. מַרְא(וֹ)ת: — 1. **vision, apparition** 1S 3_{15} (of revelation of word!); pl. w. *laylâ* Gn 46_{2}; — 2. **mirror** Ex 38_{8}.

*מֻרְאָה: sf. מֻרְאָתוֹ: **crop** (of a bird) Lv 1_{16}. †

מְרֹאן: n. loc.

מָרֵאשָׁה Jos 15_{44}, otherw. מָרֵשָׁה: n. loc.

*מְרַאֲשׁוֹת or מְרָאֲ׳: sf. מְרַאֲשֹׁתָיו: what is at the head, **head-rest** Gn $28_{11.18}$; acc. of place **at the head of** 1S $19_{13.16}$ $26_{7.11f.16}$ 1K 9_{6}. †

מֵרַב: n. pers. f.

*מַרְבַד (*b* w/o *dageš*): pl. מַרְבַדִּים: **covering** Pr 7_{16} 31_{22}. †

[מִרְבָּה Ez 23_{32}: rd מַרְבָּה (√רבה hif. pt.).]

מַרְבֶּה: — 1. Is 33_{23} *šālāl marbeh*: usu. as noun 'increase, abundance,' but syntax?; hif. pt. √*rbh*, attributive, 'numerous' (?); or rd. pual pt.?; — 2. Is 9_{6} Qr *lᵉmarbeh* 'for the increase,' but rd *lm* dittgr., *rbh* = *rabbâ*. †

מַרְבִּית: sf. מַרְבִּיתָם: — 1. **great portion, majority, multitude** 1C 12_{30} 2C 9_{6} 30_{18}; — 2. **increase**: a) (increase of) **interest** (?) Lv 25_{37}; b) *marbît bayit* next generation 1S 2_{33}. †

מַרְבֵּץ & *מַרְבָּץ Ez 25_{5}: cs. מַרְבַּץ: **fold** (for sheep) Ez 25_{5}, **lair** (for wild animals) Zp 2_{15}. †

מַרְבֵּק: **fattening**: *ʿēgel marbēq* fatted bull-calf 1S 28_{24} Je 46_{21} Am 6_{4} Ma 3_{20}. †

מַרְגּוֹעַ: **resting-place** (for *nefeš*) Je 6_{16}. †

*מַרְגְּלוֹת: sf. מַרְגְּלֹתָיו: **(place of) feet** Ru $3_{4.7f.14}$ Dn 10_{6}. †

מַרְגֵּמָה: Pr 26_{8} *kiṣrôr ʾeben bᵉmargēmâ*: usu. 'like binding a stone to a sling' or 'like a jewel on a stone-heap,' but better 'like wrapping a stone at a stoning,' i.e. to avoid injury. †

מַרְגֵּעָה: **resting-place** Is 28_{12}. †

מָרַד: **qal**: pf. מָרַד, מָ׳, מָרְדוּ, מָרַדְנוּ; impf. יִמְרֹד־, תִּמְרָד־, תִּמְרְדוּ; inf. מְר(וֹ)ד, מָרְדְכֶם; pt. מֹרְדִים, מוֹרְדֵי: **revolt, rebel**: — 1. politically Gn 14_{4}, w. *bᵉ* against 2K 18_{7}, w. *ʿal* Ne 2_{19}; — 2. against Y. Jb 24_{13}, w. *bᵉ* Nu 14_{9}.

I מֶרֶד: **rebellion** *bᵉyhwh* Jos 22_{22}. †

II מֶרֶד, מָרֶד: n. pers. 1C 4_{17f}. †

מַרְדּוּת: **rebellion** 1S 20_{30}. †

מְרֹדָךְ: **Marduk**, god of Babylon Je 50_{2}. †

מְרֹדַךְ־בַּלְאֲדָן Is 39_{1}, בְּרֹאדַךְ־ 2K 20_{12}: n. pers. king of Babylon. †

מָרְדֳּכַי, מָרְדְּכַי: n. pers.

מֻרְדָּף: **persecution** Is 14_{6}. †

מָרָה: **qal**: pf. מָ׳, מָרְתָה, מָרִיתָ, מָרוּ, מָרִינוּ; inf. abs. מָרֹה; pt. מ(וֹ)רֶה, מֹרִים: **be refractory, obstinate** Nu 20_{10}; w. *bᵉ* against Ho 14_{1}, w. *ʾēt* against Je 4_{17}; w. *ʾet-pî* against the command of 1K $13_{21.26}$.

hif.: pf. הִמְרוּ; impf. יַמְרֶה, וַתֶּמֶר, תַּמְרוּ, יַמְרוּהוּ; inf. לַמְרוֹת (< *לְהַמְ׳), הַמְּרוֹתָם; pt. מַמְרִים: **behave refractorily, obstinately** Jb 17_{2}, w. *bᵉ* Ez 20_{8}, w. *ʿim* over against Dt 9_{7}, w. acc. against Ez 5_{6}, w. *ʾet-pî* against the command of 1S 12_{14}.

I מָרָה: ↗ I מַר 2 b.

II מָרָה: loc. מָרָתָה: n. loc. Ex 15_{23} Nu 33_{8}. †

*מָרָה: cs. מֹרַת & מָרַּת: **bitterness, affliction**: w. *rûᵃḥ* Gn 26_{35}, *nefeš* Pr 14_{10}. †

מֹרֶה Dt 11_{30}: ↗ מוֹרֶה.

cj. מַרְהֵבָה Is 14_{4} for מַדְהֵבָה: **attack, assault**. †

*מָרוּד or *מָרוֹד: sf. מְרוּדִי; pl. מְרוּדִים, sf. מְרוּדֶיהָ: — 1. **homelessness** La 3_{19} sg., 1_{7} pl.; — 2. concrete: pl. (those who are) **homeless** Is 58_{7}. †

מֵרוֹז: n. loc.

*מָרוֹחַ: cs. מְרוֹחַ: **pounded, ground**: *mᵉrôᵃḥ ʾešek* s.one w. damaged testicles Lv 21_{20}. †

מָרוֹם: cs. מְרוֹם; pl. מְר(וֹ)מִים, cs. מְר(וֹ)מֵי, sf. מְרוֹמָיו: **height** (i.e. place on high): — 1. **elevation of ground** 2K 19_{23}, *rōʾš mᵉrômîm* Pr 8_{2}; — 2. highly placed location, **place on high** Is 22_{16}; = exalted Je 17_{12}; — 3. up-

ward (adv. acc.) 2K 19_{22}; — 4. **high social position** Jb 5_{11}; — 5. moral: *mimmārôm* from a high position, loftily Ps 73_8; — 6. *mārôm* = heaven: a) windows of heaven Is 24_{18}, host of h. 24_{21}; b) home of God (sg. & pl.) Is 33_5; c) to heaven *lammārôm* Is 38_{14}, from heaven *mimmārôm* 2S 22_{17}.

מֵרוֹם: n. loc.

מֵרוֹץ: **running** Ec 9_{11}. †

I ***מְרוּצָה**: cs. מְרוּצַת, מְרֻצַת, sf. מְרוּצָתָם Je 8_6 Qr (Kt ־צוֹתָם): **manner of running** 2S 18_{27}, **running** Je 8_6 23_{10}. †

II **מְרוּצָה**: **extortion** Je 22_{17}. †

***מְרוּקִים**: sf. מְרוּקֵיהֶם: **cosmetic treatment** w. massage & ointments Est 2_{12}. †

***מְרוֹרָה**: F *מְרֹרָה.

מָרוֹת: n. loc.

***מַרְזֵחַ**: cs. מַרְזַח: **cultic feast** Am 6_7, **funeral meal** Je 16_5. †

מרח: qal: impf. יִמְרְחוּ: **spread** (cake of figs) **out** (on a boil) Is 38_{21}. †

מֶרְחָב: pl. cs. מֶרְחֲבֵי: **wideness**: — 1. **wideness, extent**: *lᵉmerḥᵃbê ʾereṣ* out across the world Hb 1_6, *kᵉkebeś bammerḥāb* like a lamb in broad (pastures) Ho 4_{16}; — 2. metaph. = **open space, at large** 2S 22_{20} Ps 18_{20} 31_9 118_5. †

מֶרְחָק: pl. מֶרְחַקִּים & Je 8_{19} מַרְחַקִּים, cs. מֶרְחַקֵּי: **distance**: *ʾereṣ merḥāq* distant land Is 13_5 = *ʾereṣ hammerḥāq* Je 4_{16} & *ʾereṣ marḥaqqîm* 8_{19}; *merḥaqqê ʾereṣ* ends of the earth Is 8_9; *bamerḥaqqîm* in the distance Zc 10_9; *bêt hammerḥāq* the farthest, last house 2S 15_{17}.

מַרְחֶשֶׁת: **baking- or frying-pan** w. lid Lv 2_7 7_9. †

מרט: qal: impf. אֶמְרְטֵם, אֶמְרְטָה; inf. מָרְטָה; pt. מֹרְטִים, pass. מְרוּטָה: — 1. **pull out** (hair) Ezr 9_3 Ne 13_{25}; — 2. **burnish** (sword) Ez $21_{14 \cdot 16 \cdot 33}$; — 3. pt. pass.: (shoulder) **rubbed bare, chafed** Ez 29_{18}. †

nif.: impf. יִמָּרֵט: **become, grow bald** Lv 13_{40f}. †

pual (or qal pass.): pf. מֹרָטָה; pt. מְמוֹרָט 1K 7_{45} > מוֹרָט Is $18_{2 \cdot 7}$: — 1. **be burnished**: bronze 1K 7_{45}, sword Ez 21_{15f}; — 2. **be smooth, bare** (skin) Is $18_{2 \cdot 7}$. †

מְרִי: מֶרִי, sf. מֶרְיְךָ: — 1. **obstinacy** 1S 15_{23}; *bᵉnê merî* Nu 17_{25}, *bêt mᵉrî* Ez 2_{5f}; — 2. **obstinate** † Ez 2_8 Pr 17_{11}.

מְרִיא: pl. מְרִיאִים, cs. מְרִיאֵי, sf. מְרִיאֵיכֶם: **fattened cattle** (i.e. cattle raised for meat) 1K 1_9.

***מְרִיב**: cs. in מְרִיב בַּעַל "antagonist of Baal" as n. pers., perh. reconceived fm. F מְרִי־בַּעַל. †

I **מְרִיבָה**: cs. מְרִיבַת: **strife** Gn 13_8 Nu 27_{14}. †

II **מְרִיבָה**: n. loc.

מְרִי־בַעַל: n. pers.

מְרָיָה: n. pers.

מֹרִיָּה: n. terr. הַמֹּרִיָּה.

מְרָיוֹת: n. pers.

מִרְיָם: n. pers. f.

מְרִירוּת: **bitterness, affliction**: *bimrîrût* (sigh) bitterly Ez 21_{11}. †

מְרִירִי: **bitter** Dt 32_{24}. †

מֹרֶךְ: **despondency** Lv 26_{36}. †

מֶרְכָּב: sf. מֶרְכָּבוֹ: — 1. **saddle-seat** Lv 15_9; seat (of sedan-chair) SS 3_{10}; — 2. **war-chariot park** 1K 5_6. †

מֶרְכָּבָה: cs. מִרְכֶּבֶת, sf. מֶרְכַּבְתּוֹ; pl. מַרְכָּבוֹת, cs. מַרְכְּב(וֹ)ת, sf. מַרְכְּב(וֹ)תָיו, מַרְכְּבֹתֵיהֶם: two-wheeled vehicle, chariot: — 1. **war-chariot** 1K 10_{29}; — 2. **chariot of state** Gn 41_{43}; — 3. **chariot (for travel)** Gn 46_{29}; — 4. mythological Is 66_{15}; — 5. cultic: *markᵉbôt haššemeš* 2K 23_{11}.

***מַרְכֹּלֶת**: sf. מַרְכֻּלְתֵּךְ: **merchandizing** Ez 27_{24}. †

I **מִרְמָה**: pl. מִרְמוֹת: — 1. **fraud, deceit** Gn 27_{35}; *mōʾzᵉnê mirmâ* false balances Ho 12_8, *ʾabnê mirmâ* false weights Mi 6_{11}; *lᵉmirmâ* deceitfully Ps 24_4; **betrayal** 2K 9_{23}; pl. deceit Ps 10_7; — 2. **disappointment** † Pr $14_{8 \cdot 25}$.

II מִרְמָה: n. pers. 1C 8_{10}. †

מְרֵמוֹת: n. pers.

מִרְמָס: cs. מִרְמַס: **trampling, trampled land**: *mirmas raglêkem* what your feet have trampled Ez 34_{19}; *hāyâ lᵉmirmās* Is 5_5.

מֵרֹנֹתִי: gent. of *מֵרֹנֹת, n. loc.

מֶרֶס: n. pers.

מַרְסְנָא: n. pers.

*מֶרַע: מֶרַע: **evil, atrocity** Dn 11_{27}. †

I מֵרַע: sf. מֵרֵעֵהוּ (4×) & מְרֵעֵהוּ Pr 19_7, מֵרֵעֶךָ; pl. מֵרֵעִים: **intimate, close friend**: a) spec. at wedding Ju 14_{20} $15_{2.6}$; b) otherw. (pl.) Gn 26_{24} Ju 14_{11} 2S 3_8 Jb 6_{14} Pr 19_7. †

II *מֵרַע: ℱ I רעע hif. pt.

מִרְעֶה: cs. מִרְעֵה, sf. מִרְעֵהוּ, מִרְעֵיכֶם (sg.): **pasture** Gn 47_4.

מַרְעִית: sf. מַרְעִיתוֹ: **pasturage, grazing place** Is 49_9.

מַרְעֲלָה: n. loc.

I מַרְפֵּא & מַרְפֵּה Je 8_{15}: — 1. **healing** Je 33_6; — 2. **remedy** Pr 29_1 (but distinction fm. 1. uncert.)

II מַרְפֵּא: cs. =: — 1. **composure** Ec 10_4; *lēb marpē'* a calm heart Pr 14_{30}; — 2. **gentleness**, *marpē' lāšôn* a gentle tongue Pr 15_4. †

מַרְפֵּה Je 8_{15}: ℱ I מַרְפֵּא.

*מִרְפָּשׂ: cs. מִרְפַּשׂ: **pool muddied by trampling** Ez 34_{19}. †

מרץ: **nif.**: pf. נִמְרְצוּ; pt. נִמְרֶצֶת, נִמְרָץ: **be hurtful, painful**: subj. curse 1K 2_8 pernicious; subj. destruction Mi 2_{10}; ? Jb 6_{25} sickened? sickening? txt.? ℱ comm. †

hif.: impf. יַמְרִיצְךָ: **provoke, irritate** Jb 16_3. †

מְרָצוֹתָם Je 8_6: ℱ מְרוּצָה.

מַרְצֵעַ: **awl** Ex 21_6 Dt 15_{17}. †

מַרְצֶפֶת: **stone-pavement, -layer** 2K 16_{17} *marṣefet 'ᵃbānîm*. †

מרק: **qal**: impv. מִרְקוּ; pt. pass. מָרוּק: **polish** Je 46_4 2C 4_{16}. †

pual (or qal pass.): pf. מֹרַק: **be scoured** Lv 6_{21}. †

hif.: impf. Pr 20_{30} Qr תַּמְרִיק (Kt תַּמְרוּק noun): **cleanse**. †

מָרָק (ă): **broth** Ju 6_{19f} Is 65_4 Qr, cj Ez 24_{10}. †

*מֶרְקָח: pl. מֶרְקָחִים: **aromatic herbs** SS 5_{13}. †

מֶרְקָחָה: **ointment jar** Jb 41_{23}. †

מִרְקַחַת: **mixture of ointments** Ex 30_{25} 1C 9_{30} 2C 16_{14}. †

מרר: **qal**: pf. מַר (ℱ adj.!), מָרָ֫ה, מָר; impf. יֵמַר: — 1. **be bitter** (subj. drink) Is 24_9; — 2. **be despairing** (subj. *nefeš*) 1S 30_6 2K 4_{27}; — 3. *mar*: impers. it is bitter Je 4_{18}; *mar lî*: I am distressed Ru 1_{13}. †

piel: impf. אֲמָרֵר, יְמָרְרוּ, יְמָרֲרֻהוּ: **make bitter**: obj. life Ex 1_{14}; provoke s.one Gn 49_{23}; w. *babbekî* weep bitterly Is 22_4. †

hif.: pf. הֵמַר; impf. תַּמֵּר Ex 23_{21}; inf. הָמֵר: — 1. prepare bitterness, **afflict, trouble** Jb 27_2 Ru 1_{20}; w. *lᵉ* **embitter** Ps 106_{33}; — 2. w. *'al* weep bitterly over Zc 12_{10}. †

hitpalpel: impf. יִתְמַרְמַר: **become furious** Dn 8_7 11_{11}. †

מָרֹר & מָרוֹר: pl. מְרֹ(ו)רִים, מְרֹ(ו)רֹ(ו)ת: **bitter**: — 1. **bitter** (grapes) Dt 32_{32}; — 2. pl. *mᵉrôrîm* bitter herbs Ex 12_8 Nu 9_{11}; — 3. **bitter drink** La 3_{15}; *mᵉrōrôt* bitter experiences (? medicinal or forensic) Jb 13_{26}. †

*מְרֵרָה: sf. מְרֵרָתִי: **gall-bladder** Jb 16_{13}. †

*מְרֹרָה: cs. מְרוֹרַת, sf. מְרֹרָתוֹ: — 1. **gall-bladder** Jb 20_{25}; — 2. fluid of 1.: **poison** Jb 20_{14}. †

מְרָרִי: n. pers.

I מָרֵשָׁה: n. loc. Mi 1_{15} + 5×: ℱ מָרֵאשָׁה.

II מָרֵשָׁה: n. pers. 1C 2_{42}. †

מִרְשַׁעַת: (model of) **ungodliness**: 2C 24_7 the temptress. †

מֹרַשְׁתִּי Mi 1_1: ℱ מוֹרַשְׁתִּי.

מְרָתַיִם: "double insolence," abusive name for Babylon Je 50_{21}. †

I מַשָּׂא: sf. מַשָּׂאוֹ, מַשַּׂאֲכֶם: — 1. carrying: *le'ên maśśā'* so that it was impossible to carry away 2C 20_{25}, *'ên lakem maśśā'* you have nothing to carry 35_3; — 2. **burden** (of ass, mule, &c.) 2K 5_{17}; *bemaśśā'/bamm-* had charge of transport 1C $15_{22 \cdot 27}$ (oth.: of setting the pitch [in singing]); — 3. **burden** = **hardship** Nu 11_{11}, *hāyâ lemaśśā' 'al* be(come) a burden on s.one 2S 15_{33}; *maśśā' nafšām* longing of their soul Ez 24_{25}; — 4. play on mng. of II 'pronouncement' Je 23_{33-38}.

II מַשָּׂא: **pronouncement**: *nāśā' maśśā' 'al* 2K 9_{25}; *ḥāzâ maśśā'* Is 13_1; *maśśā' debar yhwh* Zc 9_1; *maśśā' 'al* 2C 24_{27}, *maśśā' mô'āb* pronouncement about M. Is 15_1; Je 23_{33-38} ↗ I.

III מַשָּׂא: n. (pers. &) peop. Gn 25_{14} 1C 1_{30}; Pr 31_1; 30_1 ?. †

מַשֹּׂא: *maśśō' pānîm* **partiality** 2C 19_7. †

מַשָּׂאָה: **lifting up** (of heavy clouds) Is 30_{27}. †

מַשְׂאוֹת: — 1. Ez 17_9 ? fm. ctxt. 'pulling up' (tree by roots); — 2. La 2_{14} ↗ II *maśśā'* 'pronouncement'; — 3. *maś'ôt* Gn 43_{34} & *maś'ôtêkem* Ez 20_{40} ↗ *maś'ēt* 2. 'share'. †

מַשְׂאֵת: cs. מַשְׂאַת; pl. מַשְׂאוֹת, sf. מַשְׂאוֹתֵיכֶם: — 1. **lifting up**: a) w. *kappay* lifting of hands in prayer Ps 141_2; b) *maś'at he'ānān* rising cloud of smoke Ju $20_{38 \cdot 40}$, fire-signal Je 6_1; — 2. **tax, offering** 2S 11_8; *nātan maś'ēt* grant gifts (of wheat) Est 2_{18}; *maś'at mōšeh* offering commanded by M. 2C $24_{6 \cdot 9}$; portion of honor Gn 43_{34}.

מִשְׂגָּב: cs. מִשְׂגַּב, sf. מִשְׂגַּבּוֹ: — 1. **high spot** as a refuge: rocks Is 33_{16}, walls 25_{12}; — 2. metaph. God as a **refuge** 2S 22_3.

מַשֶּׂגֶת: **overtaking**, *lemaśśeget* 1C 21_{12}; Lv 14_{21} ↗ √ *nśg* hif. †

*מְשׂוּכָה: sf. מְשׂוּכָּתוֹ: **hedge (of thorns)** Is 5_5. †

מַשּׂוֹר: **saw** Is 10_{15}. †

מְשׂוּרָה: **measure of** (liquid) **capacity** Lv 19_{35} 1C 23_{29}; *bimśûrâ* measured out Ez $4_{11 \cdot 16}$. †

I מָשׂוֹשׂ: cs. מְשׂוֹשׂ, sf. מְשׂוֹשִׂי: **joy** Is 24_8.

II *מָשׂוֹשׂ: cs. מְשׂוֹשׂ: **s.thg rotten** Jb 8_{19}; Is 8_6 ↗ √ *mss.* †

מִשְׂחָק: **laughter** Hb 1_{10}. †

מַשְׂטֵמָה: **(result of) enmity** Ho 9_{7f}. †

*מְשֻׂכָה, cs. מְשֻׂכַת Pr 15_{19} = מְשׂוּכָה & מְסוּכָה **hedge (of thorns)**. †

מַשְׂכִּיל: unclarified musical term in Ps.; sugg.: cultic-song; passage for learning; wisdom-song put to music; :: *maśkîl* 'with insight,' √ *śkl* hif. pt.

מַשְׂכִּית: sf. מַשְׂכִּ(י)תוֹ; pl. מַשְׂכִּיּוֹת, sf. מַשְׂכִּיֹּתָם: — 1. **image, sculpture** Nu 33_{52}, of silver Pr 25_{11}; *'eben maśkît* stone carved in relief Lv 26_1; *ḥadrê maśkît* image chambers Ez 8_{12}; — 2. metaph. pl., w. *lēbāb* images, imagination Pr 18_{11}. †

מַשְׂכֹּרֶת: **wages** Gn 29_{15} $31_{7 \cdot 41}$ Ru 2_{12}. †

*מַשְׂמֵרָה: pl. cs. מַשְׂמְרוֹת: **nail** (at tip of goad), metaph. Ec 12_{11}, ↗ *מַסְמֵרָה. †

מִשְׂפָּח: **breach of law** Is 5_7. †

מִשְׂרָה: **dominion** Is 9_{5f}. †

*מִשְׂרָפוֹת: cs. מִשְׂרְפוֹת: (complete) **burning**: — 1. a) *miśrefôt śîd* be burned to lime (i.e. completely) Is 33_{12}; b) *kemiśrefôt 'abôtêkā* as w. the burning of spices at burial of king Je 34_5; — 2. *miśrefôt mayim*, 'lime-kilns at the water,' n. loc. Jos 11_8 13_6. †

מַשְׂרֵקָה: n. loc.

מַשְׂרֵת: **baking- or frying-pan** 2S 13_9. †

מַשׁ: n. pers. (tribe?).

מַשָּׁא: — 1. **claim** (for repayment of debt) Ne 5_{10} 10_{32}; — 2. *nāšā' maššā' be* try to make (s.one) one's debtor Ne 5_7 (oth.: impose a burden; or impose a personal pledge). †

מֵשָׁא: n. terr.

*מַשְׁאָב: pl. מַשְׁאַבִּים: **watering-channel** Ju 5_{11}. †

*מַשָּׁאָה or *מַשָּׁאת: cs. מַשַּׁאת; pl. מַשָּׁאוֹת: **secured loan, loan based on security** Dt 24_{10} Pr 22_{26}. †

מְשָׁאָה Jb 30_3 38_{27}: F מְשׁוֹאָה.
מַשָּׁאוֹן: **deception** Pr 26_{26}. †
מַשֻּׁאוֹת: **heap of rubble** Ps 74_3. †
מִשְׁאָל: n. loc.
*מִשְׁאָלָה: pl. cs. מִשְׁאֲלוֹת, sf. מִשְׁאֲלֹתֶיךָ: **desire** Ps 20_6 37_4. †
*מִשְׁאֶרֶת: sf. מִשְׁאַרְתֶּךָ, מִשְׁאַרְתֶּךָ; pl. sf. מִשְׁאֲרוֹתֶיךָ, מִשְׁאֲרֹתָם: **kneading-trough** Ex 7_{28} Dt $28_{5\cdot17}$, **baking-pan** Ex 12_{34}. †
מִשְׁבְּצוֹת: pl. abs. & cs.: — 1. **settings** (of filigree ?) Ex $28_{11\cdot13f\cdot25}$ $39_{6\cdot13\cdot16\cdot18}$; — 2. *mišbᵉṣôt zāhāb* material w. gold thread, brocade Ps 45_{14}. †
מִשְׁבָּה: F מְשׁוּבָה*.
מַשְׁבֵּר: cs. מַשְׁבֵּר: **mouth of the womb** 2K 19_3 Is 37_3 Ho 13_{13}. †
*מִשְׁבָּר: pl. cs. מִשְׁבְּרֵי, sf. מִשְׁבָּרֶיךָ: **breakers** (of seashore) 2S 22_5 Jon 2_4 Ps 42_8 88_8 93_4. †
*מִשְׁבָּת: sf. מִשְׁבַּתֶּהָ: **cessation**, **that one is 'finished'** La 1_7. †
מִשְׁגֶּה: **inadvertent mistake, oversight** Gn 43_{12}. †
משה: **qal**: pf. מְשִׁיתִהוּ: **pull out** (of the water) Ex 2_{10}. †
מֹשֶׁה: n. pers. **Moses.**
*מַשֶּׁה: cs. מַשֵּׁה: **loan** Dt 15_2. †
מְשֹׁאָה, מְשׁוֹאָה: **desert, desolate land** Zp 1_{15} Jb 30_3 38_{27}. †
*מַשּׁוּאָה: pl. מַשּׁוּאוֹת: **deception** Ps 73_{18}. †
מְשׁוֹבָב: n. pers.
*מְשׁוּבָה & מְשֻׁבָה (5×): cs. מְשׁוּבַת, sf. מְשׁוּבָתִי, מְשׁוּבָתָם; pl. sf. מְשֻׁבוֹתַיִךְ, מְשֻׁבוֹתֵיהֶם, מְשׁוּבֹתֵיכֶם, מְשׁוּבֹתֵינוּ: **(act of) faithlessness, defection, apostasy** Je 8_5; pl. Je 2_{19}; > concrete, embodied apostasy, appos. of Isr. Je 3_6.
*מְשׁוּגָה: sf. מְשׁוּגָתִי: **offense** Jb 19_4. †
מָשׁוֹט (& *מִשּׁוֹט ? Ez 27_6): pl. sf. מְשׁוֹטַיִךְ: **oar** Ez $27_{6\cdot29}$. †
מְשׁוּסָּה Is 42_{24}: F Qr מְשִׁסָּה.
מָשַׁח: **qal**: pf. מ׳, וּמָשַׁחְתָּ, וּמְשַׁחְתּוֹ, מְשָׁחוֹ, מְשָׁחֲךָ; impf. יִמְשַׁח, תִּמְשַׁח, וַיִּמְשָׁחֲךָ, יִמְשָׁחֵם, יִמְשָׁחֻהוּ; impv. מָשְׁחֵהוּ, מִשְׁחוּ; inf. מְשֹׁחַ, מָשְׁחָה Ex 29_{29}, מָשְׁחוֹ, לְמָשְׁחֲךָ, מָשׁוֹחַ; pt. מֹשְׁחִים, pass. מָשׁוּחַ, מְשֻׁחִים: — 1. **spread a liquid** (oil, paint) **over**: wafers w. oil Ex 29_2, shield w. oil Is 21_5, house w. paint Je 22_{14}; care of body Am 6_6; — 2. obj. cult objects, **anoint** Gn 31_{13} (pillar), Ex 29_{36} (sacrificial animals); — 3. **anoint a person**: a) to be king 1K 1_{34} (*lᵉmelek*), 1_{39} (abs.); b) to be priest Ex 28_{41}; c) to be prophet 1K 19_{16}; w. *lᵉ* & inf. of his activity Is 61_1.
nif.: pf. נִמְשַׁח; inf. הִמָּשַׁח: **be anointed**: king 1C 14_8, priest Lv 6_{13}, altar Nu $7_{10\cdot84\cdot88}$. †
I מִשְׁחָה: cs. מִשְׁחַת: **anointing**: *šemen hammišḥâ* Ex 25_6.
II *מִשְׁחָה: cs. מִשְׁחַת: **portion** Lv 7_{35}. †
I *מָשְׁחָה: sf. מָשְׁחָתָם: **anointing** Ex 40_{15}. †
II מָשְׁחָה: **portion** Nu 18_{18}. †
מַשְׁחִית: sf. מַשְׁחִיתִי: — 1. **destroyer**: a) military: demolition-detachment 1S 13_{17}; b) demonic 2S 24_{16}; — 2. **destruction**: *lᵉmašḥît* Ez 5_{16}; *baʿal mašḥît* Pr 18_9 & *ʾîš mašḥît* 28_{24} scoundrel; — 3. concrete, **bird-trap** Je 5_{26}; — 4. *har hammašḥît* Je 51_{25} = Babylon; 2K 23_{13} perh. deformation of *har hammišḥâ* 'mountain of anointing.'
מִשְׁחָר: **(light before) dawn** Ps 110_3. †
*מַשְׁחֵת: sf. מַשְׁחֵתוֹ: **annihilation, destruction** Ez 9_1. †
מִשְׁחַת Is 52_{14}: ?; w. *mēʾîš* evid. 'inhumanly disfigured' Is 52_{14}. †
*מָשְׁחַת: sf. מָשְׁחָתָם: **defect** Lv 22_{25}. †
מִשְׁטוֹחַ: cs. מִשְׁטַח: **drying-yard** (for nets) Ez $26_{5\cdot14}$ 47_{10}. †
*מִשְׁטָר: sf. מִשְׁטָרוֹ: **starry sky** Jb 38_{33}. †
מֶשִׁי: trad.: silk; **fine material** (for clothing) Ez $16_{10\cdot13}$. †
מַשִׁי 1C 6_4: F מוּשִׁי.
מְשֵׁיזַבְאֵל: n. pers.
מָשִׁיחַ: cs. מְשִׁיחַ, sf. מְשִׁיחוֹ; pl. sf. מְשִׁיחָי: **anointed one**: — 1. king of Isr. (Saul,

David & his successors) 1S 24_7 Ps 2_2; — 2. Cyrus Is 45_1; — 3. priest Lv 4_3; high priest Dn 9_{26}; — 4. patriarchs Ps 105_{15}; N.B. 'Messiah' as eschatological savior-figure not in O.T.

מָשַׁךְ: **qal**: pf. מ׳, מָשַׁכְתִּי, מְשַׁכְתִּיךָ; impf. תִּמְשֹׁךְ, יִמְשְׁכוּ, אֶמְשְׁכֵם, תִּמְשְׁכֵנִי; impv. מִשְׁכוּ & מָשְׁכוּ Ez 32_{20} (txt. ?), מָשְׁכֵנִי; inf. מְשֹׁךְ, מָשְׁכוֹ; pt. מֹשֵׁךְ, מֹשְׁכִים, מֹשְׁכֵי: — 1. **seize, carry off** Ps 28_3; — 2. **pull, drag** Gn 37_{28}; w. *yād* extend one's hand Ho 7_5; w. *baqqešet,* stretch the bow 1K 22_{34}; w. *baqqeren,* blow the horn Jos 6_5; metaph. obj. *ʿāwōn* Is 5_{18}; — 3. **extend, protract**: keep long, obj. *ḥesed* Je 31_3; w/o *ḥesed*, be patient w. Ne 9_{30}; obj. *ʾaf* Ps 85_6; — 4. intrans. **go off** (+ 2nd vb., 'and take' &c.) Ex 12_{21}; w. *ʾaḥ^{a}rê* follow Jb 31_{33}; — 5. denom., go around w. a seed-pouch; pt. **sower** Am 9_{13}.

nif.: impf. יִמָּשֵׁכוּ, תִּמָּשֵׁךְ: subj. time, **be extended, delayed** Is 13_{22} Ez $12_{25.28}$. †

pual: pt. מְמֻשָּׁךְ, מְמֻשָּׁכָה: — 1. **put off, delayed** (hope) Pr 13_{12}; — 2. **lanky** (race) Is $18_{2.7}$. †

I **מֶשֶׁךְ**: **(leather) pouch, bag,** for seed Ps 126_6; for pearls & metaph. for wisdom Jb 28_{18}. †

II **מֶשֶׁךְ**: n. peop.

מִשְׁכָּב: cs. מִשְׁכַּב, sf. מִשְׁכָּבוֹ, מִשְׁכַּבְכֶם; pl. cs. מִשְׁכְּבֵי, sf. מִשְׁכְּבוֹתָם: — 1. sleeping-place, **couch, bed** 1K 1_{47}; *nāfal l^{e}miškāb* become bedridden Ex 21_{18}; *śîm miškāb* make a bed Is 57_7, *gillâ miškāb* spread (quilts for) bed 57_8; *ḥ^{a}dar miškāb* bedroom 2K 6_{12}; *ʿālâ mišk^{e}bê* climb into s.one's bed Gn 49_4; — 2. **lying,** spec. **act of lying** (sexual): *miškab dôdîm* lovebed Ez 23_{17}; *miškab zākār* lying w. a man Nu 31_{17f}, *mišk^{e}bê ʾiššâ* Lv 18_{22}; — 3. *miškab ṣoh^{o}rayim*, siesta 2S 4_5.

מֹשְׁכוֹת: **chains** (of Orion) Jb 38_{31}. †

מִשְׁכָּן: cs. מִשְׁכַּן, sf. מִשְׁכָּנוֹ; pl. מִשְׁכָּנוֹת, sf. מִשְׁכְּנוֹתָיו, מִשְׁכְּנוֹתֵינוּ: — 1. **dwelling-place, home** Nu 16_{24}; — 2. = tomb Is 22_{16}; — 3. **dwelling-place, home** of Y. Lv 15_{31}; — 4. = (central) sanctuary (74 × out of 130 ×), tabernacle Ex 25_9.

I **מָשַׁל**: **qal**: impf. יִמְשֹׁל, יִמְשְׁלוּ; impv. מְשֹׁל; pt. מֹשֵׁל, מֹשְׁלִים, מֹשְׁלֵי: — 1. **make up, repeat a** *māšāl* (i.e. saying, proverb, parable) Ez 12_{23}; — 2. spec. **use a mocking-verse** Ez 16_{44}; — 3. pt. (mocking) **speaker** Nu 21_{27}.

nif.: pf. נִמְשַׁל, נִמְשַׁלְתִּי: **become like,** w. *k^e* Ps $49_{13.21}$, w. *ʿim* 28_1 143_7, w. *ʾel* Is 14_{10}. †

piel.: pt. מְמַשֵּׁל: w. *māšāl,* **tell a riddle, speak in riddles** Ez 21_5. †

hif.: impf. תַּמְשִׁילוּנִי: w. *l^e* **compare with** Is 46_5. †

hitp.: impf. אֶתְמַשֵּׁל: **become like** s.thg Jb 30_{19}. †

II **מָשַׁל**: **qal**: pf. מ׳, מָשַׁל, מָשְׁלָה; impf. יִמְשֹׁל, יִמְשָׁל־, יִמְשְׁלוּ; impv. מְשָׁל־; inf. לִמְשֹׁל, מְשׁוֹל; pt. מֹ(ו)שֵׁל, מֹשְׁלָה, מֹשְׁלִים, מֹשְׁלֵי, מֹשְׁלוֹ (Qr ־לָיו, Kt ־לוֹ): — 1. **rule, govern**: a) w. *b^e*: subj. heavenly bodies, obj. day & night Gn 1_{18}, husband w. wife 3_{16}; b) abs. 2S 23_3; c) **gain, exercise dominion** over, w. *mōšel* Dn 11_4; d) pt. **ruler, tyrant** Ps 105_{20} (= Pharaoh), pl. Is 14_5; e) metaph.: *mōšēl b^{e}rûḥô* who controls himself Pr 16_{32}; *māšal* be empowered to Ex 21_8; — 2. subj. God Ju 8_{23}.

hif.: pf. הִמְשִׁילָם; impf. תַּמְשִׁילֵהוּ; inf. הַמְשֵׁל: — 1. **make** s.one **lord, master** over (w. *b^e*) Ps 8_7 Dn 11_{39}; — 2. *hamšēl* inf. as subj. **dominion**: *hamšel wāfaḥad* fearful dominion Jb 25_2. †

I **מָשָׁל**: cs. מְשַׁל, sf. מְשָׁלוֹ; pl. מְשָׁלִים, cs. מִשְׁלֵי: — 1. **saying** of any of var. categories, w. *māšal* Ez 12_{23}, w. *nāśāʾ* Nu 23_7 declaim one's saying; — 2. **proverb**: a) *hāyâ l^{e}māšāl* become a proverb, subj. a phrase 1S 10_{12}, subj. Isr. &c. (i.e. Isr. becomes a standard warning to others) 1K 9_{7}; b) make s.one into a *māšāl* (cf. a)), w. *nātan* Je 24_{9}, w. *śîm* Ez 14_{8}; — 3. **wisdom saying** Ez 12_{22}, simile 17_{2}; — 4. **mocking song** Mi 2_{4}; — 5. superscription of a collection, *mišlê šᵉlōmōh* Pr 1_{1}.

[II מָשָׁל 1C 6_{59}: n. loc., rd. מִשְׁאָל.]

I מֹשֶׁל: sf. מָשְׁלוֹ: 1. **similarity**, w. sf. his like Jb 41_{25}. †

II מֹשֶׁל: sf. מָשְׁלוֹ: **dominion** Zc 9_{10} Dn 11_{4}. †

מִשְׁלוֹחַ & מִשְׁלַחַ: cs. =: — 1. **sending** (portions of food as gifts) Est $9_{19.22}$; — 2. *mišlôᵃḥ yādām* upon whom one lays his hand, **sphere of influence** Is 11_{14}. †

*מִשְׁלָח: cs. מִשְׁלַח: — 1. *mišlaḥ yād* where one lays his hand, **undertaking** Dt 15_{10} 23_{21} $28_{8.20}$; gain, profit $12_{7.18}$; — 2. *mišlaḥ šôr* **pasture-land** for cattle Is 7_{25}. †

מִשְׁלַחַת: — 1. *mišlaḥat bammilḥāmâ* **leave** during (or, discharge from ?) military service Ec 8_{8}; — 2. **band, company** Ps 78_{49}. †

מְשֻׁלָּם: n. pers.

מְשִׁלֵּמוֹת: n. pers.

מְשֶׁלֶמְיָה: n. pers.

מְשֶׁלֶמְיָהוּ: n. pers.

מְשִׁלֵּמִית: n. pers.

מְשֻׁלֶּמֶת: n. pers. f.

מִשְׁלֹשׁ: *kᵉmišlōš* Gn 38_{24}, trad. *kᵉ* + *min* + *šᵉlōš(et)*, but better as noun w. *m-*, **period of three** (months). †

מְשַׁמָּה: pl. מְשַׁמּוֹת: — 1. **terror, horror** Ez 5_{15}, *šᵉmāmâ ûmᵉšammâ* 6_{14} 33_{28f} 35_{3}; — 2. *šᵉmammôt* place of horror, **desert, desolation** Is 15_{6} Je 48_{34}. †

*מִשְׁמָן: cs. מִשְׁמַן, pl. cs. מִשְׁמַנֵּי, sf. מִשְׁמַנָּיו, מִשְׁמַנֵּיהֶם: — 1. **fatness, fat** w. *bᵉśārô* Is 17_{4}; — 2. pl. concrete: **portly, distinguished people** Is 10_{16} Ps 78_{31}; — 3. pl. **rich tracts of land** Dn 11_{24}. †

מִשְׁמַנָּה: n. pers. (m. !)

מַשְׁמַנִּים: delicious **festive food** prepared w. much fat Ne 8_{10}. †

I *מִשְׁמָע: cs. מִשְׁמַע: **hearsay, rumor** Is 11_{3}.†

II מִשְׁמָע: n. (pers. &) tribe Gn 25_{14} 1C 1_{30}. †

*מִשְׁמַעַת: sf. מִשְׁמַעְתּוֹ, מִשְׁמַעְתֶּךָ: — 1. **body-guard** 1S 22_{14}; — 2. those obligated to allegiance, **subjects** 2S 23_{23} 1C 11_{25}. †

I מִשְׁמָר: cs. מִשְׁמַר, sf. מִשְׁמַרְכֶם; pl. sf. מִשְׁמָרָיו: — 1. **guard(ing), custody** Gn $40_{3f.7}$; *mikkol-mišmār* more than one is (otherwise) vigilant, w. utmost vigilance Pr 4_{23}; *bêt mišmār* prison Gn 42_{19}; — 2. **guard, sentinel** Ne 4_{3}; *'anšê mišmār* 4_{17}; w. *heḥᵉzîq* set up (or keep) a strong watch Je 51_{12}; *hāyâ lᵉmišmār* be at (s.one's) disposal Ez 38_{7}; — 3. **division, grouping of servants** Ne 12_{24}; pl. servants (at temple) Ne 13_{14} (oth.: arrangements).

II מִשְׁמָר: **muzzle** Jb 7_{12}. †

מִשְׁמֶרֶת: מִשְׁמֶרֶת; sf. מִשְׁמַרְתּוֹ; pl. מִשְׁמָרוֹת, cs. מִשְׁמְרוֹת, sf. מִשְׁמְרוֹתָם, מִשְׁמְרוֹתֵיהֶם: — 1. **what is to be preserved** Nu 18_{8}, *lᵉmišmeret* for storing Ex 16_{23}, *hāyâ lᵉmišmeret* shall be preserved Ex 12_{6}; pers. *mišmeret 'attâ* you are in safe hands 1S 22_{23}; — 2. **guard(ing), custody**: a) *šāmar mišmeret* stand guard 2K 11_{5ff}, offer allegiance 1C 12_{30} (oth.: keep loyal); b) **guard, sentinel** Is 21_{8}; *heʿᵉmîd mišmārôt* station guards Ne 7_{3}, *lᵉmišmārôt* according to the divisions of servants 12_{9}; *bêt mišmeret* detention 2S 20_{3}; — 3. a) **obligation**: *šāmar mišmartî* keep what I am obligated to do Gn 26_{5}, *mišmeret yhwh* one's obligation to Y. 1K 2_{3}; *mišmeret miṣwat yhwh* observance of the commandment of Y. Jos 22_{3}; b) **duty, service** Nu 3_{25}; w. gen. service to Nu 1_{53}; what has to be taken care of Nu 3_{7f}; *mišmeret miśśā'ām* their task of carrying Nu 4_{31f}; pl. divisions of service Ne 13_{30}.

מִשְׁנֶה: cs. מִשְׁנֵה, sf. מִשְׁנֵהוּ; pl. מִשְׁנִים: second, double: — 1. **putting a second in place of** the first: a) *kōhēn (ham)mišneh* 2K 23_4 25_{18}, deputy priest, or priest of 2nd order; *mirkebet hammišneh* second-best chariot Gn 41_{43}; — 2. > **second** Ne 11_9, *hāyâ lᵉmišneh* 1S 23_{17}, in enumeration 1C 5_{12}; *mišnēhû* his second(-born son) 1S 8_2; *mišnēh hammelek* (*lamm-*) 2C 28_7 Est 10_3 second (= 1st !) after the king; *hammišnîm* 2nd order of servants 1C 15_{18}; *hammišnîm* animals of the 2nd dropping (hence of greater value) 1S 15_9; *hammišneh* 2nd (new) area of Jerus. 2K 22_{14}; — 3. s.thg **twofold, double**: *hammišneh* = twice as much Ex 16_5, *mišneh kesef* double the money Gn 43_{15} (appos.); *hôsîf lᵉmišneh* Jb 42_{10}; — 4. **copy**: *mišnēh hattôrâ* Dt 17_{18}.

מְשִׁסָּה: pl. מְשִׁסּוֹת: **plundering** 2K 21_{14}; pl. Hb 2_7.

מִשְׁעוֹל: **narrow path** (cut through high ground) Nu 22_{24}. †

מִשְׁעִי: *lᵉmišʿî lᵉ* Ez 16_4, fm. ctxt. 'for cleansing.' †

מִשְׁעָם: n. pers.

מִשְׁעָן: cs. מִשְׁעַן: **support** (= Y.) 2S 22_{19} Ps 18_{19}; *mišʿan leḥem* Is 3_1 bread-pole (on wh. ring-shaped bread is stacked, cf. Lv 26_{26}); *mišʿan mayim*, // to 1st phr. †

מַשְׁעֵן & **מַשְׁעֵנָה**: **support** (2 words = totality), every support Is 3_1. †

מִשְׁעֶנֶת: sf. מִשְׁעַנְתּוֹ; pl. sf. מִשְׁעֲנֹתָם: **support, staff, stick**: for sick Ex 21_{19}, elderly Zc 8_4, ruler Nu 21_{18}, angel Ju 6_{21}.

מִשְׁפָּחָה (300×): cs. מִשְׁפַּחַת, sf. מִשְׁפַּחְתּוֹ; pl. מִשְׁפָּחוֹת, cs. מִשְׁפְּחוֹת, sf. מִשְׁפְּחֹתָיו, מִשְׁפְּחֹתֵיהֶם: — 1. extended family, **clan** (group in wh. there is a felt blood-relationship) Dt 29_{17}, subdivision of *šēbeṭ* (tribe) 1S 9_{21}, of *ʿām* Nu 11_{10}, of *maṭṭeh* (tribe) 36_6; as guild 1C 2_{55}; — 2. *mišpāḥôt*: **races, subdivisions**: a) of ethnic & national groups Gn 10_5 12_3; b) species of animals Gn 8_{19}; 4 kinds of disaster (sword, dogs, birds, wild beasts) Je 15_3.

מִשְׁפָּט (425×): cs. מִשְׁפַּט, sf. מִשְׁפָּטוֹ; pl. מִשְׁפָּטִים, cs. מִשְׁפְּטֵי, sf. מִשְׁפָּטַי, מִשְׁפָּטֶךָ Ps 36_7, מִשְׁפְּטֵיהֶם: decision by arbitration > legal decision > legal case > justice, right > what is in conformity to a case: — 1. **decision by arbitration, legal decision**: a) Y. gives his *mišpāṭ* Zp 2_3; *šāʾal mišpāṭ* Is 58_2; *mišpaṭ ṣedeq* just decision Dt 16_{18} = *mišpaṭ ʾᵉmet* Ez 18_8; *mišpāṭî* the judgment concerning me, my sentence Is 49_4; b) legal decisions of Y. > **legal specifications**: *hammišpāṭîm*, oft. linked w. synonyms Dt 4_8; *mišpaṭ māwet* decision demanding death penalty Dt 19_6; *bôʾ bammišpāṭ* come before the court Jb 9_{32}; — 2. **legal case, lawsuit**: *ʿāśâ mišpāṭô* win one's case Ez 39_{21}; *nātan mišpāṭ lifnê* lay one's case before 23_{24}; *mišpaṭ* (so read) *nōʾᵃfôt* law relating to adultery 16_{38}; *ʾōraḥ mišpāṭ* course of law Is 40_{14}; *baʿal mišpāṭ* legal adversary 50_8; — 3. a) **legal claim**: *mišpaṭ hammelek* 1S 8_9, *mišpaṭ habbānôt* Ex 21_9 &c.; b) (legal) claim concerning: *mišpaṭ hayruššâ, haggᵉullâ*, claim for possession & redemption Je 32_8; *kᵉmišpāṭ lô*, as is befitting to him who Ps 119_{132}; *ʿābar mišpāṭ min* his claim eludes him Is 40_{27}; — 4. **conformity**: building-plan 1K 6_{38}; mode of life, habits: *mišpaṭ hannaʿar* Ju 13_{12}; *mišpāṭô* his procedure 1S 27_{11}; *ʾîš kᵉmišpāṭô* each according to his due 1K 5_8; *kᵉmišpāṭām* as is their custom 1K 18_{28}; *mišpaṭ hāʾîš* appearance 2K 1_7; *mišpaṭ haggôyim* religion 2K 17_{33}; — 5. **justice**, oft. linked w. synonyms Is 1_{21}.

מִשְׁפְּתַיִם: **the two saddle-bags** (of pack-animal) Gn 49_{14} Ju 5_{16}. †

מֶשֶׁק: *ben mešeq* Gn 15_2, unexpl., F comm. †

***מַשָּׁק**: cs. מַשַּׁק: **onslaught** (of locusts) Is 33_4. †

***מְשֻׁקָּד**: pl. מְשֻׁקָּדִים: **shaped in the form of almond-blossoms** (cups of lampstand) Ex 25_{33f} 37_{19f}. †

מַשְׁקֶה: cs. מַשְׁקֵה, sf. מַשְׁקֵהוּ; pl. sf. מַשְׁקָיו: — 1. (pt.) **cup-bearer** Gn 40_{1ff}; — 2. (pt.) **thoroughly watered** (land) Gn 13_{10}; — 3. **drink, beverage** Lv 11_{34}, pl. 1K 10_5; w. *kelî* drinking-vessel 1K 10_{21}; — 4. office of cup-bearer Gn 40_{21}.

מִשְׁקוֹל: **weight**; *bemišqôl* weighed out exactly Ez 4_{10}. †

מַשְׁקוֹף: **lintel** (i.e. upper crosspiece of doorway) Ex $12_{7.22f}$. †

מִשְׁקָל: cs. מִשְׁקַל, sf. מִשְׁקָלוֹ: — **weight**: (:: length) Lv 19_{35}; its weight [is] Gn 24_{22}; *bemišqāl, bamm-* weighed out exactly Ez 4_{16} Lv 26_{26}; *lō' hāyâ mišqāl le* was unweighable 2K 25_{16}, so *'ên mišqāl* 1C 22_3.

***מִשְׁקֶלֶת**: מִשְׁקֶלֶת Is 28_{17} & מִשְׁקֹלֶת 2K 21_{13}: **level** (i.e. instrument for horizontal accuracy). †

***מִשְׁקָע**: cs. מִשְׁקַע: w. *mayim*, **clear water** (wh. has settled) Ez 34_{18}. †

***מִשְׁרָה**: cs. מִשְׁרַת: **liquid**: w. *'anābîm*, grape-juice or -extract Nu 6_3. †

מֵשָׁרִים Pr 1_3: ꟳ מֵישָׁרִים.

מִשְׁרָעִי: gent. of unknown *מִשְׁרָע 1C 2_{53}. †

משש: **qal**: impf. יְמֻשֵּׁנִי, יְמֻשֵּׁהוּ: **feel, touch** Gn $27_{12.22}$. †

piel: pf. מִשַּׁשְׁתָּ; impf. יְמַשֵּׁשׁ, יְמַשְׁשׁוּ; pt. מְמַשֵּׁשׁ: — 1. **feel through, rummage through** Gn $31_{34.37}$; — 2. **grope** Dt 28_{29} Jb 5_{14} 12_{25}. †

hif.: impf. יָמֵשׁ: w. *ḥōšek*, let s.one feel, ? = **touch, feel** Ex 10_{21}. †

מִשְׁתֶּה: cs. מִשְׁתֵּה sf. (all sg.) מִשְׁתֵּיהֶם, מִשְׁתָּיו, מִשְׁתֵּיכֶם: — 1. **drinking**: *mištēh yayin* drinking-bout Est 5_6; — 2. **drink(s)** (appropriate for a feast) Dn 1_5; — 3. **feast, banquet** w. wine: *'āśâ mišteh* prepare a feast Gn 19_3, arrange a feast 21_8.

מַשְׁתִּין: ꟳ שׁין hif.

מֵת: **dead**: ꟳ מות.

I ***מַת** (vocalization uncert.; *מֹת, *מְתוּ): pl. מְתִים, cs. מְתֵי, sf. מְתָיו, מְתַיִךְ: — 1. **men** (i.e. males) Dt 2_{34}; — 2. **people, persons**: *metê mispār* few people Gn 34_{30} = *metê me'āṭ* Dt 26_5; *metê šāw'* Ps 26_4; *metê 'oholî* my tent-mates Jb 31_{31}.

cj. II ***מַת** (*מֹת ?) pl. cs. Is 41_{14} (for מְתֵי): **louse** (?). †

מַתְבֵּן: **heap of straw** Is 25_{10}. †

מֶתֶג: sf. מִתְגִּי: **bridle** 2K 19_{28} Is 37_{29} Ps 32_9 Pr 26_3; 2S 8_1 n. loc. †

מָתוֹק: f. מְתוּקָה; pl. מְתוּקִים: **sweet** = pleasant, agreeable Ju 14_{14}; *lemātôq* in sweetness Ez 3_3.

מְתוּשָׁאֵל: n. pers.

מְתוּשֶׁלַח, מְתוּשָׁלַח: n. pers.

מתח: **qal**: impf. וַיִּמְתָּחֵם: **spread out** (obj. heavens) Is 40_{22}. †

מָתַי: — 1. **when?**, w. impf. Gn 30_{30}; — 2. *lemātay* in ind. qn. **when?** Ex 8_5; — 3. *'ad-mātay*, **until when?, how long?**: a) w. pf. Ex 10_3; b) w. impf. 1S 1_{14}; w. *lō'* how long, after all? Ho 8_5; c) w/o vb. Nu 14_{27}; d) w. pron. & pt. 1K 18_{21}.

מַתְכֹּנֶת: sf. מַתְכֻּנְתָּם, מַתְכֻּנְתּוֹ: **measurement, proportion**: specific number (of bricks) Ex 5_8, preparation, combination (of ingredients of oil) $30_{32.37}$; proportion (of measures) Ez 45_{11}; to its proportion = as it is proper 2C 24_{13}. †

מַתְּלָאָה Ma 1_{13}, < מַה־תְּלָאָה 'what a nuisance.' †

מְתַלְּעוֹת (3×) abs. & cs., & מַלְתְּעוֹת Ps 58_7: **jawbone** Jl 1_6 Ps 58_7 Jb 29_{27} Pr 30_{14}. †

מְתֹם: **sound, unhurt spot** Is 1_6 Ps $38_{4.8}$. †

I **מַתָּן**: **gift, present** Gn 34_{12} Pr 18_{16} 21_{14}, coll. Nu 18_{11}; *'îš mattān* generous Pr 19_6. †

II **מַתָּן**: n. pers.

I **מַתָּנָה**: cs. מַתְּנַת; pl. מַתָּנוֹת, cs. מַתְּנוֹת, sf. מַתְּנוֹתֵיכֶם, מַתְּנוֹתָם: **gift, present**: a) secular Nu 18_6; gift as a settlement Gn 25_6, to gain influence Pr 15_{27}; b) to sanctuary Ex 28_{38}.

II מַתָּנָה: ? n. loc. Nu 21_{18f}. †

מִתְנִי: gent. of unknown n. loc. *מֶתֶן or *מַתָּן: 1C 11_{43}. †

מַתְּנַי: n. pers.

מַתַּנְיָה: n. pers.

מַתַּנְיָהוּ: n. pers.

מָתְנַיִם: cs. מָתְנֵי, sf. מָתְנָיו, מָתְנֵיכֶם: the strong musculature which unites the upper & lower part of the body, lumbar region, **hips & small of the back, loins** Gn 37_{34}; *mê motnayim*, water up to the hips Ez 47_4.

מתק: **qal**: pf. מָתְקוּ; impf. יִמְתְּקוּ, יִמְתַּקוּ: **be(come) sweet** Ex 15_{25}; metaph. stolen water Pr 9_{17}, clods of earth Jb 21_{33}. †

hif.: impf. תַּמְתִּיק, נַמְתִּיק: — 1. **taste sweet**, metaph. subj. evil Jb 20_{12}; — 2. (caus.) **enjoy close fellowship** (w. *sôd*) Ps 55_{15}. †

*מָתֵק: cs. מֶתֶק: **sweetness**, w. *śᵉfātayim*, gracefulness of speech Pr 16_{21}. †

*מֹתֶק: pl. cs. מָתְקִי: **sweetness**, sweet fragrance of figtree Ju 9_{11}. †

מִתְקָה: n. loc.

מִתְרְדָת: n. pers.

*מַתַּת: cs. = or מַתַּת: **gift** 1K 13_7 Pr 25_{14} Ec 3_{13} 5_{18}; *mattat yād*, as much as he can give Ez $46_{5.11}$. †

מַתַּתָּה: n. pers.

מַתִּתְיָה: n. pers.

מַתִּתְיָהוּ: n. pers.

נ

I נָא (180×): enclitic particle of urgency, translation difficult to specify, e.g. **please** (come in), **do** (come in); **just** (listen to me); uses: — 1. w. impv.: *śā' nā' 'êneykā* just take a look Gn 13_{14}; — 2. w. 'emphatic' impv. (in *-â*): *haggîdâ-nā'* please tell me Gn 32_{30}; — 3. w. coh.: *'ᵃdabbᵉrâ-nnā'* just let me say Ps 122_8; — 4. w. juss.: *yuqqaḥ nā'* just let (a little water) be brought Gn 18_4; — 5. after sf.: *sᵉfāḥênî nā'* 1S 2_{36}; — 6. after particle: a) *hinnēh-nā'* now look Gn 12_{11}; b) *'al-nā'* w. impf. or juss.: *'al-nā' tᵉhî* (for goodness' sake) let there be no (dispute between us) Gn 13_8; alone: oh, no Gn 19_{18}; c) w. *'im*: *'im-nā' māṣā'tî* if I may find Gn 18_3; d) *'ôy-nā'* Je 4_{31}; e) *'ayyēh-nā'* where (in the world)? Ps 115_2; f) misc.: *'im yeškā-nā' maṣlîᵃḥ* if you would really lend success Gn 24_{42}.

II נָא: **raw, half-cooked** (meat) Ex 12_9. †

נֹא: n. loc.

נֹאד, נֹאוד Ju 4_{19}: sf. נֹאדְךָ; pl. נֹאדוֹת: leather 'bottle' or skin, container of animal skin, sewed & tarred, so **wineskin** Jos $9_{4.13}$ 1S 16_{20}, **skin** for milk Ju 4_{19}, for tears Ps 56_9; Ps 119_{83}. †

נאה: **qal**: (oth.: אוה *nif.*): pf. נָאווּ Is 52_7 SS 1_{10} & נַאֲוָה Ps 93_5 (?): **be lovely**. †

cj. **piel**: impf. juss. יְנָא Ps 141_5 (for [יָנִי]א): **adorn**. †

נֹאוד Ju 4_{19}: F נֹאד.

נָאוֶה: f. נָאוָה: — 1. **beautiful, lovely** Ps 147_1 SS 1_5 2_{14} 4_3 6_4; — 2. **fitting, becoming** Ps 33_1 Pr 17_7 19_{10} 26_2. †

נְאוּפִים: F נִאֻפִים.

נְאוֹת: F *נָוֶה.

נְאֻם (ca. 360×, Je ca. 120×): evid. orig. cs. of a *נָאוּם; now fixed tech. term in prophetic speech & in comb. w. oth. formulas, esp. *kōh 'āmar yhwh*: orig. **whispering**, > **declaration, decision**; usu. closing formula; at beginning Is 56_8 + 2×; in middle of oracle Am 2_{11}; *nᵉʾum-yhwh* outside the prophetic books Gn 22_{16} 1S 2_{30} 2K 9_{26} 19_{33} 22_{19} + 3×; N.B. 9× of men, e.g. *nᵉʾum-dāwid* 2S 23_{1}, evid. when understood to be under prophetic inspiration; Ps 36_{2} *nᵉʾum pešaʿ* inspiring demon ?, ℱ comm.

נאף: **qal**: impf. יִנְאָפוּ, תִּנְאַף, יִנְאַף; inf. נָא(וֹ)ף; pt. נֹאֵף, נֹאֶפֶת, נֹאֲפוֹת: — 1. **commit adultery**: a) subj. man, w. II *ʾēt* & woman (either wife or fiancée of another man) Lv 20_{10}; abs. Ex 20_{14}; b) subj. woman, abs. engage in adultery Lv 20_{10}; — 2. metaph. **commit idolatry**, w. stones & wood † Je 3_{9}.

piel: pf. נִאֲפוּ, נִאֲפָה; impf. וַיְנָאֲפוּ, תְּנָאַפְנָה; pt. מְנָאֵף, מְנָאֶפֶת, מְנָאֲפִים: w. II *ʾēt*, **commit adultery** w. a woman Je 29_{23}; abs. 3_{8}; subj. women Ho 4_{13}; pt. adulterous: men Je 9_{1}, women Is 57_{3}.

***נִאֻפִים**, נִאוּפִים Ez 23_{43}: sf. נִאֻפַיִךְ: **(commission of) adultery** Je 13_{27}; Ez 23_{43} ℱ comm. †

***נַאֲפוּפִים**: sf. נַאֲפוּפֶיהָ: **marks of adultery** Ho 2_{4}. †

נָאַץ: **qal**: pf. נָאַץ, נָאֲצוּ, נ׳; impf. יִנְאַץ, יִנְאָץ, יִנְאָצוּן: **reject** (w. scorn), **disdain** Dt 32_{19}; Je 33_{19} (*mihyōt ʿôd gôy*, so that they are no longer a nation).

piel: pf. נִאֵץ, נִאַצְתָּ, נִאֲצוּ, נִאֲצוּ, נִאֲצוּנִי; impf. יְנָאֵץ, יְנַאֲצוּנִי; inf. נַאֵץ 2S 12_{14}; pt. מְנַאֲצִי, מְנַאֲצַיִךְ: **treat disrespectfully, irreverently**: obj. God 2S 12_{14}; obj. things associated w. God 1S 2_{17} Ps 74_{10}.

hitpoel (or mixed poal & hitpoel): pt. מִנֹּאָץ (<* *mitn-*): **be reviled** Is 52_{5}. †

נְאָצָה: **shame, disgrace** 2K 19_{3} Is 37_{3}. †

***נֶאָצָה**: pl. נֶאָצוֹת, sf. נֶאָצוֹתֶיךָ: **abuse** (coll.), **aspersions** Ez 35_{12} Ne $9_{18 \cdot 26}$. †

נָאַק: **qal**: pf. נ׳; impf. יִנְאֲקוּ: **groan** Ez 30_{24} Jb 24_{12}. †

***נְאָקָה**: **groaning** Ex 2_{24} 6_{5} Ju 2_{18} Ez 30_{24}. †

נאר: **piel**: pf. נֵאֵר, נֵאַרְתָּה: **reject, disavow** Ps 89_{40} La 2_{7}. †

נֹב: n. loc.

נבא: **nif.** (ca. 85×), some forms like ל״ה vbs.: pf. נִבָּא, נִבֵּאתָ, נִבְּאוּ, נִבְּאוּ; impf. יִנָּבֵא, יִנָּבְאוּ; impv. & inf. הִנָּבֵא, inf. sf. הִנָּבְאוֹ, הִנָּבְאתוֹ Zc 13_{4}; pt. נִבָּא, (הַ)נִּבְּאִים 1S 19_{20} Je 14 &c., נִבְּאִים Ez 13_{2}, נִבְּאֵי: — 1. abs. **be in prophetic ecstasy, behave as a nābîʾ** 1K 22_{12}; w. *bᵉšēm yhwh* (by invocation of Y.'s name) Je 11_{21}; w. *babbaʿal* (driven by Baal) Je 2_{8}; w. *baššeqer, laššeqer* 5_{31} 27_{15}; — 2. **speak as a nābîʾ**: a) w. *lᵉ* & people to whom one speaks Je 14_{16}; b) w. acc. of message, e.g. *šeqer* Je 14_{6}; c) w. *lᵉ* in regard to, concerning (e.g. *rāʿâ*) Je 28_{8}; d) w. *ʾel* Je 25_{30}; — 3. 1C 25_{2} (& $_{1}$ w. emended txt.) **play** (an instrument) **while filled w.** (prophetic) **spirit**.

hitp., some forms like ל״ה vbs.: pf. הִתְנַבֵּאתִי, הִתְנַבִּיתָ; inf. הִתְנַבּוֹת; pt. מִתְנַבֵּא, מִתְנַבְּאוֹת: — 1. **behave as a nābîʾ**, oft. = **rave** 1K 18_{29}; — 2. (in later passages) **speak as a nābîʾ** Ez 37_{10}, w. *lᵉ* to Je 29_{27}, w. *ʿal* about 1K 22_{8}, against 2C 20_{37}; w. *bᵉšēm yhwh* (by invocation of Y.'s name) Je 26_{20}, w. *babbaʿal* (driven by Baal) Je 23_{13}.

I **נְבוֹ**: n. of mountain & loc.

II **נְבוֹ**: n. of Babylonian god Is 46_{1}. †

נְבוֹ Je 39_{3}: for נְבוֹ שַׂר־סְכִים rd נְבוּשַׁזְבָּן (v. 13). †

נְבוּאָה: **prophetic word, prophecy** Ne 6_{12} 2C 15_{8}, written 2C 9_{29}. †

נָבוּב: cs. נְבוּב: (spatially) **hollow** Je 52_{21}; *nᵉbûb luḥōt* hollow chest of boards Ex 27_{8} 38_{7}; *nābûb* s.one empty-headed Jb 11_{12}. †

נְבוּזַרְאֲדָן: n. pers.

נְבוּכַדְנֶאצַּר ℱ נְבוּכַדְרֶאצַּר.

נְבוּכַדְרֶאצַּר (30×), > ־נֶאצַּר (14×), נְבֻכַדְנֶאצַּר (7×), נְבֻכַדְנֶצַּר (3×): n. of king of Babylon.

נְבוּשַׁזְבָּן: n. pers.

נָבוֹת: n. pers.

נבח: **qal**: inf. לִנְבֹּחַ: **bark** (of dog) Is 56_{10}. †

I נֹבַח: n. pers. Nu 32_{42}. †
II נֹבַח: n. loc. Nu 32_{42} Ju 8_{11}. †
נִבְחַז: name of a deified altar 2K 17_{21}. †
נבט: **piel**: pf. נִבַּט: w. *le*, **glance** at, **look** at Is 5_{30}. †
hif.: pf. הִבַּטְתֶּם, הִבִּיטוּ, הִבִּיט; impf. יַבִּיט, תַּבֵּט, אַבִּיטָה; impv. הַבֵּט, הַבִּיט Ps 142_5 & La 5_1 Kt, הַבִּ֫יטָה, הַבֶּט־ Ps 142_5 Qr, הַבִּיטִי; inf. הַבִּיט, הַבִּיטָם; pt. מַבִּיט: — 1. **look** in a spec. direction: a) w. a word of direction, to the heavens Gn 15_5, to the sea 1K 18_{43}; b) **look out, gaze** (fm. a spot) Is 18_4, **look**, have a look 1K 19_6; w. following *rā'â* Is 63_{15}, w. preceding Hb 1_5; — 2. w. prep.: a) w. *'aḥarāyw* look behind onesf. Gn 19_{17}, *mē'aḥarāyw* 19_{26}; w. *'aḥarê* gaze after s.one, watch s.one (go) Ex 33_8; b) w. *'el*, look at, gaze at Ex 3_6; look at s.thg = set a value on 1S 16_7, worthy of a glance 2K 3_{14}; look at God's commandments = obey Ps 119_6; look upon weapons = trust in Is 22_8; look upon s.one = be gracious to 66_2; c) w. *be* (be pleased to) see Ps 92_{12}, (be displeased to) see 1S 2_{32}; d) w. *le* look at Ps 104_{32}, = be obedient to Ps 74_{20}; e) w. *'al* Hb 2_{15}; — 3. w. acc. **see, look at, catch sight of** 1S 17_{42}; — 4. cultic: = accept graciously Am 5_{22}.
נְבָט: n. pers.
נָבִיא (ca. 300×): sf. נְבִיאֲךָ; pl. נְבִיאִים, cs. נְבִיאֵי, sf. נְבִיאָיו, נְבִיאֵיכֶם: **prophet** Gn 20_7 1K 22_7; *benê hannebî'îm* members of prophetic guild 1K 20_{35}; in unfavorable sense Je 23_{37} Am 7_{14}.
נְבִיאָה: **prophetess**: Miriam Ex 15_{20}, wife of Isaiah (herself a prophetess?) Is 8_3.
נְבָי(וֹ)ת: n. pers. & peop.
*נֵבֶךְ: pl. cs. נִבְכֵי: **source** Jb 38_{16}, cj. Pr 8_{24}. †
I נָבֵל: **qal**: pf. נָבְלָה, נ׳; impf. יִבּוֹל, תִּבֹּל, יִבֹּלוּ, יִבּוֹלוּן; inf. נָבֹל, נְבֹל; pt. נֹבֵל, נֹבֶ֫לֶת: — 1. **wither & fall**: leaves Is 1_{30}, flowers Is 28_1, grass Ps 37_2; — 2. metaph. **wither, fall to ruin, wear out**: earth Is 24_4, men 2S 22_{46}.
II נבל: **qal**: pf. נָבַלְתָּ: **act disdainfully** Pr 30_{32}. †
piel: pf. וְנִבַּלְתִּיךְ; impf. וַיְנַבֵּל, תְּנַבֵּל; pt. מְנַבֵּל: **treat** s.one **disdainfully** Dt 32_{15} Je 14_{21} Mi 7_6 Na 3_6. †
I נָבָל: pl. נְבָלִים, f. נְבָלוֹת: **foolish** (intellectually & morally), = **godless**: — 1. a people Dt 32_6; — 2. an individual, a **fool** 2S 3_{33}; adj. Ez 13_3.
II נָבָל: n. pers.
I נֵבֶל: pl. נְבָלִים, cs. נִבְלֵי, sf. נִבְלֵיהֶם: **(storage-)jar** for wine, oil, wheat, flour 1S 1_{24} &c.; cosmic *niblê šāmayim* Jb 38_{37}.
II נֵבֶל (6×) & נֶבֶל (2×): נֵבֶל; pl. נְבָלִים-, sf. נְבָלֶיךָ: stringed instrument Am 6_5, ? **harp** F Ps 33_2; 1K 10_{12}.
נְבָלָה: — 1. **stupidity** (w. implication of disregard of God's will) 1S 25_{25}; — 2. **grave sin, sacrilege**: w. *dibber* Is 9_{16}; w. *'āśâ* specific (sexual) offense Gn 34_7.
נְבֵלָה: cs. נִבְלַת, sf. נִבְלָתְךָ, נִבְלָתָם: a) **corpse** of man 1K 13_{22}; b) **carcass** of animal Lv 5_2; c) (ironic?!) **carcass** of idols † Je 16_{18}.
נַבְלוּת: (female) **genitals** Ho 2_{12} (oth.: stupidity). †
נְבַלָּט: n. loc.
נֹבֶ֫לֶת: **withered fruit** Is 34_4 bγ. †
נבע: **qal**: pt. נֹבֵעַ: **bubble** (of brook) Pr 18_4. †
hif.: impf. יַבִּיעַ, אַבִּיעָה, יַבִּ֫יעוּ, יַבִּיעוּן, תַּבַּעְנָה: **make** s.thg **bubble forth, boil out, pour out**: obj. spirit Pr 1_{23}, speech Ps 19_3.
נִבְשָׁן: n. loc.
נֶגֶב: loc. נֶ֫גְבָּה: n. terr., the **Negeb**: — 1. **desert-land** of Negeb Gn 24_{62}; — 2. *hannegeb* southland = Egypt Dn $11_{5\text{-}40}$; — 3. **south** (as a compass-point): *pe'at negeb* south side Nu 34_3; *negeb* w. gen., south(ward) from Zc 14_{10}; *negbâ* to the south Gn 13_{14}; *negbâ le* south(ward) from Jos 17_{9f}, = *negbâ min* 18_{14}, = *minnegeb le*

Nu 34_4; *minnegeb* in the south 1S 14_5; *qēdᵉmâ mimmûl negeb* toward the southeast 1K 7_{39}.

נגד: **hif.** (ca. 320×): pf. הִגִּידָה, הִגַּדְתָּ; impf. יַגִּיד, יַגֶּד־, תַּגִּיד, אַגִּידָה, וָאַגִּד, יַגִּ(י)דוּ, תַּגִּידוּ, sf. יַגִּדָה, יַגִּידֶהָ, יַגֶּדְךָ Dt 32_7, אַגִּידֶנּוּ, נַגִּידֶנּוּ; impv. הַגֵּד, הַגֶּד־, הַגִּידָה, הַגִּידִי; inf. הַגִּיד, לַגִּיד (< לְהַ׳ 2K 9_{15} Kt), הַגֵּ(י)ד; pt. מַגִּיד, מַגֶּדֶת: put s.thg up conspicuously in front of s.one: — 1. **put forward** (an opinion &c.), **report, announce, tell,** w. *lᵉ* Gn 3_{11}; w. acc. of thing, *dᵉbārîm* Jb 26_4; w. acc. pers. 2K 7_9; w. 2 acc. (pers. & thing) Ez 43_{10}; w. *kî* that Gn 31_{20}, w. *mâ* what 29_{15}, w. *hᵃ* whether 43_6; obj. *dibrê*... = answer questions 2C 9_2; pt. *maggîd* messenger, informer 2S 15_{13}; = **speak out** in court Lv 5_1; = **denounce** s.one Je 20_{10}; — 2. w. *ḥᵃlôm*, dream Gn 41_{24} & *ḥîdâ* riddle Ju 14_{12}, **explain, solve.**

hof.: pf. הֻגַּד; impf. וַיֻּגַּד; inf. abs. הֻגֵּד: **be reported, told** 1K 10_7, w. *lᵉ* to Gn 22_{20}, w. *lēʾmōr* (that) 22_{20}, w. *kî* that 31_{22}; w. *hinnēh* 2S 19_2.

נֶגֶד (150×): loc. נֶגְדָּה (no *dagheš*), sf. נֶגְדּוֹ, נֶגְדְּךָ, נֶגְדָּם: — 1. orig. noun, **opposite, counterpart**, only in *kᵉnegdô* like his counterpart = corresponding to him Gn $2_{18 \cdot 20}$; — 2. > prep. w. gen. or sf.: a) **in the presence of, before** Gn 31_{32}; *neged haššemeš* = in broad daylight 2S 12_{12}; b) **over against** Ex 19_2; c) *rāʿâ neged lifnêkem* you have (some) evil in mind Ex 10_{10}, *neged pᵉnêkem* in your own opinion Is 5_{21}, *negdô* in his judgment 40_{17}; d) *negdô* (right) **in front of** him Jos 6_5; *negdô* straight ahead Je 31_{39}; e) **corresponding to** Ez 40_{23}; f) **against** Jb 10_{17}; — 3. *lᵉneged*: a) (motion) **in front of** Gn 33_{12}; b) **before, in front of** 2K 1_{13}; c) *lᵉnegdî* against my will Nu 22_{32}; d) *lᵉnegdî* present to my mind 2S 22_{23}; *lᵉnegdᵉkem* before your eyes Is 1_7; e) before, against Ps 54_5; f) straight ahead of Ne 12_{37}; g) w. regard to Ne 11_{22}; — 4. *minneged*: adv.: a) **opposite** Gn 21_{16}; b) **aside, aloof** 2S 18_{13}; — 5. *minneged*: prep.: a) **away from** Is 1_{16}; b) **far from** 1S 26_{20}; *hišlîk nafšô minnegdô* risked his life Ju 9_{17}; c) **before**, in front of 2S 22_{13}; d) **over against** Ne 3_{25}; e) *minneged lᵉ*: w. *hālak*, go from the path of Pr 14_7; w. *bôʾ* before Ju 20_{34}; *minneged sābîb lᵉ* all around Nu 2_2; — 6. *ʿad-neged* up to (a point) opposite Ne 3_{16}; — 7. *negdâ-nnāʾ* before Ps $116_{14 \cdot 18}$.

נָגַהּ: **qal**: pf. נ׳; impf. יִגַּהּ: **shine** (subj. light) Is 9_1 Jb 18_5 22_{28}. †

hif.: impf. יַגִּיהַּ: **let** (light) **shine** Is 13_{10}; **brighten, lighten** 2S 22_{29} Ps 18_{29}. †

I **נֹגַהּ**: sf. נָגְהָם: **gleam, shining** 2S 22_{13}.

II **נֹגַהּ**: n. pers. 1C 3_7 14_6. †

***נְגֹהָה**: pl. נְגֹהוֹת: **luster, brightness** Is 59_9. †

נגח: **qal**: impf. יִגַּח, יִגָּח: **gore** (of an ox) Ex $21_{28 \cdot 31f}$. †

piel: impf. יְנַגַּח, תְּנַגְּחוּ, נְנַגֵּחַ; pt. מְנַגֵּחַ: **butt, thrust, knock down** Dt 33_{17} 1K 22_{11} Ez 34_{21} Ps 44_6 Dn 8_4 2C 18_{12}. †

hitp.: impf. יִתְנַגַּח: **butt with** (*ʿim*), **engage in butting** with Dn 11_{40}. †

נַגָּח: **vicious, liable to gore** (ox) Ex 21_{29}. †

נָגִיד: cs. נְגִ(י)ד; pl. נְגִידִים: **chief, leader, sovereign**: — 1. **sovereign, prince,** of Tyre Ez 28_2, sg. coll. of Assyria 2C 32_{21}; — 2. in small sphere of authority: a) officers in Assyrian army alongside *śar* 2C 32_{21}, w. David 1C 13_1, commanders of cities 2C 11_{11}; b) court officials, e.g. *nāgîd lᵉbêt yᵉhûdâ* 2C 19_{11}; c) head of family 2C 11_{22}, people of rank Jb 29_{10}; — 3. cultic officials: *nāgîd bᵉbêt yhwh* = high priest Je 21_1; chief officer of contributions 2C 31_{12}; chief of doorkeepers 1C 9_{20}; — 4. leader of Isr. appointed by Y.: Saul 1S 9_{16}, David 13_{14}, Solomon 1K 1_{35} &c.; — 5. var.: *mašîᵃḥ nāgîd*, *ʿam nāgîd* Dn 9_{25f}; *nᵉgîd bᵉrît* = high priest Dn 11_{22}.

***נְגִינָה & נְגִינַת** Ps 61_{1}: sf. נְגִינָתָם; pl. נְגִינ(וֹ)ת; נְגִינוֹתַי, נְגִינוֹתָי Is 38_{2} Hb 3_{19} evid. pl. endings, not pers. sf.: — 1. **string music** Is 38_{20} La 5_{14}; — 2. **taunt-song** Ps 69_{13} Jb 30_{9} La 3_{14}; — 3. tech. musical term Hb 3_{19} Ps 4_{1} + 6× in Ps. superscriptions. †

נגן: **qal**: pt. נֹגְנִים: player on stringed-instrument, **string-player** Ps 68_{26}. †

piel: pf. נִגֵּן; impf. יְנַגֵּן; inf. נַגֵּן; pt. מְנַגֵּן: **play a stringed instrument** 2K 3_{15}.

נָגַע: **qal** (ca. 100×): pf. נ׳, נָגְעָה, נָגְעוּ, נְגָעֲנוּךָ; impf. יִגַּע, יִגְּעוּ, תִּגְּעוּ; impv. גַּע; inf. נְגֹעַ, לְנְג(וֹ)עַ, לָגַעַת, נָגְעוֹ, נָגְעֵךְ; pt. נֹגֵעַ, נֹגַעַת, נֹגַעַת, pass. נָגוּעַ: — 1. a) **touch**: w. b^e Gn 3_{3}, w. *ʾel* 1K 6_{27}, w. *ʿal* Is 6_{7}, w. acc. 52_{11}; b) touch (to do harm), w. b^e Gn 26_{29}, w. *ʾel* (obj. woman) 20_{6}; c) touch = **hurt**, w. acc. 2S 14_{10}; *nāgû*^{a}*ʿ* hit, buffeted Is 53_{4}; — 2. **reach** to, w. *ʿad* Is 16_{8}, *ʾel* Je 51_{9}; subj. *dābār* (word) came (all the way) to Jon 3_{6}; subj. month: come, arrive Ezr 3_{1}.

nif.: impf. וַיִּנָּגְעוּ: **let onesf. be beaten** (militarily) Jos 8_{15}. †

piel: pf. נִגְּעוֹ; impf. וַיְנַגַּע: **afflict** s.one (w. illness &c.) Gn 12_{17} 2K 15_{5} 2C 26_{20}. †

pual: impf. יְנֻגָּעוּ: **be afflicted** Ps 73_{5}. †

hif.: pf. הִגִּיעַ, 2. f. הִגַּעַתְּ, הִגִּיעוּ, הִגַּעְתֶּם, הִגַּעְתִּיהוּ; impf. יַגִּיעַ, וַיַּגַּע, יַגִּיעוּ, יַגִּיעֶנָּה; inf. הַגִּיעַ, הַגִּיעֵנוּ; pt. מַגִּיעַ, f. מַגַּעַת, pl. cs. מַגִּיעֵי: — 1. **touch, reach** (to): w. acc. Gn 28_{12}, w. *ʾel* Zc 14_{5}, w. *ʿal* Is 6_{7}, w. l^e Jb 20_{6}, draw near to Ps 88_{4}, w. *ʿad* Is 8_{8}; — 2. **let, make** s.thg **touch**, w. *ʾel* Ex 12_{22}, w. b^e Is 5_{8}; — 3. **throw**: *lāʾāreṣ* Is 25_{12}, w. *ʿad* Is 26_{5}, w. *ʾel* Ez 13_{14}; — 4. **reach, arrive at**: w. acc. Is 30_{4}, w. *ʾel* 1S 14_{6}, w. l^e Est 4_{14}; **happen** to (w. *ʾel*) Ec 8_{14}; — 5. subj. time, **come, arrive** Ez 7_{12}, so subj. s.one's turn Est 2_{12}; — 6. var.: *higgî*^{a}*ʿ* + l^e & inf. Est 9_{1}, were about to (be carried out); *taggîaʿ yādô* he can afford s.thg Lv 5_{7}.

נֶגַע: נֶגַע, sf. נִגְעוֹ, נִגְעֲךָ; pl. נְגָעִים, cs. נִגְעֵי: — 1. 'contact,' thus **plague, affliction** Gn 12_{17}; — 2. **blow, assault** Dt 17_{8} 2S 7_{14}; — 3. **mark, skin disease**: *negaʿ haṣṣāraʿat*, contact of *ṣāraʿat* Lv 13_{2ff}.

נָגַף: **qal**: pf. נ׳, sf. נְגָפוֹ, נְגָפָנוּ; impf. יִגֹּף, אֶגֹּף, sf. יִגְּפֶנּוּ, וַיִּגְּפֵהוּ 1S 26_{10}; inf. נְגֹף, לִנְגֹּף, נָגְפוֹ; pt. נֹגֵף: — 1. **injure** (by a blow) Ex 21_{22}; — 2. **strike** (metaph.): a) w. plague Ex 7_{21}; b) w. death 1S 25_{38}; c) w. illness 2S 12_{15}; d) w. defeat 1S 4_{3}; — 3. of foot, **stumble** against (w. b^e) Ps 91_{12}.

nif.: pf. נִגַּף, נִגְּפוּ, נִגְּפוּ; impf. וַיִּנָּגֶף, וַיִּנָּגְפוּ; inf. הִנָּגֵף, נִגֹּף: **be beaten**, w. *lifnê* before = by 1K 8_{33}; *nātan yhwh niggāfîm* let (them) suffer a defeat Dt 28_{7}.

hitp.: impf. יִתְנַגְּפוּ: **stumble** Je 13_{16}. †

נֶגֶף: נֶגֶף: — 1. **stumbling**: *ʾeben negef*, stumbling-stone Is 8_{14}; — 2. **blow, affliction** Ex 12_{13} 30_{12} Nu 8_{19} 17_{11f} 22_{17}. †

נגר: **nif.**: pf. נִגְּרָה; pt. נִגָּרִים, **flow, gush forth**: of water on ground 2S 14_{14}; of eye La 3_{49}; subj. hand Ps 77_{3} (but txt.?). †

hif.: pf. הִגַּרְתִּי; impf. וַיַּגֵּר, יַגִּרֻהוּ; impv. הַגִּרֵם: **pour out**: obj. wine Ps 75_{9}, stones Mi 1_{6}, metaph. men Je 18_{21} Ez 35_{5}. †

hof.: pt. מֻגָּרִים: **poured out** Mi 1_{4}. †

cj. ***נִגֶּרֶת**: pl. נִגָּרוֹת: **torrent** Jb 20_{28}. †

נָגַשׂ: **qal**: pf. נ׳; impf. יִגֹּשׂ, תִּנְגְּשׂוּ; pt. נֹגֵשׂ, נֹגְשִׂים, נֹגְשָׂיו, נֹגְשֵׂיהֶם: — 1. **beat, rouse up** (game) Jb 39_{7}; — 2. **exact** (contributions) 2K 23_{35}; pt. tax-collector Dn 11_{29}; — 3. w. b^e, **drive, force** (men to work) Ex 5_{6}; pt. slave-driver, task-master, overseer 5_{10}; — 4. **press** (a debtor for repayment), **dun** Dt 15_{2}; — 5. pt. a) **despot** Is $14_{2.4}$; b) pl. **government** Is 3_{12}.

nif.: pf. נִגַּשׂ: — 1. w. b^e, **jostle, crowd** each other Is 3_{5}; — 2. **be hard pressed** 1S 13_{6} Is 53_{7}. †

נגשׁ: **qal**: (pf. & pt. expressed by nif.;) impf. יִגַּשׁ, יִגַּשׁ, יִגְּשׁוּ, יִגְּשׁוּ & Jb 41_{8} יֻגְּשׁוּ, וַתִּגַּשְׁנָה; impv. גַּשׁ, גֶּשׁ־, גְּשָׁה, גֹּשִׁי, גֹּשׁוּ, גְּשׁוּ;

inf. גִּשְׁתּוֹ, גֶּשֶׁת: — 1. abs. **step up, come near** Gn 27_{21}; *geš-hālᵉʾâ* stand back, get away Gn 19_9; — 2. w. prep.: **come near**, w. *ʾel* Gn 27_{22}, **approach** 1K 18_{21}, come near to a thing Ex 28_{43}; w. *ʾel-ʾiššâ* have anything to do w. a woman Ex 19_{15}; b) w. *ʿad* come up to Gn 33_3; c) w. *lᵉ*: *gᵉšâ-llî* move over for me, make room for me Is 49_{20}; d) w. *bᵉ*, stick to, be joined to Jb 41_8; — 3. as legal term: **step forth** (in litigation): a) plaintiff to judge Gn 18_{23}; b) litigating parties to each other Is 50_8; — 4. as military term: approach Jos 8_{11}, w. *lammilḥāmâ*, draw up 2S 10_{13}.

nif. (used for qal pf. & pt.): pf. נִגַּשׁ, נִגְּשׁוּ; pt. נִגָּשִׁים: **step up, come near**: a) Gn 33_7, w. *ʾel* 1K 20_{13}; w. *bᵉ* catch up w. Am 9_{13}; b) spec.: *ʾel-mišpāṭ* go to court Dt 25_1; w. *lammilḥāmâ*, draw up 1S 7_{10}, w. *ʾel* to the city 2S 11_{20}; w. *ʾel-yhwh* draw near Ex 19_{22}.

hif.: pf. הִגִּישׁוּ, sf. הִגִּישׁוֹ; impf. יַגֵּשׁ, וַיַּגֵּשׁ Ju 6_{19}, תַּגִּישׁ, יַגִּישׁוּ, תַּגִּ(י)שׁוּן; impv. הַגִּישָׁה, הַגִּישׁוּ; pt. מַגִּישׁ, מַגִּשִׁים, מַגִּישֵׁי: — 1. **bring up** (a person or thing to s.one), **bring near** (secular use): obj. pers. Gn $48_{10\cdot13}$, food 27_{25}; metaph. present (one's case) Is 45_{21}; — 2. in legal proceedings: a) obj. pers.: **take, present** Ex 21_6; b) obj. evidence: **offer, produce** Is 41_{21}; — 3. cultic: a) **offer** (sacrifice) 1S 13_9; b) **bring out** (the ephod) 1S 23_9.

hof.: pf. הֻגְּשׁוּ; pt. מֻגָּשׁ: — 1. **be brought** (to s.thg) 2S 3_{34}; — 2. **be offered** (sacrifice) Ma 1_{11}. †

נֵד: **dam, dike** Ex 15_8 Jos $3_{13\cdot16}$ Ps 78_{13}. †

נדא: וַיַּדֵּא 2K 17_{21} Kt: rd **qal** impf. וַיִּדַּא or **hif.** וַיַּדֵּא (Qr נדח hif.): w. *mēʾaḥᵃrê*, **separate** from, **seduce from allegiance to**. †

נדב: **qal**: pf. נָדְבָה, נ׳; impf. יִדְּבֶנּוּ: **urge on, prompt**: subj. *lēb* Ex 25_2 35_{29}, *rûᵃḥ* 35_{21}. †

hitp.: pf. הִתְנַדֵּב; impf. וַיִּתְנַדְּבוּ; inf. הִתְנַדֵּב, הִתְנַדֶּב־; pt. מִתְנַדֵּב: — 1. **decide voluntarily, volunteer** w. inf. Ne 11_2; **enlist voluntarily, volunteer** (for war) Ju 5_2, **present onesf. voluntarily, volunteer** (for cult) 2C 17_{16}; — 2. **offer voluntarily, give a free-will offering**: w. acc. Ezr 3_5, abs. 1_6.

נָדָב: n. pers.

נְדָבָה: cs. נִדְבַת; pl. נְדָבוֹת, cs. נִדְבוֹת, sf. נִדְבֹתֶיךָ, נִדְבוֹתָם, נִדְבֹתֵיכֶם: — 1. **free inclination**: *bindābâ* of one's own accord Ps 54_8, = *nᵉdābâ* (adv. acc.) Ho 14_5; *gešem nᵉdābôt* plentiful rain Ps 68_{10}; — 2. **voluntary gift, free-will offering** (i.e. given spontaneously) Lv 7_{16}; *lindābâ* as a free-will offering Lv 22_{21} = *bindābâ* Nu 15_3.

נְדַבְיָה: n. pers.

נִדְגָּלוֹת: SS $6_{4\cdot10}$: 'those designated,' spec. constellation or zodiacal group (oth.: illusory phantom): ↗ II *dgl* nif. & comm. †

נדד: **qal**: pf. נָדַד, נָדְדוּ, נָדְדָה; impf. יִדּוֹד, תִּדֹּד, יְדוֹדוּן, וַתִּדַּד; inf. נְדֹד; pt. נ(וֹ)דֵד, נֹדְדִים, נוֹדֶדֶת: — 1. **flee** Is 10_{31}; metaph., sleep fled fm. my eyes Gn 31_{40}; — 2. **wander around**, w. *lᵉ* to Jb 15_{23}; — 2. **move** (obj. wing), flutter Is 10_{14}.

polel: pf. נֹדֵד (rd. נוֹדְדוּ): **flee** Na 3_{17}. †

hif.: impf. יְנִדֻהוּ: **drive out, put to flight** Jb 18_{18}. †

hof.: impf. יֻדַּד; pt. מֻנָּד (if correct): **be banished** (dream) Jb 20_8; *qôṣ munād* wind-blown shreds of wick 2S 23_6. †

נְדֻדִים: **restlessness** Jb 7_4. †

נדה: **piel**: pt. מְנַדִּים, מְנַדֵּיכֶם: — 1. force out, **exclude** Is 66_5; — 2. **believe, suppose** (s.thg to be) **far away** Am 6_3 (oth.: seek to escape fm.). †

נֵדֶה: **gift, reward** Ez 16_{33}. †

נִדָּה: cs. נִדַּת, sf. נִדָּתָהּ: — 1. **menstrual flow, menstruation** Lv 12_2; *mê niddâ* water used by menstruating woman Nu 19_9; *ʾiššâ niddâ* (*niddâ* appos.) Ez 18_6; — 2. **excretion, s.thg detestable, pollution** Lv 20_{21}; *ʾereṣ niddâ* polluted land Ezr 9_{11}; *bᵉniddat ʿammê* *hā'ᵃrāṣôt* = worship of idols Ezr 9_{11}; *hāyâ lᵉniddâ* become (nothing more than) trash Ez 7_{19}.

I נדח: **nif.**: pf. נִדְּחוּ, נִדַּחְתָּ, נִדְּחָה; impf. (F nif. דחח & דחה); pt. נִדָּח, sf. נִדָּחוֹ, נִדַּחֲךָ, נִדַּחֲכֶם, f. נִדָּחָה & נִדַּחַת; pl. נִדָּחִים, cs. נִדְּחֵי & Is 11_1 56_8 Ps 147_2 נִדְחֵי, sf. נִדָּחַי: — 1. **be scattered, go astray**: animals Dt 22_1; of men, **be banished, an outcast** 2S 14_{13f}; be chased away Jb 6_{13}; — 2. **be diverted, be led astray** Dt 4_{19}.

[**pual**: pt. מְנֻדָּח: ? rd. מֻנָּגָה Is 8_{22}. †]

hif.: pf. הִדִּיחַ, הִדַּחְתִּי, הִדִּיחוּ, הִדִּיחֲךָ, הִדַּחְתִּים, הִדַּחְתִּיו; impf. וַיַּדַּח, יַדִּיחוּ, אַדִּיחֵם, הַדִּיחֵמוֹ, וַתַּדִּחוּם; inf. הַדִּיחֲךָ, הַדִּיחִי, לְהַדִּיחַ (sf. 3. pl.): — 1. **scatter, disperse, chase apart**: animals Je 23_{2f}; people Dt 30_1; — 2. **force out** (obj. priests) 2C 13_9; — 3. **lead astray, divert**: a) from the way Dt 13_6; b) w. *mē'al*, fm. God Dt 13_{11}; — 4. **seduce**: a) subj. woman, obj. lover Pr 7_{21}; b) religious Dt 13_{14}.

hof.: pt. מֻדָּח: **scared away** (gazelle) Is 13_{14}. †

II נדח: **qal**: inf. לִנְדֹּחַ: **wield** (obj. axe), w. *'al* against Dt 20_{19}. †

nif.: pf. נִדְּחָה: (hand) is put to the axe = takes up the axe Dt 19_5. †

hif.: pf. הִדִּיחַ: **bring** (disaster), w. *'al* on 2S 15_{14}. †

[נֹדִי Ps 56_9: rd. נְדֻדַי (נְדֻדִים). †]

נָדִיב: cs. נְדִיב, f. נְדִיבָה; pl. נְדִיבִים, cs. נְדִיבֵי, sf. נְדִיבֵמוֹ (sf. 3. pl.): — 1. **willing**: *rûᵃḥ nᵉdîbâ* Ps 51_{14}; w. *lēb* Ex 35_5; *kol-nᵉdîb lēb* everyone who wished to 2C 29_{31}: — 2. (one who is) **generous, noble** 1S 2_8; *bat-nādîb* noble maiden SS 7_2; *nᵉdîbê hā'ām* Nu 21_{18}.

*נְדִיבָה: sf. נְדִיבָתִי; pl. נְדִיבוֹת: — 1. **s.thg noble** Is 32_8; — 2. **honor** Jb 30_{15}. †

I *נָדָן: sf. נְדָנָהּ: **sheath** 1C 21_{27}. †

II *נָדָן: pl. sf. נְדָנַיִךְ: **gift, wages of love** Ez 16_{33}. †

נדף: **qal**: impf. תִּנְדֹּף, יִנְדְּפֶנּוּ, תִּנְדְּפֶנּוּ: **blow away, scatter** Ps 1_4; ? Jb 32_{13} refute. †

nif.: pf. נִדַּף; inf. הִנְּדֹף Ps 68_{30} rd הִנָּדֵף; pt. נִדָּף: **be blown away** Lv 26_{36} Is 19_7 41_2 Ps 68_3 Jb 13_{25}. †

נָדַר: **qal**: pf. 'נ, נָדָרָה, נָדַרְנוּ; impf. יִדֹּר, וַיִּדַּר, תִּדֹּר, תִּדְּרוּ; impv. נִדְרוּ Ps 76_{12}; inf. לִנְדֹּר; pt. נֹדֵר: **make a vow** (promise a special deed): *nādar nēder* Gn 28_{20}; > w/o *nēder*, **vow** Lv 27_8.

נֵדֶר (5×) & נֶדֶר (20×): נֶדֶר, sf. נִדְרוֹ; pl. נְדָרִים, sf. נְדָרַי, נְדָרֶיהָ, נִדְרֵיכֶם: **vow**: — 1. wording of the vow Gn 28_{20ff}; — 2. references to kinds of vows, e.g. *nēder nāzîr* Nu 6_{2ff}; object vowed, e.g. *neder* = *zebaḥ* Lv 7_{16}; verbs, e.g. *qām nēder* the vow is valid Nu 30_5, *'āśâ nēder* perform a vow Ju 11_{39}, *šillēm nēder* pay a vow Dt 23_{22}.

נֹהַּ Ez 7_{11}: unexpl.; del. ?. †

I נָהַג: **qal**: pf. 'נ, נָהֲגוּ; impf. יִנְהַג, יִנְהָג, יִנְהָגוּ, יִנְהָגוּ, אֶנְהָגְךָ; impv. נְהַג; pt. נֹהֵג, נֹהֲגִים: — 1. **drive** (cattle) Gn 31_{18}; *nāhag wᵉhālak* drive (animals) & walk along 2K 4_{24}; drive off: cattle 1S 23_5, prisoners Is 20_4; urge on (one's horse) 2K 9_{20}; — 2. **lead, guide**: obj. men Is 60_{11}, cart 2S 6_3; w. *bᵉ* be leader of (animals) Is 11_6; lead (army) 1C 20_1.

piel: pf. נִהַג, נִהַגְתָּ; impf. יְנַהֵג, וַיְנַהֲגֵהוּ, יְנַהֶגְךָ, וַיְנַהֲגֵם: — 1. **carry off, lead away** (men) Gn 31_{26}; — 2. **lead, guide** (men) Is 49_{10}; **make** (chariot) **proceed** (laboriously) Ex 14_{25}; — 3. **lead forth** (a wind) **(to blow)** Ex 10_{13}.

cj. **pual**: pt. מְנֹהָגוֹת: **carried off, lead away** Na 2_8? †

II נהג: **piel**: pt. מְנַהֲגוֹת: **sob** Na 2_8 (oth.: I cj. pual). †

I נָהָה: **qal**: pf. 'נ; impv. נְהֵה: **lament** Ez 32_{18} Mi 2_4. †

II נהה: **nif.**: impf. וַיִּנָּהוּ: w. *'aḥᵃrê* **keep close to, stay loyal to** 1S 7_2. †

נְהִי: נְהִי: **lament** Je $9_{9.17-19}$ 31_{15} Am 5_{16} Mi 2_4. †

נהל: **piel**: pf. נִהַלְתָּ; impf. יְנַהֵל, יְנַהֲלֵם, יְנַהֲלוּם; pt. מְנַהֵל: — 1. **guide, help along, lead carefully** (esp. the handicapped) Ex 15_{13}; obj. animals w. young Is 40_{11}, those drunk 51_{18}; — 2. *baḥ^amōrîm* **help along** on asses 2C 28_{15}; w. *balleḥem* 'see s.one through,' **supply** w. bread Gn 47_{17}.

hitp.: impf. אֶתְנָהֲלָה: **move along** (intrans.) Gn 33_{14}. †

נַהֲלָל: n. loc.

I **נַהֲלֹל***: pl. נַהֲלֹלִים: **watering-place** Is 7_{19}. †

II **נַהֲלֹל**: = I; n. loc. = נַהֲלָל Ju 1_{30}. †

נהם: **qal**: pf. נָהַמְתְּ, נְהַמְתֶּם; impf. יִנְהֹם; pt. נֹהֵם: — 1. **growl** (of lion) Is 5_{29f} Pr 28_{15}; — 2. **groan** Ez 24_{23} Pr 5_{11}. †

נַ֫הַם: **growling** (of lion) Pr 19_{12} 20_{2}. †

נְהָמָה: — 1. **groaning** Ps 38_{9}; — 2. **roaring** (of sea) Is 5_{30}. †

נהק: **qal**: impf. יִנְהַק, יִנְהָקוּ: **bray** (of wild ass) Jb 6_{5}; **shriek** (of outcasts) 30_{7}. †

I **נהר**: **qal**: pf. נָהֲרוּ; impf. יִנְהֲרוּ: metaph. **stream** (of nations) Is 2_{2} Je 51_{44} Mi 4_{1}. †

II **נהר**: **qal**: pf. נָהַרְתְּ, נָהֲרוּ, נָהָרוּ: metaph. **shine, be radiant** (w. joy) Is 60_{5} Je 31_{12} Ps 34_{6}. †

נָהָר (120×): cs. נְהַר; pl. נְהָרִים (4×) & (more oft.) נְהָרוֹת; cs. נַהֲרֵי & נַהֲרוֹת, sf. נַהֲרֹתֶיךָ, נַהֲרֹתָם; du. נַהֲרַיִם: permanent watercourse: — 1. **river** Nu 24_{6}; current (in sea) Jon 2_{4}; — 2. cosmological: *nāhār yōṣēʾ mēʿēden* Gn 2_{10} (or Persian Gulf?); Y. sets the earth on *n^ehārôt* Ps 24_{2}; rivers in depths of the earth Jb 28_{11}; river around city of God Ps 46_{5}; — 3. spec. rivers: *hannāhār haggādôl* = **Euphrates** Gn 15_{18}, = **Tigris** Dn 10_{4}; *(han)nāhār* = **Euphrates** Gn 31_{21} Mi 7_{12}; *n^ehar miṣrayim* = **Nile** Gn 15_{18}.

נְהָרָה: **(bright) light** Jb 3_{4}. †

נַהֲרַיִם, נַהֲרָיִם: n. terr., alw. *ʾ^arām nah^arayim*, orig. area within great bend of Euphrates, then all central Mesopotamia Gn 24_{10}.

נוא: **qal**: impf. תְּנוּאוּן, rd Qr תְּנִיאוּן ↗ hif.: Nu 32_{7}. †

hif.: pf. הֵנִיא; impf. יָנִיא, וַיָּנִיאוּ, תְּנִיאוּן: — 1. w. acc. **hinder, prevent** (s.one fm. performing a vow) Nu $30_{6.9.12}$, counter (obj. *lēb*, one's urge to) 32_{7} Qr, $_{9}$; — 2. **thwart** (s.one's plans) Ps 33_{10}.

נוב: **qal**: impf. יָנוּב, יְנוּבוּן: **prosper, grow** Ps 62_{11} 92_{15}, w. acc. to wisdom Pr 10_{31}. †

polel: impf. יְנוֹבֵב: **make** s.one **flourish** Zc 9_{17}. †

נֹוב Is 57_{19}: rd Qr נִיב.

נֵובָי Ne 10_{20}: ↗ Qr נֵיבָי, Kt נוֹבָי.

[**נוג***: נוּגוֹת La 1_{4}: ↗ I יגה nif. pt.; נוּגֵי Zp 1_{18} rd. כְּיוֹם מוֹעֵד.]

נוד: **qal**: pf. נָדוּ; impf. יָנוּד, תָּנֻד, וַיָּנֻדוּ; impv. נֻדוּ; inf. לָנֻד; pt. נָד: — 1. **sway** (of reed in water) 1K 14_{15}; — 2. **be(come) aimless, homeless** Gn $4_{12.14}$, of bird Ps 11_{1}; — 3. *yānûd lô* **express** sympathy, **condolence to s.one** by shaking head Is 51_{19} & oft.

hif.: impf. יָנִיד, תְּנִידֵנִי; inf. הָנִיד: — 1. **make homeless** 2K 21_{8} Ps 36_{12}; — 2. **shake** (*b^erōʾšô* the head) Je 18_{16}. †

hitpolel: pf. הִתְנוֹדְדָה; impf. תִּתְנוֹדָד, יִתְנוֹדָדוּ; pt. מִתְנוֹדֵד: — 1. **sway back & forth** (earth, like a hut) Is 24_{20}; — 2. **shake** (in disapproval, disdain), w. *b^e* about (s.one) Je 48_{27} Ps 64_{9}; — 3. **lament, bemoan one's fate** Je 31_{18}. †

נוֹד: *ʾereṣ nôd*, n. terr., unknown, Gn 4_{16}. †

נוֹדָב: (n. pers. =) n. tribe.

I **נוה**: **qal**: impf. יִנְוֶה: ? reach one's goal, succeed, have enough, Hb 2_{5}, but prp. יִרְוֶה or יִבְנֶה. †

II **נוה**: **hif.**: impf. אַנְוֵהוּ (prp. piel אֲנַוֵּהוּ): **praise** Ex 15_{2}. †

נָוֶה: cs. נְוֵה, sf. נָוֵהוּ, נָוְךָ, נְוֵהֶם; ↗ נָוָה: destination of (semi-)nomadic tribe > pasturage > camping place > place of residence, home: — 1. **pasturage** 2S 7_{8}, for camels Ez 25_{5}; — 2. **abode, residence**: a) haunt (of animals) Is 34_{13}; b) = house Jb 5_3; c) Palestine is *nāweh* for Jacob/Isr. Je 10_{25} 50_{19}; *newēh šālôm*

***נָוָה**: cs. נְוַת; pl. cs. נְוֹת Zp 2_6 > נְאוֹת: — 1. **pasturage**: *ne'ôt midbār* Je 9_9, *ne'ôt rō'îm* Am 1_2, *ne'ôt deše'* (rich in grass) Ps 23_2; — 2. **abode, residence**: *newat ṣidqekā* an abode befitting you Jb 8_6; *ne'ôt haššālôm* Je 25_{37}.

נָוֹת 1S 20_1, נָוִית $19_{18f.22f}$ = Qr נָיוֹת, Kt נָוְיַת or נָוִית: not n. loc., but descriptive noun, **pasturage, residence** ↗ נָוֶה. †

נוֹזֵל: ↗ *נזל.

I **נוח**: **qal**: pf. נָחָה, וְנָחָה Is 11_2, נַחְתִּי Jb 3_{26}, וְנָחוּ Is 7_{19}, וְנַחְנוּ; impf. יָנוּחַ, וַיָּנַח (= hif.); inf. לָנוּחַ (↗ I נַחַת), נֹחָה, וְהֵחֶךְ: — 1. **settle** (intrans.): (ark on mountain) Gn 8_4, (locusts on land) Ex 10_{14}, (spirit of Elijah on Elisha) 2K 2_{15}; — 2. stay settled, **rest**: (ark) Nu 10_{36}, (hand of Y. on mountain) Is 25_{10}; — 3. **take a rest**, 'rest up': Y. Ex 20_{11}; — 4. impersonal: *yānûaḥ lî* = I have rest, am at rest Jb 3_{13}; — 5. **wait** 1S 25_9.

hif. (2 forms: הֵנִיחַ & הִנִּיחַ): I pf. הֵנִיחַ, הֲנִ(י)חֹ(וֹ)תִי; impf. וַיָּנַח, יָנִיחַ (↗ qal!), יְנִיחֵנִי, תְּנִיחֶנּוּ; impv. הָנִיחוּ; inf. הָנִיחַ, הֲנִיחִי; pt. מֵנִיחַ: — 1. **lower** (obj. one's hand) Ex 17_{11}, **let** (blessing) **come down, rest** Ez 44_{30}; — 2. **provide rest, quiet** 1K 5_{18}; — 3. **satisfy, appease** (one's anger) Ez 5_{13}; give joy, satisfaction Pr 29_{17}.

hif. II: pf. הִנִּ(י)חַ, הִנַּחְתָּ, וְהִנַּחְתָּ, הִנִּיחוּ, sf. הִנִּיחוֹ, הִנַּחְתּוֹ, הִנִּיחוּךָ; impf. יַנִּיחַ, וַיַּנַּח, יַנִּיחוּ, sf. וַיַּנִּ(י)חֵהוּ, וַיַּנִּ(י)חוּם, אַנִּיחֶנּוּ, תַּנִּחֵנוּ; impv. הַנַּח, הַנִּיחָה, הַנִּחוּ; inf. הַנִּיחוֹ; pt. מַנִּיחַ: — 1. **set, put, settle** somewhere: obj. Adam in garden Gn 2_{15}, garment beside one 39_{16}; **lay aside** = save Ex 16_{23}, deposit Dt 14_{28}; w. *bammišmār* put in custody Lv 24_{12}; **station** (troops) 2C 1_{14}; w. *lā'āreṣ* throw to the ground Is 28_2; — 2. **leave** (s.one or s.thg), **let** (s.one or s.thg) **stay**: a) obj. pers. Gn 19_{16}; b) obj. name Is 65_{15}; c) **leave (behind)** = abandon Ps 119_{121}; d) **let, allow**, w. *le* & inf. Ps 105_{14}; e) **leave alone** = let continue to exist Ju 2_{23}; f) **leave alone** = let continue to do as before 2S 16_{11}; — 3. var.: *hinnîaḥ yādô min* keep one's hand from Ec 7_{18}; *hinnîaḥ meqômô* give up one's place Ec 10_{4a}; *hinnîaḥ ḥaṭā'îm* undo (offenses) 10_{4b}.

hof.: I: pf. הוּנַח: w. *lō'* & *le* we are given no rest La 5_5. †

hof.: II (Aramaizing): pf. הֻנִּיחָה Zc 5_{11} rd. וְהִנִּיחָה (hif. I); pt. ↗ מֻנָּח. †

II **נוח**: **qal**: impf. אָנוּחַ: **groan** (in anticipation of) Hb 3_{16}. †

נוֹחַ: sf. נוֹחֶךָ: — 1. **rest** Est 9_{17f}; — 2. **place of rest** 2C 6_{41}. †.

נוֹחָה: n. pers.

נוט: **qal**: impf. תָּנוּט: **quake, shake** Ps 99_1.

נָוִית 1S $19_{18f.22f}$ 20_1: ↗ נָוֹת.

cj. ***נָוֶל**: **threads (of life)** cj. Ez 37_{11} נִגְזַר נוֹלֵנוּ, but questionable. †

נום: **qal**: pf. נָמוּ; impf. יָנוּם; inf. נוּם: **fall asleep, slumber** Is 5_{27} 56_{10} Na 3_{18} Ps 76_6 121_{3f}. †

נוּמָה: **drowsiness** Pr 23_{21}. †

נוּן & 1C 7_{27} נוֹן: n. pers.

נוס: **qal** (150×): pf. נָס, נָסָה, נַסְתֶּם, נַסְנוּ; impf. יָנוּס, וַיָּנָס, וַיָּנֹס, יָנוּסוּ, יָנֻסוּ, יְנוּסוּן, נָנוּס; impv. נֻסוּ; inf. נוּס, 2× נָס, נוּסְךָ, נוּסָם, נוֹס; pt. נָס (הַנָּיס Je 48_{44} = Qr הַנָּס Kt הַנִּיס): **flee, escape, slip away**: men Gn 19_{20}, sea Ps 114_3, shadows SS 2_{17}, metaph. vital strength Dt 34_7.

polel: pf. נֹסְסָה: **drive onward** Is 59_{19}. †

hif.: pf. הֵנִיס; impf. יָנִיסוּ; inf. הָנִיס: — 1. **put to flight** Dt 32_{30}; — 2. **flee, escape** Ju 7_{21} Je 48_{44} Kt; — 3. **get** s.thg **to safety** Ex 9_{20} Ju 6_{11}. †

hitpolel: inf. הִתְנוֹסֵס: **get** (onesf.) **to safety** Ps 60_6. †

נוע: **qal**: pf. נָעוּ, וְנָעוּ; impf. יָנוּעַ, וַיָּנַע, תָּנוּעַ, יְנוּעוּן,

יְנוּעוּן Ps 59_{16} Kt; inf. cs. נוֹעַ, לָנוּעַ; pt. נָע, נָעוֹת: — 1. **shake, tremble, totter**: people Ex 20_{18}, doorposts Is 6_4, trees 7_2, needy fm. one city to another Am 4_8; hang dangling, swing Jb 28_4; sway over Ju 9_9 = rule over?; — 2. **roam** (around) **without** shelter or home Ps 59_{16}; *nā' wānād* Gn 4_{12}.

nif.: impf. יִנּוֹעַ, יִנֹּעוּ: **be shaken**: grain in sieve Am 9_9, figs Na 3_{12}. †

hif.: pf. הֵנִיעָה, וַהֲנִעוֹתִי; impf. יָנִיעַ, יָנַע, אָנִיעָה, יָנֹעוּ, יְנִיעוּן Ps 59_{16} Qr (ꟻ qal), יְנִיעֵם, תְּנִיעֵנִי, אֲנִיעֲךָ 2S 15_{20}; impv. הֲנִיעֵמוֹ: — 1. **make** or **let** s.one **wander**, **make** s.one **unsteady** Nu 32_{13} 2S 15_{20} Qr; — 2. **shake up, disturb** (obj. bones) 2K 23_{18}; — 3. **shake**: a) the head (in disdain) 2K 19_{21}; b) (one's own) hand, fist Zp 2_{15}; c) metaph. Isr. Am 9_9.

נוֹעַדְיָה: n. pers. m. & f.

I **נוף**: **hif.**: pf. הֵנִיף, הֲנִפֹתָ, הֲנִיפוֹתִי; impf. תָּנִיף, וַיָּנֶף, יְנִיפֶהוּ; impv. הָנִיפוּ; inf. הָנִיף, הֲנִיפְכֶם; pt. מֵנִיף: — 1. **move back & forth, swing, wield, wave**: obj. sword Ex 20_{25}, saw Is 10_{15}; hand (for healing) 2K 5_{11}, (threatening) Is 13_2, (punishing) Is 11_{15}; — 2. cultic: a) w. *tᵉnûfâ*, offer the 'wave-offering,' move it back & forth in front of the altar Ex 29_{24}; b) w. *'ōmer* Lv 23_{11f} & *minḥat haqqᵉnā'ōt* Nu 5_{25} offer by waving.

hof.: pf. הוּנַף: **be dedicated by being waved** Ex 29_{27}. †

polel: impf. יְנוֹפֵף: w. *yād*, **wave one's hand threateningly** Is 10_{32}. †

II **נוף**: **qal**: pf. נַפְתִּי: **sprinkle** (bed w. myrrh) Pr 7_{17}. †

hif.: impf. תָּנִיף: **make** (rain) **fall** Ps 68_{10}. †

נוֹף: **height**, *yᵉfēh nôf* lovely in height, high-rising Ps 48_3. †

נוץ: **qal**: pf. נָצוּ: **wander off, go away** La 4_{15}. †

נוֹצָה: sf. cj. נֹצָתוֹ (for ־תָה): feathers, plumage cj. Lv 1_{16}; Ez $17_{3.7}$; for Jb 39_{13} ꟻ II נֹצָה. †

[**נוק**: **hif.**: impf. וַתְּנִקֵהוּ Ex 2_9: ꟻ ינק hif.]

[**נוש**: **qal**: impf. וָאָנוּשָׁה Ps 69_{21}: rd. וָאֲנוּשָׁה (ꟻ אָנוּשׁ).]

נזה: **qal**: impf. יִזֶּה, וַיִּז 2K 9_{33}, יִזּ Is 63_3 rd וַיִּז: **be sprinkled, spatter** (intrans.) Lv 6_{20} 2K 9_{33} Is 63_3. †

hif.: pf. הִזָּה, הִזֵּיתָ; impf. יַזֶּה, וַיַּז; impv. הַזֵּה; pt. cs. מַזֵּה: — 1. w. prep. **sprinkle** (blood &c.) on: w. *'al* Ex 29_{21}, *'el* Lv 14_{51}, *lifnê* Lv 14_{16}; — 2. w. acc. **sprinkle** (the surface of the veil at sanctuary) **with** (some of the blood, *min-haddām*) † Lv $4_{6.17}$.

נָזִיד: cs. נְזִיד: **a boiled dish** (of food) 2K $4_{38.40}$ Hg 2_{12}; = lentils Gn $25_{29.34}$; *sîr hannāzîd* cooking pot 2K 4_{39}. †

נָזִיר: cs. נְזִיר, sf. נְזִירְךָ; pl. נְזִ(י)רִים, sf. נְזִ(י)רֶיהָ: (s.one) dedicated, consecrated; — 1. *'innᵉbê nᵉzîrekā* adj. (grape-)vines given over to free growth & not harvested during sabbatical year, **unpruned vine-stem** † Lv $25_{5.11}$; — 2. noun, **Nazirite**, s.one devoted to God (*nᵉzîr 'ᵉlōhîm* Ju 13_5) w. the obligation to let hair grow & not to touch wine Nu 6_2; — 3. s.one dedicated, consecrated, **prince**, Joseph-tribe in contrast to others † Gn 49_{26} Dt 33_{16}.

נזל: **qal**: impf. יִזַּל, יִזְּלוּ; pt. נֹזְלִים: **trickle, drip down, flow**: rain Is 45_8, tears Je 9_{17}.

hif.: pf. הִזִּיל: **make** (water) **flow** Is 48_{21}. †

***נֵזֶל** & ***נוֹזֵל**: pl. נֹ(וֹ)זְלִים, sf. נֹזְלֵיהֶם: pl. **brooks, watercourses** Ps 78_{16}; **waves** † Ex 15_8.

נֶזֶם: sf. נִזְמָהּ; pl. נְזָמִים, cs. נִזְמֵי: **ring** Ex 35_{22}, nose-ring (of woman) Gn 24_{22}, ear-ring (of woman) Gn 35_4, (of man) Ex 32_2.

נֵזֶק: **burden, trouble** Est 7_4. †

נזר: **nif.**: impf. יִנָּזֵר; inf. הִנָּזֵר: — 1. undertake abstentions, **dedicate onesf. to a deity** Ho 9_{10} (ironic?); — 2. w. *mē'aḥᵃrê* separate onesf. fm. = **forsake, desert** s.one Ez 14_7; — 3. w. *min*, **treat with awe** Lv 22_2; — 4. **fast**: *hinnāzēr* adv., with fasting Zc 7_3. †

hif.: pf. הִזִּיר, הִזַּרְתֶּם; impf. יַזִּיר; inf. הַזִּירוֹ, הַזִּיר: — 1. **restrain** s.one fm. Lv 15_{31}; — 2. (denom.) **live as a nāzîr, accept the obligations of Nazirite** Nu $6_{2.5f.12}$, w. *min*, **abstain, restrain onesf.** from 6_3. †

נֵזֶר: sf. נִזְרוֹ: — 1. **consecration, ordination**: of priest Lv 21_{12}, of *nāzîr* Nu 6_7; *neder nizrô* his consecration vow Nu 6_5, *rō'š nizrô* his consecrated head (of hair) 6_9, > *nizrô* 6_{12}, *nizrēk* your **head of hair (wh. is) long** (by Nazirite consecration) Je 7_{29}; — 2. a kind of crown, **diadem, headband** (of silver or gold w. lacing-holes, as mark of being consecrated): of king 2K 11_{12}, high-priest Ex 29_6; *'abnê nēzer* precious stones of headband Zc 9_{16}.

נֹחַ: n. pers., **Noah**.

נַחְבִּי: n. pers.

נחה: **qal**: pf. נָחִיתָ, sf. נָחָם, נָחַנִי, נָחֲךָ: impf. ↗ hif.; impv. נְחֵנִי, נְחֵה: **lead**: subj. men Is 60_{11}, subj. Y. Gn 24_{27}.

hif.: pf. sf. הִנְחִיתָם, הִנְחַנִי; impf. תַּנְחֶה, sf. יַנְחוּנִי, אַנְחֶנָּה, יַנְחֶנִּי, יַנְחֵנִי; inf. לְהַנְחֹתָם > לַנְחֹ' Ex 13_{21}: **lead**: subj. men Nu 23_7, subj. Y. Gn 24_{48}.

נַחוּם: n. pers. **Nahum**.

[נְחוּם: n. pers. Ne 7_7: rd. רְחוּם Ezr 2_2.]

*נִחוּמִים Ho 11_8: ↗ נִחֻמִים.

נָחוֹר: n. pers.

נָחוּשׁ: adj. **(made) of bronze** Jb 6_{12}. †

נְחוּשָׁה (9×) & נְחֻשָׁה Lv 26_{19}: **copper, bronze**, = *n^ehōšet*, Lv 26_{19}; as gen. (made) of bronze: bow 2S 23_{35}, doors Is 45_2, forehead 48_4.

נְחִילוֹת: *'el-n^ehîlôt* Ps 5_1: unexpl., tech. hymnic or musical term: sugg. 'for flutes,' or 'against illness'; ↗ comm. †

*נָחִיר du. sf. נְחִירָיו: **nostrils** (of beast) Jb 41_{12}. †

נָחַל: **qal**: pf. נָחֲלָה, נ׳, נְחַלְתֶּם, sf. נְחָלְתָּם; impf. יִנְחַל, תִּנְחַל, יִנְחֲלוּ, יִנְחָלוּ, יִנְחָלוּהָ, יִנְחָלוּם; inf. נְחֹל: — 1. abs. **obtain, receive property** Nu 18_{20}, = *nāḥal nah^alâ* 18_{23}; — 2. *nāḥal 'ereṣ* **take possession** of land Ex 23_{30}; extended use w. obj. *šeqer* Je 16_{19}, *kābôd* Pr 3_{35} &c.; inherit Zp 2_9; — 3. subj. God, w. *b^e*, **own** (the nations as his property) Ps 82_8; **accept** (Isr. as his property) Ex 34_9; — 4. **give hereditary possession of, distribute, apportion** Nu $34_{17f.}$

piel: pf. נִחֲלוּ, נִחַל; inf. נַחֵל: **designate hereditary possession** (of land) to s.one (in a country) Nu 34_{29}; w. *n^eḥālôt* & *l^e*, **distribute, apportion** Jos 19_{51}.

hif.: pf. הִנְחַלְתִּי; impf. יַנְחִילְךָ, יַנְח(י)ל, יַנְחִילֵם, תַּנְחִילֶנָּה; inf. cs. הַנְחִיל & הַנְחֵל Dt 32_8; pt. מַנְחִיל: — 1. **give hereditary possession of**: a) w. 2 acc. 1S 2_8; b) w. 1 acc. (of property) Is 49_8; **provide for** (s.one) fm. (one's property) Ez 46_{18}; — 2. **bequeath** 1C 28_8; — 3. **apportion** (nations) **as a possession** Dt 32_8 (oth.: apportion their inheritance to the nations).

hof.: pf. הָנְחַלְתִּי: w. *lî* & acc., became possessor of = had to inherit Jb 7_3. †

hitp.: pf. הִתְנַחַלְתֶּם, sf. הִתְנַחֲלוּם; impf. תִּתְנַחֲלוּ, תִּתְנֶחָלוּ; inf. הִתְנַחֵל: — 1. **obtain, receive hereditary possession of**: w. acc. *hā'āreṣ* Nu 33_{54a} 34_{13} Ez 47_{13}; *'îš nah^alātô* Nu 32_{18}; abs. 33_{54b}; —2. **bequeath** (property) Lv 25_{46}; — 3. w. *l^e*, **take over possession of** (s.one) as (slave) Is 14_2. †

I נַחַל (140×): נָחַל, loc. נַחְלָה Nu 34_5, as nominative Ps 124_4, נַחְלָה Ez 47_{19} 48_{28}; pl. נְחָלִים, cs. נַחֲלֵי, sf. נְחָלֶיהָ; du. נַחֲלַיִם Ez 47_9 rd. נַחֲלָם or הַנַּחַל: — 1. **stream-bed, wadi**, either w. perennial stream or (oft.) stream only in rainy season, Gn 26_{19}; — 2. **stream, small river**: = Jabbok Gn 32_{24}; *nah^alê mayim* = streams full of water Dt 8_7; Euphrates divided into 7 streams Is 11_{15}; — 3. **pit, shaft**, (mining) **tunnel**: shafts dug either vertically or horizontally for graves Ne 2_{15}, for mining Jb 28_4; — 4. cosmic:

naḥ^{a}lê b^{e}liyya'al 2S 22_5, *naḥal gofrît* Is 30_{33} &c.; metaph. *naḥ^{a}lê šemen* streams of oil Mi 6_7; — 5. oft. w. spec. names of streams, ℱ *'arnôn*, III *'eškōl* &c.; spec. *naḥal miṣrayim* = *Wadî el-'Arîš* 1K 8_{65}.

II *נַחַל: נֶחַל; pl. נְחָלִים: **date-palm** Nu 24_6 (oth.: I), SS 6_{11}. †

I נַחֲלָה (ca. 250×): cs. נַחֲלַת, sf. נַחֲלָתוֹ, נַחֲלַתְכֶם, נַחֲלָתָן, נַחֲלָתֶךָ: — 1. (inalienable) **hereditary possession, heritage**, acquired by individual or family by conquest or inheritance, both property (i.e. land & buildings) & (movable) goods: *naḥ^{a}lat 'a^{a}bōtay* 1K 21_{3f}, *ḥēleq w^{e}naḥ^{a}lâ* Gn 31_{14}; w. var. vbs., e.g. *nātan* Nu 18_{21}, *he'^{e}bîr* 27_7; *naḥ^{a}lâ tippōl* 34_2; — 2. spec.: Y. is *ḥēleq & naḥ^{a}lâ* for Aaron Nu 18_{20}, for Levites Dt 10_9; Isr. is *'am naḥ^{a}lâ* for God Dt 4_{20}, cf. 1K 8_{51}; sons are *naḥ^{a}lat yhwh* (= given by Y.) Ps 127_3; *naḥ^{a}lâ* = simply 'possessions' Pr 20_{21}.

II נַחֲלָה Is 17_{11} = נַחֲלָה: I חלה nif. pt. > noun, **infirmity, ill health**. †

III נַחֲלָה Ez 47_{19} 48_{28}: ℱ I נַחַל: n. loc., usu. cj. נַחְלָה = *naḥal miṣrayim*; ℱ comm. †

נַחֲלִיאֵל: n. loc.

נֶחֱלָמִי: gent. of *נֶחֱלָם.

נחם: **nif.** (ca. 50×): pf. (ℱ piel!) נִחַם, נִחָם, נִחָמְתִּי; impf. וַיִּנָּחֵם, וַיִּנָּחֶם, אֶנָּחֵם, יִנָּחֲמוּ; inf. הִנָּחֵם; pt. נִחָם: — 1. **regret**: a) have regrets, a change of heart 1S 15_{29}; b) *niḥam 'al* allow onesf. a change of heart regarding, relent regarding Ex 32_{12}; c) abs. turn fm. former attitude, repent Jb 42_6; — 2. **(allow onesf. to) be sorry**: a) subj. God Ps 90_{13}, w. *kî* that Gn 6_{6f}; b) subj. man, w. *'el/l^e* for Ju $21_{6.15}$, abs. Je 31_{19}; — 3. **comfort, console onesf.**: a) find comfort, consolation Gn 24_{67}, w. *'al* about 2S 13_{39}; b) *niḥam min*, obtain satisfaction, take relish in Is 1_{24}; c) observe time of mourning Gn 38_{12}; d) complete the rites of mourning, be consoled Je 31_{15}.

piel: pf. (ℱ nif.!) נִחַם, נִחֲמוּ, נִחַמְתָּנִי, נִחַמְתִּים; impf. יְנַחֵם, יְנַחֲמוּן, יְנַחֲמֵנִי, אֲנַחֶמְכֶם, יְנַחֲמֻנִי; impv. נַחֵם, נַחֲמוּ; inf. נַחֵם, נַחֲמוֹ, לְנַחֲמֵנִי; pt. מְנַחֵם, מְנַחֲמִים, מְנַחֶמְכֶם: **comfort** (w. words): — 1. in case of death Gn 37_{35}; express one's condolence by a messenger 2S 10_{2f}; more genl., reassure (one's relatives) Gn 50_{21}; — 2. in other situations of comforting: a mother her child Is 66_{13}, Boaz to Ruth in her affliction Ru 2_{13}; acc. *hebel*, give empty comfort Zc 10_2; — 3. subj. God Is 12_1.

pual: pf. נֻחָמָה; impf. תְּנֻחָמוּ: **be comforted** Is 54_{11} 66_{13}. †

hitp.: pf. וְהִנֶּחָמְתִּי; < *וְהִתְנֶ׳; impf. יִתְנֶחָם, וְאֶתְנֶחָם; inf. הִתְנַחֵם; pt. מִתְנַחֵם: — 1. w. *l^e* **scheme revenge** against Gn 27_{42}, get revenge Ez 5_{13b}; — 2. **(allow onesf. to) be sorry** Nu 23_{19} Dt 32_{36} Ps 135_{14}; — 3. **be comforted, consoled** at end of time of mourning, console onesf. Ps 119_{52}. †

נַחַם: n. pers.

נֹחַם: **pity, compassion** Ho 13_{14}. †

*נֶחָמָה: sf. נֶחָמָתִי: **comfort** Ps 119_{50} Jb 6_{10}. †

נְחֶמְיָה: n. pers.

נִחֻמִים: sf. נִחוּמָי: **consolation, comfort** Is 57_{18} Ho 11_8 Zc 1_{13}. †

נַחֲמָנִי: n. pers.

נַחְנוּ: נָחְנוּ: **we** Gn 42_{11} Ex 16_{7f} Nu 32_{32} La 3_{42}. †

נַחֲנְתְּ Je 22_{23}: pf. 2. f., usu. expl. as = *נֶחַנְתְּ < *נֶאֱנַחְתְּ (אנח nif.) groan; oth.: ref. to a III חנן nif. 'groan,' or to *נחן 'groan'. †

נחץ: **qal**: pt. pass. נָחוּץ: *d^{e}bar hammelek nāḥûṣ* 1S 21_9 **urgent** (?) (oth.: confidential). †

נָחַר: **qal**: pf. נ׳: **blow** (of bellows) Je 6_{29}. †

(?) **piel**: pf. נִחֲרוּ: SS 1_6, w. *b^e* pant at (in rage? lust?), but oth.: I חרה nif. pf. become angry, ℱ comm. †

*נַחַר: **snorting** (of horse) Jb 39_{20}. †

*נַחֲרָה: cs. נַחֲרַת: **snorting** (of horse) Je 8_{16}. †

נַחְרַי: n. pers.

נחשׁ: **piel**: pf. נִחֵשׁ, נִחַשְׁתִּי; impf. יְנַחֵשׁ; inf. נַחֵשׁ; pt. מְנַחֵשׁ: **seek & give an omen, practice divination** Gn 44_{15} + 4×; Gn 30_{27} I learned through divination (oth.: read as nif., I was bewitched); 1K 20_{33} took it as an omen (i.e. good omen).

נַ֫חַשׁ: pl. נְחָשִׁים: **bewitchment, magic curse** Nu 23_{23} 24_1. †

I **נָחָשׁ**: cs. נְחַשׁ; pl. נְחָשִׁים: **snake** Gn 3_{1ff}; in sea Am 9_3 sugg.: crocodile, oth.: dragon.

II **נָחָשׁ**: n. loc., *ʿîr nāḥāš* 1C 4_{12}. †

III **נָחָשׁ**: n. pers.

נַחְשׁוֹן: n. pers.

I **נְחֹשֶׁת** (ca. 140×): sf. נְחָשְׁתִּי La 3_7, נְחָשְׁתָּהּ; du. נְחֻשְׁתַּיִם: **copper**, alloyed w. tin > **bronze**: — 1. in lists of metals Gn 4_{22} 2S 8_{10}; — 2. as material 1K 7_{14}; — 3. items made of bronze 2K 25_{13}; *neḥōšet* = fetters of bronze La 3_7, du. 2K 25_7.

II **נְחֹשֶׁת**: sf. נְחָשְׁתֵּךְ Ez 16_{36}: mng. uncert.: sugg. 'female genitals,' but more likely 'menstruation.' †

נְחֻשְׁתָּא: n. pers. f.

נְחֻשְׁתָּן: (name of) **bronze snake-idol** 2K 18_4. †

נחת: **qal**: impf. יֵחַת, תֵּחַת: — 1. tech. military term, **march down** (intrans.) Je 21_{13}; — 2. **descend** cj. Jb 17_{16} & 21_{13}; — 3. **penetrate** (more) **deeply** (than), subj. rebuke Pr 17_{10}. †

nif.: pf. נִחֲתוּ: **penetrate** (of arrow) Ps 38_3. †

piel: pf. נִחַת 2S 22_{35} & נִחֲתָה Ps 18_{35} 2. sg. f. or 3. pl. f.; inf. נַחֵת: — 1. press down (i.e. **string**?) (a bow) 2S 22_{35} Ps 18_{35}; — 3. **settle, level off** (obj. clods of earth) Ps 65_{11}. †

hif.: impv. הַנְחַת: tech. military term, **lead down, march down** (trans.) Jl 4_{11}. †

I **נַ֫חַת**: **descending** (of God's arm) Is 30_{30}. †

II **נַ֫חַת**: **rest, calmness** Is 30_{15} Pr 29_9 Ec 4_6 6_5 9_{17}. †

III **נַ֫חַת**: n. pers.

נְחִתִּים 2K 6_9: sugg. rd. נְחִתִּים coming down, marching down. †

נָטָה: **qal** (ca. 130×): pf. נָטוּ, נָטִיתִי, נָטִיתָ, נ׳, נָטָיו Ps 73_2 Qr (Kt נָטוּי); impf. יִטֶּה, יֵט, וַיֵּט, וַיֵּטוּ, וַיֵּט־; impv. נְטֵה; inf. נְטוֹתִי, נְט(וֹ)ת; pt. נֹ(וֹ)טֶה, sf. נוֹטֵיהֶם (sg.) Is 42_5, pass. נָטוּי, נְטוּיָה, נְטוּת Kt & נְטוּיוֹת Qr Is 3_{16}: — 1. **extend, stretch out**: obj. hand Ex 7_{19}, staff 9_{23}; w. *be* stretch out (the hand with) (e.g. javelin) Jos 8_{18}; — 2. **spread out**: pitch a tent Gn 12_8, ellipt. w/o *ʾōhel* Je 14_8; (obj. measuring-line) Is 44_{13}, (obj. heavens) Is 40_{22}; display (for one's choice) 1C 21_{10}; — 3. **bend down** (trans.): obj. shoulder Gn 49_{15}; *qîr nāṭûy* overhanging wall Ps 62_4; — 4. intrans.: a) **stretch out**, get longer: shadow 2K 20_{10}; w. *ʾel* bend down to Ps 40_2; *nāṭâ le* move off toward Nu 21_{15}; subj. foot, dip = slip Ps 73_2; *neṭôt yôm* the day is declining Ju 19_8; bend down = push Ju 16_{30}; b) **turn (aside)**: w. *yāmîn* to the right Nu 20_{17}, w. *be* turn in (toward) 21_{22}; w. *le* & inf. 2S 2_{19}; c) **turn away** (from) Nu 22_{33}; d) **turn toward**: w. *ʿad* Gn 38_1, *ʾel* 38_{16}, w. *ʾaḥarê* 1S 8_3; w. *le* & inf. be inclined to Ps 119_{112}; metaph. w. *ʾel* Is 66_{12}; hostile, w. *ʿal* Ps 21_{12}.

nif.: pf. נִטָּיו; impf. יִנָּטֶה, יִנָּטוּ: — 1. **be stretched** (measuring-line) Zc 1_{16}; — 2. **stretch out long**: (shadows) Je 6_4; (*neḥālîm*: wadis? date-palms?) Nu 24_6. †

hif. (75×): pf. הִטָּה, הִטִּיתִי, הִטּוּ, הִטִּיתֶם, sf. הִטָּהוּ, הִטַּתּוּ; impf. יַטֶּה, וַיֵּט, תַּט, אַט, Jb 23_{21} (but sugg. rd. אֵט qal), וָאַט, יַטּוּ, sf. יַטְּךָ, יַטֵּנוּ, וַיַּטֵּהוּ; impv. הַטֵּה, הַט, הַטִּי; inf. הַטּ(וֹ)ת, הַטֹּתָה; pt. מַטֶּה, מַטִּים: — 1. **extend, stretch out**, obj. hand Is 31_3; — 2. **spread out**, obj. sackcloth 2S 21_{10}, ellipt. make a bed = stretch out (intrans.), lie down Am 2_8; pitch a tent 2S 16_{22}; — 3. obj. *ḥesed*, extend one's love, w. *ʿad* Ezr 7_{28}; — 4. **incline, bend down**: obj. pitcher, tilt Gn 24_{12}; obj. heart = give one's loyalty Jos 24_{23}; obj. ear = listen 2K 19_{16}; — 5.

bend, obj. *mišpāṭ*, pervert, warp justice Ex 23_6; — 6. **turn aside, to the side** (trans.), **divert**: obj. ark 2S 6_{10}, *lēb* Pr 21_1; force (the innocent man) (fm. his just due) Pr 18_5, turn away (a servant) Ps 27_9; disturb (the natural order) Je 5_{25}; — 7. **mislead** Is 44_{20}; — 8. **turn**, obj. s.one else's heart, w. *'aḥ^a rê* = redirect s.one's loyalty to 1K $11_{2.4}$, = make s.one's loyalty pliable 2S 19_{15}; — 9. intrans. **turn aside** from Is 30_{11}.

hof.: pt. מֻטֶּה, מֻטּוֹת: — 1. **spread out, outspread** Is 8_8; — 2. **refused, disavowed** Ez 9_9. †

נְטֹפָתִי, נְטוֹפָתִי: gent. of נְטֹפָה n. loc.

*נָטִיל: pl. cs. נְטִילֵי: **weigher** (of silver) Zp 1_{11}. †

*נָטִיעַ: pl. נְטִעִים: **shoot** (of a plant) Ps 144_{12}. †

נְטִיפָה Ju 8_{26}: ↗ נְטִפָה.

נְטִישׁוֹת: sf. נְטִישׁוֹתֶיהָ: coll. pl. **tendrils, shoots** (of vine) Is 18_5 Je 5_{10} 48_{32}. †

נָטַל: **qal**: pf. נ׳; impf. יִטּוֹל; pt. נֹטֵל: — 1. **impose** (s.thg on s.one) 2S 24_{12} La 3_{28}; — 2. **weigh** (s.thg) Is 40_{15}. †

piel: impf. וַיְנַטְּלֵם: **lift up** Is 63_9. †

נֵטֶל: **load, burden** Pr 27_3. †

נָטַע: **qal**: pf. נ׳, נָטַע, נָטְעָה Pr 31_{16} (Qr נָטְעָה), נָטַעְתָּ, נְטַעְתֶּם, sf. נְטַעְתִּים, נְטַעְתָּם; impf. יִטַּע, תִּטְּעִי, יִטְּעוּ, יִטָּעוּ, וַיִּטָּעֵהוּ, תִּטָּעֵמוֹ; impv. נִטְעוּ; inf. לִנְטֹעַ & Ec 3_2 לָטַעַת, נְטֹעֲךָ; pt. נֹטֵעַ, cs. נוֹטַע, נֹטְעִים, pass. נָטוּעַ, נְטוּעִים: — 1. **plant**: abs. Is 65_{22}; obj. garden Gn 2_8, vineyard 9_{20}, tree Lv 19_{23}; obj. desolation Ez 36_{36}; — 2. **drive** (a nail) † Ec 12_{11}; — 3. metaph.: obj. ear (i.e. create) Ps 94_9, men Je 12_2; plant = settle (a people) 2S 7_{10}.

nif.: pf. נִטְּעוּ: **be planted** Is 40_{24}. †

נֶטַע: נֶטַע, cs. נְטַע, sf. נִטְעֵךְ, pl. cs. נִטְעֵי: — 1. **planting, plantation** Is 5_7 17_{10}; — 2. **shoot** (of plant) Jb 14_9. †

נְטָעִים: n. loc. 1C 4_{23}. †

נטף: **qal**: pf. נָטָפוּ, נָטְפוּ; impf. תִּטֹּף, תִּטֹּפְנָה, תִּטֹּפוּ; pt. נֹטְפוֹת: **drip** Ju 5_4 Ps 68_9, metaph. Jb 29_{22}; w. acc. drip with (wine, honey) Jl 4_{18} Pr 5_3 SS 4_{11} $5_{5.13}$. †

hif.: pf. הִטִּיפוּ; impf. יַטִּיפוּן, אַטִּף, תַּטִּיף, תַּטִּפוּ; impv. הַטֵּף; pt. מַטִּיף: — 1. **(let) drip, flow** Am 9_{13}; — 2. metaph. let words flow, **drivel** = prophesy ecstatically Ez $21_{2.7}$ Am 7_{16} Mi 2_{6a}, w. *l^e* about Mi $2_{6b.11}$. †

נָטָף: **drops of stacte**, i.e. resin of a shrub, sugg. *Pistacia lentiscus*, Ex 30_{34}. †

*נֶטֶף: pl. cs. נִטְפֵי: **drop** Jb 36_{27}. †

*נְטִפָה: pl. נְטִ(י)פוֹת: **earring** Ju 8_{26} Is 3_{19}. †

נְטֹפָה: n. loc.

נְטֹפָתִי: gent., ↗ נְטוֹפָתִי.

נטר: **qal**: pf. נָטַרְתִּי; impf. יִנְטֹ(ו)ר, תִּטּוֹר, אֶטּוֹר; pt. נֹטֵר, נֹטֵרָה, נֹטְרִים: — 1. **keep watch, guard** (vineyard) SS 1_6 8_{11}f; (— 2. sugg. Am 1_{11} cj. guard one's wrath, keep on being angry; but cj. open to qn.) †

נָטַשׁ: **qal**: pf. נ׳, נָטַשְׁתָּה, sf. נְטַשְׁתַּנוּ, נְטַשְׁתָּהּ, נְטַשְׁתִּיךָ; impf. יִטְּשֵׁהוּ, יִטְּשֵׁנוּ, נִטֹּשׁ, וַיִּטֹּשׁ; impv. נְטוֹשׁ; pt. pass. נְטֻשִׁים: **leave to onesf., abandon**: — 1. obj. *'ereṣ*, **leave untilled, fallow** Ex 23_{11}; — 2. **cast, throw off** † Ez 29_5 31_{12} 32_4; — 3. *ḥereb n^e ṭûšâ* drawn sword † Is 21_{15}; — 4. w. *'al* **leave with, entrust** to 1S 17_{20} = *'al-yad* 17_{22}; leave (the burden of bloodguilt) on Ho 12_{15}; — 5. **abandon** s.thg, be no longer concerned about s.thg: a) subj. man, obj. God Dt 32_{15}; b) subj. God, obj. his people 1K 8_{57}; c) subj. God, obj. 'his heritage' Je 12_7, tabernacle Ps 78_{60}, &c.; — 6. **disregard, pay no attention to** Pr 1_8; — 7. **quit** s.thg, **desist fm.** s.thg Pr 17_{14}, w. acc. **forego, renounce** Ne 10_{32}; — 8. w. acc. **give** s.one **the chance** to Gn 31_{28}.

nif.: pf. נִטְּשָׁה; impf. וַיִּנָּטְשׁוּ: **be left to onesf., abandoned**: — 1. **range out, spread out** Ju 15_9 2S $5_{18.22}$; grow luxuriantly (shoots) Is 16_8; — 2. **lie unattended** Am 5_2. †

pual: pf. נֻטַּשׁ: **be unattended** Is 32_{14}. †

[*נִי: בְּנִיהֶם Ez 27_{32}: sugg. (ב)בְּנֵיהֶם w. Verss., or = בְּנְהִיהֶם, ↗ נְהִי.]

נִיב: sf. נִיבוֹ: **fruit**, metaph. of lips Is 57_{19}; Ma 1_{12} ? gloss, ↗ comm. †

נֵיבַי: n. pers.

נִיד: **shaking of head** (as gesture of condolence); *nîd śefātay* solace of my lips Jb 16_5. †

נִידָה **shaking of head** (here as gesture of mockery); *hāyâ lenîdâ* become an object of mockery La 1_8. †

נִיח(ו)חַ: sf. נִיחֹחֲכֶם ,נִיחֹחִי; pl. sf. נִיחֹחֵיהֶם: **soothing**; alw. *rēaḥ hannîḥōaḥ* soothing odor Gn 8_{21}, otherw. attributive or in cs. w. *'iššeh*, Ex 29_{18} &c.

נִין: sf. נִינִי: **descendant** Gn 21_{23} Is 14_{22} Jb 18_{19}. †

נִינְוֵה: n. loc. **Nineveh**.

נִיס Je 48_{44}: Qr נָס (נוס pt.), Kt. נִיס inf. = noun, 'flight.' †

נִיסָן: name of month, **Nisan** = March/Apr. Est 3_7 Ne 2_1. †

נִיצוֹץ: **spark** Is 1_{31}. †

נִיר: **qal**: impv. נִירוּ: plow for the first time, **break up** (the ground), **bring into cultivation** Je 4_3 Ho 10_{12}. †

I **נִיר**, Pr 21_4 נִר ?: **light, lamp** (as symbol of what lasts) 1K 11_{36} 15_4 2K 8_{19} 2C 21_7; so also perh. Pr 21_4 (↗ נֵר). †

II **נִיר**: **ground newly broken & cleared** Je 4_3 Ho 10_{12} Pr 13_{23}. †

נֵירִי 2S 22_{29}: ↗ I נֵר.

נִירָם Nu 21_{30}: ↗ I ירה qal.

נכא: **nif.**: pf. נִכְּאוּ: **be whipped out, flogged out** Jb 30_8; Ps 109_{16} prob. rd. *נָכֵא ↗ נִכְא. †

נָכָא*: pl. נְכָאִים: **unmercifully beaten, broken** Is 16_7. †

נָכֵא*: cs. נְכֵה, f. נְכֵאָה: **beaten, broken**: *rûaḥ nekē'â* Pr 15_{13} 17_{22} 18_{14}; *nekēh-rûaḥ* Is 66_2, cj. Ps 109_{16}. †

נְכֹאת: a resin, sugg. of cistus- or rock-rose (oth.: of a shrub like *Astragalus gummifer* or *A. tragacantha*) Gn 37_{25} 43_{11}. †

נֶכֶד: sf. נֶכְדִּי: **descendant** Gn 21_{23} Is 14_{22} Jb 18_{19}. †

נכה: **nif.**: pf. נִכָּה: **be hit, be struck down** 2S 11_{15}. †

pual: pf. נֻכְּתָה ,נֻכּוּ: **be battered, ruined, destroyed** (grain by hail) Ex 9_{31f}. †

hif. (480×): pf. הִכֵּיתִי ,הִכִּיתָ(ה) ,הִכָּה, הִכִּיתוֹ ,הִכִּיתָנוּ ,הִכָּנִי ,הִכַּנִי ,הִכָּהוּ ,sf. הִכּוּ, הִכּוּנִי ,הִכּוּם ,הִכִּיתִיךָ ,הִכִּיתִיו; impf. יַכֶּה, וַיַּךְ ,וַתַּךְ ,וָאַכֶּה ,וָאַךְ ,וַיַּכּוּ ,sf. וַיַּכֵּהוּ & וַיַּכּוֹ, יַכֶּכָּה ,אַכֶּנּוּ ,נַכֵּהוּ; impv. הַכֵּה ,הַךְ ,הַכּוּ, sf. הַכֵּ(י)נִי ,הַכֵּהוּ; inf. הַכּוֹת (abs. 2K 3_{24}), הַכּוֹתָם ,הַכֵּה; pt. מַכֶּה, cs. מַכֵּה, sf. מַכֵּהוּ, pl. מַכִּים: — 1. **strike, hit, beat**: a) w. acc. 1K 20_{35}; *hakkôt mē'â* beat 100 times Pr 17_{10}; in extended sense, hit enemy in battle Gn 14_5, obj. land 1S 27_9; b) w. *be* beat on (s.thg or s.one), (virtually = a)) Ex 17_6; w.*be* = with (an instrument): w. staff Ex 17_6; w. disability (blindness) Gn 19_{11}; c) abs. strike at random, strike (in a location) Ez 9_7; — 2. **strike down**: a) = kill, **strike dead** Gn 4_{15b}; b) = **wound** 2S 10_{18}; shoot down 2K 9_{27}; c) metaph.: subj. worm, obj. plant, **attack** Jon 4_7; subj. sun & moon, strike Ps 121_6; d) batter, **destroy**, obj. house Am 3_{15}, city 2K 15_{16}; — 3. subj. God: **strike**: a) w. illness 1S 5_6, crop failure Am 4_9, &c.; b) abs. punish, chastise Is 60_{10}; — 4. var.: a) *hikkâ nefeš* take s.one's life Gn 37_{21}, strike dead Dt 19_6; *hikkâ leḥî* strike on the jaw Ps 3_8; *hikkâ be* thrust in 1S 2_{14}; b) *hikkâ makkâ (gedôlâ) be* strike w. severe plague, torment Ju 11_{33}, inflict a heavy defeat on, a great massacre 2C 13_{17}, = *hikkâ makkat ḥereb be* Est 9_5; c) *hikkâ 'arṣâ* beat on the ground 2K 13_{18}; *hikkâ kaf 'el kaf* clap one's hands Ez 21_{19} & *hikkâ (be)kaf* 2K 11_{12} Ez 6_{11}; *hikkâ bedāwid ûbaqqîr* impale D. to the wall 1S 18_{11}; *hikkâ šārāšîm* strike root Ho 14_6; *hikkâ lēb-dāwid* *'ōtô* D.'s conscience pricked him, D. reproached himsf. 1S 24_6.

hof.: pf. הֻכָּה, הוּכָּה, הֻכְּתָה, הֻכֵּיתִי, הֻכּוּ; impf. יֻכּוּ, תֻּכּוּ; pt. מֻכֶּה, cs. מֻכֵּה, pl. מֻכִּים, מֻכֵּי: — 1. *mukkēh *ᵉlōhîm* struck by God Is 53_4; — 2. **be struck down (dead)** Nu $25_{14f.18}$; be beaten (= taken) (city) Ez 33_{21} 44_1; be hit (heart, by sun) Ps 102_6. †

*נָכֶה or *נֵכֶה: cs. נְכֵה; pl. נֵכִים: struck, hit, beaten: — 1. *nᵉkēh raglayim*, **crippled** 2S 4_4 9_3; — 2. **beaten down, broken**, w. *rûªh* spirit Is 66_2, ↗ *נָכֵא. †

נְכֹה 2K & נְכוֹ Je 2C: n. pers. (Pharaoh) **Necho**.

I נָכוֹן: **kick** Jb 12_5 (oth.: II 'ready'). †

II נָכוֹן: ↗ כון nif. pt.

III נָכוֹן: n. pers. 2C 6_6. †

נֹכַח: sf. נִכְחוֹ: — 1. noun, **what lies opposite** Ez 46_9; — 2. prep.: a) **opposite** 1K 20_{29}; *nōkaḥ lᵉ* Jos 15_7; b) **in front of** (metaph.): *nōkaḥ yhwh* agreeable to Y. Ju 18_6; *nātan/śām nōkaḥ pānāyw* put before onesf. = consider agreeable Ez 14_{37}; c) w. prep. preceding: *'el nōkaḥ* in the direction of Nu 19_4; *lᵉnōkaḥ* directly in front of Gn 30_{38}; w. pray, = for Gn 25_{21}; adv. directly forward Pr 4_{25}; *'ad nōkaḥ* (to a spot) opposite Ju 19_{10}.

*נָכֹחַ: sf. נְכֹחוֹ, f. נְכֹחָה; pl. נְכֹחִים, נְכֹחוֹת: — 1. **lying straight ahead**: noun as adv., *hālak nᵉkōḥô* walk one's straight path Is 57_2; — 2. a) adj. **straight, right** 2S 15_3 Pr 8_9 24_{26}; b) f. as noun: what is straight, right: *nᵉkōḥâ* Is 59_{14} Am 3_{10}, = *nᵉkōḥôt* right(-eousness) Is 26_{10}, truth 30_{10}. †

נכל: **qal**: pt. נוֹכֵל: **act cleverly, cunningly, deceitfully** Ma 1_{14}. †

piel: pf. נִכְּלוּ: **treat cunningly, deceitfully**, w. *lᵉ* Nu 25_{18}. †

hitp.: impf. וַיִּתְנַכְּלוּ; inf. הִתְנַכֵּל: **behave cunningly, deceitfully** toward: w. acc. Gn 37_{18}, w. *bᵉ* Ps 105_{25}. †

*נֵכֶל: pl. sf. נִכְלֵיהֶם: **cunning, deceit** Nu 25_{18}. †

נְכָסִים: **wealth** Jos 22_8 Ec 5_{18} 6_2 2C $1_{11f.}$ †

נכר: [**qal** (?): impf. וָאֶכְּרֶהָ Ho 3_2; best ↗ II כרה. †]

nif.: pf. נִכְּרוּ; impf. יִנָּכֵר: — 1. **dissemble, pretend** Pr 26_{24}; — 2. **be** (considered carefully as strange & thus) **recognized** La 4_8. †

piel: pf. נִכַּר; impf. יְנַכְּרוּ, תְּנַכֵּרוּ: — 1. misjudge, **misrepresent** Dt 32_{27}; — 2. **disfigure, deface** (a place) Je 19_4; w. *bᵉyad* **deliver over** 1S 23_7; — 3. **consider carefully** Jb 21_{29} 34_{19}. †

hif.: pf. הִכִּיר, הִכִּירוֹ, הִכִּירָהוּ; impf. יַכִּיר, וַיַּכֵּר, וָאַכִּירָה, וַיַּכִּרֵם, יַכִּירָנִי Is 63_{16}, יַכִּירוּם, יַכִּירֶנּוּ; impv. הַכֶּר־, הַכִּירֵנִי; inf. הַכֵּר־, הַכִּירֵנִי; pt. מַכִּיר, sf. מַכִּירֵךְ, pl. מַכִּירִים: — 1. **investigate** (as unknown), establish or decide (judicially) Gn 31_{32}; — 2. **recognize** Gn 27_{23}; obj. a voice 1S 26_{17}, *pānîm* show consideration > partiality for s.one Dt 1_{17}; w. *lᵉṭôbâ* consider for good, kindly Je 24_5, w/o *lᵉṭôbâ* Ps 142_5; — 3. have recognized, **know** (be acquainted with, French connaître) Dt 33_9; know of s.thg Ps 103_{16}; (not) wish to know, appreciate Jb 24_{13}; abs. come to know 2S 3_{36}; — 4. w. *lᵉ* & inf. understand how to, **be able to** (French savoir) Ne 13_{24}.

hitp.: impf. יִתְנַכֵּר־, וַיִּתְנַכֵּר; pt. מִתְנַכֵּרוֹת: — 1. **disguise onesf.** 1K 14_{5f}; — 2. make onesf. a stranger to, **keep one's identity** from Gn 42_7; — 3. **make onesf. known** Pr 20_{11}. †

נֵכֶר & *נֹכֶר: sf. נָכְרוֹ: feeling of strangeness > **misfortune** Ob$_{12}$ Jb 31_3. †

נֵכָר: cs. נֵכַר־ Dt 31_{16}: **foreign land**: — 1. a) *'admat nēkār* foreign soil Ps 137_4; b) *'ēl nēkār* foreign god Dt 32_{12}, pl. *'ᵉlōhê nēkār* Gn 35_2; so *'ᵉlōªh nēkār* Dn 11_{39}, *hablê nēkār* Je 8_{19}; c) *mizbᵉḥôt hannēkār* foreign altars 2C 14_2; *kol-nēkār* everything foreign

Ne 13_{30}; — 2. *ben-nēkār* foreigner Gn 17_{12}, pl. *b*^{e}*nê nēkār* 2S 22_{45}*t*.

נָכְרִי: f. נָכְרִיָּה; pl. נָכְרִים, f. נָכְרִיּוֹת: foreign, strange (:: *gēr, zār*): — 1. adj., **foreign, alien**: vine Je 2_{21}, land Ex 2_{22}; — 2. adj. & noun, **foreigner**: *ʾîš nokrî* Dt 17_{15} > *nokrî* 1K 8_{41} (3× // *zār*); *nāšîm nokriyyôt* 1K 11_1, *nokriyyâ* Pr 2_{16}, pl. Gn 31_{15}; — 2. **strange, alien** Ps 69_9, odd, surprising Is 28_{21}.

***נְכֹת**: sf. נְכֹתֹה: *bêt n*^{e}*kōtôh* his **treasure-house** 2K 20_{13} Is 39_2. †

[**נלה**: כְּנַלֹּתְךָ Is 33_1: rd. כְּכַלֹּתְךָ. †]

[**נִמְבְזָה** 1S 15_9: rd. נִבְזָה (בזה nif. pt.). †]

נְמוּאֵל: n. pers.

נְמוּאֵלִי: gent. of נְמוּאֵל.

נְמָלָה: pl. נְמָלִים: **ant**, *Messor semirufus* Pr 6_6 30_{25}. †

[**נָמֵס**: נָמֵס אֹתָהּ 1S 15_9: rd. נִמְאֶסֶת (מאס nif.). †]

נָמֵר: pl. נְמֵרִים: **leopard, panther,** *Felis pardus* Is 11_6 Je 5_6 13_{23} Ho 13_7 Hb 1_8 SS 4_8. †

נִמְרֹ(וֹ)ד: n. pers.

נִמְרָה: n. loc.

נִמְרִים: n. terr., *mê nimrîm* Is 15_6 Je 48_{34}. †

נִמְשִׁי: n. pers.

נֵס: sf. נִסִּי: — 1. **signal pole** (w. rags tied on) Nu 21_8, *nāśāʾ nēs* Je 4_6; *hāyâ l*^{e}*nēs* become a warning Nu 26_{10}; — 2. **banner, standard**: Is 31_9, = flag 18_3; *yhwh nissî* = name of an altar Ex 17_{15}.

[**נְסִבָּה** Ez 41_7: ? סבב nif.; but prob. rd. ↗ מְסִבָּה.]

נְסִבָּה: **turn** (of events), **disposition** (from God) 2C 10_{15}. †

נסה: [cj. **nif.**: pf. נִסָּה, נִסֵּיתִי 1S $17_{39a.b}$: **be trained, accustomed** (↗ piel 1 d). †]

piel: pf. נִסָּה, נִסְּתָה, נִסִּיתִי, sf. נִסָּהוּ, נִסִּיתוֹ, נִסּוּנִי; impf. אֲנַסֶּה, וַיְנַסּוּ, תְּנַסּוּן, sf. אֲנַסֶּנּוּ, אֲנַסְּכָה, וַיְנַסֵּם; impv. נַס, נַסֵּנִי; inf. נַסּוֹת, נַסֹּתָם, נַסֹּתוֹ; pt. מְנַסֶּה: — 1. **(put s.one to the) test**: a) subj. & obj. persons 1K 10_1; b) subj. men, obj. God Ex 17_2; c) subj. God, obj. men Gn 22_1; d) give experience to, **exercise, train** s.one Ex 20_{20}, try out s.thg 1S 17_{39} (2×; cf. cj. nif.); — 2. **try**: a) w. *l*^{e} & inf. Dt 4_{34}, w. inf. 28_{56}; b) w. *b*^{e}, give a trial w. Ju 6_{39}; c) w. acc. Ec 7_{23}.

נָסָה Ps 4_7: usu. = נְשָׂא = שָׂא; oth.: rd. נָסָה (נוס 3. sg.). †

נסח: **qal**: impf. יִסַּח, יִסָּחֲךָ: — 1. **tear down** (a house) Pr 15_{25}; — 2. **tear out** (people) (from) Ps 52_7; Pr 2_{22} rd cj. ḥof. †

nif.: pf. נִסַּחְתֶּם: **be torn out** Dt 28_{63}. †

[cj. **hof.**: impf. יֻסְּחוּ Pr 2_{22}: **be torn out** (for qal). †]

I ***נָסִיךְ**: sf. נְסִיכָם; pl. sf. נְסִיכֵיהֶם: — 1. **wine contribution, drink-offering** Dt 32_{38}; — 2. **molten image, idol** Dn 11_8. †

II ***נָסִיךְ**: pl. cs. נְסִיכֵי, sf. נְסִיכֵיהֶם, נְסִיכֵמוֹ: **leader, tribal prince** Jos 13_{21} Ez 32_{30} Mi 5_4 Ps 83_{12}. †

I **נסך**: **qal**: pf. נָסַךְ, נ׳; impf. יִסְּכוּ; inf. נְסֹךְ: — 1. **pour out**: obj. wine Ho 9_4, libation Ex 30_9, drink-offering (in concluding an alliance) Is 30_1, spirit 29_{10}; — 2. **pour** = produce a molten image Is 40_{19} 44_{10}. †

[**nif.**: cj. pf. נִסַּכְתִּי: cj. Ps 2_6 (for qal): **be consecrated, exalted** (by drink-offering). †]

piel: impf. וַיְנַסֵּךְ: **pour out** (water) **as an oblation** 1C 11_{18}. †

hif.: pf. הִסְּכוּ; impf. אַסִּיךְ, וַיַּסֵּךְ, וַיַּסִּיכוּ; inf. cs. לְהַסֵּךְ Je $44_{19.25}$, abs. הַסֵּ(י)ךְ: w. *nēsek* **contribute a drink-offering** Gn 35_{14}, w. pl. Je 7_{18}; *mayim*, pour out as a contribution 2S 23_{16}.

hof.: impf. יֻסַּךְ: **be contributed as a libation** Ex 25_{29} 37_{16}. †

II **נסך**: **qal**: pt. pass. נְסוּכָה: **intertwine, weave** Is 25_7. †

nif.: pf. נִסַּכְתִּי: **be woven, formed** Pr 8_{23}. †

I **נֶסֶךְ** & **נֵסֶךְ** (3×): נֶסֶךְ, sf. נִסְכּוֹ, נִסְכָּה; pl. נְסָכִים, sf. נְסָכֶיהָ, נִסְכֵּ(י)הֶם: **drink-offering, libation**: Ps 16_4 of blood, otherw. of wine

Gn 35_{14}; in forbidden worship Is 57_6, in lawful worship 2K 16_{13}.

II *נֶסֶךְ: sf. נִסְכּוֹ; pl. sf. נִסְכֵּיכֶם, נִסְכֵּיהֶם: **molten image** Is 41_{29} 48_5 Je 10_{14} 51_{17}. †

I נסס: **qal**: pt. נֹסֵס: **falter** (?) Is 10_{18}. †

II נסס: **hitpolel**: inf. הִתְנוֹסֵס; pt. מִתְנוֹסְסוֹת: **rally around the banner** (oth.: נוס seek refuge) Ps 60_6; Zc 9_{16} rd *F* √ *nṣṣ*. †

נָסַע: **qal**: pf. נ׳, נָסָעוּ, נָסָעוּ; impf. יִסַּע, יִסְעוּ, יִסָּעוּ, וַיִּסַּע, וַיִּסְעָה, יִסָּעֵם; impv. סְעוּ; inf. נְסֹעַ, נָסְעָם; pt. נֹסֵעַ, נֹסְעִים: — 1. **tear out, pull out**, obj. gates Ju 16_3; — 2. pull up tent stakes > break camp > **start out, march on** Gn 33_{12}, retreat 2K 3_{27}; (of wind) come up, burst forth Nu 11_{31}.

nif.: pf. נִסַּע: **be torn out, pulled up** Is 38_{12} Jb 4_{21}. †

hif.: impf. וַיַּסִּעוּ, תַּסִּיעַ, תַּסִּיעִי, יַסַּע; pt. מַסִּיעַ: — 1. **take** (a plant) **away** (fm. its place) Ps 80_9 Jb 19_{10}, **quarry** (stones) 1K 5_{31} Ec 10_9, put away (jugs) 2K 4_4; — 2. **make** (people) **start out** Ps 78_{52}, make (wind) come up Ps 78_{26}. †

נִסְרֹךְ: n. of Assyrian god 2K 19_{37} Is 37_{38}. †

נֵעָה: n. loc.

נֹעָה: n. pers. f.

נַעֲוַת 1S 20_{30}: *F* עוה nif.

נְעוּרִים: sf. נְעוּרַי, נְעֻרָיו, נְעוּרַיִךְ, נְעוּרֵיהֶן: — 1. **youth** (i.e. as stage of life) Je 31_{19}; *bin'ûrāyw* as long as one is young La 3_{27}, *minne'ûrāyw* since (his) youth Gn 8_{21}; — 2. the time when a *na'ᵃrâ* is single & not engaged: *kin'ûrêhā* as in her days before engagement Lv 22_{13}, *'ēšet nᵉ'ûrîm* one who is a virgin at time of marriage Is 54_6; *ba'al nᵉ'ûrêhā* the husband (fiancé) who has married a virgin Jl 1_8, *'allûf nᵉ'ûray* confidant of a woman who was a virgin at time of marriage Je 3_4; *nᵉ'ûrîm* time when a wife was still a virgin Je 2_2.

נְעִיאֵל: n. loc.

נָעִים: cs. נְעִים; pl. נְעִ(י)מִים, נְעִמוֹת: **agreeable, pleasant, lovely**: friend 2S 1_{23}, God's name Ps 135_3; pl. as noun: m. = good ground, soil Ps 16_6, m. & f. = good fortune Jb 36_{11} Ps 16_{11}.

נָעַל: **qal**: pf. נָעַל, נ׳; impf. וָאֶנְעָלֵךְ; impv. נְעֹל; pt. pass. נָעוּל, נְעֻלוֹת: — 1. **tie** (i.e. lock) (the door w. straps) Ju 3_{23f} 2S 13_{17f} SS 4_{12}; — 2. w. 2 acc. **shoe** s.one w. s.thg (as a sandal) Ez 16_{10}. †

hif.: impf. וַיַּנְעִלוּם: **supply** s.one **w. footwear** 2C 28_{15}. †

נַעַל: נַעַל, sf. נַעֲלוֹ, נַעַלְךָ Jos 5_{15}; du. נַעֲלַיִם; pl. נְעָלִים, sf. נְעָלָיו, נַעֲלֵיכֶם, & נְעָלוֹת Jos 9_5: **sandal**, tied w. straps 1K 2_5, in var. idioms: *hišlîk na'al 'al* for taking possession Ps 60_{10}, *ḥālaṣ na'ᵃlô* in refusal of levirate marriage Dt 25_{8f}.

נעם: **qal**: pf. נָעֲמוּ, נָעֵמְתְּ, נָעַמְתָּ, נָעֵמָה; impf. יִנְעָם: — 1. **be pleasant** Gn 49_{15}; — 2. w. *lᵉ*, **be agreeable, gratifying** to Pr 2_{10}, taste good 9_{17}; — 3. w. *lᵉ*, **be dear to** s.one 2S 1_{26}; — 4. impers. *yin'am lᵉ* do well Pr 24_{25}.

*נַעַם: נַעַם: n. pers. 1C 4_{15}. †

נֹעַם: **kindness** (of God) Ps 27_4 90_{17}; name of a staff Zc $11_{7.10}$; *darkê nō'am* Pr 3_{17} & *'imrê nō'am* 15_{26} 16_{24} kindly ways, words. †

I נַעֲמָה: n. pers. f.

II נַעֲמָה: n. loc. Jos 15_{41} Jb 2_{11}. †

נָעֳמִי: n. pers. f.

נַעֲמִי: gent. of נַעֲמָן.

נַעֲמָן: n. pers.

נַעֲמָנִים: evid. distortion of epithet for Adonis; *niṭ'ê na'ᵃmānîm* gardens of A. Is 17_{10}. †

נַעֲמָתִי: gent. of II נַעֲמָה.

נַעֲצוּץ: pl. נַעֲצוּצִים: **camel-thorn**, *Alhagi camelorum* Is 7_{19} 55_{13}. †

I נער: **qal**: pf. נָעֲרוּ: **growl** (of lion) Je 51_{38}. †

II נער: **qal**: pf. נָעַרְתִּי; pt. pass. נָעוּר: **shake**: obj. hands (in refusal) Is 33_{15}, pass. be shaken out (bosom of garment) Ne 5_{13}. †

nif.: pf. נִנְעַרְתִּי; impf. אִנָּעֵר, יִנָּעֲרוּ: — 1.

shake onesf. free Ju 16_{20}; — 2. **be shaken off, out** Ps 109_{23} Jb 38_{13}. †

piel: pf. נִעֵר; impf. וַיְנַעֵר: — 1. **shake off** (*b^e* into) Ex 14_{27} Ps 136_{15}; — 2. **shake out** (*min* from) Ne 5_{13a}. †

hitp.: impv. f. הִתְנַעֲרִי: **shake onesf. free** Is 52_2. †

נַעַר (ca. 230×): נָעַר, sf. נַעֲרוֹ, נַעַרְךָ; pl. נְעָרִים, cs. נַעֲרֵי, sf. נַעֲרֵיהֶם: marriageable male while still single: — 1. **boy, youth** Gn 19_4; — 2. **young man**, pl. young people Gn 14_{24}; 400 *ʾîš-naʿar* 1S 30_{17}; — 3. **boy, (man-)servant**: of Abraham Gn 22_3, weapon-bearer 1S 14_1; pl. Jb 1_{15}; can write Ju 8_{14}; military, i.e. personal retinue 1S $21_{3.5}$; — 4. נַעֲרָ Kt נער, Qr נַעֲרָה **girl** Gn 24_{14} & oft.; *hann^eʿārîm* includes both sexes † Ru 2_{21} Jb 1_{19}.

I נַעֲרָה & נַעֲרָ (F נער 4); pl. נְעָרוֹת, cs. נַעֲרוֹת, sf. נַעֲרוֹתֶיךָ: — 1. **marriageable girl** (still virgin) 1K 1_2, coll. Ju 21_{12}; — 2. **newly married woman** (so called by her parents) Ju 9_3; — 3. **maid(servant)** Gn 24_{61}; — 4. **wench**, 'girl' † Am 2_7 (oth.: housemaid).

II נַעֲרָה: n. pers. f. 1C 4_{5f}. †

III *נַעֲרָה: n. loc.; loc. נַעֲרָתָה: Jos 16_7. †

*נְעֻרוֹת: sf. נְעֻרֹתֵיהֶם: **youth** (i.e. stage of life) Je 32_{30}. †

נַעֲרַי: n. pers. 1C 11_{37}. †

נְעַרְיָה: n. pers.

*נְעֻרִים: F נְעוּרִים.

נַעֲרָן: n. loc.

נְעֹרֶת: **tow** (flax fibers shaken free fm. raw flax by whirling or beating; used for tinder) Ju 16_9 Is 1_{31}. †

נַעֲרָתָה Jos 16_7: F III *נַעֲרָה.

נֹף: n. loc., = **Memphis**.

נֶפֶג: n. pers.

I *נָפָה: cs. נָפַת: **winnow** (i.e. a device for winnowing, such as fan or sieve); w. *šāwʾ* Is 30_{28}. †

II *נָפָה: cs. נָפַת; pl. cs. נָפוֹת: **yoke**, only in *nāfat/nāfôt dôr/dōʾr*, the hilly hinterland around Dor Jos 11_2 12_{23} 1K 4_{11}. †

נְפוּסִים Ezr 2_{50} Qr, Kt נְפִיסִים & Ne 7_{52} נְפוּשְׁסִים (mixture of *s* & *š*, & Qr *î*, Kt *û*): descendants of tribe נָפִישׁ. †

נפח: **qal**: pf. נָפַחְתִּי, נֻפְּחָה; impf. וַיִּפַּח; impv. פְּחִי; inf. פַּחַת; pt. נֹפֵחַ, pass. נָפוּחַ: — 1. **blow** Gn 2_7, w. *b^e* on Ez 37_9, w. *ʿal* 1K 17_{21}; pass. *nāfûªḥ* blown upon (by wind) Je 1_{13}; — 2. **blow (into flame)** Ez 22_{21}; — 3. **gasp** † Je 15_9.

pual (or **qal** pass.): pf. נֻפַּח: **be blown upon** (fire) Jb 20_{26}. †

hif.: pf. הִפַּחְתֶּם, הִפַּחְתִּי: metaph. **enrage** Ma 1_{13}; **make** s.one **sigh** Jb 31_{39}. †

נֹפַח: n. loc.

נְפִילִים & נְפִלִים Gn 6_4: — 1. cj. *binfilîm* for *biflilîm* Ex 21_{22} **miscarriage**, but open to qn.; — 2. **giants**, produced by miscarriages or thrown out of heaven; gigantic early population of Palestine Nu $13_{33a\beta}$, of mythical origin Gn 6_4; F comm. †

נְפִיסִים Ez 2_{50} Kt: F נְפוּסִים.

נָפִישׁ: n. (pers. &) tribe.

נֹפֶךְ: **semi-precious** (green) **stone** found in Sinai: sugg. turquoise, malachite, garnet Ex 28_{18} 39_{11} Ez 27_{16} 28_{13}. †

נָפַל: **qal** (ca. 360×): pf. נָפַל, נָפְלָה, נָפְלוּ, נ׳; impf. יִפֹּ(ו)ל, וַיִּפֹּל־, יִפְּלוּ, יִפּוֹלוּ, תִּפֹּלְנָה, נִפְּלָה; impv. נִפְלוּ; inf. נְפֹל, נְפָלוֹ & נָפְלוֹ, נָפוֹל; pt. נֹפֵל, נֹפֶלֶת, נֹפְלִים: **fall (unintentionally)**: — 1. in genl.: Gn 15_{12}; — 2. fall in battle 1S 4_{10}; fall, collapse (of state) Is 3_8, be ruined 8_{15}; w. *ʿal* on Is 54_{15}, w. *mēʿal* 2K 2_{13}; w. *l^e* fall (to s.one's possession) Nu 34_2; — 3. **be inferior** to (*min*) Jb 12_3; **turn out** (to be) Ru 3_{18}; *wayyippelû b^eʿênêhem* pride failed them Ne 6_{16}; — 4. **fall (in), collapse**: tent Ju 7_{13}, wall 1K 20_{30}, mountain Jb 14_{18}; sag, be downcast (face) Gn 4_5; *nōfēl* having fainted Nu 24_4;

metaph. *nāfal dābār* be weak, fail 1K 8_{56}; *yāmîm* lapse Nu 6_{12}; — 5. **be born** † Is 26_{18}; — 6. come to lie: *nāfal lᵉmiškāb* become bedridden Ex 21_{18}, w. *'arṣâ* lie on the ground Ju 3_{25}; — 7. **let onesf. fall** (intentionally), **throw onesf. down**: w. *'al-pānāyw* = bow w. one's face to the ground Gn 17_{3}; w. *mē'al* **get down** (quickly, attentively) from Gn 24_{64}; w. *'al-ṣawwā'rô* fling onesf. on s.one's neck Gn 33_{4}; come to rest (hand of Y.) Ez 8_{1}; subj. *tᵉḥinnâ*, w. *lifnê*, penetrate to Je 36_{7}; — 8. military: w. *bᵉ* fall on, attack Jos 11_{7}; w. *'el* invade, attack 2K 7_{2}; desert to 1S 29_{3}; w. *'al* or *'el*, surrender to Je 21_{9}; thus *nōfᵉlîm* deserters Je 39_{9}; *nāfal* abs. make a raid Jb 1_{15}; *nāfal 'al-pᵉnê* settle opposite Gn 25_{18}; *nāfal bᵉ* be encamped in Ju 7_{12}.

[**pilal**: pf. נִפְלַל Ez 28_{23}: rd נָפַל. †]

hif.: pf. הִפִּ(י)ל, הִפַּלְתָּ, הִפִּילוּ, sf. הִפִּילוֹ, הִפַּלְתִּיו; impf. יַפִּיל, וַיַּפֵּל, תַּפֵּל, יַפִּילוּ, נַפִּילָה, יַפִּילוּן, sf. יַפִּילֵם; impv. הַפִּילוּ; inf. לְהַפִּיל, לַנְפִּיל Nu 5_{22}, sf. הַפִּלְכֶם, הַפִּלָהּ; pt. מַפִּיל, מַפִּילִים: — 1. **let fall** Gn 2_{21} (deep sleep), Nu 35_{23} (stone); — 2. **bring down, make fall, fell**: tree 2K 3_{19}, man w. sword 2K 19_{7}; — 3. **make** s.thg **fall to ruin, decay** Ez 6_{4}; lay down = present (supplications) Dn 9_{18}; — 4. **make** s.one **lie down** Dt 25_{2}; **let** s.thg **sink** (into fire) Je 22_{7}; w. *miyyad* knock s.thg out of s.one's hand Ez 30_{22}; w. *gōrāl* cast lot Ps 22_{19}; w/o *gōrāl* Jb 6_{27}; w. *bên...ûbên* let the lot decide 1S 14_{42}; w. acc. & *bᵉḥebel* apportion w. a measuring line Ps 78_{55}; — 5. **throw down** (stars) Dn 8_{10}; knock out (a tooth) Ex 21_{27}; — 6. **bring** (wall) **to collapse** 2S 20_{15}; w. *pānāyw* **frown, look crossly** at Je 3_{12}; — 7. w. *min*, **leave off, give up** Ju 2_{19}; subj. *dābār*, w. *'arṣâ* allow to remain unfulfilled 1S 3_{19}; — 8. let fall = give birth to: subj. *'ereṣ*, obj. *rᵉfā'îm* Is 26_{19}.

hitp.: pf. הִתְנַפַּלְתִּי; impf. וָאֶתְנַפֵּל; inf. הִתְנַפֵּל; pt. מִתְנַפֵּל: — 1. w. *'al*, **fall on, attack** Gn 43_{18}; — 2. **throw onesf. down, lie prostrate** Dt $9_{18 \cdot 25}$, pt. upon one's knees Ezr 10_{1}. †

נֵפֶל: **miscarriage** Ps 58_{9} Jb 3_{16} Ec 6_{3}. †

נְפִלִים Gn 6_{4}: ך נְפִילִים.

I נפץ: inf. נָפוֹץ; pt. pass. נָפוּץ: **smash** (obj. jars) Ju 7_{19}; pt. pass., worth smashing Je 22_{28}. †

piel: pf. נִפֵּץ, נִפַּצְתִּי, נִפַּצְתִּים; impf. יְנַפֵּצוּ, תְּנַפְּצֵם: **smash** (obj. jars &c.) Je 13_{14} 48_{12} 51_{20-23} Ps 2_{9}; obj. babies Ps 137_{9}; **break up** (rafts) 1K 5_{23}. †

pual: pt. מְנֻפָּצוֹת: **smashed** (stones) Is 27_{9}. †

II נָפַץ: **qal**: pf. נ׳, נָפְצָה, נָפְצוּ: **spread out, be dispersed, scatter** (intrans.) Gn 9_{19}, 1S 13_{11} Is 33_{3}. †

נֶפֶץ: **pelting** (of rain) Is 30_{30}. †

נפשׁ: **nif.**: impf. וַיִּנָּפַשׁ, וַיִּנָּפֵשׁ: **exhale**, = **catch one's breath, refresh onesf.** Ex 23_{12} 31_{17} 2S 16_{14}. †

נֶפֶשׁ (ca. 750×): נֶפֶשׁ, sf. נַפְשִׁי, נַפְשְׁךָ, נַפְשֵׁנוּ (נַפְשֵׁינוּ La 5_{9}); pl. נְפָשׁ(וֹ)ת, cs. נַפְשׁוֹת, sf. נַפְשֹׁתֵינוּ, נַפְשֹׁתָם: — 1. **throat** Is 5_{14}; — 2. **neck** Ps 105_{18}; — 3. **breath** Jb 41_{13}, what makes man & animals living beings Gn 1_{20}, 'soul' (to be sharply distinguished fm. Greek idea of soul) whose seat is the blood Gn 9_{4f}; — 4. *nefeš ḥayyâ* **living being** Gn 1_{20} (= animals), 2_{7} (man); — 5. **man, men, person, people**: a) *nefeš 'ādām* **man** (i.e. person) Lv 24_{17}, = slaves Ez 27_{13}; *hōrēg nefeš* whoever kills a person Nu 31_{19}; pl. *kol-nafšôt bêtô* all the persons in his household Gn 36_{6}; *'eḥād nefeš* one (out of every 500) Nu 31_{28}; *kol-nefeš 'ādām* any person Lv 24_{17}, *nefeš bᵉhēmâ* a head of cattle 24_{18}; *'āśâ nefeš* acquire people, rear persons (slaves?) Gn 12_{5}, *qānâ nefeš* buy a slave Lv 22_{11}; b) population: *kol-nefeš* all persons, everyone Gn 46_{15}; w. numbers Gn 46_{18}; pl. *nᵉfāšôt* Ex 12_4; — 6. **personality, individuality**: a) *nafšî* (&c.), stressed **I** (myself) Gn 27_4, so *nafšēnû* we Ps 124_7; b) expression of reflexive, esp. stressed: *kᵉnafšô* like himself 1S 18_3; *ʿannôt nāfeš* self-humiliation, penance Nu 30_{14}; c) *kol-nefeš* every one = each one Ex 12_{16}, *kol-nefeš ʾᵃšer* the one who, whoever Lv 7_{27}, *hannefeš ʾᵃšer* 7_{20}, *hannefeš* w. pt. 7_{18}, *nefeš ʾᵃšer* one who 5_2; — 7. **life** (of a person, a single life): *nefeš hāʾādām* Gn 9_5, *ʿal-nafšekā* (flee) for your life 19_{17}, *biqqēš nefeš* seek (s.one's) life 1K 19_{10}; *bᵉṣēʾt nafšāh* as her (breath =) life left her Gn 35_{18}; *hikkâ nefeš* strike dead 37_{21}; *hēšîb nefeš* give (new, fresh) life Ru 4_{15}; — 8. 'soul' as seat & support of feelings & sensations: a) **desire** (even inordinate desire): (of love) SS 1_7; *nāśāʾ nefeš ʾel* have desire for Ho 4_8; *maśśāʾ nefeš* desire Ez 24_{25}; *baʿal nefeš* greedy (for food) Pr 23_2, *rᵉḥab nefeš* greedy (for possessions) 28_{25}; *nefeš* is never satisfied Ec 6_3, never quieted Ps 35_{25}; b) **mood, state of mind**: of *gēr* Ex 23_9, of cattle Pr 12_{10}; c) **feeling, taste** Nu 21_5; d) **will**: *yēš ʾet-nafšᵉkem* you are willing Gn 23_8; — 9. **someone dead**, a dead person, corpse: *śereṭ lannefeš* a slash because of the dead Lv 19_{28}; *nefeš mēt* dead body Nu 6_6, > *nefeš* (w/o *mēt*) 6_{11}; Ez $13_{18\text{-}20}$ *nafšôt*, hunted by women who prophesy, usu. of disembodied souls hunted by magic, but sugg. simply 'persons'; — 10. *bāttê hannefeš* perfume-bottles Is 3_{20}.

***נֶפֶת**: הַנָּפֶת: ? **hill** Jos 17_{11}. †

נֹפֶת: (domesticated) **honey**, (fm. combs, strained) Ps 19_{11} Pr 5_3 24_{13} 27_7 SS 4_7. †

נֶפְתּוֹחַ: n. loc.

***נַפְתּוּלִים**: cs. נַפְתּוּלֵי: **struggles**, *naftûlê ʾᵉlōhîm* Gn 30_8. †

נַפְתֻּחִים: n. (pers. =) peop.

נַפְתָּלִי: n. pers. & tribe, **Naphtali**.

I ***נֵץ**: sf. נִצָּהּ, pl. נִצָּנִים SS 2_{12}: (cluster of) **blossoms** Gn 40_{10} SS 2_{12}. †

II **נֵץ**: **falcon**, *Falco peregrinus* Lv 11_{16} Dt 14_{15} Jb 39_{26}. †

נצא נָצֹא Je 48_9: = נָצֹה (↗ נצה).

I **נצב**: **nif.**: pf. נִצַּבְתָּ, נִצָּבָה, נִצְּבָה; pt. נִצָּב, נִצָּבִים, נִצָּבוֹת, נִצֶּבֶת: — 1. **stand** = station onesf. Ex 17_9; — 2. **stand** = be standing, have taken a stand at a spot Gn 18_2; — 3. **stand** = remain standing Gn 37_7; — 4. **step up to** Ex 5_{20}; — 5. **stand firm** Ps 39_6; pt. w. *lᵉ* & inf. ready (to do s.thg) Is 3_{13}; — 6. pt. w. *ʿal* **one who is in charge** Ru 2_5; as noun, **foreman, overseer, governor** 1K 4_5; *śārê hanniṣṣābîm* chief officers 1K 5_{30}.

hif.: pf. הִצִּיב, הִצַּבְתָּ, הִצִּיבוּ; impf. יַצִּיב, וַיַּצֶּב־, וַיַּצִּיבֵהוּ; impv. הַצִּיבָה; inf. הַצִּיב, הַצִּיבִי; pt. מַצִּיב: **station, set up, establish**: set up (altar) Gn 33_{20}; establish (*yād*, dominion) 1C 18_3; set up (doors) 1K 16_{34}; put to one side (ewes) Gn 21_{28f}; take (s.one for a target) La 3_{12}; establish (boundary) Dt 32_8; bring to a standstill (water) Ps 78_{13}.

hof.: pf. הֻצַּב; pt. מֻצָּב: **be set up** (staircase) Gn 28_{12}. †

II **נצב**: **nif.**: pt. נִצָּבָה: **wretched, exhausted** (animal) Zc 11_{16}. †

I **נִצָּב**: ↗ I נצב nif. pt. 5, 6.

II **נִצָּב**: **hilt** (of sword) Ju 3_{22}. †

נְצִבֵי 1S 10_5: ↗ I נְצִיב.

נצג: **hif.** הִצִּיג, ↗ יצג.

I **נצה**: **nif.**: impf. יִנָּצוּ; pt. נִצִּים: **quarrel** 2S 14_6.

hif.: pf. הִצּוּ; inf. הַצֹּתָם, הַצּוֹתוֹ: **carry on a quarrel**, w. *ʾēt* Ps 60_2, *ʿal* Nu 26_9. †

II **נצה**: **qal**: impf. תִּצֶּינָה: **fall** (cities) Je 4_7. †

nif.: pf. נִצְּתָה Je 2_{15} Kt, Qr נִצְּתוּ: **be destroyed, devastated** Je 2_{15} 9_{11} 46_{19}. †

נִצָּה: sf. נִצָּתוֹ: **blossom** Is 18_5 Jb 15_{33}. †

I ***נֹצָה** Lv 1_{16}: ↗ *נוֹצָה.

II **נֹצָה**: **falcon** Jb 39_{13}. †

נְצוּרִים: Is 65_{4}, sugg. secret places, caves; but oth. sugg. rd. בֵּין צוּרִים. †

נצח: **nif.**: pt. נִצַּחַת: **lasting** Je 8_{5}. †

piel: inf. נַצֵּחַ; pt. מְנַצֵּחַ, מְנַצְּחִים: — 1. **supervise**, w. *ʿal*, activity connected w. the temple Ezr 3_{8}, abs. 1C 15_{21}; — 2. *lamᵉnaṣṣēᵃḥ* in superscriptions of psalms e.g. Ps 4_{1}, + Hb 3_{19}, uncert.; trad. 'for the music-director,' ↗ comm.

I **נֵצַח** (4×) & **נֶצַח** (37×): sf. נִצְחִי; pl. נְצָחִים: — 1. **luster, glory** (of God) 1C 29_{11}; Y. as *nēṣaḥ* of Isr. 1S 15_{29}; — 2. **lastingness**: a) *hāyâ neṣaḥ* become endless Je 15_{18}; b) adv. for ever Am 1_{11}; = c) w. *lᵉ* 2S 2_{26} & oft.; = *ʿad-neṣaḥ* Ps 49_{20}; — 3. (legal): *lāneṣaḥ* **successful** † Jb 23_{7} Pr 21_{28}.

II **נֵצַח**: **juice** = blood Is $63_{3.6}$. †

I **נְצִיב**: pl. נְצִ(י)בִים: — 1. **pillar** (of salt) Gn 19_{26}; — 2. (military) **post, garrison** 1K 4_{19}.

II **נְצִיב**: n. loc. Jos 15_{43}. †

נְצִיחַ: n. pers.

*__נָצִיר__, נְצִירֵי Is 49_{6} = Qr נְצוּרֵי, ↗ נצר.

נצל: **nif.**: pf. נִצַּלְנוּ: impf. יִנָּצֵל, תִּנָּצְלִי, אִנָּצְלָה, יִנָּצֵלוּ, יִנָּצְלוּ; impv. & inf. הִנָּצֵל: — 1. **be rescued, saved** Gn 32_{31} & oft.; — 2. **save onesf., escape** Dt 23_{16}.

piel: pf. (↗ nif.!) נִצַּלְתֶּם; impf. יְנַצְּלוּ: — 1. w. acc. **plunder, strip** Ex 3_{22} 12_{36}, w. *lᵉ* **snatch for onesf.** 2C 20_{25}; — 2. **pull out, extricate, rescue** Ez 14_{14}. †

hif.: (190×): pf. הִצִּיל, הִצַּלְתָּ, הִצַּלְנוּ, sf. הִצִּילַנִי, הִצִּילָם, הִצִּילָנוּ; impf. יַצִּיל, יַצֵּל, וַיַּצֵּל, וָאַצִּיל, sf. יַצִּילְךָ, יַצִּילֵם, וַיַּצִּלֵהוּ; impv. הַצֵּל, הַצִּילָה, הַצִּילֵנִי; inf. הַצִּיל, הַצִּילוֹ, הַצֵּל, הַצִּילְךָ; pt. מַצִּיל: — 1. **snatch away** Ju 11_{26}; — 2. **take away** Gn 31_{9}; — 3. **pull out, extricate, rescue** Ex 5_{23} & oft.: *hiṣṣîl nafšô* rescue onesf. Is 44_{20}; *wᵉʾên maṣṣîl* with no one to rescue, (the situation is) past help Ju 18_{28}; abs. rescue 1S 12_{21}; secure (a military position) 2S 23_{12}.

hof.: pt. מֻצָּל: **snatched away** Am 4_{11} Zc 3_{2}. †

hitp.: impf. וַיִּתְנַצְּלוּ: w. acc. **rid onesf. of** Ex 33_{6}. †

נִצָּנִים SS 2_{12}: pl. of ↗ I נֵץ.

נצע: **hif. & hof.**: ↗ יצע.

נצץ: **qal**: pt. נֹצְצִים: **sparkle** Ez 1_{7}. †

hif.: pf. הֵנֵצוּ; impf. יָנֵץ: **bloom** SS 6_{11} 7_{13} Ec 12_{5}. †

נצר: **qal**: pf. נָצַרְתִּי, נָצְרוּ, sf. נְצַרְתָּם; impf. נִצְּרָה, תִּצֹּרְנָה, יִנְצֹרוּ, יִצְּרוּ, אֶצֳּרָה, אֶצֹּר, תִּצֹּר, תִּצְּרֶךָּ, תִּנְצְרֵנִי, תִּצְּרֵנִי, תִּצְּרֶנּוּ, יִצְּרֶנְהוּ, sf. יִנְצְרוּהוּ, יִצְּרוּנִי, אֶצָּרֶנָּה, אֶצָּרְךָ, תִּנְצְרֶכָּה; impv. נְצֹר, נִצְרָה, נִצְּרָה, sf. נִצְּרֶהָ; inf. נְצֹר, נָצוֹר; pt. נֹ(וֹ)צֵר, נֹצְרִים, נֹצְרֵי, sg. sf. נֹצְרָהּ, pass. f. נְצוּרָה, cs. נְצֻרַת, pl. cs. נְצֻרֵי, f. נְצֻרוֹת: — 1. **keep watch, guard, protect** Dt 32_{10}; pt. watchman 2K 17_{9}; God is *nōṣēr hāʾādām* Jb 7_{20}; — 2. **keep, preserve**, obj. *šālôm* Is 26_{3}; — 3. **comply with, observe** (law, commandments) Ps 78_{7}; observe, keep track of (s.one's *nefeš*) Pr 24_{12}; — 4. pt. pass. *nāṣûr* (what is) **stored away, preserved, kept in reserve** Is 48_{6}; *nᵉṣurat lēb* (woman of) crafty heart Pr 7_{10}.

נֵצֶר: **sprout, shoot** (of plant) Is 11_{1} 60_{21} Dn 11_{7}; Is 14_{19} difficult, ↗ comm. †

נִצְּרָה: **watch** (i.e. guard) Ps 141_{3}. †

נקב: **qal**: pf. נָקַבְתָּ, נְקָבָה; impf. (↗ קבב) יִקְּבֵהוּ, יִקֳּבֶנּוּ, sf. יִקֹּ(וֹ)ב, יִנְקָב־, תִּקֹּ(וֹ)ב; impv. נָקְבָה; pt. נֹקֵב, pass. נָקוּב, נְקֻבֵי: — 1. **pierce** 2K 18_{21}; — 2. **stipulate, specify**: obj. wages Gn 30_{28}, name Is 62_{2}; — 3. **designate, distinguish**: *nᵉqubê* the leading citizens of Am 6_{1}; unfavorably > **curse, execrate** Pr 11_{26}; **blaspheme** (the name of God) Lv 24_{11}.

nif.: pf. נִקְּבוּ: **be designated** Nu 1_{17} Ezr 8_{20} 1C 12_{32} 16_{41} 2C 28_{15} 31_{19}. †

נֶקֶב: **tunnel**: — 1. 'pass' as n. loc. Jos 19_{33}; — 2. subterranean passage, **mine** Ez 28_{13}. †

נְקֵבָה: **female** (noun & adj.) Gn 1_{27}; of animals 6_{19}.
נָקֹד: pl. נְקֻדּוֹת ,נְקֻדִּים: **speckled, spotted** (animals) Gn 30_{32ff}.
נֹקֵד: pl. נֹקְדִים: **shepherd, sheep-breeder** 2K 3_4 Am 1_1. †
***נְקֻדָּה**: pl. נְקֻדּוֹת: small globules of silver SS 1_{11} (oth.: glass beads). †
נִקֻּדִים: — 1. **crumbling**, crumbled bread Jos $9_{5\cdot12}$; — 2. **small cake** 1K 14_3. †
נקה: **qal**: inf. abs. נָקֹּה Je 49_{12} w. nif. †
nif.: pf. נִקֵּיתִי, נִקֵּיתָ, נִקְּתָה, נִקָּתָה, נִקָּה; impf. יִנָּקֶה, תִּנָּקוּ; impv. הִנָּקִי; inf. הִנָּקֵה: — 1. w. *min*, **be free** of, **exempt** from: be free of the obligation of an oath Gn 24_8; — 2. **be without guilt, innocent** Ju 15_3; — 3. **remain unpunished** Je 25_{29}; — 4. **be emptied**: city w/o men Is 3_{26}.
piel: pf. נִקֵּיתִי Jl 4_{21} (if txt. correct); impf. יְנַקֶּה, תְּנַקֵּנִי, אֲנַקֶּךָּ; impv. נַקֵּנִי; inf. נַקֵּה: — 1. **leave unpunished** 1K 2_9; — 2. **declare** (to be) **exempt from punishment** Ps 19_{13}.
נְקוֹדָא: n. pers.
נָקֹטָה Jb 10_1: ↗ קוט nif.
נָקִי & **נָקִיא** Jl 4_{19} Jon 1_{14} La: cs. נְקִי; pl. נְקִיִּ(י)ם: — 1. w. *min*, **free** of, **exempt** from Gn 24_{41}; *ʾên nāqî* no one (was) exempt, excepted 1K 15_{22}; — 2. **innocent** 2S 14_9; pl. Gn 44_{10}, w. *min* of 2S 3_{28}; — 3. w. *dām* in various forms: *dām nāqî* 2K 24_4, *dam nāqî* 2K 21_{16} &c.; — 4. *neqî kappîm* he who has clean hands Ps 24_4.
נִקָּי(וֹ)ן: cs. נִקְי(וֹ)ן: — 1. cleanness, **whiteness** (of teeth = nothing to chew) Am 4_6; w. *yākōl* Ho 8_5 seize cleanness = make a clean sweep; — 2. **innocence**, *beniqyôn kappay* Gn 20_5, so sim. Ps 26_6 73_{13}. †
***נָקִיק**: cs. נְקִיק; pl. cs. נְקִיקֵי: **cleft, crack** (in rock) Is 7_{19} Je 13_4 16_{16}. †
נקם: **qal**: pf. sf. נְקָמַנִי; impf. יִקֹּ(וֹ)ם, תִּקֹּ(וֹ)ם; inf. נְקֹם, נָקֹם; pt. נֹקֵם, נֹקֶמֶת; qal pass. יֻקַּם ↗ hof.: **take revenge, vengeance** Lv 19_{18}; *nāqam nāqām* 26_{25}, *nāqam neqāmâ* Nu 31_2; w. acc., avenge (the blood of his servants) Dt 32_{43}, w. acc. pers. & *min* + pers., avenge s.one (= take vengeance for s.one) upon s.one 1S 24_{13}, = *mēʾēt* Nu 31_2, *ʿal* Ps 99_8.
nif.: pf. נִקַּמְתִּי, נִקְּמוּ; impf. אִנָּקְמָה, יִנָּקֵם, יִנָּקְמוּ; impv. הִנָּקְמוּ, הִנָּקֵם; inf. הִנָּקֵם: — 1. **be avenged** † Ex 21_{20}; — 2. **take revenge, avenge onesf.** Ez 25_{12}, w. *be* on 1S 18_{25}, w. *min* on 1S 14_{24}; w. *le* for & *min* on Je 15_{15}.
piel: pf. נִקַּמְתִּי: **avenge** (the blood of one's servants) 2K 9_7; abs. w. *neqāmâ* take vengeance Je 51_{36}. †
hof. (or **qal** pass.): impf. יֻקַּם, יֻקָּם: — 1. **be avenged** Gn 4_{24}; — 2. **suffer vengeance** Gn 4_{15} Ex 21_{21}. †
hitp.: impf. תִּתְנַקֵּם: **take one's vengeance** Je $5_{9\cdot29}$ 9_8. †
נָקָם: cs. נְקַם: — 1. (human) **vengeance, revenge** Ju 16_{28}; — 2. (more oft.) (divine) **requital, recompense** Ps 58_{11}; w. var. vbs., *nāqam* Ez 24_8, *lāqaḥ* Is 47_3, *ʿāśâ* Mi 5_{14}.
נְקָמָה: cs. נִקְמַת, sf. נִקְמָתְךָ, נִקְמָתֵךְ, נִקְמָתָם: — 1. (human) **vengeance, revenge** Je 20_{10}; — 2. (more oft.) (divine) **requital, recompense** (cf. *nāqām*): *niqmat dām* requital for blood Ps 79_{10}; w. var. vbs., e.g. *nāqam* Nu 31_2.
נקע: **qal**: pf. נָקְעָה: w. *min* or *mēʿal*, **disengage onesf., turn away** from s.one (in weariness w. love, satiety w. love) Ez $23_{22\cdot28}$. †
I **נקף**: **piel**: pf. נִקַּף, נִקְּפוּ: **cut down** (underbrush) Is 10_{34}; Jb 19_{26}: ? they (= one) flayed, tore up, but oth. rd. cj. nif. sg. 'flayed,' perh. txt. corr., ↗ comm. †
II **נקף**: **qal**: impf. יִנְקֹפוּ: go in a series around a circle (of the year), make a (yearly) round Is 29_1. †
hif.: pf. הִקִּיף, הִקִּיפָה, הִקַּפְתֶּם, sf. הִקִּיפוּנִי;

impf. וַיַּקֵּף, יַקִּיפוּ, וַיַּקִּפוּ; impv. sf. הַקִּיפוּהָ; inf. הַקֵּ(י)ף; pt. מַקִּפִים: — 1. **go around** (obj. city) Jos 6_{3}; go around (intrans., subj. days) Jb 1_{5}; **surround** 1K 7_{24}; of a cry, go around, penetrate Is 15_{8}; — 2. (military) **surround** (a city, to besiege) 2K 6_{14}; — 3. **trim** (hair of head) † Lv 19_{27}.

נֹקֶף: **beating** (of olives fm. tree) Is 17_{6} 24_{13}. †

נִקְפָּה: **cord, rope** (around body) Is 3_{24}. †

נקר: **qal**: impf. יִקְּרוּ; inf. נְקֹר: — 1. **put out** (s.one's eye) 1S 11_{2}; — 2. **pick out** (obj. eye, subj. raven) Pr 30_{17}. †

piel: pf. נִקַּר; impf. תְּנַקֵּר: — 1. **put out** (s.one's eye) Nu 16_{14} Ju 16_{21}; — 2. **bore out** (obj. bones; = corrode?) Jb 30_{17}. †

pual: pf. נֻקַּרְתֶּם: **be quarried** Is 51_{1}. †

***נְקָרָה**: cs. נִקְרַת; pl. cs. נִקְרוֹת: **cleft, gap** (in rock) Ex 33_{22} Is 2_{21}. †

נקשׁ: [**qal**: pt. נוֹקֵשׁ Ps 9_{17}, rd. נוֹקַשׁ, inf. nif. of יקשׁ.]

nif.: impf. תִּנָּקֵשׁ: **be caught, entangled, ensnared** Dt 12_{30}. †

piel: impf. וַיְנַקְשׁוּ: **lay snares** Ps 38_{13}. †

hitp.: pt. מִתְנַקֵּשׁ: w. b^{e} **entrap** 1S 28_{9}. †

I **נֵר**: sf. נֵרִי, נֵרָהּ; pl. נֵרֹ(ו)ת, sf. נֵרֹתֶיהָ, נֵרֹתֵיהֶם: — 1. **lamp** (small clay vessel filled w. oil, usu. w. only one spout for the wick): in house Je 25_{10}, tent Jb 18_{6}, tent of meeting Ex 25_{37}, temple 1K 7_{49}; — 2. metaph. = God 2S 22_{29}, David 2S 21_{17}.

II **נֵר**: n. pers.

נִר Pr 21_{4}: = I נִיר 'light' or II נִיר 'ground newly broken,' F comm. †

נֵרְגַל: n. of god.

נֵרְגַל שַׂר־אֶצֶר: n. pers.

נֵרְדְּ: sf. נִרְדִּי; pl. נְרָדִים: **nard**, aromatic ointment fm. Himalayan herb, *Nardostachys jatamansi* SS 1_{12} 4_{13f}. †

נֵרִיָּה: n. pers.

נֵרִיָּהוּ: n. pers.

נָשָׂא: **qal** (600×): pf. נ׳, נָשְׂאָה, נָשָׂאתָ, נָשְׂאוּ, נְשָׂאתַנִי, נְשָׂאַתְנִי, נְשָׂאֲךָ, sf. Ps 139_{20} נָשֻׂא, נָשְׂאוּ, נְשָׂאתִים (2. f., Ez 16_{58}); impf. יִשָּׂא, יִשְׂאוּ, תִּשֶּׂנָּה & תִּשֶּׂאינָה, תִּשֶּׂאנָה, תִּשָּׂאוּן, יִשָּׂאוּ, sf. וַיִּשָּׂאֵהוּ, יִשָּׂאוּנְךָ, יִשָּׂאוּם, יִשָּׂאֶנָּה, יִשָּׂאֶהָ, יִשָּׂאֵהוּ; impv. נְשָׂא Ps 10_{12}, שָׂא, שְׂאִי, שְׂאוּ, sf. שָׂאֵהוּ, שָׂאוּנִי; inf. שְׂאֵת, בִּשְׂאֵת, לָשֵׂאת, שְׂאֵתִי, 3× נְשׂ(ו)א, נְשֹׂא Ps 28_{2}, מַשְׂאוֹת Ez 17_{9} (? Aram.); pt. נֹשֵׂא, f. נֹשְׂאֵת > נֹשֵׂאת, pass. cs. נְשׂוּא, נְשֻׂא & נְשׂוּי: — 1. **lift, raise (high)**: in genl.: obj. ark Gn 7_{17}, signal Je 4_{6}; obj. feet = depart Gn 29_{1}, w/o 'feet' 1S 17_{20}; — 2. obj. *yād/kāf*, lift one's hand: b^{e} against 2S 20_{21}; in oath Ex 6_{8}, in entreaty Ps 28_{2}, in prayer Ps 63_{5}; — 3. obj. *rō'š*: a) lift or carry high one's own head = expr. of independence Zc 2_{4}; b) lift s.one else's head = legal expr., **pardon** Gn 40_{13} 2K 25_{27}; c) lift the head (of Isr. &c.) = take a headcount, census Ex 30_{12}; — 4. obj. *pānîm*, lift one's own face = expr. of confidence Jb 11_{15}, w/o *pānîm* Gn 4_{7}, w. *'el* to 2K 9_{32}, = show one's face to, dare to be in the presence of 2S 2_{22}; subj. God, be favorably disposed toward s.one Nu 6_{26}; — 5. obj. *pānîm*, lift s.one else's face: a) accept s.one kindly, be favorable to Gn 32_{21}; b) pay attention to La 4_{16}, inf. *n^{e}śô' pānîm* highly thought of, in high standing 2K 5_{1}; accept (compensation) Pr 6_{35}; c) show partiality, favoritism to(-ward) Ma 2_{9}; — 6. obj. *'ênayim* look up Gn 13_{10}; — 7. obj. *qôl* lift one's voice: to call Ju 9_{7}, rejoice Is 24_{14}, weep Gn 27_{38}; w/o *qôl* Nu 14_{1}; — 8. *qôl* replaced by oth. words: *māšāl* Nu 23_{7}, *maśśā'* 2K 9_{25}; (?) w. *'ālâ* put s.one under oath, or pronounce a curse 1K 8_{31}; — 9. *nāśā' 'al pîw* take on one's lips Ps 50_{16}, so *'al-ś^{e}fātāyw* Ps 16_{4}; *nāśā' b^{e}śārô baššinnayim* take one's flesh in the teeth = risk one's life Jb 13_{14}; — 10. *nāśā' nafšô* long for (mostly w. *'el*) Dt 24_{15}; — 11. *n^{e}śā'ô libbô* his heart drives him = he is willing Ex 35_{21}, :: *n^{e}śā'^{a}kā libbekā* your heart lifts you = misleads you

2K 14_{10}; — 12. **contain** (subj. a given fair measure) Ez 45_{11}; — 13. **carry**, obj. child 2K 4_{19}; **bear**, obj. yoke La 3_{27}; metaph. carry off (obj. *ḥesed*, favor) = win Est 2_{9}, so obj. *ḥēn* Est 2_{15}; help carry, w. *bᵉ* Nu 11_{17}, *'ēt* with Ex 18_{22}; obj. *pᵉrî* bear, yield fruit Ez 36_{8}; — 14. **support** Gn 13_{6}; **bear**, 'stand' a person, a misery Dt 1_{9} Jer 15_{15}; abs. Is 1_{14}; — 15. *nāśā' 'āwōn*: a) bear one's own guilt, load, take, bring guilt upon onesf. Ex 28_{43}, so *ḥeṭ'ô* Lv 20_{20}; = atone for guilt Ex 28_{38}, abs. bear the consequences Pr 9_{12}; b) bear s.one else's guilt, *nāśā' ḥēṭ'* Is 53_{12}, *'āwōn* Ez 4_{4}; pay penalty Pr 19_{19}; — 16. subj. *rûᵃḥ* wind, obj. locusts Ex 10_{13}; subj. ship, obj. wares 1K 10_{11}; in genl., transport Dt 14_{24}; — 17. carry away = **take** Gn 27_{3}; *nāśā' 'iššâ* take a wife, marry Ru 1_{4}, w/o *iššâ* Ezr 9_{2}; — 18. **take away**: a) 2S 5_{21}, obj. *rō'š* head, = behead (word-play on 4.) Gn 40_{19}; b) take away s.one's guilt (& punishment) Gn 50_{17}; > *nāśā' lᵉ* take away guilt = **forgive** Gn 18_{24}.

nif.: pf. נִשָּׂא; impf. יִנָּשֵׂא, אֶנָּשֵׂא, יִנָּשְׂאוּ, יִנָּשֵׂאוּ, תִּנָּשֶׂאנָה; impv. הִנָּשְׂאוּ; inf. הִנָּשֵׂא, הִנָּשְׂאָם, abs. נִשֵּׂאת 2S 19_{43}; pt. נִשָּׂא, f. נִשָּׂאָה & נִשֵּׂאת Zc 5_{7} 1C 14_{2}, נִשָּׂאִים, נִשָּׂאוֹת: — 1. **be carried** Ex 25_{28}, be carried off 2K 20_{17}; — 2. a) **raise onesf. up, rise up** Is 33_{10}, w. *bᵉ* against Ps 7_{7}; b) **rise upward** Is 40_{7}; — 3. **be exalted**: kingship Nu 24_{7}; tower over (of mountain) Is 2_{2}, pt. Is 2_{12}; raised (eyebrows) Pr 30_{13}.

piel: pf. נִשָּׂא, נִשֵּׂא, נִשְּׂאוּ (:: qal impf.!); impf. sf. יְנַשְּׂאֵהוּ, יְנַשְּׂאֵם, יְנַשְּׂאוּהוּ; impv. נַשְּׂאֵם; pt. מְנַשְּׂאִים: — 1. **lift up** Am 4_{2}; — 2. **exalt** 2S 5_{12}; raise, advance (in rank) Est 3_{1}; — 3. **carry**, **bear**: subj. God, obj. people Is 63_{9}; assist (*bᵉ* with) 1K 9_{11}; — 4. *niśśā' nafšô*, w. *lᵉ* & inf. long to, endure the longing to Je 22_{27}.

hif.: pf. sf. הִשִּׂיאוּ: burden s.one w. (guilt) Lv 22_{16}. †

hitp.: impf. יִתְנַשֵּׂא, תִּתְנַשֵּׂא > יִנָּשֵׂא, תִּנָּשֵׂא Nu 24_{7} 2C 32_{23} & יִנָּשְׂאוּ Dn 11_{14}; inf. הִתְנַשֵּׂא; pt. מִתְנַשֵּׂא: **exalt onesf.**, be ambitious 1K 1_{5}, w. *'al* Nu 16_{3}.

נשג: **hif.**: pf. הִשִּׂיג, הִשִּׂיגָה, sf. הִשִּׂיגוֹ, הִשִּׂיגָנוּ, הִשַּׂגְתָּם, הִשִּׂיגוּם; impf. יַשִּׂיג, וַיַּשֵּׂג, וַיַּשִּׂגוּ, יַשִּׂיגוּן, sf. תַּשִּׂיגוּם, אַשִּׂיגֶנּוּ, תַּשִּׂיגֵהוּ, וַיַּשִּׂ(י)גֵם; inf. הַשֵּׂג; pt. מַשִּׂיג, מַשֶּׂגֶת, sf. מַשִּׂיגֵהוּ: — 1. **overtake**, **catch up with** Gn 31_{25} & oft.; subj. blessing Dt 28_{2}, curse 28_{15}, words of Y. Zc 1_{6}; — 2. subj. *yād*, reach an amount = **be able** to put one's hand on, **to afford** Lv 5_{11}; *taśśîg yād* = come into property, become wealthy Lv 25_{47}; — 3. subj. joy &c., **appear** Is 35_{10}.

***נְשׂוּאָה**: pl. sf. נְשֻׂאֹתֵיכֶם: **burden** (portable idol) Is 46_{1}. †

I **נָשִׂיא**: cs. נְשִׂיא; pl. נְשִׂ(י)אִים, cs. נְשִׂיאֵי: **chief**, **minor king**: Abraham is *nᵉśî' 'ᵉlōhîm* Gn 23_{6}; in family of Ishmael 17_{20}, & in oth. foreign tribes, e.g. Midian Nu 25_{18}, but usu. in Isr.: leader of a given tribe of Isr. Nu 2_{3ff}.

II ***נָשִׂיא**: pl. נְשִׂאִים: **(damp) fog** Je 10_{13} 51_{16} Ps 135_{7} Pr 25_{14}. †

נשק: **nif.**: pf. נִשְּׂקָה: **be kindled, lit** (fire) Ps 78_{21}. †

hif.: pf. הִשִּׂיקוּ; impf. יַשִּׂיק: **kindle**, **light** (a fire) Is 44_{15} Ez 39_{9}.

I **נשא**: **qal**: pf. נָשִׁיתִי, נָשׁוּ־ Je 15_{10}; pt. נֹשֶׁא 2× & נֹשֶׁה 5×, נֹשְׁאִים Ne 5_{7} Kt (Qr נֹשִׁים): — 1. **lend**, **make a loan**, w. *bᵉ* to Dt 24_{11}, abs. Je 15_{10}; Is 24_{2} evid. **take a loan** from (*bᵉ*); — 2. pt. **creditor**, professional **money-lender** 2K 4_{1}; **usurer** (who collects interest) Ex 22_{24}; — 3. *nāšā' maššā' bᵉ* **practice usury** on Ne 5_{7}; — 4. *nāšā' 'ālâ bᵉ* 1K 8_{31} put a person upon an oath of purification (oth.: *nāśā'* qal 8. utter an oath).

hif.: impf. יַשֶּׁה, תַּשֶּׁה; pt. F *מַשֶּׁה: w. *bᵉ* + pers. & acc. thg., **lend** s.thg to s.one Dt 15_{2} 24_{10}. †

II נשׂא: nif.: pf. נִשְּׁאוּ: **give onesf. false hopes** Is 19_{13}. †
hif.: pf. הִשִּׁיא, הִשֵּׁאתָ, sf. הִשִּׁיאַנִי, הִשִּׁיאֲךָ, הִשִּׁיאוּךָ; impf. יַשִּׁ(י)א, יַשִּׁיאוּ, יַשִּׁאֲךָ; inf. הַשֵּׁא: **trick, deceive,** w. acc. Gn 3_{13} 2K 19_{10}, obj. *nafšô* onesf. Je 37_9, w. *lᵉ* 2K 18_{29}.
נשׁב: **qal**: pf. נָשְׁבָה: **blow** (subj. wind) Is 40_7. †
hif.: impf. יַשֵּׁב: **make** (wind) **blow** Ps 147_{18}; — 2. **scare away** (birds) Gn 15_{11}. †
I נשׁה: **qal**: pf. נָשִׁיתִי: **forget** La 3_{17}. †
nif.: impf. (w. sf.!) תִנָּשֵׁנִי: **be forgotten** (by me) Is 44_{21}. †
piel: pf. sf. נַשַּׁנִי: **make s.one forget** Gn 41_{51}. †
hif.: pf. הִשָּׁה; impf. יַשֶּׁה: **make** s.one **forget** Jb 39_{17}, **grant** (to) s.one (*lᵉ*) **forgetfulness** of (*min*) s.thg 11_6. †
II נשׁה: see forms of I נשׂא.
נָשֶׁה: *gîd hannāšeh*, nervus ischiadicus, major nerve of hip region 32_{33}. †
*נְשִׁי: 2K 4_7 Qr sf. נִשְׁיֵךְ Kt נִשְׁיְכִי: **debt.** †
נְשִׁיָּה: **forgetting,** *ʾereṣ nᵉšiyyâ* land forgotten by Y., i.e. of the dead Ps 88_{13}. †
נָשִׁים: pl. of אִשָּׁה: women.
*נְשִׁיקָה: pl. נְשִׁיקוֹת: **kiss** Pr 27_6 SS 1_2. †
I נָשַׁךְ: **qal**: pf נ׳, sf. נְשָׁכוֹ; impf. יִשֹּׁךְ, יִשָּׁךְ, sf. יִשְּׁכֶנּוּ; pt. נֹשֵׁךְ, pl. sf. נֹשְׁכֶיךָ, pass. נָשׁוּךְ: **bite**: — 1. subj. snake Gn 49_{17}; — 2. subj. men Mi 3_5 (abs. = have s.thg to eat), metaph. Hb 2_7. †
piel: pf. נִשְּׁכוּ; impf. יְנַשְּׁכוּ: subj. snake, **bite** Nu 21_6 Je 8_{17}. †
II נשׁך: **qal**: impf. יַשִּׁךְ; pt. pl. sf. נֹשְׁכֶיךָ: **borrow at interest** Dt 23_{20b} (usu. 'lend,' = hif. $_{20a}$!), pt. ? creditor (word-play w. I!) Hb 2_7. †
hif.: impf. תַּשִּׁיךְ: w. *nešek* & *lᵉ*, **give at interest,** take interest from Dt 23_{20a}, w/o *nešek* $_{21}$. †
נֶשֶׁךְ: **interest,** extra payment due on settlement of debt (oth.: loaning w. interest already deducted): of money Ex 22_{24}, of food &c. Dt 23_{20}.

נִשְׁכָּה: sf. נִשְׁכָּתוֹ; pl. נְשָׁכוֹת: **room, cell** (for storage &c.) Ne 3_{30} 12_{44} 13_7. †
נָשַׁל: **qal**: pf. נ׳; impf. יִשַּׁל; impv. שַׁל: — 1. **loosen**: take off (sandals) Ex 3_5 Jos 5_{15}, drive away, expel (peoples) Dt $7_{1.22}$ 28_{40}; — 2. (intrans.) **become detached** Dt 19_5, drop off 28_{40}. †
piel: impf. יְנַשֵּׁל: **drive away, expel** (people) 2K 16_6. †
נשׁם: **qal**: impf. אֶשֹּׁם: **pant** Is 42_{14}. †
נְשָׁמָה: cs. נִשְׁמַת, sf. נִשְׁמָתוֹ; pl. נְשָׁמוֹת: — 1. **blowing** (of God's breath) 2S 22_{16}; — 2. **breath** 1K 17_{17}; *kol-nᵉšāmâ* everything that has breath 1K 15_{29}; *nišmat ḥayyîm* Gn 2_7; — 3. pl. animated beings, 'souls' Is 57_{16}; — 4. *nišmat ʾēl* (& oth. designations of God) Jb 37_{10} 32_8.
נָשַׁף: **qal**: pf. נ׳, נָשַׁפְתָּ: subj. God, **blow** Ex 15_{10}, w. *bᵉ* on Is 40_{24}. †
נֶשֶׁף: נָשֶׁף, sf. נִשְׁפּוֹ: — 1. **twilight**: after sunset 2K 7_5, before sunrise 1S 30_{17}; — 2. (in genl.) **darkness** Je 13_{16}.
I נָשַׁק: **qal**: pf. נ׳, נָשְׁקָה, נָשְׁקוּ; impf. יִשַּׁק, יִשָּׁק, וַיִּשְּׁקוּ, אֶשְּׁקָה, יִשָּׁקוּן, sf. יִשָּׁקֵנִי; impv. וּשְׁקָה; inf. נְשָׁק־: **kiss**: a) w. acc. Gn 33_4, b) w. *lᵉ* Gn 27_{26f}; kisses are given in var. relationships: son-father Gn 27_{26}, lovers SS 8_1 &c.
[cj. **nif.**: pf. נִשָּׁקוּ: kiss each other cj. Ps 85_{11} for qal. †]
piel: impf. וַיְנַשֵּׁק, וַיְנַשֶּׁק־; impv. נַשְּׁקוּ; inf. נַשֵּׁק: **kiss** (fervently?) Gn 29_{13}.
II נשׁק: **qal**: impf. יִשַּׁק; pt. נֹשְׁקֵי: — 1. ? put onesf. in an order, accommodate onesf. Gn 41_{40} (F I qal); — 2. *nōšᵉqê qešet* **arm onesf.** w. 1C 12_2 2C 17_{17}, sim. Ps 78_9. †
hif.: pt. מַשִּׁיקוֹת: **touch each other** (of wings; w. a rustle?) Ez 3_{13}. †
I נֶשֶׁק: נֶשֶׁק, נֵשֶׁק, cs. נֵשֶׁק: — 1. **armor,** weapons 2K 10_2; — 2. battle(-array) Ps 140_8.
II נֵשֶׁק: a kind of fragrant substance 1K 10_{25} 2C 9_{24}, LXX: myrrh. †

נֶשֶׁר: נֶשֶׁר; pl. נְשָׁרִים, cs. נִשְׁרֵי: **eagle & vulture** Ex 19_4 2S 1_{23} La 4_{19}.

נשׁת: **qal**: pf. נָשָׁתָּה, נָשְׁתָה: **dry up** (intrans.), of tongue Is 41_7, metaph. of strength Je 51_{30}. †

nif.: pf. נִשְּׁתוּ; impf. יִנָּשְׁתוּ: **be dried up** (of water) Is 19_5, cj. Je 18_{14}. †

נִשְׁתְּוָן: **letter** Ezr 4_7 7_{11}. †

נְתוּנִים: Ezr 8_{17} Kt; trad. = Qr נְתִינִים, but better pt. 'stationed' √נתן. †

נתח: **piel**: pf. נִתַּח; impf. תְּנַתֵּחַ, וַיְנַתַּח, וַיְנַתְּחֵהוּ, וָאֲנַתְּחֶהָ, וַיְנַתְּחֵהוּ: **cut** (meat) **in pieces** 1K $18_{23 \cdot 33}$.

נֵתַח: pl. נְתָחִים, sf. נְתָחֶיהָ, נְתָחָיו: **piece** (of meat) Ex 29_{17}.

נָתִיב: cs. נְתִיב: **path** Ps 78_{50}.

נְתִיבָה: sf. נְתִיבָתִי; pl. נְתִיבוֹת, sf. נְתִיבֹ(וֹ)תָיו, נְתִיבוֹתֵיהֶם: **path** Ju 5_6; *bêt netîbôt* cross-roads Pr 8_2.

***נָתִין**: pl. נְתִינִים: 'those who are donated,' **temple-slaves, bondsmen** Ezr 2_{43}.

נתך: **qal**: impf. תִּתַּךְ, וַיִּתְּכוּ: **gush forth, be poured out, break forth**: water Jb 3_{24}, anger Je 42_{18}, curse Dn 9_{11}.

nif.: pf. נִתַּךְ, נִתְּכָה, נִתַּכְתֶּם; pt. נִתֶּכֶת: — 1. **gush forth, be poured out, break forth**: rain Ex 9_{33}, water 2S 21_{10}, anger Je 7_{20}; — 2. be brought to melting, **be melted** Ez 22_{21}.

hif.: pf. הִתִּיכוּ, הִתַּכְתִּי; impf. וַיַּתִּיכוּ, תַּתִּיכֵנִי; inf. הַנְתִּיךְ: — 1. **pour out** (trans.) Jb 10_{10}; pour out (money), or melt down 2K 22_9 2C 34_{17}; — 2. bring to melting, **melt** Ex 22_{20}. †

hof.: impf. תֻּתְּכוּ: **be melted** Ez 22_{22}. †

נָתַן: **qal** (1900×): pf. נ׳, נָתַן, נָתְנָה, נָתַתָּה, נָתַתָּ(ה), נָתַתְּ, נָתַתִּי (נָתַתִּי Ez 16_{18}), נָתַנּוּ, נְתַנּוּ (נָתַנּוּ Ez 27_{19}), נְתַתֶּם, נָתְנוּ, sf. נְתָנוֹ, נְתָנְךָ, נְתָנַנִי, נְתַתִּיו, נְתַתִּיהוּ; impf. וַיִּתֵּן, יִתֶּן־, וְאֶתְּנָה, נִתֵּן (נִתַּן Ju 16_5), sf. יִתְּנֶךָ, יִתְּנֵנוּ, תִּתְּנוֹ Ez 22_{29}; impv. תֵּן(־), תֶּן־, תְּנִי, תְּנִי, תְּנוּ, sf. תְּנֵהוּ, תְּנֵם, תְּנָה; inf. נְתֹן, נְתָן־, but usu. תֵּת, לָתֵת, לֶתֶת(־), לְתִתֵּן, תִּתּוֹ, תִּתִּי, תִּתֵּנוּ, abs. נָתֹ(וֹ)ן;

pt. נֹ(וֹ)תֵן, sf. נֹתֶנְךָ, pass. נָתוּן, נְתוּנִים, נְתֻנִים, נְתֻנוֹת; qal pass. ↗ hof.: — 1. **give**, w. *le* to Gn 3_6, *'el* 18_7, = deliver Ex 5_{18}, in trade Pr 31_{24}; — 2. w. 2 acc. **present** s.one w. s.thg Jos 15_{19}, = let s.one have 1K 18_{26}, = sell Gn 23_4, = cause (trouble) Pr 10_{10}, = offer (a sign) Dt 13_2, = grant (a request) 1S 1_{17}, = produce (fruit) Ps 1_3; — 3. **offer** (sacrifice) Ex 30_{14}; pt. pass. w. *le* allotted to Nu 3_9; — 4. *nātan le'iššâ* give in marriage Gn 30_4; *nātan lifnê* lay before Je 44_{10}; *nātan 'im* associate w. Gn 3_{12}; *nātan le* repay Je 17_{10}; *nātan bakkesef* turn (s.thg) into money Dt 14_{25}; *nātan be* give away for (a price) Jl 4_3; — 5. w. *šibtô* Ex 21_{19} ↗ *yšb* 3 b; w. *yād* ↗ *yād* 2 a; w. *šekobtô* &c. Lv 18_{20} &c. ↗ **šekōbet*; — 6. *mî yittēn* who will give? = if only there were...! &c.: *mî yittēn 'ereb* if only it were evening Dt 28_{67}, *mî-yittenēnî* oh, if only I had Je 9_1, *mî yittēn mûtēnû* if only we were dead Ex 16_3 &c.; otherw. Jb 14_4 who shall bring (= knows) one who?; — 7. **pass on** (knowledge) Pr 9_9, announce (a sign) 1K 13_3; — 8. w. acc. + *le* & inf. **allow, permit** Gn 20_6; *yittenēnî hāšēb rûḥî* let me catch my breath Jb 9_{18}; = *nātan le* + *le* & inf. Est 8_{11}; *nātan beyad*... + *le* & inf. commission s.one to 1C 16_7; — 9. w. *le* **surrender, deliver** La 3_{30}; *nātan bekaf* hand over to Ju 6_{13}, = *beyad* 4_7, = *nātan lifnê* (obj. land) Dt 2_{31}; *nātan libbô/nafšô*, w. *le* & inf. devote onesf. to 1C 22_{19}; — 10. *nātan rêḥô* give out fragrance SS 1_{12}, *nātan 'ênô* give out luster Pr 23_{31}; *nātan tōf* beat the timbrel Ps 81_3; — 11. *nātan pānāyw 'el* turn one's face to Dn 9_3; *nātan rō'š* w. *le* & inf. take it into one's head to Ne 9_{17} (:: abs. *nātan rō'š* choose a leader Nu 14_4); *nātan libbô le* pay attention to Ec 7_{21} (cf. 9.); *nātan tiflâ le* put blame on Jb 1_{22}; — 12. **set, put, lay** Gn 1_{17}; *nātan 'al-pîhem* put s.thg in their mouth Mi 3_{5}; *nātan ʼel-lēb* put into s.one's heart = inspire s.one Ne 7_{5}, = *b^{e}lēb* Ezr 7_{22}; *nātan ʼel-libbô* take to heart Ec 7_{2}; *nātan nōkaḥ pānāyw* set before onesf. = look w. pleasure on Ez 14_{3}; = set up Lv 26_{1}; = bring (in) Gn 41_{48}; lay (fire) = set (fire) Ez 30_{8}; = direct (shock of battering rams against) Ez 26_{9}; = add to Lv 2_{15}; *nātan b^{e}qôlô ʻal* lift one's voice against Je 12_{8}; = hold (a meeting) Ne 5_{7}; *nātan tôʻēbâ ʻal* lay (punishment for) an abomination on Ez 7_{3}; *nātan dām b^{e}* bring blood(guilt) on Dt 21_{8}, = pour out blood 1K 2_{5}, so rain Ps 105_{32}; *nātan taḥat* place s.one instead of 1K 2_{35}; — 13. w. 2 acc. make s.one (to be) s.thg: *ʼab-h^{a}môn n^{e}tattîkā* (to be) the father of a multitude Gn 17_{5}, so w. 1st obj. thg. Ps 18_{33}; w. acc. & *l^{e}*, *n^{e}tattîw l^{e}gôy* Gn 17_{20}; *nātan l^{e}-ʼālâ* make s.one become a formula for cursing Nu 5_{21}; w. acc. & *k^{e}* 1K 10_{27}; *nātan l^{e}raḥ^{a}mîm lifnê* let s.one find compassion 1K 8_{50}.

nif. (40×): pf. נִתַּן, נִתְּנָה, נִתְּנָה (Ne 13_{10}, 3. pl. f.), נִתַּתֶּם, נִתָּנוּ; impf. יִנָּתֵן, יִנָּתֶן Lv 24_{20} 2S 21_{6} Kt; inf. הִנָּתֵן, הִנָּתוֹן; pt. נִתָּן: — 1. **be given** Ex 5_{16}; be given out, issued (law) Est 3_{14}; be given into s.one's hand = power Gn 9_{2} & oft.; *nitt^{e}nâ l^{e}ʼiššâ* be given in marriage Gn 38_{14}; w. *ʻal-yad* be delivered (money) 2K 22_{7}; be given (*l^{e}*, as [a heritage]) Ez 11_{15}; w. *l^{e}* be assigned (to s.one) 2C 2_{13}; — 2. **be given away** (like grass) Is 51_{12}; be given over (to death) Ez 31_{14}, be made = become (*l^{e}*) Ez 47_{11}; w. *ʻal* be laid on Dn 8_{12}; — 3. var.: be granted Est 2_{13}, be guaranteed 5_{3}; be laid, provided for Ez 32_{23}.

(trad. **hof.**) **qal** pass: impf. יֻתַּן: **be given** 2K 5_{17}; *yuttan* (m.) *l^{e}ʼiššâ* (w. *ʼēt!*) be given in marriage 1K 2_{21}; w. *ʻal*, be put on Lv 11_{38}.

נָתָן: n. pers.

נְתַנְאֵל: n. pers.

נְתַנְיָה: n. pers.

נְתַנְיָהוּ: n. pers.

נְתַנְמֶלֶךְ: n. pers.

נתס: **qal**: pf. נָתְסוּ: **tear up** (s.one's path) Jb 30_{13}. †

נתע: **nif.**: pf. נִתָּעוּ: **be knocked out** (of teeth) Jb 4_{10}.

נָתַץ: **qal**: pf. נָתַץ, נָתָץ, נָתְצוּ, נָתָצוּ, ו׳; impf. יִתֹּץ, אֶתֹּץ, וַתִּתְּצוּ (Is 22_{10}, w. raphe), תִּתֹּצוּ, תִּתֹּצוּן, sf. יִתְּצֵנִי, יִתָּצְךָ, יִתְּצֵהוּ; impv. נְתֹץ; inf. לִנְתֹּץ; pt. pass. נְתֻצִים: **tear down, break up, demolish**: obj. altar 2K 23_{12}, house 2K 10_{27}, city Ju 9_{45}; abs. Je 1_{10}; metaph., obj. man Jb 19_{10}; obj. teeth, break Ps 58_{7}.

nif.: pf. נִתְּצוּ: **be torn down, demolished, destroyed** Je 4_{26} Ez 16_{39}. †

piel: pf. נִתַּץ, נִתַּצְתֶּם; impf. יְנַתְּצוּ: **tear down**: obj. altar Dt 12_{3} 2C 31_{1} $34_{4.7}$, high place 2C 33_{3}, wall 2C 36_{19}. †

pual: pf. נֻתַּץ: **be torn down, demolished** Ju 6_{28}. †

(**hof.**) **qal** pass.: impf. יֻתַּץ: **be torn up** (oven, stove) Lv 11_{35}. †

נתק: **qal**: pf. sf. נְתַקְנֻהוּ; impf. אֶתְּקֶנְךָ; pt. pass. נָתוּק: — 1. **tear away** (ring fm. finger) Je 22_{24}, (testicles) Lv 22_{24}; — 2. (military) **draw** (s.one) **away** Ju 20_{32}. †

nif.: pf. (ℱ piel!) נִתַּק, נִתְּקוּ, נִתָּקוּ; impf. יִנָּתֵק, יִנָּתְקוּ, יִנָּתֵקוּ: — 1. **be snapped in two** (cord, thong, &c.) Ju 16_{9} Is 5_{27}; — 2. **be pulled loose, separated** (persons) Je 6_{29}; — 3. (military) **let onesf. be drawn away** Jos 8_{16}; — 4. **be drawn out** (feet fm. river) Jos 4_{18}.

piel: pf. (ℱ nif.!) נִתַּקְתִּי, נִתְּקוּ; impf. יְנַתֵּק, תְּנַתְּקִי, אֲנַתֵּק, נְנַתְּקָה, sf. וַיְנַתְּקֵם: — 1. **tear up**: bowstrings Ju 16_{9}, rope 16_{12}, lacerate (breasts) Ez 23_{34}; — 2. **tear up, pull up** (roots) Ez 17_{9}. †

hif.: impv. הַתִּקֵם; inf. הַתִּיקֵנוּ: **pull out, separate** (sheep) Je 12_{3}; — 2. (military) **draw** s.one **away** Jos 8_{6}. †

hof.: pf. הָנְתְּקוּ (military) **be drawn away** Ju 20_{31}. †

נֶתֶק: נֶתֶק: a **skin-disease** in hair or beard, prob. ringworm (oth. sugg. eczema) Lv 13$_{30-37}$ 14$_{54}$. †

I **נתר**: **qal**: impf. יִתַּר: **fall**, metaph. of heart, i.e. heart sinks for lack of courage Jb 37$_1$ (oth. II). †

? **hif.**: impf. יַתֵּר: obj. *yādô*, **drop** = withdraw Jb 6$_9$ (oth.: stretch out). †

II **נתר**: **qal**: impf. יִתַּר: **start up, leap,** metaph. of heart Jb 37$_1$ (oth. I); cj. **leap safely** 2S 22$_{33}$ & Ps 18$_{33}$ (for וַיַּתֵּר, תּור√). †

piel: pf. נִתֵּר: **leap** (of animal) Lv 11$_{21}$. †

hif.: impf. וַיַּתֵּר: **make** (nations) **start up, jump up** Hb 3$_6$. †

III **נתר**: **hif.**: impf. וַיַּתִּירֵהוּ, יַתֵּר; impv. הַתֵּר; pt. מַתִּיר: **make** (fetters) **break up, split** Is 58$_6$, **let** (prisoners) **go free** Ps 105$_{20}$ 146$_7$. †

נֶתֶר: **natron**, mineral used as detergent Je 2$_{22}$ Pr 25$_{20}$. †

נָתַשׁ: **qal**: pf. נ׳, נְתַשְׁתִּים; impf. אֶתּוֹשׁ, וַיִּתְּשֵׁם; inf. נְתוֹשׁ, לִנְתֹּשׁ, נָתְשִׁי, abs. נָתוֹשׁ; pt. נֹתֵשׁ, sf. נֹתְשָׁם: **uproot, tear up, pull up**: subj. God, obj. *ʾašērîm* Mi 5$_{13}$; so metaph., obj. people, tear up = **drive out** 1K 14$_{15}$; abs. Jer 1$_{10}$.

nif.: impf. יִנָּתֵשׁ, יִנָּתְשׁוּ: **be uprooted, torn out** Je 31$_{40}$ Am 9$_{15}$, be smashed (of a kingdom) Dn 11$_4$. †

(trad. **hof.**) **qal** pass.: impf. וַתֻּתַּשׁ: **be uprooted, torn out** Ez 19$_{12}$. †

ס

סְאָה: pl. סְאִים; du. *סָאתַיִם > סָאתַיִם: **seah**, measure of capacity, in one estimate = approx. 7 liters, 7 1/2 quarts, Gn 18$_6$ 1S 25$_{18}$ 1K 18$_{32}$ 2K 7$_{1.16.18}$. †

סְאוֹן: **boot** (of Assyrians) Is 9$_4$. †

סאן: **qal**: pt. סֹאֵן: **tramp along** (in boots) Is 9$_4$. †

***סאסא** Is 27$_8$: ⇒ סַאסְּאָה.

סַאסְּאָה: **expulsion**; **chasing, scaring away** Is 27$_8$. †

סבא: **qal**: impf. נִסְבְּאָה; inf. סָבְאָם; pt. סֹבֵא, סֹבְאֵי: **carouse, drink hard** Is 56$_{12}$, Ho 4$_{18}$ carousing with them; pt. drunkard Dt 21$_{20}$ Pr 23$_{20f}$; Ez 23$_{42}$ Kt Na 1$_{10}$ txt. corr. †

***סֹבֶא**: sf. סָבְאֵךְ: **a drink**; Verss.: wine, but sugg. (wheat-)beer Is 1$_{22}$. †

[***סָבָא**: Ez 23$_{42}$ Qr סָבָאִים (Kt סוֹ׳, pt.?) trad. 'drunkard,' but txt. prob. corr.; Na 1$_{10}$ כְּסָבְאָם סְבוּאִים txt. corr., ⇒ comm. †]

סְבָא: (n. pers.,) n. peop.

***סְבָאִי**: pl. סְבָאִים: gent. of סְבָא Is 45$_{14}$. †

סָבַב: **qal**: pf. ס׳, סַבֹּתִי, סָבְבוּ, סַבּוֹתֶם, sf. סְבָבוּנִי, סְבָבוּם, סְבָבֻנוּ; impf. תָּסֹב, וַיָּס(ו)ב, יְסֻבֵּנִי, תְּסֻבֶּינָה, וַנָּסָב, נָסֹב, וַיִּסֹּבּוּ, יָסֹב & יְסֻבֶּנּוּ, יְסֻבְבוּהוּ; impv. סֹב, סֹבִּי, סֹבּוּ; inf. (לָ)סֹב; pt. ס(ו)בֵב, ס(ו)בְבִים: go in a circle: — 1. **turn** (in place): on hinge, door Pr 26$_{14}$; veer, of wind Ec 1$_6$, turn (sc. one's attention) 7$_{25}$; turn away Gn 42$_{24}$, turn (to go in new direction) 1S 15$_{27}$; — 2. **go around**: a) go the rounds, walk a circuit (of towns) 1S 7$_{16}$; b) **execute a** (cultic) **procession around, march around** Gn 37$_7$ Jos 6$_{3f}$; c) **sit/lie down around the table** 1S 16$_{11}$; d) **surround** (obj. person, city &c.) 1K 5$_{17}$ & oft.; of bees, buzz around Ps 118$_{12}$; e) surround = **encircle, hem in** 2K 8$_{21}$; f) **flow around** Gn 2$_{11.13}$ (oth.: wind through); g) **go around** (in evasion) Nu 21$_4$, step to the side 1S 18$_{11}$; w. *leʾāḥôr*, flow back Ps 114$_{3.5}$; w. *ʾel-aḥarê* step in behind, fall in behind 2K 9$_{18f}$, w. *derek* 2K 3$_9$; — 3. **turn** (as one goes, = change direction of motion): a) **turn off** (to go) 2S 14_{24}; roam around, wander around 2K 3_9; metaph., of kingship, turn (to become s.one else's possession) 1K 2_{15}; b) turn (= be transformed) into Zc 14_{10}.

nif.: pf. נָסַב, נָסַבָּה, נָסַבּוּ; impf. יִסַּבּוּ: — 1. **turn** = change direction: boundary Nu 34_4, wings Ez 1_9; — 2. **surround, encircle** Gn 19_4; — 3. **turn** (to become s.one's else's possession), be turned over to Je 6_{12}.

piel: inf. סַבֵּב: w. *ʾet-pᵉnê*: **put another face** (on a matter) 2S 14_{20}. †

polel: impf. תְּסוֹבֵב, אֲסֹבְבָה, sf. יְסֹבְבֵנִי, יְסֹבְבֶנְהוּ, תְּסֹבְבֵךְ: — 1. **encircle** (s.one protectively) Dt 32_{10}; — 2. **encircle** (cultically, = march around) Ps 26_6; — 3. var.: stand around, gather around Ps 7_8; flow around Jon $2_{4.6}$; roam around Ps $59_{7.15}$.

hif.: pf. הֵסֵב, הֲסִבֹּתָ, הֵסַבּוּ; impf. וַיַּסֵּב, וַיַּסֵּבּוּ, נָסֵב, וַיְסִבֵּנִי; impv. הָסֵבִּי; inf. הָסֵב; pt. מֵסֵב: change the direction of movement: — 1. spatial: a) **make** (ark) **go around** Jos 6_{11}, **make** (a wall) **surround** 2C 14_6; b) **make** s.one **turn off, lead off** Ex 13_{18}; (intrans.) turn off 2S 5_{23}; metaph. **make** s.one **change sides** (in loyalty) 2S 3_{12}; — 2. **remove** (s.thg, s.one) 1S 5_{8ff} 2S 20_{12}, fetch 1C 13_3, turn (weapons) around Je 21_4; — 3. **turn away**, obj. face 1K 21_4, = turn around (intrans.) 1K 8_{14}; obj. glance SS 6_5; — 4. **change**, obj. s.one else's heart 1K 18_{37}, a name 2K 23_{34}.

hof. (or **qal** pass.): impf. יוּסַּב; pt. מוּסַבּוֹת, מֻסַבּוֹת: — 1. be brought to turning, **be turned**: wheel Is 28_{27}, pt. Ez 41_{24} (doors) which may be turned, swinging; — 2. **be changed** (name) Nu 32_{38}; — 3. **be set** (jewels) Ex 28_{11} $39_{6.13}$. †

סִבָּה: **turning, arrangement** (= turn of affairs) 1K 12_{15}. †

סָבִיב (ca. 330×): cs. סְבִיב; pl. cs. סְבִיבֵי, sf. סְבִיבָיו & pl. סְבִיב(וֹ)ת, sf. סְבִיב(וֹ)תָיו, סְבִיב(וֹ)תֵיהֶם: I. sg.: — 1. noun, *hassābîb* ? **circuit** 1C 11_8, but txt.? F comm.; — 2. abs. as adv. **all around** 1S 31_9; so *sābîb sābîb* Ez 8_{10}; — 3. *missābîb* from all sides, all around Nu 16_{27} & oft.; — 4. *sābîb lᵉ* (to) all around Ex 16_{13} & oft.; — II. pl. — 1. a) **environs, neighborhood**: *sᵉbîbê yᵉrûšālayim* Je 32_{44}; b) w. sf. **all around** Ps 50_3; c) neighbors Ps 44_{14}; d) revolution, course (of wind) Ec 1_6.

סבך: [**qal**: pt. pass. סְבֻכִים Na 1_{10}, trad. interwoven, entangled, but txt. undoubtedly corr., F comm. †]

pual: impf. יְסֹבָכוּ: **be twisted, intertwined** Jb 8_{17}. †

סְבָךְ: pl. cs. סִבְכֵי: **underbrush, thicket** Gn 22_{13} Is 9_{17} 10_{34}. †

***סְבֹךְ**: cs. סְבָךְ־, sf. סֻבְּכוֹ: **underbrush, thicket** Je 4_7 Ps 74_5. †

סִבְּכַי: n. pers.

סבל: **qal**: pf. סָבָלְנוּ, סְבָלָם; impf. יִסְבֹּל, אֶסְבֹּל, יִסְבְּלֻהוּ; inf. לִסְבֹּל: — 1. **carry, bear**: obj. burden Gn 49_{15}, idols Is 46_7, sorrows Is $53_{4.11}$, punishment La 5_7; — 2. **support** (elderly) Is 46_4. †

pual: pt. מְסֻבָּלִים: laden = **great with young** (cattle) Ps 144_{14}. †

hitp.: impf. וְיִסְתַּבֵּל: Ec 12_5, of grasshopper, Verss. become fat, oth. sugg. drag onesf. along, or be burdened down, F comm. †

סֵבֶל: — 1. **burden** Ps 81_7 Ne 4_{11}; — 2. **forced labor** 1K 11_{28}. †

***סֹבֶל**: sf. סֻבֳּלוֹ: **burden** Is 9_3 10_{27} 14_{25}. †

סַבָּל: pl. סַבָּלִים: **porter** 1K 5_{29} Ne 4_4 2C $2_{1.17}$ 34_{13}. †

***סְבָלוֹת**: cs. סִבְלוֹת, sf. סִבְלֹתָם & סִבְלֹתֵיהֶם: **burden-carrying, forced labor** Ex 1_{11} 2_{11} 5_{4f} 6_{6f}. †

סִבֹּלֶת: Ephraimitic pronunciation of I שִׁבֹּלֶת Ju 12_6. †

סְבָרַיִם: n. loc.

סַבְתָּא 1C 1_9 & **סַבְתָּה** Gn 10_7: n. peop. or terr.

סַבְתְּכָא: (n. pers.,) n. peop. or terr.

סגד: **qal**: impf. יִסְגָּד־, יִסְגּוֹד־ (Kt יִסְגּוֹד) Is 44_{17}, יִסְגְּדוּ, אֶסְגּוֹד: **bow down** (in worship), w. l^e before Is $44_{15\cdot17\cdot19}$ 46_6. †

סְגוֹר: **enclosure**, **closing** (of the heart), i.e. chest cavity Ho 13_8. †

סָגוּר: — 1. **gold plate**, hammered thin 1K 6_{20f}; — 2. pure, fine gold 1K 7_{49} 10_{21} 2C $4_{20\cdot22}$ 9_{20}. †

סָגִים: ↗ סִיגִים.

סְגֻלָּה: cs. סְגֻלַּת, sf. סְגֻלָּתוֹ: **personal property**: — 1. secular, of David 1C 29_3, of kings &c. Ec 2_8; — 2. theological, Isr. is Y.'s *s^egullâ* Ex 19_5 Ma 3_{17} Ps 135_4, *ʿam-s^egullâ* Dt 7_6 14_2 26_{18}. †

***סֶגֶן** or ***סָגָן**: pl. סְגָנִים, sf. סְגָנֶיהָ: — 1. **governor**, official of Babylonian empire Is 41_{25}; — 2. **head** (of Jewish community) Ezr 9_2.

סָגַר: **qal**: pf. ס׳, סָגַרְתָּ, סָגְרוּ, סָגָרוּ; impf. יִסְגֹּר, נִסְגְּרָה; impv. סְגֹר, סִגְרוּ; inf. לִסְגֹּר; pt. סֹגֵר, סֹגֶרֶת, pass. סָגוּר: — 1. **shut**, **close**: a) s.thg, w. acc.: door Gn 19_6, womb 1S 1_5, breach in wall 1K 11_{27}; b) w. *baʿad* behind s.one Gn 7_{16}; *sāgar bāśār taḥat* closed it w. flesh Gn 2_{21}; c) abs. close up Is 22_{20}; a city *sōgeret ûm^esuggeret*, which closed & stayed closed Jos 6_1; — 2. w. *ʿal*, **shut** s.one **in** Ex 14_3.

nif.: pf. נִסְגַּר; impf. יִסָּגֵר, יִסָּגְרוּ; impv. הִסָּגֵר: — 1. **be shut**, **closed** (gates &c.) Ne 13_{19}; — 2. **shut onesf. in** 1S 23_7; — 3. w. *min*, **be shut out** Nu 12_{14f}.

piel: pf. סִגַּר, sf. סִגְּרַנִי; impf. יְסַגֶּרְךָ: **hand over**, **deliver** s.one 1S 17_{46} 24_{19} 26_8; abs. 2S 18_{28}. †

pual: pf. סֻגַּר, סֻגְּרוּ; pt. מְסֻגֶּרֶת: **be closed up**, **shut up** Jos 6_1 (↗ qal 1 c) Is $24_{10\cdot22}$ Je 13_{19} Ec 12_4. †

hif.: pf. הִסְגִּיר, הִסְגַּרְתִּי, sf. הִסְגִּירוֹ, הִסְגַּרְתַּנִי; impf. יַסְגִּרוּ, תַּסְגֵּר, תַּסְגִּיר, sf. יַסְגִּרֵנִי, יַסְגִּרֻנוּ; inf. הַסְגִּיר, הַסְגִּירָם: — 1. a) give into s.one's power, **hand over**, **deliver** Ob $_{14}$, w. *b^eyad* 1S 23_{11}, w. *ʾel* Dt 23_{16}, w. l^e Am 1_6; b) **surrender** s.one Dt 32_{30}; c) **arrest** Jb 11_{10}; — 2. † **separate**, **seclude** s.one Lv $13_{4\text{-}54}$, isolate (a house) $14_{38\cdot46}$.

סְגֹר Ps 35_3; usu. assume ***סָגָר**, sugg. (Scythian & Persian) double axe, but oth. sugg. (socket of) javelin, here by metonymy simply javelin. †

סַגְרִיר: **(downpour of) rain** Pr 27_{15}. †

סַד: **stocks** (blocks in whose notches a prisoner's feet are held fast by iron bolts) Jb 13_{27} 31_{11}.

סָדִין: pl. סְדִינִים: **undergarment**, ? shirt Ju 14_{12f} Is 3_{23} Pr 31_{24}. †

סְדֹם: loc. סְדֹמָה: n. loc. **Sodom**.

***סֵדֶר**: pl. סְדָרִים: **order** Jb 10_{22}, underworld is a place 'without order.' †

סַהַר: **round enclosure**, metaph. *ʾaggan hassahar*, round bowl SS 7_3. †

סֹהַר: *bêt hassōhar*, **prison** Gn 39_{20}-40_5. †

סוֹא: n. of a king of Egypt 2K 17_4. †

I **סוג**: **qal**: pf. סָג; impf. נָסוֹג; inf. סוּג Pr 14_{14} (or pt. act. or verbal adj.): **deviate**, **be disloyal**, w. *min* Ps 53_4 80_{19}; *sûg lēb* w. disloyal heart Pr 14_{14}. †

nif.: pf. נָשׂוֹג for נָסוֹג 2S 1_{22}, נְסוּגוֹתִי, נָסֹגוּ; impf. יִסֹּגוּ; inf. נָסוֹג; pt. נְסוֹגִים: — 1. w. *ʾāḥôr*, **draw back**, **shrink back**, **recoil** 2S 1_{22} & oft.; — 2. **become disloyal** Ps 78_{57}; w. *ʾāḥôr* 44_{19}, w. *mēʾaḥar/mēʾaḥ^arê* Is 59_{13} Zp 1_6.

hif.: impf. תַּסִּיג, תַּסֵּג, יַשִּׂיגוּ for יַסִּיגוּ; pt. מַסִּיג, מַסִּיגֵי: — 1. w. *g^ebûl*, **displace** (boundary-marker) Dt 19_{14}; — 2. Mi 6_{14}, *tassēg w^elōʾ taflîṭ* carry off but not save (oth.: ? press toward birth, but not give birth).

hof.: pf. הֻסַּג: **be pushed back** Is 59_{14}. †

II **סוג**: **qal**: pt. pass. f. סוּגָה: **bordered** (w. lilies) SS 7_3. †

סוּג Ez 22_{18}: ₣ Qr סִיג.

סוּגַר: **neck-stock** (of wood or iron) Ez 19_9. †

סוֹד: sf. סוֹדוֹ, סוֹדִי, סֹדָם: — 1. **confidential conversation** Am 3_7; — 2. **circle of confidants** Gn 49_6; *himtîqû sôd* cultivate intimate company Ps 55_{15}.

סוּחַ: n. pers.

סוּחָה: **offal, garbage** Is 5_{25} Ps 80_{17}. †

סוֹטַי Ne 7_{57} & **סֹטַי** Ezr 2_{55}: n. pers.

I **סוך**: **pilpel**: pf. סִכְסַכְתִּי; impf. יְסַכְסֵךְ: **stir up, provoke,** w. *b^e* against Is 9_{10} 19_2. †

II **סוך**: **qal**: סַכְתִּי, סַכְתָּ; impf. תָּסוּךְ, תָּסוּכִי, sf. וַיְסֻכוּם, וָאֲסֻכֵךְ; inf. סוּךְ: — 1. *sûk šemen*, **grease** onesf. **with oil, anoint** 2S 14_2, = (w/o *šemen*) Ru 3_3; — 2. *sûk baššemen*, **anoint s.one** Ez 16_9.

hif.: impf. וַיָּסֶךְ: **anoint onesf.** 2S 12_{20}. †

hof. (**qal** pass. ?): impf. יִיסָךְ, יֻסָּךְ: **be poured out** Ex 30_{32} 37_{16}. †

סְוֵנֵה: n. loc.

I **סוּס** (ca. 140×): pl. סוּסִים, cs. סוּסֵי, sf. סוּסַי, סוּסֵיהֶם, ₣ f. *סוּסָה: **horse** Gn 47_{17}, as war-animal Is 31_1, for chariots 1K 20_1 &c.

II **סוּס** Is 38_{14}, Je 8_7 Kt: ₣ סִיס.

***סוּסָה**: f. of I סוּס: sf. סֻסָתִי: **mare** SS 1_9; n. loc. Jos 19_5 ₣ חָצֵר B 3.

סוּסִי: n. pers. Nu 13_{11}. †

סוּף: **qal**: pf. סָפוּ, וְסָפוּ; impf. יָסוּף, יָסֻפוּ: **come to an end** Is 66_{17} Am 3_{15} Ps 73_{19} Est 9_{28}. †

[**hif.**: impf. אֲסִיפֵם Je 8_{13} rd. אָסֹף אֲסִיפָם; & אָסֵף Zp $1_{2\cdot3}$ rd. אָסֹף. †]

סוֹף: sf. סוֹפוֹ: **end** (:: beginning) Ec 3_{11} 7_2 12_{13} 2C 20_{16}; — 2. (military) **rear(-guard)** Jl 2_{20}. †

I **סוּף**: — 1. **reed** † Ex $2_{3\cdot5}$ Is 19_6, water-plants Jon 2_6; — 2. *yam-sûf*, loc. יָמָּה סוּף Ex 10_{19}: sea of reeds Ex 10_{19} 1K 9_{26} & oft.

II **סוּף**: n. loc. Dt 1_1.

I **סוּפָה**: loc. סוּפָתָה; sf. סוּפָתְךָ, pl. סוּפוֹת: (destructive) **wind** (in storm) Is 5_{28}.

II **סוּפָה**: n. loc or terr. Nu 21_{14}. †

סוֹפֶרֶת Ne 7_{57}: ₣ סֹפֶרֶת.

סוּר: **qal** (ca. 160×): pf. סָר, סָרָה, סַרְתִּי, סָרוּ, סַרְתֶּם; impf. יָסוּר, יָסַר, וַיָּסַר, תָּסוּר, אָסוּר, נָסוּרָה, נָסוּר, תָּסֻרוּ, תְּסוּרוּ, יָסוּרוּ, אָסֻרָה; impv. סוּר, סוּרָה (& סוּרָה אֵלַי Ju 4_{18}), סוּרוּ, סֹרוּ; inf. סוּר, סוֹר, שׂוּרִי Ho 9_{12}; pt. סָר, סָרָה, cs. סָרַת Pr 11_{22}; pl. cs. סָרֵי: basic meaning: turn aside in one's direction: — 1. **turn aside, off**: a) fm. road Ex 3_{3f}, to right or left 1S 6_{12}; b) *sûrâ* come over here Ru 4_1; *sār l^ebêtô* go home Ju 20_8; w. *'el* turn in at, stop at Gn 19_2; c) military, step out of line 1K 20_{39}; — 2. **go away, leave**: a) w. *min* Ex 8_{27}, b) get out of s.one's way La 4_{15}; — 3. **fall away, desert**: a) politically Is 7_{17}; b) theologically: abs., fm. God Dt 11_{16}, w. *mē'aḥ^arê* 2K 18_6; fm. path given by God Dt 9_{12}; — 4. **leave off, desist** (fm. sins) 2K 10_{29}; — 5. **keep far** from, **avoid** (evil &c.) Pr 13_{14}; — 6. **stop, cease** (to be) Is 11_{13}, disappear 1K 15_{14}.

hif. (130×): pf. הֵסִיר, הֵסִירָה, הֲסִ(י)ר(וֹ)תִי, וַהֲסִרֹתִי, הֱסִירֹךְ, הֱסִירָהּ; impf. יָסִיר, יָסֵר, וַיְסִירֵהוּ, וַיָּסִירוּ, אָסִירָה, אָסִיר, וַיָּסַר (₣ qal!), וַיְסִירֶנּוּ; impv. הָסֵר, הָסִירִי, הָסִרוּ; inf. הָסִיר, הֲסִירְכֶם, הֲסִירָהּ; pt. מֵסִיר: — 1. **clear away, get rid of**, w. *min*, *mē'al*; spec. lay aside (burnt offering) 2C 35_{12}, take off (clothes) Gn 38_{14}; = vomit (wine) 1S 1_{14}, cut off (s.one's head) 1S 17_{46}, put an end to (one's words) Is 31_2, turn away (one's face) 2C 30_9, keep (feet) far (from wicked) Pr 4_{24}; — 2. **remove** s.one: subj. God, obj. people (fm. his sight) 2K 17_{18}; subj. pers., obj. king Ju 9_{29}, obj. queen 1K 15_{13}; make (s.one) disloyal Dt 7_4.

hof.: pf. הוּסַר; impf. יוּסַר; pt. מוּסָר: — 1. **be removed** Lv $4_{31\cdot35}$; — 2. **be picked up** (offering) Dn 12_{11}; — 3. *mûsār mē'îr* cease to be a city Is 17_1.

polel: pf. סֹרֵר: La 3_{11}: trad. make depart from; but perh. denom. fm. *sîr*, scatter w. thorns.

***סוּר**: f. סוּרָה; pl. סוּרִים, cs. סוּרֵי: **disloyal, faithless** Je 17_{13} Qr, oth. occurrences dub. †

cj. ***סוּרִי**: f. סוּרִיָּה: **stinking, foul-smelling** cj Je 2_{21}. †

סות: **hif.**: pf. הֵסִית, הֵסַתָּה, הֱסִיתְךָ, sf. הֲסִיתֶךָ, הֱסִיתוּךָ; impf. יָסִית, וַיָּסֶת, יְסִיתְךָ, וַיְסִיתֵם, וַתְּסִיתֵהוּ; pt. מַסִּית: — 1. **lead astray, seduce, incite** 1K 21_{25}; — 2. (military) **draw** (enemy) **out, away** 2C 18_{31}; — 3. **stir up, provoke** (against) 1S 26_{19}.

***סוּת**: sf. סוּתֹה: **garment** Gn 49_{11}. †

סחב: **qal**: pf. סְחָבוּנוּ; impf. יִסְחָבוּם; inf. סָחוֹב, לִסְחֹב: **drag off** (dead bodies) Je 15_{3} 22_{19}; **pull away** (a town) 2S 17_{13}.

סחה: cj. **nif.**: impf. יִסָּחוּ (for יִסְּחוּ): **be swept away** cj. Pr 2_{22}. †

piel: pf. סְחֵיתִי: **sweep away** Ez 26_{4}. †

סְחִי: **sweepings** La 3_{45}. †

cj. **סְחִיפָה**: **downpour** (of rain) (wh. flattens everything) cj Jb 14_{19}, but questionable. †

סָחִישׁ: **what grows of its own accord** (after the 2nd year harvest of grain) 2K 19_{29}. †

סחף: **qal**: pt. סֹחֵף: **wash away** (of rain) Pr 28_{3}. †

nif.: pf. נִסְחַף: **be washed away, be cut down** Je 46_{15}. †

סחר: **qal**: pf. סָחֲרוּ; impf. יִסְחָרוּ, תִּסְחָרוּ; impv. sf. סְחָרוּהָ; pt. סֹ(ו)חֵר, f. sf. סֹחַרְתֵּךְ, סֹחֲרַיִךְ, סֹחֲרֶיהָ, סֹחֲרֵי, סֹחֲרִים: — 1. w. acc. *hā'āreṣ* **pass through** (as shepherds) Gn 34_{10}, **wander around** Je 14_{18b}; — 2. pt. *sōḥēr*, **merchant, buying-agent, wholesaler** (:: retailer) Gn 23_{16}; *sōḥarê hammelek*, buying-agents in service of king 1K 10_{28}.

pealal: pf. סְחַרְחַר: **keep on moving back & forth, throb** or **beat violently** (of heart) Ps 38_{11}. †

סַחַר: cs. סְחַר, sf. סַחְרָהּ: **business profit** Is $23_{3.18}$ 45_{14} Pr 3_{14} 31_{18}. †

***סְחֹרָה**: cs. סְחֹרַת **territory (of a buying-agent)** Ez 27_{15} (if txt. correct). †

סֹחֵרָה: **wall** Ps 91_{4}. †

***סֹחֶרֶת**: סֹחָרֶת: a specific **mineral** stone set among others in mosaic pavement Est 1_{6}. †

***סֵט**: pl. סֵטִים: **deviation, transgression** Ps 101_{3}. †

סִיג: pl. סִ(י)גִים, sf. סִיגַיִךְ: trad. dross, spec. **lead oxide** (PbO), produced in the refining of silver Is $1_{22.25}$ Pr 25_{4}; metaph. Ez 22_{18a} Ps 119_{119}; Pr 26_{23} ꟳ cj. *סַפְסִיג. †

סִיוָן: name of month, May/June Est 8_{9}. †

סִיחֹ(ו)ן: n. pers., king of Amorites.

I **סִין**: n. loc. in Egypt Ez 30_{15}. †

II **סִין**: n. loc. nr. Sinai Ex 16_{1} 17_{1} Nu 33_{11f}. †

סִינִי: (n. pers.) n. peop. Gn 10_{17} 1C 1_{15}. †

סִינַי: סִינָי: n. of mountain, **Sinai**.

סִינִים: n. terr., unknown Is 49_{12}. †

סִיס: Je 8_{7} Qr: name of bird, prob. **swift**, *Apus apus*; so also cj. Is 38_{14}. †

סִיסְרָא: n. pers.

סִיעָא: n. pers.

סִיעֲהָא Ezr 2_{44}, mixed form of *סִיעָה & סִיעָא: n. pers.

סִיר: pl. סִירֹ(ו)ת, sf. סִירֹתָיו: — 1. **(cooking-) pot** (for meat) 2K 4_{38ff}; — 2. **tub, basin** (for washing feet): a) metaph., *sîr raḥᵃṣî* Ps 60_{10}; b) (cultic) for ashes 1K 7_{45}.

***סִירָה**: pl. סִירוֹת Am 4_{2} & סִירִים 4×: — 1. (trad., thorn in genl.), spec. the thorny bush **burnet**, *Poterium spinosum* Is 34_{13} Ho 2_{8} Na 1_{10} Ec 7_{6}; — 2. > **barb, hook** Am 4_{2}. †

סָךְ: Ps 42_{5} *bassāk* ? in the throng; but oth. sugg. rd. סֹךְ, ꟳ comm. †

***סֹךְ** & La 2_{6} ***שֹׂךְ** (sf. שֻׂכּוֹ): sf. סֻכֹּה, סֻכּוֹ: — 1. **thicket**, as lion's den Je 25_{38} Ps 10_{9}; — 2. **hut**, shelter from sun made of leafy branches Ps 27_{5} 76_{3}; La 2_{6} ?. †

סֻכָּה: sf. סֻכָּתוֹ; pl. סֻכֹּ(ו)ת: — 1. **thicket**, as lion's den Jb 38_{40}; — 2. **hut** made of branches & mats: a) in vineyard Is 1_{8}, shelter fm. sun Is 4_{6}; for cattle Gn 33_{17}, travelers Lv 23_{43}, military camp 2S 11_{11}; metaph. for those fearing God Ps 31_{21}, for

God Ps 27_5; = David's empire Am 9_{11}; b) *ḥag hassukkôt*, feast of huts (trad. transl.: of booths, or of tabernacles) Lv 23_{34} & oft.

סֻכּוֹת: loc. סֻכֹּתָה: n. loc.

סִכּוּת: Am 5_{26}: evid. name of an Assyrian god, w. vowels of *šiqqûṣ*; in ctxt. of censure for an earlier lapse, or else (like $_{27}$) threat of punishment; but oth. sugg. rd. *sukkat*; ☞ comm. †

סֻכּוֹת בְּנוֹת: n. of Babylonian god 2K 17_{30}. †

סֻכִּיִּים: n. peop.

I **סכך**: **qal**: pf. וְסַכֹּתִי; impf. יָסֹכּוּ, sf. יְסֻכֵּהוּ; pt. סֹכְכִים, סֹ(ו)כֵךְ: — 1. **isolate, cover** (protectively): a) w. *ʿal*, subj. cherubim 1K 8_7, abs. Ez 28_{14}; b) subj. Y., w. *l*ᵉ*rōʾš* Ps 140_8, w. *b*ᵉ*ʿad* Jb 1_{10}, w. acc. Jb 40_{22}; c) w. *lāk*, wrap onesf. La 3_{44}; — 2. **put up** (a curtain) (to cover s.thg), w. *ʿal* Ex 40_3.

hif. (or **qal** also?): impf. יָסֶךְ־לָךְ, תָּסֵךְ, וַיָּסֶךְ; inf. הָסֵךְ; pt. מֵסִיךְ: **block off, cover, make unapproachable**, w. *ʿal* Ex 40_{21} Ps 5_{12}, w. *b*ᵉ Jb 38_8, w. *b*ᵉ*ʿad* Jb 3_{23}, w. *l*ᵉ Ps 91_4. †

II **סכך**: **qal**: impf. sf. תְּסֻכֵּנִי: **weave, shape** Ps 139_{13}; for pass. ☞ I נסך. †

polel: impf. sf. תְּסֹכְכֵנִי: **interweave, interlace** Jb 10_{11}. †

סֹכֵךְ: **mantelet**, i.e. portable roofing to protect besiegers Na 2_6. †

סְכָכָה: n. loc.

סכל: **nif.**: pf. נִסְכַּלְתָּ, נִסְכַּלְתִּי: **behave foolishly** 1S 13_{13} 2S 24_{10} 1C 21_8 2C 16_9. †

piel: impf. יְסַכֵּל; impv. סַכֶּל־: — 1. **make foolish, frustrate**, obj. advice 2S 15_{31}; — 2. **make a mockery of** Is 44_{25}. †

hif.: pf. הִסְכַּלְתִּי: **act foolishly** Gn 31_{28} 1S 26_{21}. †

סָכָל: **foolish, fool** Je 4_{22} 5_{21} Ec 2_{19} 7_{17} 10_{13f}. †

סֶכֶל: **foolishness** > what is foolish, **fool** Ec 10_6. †

סִכְלוּת: **foolishness** Ec $2_{3.12f}$ $10_{1.13}$ 1_{17} = שׂ׳. †

I **סכן**: **qal**: impf. יִסְכָּן־, יִסְכּ(ו)ֹן: **be of use** Jb 15_3; w. *l*ᵉ 22_{2a} 35_3, w. *ʿal* 22_{2b}, w. *b*ᵉ & inf. so that 34_9. †

nif.: impf. יִסָּכֶן: **be endangered** Ec 10_9. †

hif.: pf. הִסְכַּנְתָּה, הִסְכַּנְתִּי; impv. הַסְכֶּן־; inf. הַסְכֵּן: — 1. go around carefully > **be accustomed** to (w. *l*ᵉ & inf.) Nu 22_{30}; — 2. **be familiar with** Ps 139_3; — 3. **get along well** with (*ʿim*) Jb 22_{21}. †

II **סכן**: Is 40_{20} ☞ מְסֻכָּן.

סֹכֵן: f. סֹכֶנֶת: — 1. **steward** Is 22_{15}; — 2. f. **nurse, attendant** 1K $1_{2.4}$. †

I **סכר**: **nif.**: impf. יִסָּכֵר, יִסָּכְרוּ: **be stopped up** (of cosmic springs) Gn 8_2; of mouth, be stopped Ps 63_{12}. †

II **סכר**: **piel**: pf. סִכַּרְתִּי: **hand over** Is 19_4. †

III **סכר**: **qal**: pt. סֹכְרִים: bargain = **buy** s.one, **bribe** Ezr 4_5.

סכת: **hif.**: impv. הַסְכֵּת: **be still, silent** Dt 27_9. †

סַל: סָל; pl. סַלִּים, cs. סַלֵּי: **basket** Gn 40_{16ff}.

סלא: **pual**: pt. מְסֻלָּאִים: La 4_2 **paid** (w. fine gold). †

סַלָּא Ne 11_7 & סַלּוּ Ne 12_7 & סָלוּא Nu 25_{14} & סַלּוּא 1C 9_7: n. pers.

סִלָּא 2K 12_{21}: ? n. loc. or n. pers. †

סלד: **piel**: impf. אֲסַלְּדָה: **skip**, revel Jb 6_{10}. †

סֶלֶד: n. pers.

I **סלה**: **qal**: pf. סָלִיתָ: **treat as worthless** Ps 119_{118}. †

piel: pf. סִלָּה: **reject** La 1_{15}. †

II **סלה** = **סלא**: **pual**: impf. תְּסֻלֶּה: **be paid** Jb $28_{16.19}$. †

סֶלָה: Hb $3_{3.9.13}$ & 70× in Ps, e.g. Ps 3_3: unexpl., evid. supplementary tech. term in music or recitation; sugg.: 1. raising of voice to higher pitch; 2. 'for ever'; 3. pause (for instrumental interlude); 4. an acrostic indicating a) change of voices, or b) 'da capo'.

סַלּוּ, סָלוּא, & סַלּוּא: ☞ סַלָּא.

סִלּוֹן: pl. סִלּוֹנִים: **thorn** Ez 2_6 28_{24}. †

סלח: **qal**: pf. סָלַחְתָּ(ה); impf. יִסְלַח, אֶסְלַח, אֶסְלוֹח Je 5_7 (Qr לַח־ Kt לוֹחַ־); impv. סְלַח, סְלָחָה; inf. סְל(ו)ֹחַ; pt. סֹלֵחַ: subj.

God: **practice forbearance, pardon, forgive**: abs. 1K 8_{30}, w. *le* & pers. 1K 8_{50}; w. *le* & thg. 1K 8_{34}; w. *le* & pers. & *be* & thg. 2K 5_{18}.

nif.: pf. נִסְלַח: w. *le*, it is forgiven to s.one, i.e. he is forgiven Lv 4_{20}.

סַלָּח: of God, **ready to pardon, forgive** Ps 86_5. †

סַלָּי: n. pers.

סְלִיחָה: pl. סְלִ(י)חוֹת: (God's) **pardon, forgiveness** Ps 130_4, = pl. Dn 9_9 Ne 9_{17}. †

סַלְכָה: n. loc.

I **סלל**: **pilpel**: impv. sf. סַלְסְלֶהָ: metaph. **think highly of, cherish** Pr 4_8. †

hitpolel: pt. מִסְתּוֹלֵל: **behave haughtily, insolently**, w. *be* toward Ex 9_{17}. †

II **סלל**: **qal**: impf. וַיָּסֹלּוּ; impv. סֹלּוּ, sf. סָלּוּהָ; pt. pass. f. סְלֻלָה, סְלוּלָה: — 1. **heap up, lay out** (a road) Is 57_{14} 62_{10} Je 18_{15} Jb 19_{12} 30_{12} Pr 15_{19}; w. *le*, prepare a road (while singing) for Ps 68_5; — 2. **pile up** (sheaves) Je 50_{26}. †

סֹלְלָה, 1 × **סוֹלְלָה**: pl. סֹלְלוֹת: **siege-mound** 2K 19_{32}.

סֻלָּם: ascending series of stones, **staircase** (more prob. than ladder) Gn 28_{12}. †

***סַלְסִלָּה**: pl. סַלְסִלּוֹת Je 6_9: **(vine-)tendrils.**†

סֶלַע: סָ֫לַע, sf. סַלְעִי; pl. סְלָעִים: I. common noun: 1. (solitary) **rock** 1S 23_{25}, for tomb-chamber Is 22_{16}; phr. *šēn hasselaʿ* tooth of rock = rocky spur 1S 14_4, *rōʾš hasselaʿ* rocky peak 2C 25_{12}; — 2. **rocks**: a) sg. coll. Nu 24_{21}; b) pl. 1K 19_{11}; — 3. ? military, *salʿô* Is 31_9 his officer; — 4. God is *selaʿ* 2S 22_2.

II. n. loc.: — 1. *hasselaʿ* in Edom 2K 14_7; — 2. *selaʿ hammaḥleqôt* 1S 23_{28}; — 3. *selaʿ (hā)rimmôn* Ju 20_{45}.

סָלְעָם: (edible) **locust** Lv 11_{22}. †

סלף: **piel**: impf. יְסַלֵּף; pt. מְסַלֵּף: — 1. **twist, distort** (obj. *dābār*, a case) Ex 23_8 Dt 16_{19}; — 2. **mislead** (obj. *derek*) Pr 19_3, **ruin** Jb 12_{19} Pr 13_6 22_{12}. †

סֶלֶף: **perversity, deceit** Pr 11_3 15_4. †

סלק: **qal**: impf. אֶסַּק < *ʾislaq : **climb up** Ps 139_8. †

סֹלֶת: sf. סָלְתָּהּ: **fine**(-ground) **wheat flour**, ground fm. inner kernels of wheat Gn 18_6.

***סַם**: pl. coll. סַמִּים: *qeṭōret (has)sammîm* **fragrant perfumes** Ex 25_6.

סַמְגַּר־נְבוֹ: n. pers.

סְמָדַר: ־דָר: **blossom-cluster of vine** SS $2_{13.15}$ 7_{13}. †

סָמַךְ: **qal**: pf. ס׳, סָמְכוּ, sf. סְמָכַתְהוּ, סְמַכְתִּיו; impf. יִסְמֹךְ, sf. תִּסְמְכֵנִי; impv. sf. סָמְכֵנִי; pt. סוֹמֵךְ, pl. cs. סֹמְכֵי, pass. סָמוּךְ, סְמוּכִים: — 1. w. acc. prop up, **support** Is 59_{16}, subj. God Ps 3_6; w. *le* & pers. Ps 145_{14}; w. 2 acc., pers. & thg. (with) Gn 27_{37}; *sāmak yādô ʿal* lean against Am 5_9; — 2. a) *sāmak yādô ʿal* lay one's hand (in consecration) on Nu 27_{18}; b) *sāmak yādayim/yādô ʿal-rōʾš* lay one's hand(s) on head of sacrificial animal Ex 29_{10}, of s.one to be stoned Lv 24_{14}; — 3. *sāmak* (intrans.) *ʿal* throw onesf. against Ez 24_2, subj. God's wrath Ps 88_8; — 4. pt. pass. *sāmûk* propped up, **unshakeable** Ps 111_8.

nif.: pf. נִסְמָכוּ, נִסְמַכְתִּי; impf. יִסָּמֵךְ: w. *ʿal*, **lean against, prop onesf. up on, support onesf. on** 2K 18_{21}, on God Is 48_2.

piel: impv. sf. סַמְּכוּנִי: **refresh** SS 2_5. †

סְמַכְיָהוּ: n. pers.

סֶמֶל, **סֵמֶל**: סֵמֶל: **idol(-image)** Dt 4_{16} Ez $8_{3.5}$ 2C $33_{7.15}$. †

סמם: **hif.**: impf. וַתָּשֶׂם (for וַתָּסֶם) 2K 9_{30}: smear w. paste or perfumed ointment, **dye**. †

סמן: נִסְמָן Is 28_{25} ? **nif.** pt.; unexpl. †

סָמַר: **qal**: pf. ס׳: subj. *bāśār*, have goose-flesh, **shudder** Ps 119_{120}. †

piel: impf. תְּסַמֵּר: subj. hair, **bristle** Jb 4_{15}. †

סָמָר: **bristling** (locusts) Je 51_{27}. †

סְנָאָה: **n. terr. or loc.**

סְנָאָה 1C 9_7: ꟻ סְנוּאָה.
סַנְבַלַּט: n. pers.
סַנָּה: ꟻ קִרְיַת־סַנָּה, n. loc.
סְנֶה: **thorny shrub** Ex $3_{2\cdot4}$; Dt 33_{16} *šōkᵉnî sᵉneh* = *zeh sinay* Ju 5_5?. †
סֶנֶּה: n. loc. 1S 14_4. †
סְנוּאָה Ne 11_9, **סְנָאָה** 1C 9_7: n. pers.
סַנְוֵרִים: **dazzling light** Gn 19_{11} 2K 6_{18}. †
סַנְחֵרִיב, ־רִב 2K 19_{20}: n. pers., king of Assyria.
סַנְסַנָּה: n. loc.
***סַנְסִנָּה**: sf. סַנְסִנָּיו: **blossom-cluster** of dates (wh. becomes fruit-cluster) SS 7_9. †
סְנַפִּיר: **fin** Lv $11_{9f\cdot12}$ Dt 14_{9f}. †
סָס: (clothes-)**moth** Is 51_8. †
סִסְמַי: n. pers.
סָעַד: **qal**: pf. ס׳; impf. יִסְעָד, sf. יִסְעָדֶנּוּ, תִּסְעָדֵנִי, יִסְעָדֶךָּ; impv. ־סְעָד Ju $19_{5\cdot8}$ (ŏ!), סַעֲדוּ, וּסְעָדָה, sf. סְעָדֵנִי, סְעָדָה; inf. סַעֲדָה: — 1. **support, hold upright** Is 9_6; — 2. **strengthen** (w. food): obj. *lēb* of s.one else Ps 104_{15}, of onesf. (= reflexive) Gn 18_5 Ju $19_{5\cdot8}$, w/o *lēb* 1K 13_7. †
סעה: **qal**: pt. f. סֹעָה: **slander** (ref. to *rûᵃḥ*) Ps 55_9. †
I **סָעִיף**: cs. סְעִיף; pl. cs. סְעִיפֵי: **cleft, crack,** alw. w. *selaʿ*, fissure, space under overhanging rock Ju $15_{8\cdot11}$ Is 2_{21} 57_5. †
II **סָעִיף**: pl. sf. סְעִיפֶיהָ: **branch** (of tree) Is 17_6 27_{10}. †
סעף: **piel**: pt. מְסָעֵף: **cut down, trim** (branches) Is 10_{33}. †
***סֵעֵף**: pl. סֵעֲפִים: **divided** (in heart, mind) Ps 119_{113}. †
***סְעַפָּה**: pl. sf. סְעַפֹּתָיו: (slender) **branch** Ez $31_{6\cdot8}$. †
סְעִפִּים: **crutches** (prepared fm. tree-limbs) 1K 18_{21}. †
סער: **qal**: pt. סֹעֵר: **rage, be violent** (of sea) Jon $1_{11\cdot13}$. †
nif.: impf. יִסָּעֵר: **be stirred up** (of heart) 2K 6_{11}. †
piel: impf. sf. אֲסָעֲרֵם: **blow** s.one **off in a storm** Zc 7_{14}. †
[**poel**: impf. יְסֹעֵר Ho 13_3, rd. יְסֹעַר (pual). †]
pual: pf. סֹעֲרָה (or pt.): **be blown off, driven off** Is 54_{11}, cj. Ho 13_3 Hb 3_{14} Jb 15_{30}. †
סַעַר: **gale**, heavy windstorm Je 23_{19}.
סְעָרָה: cs. סַעֲרַת; pl. סְעָרוֹת, cs. סַעֲרוֹת: **gale,** heavy windstorm 2K 2_1.
I **סַף**: סָף; pl. סִפִּים & 2K 12_{14} סִפּוֹת (& 2S 17_{28} סַפּוֹת? ꟻ II) **bowl** or **shallow cup,** oft. of metal for cultic use Ex 12_{22} 2S 17_{28} 1K 7_{50} 2K 12_{14}; in temple Je 52_{19}; *saf raʿal*, cup of staggering Zc 12_2. †
II ***סַף**: pl. סַפּוֹת 2S 17_{28}: **wool, hide, skin**? or I? †
III **סַף**: סָף, sf. סִפָּם; pl. סִפִּים: **(door-)sill, threshold,** horizontal stone of door-frame, in wh. the door-pivots turn 1K 14_{17}; *šōmēr hassaf* = 1a) high cultic office in Jerus. Je 35_4; b) *šōmᵉrê hassaf* 3 priests in temple 2K 25_{18}; c) *šōmᵉrê hassippîm*, in 1C Levitical doorkeepers 1C 9_{19}, sim. 9_{22} 23_4; — 2. doorkeeper in Pers. palace Est 2_{21}.
IV **סַף**: n. pers. 2S 21_{18}. †
ספד: **qal**: pf. סָפְדוּ, סָפְדָה; impf. תִּסְפֹּד, אֶסְפְּדָה; impv. סִפְדוּ, סְפֹד, סְפֹדְנָה; inf. לִסְפֹּד: — 1. **beat the breast** (as sign of mourning) † Is 32_{12}; — 2. **sound a lament,** w. *ʿal* 1K 13_{30}, w. *lᵉ* Gn 23_2, cogn. acc. Gn 50_{10}. †
nif.: impf. יִסָּפְדוּ: **be mourned, lamented** Je 16_{14} 25_{23}. †
ספה: **qal**: impf. תִּסְפֶּה; inf. סְפוֹת, לִסְפּוֹתָהּ: — 1. **take, sweep, snatch away** Gn 18_{23f}; — 2. intrans. **vanish** Je 12_4.
nif.: pf. נִסְפָּה; impf. יִסָּפֶה, אֶסָּפֶה, תִּסָּפוּ; pt. נִסְפֶּה: **be swept, snatched away** Gn $19_{15\cdot17}$.
[**hif.**: impf. אַסְפֶּה Dt 32_{23} rd. אֹסִפָה (יסף hif.). †]
ספח: **qal**: impv. sf. סְפָחֵנִי: w. acc. & *ʾel*, **associate** s.one w. 1S 2_{36}. †

nif.: pf. נִסְפְּחוּ: w. *ʿal*, **join** Is 14_1. †
[**piel**: pt. מְסַפֵּחַ Hb 2_{15} rd. מִסַּף (I סַף). †]
pual: impf. יְסֻפָּחוּ: **come together**, huddle together Jb 30_7. †
hitp.: inf. הִסְתַּפֵּחַ: w. b^e, **share in, belong to** 1S 26_{19}. †

סַפַּחַת: **scales** (on skin) Lv 13_2 14_{56}. †

סַפַּי: n. pers. 1C 20_4.

I **סָפִיחַ**: cs. סְפִיחַ; pl. sf. סְפִיחֶיהָ: **after-growth**, what grows of its own accord during the sabbath-year or fm. grains that have spilled Lv $25_{5.11}$ 2K 19_{29} Is 37_{30}. †

II ***סָפִיחַ**: pl. sf. סְפִיחֶיהָ Jb 14_{19}: ₣ cj. סְחִיפָה; but perh. a noun סָפִיחַ means 'downpour.' †

סְפִינָה: **ship** (w. a deck) Jon 1_5. †

סַפִּיר: pl. סַפִּירִים: **lapis lazuli** Ex 24_{10}.

סֵפֶל: **bowl** (for water, milk) Ju 5_{25} 6_{38}. †

ספן: **qal**: impf. וַיִּסְפֹּן; pt. pass. סָפֻן, סָפוּן, pl. סְפוּנִים: **cover, roof, panel** 1K 6_9 7_3 Hg 1_4. †

סִפֻּן: **ceiling** 1K 6_{15}. †

cj. ***סַפְסִיג**: cj. pl. סַפְסִיגִים: **glaze** cj. Pr 26_{23}. †

ספף: **hitpolel**: inf. הִסְתּוֹפֵף: **lie at the threshold** (as a beggar) Ps 84_{11}. †

I **ספק**: **qal**: pf. סָפְקוּ, sf. סְפָקָם; impf. יִסְפּ(וֹ)ק; impv. סְפֹק: — 1. **clap the hands** (w. glee over s.one's misfortune, or apotropaically) Nu 24_{10} La 2_{15}; — 2. w. *ʿal-yārēk*, **slap one's thigh** (in disgust, or apotropaically) Je 31_{19} Ez 21_{17}; — 3. **box s.one's ears** (as punishment) Jb 34_{26}. †

II **סָפַק**: **qal**: pf. 'ס; impf. יִסְפּוֹק: — 1. **vomit** Je 48_{26}; — 2. Jb 34_{37} 'call into question'; oth. sugg. rd. hif., or 'jeer' I 1, ₣ comm. †

***סֶפֶק**: סֶפֶק, sf. שִׂפְקוֹ: **abundance** Jb 20_{22} 36_{18} (oth. 'jeering' I ספק 1). †

סָפַר: **qal**: pf. 'ס, סְפַרְתֶּם; impf. יִסְפּוֹר, תִּסְפָּר־, sf. אֶסְפְּרֵם; impv. סְפֹר, סִפְרוּ; inf. לִסְפֹּר; pt. ₣ סֹפֵר: — 1. **count (up)** Gn 15_5 & oft.; > measure (quantity of grain) Gn 41_{49}, (pain) Ps 56_9; — 2. w. *biktôb* count out in writing, **register** (peoples) Ps 87_6; — 3. w. acc. & l^e, **count out** Ezr 1_8; — 4. **write** only as ₣ pt. *sōfēr* writer Je 8_8.
nif.: impf. יִסָּפֵר, יִסָּפְרוּ: — 1. **be counted** 1C 23_3; — 2. (let onesf.) **be counted** Gn 16_{10} + 6×. †
piel: pf. סִפַּרְתִּי, סִפְּרוּ; impf. וַיְסַפֵּר, וַנְּסַפֶּר־, יְסַפְּרוּ, אֲסַפְּרָה, אֲסַפֵּר, וַיְסַפֶּר־, sf. וַיְסַפְּרָהּ, אֲסַפְּרֶנָּה, וַיְסַפְּרוּם; impv. סַפֵּר, סַפְּרָה, סַפְּרוּ, סַפֵּרוּ; inf. סַפֵּר; pt. מְסַפֵּר, מְסַפְּרִים: — 1. **count, check off** Ps 22_{18}; — 2. **count up, detail** Is 43_{26}; — 3. **make known, proclaim**: obj. God's name Ex 9_{16}, oth. attributes of God Ps 19_2 &c.; — 4. **report, relate, tell** Gn 24_{66} & oft.
pual: pf. סֻפַּר; impf. יְסֻפַּר: **be reported, related, told** Is 52_{15} Hb 1_5 Ps 22_{31} 88_{12} Jb 37_{20}. †

I **סֵפֶר**: sf. סִפְרְךָ, סִפְרִי; pl. סְפָרִים: — 1. **inscription** † ? Ex 17_{14}, Is 30_8 Jb 19_{23}; — 2. **writing, document, scroll**: a) phrases that specify writing: *kātab ʿal-sēfer* record in writing Dt 17_{18} & oft.; *kātab sēfer ʾel* 2S 11_{14}; *kātab bass^{e}fārîm* write in a letter 1K 21_9 &c.; b) kinds of *s^{e}fārîm*: *sēfer b^{e}rît* 2K 23_2, *sēfer ḥāzôn* Na 1_1, *sēfer ḥayyîm* book of life or of the living Ps 69_{29}, *sēfer tōl^{e}dōt* Gn 5_1, &c.; c) writing in the abstract: *(lōʾ) yādaʿ sēfer* (not to) be able to read Is 29_{11f}; // *lāšôn*: writing & language (of Chaldeans) Dn $1_{4.17}$.

II **סֵפֶר** (?): **plate, panel** (of copper or brass) Is 30_8 Jb 19_{23}, ? Ex 17_{14}, but oth.: I 1. †

סֹפֵר: ₣ ספר **qal** pt., > noun: — 1. **writer, secretary**: of commander of army 2K 25_{19}, Baruch (of Jeremiah) Je 36_{26}; — 2. **state secretary, secretary of the king** 2K 12_{11}; — 3. Ezra, **secretary for Jewish affairs** Ezr 7_{11}; — 4. **scribe** (i.e. teacher of the law) Ezr 7_6.

I **סְפָר**: **census** 2C 2_{16}. †

II ***סְפָר**: loc. סְפָרָה: n. loc. Gn 10_{30}. †

סְפָרַד: n. loc.

*סְפָרָה: sf. סִפְרָתֶךָ: **(heavenly memorandum-)book** Ps 56_9. †

סְפָרַוִם: n. loc.

סְפַרְוִים: gent. of סְפָרְוַיִם.

סְפֹרוֹת: **art of writing** Ps 71_{15}. †

סֹפְרִים 1C 2_{55}: perh. not 'scribes,' but sugg. rd. סִפְרִים, gent. pl. of קִרְיַת סֵפֶר. †

סֹפֶרֶת: הַסֹּכֶרֶת Ezr 2_{55}, סוֹפֶרֶת Ne 7_{57}; trad. n. pers.; sugg. (court office of) writer. †

cj. סֶפֶת Nu 32_{14} & Is 30_1, ≠ יסף qal inf. †

סקל: **qal**: pf. סְקַלְתֶּם, sf. סְקָלֻהוּ, סְקַלְתֻּם, סְקָלֻהָ; impf. יִסְקְלוּ, יִסְקְלֻנִי; impv. sf. סִקְלֻהוּ; inf. sf. סָקְלוֹ, abs. סָקוֹל: **stone**: w. *bāʼabānîm* 1K 21_{13}; w/o *bāʼabānîm* 1K 21_{10}.

nif.: impf. יִסָּקֵל: **be stoned** Ex $21_{28f\cdot 32}$ 19_{13} animal or man. †

piel: impf. וַיְסַקְּלֵהוּ, וַיְסַקֵּל; impv. סַקְּלוּ: — 1. **throw stones** 2S 16_{13}, w. acc. pers. 16_6; — 2. **clear** (a place) **of stones** Is 5_2; w. *mēʼeben* 62_{10}. †

pual: pf. סֻקַּל: **be stoned** 1K 21_{14}. †

סַר: f. סָרָה: **dejected, discouraged,** *rûªḥ* 1K 21_5; *sar wᵉzāʻēf* 20_{43} 21_4. †

[*סָרָב: pl. סָרָבִים: trad. 'briers,' but rd. סֹבְבִים Ez 2_6.]

סַרְגוֹן: n. of Assyrian king, **Sargon**.

סֶרֶד: n. pers.

I סָרָה: **stopping** (intrans.) Is 14_6. †

II סָרָה: disobedience, **revolt, apostasy** Dt 13_6.

סִרָה: in n. loc. בּוֹר הַסִּרָה 2S 3_{26}, = סִירָה 1. †

סָרוּחַ: (pt. or adj.), pl. סְרוּחִים, cs. סְרוּחֵי: **projecting, hanging over** Ex 26_{13}; **pendulous, flowing** Ez 23_{15}; **sprawled** Am $6_{4\cdot 7}$. †

I סרח: **qal**: impf. תִּסְרַח; pt. סֹרַחַת: — 1. **project, hang over** Ex 26_{12}; — 2. **grow luxuriantly, rankly** Ez 17_6. †

II סרח: **nif.**: pf. נִסְרְחָה: **become stinking, spoiled** Je 49_7. †

סֶרַח: **what projects, hangs over** Ex 26_{12}. †

*סִרְיוֹן: sf. סִרְיֹנוֹ; pl. סִרְיֹנוֹת: **coat of mail, scale armor** Je 46_4, 51_3, ≠ שִׁרְיֹ(וֹ)ן. †

סָרִיס: cs. סְרִיס; pl. cs. סָרִיסֵי, & pl. סָרִיסִים, sf. סָרִיסָיו: — 1. **eunuch** 2K 20_{18}; *šar/rab-sārîs*, title, chief eunuch Je 39_{13}; at Egyptian court Gn 37_{36}, Persian Est 1_{10}; — 2. (eunuch who is a) **court official** 2K 23_{11}.

I *סֶרֶן: pl. cs. סַרְנֵי: **axle** 1K 7_{30}. †

II *סֶרֶן: pl. סְרָנִים, cs. סַרְנֵי, sf. סַרְנֵיכֶם: **princes** (of 5 Philistine cities) 1S 5_8.

*סַרְעַפָּה: pl. sf. סַרְעַפֹּתָיו: **branch** (of cedar) Ez 31_5. †

סרף: **piel**: pt. sf. מְסָרְפוֹ Am 6_{10}: trad. = שׂרף, relative w. obligation of cremation & burial; but txt. clearly corr.; sugg. rd. (w. LXX) וּפָצְרוּ 'and force,' or מְגֻרָפוֹ (מַגְרֵף* 'spade') alongside דּוֹד implement of grave-digger; ≠ comm. †

סִרְפָּד: **stinging nettle** Is 55_{13}. †

I סָרַר: **qal**: pf. ס׳; pt. סוֹרֵר, סוֹרֵרָה, סֹ(וֹ)רֶרֶת: **be stubborn** Dt 21_{18}; against God Is 30_1.

II סרר: **qal**: impf. יָסֹר: **superintend** 1C 15_{22}. †

סְתָו (Qr wrongly סְתָיו): **rainy season, winter** SS 2_{11}. †

סְתוּר: n. pers.

סָתַם: **qal**: pf. ס׳; impf. וַיִּסְתְּמוּ, תִּסְתְּמוּ; impv. סְתֹם; inf. לִסְתֹּ(וֹ)ם; pt. pass. סָתֻם, סְתֻמִים: — 1. **plug up, stop up** (springs of water), **make unrecognizable** 2K $3_{19\cdot 25}$ 2C $32_{3f\cdot 30}$; — 2. **hide** (words, face), **keep secret** Dn 8_{26} $12_{4\cdot 9}$; *sātûm* **what is secret** Ez 28_3; *bᵉsātum* secretly Ps 51_8. †

nif.: inf. הִסָּתֵם: **be stopped up, closed** (breaches in wall) Ne 4_1. †

piel: pf. sf. סִתְּמוּם; impf. sf. וַיְסַתְּמוּם: **plug up, stop up** (springs of water) Gn $26_{15\cdot 18}$. †

סתר: **nif.**: pf. נִסְתַּר, נִסְתְּרָה, נִסְתָּרָה, וְנִסְתַּרְתָּ, וְנִסְתַּרְתִּי, נִסְתַּרְנוּ, נִסְתָּרְנוּ; impf. יִסָּתֵר, אֶסָּתֵר, תִּסָּתְרוּ; impv. הִסָּתֵר; inf. לְהִסָּתֵר; pt. נִסְתָּר, נִסְתָּרִים, נִסְתָּרֹ(וֹ)ת: — 1. **hide** (intrans.) Gn 4_{14}; — 2. **be hidden** Gn 31_{49}; = be unknown Ho 13_{14}, remain undiscovered

Nu 5_{13}, remain safe Zp 2_3; pt. f. s.thg hidden Dt 29_{28}; hidden fault Ps 19_{13}.

piel: impv. סַתְּרִי: **hide** (trans.) Is 16_3. †

pual: pt. מְסֻתֶּרֶת: **kept secret** Pr 27_5. †

hif.: pf. הִסְתִּיר, הִסְתַּרְתָּ, הִסְתִּירוּ, sf. הִסְתִּירָנִי; impf. אַסְתִּירָה, וַיַּסְתֵּר, יַסְתִּיר, וַיַּסְתִּירוּ, sf. יַסְתִּירֵנִי; impv. הַסְתֵּר; inf. הַסְתֵּר, לַסְתִּיר Is 29_{15} (< לְהַסְ־); pt. מַסְתִּיר: — 1. **hide**: a) s.thg 1S 20_2; b) s.one: secular use 2K 11_2; obj. those under protection of Y., fm. their persecutors Ps 17_8; — 2. obj. *pānîm*: a) subj. men, apotropaically, at holy place Ex 3_6; fm. shame Is 50_6; b) God in wrath Dt 31_{17}; man's sins have hidden God's face Is 59_2; w/o *pānîm*, inf. Is 57_{17} = while I hid my face; c) in mouth of godless, in order not to see Ps 10_{11}.

hitp.: impf. יִסְתַּתָּר; pt. מִסְתַּתֵּר: **keep (onesf.) hidden** 1S 23_{19} 26_1 Is 29_{14} 45_{15} Ps 54_2. †

סֵתֶר: סֵתֶר Pr 25_{23}, sf. סִתְרִי; pl. סְתָרִים: — 1. **hiding-place** 1S 19_2; — 2. **garment** Jb 22_{14}; *sēter pānîm*, veil 24_{15}; — 3. **refuge**: mountain 1S 25_{20}, vegetation Jb 40_{21}; — 4. **secrecy**: *debar-sēter* secret word Ju 3_{19}, *leḥem sēter* Pr 9_{17}, *lešôn sēter* secret gossip 25_{23}; *bassēter* in secret 2S 12_{12}.

סִתְרָה: **refuge** Dt 32_{38}. †

סִתְרִי: n. pers.

ע

I עָב: cs. עָב (ŏ); pl. עָבִים: uncertain archit. term, **canopy** (?) 1K 7_6 Ez 41_{25f} (oth. sugg.: 'cornice,' 'projecting roof,' 'supporting joist'). †

II עָב: cs. עָב (ā) Is 18_4; pl. עָבִים, cs. עָבֵי, sf. עָבָיו, & pl. עָבוֹת: **clouds**: a) sg. coll. 1K 18_{44}; *ʿāb ṭal*, (dewy) mist Is 18_4; b) pl. *ʿābîm* 1K 18_{45}; c) pl. *ʿābôt* 2S 23_4.

III *עָב: pl. עָבִים: **thicket** Je 4_{29}. †

עַב Ex 19_9: rd. עֲבִי.

עָבַד: **qal** (266×): pf. עָבַדְתִּי, עָבַדְתָּ, ע׳, עָבְדוּ, עָבָדוּ, עֲבָדָהּ, עֲבַדְתַּנִי, עֲבָדוּם; impf. יַעֲבֹד, אֶעֱבֹד, יַעַבְדוּ, יַעֲבְדוּ, תַּעַבְדוּן, תַּעֲבְדוּן, נַעַבְדָה, יַעַבְדֶנּוּ, אֶעֱבָדְךָ, יַעַבְדֻנִי, נַעַבְדֶךָּ; impv. עֲבֹד, עִבְדוּ, עֲבָדוּ, עִבְדֻהוּ; inf. עֲבֹד, עָבְדָם, עָבְדֵנוּ; pt. עֹבֵד, עֹבְדִים, עֹבְדֵי־, עֹבְדֵי, sf. עֹבְדָיו: — 1. abs. **work** Ex 5_{18}; — 2. w. acc. **till, cultivate** (soil, garden) Gn $2_{5.15}$; w. *be* work (w. an animal) Dt 15_{19}; — 3. w. *le*, **work** (for s.one), **serve** 2S 16_{19}; — 4. w. acc. **serve, work** (for a master) **as a slave** Ex 21_6; said of a son Ma 3_{17}, of animal Jb 39_9; political Gn 25_{23} (of a tribe), 2K 18_7 (of a king); abs. **be a slave** Ex 21_2; — 5. spec. phr.: a) *ʿōbedê hāʿîr* urban workers Ez 48_{18f}; b) *ʿābad be* work for (Rachel, i.e. to acquire her) Gn 29_{20}; c) *ʿābad be* Lv 25_{46} &c. < *ʿābad ʿabōdâ be* Ex 1_{14} **keep** (s.one) **in service, work** (s.one); d) w. acc. **yield to,** gratify 1K 12_7; e) **perform, do** Nu 4_{26}; f) **serve, do service** Nu 8_{25}; g) *ʿābad ʿabōdâ* practice a (cultic) rite Ex 13_5, do (cultic) service Nu 3_7; *ʿābad ʾēt* sacrifice to (Y.) Ex 10_{26}; — 6. **serve, worship** (a god, God) 2K 21_3 Ex 3_{12} (more properly, perform the proper rites for).

nif.: pf. נֶעֱבַד, נֶעֱבַדְתֶּם; impf. יֵעָבֵד: — 1. **be tilled, cultivated** Ez $36_{9.34}$ Ec 5_8; — 2. impers. *yēʿābēd* there is tilling Dt 21_4. †

pual: pf. עֻבַּד: — 1. subj. heifer, **be worked** Dt 21_3; — 2. subj. servitude, **be enforced** Is 14_3. †

hif.: pf. הֶעֱבַדְתִּיךָ, הֶעֱבַדְתַּנִי, הֶעֱבִיד; impf. וַיַּעֲבִדוּ, וַיַּעֲבֵד; inf. הַעֲבִיד; pt. מַעֲבִדִים: — 1. **force into labor** Ex 1_{13}; **compel** (s.one) to (do s.thg) 2C 34_{33}; — 2. **take into, keep in servitude, slavery** Ex 6_5; — 3. **make** (s.one) **subservient** Je 17_4; — 4. w. *ʿᵃbōdâ*, **make** (s.one) **do work** Ez 29_{18}.

hof.: impf. sf. תָּעָבְדֵם, נָעָבְדֵם: w. obj. sf., **allow onesf. to be brought, enticed to serve, worship** (a person, god) Ex 20_5 23_{24} Dt 5_9 13_3. †

I עֶבֶד (780×): עֶבֶד, sf. עַבְדּוֹ; pl. עֲבָדִים, cs. עַבְדֵי, sf. עֲבָדָיו, עַבְדֵיהֶם: — 1. **slave** (i.e., held in bondage) Gn 12_{16}; *bêt ʿᵃbādîm* slave-quarters Ex 13_3; *[bᵉnê] ʿabdê šᵉlōmōh* state slaves 1K 9_{27}; — 2. **servant** (for a period of time, not in bondage) 1S 29_3: military: **subordinate** Gn 14_{15}; political: **subject** Gn 20_8; formula of submission: *ʿᵃbādêkā ʾᵃnaḥnû* 2K 10_5; — 3. **servant**, i.e. a dependent in a position of trust, = minister, advisor 2K 22_{12}; — 4. formula of polite self-abasement, *ʿabdᵉkā* = 'I' Gn 18_3 &c.; — 5. indicating man's position before God, i.e. either 'slave' or 'trusted servant' Gn 24_{14} & oft.

II עֶבֶד: n. pers. Ju $9_{26\text{-}35}$, Ezr 8_6. †

*עֲבָד: pl. sf. עֲבָדֵיהֶם (cf. Aram.): **deed** Ec 9_1. †

עֹבֵד: ↗ עוֹבֵד.

עֹבֵד(־)אֱדוֹם: n. pers.

עֶבֶד־מֶלֶךְ: n. pers.

עֲבֵד נְגוֹ (& עֲבֵד נְגוֹא): n. pers.

עַבְדָּא: n. pers.

עַבְדְּאֵל: n. pers.

עֲבֹדָה & (1 & 2 C only) עֲבוֹדָה (140×): cs. עֲבֹדַת, sf. עֲבֹדָתוֹ, עֲבֹדַתְכֶם: — 1. **work, labor** Ex 5_{11}; *ʿārê ʿᵃbōdātēnû* our agricultural cities Ne 10_{38}; **forced labor** 1K 12_4; — 2. **service**: *ʿᵃbōdat yhwh* service of Y. Jos 22_{27}, *ʿᵃbōdātî* service for me Gn 30_{26}; *ʿābad ʿᵃbōdâ* do service Gn 29_{27}; esp. **(cultic) service, worship** (service): *kᵉlê hāʿᵃbōdâ* vessels of worship 1C 9_{28} &c.; — 3. (cultic) **usage** (of worship) Ex 12_{25}. †

עֲבֻדָּה: **slaves, servants** (coll.) Gn 26_{14} Jb 1_3. †

I עַבְדּוֹן: n. pers.

II עַבְדּוֹן: n. loc. Jos 21_{30} 1C 6_{59}. †

עַבְדִּי: n. pers. 1C 6_{29} 2C 29_{12} Ezr 10_{26}. †

עַבְדִּיאֵל: n. pers.

עֹבַדְיָה: n. pers.

עֹבַדְיָהוּ: n. pers.

*עַבְדֻת: sf. עַבְדֻתֵנוּ: **servitude** Ezr 9_{8f} Ne 9_{17}. †

עָבָה: **qal**: pf. עָבִיתָ, 'ע: **be thick** Dt 32_{15} 1K 12_{10} 2C 10_{10}. †

עֲבוֹט: sf. עֲבוֹטוֹ: **pledge** Dt $24_{10\text{-}13}$. †

I *עֲבוּר: alw. בַּעֲבוּר, sf. בַּעֲבוּרָהּ, בַּעֲבוּרֶךָ: — 1. prep. **for the sake of** Gn 12_{13}; — 2. w. gen. **on account of** Gn 8_{21}; *baʿᵃbûr zeh/zōʾt* because of that, therefore Ex 9_{16} 13_8; — 3. w. gen. **for** (the price of) Am 2_6; — 4. conj. w. impf. **(in order) that** Gn 21_{30}; = *baʿᵃbûr ʾᵃšer* Gn 27_{10}; *baʿᵃbûr* w. inf. **(in order) to** 2S 10_3.

II עֲבוּר: **produce** (of field) Jos 5_{11f}. †

I עָבוֹת & עָבֹת: f. עֲבֻתָּה: **(thickly) branching** (oak) Ez 6_{13}; so *ʿēṣ ʿābōt* Lv 23_{40} Ez 20_{28} Ne 8_{15}. †

II *עֲבוֹת: pl. עֲבֹתִים: **branch** (of tree) Ez 19_{11} Ps 118_{27}. †

I עבט: **qal**: impf. תַּעֲבֹט; inf. עֲבֹט: **enter into a relationship of giving & taking pledges**: — 1. (give a pledge =) **borrow** Dt 15_6; — 2. w. acc. **take a pledge from** Dt 24_{10} (better: collect a pledge from?). †

hif.: pf. הַעֲבַטְתָּ; impf. תַּעֲבִיטֶנּוּ; inf. הַעֲבֵט: w. acc. **lend on pledge to** (s.one) Dt $15_{6\text{-}8}$. †

II עבט: **piel**: impf. יְעַבְּטוּן: **change, abandon** (one's course) Jl 2_7. †

עַבְטִיט: **(indebtedness represented by) pledges** Hb 2_6. †

***עֳבִי**: cs. עֳבִי, sf. עָבְיוֹ: **thickness** 1K 7_{26} Je 52_{21} Jb 15_{26} 2C 4_5. †

I **עבר**: **qal**: pf. ע׳, עָבַר, עָבְרָה, עָבַרְתִּי, עָבְרוּ, עָבְרוּ, עֲבָרוּ; impf. יַעֲבֹר, יַעֲבָר־, תַּעֲבוּרִי, אֶעֱבֹר, אֶעְבְּרָה, אֶעֱבְרָה, יַעַבְרוּ, יַעֲבְרוּ, נַעְבְּרָה, נַעַבְרָה, נַעֲבֹר, תַּעֲבֹרְנָה, יַעַבְרֻן, sf. יַעַבְרֶנְהוּ, יַעַבְרֶנּוּ, יַעַבְרֻנְהוּ; impv. עִבְרִי, עֲבָרִי, עִבְרוּ; inf. עֲבוֹר, לַעֲבָר־, עָבְרוֹ, לְעָבְרְךָ, עָבְרְךָ, abs. עָבוֹר: pt. עֹבֵר, עֹבְרִים, עֹבְרֵי: **pass from one side (or end) to the other**: — 1. **go through, pass through** (a territory); go off through Gn 12_6; of lion, roam Mi 5_7; of prayer to God, get through La 3_{44}; — 2. subj. thing: razor Nu 6_5, wind Ps 103_{16} &c.; metaph., of wine, come over s.one = overcome s.one Je 23_9; — 3. w. *ʿal*, **pass by** (s.one or s.thg) Gn 18_5; w. *mēʿal*, **go on past** 18_3; w. *ʿal-pᵉnê* 32_{22}; — 4. (metaph. fm. 3.) **pass by, slip away, disappear**: subj. day Gn 50_4, shadow Ps 144_4; so subj. waters, flow away Jb 11_{16}; chaff, fly away Je 13_{24}; decree, be abolished Est 1_{19}; — 5. **go over, across, pass over, cross** (a river, boundary, &c.) Gn 31_{21} Je 5_{22}; abs. cross (a river) Jos 2_{23}; w. acc. go over to Je 2_{10}; — 6. w. acc. **go beyond** Gn 31_{52}, pass up, get ahead of 2S 18_{23}; w. *lifnê*, go ahead of Gn 32_{17}; w. *ʾaḥᵃrê*, go on after 2S 20_{13}; w. *min*, slip away from Is 40_{27}, withdraw from Ps 81_7; w. *mittôk*, disappear among Est 9_{28}; — 7. spec.: *ʿōbēr yām* seafaring Is 23_2; *kesef ʿōbēr* silver (at the) current (rate) Gn 23_{16}; *ʿābar wāšāb* go through ... & back Ex 32_{27}; *mōr ʿōbēr* liquid myrrh SS 5_5.

nif.: impf. יֵעָבֵר: **be crossed, forded** Ez 47_5. †

piel: pf. עִבֵּר; impf. וַיְעַבֵּר: — 1. **draw across** (it) (?) 1K 6_{21}; — 2. **mount** (obj. a female animal) Jb 21_{10}. †

hif.: pf. הֶעֱבִיר, הַעֲבַרְתָּ & הַעֲבַרְתָּ, הַעֲבַרְתֶּם, הֶעֱבִירוּ, וְהַעֲבַרְתִּי, הֶעֱבַרְתִּי, הֶעֱבִירֻנִי; impf. יַעֲבִיר, וַיַּעֲבֵר, וַיַּעֲבֶר־, אַעֲבִיר, sf. וַיַּעֲבִרֵהוּ, וַיַּעֲבִרֵנוּ, תַּעֲבִרֵנוּ, וַיַּעֲבִרוּם, וַיַּעֲבִירֵהוּ; impv. הַעֲבֵר, הַעֲבֶר־, sf. הַעֲבִירֻנִי; inf. הַעֲבִיר, לַעֲבִיר (< לְהַעֲ־), sf. הַעֲבִירוֹ; pt. מַעֲבִיר, מַעֲבִירִים: — 1. **make** (wind) **pass over, sweep across** Gn 8_1; — 2. **make** (s.one) **cross, send** (s.one) **over** Gn 32_{24}; **bring** (the king) **over** 2S 19_{16}; — 3. w. acc. & *ʿal*, **make** (s.one) **pass by, before** 1S 16_8; **let** (s.one) **pass through** Ne 2_7; — 4. w. *bᵉ*, **make** (s.one) **go through** Dn 11_{20}; — 5. **let** (sin, guilt) **pass by** = **overlook** 2S 12_{13}; **let** (time) **go by, pass** Je 46_{17}; — 6. w. acc. & *lᵉ*, **let** (inheritance) **pass to** (s.one) Nu 27_7; — 7. **let** (s.thg) **pass through** (fire) = **offer** (sacrifice) Ex 13_{12}; w. *bāʾēš*, **let** (s.one) **pass through** (the fire) = **sacrifice** (s.one) 2K 16_3; — 8. w. *min*, **transfer** (the kingship) fm. 2S 3_{10}; **get rid of, do away with** (s.thg) (out of a place) 1K 15_{12}; **take** (s.one) **down** (out of chariot) 2C 35_{23}; **turn** (one's eyes) **away** fm. Ps 119_{37}; **keep** (s.thg) **far** fm. Ec 11_{10}; **take off** (a garment) Jon 3_6; — 9. *heʿᵉbîr qôl*, **let** (the command) **go out, proclaim** Ex 36_6; *heʿᵉbîr šôfār*, **let ... resound** Lv 25_9; *heʿᵉbîr šᵉmuʿâ*, **start, spread** (a rumor) 1S 2_{24}; *heʿᵉbîr taʿar*, **go over** (the body) w. (a razor) Nu 8_7; — 10. **lead** (s.one) **by, past** (s.thg) Ez 37_2, **lead** (s.one) through Ez 46_{21}.

II **עבר**: **hitp.**: pf. הִתְעַבָּר, הִתְעַבַּרְתָּ; impf. יִתְעַבָּר, יִתְעַבֵּר; pt. מִתְעַבֵּר: **show anger, become angry** Ps 78_{21}.

I **עֵבֶר**: sf. עֶבְרוֹ; pl. cs. עֶבְרֵי, sf. עֲבָרָיו, עֶבְרֵיהֶם: — 1. **one of two sides** (opposite to each other) 1S 26_{13}; *mēʿēber hallāz* **over there** 1S 14_1; *mēhāʿēber mizzeh*, **on one side & on the other** 1S 14_4; *mikkol-ʿᵃbārāyw* fm. overy side 1K 5_4; — 2. *lᵉʿebrô*, (each) in his own direction, way Is 47_{15}; *ʾel-ʿēber pānāyw*, straight ahead (in front of it) Ez 1_9, *ʿal-ʿēber pānêhā*, over (the space) in front of it Ex 25_{37}; *ʾel-ʿēber*, on the side (belonging to) Jos 22_{11}; *miššᵉnê ʿebrêhem*, on both sides Ex 32_{15}; — 3. **side, edge** (of ephod) Ex 28_{26}; **bank** (of river), **shore** (of sea), so > **opposite side** (of sea, &c.), **over** (the sea) Dt 30_{13b}; *mēʿēber nahᵃrê kûš*, beyond the rivers of C. Is 18_1; expressions for 'beyond the Jordan' may mean east or west bank depending on where the speaker is standing: east Gn 50_{10}, west Dt 3_{20}; *ʿēber hannāhār* = beyond (i.e. west of) the Euphrates 1K 5_4, (i.e. east of it) 1K 14_{15}.

II **עֵבֶר**: n. pers., n. peop. Gn 10_{24}.

***עָבָר**: pl. עֲבָרִים = 'crossing,' but only in n. loc. Nu 21_{11} 33_{44}. †

עֶבְרָה: cs. עֶבְרַת, sf. עֶבְרָתוֹ; pl. עֲבָרוֹת, cs. עַבְרוֹת: **arrogance** Is 16_6; *ʿabrôt ʾappekā*, outbursts of anger Jb 40_{11}; **anger, rage, fury** Is 13_9.

***עֲבָרָה**: pl. cs. עַבְרוֹת 2S 15_{28} Kt: **ford, crossing** 2S 15_{28} Kt, 19_{19}. †

עִבְרִי: f. עִבְרִיָּה; pl. עִבְרִיִּים & עִבְרִים, f. עִבְרִיּ(וֹ)ת: **Hebrew** (noun & adj.) Gn 14_{13}.

עֲבָרִים: n. loc., *(har/hārê) ʿᵃbārîm* Nu 27_{12} 33_{47f} Dt 32_{49} Je 22_{20}. †

עַבְרֹנָה: n. loc.

עבשׁ: **qal**: pf. עָבְשׁוּ: **dry up, wither** Jl 1_{17}. †

עבת: **piel**: impf. sf. וַיְעַבְּתוּהָ: **twist, pervert** ? Mi 7_3, but txt. dub. †

עָבֹת: F עָבוֹת (I & II).

עֲבֹת: sf. עֲבֹתוֹ, עֲבֹתֵמוֹ, pl. עֲבֹתִים & עֲבֹ(וֹ)תֹ(וֹ)ת: — 1. **rope, cord** Ju 15_{13}; — 2. **cord, line** Ex 28_{14}: *maʿᵃśēh ʿᵃbōt*, cordage work.

עֹג: F עוֹג.

עגב: **qal**: pf. עָגְבָה, עָגָבָה; impf. וַתַּעְגַּב, וַתַּעְגְּבָה; pt. עֹגְבִים: be after (s.one) (erotically), **have (sensual) desire for**, w. *ʿal* Je 4_{30} Ez $23_{5\cdot20}$. †

עֻגָב: F עוּגָב.

***עֲגָבָה**: sf. עַגְבָתָהּ, pl. עֲגָבִים Ez 33_{32}: **sensual desire** (condemned) Ez 23_{11} 33_{32}. †

עֲגָבִים: Ez 33_{31}: sugg. rd. כְּזָבִים; 33_{32} F *עֲגָבָה. †

עֻגָה: cs. עֻגַת; pl. עֻג(וֹ)ת: (circular, flat) **bread-cake** (baked in ashes or on hot stones) Gn 18_6 Ex 12_{39} Nu 11_8 1K 17_{13} 19_6 Ez 4_{12} Ho 7_8. †

עָגוֹל: F עָגֹל.

עָגוּר: kind of bird, sugg. (short-footed) **thrush**, *Bulbul Pycnonotus*, but uncert., Is 38_{14} Je 8_7. †

עָגִיל: pl. עֲגִילִים: round ornament for both men & women, evid. **ear-ring** Nu 31_{50} Ez 16_{12}. †

cj. ***עֲגִילָה**: pl. עֲגִילוֹת: **circular shield** cj. Ps 46_{10}. †

עָגֹל & (2C 4_2) **עָגוֹל**: pl. f. עֲגֻלּוֹת: **round** 1K $7_{23\cdot31\cdot35}$ 2C 4_2. †

עֵגֶל: sf. עֶגְלְךָ; pl. עֲגָלִים, cs. עֶגְלֵי: **(bull-)calf** 1K 12_{28}.

I **עֶגְלָה**: cs. עֶגְלַת, sf. עֶגְלָתִי: **heifer, young cow** Gn 15_9.

II **עֶגְלָה**: n. pers. f. 2S 3_5 1C 3_3. †

עֲגָלָה: sf. עֶגְלָתוֹ; pl. עֲגָלוֹת, cs. עֶגְלוֹת: **wagon, cart** (not chariot) Gn 45_{19}.

I **עֶגְלוֹן**: n. pers. Ju $3_{12\text{-}17}$. †

II **עֶגְלוֹן**: n. loc.

עֶגְלַיִם: F עֵין עֶגְלַיִם.

עֶגְלַת שְׁלִשִׁיָּה: F שָׁלִישׁ.

עגם: **qal**: pf. עָגְמָה: w. *le*, **have pity on** Jb 30_{25}. †

עגן: **nif.**: impf. תֵּעָגֵנָה (< *תֵּעָגֶנָּה): subj. woman, keep onesf. fm. marital relations, **keep withdrawn** Ru 1_{13}. †

I **עַד**: some sugg. = II עַד: עַד in עוֹלָם וָעֶד: **continuing future, always**: *lāʿad* for ever Is 64_8; *minnî-ʿad* always (in the past), from the beginning Jb 20_4, *ʿᵃdê-ʿad* for ever Is 26_4; *ʿôlām wāʿed* continually & for ever, for ever & ever Ex 15_{18}, = *lāʿad leʿôlām* Ps 111_8; *ʿad-ʿôlemê-ʿad* for ever for all time Is 45_{17}; *harrê-ʿad* everlasting mountains Hb 3_6, *ʾᵃbî ʿad* father for ever Is 9_5.

II **עַד**: older form עֲדֵי: sf. עָדַי, עָדֶיךָ, עָדָיו, עֲדֵיכֶם, עַד־הֵם (rd. עֲדֵיהֶם ?) 2K 9_{18}: indicates the distance from, advance toward, movement up to > **until, up to, upon**: — 1. spatial: **to, as far as (to)** Gn 11_{31}; *ʿadê ʾereṣ* (down) to the ground Ps 147_{6}; — 2. temporal: **until**: *ʿad-habbōqer* Ju 6_{31}, *ʿad gištô* until he came near Gn 33_{3}; *ʿad-hēnnâ* until now 1S 1_{16}; *wayhî ʿad-kōh weʿad-kōh* **meanwhile** 1K 18_{45}; *ʿad ʾān, ʿad-ʾānâ, ʿad-mâ, ʿad-mātay* **how long** ? Jb 8_{2} Ex 16_{28} Nu 24_{22} Ex 10_{3}; w. inf. *ʿad-bōʾî* (until =) **before** I come Gn 48_{5}; — 3. temporal: **during**: *ʿadê regaʿ* during a moment = just for a moment Jb 20_{5}; *ʿad-zenûnê* **as long as** (harlotries continue) 2K 9_{22}; — 4. (concerning the direction of the mind, attention): **on, to**: *ʾetbōnēn ʿad* Jb 32_{12}; — 5. expresses measure or degree: *ʿad-belî-day*, to an overwhelming degree Ma 3_{10}, *ʿad meʾōd* 1K 1_{4} &c.; *lōʾ ... ʿad ʾeḥād* not a single one Ju 4_{16} &c.; — 6. in comparisons: *lōʾ ... ʿad*, not up to (the degree of) = not like 1C 4_{27}; *weʿad ... lōʾ bāʾ* did not come up to = was not his equal 2S 23_{19}; — 7. comb.: *ʿad-ʾelêhem* (all the way up) to them 2K 9_{20}; *ʿad ʾaḥar* until after Ne 13_{19}; *min ... weʿad*, (spatial) from... to Gn 13_{3}, (temporal) Ju 13_{7}; *min ... ʿad ... ʿad ... weʿad* Gn 6_{7}; *miṭṭôb ʿad-raʿ* = either good or bad Gn 31_{24}; in late passages, *ʿad le* = *ʿad* 1C 12_{17}; *ʿad lemērāḥôq* (up to) from far away Ezr 3_{13}; — 8. conj.: *ʿad yigdal* until he Gn 38_{11}, *ʿad ʾeʿebôr* while I Ps 141_{10}; w. pf. Jos 2_{22}; comb.: *ʿad ʾim* until Gn 24_{19}, *ʿad ʾašer* until 27_{44}, *ʿad ʾašer ʾim* until 28_{15}; *ʿad biltî* until ... no more Jb 14_{12}, so that ... not Nu 21_{35}; *ʿad kî* until Gn 26_{13}; *ʿad le* & inf. 1K 18_{29}, *ʿad še-* Ju 5_{7}.

III **עַד**: **prey** Gn 49_{27}. †

עֵד: sf. עֵדִי; pl. עֵדִים, עֵדֵי, sf. עֵדַי, עֵדֵיהֶם: **witness**: a) s.one who can testify personally to a fact or occurrence, in case of doubt Is 8_{2}; b) s.one who gives corroborating testimony in court Dt 5_{20}; c) s.one whose testimony is decisive in a legal case Gn 31_{50}; d) s.one whose testimony is decisive in establishing the right or wrong of a dispute Jb 16_{19} Jos 24_{22}; e) s.one who can testify on the basis of a report wh. he has heard Lv 5_{1}; witnesses in the senses of a)-e) may also be things: covenant, altar, &c. Gn 31_{44} Is 19_{20}; f) Y. as witness Gn 31_{50}; *ʿēd be* witness against Nu 5_{13}; dependable witness = *ʿēd ʾemûnâ/ʾemet/neʾemān* Is 8_{2} &c.; false witness = *ʿēd šeqer/šeqārîm/kezābîm/beliyyaʿal/šāwʾ/ḥāmās* Ex 23_{1} &c.; *ʿānâ leʿēd* testify as a witness Dt 31_{21}; *hēʿîd ʿēd* take (s.one) as a witness Is 8_{2}; *nātan ʿēdāyw* bring one's witnesses Is 43_{9}; *lepî (ʿal-pî) ʿēdîm* on the statement of witnesses Nu 35_{30} Dt 17_{6}; *ʾattem ʿēday* = formula of summoning witnesses Is 43_{10}.

עֹד: ↗ עוֹד.

עִדֹּא: n. pers.

עֹדֵד: n. pers., ↗ עוֹדֵד.

I **עָדָה**: **qal**: pf. 'ע: **walk** (over a place) Jb 28_{8}. †
hif.: pt. מַעֲדָה: **lay aside** (a garment) Pr 25_{20} (but dittgr. ?). †

II **עדה**: **qal**: pf. עָדִית; impf. תַּעְדֶּה, וַתַּעַד, תַּעְדִּי, וָאֶעְדֵּךְ; impv. עֲדֵה: **put on ornaments, adorn onesf. w.** Is 61_{10}; w. 2 acc. **adorn** (s.one) **w.** Ez 16_{11}.

עָדָה: n. pers. f. Gn 4_{19-23}; Gn 36_{2-16}. †

I **עֵדָה** (145×): cs. עֲדַת, sf. עֲדָתִי, עֲדָתְךָ: **assemblage, gathering**: — 1. *ʿadat debōrîm* **swarm** (of bees) Ju 14_{8}; — 2. **troop, gathering** (of righteous) Ps 1_{5}, **band** (of rebels) Nu 16_{5}; — 3. **company** (i.e. those gathered around a prominent person) Jb 16_{7}; **council** (of God) Ps 82_{1}; — 4. (cultic) **congregation** (of Isr.) 1K 8_{5} & oft. (esp. in P).

II **עֵדָה**: **witness** Gn 21_{30} 31_{52} Jos 24_{27}. †

***עִדָּה**: pl. עִדִּים: **(menstrual) period** Is 64_{5}. †

עִדּוֹ: n. pers., also עִדּוֹא, = עִדֹּא.

עֵדוּת & **עֵדֻת**: pl. עֵדֹת, sf. עֵדְוֹתֶיךָ, עֵדֹתֶךָ, עֵדְוֹתָיו: **warning sign, reminder** Ex 16_{34}; in many combs., e.g. *luḥōt hā'ēdut* Ex 31_{18}, *hā'ārôn lā'ēdut* 31_7 &c.; pl. **warning signs, reminders, urgings** (alw. fm. Y.) 1K 2_3.

עֲדִי: עֲדִי, sf. עֶדְיוֹ, עֶדְיֵךְ: **ornament(s)**, individual or coll. 2S 1_{24}.

עֲדָיָא: n. pers.

עֲדִיאֵל: n. pers.

עֲדָיָה: n. pers.

עֲדָיָהוּ: n. pers.

עִדִּים: ↗ *עִדָּה.

I ***עָדִין**: f. עֲדִינָה: **voluptuous** Is 47_8. †

II **עָדִין**: n. pers. Ezr 2_{15} 8_6 Ne 7_{20} 10_{17}. †

עֲדִינָא: n. pers.

עֲדִיתַיִם: n. loc.

***עַדְלַי**: עַדְלָי: n. pers.

עֲדֻלָּם: n. loc.

עֲדֻלָּמִי: gent. of עֲדֻלָּם.

עדן: **hitp.**: impf. וַיִּתְעַדְּנוּ: **luxuriate, enjoy the good life** Ne 9_{25}. †

I ***עֵדֶן** (or ***עָדָן** ?): pl. עֲדָנִים: sf. עֲדָנֶיךָ, עֲדָנָי: — 1. **joy, rapture** Ps 36_9; — 2. **ornaments, finery** 2S 1_{24}. †

II **עֵדֶן**: n. terr., **Eden**.

III **עֵדֶן**: n. pers. 2C 29_{12} 31_{15}. †

עֶדֶן: n. terr.

עֶדֶן: < ***עַד־הֵן**: **up to now**, (not) **yet** Ec 4_3. †

עַדְנָא: n. pers.

עֲדֶנָה: < ***עַד־הֵנָּה**: **up to now, still** Ec 4_2. †

עַדְנָה: n. pers.

עֶדְנָה: **(sexual) pleasure** Gn 18_{12}. †

עַדְנַח: n. pers.

עַדְעָדָה Jos 15_{22}: rd. עַרְעָרָה.

עדף: **qal**: pt. עֹדֵף, עֹדֶפֶת, עֹדְפִים: **what is** (or those who are) **left over** (food, curtains, money, people) Ex 16_{23} 26_{12f} Lv 25_{27} Nu $3_{46\cdot48f}$. †

hif.: pf. הֶעְדִּיף: **have a surplus** Ex 16_{18}. †

I **עדר**: **qal**: pt. pl. cs. עֹדְרֵי 1C 12_{39}; inf. עֲדֹר 1C 12_{34}: **flock together** (but txt. dub.). †

II **עדר**: **nif.**: impf. יֵעָדֵר, יֵעָדֵרוּן: **be weeded** Is 5_6 7_{25}. †

III **עדר**: **nif.**: pf. נֶעְדָּר, נֶעְדָּרָה; pt. נֶעְדָּר, נֶעְדֶּרֶת: **be missing, lacking** 1S 30_{19} 2S 17_{22} Is 34_{16} 40_{26} 59_{15} Zp 3_5. †

piel: impf. יְעַדְּרוּ: **let** (s.thg) **be lacking** 1K 5_7. †

I **עֵדֶר**: sf. עֶדְרוֹ; pl. עֲדָרִים, cs. עֶדְרֵי: **flock, herd** (belonging to an individual) (i.e. of sheep, goats, or cattle) Gn 29_{2f}; *hā'ēder* of king = people Je 13_{20}.

II **עֵדֶר**: n. pers. 1C 23_{23} 24_{30}. †

III **עֵדֶר**: n. loc. Jos 15_{21}. †

***עֵדֶר**: עֵדֶר: n. pers. 1C 8_{15}. †

עַדְרִיאֵל: n. pers.

עֲדָשִׁים: **lentils**, *Lens lens* Gn 25_{34} 2S 17_{28} 23_{11} Ez 4_9. †

עֵדֻת: ↗ עֵדוּת.

עַוָּא 2K 17_{24}: ↗ II עַוָּה. †

עוב: **hif.**: impf. יָעִיב: **cover with a cloud** La 2_1. †

עוֹבֵד & **עֹבֵד**: n. pers.

עוֹבָל: (n. pers.,) n. peop.

עוג: **qal**: impf. תְּעֻגֶנָּה: **bake** (obj. *'ugâ*) Ez 4_{12}. †

עוֹג & **עֹג** 1K 4_{19} †: n. pers.

עוּגָב & **עֻגָב**: sf. עֻגָבִי: **(vertical) flute** Gn 4_{21} Ps 150_4 Jb 21_{12} 30_{31}. †

עוד: [**qal**: impf. sf. אֲעוּדֵךְ Kt אֲעִידֵךְ Qr La 2_{13}: rd. אֶעֱרֹךְ or עוֹדֵךְ.]

piel: pf. sf. עִוְּדֻנִי: **surround, encircle** Ps 119_{61}. †

hif.: pf. הֵעִ(י)ד, הַעִדֹתָה, הַעִידֹתִי, הֵעִידוּ; impf. וַיָּעַד, תָּעִיד, וַתָּעַד, וָאָעֵד, וָאָעִד, וְאָעִידָה Is 8_2, וָאָעִידָה Ne 13_{21}, וַיָּעִידוּ, וַיְעִדֻהוּ 1K 21_{10} וַיְעִדֻהוּ 21_{13}; impv. הָעֵד, הָעִידוּ; inf. הָעֵד; pt. מֵעִיד: (I) **repeat**: — 1. w. *d^ebārîm b^e*, use words again & again against, **warn** Dt 32_{46}; — 2. (w/o *d^ebārîm*) **warn, admonish** Gn 43_3; **assure** (s.one about punishment) Dt 8_{19}; — (II) denom. of *'ēd*: — 1. **call** (s.one) **to witness**: w. *l^e* for Is 8_2,

w. b^e against Dt 4_{26}; — 2. **be, serve as a witness**, w. *'ēt* = for Jb 29_{11}, = against 1K 21_{10}.

hof.: pf. הוּעַד: **be warned** Ex 21_{29}. †

polel: impf. יְעוֹדֵד; pt. מְעוֹדֵד: **help** (s.one) **up, come to the aid of** Ps 146_9 147_6. †

hitpolel: impf. וַנִּתְעוֹדָד: **help each other up, hold each other up** Ps 20_9. †

עוֹד & (rarely) עֹד: sf. עוֹדְךָ, עוֹדִי, עוֹדָם, & עוֹדֶנּוּ, עוֹדֶנִּי: repetition, permanence > adv. **again, still**: — 1. noun: **permanence, constancy**: *be'ôd* as long as 2S 3_{35}, *be'ôdî* as long as I (exist) Ps 104_{33}; *be'ôd šelōšet yāmîm* within 3 days Gn 40_{13}; *mē'ôdî* all my life long 48_{15}; — 2. *wayyēbk 'ôd* wept the whole time = **continually** Gn 46_{29}; — 3. adv.: **always, still**: *'ôdî 'immāk* Ps 139_{18}, *ha'ôd ḥay* is he still alive? Gn 45_3; *'ôdennî ḥāzāq* I am still (as) strong Jos 14_{11}; *'ôd* after noun: *we'abrāhām 'ôdennû* while A. still Gn 18_{22}; — 4. **once more, again** Gn 4_{25}; — 5. **still, besides**: *'ôd mî-lekā* have you anyone else Gn 19_{12}; — 6. *lō' 'ôd*, **no one besides, no more** Gn 8_{21} Dt 34_{10}; *ha'ên ... 'ôd* is there no one else? 1K 22_7.

עוֹדֵד, עֹדֵד: n. pers.

עוה: qal: pf. עָוִינוּ, עָוְתָה: **do wrong** Est 1_{16} Dn 9_5. †

nif.: pf. נַעֲוֵיתִי; pt. cs. נַעֲוֵה, f. cs. נַעֲוַת: **be disturbed, distressed, agitated** 1S 20_{30} Is 21_3 Ps 38_7 Pr 12_8. †

piel: pf. עִוָּה: **disturb, distress, agitate** Is 24_1 La 3_9. †

hif.: pf. הֶעֱוָה, הֶעֱוֵיתִי, הֶעֱוִינוּ; inf. sf. הַעֲוֹתוֹ: — 1. **pervert** (the right) Jb 33_{27}; w. *darkô* walk the wrong way Je 3_{21}; — 2. abs. **do wrong** 2S 7_{14} 19_{20} 24_{17} 1K 8_{47} Je 9_4 Ps 106_6 2C 6_{37}. †

I עַוָּה: **wreckage, rubble** Ez 21_{32}. †

II עַוָּה, עִוָּה: n. loc. 2K 17_{24} 18_{34} Is 37_{13}. †

עָוֹן: ℱ עָוֹן.

עוז: **qal**: impf. יָעוֹז; inf. עוֹז: **take refuge** Is 30_2 Ps 52_9. †

hif.: pf. הֵעִיזוּ; impv. הָעֵז, הָעִיזוּ: **bring to refuge, shelter** Ex 9_{19} Is 10_{31} Je 4_6 6_1. †

עוֹז: ℱ עֹז.

עֲוִיל: pl. עֲוִילִים, sf. עֲוִילֵיהֶם: **boy** Jb 16_{11} 19_{18} 21_{11}. †

עַוִּים: n. peop.

עֲוִית: n. loc.

I עול: **piel**: impf. יְעַוֵּל; pt. מְעַוֵּל: **act wrongly** Is 26_{10} Ps 71_4. †

II עול: **qal**: pt. pl. f. עָלוֹת: subj., female animals, **nurse, suckle** (young) Gn 33_{13} 1S $6_{7.10}$ Is 40_{11} Ps 78_{71}. †

עוּל, עֻל: sf. עוּלָהּ: **nursing baby, nursling** Is 49_{15} 65_{20}. †

עָוֶל: cs. עֶוֶל, sf. עַוְלוֹ: **wrong, injustice** Dt 25_{16}; *'îš 'āwel* Pr 29_{27}; God is *'ên 'āwel* Dt 32_4.

עַוָּל: **evildoer, transgressor, criminal** Jb 18_{21} 27_7 29_{17} 31_3. †

עַוְלָה > I עוֹלָה Is 61_8 (> ℱ I עַלְוָה Ho 10_9): loc. עַוְלָתָה Ez 28_{15} Ho 10_{13} Ps 125_3 92_{16} Qr, > עֹלָתָה Jb 5_{16}: **perversity, wickedness** Is 59_3.

I עוֹלָה: ℱ עַוְלָה.

II עוֹלָה: ℱ עֹלָה.

עוֹלֵל: pl. עֹ(וֹ)לְלִים, cs. עֹלְלֵי, sf. עֹלְלֵיהֶם: **child** 2K 8_{12}.

עוֹלָל: pl. עוֹלָלִים, sf. עוֹלָלֶיהָ, עוֹלָלַיִךְ: **child** Je 6_{11}.

עוֹלֵלוֹת: ℱ עֹלֵלוֹת.

עוֹלָם & (14×) עֹלָם (437×): sf. עֹלָמוֹ Ec 12_5; pl. עֹ(וֹ)לָמִים, cs. עוֹלְמֵי: — 1. **long time, constancy, all** (coming) **time** (in Eng. usu. 'eternity,' 'eternal,' but not to be understood in philosophical sense): *'ebed 'ôlām* 1S 27_{12} = David's lifetime; so in many comb.: *berît 'ôlām* Gn 9_{16} &c.; — 2. adv. **for all time, for ever** Ps 61_8, = *le'ôlām* Gn 3_{22}, = *'ad-'ôlām* 13_{15} & *'ad-le'ôlām* 1C 23_{25}; — 3. **long time ago, the dim past**: *gib'ōt 'ôlām* Gn 49_{26}; *mē'ôlām* Gn 6_4; so *mēhāʿôlām weʿad-hāʿôlām* Ps 41_{14} &c.; — 4. *ʿôlām* referring to God: *ʾel ʿôlām* Gn 21_{33} & sim. phr.; — 5. spec.: *bêt ʿôlāmô* house for ever = grave Ec 12_5; *mētê ʿôlām* those long dead Ps 143_3; pl. *ʿôlāmîm* = times to come 1K 8_{13}; = times past Ec 1_{10}.

עָוֹן, less frequently עָווֹן: cs. עֲוֹן, עֲווֹן, sf. עֲוֹנוֹ, עֲוֹנְךָ, עֲוֹנֵכִי Ps 103_3; pl. עֲוֹנֹ(וֹ)ת, עֲוֹנֹתָיו, עֲוֹנֹ(וֹ)תֵיכֶם, עֲוֹנֹתָם; occasional forms like עֲוֹנֶיךָ, עֲוֹנֵינוּ: 231 ×: **activity that is crooked or wrong**: — 1. (conscious, intentional) **offense, sin** 2S 22_{24}; — 2. > **guilt** (incurred by offense, sin) Gn 15_{16}; phr.: *ʿawōnāh bāh* her guilt (lies) upon her Nu 15_{31}, *nāśāʾ ʿawōnāh* (her husband) bears her guilt 30_{16}; *bî-ʾanî heʿāwôn* I am (the only one) guilty 1S 25_{24} &c.; — 3. > **punishment** (for guilt) Gn 4_{13}.

עִוְעִים: coll. pl.: **staggering** Is 19_{14}. †

I **עוף**: **qal**: pf. עָפוּ; impf. וַיָּעָף, יָעוּף, וַיָּעֹף, וַנָּעֻפָה, תְּעוּפֶינָה, יָעֻפוּ, אָעוּפָה; inf. עוּף; pt. f. עָפָה, עָפוֹת: — 1. **fly**: birds Dt 4_{17}; Y. 2S 22_{11}; — 2. **fly off, away** † Ps 90_{10} Jb 20_8.

hif.: impf. תָּעִיף: w. *ʿênayim be*, **let** (eyes) **fly** = **let** (eyes) **glance at** Pr 23_5 Qr. †

polel: impf. יְעוֹפֵף; pt. מְעוֹפֵף: **fly, soar** Gn 1_{20} Is 6_2 14_{29} 30_6. †

hitpolel: impf. יִתְעוֹפֵף: **fly off, away** Ho 9_{11}. †

[II **עוף**: **qal**: impf. תָּעֻפָה Jb 11_{17}: rd F cj. תְּעָפָה.]

עוֹף (70×): coll.: flying creatures: **birds** (& **insects**) Gn 1_{20}.

עוֹפַי Je 40_8: rd Qr עֵיפַי.

עוֹפֶרֶת: F עֹפֶרֶת.

עוץ: **qal**: impv. עֻצוּ: *ʿuṣû ʿēṣâ* **form a plan** Is 8_{10} (& Ju 19_{30}). †

I **עוּץ**: n. pers.

II **עוּץ**: n. terr. Je 25_{20} Jb 1_1 La 4_{21}. †

עוק: **qal**: impf. תָּעִיק: **be hindered, totter** Am 2_{13b} (recent sugg.: be bogged down.) †

hif.: pt. מֵעִיק: **make** (s.thg) **be hindered, make totter** Am 2_{13a} (recent sugg.: make bog down). †

I **עור**: **piel**: pf. עִוֵּר; impf. יְעַוֵּר: **blind** (s.one's eyes), **put out** (s.one's eyes) 2K 25_7 Je 39_7 52_{11}; metaph. **blind** (subj. bribe, wh. blinds an official) Ex 23_8 Dt 16_{19}. †

[II **עור**: **nif.**: impf. תֵּעוֹר Hb 3_9: rd. תְּעָרֶה (√ערה piel). †]

III **עור**: **qal**: impv. עוּרָה, עוּרִי; pt. עֵר; for Jb 41_2 Qr rd Kt (hif.): **stir onesf. up, be awake, astir, lively** Ju 5_{12}; subj. Y. Ps 7_7, wind SS 4_{16}.

nif.: pf. נֵעוֹר; impf. יֵעוֹר, יֵעֹ(וֹ)רוּ: **be stirred up, be set in motion**: people Je 6_{22}, storm 25_{32}.

polel: pf. עוֹרֵר, עוֹרַרְתִּי, עוֹרַרְתִּיךָ; impf. תְּעוֹרֵר, תְּעוֹרְרוּ; impv. עוֹרְרָה; inf. עוֹרֵר: — 1. **set in motion, arouse** SS 2_7; — 2. **stir up, rouse up, disturb** Is 14_9; — 3. **let onesf. be stirred up** Ps 80_3; — 4. **brandish** (a weapon) 2S 23_{18}.

hif.: הֵעִיר, הַעִירוֹתִי, הַעִירֹתִהוּ; impf. יָעִיר, יָעֵר, וַיָּעַר, אָעִירָה, תָּעִירוּ, sf. וַיְעִירֵנִי, יְעִירֶנּוּ Jb 41_2 Kt; impv. הָעִירָה, הָעִירוּ; inf. בָּעִיר (< *בְּהָעִיר); pt. מֵעִיר, sf. מְעִירָם: — 1. **rouse, wake up** Zc 4_1; **disturb** Dt 32_{11}; **stir up, set in motion** Is 41_2; **summon, order out** (warriors) Jl 4_9; stir up (fire) Ho 7_4; **let** (one's rage) **be stirred up** Ps 78_{38}; — 2. **awake** (intrans.) Is 42_{13}.

hitpolel: impf. יִתְעוֹרֵר; impv. הִתְעוֹרְרִי; pt. מִתְעוֹרֵר: **rouse onesf.**, get going Is 51_{17} 64_{16}; **be stirred up** Jb 17_8. †

pilpel: impf. יְעֹעֵרוּ, rd. יְעַרְעֵרוּ: **keep up** (obj. a cry) Is 15_5. †

עוֹר: sf. עֹ(וֹ)רוֹ; pl. עוֹרוֹת: — 1. **skin** (of man) Ex 22_{26}; (of bullock, crocodile &c.) Ex 29_{14} Jb 40_{31}; **hide** (of kids) Gn 27_{16}; *kotnôt ʿôr* garments of skin 3_{21}; — **leather** Lv 11_{32}.

עִוֵּר: pl. עִוְרִים, עִוְרוֹת: **blind** (in one eye or both eyes) 2S $5_{6.8}$.

עוֹרֵב: F I עֹרֵב.

עִוָּרוֹן: **blinding, blindness** Dt 28_{28} Zc 12_4. †

עֲוָרִים Is 30_6: F עַיִר.

עַוֶּרֶת: **blindness** Lv 22_{22}. †

[**עוש**: **qal**: impv. עוּשׁוּ: rd חוּשׁוּ or עוּרוּ. †]

עות: **piel**: pf. sf. עִוְּתוֹ, עִוְּתָנִי, עִוְּתוּנִי; impf. יְעַוֵּת־, יְעַוֵּת; inf. עַוֵּת: **make crooked, pervert** Jb 8_3; **falsify** (balances) Am 8_5; mislead Ps 119_{78}.

pual: pt. מְעֻוָּת: **what is bent, crooked** Ec 1_{15}. †

hitp.: pf. הִתְעַוְּתוּ: **bend** (intrans.) Ec 12_3. †

עות Is 50_4: rd. לַעֲנֹת.

***עַוָּתָה**: sf. עַוָּתָתִי: **oppression** La 3_{59}. †

עוּתַי: n. pers.

עַז: עָז, f. עַזָּה; pl. עַזִּים, cs. עַזֵּי: — 1. **strong**: person Ju 14_{14}, wrath Gn 49_7, &c.; *ʿaz nefeš* covetous Is 56_{11}; — 2. † **defiant, shameless**: *ʿaz pānîm* Dt 28_{50} Dn 8_{23}; *ʿazzôt* adv. insolently Pr 18_{23}.

עָז: **power, strength** Gn 49_3. †

עֵז: pl. עִזִּים, sf. עִזֶּיךָ: — 1. **goat** Gn 27_9; — 2. **goathair** (for felt & fabric) Ex 25_4.

עֹז, rarely עוֹז: עֹז־, עָז־, sf. עֻזּוֹ, עֻזָּה, עָזְּךָ, עֻזֵּךְ, עֻזְּךָ, עֻזֵּךְ, עֻזִּי, עָזִּי, עֻזֵּנוּ, עוּזֵנוּ, עֻזְּכֶם, עֻזָּמוֹ: — 1. **strength, power** 1S 2_{10}; adv. w. strength Ju 5_{21}; in comb., = **strong**: *migdal-ʿōz* Ju 9_{51} &c.; *ʿōz pānāyw* his stern face Ec 8_1; — 2. said of God: *ʿōz yhwh* Mi 5_3 & many comb.; — Note: Koehler-Baumgartner (first edition) proposes a II *ʿōz* 'protection, refuge, shelter,' w. forms identical w. I *ʿōz* 'strength,' but derived fm. √ *ʿwz* 'take shelter' rather than fm. √ *ʿzz* 'be strong'; this proposal has not won acceptance, and recently oth. have sugg. for the cited passages the mng. 'fortress'; therefore 3. **fortress** Ps 59_{18}.

עֻזָּא: n. pers.

עֲזָאזֵל: a desert demon Lv $16_{8\cdot10\cdot26}$. †

I **עָזַב**: **qal** (200×): pf. ע׳, עָזַב, עָזְבָה, עָזַבְתִּי, עֲזַבְתִּים, עֲזַבְתָּנִי, עֲזָבוּנִי, עֲזָבַנִי, עֲזָבוֹ, sf. עֲזָבוּ, עֲזָבוּךְ; impf. יַעֲזֹב, יַעֲזָב־, אֶעֱזָבָה, יַעַזְבוּ, אֶעֶזְבְךָ, תַּעַזְבֶהָ, יַעַזְבֵנוּ, sf. נַעַזְבָה, יַעַזְבוּ, אֶעֱזָבְךָ, יַעַזְבְךָ, impv. עִזְבָה Je 49_{11}, עִזְבוּ, sf. עִזְבוּהָ; inf. עֲזֹב, עָזְבֵךְ, abs. עָזֹב; pt. עֹזֵב, עֹזֶבֶת, pl. cs. עֹזְבֵי, sf. עֹזְבֶיךָ, pass. עָזוּב, f. עֲזוּבָה, f. cs. עֲזוּבַת, f. pl. עֲזֻבוֹת: — 1. **leave, abandon** Gn 2_{24}; *ʿᵃzûbâ* abandoned wife Is 60_{15}; forsake (advice) 1K 12_8; in religious sense: subj. God, obj. man Gn 28_{15}; subj. man, obj. Y.'s covenant 1K 19_{10} &c.; — 2. **leave behind**: obj. clothes Gn 39_{12}, tent 2K 7_7, wrath Ps 37_8; — 3. **leave** (s.thg) **over, leave** (s.thg) **remain** (for s.one else) Lv 19_{10}; — 4. **leave** (s.one) **(lie)** (naked) Ez 23_{29}; let (harlotry) be, **give up** Ez 23_9; let (s.thg) go Jb 20_{13}; **set free** 2C 28_{14}; give (s.one) up to (*le*) Ps 16_{10}, (*ʿal*) 10_{14}; *ʿāzab mēʿim*, be wanting in Gn 24_{27}; — 5. spec.: *ʿāzab pānāyw* change one's (facial) expression Jb 9_{27}; *ʿāzab maśśāʾ* desist fm. a claim Ne 5_{10}.

nif.: pf. נֶעֱזָב, נֶעֶזְבָה; impf. תֵּעָזֵב, יֵעָזְבוּ; pt. נֶעֱזָב, pl. f. נֶעֱזָבוֹת: — 1. **be abandoned** Lv 26_{43} Is 7_{16} 27_{10} 62_{12} Ez 36_4 Jb 18_4; — 2. **be neglected** Ne 13_{11}; **be left in the lurch** Ps 37_{25}; — 3. w. *le* **be left** to Is 18_6. †

pual (or **qal** pass.): pf. עֻזַּב, עֻזְּבָה: **be abandoned, deserted** Is 32_{14} Je 49_{25}. †

II **עזב**: impf. וַיַּעַזְבוּ: **pave**? (oth. sugg.: renovate) Ne $3_{8\cdot34}$. †

***עִזְבוֹנִים** (*b* w/o *dageš*): sf. עִזְבוֹנַיִךְ, ־נַיִךְ: what is left by caravans or ships, to be sold: **good, stores** Ez $27_{12\cdot14\cdot16\cdot19\cdot27\cdot33}$. †

עַזְבּוּק: n. pers.

עַזְגָּד: n. pers.

עַזָּה: loc. עַזָּתָה: n. loc., **Gaza**.

עֻזָּה: n. pers.

עֲזוּבָה: n. pers. f. 1K 22_{42} = 2C 20_{31}, 1C 2_{18f}. †

***עֱזוּז**: cs. עֱזוּז, sf. עֱזוּזוֹ: **strength, power** Is 42_{25} Ps 78_4 145_6. †

עִזּוּז: **powerful** Ps 24_8, coll. Is 43_{17}. †

עזור: F עַזֻּר.

עזז: **qal**: impf. וַתָּעָז, תָּעֹז, יָעֹז: — 1. **(turn out to) be strong** Ju 3_{10} 6_{2} Ps 89_{14} Ec 7_{19} Dn 11_{12}; — 2. **defy** Ps 9_{20}. †

[**nif.**: pf. נוֹעָז: trad. 'defiant,' but sugg. rd. לוֹעֵז Is 33_{19}. †]

cj. **piel**: inf. sf. עַזְּזוֹ: **make** (springs) **strong** Pr 8_{28}. †

hif.: pf. הֵעֵז, הֵעֵזָה: w. *pānîm*, **show a defiant, shameless** (face) Pr 7_{13}, so w. *bepānîm* appear w. a defiant, shameless (face) 21_{29}. †

עָזָז: n. pers.

עֲזַזְיָהוּ: n. pers.

עֻזִּי: n. pers. 1C 5_{31f} 6_{36} Ezr 7_{4}; 1C $7_{2f\cdot7}$ 9_{8} Ne 11_{22} $12_{19\cdot42}$. †

עֻזִּיָּא: n. pers.

עֲזִיאֵל: n. pers.

עֻזִּיאֵל: n. pers.

עָזִּיאֵלִי: gent. of עֻזִּיאֵל.

עֻזִּיָּה: n. pers.

עֻזִּיָּהוּ: n. pers.

עֲזִיזָא: n. pers.

עַזְמָוֶת: n. pers.

עַזָּן: n. pers.

עָזְנִיָּה: a bird, perh. **black vulture**, *Aegypius monachus* Lv 11_{13} Dt 14_{12}. †

עזק: **piel**: impf. sf. וַיְעַזְּקֵהוּ: **hoe, weed** (a vineyard) Is 5_{2}. †

עֲזֵקָה: n. loc.

עזר: qal (80×): pf. עָזַרְתָּ, עָזְרוּ, sf. עֲזָרֶנִי, עֲזָרָם, עֲזָרֶךָ; impf. יַעֲזָר־, יַעְזְרוּ, וַיַּעְזְרוּ, sf. וַיַּעְזְרֵם, יַעְזְרֻכֶם, יַעְזְרֵנִי, יַעְזְרֶךָּ, יַעְזְרֶהָ; impv. sf. עָזְרֵנִי, עִזְרֵנִי; inf. לַעְז(וֹ)ר, בְּעָזוֹר 1C 15_{26}, sf. לְעָזְרוֹ, לְעָזְרֵנִי; pt. עֹ(וֹ)זֵר, sf. עֹזְרֶךָ, pl. cs. עֹזְרֵי, sf. עֹזְרַי, עֹזְרֶיהָ, pass. עָזֻר: — 1. **help, support**: subj. God, obj. men Gn 49_{25}, subj. a nation, obj. others in war 2S 8_{5}; come to help 1K 20_{16}; abs. 2C 14_{10}, esp. pt. helper Is 31_{3}; — 2. *'āzar le* **come to the aid of** 2K 14_{26}, so w. *'im* 1C 12_{22}; w. *'aḥarê*, stand by (s.one) 1K 1_{7}.

nif.: pf. נֶעֱזַרְתִּי; impf. יֵעָזְרוּ; inf. הֵעָזֵר: **find help** Ps 28_{7} Dn 11_{34} 1C 5_{20} 2C 26_{15}. †

[**hif.**: for לעזיר 2S 18_{3} Kt, rd Qr לַעֲזוֹר; for מַעְזְרִים 2C 28_{23} rd. עֹזְרִים. †]

I **עֵזֶר, עֶזֶר**: sf. עֶזְרֶךָ, עֶזְרֹה, עֶזְרוֹ: — 1. **help, support** Is 30_{5}; — 2. > a **helper** Gn $2_{18\cdot20}$; said of God Ex 18_{4}.

II **עֵזֶר**: n. pers. Ne 3_{19} 1C 4_{4} 12_{10}. †

I ***עֶזֶר**: עֵזֶר: in n. loc. אֶבֶן הָעֵזֶר 1S 7_{12}; so in 1S 4_{1} 5_{1} rd הָעֵזֶר. †

II **עֵזֶר**: n. pers. Ne 12_{42} 1C 7_{21}.

עָזוּר, עַזֻּר: n. pers.

עֶזְרָא: n. pers.

עֲזַרְאֵל: n. pers.

I **עֶזְרָה**: עֶזְרָת Ps 60_{13} 108_{13}, = עֶזְרָתָה; cs. עֶזְרַת, sf. עֶזְרָתִי, עֶזְרָתֵנוּ: **support, help** Is 10_{3}; coll. = helpers Ju 5_{23}.

II **עֶזְרָה**: n. pers. 1C 4_{17}. †

עֲזָרָה: — 1. **barrier, enclosure** (around the altar) Ez $43_{14\cdot17\cdot20}$ 45_{19}; — 2. **enclosure, court** 2C 4_{9} 6_{13}. †

עֶזְרִי: n. pers. 1C 27_{26}. †

עַזְרִיאֵל: n. pers.

עֲזַרְיָה: n. pers.

עֲזַרְיָהוּ: n. pers.

עַזְרִיקָם: n. pers.

עֶזְרָת: ↗ I עֶזְרָה.

עַזָּתִי: gent. of עַזָּה.

עֵט: **stylus** Je 8_{8} 17_{1} Ps 45_{2} Jb 19_{24}. †

I **עטה**: **qal**: pf. עָטוּ; impf. תַּעֲטֶה, וַיַּעַט, יַעְטֶה, תַּעְטוּ; pt. עֹטֶה: — 1. w. *'al*, **wrap, cover** Lv 13_{45}; — 2. w. acc. **wrap onesf. with, cover onesf. with** 1S 28_{14}.

hif.: pf. הֶעֱטִיתָ; impf. יַעְטֶה, sf. cj. יַעְטֵנִי Is 61_{10}: w. 2 acc. **wrap** (s.one) **in** (a garment) Is 61_{10}; w. acc. & *'al*, **wrap** (s.one) **up** w. (s.thg) Ps 89_{46}; ? Ps 84_{7}. †

II **עָטָה**: **qal**: pf. ע׳; impf. יַעֲטֶה; inf. עָטֹה; pt. sf. עֹטְךָ: — 1. **grasp** Is 22_{17}; — 2. **delouse** Je 43_{12}. †

***עָטוּף**, ***עָטֵף**: pl. עֲטֻפִים, עֲטוּפִים: — 1. **weakened** La 2_{19}; — 2. **feeble, sickly** (cattle) Gn 30_{42}. †

***עֲטִין**: pl. sf. עֲטִינָיו: rd. עֲטָמָיו. †

***עֲטִשָׁה**: pl. sf. עֲטִישֹׁתָיו: **sneezing** Jb 41_{10}. †

עֲטַלֵּף: pl. עֲטַלֵּפִים: **bat** Lv 11_{19} Dt 14_{18} Is 2_{20}. †

cj. ***עָטָם**: pl. sf. עֲטָמָיו: **thigh** cj. Jb 21_{24}. †

I **עטף**: **qal**: impf. יַעְטֹף ,יַעֲטֹף־ ,יַעַטְפוּ: — 1. **turn aside** Jb 23_9; — 2. w. acc. **wrap onesf. in** Ps 65_{14}; — 3. w. *le*, **wrap** (s.one) Ps 73_6. †

II **עטף**: **qal**: impf. יַעֲטֹף; inf. עֲטֹף: **grow weak** Is 57_{16} Ps 61_3 102_1. †

nif.: inf. בֵּעָטֵף < *בְּהֵעָטֵף: **faint** La 2_{11}. †

hif.: inf. הַעֲטִיף: **be feeble** Gn 30_{42}. †

hitp.: impf. תִּתְעַטֵּף ,תִּתְעַטָּף; inf. הִתְעַטֵּף: **feel faint** Jon 2_8 Ps 77_4 107_5 142_4 143_4. †

עטר: **qal**: impf. sf. תַּעְטְרֶנּוּ; pt. עֹטְרִים: — 1. w. *'el*, **close in** on (s.one to capture him) 1S 23_{26}; — 2. w. 2 acc. **surround** (s.one) with (favor) Ps 5_{13}. †

piel: pf. עִטְּרָה ,עִטַּרְתָּ; impf. sf. תְּעַטְּרֵהוּ; pt. sf. מְעַטְּרֵכִי: — 1. w. 2 acc. **crown** (s.one) with Ps 8_6 65_{12} 103_4; — 2. *'iṭṭēr 'aṭārâ*, **make a crown, wreath** SS 3_{11}. †

hif.: pt. f. מַעֲטִירָה: **bestow crowns** Is 23_8. †

I **עֲטָרָה**: cs. עֲטֶרֶת; pl. עֲטָר(וֹ)ת: **crown, wreath**: for pagan god 2S 12_{30}, king Ez 21_{31}, drinkers Is 28_1 &c.

II **עֲטָרָה**: n. pers. f. 1C 2_{26}. †

עֲטָרוֹת: cs. עַטְר(וֹ)ת: n. loc., & component of var. comb. n. loc., thus *'aṭrôt 'addād* Jos 16_5, *'aṭrôt bêt yô'āb* 1C 2_{54}, & *'aṭrōt šôfān* Nu 32_{35}.

***עַי**: n. loc., always הָעַי ,הָעָי: **Ai.**

עִי: pl. עִיִּים, > עִיִּין: **heap of stones, of rubble** Je 26_{18} Mi 1_6 3_{12} Ps 79_1. †

עיב: ↗ עוב.

I **עֵיבָל**: n. of mountain Dt 11_{29} $27_{4.13}$ Jos $8_{30.33}$. †

II **עֵיבָל**: n. pers. Gn 36_{23} 1C 1_{40}. †

עַיָּה: 1C 7_{28}, עַיַּת Is 10_{28}: n. loc. †

עִיּוֹן: n. loc.

עיט: **qal**: impf. וַיַּעַט ,וַתַּעַט 1S 15_{19} (sugg. rd. וַתָּעַט): — 1. w. *be*, **yell** at, **shriek at** 1S 24_{15}; — 2. w. *'el*, **swoop down (w. shrieks)** on 1S 15_{19}, cj. 14_{32}. †

cj. **hif.**: impf. יָעִיטוּ: (they) **cry** (trouble upon me) cj. Ps 55_4 (but dub.). †

עַיִט: cs. עֵיט: coll. **birds of prey** Gn 15_{11} Is 18_6 46_{11} Je 12_9 Ez 39_4 Jb 28_7. †

עֵיטָם: n. loc.

עִיִּים: cs. עִיֵּי: n. loc.

[**עִילוֹם** 2C 33_7: rd. עוֹלָם. †]

עִילַי: n. pers.

עֵילָם: n. pers., terr., peop. **Elam.**

עין: **(qal)**: pt. עֹוֵן 1S 18_9 Kt, Qr עוֹיֵן: **eye, treat with suspicion** 1S 18_9. †

עַיִן (860×): עָיִן, loc. הָעַיְנָה, cs. עֵין, sf. עֵינִי, עֵינוֹ, du. עֵינַיִם, cs. עֵינֵי (עֲנֵי Is 3_8), sf. עֵינַי, עֵינֵיהוּ ,עֵינֵמוֹ ,עֵינֵ(י)כֶם Jb 24_{23}; pl. (= 'springs') עֲיָנוֹת, cs. עֵינוֹת ,עֵינוֹת: — 1. **eye** (of man & animal) Gn 27_1; *nāśā' 'ênāyw* raise one's eyes 18_2 & many such phr.; *bat 'ayin* **pupil** Ps 17_8; — 2. **look, appearance** Lv 13_{55}; — 3. **spring, fountain** Gn 16_7, pl. Nu 33_9; — 4. many n. loc. in comb.: a) שַׁעַר הָעַיִן Fountain Gate Ne 2_{14}; b) עֵין אָדָם; c) עֵין גֶּדִי; d) עֵין גַּנִּים; e) עֵין דֹּאר = עֵין ד(וֹ)ר; f) עֵין חַדָּה; g) עֵין חָצוֹר; h) עֵין חֲרֹד; i) עֵין מִשְׁפָּט; j) עֵין עֶגְלַיִם; k) עֵין הַקּוֹרֵא; l) עֵין רֹגֵל; m) עֵין רִמּוֹן; n) עֵין שֶׁמֶשׁ; o) עֵין הַתַּנִּין; p) עֵין תַּפּוּחַ.

עֵינוֹן: ↗ חֲצַר עֵינוֹן.

עֵינַיִם: n. loc.

עֵינָם: n. loc.

עֵינָן: n. pers.

עיף: **qal**: pf. עָיְפָה; impf. וַיָּעַף: if true rdg., = יָעֵף **be weary**; but texts doubtful; Ju 4_{21} 1S $14_{28.31}$ 2S 21_{15}. †

עיף: וְעִיף: Pr 23_5: rd Qr יָעוּף. †

עָיֵף: f. עֲיֵפָה; pl. עֲיֵפִים: **exhausted, faint** Gn 25_{29f}; *'ereṣ 'ayēfâ* exhausted land Is 32_2.

I **עֵיפָה**: loc. עֵיפָתָה: **darkness** Am 4_{13} Jb 10_{22}. †

II **עֵיפָה**: n. loc. Is 60_6. †

III **עֵיפָה**: n. pers.

עֵיפַי: n. pers. Je 40_8 Qr. †

עֵיפָתָה: ↗ I עֵיפָה.

I **עִיר** (1090×): loc. הָעִ֫ירָה, sf. עִירִי, עִירוֹ, עִירֹה; pl. עָרִים (rd. עָרִים for 2nd עֲיָרִים Ju 10_4), cs. עָרֵי, sf. עָרָיו; f.: — 1. permanent settlement, **city** (w/o respect to size or claims) Gn 4_{17}; *ʿîr nāḥôr* city where N. lives 24_{10}; is walled Lv 25_{29}, has unwalled villages belonging to it Jos 13_{23}; *ʿîr ʿamāleq* capital of A. 1S 15_5; — 2. a **quarter** in the city: *ʿîr hammayim* 2S 12_{27}, *ʿîr dāwîd* 2S 5_7 †; — 3. city = **population** of the city: *kol-hāʿîr* 1S 4_{13}; — 4. phrases: *ʿîr haṣṣedeq* Is 1_{26}; *(hā)ʿîr* = Jerusalem Ez 7_{23} Is 66_6; — 5. n. loc. w. *ʿîr*: in each case refer to the other element in the comb.: a) עִיר־הַהֶרֶס; b) עִיר־הַחֶרֶס; c) עִיר־הַמֶּלַח; d) עִיר־נָחָשׁ (↗ II נָחָשׁ); e) עִיר־שֶׁמֶשׁ; f) עִיר־הַתְּמָרִים; g) הָעִיר אֲשֶׁר בַּנַּחַל.

II **עִיר**: **agitation** Je 15_8. †

III **עִיר**: n. pers. 1C 7_{12}. †

IV **עִיר**: sf עִירֹה: (stallion of) **ass** Gn 49_{11}. †

עַיִר: pl. עֲיָרִים: **stallion**: of ass Gn 32_{16}; of zebra Jb 11_{12}.

עִירָא: n. pers.

עִירָד: n. pers.

עִירוּ: n. pers. 1C 4_{15}; txt.? †

עִירִי: n. pers. 1C 7_7. †

עִירָם: n. pers. Gn 36_{43} 1C 1_{54}. †

עֵירֹם, עֵרֹם: pl. עֵירֻמִּים: — 1. adj. **naked, unclothed** Gn $3_{7.10f}$; — 2. subst. **nakedness** Dt 28_{48}.

עַיִשׁ: **lioness** (constellation, evid. = modern Leo plus some stars of Cancer; the Arabs see 4 stars of Virgo as dogs barking at the lion) Jb 38_{32}. †

עַיִת: ↗ עַיָּה.

עַכְבּוֹר: n. pers.

עַכָּבִישׁ: **spider** Is 59_5 Jb 8_{14}. †

עַכְבָּר: pl. cs. עַכְבְּרֵי, sf. עַכְבְּרֵיכֶם: (male) **jerboa**, *Jaculus jaculus* (= *Dipus aegypticus*) 1S 6_{4f}.

עַכּוֹ: n. loc. **Acco**.

עָכוֹר: n. loc.

עָכָן: n. pers.

עכס: **piel**: impf. תְּעַכַּסְנָה: **jingle** (w. anklets) Is 3_{16}. †

עֶכֶס: pl. עֲכָסִים: **anklet** Is 3_{18}.

עַכְסָה: n. pers. f.

עָכַר: **qal**: pf. ע׳, עָכַרְתִּי, עֲכַרְתֶּם, עֲכַרְתָּנוּ; impf. יַעְכָּרְךָ; pt. עוֹכֵר, pl. sf. עֹכְרַי: **make** s.one **taboo**, **cut** s.one **off** (fm. social life) Gn 34_{30} 1K 18_{17f}.
nif.: pf. נֶעְכַּר; pt. f. נֶעְכֶּרֶת: **become taboo, untouchable** Ps 39_3.

עָכָר: n. pers.

עַכְרָן: n. pers.

עַכְשׁוּב: **horned viper** *Cerastes cornutus* Ps 140_4. †

I **עַל**: עֵל: **height**: *šāmayim mēʿāl* heaven above Gn 27_{39}, *huqam ʿāl* be raised on high 2S 23_1; > **amount** Is 59_{18}.

II **עַל**: sf. עָלַי, עָלָי, עָלֶיךָ, עָלַיִכִי, עָלָיו, הֶעָלֶיהָ 1S 9_{24}, עָלֵינוּ, עֲלֵיהֶם & עֲלֵהֶם, עָלֵימוֹ; עֲלֵי: — 1. higher than > **on, over**: *šākab ʿal* 2S 4_7; > **in front of** (if one person is standing & the other sitting): *dibber ʿal* Je 6_{10}, *ʿāmad ʿal* Gn 18_8; garment on s.one Gn 37_{23}; metaph. load (bride-price) on s.one Gn 34_{12}: duty: it is for me to (w. *lᵉ* & inf.) 2S 18_{11}; *ʿal* w. *ṣiwwâ, pāqad*: order s.one to; w. sensual & emotion impressions: *mātôq ʿal* sweet to (your taste) Pr 24_{13}; on = (supported) by: *ḥāyâ ʿal* live by Gn 27_{40}; — 2. upon = **because of**: *ʿal-zōʾt, ʿal-kēn* therefore; *ʿal-rāʿātām* because of ... Je 1_{16}; — 3. **with regard to, concerning**: w. regard to redemption Ru 4_7; — 4. **according to**, *ʿal-dibrātî* according to the manner Ps 110_4; *ʿal-pî* = according to; — 5. **over against**: *ʿal-pānay* over against me = in defiance of me Ex 20_3; > in spite of: *ʿal-daʿtᵉkā* in spite of your knowing Jb 10_7; — 6. (w. expr. of motion) **onto**: *ʿal-hammizbēᵃḥ*

Lv 1_{7}; *ʿālâ ʿal-lēb* comes to mind Je 3_{16}; — 7. upon = **in addition to**: w. *yāsaf* Dt 19_{9}; *šeqer ʿal šeqer* lie upon lie Je 4_{20}; *lāqaḥ ʿal* take (as a wife) in addition to Gn 28_{9}; therefore *ʿal* is used w. verbs of preferring, surpassing; *gābar ʿal* surpass Gn 49_{26}; — 8. above = **against**, face to face w.: *niqrâ ʿālênû* meet with us Ex 3_{18}; implies weight, predominance, but shades into *ʾel*; — 9. *kᵉʿal*: *kᵉʿal-kōl* according to all Is 63_{7}; — 10. *mēʿal* from (upon), **down from** Gn 24_{64}, off (from) Jb 19_{9}; *lēk mēʿālay* get away from me! Ex 10_{28}; *mēʿal lᵉ* up over Jon 4_{6}; *ʿad mēʿal* to above Ez 41_{20}; — 11. conj.: *ʿal-bᵉlî* in that ... not Gn 31_{20}; *ʿal lōʾ* because ... not Ps 119_{136}, although ... not Is 53_{9}; *ʿal-ʾašer* because Ex 32_{35}; *ʿal kî* because Dt 31_{17}.

עֹל: sf. עֻלֵּנוּ, עֻלּוֹ: **yoke**: of wood Gn 27_{40} & oft.; of iron Dt 28_{48}.

עַל: ↗ עוּל.

עֻלָּא: n. pers.

עַלְבוֹן: ↗ אֲבִי־עַלְבוֹן.

***עִלֵּג**: pl. עִלְּגִים: **stammerer** Is 32_{4}. †

עָלָה: **qal**: pf. עָלִינוּ, עָלִיתָ, עָלָתָה, עָלְתָה, ע׳; impf. וַתַּעֲלֶ(י)נָה, יֶעַל, וַיַּעַל, יַעֲלֶה; impv. עֲלוּ, עֲלִי, עֲלֵה; inf. עֲל(וֹ)ת, sf. עָלֹה, עֲלֹתוֹ; pt. עֹל(וֹ)ת, עֹלִים, עֹלָה, עֹ(וֹ)לֶה: — 1. **go up, ascend** (intrans.): man Is 14_{14}, plant Gn 41_{22}, smoke Gn 19_{28}, road Ju 21_{19}; — 2. **go up** (on journey, pilgrimage) Gn 13_{1}; — 3. **climb** (trans.) Nu 13_{17}; — 4. **mount** (w. *ʿal*): for mating Gn 31_{10}; mount above Dt 28_{43}; — 5. spec.: (in war) go up (*ʿal* against) 1K 20_{22}, (*ʾel*) 1S 7_{7}; (*mēʿal*) go away from 2K 12_{19}; *ʿālᵉtâ milḥāmâ* became more violent 1K 22_{35}; (of a well) spring up Nu 21_{17}; (of [new] flesh) cover (over a wound) Ez 37_{8} Je 8_{22}; (of a lot) come out Lv 16_{9}; *ʿālâ ʿal-lēb*, *ʿal-rûᵃḥ* come to mind; *ʿālâ bᵉ* amount to 1K 10_{29}.

nif.: pf. נַעֲלֵיתָ, נַעֲלָה; impf. וַיֵּעָלוּ, יֵעָלֶה, וַתֵּעָלוּ; impv. הֵעָלוּ; inf. הֵעָלוֹת, sf. הֵעָלֹתוֹ: — 1. **be taken up** (of cloud) Ex 40_{36}; — 2. **be exalted** (God) Ps 47_{10}; — 3. **get away**: (*mēʿal*) Nu 16_{24}, (*mēʾaḥᵃrê*) 2S 2_{27}; **withdraw** Je 37_{5}; — 4. **be led up** Ezr 1_{11}; — 5. w. *ʿal-śᵉfat* **be made the subject of talk** Ez 36_{3}.

hif.: pf. הֶעֱלָה > הֶעֱלָה Hb 1_{15}, וְהַעֲלִתָה, הַעֲלִיתֶם, הֶעֱלוּ, וְהַעֲלֵיתָ, הֶעֱלֵיתָ & הֶעֱלִיתָ, הֶעֱלִיתָנוּ, הֶעֱלָתַם, הֶעֱלָנוּ, הֶעֱלְךָ; impf. יַעֲלֶה, יַעַל, וַיַּעַל, וַיַּעַל, וַתַּעֲלִי, אַעֲלֶה, וַיַּעֲלוּ, וַיַּעֲלֿ Ezr 3_{3}, תַּעֲלֶנָּה, וַיַּעֲלֵנִי, יַעֲלֵם; impv. הַעַל, הַעֲלוּ, הַעֲלִי, הַעֲלֵהוּ; inf. הַעֲלֹתִי, הַעֲל(וֹ)ת, הַעֲלֵה; pt. מַעֲלֶה, cs. מַעַלְךָ, מַעֲלֵה, f. מַעֲלָה, cs. מַעֲלַת, pl. מַעֲלֵי, מַעֲלִים: — 1. **bring up, lead up** Gn 46_{4}; sacrifices to altar Gn 8_{20}; — 2. **bring over** s.thg, s.one: frogs upon land Ex 8_{1}; cause (healing) to grow Je 30_{17}; — 3. **make high, bring** (high) **up, make** s.thg **go up**: make s.one get up (into chariot) 1K 20_{33}; make (stench) rise Am 4_{10}; chew (cud) Lv 11_{3}; conjure up (spirit of dead) 1S 28_{8}; cover (w. gold) 1K 10_{16f}; shape (wings) Is 40_{31}; raise, rear (a cub) Ez 19_{3}; raise (a levy) 1K 5_{27}; *heʿᵉlâ ʾaf* stir up anger Pr 15_{1}; *heʿᵉlâ ʿal-lēb* take into one's heart Ez 14_{3}; God subj.: **take up** 2K 2_{1}, take away (in death) Ps 102_{25}.

hof.: pf. הֹעֲלָה, הָעַלְתָה: — 1. **be offered** Ju 6_{28}; — 2. **be carried away** Na 2_{8}; — 3. **be contained** (in a book) 2C 20_{34}. †

hitp.: impf. יִתְעַל: **raise onesf. up** Je 51_{3}. †

עָלֶה: cs. עֲלֵי, עֲלֵה, sf. עָלֶהָ, עָלֵהוּ: **leaves, foliage** Gn 3_{7}.

I **עֹלָה** (280×), rarely עוֹלָה; cs. ע(וֹ)לַת, sf. עֹלָתְךָ, עֹלָתוֹ; pl. ע(וֹ)ל(וֹ)ת, sf. עֹלֹתֶיךָ, עֹלֹתֵיהֶם: — 1. **burnt offering**, an offering completely burned on altar: oft. w. vb. *heʿᵉlâ*: *heʿᵉlâ ʿōlōt* Gn 8_{20}, *heʿᵉlâ lᵉʿōlōt* Gn 22_{2}; = *ʿōlâ kālîl* 1S 7_{9}; — 2. **animal** to be offered in burnt offering Lv 1_{4}.

II **עֹלָה**: ↗ עַוְלָה.

I עַלְוָה: **unruliness** Ho 10_9. †
II עַלְוָה: n. loc. Gn 36_{40}. †
*עֲלוּמִים: sf. עֲלוּמֶיךָ, עֲלוּמָו, עֲלוּמָיו: — 1. (time of) **youth** Is 54_4 Ps 89_{46} Jb 33_{25}; — 2. **vigor of youth** Jb 20_{11}. †
עַלְוָן: n. pers.
עֲלוּקָה: **leech** Pr 30_{15}. †
עלז: **qal**: impf. יַעֲלֹז, תַּעֲלֹזִי, אֶעֱלֹזָה, יַעְלֹזוּ, יַעֲלֹזוּ, תַּעֲלֹזְנָה, תַּעְלֹזְנָה; impv. עִלְזִי, עִלְזוּ; inf. עֲלוֹז: **exult** 2S 1_{20}.
עָלֵז: **exultant** Is 5_{14}. †
עֲלָטָה: **darkness** Gn 15_{17} Ez $12_{6f \cdot 12}$. †
עֵלִי: n. pers. **Eli**.
עֱלִי: **pestle** Pr 27_{22}. †
עִלִּי: f. עִלִּית, pl. עִלִּיּוֹת: (the) **upper** Jos 15_{19} Ju 1_{15}. †
עַלְיָה: n. loc.
עֲלִיָּה: cs. עֲלִיַּת, sf. עֲלִיָּתוֹ; pl. עֲלִיּוֹת: **upper room, roof-chamber** Ju 3_{20}; (over city-gate) 2S 19_1; (in heaven) Ps 104_{13}.
עֶלְיוֹן: f. עֶלְיוֹנָה; pl. f. עֶלְיוֹנֹת:
I. in genl., (the) **upper** Gn 40_{17}; gate 2K 15_{35}, pool 2K 18_{17}.
II. designation of God: compound with high god El: *ʾēl-ʿelyôn* (‘God Most High’) Gn 14_{18-20}, identified w. Y. 14_{22}; **Most High,** // *ʾēl* Nu 24_{16}.
עַלִּיז: f. עַלִּיזָה; pl. עַלִּיזִים, עַלִּיזֵי: — 1. **exultant** Is 24_8; — 2. **wild, haughty, wanton** Is 22_2.
עֲלִיל: **entrance** Ps 12_7; but text corr.? ↗ comm. †
עֲלִילָה: pl. עֲלִילֹ(וֹ)ת, sf. עֲלִילֹתָיו, עֲלִילוֹתֵיכֶם: **deed, action**: of faithful Ez 14_{22}, of unfaithful 1S 2_3, of God Is 12_4; *śām ʿalîlōt dᵉbārîm lᵉ* charge s.one w. shameful conduct Dt $22_{14 \cdot 17}$.
עֲלִילִיָּה Je 32_{19}: rd. עֲלִילָה. †
עַלְיָן: n. pers.
cj עָלִיץ: = עָלִיז **haughty**: cj Ps 37_{35}. †
*עֲלִיצֻת: sf. עֲלִיצֻתָם: **haughtiness, presumption** Hb 3_{14}. †

עַל־כֵּן: עַל + II כֵּן: — 1. thereover, **over them** Hb 1_{15}; — 2. **therefore** (135 ×) Gn 2_{24}; comb.: *haʿal-kēn* shall (he) ... therefore? Hb 1_{17}; *ʿal ʾᵃšer ... ʿal-kēn* because ... therefore 1K 9_9; = *yaʿan ʾᵃšer ... ʿal-kēn* Ez 44_{12}; *kî ʿal-kēn* for that is why Gn 18_5; inasmuch as 19_8.
I עלל: **poel**: pf. עוֹלַלְתָּ, עוֹלְלָה; impf. תְּעוֹלֵל, יְעוֹלְלוּ, וַיְעֹלְלֻהוּ; impv. עוֹלֵל; inf. עוֹלֵל; pt. מְעוֹלֵל: — 1. **deal with, treat** s. one La 1_{22} 2_{20}; — 2. spec.: **glean** (grain, olives) Lv 19_{10}; metaph., obj. remnant of Israel Je 6_9.
poal: pf. עוֹלַל: w. *lᵉ*, **be inflicted** on La 1_{12}. †
hitpael: pf. הִתְעַלֵּל, הִתְעַלַּלְתְּ, הִתְעַלְּלוּ; impf. וַיִּתְעַלְּלוּ: w. *bᵉ*, **make a fool** of s.one Ex 10_2 1S 6_6; (sexually) **abuse** (a woman) Ju 19_{25}.
hitpoel: inf. הִתְעוֹלֵל: **act mischievously** Ps 141_4. †
II עלל: **poel**: pf. עוֹלַלְתִּי: **thrust** in Jb 16_{15}. †
עֹלֵלוֹת: cs. עֹלְלֹת: **gleaning (s)** Ju 8_2.
עלם: **qal**: pt. pass. sf. עֲלֻמֵנוּ: hidden (things), **secrets** = faults Ps 90_8. †
nif.: pf. נֶעְלַם, נֶעְלְמָה; pt. נֶעְלָם, נַעֲלָמִים: **be hidden** 1K 10_3; pt. pl. those who are hidden, reserved? Ps 26_4.
hif.: pf. הֶעְלִים, הֶעֱלִימוּ; impf. תַּעְלֵם, אַעְלִים, יַעְלִימוּ; inf. הַעְלֵם; pt. מַעְלִים: **hide** (trans.), **cover up** 1S 12_3.
hitp.: pf. הִתְעַלַּמְתָּ; impf. יִתְעַלֶּם־, תִּתְעַלָּם, תִּתְעַלֵּם; inf. הִתְעַלֵּם: **hide** (onesf.), **withdraw** Dt $22_{1 \cdot 3f}$.
עֶלֶם: עֶלֶם: **young man** 1S 17_{56} 20_{22}.
עֹלָם: ↗ עוֹלָם.
עַלְמָה: pl. עֲלָמוֹת: **girl** (of marriageable age), **young woman** (until the birth of first child) Gn 24_{43} Is 7_{14}; unexplained term in performance Ps 46_1 1C 15_{20}.
עַלְמוֹן: n. loc.
עַל־מוּת: unexplained technical notation Ps 9_1 48_{15}. †

I **עָלֶמֶת**: n. loc. 1C 6_{45}. †
II **עָלֶמֶת**: n. pers.
עלס: **qal**: impf. יַעֲלֹס: w. b^e, **enjoy** s.thg Jb 20_{18}. †
nif.: pf. נֶעֱלָסָה: **appear glad** Jb 39_{13}. †
hitp.: impf. נִתְעַלְּסָה: **enjoy onesf.** with Pr 7_{18}. †
[**עלע**: יְעַלְעוּ Jb 39_{30}: text corr.; ℱ comm. †]
עלף: **pual**: pf. עֻלְּפוּ; pt. מְעֻלֶּפֶת: — 1. **be covered, enveloped** SS 5_{14}; — 2. metaph. lose one's senses, **faint** Is 51_{20}. †
hitp.: impf. תִּתְעַלַּפְנָה, וַיִּתְעַלָּף: — 1. **wrap onesf.** Gn 38_{14}; — 2. metaph. **faint** Am 8_{13} Jon 4_8. †
עֻלְפֶּה Ez 31_{15} text ? ℱ comm. †
עלץ: **qal**: pf. ע׳; impf. יַעֲלֹץ, אֶעֶלְצָה, יַעְלְצוּ, יַעֲלֹצוּ; inf. עֲלֹץ: **rejoice** 1S 2_1.
***עלק**: ℱ עֲלוּקָה.
עֹלָתָה Jb 5_{16}: ℱ עַוְלָה.
I **עַם**: sf. עַמִּי; pl. sf. עַמָּיו, עַמֶּיהָ, עַמֶּיךָ: [father's brother, f.'s relative >] **relative**: sg. in name, Gn 19_{38}; coll. **father's relatives** Je 37_{12}; pl. **father's relatives**: Gn 25_8.
II **עַם**: עָם, הָעָם; sf. עַמּוֹ, עַמְּךָ; pl. עַמִּים, עֲמָמִים, cs. עַמֵּי, עַמְמֵי, sf. עֲמָמֶיךָ, m.: — 1. (a whole) **people** (emphasis on internal ethnic solidarity) Gn 11_6; *lō' 'ām* non-people Dt 32_{21}; people to whom s.one belongs: *bᵉnê 'ammām* fellow-countrymen Lv 20_{17}; of animals: community of ants, coneys Pr 30_{25f}; — 2. pl. **peoples** Gn 28_3; — 3. oft. not a whole people but a portion: **people, inhabitants**: *'am yᵉrûšālayim* 2C 32_{18}; people attached to an individual Gn 32_8; *hā'ām haddallîm* common people Je 39_{10}; *hā'ām* mankind Is 42_5; = garrison Is 36_{11}; — 4. *'am hā'āreṣ* **citizens** (w. full civil rights) 2K 11_{14}; — 5. *'ammê hā'āreṣ* the (non-Israelite) **people(s) of the land** Ezr 10_2.
עִם: sf. עִמּוֹ, עִמָּהּ, עִמְּךָ, עִמְּכָה 1S 1_{26}, עִמָּךְ, עִמָּנוּ, עִמָּכֶם, עִמָּם, עִמִּי; prep.: — 1. **(in common) with, (together) with**: *'ākal 'im* 1S 9_{24}, *hālak 'im* Gn 18_{16}; even w. hostility: Ps 94_{16}; *wᵉ'im zeh* and with it = **nevertheless** Ne 5_{18}; — 2. (compared) with = **as well as**, just as much as Gn 18_{23}; = **like** Ps 73_5 Jb 9_{26}; — 3. (together) with > **at the same time as** 2S 1_{24}; *'im hassēfer* at the same time in writing Est 9_{25}; — 4. *mē'im* (72×) away from (being) with > **away from** Gn 26_{16}; *nāqî mē'im* guiltless before Y. (i.e. fm. Y.'s point of view) 2S 3_{28}; oft.: fm. (Y.'s) side 1K 2_{33}; *mē'immô* (more) than with him 2C 32_7.
עמד: **qal** (430×): pf. ע׳, עָמַד, עָמְדָה, עָמַדְתָּ, עֲמַדְתֶּן, עָמָדוּ, עָמְדוּ; impf. יַעֲמֹד, יַעֲמָד־, יַעַמְדוּ, יַעֲמֹדוּ, תַּעַמְדִי, אֶעֱמֹד, אֶעֱמְדָה Hb 2_1, נַעַמְדָה, נַעֲמֹד, יַעֲמֹדְנָה Dn 8_{22}, תַּעֲמֹדְנָה; impv. עֲמֹד, עִמְדִי, עִמְדוּ, עֲמֹדוּ, עֲמֹדְנָה; inf. עֲמֹד, עָמְדוֹ, עָמְדְךָ, עֲמֹד; pt. עֹ(וֹ)מֵד, עֹ(וֹ)מֶדֶת, עֹמֶדֶת, עֹמְדִים, עֹמְדוֹת: — 1. (move to) **stand** Ex 33_9, **take one's stand** 2K 23_3; (late:) **stand up** Ne 8_5; step up (*'el*, to) 1S 17_{51}; stand waiting (*lᵉ*, for) 1K 20_{38}; w. *yaḥad* oppose each other (in lawsuit) Is 50_8; — 2. **stand** (= be standing motionless) Ex 33_{10}, w. *'al* beside Gn 18_8; w. *'al-'ereṣ* inhabit a land Ex 8_{18}; w. *lifnê* stand (w. respect) before 1K 1_{28}, (as servant) Gn 41_{46}; *lifnê yhwh* 1K 17_1; *'āmad 'al* be leader over Nu 7_2, *'āmad 'al nefeš* protect, defend (one's life) Est 8_{11}; *'āmad 'al-ḥereb* rely on, resort to, the sword Ez 33_{26}; — 3. **stand still, stop moving** Gn 19_{17}; (of sea) stop raging Jon 1_{15}; **stay** Ex 9_{28}; be preserved Je 32_{14}; stay alive Ex 21_{21}.
hif. (80×, mostly late): pf. הֶעֱמִיד, הֶעֱמִידוֹ, הַעֲמַדְתָּ, הֶעֱמַדְתָּ (הֶעֱמַדְתָּה Ps 30_8), הֶעֱמַדְתִּיךָ, הַעֲמַדְתִּיהוּ, הֶעֱמִדָה; impf. יַעֲמִיד, יַעֲמִידֵנִי, וָאַעֲמִידָה, וָאַעֲמִיד, וַיַּעֲמֶד־, וַיַּעֲמֵד; impv. הַעֲמֵד, הַעֲמִידָה; inf. הַעֲמִיד, הַעֲמֵד; pt. מַעֲמִיד: — 1. **set** (s.one standing): *'al-raglay* Ez 2_2; — 2. **station, set**: s.one Lv 14_{11}, stars Ps 148_6; — 3. cause (s.one, s.thg) to

stand, **maintain** Ex 9_{16}, 1K 15_4; give stability Pr 29_4; — 4. **appoint, designate** 1K 12_{32}; set up (gods) 2C 25_{14}; — 5. **restore** Ezr 9_9; — 6. var.: w. *lifnê* present (s.one to) Gn 47_7; w. *pānāyw* stare straight ahead 2K 8_{11}; confirm Ps 105_{10}.

hof.: impf. יָעֳמַד; pt. מָעֳמָד: — 1. **be presented** Lv 16_{10}; — 2. **be set upright** 1K 22_{35}. †

עֹמֶד: sf. עָמְדוֹ, עָמְדֶךָ: **place** (where one normally stands or is stationed) Ne 8_7.

עַמֻּד: ↗ עַמּוּד.

*עִמָּד: only sf. עִמָּדִי (alternating w. עִמִּי): **my company** Gn 3_{12}; adv. in my company 1S 22_{23}; — 2. **with me, in my presence** Gn 31_{32}; connotation of helping: Gn 28_{20}; connotation of injury: Gn 20_9.

*עֶמְדָּה: sf. עֶמְדָּתוֹ: **place to stand** Mi 1_{11}. †

I *עֻמָּה: cs. עֻמַּת; sf. עֻמָּתוֹ, עֻמָּתָם: alw. w. *le*: — 1. **close to** Ex 25_{27}; *milleʿummat* close beside 1K 7_{20}; — 2. (close and) **parallel to** 2S 16_{13}; — 3. **corresponding to** Ex 38_{18}; — 4. **just like, along with** Ez 1_{20}.

II עֻמָּה: n. loc. Jos 19_{30}; text corr.?

עַמּוּד (98×), עַמֻּד Je 52_{21}: cs. עַמּוּד Nu 14_{14}; sf. עַמּוּדוֹ; pl. עַמּוּדִים, עַמֻּדִים, cs. עַמֻּדֵי, sf. עַמּוּדַי, עַמֻּדָיו: — 1. **tent-pole, post** Ex 26_{32}; — 2. **column, pillar** (of house) Ju 16_{25f} 1K 7_2; — 3. (free-standing) **column** 1K 7_{15ff}; — 4. *ʾûlām hāʿammûdîm* **hall of pillars** 1K 7_6; — 5. **post** (of sedan-chair) SS 3_{10}; — 6. **column** of smoke Ju 20_{40}, of fire Ex 13_{22}, of clouds Ex 13_{21f}; — 7. **pillars** of earth Ps 75_4, of heaven Jb 26_{11}.

עַמּוֹן: n. people, **Ammon**.

עַמּוֹנִי, עַמֹּנִי: gent. of בְּנֵי עַמּוֹן; f. עַמּוֹנִית; pl. עַמֹּנִים, f. עַמֳּנִיּוֹת, עַמּוֹנִיּוֹת Ne 13_{23}, עַמָּנִיּוֹת 1K 11_1: **Ammonite**.

עָמוֹס: n. pers.: prophet **Amos**.

עָמוֹק: n. pers.

עַמִּיאֵל: n. pers.

עַמִּיהוּד: n. pers.

עַמִּיזָבָד: n. pers.

עַמִּיחוּר: n. pers.

עַמִּינָדָב: n. pers.

עָמִיר: (newly) **cut grain** Je 9_{21} Am 2_{13}.

עַמִּישַׁדָּי: n. pers.

*עָמִית: sf. עֲמִיתִי, עֲמִיתְךָ, עֲמִיתוֹ: **fellow, comrade** Lv 5_{21}.

עָמַל: **qal**: pf. עָמַלְתָּ, עָ׳, עָמְלוּ; impf. יַעֲמֹל: **exert onesf., labor** Jon 4_{10} Ec 2_{21}.

I עָמָל: cs. עֲמַל; sf. עֲמָלוֹ, עֲמָלְךָ: — 1. **distress, trouble** Gn 41_{51}, Is 53_{11}; — 2. **what is gained by toil** (i.e. land & produce) Ps 105_{44}; — 3. **toil, effort** Ec 1_3; — 4. **misfortune** Nu 23_{21}; — 5. **disaster, evil** Ps 7_{15}.

II עָמָל: n. pers. 1C 7_{35}. †

עָמֵל: pl. עֲמֵלִים: — 1. **wretched**, in distress Jb 3_{20}; — 2. toiling, **laboring** Ec 2_{18}; — 3. **laborer, workman** Ju 5_{26}.

עֲמָלֵק: n. peop. (n. pers.) **Amalek(ite)**.

עֲמָלֵקִי: gent. of עֲמָלֵק.

I עמם: **qal**: pf. עֲמָמֻךָ, עֲמָמֻהוּ: **be equal to** Ez 28_3 31_8. †

II עמם: **hof.**: impf. יוּעַם: **become dark, black** La 4_1. †

עֲמָמִים: ↗ II עַם.

עִמָּנוּ אֵל: n. pers. Is 7_{14} 8_8. †

עַמֹּנִי: ↗ עַמּוֹנִי.

עמס: **qal**: impf. יַעֲמָס־, יַעֲמֹס; pt. pl. עֹמְשִׂים Ne 4_{11} = עֹמְסִים, sf. עֹמְסָהּ, pass. עֲמֻסִים, f. עֲמוּסוֹת: **load** (an animal) Gn 44_{13}; **carry** (a load) Is 46_3; **lift** (a load) Zc 12_3; pt. pass. **a load, luggage** Is 46_1.

hif.: pf. הֶעְמִיס: **lay a heavy yoke upon** (w. *ʿōl*) 1K 12_{11} 2C 10_{11}. †

עֲמַסְיָה: n. pers.

עַמְעָד: n. loc.

עמק: **qal**: pf. עָמְקוּ: **be deep, mysterious** Ps 92_6. †

hif.: pf. הֶעֱמִיק, הֶעְמִיקוּ; inf. הַעֲמֵק; pt. מַעֲמִיקִים: — 1. abs. **make deep** Is 30_{33}; — 2. w. other vbs., best transl. adverbially: w. *hastîr* hide deep Is 29_{15}; w. *yāšab* dwell in the depths Je 49_{8}.

עֵמֶק: sf. עִמְקֵךְ; pl. עֲמָקִים, sf. עֲמָקַיִךְ: — 1. **valley**, (low-lying) **plain** Nu 14_{25} 1S 6_{13}; *'ereṣ hā'ēmeq* flat country Jos 17_{16}; — 2. *'ēmeq* in various proper names: a) בֵּית הָעֵמֶק; b) הַר הָעֵמֶק; c) עֵמֶק אַיָּלוֹן; d) הָעֵמֶק אֲשֶׁר לְבֵית רְחוֹב; e) עֵמֶק בְּגִבְעוֹן; f) עֵמֶק בְּרָכָה; g) עֵמֶק הָאֵלָה; h) עֵמֶק הַבָּכָא; i) עֵמֶק הֶחָרוּץ; j) עֵמֶק הַמֶּלֶךְ; k) עֵמֶק הַשִּׂדִּים; l) עֵמֶק חֶבְרוֹן; m) עֵמֶק יְהוֹשָׁפָט; n) עֵמֶק יִזְרְעֶאל; o) עֵמֶק סֻכּוֹת; p) עֵמֶק עָכוֹר; q) עֵמֶק קְצִיץ; r) עֵמֶק רְפָאִים; s) עֵמֶק שָׁוֵה.

עָמֹק: f. עֲמֻקָּה; pl. עֲמֻקִּים, עֲמֻקּוֹת: — 1. **deep**: waters Pr 18_{4}, cup Ez 23_{32}; — 2. **gone deep** (of diseased spot of skin) Lv 13_{3f}; — 3. **impenetrable** (*lēb*) Ps 64_{7}; — 4. **mysterious** (limit of God) Jb 11_{8}.

עֹמֶק: pl. cs. עִמְקֵי (to *עָמֵק ?): **depth** Pr 9_{18} 25_{3}. †

***עָמֵק**: pl. cs. עִמְקֵי: *'imqê śāfâ* **unintelligible** Is 33_{19} Ez 3_{5f}. †

I **עמר**: **piel**: pt. מְעַמֵּר: **gather (newly cut grain)** Ps 129_{7}. †

II **עמר**: **hitp.**: pf. הִתְעַמֶּר־; impf. תִּתְעַמֵּר: w. *b^e*, **treat** s.one **brutally** Dt 21_{14} 24_{7}. †

I **עֹמֶר**: pl. עֳמָרִים: (newly) cut **ears of grain** (not sheaves; the stalks were cut off right under the ears) Lv 23_{10ff}.

II **עֹמֶר**: **omer**, a measure of grain (approx. 2 liters or quarts) Ex 16_{16}.

עֲמֹרָה: n. loc. **Gomorrah**.

עָמְרִי: n. pers. **Omri**.

עַמְרָם: n. pers.

עַמְרָמִי: gent. of עַמְרָם.

עמשׂ: עֹמְשִׂים Ne 4_{11} F עמס.

עֲמָשָׂא: n. pers.

עֲמָשַׂי: n. pers.

עֲמַשְׁסַי: n. pers.

עֲנָב: n. loc.

עֵנָב: pl. עֲנָבִים, cs. עִנְּבֵי, sf. עֲנָבֵמוֹ: **grape** Gn 40_{10}; w. *'āśâ* yield Is 5_{2}; *'eškôl 'anābîm* cluster, bunch of grapes Nu 13_{23}.

ענג: **pual**: pt. מְעֻנָּגָה: **pampered, spoiled** Je 6_{2} †

hitp.: pf. הִתְעַנַּגְתֶּם; impf. תִּתְעַנַּג, תִּתְעַנָּג; impv. הִתְעַנַּג; inf. הִתְעַנֵּג: — 1. **pamper onesf., be fastidious**: of a woman Dt 28_{56}; — 2. **take great delight in** (*b^e*, *'al*) Is 55_{2}; **refresh onesf.** w. (*min*) Is 66_{11}; — 3. **make merry over** (*'al*) Is 57_{4}.

עֹנֶג: **enjoyment, pleasure, delight** Is 13_{22} 58_{13}. †

עָנֹג: f. עֲנֻגָּה: **spoiled, pampered** Dt $28_{54.56}$ Is 47_{1}. †

ענד: **qal**: impf. אֶעֶנְדֶנּוּ; impv. עָנְדֵם: **wind** s.thg **around, tie** s.thg **on** Jb 31_{36} Pr 6_{21}. †

I **עָנָה**: **qal** (305 ×): pf. עָנוּ, עָנִיתִי, עֲנִתָה, ע׳, עֲנִיתֶם, עָנָנִי, עָנָךְ, עָנָהוּ; impf. וַיַּעַן, יַעֲנֶה, וַיַּעֲנֵנִי, וַתַּעֲנֶינָה, יַעֲנוּ, וָאַעַן, אֶעֱנֶה, תַּעַן, תַּעֲנֶה, יַעֲנֶנּוּ, אֶעֱנֶנּוּ, תַּעַנְךָ, תַּעֲנֶנּוּ, תַּעֲנֵנוּ; impv. עֲנֵה, עֲנוּ, עֲנֵנִי; inf. עֲנוֹת; pt. עֹ(ו)נֶה, עֹנֵהוּ, עוֹנֶךָ Jb 5_{1}: — 1. **answer** (w. acc. of pers.) Gn 23_{14}; (w. acc. of thing: a word) 1K 18_{21}; oft.: *wayya'an wayyō'mer* he answered & said Jb 40_{1}; — 2. **answer, return** (a greeting) 2K 4_{29}; *'ānâ l^e'ēd* confront as a witness Dt 31_{21}; — 3. **let** s.one **know** 1S 9_{17}; (of God) answer = give favorable hearing to Is 30_{19}; — 4. **answer** for (*b^e*) s.one, **testify** for Gn 30_{33}; against 2S 1_{16}.

nif.: pf. נַעֲנֵיתִי; impf. אֵעָנֶה, יֵעָנֶה; pt. נַעֲנֶה: — 1. **be brought to answer** (of God) Ez $14_{4.7}$; — 2. **be provided with an answer** Pr 21_{13}.

hif.: pt. מַעֲנֶה: **pay attention to** s.thg Pr 29_{19}. †

II **ענה**: **qal**: pf. עָנִיתִי; impf. יַעֲנוּ, אֶעֱנֶה, יַעֲנֶה: **bend down, be wretched, pitiful**: sheep w/o a shepherd Zc 10_{2}; **stoop** (lion before hunter) Is 31_{4}; **be bowed down** Ps 116_{10} 119_{67}. †

nif.: pf. נַעֲנֵיתִי; inf. לַעֲנֹת (< לְהֵעָנֹת*); pt. נַעֲנֶה, f. נַעֲנָה: — 1. **bow down, humble onesf.** Ex 10_{3}; — 2. **be humbled** Is 58_{10}.

piel: pf. עִנָּה, עִנִּינוּ, עִנִּיתֶם, עִנּוּ, עִנֵּיתִי, עִנָּה, עִנִּיתָנוּ, עִנִּתְךָ Na 1_{12}; impf. אֲעַנֶּה, תְּעַנֶּה

1K 11_{39} rd וַיְעַנֶּהָ, תְּעַנּוּן, תְּעַנּוּ, יְעַנּוּ, וַאֲעַנֶּה, וַיְעַנּוּהוּ, אֲעַנֵּךְ, תְּעַנֵּנִי, יְעַנֻּהוּ; impv. עַנֵּה, עַנּוּ; inf. sf. עַנֹּתוֹ, עַנּוֹתֶךָ; pt. pl. sf. מְעַנַּיִךְ: — 1. **oppress, make** s.one **feel his dependence** Gn 15_{13} & oft.; **humiliate** Nu 24_{24}, (of God) **humble, subdue** 1K 11_{39}; *ʿinnâ mišpāṭ* violate justice Jb 37_{23}; humiliate (a woman by forced marriage) Dt 21_{14}; *ʿinnâ nafšô*, **humble onesf., mortify onesf.** (by fasting) Lv 16_{29}; — 2. **violate, rape** (a woman) Gn 34_{2}; — 3. **overpower** Ju 16_{5f}; **force** s.one into (*b^e^*) s.thg Ps 105_{18}.

pual: pf. עֻנֵּיתִי; impf. תְּעֻנֶּה; inf. sf. עֻנּוֹתוֹ; pt. מְעֻנֶּה: — 1. **be humbled** Is 53_{4}; — 2. **humble onesf.** Ps 132_{1}; mortify onesf. Lv 23_{29}.

hitp.: pf. הִתְעַנָּה, הִתְעַנִּיתָ; impf. יִתְעַנּוּ; impv. הִתְעַנִּי; inf. הִתְעַנּוֹת: — 1. **bow humbly down, submit** Gn 16_{9} 1K 2_{26}; — 2. **be tormented** Ps 107_{17}.

III ענה: **qal**: inf. עֲנוֹת: w. *b^e^* **be concerned about, worried about** Ec 1_{13} 3_{10}. †

hif.: pt. מַעֲנֶה: **keep s.one busy** (*b^e^* with) Ec 5_{19}. †

IV ענה: **qal**: pf. עָנוּ; impf. יַעֲנֶה, תַּעַן, וַתַּעַן, יַעֲנוּ, וַיַּעֲנוּ, וַתַּעֲנֶינָה; impv. עֱנוּ; inf. עֲנוֹת: **sing** 1S 18_{7}; inf. *ʿanôt* w. gen. **singing, noise** of Ex 32_{18}; **howl** (of animals) Is 13_{22}.

piel: impv. עַנּוּ; inf. עַנּוֹת: — 1. **sing to** (w. *l^e^*) Is 27_{2}; — 2. *l^e^ʿannôt* Ps 88_{1} for singing? or II *ʿanh* ?

*עֹנָה: sf. עֹנָתָהּ: **marital intercourse** (oth.: right to motherhood) Ex 21_{10}. †

עֲנָה: n. pers.

עָנָו: N.B. עָנִי & עָנָו alternate in Kt-Qr, ↗ עָנִי; pl. עֲנָוִים, cs. עַנְוֵי: (one who understands himsf. to be) **low, humble, gentle** (before God): Nu 12_{3}, oft. in Ps.

עָנוֹ Ne 12_{9} Kt: rd Qr עֻנִּי. †

עָנוּב: n. pers.

עֲנָוָה: **humility** Zp 2_{3} Pr 15_{33} 18_{12} 22_{4}. †

עַנְוָה Ps 45_{5}: rd וְיַעַן הַצֶּדֶק. †

עֲנוּק: n. pers.

עֲנוּשִׁים: **fines** Am 2_{8}. †

עֲנוֹת: n. of deity.

עֱנוּת Ps 22_{25}: rd עֲנוֹת (I עָנָה). †

עָנִי: f. עֲנִיָּה, sf. עֲנִיֶּךָ; pl. עֲנִיִּים, cs. עֲנִיֵּי, sf. עֲנִיָּיו, עֲנִיֶּיךָ: **overwhelmed by want, poor, wretched**: — 1. (in secular sense) **unfortunate, wretched** Dt 24_{15} Ps 10_{2} & oft.; — 2. **humble** Is 49_{13} (of Y.); = Jerusalem Is 51_{21}.

עֳנִי: עָנְיִי & עֹנִי; sf. עָנְיוֹ, עָנְיִי: **misery,** (situation of) **affliction** Gn 16_{11}.

עֻנִּי: n. pers.

עֲנָיָה: n. pers.

עָנָיו Nu 12_{3} Qr: = עָנָו. †

עָנִים: n. loc. Jos 15_{50}. †

עִנְיָן: sf. עִנְיָנוֹ: **occupation, task** Ec 1_{13}.

עָנֵם: n. loc.

עֲנָמִים: n. peop.

עֲנַמֶּלֶךְ: n. of deity.

ענן: **piel**: inf. sf. עַנְנִי: **cause** s.thg **to make an appearance** Gn 9_{14}. †

poel: pf. עוֹנֵן; impf. תְּעוֹנֵנוּ; pt. מְעוֹנֵן, f. עֹנְנָה (<* מְעֹנְנָה), pl. מְעֹנְנִים > עֹנְנִים, sf. עֹנְנֵיכֶם: **cause** s.thg **to make an appearance, conjure up** (spirits), **practice magic** 2K 21_{6}.

I עָנָן: הֶעָנָן, cs. עֲנַן, sf. עֲנָנְךָ: (mass of) **clouds** Gn 9_{13f}; *ʿanan yhwh* Ex 40_{38}.

II עָנָן: n. pers. Ne 10_{27}. †

עֲנָנָה: pl. עֲנָנִים: **rain-cloud** Je 4_{13} Jb 35_{5}. †

עֲנָנִי: n. pers.

I עֲנַנְיָה: n. pers. Ne 3_{23}. †

II עֲנַנְיָה: n. loc. Ne 11_{32}. †

עָנָף: cs. עֲנַף, sf. עַנְפְּכֶם; pl. sf. עֲנָפֶיהָ: sg. coll. **branches** Ez 17_{8}, pl. Ps 80_{11}.

*עָנֵף: f. עֲנֵפָה: **full of branches** Ez 19_{10}. †

ענק: **qal**: pf. עֲנָקַתְמוֹ: **put on as a necklace** Ps 73_{6}. †

hif.: impf. תַּעֲנִיק; inf. הַעֲנֵיק: put around one's neck, thus **outfit** w., **provide** w. Dt 15_{14}. †

I עֲנָק: pl. עֲנָקוֹת, עֲנָקִים: **necklace**: for women Pr 1_9 SS 4_9, for camels Ju 8_{26}. †

II עֲנָק: pl. עֲנָקִים: n. peop. **Anak, Anakim**.

I עָנֵר: n. pers. Gn $14_{13\cdot24}$. †

II עָנֵר: n. loc. 1C 6_{55}. †

ענשׁ: **qal**: pf. עָנְשׁוּ; inf. עֲנוֹשׁ, עֲנֹשׁ־, עָנוֹשׁ: **fine** s.one Ex 21_{22}.

nif.: pf. נֶעֶנְשׁוּ; impf. יֵעָנֵשׁ: — 1. **be fined** (an amount) Ex 21_{22}; — 2. **have to pay a penalty** (= be punished in genl.) Pr 22_3 27_{12}. †

עֹנֶשׁ: — 1. **fine** 2K 23_{33}; — 2. *nāśā' 'ōneš* **have to pay a penalty** (= make amends in genl.) Pr 19_{19}. †

עֲנָת: n. pers. & deity.

I עֲנָתוֹת & עֲנָתֹת: n. loc.

II עֲנָתוֹת: n. pers. (& tribe?) 1C 7_8 Ne 10_{20}. †

עַנְּתֹתִי & עַנְתֹתִי: gent. of עֲנָתוֹת.

עַנְתֹתִיָּה: n. pers.

עָסִיס: עֲסִיס: **grape-juice** (freshly pressed, unfermented) Is 49_{26} Am 9_{13}.

עסס: **qal**: pf. עַסּוֹתֶם: **tread down** Ma 3_{21}. †

[ערער: יְעֹעֵרוּ Is 15_5, rd. יְעַרְעֵרוּ pilpel III עור.]

*עֳפִי: pl. עֳפָאִים (Kt עֳפָאִים or עֲ׳, Qr עֳפָיִם): **thick foliage** Ps 104_{12}. †

עפל: [**pual**: pf. עֻפְּלָה Hb 2_4: text corr.] †

hif.: impf. וַיַּעְפִּלוּ: w. *le* & inf. **have the audacity to** Nu 14_{44}. †

I עֹפֶל: pl. עֳפָלִים (Qr rd. טְחֹרִים), cs. עָפְלֵי, sf. עָפְלֵיכֶם: **boils, abscesses** (at the anus); buboes from plague? 1S $5_{6\cdot9\cdot12}$.

II עֹפֶל: n. loc. **Ophel**.

עָפְנִי: Jos 18_{24} וְהָעָפְנִי: delete. †

*עַפְעַפַּיִם: cs. עַפְעַפֵּי, sf. עַפְעַפָּיו, עַפְעַפֶּיהָ: trad: eyelids, but better: **rays**, gleam, **flashing glance of the eye** Je 9_{17}, of Y. Ps 11_4.

עפף: **poel**: inf. sf. עוֹפְפִי: **double** Ez 32_{10}. †

עפר: **piel**: pf. עִפַּר: **throw** (dirt) **at** 2S 16_{13}. †

עָפָר (109×): cs. עֲפַר, sf. עֲפָרוֹ; pl. cs. עַפְר(וֹ)ת: — 1. **dry, fine particles of dirt, dust**: *'afar hā'āreṣ* Gn 13_{16}; — 2. **loose soil** Is 34_7; — 3. **rubble** 1K 20_{10}; — 4. (disintegrated) **coating** or **plaster** of wall of a house Lv 14_{41}; **dust** of an idol that has been ground up Dt 9_{21}; (gold-)dust Jb 28_6; — 5. *'āfār* = realm of the humble & undeserving 1K 16_2; — 6. *'āfār* = realm of what is perishable & transitory Gn 3_{19}.

עֵפֶר: n. pers.

עֹפֶר: pl. עֳפָרִים: **fawn** of gazelle, deer SS 2_9.

I עָפְרָה: n. pers. 1C 4_{14}. †

II עָפְרָה: n. loc.; cs. עָפְרָת rd עָפְרַת Ju 6_{24}; loc. עָפְרָתָה.

עַפְרָה: n. loc.: בֵּית לְעַפְרָה.

I עֶפְרוֹן: n. pers. Gn $23_{8\text{-}17}$ 25_9 49_{29f} 50_{13}. †

II עֶפְרוֹן: n. loc.

*עֶפְרַיִם cj. 2S 13_{23} & עֶפְרַיִן 2C 13_{19} Qr: ↗ II עֶפְרוֹן.

עוֹפֶרֶת & עֹפֶרֶת: עֹפָרֶת: **lead** Nu 31_{22}.

עֵפָתָה: ↗ I עֵיפָה.

עֵץ (325×): sf. עֵצָהּ, עֵצְךָ; pl. עֵצִים, cs. עֲצֵי, sf. עֵצָיו, עֵצֶיךָ: — 1. sg. coll. **trees** (in genl.): Gn 1_{11}; *'ēṣ hā'āreṣ* Lv 26_{20}; *'ēṣāh* its (stock of) trees Dt 20_{19}; — 2. (a single) **tree** *'ēṣ (ha)ḥayyîm* Gn 2_9; *kol-'ēṣ* any tree Dt 22_6; — 3. pl. **trees**: *'aṣê yhwh* Ps 104_{16}; — 4. (specific kind of) **tree**: *'ēṣ hazzayit* Hg 2_{19}; — 5. **wood** (as a material): *kol-'ēṣ* any kind of wood Dt 16_{21}; *ḥārāšê 'ēṣ* carpenters 2S 5_{11}; *'ēṣ* **timber** Hg 1_8; *'ēṣ* piece of wood, stick Ez 37_{16f}; *'ēṣ* gallows, pole Gn 40_{19}; — 6. pl. **pieces of wood**, sticks 1K 17_{12}; logs (for fire) Gn 22_3; vessels of wood Ex 7_{19}; wooden parts of house Lv 14_{45}.

I עצב: **piel**: pf. עִצְּבוּנִי: **shape** (of God's hands, obj. man) Jb 10_8. †

hif.: inf. sf. לְהַעֲצִבָהּ (MT לְהַעֲצִבָה): **copy** (an image) Je 44_{19}. †

II עצב: **qal**: pf. עֲצָבוֹ; inf. sf. עָצְבִּי; pt. pass. f. cs. עֲצוּבַת: — 1. **find fault with** 1K 1_6; — 2. **hurt, trouble** 1C 4_{10}; *'aṣûbat rûaḥ* deeply grieved in spirit Is 54_6. †

nif.: pf. נֶעֱצַב & נֶעְצַב; impf. יֵעָצֵב, תֵּעָצְבוּ, תֵּעָצְבוּ: — 1. **be distressed, worried** 1S 20$_{3\cdot 34}$; — 2. **grieve** (intrans.) Gn 45$_5$; — 3. **hurt onesf.** Ec 10$_9$. †

piel: pf. עִצְּבוּ; impf. יְעַצְּבוּ: **grieve, offend** (trans.) Ps 56$_6$ Is 63$_{10}$. †

hif.: impf. יַעֲצִיבוּהוּ: **grieve, offend** Ps 78$_{40}$. †

hitp.: impf. וַיִּתְעַצֵּב, וַיִּתְעַצְּבוּ: **feel grieved, outraged** Gn 6$_6$ 34$_7$. †

*עָצָב: pl. עֲצַבִּים, cs. עֲצַבֵּי, sf. עֲצַבֶּיהָ, עֲצַבֵּיהֶם: (disparaging term) **image, idol** 1S 31$_9$.

*עַצָּב: pl. sf. עַצְּבֵיכֶם: Is 58$_3$ **(heavy) worker**, but sugg. text corr. †

I עֶצֶב: **form, creation** Je 22$_{28}$. †

II עֶצֶב: pl. עֲצָבִים, sf. עֲצָבֶיךָ: — 1. **hardship, pain** Gn 3$_{16}$; — 2. **offending** Pr 15$_1$; — 3. **hard-won acquisition** Pr 5$_{10}$. †

I *עֹצֶב: sf. עָצְבִּי: **idol** Is 48$_5$. †

II עֹצֶב: sf. עָצְבְּךָ: **hardship, pain, distress** Is 14$_3$.

עִצָּבוֹן: cs. עִצְּבוֹן, sf. עִצְּבוֹנֵךְ: **hardship, pain, distress** Gn 3$_{16f}$ 5$_{29}$. †

עַצֶּבֶת: עַצֶּבֶת, cs. עַצְּבַת!; pl. sf. עַצְּבֹתָי, עַצְּבוֹתָם: **pain** Ps 16$_4$; **painful spot** Ps 147$_3$. †

עצה: **qal**: pt. עֹצֶה: w. *ʿênāyw*: **contract, narrow** (one's eyes) Pr 16$_{30}$. †

עָצֶה: **tail-bone**, spec. *os sacrum*, bone associated w. fat-tail Lv 3$_9$. †

I עֵצָה (80×): cs. עֲצַת, sf. עֲצָתוֹ, עֲצָתְךָ; pl. עֵצוֹת: — 1. **advice** 1K 12$_{14}$; *ʾanšê ʿaṣātî* = 'my men of advice,' i.e. my counsellors Ps 119$_{24}$; — 2. **plan, scheme** 2K 18$_{20}$; *tābôʾ ʿēṣâ* plan be fulfilled Is 5$_{19}$; *ʾîš ʿaṣātô* one who carries out his plan Is 46$_{11}$; *beʿēṣâ* on purpose 1C 12$_{20}$.

II *עֵצָה: cs. עֲצַת, sf. עֲצָתָם; pl. עֵצוֹת: **disobedience** Ps 106$_{43}$; **revolt, resistance** Ps 13$_3$. †

III עֵצָה: coll. **wood** Je 6$_6$. †

עָצוּם: pl. עֲצֻמִים, עֲצוּמִים: **mighty, vast** (connotation of numbers or quantity): people Gn 18$_{18}$, cattle Nu 32$_1$, water Is 8$_7$; subst.: strong (men) Is 53$_{12}$.

עֶצְיוֹן־גֶּבֶר: n. loc.

עצל: **nif.**: impf. תֵּעָצְלוּ: **be slow, hesitate** Ju 18$_9$. †

עָצֵל: **slow, lazy** Pr 6$_{6\cdot 9}$.

עַצְלָה: **laziness** Pr 19$_{15}$. †

עַצְלוּת **laziness** Pr 31$_{27}$. †

עֲצַלְתַּיִם: extreme laziness, **indolence** Ec 10$_{18}$. †

I עצם: **qal**: pf. עָצְמוּ, עָצֵמוּ, ע׳; impf. וַיַּעַצְמוּ; inf. עָצְמוֹ: — 1. **be mighty, vast, numerous** (of a people &c.) Gn 26$_{16}$; — 2. be strong (ram, he-goat, king) Dn 8$_{8\cdot 24}$ 11$_{23}$.

piel (denom. of I עֶצֶם): pf. עִצְּמוֹ: **gnaw, pick a bone** Je 50$_{17}$. †

hif.: impf. וַיַּעֲצִמֵהוּ: (w. *min*) **make strong**(er than) Ps 105$_{24}$. †

II עצם: **qal**: pt. עֹצֵם: w. *ʿênāyw*: **close** (one's eyes) Is 33$_{15}$. †

piel: impf. וַיְעַצֵּם: w. *ʿēnayim*: **close** (one's eyes) Is 29$_{10}$. †

I עֶצֶם (124×): עֶצֶם, sf. עַצְמוֹ, עַצְמְכֶם; pl. עֲצָמִים, sf. עֲצָמַי, עֲצָמֵינוּ, & עֲצָמוֹת, cs. עַצְמוֹת, sf. עַצְמֹתַי, עַצְמֹתֵיהֶם: — 1. sg.: **bone**, or coll. **bones** Gn 2$_{23}$; skeleton Nu 19$_{18}$; — 2. pl.: **bones** Gn 2$_{23}$ 1K 13$_2$; = corpse Gn 50$_{25}$; — 3. sg. & pl. seat of perceptions Je 20$_9$; — 4. *ʿeṣem ûbāśār* expresses the total being Gn 29$_{14}$; — 4. thus *ʿeṣem* expresses complete identity: *keʿeṣem haššāmayim* like the very heavens Ex 24$_{10}$; *beʿeṣem hayyôm hazzeh* on this very day Gn 7$_{13}$.

II עֶצֶם: n. loc. Jos 15$_{29}$ 19$_3$ 1C 4$_{29}$. †

I עֹצֶם: **full power** Dt 8$_{17}$.

II עֹצֶם: sf. עָצְמִי: **bones** Ps 139$_{15}$. †

*עַצְמָה: pl. cs. עַצְמוֹת, sf. עַצְמוֹתַי: — 1. **evil deeds** Ps 53$_6$; — 2. **severe sufferings** Ps 22$_{18}$ Jb 7$_{15}$. †

עָצְמָה: cs. עָצְמַת: **full power** Is 40$_{29}$.

עַצְמוֹן: n. loc.
***עֲצֻמוֹת**: sf. עֲצֻמוֹתֵיכֶם: strong words > **proofs** Is 41_{21}. †
***עֵצֶן**, sf. עֶצְנוֹ 2S 23_8: text corr.
עָצַר: **qal**: pf. ע׳, עֲצָרַנִי, עָצַרְתִּי; impf. יַעְצֹר, תַּעְצְרֵנִי, יַעֲצָרְכָה, נַעְצְרָה, אֶעְצֹר, יַעֲצָר־; inf. לַעְצֹר 2C 22_9, וַעְצֹר ! Jb 4_2, עָצוֹר; pt. pass. עָצוּר, עָצֻר, עֲצֻרָה: **hold back, hinder**: — 1. **detain** 1K 18_{44}; w. *bᵉ* restrain Jb 4_2; — 2. **imprison** 2K 17_4, keep away 1C 12_1; — 3. **keep imprisoned** Je 33_1, **shut up** Je 20_9; — 4. **keep, retain** (strength) Dn $10_{8 \cdot 16}$; — 5. **close, shut**: womb Gn 20_{18} (w. *bᵉʿad*), Is 66_9 (w. acc.); w. acc. & *milledet* prevent s.one fm. bearing Gn 16_2; *ʾiššâ ʿᵃṣûrâ* woman removed (fm. sexual relations) 1S 21_6; — 6. **keep within bounds** = rule 1S 9_{17}; — 7. **check** (riding) 2K 4_{24}; — 8. *ʿāṣûr wᵉʿāzûb* 1K 14_{10} mng. uncert.: slave & free? married man & bachelor? minor & of age? ℱ comm.

nif.: pf. נֶעֶצְרָה; impf. תֵּעָצַר; inf. הֵעָצֵר; pt. נֶעְצָר: — 1. **be detained** 1S 21_8; **be brought to a standstill** (of plague) 2S $24_{21 \cdot 25}$; — 2. **be shut** (of heavens, i.e. no rain) 1K 8_{35}.
עֶצֶר: **oppression** Ju 18_7 (rd. וְאֵין יוֹרֵשׁ וָעֶצֶר). †
עֹצֶר: — 1. **barrenness** (lit.: closedness) (of womb) Pr 30_{16}; — 2. **oppression** Is 53_8 Ps 107_{39}. †
עֲצָרָה & עֲצֶרֶת: עֲצֶרֶת; pl. sf. עַצְּרֹתֵיכֶם: stopping of work > **festive assembly** Jl 1_{14}, *qiddēš ʿᵃṣārâ* = prepare for a festive assembly by rites of purification 2K 10_{20}.
עָקַב: **qal**: pf. ע׳; impf. יַעְקֹב, וַיַּעְקְבֵנִי; inf. עָקוֹב: **grasp by the heel, cheat** Gn 27_{36} Je 9_3 Ho 12_4. †

piel: impf. יְעַקְּבֵם: **hold by the heel, restrain** Jb 37_4. †
עָקֵב: cs. עֲקֵב, sf. עֲקֵבוֹ; pl. cs. עִקְּבֵי & עִקְּבוֹת, sf. עֲקֵבַי, עִקְּבוֹתֶיךָ: — 1. **heel** Gn 3_{15}; euphem. for genitals Je 13_{22}; — 2. *ʿiqbê sûs* **hooves** Gn 49_{17}; — 3. pl. **footprints** Ps 77_{20}; — 4. **rear-guard** (of army) Jos 8_{13}.
עֵקֶב: — 1. last, end: *ʿēqeb* **to the end** Ps 119_{33}; — 2. > result, **reward** Is 5_{23}; — 3. > conj. *ʿal-ʿēqeb* **because of** Ps 40_{16}; *ʿēqeb* **because** Nu 14_{24}, = *ʿēqeb ʾᵃšer* Gn 22_{18} 26_5 2S 12_6 = *ʿēqeb kî* 2S 12_{10} Am 4_{12}.
עָקֹב: **uneven, bumpy ground** Is 40_4; > **tough, crafty** (heart) Je 17_9. †
עָקְבָה: **cunning, craftiness** 2K 10_{19}. †
עקד: **qal**: impf. וַיַּעֲקֹד: **tie up** (feet of sacrificial victim) Gn 22_9. †
עָקֹד: pl. עֲקֻדִּים: **with twisted tail** Gn $30_{35 \cdot 39f}$ $31_{8 \cdot 12}$. †
***עָקָה**: cs. עָקַת: **pressure** Ps 55_4. †
עַקּוּב: n. pers.
עקל: **pual**: pt. מְעֻקָּל: **distorted** Hb 1_4. †
***עֲקַלְקַל**: pl. f. עֲקַלְקַלּוֹת, sf. ־תָם: **twisted, winding** (paths) Ju 5_6 Ps 125_5. †
עֲקַלָּתוֹן: **twisting** (serpent) Is 27_1. †
עֲקָן: n. pers.
עקר: **qal**: inf. עֲקוֹר: **pull up by the roots, weed** Ec 3_2. †

nif.: impf. תֵּעָקֵר: **be uprooted** Zp 2_4. †

piel: pf. עִקֵּר; impf. וַיְעַקֵּר: **hamstring, cripple** Gn 49_6 2S 8_4.
עָקָר: f. עֲקָרָה, עֲקֶרֶת: **barren, without offspring** Gn 11_{30}; masc. form Dt 7_{14}.
I **עֵקֶר**: עֵקֶר מִשְׁפַּחַת גֵּר Lv 25_{47} **offspring**. †
II **עֵקֶר**: n. pers. 1C 2_{27}. †
עַקְרָב: pl. עַקְרַבִּים: — 1. **scorpion**, *Buthus quinquestriatus* (& 3 other species of *Buthus*), *Scorpio testaceus* Dt 8_{15}; — 2. (particularly painful kind of) **scourge** 1K $12_{11 \cdot 14}$.
עֶקְרוֹן: n. loc.
עֶקְרוֹנִי: gent. of עֶקְרוֹן.
עקשׁ: **nif.**: pt. cs. נֶעְקַשׁ: w. *dᵉrākayim*: **one who walks crooked paths** Pr 28_{18}. †

piel: pf. עִקְּשׁוּ; impf. יְעַקֵּשׁ; inf. עַקֵּשׁ; pt. מְעַקֵּשׁ: — 1. **distort, pervert** Mi 3_9; — 2. w.

derek, netîbâ: **choose crooked paths** Is 59_8.

hif.: impf. וַיַּעְקְשֵׁנִי: **declare** s.one **crooked, guilty** Jb 9_{20}. †

I **עִקֵּשׁ**: cs. עִקֶּשׁ־; pl. cs. עִקְּשֵׁי: **perverted, false** 2S 22_{27}.

II **עִקֵּשׁ**: n. pers. 2S 23_{26} 1C 11_{28} 27_9. †

עִקְּשׁוּת: **perversion, falsehood** Pr 4_{24} 6_{12}. †

***עָר**: עָרֶךָ 1S 28_{16} text corr.; עָרֶיךָ Ps 139_{20} text corr. †

עָר: n. terr.

עֵר: n. pers.

I **עָרַב**: **qal**: pf. עָרַבְתָּ, ע׳; impf. אֶעֶרְבֶנּוּ; inf. עֲרֹב, עָרְבֵנוּ; pt. עֹרֵב, עֹרְבִים, עֹרְבֵי: — 1. w. acc. **stand surety** for Gn 43_9 44_{32}; **step in for** Is 38_{14}; w. *libbô* risk one's life Je 30_{21}; — 2. **mortgage** Ne 5_3; *ʿārab maʿarāb* **barter** Ez $27_{9\cdot 27}$; w. *maššāʾôt* **pledge onesf.** as surety for debts Pr 22_{26}, w. *ʿarubbâ lifnê* give security before Pr 17_{18}; — 3. w. *le* **give security** on behalf of Pr 6_1.

hitp.: impv. הִתְעָרֶב־: **make a wager** 2K 18_{23} Is 36_8. †

II **ערב**: **hitp.**: pf. הִתְעָרְבוּ; impf. תִּתְעָרַב, תִּתְעָרָב: — 1. w. *le*: **associate** with Pr 20_{19}; — 2. w. *be*: **mingle** with Ps 106_{35} Ezr 9_2; — 3. w. *be*: **be intermixed** with Pr 14_{10}. †

III **ערב**: **qal**: pf. עָרְבָה, עָרַבְתְּ; impf. יֶעֱרַב, יֶעֶרְבוּ: **be pleasing, be to one's tastes** Je 6_{20}.

IV **ערב**: **qal**: inf. עֲרוֹב: **become evening** Ju 19_9. †

hif.: inf. הַעֲרֵב: **do s.thg in the evening, do s.thg late** 1S 17_{16}. †

I **עֶרֶב**: Je 25_{24} dittgr.; 1K 10_{15} rd עֲרַב. †

II **עֶרֶב**: עָרֶב, du. עַרְבַּיִם: **evening** (sunset) Gn 1_5; *ʿereb* in the eve. Ex 16_6; var. expr. w. prep., e.g. *bāʿereb* in the eve. Gn 19_1, *lifnôt-ʿāreb* towards eve. Gn 24_{63}, *bāʿereb bāʿereb* every eve. 2C 13_{11}; du. *bên hāʿarbayim* (P only) in the dusk, twilight Ex 12_6.

III **עֶרֶב**: ↗ II עֵרֶב.

I **עֵרֶב**: הָעֵרֶב: Lv $13_{48\text{-}59}$ weaver's tech. term: trad. woof, but uncert.; simply what is woven?

II **עֵרֶב**, **עֶרֶב**: **mixed people or race** Ex 12_{38}.

I **עֲרַב**: **עֲרָב**: n. peop. **Arabs** Je 25_{24}.

II ***עֲרַב**: Is 21_{13} בַּעְרַב & בְּעֶרֶב: = II עֲרָבָה. †

עָרֵב: **pleasant** Pr 20_{17} SS 2_{14}. †

I **עֹרֵב**, **עוֹרֵב**: pl. עֹרְבִים, cs. עֹרְבֵי: **raven** (of var. species), *Corvus* Gn 8_7 1K $17_{4\cdot 6}$.

II **עֹרֵב**: n. pers. Ju 7_{25} 8_3 Is 10_{26} Ps 83_{12}. †

עָרֹב: swarm of noxious insects, unidentifiable Ex 8_{17ff}.

I ***עֲרָבָה**: pl. עֲרָבִים, cs. עַרְבֵי: **(Euphrates) poplar**, *Populus euphratica Oliv.* Is 44_4; *naḥal hāʿarābîm* n. of river Is 15_7.

II **עֲרָבָה**: loc. הָעֲרָבָתָה, sf. עֲרָבָתָהּ; pl. עֲרָבוֹת, cs. עַרְבֹ(וֹ)ת: **desert** (waterless region) Je 2_6, esp. in Jordan valley, on east side of Jordan or S. of Judah Jos 12_1 1S 23_{24}; *yām hāʿarābâ* Dead Sea Dt 3_{17}.

עֲרֻבָּה: sf. עֲרֻבָּתָם: — 1. **security, pledge** Pr 17_{18}; — 2. **token** (evidence that errand was carried out) 1S 17_{18}. †

עֵרָבוֹן: security, **pledge** Gn $38_{17f\cdot 20}$. †

עַרְבִי: gent. of עֲרַב: pl. עַרְבִי(י)ם, עַרְבִיאִים 2C 17_{11}: **Arabs**, desert **Bedouin**.

עֲרָבִי: gent. of עֲרַב, = עַרְבִי.

עַרְבָתִי: gent. of בֵּית הָעֲרָבָה.

ערג: **qal**: impf. תַּעֲרֹ(וֹ)ג: **pant for, long for** Ps 42_2 Jl 1_{20}. †

I **עֵרָד**: n. pers. 1C 8_{15}. †

II **עֲרָד**: n. loc.

ערה: **nif.**: יֵעָרֶה: **be poured out** (*rûaḥ*) Is 32_{15}. †

piel: pf. עֵרָה; impf. יְעָרֶה, תְּעַר, וַיְעָרוּ; impv. עָרוּ; inf. עָרוֹת: — 1. **lay bare** Is 3_{17}; **uncover** (shield) Is 22_6; — 2. **empty out** Gn 24_{20}; — 3. **pour out** (*nefeš*) Ps 141_8.

hif.: pf. הֶעֱרָה: make naked, **expose** Lv 20_{18f}; w. *lammāwet nafšô* **abandon to death** Is 53_{12}. †

hitp.: impf. תִּתְעָרִי; pt. מִתְעָרֶה: **show onesf. naked** La 4_{21}; Ps 37_{35} text?. †

*עָרָה: pl. עָרוֹת: **(bul)rushes** Is 19_7. †

עֲרוּגָה: cs. עֲרוּגַת; pl. עֲרֻג(וֹ)ת: **bed** (of plants) Ez $17_{7.10}$ SS 5_{13} 6_2. †

עָרוֹד: **wild ass**, *Asinus hemippus* Jb 39_5. †

עֶרְוָה: cs. עֶרְוַת, sf. עֶרְוָתְךָ, עֶרְוָתֵךְ: **nakedness, genital area** (of both sexes) Gn 9_{22f}; in curse, *l^{e}bōšet ʿerwat ʾimmekā* to the disgrace of your mother's nakedness 1S 20_{30}; *ʿerwat hāʾāreṣ* = undefended areas of the land Gn $42_{9.12}$; *ʿerwat dābār* s.thg indecent Dt 23_{15}.

עָרֹם, עָרוֹם: f. עֲרֻמָּה; pl. עֲרֻמִּים: **naked, undressed** Gn 2_{25} 1S 19_{24}.

עָרוּם: pl. עֲרוּמִים: **subtle, shrewd, clever** Gn 3_1.

I עֲרוֹעֵר Je 48_6: text corr. †

II עֲרוֹעֵר, עֲרֹעֵר: n. loc.

*עָרוּץ: cs. עֲרוּץ: **slope** Jb 30_6. †

עָרוֹת Is 19_7: ↗ *עָרָה. †

I עֵרִי: n. pers.

II עֵרִי: gent. of I עֵרִי Nu 26_{16}. †

עֶרְיָה: **bareness, nakedness** Ez $16_{7.22.39}$ 23_{29}. †

*עֲרִיסָה: pl. sf. עֲרִיסֹתֵינוּ, ־תֵ(י)כֶם: mixed dough, **dough at the first stage** Nu 15_{20f}.

*עֲרִיפִים: sf. עֲרִיפֶיהָ: **trickling**, drops (from clouds) (text?) Is 5_{30}. †

עָרִיץ: pl. עָרִיצִים, cs. עָרִיצֵי: — 1. one in authority, **master** Je 20_{11}; — 2. **violent, tyrant** Is 29_{20}.

עֲרִירִי: **childless** Gn 15_2.

עָרַךְ: **qal**: pf. עָרַכְתָּ, ע׳; impf. יַעֲרֹךְ, אֶעֱרָךְ־, יַעַרְכוּנִי, יַעַרְכֶנּוּ, יַעַרְכֶהָ, תַּעַרְכוּ, אֶעֶרְכָה; impv. עֶרְכָה, עִרְכוּ; inf. עֲרֹךְ, עָרֹךְ; pt. עֹרְכִים, עֹרְכֵי, pass. עָרוּךְ, cs. עֲרוּךְ, f. עֲרוּכָה, pl. עֲרֻכוֹת: — 1. w. pl. acc. **lay, put, set in rows, layers; stack, set out**: logs Gn 22_9, cakes Lv 24_8, altars Nu 23_4; cogn. acc. *ʿārak ʿērek* Ex 40_4; — 2. w. sg. acc. **prepare, put in order**: set table Is 21_5, burnt-offering Lv 24_3; **keep ready** (shield) 1C 12_9; *ʿ^{a}rûkâ bakkōl* all in order 2S 23_5; — 3. tech. term *ʿārak milḥāmâ* **draw up in battle order, enter into battle** Gn 14_8; w/o *milḥāmâ* 1S 4_2; *ʿārûk lammilḥāmâ* drawn up for battle Je 6_{23}, = *ʿ^{e}rûk milḥāmâ* Jl 2_5; *ʿārak* (w. *l^e*, *ʿal*) **form up** against Je $50_{9.14}$; — 4. therefore: *ʿārak lî* **confront** me (w. s.thg) Is 44_7; > **compare** Ps 40_6; — 5. (< 2) **lay** (a case before s.one) Ps 50_{21} Jb 13_{18}; w. *millîn ʾel* put forth (words against s.one) Jb 32_{14}, w/o *millîn* 33_5.

hif.: pf. הֶעֱרִיךְ, הֶעֱרִיכוֹ; impf. יַעֲרִיךְ, יַעֲרִיכֶנּוּ: **assess (value)** 2K 23_{35}.

עֵרֶךְ: sf. עֶרְכּוֹ: — 1. **layer, row, suitable number of pieces**: *ʿērek leḥem* Ex 40_{23}; *ʿerkô* **its** equipment, **accessories** Ex 40_4; — 2. *ʿerkî* one who fits me, my equal Ps 55_{14}; — 3. what is adequate, **(estimated) value** Lv 5_{15}; the sf. *-kā* has become meaningless, so that even *hāʿerk^{e}kā* Lv 27_{23} is possible; *ʿerk^{e}kā hakkōhēn* value estimated by the priest Lv 27_{12}; *kesef ʿērek* amount of valuation Lv 27_{15}.

ערל: **qal**: pf. עֲרַלְתֶּם: *ʿāral ʿorlâ* leave the foreskin uncircumcised, i.e. **leave unharvested** Lv 19_{23}. †

nif.: impv. הֵעָרֵל: text corr. Hb 2_{16}. †

עָרֵל: cs. עֲרֵל, עֶרֶל Ez 44_9; f. עֲרֵלָה; pl. עֲרֵלִים, cs. עַרְלֵי: — 1. **having a foreskin, uncircumcised** Gn 17_{14}; — 2. metaph. *ʿerel lēb* Ez 44_9, *ʿarlê lēb* 44_7, *l^{e}bābām heʿārēl*; sim. *ʿ^{a}ral ś^{e}fātāyim* Ex $6_{12.30}$ uninitiated, unskilled in speaking, & *ʿ^{a}rēlâ ʾoznām* unfit for hearing Je 6_{10}; of trees whose fruit is not yet to be eaten Lv 19_{23}; — 3. (only Ez) *šākab ʾet-/b^{e}tôk ʿ^{a}rēlîm* = the slain in Sheol 31_{18}.

עָרְלָה: cs. עָרְלַת, sf. עָרְלָתוֹ; pl. עֲרָלוֹת, cs. עָרְלוֹת, sf. עָרְלֹתֵיכֶם: — 1. **foreskin** Gn 17_{11}; = the whole penis 1S $18_{25.27}$; — 2. metaph. *ʿorlat lēbāb* Dt 10_{16}; of a tree = fruit not yet to be eaten Lv 19_{23}.

I ערם: **nif.**: pf. נֶעֶרְמוּ: gather (intrans.), **be dammed up, rise** (of water) Ex 15_8. †

II ערם: qal: impf. יַעְרִם!; inf. עָרוֹם, עָרְמָם: be(come) subtle, shrewd, clever Pr 15_{5}; be crafty, cunning 1S 23_{22}.

hif.: impf. יַעֲרִימוּ: w. *sôd*, have a sly discussion Ps 83_{4}. †

עָרֹם: ʄ עָרוֹם.

עֵרֹם: ʄ עֵירֹם.

עָרְמָה: (noun) cunning Ex 21_{14} Jos 9_{4}.

עֲרֵמָה: cs. עֲרֵמַת; pl. עֲרֵמוֹת, עֲרֵמִים: heap: of wheat Hg 2_{16}, fruit 2C 31_{6ff}, rubble Ne 3_{34}.

עַרְמוֹן: pl. עַרְמֹנִים: plane-tree, *Platanus orientalis L.* Gn 30_{37} Ez 31_{8}. †

עֵרָן: n. pers.

עֵרָנִי: gent. of עֵרָן.

עַרְעוֹר Ju 11_{26}: rd. עֲרוֹעֵר.

עַרְעָר: — 1. coll. the naked, stripped Ps 102_{18}; — 2. juniper, *Juniperus oxycedrus & phoenicia* Je 17_{6}. †

עֲרֹעֵר: ʄ עֲרוֹעֵר.

עֲרֹעֵרִי: gent. of עֲרוֹעֵר.

I ערף: qal: impf יַעֲרֹף, יַעַרְפוּ: trickle, drip Dt 32_{2} 33_{28}. †

II ערף: qal: pf. עָרְפוּ, עֲרַפְתּוֹ; impf. יַעֲרֹף; pt. עֹרֵף, pass. f. עֲרוּפָה: break the neck (of an animal) Ex 13_{13}; break (altars) Ho 10_{2}.

עֹרֶף: sf. עָרְפּוֹ: area of hair (on top of head) & back of neck, spec. back of neck, neck (in genl.) Gn 49_{8}; oft. w. *qāšeh* stiff Dt 31_{27}, esp. *qešēh ʿōref* stiff-necked, obstinate Ex 32_{9}, *hiqšâ ʿōref* stiffen the neck, be obstinate 2K 17_{14}; w. verbs of turning or showing: *hāfak ʿōref lifnê* turn one's back before Jos 7_{8}, *pānâ ʿōref ʾel* Je 2_{27}, *nātan ʾōtô ʿōref ʾel* make him turn his back on Ex 23_{27} 2S 22_{41}.

עָרְפָּה: n. pers. f.

עֲרָפֶל: darkness, gloom Is 60_{2}; enveloping God 1K 8_{12}.

ערץ: qal: impf. תַּעֲרֹץ, תַּעַרְצִי, אֶעֱרוֹץ, תַּעַרְצוּ, תַּעַרְצוּן; inf. עֲרוֹץ: — 1. be terrified Dt 1_{29}; — 2. terrify Is 47_{12}.

nif.: pt. נַעֲרָץ: inspiring terror, dreadful Ps 89_{8}. †

hif.: impf. יַעֲרִיצוּ; pt. sf. מַעֲרִיצְכֶם: — 1. terrify Is 8_{13}; — 2. be in terror, dread before Is 8_{12} 29_{23}. †

ערק: qal: pt. עֹרְקִים, sf. עֹרְקַי: Jb 30_{17} *ʿōreqay* those that gnaw me = my pains (?); Jb 30_{3} *hāʿōreqîm* those who gnaw, text corr.

עַרְקִי: n. peop.

ערר: qal: impv. pl. f. עֹרָה: strip onesf. Is 32_{11}. †

poel: impv. עֹרְרוּ Is 23_{13}: lay bare (text?). †

pilpel: inf. עַרְעֵר: lay bare, demolish Je 51_{58}. †

hitpalpel: impf. תִּתְעַרְעָר: be demolished Je 51_{58}. †

עֶרֶשׂ: עֶרֶשׂ; sf. עַרְשׂוֹ, עַרְשֵׂנוּ; pl. sf. עַרְשׂוֹתָם, f.: bedstead, couch: Dt 3_{11} Am 3_{12}; of branches SS 1_{16}.

עֵשֶׂב: sf. עֶשְׂבָּם; pl. cs. עִשְּׂבוֹת: coll. green plants: weeds, grass, vegetables, cereals, growing during rainy season, not perennials Gn 1_{30}; oft. *ʿēśeb haśśādeh* Gn 3_{18}; learned terms *ʿēśeb mazrîaʿ zeraʿ* seed-producing plants Gn 1_{11} & *ʿēśeb zōrēaʿ zeraʿ* seed-bearing plants 1_{29}; *ʿēśeb* symbol of transitoriness Ps 102_{5} & of abundant growth Ps 72_{16}.

עשׂה (2600×): qal: pf. ע׳, עָשְׂתָה, עָשָׂת Lv 25_{21}, עָשִׂיתָ, עָשִׂית, עָשׂוּ, עֲשִׂיתֶן, עָשִׂינוּ, sf. עָשָׂהוּ, עָשָׂךְ, עָשָׂתְנִי, עֲשִׂיתִיהוּ, עֲשִׂיתִנִי; impf. יַעֲשֶׂה, יַעַשׂ, וַיַּעַשׂ, תַּעֲשֶׂה, תַּעֲשֶׂה Jos 7_{9} & 2S 13_{12} & תַּעַשׂ Je 40_{16} Qr, תַּעַשׂ, תַּעֲשִׂי, אֶעֱשֶׂה, יַעֲשׂוּ, תַּעֲשֶׂינָה, נַעֲשֶׂה, וְנַעֲשֶׂה! Jos 9_{24}, sf. יַעֲשֵׂהוּ, יַעֲשֵׂם, אֶעֶשְׂךָ, אֶעֱשֶׂנָּה; impv. עֲשֵׂה, עֲשֵׂי, עֲשׂוּ, עֲשׂוּ; inf. עֲשׂוֹת, עֲשׂה, עָשׂוֹ, sf. עֲשֹׂהוּ, עֲשֹׂתָהּ, abs. עָשֹׂה; pt. עֹ(וֹ)שֶׂה, cs. עֹ(וֹ)שֵׂה, f. עֹשָׂה, pl. עֹשִׂים, cs. עֹשֵׂי, f. עֹשׂוֹת, sf. עֹשֵׂהוּ, עֹשָׂיו, עֹשַׂי, pass. עָשׂוּי, > עָשׂוּ Jb 41_{25}, f. עֲשׂוּיָה, עֲשֻׂיָה, pl. עֲשׂוּיִם, f. עֲשׂוּוֹת Kt עֲשׂוּיוֹת Qr 1S 25_{18}: — 1. make, manufacture Gn 3_{21}, lay out (garden) Am 9_{14}; — 2.

make, **apply** Ex 39_{24} (w. *ʿal*), Ez 41_{19} (w. *ʾel*); — 3. **make** s.thg (acc.) into **s.thg** (*le*) Is 44_{17}; w. 2 acc. 2K 3_{16}; **make** s.thg out of s.thg. (material) (2 acc.) Ex 37_{24}; make s.thg with s.thg (*be*) 1C 18_{8}; — 4. God as subj., = create Gn 1_{7}; pt. pass. created Jb 41_{25}, pt. act. maker = creator Jb 4_{17}; — 5. derived mng.: **effect**, **produce**, **do**: a wonder Ex 11_{10}, cogn. acc. deed Gn 20_{9}; of cow, produce (milk) Is 7_{22}, of man, put on (fat) Jb 15_{27}, of plants, bear (fruit) Gn 1_{11}; **acquire**, **win** (glory) Gn 31_{1}, (*nefeš* = slaves) Gn 12_{5}; *ʿōśê śeker* hired laborers Is 19_{10}; — 6. **prepare** (food) Gn 18_{7f}, *ʿāśûy* dressed (sheep) 1S 25_{18}; **take care of** (feet, beard) 2S 19_{25}; prepare s.thg for sacrifice 1K 18_{23}; **officiate** 2K 17_{32}; — 7. **make** (appoint) s.one (*le*, to be ...) Gn 12_{2}; — 8. var.: *ʿāśâ šālôm le* make peace w. Is 27_{5}; *ʿāśâ milḥāmâ* wage war Gn 14_{2}; *ʿāśâ yāmîm* spend days Ec 6_{12}; — 9. **perform, carry out** (orders) Ps 111_{8}, (*debārîm*) Is 42_{16}, (plan) Is 30_{1}; **keep** (Passover) Ex 12_{48}; — 10. w. *melāʾkâ* **do work** 1K 11_{28}, *ʿōśê melāʾkâ* workmen 2K 12_{12}; — 11. abs. **act, step in** Gn 41_{34} 1S 14_{6}; — 12. w. *ʾašer* **cause** s.thg to be done Ez 36_{27}, w. *še-* Ec 3_{14}; — 13. **work** Gn 30_{30}; *ʿāśâ betôk* work s.thg into Ex 39_{3}; **be busy** 1K 20_{40}; *ʿāśâ ṭôb* enjoy onesf. † Ec 3_{12}; — 14. w. *ṣedāqâ* exercise justice Gn 18_{19}, w. *nebālâ* commit an outrage Gn 34_{7}, w. *ḥesed* show kindness Gn 24_{12}; — 15. **do**: what have you done to (*le*) us? Gn 20_{9}; oath-formula: *kōh yaʿaśeh-lekā ʾelōhîm* ... 1S 3_{17}; — 16. reflects mng. of previous vb., **do, manage** Je 12_{5}.

nif. (95×): pf. נַעֲשָׂה, נֶעֶשְׂתָה, נֶעֱשָׂתָה, נַעֲשׂוּ; impf. יֵעָשֶׂה, תֵּיעָשֶׂה Ex 25_{31} rd. תֵּעָשֶׂה, תֵּעָשֶׂינָה, יֵעָשׂוּ, תֵּעָשׂ; inf. הֵעָשׂוֹת, sf. הֵעָשׂוֹתוֹ; pt. נַעֲשֶׂה, f. נַעֲשָׂה, pl. נַעֲשִׂים: — 1. **be done**: *maʿaśîm* Gn 20_{9}; be followed, carried out: advice 2S 17_{23}; impers. *yēʿāśeh le* it shall be done to 1S 11_{7}; — 2. **be made, manufactured, prepared**: food Ex 12_{16}, ark (of covt.) Je 3_{16}, sacrifice Ez 43_{18}; be kept: Passover 2K 23_{22f}; be made = created: heavens Ps 33_{6}; *yēʿāśeh le* is used for Ez 15_{5}.

piel: pf. עִשּׂוּ, cj. inf. עַשּׂוֹת: **press, squeeze** Ez $23_{3.8}$ cj. $_{21}$. †

pual (pass. qal): pf. עֻשֵּׂיתִי: **I was made = created** Ps 139_{15}. †

עֲשָׂהאֵל, עֲשָׂה־אֵל: n. pers.

עֵשָׂו: n. pers. **Esau.**

עָשׂוֹר: — 1. (a group of) **ten**: of days Gn 24_{55}; *nēbel ʿāśôr* w. ten strings Ps 33_{2}, *ʿāśôr* || *nēbel* Ps 92_{4}; — 2. date formula *beʿāśôr laḥōdeš* on the 10th day of the month 2K 25_{1}.

עֲשִׂיאֵל: n. pers.

עֲשָׂיָה: n. pers.

עֲשִׂירִי, עֲשִׂרִי: f. עֲשִׂירִית & עֲשִׂרִיָּה: ord. **tenth**: month Gn 8_{5}; *bāʿaśîrî* in the 10th month Gn 8_{5}; day Nu 7_{66}; part Ex 16_{36}; generation Dt 23_{3f}; 10th of a series 1C 12_{14}; 1/10 Is 6_{13}.

עשק: **hitp.**: pf. הִתְעַשְּׂקוּ: **quarrel** Gn 26_{20}. †

עֵשֶׂק: n. loc.

עשׂר: **qal**: impf. יַעְשֹׂר: **confiscate one-tenth of** 1S $8_{15.17}$. †

piel: impf. תְּעַשֵּׂר, אֲעַשְּׂרֶנּוּ; inf. עַשֵּׂר; pt. מְעַשְּׂרִים: — 1. **give one-tenth of, tithe** Gn 28_{22} Dt 14_{22}; — 2. **collect the tithe of** Ne 10_{38}. †

hif.: inf. לַעְשֵׂר Dt 26_{12}, בַּעְשֵׂר Ne 10_{39}: — 1. **tithe** Dt 26_{12}; — 2. **collect the tithe of** Ne 10_{39}. †

עֶשֶׂר (54×): **(a group of) ten**: she-asses Gn 45_{23}, cities Jos 15_{57}, cubits 1K 6_{3}.

עָשָׂר (200×): combining form for numbers fm. 11-19 w. m. nouns, cf. עֶשְׂרֵה: *ʾaḥad ʿāśār* eleven Gn 32_{23} &c.; ↗ gramm.

עֶשְׂרֵה (144×): combining form for numbers fm. 11-19 w. f. nouns, cf. עָשָׂר: *ʾaḥat ʿeśrēh* eleven 2K 23_{36} &c.; ↗ gramm.

עֲשָׂרָה: (group of) **ten** (noun) Gn 18_{32}; **ten** (adj.) Gn 24_{10}.

עִשָּׂרוֹן: pl. עֶשְׂרֹנִים: **tenth part** (of an ephah; dry measure) (P only) Ex 29_{40}.

עֲשִׂרִי: ☞ עֲשִׂירִי.

עֶשְׂרִים (315×): **twenty** Gn 31_{38}; in higher comb. Gn 11_{24}.

עֲשֶׂרֶת (50×): pl. עֲשָׂרֹת: (group of) **ten**: pl. Ex 18_{21}; **ten**: *ʻᵃśeret dᵉbārîm* 10 Commandments Ex 34_{28}; *ʻᵃśeret [šeqel] kesef* Ju 17_{10}.

I **עָשׁ**: **(clothes-)moth** Is 50_9.

II **עָשׁ**: **pus** Ho 5_{12}. †

III **עָשׁ**: (constellation of) **Leo** Jb 9_9. †

עָשׁוֹק: **oppressor** Je 22_3. †

עֲשׁוּקִים Am 3_9 & **עֲשֻׁקִים** Ec 4_1: **oppression**. †

עָשׁוֹת: **wrought** (iron) Ez 27_{19}.

עַשְׁוָת: n. pers.

עָשִׁיר: pl. עֲשִׁירִים, cs. עֲשִׁירֵי, sf. עֲשִׁירֶיהָ: **wealthy, rich** 2S $12_{1f.4}$; as type Je 9_{22}.

עָשַׁן: **qal**: pf. ע׳; impf. יֶעְשַׁן, יֶעֶשְׁנוּ: **be wrapped in smoke, smoke** (vb.): mountain Ex 19_{18}; *ʼaf-yhwh* Dt 29_{19}.

I **עָשָׁן**: cs. עֶשֶׁן & עֲשַׁן, sf. עֲשָׁנוֹ, עֲשָׁנָהּ: — 1. (ascending) **smoke** Gn 15_{17}; — 2. smoke envelops God in theophany 2S 22_9; — 3. = breath of crocodile Jb 41_{12}.

II **עָשָׁן**: n. loc., ☞ בּוֹר עָשָׁן.

עָשֵׁן: pl. עֲשֵׁנִים: **smoking**, mountain Ex 20_{18}, logs Is 7_4. †

עָשַׁק: **qal**: pf. עֲשַׁקְתָּנוּ, עֲשָׁקוּ, עָשַׁקְתִּי, עָשַׁק, ע׳; impf. יַעַשְׁקֻנִי, תַּעֲשְׁקוּ, תַּעֲשֹׁק; inf. sf. עָשְׁקָם; pt. עֲשׁוּקִים, עָשׁוּק, עֹשְׁקֵי, עֲשֻׁקוֹת, עוֹשֵׁק, pass. — 1. **oppress, wrong** s.one 1S 12_{3f}; *ʻāšûq bᵉdam* burdened w. the blood of Pr 28_{17}; — 2. **extort, exploit** Lv 5_{21}; cogn. acc. *ʻāšaq ʻošeq* Lv 5_{23}.

pual: pt. מְעֻשָּׁקָה: **abused** Is 23_{12}. †

עֵשֶׁק: n. pers.

עֹשֶׁק: — 1. **oppression** Is 54_{14}; — 2. **extortion** Lv 5_{23}.

עָשְׁקָה: **oppression** Is 38_{14}. †

עֲשֻׁקִים: ☞ עֲשׁוּקִים.

עָשַׁר: **qal**: pf. עָשַׁרְתִּי; impf. יֶעְשַׁר: **become rich** Ho 12_9 Jb 15_{29}. †

hif.: pf. הֶעֱשַׁרְתִּי; impf. יַעֲשִׁר, תַּעֲשִׁיר, וָאַעְשִׁר Zc 11_5, וַיַּעֲשִׁירוּ, תַּעְשְׁרֶנָּה Ps 65_{10}, יַעְשְׁרֶנּוּ 1S 17_{25}; pt. מַעֲשִׁיר: — 1. **make** s.one **rich** Gn 14_{23}; — 2. abs. **gain riches** Je 5_{27}.

hitp.: pt. מִתְעַשֵּׁר: **pretend to be rich** Pr 13_7. †

עֹשֶׁר: sf. עָשְׁרוֹ: **riches** Gn 31_{16}; *ʻāśâ ʻōšer* gain riches Je 17_{11}.

עשׁשׁ: **qal**: pf. עָשְׁשָׁה, עָשֵׁשׁוּ: **become weak** Ps 6_8 31_{10}; **dissolve** Ps 31_{11}. †

[I **עשׁת**: **qal**: pf. עָשְׁתוּ Je 5_{28} text corr. †]

II **עשׁת**: **hitp.**: impf. יִתְעַשֵּׁת: w. *lᵉ* **turn out to take notice** of Jon 1_6. †

***עֶשֶׁת**: cs. עֶשֶׁת: **slab** SS 5_{14}. †

עַשְׁתּוּת: **thought** (?) Jb 12_5. †

עַשְׁתֵּי: f. עַשְׁתֵּין: combining form with *ʻāśār/ʻeśrē*, **eleven(th)** 2K 25_2; ☞ gramm.

***עֶשְׁתֹּנֶת**: pl. sf. עֶשְׁתֹּנֹתָיו: **thought, plan** Ps 146_4.

עַשְׁתָּרוֹת: ☞ עַשְׁתָּרֹת.

עַשְׁתֹּרֶת: n. of goddess, **Astarte, Ashtoreth** 1K 11_5.

***עַשְׁתֶּרֶת**: pl. cs. עַשְׁתְּרֹת: *ʻaštᵉrōt ṣōʼnekā* Dt 7_{13} $28_{4.18.51}$ **increase** (oth.: ewes & she-goats) of your flock. †

עַשְׁתָּרֹת & עַשְׁתָּרוֹת: n. loc.

עַשְׁתְּרָתִי (so vocal. in KBH₃; oth.: ע׳): gent. of עַשְׁתָּרֹת 1C 11_{44}. †

עֵת (290×): עֶת־ Je 51_{33}, עֵת־, sf. עִתּוֹ, עִתָּם; pl. עִתִּים, sf. עִתֶּיךָ & עִתּוֹת, sf. עִתּוֹתַי; f., later m.: — 1. **time**: both a **point of time** & a **lapse of time**: *ʻēt wāfegaʻ* time & chance Ec 9_{11}; *ʻēt ʻereb* time of evening Gn 8_{11}, *ʻēt pᵉquddātām* time of their punishment Je 8_{12}; — 2. *ʻēt* preceding dependent vb.: a) inf.: *ʻēt ṣēʼt šōʼᵉbôt* = time when the women come forth to draw water Gn 24_{11}; b) fin. vb. *ʻēt tāmûṭ raglām* Dt 32_{35}; c) clause *ʻēt yôlēdâ yālādâ* time when she who is to give birth gives birth Mi 5_2; — 3. *ʻēt* + *lᵉ* & inf.: Ec 3_{2-8}, cf. *ʻet-bêt-yhwh lᵉhibbānôt* time when … is built Hg 1_2; — 4. idioms: *bāʿēt hahîʾ* at that time Gn 21_{22}; *kāʿēt māḥār* & *māḥār kāʿēt hazzōʾt* tomorrow at this time Ex 9_{18} Jos 11_6; *kāʿēt ḥayyâ* next year at this time Gn $18_{10 \cdot 14}$ 2K 4_{16f}; *kāʿēt* now Nu 23_{23}, *bāʿēt* at the right time Ec 10_{17}; *weloʾ-ʿēt* before the time Jb 22_{16}; *leʿet yôm beyôm* from day to day 1C 12_{23}; — 5. **(the right) time** (for an event): who gives the rain *beʿittô* in its time Je 5_{24}; why should you die *belōʾ ittekā* before your time? Ec 7_{17}; — 6. **(the eschatological**, end-) **time**: *ʿittāh* of Babylon Is 13_{22}; — 7. pl. *ʿittîm* : *bāʿittîm hāhēm* in those times Dn 11_{14}; **epochs** Est 1_{13}; **periods** (of trouble) Ps 9_{10}.

עֵת* קָצִין: loc. עִתָּה ק׳: n. loc. Jos 19_{13}. †

עתד: **piel**: impv. sf. עַתְּדָהּ: **take care of** Pr 24_{27}. †

hitp.: pf. הִתְעַתְּדוּ: **prove** prepared, **destined** Jb 15_{28}. †

עֲתִדֹת: F עָתִיד.

עַתָּה (425×): Ez 23_{43} Ps 74_6 Kt עַתְּ, עֱתָּה: — 1. **now** (at the present moment) Nu 24_{17}; — 2. (so) **now** (in the present situation) Gn 19_9; — 3. **now** (after what has happened) Gn 22_{12}; — 4. *weʿattâ* **and now** (frequent introduction of new thought or section) Gn 3_{22}; **but now** Gn 32_{11}; — 5. *ʿad-ʿattâ* **until now** Gn 32_5; **until then** 2K 13_{23}; — 6. *mēʿattâ* **from now on** Is 48_6; — 7. spec.: *ʿattâ* now = already Ex 5_5; = therefore Gn 31_{28}; = so now (admission) Gn 26_{29}; *lōʾ ʿattâ* = no more now Is 29_{22}; *ʿattâ zeh* now therefore 1K 17_{24}, just now 2K 5_{22}; *kî ʿattâ* surely now Gn 31_{42}, but now 1S 14_{30}.

***עָתוּד**: pl. עֲתוּדִים (Qr עֲתִידִים), f. sf. עֲתוּדֹתֵיהֶם (Kt עֲתִידֹתֵיהֶם): — 1. **ready** Est 8_{13}; — 2. pl. f. **supplies** Is 10_{13} Qr. †

***עַתּוּד**: pl. עַתּוּדִים, עַתֻּדִים, cs. עַתּוּדֵי: **ram, he-goat** Gn $31_{10 \cdot 12}$; metaph. **leader** Is 14_9.

עִתִּי: **available** Lv 16_{21}. †

עַתַּי: n. pers.

עָתִיד: pl. עֲתִידִים, עֲתִ(י)דֹת (F עָתוּד): — 1. **ready** Jb 15_{24}, w. inf. Jb 3_8; — 2. pl. f. things prepared = **events to come** Dt 32_{35}; supplies, **treasury** Is 10_{13} Kt.

עֲתָיָה: n. pers.

עָתִיק: **select, choice** Is 23_{18}. †

***עַתִּיק**: pl. עַתִּיקִים, cs. עַתִּיקֵי: — 1. removed, **weaned** Is 28_9; — 2. **handed down from antiquity** 1C 4_{22}. †

עֲתָךְ: n. loc.

עַתְלַי: n. pers.

עֲתַלְיָה: n. pers. m. & f.

עֲתַלְיָהוּ: n. pers. f.

עתם: **nif.** נֶעְתַּם Is 9_{18}; many emend, but recent sugg.: *nʿt-m* (F *nwʿ* qal pf. 3. sg. f. + enclitic F *-m*, thus: writhe. †

עָתְנִי: n. pers.

עָתְנִיאֵל: n. pers.

עתק: **qal**: pf. עָתְקוּ, עָתְקָה; impf. יֶעְתַּק: — 1. **move on** fm. (*min*) Jb 14_{18} 18_4; — 2. **grow old** Jb 21_7; **grow weak** (?) Ps 6_8. †

hif.: pf. הֶעְתִּיקוּ; impf. וַיַּעְתֵּק; pt. מַעְתִּיק: — 1. **move on** Gn 12_8 26_{22}; w. *min* **leave** s.one **in the lurch, fail** Jb 32_{15}; — 2. **remove** s.thg **fm. its place** Jb 9_5; — 3. **transcribe, copy** Pr 25_1. †

עָתָק: (severed fm. custom) **forward, insolent** 1S 2_3 Ps 31_{19} 75_6 94_4. †

עָתֵק: **hereditary** Pr 8_{18}. †

עֵת* קָצִין: F after עֵת.

עתר: **qal**: impf. יֶעְתַּר: **pray, plead**: w. *le* Gn 25_{21}, w. *ʾel* Ex 8_{26}.

nif.: pf. נֶעְתַּר; impf. וַיֵּעָתֵר, וַיֵּעָתֶר; inf. הֵעָתֵר־, נַעְתּוֹר: **be moved by entreaties**, (*le* of) Gn 25_{21}, (*le* for) 2S 21_{14}.

hif.: pf. הַעְתַּרְתִּי; impf. תַּעְתִּיר, אַעְתִּיר; impv. הַעְתִּירוּ: **pray, plead**, (*le* for) Ex 8_5, (*le* before) Ex 10_{17}, (*ʾel*) Ex 8_4.

***עָתָר**: cs. עֲתַר: **fragrance** Ez 8_{11}. †

עֶתֶר: n. loc.

עֲתֶרֶת: Je 33_6: text? †

פ

פּא: ↗ פֹּה.

פאה: **hif.**: impf. אַפְאֵיהֶם: **dash to pieces** Dt 32_{26}, but text dub. †

I **פֵּאָה** (83×, 47× Ez, 32× P): cs. פְּאַת; du. cs. פַּאֲתֵי Nu 24_{17}; pl. פֵּאֹת: **side, edge**: of field Lv 19_9; of head = temple Lv 19_{27}; of beard 19_{27}; spec. side of courtyard: *pe'at negeb* S. side Ex 27_9 (& oth. directions $_{11\cdot12\cdot13}$).

II **פֵּאָה**: **piece, part** Ne 9_{22}. †

III **פֵּאָה**: cs. פְּאַת: **luxury** (of a couch) = luxurious Am 3_{12}. †

I **פאר**: **piel**: impf. תְּפָאֵר: trad.: go over (the branches of olive-tree) again Dt 24_{20}; but better: **knock down** (olives) **with a stick**. †

II **פאר**: **piel**: pf. פֵּאֲרָךְ; impf. יְפָאֵר, אֲפָאֵר; inf. פָּאֵר: **endow** s.one **with glory**, **glorify**, **exalt** Is 55_5.

hitp.: impf. יִתְפָּאֵר, יִתְפָּאַר, אֶתְפָּאָר; impv. & inf. הִתְפָּאֵר: — 1. **manifest one's glory** in/on Is 44_{23}; — 2. **boast**, vaunt onesf. before (*'al*) Ju 7_2 Is 10_{15}; — 3. spec. phr. *hitpā'ēr 'ālay* Ex 8_5: prove yourself glorious before me = please determine for me? (oth.: text corr.).

פְּאֵר: sf. פְּאֵרְךָ; pl. פְּאֵרִים, cs. פַּאֲרֵי, sf. פַּאֲרֵכֶם: **head-dress**: for women Is 3_{20}, men Ez 24_{17}, priests Ex 39_{28}.

***פֹּארָה**: pl. פֹּארֹת (Ez 17_6 פארות), sf. פֹּארֹתָיו: **shoots** (of a vine) Ez 17_6; **branches** (of a tree) Ez $31_{5f\cdot8\cdot12f}$. †

פֻּארָה: coll. **branches** Is 10_{33}. †

פָּארוּר: **heat**: *qibbēṣ pā'rûr* gather heat = **glow** (in agitation) (of face) Jl 2_6 Na 2_{11}. †

פָּארָן: n. terr.

***פַּג**, or rather prob. *פַּגָּה: pl. sf. פַּגֶּיהָ: **unripe fig** SS 2_{13}. †

פִּגּוּל: **meat fm. sacrifice which has become unclean** because not eaten within specified time Lv 7_{18}.

פָּגַע: **qal**: pf. פ׳, וּפָגַעְתָּ, פָּגְעוּ; impf. וַיִּפְגַּע, יִפְגָּעֶנּוּ, תִּפְגְּעוּ, יִפְגְּעוּן; impv. פְּגַע, פִּגְעוּ; inf. פְּגֹעַ, לִפְגֹּעַ: — 1. w. *be*: **encounter** s.one Gn 32_2; — 2. w. acc.: **meet, fall in with** 1S 10_5; — 3. w. *be*: **reach** a place Gn 28_{11}; — 4. w. *be*: **fall upon, attack** s.one 1K 2_{25}; **molest** (a woman) Ru 2_{22}; — 5. w. acc.: **assail, attack** Ex 5_3; — 6. w. *be*: **put pressure on** s.one, **urge strongly on** s.one (*le* on behalf of) Gn 23_8; = intercede with, pray to Je 7_{16}; — 7. *pāga' gebûl be* the border touches Jos 16_7.

hif.: pf. הִפְגִּיעַ, הִפְגַּעְתִּי, הִפְגִּעוּ; impf. יַפְגִּיעַ; pt. מַפְגִּיעַ: — 1. w. acc. of thg. & *be* + pers., **let** s.thg **strike** s.one Is 53_6; — 2. w. *le* **intercede** for Is 53_{12}, abs. 59_{16}; — 3. **urge strongly** on s.one Je 36_{25}. †

פֶּגַע: **occurrence**, chance 1K 5_{18} Ec 9_{11}. †

פַּגְעִיאֵל: n. pers.

פגר: **piel**: pf. פִּגְּרוּ: w. *min* & inf. **be too feeble, tired** to ... 1S $30_{10\cdot21}$. †

פֶּגֶר: פֶּגֶר; pl. פְּגָרִים, cs. פִּגְרֵי, sf. פִּגְרֵיכֶם: **corpse** (of man) Lv 26_{30}, **carcass** (of animal) Gn 15_{11}; metaph. of lifeless idols Lv 26_{30}; *pegārîm mētîm* 2K 19_{35}.

פגשׁ: **qal**: pf. פָּגַשְׁתִּי, פָּגְשׁוּ; impf. יִפְגָּשְׁךָ, וַתִּפְגֹּשׁ, אֶפְגְּשֵׁם, וַיִּפְגְּשֵׁהוּ; inf. פְּגֹשׁ: w. acc. or *be*, **fall in with, meet** Gn 32_{18}.

nif.: pf. נִפְגָּשׁוּ: **meet** (each other) Ps 85_{11} Pr 22_2 29_{13}. †

piel: impf. יְפַגְּשׁוּ: **meet** Jb 5_{14}. †

פָּדָה: qal: pf. פְּדִיתִיךָ, פֶּדְךָ, פָּדָם, פָּדִיתָ(ה), פ׳, פְּדִיתִים; impf. וַיִּפְדְּךָ, וַיִּפְדּוּ, אֶפְדֶּה, תִּפְדֶּה, תִּפְדּוּנִי, אֶפְדֵּם; impv. פְּדֵנוּ, פְּדֵנִי, פְּדֵה; inf. פְּדוֹת, abs. פָּדֹה; pt. פֹּדֶה, sf. הַפֹּדְךָ (sf. w. art.!) Dt 13_6, pass. pl. cs. פְּדוּיֵי, sf. פְּדוּיָו: — 1. **ransom, redeem**: the first-born Ex 13_{13}; Jonathan 1S 14_{45}; God ransoms, redeems his people 2S 7_{23}; — 2. (idea of 'ransom' recedes): **redeem, deliver** (genl. theol. affirmation) 1K 1_{29}.

nif.: pf. נִפְדָּתָה; impf. יִפָּדֶה: — 1. **be ransomed**: female slave Lv 19_{20}, cf. 27_{29}; — 2. **be redeemed**: Zion Is 1_{27}. †

hif.: pf. הֶפְדָּהּ: **let** s.one **be ransomed** Ex 21_8. †

hof.: inf. הָפְדֵּה: **be brought to ransom** Lv 19_{20}. †

פְּדַהְאֵל: n. pers.

פְּדָהצוּר: n. pers.

פְּדוּיִם: Kt פְּדֻיִם Nu 3_{51} † : cs. פְּדוּיֵי: plural form only, **ransom** Nu $3_{46 \cdot 48f \cdot 51}$. †

פָּדוֹן: n. pers.

פְּדוּת & Ex 8_{19} † פְּדֻת: **redemption** Ps 111_9 130_7; Ex 8_{19} txt. corr.?. †

פְּדָיָה: n. pers.

פְּדָיָהוּ: n. pers.

פִּדְיוֹם: **ransom** Nu 3_{49}. †

***פִּדְיוֹן**, ***פִּדְיֹן** (or ***פִּדְי(ו)ן**): cs. פִּדְי(וֹ)ן: **ransom money** Ex 21_{30} Ps 49_9. †

פַּדָּן: cs. פַּדַּן; loc. פַּדֶּנָה; n. loc., mostly w. אֲרָם.

[**פדע**: Jb 33_{24} פְּדָעֵהוּ: text corr.; some mss. rd. פְּרָעֵהוּ. †]

פֶּדֶר: פֶּדֶר; sf. פִּדְרוֹ: **suet** Lv $1_{8 \cdot 12}$ 8_{20}. †

פֶּה (490×): cs. פִּי, sf. פִּיהוּ > פִּיו, פִּיךָ, פִּי, פִּימוֹ, פִּינוּ, פִּיהֶם; pl. פִּיּוֹת Pr 5_4, פֵּיוֹת Ju 3_{16}: — 1. **mouth** (of man or animal): man Ex 4_{16}, ass Nu 22_{28}, beak of bird Gn 8_{11}; — 2. metaph. of openings: mouth of well Gn 29_2, of sack 42_{27}, of cave Jos 10_{18}; = collar Jb 30_{18}; — 3. *pî ḥereb* = **edge** of sword Gn 34_{26}; — 4. phr.: *peh ʾaḥad* unanimously Jos 9_2; *peh ʾel-peh* mouth to mouth = face to face Nu 12_8; *mippeh ʾel-peh* from one end to the other Ezr 9_{11}; *bᵉkol-peh* with open mouth Is 9_{11}; *šāʾal ʾet-pîhā* ask what **she** thinks Gn 24_{57}; — 5. *pî yhwh* **mouth of Y.**, in many ctxts.: *dibber bᵉpîw* 1K 8_{15}, *rûᵃḥ pîw* Ps 33_6; — 6. mouth = **statement, decision, command**: *ʿal-pîkā* Gn 41_{40}; *pî ʿēdîm* statement of witnesses Nu 35_{30}; oft. of command of Y. (F 5) 1S 15_{24}; — 7. w. preps.: a) *kᵉfî* **according to** Lv 25_{52}; *kᵉfîkā* as much as you Jb 33_6; *kᵉfî ʾᵃšer* inasmuch as Ma 2_9; b) *lᵉfî* **according to**: *lᵉfîhen* according to them Lv 25_{51}; *lᵉfî rōb haššānîm* the more the years are Lv 25_{16}; c) *ʿal-pî* **according to** Gn 43_7, *ʿal-pî ʾᵃšer* according to what Lv 27_8; — 8. *pî šᵉnayim* **two parts** Dt 21_{17}; = 2/3 2K 2_9.

פֹּה (54×), פוֹ Ez $40_{10 \cdot 26}$, פֹּא Jb 38_{11} †: **here** Gn 19_{12}; **(to) here** 2K 2_2; *mippōh, mippô* on this/that side Ez 40_{10}; *ʿad-pōh* this far Jb 38_{11}.

פּוּאָה: n. pers.

פוג: **qal**: impf. וַיָּפָג, תָּפוּג: **be feeble, numb, cold** Gn 45_{26} Hb 1_4 Ps 77_3. †

nif.: pf. נְפוּגוֹתִי: **be prostrated, powerless** Ps 38_9. †

***פוּגָה**: cs. פוּגַת: **slackening, relaxation** La 2_{18}. †

פּוּוָה: n. pers.

I **פוח**: **qal**: impf. יָפוּחַ: **blow** (of day), evid. ref. to evening breeze SS 2_{17} 4_6. †

hif.: impv. הָפִיחִי: **let** (garden) **send forth fragrance** SS4_{16}. †

II **פוח**: identical with I פוח?: **qal**: impf. יָפִיחַ, אָפִיחַ, יָפִיחוּ: — 1. w. *ʿal* Ez 21_{36} & *bᵉ* Ps 10_5: blow heavily, **blast**; — 2. w. acc. **knock out, produce** Pr 6_{19}.

פּוּט: n. peop., (portion of) **Libyans** Gn 10_6.

פּוּטִיאֵל: n. pers.

פּוֹטִיפַר: n. pers.

פּוֹטִי פֶרַע: n. pers.; > פּוֹטִיפַר.

פּוּךְ: — 1. **black eye-paint** (lead sulfide) 2K 9_{30}; — 2. a special kind of **hard** (black?) **cement** Is 54_{11}.

פּוֹל: **broad beans, horse-beans,** *Vicia faba L.* 2S 17_{28} Ez 4_9. †

I **פּוּל**: n. peop., unknown, Is 66_{19}. †

II **פּוּל**: n. pers., = Tiglath-Pileser III 2K 15_9 1C 5_{26}. †

פּוּן: **qal**: impf. אָפוּנָה: Ps 88_{16}, txt. corr.?, ℱ comm. †

פּוּנֶה: הַפּוּנֶה 2C 25_{23}, rd. הַפִּנָּה. †

פּוּנִי: gent. of פֻּוָּה Nu 26_{23}. †

פּוּנֹן: n. loc.

פּוּעָה: n. pers. f.

פּוּץ: **qal**: impf. נָפוּץ, תְּפוּצֶינָה, תְּפֻצֶין, יָפֻצוּ; impv. פֻּצוּ: — 1. **scatter, disperse** (intrans.): of men Gn 11_4, animals Ez 34_5; — 2. w. *min*, **be pushed out** (fm. property) Ez 46_{18}; — 3. **overflow** Pr 5_{16}.

nif.: pf. נָפוֹצָה, נָפֹצוּ, נְפוֹצוֹתֶם; pt. f. נָפֹצֶת (Kt. נפצית) 2S 18_8, pl. נְפֹצוֹת, נְפוֹצִים: — 1. **be scattered, dispersed**: nations Gn 10_{18}, animals 1K 22_{17}; — 2. **spread out** (intrans.), **get scattered** (of battle) 2S 18_8.

hif.: pf. הֱפִיצְךָ, הֱפִ(י)צֹתֶם, הֲפִצֹתִי, הֵפִיץ, הֱפִיצָהוּ, הֱפִיצָם, הֲפִיצוֹתִים, הֲפִצוֹתִיךָ; impf. אֲפִיצֵם, וַיְפִיצֵם, וָאָפִיץ, וַיָּפֶץ, יָפֵץ, יָפִיץ; impv. הָפֵץ; inf. הָפִיץ, sf. הֲפִיצֵנִי, הֲפִיצִי; pt. מְפִיצִים, מֵפִיץ: — 1. w. acc. **scatter, disperse** Gn 11_{8f}; **let** s.thg **pour out, gush out** Jb 40_{11}; — 2. **strew, scatter**: arrows 2S 22_{15}; — 3. w. acc. **chase** Jb 18_{11}; — 4. **be scattered** 1S 13_8.

פּוּצַי Zp 3_{10} txt. corr., ℱ comm. †

פּוּק: **qal**: pf. פָּקוּ ! **stagger** Is 28_7. †

hif.: impf. וַיָּפֶק, תָּפֵק, יָפִיק; pt. pl. מְפִיקִים: — 1. **wobble** Je 10_4; — 2. meet, **gain** Pr 3_{13}; — 3. **let** s.one **find, grant** Ps 144_{13}; w. *nafšekā* your desire Is 58_{10}.

פּוּקָה: **stumbling** (i.e. pang of conscience) 1S 25_{31}. †

פּוּר: **hif.**: pf. הֵפִיר: **destroy** Ez 17_{19} Ps 33_{10}. †

פּוּר: **lot** Est 3_7; therefore פּוּרִים, פֻּרִים **Purim** Est 9_{26}.

פּוּרָה: **trough of wine-press** Is 63_3 Hg 2_{16}. †

פּוֹרָתָא: n. pers.

פּוּשׁ: **qal**: pf. פִּשְׁתֶּם, וּפָשׁוּ; impf. תָּפוּשׁוּ Qr, תָּפוּשִׁי Kt Je 50_{11}: **frisk, paw the ground** Je 50_{11} Hb 1_8 Ma 3_{20}. †

nif.: pf. נָפֹשׁוּ Na 3_{18}: txt. corr. †

פּוּתִי: gent. 1C 2_{53}. †

פַּז: פָּז: trad. **pure gold**; but perh. **chrysolite** (olivine), confused w. topaz in antiquity Is 13_{11}.

I **פזז**: **hof.**: pt. מוּפָז: denom. of פָּז: set with pure gold? chrysolite? 1K 10_{18}. †

II **פזז**: **qal**: impf. וַיָּפֹזּוּ: **be nimble** Gn 49_{24}. †

piel: pt. מְפַזֵּז: **leap** 2S 6_{16}. †

פזר: **qal**: pt. pass. פְּזוּרָה: **isolated, dispersed** Je 50_{17}. †

nif.: pf. נִפְזְרוּ: **be scattered** Ps 141_7. †

piel: pf. פִּזַּר, פִּזַּרְתָּ, פִּזְּרוּ; impf. יְפַזֵּר, וַתְּפַזְּרִי; pt. מְפַזֵּר: **disperse, scatter** Jl 4_2 Ps 53_6; **strew, scatter** Ps 147_{16}.

pual: pt. מְפֻזָּר: **scattered** Est 3_8. †

I **פַּח**: פַּח; pl. פַּחִים: (self-springing) **birdtrap** Is 24_{17}; many phr., e.g. *hāyâ leppaḥ* Jos 23_{13}.

II **פַּח***: pl. פַּחִים, cs. פַּחֵי: **leaf** (of gold) Ex 39_3, (thin) **plate** Nu 17_3. †

פָּחַד: **qal**: pf. פָּחֲדוּ, פָּחֲדוּ, פ׳; impf. תִּפְחַד, יִפְחֲדוּ, אֶפְחַד: **tremble** (in terror) Dt 28_{66}; cogn. acc. *pāḥad paḥad* tremble Dt 28_{67}; *pāḥad ʾel* come trembling to Ho 3_5; tremble (with joy) Is 60_5.

piel: impf. וַתְּפַחֵד; pt. מְפַחֵד: **be trembling, be in dread** Is 51_{13} Pr 28_{14}. †

hif.: pf. הִפְחִיד: **make** s.thg **shake** Jb 4_{14}. †

I **פַּחַד**: פַּחַד; sf. פַּחְדּוֹ, פַּחְדְּךָ; pl. פְּחָדִים: **trembling, terror** Ex 15_{16}; *paḥad le* terror of Ps 31_{12}; w. gen. or sf. of cause of terror, *paḥad ʾôyēb* terror (one has) of the enemy Ps 64_2; — 2. terror caused by God: *paḥad yhwh* 1S 11_7, *paḥdekā* Ps 119_{120}; — 3. *paḥad yiṣḥāq* a designation of God Gn $31_{42.53}$.

II *פַּחַד: pl. sf. פַּחֲדָו: **thigh** Jb 40_{17}. †

*פַּחְדָּה: sf. פַּחְדָּתִי Je 2_{19}: txt. corr., rd. perh. פְּחַדְתִּי. †

פֶּחָה: cs. פַּחַת 2K 18_{24} & פַּחַת Hg 2_{21}, sf. פֶּחָתֶךָ; pl. פַּחוֹת, cs. פַּחֲוֹת, sf. פַּחֲוֹתֶיהָ: **governor** (a rather vague title) 1K 10_{15}.

פחז: **qal**: pt. פֹּחֲזִים: **be insolent, undisciplined** Ju 9_4 Zp 3_4. †

פַּחַז: Gn 49_4: trad. noun **recklessness**, or adj. **reckless** (= overflowing); but txt. corr. ? †

*פַּחֲזוּת: sf. פַּחֲזוּתָם: **loose talk, boastful tales** Je 23_{32}. †

פחח: **hif.**: inf. הָפֵחַ: ctxt. demands **hof.**: **be captured, chained** Is 42_{22}. †

פֶּחָם: **charcoal** (when not glowing) Is 44_{12} 54_{16} Pr 26_{21}. †

פַּחַת: פַּחַת; pl. פְּחָתִים: **pit** 2S 17_9.

פַּחַת מוֹאָב: n. pers.

פְּחֶתֶת: **hollow (eaten away)** Lv 13_{55}. †

פִּטְדָה: **chrysolith** Ex 28_{17}.

פטירים: 1C 9_{33} Kt: ↗ פָּטַר qal 3.

פַּטִּישׁ: **sledge-hammer** Is 41_7 Je 23_{29} 50_{23}. †

פָּטַר: **qal**: pf. פ׳; impf. וַיִּפְטַר; pt. פּוֹטֵר, pass. pl. פְּטֻרֵי, פְּטוּרִים: — 1. w. *mippᵉnê*: **vanish, escape** 1S 19_{10}; — 2. w. *mayim*: **let out** (water through irrigation gate or the like) Pr 17_{14}; — 3. **let s.one off duty** 2C 23_8; — 4. *pᵉṭûrê ṣîṣîm* garlands? buds? 1K 6_{18}.

hif.: impf. יַפְטִירוּ: w. *bᵉśāfâ*: **make a wry mouth** (in contempt) Ps 22_8. †

פֶּטֶר: what opens a mother's womb, **first-born** Ex 13_2.

*פִּטְרָה: cs. פִּטְרַת: **first-born** (no distinction w. *peṭer*) Nu 8_{16}. †

פִּי: ↗ פֶּה.

פִּי־בֶסֶת: n. loc.

פִּיד: sf. פִּידוֹ: **ruin, destruction** Pr 24_{22}.

פִּי(־)הַחִירֹ(וֹ)ת: n. loc.

פֵּיוֹת: ↗ פֶּה.

פִּיחַ: **soot** Ex $9_{8.10}$. †

פִּיכֹל: n. pers.

פִּילֶגֶשׁ: ↗ פִּלֶגֶשׁ.

פִּים: a weight, **pim**, ca. 7 1/2 gm. = 1/4 oz. 1S 13_{21}. †

פִּימָה: **fat** Jb 15_{27}. †

פִּינְחָס, פִּנְחָס 1S 1_3 †: n. pers.

פִּינֹן: n. pers.

פִּיפִיּוֹת: **with double edge(s)**: threshing-sledge Is 41_{15}, sword Ps 149_6. †

פִּישׁוֹן: n. river.

פִּיתוֹן: n. pers.

פַּךְ: **juglet** 1S 10_1 2K $9_{1.3}$. †

פכה: **piel**: pt. מְפַכִּים: **trickle** Ez 47_2. †

פֹּכֶרֶת הַצְּבָיִים: n. pers.

פלא: **nif.**: pf. נִפְלֵאת 3 f. sg. Dt 30_{11}, נִפְלָאתָה (txt.?) 2S 1_{26}, נִפְלְאוּ; impf. יִפָּלֵא; pt. נִפְלָאִים, נִפְלָאוֹת, sf. נִפְלְאוֹתָיו: — 1. be treated as different, unsuitable > **be too hard, difficult**, w. *min* for Gn 18_{14}; — 2. **be extraordinary, marvellous** 2S 1_{26}, w. *min* be too marvellous for Pr 30_{18}; — 3. *niflā'ôt*: w. *dibber* speak unheard-of words Dn 11_{36}: marvellous deeds Jb 37_{14}, esp. **wonders** Ex 3_{20}.

piel: inf. פַּלֵּא: w. *neder* fulfill a special vow Lv 22_{21}. †

hif.: pf. הִפְלָא, הִפְלִ(י)א Dt 28_{59}; impf. יַפְלִא; impv. הַפְלֵה!; inf. הַפְלִיא, הַפְלֵא; pt. מַפְלִא: — 1. w. acc. **do** s.thg **in a surprising, strange way**: w. *makkôt*, inflict especially severe plagues Dt 28_{59}, w. *ḥesed*, show marvellous solidarity Ps 31_{22}; — 2. w. *lᵉ* & inf.: *maflî' laᵃ'śôt* who does wonderful things Ju 13_{19}; *hiflî' lᵉhē'āzēr* he is marvellously helped 2C 26_{15}; — 3. act wonderfully Is 29_{14}; — 4. adv. *haflē'* in a wonderful way Is 29_{14}.

פֶּלֶא: sf. פִּלְאֲךָ, פִּלְאֶךָ; pl. פְּלָאִים & פְּלָאוֹת: — 1. **s.thg extraordinary, marvel** Ex 15_{11}; *pele' yô'ēṣ* a marvel of a counsellor Is 9_5; — 2. pl. *pᵉlā'îm* adv. in an astonishing manner La 1_9; *pᵉlā'ôt* marvels Ps 119_{129}.

פִּלְאִי: Qr פֶּלִ(א)י, rd. Kt פִּלְאִי Ju 13_{18}; f. פְּלִאִיָּה = Qr פְּלִיאָה, rd Kt פְּלִאִיָּה Ps 139_6: **wonderful, marvellous.** †

פַּלְאִי: gent. of **פַּלּוּא**.

פְּלָאיָה: n. pers.

פלג: **nif.**: pf. **נִפְלְגָה**: **be divided** Gn 10_{25} 1C 1_{19}. †

piel: pf. **פִּלַּג**: **cut open, split** (channel) Jb 38_{25}; for *pallag* Ps 55_{10} rd. *peleg* 'split.' †

I **פֶּלֶג**: pl. **פְּלָגִים**, cs. **פַּלְגֵי**, sf. **פְּלָגָיו**: **artificial water-channel, canal** Is 30_{25}; metaph. *palgê šemen* Jb 29_6.

II **פֶּלֶג**: n. pers. Gn 10_{25} 11_{16-19} 1C $1_{19.25}$. †

***פְּלַגָּה**: pl. **פְּלַגּוֹת**: — 1. **division** Ju 5_{15f}; — 2. **watercourse** Jb 20_{17}. †

***פְּלֻגָּה**: pl. **פְּלֻגּוֹת**: **division** 2C 35_5. †

פִּילֶגֶשׁ, **פִּלֶגֶשׁ**: sf. **פִּילַגְשׁוֹ**, **פִּילַגְשֵׁהוּ**; pl. **פִּ(י)לַגְשִׁים**, cs. **פִּלַגְשֵׁי**, sf. **פִּילַגְשָׁיו**, **פִּלַגְשֵׁיהֶם**: **concubine** Gn 22_{24}.

פִּלְדָּשׁ: n. pers.

פְּלָדֹת: Na 2_4: many assume 'steel,' but txt. corr. †

פלה: **nif.**: pf. **נִפְלֵיתִי**, **נִפְלֵינוּ**: w. *min*, **be treated differently, be distinguished** Ex 33_{16}; Ps 139_{14} txt. corr.? †

hif.: pf. **הִפְלָה**, **הִפְלֵיתִי**; impf. **יַפְלֶה**; impv. **הַפְלֵה**, ꟳ *pl'* hif.: **treat with distinction, differently** Ex 8_{18}; w. *bên* … *ûbên* make a distinction between … and Ex 9_4 11_7. †

פַּלּוּא: n. pers.

פלח: **qal**: pt. **פֹּלֵחַ**: trad. split, but txt. corr.? †

piel: impf. **יְפַלַּח**, **תְּפַלַּחְנָה**: **split open** (trans.) Pr 7_{23} Jb 16_{13}; — 2. **cut into slices** 2K 4_{39}; — 3. (split the mouth of the womb), **bring forth** (young) Jb 39_3. †

פֶּלַח: — 1. **slice** (of cake of figs) 1S 30_{12}, (of pomegranate) SS 4_3 6_7; — 2. (upper) **millstone** Ju 9_{53} 2S 11_{21}, *pelaḥ taḥtît* lower millstone Jb 41_{16}. †

פִּלְחָא: n. pers.

פלט: **qal**: pf. **פָּלְטוּ**: **escape** Ez 7_{16}. †

piel: impf. **תְּפַלְּטֵנִי**, **יְפַלְּטֵהוּ**, **תְּפַלֵּט**, **פַּלְּטוּ**, **אֲפַלְּטֵהוּ**, **וַתְּפַלְּטֵמוֹ**; impv. **פַּלְּטָה**, **פַּלְּטֵנִי**; inf. **פַּלֵּט**; pt. **מְפַלְּטִי**: — 1. **bring to safety** 2S 22_{44}; w. *mišpāṭô* carry one's case through Jb 23_7; *mᵉfallᵉṭî* my deliverer 2S 22_2; — 2. (of cow) **bring forth** (young) = calve Jb 21_{10}.

hif.: impf. **יַפְלִיט**: **bring to safety** Is 5_{29} Mi 6_{14}. †

פֶּלֶט: n. pers.

I **פַּלְטִי**: n. pers. Nu 13_9 1S 25_{44}. †

II **פַּלְטִי**: gent. of **בֵּית פֶּלֶט**.

פִּלְטַי: n. pers.

פַּלְטִיאֵל: n. pers.

פְּלַטְיָה: n. pers.

פְּלַטְיָהוּ: n. pers.

פְּלִיאָה, **פֶּלִא**, **פֶּלִי** & **פִּלְאִי**: ꟳ **פֶּלֶא**.

פְּלָיָה: n. pers.

פָּלִיט: pl. cs. **פְּלִטֵי**, sf. **פְּלִטָיו**: **fugitive** (fm. danger) Gn 14_{13}, oft. coll. Jos 8_{22}.

***פָּלֵיט**: pl. **פְּלֵ(י)טִ(י)ם**: **fugitives**, those **spared** Nu 21_{29}.

פְּלֵטָה, **פְּלֵיטָה**: cs. **פְּלֵטַת**: — 1. what has **escaped**, what is **spared** Ex 10_5 2K 19_{30f}; *hāyâ liflêṭâ* be able to escape Gn 32_9; — 2. **escape, deliverance** Gn 45_7.

***פָּלִיל**: pl. **פְּלִילִים**: **judges** Dt 32_{31}.

פְּלִילָה: **decision** Is 16_3. †

פְּלִילִי: s.thg **calling for judgment** Jb 31_{28}. †

פְּלִילִיָּה: **decision, judgment** Is 28_7. †

I **פֶּלֶךְ**: **spindle-whorl** 2S 3_{29} Pr 31_{19}. †

II **פֶּלֶךְ**: **district** Ne 3_{9-18}. †

I **פלל**: **piel**: pf. **פִּלְלוֹ**, **פִּלַּלְתְּ**, **פִּלָּלְתִּי**; impf. **וַיְפַלֵּל**: — 1. **sit in judgment** Ps 106_{30}; — 2. **arbitrate** 1S 2_{25}; — 3. decide in favor of an opinion > **expect** (obj.: to see) Gn 48_{11}; — 4. w. *lᵉ* **stand up** (as a guarantee) for Ez 16_{52}. †

II **פלל**: **hitp.**: pf. **הִתְפַּלֵּל**, **הִתְפַּלַּלְתִּי**, **הִתְפַּלַּלְתֶּם**; impf. **יִתְפַּלֵּל**, **אֶתְפַּלֵּל**, **וָאֶתְפַּלֵּל**, **וָאֶתְפַּלְלָה** Dn 9_4; impv. & inf. **הִתְפַּלֵּל**, **הִתְפַּלֶּל-**, pt. **מִתְפַּלֵּל**: — 1. 1S 2_{25} rd. *yᵉfallel-* (I *pll*); — 2. **pray**: w. *bᵉʿad* for Gn 20_7, w. *ʿal* for Jb 42_8; w. *ʾel* to (God) Gn 20_{17}, w. *lifnê* before (God) 1K 8_{28}; w/o prep. **pray** 2K 6_{17}; w. *'el* toward (a place) 1K 8_{29f}.

פָּלָל: n. pers.

פְּלַלְיָה: n. pers.

פַּלְמֹנִי: **a certain one** Dn 8_{13}. †

פְּלֹנִי: **a certain one** 2K 6_8.

I פלס: **piel**: impf. יְפַלֵּס, תְּפַלֵּסוּן; impv. פַּלֵּס: obj. path, **clear, smooth, level** Is 26_7; abs. **make a path** Ps 58_3.

II פלס: **piel**: impf. תְּפַלֵּס: **observe** Pr $5_{6\cdot21}$. †

פֶּלֶס: **pointer of a balance** Is 40_{12} Pr 16_{11}. †

פלץ: **hitp.**: impf. יִתְפַּלָּצוּן: **shake** Jb 9_6. †

פַּלָּצוּת: **shaking, shuddering** Is 21_4.

פלשׁ: **hitp.**: pf. הִתְפַּלָּשְׁתִּי Mi 1_{10} Kt; impf. יִתְפַּלָּשׁוּ; impv. הִתְפַּלְּשִׁי, הִתְפַּלְּשׁוּ: **roll** (intrans.) Je 25_{34}.

פְּלֶשֶׁת: n. terr.: **land & territory of Philistines** Ex 15_{14}.

פְּלִשְׁתִּי: n. peop.: pl. פְּלִשְׁתִּים: **Philistine(s)** Gn 10_{14}.

פֶּלֶת: n. pers.

פְּלֵתִי: unexplained; alw. w. *kerēti*, e.g. 2S 8_8.

פֶּן־ (133×), conj. :— 1. w. impf. (106×), prevention of a theoretically possible event: **lest, so that ... not**; *pen-yišlaḥ* so that he does not stretch out Gn 3_{22}; — 2. w. impf., prevention of an otherwise predictable event: **otherwise**; *pen-tidbāqanî* otherwise (disaster) will overtake me Gn 19_{19}, so $26_{7\cdot9}$ & oft.; — 3. *pen mah-* (w/o *maqqēf*) **what else** Pr 25_8; — 4. w. pf., *pen-nesā'ô* **otherwise** (if they do not find him) ... has carried him away 2K 2_{16}; *pen-māṣā'* otherwise he will find 2S 20_6.

פַּנַּג: unexpl.; a kind of food Ez 27_{17}. †

פָּנָה: **qal**: pf. פָּנִינוּ, פָּנוּ, פָּנִיתָ, פ׳; impf. יִפְנֶה, וַיִּפֶן, תֵּפֶן, וָאֵפֶן, וַיִּפְנוּ; impv. פְּנֵה, פְּנוּ; inf. פְּנוֹת, פְּנוֹתָם Ez 29_{16}, abs. פָּנֹה; pt. פֹּ(ו)נֶה, פֹּנִים: — 1. **turn to the side, take a** (specific) **direction** 1K 2_3; — 2. w. *'el*, **turn** towards s.one Lv 19_4; **turn** towards s.thg Ex 16_{10}; > **concern onesf., worry about** 2S 9_8; **wait** (anxiously) for Hg 1_9; — 3. *pānâ 'aḥarāyw* **turn** (and go) **back** 2K 2_{24}; — 4. **turn around** (in place) 1K 10_{13}; turn > **go on** Gn 18_{22}; — 5. *pānâ* + *'aḥarê* **join, attach onesf. to** Ez 29_{16}; + *be* **pay attention to** Jb 6_{28}; — 6. turn away = **slip away, pass on**: *lifnôt 'ereb* as evening was coming on Gn 24_{63}; so *lifnôt bōqer* Ex 14_{27}; *pānâ hayyôm* day is coming to a close Je 6_4; — 7. *pānâ* + *'ōref* **turn the back** (of neck) Jos 7_{12}.

piel: pf. פִּנָּה, פִּנִּיתָ, פִּנּוּ; impv. פַּנּוּ: — 1. **get rid of** Zp 3_{15}; — 2. **clear up** Ps 80_{10}; obj. house Gn 24_{31}; — 3. obj. *derek*, **clear** (the way) Is 40_3.

hif.: pf. הִפְנָה, הִפְנְתָה, הִפְנוּ; impf. וַיֶּפֶן; inf. הַפְנוֹתוֹ; pt. מַפְנֶה: — 1. **turn** (intrans.) Je 47_3, **retreat** (in battle) Je 46_{21}; — 2. w. *'ōref* **turn the back** (of neck) Je 48_{39}; w. *šikmô* turn one's shoulder = turn away 1S 10_9.

hof.: impv. הָפְנוּ; pt. מָפְנֶה: **be pushed back** Je 49_8; be turned Ez 9_2. †

*פָּנֶה (2100×): only pl. פָּנִים, cs. פְּנֵי, sf. פָּנָיו, פָּנֶיךָ, פְּנֵיכֶם, פָּנֵימוֹ Ps 11_7; m.: — 1. **face** Gn 31_2, pl. Ez 1_6; *nāfal 'al-pānāyw* (in submission) Gn 17_3; *hēsēb pānāyw* turn one's face away 1K 21_4; *śām pānāyw* direct one's face toward, head toward Gn 31_{21}; *pānîm befānîm* face to face Dt 5_4; *nātan pānāyw* set one's face to, set one's intention to 2C 20_3; — 2. **(features of) face**: *wayyippelû pānāyw* his face fell = he was downcast Gn 4_5; *penêkem rā'îm* you look bad Gn 40_7; *penê dābār* appearance of the matter 2S 14_{20}; — 3. metaph. face = **visible side**: **surface** *penê hā'adāmâ* Gn 2_6, *penê tehôm* Gn 1_2, *penê hammayim* 1_2; *penê lebûš* outer garment Jb 41_5; — 4. face = **front** (side): *penê hā'ōhel* Ex 26_9; *mippānîm* in front 2S 10_9; *penê milḥāmâ* **attack, assault** 2S 10_9; — 5. *panîm* in front = **formerly**: *lefānîm*

1S 9_9, *millᵉfānîm* from the beginning = at all times Is 41_{26}; — 6. **face of God** Gn 33_{10} & oft.; — 7. *šulḥan (leḥem) happānîm* table of the (bread of the) Presence Nu 4_7; — 8. face = a person's **self**: *pānéká* you yourself (in person) 2S 17_{11}; — 9. *'el-pᵉnê* **before** (w. vb. of motion) Lv 9_5; — 10. *'et-pᵉnê* with the face of = **before** Gn 19_{13}; w. vb. of motion 1S 22_4; *mē'ēt pᵉnê* away from Gn 27_{30}; — 11. *bifnê* **before, against** Jos 10_8; — 12. *lifnê* **before**: a) spatial, no motion Gn 23_{12}, motion 2K 4_{43}; b) temporal: *lifnê môtî* before I die Gn 27_7, *lᵉfānay* before I came Gn 30_{30}; before = faster than Jb 4_{19}; c) indicating rank Gn 43_{14}; *lᵉfānéká* at your disposal Gn 13_9; — 13. *millifnê* away from Gn 47_{10}; *kātab millifnê* copy from Dt 17_{18}; out of the reach of Gn 4_{16}; w. *yārē'* stand in fear of Ec 8_{13}, cf. 1K 21_{29}; *millifnê* **on account of** 1S 8_{18}; — 14. *mippᵉnê* **away from, out from** Gn 16_8; > **on account of** Gn 6_{13}; *mippᵉnê 'ᵃšer* because Ex 19_{18}; — 15. *'al-pᵉnê* **in the face of, in the sight of, before** 2S 15_{18}; **in front of** 1K 6_3; **opposite to** Gn 23_{19}; against = to the disadvantage of Dt 21_{16}.

פִּנָּה: cs. פִּנַּת, sf. פִּנָּתָהּ; pl. פִּנּוֹת, sf. פִּנֹּתָיו; pl. also פִּנִּים Zc 14_{10} †; — 1. **corner**, of house Jb 1_{19}, altar Ex 27_2, street Pr 7_8; *'eben pinnâ* cornerstone Jb 38_6 > *pinnâ* Is 28_{16}; — 2. **corner-tower** Zp 1_{16}; therefore *ša'ar happinnâ* 2K 14_{13}; — 3. metaph. corner-tower = **leader** 1S 14_{38}.

I **פְּנוּאֵל**: n. pers. 1C 4_4 8_{25} Qr. †

II **פְּנוּאֵל**: n. loc.

פִּנְחָס: F פִּינְחָס.

I **פְּנִיאֵל**: n. pers. 1C 8_{25} Kt. †

II **פְּנִיאֵל**: n. loc.

פְּנִיִּים: F פְּנִינִים.

פָּנִים: F *פָּנֶה.

פְּנִימָה: — 1. (to the) **inside** Lv 10_{18}; — 2. **inside** 1K $6_{18f.21}$; — 3. *lifnîmâ* **inside** 1K 6_{30}; (to the) inside, **inwards** Ez 40_{16}; — 4. *mippᵉnîmâ* **inside** 2C 3_4.

פְּנִימִי: f. פְּנִימִית; pl. פְּנִימִים, f. פְּנִימִיּוֹת: adj. **inner** 1K 6_{27}.

פְּנִינִים: **corals** Pr 8_{11} La 4_7.

פְּנִנָּה: n. pers. f.

פנק: **piel**: pt. מְפַנֵּק Pr 29_{21} **pamper**; but perh. to be vocal. as **pual**. †

***פַּס**: pl. פַּסִּים: *kᵉtōnet passîm* Gn 37_3 2S 13_{18} & *kᵉtōnet happassîm* Gn $37_{23.32}$ 2S 13_{19}: tunic of pieces of various colors? tunic reaching to ankles?. †

פסג: **piel**: impv. פַּסְּגוּ Ps 48_{14} unexpl. †

פִּסְגָּה: alw. w. art.: n. of mountain.

***פִּסָּה**: cs. פִּסַּת: Ps 72_{16} unexpl.; **portion**??. †

פָּסַח: **qal**: pf. 'פ, פָּסַחְתִּי; inf. פָּסוֹחַ; pt. פֹּסְחִים: — 1. **be lame, limp** 1K 18_{21}; — 2. w. *'al* **skip by, spare** Ex $12_{13.23.27}$ Is 31_5. †
nif.: impf. יִפָּסֵחַ: **become lame** 2S 4_4. †
piel: impf. וַיְפַסְּחוּ: **limp around** (in cultic observance) 1K 18_{26}. †

פֶּסַח; פָּסַח; pl. פְּסָחִים: **Passover**: — 1. usu. the festival 2K 23_{21}; — 2. sacrifice 2C 30_{18}.

פָּסֵחַ: n. pers.

פִּסֵּחַ: pl. פִּסְחִים: **lame**, person 2S 9_{13}, thus unfit for priesthood Lv 21_{18}; animal (unfit for sacrifice) Dt 15_{21}.

***פָּסִיל**: pl. פְּסִילִים, cs. פְּסִילֵי, sf. פְּסִילֶיךָ: **idol** 2K 17_{41}.

פָּסַךְ: n. pers.

פסל: **qal**: pf. פָּסַלוּ; impf. יִפְסֹל; impv. פְּסָל־: **hew out, dress** (stone) 1K 5_{32}.

פֶּסֶל: פֶּסֶל; sf. פִּסְלוֹ: **idol** (of stone, clay, wood, or metal), 2K 21_7.

פסס: **qal**: pf. פַּסּוּ Ps 12_2; txt. ?. †

פִּסְפָּה: n. pers.

פעה: **qal**: impf. אֶפְעֶה: **groan** (in childbirth) Is 42_{14}. †

פָּעוּ: n. loc. Gn 36_{39}. †

פְּעוֹר: n. loc.; (*ba'al*) *pᵉ'ôr* n. of deity; *pᵉ'ôr* n. of mountain; F comm.

פָּעִי: n. pers.

פָּעַל: **qal**: pf. פָּעַל, פ׳, פָּעֲלוּ, פָּעַלְתָּ, פָּעֲלוּ; impf. אֶפְעַל, תִּפְעַל־, יִפְעַל, יִפְעָל Jb 35_6, inf. פָּעֳלָם Jb 37_{12}; pt. פֹּעֵל, sf. פֹּעֲלִי, pl. cs. פֹּעֲלֵי: — 1. **make** Is 41_4; w. acc. & l^e make s.thg (into) s.thg Ps 7_{14}; **commit, practice,** obj. *šeqer* Ho 7_1, *ṣedeq* Ps 15_2, &c.; *pāʿal bᵉ* **work** (a material w.) Is 44_{12}; — 2. abs. **do** Jb 11_8, w. l^e do Jb 7_{20}; **accomplish, perform** Ps 11_3; — 3. subj. God, usu. w. acc. & l^e **make** s.thg (into) s.thg Ex 15_{17}, **do** Nu 23_{23}; *pōʿᵃlî* my maker = creator Jb 36_3; — 4. **get, acquire** Pr 21_6.

פֹּעַל: sf. פָּעֳלְךָ (*poʿolᵉkā*), פָּעֳלָהּ, פֹּעֲלוֹ, פָּעֳלוֹ, פָּעֳלֶךָ; pl. פְּעָלִים: — 1. **deed** Is 59_6, **work** (= activity) Ps 104_{23}; — 2. **work** (= achievement) Is 1_{31}; — 3. **doing, working** Dt 32_4; — 4. **management** (of God) Is 5_{12}; — 5. **conduct, behavior** Pr 20_{11}; — 6. **wages** Je 22_{13}.

פְּעֻלָּה: cs. פְּעֻלַּת, sf. פְּעֻלָּתוֹ, פְּעֻלַּתְכֶם; pl. פְּעֻל(וֹ)ת: — 1. **work** Je 31_{16}; — 2. pl. **deeds** Ps 17_4; — 3. (positive) **reward** Is 40_{10}; — 4. **wages** Lv 19_{13}; — 5. **reward** (of sin), **punishment** Is 65_7.

פְּעֻלְּתַי: n. pers.

פעם: **qal**: inf. פַּעֲמוֹ: **impel, push** Ju 13_{25}. †
nif.: pf. נִפְעַמְתִּי; impf. וַתִּפָּעֶם: **be disturbed** Gn 41_8 Ps 77_5 Dn 2_3. †
hitp.: impf. וַתִּתְפָּעֶם: **feel disturbed** Dn 2_1. †

פַּעַם (117×): פָּעַם; pl. פְּעָמִים, cs. פַּעֲמֵי, sf. פְּעָמָיו, פְּעָמֶיךָ, פַּעֲמֹתָיו, du. פַּעֲמַיִם, פַּעֲמָיִם; f.: — 1. **foot** (of person) Ps 58_{11}; *kaf pᵉʿāmay* sole of my foot 2K 19_{24}; — 2. **foot** (of furniture) Ex 25_{12}; — 3. **step, pace** Ju 5_{28}; *paʿam ʾaḥat* w. one stroke 1S 26_8; — 4. **anvil** Is 41_7; — 5. **time** (= occurrence) *bappaʿam hazzōʾt* this time Ex 8_{28}; *happaʿam* once = at last Gn 2_{23}; *ʾak happaʿam* just this once Gn 18_{32}; *paʿam … paʿam* now … now Pr 7_{12}; *paʿam ûšᵉtayim* once or twice Ne 13_{20}; *kᵉfaʿam bᵉfaʿam* as at other times 1S 3_{10}; — 6. du. *zeh paʿᵃmayim* now twice Gn 27_{36}; — 7. *šēš pᵉʿāmîm* 6 times 2K 13_{19}; *ʿad-kammeh pᵉʿāmîm* how many times? 1K 22_{16}.

פַּעֲמֹן: (small) **bell** (on priest's robe) Ex 28_{33f} 39_{25f}. †

פַּעְנֵחַ: ↗ צָפְנַת.

פער: **qal**: pf. פָּעֲרָה, פָּעַרְתִּי, פָּעֲרוּ: **open wide** (mouth) Is 5_{14}.

פַּעֲרַי: n. pers.

פצה: **qal**: pf. פָּצְתָה, פָּצִיתִי, פָּצוּ; impf. יִפְצֶה; impv. פְּצֵנִי; pt. פּוֹצֶה: — 1. **open up** (mouth, to gulp) Gn 4_{11}; (of bird) Is 10_{14}; (mouth, to speak) Ju 11_{35f}; w. *ʿal* against (threatening gesture) Ps 22_{14}; — 2. *pāṣû śᵉfātayim* lips open Ps 66_{14}; — 3. w. acc. (Aramaism) **set free** Ps $144_{7.10f}$.

I **פצח**: **qal**: pf. פָּצְחוּ; impf. יִפְצְחוּ; impv. פִּצְחוּ, פִּצְחִי: **be serene** Is 14_7.

II **פצח**: **piel**: pf. פִּצֵּחוּ: **break in pieces** Mi 3_3. †

פְּצִירָה: **sharpening** (of plowshare) 1S 13_{21}. †

פצל: **piel**: pf. פִּצֵּל; impf. יְפַצֵּל: **strip off, peel** (bark) Gn 30_{37f}. †

פְּצָלוֹת: **peeled strips** (of bark) Gn 30_{37}. †

פצם: **qal**: pf. פְּצַמְתָּהּ: **split open** (the earth) Ps 60_4. †

פצע: **qal**: pf. פְּצָעוּנִי; inf. פָּצוֹעַ; pt. pass. cs. פְּצוּעַ: **inflict bruises** 1K 20_{37} SS 5_7; *pᵉṣûaʿ-dakkāʾ* **emasculated by crushing** (of testicles) Dt 23_2.

פצץ: **polel**: impf. יְפֹצֵץ: **shatter** (rock) Je 23_{29}. †
hitpolel: impf. וַיִּתְפֹּצְצוּ: **be shattered** Hb 3_6. †
pilpel: impf. יְפַצְפְּצֵנִי: **smash** Jb 16_{12}. †

הַפִּצֵּץ: n. pers.

פצר: **qal**: impf. וַיִּפְצְרוּ, וַיִּפְצַר: w. b^e **urge** s.one **strongly** Gn $19_{3.9}$.
hif.: inf. הַפְצַר: **refractoriness** (?) 1S 15_{23}. †

***פֹּק**: cs. פַּק: **shaking** Na 2_{11}. †

פָּקַד: **qal** (230×): pf. פָּקְדוּ, פָּקַדְתָּ, פ׳, פְּקַדְתִּים, פְּקָדוּךָ; impf. יִפְקֹד, אֶפְקָד־, וַתִּפְקְדֵנוּ, וַיִּפְקְדֵם, יִפְקְדוּ, וָאֶפְקֹד; impv. פִּקְדוּ; inf. פְּקֹד, פָּקְדִי, abs. פָּקֹד; pt. פֹּקֵד, pass. פְּקוּדֵי, פְּקֻדִים, sf. פְּקֻדֵיכֶם: — 1. **miss** s.one 1S 20_{6}; — 2. **make a search, have a look** 1S 14_{17}; — 3. **hunt up, seek out** Ju 15_{1}; w. *lešālôm* look after s.one's condition, health 1S 17_{18}; — 4. **take care of** 2K 9_{34}; — 5. **long for** Ez 23_{21}; — 6. subj. God: **take care of, take up the cause of** Gn 21_{1} & oft.; — 7. **call up** (for duty), **muster** 1K 20_{15}; — 8. *pāqûd* one **entrusted** w. a task, **commissioned** 2K 11_{15}; — 9. therefore: **appoint** Gn 40_{4}; — 10. **call** s.one **to account** Je 6_{15}; — 11. therefore: **avenge** 1S 15_{2}; — 12. (= 11. w/o obj.) **call to account** (for) Is 10_{12}; — 13. *pāqad be* **avenge on** Je 9_{8}; — 14. spec.: *pāqad (babbayit)* **put** s.thg **away** 2S 5_{24}; *pāqad bešēmôt* **list by name** Nu 4_{32}.

nif.: pf. נִפְקַד, נִפְקַדְתָּ; impf. יִפָּקֵד, יִפָּקֵד, יִפָּקְדוּ; inf. הִפָּקֵד: — 1. **be missed, be lacking** 1K 20_{39}; **remain empty** (seat) 1S 20_{18}; **be missing** 1S 25_{7}; — 2. **be called up** Ez 38_{8}; **be installed** (in office) Ne 7_{1}; **be called to account** Is 24_{22}; — 3. *nifqad ʿal* **befall** s.one Nu 16_{29}; — 4. **be touched by** (*rāʿ*) Ps 19_{23}.

piel: pt. מְפַקֵּד: **muster** Is 13_{4}. †

pual: pf. פֻּקַּדְתִּי, פֻּקַּד: — 1. **be summoned** Is 38_{10}; — 2. **be determined, counted** Ex 38_{21}. †

hif.: pf. הִפְקַדְתּוֹ, הִפְקַדְתִּי, הִפְקִיד; impf. יַפְקִיד, יַפְקֵד, יַפְקִדֵהוּ; impv. הַפְקֵד, הַפְקִידוּ: — 1. **order, appoint** Gn 39_{4f}; — 2. w. acc. & *le* **entrust** s.thg to s.one 1K 11_{28}; w. acc. & *beyad* **commit** s.thg to the hands of 1K 14_{27}; — 3. w. acc. **assign** (a place) 1S 29_{4}; **leave, store** Is 10_{28}; **entrust** Je 36_{20}; — 4. w. acc. & *ʿal*: **decree** (a punishment on s.one) Lv 26_{16}.

hof.: pf. הָפְקַד; pt. מֻפְקָדִים: — 1. **be appointed, entrusted** 2K 22_{5}; — 2. **be deposited** Lv 5_{23}.

hitp.: pf. הִתְפָּקְדוּ; impf. וַיִּתְפָּקֵד: **be mustered, counted** Ju $20_{15\cdot17}$ 21_{9}. †

hotpaal: pf. הָתְפָּקְדוּ: **be mustered, counted** Nu 1_{47} 2_{33} 26_{62} 1K 20_{27}. †

פְּקֻדָּה: cs. פְּקֻדַּת; sf. פְּקֻדָּתְךָ; pl. פְּקֻדּ(וֹ)ת: — 1. **appointment, service, office** Nu 3_{36}; — 2. **guard, sentry** 2K 11_{18}; *pequddat yiśrāʾēl* **administration** of Isr. 1C 26_{30}; — 3. **vengeance, visitation** Is 10_{3}; — 4. **fate** Nu 16_{29}; — 5. **mustering** 2C 26_{11}; — 6. **what is stored up** Is 15_{7}.

פִּקָּדוֹן: — 1. **deposit** Lv $5_{21\cdot23}$; — 2. **(reserve) supply**, stores Gn 41_{36}. †

פְּקִדֻת: *baʿal peqidut* **commander of the guard** Je 37_{13}. †

פְּקוֹד: n. terr.

***פִּקּוּדִים**; cs. פִּקּוּדֵי, sf. פִּקּוּדָיו: **directions, orders** Ps 19_{9}.

פָּקַח: **qal**: pf. פָּקַחְתָּ, פ׳; impf. יִפְקַח; impv. פְּקַח, פְּקָחָה Dn 9_{18} Kt; inf. פָּקוֹחַ; pt. פֹּקֵחַ, pass. פְּקֻחוֹת: w. *ʿênayim* **open** (the eyes) Gn 21_{19}; w. *ʾoznayim* Is 42_{20}.

nif.: pf. נִפְקְחוּ; impf. תִּפָּקַחְנָה: **be opened** (eyes) Gn $3_{5\cdot7}$ Is 35_{5}. †

פֶּקַח: n. pers.

פִּקֵּחַ: pl. פִּקְחִים: **clear-sighted** (person) Ex 4_{11} 23_{8}. †

פְּקַחְיָה: n. pers.

פְּקַח־קוֹחַ: **opening** (of eyesight) Is 61_{1}. †

פָּקִיד: cs. פְּקִיד; pl. פְּקִידִים: **commissioner, officer** Gn 41_{34}.

פְּקָעִים: **gourd-shaped ornaments** 1K 6_{18} 7_{24}. †

פַּקֻּעֹת: **(wild) gourd**, *Colocynthis vulgaris* 2K 4_{39}. †

פַּר (132×): פַּר וָאַיִל, פָּר Nu $23_{2\cdot4}$, הַפָּר, בַּפָּר &c.; pl. פָּרִים, sf. פָּרֶיהָ: **young bull** Gn 32_{16}, oft. w. *ben-bāqār* added, Ex 29_{1}; in sacrifice Lv 4_{3}.

פרא: **hif.**: impf. יַפְרִיא: **thrive in fruitfulness** Ho 13_{15}. †

פֶּרֶא: pl. פְּרָאִים: **zebra** (oth.: **wild ass, onager**) Gn 16_{12}.

פְּרָאם: n. pers.
פַּרְבָּר: 1C 26_{18}; pl. פַּרְוָרִים 2K 23_{11}: **court.** †
פרד: **qal**: pt. pass. פְּרֻדוֹת: **outspread** (wings) Ez 1_{11}. †
nif.: pf. נִפְרַדוּ, נִפְרָדוּ; impf. יִפָּרֵד, יִפָּרְדוּ, יִפָּרֵדוּ; impv. הִפָּרֶד; pt. נִפְרָד, נִפְרָדִים: — 1. **divide** (into; river) Gn 2_{10}; **branch off** (family groups genealogically) Gn 10_5; — 2. **separate** (intrans.); w. *ʿal* Gn $13_{9\cdot11}$, w. *min* Ju 4_{11}; — 3. **be separated** Pr 28_1; — 4. **be apart, be cut off** (fm. each other) Gn 25_{23}.
piel: impf. יְפָרֵדוּ: separate, **go off** (w. s.one) Ho 4_{14}. †
pual: pt. מְפֹרָד: **separated** Est 3_8. †
hif.: pf. הִפְרִיד; impf. יַפְרִיד, יַפְרִידוּ; inf. הַפְרִידוֹ; pt. מַפְרִיד: — 1. **separate** (trans.), **keep for onesf.** Gn 30_{40}; — 2. *hifrîd bên ... ûbên* **separate** (trans.) **... fm. each other** Ru 1_{17}.
hitp.: pf. הִתְפָּרְדוּ; impf. יִתְפָּרְדוּ, יִתְפָּרָדוּ: — 1. **separate** (intrans.) **fm. each other** Ps 22_{15}; — 2. **be separated, scattered fm. each other** Ps 92_{10} Jb 4_{11} 41_9. †
פֶּרֶד: sf. פִּרְדּוֹ; pl. פְּרָדִים, sf. פִּרְדֵיהֶם: **mule** 1K 10_{25}.
פִּרְדָּה: **she-mule** 1K $1_{33\cdot38\cdot44}$. †
פְּרֻדֹת: **dried figs** Jl 1_{17}. †
פַּרְדֵּס: **park, forest** SS 4_{13} Ec 2_5 Ne 2_8. †
פרה: **qal**: pf. פָּרוּ, פְּרִיתֶם, פָּרִינוּ; impf. יִפְרֶה, יִפְרוּ; impv. פְּרוּ, פְּרֵה; pt. פֹּרֶה, f. פֹּרִיָּה & פֹּרָה: — 1. **bear fruit** (subj. plants) Dt 29_{17}; — 2. **be fruitful** (subj. men) Gn 26_{22}, & esp. *pārâ werābâ* be fruitful & multiply Gn 1_{22}.
hif.: pf. הִפְרַנִי, הִפְרֵ(י)תִי; impf. וַיֶּפֶר, יַפְרְךָ; pt. מַפְרְךָ: **make fruitful** Gn 17_6.
I **פָּרָה**: sf. פָּרָתוֹ; pl. פָּרוֹת: **cow** Gn 32_{16}.
II **פָּרָה**: n. loc. (הַפָּרָה): Jos 18_{23}. †
פֶּרֶה Je 2_{24}: prob. = ☞ פֶּרֶא. †
פֻּרָה: n. pers.
פְּרוּדָא: n. pers.
פֵּרוֹת Is 2_{20}: ☞ *חֲפַרְפָּרָה. †

***פְּרוֹזִים** Est 9_{19} Kt, Qr פְּרָזִים, ☞ פְּרָזִי. †
פָּרוּחַ: n. pers.
פַּרְוַיִם: n. terr.
***פַּרְוָר**: ☞ פַּרְבָּר.
פָּרוּר: (earthenware) **cooking pot** 1S 2_{14}.
***פָּרָז** or ***פֶּרֶז**: pl. sf. פְּרָזָו Hb 3_{14}: txt. corr. †
פְּרָזוֹן: sf. פִּרְזוֹנוֹ: **people** who live **in open country** Ju $5_{7\cdot11}$. †
פְּרָזוֹת: **open, rural country** Ez 38_{11} Zc 2_8 Est 9_{19}. †
פְּרָזִי: pl. פְּרָזִים: — 1. **open, rural country** Dt 3_5 1S 6_{18}; — 2. pl. Est 9_{19} Qr **those living in open country**. †
פְּרִזִּי: n. peop. **Perizzite(s)**.
I **פָּרַח**: **qal**: pf. פָּרְחָה, פָּרָחָה, פּ׳; impf. יִפְרַח, יַפְרִ(י)חַ & תִּפְרַחְנָה, יִפְרְחוּ, יִפְרָחוּ, יִפְרָח, יַפְרִיחוּ; inf. פְּרֹחַ, פָּרֹחַ; pt. פֹּרַחַת, פֹּרֵחַ: — 1. **sprout**: of tree Jb 14_9, of rod Nu 17_{20}; metaph., of Isr. Is 27_6; — 2. **bud**, of vine Gn 40_{10}; **bloom** Is 35_2; — 3. **break out**, of skin disease Lv 13_{20}; — 4. **break open**, of boil Ex 9_{9f}.
hif.: pf. הִפְרַחְתִּי; impf. תַּפְרִיחִי: **bring to bud, bloom** Is 17_{11} Ez 17_{24}. †
II **פרח**: pt. pl. f. פֹּרְח(וֹ)ת Ez 13_{20}: unexpl. †
פֶּרַח: פֶּרַח; sf. פִּרְחָם; pl. sf. פְּרָחֶיהָ: — 1. **bud, flower** 1K 7_{26}; — 2. **bud- or flower-shaped ornament** 1K 7_{49}.
פִּרְחַח: Jb 30_{12}: unexpl. †
פרט: **qal**: pt. pl. פֹּרְטִים: **improvise** (in playing an instrument) Am 6_5. †
פֶּרֶט: coll. **fallen grapes** Lv 19_{10}. †
פְּרִי (120×): פֶּרִי; sf. פִּרְיוֹ, פֶּרְיְךָ, פִּרְיֵךְ, פִּרְיִי, פִּרְיָמוֹ, פִּרְיְהֶם, פֶּרְיְכֶם: — 1. **fruit**: of tree Gn 1_{29}, vine Zc 8_{12}; *ʿēṣ perî* tree(s) bearing fruit Gn 1_{11}; *ʾereṣ perî* fruitful land Ps 107_{34}; — 2. fruit of body = **offspring** Gn 30_2; — 3. fruit = **result** of action or attitude: *perî maʿalāl* Is 3_{10}.
פְּרִידָא: n. pers.

I *פָּרִיץ: cs. פְּרִיץ: **ravenous** (one) (|| lion) Is 35_9. †

II פָּרִיץ: pl. פָּרִיצִים, cs. פָּרִיצֵי: **burglar, robber** Je 7_{11}.

פֶּרֶךְ: פֶּרֶךְ: (deed of) **violence, torment** Ex 1_{13f}.

פָּרֹכֶת: **curtain** (in front of the most holy place) Ex 26_{31}.

פרם: **qal**: impf. יִפְרֹם, תִּפְרֹמוּ; pt. pass. פְּרֻמִים: **tear** (clothes) **to pieces** Lv 10_6 13_{45} 21_{10}. †

פַּרְמַשְׁתָּא: n. pers.

פַּרְנָךְ: n. pers.

פרס: **qal**: impf. יִפְרְסוּ; inf. פָּרֹס: w. *leḥem* **break** (bread) Is 58_7 Je 16_7. †

hif. (denom. of פַּרְסָה): pf. הִפְרִיסָה, הִפְרִיסוּ; impf. יַפְרִיס; pt. מַפְרִיס, מַפְרֶסֶת, pl. cs. מַפְרִסֵי: *mafrîs parsâ* (animal) **having divided hoofs** Lv 11_3; w/o *parsâ* Ps 69_{32}.

פֶּרֶס: an unclean bird Lv 11_{13} Dt 14_{12}; ? **lammergeier** (great bearded vulture), *Gypaëtus barbatus*. †

פָּרַס: n. peop. **Persia**.

פַּרְסָה: pl. פְּרָסֹת, cs. פַּרְסוֹת, sf. פַּרְסֹתַיִךְ, פַּרְסֵיהֶן: (divided) **hoof** Lv 11_3, so **hoof** in genl. Is 5_{28}; *lōʾ* ... *parsâ* = nothing at all Ex 10_{26}.

פַּרְסִי: gent. of פָּרַס **Persian**.

פָּרַע: **qal**: pf. פָּרְעָה, פּ׳; impf. יִפְרַע, אֶפְרַע, תִּפְרְעוּ, תִּפְרָעוּ; impv. פְּרָעֵהוּ; inf. פְּרוֹעַ; pt. פּוֹרֵעַ, pass. פָּרֻעַ: — 1. **let** s.one **(hang) loose** Jb 33_{24} (if mss. correct); oft. w. *rōʾš* **let** the hair of the head **hang** loose Lv 10_6; **untie** (or **unbraid**) the hair Nu 5_{18}; cogn. acc. Ju 5_2; — 2. w. acc. **let** s.one **go out of control, run wild** Ex 32_{25}; — 3. w. acc. **ignore, neglect** Pr 1_{25}.

hif.: pf. הִפְרִיעַ; impf. תַּפְרִיעוּ: — 1. w. acc. & *min*: **make (let)** s.one **be negligent** of Ex 5_4; — 2. abs. **allow depravity to spread** 2C 28_{19}. †

פֶּרַע: pl. פְּרָעוֹת, cs. פַּרְעוֹת: **loose** (or **un-braided**) **hair** of the head Nu 6_5 Dt 32_{42} Ju 5_2 Ez 44_{20}. †

פֶּרַע Gn $41_{45.51}$ 46_{20}: F פּוֹטִי. †

פַּרְעֹה (275×): **Pharaoh** Gn 12_{15}.

I פַּרְעֹשׁ: **flea,** *Pulex irritans* 1S 24_{15} 26_{20}. †

II פַּרְעֹשׁ: n. pers.

פִּרְעָתוֹן: n. loc.

פִּרְעָתוֹנִי: gent. of פִּרְעָתוֹן.

פַּרְפַּר: n. of river.

פָּרַץ: **qal**: pf. פָּרַצְתָּ, פּ׳, פְּרַצְתָּנוּ; impf. יִפְרֹץ, יִפְרָץ־, יִפְרְצוּ, יִפְרֹצוּ, יִפְרְצֵנִי; inf. פְּרוֹץ, פָּרֹץ; pt. פֹּרֵץ, pass. פְּרוּצָה: — 1. in genl. **make a breach, burst out** Gn 38_{29} 2S 6_8; **make a breach** in a wall 2K 14_{13}; *ʿîr perûṣâ* breached city Pr 25_{28}; *perûṣîm* **breaches** Ne 2_{13}; — 2. w. acc. **tear down** (wall) Is 5_5; — 3. w. *naḥal* **sink** (shaft) Jb 28_4; w. *bayit* **break into** (house) 2C 24_7; — 4. abs. **break through** Mi 2_{13}; **overflow** Pr 3_{10}; — 5. *pāraṣ be* Ex $19_{22.24}$ break out among? against?; 2K 5_{23} **urge** s.one; — 6. break over (in fullness, numbers), **spread out, increase** Gn 28_{14}.

nif.: pt. נִפְרָץ: **be ordered, orderly** 1S 3_1. †

pual: pt. f. מְפֹרֶצֶת: **broken down** (wall) Ne 1_3. †

hitp.: pt. pl. מִתְפָּרְצִים: **break loose, away** (intrans.) 1S 25_{10}. †

I פֶּרֶץ: פָּרֶץ; pl. פְּרָצִים, sf. פִּרְצֵיהֶן: **gap, breach** (in a wall) 1K 11_{27}; *pereṣ mayim* **breach of a dike** (or dam) 2S 5_{20}; (perineal) **rupture** (of woman in childbirth) Gn 38_{29}; **rupture** (of relations betw. tribes) Ju 21_{15}; = death Ps 144_{14}.

II פֶּרֶץ: n. pers.

פַּרְצִי: gent. of II פֶּרֶץ.

פְּרָצִים: n. loc.: הַר־פְּרָצִים & בַּעַל־פְּרָצִים.

פֶּרֶץ עֻזָּה: n. loc.

פרק: **qal**: pf. פָּרַקְתָּ; impf. וַיִּפְרְקֵנוּ; pt. פֹּרֵק: w. *min* or *mēʿal* **pull off, away; tear off, away** Gn 27_{40}.

piel: impf. יְפָרֵק; impv. פָּרְקוּ; pt. מְפָרֵק:

pull off, tear off Ex 32_{2}; break up, split 1K 19_{11}.

hitp.: pf. הִתְפָּרְקוּ, הִתְפָּרֲקוּ; impf. וַיִּתְפָּרְקוּ: — 1. w. acc. **pull off, tear off fm. onesf.** Ex $32_{3.24}$; — 2. **be pulled off, torn off** Ez 19_{12}. †

פֶּרֶק: — 1. **crossroad(s)** Ob $_{14}$; — 2. **plunder** Na 3_{1}. †

***פָּרָק**: cs. פְּרַק: **bread crumbled** (into broth) Is 65_{4} Kt, but rd. Qr מְרַק. †

I **פרר**: **hif.**: pf. הֵפַר, הֵפֵר Gn 17_{14} & הֵפִיר Ez 17_{19} Ps 33_{10}, הֵפַרְתָּה, הֵפֵרוּ, הֲפֵרָם; impf. יָפֵר, וַיָּפֶר, אָפֵר, יְפֵרֶנּוּ; impv. הָפֵר, הָפֵרָה; inf. הָפֵר & הָפִיר Zc 11_{10}, הַפְרְכֶם; pt. מֵפֵר: — 1. — intrans., of fruit, **break out, burst forth** Ec 12_{5}; — 2. w. acc. **break, destroy, put an end to, frustrate, invalidate**: w. *b^e^rît* Gn 17_{14}; w. counsel 2S 15_{34}.

hof.: impf. תֻּפַר, תֻּפָר: **be broken, invalidated, frustrated**: counsel Is 8_{10}, *b^e^rît* Je 33_{21} Zc 11_{11}. †

II **פרר**: **qal**: inf. פּוֹר, ↗ **hitpolel**: Is 24_{19}. †

polel: pf. פּוֹרַרְתָּ: **rouse up** Ps 74_{13}. †

hitpolel: pf. הִתְפּוֹרְרָה: w. qal inf.: **shake to and fro** Is 24_{19}. †

pilpel: impf. וַיְפַרְפְּרֵנִי: **shake, bewilder** Jb 16_{12}. †

פָּרַשׂ: **qal**: pf. פָּרַשְׂתִּי, פ׳; impf. יִפְרֹשׂ, וַיִּפְרְשֵׂהוּ, וְאֶפְרְשָׂה; pt. פֹּ(וֹ)רֵשׂ, pl. cs. פֹּרְשֵׂי, pass. פָּרֻשׂ, פְּרֻשִׂים: — 1. **spread out** (trans.): obj. wings 1K 6_{27}, tent Ex 40_{19}; metaph. **flaunt** (obj. folly) Pr 13_{16}; — 2. *pāraś kappayim* **spread** the hands (in prayer) 1K 8_{38}; — 3. obj. *yādô* **stretch out** one's hand (to seize) La 1_{10}, obj. *kappāh* (to help) Pr 31_{20}; — 4. *pāraś* = *pāras*: **break** (bread) La 4_{4}, **break** (bones) **to pieces** Mi 3_{3}.

nif.: impf. יִפָּרֵשׂוּ: **be scattered** Ez 17_{21}. †

piel: pf. פֵּרַשׂ, פֵּרְשָׂה, פֵּרַשְׂתִּי; impf. יְפָרֵשׂ; inf. פָּרֵשׂ, פָּרְשְׂכֶם: — 1. obj. hands: **spread out** (to swim) Is 25_{11}; (of God, in invitation) Is 65_{2}; (in prayer) Is 1_{15}; — 2. **scatter** Zc 2_{10}.

פרשז: Jb 26_{9}, mixed form, פרז & פרשׂ; rd. פָּרַשׂ. †

פרשׁ: **qal**: inf. פְּרֹשׁ: **inform precisely** Lv 24_{12}.

[**nif.**: pt. pl. נִפְרָשׁוֹת Ez 34_{12}, rd. ־שׂ־. †]

pual: pf. פֹּרַשׁ; pt. מְפֹרָשׁ: — 1. **be explained, decided** Nu 15_{34}; — 2. **be divided into sections** (oth.: expounded ex tempore, or, translated) Ne 8_{8}. †

hif.: impf. יַפְרִשׁ: **secrete** (poison) Pr 23_{32}. †

I **פֶּרֶשׁ**: sf. פִּרְשׁוֹ: **contents of the stomach** (usu. of ruminant animals); (oth.: **dung**) Ex 29_{14}.

II **פֶּרֶשׁ**: n. pers. 1C 7_{16}. †

פָּרָשׁ: cs. פָּרַשׁ Ez 26_{10}; pl. פָּרָשִׁים, sf. פָּרָשָׁיו: — 1. **horseman, rider** Gn 50_{9} & oft.; — 2. (riding-)**horse** (in earlier Semitic a slightly different word, now a homonym w. 1.; in following passages only:) 1S 8_{18} Is 22_{6} 28_{28} Ez 27_{14} Jl 2_{4} Na 3_{3} Hb 1_{8}.

***פַּרְשְׁדֹן**: loc. פַּרְשְׁדֹנָה: **loop-hole** (for escape) Ju 3_{22}. †

***פָּרָשָׁה**: cs. פָּרָשַׁת: **exact statement** Est 4_{7} 10_{2}. †

פרשז: Jb 26_{9}: ↗ פרשׂז.

פַּרְשַׁנְדָּתָא: n. pers.

פְּרָת: n. river, **Euphrates**; loc. פְּרָתָה.

פֹּרָת: Gn 49_{22}, ↗ פרה qal. †

פַּרְתְּמִים: pl. **nobles** Est 1_{3} 6_{9} Dn 1_{3}. †

פָּשָׂה: **qal**: pf. פָּשְׂתָה, פָּשָׂתָה, פ׳; impf. יִפְשֶׂה; inf. פְּשׂה: (of symptoms of disease) **spread** Lv 13_{5}.

פשׂע: **qal**: impf. אֶפְשְׂעָה: **step forth** Is 27_{4}. †

פֶּשַׂע: **step** 1S 20_{3}. †

פשׂק: **qal**: pt. פֹּשֵׂק: w. *ś^e^fātāyw*, **distort the lips (smirk)** Pr 13_{3}. †

piel: impf. וַתְּפַשְּׂקִי: w. *raglayim*, **spread one's legs** Ez 16_{25}. †

פַּשׁ: Jb 35_{15} txt. corr.; rd. פֶּשַׁע. †

פשׁח: **piel**: impf. וַיְפַשְּׁחֵנִי: **leave fallow** La 3_{11}. †

פַּשְׁחוּר: n. pers.

פָּשַׁט: **qal**: pf. פ׳, פְּשַׁטְתֶּם; impf. יִפְשְׁטוּ, וַיִּפְשַׁט, יִפְשְׁטוּ! 1S 19_{24}; impv. פְּשֹׁטָה; pt. פֹּשְׁטִים: — 1. obj. clothes: **take off** (fm. onesf.) Lv 6_{4}, **strip off** 1S 19_{24}; — 2. abs. **undress** Is 32_{11}; of locust, **strip off skin, emerge fm. cocoon** Na 3_{16}; — 3. w. *'al* **cut loose, rush out, dash out** (against enemy) 1S 23_{27}; abs. **make a raid** 1S 27_{10}.

piel: inf. פַּשֵּׁט: **strip** (slain enemy) 1S 31_{8} 2S 23_{10} 1C 10_{8}. †

hif.: pf. הִפְשִׁיטוּ, הִפְשִׁיט, הִפְשִׁיטוּךָ; impf. אַפְשִׁיטֶנָּה, תַּפְשִׁיטוּן, וַיַּפְשִׁיטוּ, וַיַּפְשֵׁט, תַּפְשִׁיט, וַיַּפְשִׁיטֵהוּ; inf. הַפְשֵׁט; pt. מַפְשִׁיטִים: — 1. obj. clothes or armor, **take off, strip off** (fm. s.one else) Gn 37_{23}; — 2. **strip off** (skin) Mi 3_{3}; abs. **flay** 2C 35_{11}; — 3. obj. pers. **strip** s.one Ho 2_{5} 1C 10_{9}.

hitp.: impf. וַיִּתְפַּשֵּׁט: w. acc. **strip off** (robe fm. onesf.) 1S 18_{4}. †

פָּשַׁע: **qal**: pf. פ׳, 2 sg. f. פָּשַׁעַתְּ (= פָּשַׁעְתְּ or פָּשַׁעַת), פְּשַׁעְתֶּם, פָּשַׁעַתְּ; impf. יִפְשַׁע; impv. פִּשְׁעוּ; inf. פְּשֹׁעַ, פֶּשַׁע; pt. פֹּשְׁעִים, פֹּשֵׁעַ: — 1. **revolt, rebel** (*b^e*, against) 1K 12_{19}; esp. against God 1K 8_{50}; — 2. abs. **revolt, rebel** Am 4_{4}; pt. *pōšēa'* rebel Is 1_{28}.

nif.: pt. נִפְשָׁע: **suffer revolt**? Pr 18_{19}. †

פֶּשַׁע: פָּשַׁע; sf. פִּשְׁעוֹ; pl. פְּשָׁעִים, cs. פִּשְׁעֵי, sf. פִּשְׁעֵיכֶם, פְּשָׁעַי: — 1. **rebellion, revolt** 1K 12_{19}; rebellion against community solidarity Gn 31_{36} or against God Je 5_{6}; *nāśā' l^efeša'* forgive the offense of 1S 25_{28}; — 2. † **contesting of ownership** Ex 22_{8}.

פֵּשֶׁר: **interpretation** Ec 8_{1}. †

***פֵּשֶׁת**: sf. פִּשְׁתִּי; pl. פִּשְׁתִּים, cs. פִּשְׁתֵּי: **flax, linen** Dt 22_{11}; *pištê 'ēṣ* stalks of flax Jos 2_{6}.

פִּשְׁתָּה: — 1. **flax, linen** Ex 9_{31}; — 2. **wick** of flax Is 42_{3} 43_{17}. †

פַּת: sf. פִּתִּי; pl. פִּתִּים; f.: *pat leḥem* (small) **piece, bit**, morsel (of bread) Gn 18_{5}; > *pat* (w/o *leḥem* &c). 2S 12_{3}; metaph. for hail Ps 147_{17}.

***פֹּת**: sf. פָּתְהֵן; pl. פֹּתוֹת: — 1. **forehead** Is 3_{17}; — 2. **front, façade** 1K 7_{50}. †

פְּתָאִים: ↗ פֶּתִי.

פִּתְאֹם, פִּתְאוֹם: **suddenly, surprisingly** Nu 12_{4}; = *b^efit'ōm* 2C 29_{36}; *peta' pit'ōm* all of a sudden Nu 6_{9}, *pit'ōm l^efeta'* in an instant Is 30_{13}; *paḥad pit'ōm* sudden terror Pr 3_{25}.

פַּת־בַּג: sf. פַּת־בָּגוֹ: **(fine) food** Dn 1_{5}.

פִּתְגָם: **decree, decision, statement** Ec 8_{11} Est 1_{20}. †

I **פתה**: **qal**: impf. וַיִּפְתְּ, יִפְתֶּה; pt. פֹּתֶה, פּוֹתָה: **be inexperienced, fool onesf., be naïve, be open to deception** Dt 11_{16} Ho 7_{11}, Jb 5_{2} 31_{27}; *pōteh ś^efātāyw* silly chatterer Pr 20_{19}. †

nif.: pf. נִפְתָּה; impf. וָאֶפָּת: **let onesf. be fooled, be made a fool of** Je 20_{7} Jb 31_{9}. †

piel: pf. פִּתִּיתַנִי, פִּתִּיתָ, פִּתֵּיתִי; impf. יְפַתֶּה, אֲפַתֶּנּוּ, יְפַתּוּךָ; impv. פַּתִּי; inf. פַּתֹּתְךָ; pt. מְפַתֶּיהָ: — 1. **fool, deceive** s.one 1K $22_{20\text{-}22}$; **seduce** a virgin Ex 22_{15}; — 2. **persuade** Ho 2_{16}.

pual: impf. יְפֻתֶּה: **let onesf. be seduced, corrupted; be seducible, corruptible** Je 20_{10} Ez 14_{9} Pr 25_{15}. †

II **פתה** **hif.**: impf. יַפְתְּ: **provide ample space** Gn 9_{27}. †

פְּתוּאֵל: n. pers.

פִּתּוּחַ: sf. פִּתּוּחָהּ; pl. פִּתּוּחִים, cs. פִּתּוּחֵי, sf. פִּתּוּחֶיהָ: **engraving**: on wood 1K 6_{29}, stone Ex 28_{11}, gold Ex 28_{36}.

פְּתוֹר: n. loc.; loc. פְּתוֹרָה.

***פְּתוֹת**: pl. cs. פְּתוֹתֵי: **piece, morsel** (of bread) Ez 13_{19}. †

I **פָּתַח**: **qal**: pf. פ׳, פָּתַח; impf. וָאֶפְתַּח, יִפְתַּח, וַיִּפְתְּחוּ, וְנִפְתְּחָה, יִפְתָּחוּם; impv. פְּתַח, פִּתְחוּ; inf. לִפְתֹּחַ, פְּתֹחַ, abs. פָּתוֹחַ; pt. פּ(וֹ)תֵחַ, pass. פָּתוּחַ, פְּתֻחָה, פְּתֻחֹת: — 1. **open**: abs. (city understood) 2K 15_{16}; w. acc. window Gn 8_{6}, room Gn 41_{56}, cistern Ex 21_{33}, letter Ne 6_{5}; hand Ps 104_{28}, womb Gn 29_{31}; *'ênayim p^etuḥōt* eyes open 1K 8_{29}; — 2.

spec.: obj. rivers, open = **cause to flow** Is 41_{18}; *pāṯaḥ bār* **offer** wheat **for sale** Am 8_{5}; *pāṯaḥ 'îr* (obj.) **conquer** Je 13_{19}, *'îr* subj., **surrender** 2K15_{16}; *pāṯaḥ ḥereb* **draw** a sword Ez 21_{33}.

nif.: pf. נִפְתַּח, נִפְתָּח, נִפְתְּחוּ; impf. יִפָּתֵחַ, יִפָּתַח, יִפָּתְחוּ; inf. הִפָּתַח; pt. נִפְתָּח: — 1. **be opened** Gn 7_{11}; — 2. **open (up)** (intrans.) Ez 1_{1}; — 3. **be set free** (person from prison, evil into land) Is 51_{14} Je 1_{14}; — 4. subj. wine, be given air Jb 32_{19}.

piel: pf. פִּתַּח, פִּתֵּחַ Jb 30_{11}, פִּתַּחְתִּיךְ; impf. יְפַתַּח, יְפַתֵּחַ, יְפַתְּחֵהוּ; inf. פַּתֵּחַ; pt. מְפַתֵּחַ: — 1. **unsaddle** (camels in evening) Gn 24_{32}; **loosen** (sackcloth on loins) Is 20_{2}, **take off** (armor) 1K 20_{11}; — 2. (of flowers) **open, bloom** SS 7_{13}; **break up** (ground) Is 28_{24}.

hitp.: impv. הִתְפַּתְּחִי (Kt ־חוּ) **loosen for onesf.** Is 52_{2}. †

II פתח: **piel**: pf. פִּתַּח, פִּתַּחְתָּ; impf. יְפַתַּח; inf. פַּתֵּחַ, pt. מְפַתֵּחַ: — 1. w. *'al* **engrave** on (material): tablets 1K 7_{36}, stone Ex 28_{9}, gold 28_{36}; — 2. **decorate** s.thg w. engraving Ex 28_{11}; — 3. w. acc. & *'al* **engrave** s.thg on (wood) 2C 3_{7}.

פֶּתַח (164×): פֶּתַח; sf. פִּתְחוֹ, loc. הַפֶּתְחָה; pl. פְּתָחִים, cs. פִּתְחֵי, sf. פְּתָחֵינוּ: **opening, entrance**: of tent Gn 18_{1}, city 1K 17_{10}; *lappeṯaḥ* at the entrance Gn 4_{7}.

*פֵּתַח: cs. פֵּתַח: **disclosure, communication** Ps 119_{130}. †

פְּתִחָה: → *פְּתִיחָה.

*פִּתָּחוֹן: cs. פִּתְחוֹן: **opening** (of the mouth) = occasion for speaking Ez 16_{63} 29_{21}. †

פְּתַחְיָה: n. pers.

I פֶּתִי: pl. פְּתָאִים, פְּתָיִ(י)ם (!): **young, naïve person**, easily deceived Pr 14_{15}.

II פְּתִי: **simplemindedness, naïveté** Pr 1_{22}. †

פְּתִיגִיל: **fine garment** Is 3_{24}. †

פְּתַיּוּת: Pr 9_{23} txt. corr.; rd. וּמְפַתָּה. †

*פְּתִיחָה: pl. פְּתִחוֹת: **drawn sword** or **dagger** Ps 55_{22}. †

פָּתִיל: cs. פְּתִיל; pl. פְּתִילִים: (twisted) **thread**, of gold Ex 39_{3}; **cord** Gn 38_{18}; **skein** (of tow) Ju 16_{9}.

פתל: **nif.**: pf. נִפְתַּלְתִּי; pt. נִפְתָּל: — 1. **twist** (intrans.), **wrestle** ? Gn 30_{8}; — 2. **be tortuous, subtle** Pr 8_{8} Jb 5_{13}. †

hitp.: impf. תִּתְפַּתָּל: **prove** (onesf.) **tortuous, subtle** Ps 18_{27}. †

פְּתַלְתֹּל: **tortuous**, perverse Dt 32_{5}. †

פִּתֹם: n. loc.

פֶּתֶן: פֶּתֶן; pl. פְּתָנִים: (African) **cobra** or **asp**, *Naja haje* Dt 32_{33} (oth.: **horned viper**, *Cerastes cornutus*).

פֶּתַע: **instant**: *beфeta'*, *lefeta'* Nu 6_{9}; w/o prep., adv. **suddenly** Hb 2_{7}.

פתר: **qal**: pf. 'פָּתַר, פָּתַר־ פ Gn 41_{13}; impf. וַיִּפְתָּר־; inf. לִפְתֹּר; pt. פֹּתֵר: **interpret, explain** (dream) Gn 40_{8}.

פִּתְרוֹן: cs. פִּתְרוֹן; sf. פִּתְרֹנוֹ; pl. פִּתְרֹנִים: **interpretation** (of a dream) Gn 40_{5}.

פַּתְרוֹס: n. terr., **Upper Egypt**.

פַּתְרֻסִים: n. peop., inhab. of פַּתְרוֹס, **Upper Egypt**.

פַּתְשֶׁגֶן: **copy** Est 3_{14} 4_{8} 8_{13}. †

פתת: **qal**: inf. פָּתוֹת: **crumble** (sacrificial cake) Lv 2_{6}. †

צ

צֵא: **dirt, filth** Is 30_{22}. †

*צֵאָה: cs. צֵאַת; sf. צֵאָתֶךָ: **dung, excrement** Dt 23_{14} Ez 4_{12}. †

צֹאָה: צֹאַת; sf. צֹאָתוֹ, צוֹאָתָם 2K 18_{27} Qr: **dung, excrement** 2K 18_{27} Qr, Is 4_{4}; phrase *qî' ṣō'â* loathsome vomit Is 28_{8}.

צֹאִי*: pl. צ(ו)אִים: **filthy, befouled** (w. excrement) Zc $3_{3f.}$ †

צֶאֱלִים: a specific species of **thorny shrub** related to buckthorn, *Zizyphus lotus* Jb 40_{21}. †

צֹאן (273×): sf. צֹאנוֹ, צֹאנֵינוּ Ne 10_{37}, צֹאונֵנוּ Ps 144_{13}; f.: coll. **small cattle, i.e. sheep & goats** Gn 4_2; sheep only 1S 25_2; males only (thus m.) Gn 30_{40}; *bᵉnê ṣō'n* individual animals Ps 114_4; metaph. = Isr. 2S 24_{17}.

צַאֲנָן: n. loc.

צֶאֱצָאִים: cs. צֶאֱצָאֵי, sf. צֶאֱצָאֵיהֶם: **offspring** Is 34_1; **descendants** Is 44_3.

I **צָב**: pl. צַבִּים: **covered wagon** Nu 7_3 Is 66_{20}. †

II **צָב**: a **lizard** w. a spiny-scaled tail, *Uromastix spinipes* Lv 11_{29}. †

צבא: **qal**: pf. צָבְאוּ; impf. וַיִּצְבְּאוּ; inf. לִצְבֹּא & לִצְבָא; pt. צֹבְאִים, צֹבְאֹת: — 1. **go to war** Nu 31_{42}, w. *'al* against Nu 31_7; — 2. **serve** (in the cult): men Nu 4_{23}, women 1S 2_{22}.

hif.: pt. מַצְבִּא: **muster, conscript** 2K 25_{19} Je 52_{25}. †

I **צָבָא** (479×, 279× צְבָאוֹת in designation of Y.): A: aside fm. צְבָאוֹת for Y.: cs. צְבָא, sf. צְבָאִי; pl. צְבָאוֹת, cs. צִבְאוֹת, sf. צִבְאֹתָם, צִבְאוֹתֵיכֶם: — 1. **army service**: *yāṣā' ṣābā'* Nu 1_3; *ṣᵉbā' milḥāmâ* **warfare** Nu 31_{14}; — 2. **army, warriors** 2S 3_{23}; pl. Ex 6_{26}; *śar ṣᵉbā'ô* Gn 21_{22}; — 3. w. ref. to Y.: *ṣib'ôt yhwh* = Isr. Ex 12_{41}; *ṣar ṣᵉbā' yhwh* = angel Jos $5_{14f.}$; — 4. *ṣᵉbā' haššāmayim* = stars 2K 17_{16}; = attendants of God 1K 22_{19}; — 5. *ṣᵉbā' hammārôm* = *ṣᵉbā' haššāmayim* Is 24_{21}; — 6. army service > **cultic service** Nu 4_3, *ṣᵉbā' hā'ᵃbōdâ* Nu 8_{25}; — 7. army service > **compulsory service** (to pay off a debt) Is 40_2; —
B: *ṣᵉbā'ôt* **hosts** as designation of God; *yhwh ('ᵉlōhê) (haṣ)ṣᵉbā'ôt* Ho 12_6; *ṣᵉbā'ôt* = Isr.'s warriors? angels? stars?

II **צְבָא***: pl. צְבָאִים: **gazelle** 1C 12_9. †

צְבָאָה*: pl. צְבָאוֹת: female **gazelle** SS 2_7 3_5. †

צְבָאוֹת: ↗ I צָבָא & צְבָאָה*.

צְבֹאִים Ho 11_8 Kt, Qr צְבוֹיִם, צְבֹיִם Gn 10_{19}, צְבֹיִּים Gn $14_{2.8}$ Dt 29_{22}: n. loc.

הַצֹּבֵבָה: n. pers.

צבה: **qal**: pf. צָבְתָה: **swell up** Nu 5_{27}. †

hif.: inf. לַצְבּוֹת < לְהַצְבּוֹת: **make s.thg swell up** Nu 5_{22}. †

צֹבָה: n. loc.: ↗ צוֹבָה.

צֶבֶה*: pl. sf. צֹבֶיהָ Is 29_7: txt. corr., rd. צֹבְאֶיהָ ?. †

צָבֶה*: f. צָבָה, adj.: **swollen** Nu 5_{21}. †

צָבוּעַ: **hyena**, *Hyaena hyaena* Je 12_9. †

צבט: **qal**: impf. וַיִּצְבָּט־: **give, pass s.thg to s.one** Ru 2_{14}. †

I **צְבִי**: צְבִי; pl. cs. צִבְאוֹת: **ornament, glory** 2S 1_{19}; *ṣᵉbî ṣib'ôt* Je 3_{19}; — 2. *haṣṣᵉbî* = Jerus. Dn 8_9, *'ereṣ haṣṣᵉbî* = Palestine Dn 11_{16}.

II **צְבִי**: pl. צְבָיִם: generic term for var. types of **gazelle** 1K 5_3.

צִבְיָא: n. pers.

צִבְיָה: n. pers. f.

צְבִיָּה: female **gazelle** SS 4_5 7_4. †

צְבֹיִ(י)ם: ↗ צְבֹאִים.

צבע*: cj **hitp.**: וְתִצְטַבַּע: **turn out to be dyed** cj Jb 38_{14}. †

צֶבַע*: pl. צְבָעִים: **colored, dyed fabric** Ju 5_{30}. †

צִבְעוֹן: n. pers.

צְבֹעִים: n. loc.

צבר: **qal**: impf. וַיִּצְבְּרוּ, יִצְבָּר־, יִצְבֹּר: **pile up**, grain Gn $41_{35.49}$, dead frogs Ex 8_{10}.

צִבֻּר*: pl. צִבֻּרִים: **heap, pile** 2K 10_8. †

צֶבֶת*: pl. צְבָתִים: **bundle of grain** (handful cut together) Ru 2_{16}. †

I **צַד**: sf. צִדּוֹ; pl. cs. צִדֵּי, sf. צְדָדָיו: **side** (of an obj.) Gn 6_{16}; (of a man) 2S 2_{16}; *miṣṣad* at the side of 1S 6_8.

II **צַד***: pl. צִדִּים: **snare** Ju 2_3. †

צְדָד* or **צְדָד***: n. loc.; loc. צְדָדָה.

I **צדה**: **qal**: pf. צ׳; pt. צֹדֶה: **lie in wait for** Ex 21_{13} 1S 24_{12}. †

II **צדה**: **nif.**: pf. נִצְדּוּ: **be devastated** Zp 3_6. †

צָדָה: ↗ צֵידָה.

צָדוֹק: n. pers.

צְדִיָּה: **ambush, malice aforethought** Nu $35_{20\cdot22}$. †

צִדִּים: n. loc. Jos 19_{35} txt.?. †

צַדִּיק (205×): pl. צַדִּיקִ(י)ם: — 1. a thing examined and found to be in order, right: *wenō'mar ṣaddîq* we say, 'it is (all) right' Is 41_{26}; — 2. (legally: a person whose conduct is examined and found to be unobjectionable): **not guilty, innocent, in the right** 2K 10_9; — 3. (morally in the right): **innocent, guiltless** 2S 4_{11}; *ṣaddîq min* more upright than 1S 24_{18}; — 4. therefore: **just, righteous** (character or conduct) 2S 23_3; — 5. (religiously) **righteous, godly** Gn 6_9; — 6. said of God, **in the right** Ex 9_{27}; **righteous, just** Ps 7_{10}.

צֵדֹנִית: ↗ צִידוֹנִי.

צדק: **qal**: pf. צָדַקְתִּי, צָדְקָה; impf. יִצְדַּק, יִצְדָּקוּ, יִצְדְּקוּ, יִצְדָּק: — 1. **be in the right, be right, have a just case** Is $43_{9\cdot26}$; w. *min* before Gn 38_{26}; — 2. **carry one's point, be vindicated** Jb 11_2; — 3. **be just, righteous** Ps 19_{10}.

nif.: pf. נִצְדַּק: **be brought** (back) **to its rights, be vindicated** Dn 8_{14}. †

piel: pf. צִדְּקָה; impf. וַתְּצַדְּקִי; inf. sf. צַדְּקֵךְ, צַדְּקוֹ: — 1. make s.one **appear righteous, innocent** Ez 16_{51f}; — 2. *ṣiddeqâ nafšô min* **prove more just, righteous than** Je 3_{11}; **consider onesf. in the right** compared w. Jb 32_2; — 3. **declare** s.one **to be in the right** Jb 33_{32}. †

hif.: pf. הִצְדַּקְתִּיו, הִצְדִּיקוּ; impf. יַצְדִּיק; impv. הַצְדִּיקוּ; inf. הַצְדִּיק; pt. מַצְדִּיק, sf. מַצְדִּיקִי: — 1. **give** s.one **justice, bring justice** 2S 15_4; **acknowledge that s.one is right** Jb 27_5; **pronounce** s.one **not guilty, innocent** 1K 8_{32}; **treat** s.one **as not guilty, innocent** Ex 23_7; — 2. **help** s.one **gain his rights** Is 53_{11}.

hitp.: impf. נִצְטַדָּק: **prove onesf. to be innocent** Gn 44_{16}. †

צֶדֶק: sf. צִדְקֶךָ, צִדְקוֹ: — 1. **(what is) right, normal**: just weights Dt 25_{15}; *'ēlê haṣṣedeq* evergreen trees Is 61_3; what is **right, just** = suitable Is 45_{19}, = trustworthy Ps 23_3; — 2. **(legal) rightness** Dt 16_{20}; *ṣidqî* my legal right Jb 6_{29}; — 3. **justice** Dt 1_{16}; adj. **just, righteous** Dt 16_{18}; *ṣedeq* adv. Ps 119_{138}; — 4. justice done to s.one = **success** Is 41_2; — 5. *beṣedeq* through success given by God = **by grace** Is 42_6.

צְדָקָה (157×): cs. צִדְקַת, sf. צִדְקָתִי; pl. צְדָקוֹת, cs. צִדְקֹת, sf. צִדְקֹתֵינוּ: — 1. righteousness = **blameless behavior, honesty** Gn 30_{33}; *biṣdāqâ* in honesty Is 48_1 Je 4_2; — 2. **righteousness** (of the whole being) Pr 15_9; — 3. **justice** (of a human judge) Gn 18_{19}; — 4. **justice** (characteristic of God the divine judge) Is 5_{16}; — 5. **righteousness** (as religious attitude =) **godliness** 2S $22_{21\cdot25}$; — 6. **righteousness** (= behavior wh. God expects man to show to God) Gn 15_6; — 7. (God's) **justice**: a) wh. God expects for man's conduct w. man Dt 33_{21}; b) **what is reliable**; truth Is 45_{23}; c) what God gives = **salvation, deliverance** Is 46_{12}; — 8. pl.: a) **legal claims** Je 51_{10}; b) God's **acts of justice** 1S 12_7; c) just acts of men Is 33_{15}; godliness Ez 18_{24}; — 9. var.: *ṣedāqâ* **legal claim** 2S 19_{29}, **blamelessness** Is 5_{23}.

צִדְקִיָּה: n. pers.

צִדְקִיָּהוּ: n. pers.

צהב: **hof.**: pt. מֻצְהָב: **gleaming red** (bronze) Ezr 8_{27}. †

צָהֹב: **gleaming red** (hair) Lv $13_{30\cdot32\cdot36}$. †

I **צהל**: **qal**: pf. צָהֲלוּ, צָהֲלָה; impf. יִצְהֲלוּ, תִּצְהַלוּ; impv. צַהֲלִי: — 1. **neigh** (of stallion) Je 5_8; — 2. **shout** (for joy) Is 12_6.

piel: impv. צַהֲלִי (identical w. qal): **make** s.thg (i.e. voice) **yell** Is 10_{30}. †

II **צהל**: **hif.**: inf. הַצְהִיל: **make** s.thg **shine** Ps 104_{15}. †

צהר: **hif.**: impf. יַצְהִירוּ: some: denom. of *yiṣhār*, **press out oil**; oth.: denom. of *ṣohᵒrayim*, **spend noonday** Jb 24_{11}. †

צֹהַר: **covering, roof** (of ark) Gn 6_{16}. †

צָהֳרַיִם: צָהֳרָיִם: **midday, noontime** Gn 43_{16}; *bᵉtôk ṣohᵒrayim* in broad noonday Is 16_{3}; *miškab haṣṣohᵒrayim* **siesta** 2S 4_{5}.

צַו: צָו: syllable mimicking prophetic speech Is $28_{10\cdot 13}$. †

***צוֹאָה**: *F* *צֹאָה.

צַוָּאר: cs. צַוַּאר, sf. צַוָּ(א)רָם; pl. cs. צַוְּארֵי, sf. צַוְּארֹתֵיכֶם, צַוָּארָיו: **neck** (spec. **back of neck** Je 27_{8}): of man Gn 27_{16}, of animal Gn 27_{40}; *bᵉṣawwāʾr* w. stiff neck Jb 15_{26}.

צוֹבָה & **צֹבָה**: n. loc.

צוד: **qal**: pf. צָדוּ, צָדוּנִי, צָדוּם; impf. יָצוּד, תְּצוּדֵנִי, יְצוּדֻנוּ, יָצוּדוּ; impv. צוּדָה; inf. cs. צוּד, abs. צוֹד; pt. צָד: — 1. **hunt** Gn 27_{3} (obj. animal), La 3_{52} (obj. bird); — 2. metaph. **hunt** (obj. men), **lie in wait for** Mi 7_{2}.

pilpel: inf. צוֹדֵד pt. מְצֹדְדוֹת: (obj. *nᵉfāšôt* 'souls') (hunt and) **catch** Ez $13_{18\cdot 20}$. †

צוה (485×): **piel**: pf. צִוָּה, צִוְּתָה, צִוִּיתָה, צִוַּנִי, צִוֻּנִי, צִוְּךָ, צִוָּהוּ, צִוָּם, sf. צִוִּיתִי, צִוִּיתִי, וְאֲצַוֶּה, וַיְצַו, יְצַו, יְצַוֶּה; impf. צִוִּית(י)ךָ, צִוִּתָה, אֲצַוְּךָ, תְּצַוֶּנּוּ, וִיצַוְּךָ, וַיְצַוֵּהוּ, יְצַוֵּם, sf. וַיְצַוּוּ, צַוֵּנִי; impv. צַוֵּה, צַו, צַוּוּ; inf. צַוּוֹת, sf. צַוֹּתוֹ; pt. מְצַוֶּה, cs. מְצַוֵּה, f. מְצַוָּה, sf. מְצַוְּךָ, מְצַוֶּךָ: — 1. **order, direct, appoint** (s.one to do s.thg) 1K 1_{35} 17_{9}; — 2. **order, direct, appoint** (s.thg [to do s.thg]): obj. blessing Lv 25_{21}; obj. serpent, sword Am $9_{3\cdot 4}$; — 3. **command, order** s.one: contents of order var. expressed: a) in indep. clause: and he shall keep = that he should keep Gn 18_{19}; b) sim.: *wayṣawwēhû wayyōʾmer* Gn 28_{1}; c) *lēʾmōr* & indep. clause Gn 26_{11}; d) w. *lᵉ* & inf. Gn 50_{2}; e) *lᵉbiltî* **forbid** Gn 3_{11}; f) (late) *ʾᵃšer* Est 2_{10}; — 4. **give an order, order** w. *ʿal*, *ʾel*, or *lᵉ* & pers. Gn 2_{16}; — 5. **charge** s.one (to do s.thg) Gn 6_{22}; — 6. var.: *mᵉṣawwēh lᵉʾummîm* **commander** of the nations Is 55_{4}; *ṣiwwâ ʾel-* (or *lᵉ*) *bêtô* **set** one's house **in order** (= prepare for death) 2K 20_{1}.

pual: pf. צֻוֵּיתִי, צֻוֵּיתָ, צֻוָּה; impf. יְצֻוֶּה: **be ordered, receive a command** Ex 34_{34}.

צוח: **qal**: impf. יִצְוָחוּ: **shout** Is 42_{11}. †

צְוָחָה: cs. צִוְחַת, sf. צִוְחָתֵךְ: **wail** Is 24_{11}.

צוּלָה: **abyss** (of sea) Is 44_{27}. †

צום: **qal**: pf. צַמְתֶּם, צַמְתָּ, צַמְנוּ, צַמְתֻּנִי; impf. וַיָּצֻם, וַיָּצוּם, אָצוּם, יָצְמוּ, impv. צוּמוּ; inf. צוֹם; pt. צָם; **fast,** i.e. abstain fm. food & drink in time of penitence or mourning 1K 21_{27}, cogn. acc. 2S 12_{16}; trans.! *ṣamtunî* you have fasted for (= to please) me (= God) Zc 7_{5}.

צוֹם: sf. צוֹמְכֶם; pl. צוֹמוֹת: (act of) **fasting,** (time of) **fasting, fast** 1K $21_{9\cdot 12}$.

צוּעָר: n. pers.

צוֹעַר: *F* צֹעַר.

צוף: **qal**: pf. צָפוּ: **flood, rise up** (waters) La 3_{54}. †

hif.: pf. הֵצִיף; impf. וַיָּצֶף: — 1. **make** (waters) **flood** Dt 11_{4}; — 2. **make** (iron) **float** 2K 6_{6}. †

I **צוּף**: pl. צוּפִים: **(honey-)comb** (wh. is dripping w. honey) Ps 19_{11} Pr 16_{24}. †

II **צוּף**: n. pers.

צוֹפַח: n. pers.

צוֹפַי: n. pers.

צוֹפִים 1S 1_{1}: rd. צוֹפִי. †

צוֹפַר & **צֹפַר**: n. pers.

I **צוץ**: **qal**: pf. צָץ: **sprout, bloom** (subj. *maṭṭeh*; txt.?) Ez 7_{10}. †

hif. (or **qal**?): impf. וַיָּצֵץ, יָצִיץ, יָצִיצוּ: **produce blossoms** Nu 17_{23}.

II **צוץ**: **hif.**: pt. מֵצִיץ: **look** (through windows) SS 2_{9}. †

צוק: **hif.**: pf. הֵצִיקָה, הֲצִיקוֹתִי, הֱצִיקַתְהוּ,

הֱצִיקַתְנִי; impf. יָצִיק; pt. מֵצִיק: **oppress** s.one, **press** s.one **hard**: w. *le* Dt 28_{53}, w. acc. Ju 14_{17}; *mēṣîq* **oppressor** Is 51_{13}.

צוֹק Dn 9_{25}: trad. **oppression**, but txt. corr.?. †

צוּקָה: **oppression, distress** Is 8_{22} 30_6 Pr 1_{27}. †

I צוּר: **qal**: pf. צַרְתָּ, צַרְתַּנִי; impf. וַיָּצַר, תָּצוּר, וַיָּצֻרוּ; impv. צוּרִי; inf. צוּר, pt. צָרִים: — 1. **tie up** (silver in bags) 2K 5_{23}; w. *be* & acc. **clasp** (silver in hand) Dt 14_{25}; **collect** (population against …) Ju 9_{31}; — 2. *ṣar muṣṣāb* **post** (sentries) **around** Is 29_3; — 3. w. *'el* **enclose, invest** (town &c. in siege) 1S 23_8; w. *'al* **besiege** 1K 15_{27} & oft.; — 4. w. *'al* **barricade** SS 8_9.

nif.: pt. f. cj נְצוּרָה **enclosed** cj Is 1_8. †

II צוּר: **qal**: pf. צַרְתִּי; impf. תָּצַר, תְּצֻרֵם; inf. צוּר, pt. pl. צָרִים: **oppress, press** s.one **hard** Ex 23_{22} Dt $2_{9.19}$ Ps 89_{44} Est 8_{11} (II = I?). †

III צוּר: **qal**: impf. וַיָּצַר: **cast** (metal) Ex 32_4 1K 7_{15}. †

אֶצָּוֹרְךָ Je 1_5 ↗ יָצַר. †

I צוּר: sf. צוּרִי, pl. צוּרִים, צֻרִים, צוּרוֹת: — 1. **boulder**, (large) **rock** 2S 21_{10}; — 2. w. n. loc.: *ṣûr 'ôrēb, bêt ṣûr, ṣûrê hay'ēlîm*; — 3. **rock** = God 1S 2_2 & oft.

צֻרִם Jos 5_2f: ↗ צֹר.

II צוּר: **pebble, flint** Jb 22_{24}. †

III צוּר: n. pers. Nu 25_{15} 31_8 Jos 13_{21} 1C 8_{30} 9_{36}. †

IV צוּר: name of deity (in n. loc. *bêt ṣûr*).

צוֹר: n. loc. **Tyre**, ↗ צֹר.

*צַוָּר: ↗ צַוָּאר.

*צוּרָה: cs. צוּרַת, sf. צוּרָתוֹ: **design, plan** Ez 43_{11}. †

צוּרִיאֵל: n. pers.

צוּרִישַׁדַּי: n. pers.

*צַוְּרֹנִים: sf. צַוְּרֹנָיִךְ: **necklace** SS 4_9. †

צות: **hif.**: impf. אֲצִיתֶנָּה: **set on fire** Is 27_4. †

צַח: pl. f. צַחוֹת: — 1. **dazzling, vibrating** (hot wind) Is 18_4 Je 4_{11}; — 2. **splendid, bright** SS 5_{10}; — 3. **clear** Is 32_4. †

צִחָא: ↗ צִיחָא.

*צִחֶה: cs. צְחֵה: **parched** Is 5_{13}. †

צחח: **qal**: pf. צַחוּ: **be white** La 4_7. †

*צְחִחִי: ↗ *צְחִיחַ.

*צְחִיחַ: cs. צְחִיחַ: **brilliant, bare surface** (of a rock) Ez 24_7 $26_{4.14}$; pl. Ne 4_7 **bare places**. †

צְחִיחָה: **bare, scorched land** Ps 68_7. †

*צַחֲנָה: sf. צַחֲנָתוֹ: **stench** (of putrefaction) Jl 2_{20}. †

צַחְצָחוֹת: **scorched land** Is 58_{11}. †

צחק: **qal**: pf. צָחֲקָה, צָחַקְתְּ; impf. יִצְחַק־ Gn 21_6, וַתִּצְחַק, וַיִּצְחַק: **laugh** Gn 17_{17} $18_{12f.15}$, w. *le* at 21_6.

piel: impf. וַיְצַחֵק; inf. לְצַחֵק, לְצַחֶק; pt. מְצַחֵק: — 1. abs. **joke** Gn 19_{14}, **play** 21_9, **amuse onesf.** Ex 32_6; — 2. w. *'ēt* **fondle** (a woman) Gn 26_8; w. *be* **play around with** $39_{14.17}$; w. *lifnê* **amuse onesf.** before Ju 16_{25}. †

צְחֹק: **laughter** Gn 21_6 Ez 23_{32}. †

צַחַר: n. loc.

*צָחֹר: pl. f. צְחֹרוֹת: **tawny, yellowish-red** (asses) Ju 5_{10}. †

צֹחַר: n. pers.

I צִי: pl. צִים, צִיִּים: **ship** Nu 24_{24} Is 33_{21} Dn 11_{30}. †

II צִי: pl. צִיִּים: **demon** (dweller in *ṣiyyâ*) Is 13_{21} 23_{13} 34_{14} Je 50_{39}. †

צִיבָא: n. pers.

ציד: **hitp.**: pf. הִצְטַיָּדְנוּ: **take for one's provisions** Jos 9_{12}, cj $_4$. †

I צַיִד: צֵיד, cs. צֵיד, sf. צֵידוֹ: — 1. **hunting** Gn 10_9; — 2. **game** Gn 25_{28}.

II צַיִד: צֵיד, sf. צֵידָם: **provisions** (for journey) Jos $9_{5.14}$; food (for birds) Jb 38_{41}, (for men) Ps 132_{15} Ne 13_{15}. †

צַיָּד: **hunter** Je 16_{16}; cj Pr 6_5. †

צֵידָה & צֵדָה: **provisions** (for journey) Gn 42_{25}.

צִיד(וֹ)ן: n. loc. **Sidon**.

צִידֹנִי: gent. of צִידוֹן: pl. צִידֹנִים, f. צֵדְנִית: **Sidonian**.

צִיָּה: pl. צִיּוֹת: **dry country, waterless region**, *'ereṣ ṣiyyâ* Is 41_{18}.

צָיוֹן: **waterless land** Is 25_5 32_2. †

צִיּוֹן: n. loc.; loc. צִיּ֫וֹנָה: **Zion**.

צִיּוּן: **stone landmark** (cairn or single upright stone) Ez 39_{15}; **gravestone** 2K 23_{17}; **road-mark** Je 31_{21}. †

צִיחָא: n. pers.

צִיִּים: ↗ צִי.

צִין: ↗ צִן.

צִינֹק: **iron collar** Je 29_{26}. †

צִיעֹר: n. loc.

צִיף: ↗ II צוּף.

I **צִיץ**: pl. צִצִּים: — 1. **blossoms** Nu 17_{23}; — 2. (artificial) **flower** 1K 6_{18}, as ornament on forehead of priest Ex 28_{36}.

II **צִיץ**: הַצִּיץ: n. loc. 2C 20_{16}. †

***צִיצָה**: cs. צִיצַת: **flower** Is 28_4. †

צִיצִת: — 1. *ṣîṣit rō'š* **lock** (of hair on head) Ez 8_3; — 2. **tuft, fringe, tassel** Nu 15_{38}. †

צִיקְלַג: ↗ צִקְלַג.

[**צִיר**: **qal**: pt. צָר Is 59_{19}, ↗ I צור. †

hitp.: impf. וַיִּצְטַיָּרוּ Jos 9_4, rd. וַיִּצְטַיָּדוּ. †]

I **צִיר**: **(door-)pivot** Pr 26_{14}. †

II **צִיר** & ***צִר**: pl. צִירִים, sf. צִרַיִךְ: **messenger** Is 18_2.

III ***צִיר**: pl. צִירִים, sf. צִירֶיהָ, צִרַי: **pangs, convulsions** 1S 4_{19}.

IV ***צִיר**: pl. צִירִים: Is 45_{16} trad. **idols**, but txt. corr.?; *ṣîrām* Ps 49_{15} txt.?. †

צֵל: cs. =, sf. צִלּוֹ, צִלְלוֹ Jb 40_{22}; pl. צְלָלִים, cs. צִלְלֵי: **shadow, shade**: — 1. lit., of roof Gn 19_8, of tree Ju 9_{15}, of cloud Is 25_5; — 2. metaph., of God's protection Is 49_2; — 3. = **protection** (of men) Nu 14_9.

צלה: **qal**: impf. יִצְלֶה, אֶצְלֶה; inf. צְלוֹת: **roast** (meat) 1S 2_{15} Is $44_{16.19}$. †

צִלָּה: n. pers. f.

***צְלוֹל** Kt, Qr צְלִיל: cs. צְלוֹל *ṣelûl leḥem* (disk-shaped) **loaf** (of bread) Ju 7_{13}. †

צלח: **qal**: pf. צָלְחָה, צָלֵחָה; impf. יִצְלַח, יִצְלָח, וַתִּצְלְחִי: — 1. **be strong, effective, powerful**, of *rûᵃḥ* 1S 10_6; — 2. **be of use** Is 54_{17}; — 3. **succeed** Nu 14_{41}, **be successful** Je 12_1.

hif.: pf. הִצְלַחְתָּ, הִצְלִיחָה, הִצְלִיחַ, הִצְלִיחוֹ; impf. יַצְלִיחַ, וַיַּצְלַח, תַּצְלִיחִי; impv. הַצְלַח, הַצְלִיחָה; pt. מַצְלִיחַ: — 1. **be successful, succeed, enjoy success** 1K 22_{12}; *'îš maṣlîᵃḥ* successful man Gn 39_2; w. acc. in s.thg Dt 28_{29}; — 2. w. acc. **make** s.thg **succeed, bring** s.thg **to successful conclusion** Gn 24_{21}; — 3. **make** s.one **prosper** 2C 26_5.

צְלֹחִית: (shallow) **bowl** 2K 2_{20}. †

צַלַּחַת: pl. צְלָחוֹת: (shallow) **bowl** 2K 21_{13}.

***צֵלַחַת**: pl. צְלָחוֹת: ↗ צַלַּחַת.

צָלִי: cs. צְלִי: **roasted (meat)** Ex 12_{8f} Is 44_{16}. †

צְלִיל: ↗ צְלוֹל.

I **צלל**: **qal**: pf. צָלְלוּ; impf. תְּצִלֶּינָה, תְּצִלֶּנָה: (of ears) **ring** 1S 3_{11} 2K 21_{12} Je 19_3; (of lips) **quiver** Hb 3_{16}. †

II **צלל**: **qal**: pf. צָלֲלוּ: **sink** (down) Ex 15_{10}. †

III **צלל**: **qal**: pf. צָלְלוּ: **become shady, dark** Ne 13_{19}. †

hif.: pt. מֵצַל, cj. inf. הָצֵל: **give shade** Ez 31_3, cj. Jon 4_6. †

צִלּוֹ, צִלְלֵי, צְלָלִים: ↗ צֵל.

I **צֶלֶם**: sf. צַלְמוֹ, צַלְמֵנוּ; pl. cs. צַלְמֵי, sf. צְלָמָיו, צַלְמֵיכֶם: — 1. **statue** 2K 11_{18}; *ṣalmê massēkōt* cast-metal statues Nu 33_{52}; — 2. **image, model** 1S 6_5; **image, drawing** Ez 23_{14}; — 3. **image** (i.e. man in image of God) Gn 1_{26f}.

II **צֶלֶם**: sf. צַלְמָם: **shadow, s.thg shadowy,** form w/o substance Ps 39_7 73_{20}. †

I **צַלְמוֹן**: n. pers. 2S 23_{28}. †

II **צַלְמוֹן**: n. of mountain Ju 9_{48} Ps 68_{15}. †

צַלְמָוֶת: **darkness** Ps 23_4.

צַלְמֹנָה: n. loc.

צַלְמֻנָּע: n. pers.

צלע: **qal**: pt. צֹלֵעַ, f. צֹלֵעָה: — 1. **limp** Gn 32_{32}; — 2. **be lame** (animals) Mi 4_{6f} Zp 3_{19}. †

צֶלַע: sf. צַלְעִי: **stumbling** Je 20_{10} Ps 35_{15} 38_{18} Jb 18_{12}. †

I **צֵלָע**: cs. צֶלַע & צְלַע, sf. צַלְעוֹ; pl. צְלָעוֹת, cs. צַלְעֹת & צְלָעִים 1K 6_{34}; f.: — 1. **rib**

Gn $2_{21}f$; — 2. **side** (of mountain) 2S 16_{13}; (of obj., opp. back & front) Ex 25_{12}; — 3. **side-rooms, story** (= floor) 1K 6_5; **wing** (of building) Ez 41_5; — 4. **plank** 1K $6_{15}f$; — 5. **leaf** (of door) 1K 6_{34}; — 6. **supporting beam** 1K 7_3.

II **צֵלַע**: n. loc. Jos 18_{28} 2S 21_{14}. †

צָלָף: n. pers.

צְלָפְחָד: n. pers.

צֶלְצַח: n. loc.

צְלָצַל: cs. צִלְצַל: (swarm of) (mole-) **crickets**, *Gryllotalpa vulgaris*, very destructive to plants Dt 28_{42}; *'ereṣ ṣilṣal kᵉnāfayim* country of winged crickets Is 18_1. †

***צִלְצָל**: cs. צִלְצַל: *ṣilṣal dāgîm* **fishing spear**; Is 18_1, F *ṣᵉlāṣal*. †

צֶלְצְלִים: cs. צִלְצְלֵי: **cymbals** 2S 6_5; *ṣilṣᵉlê šāmaʿ* small, vertically-held cymbals; *ṣilṣᵉlê tᵉrûʿâ* large, horizontally-held cymbals Ps 150_5. †

צֶלֶק: n. pers.

צִלְּתַי: n. pers.

צמא: **qal**: pf. צָמְאוּ, צָמֵ(א)תִי, צָמֵת, צָמְאָה; impf. וַיִּצְמָא, וַיִּצְמְאוּ: **be thirsty** Ju 4_{19}; *lᵉ* for (water) Ex 17_3, (God) Ps 42_3.

צָמָא: sf. צְמָאִי: **thirst** Ex 17_3.

צָמֵא: f. צְמֵאָה; pl. צְמֵאִים: — 1. **thirsty** 2S 17_{29}; — 2. *haṣṣᵉmēʾâ* **thirsty, arid** (country) Dt 29_{18}.

צִמְאָה: **thirst** Je 2_{25}. †

צִמָּאוֹן: **thirsty, waterless region** Dt 8_{15} Is 35_7 Ps 107_{33}. †

צמד: **nif.**: impf. וַיִּצָּמֶד, וַיִּצָּמְדוּ; pt. נִצְמָדִים: w. *lᵉ* **commit onesf. to, attach onesf. to** Nu $25_{3\cdot5}$ Ps 106_{28}. †

pual: pt. מְצֻמֶּדֶת: **fastened** 2S 20_8. †

hif.: impf. תַּצְמִיד: **hitch up** (animal: here metaph.) Ps 50_{19}. †

צֶמֶד: sf. צִמְדּוֹ; pl. צְמָדִים, cs. צִמְדֵּי: — 1. **yoke, team** (= 2 animals): *bāqār* 1K 19_{21}, *ḥᵃmōrîm* 2S 16_1; — 2. area of land wh. a team can plow in a day, **acre** 1S 14_{14}.

***צַמָּה**: sf. צַמָּתֵךְ: **veil** (for face) Is 47_2 SS $4_{1\cdot3}$ 6_7. †

צִמֻּקִים, צִמּוּקִים: **cakes of raisins** 1S 25_{18} 30_{12} 2S 16_1 1C 12_{41}. †

צמח: **qal**: pf. צָמַח־, צָמְחוּ; impf. וַיִּצְמַח, יִצְמָח, יִצְמְחוּ, תִּצְמַחְנָה; pt. צֹמֵחַ, צֹמְחוֹת: **sprout, spring up**: plants Gn 2_5, new flesh in healing wound Is 58_8, men Is 44_4, metaph. events Is 42_9.

piel: pf. צִמַּח; impf. יְצַמֵּחַ; inf. צַמֵּחַ: **grow** (thickly) (of hair, beard) 2S 10_5.

hif.: pf. הִצְמִיחָה; impf. יַצְמִיחַ, תַּצְמִחַ, וַיַּצְמַח; inf. הַצְמִיחַ; pt. מַצְמִיחַ: — 1. (subj. God) **make** (plants) **grow, sprout** Gn 2_9; metaph. **make** s.thg **prosper** 2S 23_5; — 2. (subj. earth) **make** (plants) **sprout** Is 55_{10}; — 3. 2 acc. (God subj.) **make** (mountains) **grow** (grass) Ps 147_8.

צֶמַח: sf. צִמְחָהּ: — 1. coll. **growth, what sprouts** Gn 19_{25}; *ṭarpê ṣimḥāh* its fresh shoots Ez 17_9; — 2. (the individual) **shoot, bud**: metaph. of Messianic king Je 23_5.

I **צָמִיד**: pl. צְמִידִים: (woman's) **bracelet** Gn 24_{22}.

II **צָמִיד**: **lid, cover** Nu 19_{15}. †

צַמִּים: Jb 5_5 txt. corr., rd. צְמֵאִים?; Jb 18_9 **snare** ?. †

צְמִיתֻת: F צְמִתֻת.

צמק: **qal**: pt. צֹמְקִים: **dry up, shrivel** (of breasts) Ho 9_{14}. †

צִמֻּקִים: F צִמּוּקִים.

צֶמֶר: **wool** 2K 3_4.

צְמָרִי: n. peop. Gn 10_{18}.

צְמָרַיִם: n. of mountain.

צַמֶּרֶת: sf. צַמַּרְתּוֹ: **(tree-)top** Ez 17_3.

צמת: **qal**: pf. צָמְתוּ: **silence** s.thg La 3_{53}. †

nif.: pf. נִצְמְתוּ, נִצְמַתִּי: **be silenced** Jb 6_{17} 23_{17}. †

pilpel: pf. צִמְּתוּתֻנִי: **silence** Ps 88_{17}. †

hif.: pf. הִצְמַתָּה; impf. תַּצְמִית, אַצְמִיתֵם; impv. הַצְמִיתֵם: **silence** 2S 22_{41}.

צְמִתֻת Lv 25_{23} & צְמִיתֻת 25_{30}: **forfeiture of the right of repurchase**. †

***צֵן**: pl. צִנִּים Pr 22_5 Jb 5_5 & צִנּוֹת Am 4_2: **butcher's hook**?. †

צִן: n. loc.: מִדְבַּר־צִן Nu 13_{21}; loc. צִנָּה Nu 34_4.

***צֹנֶא**: for צֹנַאֲכֶם Nu 32_{24} rd. צֹאנְכֶם.

צֹנֶה: **small cattle** (sheep & goats) Ps 8_8. †

I ***צִנָּה**: cs. צִנַּת: **cold** (abstract noun) Pr 25_{13}. †

II **צִנָּה**: pl. צִנּוֹת: (large rectangular) **shield** 1K 10_{16}.

[III ***צִנָּה**: pl. צִנּוֹת Am 4_2: ↗ ***צֵן**.]

***צָנוּעַ**: pl. צְנוּעִים: **humble** Pr 11_2. †

צנוף Is 62_3: ↗ צָנִיף.

צִנּוֹר: pl. sf. צִנּוֹרֶיךָ: Ps 42_8 **water-spout**? **cataract**? **trident**? **thunderbolt**?; 2S 5_8 **water-shaft**?.

צנח: **qal**: impf. וַתִּצְנַח: — 1. **clap one's hands** (to attract attention) Jos 15_{18} Ju 1_{14}; — 2. **drive** (tent-peg) Ju 4_{21}. †

צְנִינִים: **thorns** Nu 33_{55} Jos 23_{13}. †

צָנִיף: cs. צְנִיף: **turban** Is 62_3 Zc 3_5 Jb 29_{14}. †

***צְנִיפָה**: pl. צְנִיפוֹת: (woman's) **turban** Is 3_{23}. †

***צָנֻם**: pl. f. צְנֻמוֹת: **hard, barren** (ears of grain) Gn 41_{23}. †

צנע: **hif.**: inf. הַצְנֵעַ: **live cautiously, carefully** Mi 6_8. †

צנף: **qal**: impf. יִצְנָפְךָ, יִצְנֹף; inf. צָנֹף: — 1. **wind around, wrap around** Is 22_{18}; — 2. **wrap** (and fasten) (turban) Lv 16_4. †

צְנֵפָה: **winding** Is 22_{18}. †

צִנְצֶנֶת: **receptacle** Ex 16_{33}. †

***צַנְתָּרוֹת**: cs. צַנְתְּרוֹת: **pipes** Zc 4_{12}. †

צעד: **qal**: pf. צָעֲדוּ, צָעֲדָה, צָעֲדוּ; impf. יִצְעַד, תִּצְעַד; inf. צַעְדְּךָ: **walk, step** 2S 6_{13}; Gn 49_{22} (?); subj. Y. Ju 5_4, gods Je 10_5.

hif.: impf. תַּצְעִדֵהוּ: **make** s.one **walk** Jb 18_{14}. †

***צַעַד**: צַעַד, sf. צַעֲדוֹ; pl. צְעָדִים, cs. צַעֲדֵי, sf. צְעָדֶיהָ, צְעָדָיו: — 1. sg. **walking** 2S 22_{37}; — 2. pl. **steps** 2S 6_{13}.

צְעָדָה: pl. צְעָדוֹת: — 1. **marching** (of God) 2S 5_{24} 1C 14_{15}; — 2. pl. **anklets, ankle bracelets** Is 3_{20}. †

צעה: **qal**: pt. צֹעֶה, צֹעָה, צֹעִים: — 1. s.one **in chains, cowering in prison** Is 51_{14}; — 2. **sprawl** (of prostitute) Je 2_{20}; — 3. trans. **tip, tilt** (wine-jars), **be a cellarman** Je 48_{12}. †

piel: pf. צֵעֻהוּ: **decant** (wine) Je 48_{12}. †

***צָעוֹר**: sf. צְעוֹרֶיהָ, צְעוֹרֵיהֶם Je 14_3 48_4; ↗ I צָעִיר. †

צָעִיף: sf. צְעִיפָהּ: **wrapper, shawl** Gn 24_{65} $38_{14 \cdot 19}$. †

I **צָעִיר**: f. צְעִ(י)רָה, m. sf. צְעִירוֹ; pl. cs. צְעִירֵי, sf. Je 14_3 Kt צְעוֹרֶהָ, Qr צְעִירֶיהָ: — 1. **little, small (-er, -est)** 1S 9_{21}; w. *lᵉ* & inf. too little to ... Mi 5_1; — 2. **young (-er, -est)** Gn 19_{31}; — 3. (young & therefore) **trifling, insignificant** Ps 68_{28}; — 4. pl. youths = **servants** Je 14_3.

II **צָעִיר**: n. loc.; loc. צָעִירָה: 2K 8_{21}. †

***צְעִירָה**: sf. צְעִירָתוֹ: (comparative) **youth** Gn 43_{33}. †

צען: **qal**: impf. יִצְעַן: (have to) **pack up** Is 33_{20}. †

צֹעַן: n. loc.

צַעֲנַנִּים: n. loc.

צַעֲצֻעִים: pl. coll. **casting, things formed by metal-casting** 2C 3_{10}. †

צָעַק: **qal**: pf. צ׳, צָעֲקָה, צָעַק; impf. וַיִּצְעַק, אֶצְעַק, אֶצְעֲקָה, תִּצְעֲקוּ; impv. צַעֲקִי, צְעַקִי Je 22_{20}, צַעֲקָנָה; inf. cs. צְעֹק, abs. צָעֹק; pt. צֹעֶקֶת, צֹעֲקִים: **cry out, raise a cry of wailing, call for help** (mostly to God) Gn 4_{10}.

nif.: impf. וַיִּצָּעֵק, וַיִּצָּעֲקוּ: **be summoned, called together** 2K 3_{21}.

piel: pt. מְצַעֵק: **keep crying** 2K 2_{12}. †

hif.: impf. וַיַּצְעֵק: **summon, call together** 1S 10_{17}. †

צְעָקָה: cs. צַעֲקַת, sf. צַעֲקָתוֹ: — 1. **cry of wailing, call for help** Gn 18_{21}; *ṣᵉʿāqâ gᵉdôlâ ûmārâ* loud & bitter cry Gn 27_{34}; — 2. **outcry, wailing** 1S 4_{14}.

צער: **qal**: impf. יִצְעָרוּ, יִצְעָרוּ; pt. צֹעֲרִים: **be trifling, insignificant** Je 30_{19}; **become trifling,**

insignificant Jb 14_{21}; pt. **shepherd-boy** Zc 13_7.

צֹעַר & **צוֹעַר**: n. loc.; loc. צֹעֲרָה.

צָפַד: **qal**: pf. צ׳: **shrivel** (of skin) La 4_8. †

I **צפה**: **qal**: impf. יִצֶף, תְּצַפֶּינָה; pt. צֹפֶה, צֹפִים, sf. צֹפַיִךְ, צֹפָו Is 56_{10} Kt, f. צֹפִיָּה, צֹפוֹת: — 1. **keep guard** (*bên* between) Gn 31_{49}; — 2. **observe attentively, watch** 2K 9_{17f}; — 3. **lie in wait** (ambush) for Ps 37_{32}.

piel: pf. צִפִּינוּ; impf. אֲצַפֶּה; impv. צַפֵּה, צַפִּי; pt. מְצַפֶּה: **watch** (= wait expectantly) 1S 4_{13}; w. b^e for Na 2_2.

II **צפה**: **qal**: inf. צָפֹה: **arrange** (order of seating) Is 21_5. †

piel: pf. צִפָּה, צִפִּיתָ, וַיְצַף; impf. תְּצַפֶּה, וַיְצַפֵּם, תְּצַפֶּנּוּ, וַיְצַפֵּהוּ: **overlay, plate** s.thg 2K 18_{16}; *zāhāb* w. gold (w/o prep.) 1K 6_{20}.

pual: pt. מְצֻפֶּה, מְצֻפִּים: **overlaid** Ex 26_{32} *zāhāb* w. gold; **glazed** Pr 26_{23}. †

***צָפָה**: sf. צָפָתְךָ: **discharge**? or rd. צֹאָתְךָ **pus**? Ez 32_6. †

צְפוֹ: n. peop. Gn $36_{11 \cdot 15}$; = צְפִי 1C 1_{36}. †

צִפּוּי: (metal) **plating** Ex $38_{17 \cdot 19}$ Nu 17_{3f} Is 30_{22}. †

I **צָפוֹן** (152×): w. art. הַצָּפוֹן & הַצָּפוֹנָה; cs. צְפוֹן, loc. צָפוֹנָה (oft. instead of צָפוֹן), צְפוֹנָה Ju 21_{19}: — 1. **north**: p^{e}'*at ṣāfôn* north side Ex 26_{20}; — 2. along w. oth. directions Gn 13_{14}; — 3. to the north, **northwards** *ṣāfônâ* Ex 40_{22}, *'el-haṣṣ.* Ez 8_{14}, *laṣṣāfôn* 40_{23}; from the north *miṣṣāfôn* Is 14_{31} &c.; — 4. north as source of evil Je 1_{14}; — 5. **north-wind** SS 4_{16}; — 5. *yark^etê ṣāfôn* Is 14_{13} Ps 48_3 = on the top of Mt. Zaphon (Mons Cassius); so *ṣāfôn* alone = Mt. Zaphon Ps 89_{13} Jb 26_7 Ez 32_{30}.

II **צָפוֹן**: n. loc.; loc. צָפוֹנָה: Jos 13_{27} Ju 12_1. †

צָפוֹן: n. pers.

I **צְפוֹנִי**: **northerner** (☞ I *ṣāfôn* 4) Jl 2_{20}; but perh. rd. צִפְצְפוֹנִי **chirper**.

II **צְפוֹנִי**: gent. of צָפוֹן.

צָפוּעַ: Ez 4_{15} Kt; ☞ צָפִיעַ. †

I **צִפּוֹר** & **צִפֹּר**: pl. צִפֳּרִים, f.: — 1. coll. **birds**, (creatures) **with wings** Gn 7_{14}; — 2. (individual) **bird** Dt 14_{11}; — 3. Jb 40_{29} perh. **crocodile bird**, *Pluvianus Aegyptius*, which picks parasites from the mouth of the crocodile.

II **צִפּוֹר** & **צִפֹּר**: n. pers. Nu $22_{2 \cdot 4 \cdot 10 \cdot 16}$ 23_{18} Jos 24_9 Ju 11_{25}. †

צַפַּחַת: small convex vessel for water & oil, **jar, jug(let)** 1K 17_{12}.

צְפִי 1C 1_{36}: ☞ צְפוֹ.

***צְפִיָּה**: sf. צְפִיָּתֵנוּ: watch-tower, **lookout** La 4_{17}.

צִפְיוֹן: n. pers.

צַפִּיחִת: **flat cake, wafer** Ex 16_{31}. †

***צָפִין**: sf. צְפִינְךָ Ps 17_{14} rd. צְפוּנְךָ ☞ צפן qal pt. pass.

***צָפִיעַ**: pl. cs. צְפִיעֵי: **dung** Ez 4_{15} Qr. †

***צְפִיעָה**: pl. צְפִעוֹת Is 22_{24}: **leaf.** †

צָפִיר: cs. צְפִיר, pl. cs. צְפִירֵי: **he-goat** Dn 8_5.

צְפִירָה & **צְפִרָה**: cs. צְפִירַת: **wreath, crown** Is 28_5; Ez $7_{7 \cdot 10}$ unexpl., evid. vivid synonym for 'end.' †

צָפִית: **order of seating** (at table) Is 21_5. †

צָפַן: **qal**: pf. צ׳, צָפַנְתִּי; impf. תִּצְפֹּן, נִצְפְּנָה, יִצְפְּנֵנִי, וַתִּצְפְּנוֹ; pt. sf. צֹפְנֶיהָ, pass. צָפוּן, צְפוּנָה, sf. צְפוּנִי, צְפוּנֶיךָ: — 1. **hide** Ex 2_2; — 2. **shelter** Ps 27_5; — 3. **store up, treasure up** Ho 13_{12}; — 4. **keep** s.thg **away from** (w. *min*) Jb 17_4; — 5. *ṣ^efûnî* my (= Y.'s) hidden things = **treasure** Ez 7_{22}.

nif.: pf. נִצְפַּן, נִצְפְּנוּ: — 1. **be hidden** Je 16_{17} Jb 24_1; — 2. **be stored up, treasured up** Jb 15_{20}. †

hif.: impf. תַּצְפִּינֵנִי; inf. הַצְפִּינוֹ (!): **hide** Ex 2_3.

צְפַנְיָה: n. pers.

צְפַנְיָהוּ: n. pers.

צָפְנַת פַּעְנֵחַ: n. pers. (Egyp. name of Joseph) Gn 41_{45}. †

צֶפַע: a poisonous **snake**, **(Aegean) viper**, *Vipera xanthina* Is 14_{29}. †

***צְפִעָה**: F *צְפִיעָה.

צִפְעֹנִי: pl. צִפְעֹנִים: = *ṣefaʿ*, a poisonous **snake, viper** Is 11_8 59_5 Je 8_{17} Pr 23_{32}. †

צפף: **pilpel**: impf. תְּצַפְצֵף, אֲצַפְצֵף; pt. מְצַפְצֵף, מְצַפְצְפִים: **chirp**, **whisper** (as a sorcerer) Is 8_{19} 10_{14} 29_4 38_{14}. †

צַפְצָפָה: **willow**, *Salix* Ez 17_5. †

[**צפר**: וְיִצְפֹּר מֵהַר Ju 7_3: txt. corr., rd. וַיִּצְרְפֵם. †]

צֹפַר: F צוֹפַר.

צִפֹּר: F צִפּוֹר.

צְפַרְדֵּעַ: pl. צְפַרְדְּעִים: **frogs** coll. Ex 8_2, pl. Ex 7_{27}.

צְפֹרָה: F צְפִירָה.

צִפֹּרָה: n. pers. f.

צִפֹּרֶן: pl. sf. צִפָּרְנֶיהָ: — 1. **nail** (of finger, toe) Dt 21_{12}; — 2. *ṣippōren šāmîr* **diamond point** (for writing) Je 17_1. †

צֶפֶת: **capital** (of pillar) 2C 3_{15}. †

צְפַת: n. loc.

צְפָתָה 2C 14_9: rd. צְפוֹנָה. †

צִצִּים: F צִיץ.

צָקוּן Is 26_{16}: unexpl.; vb. צוק?

צִיקְלַג, צִקְלַג, צִקְלָג: n. loc.

***צִקָּלוֹן**: sf. צִקְלֹנוֹ 2K 4_{42}: txt. corr., rd. קַלַּעַת. †

I **צַר**: צָר, f. צָרָה: — 1. adj. **narrow** Nu 22_{26}, **scarce** Pr 24_{10}, *ṣar min*, too narrow for 2K 6_1; — 2. noun, **narrowness, distress, dread** Jb 7_{11}; **distress, want** Is 5_{30}.

II **צַר**: צָר, sf. צָרִי; pl. cs. צָרֵי, sf. צָרָיו, צָרֵיהֶם, צָרֵימוֹ Dt 32_{27}: **oppressor, adversary, enemy** 2S 24_{13}.

III **צַר**: Is 5_{28} rd. כַּצֹּר. †

צֵר: n. loc. Jos 19_{35}; txt.?. †

צִר: F II צִיר.

***צָר**: F II צוּר.

I **צֹר**: pl. צֻרִים: — 1. **pebble, flint** Ez 3_9; — 2. **flint knife** Ex 4_{25} Jos 5_{2f}. †

II **צֹר** & (5×) **צוֹר**: n. loc., **Tyre**.

צרב: **nif.**: pf. נִצְרְבוּ: **be scorched** Ez 21_3. †

***צָרָב**: f. צָרֶבֶת: **scorching** Pr 16_{27}. †

צָרֶבֶת: **scar** (= scorching) Lv $13_{23.28}$. †

צְרֵדָה: n. loc.; loc. צְרֵדָתָה.

I **צָרָה** (69×): cs. צָרַת, sf. צָרָתוֹ, צָרַתְכֶם; pl. צָרוֹת, sf. צָרוֹתָם, צָרוֹתֵיכֶם; w. -*â* Ps 120_1 צָרָתָה: **distress** Gn 35_3.

II **צָרָה**: **rival-wife** (e.g. Rachel's *ṣārâ* is Leah) 1S 1_6. †

cj. **צָרָה**: (sheep-)**fold** cj. Mi 2_{12}. †

צְרוּיָה & **צְרֻיָה**: n. pers. f.

צְרוּעָה: n. pers. f.

I **צְרוֹר**: pl. צְרֹרוֹת: **pouch, bag** (for silver) Gn 42_{35}.

II **צְרוֹר**: **pebble** 2S 17_{13} Am 9_9. †

III **צְרוֹר**: n. pers. 1S 9_1. †

צרח: **qal**: pt. צֹרֵחַ: **yell, call shrilly** Zp 1_{14}. †
hif.: impf. יַצְרִיחַ: **raise the war-cry** Is 42_{13}. †

cj. **צָרַח**: **war-cry** cj Ez 21_{27}, **shriek** cj Je 4_{31}. †

צֹרִי: pl. צֹרִים: gent. of II צֹר.

צֳרִי & צְרִי Gn 37_{25}: **mastic**, resin of *Pistacia mutica* Gn 37_{25} 43_{11}.

צְרִי: n. pers.

צְרֻיָה: F צְרוּיָה.

צְרִיחַ: pl. צְרִיחִים: **cellar, vault** Ju $9_{46.49}$ 1S 13_6 (oth.: rock-cut cave). †

***צֹרֶךְ**: sf. צָרְכֶּךָ: **need** 2C 2_{15}. †

צרע: **qal**: pt. pass צָרוּעַ: **suffering fm. a skin eruption, struck w. a skin disease** (scarcely leprosy) Lv 13_{44f}.
pual: pt. מְצֹרָע, f. מְצֹרַעַת, מְצֹרַעַת, pl. מְצֹרָעִים: **struck w. a skin disease** 2K 5_1.

צָרְעָה: n. loc.

צִרְעָה: **depression, discouragement** Ex 23_{28} Dt 7_{20} Jos 24_{12}. †

צָרְעִי: gent. of צָרְעָה.

צָרַעַת: צָרַעַת, sf. צָרַעְתּוֹ: **skin-disease** (not leprosy: leucodermia & related diseases) 2K 5_3; similar appearances on garment Lv 13_{47}, leather 14_{55}, wall 14_{44}.

צָרְעָתִי: gent. of צָרְעָה.

צָרַף: **qal**: pf. צְרַפְתַּנִי, צְרָפַתְהוּ, צְרַפְתָּנוּ, צ׳; impf. אֶצְרְפֶנּוּ, אֶצְרֹף; impv. צָרְפָה (Kt צורפה) Ps 26_{2}; inf. צְרָף־, צְרֹף, abs. צָרוֹף; pt. צֹ(וֹ)רֵף, sf. צֹרְפָם, pass. צְרוּפָה, צָרוּף: — 1. **smelt** (metal) Is 1_{25}; *ṣōrēf* **gold-, silversmith** Ju 17_{4}; — 2. **refine** (by smelting) 2S 22_{31}; — 3. **test** Ju 7_{4}.

nif.: impf. וְיִצָּרְפוּ: **be refined** Dn 12_{10}. †

piel: pt. מְצָרֵף: **smelter, refiner** Ma 3_{2}. †

צֹרְפִי: **goldsmith's guild**: *ben-ṣōrᵉfî* Ne 3_{31}. †

צָרְפַת: n. loc.; loc. צָרְפָ֫תָה.

I **צרר**: **qal** I (trans.): pf. צָרַר; impv. צוֹר (!); inf. צְרוֹר; pt. צֹרֵר, pass. צְרוּרָה, צָרוּר, צְרֻרֹת: — 1. **wrap up** Ex 12_{34}, **tie up** (w. *nefeš*!) 1S 25_{29}; — 2. **shut away**, obj. wives kept fm. intercourse 2S 20_{3}.

qal II (intrans.): pf. צָרָה, צַר; impf. יֵצַר, יֵצְרוּ, תֵּצְרִי, וַיֵּ֫צֶר, יֵ֫צֶר: — 1. **be (too) narrow, cramped** Is 49_{19}; — 2. **be hampered, impeded** (of steps) Pr 4_{12}; — 3. **be hard pressed, in distress**: *wayyēṣer lô* he became anxious Gn 32_{8}; — 4. **be oppressed, afflicted** 2S 1_{26}.

pual: pt. מְצֹרָרִים: **tied up** (and thus mended) Jos 9_{4}. †

hif.: pf. הֲצֵרֹתִי, הֵצַר; impf. וַיָּצַר, יָצֵר־, וַיָּצֵרוּ; inf. הָצֵר; pt. f. מְצֵרָה: — 1. w. *lᵉ*, **oppress, afflict** 1K 8_{37}; — 2. (of woman) **be in labor** Je 48_{41}.

II **צרר**: **qal**: pf. צְרָרוּנִי, צְרָרוּ, צַרְתִּי, צַר; impf. יָצֹר; inf. צְרֹר, abs צָרֹר; pt. צֹרֵר, צֹרְרֵי, צֹרְרִים, sf. צוֹרְרֶיךָ, צֹרְרָיו: — 1. **be hostile toward, be in state of conflict w.** Ex 23_{22}; — 2. (denom. of II *ṣārâ*): **be a rival-wife** Lv 18_{18}.

צְרֹר: ↗ צְרוֹר.

צְרֵרָה Ju 7_{22}: rd. צְרֵדָה. †

צֶרֶת: n. pers.

צֶרֶת הַשַּׁחַר: n. loc.

צָרְתָן: n. loc.; loc. צָרְתָנָה.

ק

***קֵא**: sf. קֵאוֹ: **vomit** Pr 26_{11}.

קָאָת, קָאַת: cs. קְאַת: some unclean species of bird: species of owl, e.g. (European) little owl, *Athene noctua lilith*? jackdaw? Dt 14_{17}.

קַב: a measure of capacity, about 1 1/2 liters or 1 1/3 quarts, 2K 6_{25}. †

קבב: **qal**: pf. קַבֹּתוֹ; impf. יִקְּבֻהוּ, אֶקֹּ(וֹ)ב, תִּקֳּבֶנּוּ; impv. קָבְנוֹ, קָבָה־; inf. קֹב: **curse** Nu 22_{11}.

קֵבָה: sf. קֵבָתָהּ: — 1. **maw**, i.e. 4th stomach of ruminants Dt 18_{3}; — 2. Nu 25_{8}, more genl., **belly**. †

קֻבָּה: **women's quarters** (in tent) Nu 25_{8}. †

***קִבּוּץ**: pl. sf. קִבּוּצַיִךְ Is 57_{13}: unexpl.; most rd. שִׁקּוּצַיִךְ. †

קְבוּרָה: cs. קְבֻרַת, sf. קְבֻרָתוֹ: — 1. **burial** Je 22_{19}; — 2. **grave** Gn 47_{30}; *qᵉbûrat-rāḥēl* Gn 35_{20}.

קבל: **piel**: pf. קִבְּלְ, קִבֵּל Est 9_{27}, קִבְּלוּ; impf. וַיְקַבְּלֵם, נְקַבֵּל; impv. קַבֶּל־, קַבֵּל: **accept, receive**: gift Est 4_{4}, instruction Pr 19_{20}; **choose** (to accept) 1C 21_{11}.

hif.: pt. f. pl. מַקְבִּילֹת: **match, correspond** Ex 26_{5} 36_{12}. †

***קֹבֶל**: sf. קָבֳלוֹ: tech. term for a siege device: **battering-ram**? Ez 26_{9}. †

קָבַע: perh. metathesis of עקב to avoid assonance of יַעֲקֹב:

qal: pf. קְבַעֲנוּךָ, ק׳; impf. יִקְבַּע; pt. קֹבְעֵיהֶם, קֹבְעִים: **deceive** Ma 3_{8f} Pr 22_{23}; or perh. **rob**.

קֻבַּעַת: **cup** Is $51_{17\cdot 22}$. †

קבץ: **qal**: pf. ׳ק; impf. תִּקְבֹּץ, יִקְבָּץ־, אֶקְבְּצָה, וָאֶקְבְּצֵם, יִקְבְּצֵנוּ; impv. קְבֹץ, קִבְצוּ; inf. לְקָבְצִי; pt. קֹבֵץ, pass. קְבוּצִים: — 1. **collect**: food Gn 41_{35}, booty Dt 13_{17}; — 2. *qābaṣ ḥêlô* **concentrate** (one's forces) 1K 20_1; — 3. **gather, assemble** (obj. men, soldiers) 1K 22_6.

nif.: pf. נִקְבָּצוּ, נִקְבְּצוּ; impv. הִקָּבְצוּ; inf. הִקָּבֵץ; pt. נִקְבָּצִים, sf. נִקְבָּצָיו: — 1. **be gathered** (together) Is 56_8; — 2. **gather, assemble** (intrans.) Gn 49_2.

piel: pf. קִבַּצְתִּי, קִבֶּצְךָ, קִבְּצָן; impf. יְקַבֵּץ, אֲקַבֵּצָה, וַתְּקַבְּצוּ, יְקַבֶּצְךָ, אֲקַבֶּצְךָ; impv. קַבְּצֵנוּ; inf. קַבֵּץ, קַבְּצִי; pt. מְקַבֵּץ, sf. מְקַבְּצָם, pl. sf. מְקַבְּצָיו: — 1. **gather together**: sheep Is 13_{14}, & esp. exiles Dt 30_{3f}; — 2. **assemble** (people) Ez 16_{37}; — 3. *qibbēṣ tîrôš* **harvest** (wine) Is 62_9; — 4. *qibbēṣ pā'rûr* (gather a glow), **glow** (of face in excitement) Jl 2_6 Na 2_{11}.

pual: pf. cj. קֻבָּצוּ Mi 1_7; pt. מְקֻבֶּצֶת: **be gathered together** Ez 38_8, cj Mi 1_7. †

hitp.: pf. הִתְקַבְּצוּ; impf. יִתְקַבְּצוּ; impv. הִתְקַבְּצוּ: **assemble together** (intrans.) 1S 7_7.

קַבְצְאֵל: n. loc.

***קְבֻצָה**: cs. קְבֻצַת: **gathering** Ez 22_{20}. †

קִבְצַיִם: n. loc.

קבר: **qal** (86×): pf. ׳ק, קְבָרוּ, קְבַרְתַּנִי, קְבָרוּם; impf. תִּקְבְּרֵנִי, וַיִּקְבְּרוּ, אֶקְבְּרָה, תִּקְבְּרֵנוּ, וָאֶקְבְּרֶהָ; impv. קְבֹר, קִבְרוּ, קִבְרוּהָ; inf. קְבוֹר, קָבְרוֹ, abs. קָבוֹר; pt. קֹבְרִים, pass. קְבוּר, קְבֻרִים: **bury** Gn 23_4.

nif.: impf. יִקָּבֵר, יִקָּבְרוּ: **be buried** Gn 15_{15}.

piel: impf. תְּקַבְּרֵם; inf. קַבֵּר; pt. מְקַבֵּר: **bury** (many at once, mass burial) 1K 11_{15}.

pual: pf. קֻבַּר: **be buried** (of Abraham & Sarah) Gn 25_{10}. †

קֶבֶר (ca. 67×): קֶבֶר, sf. קִבְרוֹ; pl. קְבָרִים, cs. קִבְרֵי, sf. קִבְרֵיהֶם & קְבָרוֹת, cs. קִבְרוֹת, sf. קִבְרוֹתֵיכֶם, קִבְרֹתֶיהָ: **grave, burial ground**: individual Gn 23_4, for family 1K 13_{22}; = Underworld Ps 88_{12}.

קִבְרוֹת הַתַּאֲוָה: n. loc.

קדד: **qal**: impf. יִקֹּד, אֶקֹּד, יִקְּדוּ: **bow down, kneel down** (alw. followed by *hištaḥawâ*) Gn 24_{26}.

קִדָּה: **cassia-buds**, *Flores Cassiae* Ex 30_{24} Ez 27_{19}. †

קְדוּמִים: נַחַל קְדוּמִים Ju 5_{21}, unexpl., F comm. †

קָדוֹשׁ & קָדֹשׁ (115×): cs. קְד(וֹ)שׁ, sf. קְדשׁוֹ; pl. קְד(וֹ)שִׁים, sf. קְדשָׁיו: — 1. **holy**: of things, awe-inspiring, to be treated w. caution, kept fm. profane (*ḥōl*) use: place Ex 29_{31}, day Ne 8_{11}, waters Nu 5_{17}; — 2. **holy**: of persons, w/o particular ref. to God: *nāzîr* Nu 6_5 (cf. $_8$!); — 3. **holy**: singled out, ordained, for (*le*): a) priest, for the people Lv 21_8; b) sabbath Is 58_{13}; Israel, for God Nu 15_{40}; — 4. (fm. 3.) individuals are called **holy**: of Isr. Lv 11_{44}; — 5. God is **holy**: *qedôš yiśrā'ēl* Is 1_4; 6_3; his name is holy Is 57_{15}; — 6. pl. **holy** = heavenly beings Zc 14_5, sg. Dn 8_{13}.

קדח: **qal**: pf. קָדְחָה, קְדַחְתֶּם; inf. קְדֹחַ; pt. pl. cs. קֹדְחֵי: — 1. **break out** (of fire) Je 15_{14}; — 2. **light** (obj. fire) Is 50_{11}.

קַדַּחַת: **inflammation, fever** Lv 26_{16} Dt 28_{22}. †

קָדִים: loc. קָדִ(י)מָה: — 1. **east side, east** Ez 40_{23}; *qādîmâ* to the east Ez 11_1 &c.; — 2. *rûaḥ (haq)qādîm* **east wind** Ex 10_{13}; > *qādîm* east wind Gn 41_6.

קדם: **piel**: pf. קִדַּמְתִּי, קִדְּמוּ, קִדְּמֻנִי; impf. יְקַדְּמוּנוּ, תְּקַדְּמֶךָּ, יְקַדְּמֵנִי, נְקַדְּמָה, אֲקַדֵּם; impv. קַדְּמָה: — 1. **be in front, walk at the head** (of procession) Ps 68_{26}; **be** (sitting) **opposite** cj 1S 20_{25}; — 2. w. acc. step up to, **meet** 2S 22_6; — 3. w. 2 acc. **meet** s.one w. s.thg 2K 19_{32}; — 4. **reach** s.one cj Am 9_{10}; — 5. *qiddēm penê* **confront** Ps 17_{13}; w. *le* & inf. anticipate doing, **do** s.thg **for the first time** Jon 4_2; — 7. be early, **do** s.thg **early** Ps 119_{147}.

[hif.: Am 9_{10} Jb 41_3 rd. piel.]

קֶדֶם: pl. cs. קַדְמֵי Pr 8_{23}: — 1. **in front** Ps 139_5; *miqqedem* **from the front** Is 9_{11}; — 2. in front = **east**: in the east Gn 2_8; eastward Gn 13_{11}; *miqqedem* from the east Is 2_6, *miqqedem le* east of Gn 3_{24}; — 3. **east** (as a geographical region) Gn 25_6; *benê qedem* Easterners Gn 29_1; *har haqqedem* Eastern Mountains = northern border of Sinai Gn 10_{30}; — 4. temporal: **before, earlier, ancient times** (adv.) *keqedem* as of old Je 30_{20}; *miqqedem* for the first time Ne 12_{46}, from ancient times Is 45_{21}; — 5. (noun) **antiquity, primeval times**: *'elōhê qedem* God from primeval times = eternal God Dt 33_{27}.

*קֵדֶם: only loc. קֵ֫דְמָה: **eastward** Gn 13_{14}.

*קַדְמָה: sf. קַדְמָתָהּ, קַדְמַתְכֶן; pl. sf. קַדְמֹתֵיכֶם: — 1. **origin** Is 23_7; — 2. **former condition** Ez 16_{55}; — 3. pl. **former situation** Ez 36_{11}. †

*קִדְמָה: cs. קִדְמַת: **in front of, opposite** Gn 2_{14} 4_{16} 1S 13_5 Ez 39_{11}. †

I קֵ֫דְמָה: ↗ *קֵדֶם.

II קֵדְמָה: n. pers. (& peop.) Gn 25_{15} 1C 1_{31}. †

*קַדְמוֹן: f. קַדְמוֹנָה: **eastern** Ez 47_8. †

קַדְמוֹנִי: ↗ קַדְמֹנִי.

קְדֵמוֹת: n. loc.

קַדְמִיאֵל: n. pers.

I קַדְמֹנִי & קַדְמוֹנִי: pl. קַדְמֹנִים, f. קַדְמוֹנִיּוֹת: — 1. **eastern** Ez 10_{19}; pl. inhabitants of the east Jb 18_{20}; — 2. **former** Ez 38_{17}; coll. **the ancients** 1S 24_{14}, f. **former things** Is 43_{18}. †

II קַדְמֹנִי: n. peop. **the Easterners** Gn 15_{19}. †

קָדְקֹד: **crown of head**, spec.: — 1. *qodqōd śēʿār* spot where hair grows in a whorl Ps 68_{22}; — 2. line of parting the hair Gn 49_{26}; *mikkaf hāregel weʿad haqqodqōd* 2S 14_{25}.

קדר: **qal**: pf. קָדַרְתִּי, ק׳; pt. קֹדֵר: — 1. **grow dark** (as of an eclipse): sun & moon Jl 2_{10}, day Mi 3_6; — 2. **grow dark, turbid** (of stream, w. ice) Jb 6_{16}; — 3. **be dirty, unkempt, dressed in mourning attire** Je 8_{21}.

hif.: pf. הִקְדַּרְתִּי; impf. וָאַקְדִּר, אַקְדִּירֵם: **darken** Ez 31_{15} $32_{7.8}$. †

hitp.: pf. הִתְקַדְּרוּ: **grow dark** 1K 18_{45}. †

קֵדָר: n. pers., peop.

קִדְרוֹן: n. river.

קַדְרוּת: **darkening, blackness** Is 50_3. †

קְדֹרַנִּית: unkempt, **dressed in mourning attire** Ma 3_{14}. †

קדשׁ: **qal**: pf. קָדְשׁוּ, ק׳; impf. יִקְדָּשׁ, יִקְדַּשׁ, וַיִּקְדְּשׁוּ: **be holy**, withheld from ordinary use, treated w. special care, belonging to the sanctuary, e.g. priest & his garment Ex 29_{21}, things touching the altar 29_{37}, warriors in a campaign 1S 21_6.

nif.: pf. נִקְדַּשׁ; impf. אֶקָּדֵשׁ; inf. sf. הִקָּדְשִׁי: — 1. **show, prove onesf. holy** (of God): w. *be* among Lv 10_3; — 2. **be treated as holy**, w. *be* by Ex 29_{43}.

piel: pf. קִדַּשׁ, קִדַּשְׁתֶּם, קִדְּשׁוֹ, קִדְּשׁוּהוּ, קִדַּשְׁתָּם; impf. וַיְקַדֵּשׁ, אֲקַדֵּשׁ, וַיְקַדְּשֵׁהוּ; impv. קַדֵּשׁ, קַדֶּשׁ־, קַדְּשׁוּ, קַדְּשׁוֹ; inf. קַדֵּשׁ, קַדְּשָׁם; pt. sf. מְקַדִּשְׁכֶם (!): — 1. put s.thg into a state of holiness, i.e. treat according to the procedures of worship, **pronounce** s.thg **(to be) holy**: sabbath Gn 2_3, a place 1K 8_{64}; — 2. put s.one into a state of holiness, **consecrate, dedicate**: priest 1S 7_1, first-born Dt 15_{19}; Job purifies his sons, absolves them from sin Jb 1_5; — 3. **establish, appoint a holy day** or **period of time** (characterized by special cultic procedures) 2K 10_{20} (to Baal); a fast Jl 1_{14}; war = period of holy war Je 6_4; — 4. subj. God: put (s.one or s.thg) into a state of holiness, consecration, inviolability, **consecrate, dedicate**: obj. Isr. Ex 31_{13}, sanctuary Lv 21_{23}, Y.'s name Ez 36_{23}; — 5. make (s.one) holy (by having them touch s.thg consecrated), **transfer** or **convey holiness** to s.one Ez 44_{19}; — 6. **treat** (s.one or s.thg) **as holy, conse-**

crated, dedicated: sabbath Ex 20_8, God Dt 32_{51}.

pual: pt. מְקֻדָּשִׁים ,מְקֻדָּשַׁי: **be made holy, consecrated, dedicated**: priest Ez 48_{11}, warriors Is 13_3.

hif.: pf. הִקְדַּשְׁנוּ ,הִקְדַּשְׁתִּי ,הִקְדִּישׁ, הִקְדַּשְׁתִּיךָ; impf. יַקְדִּ(י)שׁ; impv. sf. הַקְדִּישֵׁנִי: inf. הַקְדִּישׁ, abs. הַקְדֵּשׁ; pt. מַקְדִּישׁ ,מַקְדִּשִׁים: — 1. **designate** (s.one or s.thg) **as made holy, consecrated, dedicated**: prophet Je 1_5, temple 1K 9_3, sheep for slaughter Je 12_3; — 2. **treat** (s.one or s.thg), **offer up, as made holy, consecrated, dedicated**: votive gifts 2K 12_{19}, field Lv 27_{16}, silver 2S 8_{11}; — 3. subj. God: **declare** (s.one or s.thg) **to be holy to him, consecrated** or **dedicated to him**: temple (to his name) 1K 9_7; — 4. obj. God: **treat** God **as holy, take** him **to be holy** Nu 20_{12}; — 5. **give as votive offerings** Ne 12_{47}; **(re)consecrate** 2C 29_{19}.

hitp.: pf. הִתְקַדְּשׁוּ ,הִתְקַדַּשְׁתִּי ,הִתְקַדֶּשׁ־, הִתְקַדִּשְׁתֶּם; impf. יִתְקַדָּשׁוּ; impv. הִתְקַדְּשׁוּ; pt. מִתְקַדֶּשֶׁת ,מִתְקַדְּשִׁים: — 1. **behave as** (people who have been) **consecrated, made holy** Ex 19_{22}; — 2. **prove onesf.** (to be) **holy** (subj. Y.) Ez 38_{23}; — 3. **put onesf.** (or each other) **into the state of dedication** or **cultic purity** 1S 16_5, of a woman after menstruation 2S 11_4.

I קָדֵשׁ: pl. קְדֵשִׁים; f. קְדֵשָׁה, pl. קְדֵשׁוֹת: **consecrated person, cult prostitute**: male 1K 14_{24}, female Gn 38_{21f}.

II קָדֵשׁ: loc. קָדֵשָׁה: n. loc. **Kadesh**.

קָדֹשׁ: ⇒ קָדוֹשׁ.

קֶדֶשׁ: loc. קֶדְשָׁה: n. loc.

קֹדֶשׁ & (Dn 11_{30} †) קוֹדֶשׁ: sf. קָדְשִׁי ,קָדְשֶׁךָ; pl. קֳדָשִׁים, ($q^od\bar{a}$-; alw. w. art.) & קָדָשִׁים (prob. $qod\bar{a}$-), cs. קָדְשֵׁי, sf. קָדָשַׁי ,קָדָשָׁיו, קָדְשֵׁיכֶם: — 1. **a holy thing**, a thing to which holiness adheres & wh. must thus be treated w. care: contrasted w. *ḥōl* (common, ordinary) 1S 21_5; what is holy Lv 22_{10}; the following may be holy: warriors in (holy) war 1S 21_6, food Ex 29_{33}, sabbath Ex 31_{14}, priest Lv 21_6, Jerus. Jl 4_{17}; *haqqōdeš* everything holy Lv 5_{16}, *kol-qōdeš* anything holy Lv 12_4, all holy things 1C 23_{28}; = spec. set apart for the cult Dt 26_{13}!; — 2. pl. *$q^od\bar{a}\check{s}\hat{\imath}m$* **votive gifts, offerings** 1K 7_{51}: *kesef haqq^{o}dāšîm* money for votive gifts 2K 12_5; — 3. the **holiness** adhering to God (& requiring spec. respect): Y. swears by his h. Am 4_2; — 4. the **holiness** adhering to a thing: to Y.'s house Ps 93_5, thus *qodšî* &c. as attribute of s.thg possessed by God: *šēm qodšî* name of my h. = my (Y.'s) holy name Lv 20_3 & oft.; so mountain Is 11_9, people Is 62_{12}, throne Ps 47_9, spirit Is 63_{10}; *'abnê qōdeš* talismans La 4_1; — 5. *qōdeš* = **holy area** Ez 45_1; *haqqōdeš* the holy place (:: most holy place) Ex 26_{33}, in Temple 1K 8_8, a holy place Ob $_{17}$; *qodšô* his holy place Ps 20_3 (= Judah Ps 114_2), pl. Ez 22_8; — 6. *qōdeš q^{o}dāšîm* **s.thg most holy**: area for priests Ez 48_{12}; = Temple Dn 9_{24}; var. sacrificial offerings, e.g. *minḥâ* Lv 2_3; interior of tent of meeting Ex 26_{33}, of Temple 1K 6_{16} (|| *d^{e}bîr*); most holy offerings Nu 18_9.

קְדֵשָׁה: ⇒ קָדֵשׁ.

קהה: **qal**: impf. תִּקְהֶינָה: **become blunt, numb** (of teeth) Je 31_{29f} Ez 18_2. †

piel: pf. קֵהָה: **become blunt** (of iron) Ec 10_{10}. †

קהל: **nif.**: pf. נִקְהֲלוּ; impf. וַיִּקָּהֵל ,וַיִּקָּהֲלוּ Kt ויקלהו 2S 20_{14} (rd Qr); inf. הִקָּהֵל; pt. נִקְהָלִים: **assemble** (intrans.): w. *'el* 1K 8_2, w. *l^e* † 2C 20_{26}, w. *'al* Ex 32_1.

hif.: pf. הִקְהִילוּ ,הִקְהַלְתָּ; impf. יַקְהֵל, יַקְהִיל 2C 5_2, וַיַּקְהִלוּ; impv. הַקְהֵל־ ,הַקְהֵל; inf. הַקְהִיל: **assemble** (trans.), **summon** 1K 8_1.

קָהָל: cs. קְהַל, sf. קְהַלְכֶם ,קְהָלֵךְ: — 1. **convocation, assembly**: Gn 49_6; *q^{e}hal 'ammîm*

Gn 28_3; *yôm haqqāhāl* Dt 9_{10}; — 2. **convocation of the people**, esp. of Isr. 1K 8_{14}; *kol-haqqāhāl* = Isr. 1S 17_{47}; = (Jewish) cultic congregation Ps 22_{23}; — 3. (occasional or special) **convocation, company**: *qᵉhal mᵉrēʿîm* Ps 26_5, *qᵉhal qᵉdōšîm* = angels Ps 89_6; *(haq)qāhāl* = law-court assembly † Ez 23_{47} Pr 26_{26}.

קְהִלָּה: **convocation, congregation** Dt 33_4 Ne 5_7. †

קֹהֶלֶת: qal pt. f. of קהל: **speaker** (in assembly) Ec $1_{1f.12}$ $12_{8ff.}$ †

קְהֵלָ֫תָה: n. loc.

קְהָת & קֳהָת: n. pers.

קֳהָתִי & קְהָתִי: gent. of קְהָת; pl. קְהָתִים.

I **קַו & קָו**; oft. Qr קַו, קָו & Kt קָוֶה, קְוֵה: cs. קַו, sf. קַוָּם (F 4.): — 1. **cord** (context: for measuring) 1K 7_{23} Qr; — 2. *qaw hammiddâ* **measuring-line** Je 31_{39}; > — 3. *qāw/qaw* alone = **measuring-line** 2K 21_{13}; — 4. *qawwām* Ps 19_5: some rd *qôlām*, but oth.: *qawwām* itself = 'their call,' √ II *qwh* 'collect,' F comm.

II **קַו & קָו**: *qaw-qāw* is a designation of *kûš*, Is $18_{2.7}$; rd. as one word: **suppleness, expansiveness**.

III **קַו**: syllable imitating prophetic speech Is $28_{10.13}$. †

קְוֵא 2C 1_{16}: F קְוֵה. †

קוֹבַע: = F כּוֹבַע: **helmet** 1S 17_{38} Ez 23_{24}. †

קוֹדֶשׁ Dn 11_{30}: F קֹדֶשׁ. †

I **קוה**: **qal**: pt. pl. cs. קֹוֵי, sf. קֹוֶיךָ, קֹוָי, קֹוָו (<* קֹוָיו): **wait** (for Y.) Is 40_{31}.

piel: pf. קִוִּיתָה, קִוִּיתִי, קִוֵּיתִי, קִוּוּ, קִוִּינוּ, sf. קִוִּיתִיךָ, קִוִּינוּךָ, קִוִּנֻהוּ; impf. יְקַוֶּה, יְקַו, נְקַוֶּה, יְקַוּוּ, וָאֲקַוֶּה; inf. abs. קַוֹּה & קַוֵּה: **wait for** (**w.** implication of **tenseness, eagerness**): — 1. w. *lᵉ* Gn 49_{18}; lie in wait Ps 119_{95}; — 2. w. *ʾel* Is 51_5; — 3. w. acc. Is 26_8; = expect s.thg (terrible) Is 64_2; — 4. w. *nefeš* seek s.one's life Ps 56_7.

II **קוה**: **nif.**: pf. נִקְווּ; impf. יִקָּווּ: **collect** (intrans.) Gn 1_9, **gather** (intrans.) Je 3_{17} (both. w. *ʾel*). †

***קָוֶה**: cs. קְוֵה: Kt = I קַו: 1K 7_{23} Je 31_{39} Zc 1_{16}. †

cj. **קְוֵה** 1K 10_{28} & קְוֵא 2C 1_{16}: n. terr. **Cilicia**. †

קוֹחַ Is 61_1: F פְּקַח־קוֹחַ.

קוט: [**qal**: impf. אָקוּט Ps 95_{10} rd. nif. ? if qal, mng. identical.]

nif.: pf. נָקֹטוּ, נְקֹטֹתֶם, also 3 sg f. נָקְטָה (as if √ *nqṭ*); impf. cj. אָקוֹט Ps 95_{10}: w. *bᵉ*, **feel a disgust** for Ez 6_9 20_{43} 36_{31} Jb 10_1. †

hitpolal: impf. אֶתְקוֹטָט, וָאֶתְקוֹטְטָה: **loathe** Ps 119_{158} 139_{21}. †

קוֹל, rarely קֹל (560×): sf. קֹ(ו)לִי, קֹ(ו)לְךָ, קוֹלָן; pl. קֹ(ו)לֹ(ו)ת (cs. =): — 1. **sound, voice, call**: of a man Jos 10_{14}, sheep 1S 15_{14}, flute Jb 21_{12}; metaph. of bloodshed Gn 4_{10}; — 2. **noise, sound**: of battle Ex 32_{17}, ram's horn Ex 19_{16}, words Dt 1_{34} &c.; — 3. **voice** of God Gn 3_8; — 4. phr.: *nāśāʾ qôlô* Gn 21_{16}, *hērîm qôlô* Gn 39_{15}, *nātan qôlô bibkî* Gn 45_2 &c.; *qôl gādôl* loud voice Gn 39_{14}; — 5. pl. *qōlōt* **thunder** 1S 12_{17f}; — 6. spec.: **report, rumor** Gn 45_{16}; *qōl hāʾōt* voice (= meaning) of the sign Ex 4_8; *qôl nitpᵉśâ bābel* the shout 'Babylon is taken!' Je 50_{46}; *qôlî ʾeqrāʾ* I call w. full voice Ps 3_5; *qôl* interj. 'listen!' (?) Is $40_{3.6}$.

קוֹלָיָה: n. pers.

קוּם: **qal** (460×): pf. קָם, קָאם Ho 10_{14}, קָ֫מָה, קַמְתָּ, קַמְתִּי, קָ֫מוּ, קַמְתֶּם, קַמְנוּ; impf. יָקוּם, וָאָקֻם, אָקוּמָה, וַיָּ֫קָם, וַיָּקָם Jb 22_{28}, יָקֻם, וַיָּקֻמוּ, יְקוּמוּן, תָּקֻמוּ, נָקוּמָה; impv. קוּם, קוּמָה, קוּמִי, קוּמוּ, קֻמָה; inf. cs. קוּם, sf. קֻמָהּ, abs. קוֹם; pt. קָם, קָמָה, קָמִים, קוֹמִים 2K 16_7, sf. קָמָיו, קָמֵיהֶם: — 1. **stand up, get up**: in the morning Gn 24_{54}, :: *šākab* (lie) Gn 19_{33}, :: *yāšab* (sit) Ps 139_2; w. *mēʿal* Gn 23_3 & oth. preps.; — 2. oft. w. a 2nd vb. merely to make an action vivid (cf. Eng.

'so he went & told her' &c.): *wayyāqom … wayyahargēhû* Gn 4$_{8}$; even: *wattāqom … wattiškab* (lie = sexual relations) Gn 19$_{35}$; esp. in impv.: *qûm qaḥ* Gn 19$_{15}$; — 3. derived mngs.: a) **stand upright**: of sheaf Gn 37$_{7}$; b) **arise** = appear (of a prophet) Dt 13$_{2}$; appear (of years) = almost follow, come Gn 41$_{30}$; arise (from one's place) = move Ex 10$_{23}$; arise (in one's place) = replace 1K 8$_{20}$; c) w. preps.: of hostility: w. *bᵉ* or *ʿal* arise against Mi 7$_{6}$ Ju 9$_{18}$; thus pt. *qāmîm* enemies: w. *ʿal* 2S 18$_{31}$, w/o *ʿal* Ex 15$_{7}$; w. *mēʾaḥᵃrê* rise up after you = follow you (in time) Dt 29$_{21}$; *qāmâ rûᵃḥ mippᵉnê* courage awakes against Jos 2$_{11}$; — 4. God subj.: **rise up** (in action) Is 2$_{19}$; *qûmâ yhwh* = step in Ps 3$_{8}$; man subj., sim. mng. of 'interfere' Ob $_{1}$; — 5. (of an event) **come about** Is 7$_{7}$; of Y.'s counsel Is 46$_{10}$; — 6. stand = **last, continue** 1S 13$_{14}$; = **be valid** (of a vow) Nu 30$_{5}$; — 7. w. *lᵉ* **belong** Lv 25$_{30}$; *qām lᵉmiqnâ lᵉ* pass over by purchase to Gn 23$_{17f}$; — 8. stand (at) = **cost** Lv 27$_{14\cdot17}$; — 9. *qāmû ʿênāyw* were motionless 1K 14$_{4}$; — 10. get up = **recover** Ex 21$_{19}$; — 11. *lēb qāmay* Je 51$_{1}$ is athbash for *kaśdîm* (↗ comm.).

piel (late): pf. קִיַּם, קִיְּמוּ; impf. וָאֲקַיְּמָה; impv. sf. קַיְּמֵנִי; inf. קַיֵּם: put in place, set up: — 1. **make** (a word) **come true** Ez 13$_{6}$, **confirm** (an oath) Ps 119$_{106}$, (letter) Est 9$_{29}$; — 2. *qiyyēm ʿal* **impose** (an obligation) **on** (s.one) Est 9$_{31}$, w. *lᵉ* & inf. Est 9$_{21\cdot27}$; — 3. **institute, direct** Est 9$_{31f}$; — 4. **support, strengthen** Ps 119$_{28}$. †

polel: impf. תְּקוֹמֵם, אֲקוֹמֵם, יְקוֹמֵמוּ: **raise up** (ruins) Is 44$_{26}$ 58$_{12}$ 61$_{4}$. †

hif. (146×): pf. הֵקִים, הֲקֵמֹתָ, הֲקִ(י)מֹ(ו)תִי, הֵקִימוּ, הֲקִמֹנוּ, sf. הֲקִמֹתוֹ; impf. יָקִים, יָקֵם, וַיָּקֶם, אָקִים, יָקִימוּ, יְקִימוּן, תְּקִימֶנָה Je 44$_{25}$, sf. יְקִימְךָ, יְקִימֵנוּ, וַיְקִימֶהָ; impv. הָקֵם, הָקִימוּ, הֲקִמֵנִי; inf. cs. הָקִים, הֲקִימוֹ, abs. הָקֵם, הָקִים; pt. מֵקִים, cs. מְקִימִי (!) Ps 113$_{7}$, sf. מְקִימָהּ: — 1. **set up, erect**: pillar 1K 7$_{21}$, booth Am 9$_{11}$; — 2. obj. word, vow &c., **carry out, perform** Dt 9$_{5}$; subj. oft. God 1K 2$_{4}$; obj. *bᵉrît* Gn 6$_{18}$; — 3. > *hēqîm* abs. **keep one's word** 1S 3$_{12}$; — 4. **command** (s.one) **to stand** 2K 9$_{2}$; **make** (s.one) **stand** Is 14$_{9}$; **rouse** (a lion) Gn 49$_{9}$; — 5. **raise up, help up**: fallen animal Dt 22$_{4}$, the poor 1S 2$_{8}$; — 6. set up s.one = **appoint, install, entrust w. a commission**: *śāṭān* (adversary) 1K 11$_{14}$, priest 1S 2$_{35}$, oft. w. *lᵉ* Am 2$_{11}$; — 7. cause to arise = **establish, provide**: *zeraʿ* Gn 38$_{8}$, *rāʿâ* 2S 12$_{11}$; — 8. spec.: *hēqîm taḥat* set (children) in the place of (their parents) Jos 5$_{7}$; *hēqîm* establish (the ends of the earth) = create Pr 30$_{4}$; *hēqîm šēm mēt* = revive Ru 4$_{5\cdot10}$; *hēqîm bammilḥāmâ* allow to rise (= gain ground) in battle Ps 89$_{44}$; *hēqîm lidmāmâ* bring to silence Ps 107$_{29}$.

hof.: pf. הוּקַם, הֻקַם: — 1. **be erected** (tabernacle) Ex 40$_{17}$; — 2. **be carried out** (word) Je 35$_{14}$; — 3. **be appointed** 2S 23$_{1}$. †

hitpolel: pt. m. sf. מִתְקוֹמְמִי, f. מִתְקוֹמָמָה, pl. sf. מִתְקוֹמְמַי: **rise up, rebel** against (w. *lᵉ* or sf.) Ps 17$_{7}$ 59$_{2}$ Jb 20$_{27}$ 27$_{7}$. †

קוֹמָה & קֹמָה: cs. קוֹמַת, sf. קֹמָתוֹ, קוֹמָתָהּ: — 1. **height** (as measurement of ark &c.) Gn 6$_{15}$; — 2. **height** (= stature of person) 1S 16$_{7}$; *mᵉlōʾ qômātô* his full length (on the ground) 1S 28$_{20}$; *qômat ʾᵃrāzāyw* = its (Lebanon's) tall(est) cedars 2K 19$_{23}$.

קוֹמְמִיּוּת: adv. (walk) **erect, w. head high** Lv 26$_{13}$. †

קוֹנֵן: ↗ קין.

קוֹעַ: n. peop.

***קוֹף & *קֹף**: pl. קֹ(וֹ)פִים: **ape**, *Papio Hamadrias Arabicus*? 1K 10$_{22}$ 2C 9$_{21}$. †

I **קוץ**: **qal**: pf. קַצְתִּי, קָ֫צָה; impf. תָּקֹץ, וַיָּקָץ, וַיָּקֻצוּ, וָאָקוּץ; pt. קָץ: w. *bᵉ*: **feel a disgust** for Gn 27_{46} 1K 11_{25}; w. *mippenê* feel a horror of Ex 1_{12}.

II קוץ: **hif.**: impf. יָקִיצוּ, sf. יְקִיצֶנָּה: — 1. intrans.: **tear apart** Jb 14_{12} (w. neg. = stay sewn together); — 2. trans. **tear apart** Is 7_6. †

I קוֹץ: pl. קֹ(ו)צִים, קוֹצֵי: **thorn-bush** Gn 3_{18}.

II קוֹץ: **shreds of a wick** 2S 23_6. †

III קוֹץ: n. pers.

*קְוֻצּוֹת: sf. קְוֻצּוֹתַי, קְוֻצּוֹתָיו: **locks** (of hair) SS $5_{2.11}$. †

קור: **qal**: pf. קַרְתִּי: **dig** (for water) 2K 19_{24} Is 37_{25}. †

*קוּר: pl. cs. קוּרֵי, sf. קוּרֵיהֶם: **thread**: of spiderweb Is 59_{5f}. †

קוֹרֵא ↗ II קֹרֵא.

קוֹרָה: pt. of קרה: sf. קֹרָתִי, קֹרוֹת: **beam** 2K $6_{2.5}$; beams (of house) SS 1_{17} 2C 3_7; = house itself Gn 19_8. †

קוש: **qal**: impf. יְקֹשׁוּן: **set snares** (for bird; metaph. for person) Is 29_{21}. †

קוּשָׁיָהוּ: n. pers.

קַח: **willow**, *Salix* Ez 17_5. †

קַט Ez 16_{47}: trad. 'little,' but prob. dittgr. †

קֶטֶב & קֹטֶב: קֶטֶב; sf. קָטָבְךָ (*qotobkā*) Ho 13_{14}: — 1. **sting, prick** Ho 13_{14}; *śaʿar qeṭeb* Is 28_2; — 2. sting (as name of disease, measles?) Dt 32_{24} Ps 91_6 (later a demon). †

קְטוֹרָה: **smoking** (of sacrifice) Dt 33_{10}. †

קְטוּרָה: n. pers. f.

קטל: **qal**: impf. יִקְטֹל־, תִּקְטֹל, יִקְטְלֵנִי: **kill** Ps 139_{19} Jb 13_{15} 24_{14}. †

*קֶטֶל: קֶטֶל: **murder** Ob 9. †

קטן: **qal**: pf. קָטֹנְתִּי; impf. וַתִּקְטַן: **be small, trifling** 2S 7_{19} 1C 17_{17}; w. *min*, be too unworthy for Gn 32_{11}. †

hif.: inf. הַקְטִין: **make** (s.thg) **small** Am 8_5. †

*קֹטֶן: sf. קָטָנִּי (*qoṭonnî*): trad. my little **finger**, but perh. my **penis** 1K 12_{10} 2C 10_{10}. †

I קָטָן: sf. קְטַנָּם, f. קְטַנָּה; pl. קְטַנִּים, cs. קְטַנֵּי, f. קְטַנּוֹת: — 1. **little, small** 1K 17_{13}; modest (request) 1K 2_{20}; *qeṭannâ* s.thg small Nu 22_{18}; = insignificant (in rank) 2K 18_{24}; — 2. **young (-er, -est)** Gn 9_{24}; *yeled zeqûnîm qāṭān* young child of his old age Gn 44_{20}.

II קָטָן: n. pers. Ezr 8_{12}. †

קָטֹן: cs. קְטֹן: — 1. **small, trifling, insignificant** Gn 1_{16} 1S 20_2; w. *min* & inf. too small to 1K 8_{64}; — 2. **young(est)** Gn 42_{13}.

קטף: **qal**: pf. קָטַף, קָטַפְתָּ; impf. אֶקְטֹף; pt. קֹטְפִים: **pick, pluck** (ears of grain) Dt 23_{26}, **break off** (twigs) Ez $17_{4.22}$, pick (mallow) Jb 30_4. †

nif.: impf. יִקָּטֵף: **be picked** (of flowers) Jb 8_{12}. †

קטר: **piel**: קִטְּרוּ, קִטַּרְתֶּם; impf. וַיְקַטֵּר, יְקַטְּרוּ, יְקַטֵּרוּן, וַיְקַטְּירוּ (Qr piel, Kt hif.) 2C 34_{25}; inf. קַטֵּר; pt. מְקַטְּרוֹת: **let** (sacrifice) **go up in smoke**: not in Gn-Ju; 1S 2_{16}; *qaṭṭēr tôdâ* Am 4_5; otherw. of forbidden cult 2K 17_{11}.

pual: pt. f. מְקֻטֶּרֶת: **perfumed** SS 3_6. †

hif.: pf. הִקְטִיר, הִקְטַרְתָּ, sf. הִקְטִירוֹ; impf. וַיַּקְטֵר, תַּקְטִיר, יַקְטִירוּן, יַקְטִירֶנָּה; pt. מַקְטִיר: **make** (sacrifices) **go up in smoke**, usu. of worship of Y.: — 1. 43× Ex-Dt: Ex 29_{13}; — 2. outside Ex-Dt 1K 3_3; less oft. of worship of oth. gods 1K 11_8.

hof.: impf. תָּקְטַר; pt. מֻקְטָר: (of sacrifice) **be made to go up in smoke** Lv 6_{15} Ma 1_{11}. †

קִטֵּר Je 44_{21}: rd קְטֹרֶת.

קִטְרוֹן: n. loc.

קְטֻרוֹת Ez 46_{22}: rd. קְטַנּוֹת.

קְטֹרֶת: sf. קְטָרְתִּי: — 1. **smoke** of burning sacrifice 1S 2_{28} Is 1_{13} (to 2. ?) Ps 66_{15} †; — 2. **incense** Ex 25_6 & oft.

קַטָּת: n. loc.

קיא: **qal**: pf. קָאָה; impv. קְיוּ: **vomit** (obj. nation) Lv 18_{28}; abs. Je 25_{27}. †

hif.: pf. sf. הֱקִיאַתוּ; impf. תָּקִא, תָּקִיא, וַתָּקִא, sf. וַיְקִאֵנוּ, תְּקִיאֶנָּה: **vomit** s.thg; subj. man, obj. mouthfuls Pr 23_8, riches

Jb 20_{15}; subj. fish Jon 2_{11}, subj. land, obj. inhabitants Lv 18_{25}.

קִיא: sf. קִיאוֹ: **vomit** Is 19_{14} 28_8 Je 48_{26}. †

*קִיה: ↗ קיא qal.

cj. *קַיִט: **summer**: *qiššurê *qayiṭ* gossamer Jb 8_{14} (for ↗ *yāqôṭ*; ↗ comm.). †

קִיטוֹר & קִיטֹר: **smoke** Gn 19_{28} Ps 119_{83}. †

*קִים: sf. קִימָנוּ: **adversary** Jb 22_{20}. †

*קִימָה: sf. קִימָתָם: **standing (up)** La 3_{63}. †

קין: **polel**: pf. קוֹנְנוּ, sf. קוֹנְנוּהָ; impf. וַיְקוֹנֵן, תְּקוֹנֵנָּה Ez 32_{16}; pt. מְקוֹנְנוֹת: **sing a dirge** (*qînâ*) 2S 1_{17}.

I *קַיִן: sf. קֵינוֹ: trad. **spear** 2S 21_{16}. †

II קַיִן: n. pers.; קָיִן: **Cain**.

III קַיִן: n. peop.; = II? Nu 24_{22} Ju 4_{11}. †

IV קַיִן: n. loc. Jos 15_{57}. †

I קִינָה: pl. קִינִים & קִינוֹת, sf. קִינוֹתֵיהֶם: **dirge** 2S 1_{17}.

II קִינָה: n. loc. Jos 15_{22}. †

קֵינִי: הַקֵּינִי, pl. הַקִּינִים 1C 2_{55}: n. peop. (II & III *qayin*) **Kenite**.

קֵינִים 1C 2_{55}: ↗ קֵינִי.

קֵינָן: n. pers.

קיץ: **qal**: pf. קָץ **spend the summer** Is 18_6. †

hif.: pf. הֵקִיץ, הֱקִיצוֹתָ, הֱקִיצוֹתִי; impf. יָקִיצוּ; impv. הָקִיצוּ, הָקִיצָה; pt. מֵקִיץ: intrans. **awake**: from sleep 1S 26_{12}, from expected death 2K 4_{31}, from drunkenness Jl 1_5; impv., voc. God = be active Ps 35_{23}.

קַיִץ: קָיִץ, sf. קֵיצֵךְ: — 1. **summer** Gn 8_{22}; — 2. **summer-fruit** (esp. figs) 2S 16_1.

*קִיצוֹן: f. קִיצוֹנָה: **outermost** Ex $26_{4.10}$ $36_{11.17}$. †

קִיקָיוֹן: prob. **castor-oil plant**, *Ricinus communis*; oth.: a kind of cucumber Jon $4_{6\text{-}10}$. †

קִיקָלוֹן: **disgrace** Hb 2_{16}. †

I קִיר (74×, 20× Ez): pl. קִירוֹ(ו)ת, sf. קִירוֹתֶיהָ: — 1. **wall** of a house 1K 6_5, of temple Ez 41_{20}; metaph., of heart Je 4_{19}; — 2. > (stone) **wall** of city Nu 35_4.

II קִיר: n. loc., in compound w. var. forms of √ *ḥrś* or *ḥrš*, e.g. *qîr-ḥ^arāšet* 2K 3_{25}; all forms refer to same town, a capital of Moab.

III קִיר: n. terr., loc. קִירָה: 2K 16_9 Is 22_6 Am 1_5 9_7. †

קֵירֹס: n. pers. Ne 7_{47}, = קֵרֹס. †

קִישׁ: n. pers.

קִישׁוֹן: n. river.

קִישִׁי: n. pers.

קַל: קַל, קָל, קַל; f. קַלָּה; pl. קַלִּים: **light, agile, quick**: messengers Is 18_2, cloud 19_1; *qal b^eraglāyw* swift-footed 2S 2_{18}; as noun, swift warrior Am 2_{14}, swift horse Is 30_{16}; adv. Is 5_{26}.

I קֹל: **lightness** = lightheartedness Je 3_9. †

II קֹל: ↗ קוֹל.

קלה: 2S 20_{14} וַיִּקָּלֲהוּ: Kt ?, rd Qr וַיִּקָּהֲלוּ ↗ קהל. †

I קלה: **qal**: pf. sf. קָלָם; pt. pass. קָלוּי: **roast** (obj. men) Je 29_{22}; **parch** (obj. grain) Lv 2_{14}; *qālûy* alone = parched grain Jos 5_{11}. †

nif.: pt. נִקְלֶה: **burning** (= fever) Ps 38_8. †

II קלה: **nif.**: pf. נִקְלָה; pt. נִקְלֶה: **be(come) of low esteem, of little account** Dt 25_3 1S 18_{23} Is 3_5 16_4 Pr 12_9. †

hif.: pt. מַקְלֶה: **treat with contempt** Dt 27_{16}. †

קָלוֹן: cs. קְלוֹן, sf. קְלוֹנֵךְ: **shame, dishonor** Is 22_{18}.

קַלַּחַת: קַלָּחַת: (large cooking-)**pot, caldron** 1S 2_{14} Mi 3_3. †

קלט: **qal**: pt. pass. קָלוּט: ref. to a bodily defect in an animal; Verss.: stunted; or, w. shortened tail Lv 22_{23}. †

קָלִי(א): **parched grain** (roasted whole grains) Lv 23_{14} 1S 17_{17} 25_{18} 2S 17_{28} Ru 2_{14}. †

קַלַּי: n. pers.

קֵלָיָה: n. pers.

קְלִיטָא: n. pers.

קלל: **qal**: pf. קַל, קַלּוֹתָ, קַלּוֹתִי, קַלּוּ; impf.

יֵקַלּוּ, וָאֵקַל, וַתֵּקַל: — 1. **be small, of little account** 1S 2_{30} Jb 40_4; (of water) become low(er) = go down Gn $8_{8\cdot11}$; — 2. w. *min* **be swifter** than 2S 1_{23}; — 3. w. *beʻênê* **be of no account** in the eyes of Gn 16_{4f}.

nif.: pf. נְקַלֹּתִי, וְנָקַל, נָקֵל; impf. יֵקַלּוּ; pt. נָקֵל, נָקֵל, f. נְקַלָּה: — 1. **prove swift** Is 30_{16}; — 2. **humble onesf., demean onesf.** 2S 6_{22}; — 3. w. *beʻênê* be a small (= too small a) matter to s.one 1S 18_{23} 2K 3_{18}; w. inf. be a small (the smallest) matter that ... Is 49_6; — 4. w. *le* & inf.: **be easy to ...** 2K 20_{10}; — 5. w. *min* & inf.: **be too light a thing to ...** Ez 8_{17}; — 6. abs.: **be easy** Pr 14_6; *ʻal-neqallâ* **superficially** Je 6_{14} 8_{11}.

piel: pf. קִלֵּל, קִלַּלְתָּ, sf. קִלְלַנִי; impf. יְקַלֵּל, וַיְקַלְלוּ, sf. יְקַלֶּלְךָ, וַאֲקַלְלֵם; impv. קַלֵּל; inf. קַלֵּל, קַלְלוֹ, קַלֶּלְךָ; pt. מְקַלֵּל, sf. מְקַלֶּלְךָ, מְקַלְלַונִי (txt. corr.) Je 15_{10}: — 1. **declare** s.one *ʼārûr*, **cursed**: man subj. & obj. Gn 12_3, obj. father & m. Ex 21_{17} &c.; God subj., obj. field Gn 8_{21}; abs. 2S 16_5; — 2. w. *bešēm yhwh*: declared cursed by invoking the name of Y. 2K 2_{24}; *bēʼlōhāyw* 1S 17_{43}; *qillēl qelālâ* + acc. call a curse-formula upon 1K 2_8; = *qillēl be* Is 8_{21}.

pual: impf. יְקֻלָּל, תְּקֻלָּל; pt. sf. מְקֻלָּלָיו: **be declared cursed** Is 65_{20} Ps 37_{22} Jb 24_{18}. †

hif.: pf. הֵקַל, הֵקַלּוּ, sf. הֱקַלַּתְנִי; impf. יָקֵל; impv. & inf. הָקֵל: — 1. **lighten** (make lighter in weight) (w. *mēʻal*): obj. yoke 1K 12_{10}, ship Jon 1_5; — 2. **treat** s.one **triflingly, w. contempt** 2S 19_{44}.

pilpel: pf. קִלְקַל: — 1. **whet** (edges of metal) Ec 10_{10}; — 2. **shake** (arrows for casting lots) Ez 21_{26}. †

hitpalpel: pf. הִתְקַלְקְלוּ: **be shaken** (back & forth) Je 4_{24}. †

קָלָל: adj. **polished** (metal) Ez 1_7 Dn 10_6. †

קְלָלָה: cs. קִלְלַת, sf. קִלְלָתְךָ; pl. קְלָלוֹת: **curse** (both action & formula of cursing) Gn 27_{12}; *nātan liqlālâ* make s.one('s name into) a curse-formula Je 24_9, *hāyâ liqlālâ* become a curse-formula 2K 22_{19} (not 'an obj. of cursing'); gen. is both subjective (*qillat yôtām* the curse spoken by J. Ju 9_{57}) and objective (*ʻalay qillātekā* upon me be the curse spoken against you Gn 27_{13}).

קלס: **piel**: inf. קַלֵּס: **disdain** (prostitute's pay) Ez 16_{31}. †

hitp.: impf. יִתְקַלָּס, יִתְקַלְּסוּ: **make fun of** 2K 2_{23} Ez 22_5 Hb 1_{10}. †

קֶלֶס: (source of) **ridicule** Je 20_8 Ps 44_{14} 79_4. †

קַלָּסָה: **laughing-stock** Ez 22_4. †

I **קלע**: **qal**: pt. קֹלֵעַ: **sling** (w. *be* & 'stones') Ju 20_{16}; w. acc. **sling out** (men) Je 10_{18}. †

piel: impf. וַיְקַלַּע, sf. וַיְקַלְּעֶנָּה: abs. **sling** (i.e. a stone) 1S 17_{49}; acc. lives 25_{29}. †

II **קָלַע**: **qal**: pf. 'ק: **carve** 1K $6_{29\cdot32\cdot35}$. †

I **קֶלַע**: קָלַע, sf. קַלְעוֹ; pl. קְלָעִים: **sling** 1S $17_{40\cdot50}$; *kaf-haqqelaʻ* hollow of sling 1S 25_{29}, *ʼabnê-qelaʻ* sling-stones Zc 9_{15} Jb 41_{20} 2C 26_{14}. †

II ***קֶלַע**: pl. קְלָעִים, cs. קַלְעֵי: **curtain** Ex 27_9.

***קַלָּע**: pl. קַלָּעִים: **slinger** 2K 3_{25}. †

קְלֹקֵל: *leḥem haqqelōqēl* Nu 21_5 trad. **starvation rations, wretched food**; but cogn. languages suggest a spec. (unappetizing) leguminous plant. †

קִלְּשׁוֹן: sharpened iron, *šeloš qillešôn* 1S 13_{21} **trident**; but txt. prob. corr. †

קָמָה: cs. קָמַת: **standing grain** Ex 22_5.

קָמָה: ↗ קוֹמָה.

קְמוּאֵל: n. pers.

קָמוֹן: n. loc.

קִמּוֹשׂ: pl. קִמְּשֹׂנִים (!): **weeds** (spec.: **nettles**?) Is 34_{13} Ho 9_6; pl. all kinds of weeds Pr 24_{31}. †

קֶמַח: קֶמַח: **flour** Gn 18_6.

קמט: **qal**: impf. וַתִּקְמְטֵנִי: **seize** Jb 16_8. †

pual: pf. קֻמְּטוּ: **be seized** Jb 22_{16}. †

קָמַל: **qal**: pf. 'ק, קָמֵל, קָמְלוּ: **become infested w. injurious insects** Is 19_6 33_9. †

קָמַץ: **qal**: pf. ׳ק: **take a handful** Lv 2_{2} 5_{12} Nu 5_{26}. †

***קֹמֶץ**: sf. קֻמְצוֹ; pl. קְמָצִים: **a handful** Lv 2_{2} 5_{12} 6_{8}; pl. handfuls (= abundance) Gn 41_{47}. †

קֵן: cs. קַן Dt 22_{6}, sf. קִנּוֹ; pl. קִנִּים: — 1. **nest** Nu 24_{21}; — 2. pl. **compartments** † Gn 6_{14}.

קנא: **piel**: pf. קִנֵּא, קִנֵּאתִי, sf. קִנְאוּנִי Dt 32_{21}; impf. יְקַנֵּא, וַיְקַנְאוּ, sf. וַיְקַנְאֻהוּ; inf. cs. קַנְּאוֹ, קַנְּאתוֹ, abs. קַנֹּא; pt. מְקַנֵּא: — 1. **be envious of** Gn 26_{14} w. acc., Gn 30_{1} w. *b^e*; — 2. w. acc. & *b^e* **arouse s.one's** (God's) **jealousy** by 1K 14_{22}; — 3. w. *l^e* **be** (greatly) **eager, zealous** for (= on behalf of) 1K $19_{10\cdot14}$; — 4. *qinnēʾ qinʾâ l^e* **be furious** for (= on behalf of) Zc 8_{2}.

hif.: impf. sf. יַקְנִיאוּהוּ, יַקְנִאֻהוּ, אַקְנִיאֵם; pt. מַקְנֶה: — 1. w. sf. & *b^e*: **arouse s.one's jealousy** by Dt $32_{16\cdot21}$ Ps 78_{58}; — 2. pt. arousing jealousy Ez 8_{3}. †

קַנָּא: **jealous** (ref. to God) Ex 20_{5}.

קִנְאָה: cs. קִנְאַת, sf. קִנְאָתוֹ; pl. קְנָאֹת: — 1. **passion**, **ardor**: (of man for God) 2K 10_{16}, (of God for Isr.) Is 26_{11}; **passion** (of sexual attraction) SS 8_{6}; w. *min*, **envy** of Ec 4_{4}; *qinʾat yhwh* = Y.'s jealous love 2K 19_{31}; — 2. **jealousy** Is 11_{13}, *rûᵃḥ qinʾâ* Nu 5_{14}; pl. *minḥat qinʾōt* 'offering of jealousy,' offering for case of suspected adultery Nu $5_{15\cdot18\cdot25}$.

I **קנה**: **qal**: pf. ׳ק, קָנְתָה, קָנִיתָ, קָנִיתִי, Ru 4_{5} (= Qr ־תָ, Kt ־תִי), קָנִינוּ, sf. קָנָהוּ, קָנֶךָ; impf. יִקְנֶה, וַיִּקֶן, וְאֶקְנֶה, יִקְנוּ, sf. וַיִּקְנֵהוּ; impv. קְנֵה; inf. cs. קְנֹה, קְנוֹת, abs. קָנֹה, קָנוֹ 2S 24_{24}; pt. קֹ(וֹ)נֶה, cs. קֹנֵה, sf. קֹנֵיהֶן, קֹנֵהוּ: — 1. **acquire**: field Gn 33_{19}, servant 39_{1}; — 2. **buy** Gn 47_{20}; — 3. spec.: *qānâ lᵉʾiššâ* buy as a wife Ru 4_{10}; ransom, redeem slaves Ne 5_{8}; acquire wisdom &c. Pr 4_{5}; — 4. God subj.: redeem Is 11_{11}.

nif.: pf. נִקְנָה; impf. יִקָּנוּ: **be bought** Je $32_{15\cdot43}$. †

[**hif.**: pf. sf. הִקְנַנִי Zc 13_{5} rd אֲדָמָה קִנְיָנִי; pt. מַקְנֶה Ez 8_{3} ↗ קנא hif.]

II **קנה**: **qal**: pf. קָנִיתִי, קָנִיתָ, קָנְתָה, sf. קָנֶךָ; pt. cs. קֹנֵה: — 1. subj. God: **create** Gn $14_{19\cdot22}$ Ex 15_{16} Dt 32_{6} Ps 78_{54} 139_{13}; — 2. subj. Eve: **produce** Gn 4_{1}. †

קָנֶה: cs. קְנֵה, sf. קָנָהּ, קָנֶה Jb 31_{22}; pl. קָנִים, cs. קְנֵי, sf. קְנֹתָם: — 1. **(giant) reed**, *Arundo donax* 1K 14_{15}; — 2. *qāneh haṭṭôb*, a variety of **oil-grass** (↗ II *ṭôb*) Je 6_{20}, > *qāneh* Is 43_{24}; — 3. *qᵉnēh bōśem* **sweet cane** (↗ *bōśem*) Ex 30_{23}; — 4. tube-shaped objects: *qᵉnēh hammiddâ* **measuring reed** † Ez $40_{3\cdot5}$ $42_{16\cdot19}$; — 5. > linear measure, 'reed,' = 6 long cubits (= 3 meters, or 10′4″) Ez 40_{5}, pl. 42_{16}; — 6. **stalk** Gn $41_{5\cdot22}$; — 7. **shaft** (of candlestick) Ex 25_{31}; — 8. **bone of upper arm** Jb 31_{22}; — 9. (beam of scales) > **scales** Is 46_{6}.

קָנָה: n. loc.

קַנּוֹא: **jealous** Jos 24_{19} Na 1_{2}. †

קְנַז: (n. pers.,) n. peop.

קְנִזִּי: gent. of קְנַז.

קִנְיָן: cs. קִנְיַן, sf. קִנְיָנְךָ, קִנְיָנֶךָ: **(personal) property**: flock Gn 31_{18}, movable goods 34_{23}; *qinyan kaspô* acquired by his own silver Lv 22_{11}.

קִנָּמוֹן, cs. ־קִנְּמָן: (Chinese) **cinnamon** Ex 30_{23} Pr 7_{17} SS 4_{14}. †

קנן: **piel**: pf. קִנְּנָה; impf. תְּקַנֵּן, יְקַנְּנוּ: **nest, make a nest** Is 34_{15} Je 48_{28} Ez 31_{6} Ps 104_{17}. †

pual: pt. מְקֻנַּנְתְּי Je 22_{23} Qr מְקֻנֶּנֶת: **nested** (= having been nested). †

***קֶנֶץ**: pl. cs. קִנְצֵי Jb 18_{2}, < קִצֵּי, ↗ קֵץ. †

קְנָת: n. loc.

קסם: **qal**: impf. יִקְסֹמוּ, וַיִּקְסְמוּ, תִּקְסַמְנָה; impv. f. sg. קָסֳמִי 1S 28_{8} Qr (Kt קְסוּמִי), inf. ־קְסָם: **practice divination** (by consulting lots which have been cast) 2K 17_{17}.

קֶסֶם: pl. קְסָמִים: — 1. **divination** (by casting lots) 2K 17_{17}; — 2. **result, decision** (produced by casting lots) † Pr 16_{10}.

קסס: **polel**: impf. יְקוֹסֵס: **make** (grapes) **scaly** Ez 17_9 (?); but perh. trad.: **strip off.** †

קֶסֶת: **writing-case** Ez $9_{2f.11}$. †

קְע(י)לָה: n. loc.

קַעֲקַע: **tattoo** Lv 19_{28}. †

קְעָרָה: cs. קַעֲרַת; pl. קְעָרֹת, cs. קַעֲרֹת, sf. קְעָרֹתָיו: **dish** Ex 25_{29}.

***קֹף**: ↗ קוֹף.

קפא: **qal**: pf. קָפְאוּ; impf. ↗ nif.; pt. קֹפְאִים: intrans. **congeal** Ex 15_8, **thicken** Zp 1_{12}. †

[**nif.**: impf. יְקְפָּאוּן (or qal יִקְפָּאוּן) Zc 14_6 Kt; rd Qr וְקִפָּאוֹן.]

hif.: impf. תַּקְפִּיאֵנִי: trans. **curdle** (cheese) Jb 10_{10}. †

קִפָּאוֹן: **frost** Zc 14_6 Qr. †

קפד: **piel**: pf. קִפַּדְתִּי: **roll up** (as a weaver his cloth) Is 38_{12}. †

קִפֹּד & **קִפּוֹד**: — 1. trad. **hedgehog,** *Erinaceus auritus & E. sacer* Is 14_{23} 34_{11}; — 2. (short-eared) **owl**, *Asio flammens* Zp 2_{14} (also Is 34_{11} ?). †

קְפָדָה: **anguish** Ez 7_{25}. †

קִפּוֹד: קִפֹּד.

קִפּוֹז: some: a type of small **tree-snake** (*Coluber jugularis? C. najadum? C. nummifer?*); oth.: a kind of **owl** (*Syrnium aluco* or *Scops giu*) Is 34_{15}. †

קָפַץ: **qal**: pf. קָ׳, קָפְצָה; impf. תִּקְפֹּץ, יִקְפְּצוּ: **draw together, shut**: obj. hand Dt 15_7, mouth Is 52_{15} Ps 107_{42} Jb 5_{16}, compassion Ps 77_{10}. †

nif.: impf. יִקָּפֵצוּן Jb 24_{24}: **be drawn together** (in death)?. †

piel: pt. מְקַפֵּץ: **leap** SS 2_8. †

קֵץ: sf. קִצּוֹ, קִצָּהּ, קִצֵּנוּ; pl. cs. קִנְצֵי < *קִצֵּי Jb 18_2: — 1. **end** (of s.one's existence) Gn 6_{13}; — 2. (absolute) **end** Am 8_2; — 3. **limit, boundary** (to perfection, empty words) Ps 119_{96} Jb 16_3; — 4. **limit** (of one's endurance) Jb 6_{11}; — 5. *qēṣ hayyāmîn* (eschatological) end of the days Dn 12_{13}; — 6. after a noun, **farthest** 2K 19_{23}; — 7. *'ên qēṣ* without end Is 9_6; — 8. *'ēt qēṣ* (eschatological) end-time Dn 8_{17}; > *qēṣ* end-time Dn 8_{19}; — 9. *miqqēṣ yāmîm* sometime later Gn 4_3 1K 17_7, *miqqēṣ yāmîm layyāmîm* at the end of every year 2S 14_{26}; ***miqqēṣ* at the end of, after** Gn 8_6 & oft.; *miqqēṣ hᵉyôt* after he had been Est 2_{12}; — 10. *lᵉqēṣ šānîm* after some years Dn 11_6, *lᵉqēṣ yāmîm* some time later Ne 13_6; — 11. *haqqēṣ lᵉyāmîm šᵉnayim* at the end of 2 years 2C 21_{19}.

קֹץ: ↗ I קוֹץ.

קצב: **qal**: impf. וַיִּקְצָב־; pt. pass. קְצוּבָה: **cut off** (obj. a stick) 2K 6_6; pt. pass. **shorn** (ewes) SS 4_2. †

קֶצֶב, קֶצֶב: pl. cs. קִצְבֵי: **shape** 1K 6_{25} 7_{37}; pl. (cut, start >) **foundations**? *qiṣbê hārîm* Jon 2_7. †

קצה: [**qal**: inf. קְצוֹת Hb 2_{10} txt. corr.; sugg. rd. קַצּוֹת.]

piel: inf. קַצּוֹת; pt. מְקַצֶּה: **trim off** (piece by piece) 2K 10_{32}; **maim** (feet) Pr 26_6; if Hb 2_{10} (↗ qal) is here, **shorten** (one's life).

[**hif.**: pf. הִקְצוֹ; inf. הִקְצוֹת; rd. √ *qṣ'* Lv $14_{41.43}$.]

קָצֶה (92×): cs. קְצֵה, sf. קָצֵהוּ, קְצֵיהֶם: — 1. spatial: **end, edge, border, extremity**: of field Gn 23_9, wilderness Ex 13_{20}; *miqṣēh ṣāfônâ* in the far north Ez 48_1; *qᵉṣēh hammaṭṭeh* end, tip of staff 1S 14_{27}; *'el-qᵉṣēh haḥᵃmušîm* to the outposts of … Ju 7_{11}; — 2. temporal: **end**: *miqṣēh šālôš šānîm* at the end of 3 years Dt 14_{28}; — 3. w. prep.: *miqqāṣeh* 'from (the) edge' = to the last man Gn 19_4, *miqqᵉṣēh 'eḥāyw* 47_2; *miqṣēh … wᵉ'ad-qāṣēhû* from one end to the other Gn 47_{21}.

קָצָה: (f. of קָצֶה): pl. cs. קְצוֹת, sf. קְצוֹתָם, קְ׳ קְצוֹתָיו (Qr Ex 37_8 & 39_4; Kt קְצוֹוֹתָו or קְ׳, ↗ קָצַת): **end, edge, border, extremity**: of the *kappōret* Ex 25_{18}, breast piece of priest 28_{23}; of the earth Is 40_{28}, heavens Je 49_{36};

qᵉṣôt dᵉrākāyw outskirts of his (God's) ways Jb 26_{14}.

קֵצֶה: alw. *ʾên qēṣeh* **without end** Is 2_7 Na 2_{10} $3_{3.9}$. †

*קָצוּ: pl. cs. קַצְוֵי: *qaṣwê-ʾereṣ* (-*ʾāreṣ*) **ends of the earth** Is 26_{15} Ps 48_{11} 65_6. †

*קָצוּר: pl. f. קְצֻרוֹת: **shortened** Ez 42_5. †

*קְצוֹת: pl. of קָצָה?; sf. קְצוֹתָם: **end** Ps 19_7, **tip** (of wing) 1K 6_{24}; *miqṣôtām* from (among, the whole of) them Ju 18_2 1K 12_{31} 13_{33} 2K 17_{32}. †

קְצָוֹת: ↗ קְצָת.

קֶצַח: **black cummin**, *Nigella sativa L.* Is $28_{25.27}$. †

קָצִין: cs. קְצִין; pl. cs. קְצִינֵי, sf. קְצִינַיִךְ: **leader** Jos 10_{24}.

I *קְצִיעָה: pl. קְצִיעוֹת: **cassia, cinnamon-flowers** (dried for incense) Ps 45_9. †

II קְצִיעָה: n. pers. f.

קְצִיץ: n. loc. עֵמֶק קְצִיץ.

I קָצִיר: cs. קְצִיר, sf. קְצִירֵךְ: — 1. (activity of) **grain harvest** (Apr.-June): *yᵉmê qāṣîr* 2S 21_9, *zeraʿ wᵉqāṣîr* Gn 8_{22}; *qāṣîr* + *qayiṣ* = whole season of harvest Je 8_{20}; — 2. **yield of harvest** 1S 8_{12}.

II קָצִיר: sf. קְצִירוֹ, קְצִירָהּ: **bough** Is 27_{11} Ps 80_{12} Jb 14_9 18_{16} 29_{19}. †

I קצע: **hif.**: impf. יַקְצִעַ: **scrape off** Lv 14_{41}. †

II קצע: **pual**: pt. f. pl. cs. מְקֻצְעֹת: **made with corners** Ex 26_{23} 36_{28}. †

hof.: pt. מְהֻקְצָעוֹת: **made with corners** Ez 46_{22} (if txt. correct). †

קצף: **qal**: pf. ק׳, קָצַפְתִּי; impf. יִקְצֹף; inf. קְצֹף: **be(come) angry** 2K 5_{11}; prep. *ʾel* with Jos 22_{18}, *ʿal* with Gn 40_2, on account of Ec 5_5; subj. God Dt 1_{34}.

hif.: pf. הִקְצַפְתָּ; impf. וַיַּקְצִיפוּ; inf. הַקְצִיף; pt. מַקְצִפִים: **provoke** (God) **to anger** Dt $9_{7f.22}$ Zc 8_4 Ps 106_{32}. †

hitp.: impf. וְהִתְקַצֵּף: **fly into a rage** Is 8_{21}. †

I קֶצֶף: קֶצֶף; sf. קִצְפִּי, קִצְפְּךָ, קִצְפֵּךְ: **anger, rage**: mostly of God Je 50_{13}; *hāyâ qeṣef ʿal* 2K 3_{27}; of man † Est 1_{18} Ec 5_{16}.

II קֶצֶף: **twig broken off** Ho 10_7. †

קְצָפָה: **stump** Jl 1_7. †

קצץ: **qal**: pf. קַצֹּתָה; pt. pass. pl. cs. קְצוּצֵי: **cut off** (obj. hand) Dt 25_{12}; **trim** (hair) Je 9_{25} 25_{23} 49_{32}. †

piel: pf. קִצֵּץ; impf. וַיְקַצֵּץ: **cut up** 2K 16_{17}, **cut in pieces** 2K 24_{13}, **cut off** (hands & feet) 2S 4_{12}.

pual: pt. מְקֻצָּצִים: **maimed** (in having thumbs & big toes cut off) Ju 1_7. †

I קצר: **qal**: pf. קָצְרוּ, קְצַרְתֶּם; impf. יִקְצוֹר־ (Qr ־צָר־, Kt ־צוֹר) Pr 22_8, יִקְצִירוּ, יִקְצְרוּן, יִקְצְרוּ, תִּקְצ(ו)ר (rd. Qr יִקְצוֹרוּ) Jb 24_6, sf. יִקְצְרֻהוּ; impv. קִצְרוּ; inf. קְצֹר, קָצְרְכֶם; pt. קוֹצֵר: — 1. w. cogn. acc. *qāṣar qāṣîr* **reap the harvest** 1S 6_{13}; > *qāṣar* abs. 2K 19_{29}; — 2. w. oth. acc. **reap, harvest** Lv 25_5; metaph., obj. whirlwird Ho 8_7, injustice 10_{13}.

[**hif.**: impf. יַקְצִירוּ Jb 24_6 Kt, rd Qr. †]

II קצר: **qal**: pf. ק׳, קָצְרָה; impf. וַתִּקְצַר, תִּקְצַרְנָה! תִּקְצַר Pr 10_{27}; inf. abs. קָצוֹר: — 1. **be (too) short** Nu 11_{23}; w. *min*, be too short to ... Is 28_{20}; **be shortened** (years) Pr 10_{27}; — 2. subj. *nefeš* = be/grow impatient Ju 10_{16}; subj. *rûᵃḥ* = become annoyed Mi 2_7.

[**piel**: pf. קִצַּר Ps 102_{24}, rd קֹצֶר.]

hif.: impf. הִקְצַרְתָּ: **shorten** Ps 89_{46}. †

קֹצֶר: *qōṣer rûᵃḥ* **despondency** (of spirit) Ex 6_9.

*קָצֵר: cs. קְצַר; pl. cs. קִצְרֵי: **short(ened)**: only in cs.: *qiṣrê yād* powerless 2K 19_{26} Is 37_{27}; *qᵉṣar ʾappayim* irascible Pr 14_{17}; *qᵉṣar rûᵃḥ* impatient Pr 14_{29}; *qᵉṣar yāmîm* short-lived Jb 14_1. †

*קְצָת: cs. קְצָת, sf. קְצָתָם; pl. קְצוֹת, sf. קְצוֹתָו (or קְ־) Kt Ex 37_8 & 39_4: **end, extremity**: pl. of earth Ps 65_9, of *kappōret* Ex 37_8; *miqṣāt* w. gen. or sf. at the end of Dn 1_5; = a portion of, some of Dn 1_2.

קַר: pl. קָרִים: adj. **cool**: water Je 18_{14} Pr 25_{25}; *qar rûaḥ* cool of spirit = composed Pr 17_{27} Kt. †

קִר: ↗ קִיר.

קֹר: **cold** Gn 8_{22}. †

I **קָרָא**: **qal**: pf. ק׳, קָרָאת 3 sg. f. Is 7_{14}, קָרָאתָ, קְרָאתֶם, קְרָאֲךָ, קְרָאתִיו; impf. יִקְרָא, וָאֶקְרָא, וָאֶקְרָאֶה 1S 28_{15} (txt. error; rd. ־רֶא or ־רָא), יִקְרָאוּ, יִקְרְאוּ, יִקְרָאוֹ > יִקְרָאֵהוּ, וַתִּקְרֶאךָ, תִּקְרֶאנָה Je 23_6, תִּקְרָאֵם, אֶקְרָאֶךָ, יִקְרָאֻהוּ, יִקְרָאֻנְנִי Pr 1_{28}; impv. קְרָא, קִרְאוּ, קְרֶאוּ, קְרֶאןָ Ru 1_{20}, קְרֶאןָ Ex 2_{20}, קְרָאֵנִי, קְרָאֶנָּה; inf. קְרֹא, קְרֹאות Ju 8_1, קָרְאִי; pt. קֹ(וֹ)רֵא, קֹרְאִים, קֹרְאִים Ps 99_6, קֹרְאָיו, pass. קָרוּא, pl. sf. קְרֻאֶיהָ: — 1. *qārā' le*: **call** Gn 12_{18}; *qārā'* + acc. 27_1, abs. 39_{15}, w. *'el* 3_9; the message follows as acc. Ex 34_6; — 2. *qārā' šēm le*: **give a name to** Gn 2_{20}, > *qārā' le* call (= name) (the light 'day') Gn 1_5; *qārā' šemô* + acc. call his name, call him so-and-so Gn 3_{20}; — 3. *qārā' bešēm* + gen. **invoke** (the name of Y.) Gn 4_{26}; *qārā' bešēm* + acc. **call** s.one by name Nu 32_{38}, **summon** Ex 31_2; *qārā' 'al-šemô* call (a village) after one's own name Dt 3_{14}; *qārā' šēmôt le* give names to (the stars) Ps 147_7; — 4. **call, summon** (obj. convocation, assembly) Lv 23_{24}; — 5. **proclaim**: obj. release Is 61_1, fast 1K 21_9; — 6. *qārā' lifnê* call in front of s.one Gn 41_{43}; *qārā' be'oznê* call loudly to Ez 8_{18}; — 7. obj. of calling is God: **call on, appeal to**: w. *'el* 1K 8_{52}, w. *le* 1C 4_{10}; w. *bešēm-'elōhê* 1K 18_{24}, sf. Ps 86_5; — 8. **invite** 1K 1_{9f}; *qārû' lāh* invited by her Est 5_{12}, *qerû'îm* 1S 9_{13}; — 9. spec.: *qārā' lešālôm 'el-'îr* offer terms of peace to Dt 20_{10}; *qārā' qerî'â 'el* proclaim a message to Jon 3_2; *qārā' šemô be* make one's name known in Ru 4_{11}; — 10. *qārā' be* **recite** from, **read aloud** from (book, scroll) Dt 17_{19}; *qārā' be'oznê* read aloud to Ex 24_7; *qārā'* + acc. read (a letter &c.) 2K 5_7.

nif.: pf. נִקְרָא, נִקְרְאָה, נִקְרְאוּ; impf. יִקָּרֵא, תִּקָּרְאוּ; pt. נִקְרָא, נִקְרָאִים: — 1. subj. person: **be called** (= be addressed, summoned) Est 3_{12}; w. *bešēm* by name Est 2_{14}; w. *'al* **be summoned** against Is 31_4; — 2. subj. (news of) disaster: **be cried out, exclaimed** Je 4_{20}; subj. name: **be invoked** Je 44_{26}; *niqrā' šemô* = it is known to exist Ec 6_{10}; *yiqqārē' lekā zera' be* your descendants will be called = identified through Gn 21_{12}; — 3. naming: *yiqqārē' le* : *lezō't yiqqārē' 'iššâ* (lit.: ''iššâ' shall be called to her =) she shall be called ''iššâ' Gn 2_{23}; *niqrā' (šemô)* his name is Gn 17_5 Is 54_5; — 4. *niqrā' šemô 'al* one's name is used over (= guardianship, dominion): over women Is 4_1, city 2S 12_{28}, temple 1K 8_{43}; — 5. *niqrā' min*, is named after Is 48_2; — 6. *niqrā' 'al-šēm* be called by the name of Gn 48_6; = *niqrā' bešēm* Is 43_7; — 7. *niqrā' 'al* be called (= counted) among 1C 23_{14}; — 8. **be read**: subj. message Ne 13_1, subj. book Est 6_1.

pual (or **qal** pass.): pf. קֹרָא; pt. sf. מְקֹרָאִי: **be called, named** (by God's name) Is 62_2 65_1; *qōrā' lî* I am named Is 48_8 58_{12} 61_3 Ez 10_{13}; pt. my called one = the one I called Is 48_{12}. †

II **קרא**: **qal**: pf. קָרָאת, sf. קְרָאָהוּ, קְרָאַנִי, קְרָאֻנִי; impf. יִקְרָא, תִּקְרֶאנָה, יִקְרָאֵהוּ, יִקְרָאֻנּוּ; inf. לִקְרַאת, לִקְרָאתוֹ, לִקְרָאתְךָ, לִקְרָאתֵךְ, לִקְרַאתְכֶם; pt. f. pl. w. sf. קֹרְאֹתַיִךְ: — 1. w. acc. pers. **happen** to s.one, **come** to s.one: subj. disaster Gn 42_4, (neutral) Gn 49_1; pt. *qōre'ōtayik* your experiences Is 51_{19}, *qārā' milḥāmâ* expose onesf. to a battle w. Jos 11_{20}; — 2. *le* & inf. cs. > prep., usu. w. vb. of motion, context of war, battle: **against** Gn 14_{17} (120×).

***קְרָא**: F ***קָרִיא**.

I **קֹרֵא**: **partridge,** *Alectoris graeca* or *Ammoperdrix hayi* 1S 26_{20} Je 17_{11}. †

II **קֹרֵא & קוֹרֵא**: n. pers. 1C 9_{19} 26_1 2C 31_{14}. †

קרב: qal: pf. קָרַב, קָרְבָה, קָרַבְתָּ; impf. יִקְרַב, תִּקְרַב, יִקְרְבוּ, וַתִּקְרַבְנָה, נִקְרְבָה; impv. קְרַב, קִרְבָה, קִרְבוּ; inf. cs. לְקָרְבָה, קָרְבְכֶם (*qorobkem*), קָרְבָתָם, abs. קָרוֹב: — 1. abs., subj. time: **draw near, approach** Gn 27_{41}; subj. person: **come near** Dt 4_{11}, subj. God La 3_{57}; *wattiqrab hammilḥāmâ* the battle was joined 1K 20_{29}; — 2. w. *'el*: **come near** Gn 37_{18}; to a task Ex 36_2; to a woman (for sexual intercourse) Gn 20_4; to God 1S 14_{36}; — 3. w. *be* come near to = get to Ju 19_{13}; — 4. w. *be* **draw near** to Jb 33_{22}, w. *lifnê* **step up** before Ex 16_9, w. *lemišpāṭ* for judgment Is 41_1; w. *liqra't* **come up** against 1S 17_{48}, w. *le* & inf. 2S 15_5, w. *'al* **assail** Ps 27_2; — 5. *qerab 'ēlêkā* stay by yourself (?) Is 65_5.

nif.: pf. נִקְרַב, נִקְרַבְתֶּם: — 1. **be brought near** Ex 22_7; — 2. bring onesf. near = **come near** Jos 7_{14}. †

piel: pf. קֵרַבְתִּי, קֵרְבוּ; impf. תְּקָרֵב, אֲקָרְבֶנּוּ; impv. קָרֵב Ez 37_{17}, קָרְבוּ: — 1. **bring up** (= forward) (obj. proofs) Is 41_{21}, **bring near** (deliverance) 46_{13}; — 2. bring near (to each oth.) = **join** Ez 37_{17}; — 3. **bring** (the faithful) **near** (to God) Ps 65_5; — 4. w. acc. **approach** Jb 31_{37}; — 5. w. *le* & inf. **be about to ...** Ez 36_8. †

hif. (172×): הִקְרִיב, הִקְרִיבָה, הִקְרַבְתָּ, הִקְרִיבוּ, הִקְרִיבָם, הִקְרַבְתִּיו; impf. יַקְרִיב, יַקְרִיבֻהוּ, וַנַּקְרֵב, תַּקְרֵב, וַיַּקְרֵב; impv. הַקְרֵב, הַקְרִיבֵהוּ; inf. הַקְרִיב, הַקְרִיבְכֶם; pt. מַקְרִיב, pl. cs. מַקְרִיבֵי: — 1. obj. thing: **bring (near)**: gift Ju 3_{17f}, legal case Nu 27_5 (*mišpāṭ*), Dt 1_{17} (*dābār*); oft. in P &c., **offer** (s.thg for sacrifice) Ex 29_3; in P, *hiqrîb qorbān* Lv 1_2; *hiqrîb yāmāyw* bring near one's days (of judgment) Ez 22_4; — † 2. w. *le* & inf. **be about to ...** Gn 12_{11} Is 26_{17}; w. *'el* or abs. **draw near** Ex 14_{10} Nu $16_{5.9f}$; — 3. obj. pers. or animal: **bring near, make ... come near** 1S 10_{20f}; — 4. *hiqrîb śādeh beśādeh* join field to f. Is 5_8.

קָרֵב: pl. קְרֵבִים: (person) **approaching** 1K 5_7; *hōlēk weqārēb* come nearer & nearer 1S 17_{41}; *qerēbîm lammilḥāmâ* those about to join battle Dt 20_3.

קְרָב: pl. קְרָבוֹת: (hostile) approach = **battle** Ps 55_{22}.

קֶרֶב (222×): sf. קִרְבּוֹ, קִרְבֵּךְ, קִרְבֶּנָה Gn 41_{21}; pl. sf. קְרָבַי: — 1. the **inward part** of body, considered the seat of laughter Gn 18_{12} (thus *beqirbāh* = 'to herself'), the *nefeš* 1K 17_{21}, *rûaḥ* Is 19_3, thoughts Je 4_{14}; **body, corpse** (of cows) Gn 41_{21}; = womb (of pregnant woman) 25_{22}; **inner parts** of sacrificial animal Ex 12_9; **interior, middle**: of city Gn 18_{24}, land 45_6, people Ex 34_{12}; **midst** of a group 1S 16_{13}, *beqirbô* in the midst of them Gn 24_3; — 2. prep. *beqereb*: **in (the midst of)**: obj. years Hb 3_2; *miqqereb* **from (among)** Nu 14_{13} & oft.; — 3. pl.: *kol-qerābay* all this is in me † Ps 103_1; — 4. ref. to God: he is *beqereb hā'āreṣ* Ex 8_{18}, *beqirbēnû* 17_7 &c.

קָרֹב: F **קָרוֹב**.

***קִרְבָה**: cs. קִרְבַת: functions as inf.: **to draw near** (to God) Is 58_2 Ps 73_{28}. †

קָרְבָּן: cs. קָרְבַּן, sf. קָרְבָּנוֹ, קָרְבָּנְךָ: **offering, gift** (in the vaguest & most genl. sense) Lv 1_2 (all P + 2× Ex).

***קֻרְבָּן**: cs. קֻרְבַּן: **supply** (of wood) Ne 10_{35} 13_{31}. †

קַרְדֹּם: sf. קַרְדֻּמּוֹ; pl. קַרְדֻּמִּים, קַרְדֻּמּוֹת: adze & axe Ju 9_{48} 1S 13_{20f} Je 46_{22} Ps 74_5. †

קרה: qal: pf.sf. קָרָהוּ, קָרָךְ; impf. יִקְרֶה, יִקְרָה Dn 10_{14} (= Qr יִקְרָא, Kt יִקְרֶה), וַיִּקֶר, תִּקְרֶינָה, sf. יִקְרֵנִי, יִקְרְךָ, יִקְרֵךְ 1S 28_{10}; pt. pl. f. קֹרֹת: — 1. w. acc.: **happen, come** (to s.one): subj. harm Gn 44_{29}, (neutral)

Gn 42_{29}; *yiqrᵉkā dᵉbārî* my (= Y.'s) word comes true for you Nu 11_{23}; *wayyiqer miqrehā* she happened to come on Ru 2_3; — 2. abs.: *ʾᵃšer tiqrénâ* what is to happen Is 41_{22}; — 3. w. *lᵉ* **happen** to Dn 10_{14}.

nif.: pf. נִקְרָה, נִקְרֵיתִי; impf. יִקָּרֶה, וַיִּקָּר, אֶקָּרֶה: — 1. **make onesf. available to**, w. *ʿal* Ex 3_{18}, w. *ʾel* Nu $23_{4.16}$, w. *liqraʾt* 23_3, with *kōh* (over there) 23_{15}; — 2. w. *bᵉ*: **happen to be** (at a place) 2S 1_6. †

piel (denom. of קוֹרָה): pf. sf. קֵרוּהוּ; inf. קָרוֹת; pt. מְקָרֶה: **timber, build w. beams** Ps 104_3 Ne 2_8 $3_{3.6}$ 2C 34_{11}. †

hif.: pf. הִקְרָה, הִקְרִיתֶם; impv. הַקְרֵה: — 1. let s.thg happen = **ordain, direct**: w. *lᵉfānay* for me Gn 24_{12} 27_{20}; — 2. w. *lᵉ*: let fall to one's lot = **select** for onesf. Nu 35_{11}. †

*קְרֵה: cs. קְרֵה: event, *qᵉrēh laylâ* = **nocturnal emission** Dt 23_{11}. †

קָרָה: **cold** Na 3_{17} Ps 147_{17} Pr 25_{20} Jb 24_7 37_9. †

קָרָה: ↗ קוֹרָה.

קָרוֹב, קָרֹב (73×): adj.: sf. קְרוֹבוֹ, f. קְרֹ(וֹ)בָה; pl. קְרֹבִים, sf. קְרוֹבַי, f. קְרֹבוֹת: — 1. spatial: **near** Gn 19_{20}; *qārôb ʾel* Gn 45_{10}; *miqqārôb* (from) nearby Je 23_{23}; — 2. temporal: **near, imminent** Dt 32_{35}; *qārôb lābôʾ* near (to come = at hand) Is 13_{22}; *miqqārôb* shortly Ez 7_8, (of) short (duration) Jb 20_5; — 3. in human relationship: **near**: *qārôb hammelek ʾēlay* the king is closely related to me 2S 19_{43}; *qᵉrôbô* his relation(s) Ex 32_{27}; — 4. in relation to God: *qᵉrōbay* those who are near to me (= Y.) Lv 10_3; *yihyû dᵉbāray qᵉrōbîm ʾel-yhwh* let my words be near (= present) to Y. 1K 8_{59}.

cj. קָרוּת: cold cj. Zc 14_6. †

קרח: **qal**: impf. יִקְרְחָה; impv. קָרְחִי: **shave bald** Lv 21_5 Mi 1_{16} (in both cases, obj. 'onesf.' is implied). †

nif.: impf. יִקָּרֵחַ: **shave onesf. bald** Je 16_6. †

hif.: pf. הִקְרִיחוּ: **shave onesf. bald** Ez 27_{31}. †

hof.: pt. מֻקְרָח: **shaved bald** Ez 29_{18}. †

קֶרַח: קֶרַח, sf. קַרְחוֹ: — 1. **frost** Gn 31_{40}; — 2. **ice** Ps 147_{17}.

קֵרֵחַ: **bald** (on the back of the head) Lv 13_{40} 2K 2_{23}. †

קֹרַח: n. pers.

קֹרַח: n. pers.

קָרְחָא: ↗ קָרְחָה.

קָרְחָה & Ez 27_{31} קָרְחָא: **baldness** (act undertaken as a sign of mourning) Is 3_{24}.

קָרְחִי: gent. of קֹרַח; pl. קָרְחִים.

קָרַחַת: **bald spot** (on back of head) Lv 13_{42f}, **bare spot** (on the back of textile or leather) 13_{55}. †

*קְרִי: קֶרִי: (hostile) **encounter**: spec.: *hālāk ʿim … (bᵉ)qerî* **resist, set oneself against** Lv $26_{21.26}$; *hālak ʿim … baḥᵃmat-qerî* **resist furiously** Lv 26_{28}.

*קָרִיא: pl. cs. קְרִ(י)אֵי: **summoned** Nu 1_{16} Qr, 16_2, 26_9 Kt. †

קְרִיאָה: **call, appeal** Jon 3_2. †

קִרְיָה: cs. קִרְיַת; pl. קִרְיוֹת: I. **city, town** 1K 1_{41}; oft. = Jerus. Is 1_{21}; — II. **city, town** in n. loc.: 1) קִרְיַת אַרְבַּע; 2) קִרְיַת־בַּעַל; 3) קִרְיַת חֻצוֹת; 4) קִרְיַת יְעָרִים; 5) קִרְיַת־סַנָּה; 6) קִרְיַת־סֵפֶר.

קְרִיּוֹת: n. loc.

קִרְיָתַיִם: n. loc.

קרם: **qal**: pf. קָרַמְתִּי: **cover over with, spread over** (obj. skin, on bones) Ez 37_6. †

[**nif.**: cj. וַיִּקָּרֵם: **be spread over** Ez 37_8 (so some mss., Verss.). †]

קרן: **qal**: pf. ק׳: **shine, be radiant** (of face) Ex $34_{29f.35}$. †

hif.: pt. מַקְרִין: **be with horns** Ps 69_{32}. †

קֶרֶן: sf. קַרְנִי; du. קַרְנַיִם, קְרָנַיִם, קַרְנַיִם, cs. קַרְנֵי, sf. קַרְנָיו, קַרְנֵינוּ; pl. קְרָנוֹת, cs. קַרְנ(וֹ)ת, sf. קַרְנֹתָיו: **horn** (part of body, not the material): — 1. of an animal Gn 22_{13}; tusks mistaken for horns Ez 27_{15}; iron imitation 1K 22_{11}; as wind instrument Jos 6_5; — 2. **horns** (of altar = protrusions at corners) 1K 1_{50f}; — 3. **horn** = receptacle for oil 1K 1_{39}; — 4. = **ray** (of brightness, cf. √*qrn* qal) Hb 3_4; — 5. = **hillside** Is 5_1; — 6. as symbol of strength & power: *qeren mô'āb* Je 48_{25}, *qeren mešîḥô* 1S 2_{10}; = God 2S 22_3; = insolence Ps 75_5, = grace Ps 89_{18}.

קֶרֶן הַפּוּךְ: n. pers. f. Jb 42_{14}. †

קַרְנַיִם: n. loc. Am 6_{13}. †

קרס: **qal**: pf. קָרְסוּ; pt קֹרֵס: **bend over, cringe** Is 46_{1f}. †

*קֶרֶס: pl. קְרָסִים, cs. קַרְסֵי, sf. קְרָסָיו: **hook** Ex 26_6.

*קַרְסֹל: du. sf. קַרְסֻלָּי: **ankle** 2S 22_{37} Ps 18_{37}. †

קרע: **qal**: pf. קָרַעְתִּי, קָרְעָה, ק׳; impf. אֶקְרְעֶנָּה, וַיִּקְרָעֶהָ, אֶקְרַע, אֶקְרָע, וַיִּקְרַע; impv. קִרְעוּ; inf. cs. קְרוֹעַ, קָרְעִי, abs. קָרֹעַ; pt. קֹרֵעַ, pass. קְרֻעִים: — 1. **tear up**: garment Gn 37_{29}, scroll Je 36_{23}, metaph. heart Jl 2_{13}, heavens Is 63_{19}; — 2. **tear away**: obj. kingdom 1K 11_{11}; — 3. **tear** (into specific number of pieces) 1K 11_{30}; — 4. **enlarge** (the eyes with) (cosmetics) Je 4_{30}; *qāra' ḥallôn* cut out a window? Je 22_{14}.

nif.: pf. נִקְרַע; impf. יִקָּרֵעַ, יִקָּרַע: **be torn up** Ex 28_{32} 29_{23} 1S 15_{27} 1K $13_{3.5}$. †

קְרָעִים: torn pieces of material, **rags** 1K 11_{30f} 2K 2_{12} Pr 23_{21}. †

קרץ: **qal**: impf. יִקְרְצוּ; pt. קֹרֵץ: — 1. *qāraṣ 'ayin* Ps 35_{19} Pr 10_{10} & *qāraṣ be'ênāyw* Pr 6_{13} **wink** (i.e. in maliciousness); — 2. *qāraṣ śefātāyw* **purse** (one's lips) Pr 16_{30}. †

pual: pf. קֹרַצְתִּי: **be** pinched off, **formed** Jb 33_6. †

קֶרֶץ: **mosquito** Je 46_{20}. †

I קַרְקַע: — 1. **floor, bottom** (of sea) Am 9_3; — 2. **floor** (of building) Nu 5_{17} 1K $6_{15f.30}$ 7_7.

II קַרְקַע: n. loc. Jos 15_3. †

קַרְקַר Nu 24_{17}: rd קָדְקֹד.

קַרְקֹר: n. loc.

קרר: **pilpel**: pt. מְקַרְקַר: Is 22_5 unexplained; usu. 'tear down,' but dub. †

hif.: pf. הֵקֵרָה; inf. הָקִיר: **keep cool** (obj. water) Je 6_7. †

קֶרֶשׁ: קֶרֶשׁ; pl. קְרָשִׁים, cs. קַרְשֵׁי, sf. קְרָשָׁיו: **plank** Ex 26_{15}; Ez 27_6 prow? deck?.

קֶרֶת: קֶרֶת: **city, town** Pr 8_3 $9_{3.11}$ 11_{14} Jb 29_7. †

קַרְתָּה: n. loc.

קַרְתָּן: n. loc.

*קַשְׂוָה: pl. קְשָׂוֹת, cs. קְשׂוֹת, sf. קְשׂוֹתָיו: **jar** (for libation) Ex 25_{29} 37_{16} Nu 4_7 1C 28_{17}. †

קְשִׂיטָה: old measure of weight, amount unknown Gn 33_{19} Jos 24_{32} Jb 42_{11}. †

קַשְׂקֶשֶׂת: pl. קַשְׂקַשִּׂים, sf. קַשְׂקְשֹׂתֶיךָ: **scale** (i.e. of a fish) Dt 14_{9f}; *širyôn qaśqaśśîm* scale-armor 1S 17_5.

קַשׁ: **stubble** Ex 15_7.

*קִשֻּׁאָה: pl. קִשֻּׁאִים: (Egyptian) **cucumber**, *Cucumis melo, chate* Nu 11_5. †

קשב: **qal**: impf. תִּקְשַׁבְנָה: **be** sharp, **attentive** (of ears) Is 32_3. †

hif.: pf. הִקְשִׁיב, הִקְשַׁבְתָּ, הִקְשִׁיבוּ; impf. יַקְשֵׁב, וַיַּקְשֵׁב, תַּקְשִׁיב, נַקְשִׁיבָה; impv. הַקְשֵׁב, הַקְשִׁיבָה, הַקְשִׁיבָה Dn 9_{19}, הַקְשִׁיבִי; inf. cs. הַקְשִׁיב; pt. מַקְשִׁיב, מַקְשֶׁבֶת: **pay attention, listen (carefully)** 1S 15_{22}: w. *'el* Is 51_4, w. *le* Is 48_{18}, w. *'al* Je 6_{19}, w. *be* Ps 66_{19}; Y. subj. Ps 5_3.

קֶשֶׁב: קֶשֶׁב: **attentiveness, paying attention** 1K 18_{29} 2K 4_{31} Is 21_7. †

*קַשָּׁב: f. קַשֶּׁבֶת: **attentive** Ne $1_{6.11}$. †

*קַשֻּׁב: pl. f. קַשֻּׁבוֹת: **attentive** (*le*) Ps 130_2 2C 6_{40} 7_{15}. †

קשה: **qal**: pf. קָשְׁתָה, קָשָׁתָה; impf. יִקְשֶׁה, וַיִּקֶשׁ: **be heavy, hard, fierce**: subj. hand 1S 5_7, anger Gn 49_7, word(s) 2S 19_{44}, thing Dt 1_{17} 15_{18}. †

nif.: pt. נִקְשֶׁה: **oppressed** Is 8_{21}. †

piel: impf. וַתְּקַשׁ: **have hard labor, severe pains** (in childbirth) Gn 35_{16}. †

hif.: pf. הִקְשָׁה, הִקְשִׁיתָ; impf. וַיֶּקֶשׁ,

תַּקְשׁוּ, אַקְשֶׁה; inf. sf. הַקְשֹׁתָהּ: — 1. **make hard, heavy**: obj. yoke 1K 12_4; **harden**: obj. s.one's *rûaḥ* Dt 2_{30}, s.one's *lēb* Ex 7_3; obj. one's neck (*ʿorpô*) = **be(come) stiff-necked, stubborn** 2K 17_{14}; — 2. w. *l*^{e} & inf.: *liš'ôl* **ask s.thg difficult** 2K 2_{10}; w. *b*^{e} & inf.: *b*^{e}*lidtāh* **had hard labor** Gn 35_{17}.

קָשֶׁה: cs. קְשֵׁה, f. קָשָׁה, cs. קְשַׁת; pl. קָשִׁים, cs. קְשֵׁי, f. קָשׁוֹת: — 1. **hard, difficult, heavy**: hand Ju 4_{24}, work 1K 12_4, battle 2S 2_{17}, *qāšâ* hard things Ps 60_5; *q*^{e}*šēh yôm* him whose day is hard Jb 30_{25}; — 2. **hard, severe** (person): 1S 25_3, pl. 2S 3_{39}; *ʿānâ qāšâ* answer severely 1K 12_{13}, *dibber qāšôt* speak harshly Gn 42_7, *šālûaḥ qāšâ* sent with bad news 1K 14_6; *ʿōref qāšeh* stiff-necked, stubborn Dt 31_{27} = *q*^{e}*šēh ʿōref* Ex 32_9 > *qāšeh* Is 48_4 cf. Ju 2_{19}; — 3. **difficult**: *dābār qāšeh* Ex 18_{26}; — 4. > **shameless**, insolent: *q*^{e}*šê pānîm* Ez 2_4, *q*^{e}*šê lēb* 3_7.

קשׁח: **hif.**: pf. הִקְשִׁיחַ; impf. תַּקְשִׁיחַ: — 1. **treat roughly** Jb 39_{16}; — 2. **harden** (obj. s.one's heart) Is 63_{17}. †

קֹשְׁטְ: **truth** Pr 22_{21}. †

קֹשֶׁט: **bow** (weapon) Ps 60_6. †

קְשִׁי: (stiff-neckedness =) **stubbornness** Dt 9_{27}. †

קִשְׁיוֹן: n. loc.

קָשַׁר: **qal**: pf. ק׳, קָשַׁר, קָשַׁרְתִּי, קְשַׁרְתֶּם; impf. תִּקְשֹׁר, הֲתִקְשָׁר־, תִּקְשְׁרִי, תִּקְשְׁרֵנוּ; impv. קָשְׁרֵם; pt. קֹשְׁרִים, pass. קְשׁוּרָה, קְשֻׁרִים: — 1. **tie up**: obj. cord Gn 38_{28} (w. *ʿal*); *nafšô q*^{e}*šûrâ* **his life is bound up** (w. *b*^{e}) Gn 44_{30}; — 2. *qāšar ʿal* **be allied together, conspire** 1K 15_{27}; *qāšar qešer* **form a conspiracy, make a plot** 1K 16_{20}; — 3. pt. pass. **sturdy** (animals) Gn 30_{42}.

nif.: pf. נִקְשְׁרָה; impf. וַתִּקָּשֵׁר: — 1. w. *b*^{e}: **bind onesf., be bound** (to) 1S 18_1; — 2. **be joined together** (subj. wall) Ne 3_{38}. †

[**hif.**: cj. impf. תַּקְשִׁירוּ Is 8_{13}: **designate as conspiracy** (oth.: consider implicated). †]

piel: impf. תְּקַשֵּׁר, תְּקַשְּׁרֵם: — 1. **bind** Jb 38_{31}; — 2. **bind on, tie on** (ornaments) Is 49_{18}. †

pual: pt. מְקֻשָּׁרוֹת: **sturdy** (↗ qal 3.) Gn 30_{41}. †

hitp.: impf. וַיִּתְקַשֵּׁר; pt. מִתְקַשְּׁרִים: **form a conspiracy** 2K 9_{14} 2C 24_{25f}. †

קֶשֶׁר: קֶשֶׁר, sf. קִשְׁרוֹ: alliance, **conspiracy** 2K 11_{14}; *qāšar qešer* ↗ *qāšar* qal 2.

קִשֻּׁרִים: cj. cs. קִשֻּׁרֵי, sf. קִשֻּׁרֶיהָ: — 1. **breast-bands**? (or some other sash or tie in women's dress) Is 3_{20} Je 2_{32}; — 2. cj. *qiššurê qayiṭ* **gossamer** cj Jb 8_{14}. †

קשׁשׁ: **qal**: impv. קוֹשׁוּ: **assemble**? Zp 2_1. †

polel: pf. קֹשְׁשׁוּ; inf. קֹשֵׁשׁ; pt. מְקֹשֵׁשׁ, מְקֹשֶׁשֶׁת: **collect**: stubble Ex $5_{7.12}$, pieces of wood Nu 15_{32f} 1K $17_{10.12}$. †

hitpolel: impv. הִתְקוֹשְׁשׁוּ: **gather yourselves together**? Zp 2_1. †

קֶשֶׁת: קֶשֶׁת, sf. קַשְׁתּוֹ; pl. קְשָׁתוֹת, sf. קַשְּׁתֹתָיו Is 5_{28}, קַשְּׁתוֹתָם Je 51_{56}; f.: — 1. **bow** (weapon): of hunter Gn 27_3, warrior Ho 2_{20}; *ben-qešet* = arrow Jb 41_{20}; *m*^{e}*ṭaḥ*^{a}*wê qešet* bowshot = measure of distance Gn 21_{16}; — 2. metaph. = **rainbow** Gn $9_{13f.16}$.

קַשָּׁת: **bowman** Gn 21_{20}, but txt.?. †

ר

רָאָה: **qal** (1140×): pf. רָאָה, ר׳, רָאֲתָה, רָאִיתָ, רָאוּ, רְאִיתֶם, רָאִינוּ, sf. רָאָהוּ, רָאֲתְךָ, רְאִיתִיו; impf. יִרְאֶה, יֵרֶא, וַיַּרְא (= **hif.** impf.), תִּרְאֶה, וַתֵּרֶא, תֵּרָאֶה Dn 1_{13}, יִרְאוּ, וַיִּרְאֶה, תִּרְאֶינָה, תִּרְאֶינָּה Mi 7_{10}, unique forms וַיִּרְאֶה Ez 18_{28}, וַיַּרְאֶ Jb 42_{16}, וַתֵּרְאֶה (= Kt וַתִּרְאֶה,

Qr וַתֵּרֶא) Je 3_7, sf. יִרְאַנִי, נִרְאֵהוּ, תִּרְאֵנִי, וַיִּרְאֵנִי; impv. רְאֵה, רְאִי, רְאוּ, רְאֶינָה; inf. cs. רְאוֹ, רְאוֹת, רַאֲוָה, רְאוֹתֶךָ, רְאֹתוֹ, abs. רָאֹה, רָאוֹ; pt. רֹאֶה, cs. רֹאֵה, sf. רֹאִי, רֹאֵנִי, pl. רֹאִים, cs. רֹאֵי, pass. רְאֻיוֹת: — 1. **see** (no obj.): subj. eye(s) Gn 27_1; subj. *'ereṣ* Ps 97_4; see:: *yāda'* perceive Is 6_9; — 2. *rā'â l*^{e} **see** Ps 64_6; *rā'â la'ênayim* look at outside appearances 1S 16_7; — 3. *rā'â* & 2 acc. see that s.one is righteous (forsaken &c.) Gn 7_1 Ps 37_{25}; — 4. *rā'â k*^{e} see s.thg/s.one as if it is ... Ju 9_{36}; — 5. obj. of *rā'â* is an indep. clause (w/o. conj.): *r*^{e}*'îtem 'āśîtî* you have seen me do Ju 9_{48}; — 6. foll. by *kî* & clause, **see that** Gn 38_{14}; oft. obj. of *rā'â* = subj. of *kî*-clause: saw the light, that it was good = saw that the light was g. (oth.: saw how good the light is) Gn 1_4 (↗ *kî* 6.); — 7. *rā'â še* Ec 2_{13} = *rā'â kî*; — 8. *l*^{e} & inf. as (preceding) obj. of *rā'â* La 3_{34-36}; — 9. *rā'â* in extended mngs.: **perceive, become aware of** Ho 9_{10}; = **know** (a person, French connaître) Dt 33_9; **look at, consider** Gn 11_5; **take any trouble about** Gn 39_{23}, subj. God Ex 4_{31}, abs. Ps 10_{11}; *rā'â h*^{a} see whether Ex 4_{18}, *rā'â mâ* see what 2C 19_6; — 10. *rā'â b*^{e}, **see** (w. emotion): **gaze at** SS 6_{11}; **enjoy looking at** 1S 6_{19}; **gloat over** Ps 22_{18}; **look w. sorrow at** Gn 21_{16}; subj. God, see (s.one's affliction) **w. concern** Gn 29_{32}; *rā'â bakkābēd* examine the liver (for divination) in suspense Ez 21_{26}; — 11. **see (visions)** Is 30_{10}, ↗ *rō'eh, mar'eh*; *rā'â baḥ*^{a}*lom* Gn 41_{22}; — 12. impv. *r*^{e}*'ēh* **see!** (almost interj., > *hinneh*) Gn 27_{27}; sg. even in addressing plural Dt 1_8; so other forms of *rā'â* as means of arousing attention 1K 20_{13}; *da' ûr*^{e}*'ēh* 1K 20_7; — 13. *rā'â* w. acc. **look at** (w. disdain, inquisitiveness) SS 1_6; — 14. see = **visit** 2K 8_{29}; — 15. see = **choose, select** Gn 22_8 2K 10_3; *r*^{e}*'uyâ* chosen Est 2_9; — 16. **perceive** (not w. eyes) Gn 2_{19}, **notice** 1K 10_4, subj. *lēb* Ec 1_{16}; *rā'îtî 'ûr* I have seen (= felt, experienced) the fire Is 44_{16}; = **get to know, become acquainted with**: obj. famine Je 5_{12}, life Ec 9_9; — 17. w. spec. obj.: God Gn 32_{31}, face of God 33_{10}, face of king 2K 25_{19}; — 18. prep.: *'el* Is 17_7; *b*^{e} ↗ 10.; *rā'â bên* ... *l*^{e} **see the difference** between ... & Ma 3_{18}; *rā'â min* **watch** s.one (& so learn from him) Ju 7_{17}; *rā'â 'al* **look (reproachfully)** at (s.one) Ex 5_{21}.

nif.: pf. נִרְאָה, נִרְאֲתָה, נִרְאוּ; impf. יֵרָאֶה, יֵרָא, וַיֵּרָא, וָאֵרָא; impv. הֵרָאֵה; inf. הֵרָאֹה, הֵרָאוֹת, לֵרָאוֹת Is 1_{12} (< לְהֵ'); pt. נִרְאֶה, נִרְאָה: — 1. **appear, become visible**: dry land Gn 1_9, no stone (in building) 1K 6_{18}; **make one's appearance** 1K 18_{1f} (w. *'el*); — 2. subj. God: **appear** (w. *'el*) Gn 12_7; — 3. *nir'â et-p*^{e}*nê [yhwh]* etc. 1S 1_{22} & elsewh.: w. nif., appear before the presence of Y., but perh. orig. qal, 'see the face of Y.,' text then changed for theological reasons.

pual (qal pass.): pf. רֻאוּ: **be seen** Jb 33_{21}. †

hif.: pf. הֶרְאָה, הִרְאִיתָ, הַרְאֵיתִי, sf. הִרְאַנִי, הֶרְאִיתִיךָ, הֶרְאָנוּ, הֶרְאָם, הֶרְאֲךָ, הֶרְאֵנִי, הִרְאִיתַנִי, הִרְאִיתִים Ps 71_{20} Qr; impf. יַרְאֶה, וַיַּרְא (like qal!), sf. יַרְאֵנִי, אַרְאֵהוּ, אַרְאֶךָּ, וַיַּרְאוּם; impv. sf. הַרְאֵנִי, הַרְאִינִי; inf. הַרְאוֹת, הַרְאוֹתָם, הַרְאוֹתְכָה, לַרְאֹתְכֶם (< לְהַ'); pt. מַרְאֶה: — 1. **let, make** s.one **see, show** Gn 12_1; subj. God, obj. prophets Je 24_1; — 2. **make** s.one **experience** Ps 71_{20}; — 3. spec.: **render** s.one **able to see** Dt 1_{33}; w. *kî, mâ*, **show** s.one that/what 2K 8_{10} Zc 1_9; w. acc. & *b*^{e} let me look w. pleasure on (enemies &c.) Ps 59_{11}; w. 3 acc. **cause** s.one **to see** s.one else **as, show** s.one s.one else as 2K 8_{13}.

hof.: pf. הָרְאָה, הָרְאֵתָה, הָרְאֵיתָה; pt. מָרְאֶה: **be shown, be made to see** s.thg: subj. person, obj. thing Ex 25_{40} 26_{30} Dt 4_{35};

be shown to s.one: subj. thing, *'ēt* + person Lv 13_{49}. †
hitp.: impf. נִתְרָאֶה, תִּתְרָאוּ, וַיִּתְרָאוּ: — 1. **look at each other** Gn 42_1; — 2. face each other = **try our/their strength** w. each other (in battle) 2K $14_{8\cdot11}$ 2C $25_{17\cdot21}$. †
רָאָה: Dt 14_{13} (rd דָּאָה w. mss.?) **kite**, *Milvus milvus*. †
[**רָאֶה***: trad. cs. רְאֵה **seeing** Jb 10_{15}; but rd. רְוֵה.]
I **רֹאֶה**: pl. רֹאִים: **seer** 1S 9_9.
II **רֹאֶה**: **vision** Is 28_7. †
רְאוּבֵן: n. pers. & peop. **Reuben**.
רְאוּבֵנִי: gent. of רְאוּבֵן.
רַאֲוָה: **seeing** Ez 28_{17}. †
רְאוּמָה: n. pers. f.
רְאוּת Ec 5_{10} Qr: ‡ רְאִית.
רְאִי: **mirror** Jb 37_{18}. †
רֳאִי: רְאִי: — 1. **appearance**: *ṭôb rō'î* = handsome 1S 16_{12}; **appearing**: his flesh wastes away from sight Jb 33_{21}; I will make you a **spectacle** (for contempt) Na 3_6; — 2. *'el ro'î* Gn 16_{13a}, *laḥay rō'î* 16_{14} 25_{11} unexplained, ‡ comm.; Gn 16_{13b} txt.?. †
רְאָיָה: n. pers.
רְאֵים: ‡ רְאֵם.
רִאישׁ(וֹ)ן: ‡ רִאשׁוֹן.
רְאִית (Kt רְאִית, Qr רְאוּת): **look, sight** Ec 5_{10}. †
ראם: **qal**: pf. רָאֲמָה: **tower high** Zc 14_{10}. †
רְאֵם: > רֵים Jb 39_{9f}; pl. רְאֵמִים, > רֵמִים Ps 22_{22}: **wild ox**, *Bos primigenius Bojanus* Nu 23_{22}.
I **רָאמוֹת**: Ez 27_{16} Jb 28_{18} Pr 24_7: uncert.; Ez 27_{16} = Jb 28_{18}, perh. **coral**; Pr 24_7 txt. dub., ‡ comm. †
II **רָאמוֹת**: n. loc.
ראשׁ = 'be poor': ‡ רושׁ.
רָאשׁ: ‡ רֵישׁ.
I **רֹאשׁ** (599×): sf. רֹאשׁוֹ, רֹאשְׁךָ, רֹאשְׁכֶם; pl. רָאשִׁים, cs. רָאשֵׁי, sf. רָאשָׁיו רֹאשָׁיו Is 15_2, רָאשֵׁיהֶם: — 1. **head** (part of body) Gn 3_{15}; *lᵉmaʿᵃlâ rō'š* above one's head Ezr 9_6; *nāśā' rō'š* lift up s.one's head Gn 40_{20} = reaccept (oth.: take notice of); var. phrases w. vbs., e.g. *hēnîᵃʿ rō'šô 'aḥᵃrê* wag head behind 2K 19_{21}; *nātan bᵉrō'šô* = pay s.one back (for his deeds) Ez 9_{10}; *nātan rō'š lᵉ* take it into one's head to Ne 9_{17}; — 2. **hair of the head** Nu 6_9; — 3. **top** (of mountain, tower &c.) Gn 8_5; *hārō'š* = top of the hill 2S 15_{32}; — 4. **beginning**: of month Ex 12_2, year Ez 40_1, street Is 51_{20}; *rō'š* for the first time 1C 16_7; *mērō'š* from the beginning Is 40_{21}; — 5. **choicest**: myrrh Ex 30_{23}; head of the guests = head of the table 1S 9_{22}; highest (joy) Ps 137_6; — 6. **head, chief, leader** Dt 20_9; so *hārō'š* Ez 10_{11}; *rā'šê hā'ābôt* heads of the families 1C 24_{31}; chiefs 1K 8_1; (musical) conductor Ne 11_{17}; *(hak)kōhēn hārō'š* chief priest 2K 25_{18} Ezr 7_5; — 7. **total amount** Pr 8_{26}; *lᵉrō'š geber* = for each man Ju 5_{30}, pl. 1C 24_4; *nāśā' rō'š* establish the total Ex 30_{12}; *bᵉrō'šô* in full Lv 5_{24}; *rō'š dᵉbārᵉkā* sum total of = essence of Ps 119_{160}; — 8. **branch** (of river) Gn 2_{10}; **company** (of soldiers) 1S 11_{11}; — 9. spec.: *rō'š pinnâ* main cornerstone Ps 118_{22}; *rō'š kōkābîm* the highest star? sum of the stars? Jb 22_{12}; *rō'š keleb* = insult 2S 3_8.
II **רֹאשׁ** & **רוֹשׁ** Dt 32_{32}: unspecified **poisonous plant** Dt 29_{17}; > **poison**: *mê rō'š* Je 8_{14}; (snake) venom Dt 32_{33}.
III **רֹאשׁ**: n. pers. Gn 46_{21}, but txt. corr. †
IV **רֹאשׁ**: n. peop. Ez 38_{2f} 39_1. †
רִאשָׁה*: pl. sf. רִאשֹׁתֵיכֶם: your former situation Ez 36_{11}. †
רֹאשָׁה: f. **uppermost**: *hā'eben hārō'šâ* the capstone? Zc 4_7. †
רִאשׁוֹן & **רִישׁוֹן** Jb 8_8 (רִאישׁוֹן Jb 15_7 & רִאישֹׁנָה Jos 21_{10}) (180×): f. רִאשֹׁנָה; pl. רִאשֹׁנִים, רִאשֹׁנוֹת: — 1. **the first** (in series) Gn 25_{25}, pl. 2K 1_{14}; *haḥōdeš hāri'šôn* the 1st month Ex 40_2, so *hayyôm hār.* Ex 12_{15};

bāri'šôn = in the 1st month Gn 8_{13}, *bāri'šônîm* in the 1st days 2S 21_{9}; *bāri'šônâ* for the 1st time Nu 10_{13}; *(bā)ri'šônâ* first (adv.) Gn 38_{28} Dt 13_{10}, *kāri'šônâ* as at the 1st Dt 9_{18} = *kebāri'šônâ* Ju 20_{32}; God is *ri'šôn* Is 41_{4}; — 2. **preceding, former** Gn 40_{13}; many contexts, e.g. *'îšî hāri'šôn* my former husband Ho 2_{9}; *ri'šônîm* ancestors Dt 19_{14}; *ri'šônôt* former things Is 41_{22}; *ri'šônâ* preceding = in front Gn 33_{2}.

***רִאשׁוֹנִי**: f. רִאשֹׁנִית: *haššānâ hāri'šōnît* the **first** year (= accession year) Je 25_{1}. †

רַאֲשׁוֹת: F מְרַאֲשׁוֹת.

רֵאשִׁית, רֵשִׁית Dt 11_{12}: sf. רֵאשִׁיתְךָ, רֵאשִׁיתוֹ: — 1. what is first, **beginning** Is 46_{10}; — 2. **beginning, starting-point**: time Gn 1_{1}; metaph.: *rēšît ḥokmâ* Ps 111_{10}; — 3. **first, best**: *rē'šît 'ônî* first of my strength = first-born Gn 49_{3}; *rē'šît gôyyim* Nu 24_{20}; *rē'šît kol-minḥâ* 1S 2_{29}; — 4. **first-fruits**: *hārē'šît* offering of firstfruits Ne 12_{44}, so Je 2_{3}.

I **רַב** (420×): רָב, f. רַבָּה, cs. רַבַּת, רַבָּתִי; pl. רַבִּים, cs. רַבֵּי, f. רַבּוֹת: — 1. sg. (w. sg. noun) **numerous**: *ʿam rab* Gn 50_{20}; esp. w. coll. sg.: *zeraʿ rab* **much** seed Dt 28_{38}, *miqneh rab* much cattle Nu 32_{1}; *rabbat baqqāhāl* many in the congreg. 2C 30_{17}, *rabbat min* many of 30_{18}; — 2. pl. (w. pl. noun): **many**: *yāmîm rabbîm* Gn 21_{34}; abs. *rabbîm* the many, the rank & file (of people) Ex 23_{2}; *rabbôt* many things Is 42_{20}; — 3. pl. (w. coll. sg.): *ṣō'n rabbôt* = large flocks Gn 30_{43}; *rabbîm ʿam hā'āreṣ* is numerous Ex 5_{5}; *mayim rabbîm* Nu 20_{11} &c.; — 4. sg. numerous, manifold > **great** (in extent, quantity): space 1S 26_{13}; = long (journey) 1K 19_{7}; = vast (kingdom) Est 1_{20}; *tehôm* Gn 7_{11}; city: Sidon Jos 11_{8}, Hamath Am 6_{2}; *melek rāb* = God Ps 48_{3}; *wayyēlek hālôk wārāb* (noise) became louder & louder 1S 14_{19}; — 5. sg. abs. **much, plentiful, enough**: straw & fodder Gn 24_{25}; *yeš-lî rāb* I have enough 33_{9}; (wickedness is) **abundant** Gn 6_{5}; — 6. *rab* w. gen. **abounding in** (or rephrase): *rabbat bānîm* with many sons 1S 2_{5}; *rab peʿālîm* of many exploits 2S 23_{20}; *rab ḥesed* Ex 34_{6}; — 7. adv. *rabbat* **abundantly** Ps 65_{10}; (for) **too long** (a time) 120_{6}; — 8. **enough** Gn 45_{28} 1K 19_{4}; *rab miheyôt qōlōt* (there has been) enough thunder Ex 9_{28}; *rab lākem min*, too much for you to ... 1K 12_{28}.

II **רַב**: **captain, chief**, in phr.: *rab māg*; *rab-sārîs, rab-šāqēh* 2K 18_{17} &c.; pl. *rabbê hammelek, rabbê melek bābel* Je 39_{13} 41_{1}.

III ***רַב**: pl. sf. רַבָּיו Jb 16_{13}: sugg. his arrows, oth. his archers; Je 50_{29} F comm. †

רָב: F רִיב.

רֹב, רוֹב: cs. רֹב, רָב־, sf. רֻבְּכֶם, pl. cs. רֻבֵּי Ho 8_{12} (?): **great number** (e.g. of people), **abundance** Gn 16_{10}; *rōb derek* long way Jos 9_{13}, *rōb yāmîm* long time Is 24_{22}, *rōb kōḥô* greatness of his strength Is 63_{1}; *lārōb* abundantly Gn 30_{30}, so: greatly, much 1C 4_{38} 2C 27_{3}.

I **רבב**: **qal**: pf. רַבֹּה Ex 23_{29}, רָבָּה Gn 18_{20}, רַבּוּ 1S 25_{10}, רָבּוּ Is 22_{9}; inf. רֹב, לָרֹב, רֻבָּם, רֻבְּכֶם: **be(come) numerous, much, great** Gn 6_{1}; w. *min* more than Dt 7_{7}.

pual: pt. pl. f. מְרֻבָּבוֹת: **increased ten-thousand-fold** Ps 144_{13}. †

II **רבב**: **qal**: רֹבּוּ: **shoot** (arrows) Gn 49_{23}. †

רְבָבָה: **very great multitude, legion > ten thousand** 1S 18_{7f}; as indefinitely large number Nu 10_{36}.

רְבָבִים: F רְבִיבִים.

רבד: **qal**: pf. רָבַדְתִּי: **prepare** (a couch) Pr 7_{16}. †

I **רבה**: **qal**: pf. רָבְתָה, רָבִית, רָבוּ, רְבִיתֶם; impf. יִרְבֶּה, יִרֶב, וַיִּרֶב, וַתֵּרֶב, וַתִּרְבִּי, יִרְבּוּ, יִרְבְּיֻן, תִּרְבּוּן, וַתִּרְבֶּינָה; impv. רְבֵה, רְבוּ; inf. רְבוֹת: — 1. **become numerous** Gn 1_{22}; — 2. **be(come) great**: waters Gn 7_{17f}, glory of s.one's house Ps 49_{17}, slaughter 1S 14_{30}; w.

min be greater than Gn 43_{34}; way is too long from you (to cult center) Dt 14_{24}.

piel: pf. רִבְּתָה, רִבִּיתָ; impv. רַבֵּה Ju 9_{29}: — 1. **increase** (obj. army) Ju 9_{29}; — 2. **bring up** (obj. children) Ez 19_2 La 2_{22}; — 3. **make a profit** Ps 44_{13}. †

hif. (160×): pf. הִרְבָּה, הִרְבְּתָה, הִרְבִּיתָ, הִרְבֵּיתִי, הִרְבּוּ, הִרְבֵּיתֶם, הִרְבִּינוּ, sf. הִרְבְּךָ, הִרְבִּיתִךְ, הִרְבַּתִּים; impf. יַרְבֶּה, יֶרֶב, וַיֶּרֶב, יַרְבּוּ, תַּרְבִּי, וָאַרְבֶּה (Kt), וָאֶרֶב (Qr) Jos 24_3, תַּרְבֶּינָה, sf. יַרְבְּךָ, אַרְבֵּהוּ, תַּרְבֵּנִי; impv. הַרְבֵּה > הֶרֶב Ps 51_4 Qr, הַרְבִּי, הַרְבּוּ; inf. cs. הַרְבּוֹת (2S 14_{11} Kt הַרְבִּית), abs. הַרְבֵּה & הַרְבָּה; pt. מַרְבֶּה, cs. מַרְבֵּה, f. מַרְבָּה, pl. מַרְבִּים: — 1. **make many** Ho 8_{11}; obj. *yāmîm* = live long Jb 29_{18}; — 2. **make great**: obj. king 2S 22_{36}, reward Gn 15_1; — 3. spec.: *hirbâ min* **make** s.thg **more than** Ez 16_{51}; *hirbâ bānîm* have many children 1C 7_4, *hirbâ ʿad* 1C 4_{27}; *marbēh raglayim* with many feet Lv 11_{42}; *hirbâ lᵉ* obtain, supply in large quantity for Dt 17_{16f}; *hirbâ mōhar* set a high bridal payment Gn 34_{12}; obj. wealth: **increase** Pr 13_{11}; *hirbâ* w. *lᵉ* & inf. **do** s.thg **frequently, copiously, continually** 1S 1_{12} 2S 14_{11} 2K 21_6; w. *min* **do more frequently** than 2S 18_8; *hirbâ* > adj. diverse Ne 4_{13}; — 4. *hirbâ* in asyndeton w. other vbs.: *tarbû tᵉdabbᵉrû* you speak much 1S 2_3 &c.

II רבה: **qal**: pt. רֹבֶה **archer** Gn 21_{20} (as text stands, *qaššāt* is a gloss).

רַבָּה: n. loc.

רִבּוֹ(א): pl. רִבֹּאוֹת > רִבּוֹת Ne 7_{70}, du. רִבֹּתַיִם: countless host, **ten thousand** Jon 4_{11}.

רְבִבִים, רְבִיבִים: coll. pl. **mild rain** Dt 32_2.

רָבִיד: cs. רְבִד: **necklace** Gn 41_{42} Ez 16_{11}. †

רְבִיעִי, רְבִעִי: f. רְבִיעִ(י)ת; pl. רְבִ(י)עִים: — 1. **fourth**: day Gn 1_{19}, river 2_{14}, generation 15_{16}; *hārᵉbîʿî* = 4th month Zc 8_{19}; '4th year' is *haššānâ hārᵉbîʿît* 1K 6_1 or *šᵉnat hārᵉbîʿît* Je 46_2; — 2. f. *rᵉbîʿît* **one-fourth** (fraction) Ex 29_{40}; — 3. pl. *bᵉnê rᵉbîʿîm* sons of the 4th generation 2K 10_{30}.

רַבִּית: n. loc.

רבך: **hof.**: pt. מֻרְבֶּכֶת, ־בֶּכֶת: **stirred, mixed** (dough) Lv 6_{14} 7_{12} 1C 23_{29}. †

רִבְלָה: n. loc.; loc. רִבְלָתָה.

רַב מָג: ↗ מָג & II רַב.

רַב־סָרִיס: ↗ סָרִיס & II רַב.

I רבע: **qal**: inf. רִבְעָהּ, רְבִעִי, inf. f. רִבְעָה: — 1. **be lying** (stretched out) Ps 139_3; — 2. w. acc.: **lie with** (copulate w.) (obj. beast) Lv 18_{23} 20_{16}. †

hif.: impf. תַּרְבִּיעַ: **crossbreed** (cattle) Lv 19_{19}. †

II רבע: **qal**: pt. pass. רָבוּעַ, רְבֻעָה, רְבֻעִים: **square(d)** (altar, breastplate, &c.) 1K 7_5.

pual: pt. מְרֻבָּע, מְרֻבַּעַת, מְרֻבָּעוֹת: **square** 1K 7_{31} Ez 40_{47} 45_2. †

I רֶבַע: pl. sf. רְבָעָיו, רְבָעֶיהָ, רִבְעֵיהֶן: — 1. **one-fourth** (fraction) 1S 9_8; — 2. **side** (of s.thg square) Ez 1_8.

II רֶבַע: n. pers. Nu 31_8 Jos 13_{21}. †

I רֹבַע: **one-fourth** (fraction) 2K 6_{25}. †

II רֹבַע: **dust, rubbish** (oth.: dust-cloud) Nu 23_{10}. †

*רִבֵּעַ: pl. רִבֵּעִים: **member of the fourth generation** Ex 20_5 34_7 Nu 14_{18} Dt 5_9. †

רְבִעִי: ↗ רְבִיעִי.

cj. רְבַעַת: **(four-)square** (for רְבִעִית) Ez 48_{20}. †

רָבַץ: **qal**: pf. ר׳, רָבְצָה, רָבָצָה; impf. יִרְבַּץ, וַתִּרְבַּץ, יִרְבְּצוּ, יִרְבָּצוּן, תִּרְבַּצְנָה; pt. רֹבֵץ, רֹבֶצֶת, רֹבְצִים: — 1. **lie down; couch** (i.e. of animals, w. chest to the ground): herds Gn 29_2, lion 49_9, mother-bird protecting brood Dt 22_6; — 2. **be lying** (stretched out): exhausted beast of burden Ex 23_5, men Is 14_{30}, *tᵉhôm* Gn 49_{25}; — 3. w. *bᵉ*: subj. curse, **settle** on Dt 29_{19}; — 4. Gn 4_7 context unclear; either rd. *tirbōṣ* (dittgr.) or (w. oth.) rd. *rōbēṣ* as name of demon, ↗ comm.

hif.: impf. יַרְבִּיצֵנִי, יַרְבִּצוּ, תַּרְבִּיץ, אַרְבִּיצֵם; pt. מַרְבִּיץ, מַרְבִּצִים: — 1. **let** (a flock) **lie down** Ps 23_{2}; — 2. **cover** (stones w. jewels) Is 54_{11}.

רֵבֶץ: sf. רִבְצוֹ, רִבְצָם: **resting-place** (for animals) Is 65_{10} Je 50_{6} Pr 24_{15}.

רִבְקָה: n. pers. f. **Rebekah**.

רַב־שָׁקֵה (רַבְשָׁקֵה): evid. Assyrian office 'cup-bearer' 2K 18_{17}.

רַבַּת, רַבָּתִי: ↗ רַב I.

***רֶגֶב**: pl. רְגָבִים, cs. רִגְבֵי: **clod** Jb 21_{33} 38_{38}. †

רָגַז: **qal**: pf. ר׳, רָגְזָה; impf. יִרְגַּז, וַיִּרְגְּזוּ, יִרְגָּזוּ, תִּרְגַּזְנָה, יִרְגָּזוּן; impv. רִגְזוּ, f. רְגָזָה Is 32_{11}: — 1. intrans. **shake, quake**: subj. earth 1S 14_{15}, heavens 2S 22_{8}, belly Hb 3_{16}; — 2. metaph. **tremble**, in fear 2S 7_{10}, joy Je 33_{9}, grief 2S 19_{1}; — 3. *rāgaz min* **come out trembling** from Mi 7_{17}; — 4. **be upset** (of emotion) Gn 45_{24}, **fly into a passion** (of Y.) Is 28_{21}.

hif.: pf. הִרְגִּיז, הִרְגַּזְתַּנִי; impf. אַרְגִּיז; pt. מַרְגִּיז: — 1. **make** (earth, heavens) **shake, quake** Is 13_{13} 14_{16}, **agitate** (nations) Is 23_{11}; **rouse up** (the dead Samuel) 1S 28_{15}; — 2. w. *le* **work agitation** on Je 50_{34}.

hitp.: inf. הִתְרַגֶּזְךָ: **excite onesf.** 2K 19_{27f} Is 37_{28f}. †

רֹגֶז: sf. רָגְזְךָ: — 1. **excitement**: of horse Jb 39_{24}; of a sound = thunder Jb 37_{2}; > wrath Hb 3_{2}; — 2. **turmoil** Is 14_{3} Jb $3_{17.26}$ 14_{1}. †

רַגָּז: **agitated, trembling** (*lēb*) Dt 28_{65}. †

רָגְזָה: **agitation** Ez 12_{18}. †

רָגַל: **qal**: pf. ר׳: **slander, gossip** Ps 15_{3}. †

piel: impf. וַיְרַגֵּל; impv. רַגְּלוּ, sf. רַגְּלָהּ; inf. רַגֵּל; pt. מְרַגְּלִים: — 1. roam (a land &c.) > **spy out** 2S 10_{3}; pt. **spy** Gn 42_{9}; — 2. **slander** (*be*) s.one to (*'el*) s.one else 2S 19_{28}.

tifil: תִּרְגַּלְתִּי: **teach** s.one **to walk** Ho 11_{3}. †

רֶגֶל (245×): sf. רַגְלְךָ, רַגְלֵנוּ, רַגְלוֹ Qr (so rd) Ec 4_{17}; du. רַגְלַיִם, רַגְלָיִם, cs. רַגְלֵי, sf. רַגְלָיו, רַגְלֵיהֶם; pl. רְגָלִים Ex 23_{14}: — 1. **foot**: of man Gn 18_{4}, animal Ez 29_{11}, dove Gn 8_{9}, God 2S 22_{10}; — 2. phr.: *kaf regel* = **sole** Dt 2_{5}, *bōhen regel* = great toe Ex 29_{20}, *'eṣbe'ôt raglāyw* his toes 2S 21_{20}; — 3. extended mng.: a) = **leg** 1S 17_{6}; b) euphem. for genital area: *mê(mê) raglêhem* Qr 2K 18_{27} (|| Is 36_{12}) **urine**; *śa'ar hāraglāyim* = pubic hair Is 7_{20}; cf. Dt 28_{57} Is 6_{2}; — 4. vb. phr.: *'āśâ raglāyw* care for one's feet 2S 19_{25}; *nāśā' raglāyw* (evid.) resume one's journey Gn 29_{1}; oth. phr.: *mikkaf regel we'ad qodqōd* Dt 28_{35} & sim.; *qal beraglāyw* swift-footed 2S 2_{18}; *(hithallēk) beraglê* follow behind s.one 1S 25_{27} = *leraglô, leraglāyw* Is 41_{2} Hb 3_{5}; *beraglayim* straight through Dt 2_{28}, *beregel, beraglāyw* on foot Ps 66_{6} Ju 4_{15}; *regel beregel, regel taḥat regel* foot for foot Dt 19_{21} Ex 21_{24}; — 5. **foot** (metaph.): of Isr. 2K 21_{8}, of arrogance Ps 36_{12}, of table Ex 25_{26}; — 6. pl. **times** (= occurrences) Ex 23_{14}; — 7. spec.: *leraglî* Gn 30_{30} because I am here; *leregel* Gn 33_{14} as is suitable to the foot (oth. assume 'in my wake,' 'in the wake of' for both passages).

רַגְלִי: pl. רַגְלִים: (man) **on foot** Ex 12_{37}, esp. **foot-soldier** 1K 20_{29}.

רֹגְלִים: n. loc.

רגם: **qal**: pf. רָגְמוּ, רְגָמֻהוּ; impf. יִרְגְּמוּ, יִרְגְּמֻהוּ; inf. רָגוֹ(ו)ם, לִרְגּוֹם: **stone** s.one: usu. w. *'eben*, either *rāgam* + acc. pers. + *be'eben* Lv 20_{2} or *rāgam 'eben be* + pers. 1K 12_{18}.

רֶגֶם: n. pers.

***רִגְמָה**: sf. רִגְמָתָם: **noisy crowd** Ps 68_{28}. †

רֶגֶם מֶלֶךְ Zc 7_{2}: trad. n. pers.; but prob. rd. רַב־מַג הַמֶּלֶךְ. †

רגן: **qal**: pt. רֹגְנִים: **find fault, grumble** Is 29_{24}. †

nif.: impf. וַיֵּרָגְנוּ; pt. נִרְגָּן: **appear sullen, backbite** Dt 1_{27}; pt. tale-bearer Pr 16_{28}.

רָגַע: **qal**: pf. ר׳; pt. cs. רֹגַע: — 1. intrans. **crust over** (of skin) Jb 7_{5}; — 2. trans., obj. sea: **stir up** Jb 26_{12} (oth.: 'still'), Is 51_{15} = Je 31_{35}. †

nif.: impv. הֵרָגְעִי: **stop, keep quiet** Je 47_6. †

hif.: pf. הִרְגִּיעַ, הִרְגִּיעָה; impf. תַּרְגִּיעַ, אַרְגִּיעָה; inf. הַרְגִּיעוֹ: — 1. **come to rest, stop** Dt 28_{65}; — 2. subj. Y., acc. pers.: **provide rest to** s.one Je 50_{34}; — 3. *weʿad-ʾargîʿâ* as long as I grant rest = for a moment Pr 12_{19}; — 4. denom. of *regaʿ*: **do** s.thg **in a moment**: *hirgîaʿ hērîṣ* suddenly make s.one run Je 49_{19}.

***רָגֵעַ**: pl. cs. רִגְעֵי: **quiet, resting** Ps 35_{20}. †

רֶגַע: רָגַע; pl. רְגָעִים: — 1. **tranquillity** Jb 21_{13}; — 2. **while, period** (of time) Is 54_8; *regaʿ* ... *weregaʿ* at one moment ... at another m. Je 18_{7-9}; *kimʿat regaʿ*, *beregaʿ qāṭôn* for a moment, short while Is 26_{20} 54_7; — 3. > **moment, instant** Ex 33_5; *regaʿ* **suddenly** Is 47_9; — 4. *lirgāʿîm* **every moment** Is 27_3.

רגשׁ: **qal**: pf. רָגְשׁוּ: **be restless** Ps 2_1. †

***רֶגֶשׁ**: רֶגֶשׁ: **unrest** Ps 55_{15}. †

***רִגְשָׁה**: cs. רִגְשַׁת: **unrest, emotion** Ps 64_3. †

רדד: **qal**: inf. רַד; pt. רוֹדֵד; cj. impf. יָרֹד or יָרֹד Is 41_2?: **repel, subdue** Is 45_1 Ps 144_2; cj. Is 41_2. †

hif.: impf. וַיָּרֶד: **have** s.one **hammer out** (gold leaf) 1K 6_{32}; תָּרִיד < *תָּרֵד **obtain control** Gn 27_{40}. †

cj. **pual/hof.** (**qal** pass.): pf. רֻדְּדוּ; impf. אוּרַד: **be subdued** cj. Je 2_{31}, cj Ps. 55_3 (?). †

I **רדה**: **qal**: pf. רָדוּ, רְדִיתֶם; impf. תִּרְדֶּה, יִרְדְּנוּ, וְיִרְדּוּ, וְיֵרְדְּ; impv. רְדֵה, רְדוּ; inf. רְדוֹת; pt. רֹדֶה, רֹדִים: — 1. **tread** (in the wine-press) Jl 4_{13}; — 2. **rule, govern** abs. Ps 72_8, w. *be* over Gn 1_{26}.

[**hif.**: impf. יַרְדְּ Is 41_2; rd perh. √*rdd*, or txt. corr. †]

II **רָדָה**: **qal**: pf. ר׳; impf. יִרְדּוּ, sf. וַיִּרְדֵּהוּ: **scrape out** (honeycomb) Ju 14_9; w. *ʿal-yedêhem*: some: 'take into their own hands,' oth.: scrape out Je 5_{31}. †

רַדַּי: n. pers.

רְדִיד: sf. רְדִידִי; pl. רְדִידִים: item of clothing, perh. a **wrapper** (like a stole) for summer wear Is 3_{23} SS 5_7. †

רדם: **nif.**: pf. נִרְדַּמְתִּי; impf. וַיֵּרָדַם; pt. נִרְדָּם: **snore, be in deep sleep, lie stupefied** Ju 4_{21}.

***רֹדָן**: n. peop. **Rhodians**: pl. רוֹדָנִים 1C 1_7 (so rd. Gn 10_4); rd. sg. Ez 27_{15}. †

רָדַף: **qal** (124×): pf. ר׳, רָדְפוּ, רְדַפְתֶּם, רְדָפוּנִי, רְדָפוּךָ; impf. יִרְדֹּף, יִרְדָּף־, יִרְדֹּף Ps 7_6 = either יִרְדֹּף or יְרַדֵּף, אֶרְדְּפָה, יִרְדְּפֶךָּ, יִרְדְּפוּ, וַיִּרְדְּפֵהוּ, נִרְדְּפָה, יִרְדְּפָה, יִרְדְּפוּ, וַיִּרְדְּפוּם, תִּרְדְּפוּנִי; impv. רְדֹף, רִדְפוּ; inf. רְדֹף, לִרְדֹּף, לְרָדְפְךָ, רָדְופִי Ps 38_{21} = Kt רְדוֹפִי & Qr רָדְפִי; pt. רֹ(ו)דֵף, sf. רֹדְפָם, רֹדְפֶךָ, pl. רֹדְפִים, רֹדְפֵי, sf. רֹדְפַי, רֹדְפֵיכֶם: — 1. w. *ʾaḥarê*: **pursue, set off** after s.one (to catch up w. him, oft. hostile) Gn 44_4, abs. Gn 14_{14}; — 2. w. acc.: **pursue** (oft. sim. to 1) Gn 14_{15}, **persecute** Am 1_{11}; subj. inanimate: blood Ez 35_6, disease Dt 28_{22}, goodness & steadfast love Ps 23_6; obj. east wind Ho 12_2; pt. **pursuer** Lv 26_{35} & oft.; subj. God Jb 19_{22}; — 3. w. *le* **pursue** Jb 19_{28}; w. *le* & inf. **push on** to (know) Ho 6_3.

nif.: pf. נִרְדָּפְנוּ; pt. נִרְדָּף: **be chased, pursued** La 5_5; **have vanished** Ec 3_{15}. †

piel: pf. רִדְּפוּ; impf. תְּרַדֵּף; pt. מְרַדֵּף: **chase, hunt** Ho 2_9; **pursue** Pr 13_{21}.

pual: pf. רֻדַּף: **be driven out** Is 17_{13}.

[**hif.** pf. sf. הִרְדִּיפֻהוּ Ju 20_{43}: txt. corr., rd. qal. †]

רהב: **qal**: impf. יִרְהֲבוּ; impv. רְהַב: **assail, press** (s.one hard), **pester**: w. *be* Is 3_5, w. acc. Pr 6_3.

hif.: pf. הִרְהִיבֻנִי; impf. sf. תַּרְהִבֵנִי (Ps 138_3; but txt. corr.? F comm.): **alarm, confuse** SS 6_5; Ps 138_3?. †

רַהַב: רְהַב; pl. רְהָבִים (never w. art.): **afflicter** (oth.: arrogant); sg. = Egypt Ps 87_4; pl. = idols Ps 40_5.

***רֹהַב**: sf. רָהְבָּם: **crowding, hurry** Ps 90_{10}.

רָהֲגָה (Qr) & רוֹהֲגָה (Kt): n. pers. 1C 7_{34}. †

***רַהַט**: pl. רְהָטִים: **watering trough** Gn $30_{38 \cdot 41}$ Ex 2_{16} SS 7_6. †

***רָהִיט**: pl. Qr רָהִיטֵנוּ, Kt רָחִיטֵנוּ (!) SS 1_{17}: **rafter.** †

רוֹב: F רֹב.

רוּב: F רִיב.

רוּד: **qal**: pf. רַדְנוּ Je 2_{31}; pt. רָד Ho 12_1: **roam** (but txt. questionable). †

hif.: impf. תָּרִיד (< *תָּרֵד hif. רדד?) Gn 27_{40}, אָרִיד (rd. אוּרַד hof. רדד?) Ps 55_3 uncert. †

רוֹדָנִים: n. peop. F *רֹדָן.

רוה: **qal**: pf. רָוְתָה; impf. נִרְוֶה, יִרְוְיֻן: **drink one's fill**: w. acc. (of) Pr 7_{18} (metaph.), w. *min* (of) Je 46_{10} Ps 36_9. †

cj. **nif.**: impf. יֵרָוֶה: **be given one's fill to drink** cj. Pr 11_{25}. †

piel: pf. רִוְּתָה, רִוֵּיתִי; impf. יְרַוֶּךָ, אֲרַיָּוֶךְ < *אֲרַוֶּיךְ Is 16_9; inf. רַוֵּה: **give s.one his fill to drink, drench**: obj. furrows Ps 65_{11}, obj. pers., metaph. Pr 5_{19}; w. acc. of what is drunk: tears Is 16_9, fatness Je 31_{14}. †

hif.: pf. הִרְוָה, הִרְוֵיתִי, sf. הִרְוַנִי, הִרְוִיתַנִי; cj. impf. יַרְוֶה Ho 6_3; pt. מַרְוֶה: **give s.one his fill to drink, drench**: Is 55_{10} Je 31_{25} Pr 11_{25} cj Ho 6_3; w. acc. of what is drunk Is 43_{24} La 3_{15}. †

hof.: impf. יוֹרֶא < יוֹרֶה = יוּרֶה: **be given one's fill to drink** Pr 11_{25}; but F cj. nif. †

רָוֶה: cs. cj. רְוֵה, f. רָוָה: **drenched, (well)-watered**: garden Is 58_{11} Je 31_{12}, land Dt 29_{18}; cj. *rᵉwēh ʼōnî* Jb 10_{15}. †

רוֹהֲגָה: F רָהְגָּה.

רוח: **qal**: pf. רָוַח; impf. יִרְוַח: w. *lô*: it becomes wide for him = **he feels relieved** 1S 16_{23} Jb 32_{20}. †

pual: pt. מְרֻוָּחִים: **spacious** Je 22_{14}. †

hif.: impf. יָרִיחַ, יָרַח, וַיָּרַח, אָרִיחַ, יְרִיחוּן, יְרִיחֻן; inf. לָרִיחַ (< *לְהָרִיחַ) הֲרִיחוֹ: **smell** s.thg Gn 8_{21}; w. *bᵉ* **enjoy** (or **suffer**) **the smell of** Ex 30_{38}; abs.: (the gods are not able to) smell Dt 4_{28}.

רֶוַח: **space, interval** Gn 32_{17}, > **liberation** Est 4_{14}. †

רוּחַ (377× esp. Is Ez Ps): **air in motion, blowing, wind, what is empty or transitory, spirit, mind**; usu. f., but quite oft. m.: — 1. **breath** Ez 37_5; *rûᵃḥ śᵉfātāyw* Is 11_4; of God Jb 27_3; **air** (for breathing) Je 14_6; *šābâ rûḥô* = he came to his senses 1S 30_{12}; *hēšîb rûḥô* catch one's breath Jb 9_{18}; *lōʼ hāyâ bāh rûᵃḥ* = left her breathless (w. astonishment) 1K 10_5; *rûᵃḥ ʼappô* breath of his (God's) wrath Jb 4_9; *hārûḥōt lᵉkol-bāśār* the totality of breath within all individual creatures of flesh = the breath of life within all flesh Nu 16_{22}; — 2. **breath** as transitory Jb 7_7, so *rûᵃḥ hōlēk* Ps 78_{39}; > **what is empty or transitory**: *hāyâ lᵉrûᵃḥ* Je 5_{13}; *dibrê rûᵃḥ* Jb 16_3; *rûᵃḥ* = nothing Pr 11_{29}; *lᵉrûᵃḥ* for nothing Jb 6_{26}; — 3. **wind** (over 100×): *rûᵃḥ hayyôm* evening (or morning?) breeze Gn 3_8; *rûᵃḥ qādîm* east-wind Ex 10_{13} &c.; *kanfê rûᵃḥ* wings of the wind 2S 22_{11}; — 4. wind > (one of the 4 compass-)**direction[s]**: Ez 42_{16ff}; — 5. wind associated w. God: *heʻᵉbîr rûᵃḥ* (God) made a wind blow Gn 8_1 &c.; — 6. (breath, the bearer of life = the natural) **spirit** (of man, or of all flesh): *rûᵃḥ ḥayyîm* (*bᵉkol-bāśār*) Gn 6_3; *rûᵃḥ* of Pharaoh Gn 41_8, of Egypt Is 19_3; God gathers *rûᵃḥ ʼādām* (i.e. they die) Ps 104_{29}; God weighs the *rûᵃḥ* Pr 16_2; *hārûᵃḥ* produces life Ez 37_9; — 7. (natural spirit of man as) **mind, disposition, temper**: mind, specific spirit Ps 32_2, disposition 1K 21_5, courage Jos 2_{11}; *mōšēl bᵉrûḥô* s.one w. self-control Pr 16_{32}; — 8. spirit of Y. 1K 18_{12} & oft.; — 9. spirit of God 1S 10_{10}, *hāyâ ʻal/ʼel* 1S $16_{16 \cdot 23}$; — 10. holy spirit: *rûᵃḥ qodšô* Is 63_{10f}; — 11. *(hā)rûᵃḥ* = the spirit of God Nu 11_{17} Ez 2_2; = spirit indep.

of God 1K 22_{21}; — 12. granting of the spirit: *rûaḥ bô* (Joshua) Nu 27_{18}; from Elijah to Elisha 2K 2_{9}; into king of Assyria 2K 19_{7}; — 13. spec. kinds of spirit: *rûaḥ rāʿâ mēʾēt yhwh* 1S 16_{14}; *rûaḥ šeqer* 1K 22_{22}; *rûaḥ ḥokmâ* (= skill) Ex 31_{3}; *rûaḥ mišpāṭ* Is 4_{4} &c.; — 14. *rûaḥ : : bāśār = ʾēl : : ʾādām* Is 31_{3}.

רְוָחָה: sf. רַוְחָתִי: **respite, relief** Ex 8_{11} La 3_{56}. †

רְוָיָה: **overflow, superabundance** Ps 23_{5}. †

רוּם: **qal**: pf. רָם, רָ֫מָה, רָמוּ Jb 22_{12}; impf. יָרוּם, יָרֻם, יָרֹם, וַיָּרֻם (וַיָּרֻם Ex 16_{20} ⟋ I רמם), יָרוּם, יְרֻמוּן, יְרוּמוּ, אָרוּם, יָרוּם Dn 11_{12} = יָרוּם (Kt) & וְרָם (Qr); impv. ר֫וּמָה; inf. רוּם, רֻם, sf. רוּמָם; pt. רָם, רָמָה, רָמִים, רָמֵי, רָמוֹת: — 1. **be high (above)**: subj. stars Jb 22_{12}; **reach high**: subj. hand(s) Dt 32_{27}, horn (= strength) 1S 2_{1}, ark (*mēʿal-hāʾāreṣ*) Gn 7_{17}; — 2. subj. God: **be exalted** 2S 22_{47}; so *ʿebed yhwh* Is 52_{13}; — 3. **arise**: subj. glory of Y. Ez 10_{4}; so God Ps 108_{6}, oth. subj. Pr 11_{11}; — 4. **be overbearing, boast**: subj. man's heart (*lēb*) Dt 8_{14}; **be haughty**, subj. eyes Ps 131_{1}; — 5. pt.: a) **high**: mountain Dt 12_{2} &c.; **loud** (voice) Dt 27_{14}; **tall** Dt 1_{28}; **haughty** (eyes) Ps 18_{28}, (people) 2S 22_{28}; **uplifted** (arm) Jb 38_{15}, (hand = intentionally) Nu 15_{30}; b) **exalted**: God Ps 99_{2}, pl. = heavenly beings Jb 21_{22}.

[**nif.**: ⟋ II רמם.]

polel: pf. רוֹמַמְתִּי, sf. רֹמְמָתְהוּ; impf. תְּרוֹמְמֶךָ, יְרוֹמְמֶךָ, נְרוֹמְמָה, וַתְּרוֹמֵם, יְרוֹמֵם, וִירוֹמְמוּהוּ, אֲרוֹמִמְךָ, אֲרֹמְמֶנְהוּ, תְּרוֹמְמֵנִי; impv. רוֹמְמוּ; inf. רוֹמֵם, pt. מְרוֹמֵם, f. רוֹמֵמָה (w/o ־מ) Ps 118_{16}, sf. מְרוֹמְמִי: — 1. **raise** (obj. children) Is 1_{2}, **make** (tree) **grow tall** Ez 31_{4}, **heap up** (waves) Ps 107_{25}, **set up** (temple) Ezr 9_{9}, **lift** (s.one) **high** Ps 27_{5}; — 2. **exalt** (men in their position) 1S 2_{7}; — 3. **exalt, extol** (God) Ex 15_{2}.

polal: impf. תְּרוֹמַמְנָה; pt. מְרוֹמָם (rd. ־מָם) Ne 9_{5}: **be exalted** Ps 75_{11} Ne 9_{5}. †

hif.: pf. הֵרִים, הֲרִימוֹתָ(ה), הֲרֵמֹתָ, הֲרִימֹתִי, הֲרֵמֹתִיךָ, הֲרֵמֹתֶם, הֵרִימוּ; impf. יָרִים, יָרֵם, וַיְרִימֶהָ, תָּרִימוּ, וַיָּרֶם; impv. הָרִים Ez 21_{31} (rd הָרֵם?), הָ֫רֶם, הָרֵם 2K 6_{7}, הָרִימָה, הָרִימוּ; inf. הָרִים, הֲרִימִי, הֲרִימְכֶם; pt. מֵרִים, pl. sf. מְרִימָיו: — 1. **raise, lift up**: obj. hand Gn 14_{22}; voice = speak, call loudly Gn 39_{15}; **pick up, lift up**: rod Ex 14_{16}, stone Jos 4_{5}; — 2. **put up, erect**: stone Gn 31_{45}, signal Is 49_{22}, throne Is 14_{13}; **take up, serve** (food) 1S 9_{24}; **build** (nest) **in the heights** Jb 39_{27}; *hērîm bᵉ* lift up Ex 7_{20}; **exalt, raise up, elevate** (a person, in station) 1K 14_{7}; *hērîm rōʾš*: lift up s.one's head = treat w. distinction Ps 3_{4}; lift up one's head = carry one's head high Ps 110_{7}; *hērîm qeren* = treat w. distinction 1S 2_{10}, *hērîm qarnô* = revolt Ps 75_{5}; *hērîm yᵉmînô* = treat w. distinction Ps 89_{43}; — 3. **pick up, take away**: ashes Lv 6_{3}, yoke Ho 11_{4}; **stop** (expropriations) Ez 45_{9}; — 4. **(pick out and) present, offer** (a portion of sacrifice &c.) Lv 2_{9}; *hērîm lᵉ* contribute for 2C 30_{24}.

hof.: pf. הוּרַם Dn 8_{11} Qr, הוּרָם; impf. יוּרַם; pt. מוּרָם: — 1. **be exalted** cj Je 17_{12}; — 2. **be removed** Dn 8_{11} Qr; — 3. **be (picked out and) presented** Ex 29_{27} Lv 4_{10}. †

hitpolel: impf. יִתְרוֹמֵם, אֲרוֹמָם (< *אֶתְרוֹמָם: — sic ־מָ־): **assume proud superiority** Is 33_{10} Dn 11_{36}. †

רוּם, רֻם: = inf. רוּם: — 1. **height** Pr 25_{3}; — 2. something (anyth.) high Is $2_{11.17}$; *rum lēb* **haughtiness** (of heart) Je 48_{29}; *rûm ʿênayim* haughtiness (of eyes) Is 10_{12} Pr 21_{4}. †

רוּם Hb 3_{10}: txt. & mng. doubtful. †

רוּמָה: n. loc. 2K 23_{36}. †

רוֹמָה: *hālak rômâ* **walk haughtily** Mi 2_{3}. †

***רוֹמָם**: pl. cs. רוֹמְמוֹת: pl. **extolling, praising** Ps 149_{6}. †

***רוֹמֵמֻת**: sf. רוֹמְמֻתֶךָ Is 33_{3}: trad. lifting up; but txt.?. †

רון: **hitpolel**: pt. מִתְרוֹנֵן: **sober up** (after drinking wine) Ps 78_{65}. †

רוע: **hif.**: pf. הֵרִיעוּ, הֲרִיעֹתֶם, הֲרֵעֹתֶם Nu 10_{9}; impf. יָרִיעַ, וַיָּרַע, תָּרִיעִי, וַיָּרִ(י)עוּ, נָרִיעַ, נָרִיעָה; impv. הָרִיעִי, הָרִיעוּ; inf. הָרִיעַ; pt. מְרִיעִים: subj. alw. pl. or coll.: — 1. **shout** (in alarm) Ju 7_{21}; (in triumph) 15_{14} (w. *liqrā'tô*: ran shouting towards him); (in acclamation) 1S 10_{24}; — 2. *hērî'û terû'â gedôlâ* **give a great shout** 1S 4_{5}; — 3. **shout a war-cry** 1S 17_{52}, w. *terû'â gedôlâ* a loud war-cry Jos 6_{5}; — 4. *hērî'û bammilḥāmâ* **shout a war-cry** 1S 17_{20}, *'al* against Je 50_{15}; — 5. *hērî'û (baḥaṣōṣerôt)* **sound the signal for battle** Nu $10_{7.9}$; — 6. **shout in triumph** Is 44_{23}; — 7. *hērî'û rēa'* **shout loudly** Mi 4_{9}.

רוץ: **qal**: pf. רָץ, רַצְתָּה, רָצוּ; impf. יָרוּץ, וַיָּרָץ, וַיָּרֹץ, אָרוּצָה, יָרוּצוּ, וַיָּרֻצוּ, יְרוּצוּן, נָרוּצָה, יְרֻצוּן; impv. רוּץ, רֻץ; inf. רוּץ; pt. רָץ, רָצִים > רָצִין 2K 11_{13} (gloss): — 1. **run**: man Gn 18_{7}, horse Am 6_{12}; — 2. pt. *rāṣ* **runner** (of the king) 1K 1_{5}, > (mounted) courier Est 8_{10}; — 3. spec.: *rûṣ 'ōraḥ*, *rûṣ derek* run one's way Ps 19_{6} 119_{32}; subj. *dābār* Ps 147_{15}; *rûṣ gedûd* go on a raid 2S 22_{30}; *rûṣ le* **be busy** w. Hg 1_{9}; (read) **fluently** Hb 2_{2}.

polel: impf. יְרוֹצֵצוּ: **dash to and fro** Na 2_{5}. †

hif.: impf. אֲרִיצֵנּוּ, וַיְרִיצֻהוּ, וַיָּרִיצוּ; impv. הָרֵץ; (note: see also forms of רצץ): — 1. **make** s.one **run, chase** s.one **quickly off** Je 49_{19} 50_{44} Qr; — 2. **bring** s.one **quickly** Gn 41_{14} 1S 17_{17} 2C 35_{13}. †

רוק: ↗ ריק.

רור: ↗ ריר.

רוש: **qal**: pf. רָשׁוּ; pt. רָ(א)שׁ, pl. רָ(א)שִׁים: **be poor** 1S 18_{23}.

[**hif., hof.**: ↗ ירש.]

hitpolel: pt. מִתְרוֹשֵׁשׁ: **pretend to be poor** Pr 13_{7}. †

רוש: ↗ II ראש.

רוּת: n. pers. f. **Ruth**.

רָזָה: **qal**: pf. ר׳ Zp 2_{11}: dub.; sugg. rd. piel; ↗ comm. †

nif.: impf. יֵרָזֶה: **shrink away** Is 17_{4}. †

cj. **piel**: impf. יְרַזֶּה: let shrink away cj. Zp 2_{11}.

***רָזֶה**: f. רָזָה: **lean**: soil Nu 13_{20}, sheep Ez 34_{20}. †

I **רָזוֹן**: **emaciation** Is 10_{16} Ps 106_{15}, *'êfat rāzôn* scant ephah Mi 6_{10}. †

II **רָזוֹן**: **dignitary** Pr 14_{28}. †

רְזוֹן: n.pers.

רָזִי: רָזִי־לִי Is 24_{16} unexpl. †

רזם: **qal**: impf. יִרְזְמוּן: **wink** Jb 15_{12}. †

רזן: **qal**: pt. pl. ר(וֹ)זְנִים: **dignitary** Ju 5_{3}.

רָחַב: **qal**: pf. ר׳, רָחֲבָה: intrans. **open wide** 1S 2_{1}, **broaden** Ez 41_{7}. †

nif.: pt. נִרְחָב: **broad** Is 30_{23}. †

hif.: pf. הִרְח(י)ב, הִרְחִיבָה, הִרְחַבְתִּי; impf. יַרְחִיב, תַּרְחִיבוּ; impv. הַרְחֶב־, הַרְחִיבִי; inf. הַרְחִיב; pt. מַרְחִיב: — 1. **make wide** Is 30_{33}, **extend** (territory) Ex 34_{24}, (place for tent) Is 54_{2}; obj. *nefeš* or *peh*: **open wide** Is 5_{14} 57_{4}; **make wide room for** 2S 22_{37}; *hirḥîb libbî* gives me open space = confidence Ps 119_{32}; *hirḥîb ṣārôt* alleviates troubles Ps 25_{17}; — 2. *hirḥîb le* **provide wide room for** Gn 26_{22}.

רֹחַב: sf. רָחְבּוֹ, רָחְבָּן: — 1. **width** Gn 6_{15} (here of ark, elsewh. of oth. objs.); — 2. **breadth** (of land) Gn 13_{17}, *rōḥab mayim* (broad) expanse of water Jb 37_{10}; *rōḥab lēb* wide-ranging understanding (or intelligence) 1K 5_{9}.

I **רָחָב**: cs. רְחַב, f. רְחָבָה, cs. רַחֲבַת; m. pl. cs. רַחֲבֵי: — 1. **wide, broad, extended**: land Ex 3_{8}, wall Je 51_{58}; as noun, *hārehābâ* **the open** Ps 119_{45}; *reḥab (raḥabat, raḥebê) yādayim* extended on both (every) side

Gn 34_{21} &c.; — 2. **extensive, comprehensive** Ps 119_{96}; — 3. *reḥab lēb* **arrogant** Ps 101_5; = *reḥab nefeš* Pr 28_{25}.

II רָחָב: n. pers. f.

I רְחֹב, רְחוֹב: sf. רְחוֹבָהּ; pl. רְחֹבוֹת, sf. רְחֹבֹתֶיהָ, רְחוֹבֹתֵינוּ: (open) **square, plaza** (of town, village) Gn 19_2.

II רְחֹב: n. loc. Jos $19_{28\cdot30}$ 21_{31} Ju 1_{31} 1C 6_{60}. †

III רְחֹב: n. pers. 2S $8_{3\cdot12}$ Ne 10_{12}. †

רְחֹב(וֹ)ת: n. loc. Gn 10_{11} 26_{22} 36_{37} 1C 1_{48}. †

רְחַבְיָה: n. pers.

רְחַבְיָהוּ: n. pers.

רְחַבְעָם: n. pers. **Rehoboam**.

רְחוֹב: ↗ רְחֹב.

רְחוּם: n. pers.

רַחוּם: **compassionate**: of God Dt 4_{31}, only 1x of man Ps 112_4.

רָחוֹק, רָחֹק: f. רְחוֹקָה; pl. רְחוֹקִים, f. רְח(וֹ)ק(וֹ)ת: — 1. **distant, remote**: land 1K 8_{41}, nation Jl 4_8; *ʿad-rāḥôq* off into the distance Mi 4_3; — 2. **far** from (*min*): in space Jos 9_{22}; metaph. Je 12_2 (thou art far from their heart), (commandment beyond your reach) Dt 30_{11}; (her value is) far above (jewels) Pr 31_{10}; — 3. *rāḥôq bên ... ûbên* **distance** between ... and Jos 3_4; *derek reḥôqâ* distant journey Nu 9_{10} cf. *derek mērāḥôq* Pr 7_{19}; (stand) *mērāḥôq* at a distance 2K 2_7, far away Is 59_{14}; (see s.thg/s.one) far away Gn 22_4 37_{18}; *lemērāḥôq* from afar Jb 36_3, *ʿad-lemērāḥôq* (to) far off Ezr 3_{13}; — 4. (temporal) *ʿittîm reḥōqôt* times **far off** (in the future) Ez 12_{27}; *mērāḥôq* **long ago** Is 22_{11}, so *lemērāḥôq* 2K 19_{25}, = for a long time to come 1C 17_{17}; — 5. distant = unapproachable, mysterious Ec 7_{24}.

*רָחִיט SS 1_{17}: rd רָהִיט. †

רֵחַיִם: du. (sg. *רֵחֶה (?)); רֵחָיִם: (pair of mill-stones), **hand-mill** Ex 11_5 Nu 11_8 Dt 24_6 Is 47_2 Je 25_{10}. †

I רָחֵל: pl. רְחֵלִים, sf. רְחֵלֶיךָ: **ewe** Gn 31_{38} 32_{15} Is 53_7 SS 6_6. †

II רָחֵל: n. pers. f. **Rachel**.

רחם: [**qal**: impf. אֶרְחָמְךָ Ps 18_2: sugg. אֲרֹמִמְךָ.]

piel: pf. רִחַם, וְרִחַמְתִּי, רִחַמְךָ, רִחֲמֶךָ, רִחֲמוּם, רִחַמְתִּים; impf. יְרַחֵם, אֲרַחֵם, יְרַחֲמוּ, יְרַחֲמֵהוּ, אֲרַחֲמֶנּוּ, יְרַחֲמֵנוּ; inf. רַחֵם, רַחֶמְכֶם; pt. מְרַחֵם, sf. מְרַחֲמֵךְ, מְרַחֲמָם: — 1. w. acc. **show love for, have compassion on**: subj. man 1K 8_{50} (+ 5×), God 2K 13_{23} (+ ca. 30×); w. *ʿal* Ps 103_{13}; abs. **be compassionate** Hb 3_2.

pual: pf. רֻחָמָה; impf. יְרֻחָם, יְרֻחָם: **experience compassion, pity, love** Ho 1_6.

רָחָם: **carrion-vulture**, *Vultur percnopterus* Lv 11_{18}. †

I רַחַם: n. pers. 1C 2_{44}. †

II רַחַם: ↗ רֶחֶם.

רֶחֶם & (II) רַחַם: רֶחֶם, (רַחַם >) רָחֶם Gn 49_{25} Pr 30_{16}, sf. רַחְמָהּ; [pl. ↗ רַחֲמִים; du. רַחֲמָתַיִם ↗ רַחֲמָה*]: **womb** Gn 20_{18}; Ju 5_{30} ↗ רַחֲמָה*.

רָחָמָה: (f. of רָחָם): **carrion-vulture** Dt 14_{17}. †

*רַחֲמָה: f. of רַחַם (רֶחֶם): du. רַחֲמָתַיִם: Ju 5_{30} *raḥam raḥamātayim*: coarse soldiers' slang: a womb or two = a bedmate or two. †

רַחֲמִים: pl. of רַחַם (רֶחֶם): cs. רַחֲמֵי, sf. רַחֲמָיו: **loving feeling, compassion** Gn 43_{30}; many vb. phrs., e.g. *nātan lākem raḥamîm lifnê* (may he) grant you mercy before ... Gn 43_{14}, *nātan leraḥamîm lifnê* 1K 8_{50}; *śîm raḥamîm le* Is 47_6 &c.

*רַחֲמָנִי (or *רַחֲמָן): pl. f. רַחֲמָנִיּוֹת: **compassionate, affectionate** La 4_{10}. †

רחף: **qal**: pf. רָחֲפוּ: *rāḥafû ʿaṣmôtay* Je 23_9 **shake, tremble**. †

piel: impf. יְרַחֵף; pt. f. מְרַחֶפֶת: **hover (tremulously)** Gn 1_2 Dt 32_{11}. †

רחץ: **qal**: pf. ר׳, רָחַצְתְּ, רָחֲצוּ, רָחָצוּ; impf. יִרְחַץ, יִרְחָץ, יִרְחֲצוּ, וָאֶרְחָצֵךְ; impv. רְחַץ,

רַחֲצוּ; inf. רָחְצָה ,רְחֹץ Ex 30_{18}; pt. רֹחֶצֶת, רֹחֲצוֹת: — 1. w. acc. of thing: **wash** (in water), **rinse**: obj. feet Gn 18_{4}, face Gn 43_{31}, portions of sacrificial animals Ex 29_{17}; — 2. abs. **bathe, wash** (onesf.) Ex 2_{5} 1K 22_{38}; — 3. *rāḥaṣ bammayim*: **wash** (s.thg, s.one) **w. water** Ex 29_{4}, **wash onesf.** Lv 14_{8}; *rāḥaṣ mayim* wash onesf. Ex 30_{20}.

pual: pf. רֻחַצְתְּ ,רֻחָץ: **be washed** Ez 16_{4} Pr 30_{12}. †

hitp.: pf. הִתְרָחַצְתִּי: **take a bath** Jb 9_{30}. †

***רַחַץ**: sf. רַחְצִי: **washing**: *sîr raḥṣî* my wash-basin Ps 60_{10} 108_{10}. †

רַחְצָה: **washing, dipping** (of sheep) SS 4_{2} 6_{6}. †

רָחַק: **qal**: pf. רַחֲקָה ,ר׳ ,רָחֲקוּ; impf. יִרְחַק, תִּרְחָק; impv. רַחֲקוּ; inf. רָחְקָה ,רְחֹק Ez 8_{6}, רָחוֹק: — 1. **be far (away), distant**: subj. place Dt 12_{21}, justice Is 59_{9}; — 2. become distant: **drift away from, wander from** (*mēʿal*, obj. God) Je 2_{5}; **keep** (onesf.) **far from, stay far** (away) **from** Ex 23_{7}.

nif.: impf. יֵרָחֵק: **be removed, taken away** Ec 12_{6}. †

piel: pf. רִחַקְתָּ ,רִחַק; impf. יְרַחֲקוּ: completely remove, **send far away** Is 6_{12} Ez 43_{9}; **extend** (obj. borders) Is 29_{13}. †

hif.: pf. הִרְחַקְתִּים ,הִרְחִיקוּ ,הִרְחִיק; impf. יַרְחִיקֻנָּה ,תַּרְחִיקוּ ,אַרְחִיק; impv. הַרְחֵק, הַרְחַק Jb 13_{21}; inf. הַרְחִיקָם ,הַרְחִיק ,הַרְחֵק: — 1. **remove, move** (s.one) **far** (away) Je 27_{10}; **keep** (s.thg) **far away** Pr 5_{8}; — 2. **go far away** Gn 44_{4}, so *hirḥîq lāleket* Ex 8_{24}; inf. adv. **far off, at a good distance** Gn 21_{16}.

***רָחֵק**: pl. sf. רְחֵקֶיךָ: **he who stays far away** Ps 73_{27}. †

רָחֹק: ↗ רָחוֹק.

רָחַשׁ: **qal**: pf. ר׳: **be stirred up** (subj. *lēb*) Ps 45_{2}. †

רַחַת: **winnowing-shovel** Is 30_{24}. †

רטב: **qal**: impf. יִרְטָבוּ: **be(come) wet** Jb 24_{8}. †

רָטֹב: **full of sap** (as a plant) Jb 8_{16}. †

[**רטה**: **qal**: impf. sf. יִרְטֵנִי: rd. יָרְטֵנִי (ירט) Jb 16_{11}. †]

רֶטֶט: **panic** Je 49_{24}. †

[**רטפשׁ**: **qal**: pf. pass. רֻטֲפַשׁ Jb 33_{25}: rd יִטְפַּשׁ. †]

רטשׁ: **piel**: impf. תְּרַטֵּשְׁנָה ,תְּרַטֵּשׁ: **smash** (in pieces) (obj. children, i.e. on rocks) 2K 8_{12} Is 13_{18}. †

pual: pf. רֻטָּשָׁה; impf. יְרֻטָּשׁוּ ,יְרֻטְּשׁוּ: **be smashed** (in pieces) Is 13_{16} Ho 10_{14} 14_{1} Na 3_{10}. †

רִי: **moisture** Jb 37_{11}. †

ריב: **qal**: pf. רַבְתָּ ,רָב & רִיבוֹתָ Jb 33_{13}, רָבוּ; impf. וָאָרִיבָה ,אָרִיב ,וַיָּרֶב ,יָרֶב ,יָרֵב ,יָרִיב, תְּרִיבֵהוּ ,יְרִיבֵךְ ,תְּרִיבוּן ,יְרִיבֻן ,וַיָּרִיבוּ, תְּרִיבֶנִי ,תְּרִיבֶכָּה; impv. רִיבוּ ,רִיבָה ,רִיב; inf. ר(ו)ב ,רִ(י)ב; pt. רָב: — 1. **dispute, quarrel** (in public, w. words, complaints, assertions, reproaches); **conduct a** (legal) **case, lawsuit**: abs. Gn 26_{21} (*ʿal* about s.thg); w. *ʾēt* with, against (s.one) Nu 20_{13}; w. *ʿim* with, against (s.one) Gn 26_{20}; sim. w. *ʿimmād* Jb 13_{19}, *ʾel* Jb 33_{13}; *le* for Dt 33_{7}; — 2. *rāb rîb* (cs. followed by pers., or w. sf. of pers.) **conduct the case, lawsuit of** s.one; **defend, plead the case of** s.one 1S 24_{16}; — 3. *rāb* + acc. = 2.: Is 1_{17}; — 4. *rāb ʾel* **put, lay a case, lawsuit** before s.one Je 2_{29}; — 5. *rāb be* **attack** s.one (w. reproaches) Dt 33_{8}; — 6. spec., God subj.: 1S 24_{16} (as 2.) & oft.

רִיב ,רָב: sf. רִיבוֹ ,רִיבָם; pl. cs. רִיבֵי: (legal) **dispute, case, lawsuit**: — 1. w. corresponding vb., *rāb rîb*, ↗ qal 2.; — 2. *hāyâ rîb bên ... ûbên* Gn 13_{7}; *qārab rîb* bring forth one's case Is 41_{21}; *rîb lô be* has a case against Je 25_{31}, *ʿim* Ho 4_{1}, *ribām ʿimmādî* their case against me Jb 31_{13}; *ʾîš rîbî* my adversary (in a case) Jb 31_{35}, pl. *ʾanšê rîbekā* Is 41_{11}; *hāyâ ʾîš rîb* have a feud Ju 12_{2}; *gillâ rîbô ʾel* submit one's case to, leave one's case in the hands of Je 11_{20}.

***רִיבָה**: pl. רִיבֹת, רִבוֹת: **legal case** Dt 17_8, **speech** in a case Jb 13_6. †

רִיבַי: n. pers.

ריה Is 16_9: ↗ רוה piel.

רִיחַ: ↗ רוּחַ.

רֵיחַ: sf. רֵיחוֹ: **odor, scent**: of clothes Gn 27_{27}, water Jb 14_9, oil SS 1_3, breath SS 7_9; *nātan rēaḥ* give forth fragrance SS 1_{12}; *hibʾîš rēaḥ* = bring s.one into bad odor Ex 5_{21}.

רֵים: ↗ רְאֵם.

רֵיעַ Jb 6_{27}: ↗ רֵעַ.

רִיפוֹת Pr 27_{22}, רִפוֹת 2S 17_{19}: sugg. rd. ↗ חֲרִיפוֹת. †

רִיפַת: (n. pers.) n. peop.

ריק: **hif.**: pf. הֲרִיקֹתִי, הֵרִיקוּ; impf. יָרִיק, וַיָּרֶק; impv. הָרֵק; inf. הָרִיק; pt. מְרִיקִים: — 1. **empty out**: obj. sack Gn 42_{35}, vessel Je 48_{12}; — 2. **pour out**: obj. gold (or oil?) Zc 4_{12}; — 3. *hērîq ḥereb* **draw** a sword Ex 15_9; — 4. **leave** s.one **unfed** Is 32_6.

hof.: pf. הוּרַק: (of oil) **be poured out** (from vessel to vessel), (and so) **clarified** Je 48_{11}. †

רִיק: noun: **emptiness, worthlessness**, in cs. chain like adj. **empty, worthless**: *kelî rîq* **empty** Je 51_{34}; what is empty Ps 4_3, what is worthless, idle Ps 2_1; *lerîq, lārîq* **in vain** Is 49_4 65_{23}; *bedê rîq* for nothing = for no purpose Je 51_{58}.

רֵיק, רֵק: f. רֵיקָה; pl. רֵ(י)קִים, f. רֵקוֹת: — 1. **empty**: pit Gn 37_{24}, vessel 2K 4_3, ears of grain Gn 41_{27}; w. *nefeš*, **unsatisfied** (hunger) Is 29_8; — 2. metaph., of men, empty = **unprincipled, reckless** 2S 6_{20}; — 3. **vain, idle**: word Dt 32_{47}; pl. worthless things Pr 12_{11}.

רֵיקָם: — 1. **empty-handed(ly), without a gift or offering** Gn 31_{42}; — 2. **without success, without booty** 2S 1_{22} Je 50_9; — 3. **without property, without family** Ru 1_{21}; — 4. **without cause** Ps 7_5.

ריר: **qal**: pf. רָר: **let** (a bodily discharge) **flow, run with** Lv 15_3. †

רִיר: **spittle** 1S 21_{14}; **slime** (of bugloss) Jb 6_6. †

רֵאשׁ, רִישׁ, רֵישׁ: sf. רֵישׁוֹ, רֵאשֶׁךָ, רֵישָׁם: **poverty** Pr 6_{11}.

רִישׁוֹן: ↗ רִאשׁוֹן.

רֹךְ: quality of being soft, weak, tender: **softness** &c. Dt 28_{56}. †

רַךְ: f. רַכָּה; pl. רַכִּים, f. רַכּוֹת: — 1. **tender, frail, weak**: child Gn 33_{13}, calf 18_7; — 2. **tender, sensitive, delicate**: eyes Gn 29_{17}, old man 2S 3_{39}; — 3. **pampered, tender** (in sensibility): man Dt 28_{54}, woman 28_{56}; — 4. **soft**: tongue Pr 25_{15}, answer 15_1; *rakkôt* soft words Jb 40_{27}; — 5. **timid** Dt 20_8.

רָכַב: **qal**: pf. רָכְבוּ, ר׳; impf. יִרְכַּב, יִרְכָּבוּ, וַתִּרְכַּבְנָה, נִרְכָּב; impv. רְכַב; inf. לִרְכֹּב; pt. רֹכֵב, רֹכֶבֶת, sf. רֹכְבוֹ, pl. רֹכְבִים, רֹכְבֵי, sf. רֹכְבֵיהֶם: — 1. **ride** (upon an animal), usu. w. *ʿal*: camel Gn 24_{61}, ass 1S 25_{20}, horse Gn 49_{17}; *rōkēb (has)sûs* horseman 2K 9_{18f}; — 2. **ride** (in a chariot &c.) Je 17_{25}; on horse or in vehicle? † 1K 18_{45} 2K 9_{16}; — 3. subj. God, phr.: *rōkēb šāmayim* Dt 33_{26}, *rōkēb ʿal-kerûb* 2S 22_{11} &c.

hif.: pf. הִרְכַּבְתָּ, הִרְכַּבְתִּיךָ, הִרְכִּיבֻהוּ; impf. אַרְכִּיב, וַיַּרְכֵּב, וַיַּרְכִּבֵהוּ, יַרְכִּיבֻהוּ; impv. הַרְכֵּב: — 1. **mount** (s.one) on (*ʿal*) (an animal to ride) 1K 1_{33}; — 2. **have, make** (s.one) **ride** in (*be*) (a chariot &c.) Gn 41_{43}; subj. God Dt 32_{13}; — 3. **carry** (s.one dead) in a chariot 2K 9_{28}; — 4. **put** (an animal) **to** (i.e. the yoke) Ho 10_{11}; — 5. *hirkîb yād ʿal-qešet* mount the hand on the bow = **draw** the bow 2K 13_{16}; — 6. *hirkîb ʾenôš lerōʾšô* causes people to ride ('dance') on his head Ps 66_{12}.

רֶכֶב (120×): רֶכֶב; sf. רִכְבּוֹ; pl. cs. רִכְבֵי: — 1. coll. **chariotry**, (group of) **chariots** Gn 50_9, esp. **war-chariots** 1K 1_5; *ʿārê rekeb* = (storage) cities for chariots 1K 9_{19}; — 2.

train of chariots > **train** (of animals): *rekeb ḥ^{a}môr, rekeb gāmāl* Is 21$_{7}$; — 3. *rekeb* = (a single) **chariot** 1K 22$_{35}$; pl. SS 1$_{9}$; — 4. **upper millstone** 2S 11$_{21}$.

רַכָּב: sf. רַכָּבוֹ: **charioteer** 1K 22$_{34}$ 2C 18$_{33}$; **horseman** 2K 9$_{17}$. †

רֵכָב: n. pers.

רִכְבָּה: (act of) **riding** (or driving) Ez 27$_{20}$. †

*רֵכָבִי: gent. of רֵכָב: pl. רֵכָבִים: **Rechabite**.

רֵכָה: n. loc. 1C 4$_{12}$, but txt.?. †

*רְכוּב: sf. רְכוּבוֹ: **vehicle, chariot** Ps 104$_{3}$. †

רְכוּשׁ, רְכֻשׁ: sf. רְכֻשׁוֹ, רְכוּשָׁם: **property, goods** (gained by work, not by purchase): — 1. **goods** (furnishings, gear, utensils) Gn 12$_{5}$; — 2. **goods, outfit, equipment** (of warriors) Dn 11$_{24}$, **baggage-train** 11$_{13}$; — 3. **personal property, domain** (of king) 1C 27$_{31}$.

רָכִיל: *'anšê rākîl* **slanderers** Ez 22$_{9}$, *hālak rākîl* **practice slander** Je 6$_{28}$.

רכך: **qal**: pf. רַךְ, רַכּוּ; impf. יֵרַךְ: **be tender, gentle**: word Ps 55$_{22}$; **be timid**: heart 2K 22$_{19}$.

pual: pf. רֻכְּכָה: **be softened** Is 1$_{6}$. †

hif.: pf. הֵרַךְ: **make** (s.one's heart) **timid** Jb 23$_{16}$. †

רכל: **qal**: pt. רוֹכֵל, f. רֹכֶלֶת, sf. רֹכַלְתֵּךְ; pl. רֹכְלִים, רֹכְלֵי, sf. רֹכְלַיִךְ: **merchant, tradesman** 1K 10$_{15}$; f. **tradeswoman** Ez 27$_{3}$.

רָכָל: n. loc. 1S 30$_{29}$; but rd. בְּכַרְמֶל. †

*רְכֻלָּה: sf. רְכֻלָּתֵךְ, רְכֻלָּתְךָ: **trade** Ez 28$_{5.16.18}$; **merchandise** 26$_{12}$. †

רכס: **qal**: impf. וַיִּרְכְּסוּ: **bind, tie** Ex 28$_{28}$ 39$_{21}$. †

*רֶכֶס: pl. רְכָסִים: **protruding ground, rugged ground** Is 40$_{4}$. †

*רֹכֶס: pl. cs. רֻכְסֵי Ps 31$_{21}$: sugg. rd. רִכְלֵי ↗ רָכִיל. †

רכשׁ: **qal**: pf. ר׳, רָכַשׁ, רָכָשׁוּ: **gather, acquire** (property) Gn 12$_{5}$ 31$_{18}$ 36$_{6}$ 46$_{6}$. †

רֶכֶשׁ: רֶכֶשׁ: **team of horses** 1K 5$_{8}$ Mi 1$_{13}$, **post-horses** Est 8$_{10.14}$. †

I רָם: ↗ רום.

II רָם: n. pers.

רֵם: ↗ רְאֵם.

רָם: ↗ רום.

I רָמָה: **qal**: pf. ר׳; pt. cs. רֹמֵה, pl. cs. רֹמֵי: — 1. **throw** (obj. horse & rider) Ex 15$_{1.21}$; — 2. **shoot**: *rōmēh qešet* archer Je 4$_{29}$. †

II רמה: **piel**: pf. רִמָּה, רִמִּיתֶם, רִמָּנִי, רִמִּתָנִי, רִמִּיתִנִי, רִמּוּנִי; inf. sf. רַמּוֹתֵנִי: — 1. **leave** (s.one) **in the lurch** La 1$_{19}$; — 2. **deceive** Gn 29$_{25}$; — 3. w. *l^{e}* **betray to** 1C 12$_{18}$.

I רָמָה: pt. f. רום: sf. רָמָתֵךְ; pl. sf. רָמֹתַיִךְ: — 1. **height, high ground** 1S 22$_{6}$; — 2. **high spot** (= 1.) artificially built up by the harlot Ez 16$_{24f.31.39}$. †

II רָמָה: n. loc.

רִמָּה: **maggot**: in rotting food Ex 16$_{24}$, in decaying corpse Jb 7$_{5}$.

I רִמּוֹן: pl. רִמֹּ(וֹ)נִים, cs. רִמּוֹנֵי: **pomegranate**, *Punica granatum L.*: — 1. tree 1S 14$_{2}$; — 2. fruit Nu 13$_{23}$; — 3. (artificial) pomegranate Ex 28$_{33}$, of metal 1K 7$_{18}$.

II רִמּוֹן: n. pers. 2S 4$_{2.5.9}$. †

III רִמּוֹן, רִמֹּן: n. loc.

IV רִמּוֹן: n. of deity 2K 5$_{18}$. †

רִמּוֹנוֹ 1C 6$_{62}$: rd. רִמּוֹנָה ↗ III רִמּוֹן. †

רָמ(וֹ)ת: ↗ II רָמָה.

*רָמוּת: sf. רָמוּתֶךָ Ez 32$_{5}$: **rubbish**? or rd. רִמָּתֶךָ ? †

*רֹמַח: pl. רְמָחִים, sf. רָמְחֵיהֶם: **lance** (spear w. long shaft) 1K 18$_{28}$.

רַמְיָה: n. pers.

I רְמִיָּה: **slackness, looseness** Pr 12$_{27}$; *qešet r^{e}miyyâ* slack, loose bow Ho 7$_{16}$ Ps 78$_{57}$, *yad/kaf r^{e}miyyâ* slack, lazy hand Pr 12$_{24}$ 10$_{4}$; *nefeš r^{e}miyyâ* lazy creature 19$_{15}$; adv.: *'āśâ r^{e}miyyâ* manage lazily Je 48$_{10}$. †

II רְמִיָּה (= I?): **deceit** Mi 6$_{12}$.

רַמִּים: הָרַמִּים 2C 22$_{5}$: rd. הָאֲרַמִּים. †

*רַמָּכָה: pl. רַמָּכִים: (swift) **mare** Est 8$_{10}$. †

רְמַלְיָהוּ: n. pers.

I רמם: **qal**: impf. וַיָּרֻם: **rot**; w. *tôlāʿîm* become full of worms Ex 16_{20}. †

II רמם: **qal**: pf. רוֹמּוּ Jb 24_{24}: rd רָמוּ. †

nif.: impf. וַיֵּרֹמּוּ, יֵרוֹמּוּ; impv. הֵרֹמּוּ: **rise up** Ez $10_{15 \cdot 17 \cdot 19}$; w. *min*, **get away** from Nu 17_{10}. †

רֹמַמְתִּי עֶזֶר (עֶזֶר · · ·): artificial n. pers. 1C $25_{4 \cdot 31}$. †

רִמֹּן: ↗ III רִמּוֹן.

רָמַס: **qal**: pf. ר׳; impf. וַיִּרְמְסוּ, יִרְמָס־, יִרְמֹס, וַיִּרְמְסֵהוּ, וַיִּרְמְסֶנָּה, וָאֶרְמְסֵם, אֶרְמְסֵהוּ; impv. רְמֹס, רָמְסִי; pt. רֹמֵס: **trample** (down, out), **tread**: obj. potter's clay Is 41_{25}, grapes 63_3, ground Is 1_{12}, men 2K 7_{17}; subj. horses 2K 9_{33}.

nif.: תֵּרָמַסְנָה: **be trampled** (crown[s]). Is 28_3. †

רמשׂ: **qal**: impf. תִּרְמֹשׂ; pt. ר(ו)מֵשׂ, רֹמֶשֶׂת: **swarm, teem** (of vast numbers of creatures in water, on ground, in woods; in random movement) Gn 1_{26}.

רֶמֶשׂ: of animal world exc. large animals & birds: coll. **small animals, reptiles** Gn 1_{24ff}.

רָמֹת: ↗ II רָמָה.

רֶמֶת: n. loc.

רָמָתִי: gent. of II רָמָה.

*רֹן: pl. cs. רָנֵּי Ps 32_7: sugg. del. dittgr.; ↗ comm. †

רנה: **qal**: impf. תִּרְנֶה: **rattle** Jb 39_{23}. †

I רִנָּה: sf. רִנָּתִי, רִנָּתָם: loud inarticulate cry, yell: — 1. **shout of joy** Is 14_7; — 2. **cry of lamentation, moaning** 1K 8_{28}; — 3. *hārinnâ* w. masc. vb. 1K 22_{36}, rd. *hāranneh* **herald**?

II רִנָּה: n. pers.

רנן: **qal**: impf. יָרוֹן Pr 29_6, תָּרֹן, יָרֹנּוּ; impv. רָנִּי, רֹנּוּ, רָנּוּ; inf. רָן־: **yell**: — 1. **shout with joy** Is 12_6; — 2. **whimper, moan** La 2_{19}.

piel: pf. רִנְּנוּ; impf. תְּרַנֵּן, אֲרַנֵּן, יְרַנְּנוּ, יְרַנֵּנוּ, תְּרַנֵּנָּה, נְרַנְּנָה; impv. רַנְּנוּ; inf. רַנֵּן: **shout with joy** Is 26_{19}; (w. *bᵉ* because of) Ps 92_5; w. acc. **proclaim in shouts of joy** Ps 51_{16}; w. *ʾel*, *lᵉ* Ps 84_3 95_1.

pual: impf. יְרֻנַּן: **there are joyful shouts** Is 16_{10}. †

hif.: impf. אַרְנִן, תַּרְנִין; impv. הַרְנִינוּ: — 1. **make** (s.one) **shout with joy** Dt 32_{43}; — 2. **ring out a shout of joy** Ps 32_{11}; w. *lᵉ* Ps 81_2.

[**hitp.**: ↗ רון.]

רְנָנָה: cs. רִנְנַת; pl. רְנָנוֹת: **shout of joy** Ps 63_6 100_2 Jb 3_7 20_5. †

רְנָנִים: sg. *רְנָנָה?: **female ostriches** Jb 39_{13}. †

רִסָּה: n. loc.

I *רָסִיס: pl. cs. רְסִיסֵי: **drop** (of moisture) SS 5_2. †

II *רָסִיס: pl. רְסִיסִים: **(piece of) rubble** Am 6_{11}. †

I רֶסֶן: **bridle** Is 30_{28} Ps 32_9 Jb 30_{11}. †

II רֶסֶן: n. loc.

רסס: **qal**: inf. רֹס: **moisten, sprinkle on** Ez 46_{14}. †

רַע, רָע (225×): f. רָעָה; pl. רָעִים, cs. רָעֵי, f. רָעוֹת; adj.: — 1. **of bad quality, inferior**: cattle Gn 41_{20}, water 2K 2_{19}; *marʾeh* **ugly** Gn 41_3; — 2. **disagreeable, unwholesome**: lifetime Gn 47_9, region Nu 20_5; *bᵉrāʿâ* in unfavorable circumstances 2K 14_{10}; — 3. **bad, of no value, contemptible**: name Dt 22_{14}; — 4. **bad-tempered, evil, morally depraved**: *maḥšābâ* (scheme) Gn 6_5; *derek rāʿâ* 1K 13_{33}; — 5. *raʿ bᵉʿênê* bad in the eyes (= judgment) of = **disagreeable, displeasing** Gn 28_8, = **undesirable, annoying** Nu 11_{10}, = **objectionable, disapproved of** 1K 11_6; *raʿ ʿal* annoying to Ec 2_{17}; — 6. bad = **vicious, harmful**: boils Dt 28_{35}, wild animal Gn 37_{33}; *dābār raʿ* something unwholesome 2K 4_{41}; *rûªḥ rāʿâ* harmful, destructive spirit 1S 16_{14}; *raʿ ʿayin* envious Pr 23_6; — 7. **evil, adverse**: *yôm rāʿ* fatal day Am 6_3; *rāʿ* disaster Gn 44_{34}; *bᵉrāʿ* in a bad situation Ex 5_9; *lᵉraʿ lākem* to your harm Je 7_6; — 8. **bad, evil** (in the absolute, ethical sense) Gn 2_9 1K 3_9; — 9. **in a bad mood,** cross, discontented: *pānêkā rā'îm* you look out of sorts Gn 40_7; — 10. *ra'* > noun: (I fear no) **evil** Ps 23_4; *'anšê rā'* wicked men Pr 28_5; — 11. spec.: *b^{e}rā' hû'* he is prone to evil Ex 32_{22}; *'āśâ rā'â* cause disaster? do harm to onesf. ? 2S 12_{18}.

I רֵעַ: sf. רֵעוֹ, רֵעֹה: **shouting** Ex 32_{17} Mi 4_9 Jb 36_{33}. †

II רֵעַ (179×): sf. רֵעוֹ, רֵעֵהוּ (or ↗ רֵעֶה ?), רֵעָהּ, רֵעֶךָ, רֵעֲךָ, רֵיעֲכֶם for רֵעֲכֶם Jb 6_{27}; pl. רֵעִים, cs. רֵעֵי, sf. רֵעָיו & רֵעֵהוּ! 1K 16_{11} & Jb 42_{10}, רֵעַי, רֵעַי, רֵעֶיךָ, רֵעֶיךָ, רֵעֶיהָ, רֵיעֵהֶם: — 1. **comrade, companion, friend, fellow** Gn 38_{12}; *rē'îm* of a woman Je 3_1; — 2. 'neighbor' in expressions of reciprocity: *lō' yišm^e'û 'îš ś^{e}fat rē'ēhû* they will not understand each his neighbor's speech Gn 11_7; *'îš mērē'ēhû* each from the other 31_{49}; *'îš 'el-rē'ēhû* to each other Gn 11_3, *'îš 'et-rē'ēhû* Ex 21_{18} &c.; *'ēšet rē'ēhû* someone else's wife Ex 20_{17}; *l^{e}rē'^{a}kā l^{e}dāwid* to someone else, [namely] David 1S 28_{17}; *l^{e}rē'ekā* (corr. for *l^{e}rē'ékā*) to someone else (than you) 2S 12_{11}; *rē^a' hammelek* = a courtier 1C 27_{33}.

III *רֵעַ: sf. רֵעִי; pl. sf. רֵעֶיךָ: **intention, thought** (w. wh. one's mind is occupied) Ps $139_{2.17}$. †

רֹעַ: — 1. **bad quality** Je 24_2 (figs); — 2. **ugliness** Gn 41_{19}; — 3. *rō^a' pānîm* **bad humor, crossness** Ec 7_3; — 4. **perverseness, malice** Dt 28_{20}.

רָעֵב: **qal**: pf. ר׳; impf. יִרְעַב, יִרְעָב: **be hungry**: subj. land Gn 41_{55}, people Is 8_{21}.

hif.: impf. יַרְעִיב, יַרְעִיבְךָ: **let** (s.one) **be hungry** (subj. God) Dt 8_3 Pr 10_3. †

רָעָב (101×): sf. רְעָבָם: **hunger** Dt 28_{48}; w. *l^e* for Am 8_{11}; **famine** Gn 12_{10}.

רָעֵב adj.: f. רְעֵבָה; pl. רְעֵבִים: **hungry** 2K 7_{12}; *nefeš r^e'ēbâ* Ps 107_9.

רְעָבוֹן: cs. רַעֲבוֹן: **hunger** Gn $42_{19.33}$ Ps 37_{19}. †

רעד: **qal**: impf. וַתִּרְעַד: **tremble** (subj. earth) Ps 104_{32}. †

hif.: pt. מַרְעִיד, מַרְעִידִים: **tremble, shake** Dn 10_{11} Ezr 10_9. †

רַעַד: רָעַד: **trembling, shaking** Ex 15_{15} Ps 55_6. †

רְעָדָה: **trembling, shaking** Is 33_{14} Ps 2_{11} 48_7 Jb 4_{14}. †

I רעה: **qal** (167×): pf. ר׳, רָעוּ, רְעִיתִים, רָעוּם; impf. יִרְעֶה (יֵרַע Jb 20_{26} ↗ I רעע nif.), יִרְעוּ, וָאֶרְעֶה, וַתִּרְעֶינָה, sf. יִרְעֵם, יִרְעֶנָּה, יִרְעוּךְ; impv. רְעֵה, רְעִי, רְעוּ, sf. רְעֵם; inf. רְעוֹת, sf. רְעֹתוֹ; pt. רֹ(וֹ)עֶה, cs. רֹעֵה, f. רֹעָה, sf. רֹעִי, pl. רֹעִים, cs. רוֹעֵי, sf. רֹעֶיךָ, רֹעַי, רֹעֵיהֶם, f. רֹעוֹת: — 1. subj. cattle, flocks &c., obj. land: **graze** Gn 41_2; metaph., w. a sword Mi 5_5; — 2. subj. shepherds &c., obj. flocks &c.: **pasture** Jb 24_2; — 3. more generally, **tend, keep** (flocks), **shepherd** Ex 3_1 (acc. *ṣō'n*), Gn 37_2 (*baṣṣō'n*); — 4. pt. *rō'eh* **shepherd** Gn 4_2, **herdsman** 13_7; f. *rō'â* **shepherdess** 29_9; — 5. metaph.: **shepherd, tend, lead** (obj. people) 2S 5_2; pt. pl. *rō'îm* **keepers,** (responsible) **rulers** Je 2_8; *rō'î* the ruler whom I have appointed Is 44_{28}; — 6. subj. God Gn 48_{15}; — 7. metaph. subj.: death Ps 49_{15}; *rû^{a}ḥ* Je 22_{22}; pasture = refresh Pr 10_{21}; = be occupied w. 15_{14}.

II רעה: **qal**: pt. רֹעֶה: w. acc. **have dealings with** (s.one) Pr 13_{20} 28_7 29_3 Jb 24_{21}, also Is 44_{20} Ho 12_2 (usu. ref. to I). †

piel: pf. רֵעָה: **be 'best man'** (at a wedding) Ju 14_{20}. †

hitp.: impf. תִּתְרַע, cj. תִּתְרָעֶינָה: w. *'el* **make friends** with Pr 22_{24}; cj. abs. **make friends** Is 11_7. †

רָעָה: noun, f. of רַע (ca. 300×, difficult to distinguish fm. adj. f.): cs. רָעַת, sf. רָעָתִי, רָעָתֵךְ, רָעָתֵכִי Je 11_{15}, רָעַתְכֶם; pl. רָע(וֹ)ת, sf. רָע(וֹ)תֵיכֶם: — 1. (intended) **evil, harm** (to s.one) Gn 26_{29}; *hārā'â* evil (plan) 1S 23_9; *rā'ātî* harm to me Ps 35_4; *'anšê rā'â* evil men Pr 24_1; *l^{e}rā'â* w. evil intent 2S 18_{32}; —

2. **wickedness, perverseness** Gn 6_5; **crime** Ju 9_{56}; — 3. **misery, trouble, disaster** Gn 19_{19}; *yôm rā'â* fatal day Pr 27_5; God brings *rā'â* 1K 14_{10}; **evil** (in a weakened sense) Ec 5_{12}; — 4. *wayyēra' rā'â gᵉdōlâ* it displeased him greatly Ne 2_{10}.

רֵעֶה: cs. =; sf. sg. רֵעֶיךָ: **friend, fellow** 2S 12_{11} 15_{37} 16_{16} 1K 4_5 (↗ *rēa'*, end) Pr 3_{28} (Kt) 27_{10}. †

***רֵעָה**: f. of רֵעֶה; pl. sf. רֵעוֹתֶיהָ, רֵעיֹתָי < Qr רֵעוֹתַי: (female) **companion** (of maidens) Ju 11_{37}f Ps 45_{15}. †

[**רֹעָה**: Is 24_{19} rd רֹעַ (II רעע); Pr 25_{19} ↗ II רעע.]

רְעוּ: n. pers.

רְעוּאֵל: n. pers.

I ***רְעוּת**: sf. רְעוּתָהּ: (female) **neighbor** in reciprocal expr.: *'iššâ mē'ēt rᵉ'ûtāh* each (woman) from her neighbor Ex 11_2; *'iššâ rᵉ'ûtāh* each other Je 9_{19}; *lir'ûtāh haṭṭôbâ mimmennâ* to s.one better than she Est 1_{19}.

II **רְעוּת**: **striving, aspiration** (*rûᵃḥ* after wind = emptiness) Ec 1_{14}.

רְעִי: **pasture**: *bāqār rᵉ'î* pasture-fed (not stall-fed) cattle 1K 5_3. †

רֵעִי: n. pers.

***רַעְיָה**: sf. רַעְיָתִי: (female) **companion** = **beloved** SS 1_9.

***רֵעְיָה**: pl. sf. רֵעיֹתָי (Kt רֵעְיָתָי ?) Ju 11_{37}: ↗ *רֵעָה. †

רַעְיוֹן: **striving** Ec 1_{17} 4_{16}; w. *libbô* 2_{22}. †

רעל: cj. **nif.**: impv. הֵרָעֵל: **stagger** cj. Hb 2_{16}. †.

hof.: pf. הָרְעָלוּ: **be made to quiver** Na 2_4. †

רַעַל: **staggering** Zc 12_2. †

***רְעָלָה**: pl. רְעָלוֹת: **veil** Is 3_{19}. †

רְעֵלָיָה: n. pers.

I **רעם**: **qal**: impf. יִרְעַם: subj. sea: **storm, thunder** Ps 96_{11} 98_7 1C 16_{32}. †

hif.: pf. הִרְעִים; impf. יַרְעֵם: subj. Y.: (cause it to) **thunder, storm** 1S 2_{10}.

II **רעם**: **qal**: pf. רָעֲמוּ: subj. *pānîm*: **be agitated, confused** Ez 27_{35}. †

hif.: inf. הַרְּעִימָהּ (sic!) (< *הַרְעִימָהּ): **appear upset, disturbed** 1S 1_6. †

רַעַם: sf. רַעַמְךָ: **uproar, thunder** Is 29_6; *sēter ra'am* thunder-cloud Ps 81_8. †

רַעְמָא: ↗ II רַעְמָה.

I **רַעְמָה**: **mane** (of horse) Jb 39_{19}. †

II **רַעְמָה** = **רַעְמָא**: n. pers.

רַעַמְיָה: n. pers.

רַעַמְסֵס & **רַעְמְסֵס**: n. loc.

רען: **palel**: pf. רַעֲנָנָה: **be luxuriant** Jb 15_{32}.†

רַעֲנָן: f. רַעֲנָנָה; pl. רַעֲנַנִּים: **luxuriant, full of leaves** 1K 14_{23}.

I **רעע**: **qal**: pf. רַע, רָעָה, וְרָעָה, רָעוּ; impf. יֵרַע, וַיֵּרַע, יֵרְעוּ; impv. רֹעוּ Is 8_9 (but rd דְּעוּ ?); inf. רֹעַ: — 1. **be bad, of no more use** (of boughs) Je 11_{16} (if txt. good); — 2. *ra' bᵉ'ênê* **be displeasing to** Gn 21_{11}f; *wayyēra' lᵉ* Ne 2_{10}, *'el* Jon 4_1; — 3. *rā'â 'ênô bᵉ* **look coldly on** (s.one) Dt 15_9; — 4. *yēra' lᵉbābô* **is discontented** 1S 1_8; — 5. *wayyēra' lô* **things went wrong** for Ps 106_{32}; — 6. *yērᵉ'û pānay* **I look sad** Ne 2_3;— 7. *ra' lᵉ ...min ...* **it is worse** for ... than ... 2S 19_8.

nif.: impf. יֵרֹעַ: **be treated badly, suffer** Pr 11_{15} 13_{20}. †

hif.: pf. הֵרַעְתִּי, הֲרֵעֹתָה, הֲרֵעוֹתָ, הֵרַע, הֵרֵעוּ, הֲרֵעֹתֶם; impf. יָרֵעַ, וַיָּרַע, אָרַע, יָרֵעוּ, נָרַע, תָּרֵעוּ; inf. הָרֵעַ, הָרַע; pt. מֵרַע, pl. מְרֵעִים: — 1. **do evil, behave objectionably** Gn 19_7; — 2. *hēra' lᵉ* **hurt, injure** s.one Gn 19_9; — 3. *hēra'* w. acc. **treat** s.one **badly** 1S 25_{34}; — 4. *hēra'* **harm** s.one, w. *'immad* Gn 31_7, w. *bᵉ* 1C 16_{22}; — 5. **bring calamity** on (*'al*) 1K 17_{20}; — 6. pt. *mēra'* **evil-doer** Is 1_4; — 7. *hēra'* abs. **cause damage**: subj. animals Is 11_9, subj. God Je 25_{29}; — 8. *hēra' ma'ᵃlāl* **commit an evil deed** Mi 3_4; *hēra' la'ᵃśôt* **act wickedly** 1K 14_9.

II **רעע**: **qal**: pf. רָעוּ; impf. יָרֹעַ, sf. תְּרֹעֵם;

cj. inf. רֹעַ Is 24_{19}: **break** Je 15_{12} Mi 5_5 Ps 2_9 Jb 34_{24}. †

hitpolel: pf. הִתְרֹעֲעָה; inf. הִתְרֹעֵעַ: **be smashed up, split up** Is 24_{19}; **beat each other up, destroy each other** Pr 18_{24}. †

רעף: **qal**: impf. יִרְעֲפוּן, יִרְעֲפוּ: **drip** Ps 65_{12} Pr 3_{20} Jb 36_{28}. †

hif.: impv. הַרְעִיפוּ: **let drip** Is 45_8. †

רעץ: **qal**: impf. תִּרְעַץ, תִּרְעֲצוּ: **beat down** Ex 15_6 Ju 10_8. †

I **רעשׁ**: **qal**: pf. רָעֲשָׁה, רָעֲשָׁה, רָעֲשׁוּ; impf. תִּרְעַשׁ, וַיִּרְעֲשׁוּ, תִּרְעַשְׁנָה; pt. pl. רֹעֲשִׁים: **quake, shake** (intrans.): earth 2S 22_8, heavens Jl 2_{10}, animals & men Ez 27_{28}.

[**nif.**: pf. נִרְעֲשָׁה rd qal Je 50_{46}. †]

hif.: pf. הִרְעַשְׁתָּה, הִרְעַשְׁתִּי; pt. הַרְעִישׁ **shake** (violently), **cause to quake** Is 14_{16}; **make** (horse) **leap** Jb 39_{20}.

II **רעשׁ**: **qal**: impf. יִרְעַשׁ: **be abundant** Ps 72_{16}. †

רַעַשׁ: רַעַשׁ **quaking** 1K 19_{11}f; **roar, clatter, commotion** Je 10_{22} 47_3.

רפא: **qal**: pf. ר׳, sf. רְפָאתִיו, רְפָאתִים; impf. יִרְפָּא, אֶרְפָּא > אֶרְפָּה Je 3_{22}, תִּרְפֶּינָה Jb 5_{18}, sf. וַתִּרְפָּאֵנִי, אֶרְפָּאֵהוּ; impv. רְפָא > רְפָה Ps 60_4, רְפָאָה, sf. רְפָאֵנִי; inf. לִרְפֹּא, רָפְאִי, abs. רָפוֹא; pt. רוֹפֵא & רֹפֵא (ל״א > ל״ה) 2K 20_5, sf. רֹפְאֶךָ, pl. רֹפְאִים: — 1. w. l^e: **heal** (s.one) 2K 20_5; — 2. w. acc.: **heal** Gn 20_{17}; — 3. abs. **heal** Dt 32_{39}; — 4. pt. **healer, surgeon, doctor** Gn 50_2; *rōfeʾê ʾelîl* bungling healers (quacks) Jb 13_4.

nif.: pf. נִרְפָּא, (many forms ל״ה) נִרְפְּתָה, נִרְפּאוּ (pronunciation w/o א) Ez 47_8; impf. אֵרָפֵא, וַיֵּרָפְאוּ > וַיֵּרָפוּ 2K 2_{22}; inf. הֵרָפֵא > הֵרָפֵה Je 19_{11}: — 1. impersonal w. l^e: *nirpāʾ lānû* we are healed Is 53_5; — 2. subj. flesh, wound &c.: **become healed, restored, sound** Lv 13_{18} Je 15_{18}; subj. unhealthy water 2K 2_{22}.

piel: pf. רִפֵּאתִי, רִפְּאנוּ, רִפֵּאתֶם (ל״א > ל״ה) Ez 34_4; impf. יְרַפֵּא, וַיְרַפְּאוּ > וַיְרַפּוּ Je 8_{11}; inf. רַפֹּא: — 1. w. l^e: **make healthy, drinkable** 2K 2_{21}; — 2. w. acc.: **heal** 1K 18_{30}; — 3. abs. **pay for** s.one's **cure** Ex 21_{19}.

hitp.: inf. הִתְרַפֵּא: **get healed** 2K 8_{29} 9_{15} 2C 22_6. †

רָפָא **piel**: ↗ also רָפָה.

רָפָא: n. pers.

רִפְאוּת: **healing** Pr 3_8. †

I **רְפָאִים**: **ghosts** (of the dead) Is 26_{14}.

II **רְפָאִים**: n. peop.; sg. רָפָא 1C $20_{6.8}$; = I ?: Gn 15_{20} &c.: legendary pre-Israelite inhabitants of Palestine; ↗ II רָפָה.

רְפָאֵל: n. pers.

רפד: **qal**: impf. יִרְפַּד: **stretch out** (intrans.) Jb 41_{22}. †

piel: pf. רִפַּדְתִּי; impv. רַפְּדוּנִי: **spread out** (trans.) Jb 17_{13}; **support, refresh** SS 2_5. †

רָפָה: **qal**: pf. ר׳, רָפְתָה, רָפוּ; impf. יִרְפֶּה, וַיִּרֶף, יִרְפּוּ, תִּרְפֶּינָה: — 1. **become slack, relax, desist** (*min*, from) Ex 4_{26}, (*mēʿal*) Ju 8_3; of daylight, **fade away** Ju 19_9; — 2. w. *yādayim*: the hands relax, drop = one **loses heart, courage** 2S 4_1: > w/o *yādayim* Je 49_{24}; — 3. of dry grass, **sink down** (in flame) Is 5_{24}.

nif.: pt. pl. נִרְפִּים: **slack, idle** Ex $5_{8.17}$. †

piel: pf. רִפָּה; impf. תְּרַפֶּינָה; pt. מְרַפֵּא (< *מְרַפֶּה), pl. מְרַפִּים: — 1. **make slack, loose** Jb 12_{21}; **let** (wings) **drop** Ez 1_{24}f; — 2. obj. *yādayim*: **demoralize, discourage** Je 38_4 Ezr 4_4. †

hif.: impf. תֶּרֶף, sf. יַרְפְּךָ, תַּרְפֵּנִי, אַרְפֶּנּוּ; impv. הֶרֶף, הַרְפֵּה, הַרְפּוּ: — 1. **abandon** Dt 4_{31}; **forsake, leave in the lurch** Ps 138_8; c. *min*: **desist** from s.one, **leave** s.one **alone** Dt 9_{14}; *hirpâ yādāyw min* = **abandon** Jos 10_6; abs. **leave off, stop** 1S 15_{16}; — 2. **leave** s.one **alone** (= not bother) Jb 7_{19}; **stop** (work) Ne 6_3; w. *min*, **let** s.one **alone**

= **give time** Ju 11_{37} = w. *le* 2K 4_{27}; — 3. *hirpâ yādô* **drop one's hand** 2S 24_{16}.

hitp.: pf. הִתְרַפִּיתָ; pt. מִתְרַפֶּה, מִתְרַפִּים: — 1. **show** onesf. **lazy** Jos 18_3 Pr 18_9; — 2. **show** onesf. **discouraged** Pr 24_{10}. †

רָפֶה: cs. רְפֵה; pl. f. רָפוֹת: **slack, feeble** Nu 13_{18}; *yādayim rāfôt* Is 35_3 Jb 4_3; *refēh yādayim* **discouraged** 2S 17_2. †

I **רָפָה**: n. pers. 1C 8_{37}. †

II **רָפָה**: הָרָפָה: n. pers., presumed ancestor of רְפָאִים 2S $21_{16·18·20·22}$; > הָרָפָא 1C $20_{6·8}$.†

רָפוּא: n. pers.

*__רְפוּאָה__: pl. רְפֻאוֹת: **healing** Je 30_{13} 46_{11} Ez 30_{21}. †

רְפוֹת: F רִיפוֹת.

רֶפַח: n. pers.

*__רְפִידָה__: sf. רְפִידָתוֹ: **support** (of litter); oth.: covering SS 3_{10}. †

רְפִידִים: n. loc.

רְפָיָה: n. pers.

*__רִפָּיוֹן__ or *__רִפְיוֹן__: cs. רִפְיוֹן: **slackness**: w. *yādayim* **discouragement, despondency** Je 47_3. †

רפס: F רפשׂ.

רַפְסֹדוֹת: **rafts** 2C 2_{15}. †

רפף: **poal**: impf. יְרוֹפָפוּ: **shake** (intrans.) Jb 26_{11}. †

רפק: **hitp.**: pt. f. מִתְרַפֶּקֶת: **lean** SS 8_5. †

רפשׂ, **רפס**: **qal**: impf. תִּרְפֹּס, תִּרְפֹּשׂוּן: **muddy** (obj. waters) (by trampling) Ez 32_2 34_{18}. †

nif.: pt. נִרְפָּשׂ: **muddied** (water) Pr 25_{26}. †

hitp.: impv. הִתְרַפֵּס; pt. מִתְרַפֵּס: **trample** Ps 68_{31}, **trample onesf. down** Pr 6_3; but txt. of one or both may be corr. †

רֶפֶשׁ: **slime and seaweed** Is 57_{20}. †

*__רֶפֶת__: pl. רְפָתִים: **enclosure** (for cattle) Hb 3_{17}. †

*__רַץ__: pl. cs. רַצֵּי: *beraṣṣê-kāsef* Ps 68_{31} txt. corr., F comm. †

*__רָץ__: pl. (Aram.) רָצִין 2K 11_{13}: F רוץ.

I **רצא**: **qal**: inf. רָצוֹא: rd. רוץ ? Ez 1_{14}. †

II **רצא**: F I רָצָה.

רצד: **piel**: impf. תְּרַצְּדוּן: **keep one's eyes on, watch w. hostility** Ps 68_{17}. †

I **רָצָה**: **qal**: pf. ר׳, רָצְתָה, רָצִיתָ, רָצָאתִי (!) Ez 43_{27}, רָצוּ, sf. רָצָם, רְצִיתָם; impf. יִרְצֶה, וַתִּרֶץ, אֶרְצֶה, *אֶרֶץ (for אָרֶץ) 2S 3_{12}, יִרְצוּ, תִּרֹצְנָה (Qr תִּצֹּרְנָה) rd Kt תִּרְצֶינָה Pr 23_{26}, sf. וַיִּרְצֵהוּ, יִרְצְךָ, יִרְצֶךָּ, וַתִּרְצֵנִי, אֶרְצֵם; impv. רְצֵה; inf. רְצוֹת, sf. רְצֹתוֹ; pt. רוֹצֶה, sf. רֹצָם, pass. רָצוּי, cs. רְצוּי; (30× out of 40, subj. God): — 1. w. acc.: **be pleased with, well-disposed toward, favorable to** s.one Gn 33_{10}; > **like** s.one or s.thg Am 5_{22}; **treat** (a land) **favorably** Ps 85_2; *reṣûy 'eḥāyw* **favorite** of his brothers Dt 33_{24}; *rāṣûy lerōb* **popular** w. the multitude Est 10_3; *rāṣâ yômô* **enjoys** his day Jb 14_6; — 2. w. *be*: **be pleased with** Mi 6_7; **be favorable to** Ps 149_4; — 3. *rāṣâ 'im* **make friends with** Ps 50_{18}; — 4. w. *le* & inf.: **be pleased to** Ps 62_5; w. stressed obj.: *bî rāṣâ le* it was I whom he chose to … 1C 28_4.

nif.: pf. נִרְצָה; impf. יֵרָצֶה: **be treated as acceptable** Lv 7_{18}, w. *le* for the benefit of Lv 1_4.

piel: impf. יְרַצּוּ: **put** s.one **in a benevolent mood, beg from** s.one Jb 20_{10} (oth.: conciliate, F comm.). †

hitp.: impf. יִתְרַצֶּה: w. *'el*: **make onesf. pleasing** to 1S 29_4. †

II **רצה**: **qal**: pf. רָצְתָה; impf. תִּרְצֶה, תִּרֶץ, יִרְצוּ: **count**: =: — 1. **pay for** (one's sins) Lv $26_{41·43}$; — 2. **make good** (obj. sabbaths wh. were neglected) Lv 26_{34} 2C 36_{21}. †

nif.: pf. נִרְצָה: **be paid off** (debt or guilt) Is 40_2. †

hif.: pf. 3. sg. f. הִרְצָת (< *הִרְצְתָה): **cause to be paid off, make good** Lv 26_{34}. †

cj. **hof.**: impf. יֻרְצוּ: **be counted** cj. Ps 139_{16}. †

רָצוֹן: cs. רְצוֹן, sf. רְצֹ(וֹ)נוֹ: — 1. secular use:

reṣôn melek **favor** of the king Pr 14_{35}, **desire** Ps 145_{19}, **what is acceptable** Pr 10_{32}; **good understanding** (among men) Pr 14_9; (one's) **liking** Est 1_8; *birṣônām* **arbitrarily**, without permission Gn 49_6; — 2. religious use: a) **favor** (of God) wh. men seek Ex 28_{38}; *yôm rāṣôn* Is 58_5, *ʿêt rāṣôn* Ps 69_{14}; b) **favor** granted by God to men in blessings Dt 33_{16}; *ʿêt rāṣôn* Is 49_8, *šenat rāṣôn* 61_2.

רצח: **qal**: pf. ר׳, רָצַחְתָּ, רְצָחוֹ; impf. תִּרְצַח, תִּרְצָֽח; inf. רְצֹחַ; pt. ר(ו)צֵחַ: **kill** 1K 21_{19}; pt. **manslayer** Nu 35_6 (no distinction betw. premeditated & involuntary killing).

nif.: impf. אֵרָצֵחַ; pt. נִרְצָחָה: **be killed** Ju 20_4; of animal Pr 22_{13}. †

piel: impf. יְרַצֵּחוּ; pt. מְרַצֵּחַ, מְרַצְּחִים: **murder, slay** 2K 6_{32} Is 1_{21} Ho 6_9 Ps 94_6. †

[**רֶצַח**: trad. **murder**, but Ps 42_{11} uncert., & in Ez 21_{27} rd בְּצֶרַח. †]

רִצְיָא: n. pers.

רְצִין: n. pers. **Rezin**, but prob. word-play on *Rāṣon*: 2K 15_{37} &c.

רָצִין 2K 11_{13}: ↗ רָץ.

רצע: **qal**: pf. ר׳: **pierce** Ex 21_6. †

רצף: **qal**: pt. pass. רָצוּף: **inlaid** SS 3_{10}. †

I **רֶצֶף**: רִצְפָּה unit; pl. רְצָפִים: **live coal** (from the altar) Is 6_6; *ʿugat reṣafîm* baked on hot stones 1K 19_6. †

II **רֶצֶף**: n. loc.

I **רִצְפָּה**: ↗ I רֶצֶף.

II **רִצְפָּה**: n. pers. f.

רִצְפָה: cs. רִצְפַת: **pavement** (of stones) Ez 40_{17f} 42_3 2C 7_3; (mosaic) **pavement** Est 1_6. †

רצץ: **qal**: pf. רַצּוֹתִי, רַצּוֹתָנוּ; impf. וַיָּרָץ 2K 23_{12}, [יָרוֹץ Is 42_4 rd יֵרוֹץ], [sf. Kt ארוצם Je 50_{44} rd Qr אֲרִיצֵם (ארוץ)]; pt. pl. f. רֹצְצוֹת Am 4_1, pass. רָצוּץ, cs. רְצוּץ, pl. רְצוּצִים: **smash up** 2K 23_{12}; **ill-treat, abuse** 1S 12_{3f}; *qāneh rāṣûṣ* crushed reed 2K 18_{21}.

nif.: pf. נָרוֹץ; impf. תֵּרוֹץ: **crack, break** (intrans.) Is 42_4 (rd יֵרוֹץ) Ez 29_7 Ec 12_6. †

hif.: impf. וַתָּרִץ (oth.: qal): **crush in pieces** Ju 9_{53}. †

piel: pf. רִצַּצְתָּ, רִצַּץ; impf. וַיְרַצֵּץ: **crush in pieces** Ps 74_{14} Jb 20_{19} 2C 16_{10}. †

polel: impf. וַיְרֹצְצוּ: **oppress** Ju 10_8. †

hitpolel: impf. וַיִּתְרֹצְצוּ: **push each other around** Gn 25_{22}. †

I ***רַק**: pl. f. רַקּוֹת: **thin, lank** (cows) Gn $41_{19f.27}$. †

II **רַק** (100×); = I, adv.: in a slight way > **only**: *raq raʿ* only (= exclusively) evil Gn 6_5; *raq ʾašer* only what Gn 14_{24}; *raq* … *lōʾ* except that (= but) … not Gn 24_8; *haraq ʾak* has he indeed only …? Nu 12_2; *raq ʾên dābār* only … without [doing] anything [more] Nu 20_{19}; *raq bekol-* yet … according to any … Dt 12_{15} &c.

רֵק: ↗ רֵיק.

רֹק: sf. רֻקִּי: **spittle** Is 50_6 Jb 7_{19} 30_{10}. †

רקב: **qal**: pf. ר׳; impf. יִרְקָבוּ, יִרְקָב, יִרְקַב; inf. רְקוֹב: **rot, become worm-eaten** Is 40_{20} Pr 10_7. †

רָקָב: cs. רְקַב: **rottenness** (in bones) Hb 3_{16} Pr 12_4 14_{30}. †

cj. **רֹקֶב**: **wine-skin** cj. Jb 13_{28}. †

רִקָּבוֹן: **rottenness** Jb 41_{19}. †

רקד: **qal**: pf. רָקְדוּ; impf. תִּרְקְדוּ; inf. רְקוֹד: **skip about** Ps $114_{4.6}$ Ec 3_4. †

piel: impf. יְרַקְּדוּ, יְרַקֵּדוּן; pt. מְרַקֵּד, מְרַקֵּדָה: **dance** Is 13_{21}.

hif.: impf. וַיַּרְקִידֵם: **make** s.thg **skip about** Ps 29_6. †

***רַקָּה**: sf. רַקָּתוֹ, רַקָּתֵךְ: **temple** (of head) Ju 4_{21f} 5_{26} SS 4_3 6_7. †

(הָ)רַקּוֹן: n. loc.

רקח: **qal**: impf. יִרְקַח; pt. ר(ו)קֵחַ, pl. cs. רֹקְחֵי: **blend, mix ointment** (oil for anointing, perfume) Ex $20_{25.33.35}$ Ec 10_1 1C 9_{30}. †

pual: pt. pl. מְרֻקָּחִים: **mixed, blended** (of ointments) 2C 16_{14}. †

[**hif.**: impv. הַרְקַח: rd. הָרֵק הַמָּרָק Ez 24_{10}. †]

רֶקַח: **spice** (powdered & added to wine) SS 8_2. †

רֹקַח: **spice** Ex $30_{25 \cdot 35}$. †

*רַקָּח: pl. רַקָּחִים, f. רַקָּחוֹת: **ointment-mixer, perfumer** (male & female) 1S 8_{13} Ne 3_8. †

*רִקֻּחַ: pl. רִקֻּחַיִךְ: **ointment, perfume** (of oil-base) Is 57_9. †

רָקִיעַ: cs. רְקִיעַ: (beaten, [metal]) **plate, firmament** (i.e. vault of heaven, understood as a solid dome) Gn 1_6.

רָקִיק: cs. רְקִיק; pl. cs. רְקִיקֵי: (thin, flat) **cake, wafer** Ex 29_{23}; w. *maṣṣâ, -ôt* Ex 29_2.

רקם: **qal**: pt. רֹקֵם: **weaver of colored fabric, embroiderer** Ex 26_{36}.

pual: pf. רֻקַּמְתִּי: **I was** (intricately) **woven** (as an embryo) Ps 139_{15}. †

I רֶקֶם: n. loc. Jos 11_{27}. †

II רֶקֶם: רֶקֶם: n. pers.

רִקְמָה: sf. רִקְמָתֵךְ; pl. רְקָמוֹת; du. רִקְמָתַיִם: **fabric of** (variety of) colors Ez 16_{10}; **variegated plumage** Ez 17_3; *riqmātayim*: some: 2 pieces of fabric, oth.: fabric embroidered on both sides, Ju 5_{30}; *'abnê riqmâ* mosaic stones 1C 29_2.

רקע: **qal**: impf. אֶרְקָעֵם; impv. רְקַע, inf. רַקְעֲךָ; pt. cs. רֹקַע: **stamp** (obj. foot) Ez 6_{11} 25_6, **stamp down** (obj. enemies) 2S 22_{43}; **spread out** Is 42_5 44_{24} Ps 136_6. †

piel: impf. וַיְרַקְּעוּם, יְרַקְּעֶנּוּ, וַיְרַקְּעוּ: **hammer out** Ex 39_3 Nu 17_4; **overlay** (obj. metal) Is 40_{19}.

pual: pt. מְרֻקָּע: **hammered out, beaten into plates** Je 10_9. †

hif.: impf. תַּרְקִיעַ: **hammer out** Jb 37_{18}. †

*רִקֻּעַ: pl. cs. רִקֻּעֵי: **hammered out, beaten into plates** Nu 17_3. †

רקק: **qal**: impf. יָרֹק: **spit** Lv 15_8. †

רַקַּת: n. loc.

רָשׁ: **poor**: ↗ רוּשׁ.

cj. רֹשׁ: n. peop.: ↗ IV רֹאשׁ n. peop.

*רִשְׁיוֹן: **authorization** Ezr 3_7. †

רֵשִׁית: ↗ רֵאשִׁית.

רשם: **qal**: pt. pass. רָשׁוּם: **registered** Dn 10_{21}. †

רשע: **qal**: pf. רָשַׁעְתִּי, רָשָׁעְנוּ; impf. תִּרְשַׁע, אֶרְשָׁע: **be (come) guilty** 1K 8_{47}, w. *min* towards 2S 22_{22}.

hif.: הִרְשִׁיעַ, הִרְשִׁיעוּ, הִרְשַׁעְנוּ; impf. יַרְשִׁיעֻנִי, יַרְשִׁיעֻן, יַרְשִׁיעוּ, תַּרְשִׁיעִי, יַרְשִׁעַ, יַרְשִׁיעֶנּוּ; inf. הַרְשִׁיעַ; pt. מַרְשִׁיעַ, pl. cs. מַרְשִׁיעֵי: — 1. **make onesf. guilty** Ps 106_6, w. acc. in regard to Dn 11_{32}; **lead a delinquent life** 2C 22_3; w. *la'ăśôt* **act culpably** 2C 20_{35}; — 2. w. acc.: **declare, pronounce** s.one **guilty** 1K 8_{32} & oft.; — 3. w. acc.: **let** s.one **be condemned** Ps 37_{33}.

רֶשַׁע: רֶשַׁע; sf. רִשְׁעוֹ; pl. רְשָׁעִים † Ez 21_{34}: **wrong, injustice, guilt** 1S 24_{14}; *'āśâ reša'* do wrong Pr 16_{12}; *'anšê reša'* wrongdoers Jb 34_8; *'ōṣerôt reša'* treasures gained by wrongdoing Mi 6_{10}; *mō'znê reša'* false balances Mi 6_{11}.

רָשָׁע: f. רְשָׁעָה; pl. רְשָׁעִים, cs. רִשְׁעֵי: — 1. **guilty** (in a single instance), **in the wrong** Ex 2_{13}; *rāšā' lāmût* guilty and deserving death Nu 35_{31}; — 2. **guilty** (in genl., essentially, before God), **transgressor** Gn 18_{23} 1K 8_{32}; — 3. *mal'āk rāšā'* Pr 13_{17} & *darkô hārešā'â* Ez 3_{18f} guilty > **impious**; *'anāšîm rešā'îm* impious men 2S 4_{11}.

רִשְׁעָה: cs. רִשְׁעַת; sf. רִשְׁעָתוֹ: **guilt** Dt 9_{4f}; *riš'at rāšā'* Ez 18_{20}; *'āśâ riš'â* Ma 1_4; personified Zc 5_8; *leriš'â min*, more guilty than Ez 5_6.

רִשְׁעָתַיִם: ↗ כּוּשַׁן.

I רֶשֶׁף: pl. רְשָׁפִים, cs. רִשְׁפֵּי & רִשְׁפֵי, sf. רְשָׁפֶיהָ: — 1. **flame** (i.e. of love) SS 8_6; — 2. *rišfê qešet* **flames** of the bow Ps 76_4; — 3. = **pestilence** Dt 32_{24}.

II רֶשֶׁף: n. pers. 1C 7_{25}. †

רשש: **polel**: impf. יְרֹשֵׁשׁ: **batter down, shatter** Je 5_{17}. †

pual: pf. רֻשַּׁשְׁנוּ: **be shattered** Ma 1_4. †

רֶשֶׁת: רֶשֶׁת; sf. רִשְׁתּוֹ: — 1. **net** (for catching

game & birds) Ez 12_{13}; — 2. **network** Ex 27_4.

[רַתּוֹק: pl. Qr רַתּוּקוֹת rd רַתִּיקֹת 1K 6_{21}; Ez 7_{23} rd הַבַּתּוּק.]

רתח: **piel**: impv. רַתַּח: **(bring to) boil** Ez 24_5. †

pual: pf. רֻתְּחוּ: **be boiled, brought to boil** Jb 30_{27}. †

hif.: impf. יַרְתִּיחַ: **(bring to) boil** Jb 41_{23}. †

[*רֶתַח: pl. sf. רְתָחֶיהָ: rd (w. 2 mss.) נְתָחֶיהָ Ez 24_5. †]

cj. *רַתִּיקָה: cs. רַתִּיקַת: **chain** cj. 1K 6_{21}. †

רתם: **qal**: impv. רְתֹם: **tie up**? Mi 1_{13}. †

רֹתֶם: pl. רְתָמִים: **broom** (shrub), *Retama raetam* 1K 19_{4f} Ps 120_4 Jb 30_4. †

רִתְמָה: n. loc.

רתק: [**nif.**: impf. יֵרָתֵק: rd. יִנָּתֵק Ec 12_6. †]

pual: pf. רֻתְּקוּ: **be fettered, bound in chains** Na 3_{10}. †

רְתֻקוֹת: **chains** Is 40_{19}. †

רְתֵת: **terror, trembling** Ho 13_1. †

שׂ

שְׂאֹר: **leaven** Ex $12_{15 \cdot 19}$ 13_7 Lv 2_{11} Dt 16_4. †

I **שְׂאֵת**: sf. שֵׂאתוֹ > שְׂאֵתוֹ Jb 41_{17}: **raising onesf. up** Jb 41_{17}, **dignity, nobility** Gn 49_3 Jb 31_{23}, ? Hb 1_7; Gn 4_7 **exaltation** (?) ꟳ comm.; Jb 13_{11} Ps 62_5 txt. corr.; cj. Nu 24_{17} (ꟳ III *šēt*). †

II **שְׂאֵת**: **swelling, blotch** Lv $13_{2 \cdot 10 \cdot 19 \cdot 28 \cdot 43}$ 14_{56}. †

שָׂב: ꟳ שׂיב.

שְׂבָכָה: pl. שְׂבָכִים 1K 7_{17} & שְׂבָכוֹת 7_{41f}: — 1. **net** Jb 18_8; — 2. **lattice, screen-work** 2K 1_2; — 3. (ornamental) **grating** 1K 7_{17}.

שְׂבָם: n. loc.

שִׂבְמָה: n. loc.

שָׂבַע: **qal**: pf. שָׂבֵעְתָּ) שָׂבַעְתָּ, שָׂבַעְתָּ, שָׂבְעָה, שׂ׳ or שָׂבַעַת), שָׂבְעוּ, שְׂבַעְתֶּם, שָׂבָעוּ, שָׂבָעְנוּ; impf. יִשְׂבַּע, יִשְׂבְּעוּ, יִשְׂבָּעוּן, אֶשְׂבְּעָה, תִּשְׂבַּע, יִשְׂבָּע, תִּשְׂבַּעְנָה, sf. יִשְׂבָּעֶךָּ, יִשְׂבָּעֶנּוּ, תִּשְׂבָּעֶנּוּ; impv. שְׂבַע; inf. שָׂבוֹעַ, שָׂבְעָתֵךְ, לִשְׂבֹּעַ: **be satiated, have had enough**: — 1. **be satiated w. food, have had enough to eat** Ex 16_8; — 2. **be satiated w. drink, have had enough to drink** Is 66_{11}; — 3. w. acc.: **satisfy one's hunger** w., **have had enough** (food &c.): bread Ex 16_{12}; *ṭûb* Je 31_{14} &c.; *śāba' yāmîm* satiated w., weary of life 1C 23_1; — 4. w. acc.: **have had enough, can take no more** (of s.thg wh. becomes disgusting) Is 1_{11}; — 5. w. *b^e*: **satisfy one's hunger** w. Is 53_{11}, **have had enough, can take no more** Ps 88_4; — 6. w. *min*: **get one's fill** of Pr 1_{31}, **become satiated** w. Ps 18_{20}; — 7. *śāba' lir'ôt* **see enough** Ec 1_8; — 8. spec. subj.: sword Je 46_{10}, animals Ez 39_{20}, death Hb 2_5.

nif.: pt. נִשְׂבָּע **sated, filled** (w. meat) Jb 31_{31}. †

piel: impf. יְשַׂבֵּעוּ; impv. שַׂבְּעֵנוּ: **satisfy** s.one, **give** s.one **enough** Ez 7_{19}, w. 2 acc. (pers. & thg.) Ps 90_{14}. †

hif.: pf. הִשְׂבִּיעַ, הִשְׂבַּעַתְּ (־בַּעְתְּ or ־בַּעַת) Ez 27_{33}, הִשְׂבַּעְתִּי, הִשְׂבִּיעַנִי; impf. תַּשְׂבִּיעַ, אַשְׂבִּיעֶךָ, אַשְׂבִּיעֵהוּ, יַשְׂבִּיעֵם, יַשְׂבִּעֵנִי; inf. הַשְׂבִּיעַ; pt. מַשְׂבִּיעַ: — 1. w. acc.: **satisfy** s.one('s hunger), **fill** Je 5_7; w. 2 acc.: with (food &c.) Ps 81_{17}; — 2. w. *b^e* with Ps 103_5; — 3. w. *l^e* (+ creature) & acc. (of thing): **satisfy** one with Ps 145_{16}.

שָׂבָע: **satiation, plenty** Gn 41_{29ff} Pr 3_{10} Ec 5_{11}. †

שֹׂבַע: sf. שָׂבְעֲךָ, שָׂבְעָה: **satiation, plenty** Ex 16_3.

שָׂבֵעַ: cs. שְׂבַע, f. שְׂבֵעָה; pl. שְׂבֵעִים: **full, sati-**

ated, satisfied 1S 2_5; *śᵉbaʿ yāmîm* **sated w. days** Gn 35_{29}; > *śābēaʿ* Gn 25_8.

שָׂבְעָה: sf. שָׂבְעָתֵךְ: **satiation, plenty** Is 23_{18}.

***שִׂבְעָה**: cs. שִׂבְעַת: **satiation, plenty** Ez 16_{49}. †

שׂבר: **qal**: pt. שֹׂבֵר: w. *bᵉ*, **examine, inspect** Ne $2_{13\cdot15}$. †

piel: pf. שִׂבַּרְתִּי, שִׂבְּרוּ; impf. יְשַׂבְּרוּ, תְּשַׂבֵּרְנָה, יְשַׂבְּרוּן: **hope, wait**, w. *ʾel* for Is 38_{18}, = w. *lᵉ* Ps 119_{166}, w. *ʿad ʾᵃšer* until Ru 1_{13}, w. *lᵉ* & inf. hope to ... Est 9_1.

***שֵׂבֶר**: sf. שִׂבְרוֹ: **hope** Ps 119_{116} 146_5. †

שׂגא: **qal**: impf. יִשְׂגֶּא: **grow** Jb 8_{11}. †

hif.: impf. תַּשְׂגִּיא; pt. מַשְׂגִּיא: — 1. call s.thg great, **extol** Jb 36_{24}; — 2. w. *lᵉ* **make** (nations) **great** Jb 12_{23}. †

שׂגב: **qal**: pf. שָׂגְבוּ, שָׂגְבָה: w. *min*: **be too high, fortified for** Dt 2_{36}; *śagᵉbû yešaʿ* **have high success** Jb 5_{11}. †

nif.: pf. נִשְׂגַּב, נִשְׂגְּבָה, נִשְׂגָּב; pt. נִשְׂגָּב, נִשְׂגָּבָה: — 1. **be high, inaccessible**: wall Is 30_{13}, city Is 26_5; — 2. of God, **be exalted** Is 2_{11}; his name Is 12_4; — 3. of knowledge, **be unattainable** Ps 139_6; — 4. **be high, safe** Pr 18_{10}.

piel: impf. אֲשַׂגְּבֵהוּ, תְּשַׂגְּבֵנִי, יְשַׂגֶּבְךָ, וַיְשַׂגֵּב: **make high, inaccessible, protect** Ps 20_2; w. acc. & *ʿal*, **make great** against Is 9_{10}.

pual: impf. יְשֻׂגָּב: **be protected** Pr 29_{25}. †

hif.: impf. יַשְׂגִּיב: **prove to be great** Jb 36_{22}. †

שׂגה: **qal**: impf. יִשְׂגֶּה: **grow great** Ps 92_{13} Jb 8_{11}.

hif.: pf. הִשְׂגּוּ: **make great** Ps 73_{12}.

שְׂגוּב: n. pers.

שַׂגִּיא: **exalted** (of God) Jb 36_{26} 37_{23}. †

שְׂגִיב: 1K 16_{34} Kt F שְׂגוּב.

שִׂגְשֵׂג Is 17_{11}: F II שׂוג.

שׂדד: **piel**: impf. יְשַׂדֵּד, יְשַׂדֶּד־: **draw a boundary furrow** (oth: **harrow**) Is 28_{24} Ho 10_{11} Jb 39_{10}. †

שָׂדֶה: cs. שְׂדֵה & שְׂדֵי, sf. שָׂדֵהוּ, שָׂדְךָ, שָׂדֶךָ, שָׂדִי; pl. שָׂד(וֹ)ת, cs. שְׂדוֹת, sf. שְׂדֹתָם, שְׂדֹתֶיהָ, שְׂדוֹתֵינוּ, שְׂדוֹתֵיהֶם, & cs. pl. (= sg.!) שְׂדֵי, sf. שָׂדֵינוּ (sg.?) Mi 2_4: — 1. **open country, open field**: opp. city Gn 34_{28}; *baśśādeh* in the open Gn 4_8 & oft.; *haśśādeh* into the open Gn 27_3; *ʿārê haśśādeh* towns in the (open) country 1S 27_5; *rêaḥ śādeh* smell of the fields Gn 27_{27}; — 2. **fields** (in the territory of a city &c.), **domain** (of city &c.): *śᵉdēh hāʿîr* Jos 21_{12}; *śᵉdēh ʾᵉdôm* Gn 32_4; — 3. (arable) land, > **plot** (of land), **field** (of an individual) Gn 23_9; *ḥelqat haśśādeh* Gn 33_{19}; — 4. particular, named fields: *śᵉdēh hammakpēlâ* Gn 23_{19} &c.; — 5. spec.: *śādeh neʿᵉbār* tilled field Ec 5_8.

שָׂדַי: older form of שָׂדֶה: שָׂדָי, cs. שְׂדֵי F שָׂדֶה: **open country, open field** Dt 32_{13}.

הַשִּׂדִּים: שִׂדִּים: n. loc.

***שְׂדֵרָה**: pl. שְׂדֵר(וֹ)ת: unexpl. archit. term; perh. = *sᵉdērôt* **aligned beams** 1K 6_9 2K $11_{8\cdot15}$ 2C 23_{14}. †

שֶׂה: cs. שֵׂה, sf. שֵׂיֵהוּ & שֵׂיוֹ: **lamb** or **kid**, i.e. young of either sheep or goat Gn 22_7.

***שָׂהֵד**: sf. שָׂהֲדִי: **witness** Jb 16_{19}. †

שָׂהֲדוּתָא Gn 31_{47}: F Aram. שָׂהֲדוּ. †

שַׂהֲרֹנִים: **crescents** (ornaments) Ju $8_{21\cdot26}$ Is 3_{18}. †

שׂוֹא: F נשא.

שׂוֹבֶךְ: **tangle of branches** 2S 18_9. †

I **שׂוג**: F I סוג nif. & hif.

II **שׂוג**: = II סוג?: **pilpel**: impf. תְּשַׂגְשֵׂגִי: **fence in? raise** (plants) ? Is 17_{11}. †

שׂוח: **qal**: inf. לָשׂוּחַ: unexpl.; transls. are only guesswork Gn 24_{63}. †

שׂוט: **qal**: pt. pl. cs. שָׂטֵי: w. *kāzāb*: **become entangled in falsehood** Ps 40_5. †

cj. **pilpel**: impf. יְשַׂטְטוּ: **turn apostate** cj. Dn 12_4. †

שׂוך: **qal**: pf. שַׂכְתָּ; pt. שָׂךְ: **hedge** (w. thornbushes), **shut in** Ho 2_8, w. *bᵉʿad* Jb 1_{10}. †

[***שׂוֹךְ**: sf. שׂוֹכֹה: rd F שׂוֹכָה or שׂוֹכָתוֹ Ju 9_{49}. †]

***שׂוֹכָה**: cs. שׂוֹכַת: **brushwood** Ju 9_{48} cj $_{49}$. †

שׂוֹכֹה, שֹׂכֹה, & שׂוֹכוֹ: n. loc.
***שׂוֹכָתִי**: gent. of unknown n. loc. *שׂוֹכָה; pl. שׂוּכָתִים 1C 2_{55}. †
שׂוּם: → שִׂים.
[**שׂוּר**: **qal**: impf. וַיָּשַׂר rd. וַיִּשַׂר (√שרה) Ho 12_5, rd וַיָּשֶׂם (as 2S 12_{31}) 1C 20_3; inf. שׂוּרִי = סוּרִי (√סור) Ho 9_{12}. †
hif.: pf. הֵשִׂירוּ Ho 8_4 → שׂרר.]
שׂוֹרָה: **millet** ? Is 28_{25}. †
I **שׂוֹרֵק**: n. loc. Ju 16_4. †
II **שׂוֹרֵק**: → שֹׂרֵק.
שׂוּשׂ & שִׂישׂ: **qal**: pf. שָׂשׂוּ, שַׂשְׂתִּי, שָׂשׂ; impf. יְשִׂישׂוּם, יָשִׂישׂוּ, יָשִׂישׂ Is 35_1, נָשִׂישָׂה; impv. שִׂישִׂי, שִׂישׂוּ; inf. cs. שׂוּשׂ, abs. שׂוֹשׂ; pt. שָׂשׂ: **rejoice** Is 35_1, w. b^e in Is 61_{10}, w. l^e & inf. Dt 28_{63}.
***שֵׂחַ**: sf. [מַה־]שֵּׂחוֹ: usu.: his thoughts; oth.: txt. corr. Am 4_{13}. †
שׂחה: **qal**: inf. שְׂחוֹת; pt. שׂוֹחֶה: **swim** Is 25_{11}. †
hif.: impf. אַשְׂחֶה: make swim, **flood** Ps 6_7. †
שָׂחוּ: **swimming** = (water) deep enough for swimming Ez 47_5. †
שְׂחוֹק: — 1. **laughter** Ps 126_2; — 2. **fun, sport** Pr 10_{23}; — 3. **mockery, laughingstock** Je 20_7.
שׂחט: **qal**: impf. וָאֶשְׂחַט: **squeeze out** (grapes) Gn 40_{11}. †
***שָׂחִיף**: cs. שְׂחִיף: unexpl. Ez 41_{16}, evid. tech. term in handicraft; sugg.: a species of wood, or facing?. †
שָׂחַק: **qal**: pf. שָׂחֲקוּ, שׂ׳; impf. יִשְׂחַק, יִשְׂחָק, יִשְׂחָקוּ; inf. שְׂחוֹק: — 1. **play, act clumsy**, 'carry on' (for others' amusement) Ju 16_{27}; — 2. **laugh** Pr 29_9; w. l^e at Ps 2_4; Pr 31_{25} she laughs at (a threat) = is unconcerned about; w. *'al* Ps 52_8, w. b^e Pr 1_{26}; w. *'el* **smile** at, on s.one Jb 29_{24}.
piel: pf. שִׂחַקְתִּי; impf. וַיְשַׂחֵק־, וַיְשַׂחֲקוּ; inf. שַׂחֵק־; pt. מְשַׂחֵק, מְשַׂחֶקֶת, מְשַׂחֲקִים, מְשַׂחֲקוֹת: — 1. **be happy** Je 30_{19}; **joke** Je 15_{17}; w. b^e **play** with Ps 104_{26}; — 2. **amuse, entertain** Ju 16_{25}; — 3. **dance, play** 1S 18_7; **hold a tournament, contest** 2S 2_{14}.
hif.: pt. מַשְׂחִיקִים: w. *'al*, **make fun** of (s.one) 2C 30_{10}. †
cj. **שַׂחַת** Jb 9_{31} **filth**: → סוּחָה.
[***שֵׂט**: pl. שֵׂטִים: rd. נַחַל הַשִּׁטִּים Ho 5_2. †]
שׂטה: **qal**: pf. שָׂטִית; impf. תִּשְׂטֶה, יֵשְׂטְ; impv. שְׂטֵה: — 1. **go astray**: of wife: abs. Nu 5_{12}; w. *taḥat*, to Nu $5_{19f.29}$; — 2. **turn aside, away**, w. *mē'al* from Pr 4_{15}, w. *'el* to Pr 7_{25}. †
שׂטם: **qal**: impf. וַיִּשְׂטֹם, יִשְׂטְמֵנוּ, תִּשְׂטְמֵנִי, יִשְׂטְמוּנִי: w. acc. or *'al*: **bear a grudge** against, **harbor animosity** toward Gn 27_{41}.
שׂטן: **qal**: impf. יִשְׂטְנוּנִי; inf. שִׂטְנוֹ; pt. pl. cs. שֹׂטְנֵי, sf. שֹׂטְנַי: **bear a grudge** against, **harbor animosity** toward Ps 38_{21}.
שָׂטָן: — 1. **accuser, adversary**: a) human: 1K 5_{18}; b) *mal'ak yhwh* † Nu $22_{22.32}$; — 2. spec. supernatural figure: *haśśāṭān*, **the Satan** † Zc 3_{1f} Jb 1_6-2_7 (14×); > *śāṭān* (proper name) † 1C 21_1.
I **שִׂטְנָה**: **accusation** Ezr 4_6. †
II **שִׂטְנָה**: n. loc. Gn 26_{21}. †
***שִׂיא**: sf. שִׂיאוֹ: **height** Jb 20_6. †
שִׂיאֹן: n. of mountain.
שׂיב: **qal**: pf. שַׂבְתִּי; pt. שָׂב: **be gray, old** 1S 12_2 Jb 15_{10}. †
***שֵׂיב**: sf. שֵׂיבוֹ: gray-headedness, **old age** 1K 14_4. †
שֵׂיבָה: cs. שֵׂיבַת, sf. שֵׂיבָתוֹ, שֵׂיבָתֵךְ: **gray-headedness, old age** Gn 42_{38}; *'îš śêbâ* Dt 32_{25} > *śêbâ* Lv 19_{32} **gray-headed** person; *b^eśêbâ ṭôbâ* in a good old age Gn 15_{15}.
שִׂיג: **bowel movement** 1K 18_{27}. †
שׂיד: **qal**: pf. שַׂדְתָּ: **plaster, whitewash** Dt $27_{2.4}$. †
שִׂיד: **plaster, whitewash, lime** Dt $27_{2.4}$ Is 33_{12} Am 2_1. †
שֵׂיו, שֵׂיהוּ: → שֶׂה.
שׂיח: **qal**: impf. תָּשִׂיחַ, יָשִׂיחַ, אָשִׂיחָה, יָשִׂיחוּ, תְּשִׂיחֶךָ; impv. שִׂיחַ, שִׂיחוּ; inf. שִׂיחַ: **be(come) concerned** w., **occupy one's attention** w., s.thg:

a) in thought, consideration Ps 77_{4}, w. b^{e} Ps 77_{13}; b) in complaint Ps 55_{18}; c) in speaking Ps 69_{13}.

polel: impf. יְשׂוֹחֵחַ, אֲשׂוֹחֵחַ: **occupy oneself** w., **consider** Is 53_{8} Ps 143_{5}. †

I שִׂיחַ: pl. שִׂיחִים: **shrub, bush** Gn 2_{5} 21_{15} Jb $30_{4.7}$. †

II שִׂיחַ: sf. שִׂיחוֹ: **(object of) concern, object of interest** 1S 1_{16} Ps 55_{3}; > **babble** 2K 9_{11}; *śîaḥ lô* has to attend to business (= relieve himself) 1K 18_{27}.

שִׂיחָה: sf. שִׂיחָתִי: **occupation, concern** (of one's thoughts, mind) Ps $119_{97.99}$ Jb 15_{4}. †

(I) שִׂים (580×): **qal**: pf. שָׂם, שָׂמָה, שַׂמְתָּ, שַׂמְתֶּם, sf. שָׂמָהוּ > שָׂמוֹ, שָׂמְתְהוּ, שַׂמַתְנִי, וַיָּשֶׂם, יָשֵׂם, יָשִׂ(י)ם; impf. שָׂמוּךָ, שַׂמְתִּיו, שַׂמְתּוֹ, יָשׂוּם Ex 4_{11}, (וַ)תָּשִׂימִי, אָשִׂים, וָאָשִׂם, Ju 12_{3} rd וָאָשִׂימָה, יָשִׂימוּ, נָשִׂימָה, sf. וַיְשִׂימֵהוּ, יְשִׂימֵנִי, וַיְשִׂימְךָ, יְשִׂימֵם, אֲשִׂימֶנּוּ, אֲשִׂימְךָ; impv. שִׂים, שִׂימָה, שִׂימוּ; inf. cs. שׂוּם, שִׂים, sf. שׂוּמִי, שֻׂמוֹ, שׂוּמוֹ Qr Is 10_{6}, abs. שׂוֹם; pt. שָׂם, שָׂמִים, pass. שִׂים Nu 24_{21}, f. שִׂימָה Kt 2S 13_{32}: — 1. **put, set, place** (s.thg in a location) Gn 2_{8}; — 2. **set up**: obj. stone 1S 7_{12}, ambush Je 9_{7}; obj. *rā'šîm* put in companies 1S 11_{11}; obj. *māṣôr* lay siege Mi 4_{14}; *śâm 'al* **attack** (a town) 1K 20_{12}; *śâm badderek* l^{e} stand in s.one's way 1S 15_{2}; — 3. *śâm 'al* **impose** (a time on s.one) Jb 34_{23}; **set over** Ex 1_{11}; = *śâm 'el* 2S 23_{23}; — 4. set up = **appoint**: w. *melek* 1S 8_{5}; w. *l^{e}'ādôn* Gn 45_{9}; — 5. *śâm lithillâ* bring to honor Zp 3_{19}; *śâm l^{e}negdô* set before them Ps 54_{5}; — 6. **lay, put** Gn 31_{34}; — 7. *śâm derek bên* leave a distance between Gn 30_{36}; *śâm toh^{o}lâ* b^{e} charge w. error Jb 4_{18}, *śâm simlâ 'al* put (a mantle) on Ru 3_{3}; — 8. *śâm b^{e}yādô* **put** in s.one else's hand (= power) Ex 4_{21}; **pick up** (in one's own hand) Ju 4_{21} 1K 20_{6}; = *śâm b^{e}kappô* Ju 12_{3}; *śâm b^{e}fîhā* put in her mouth 2S 14_{3} &c.; — 9. *śâm ('ērābôn)* **deposit** (a pledge) Jb 17_{3}; *śâm 'āšām* give as atonement Is 53_{10}; — 10. *śâm* b^{e} **inflict** (diseases) on Dt 7_{15}, = w. *'al* Ps 109_{5}; *śâm* l^{e} **charge** s.one w. Dt 22_{14}, = w. b^{e} 1S 22_{15}; *śâm dāmîm* b^{e} bring bloodguilt on Dt 22_{8}; — 11. *śâm šēm* l^{e} give a name to Dn 1_{7}; *śâm dibrātô 'el* commit one's cause to Jb 5_{8}, *śâm lifnê* put before Ex 21_{1}, *śâm b^{e}'oznê* enjoin on Ex 17_{14} &c.; — 12. *śâm* w. *'al-libbô* Is 47_{7}, w. *'el-libbô* 2S 13_{33}, w. *b^{e}libbô* 1S 21_{13} take to heart, pay attention to, > *śâm libbô* pay attention to Is 41_{22} > *śâm* Is 41_{20}; — 13. *śâm yādayim* l^{e} seize, **arrest** 2K 11_{16}; — 14. **fix** Gn 24_{47}; — 15. *śâm ḥiṭṭâ* **plant** wheat Is 28_{25}; *śâm dešen* heap up Lv 6_{3}; *śâm mārāq* pour (broth) Ju 6_{19}; — 16. place = **make** Ex 4_{11}; w. 2 acc. make s.thg (into) s.thg Jos 8_{28}; = w. acc. & l^{e} Gn 21_{13}; w. acc. & k^{e} make like Gn 13_{16}; — 17. **fix, define**: boundary Ps 104_{9}, place Ex 21_{13}; w. acc. & l^{e} **assign** s.thg to s.one 1K 20_{34}, **preserve** Gn 45_{7}, give (glory) to Jos 7_{19}, **order** for Ex 8_{8}.

[**hif.**: no form certain; all cited forms txt. prob. corr.: Ez 14_{8} 21_{21} Jb 4_{20}. †]

hof. (or pass. **qal**): impf. וַיּוּשַׂם (for וַיִּישֶׂם Gn 24_{33} & for וַיִּישֶׂם 50_{26}) **be put, laid.** †

[II שִׂים: וְתָשֵׂם Jb 13_{27} & וַתָּשֶׂם: שׂמם ꟻ סמם.]

שִׂישׂ: ꟻ שׂוּשׂ.

*שֵׂךְ: pl. שִׂכִּים: **thorn, splinter** Nu 33_{55}. †

*שֹׂךְ: sf. שֻׂכּוֹ La 2_{6}: fence? garden? but sugg. txt. corr., rd בְּאֻשּׁוֹ. †

cj. שׂכה: **qal**: pf. שָׂכוּ: w. l^{e} **lie in wait for** cj Ps 35_{12}. †

*שֻׂכָּה: pl. שֻׂכּוֹת: **harpoon** Jb 40_{31}. †

שֹׂכֹה: n. loc. ꟻ שׂוֹכֹה.

שֶׂכוּ 1S 19_{22}: rd. שְׁפִי. †

שֶׂכְוִי: **cock** Jb 38_{36}. †

שְׂכַיָה: n. pers.

*שְׂכִיָּה: pl. שְׂכִיּוֹת: **ship** Is 2_{16}. †

שַׂכִּין: **knife** Pr 23_{2}. †

שָׂכִיר: cs. שְׂכִיר, sf. שְׂכִירֶךָ, f. שְׂכִירָה; pl. sf. שְׂכִירֶיהָ: — 1. adj.: rented, hired: animal

Ex 22_{14}, knife Is 7_{20}, soldier (i.e. mercenary) Je 46_{21}; — 2. noun: **day-laborer, hired laborer, wage-earner** Ex 12_{45}; for a year Lv 25_{53}; *śᵉkar śākîr* Dt 15_{18}.

שׂכךְ: **qal**: pf. וְשַׂכֹּתִי: **hold** (one's hand) **to block, screen off** (a view) Ex 33_{22}. †

polel: impf. sf. תְּשֹׂכְכֵנִי: **interlace, weave together** Jb 10_{11}. †

I **שָׂכַל**: **qal**: pf. ׳שׂ: **have success** 1S 18_{30} (but txt. ?). †

piel: יְשַׂכֵּל Is 44_{25} F סכל. †

hif.: pf. הִשְׂכִּיל, הִשְׂכַּלְתִּי, הִשְׂכִּילוּ; impf. תַּשְׂכִּיל, תַּשְׂכֵּל, אַשְׂכִּילָה, אַשְׂכִּילְךָ; impv. הַשְׂכִּילוּ; inf. הַשְׂכִּיל, הַשְׂכִּילְךָ, abs. הַשְׂכֵּ(י)ל; pt. מַשְׂכִּיל, מַשְׂכֶּלֶת, מַשְׂכִּ(י)לִים: — 1. **understand, see** (= have insight) Dt 32_{29}; w. *'el* gain insight into Ne 8_{13}, w. *bᵉ*, *'al* pay close attention to Dn 9_{13} Pr 16_{20}; — 2. abs. **understand, see** (= have insight) Is 41_{20}; *'iššâ maśkelet* sensible, intelligent wife Pr 19_{14}; *haśkîl* (w.) insight Je 3_{15} Pr 21_{11}; = *haśkêl* Pr 1_3; — 3. **make** (s.one) **keen, clever** Gn 3_6; — 4. **have success** 1S 18_5; w. acc. in s.thg 1K 2_3, = w. *bᵉ* 2K 18_7; — 5. **act w.** (religious) **insight, devotion, piety** Is 52_{13}; w. *lᵉ* **show onesf. devoted to, fit for** 2C 30_{22}.

II **שׂכל**: **piel**: pf. שִׂכֵּל: **cross** (= lay crosswise) Gn 48_{14}. †

שֶׂכֶל (5×) & **שֵׂכֶל** (8×): שֶׂכֶל; sf. שִׂכְלוֹ: **insight, understanding** Pr 12_8; in bad sense Dn 8_{25}; *'îš śekel* sensible man Ezr 8_{18}, *śekel millîm* sensible words Pr 23_9.

שִׂכְלוּת: = סִכְלוּת Ec 1_{17}. †

שָׂכַר: **qal**: pf. ׳שׂ, sf. שְׂכָרוֹ, שְׂכַרְתִּיךָ; impf. וַיִּשְׂכֹּר, וַיִּשְׂכְּרֵנִי; inf. לִשְׂכֹּר, שָׂכֹר; pt. שֹׂכֵר, שֹׂכְרִים, = סֹכְרִים Ezr 4_5, pass. שָׂכוּר: **hire** (s.one for wages) 2K 7_6; w. *bᵉ* + wages Gn 30_{16}.

nif.: pf. נִשְׂכָּרוּ: **(have to) hire onesf. out**, w. *bᵉ* + wages 1S 2_5. †

hitp.: pt. מִשְׂתַּכֵּר: **hire onesf. out** Hg 1_6. †

I **שָׂכָר**: cs. שְׂכַר, sf. שְׂכָרוֹ, שְׂכָרֵךְ: **wages** Gn 30_{32f}; *śᵉkārᵉkā 'ālay* your wages I shall give 30_{28}; **reward** (given by God) Gn 15_1; *bā' biśkārô* it is reckoned in his wages Ex 22_{14}; **fare** (for journey) Jon 1_3; **expenses, maintenance** Zc 8_{10}.

II **שָׂכָר**: n. pers. 1C 11_{35} 26_4. †

שֶׂכֶר: **wages** Pr 11_{18}; *'ōśê śeker* **hired laborers** Is 19_{10}. †

שְׂלָו (Qr שְׂלָיו): pl. שַׂלְוִים: **quail**, *Coturnix coturnix* Ex 16_{13} Nu 11_{31f} Ps 105_{40}. †

שַׂלְמָא: n. pers.

I **שַׂלְמָה**: cs. שַׂלְמַת, sf. שַׂלְמָתוֹ; pl. שַׂלְמוֹת, sf. שַׂלְמֹתַי, שַׂלְמוֹתֵיכֶם: **mantle, wrapper** (as covering for sleep) 1K 10_{25}.

II **שַׂלְמָה**: n. pers. Ru 4_{20}. †

שַׂלְמוֹן: n. pers.

שַׂלְמַי, **שַׂלְמָי**: n. pers.

שְׂמֹאל & **שְׂמֹאול**: sf. שְׂמֹאלוֹ, שְׂמֹאלָם, שְׂמֹאלֶךָ: — 1. **left (side)** Jon 4_{11}; *miśśᵉmō'l* on the left Ex 14_{22}, *(haś)śᵉmō'l* to the left Gn 13_9 2K 22_2; *'al-śᵉmō'lekā* to the left 2S 2_{21}, &c.; — 2. *yad śᵉmō'lô* his **left hand** Ju 3_{21} > *śᵉmō'lô* his left hand Gn 48_{14}; — 3. unwholesome, **unlucky** Ec 10_2; — 4. **northwards**: *'el-miśśᵉmō'l* Jos 19_{27}; *śᵉmō'l* Is 54_3; *'al-śᵉmō'lēk* north of you Ez 16_{46}.

שׂמאל: **hif.**: impf. אַשְׂמְאִילָה, תַּשְׂמְאִילוּ; impv. הַשְׂמִילִי; inf. הַשְׂמִיל; pt. מַשְׂמְאלִים: — 1. **go to the left** Gn 13_9 2S 14_{19} Is 30_{21} Ez 21_{21}; — 2. **use the left hand** 1C 12_2. †

שְׂמָאלִי: f. שְׂמָאלִית: **(on the) left** 1K 7_{21}.

שָׂמַח: **qal**: pf. ׳שׂ, שָׂמֵחַ, שָׂמֵחָה, שָׂמַחְתִּי, שָׂמֵחוּ, שְׂמַחְתֶּם, שָׂמֵחוּ; impf. יִשְׂמַח, וַתִּשְׂמַח, תִּשְׂמְחִי, נִשְׂמְחָה, תִּשְׂמַחְנָה, יִשְׂמָחוּ, אֶשְׂמְחָה, אֶשְׂמַח; impv. שְׂמַח, שִׂמְחִי, שְׂמֵחִי, שִׂמְחוּ; inf. שְׂמֹ(ו)חַ: — 1. **rejoice** 1S 11_9, w. *bᵉ* in Dt 33_{18}; = w. *lᵉ* Is 14_8, *'al* Is 39_2; w. *lᵉ* + inf. 1S 6_{13}; *wayyiśmaḥ liqra't* went with joy to meet Ju 19_3; subj. Y. Ps 104_{31}; *bᵉ* + Y. Ps 32_{11}; — 2. **be joyful, glad** Dt 12_7; *lifnê yhwh* Dt 12_{12}.

piel: pf. שִׂמַּח, שִׂמַּחְתָּ, sf. שִׂמְּחָהוּ, שִׂמַּחְתִּים,

שִׂמְּחוּךָ; impf. יְשַׂמַּח, יְשַׂמְּחוּ, יְשַׂמְּחֶנָּה; impv. שַׂמַּח, שַׂמְּחֵנוּ; inf. שַׂמֵּחַ; pt. מְשַׂמֵּחַ, pl. cs. מְשַׂמְּחֵי: — 1. **make** (s.one or s.thg) **glad**: obj. pers. Je 20_{15}, obj. *lēb* Ps 19_{9}; subj. wine Ec 10_{19}, subj. God Is 56_{7}; — 2. **allow** (s.one) **to rejoice** La 2_{17}.

hif.: pf. הִשְׂמַחְתָּ: **make** (s.one) **rejoice** Ps 89_{43}. †

שָׂמֵחַ: f. שְׂמֵחָה; pl. שְׂמֵחִים, cs. שְׂמֵחֵי & שִׂמְחֵי Is 24_{7}: **filled w. joy, glad** 1K 1_{40}; *śāmē^{a}ḥ lēb* Pr 15_{13}; w. *l^{e}* over Am 6_{13}, = w. gen. Ps 35_{26}; w. *l^{e}* + inf. Pr 2_{14}.

שִׂמְחָה: cs. שִׂמְחַת, sf. שִׂמְחָתוֹ; pl. שְׂמָח(וֹ)ת: **joy** (both emotion & its manifestation) Is 16_{10}; *ʿāśâ śimḥâ* **hold a feast** Ne 8_{12}.

שְׂמִיכָה: **curtain** (separating women's section of tent) (oth.: **rug** or the like) Ju 4_{18}. †

***שׂמל** **hif.**: ⟶ שמאל.

שַׂמְלָה: n. pers.

שִׂמְלָה: cs. שִׂמְלַת, sf. שִׂמְלָתוֹ; pl. שְׂמָלוֹת, sf. שִׂמְלֹתָיו: **mantle, wrapper** (both garment and under-blanket) Gn 9_{23}.

שַׂמְלַי: n. pers.

שׂמם: **hif.**: impf. וַתָּשֶׂם 2K 9_{30} (not שׂוּם!): ⟶ סמם.

שְׂמָמִית: **gecko**, *Hemidactylus turcicus* & oth. Pr 30_{28}. †

שָׂנֵא: **qal**: pf. שׂ׳, שָׂנֵאת, שָׂנֵאתִי, שָׂנְאוּ, שְׂנֵאתֶם, sf. שְׂנֵאָהּ, שְׂנֵאתִיהָ, שְׂנֵאתַנִי, שְׂנֵאתִים, שְׂנֵאָהוּ, שְׂנֵאוּנִי; impf. יִשְׂנָא, אֶשְׂנָא, יִשְׂנְאוּ, יִשְׂנָאֶךָ; impv. שִׂנְאוּ; inf. שְׂנֹא, > שִׂנְאַת Pr 8_{13}, שָׂנֹא; pt. שׂ(וֹ)נֵא, sf. שֹׂנְאוֹ, pl. cs. שֹׂנְאֵי, sf. שֹׂנְאָיו, שֹׂנְאֵינוּ, שֹׂנְאֵיכֶם, pl. f. sf. שֹׂנְאֹתַיִךְ, pass. f. שְׂנוּאָה: — 1. **hate** Gn 26_{27}; obj. God Ex 20_{5}, subj. God Dt 12_{31}; subj. *nefeš* 2S 5_{8}, of God Ps 11_{5}; — 2. **be unable** (or **unwilling**) **to put up with, slight** (one's wife) Dt 22_{13}; *ś^{e}nû'â* Gn 29_{31}; — 3. *śōnē'* **enemy** Gn 24_{60}; *śōn^{e}'ê yhwh* 2C 19_{2}; *śōnē' lô* one of his enemies Dt 4_{42}; — 4. *śōn^{e}'ê beṣaʿ* those who disdain profit Ex 18_{21}.

nif.: impf. יִשָּׂנֵא: **be hated** Pr 14_{20}. †

piel: pt. sf. מְשַׂנְאִי, pl. cs. מְשַׂנְאֵי, sf. מְשַׂנְאֶיךָ, מְשַׂנְאָיו: **enemy** 2S 22_{41}.

שִׂנְאָה: cs. שִׂנְאַת, sf. שִׂנְאָתוֹ, שִׂנְאָתֶיךָ Ez 35_{11}: **hate, hatred** Ps 109_{5}; *miśśin'ātô 'ōtām* because he hates them Dt 9_{28}.

שָׂנִיא*: f. שְׂנִיאָה: **slighted, disdained** Dt 21_{15}. †

שְׂנִיר: n. of mountain.

I **שֵׂעָר, שָׂעִיר**: pl. f. שְׂעִרֹת: **hairy** Gn 27_{11}; **shaggy** Dn 8_{21}. †

II **שָׂעִיר**: = I: cs. שְׂעִיר; pl. שְׂעִירִים, cs. שְׂעִירֵי: **he-goat**; oft. *ś^{e}ʿîr ʿizzîm* Gn 37_{31}.

III **שָׂעִיר**: = I: pl. שְׂעִיר(י)ם: (hairy) **demon** (in shape of he-goat) Lv 17_{7} Is 13_{21} 34_{14} 2C 11_{15}. †

IV ***שָׂעִיר**: pl. שְׂעִירִים: **rain-showers** Dt 32_{2}. †

I **שֵׂעִיר**: n. of mountain: **Seir** (in Edom).

II **שֵׂעִיר**: n. of mountain in Judah Jos 15_{10}. †

III **שֵׂעִיר**: n. pers. Gn 36_{20f} 1C 1_{38} 2C $25_{11.14}$. †

I **שְׂעִירָה**: cs. שְׂעִירַת: w. *ʿizzîm*, **(she-)goat** Lv 4_{28} 5_{6}. †

II ***שְׂעִירָה**: loc. שְׂעִירָתָה: n. loc. Jos 3_{26}. †

שְׂעִפִּים: sf. שְׂעִפַּי: **disquieting thoughts** Jb 4_{13} 20_{2}. †

I **שׂער**: **qal**: pf. שָׂעֲרוּ; impf. יִשְׂעֲרוּ; impv. שַׂעֲרוּ: **suffer one's hair to stand on end, bristle** (w. horror) Je 2_{12} Ez 27_{35} 32_{10}. †

II **שׂער**: **qal**: impf. sf. יִשְׂעָרֶנּוּ: carry off in a gale? Ps 58_{10}. †

nif.: pf. נִשְׂעֲרָה: **it is stormy** (weather) Ps 50_{3}. †

piel: impf. וִישָׂעֲרֵהוּ: **sweep away in a gale** Jb 27_{21}. †

hitp.: impf. יִשְׂתָּעֵר: w. *ʿal* **rush in upon** Dn 11_{40}. †

III **שׂער**: **qal**: pf. שְׂעָרוּם: **know about** Dt 32_{17}. †

I **שַׂעַר**: שָׂעַר: **bristling, shudder(ing)** Ez 27_{35} 32_{10} Jb 18_{20}. †

II **שַׂעַר**: **gale** Is 28_{2}. †

שָׂעָר: ⟶ שָׂעִיר.

שֵׂעָר: cs. שַׂעַר & שְׂעַר, sf. שְׂעָרוֹ, שְׂעָרָהּ >

שְׂעָרָה (!) Lv 13$_{4}$, שְׂעָרֵךְ & שַׂעְרֵךְ SS 4$_{1}$ 6$_{5}$: **hair** (collective): of head 2S 14$_{26}$ & oft.; *śa'ar hāraglayim* pubic hair Is 7$_{20}$, > *śē'ār* Ez 16$_{7}$; *ba'al sē'ār* 2K 1$_{8}$ hairy man? man w. hair-garment?; *'addeṛet śē'ār* hair-garment Gn 25$_{25}$.

שַׂעֲרָה: cs. שַׂעֲרַת, sf. שַׂעֲרָתוֹ: **(a single) hair** 1K 1$_{52}$.

שְׂעָרָה: **gale** Na 1$_{3}$ Jb 9$_{17}$. †

שְׂעֹרָה: pl. שְׂעֹרִים: **barley**, *Hordeum sativum*: the plant Ex 9$_{31}$, the kind of grain sg. Dt 8$_{8}$, pl. 2S 14$_{30}$, grains 1K 5$_{8}$, kind of flour 2K 4$_{42}$; *qeṣîr śe'ōrîm* barley harvest 2S 21$_{9}$.

שְׂעֹרִים: n. pers. 1C 24$_{8}$. †

שָׂפָה: cs. שְׂפַת, sf. שְׂפָתוֹ; du. שְׂפָתַיִם, שְׂפָתָיִם, cs. שִׂפְתֵי, sf. שְׂפָתֵיהֶם, שְׂפָתֵימוֹ, שְׂפָתָיו, also pl. cs. שִׂפְתוֹת, sf. שִׂפְתוֹתֶיךָ: — 1. **lip** (as physical organ) Is 6$_{7}$; — 2. **lip** (as organ of speech) 2K 18$_{20}$; — 3. lip = manner of speaking, **language** Gn 11$_{1}$, *śefat kena'an* Is 19$_{18}$; *śefat lāšôn* (idle) talk of tongues Ez 36$_{3}$; *śefat lō' yāda'tî* language that I did not understand Ps 81$_{6}$; — 4. **shore, bank** (of river): *śefat hayyām* Gn 22$_{17}$, *śefat hayyardēn* 2K 2$_{13}$; **edge** (of altar, curtains) Ex 26$_{4}$; **brim** (of vessel) 1K 7$_{23}$.

שׂפח: **piel**: pf. שִׂפַּח: **make scabby** Is 3$_{17}$. †

שָׂפָם: sf. שְׂפָמוֹ: **moustache** Lv 13$_{45}$ Ez 24$_{17.22}$ Mi 3$_{7}$, w. *'āśâ* trim 2S 19$_{25}$. †

שִׂפְמוֹת: n. loc.

שׂפן: **qal**: pt. pass. pl. cs. שְׂפֻנֵי: **conceal, hide** Dt 33$_{19}$. †

I שׂפק: **qal**: impf. יִשְׂפֹּק: w. *kappayim*, **clap** one's hands (in malice) Jb 27$_{23}$. †

hif.: impf. יַשְׂפִּיקוּ: **strike** hands w. (in bargain) ? Is 2$_{6}$; ↗ II & comm. †

II שׂפק: **qal**: impf. יִשְׂפֹּק: w. *le*, **suffice, be enough** for 1K 20$_{10}$. †

? **hif.**: impf. יַשְׂפִּיקוּ: **abound** ? Is 2$_{6}$; ↗ I. †

*שֶׂפֶק: sf. שִׂפְקוֹ: ↗ *סֶפֶק.

שַׂק: שָׂק, sf. שַׂקּוֹ; pl. שַׂקִּים, sf. שַׂקֵּיהֶם: poor quality material of goat-hair: — 1. **sack-cloth** (as a material) 2S 21$_{10}$; — 2. **sack-cloth** (as garment covering bare loins during mourning) Gn 37$_{34}$; — 3. **sack** Gn 42$_{25}$.

שׂקד: **nif.**: pf. נִשְׂקַד La 1$_{14}$: rd נִשְׁקַד (27 mss.). †

שׂקר: **piel**: pt. מְשַׂקְּרוֹת: w. *'ênayim*: **toss seductive glances** Is 3$_{16}$. †

שַׂר (420×): sf. שַׂרְכֶם; pl. שָׂרִים, cs. שָׂרֵי, sf. שָׂרָיו: (I) outside Isr.: — 1. representative of the king, **official** Gn 12$_{15}$; — 2. **chief, ruler** 1S 18$_{30}$; — 3. **leader** of a group, profession, district Gn 21$_{22}$; — (II) in Isr.: — 4. leading person, **chief** (in series of named offices) 2S 3$_{38}$; — 5. **leader, official** of place, group 1K 4$_{2}$; — 6. oft. leader of a military group of spec. size 1S 17$_{18}$, or of temple or priests 1C 24$_{5}$ Ezr 8$_{24}$; — 7. spec.: *hāyâ leśar 'al/le* 1S 22$_{2}$ 2S 23$_{19}$; — (III) † higher being, guardian angel Dn 10$_{20f}$ 12$_{1}$; God is *śar śārîm* Dn 8$_{25}$; cf. Jos 5$_{14f}$.

שַׂרְאֶצֶר: n. pers.

שׂרג: **pual**: impf. יְשֹׂרָגוּ: **be intertwined, interlaced** Jb 40$_{17}$. †

hitp.: impf. יִשְׂתָּרְגוּ: **intertwine onesf.** La 1$_{14}$. †

שׂרד: **qal**: pf. שָׂרְדוּ: **run away** Jos 10$_{20}$. †

שְׂרָד: *bigdê (haś)śerād*, special kind of woven material, corduroy? Ex 31$_{10}$ 35$_{19}$ 39$_{1.41}$. †

שֶׂרֶד: some kind of marker, sugg. **reddle (red chalk)** Is 44$_{13}$. †

שָׂרָה: **qal**: pf. שׂ׳, שָׂרִיתָ; impf. cj. וַיָּשַׂר Ho 12$_{5}$: **contend, strive with**: w. *'im* Gn 32$_{29}$, *'ēt* Ho 12$_{4}$, *'el* cj Ho 12$_{5}$. †

I שָׂרָה: cs. שָׂרָתִי La 1$_{1}$; pl. שָׂרוֹת, sf. שָׂרוֹתֶיהָ, שָׂרוֹתֵיהֶם: **lady, gentlewoman** Ju 5$_{29}$ 1K 11$_{3}$ Is 49$_{23}$ La 1$_{1}$ Est 1$_{18}$. †

II שָׂרָה: n. pers. f. **Sarah**.

שְׂרוּג: n. pers.

שְׂרוֹךְ: *śerôk na'al* **sandal-thong** Is 5$_{27}$, > obj. of minimum value Gn 14$_{23}$. †

שְׂרוּקִים: ↗ שָׂרֹק.

שֶׂרַח: n. pers. f.

שׂרט: **qal**: impf. יִשְׂרְטוּ; inf. שָׂרוֹט: **make incisions, tattoo** Lv 21_5. †

nif.: impf. יִשָּׂרֵטוּ: **get (one's skin) torn up** Zc 12_3. †

שֶׂרֶט: **incision, tattoo** Lv 19_{28}. †

***שָׂרֶטֶת**: שָׂרֶטֶת: **incision, tattoo** Lv 21_5. †

שָׂרַי: שָׂרַי: n. pers. f. **Sarai**; > ℱ II שָׂרָה.

***שָׂרִיג**: pl. שָׂרִיגִים, sf. שָׂרִיגֶיהָ: **branch** (of vine) Gn $40_{10 \cdot 12}$ Jl 1_7. †

I **שָׂרִיד**: pl. שְׂרִידִים, cs. שְׂרִידֵי, sf. שְׂרִידָיו: **survivor** (of battle, then in genl.) 2K 10_{11}; *śe͏rîdê ḥāreb* Je 31_2.

II **שָׂרִיד**: n. loc. Jos $19_{10 \cdot 12}$. †

שְׂרָיָה: n. pers.

שְׂרָיָהוּ: n. pers.

שִׂרְי(וֹ)ן: n. of mountain, = Hermon.

***שָׂרִיק**: pl. f. שְׂרִיקוֹת: **carded** (flax) Is 19_9, but txt? cj. rd. pt., ℱ cj I שׂרק. †

שׂרך: **piel**: pt. f. מְשָׂרֶכֶת: w. *de͏rākîm* **interweave** (tracks) Je 2_{23}. †

שַׂר־סְכִים: n. pers.

שׂרע: **qal**: pt. pass. שָׂרוּעַ: a kind of bodily mutilation or deformity, of men Lv 21_{18} & animals Lv 22_{23}, trad. mutilated or deformed ear or nose. †

hitp.: inf. הִשְׂתָּרֵעַ: **stretch** (onesf.) **out** Is 28_{20}. †

***שַׂרְעַפִּים**: sf. שַׂרְעַפַּי: **disquieting thoughts** Ps 94_{19} 139_{23}. †

שָׂרַף: **qal**: pf. ׳שׂ, שָׂרַפְתִּי, שָׂרְפוּ, sf. שְׂרָפָהּ, שְׂרָפָהָ, שְׂרָפְתָם; impf. תִּשְׂרֹף, וָאֶשְׂרֹף, יִשְׂרְפוּ, תִּשְׂרְפֶנּוּ, וַיִּשְׂרְפָה, נִשְׂרְפָה, תִּשְׂרְפוּן, תִּשְׂרְפוּ, וַיִּשְׂרְפוּהָ; inf. שְׂרֹף, שָׂרְפוֹ, שָׂרוֹף; pt. שֹׂרֵף, pass. שְׂרֻפָה, שְׂרוּפָה, שְׂרֻפִים, שְׂרֻפוֹת: — 1. **burn** (trans.): bones 1K 13_2, children (as religious act) Dt 12_{31}, town Dt 13_{17}; oft. w. *bā'ēš* Ex 29_{14}; **cauterize** (spot on skin) Lv 13_{55}; — 2. cogn. acc. Lv 10_6; — 3. *śāraf le͏bênîm liśfērâ* burn bricks thoroughly (i.e. not dry them in sun) Gn 11_3.

nif.: impf. יִשָּׂרֵף, יִשָּׂרְפוּ, תִּשָּׂרַפְנָה: **be burned** (oft. w. *bā'ēš*) Gn 38_{24}.

pual (qal pass.?): pf. שֹׂרַף: **be burned** (of animal) Lv 10_{16}. †

I **שָׂרָף**: pl. שְׂרָפִים: *nāḥāš śārāf* **fiery serpent** Dt 8_{15}, pl. Nu 21_6; *śārāf me͏'ôfēf* Is 14_{29} 30_6 winged serpent (unidentifiable); — 2. bronze serpent Nu 21_8; — 3. **seraph**, mythological six-winged creature Is $6_{2 \cdot 6}$. †

II **שָׂרָף**: n. pers. 1C 4_{22}. †

שְׂרֵפָה: cs. שְׂרֵפַת: — 1. **burning, conflagration** Is 9_4; *har śe͏rēfâ* burned-out mountain Je 51_{25}; — 2. Gn 11_3 fire-hardened bricks; — 3. cremation fire 2C 16_{14}; — 4. **burned-out place** Dt 29_{22}.

cj **שׂרק**: cj **qal**: pt. pl. f. שֹׂרְקוֹת: **card** (flax) cj Is 19_9. †

***שָׂרֹק**: pl. שְׂרֻקִּים, sf. שְׂרוּקֶּיהָ: a color of grapes Is 16_8 & horses Zc 1_8; some: bright red; oth. pale yellow, chestnut. †

שׂוֹרֵק, שֹׂרֵק: **choice** (kind of) **grapes** of spec. color, ℱ *שָׂרֹק Is 5_2 Je 2_{21}. †

שֹׂרֵקָה: **vine w. choice grapes** of spec. color, ℱ *שָׂרֹק Gn 49_{11}. †

שׂרר: **qal**: impf. יָסֹר (mss. יָשֹׂר) 1C 15_{22}, וַיָּשַׂר, יָשֹׂרוּ; pt. שֹׂרֵר: — 1. **rule** Ju 9_{22} Is 32_1 Pr 8_{16} Est 1_{22}; — 2. **direct, superintend** 1C 15_{22}. †

hif.: pf. הֵשִׂירוּ (!): **make, appoint a** *śar* Ho 8_4. †

hitp.: impf. תִּשְׂתָּרֵר; inf. הִשְׂתָּרֵר: **lord it** (over s.one) Nu 16_{13}. †

שָׂשׂוֹן: cs. שְׂשׂוֹן: **joy, exultation** Is 22_{13}.

שֵׂת: < ℱ שְׂאֵת.

שָׂתַם: **qal**: pf. ׳שׂ: **obstruct** (the way for s.thg) La 3_8; cj. pt. pass. cs. שְׂתֻם [הָעָיִן] w. closed eye Nu $24_{3 \cdot 15}$. †

שׂתר: **nif.**: impf. וַיִּשָּׂתְרוּ: **break out** (subj. tumors) 1S 5_9. †

שׂ

שֶׁ w. doubling of following cons., שָׁ, שֶׁ if doubling impossible, or before $\bar{a}$ or $\bar{o}$, > שְׁ before הֵם Ec 3_{18}; alw. proclitic: 139 × : Ec 68 ×, SS 32 × ; usage identical w. אֲשֶׁר: a) introducing nominal clause after noun: *kaḥōl šeʿal* like the sand wh. is upon Ju 7_{12}; *šellî* my SS 1_{6}, *bešellî* for my sake Jon 1_{12}; b) introducing verbal clause: *šehikkâ* who struck down Ps 135_{8}; c) in rel. clause w. deferred adv. or prep. + sf.: *še- … bāh* where SS 8_{8}, *šeʿiṭṭerâ lô* w. wh. she crowned him SS 3_{11}; w. preceding *ke* Ec 12_{7}; note also *šekkullām* who all, all of whom SS 4_{2} 6_{6}; d) after vb. of saying, knowing, &c.: **that**: *šāʾattâ* that it is thou Ju 6_{17}; *ʿad-ša* **until** Ju 5_{7}; > **for** SS 5_{7}.

שָׁ, שֶׁ, שְׁ: ⸢ שַׁ.

שׂא: ⸢ שׂוֹא.

שׁאב: **qal**: pf. שְׁאַבְתֶּם; impf. וַתִּשְׁאַב, וַתִּשְׁאָב, יִשְׁאֲבוּן, וַיִּשְׁאֲבוּ, אֶשְׁאָב; impv. שַׁאֲבִי; inf. שְׁאֹב; pt. שֹׁאֵב, pl. cs. שֹׁאֲבֵי, f. שֹׁאֲבֹת: obj. *mayim*, **draw** (water) Gn 24_{13}; abs. Gn 24_{11}.

שׁאג: **qal**: pf. שָׁאָג; impf. יִשְׁאַג, יִשְׁאָג, יִשְׁאֲגוּ, יִשְׁאָגוּ; inf. שָׁאֹג; pt. שׁ(וֹ)אֵג, שֹׁאֲגִים: **roar** (of lion) Ju 14_{5}; metaph. of Y. Am 1_{2}, of foes Ps 74_{4}, of thunder Jb 37_{4}.

שְׁאָגָה: cs. שַׁאֲגַת, sf. שַׁאֲגָתִי; pl. sf. שַׁאֲגֹתַי: — 1. **roaring** (of lion) Is 5_{29}; — 2. **bawling, groaning** (of s.one praying) Ps 22_{2}, pl. Jb 3_{24}.

I **שׁאה**: **qal**: pf. שָׁאוּ: **lie desolate** Is 6_{11}. †
nif.: impf. תִּשָּׁאֶה, cj. וַתִּשָּׁא: **be laid waste** Is 6_{11} (but txt.?), cj. Na 1_{5}. †
hif.: inf. הַשְׁאוֹת Is 37_{26}, > לַהְשׁוֹת 2K 19_{25}: w. acc. & *gallîm*, **turn** s.thg **into desolate** (heaps of stones). †

II **שׁאה**: **nif.**: impf. יִשָּׁאוּן: **be in an uproar** Is 17_{12f}. †

III **שׁאה**: **hitp.**: pt. cs. מִשְׁתָּאֵה: **stand gazing** Gn 24_{21}. †

שֹׁאָה: ⸢ שׁוֹאָה.

שׁאוה Pr 1_{27}: rd שׁוֹאָה Qr.

שְׁאוֹל & 1K 2_{6} Jb 17_{16} שְׁאֹל: loc. שְׁאוֹלָה; f.: **Sheol, underworld**, abode of the dead Gn 37_{35}.

שָׁאוּל: n. pers., **Saul**.

שָׁאוּלִי: gent. of שָׁאוּל.

I **שָׁאוֹן**: **desolation, waste** Ps 40_{3}. †

II **שָׁאוֹן**: cs. שְׁאוֹן, sf. שְׁאוֹנָהּ: **din, uproar**: of crowd Is 5_{14}, water Is 17_{13}.

שְׁאָט: ⸢ II שׁוּט.

שְׁאָט: sf. שָׁאטְךָ < *שְׁאָטְךָ: **scorn** Ez $25_{6 \cdot 15}$ 36_{5}. †

שְׁאִיָּה: **desolation** Is 24_{12}. †

שָׁאַל: **qal**: pf. שָׁאַלְתְּ, שָׁאֲלָה, שְׁאֵלָה, שָׁאָל, ש׳, שְׁאֵלְךָ, שְׁאֶלְךָ, sf. שְׁאֶלְתֶּם, שָׁאֲלוּ, שְׁאֵלוּ, שְׁאֵלוּנוּ, שְׁאִלְתִּיו, שְׁאִלְתִּיהוּ; impf. יִשְׁאַל, יִשְׁאָלוּן, יִשְׁאֲלוּ, אֶשְׁאֲלָה, אֶשְׁאַל, תִּשְׁאַל, יִשְׁאָלוּנִי, וָאֶשְׁאָלֵם, יִשְׁאָלְךָ, נִשְׁאֲלָה; impv. לִשְׁאָל־, שְׁאוֹל, שְׁאָלוּנִי, שַׁאֲלוּ, שַׁאֲלִי, שְׁאַל; inf. שָׁאוֹל; pt. שֹׁאֵל, שֹׁאֶלֶת, שֹׁאֲלִים, pass. שָׁאוּל; יִשָּׁאֵל Pr 20_{4} = יִשְׁאַל Kt & וְשָׁאַל Qr: — 1. **ask** (a question): obj. pers. to whom qn. is asked Gn 32_{18}; obj. *pî yhwh* Jos 9_{14}, *ʾôb* Dt 18_{11}; w. 2 acc. (pers. & thing) Ps 137_{3}; w. *lēʾmōr* Gn 38_{21}; followed by indir. qn. Ju 13_{6}; w. *ʿal* about Is 45_{11}, w. *le* for Gn 32_{30}; w. *le* + pers. 2K 8_{6}; *šāʾal lô lešālôm* ask how he is Gn 43_{27}; abs. Dt 13_{15}; — 2. *šāʾal be* **inquire of, consult**: *bāʾôb* 1C 10_{13}; *beyhwh*: actually, ask by invoking Y. 1S 10_{22}; *bidbar hāʾelōhîm* 2S 16_{23}; *šāʾal* *lô b^{e}mišpāṭ hā'ûrîm* ask him for the decision of the U. Nu 27_{21}; — 3. **ask** for s.thg, **request, demand**: son 2K 4_{28}, water Ju 5_{25} &c.; from s.one: *min* Ps 2_8, *mē'im* Dt 18_{16}, *mē'ēt* Jos 15_{18}; *hiqšâ liš'ôl* ask s.thg difficult 2K 2_{10}; w. 2 acc. ask s.thg of s.one Is 58_2; — 4. **wish for, desire**: obj. *šālôm* wish for prosperity for s.one Ps 122_6; *wayyiš'al 'et-nafšô lāmût* wished he might die 1K 19_4; — 5. *šā'ûl* **borrowed** 2K 6_5.

nif.: pf. נִשְׁאַל, נִשְׁאַלְתִּי; inf. נִשְׁאֹל: **ask** (for onesf.) **leave of absence** 1S $20_{6.28}$ Ne 13_6. †

piel: pf. שִׁאֲלוּ; impf. יְשָׁאֲלוּ: **inquire** 2S 20_{18}; — 2. **beg** (for alms) Ps 109_{10}. †

hif.: pf. sf. הִשְׁאִלְתִּהוּ; impf. וַיַּשְׁאִלוּם: let (s.one) ask; therefore **let (s.one) have what he asks** Ex 12_{36}; **lend** (s.one) to (*l^e*) s.one (whether or not the latter asks) 1S 1_{28}. †

שָׁאֻל: n. pers.

שְׁאָלָה Is 7_{11}: rd. שְׁאֹלָה.

שְׁאֵלָה: sf. שְׁאֵלָתִי, שֶׁאֱלָתִי, שְׁאֵלָתֵךְ > 1S 1_{17} שֶׁאֱלָתָם, שֵׁלָתֵךְ: **request**: w. *šā'al* 1K 2_{16}; *nātan š^e'ēlâ* grant a request 1S 1_{27}; *tābô' š^e'ēlâ* request is granted Jb 6_8.

שְׁאַלְתִּיאֵל: n. pers.

שׁאן: **palal**: pf. שַׁאֲנַן, שַׁאֲנָנוּ: **be at ease, untroubled** Je 30_{10}.

שְׁאָן: ↗ n. loc. בֵּית־שְׁאָן.

שַׁאֲנָן: pl. שַׁאֲנַנִּים, f. שַׁאֲנַנּוֹת: **at ease, untroubled** Is 32_9, **undisturbed** Is 32_{18}.

***שׁאס**: שֹׁאסַיִךְ Je 30_{16}; ↗ שׁסס.

שׁאף: **qal**: pf. שָׁאֲפָה, שָׁאֲפוּ, sf. שְׁאָפַנִי; impf. יִשְׁאַף, אֶשְׁאַף, וְאֶשְׁאֲפָה; inf. שְׁאֹף; pt. שֹׁאֲפִים: **gasp, pant for**: obj. breath Je 2_{24}, ellipt. Is 42_{14}; obj. shadow Jb 7_2, night Jb 36_{20}; **snap at** s.one, **hound** Ps 56_2.

שָׁאַר: **qal**: pf. 'שׁ: **remain** (= be left over) 1S 16_{11}. †

nif. (90×): pf. נִשְׁאַר, נִשְׁאַר, נִשְׁאֲרָה, נִשְׁאֲרָה, נִשְׁאַרְתִּי, נִשְׁאֲרוּ; impf. יִשָּׁאֵר, יִשָּׁאֵר, וַיִּשָּׁאֲרוּ, תִּשָּׁאַרְנָה; וְנִאשֲׁאַר Ez 9_8 = וָאֶשָּׁאֵר or וְנִשְׁאָר; וָאֵשֵׁר Ez 3_{15} ↗ below; pt. נִשְׁאָר, נִשְׁאֶרֶת, נִשְׁאֶרֶת, נִשְׁאָרִים, נִשְׁאָרוֹת: **be left over, remain** Gn 7_{23}; *hanniš'ār baddām* what remains of the blood Lv 5_9; *wā'ēšēr* < **wā'eššā'ēr* I restrained myself, held back (?) Ez 3_{15}.

hif.: pf. הִשְׁאִיר, הִשְׁאַרְתִּי, הִשְׁאִירוּ, הִשְׁאַרְנוּ; impf. יַשְׁאִיר, יַשְׁאִ(י)רוּ, נַשְׁאֵר; inf. הַשְׁאִיר: **leave** (s.thg or s.one remaining) 1K 15_{29}; **have left** Am 5_3.

שְׁאָר (favorite word of Is.): **remainder, remnant**: of trees Is 10_{19}, of Isr. 10_{20}; in end-time Is 10_{21f}.

שְׁאֵר: sf. שְׁאֵרוֹ, שְׁאֵרֶךָ: — 1. **flesh, body, self** (indistinguishable fm. *bāśār*): flesh (of one's body) Mi 3_2; = self Pr 11_{17}; — 2. meat = **food** Ex 21_{10}; — 3. one's flesh = **blood-relation** Lv 18_6, spec. w. *'ābîkā* & *imm^{e}kā* on father's/mother's side Lv 18_{12f}.

שַׁאֲרָה Lv 18_{17}: rd. שְׁאֵרָהּ. †

שֶׁאֱרָה: n. pers. f.

שְׁאָר יָשׁוּב: symb. n. pers. Is 7_3, ↗ 10_{21f}. †

שְׁאֵרִית: sf. שְׁאֵרִיתוֹ: — 1. **remainder, remnant, what is left**: of a tree Is 44_{17}; — 2. **remnant** (of a people who have been [or are to be] destroyed) 2K 19_4: of Edom Am 9_{12}, of Jerusalem Je 15_9; — 3. **remnant** (who are to be saved) Je 6_9; *śām š^e'ērît l^e* make sure there are survivors for Gn 45_7.

שְׁאֵת: **desolation** La 3_{47}. †

שְׁבָא: n. peop. (& pers.) **Sheba**.

שְׁבָאִים: n. peop., **men of Sheba** Jl 4_8. †

שְׁבְאֵל: ↗ שְׁבוּאֵל.

שְׁבָבִים: **wood-shavings, splinters** (?) Ho 8_6. †

שָׁבָה: **qal**: pf. 'שׁ, שָׁבִיתָ, שָׁבוּ, sf. שְׁבָם, שְׁבוּם; impf. וַיִּשְׁבְּ, וַיִּשְׁבּוּ, sf. וַיִּשְׁבֵּם, תִּשְׁבְּךָ; impv. (ו)שְׁבֵה; inf. שְׁב(ו)ת; pt. שֹׁבִים, sf. שֹׁבֵינוּ, pass. שְׁבוּיִם, שְׁבֻיוֹת: **take captive** (in war): obj. persons Gn 34_{29}, men & animals Nu 31_9, cogn. acc. Nu 21_1.

nif.: pf. נִשְׁבּוּ, נִשְׁבָּה: **be taken captive**: person Gn 14_{14}, animal Ex 22_9.

שְׁבוֹ: a precious stone, trad. agate Ex 28_{19} 39_{12}. †

שְׁבוּאֵל, שְׁבָאֵל: n. pers.

*שְׁבוֹל Je 18_{15} Kt: F שְׁבִיל. †

שָׁבוּעַ: cs. שְׁבֻעַ; du. שְׁבֻעַיִם; pl. שָׁבֻעִים, cs. שְׁבֻעֵי Ez 21_{28}, & שָׁבֻעֹ(וֹ)ת, cs. שְׁבֻעוֹת, sf. שָׁבֻעֹתֵיכֶם: unit (period) of seven: — 1. seven days, **a week** Dn 9_{27}; *šebua‘ zôʾt* (bridal) week of this (woman) Gn 29_{27f}; — 2. *ḥag šābu‘ōt* **feast of weeks** (i.e. 7 weeks after Passover) Ex 34_{22}; > *šābu‘ōt* Nu 28_{26}.

שְׁבוּעָה, שְׁבֻעָה: cs. שְׁבֻעַת, sf. שְׁבֻעָתוֹ: **oath** 2C 15_{15}; *nišba‘ šebû‘â* Nu 30_3; *šebu‘at yhwh* oath in wh. Y. is invoked 1K 2_{43}; *šebu‘at ʾālâ* imprecatory oath Nu 5_{21}; *šebu‘at ʾissār* binding oath Nu 30_{14}; *šebû‘â … bên* oath (of friendship) between 2S 21_7; *ba‘alê šebû‘â lô* those bound to him by oath Ne 6_{18}; *šebû‘â* = curse 1S 14_{26}; *hāyâ lišbû‘â* (a name) serves as a curse-word Is 65_{15}; *hêqîm šebû‘â* fulfill an oath Gn 26_3; *niqqâ miššebû‘â* be free of the obligation of an oath Gn 24_8.

שָׁבוּר: **fracture** (of arm or leg) Lv 22_{22}. †

שְׁבוּת (17×), שְׁבִית (6×), & mixed forms שְׁבִות (3×) & שְׁבִית (2×): sf. שְׁבוּתָם, שְׁבִיתֵךְ: **carrying off to captivity, imprisonment**; w. vb. *hēšîb* Je 32_{44} or *šāb* (F √II *šwb*) Dt 30_3 lift the sentence of imprisonment, **turn one's fortune** (to the good); but oth. believe the basic mng. of phrase is 'bring about a restoration'.

שְׁבוּת: F שְׁבוּת.

I שׁבח: **piel**: pf. שִׁבַּחְתִּי; impf. יְשַׁבַּח, sf. יְשַׁבְּחוּנְךָ; impv. שַׁבְּחִי, sf. שַׁבְּחוּהוּ; inf. שַׁבֵּחַ: **praise, glorify**: obj. God Ps 63_4, joy Ec 8_{15}; **congratulate** Ec 4_2.

hitp.: inf. הִשְׁתַּבֵּחַ: w. *be*, **glory in** Ps 106_{47} 1C 16_{35}. †

II שׁבח: **piel**: impf. תְּשַׁבְּחֵם: **hush** Ps 89_{10}. †

hif.: pt. מַשְׁבִּיחַ: **soothe, quiet** Ps 65_8. †

שֵׁבֶט (189×): שָׁבֶט, sf. שִׁבְטוֹ; pl. שְׁבָטִים, cs. שִׁבְטֵי, sf. שְׁבָטֶיךָ, שִׁבְטֵיכֶם: — 1. **stick, staff, rod**: of shepherd Lv 27_{32}, teacher 2S 7_{14}; scepter Zc 10_{11}; as weapon 2S 23_{21}, tool Is 28_{27}; *šēbeṭ ʾappî* (of God) Is 10_5; *šēbeṭ pîw* (of Messiah) Is 11_4; — 2. **tribe** (143×), esp. of Isr. Gn 49_{16}.

שְׁבָט: name of 11th month (Feb.-Mar.) Zc 1_7. †

שְׁבִי: שֶׁבִי; sf. שִׁבְיוֹ, שִׁבְיָם: **those who are** (or **that which is**) **taken captive**: people & animals Nu 31_{26}; *šābâ šebî* take (s.one) captive Dt 21_{10}; *hālak (baš)šebî* go into captivity Dt 28_{41} La 1_5; *luqqaḥ baššebî* Je 48_{46}; *nātan laššebî* give into captivity Ps 78_{61}.

שֹׁבִי: n. pers.

שֹׁבָי: n. pers.

*שָׁבִיב: cs. שְׁבִיב: **spark** Jb 18_5. †

שִׁבְיָה: **captives** (in war) (coll.) Dt 21_{11}; > **captivity** † Ne 3_{36}.

שִׁבְיָּה: (one taken) **captive** Is 52_{2b}. †

*שְׁבִיל: sf. שְׁבִילְךָ Ps 77_{20} Qr; pl. cs. שְׁבִילֵי, sf. שְׁבִילֶיךָ Ps 77_{20} Kt: **path** Je 18_{15} Ps 77_{20}. †

*שָׁבִיס: pl. שְׁבִיסִים: **head-band** (of gold-foil or silver) Is 3_{18} (oth: small replicas of the sun). †

שְׁבִיעִי (95×): f. שְׁבִ(י)עִ(י)ת: seventh Gn 2_2; *baššebî‘it* (at) the 7th time 1K 18_{44}, in the 7th year Ex 21_2; *ṣôm haššebî‘î* fast of the 7th month Zc 8_{19}; *haššebi‘î* the 7th son 1C 2_{15}.

שְׁבִית: — 1. **captivity** Nu 21_{29}; — 2. F שְׁבוּת.

שְׁבִית: F שְׁבוּת.

שֹׁבֶל: **flowing skirt, hem of skirt** Is 47_2. †

שַׁבְּלוּל: trad. 'snail'; but sugg. **miscarriage** Ps 58_9; F comm. †

I שִׁבֹּלֶת: pl. שִׁבֳּלִים, cs. שִׁבֳּלֵי: **ear of grain** Gn 41_{5ff}; Ju 12_6 F II & סִבֹּלֶת; **bunch of twigs** † Zc 4_{12}.

II שִׁבֹּלֶת: **torrent, undulation** (of water) Is 27_{12} Ps $69_{3.16}$; Ju 12_6 F I & סִבֹּלֶת. †

שֶׁבְנָא: n. pers.
שֶׁבְנָה: n. pers.; = F שֶׁבְנָא.
שְׁבַנְיָה: n. pers.
שְׁבַנְיָהוּ: n. pers.
שׁבע: **qal**: F שְׁבוּעָה.

nif. (150×): pf. נִשְׁבַּע, נִשְׁבַּעְתָּ, נִשְׁבְּעוּ, נִשְׁבַּעְנוּ; impf. יִשָּׁבַע, תִּשָּׁבַע, אִשָּׁבַע, וָאִשָּׁבַע, תִּשָּׁבְעוּ; impv. הִשָּׁבְעָה, הִשָּׁבְעוּ; inf. הִשָּׁבֵעַ, הִשָּׁבַע; pt. נִשְׁבָּע, נִשְׁבָּעִים, נִשְׁבָּעוֹת: **swear** (i.e. make a statement or promise, with an oath, invoking God, pledging s.thg valuable): — 1. w. *le*, **swear** to (s.one) Gn 21_{23}; abs. Gn 21_{24}; *nišbaʿ šebuʿâ* swear an oath Gn 26_3; content of oath after *lēʾmōr* Gn 24_7; indir. discourse, w. *ʾim* **that not** Gn 21_{23}, w. *ʾim lōʾ* **that** Jos 14_9, w. *kî* **that** Gn 22_{16f}, w. *le* + inf. Ex 13_5, w. *min* + inf. **that ... no more** Is 54_9, w. *lebiltî* that not Dt 4_{21}; — 2. w. *be* + obj. pledged: (God) swears *benafšô* by his life Je 51_{14}; *nišbaʿ ḥay yhwh* swears, Y. shall not live, if/unless 1S 19_6; — 3. w. *be* + deity invoked: *bēʾlōhîm* Gn 21_{23}, *bešēm*... 1S 20_{42}, *beyhwh* 1K 1_{17}; God swears by himself (*bî*) Gn 22_{16}, (*bāk*) Ex 32_{13}; — 4. var.: *nišbaʿ le* **adjure**, **urge** (w. an oath) 2S 21_{17}; swear to = swear allegiance to Is 19_{18}; *nišbaʿ ʿal* swear concerning Gn 24_9.

hif.: pf. הִשְׁבִּיעַ, הִשְׁבַּעְתִּי, sf. הִשְׁבִּיעוֹ, הִשְׁבַּעְתִּיךָ, הִשְׁבַּעְתַּנִי, הִשְׁבִּיעָנִי, הִשְׁבִּיעֶךָ; impf. וַיַּשְׁבַּע, תַּשְׁבִּיעוּ, וַיַּשְׁבִּיעֵנִי, אַשְׁבִּיעֲךָ, וָאַשְׁבִּיעֵם; inf. הַשְׁבִּיעַ, abs. הַשְׁבֵּעַ; pt. sf. מַשְׁבִּיעֶךָ: — 1. w. acc.: **make** (s.one) **swear** Gn 24_{37}, w. *be* by (F nif. 3); *hišbîaʿ bišbuʿat hāʾālâ* make s.one take the oath of the curse Nu 5_{21}; — 2. w. acc. & *be*, **adjure** s.one, **urgently beg** s.one by (obj. pledged) SS 2_7; — 3. *hišbîaʿ* w. *ʾim* that not Ne 13_{25}, w. *ʾašer* that Gn 24_3, w. *kî* that 1K 18_{10}; w. *lēʾmōr* Gn 24_{37}, w. *le* & inf. Ezr 10_5.

I **שֶׁבַע**: cs. שֶׁבַע, שְׁבַע וּשְׁבַע 1K 14_{21}, f. שִׁבְעָה, cs. שִׁבְעַת, sf. שִׁבְעָתָם (Kt שִׁבְעָתַיִם, Qr שִׁבְעָתָם 2S 21_9): — 1. **seven**: *šebaʿ šānîm* Gn 5_7; *šebaʿ ʿeśrēh* 17 Gn 37_2; — 2. *šibʿâ šibʿâ* 7 and 7 Gn 7_2; *šibʿātayim* 7-fold Gn 4_{15}, *šebaʿ* 7 times Lv 26_{18}; — 3. pl. *šibʿîm* 70 Gn 50_3; *šibʿîm wešibʿâ* 77 times Gn 4_{24}; — 4. dates: *bešibʿâ laḥōdeš* on the 7th day of the month Ez 30_{20}; — 5. *lešibʿâ ʿāśār* the 17th (lot) 1C 25_{24}; for complete use of number, F gramm.

II **שֶׁבַע**: n. pers.
III **שֶׁבַע**: n. loc. Jos 19_2. †
שִׁבְעָה: n. loc. Gn 26_{33}. †
שְׁבֻעָה: F שְׁבוּעָה.
שִׁבְעָנָה: mixed form, שִׁבְעָה 7 & שִׁבְעָן twice 7 times, Jb 42_{13}. †
שׁבץ: **piel**: pf. שִׁבַּצְתָּ: **weave in patterns** Ex 28_{39}. †

pual: pt. מְשֻׁבָּצִים: (precious stones) **set** (in gold) Ex 28_{20}. †

שָׁבָץ: **seizure of weakness**? **cramp**? 2S 1_9. †

I **שָׁבַר**: **qal**: pf. שָׁבַר, שׁ׳, שָׁבַרְתָּ, sf. שְׁבָרָהּ; impf. יִשְׁבֹּר, תִּשְׁבָּר־, תִּשְׁבְּרוּ, וַיְּשַׁבְּרֵהוּ; impv. שְׁבֹר, sf. שָׁבְרֵם; inf. שָׁבוֹר, לִשְׁבֹּר, sf. שִׁבְרִי; pt. שֹׁבֵר, pass. שְׁבוּרֵי: **break**, **break down**, **break up** (trans.): obj. door Gn 19_9, bone Ex 12_{46}, weapon Je 49_{35}; subj. lion, obj. body, tear to pieces 1K 13_{26}; obj. ship, wreck Ez 27_{26}; obj. people, destroy, break up Is 14_{25}; metaph. break down: obj. *lēb* courage, confidence Ps 69_{21}.

nif.: pf. נִשְׁבַּר, נִשְׁבָּר, נִשְׁבְּרָה, נִשְׁבָּרוּ, נִשְׁבְּרָה (־רָה or ־רוּ 1K 22_{49}); impf. יִשָּׁבֵר, תִּשָּׁבֵר Ez 32_{28}, יִשָּׁבֵרוּ, תִּשָּׁבַרְנָה; inf. הִשָּׁבֵר; pt. נִשְׁבָּר, נִשְׁבָּרָה, נִשְׁבֶּרֶת, נִשְׁבָּרִים, נִשְׁבָּרֵי: **be broken (up)**: arm or leg Ez 34_4, vessel Lv 6_{21} &c.; of cisterns, be cracked Je 2_{13}; of snare, be torn Ps 124_7; of ship, be wrecked 1K 22_{49}; of courage, confidence Is 61_1.

piel: pf. שִׁבֵּר, שִׁבַּר, שִׁבַּרְתָּ, שִׁבְּרוּ; impf. יְשַׁבֵּר, וָאֲשַׁבְּרָה, תְּשַׁבֵּרוּ, תְּשַׁבֵּרוּן, וָאֲשַׁבְּרֵם; inf. שַׁבֵּר; pt. מְשַׁבֵּר: **smash**, **shatter** (to pieces): sacred pillar 2K 18_4, tablets Ex 32_{19}, door Is 45_2, ships Ps 48_8.

hif.: impf. אַשְׁבִּיר: make to break through = **bring to birth** Is 66_9. †

hof.: pf. הָשְׁבַּרְתִּי: **be broken**, be brought to breaking Je 8_{21}. †

II שׁבר: **qal**: impf. תִּשְׁבְּרוּ, נִשְׁבְּרָה; impv. שִׁבְרוּ; inf. לִשְׁבֹּר, לִשְׁבָּר־; pt. שֹׁבְרִים: **buy grain**: *šābar šeber* Gn 47_{14}, *šābar bar* 42_3, abs. 41_{57}; more generally, **buy**, obj. food Gn 42_7, wine & milk Is 55_1.

hif.: impf. תַּשְׁבִּרֵנִי, נַשְׁבִּירָה, נַשְׁבִּיר; pt. מַשְׁבִּיר: **sell** (lit. let s.one buy) **grain**: *šeber* Am 8_5, *bar* 8_6; more generally, food Dt 2_{28}.

I שֶׁבֶר, שֵׁבֶר (Is 65_{14} Am 6_6): שֶׁבֶר, sf. שִׁבְרָהּ, שִׁבְרֵךְ; pl. sf. שְׁבָרֶיהָ: — 1. (concrete) **breaking**: **fracture** of foot, hand Lv 21_{19}; breaking of vessel Is 30_{14}, of wall 30_{13}; pl. fractures, breaches of earth Ps 60_4; — 2. metaph. **crushing**, **depression** of spirit Is 65_{14}; — 3. genl., **collapse**, **breakdown** Is 1_{28}.

II שֶׁבֶר: **grain** for sale Gn 42_{1f}.

III שֶׁבֶר: n. pers. 1C 2_{48}. †

*שֶׁבֶר: sf. שִׁבְרוֹ: **interpretation** (of dream) Ju 7_{15}. †

שִׁבָּרוֹן: cs. שִׁבְרוֹן: — 1. **collapse**, **breakdown** Je 17_{18}; — 2. *šibrôn motnayim* broken loins (= emotional distress) Ez 21_{11}. †

שְׁבָרִים: n. loc. Jos 7_5. †

שׁבת: **qal**: pf. שָׁבָתוּ, שָׁבָתָה, שָׁבְתָה, שׁ׳; impf. יִשְׁבֹּתוּ, תִּשְׁבַּת, תִּשְׁבֹּת, יִשְׁבּוֹת: — 1. **cease**, **stop**, **be at a standstill** (intrans.) Gn 8_{22}; w. *min* Gn 2_{2f}, w. *min* + inf. Je 31_{36}; w. *min* stay away from La 5_{14}; — 2. **stop working**, **take a holiday** Ex 16_{30}; subj. land Lv 26_{34f}; = keep sabbath Ex 23_{12}; *šābat šabbāt* keep sabbath Lv 23_{32}.

nif.: pf. נִשְׁבְּתוּ, נִשְׁבַּת: **be brought to a stop**, **disappear** Is 17_3 Ez 6_6 30_{18} 33_{28}. †

hif.: pf. הִשְׁבִּית, הִשְׁבַּתִּי, sf. הִשְׁבַּתִּים; impf. וַיַּשְׁבֵּת, תַּשְׁבִּית, אַשְׁבִּיתָה; impv. הַשְׁבִּיתוּ; inf. לַשְׁבִּית < *לְהַשְׁבִּית; pt. מַשְׁבִּית: — 1. **put an end to, bring to a stop**: obj. vintage shout Is 16_{10}, kingdom Ho 1_4; discontinue (work) Ne 4_5; — 2. **remove** (priests) 2K 23_5; — 3. **let** (s.thg) **be lacking** Lv 2_{13}; **make** (s.thg) **disappear** Je 7_{34}; — 4. w. *min*, **make** (s.one) **rest** from Ex 5_5; w. *min* & inf. **make** (s.one) **stop** (doing s.thg) Ez 34_{10}; — 5. w. acc. of thg. & *min* + pers., make (s.thg) cease (from [among]) Dt 32_{26}; — 6. w. acc. & *l^ebiltî* **make** (s.one) **stop** (doing s.thg) Jos 22_{25}; — 7. w. acc. & *mipp^enê* + pers. **not bother** (s.one) **with** Is 30_{11}.

cj. hof.: pt. מָשְׁבָּת: **be brought to a standstill, removed** cj Is 30_7. †

שֶׁבֶת: שֶׁבֶת, sf. שִׁבְתּוֹ: **sitting quiet(ly)**, **inaction**; (caused by injury) Ex 21_{19}; Pr 20_3.

שַׁבָּת (101 ×): cs. שַׁבַּת, sf. שַׁבַּתּוֹ, שַׁבַּתָּהּ; pl. שַׁבָּתוֹת, cs. שַׁבְּתֹת, sf. שַׁבְּתוֹתַי, שַׁבְּתֹתֵיכֶם; m. & f. (cf. Lv 16_{31} 22_{32}): — 1. *yôm haššabbāt* **day of rest, sabbath** Ex 20_8; — 2. > *šabbāt* **day of rest, sabbath** 2K 4_{23}; *šabbat baššabbattô* Nu 28_{10} & *šabbat šabbāt* 1C 9_{32} sabbath after sab.; — 3. pl. Ex 31_{13}; — 4. *haššabbātôt* the sabbath days Ne 10_{34}; — 5. *šabbat šabbātôn* ⸗ *šabbātôn*; — 6. pl. **weeks** (i.e. from one sabbath to next) Lv 23_{15}; *šabb^etōt šānîm* weeks of years = 7 years each Lv 25_8; — 7. metaph.: land keeps sabbath (by remaining fallow) Lv 25_6, pl. 26_{34}.

שַׁבָּתוֹן: **sabbath feast** Ex 16_{23}; *š^enat šabbātôn* sabbatical year Lv 25_5; *šabbat šabbātôn* most solemn sabbath Ex 35_2.

שַׁבְּתַי: n. pers.

שׁגג: **qal**: pf. שָׁגַג; inf. sf. (?) בְּשַׁגָּם Gn 6_3; pt. שֹׁגֵג, f. שֹׁגֶגֶת: **commit error, sin inadvertently** Gn 6_3 (?) Lv 5_{18} Nu 15_{28} Ps 119_{67} Jb 12_{16}. †

שְׁגָגָה: sf. שִׁגְגָתוֹ: **error, inadvertence** Jos 20_3.

שׁגה: **qal**: pf. שָׁגִיתִי, שָׁגוּ; impf. תִּשְׁגֶּה, יִשְׁגּוּ; inf. שְׁגוֹת; pt. שֹׁגֶה, שֹׁגִים: — 1. **stray, go astray**:

sheep Ez 34_6, fool Pr 5_{23}; err 1S 26_{21}; — 2. **stagger, be unable to walk straight**: w. *bᵉ* because of or with: drinking Is 28_7, a vision 28_7, love Pr 5_{19}; — 3. **go wrong, do wrong** (involuntarily) Lv 4_{13}; w. *min* against Ps 119_{21}.

hif.: impf. sf. תַּשְׁגֵּנִי; pt. מַשְׁגֶּה: — 1. **let** (s.one) **stray** Ps 119_{10}; — 2. **lead** (s.one) **astray, mislead** Dt 27_{18} Pr 28_{10} Jb 12_{16}. †

שָׁגֵה: n. pers.

שגח: **hif.**: pf. הִשְׁגִּיחַ; impf. יַשְׁגִּיחוּ; pt. מַשְׁגִּיחַ: **gaze, stare** SS 2_9, w. *ʾel* at Is 14_{16} Ps 33_{14}. †

***שְׁגִיאָה**: pl. שְׁגִיאוֹת: **lapse, error** (from ignorance) Ps 19_{13}. †

שִׁגָּיוֹן: pl. שִׁגְיֹנוֹת: obscure superscription Ps 7_1 Hb 3_1. †

שׁגל: (this vb. considered obscene by Masoretes, and *šākab* everywhere substituted):

qal: impf. יִשְׁגָּלֶנָּה: **lie with** (a woman) Dt 28_{30}. †

nif.: impf. תִּשָּׁגַלְנָה: **be lain with** Is 13_{16} Zc 14_2. †

pual (**qal** pass.): pf. שֻׁגַּלְתְּ: **be lain with** Je 3_2. †

שֵׁגָל: trad. **queen** Ps 45_{10} Ne 2_6, but sugg. 'favorite of harem'. †

שׁגע: **pual**: pt. מְשֻׁגָּע, מְשֻׁגָּעִים: **raving, crazy** (alw. used contemptuously) 2K 9_{11}.

hitp.: inf. הִשְׁתַּגֵּעַ; pt. מִשְׁתַּגֵּעַ: **behave like a madman** 1S 21_{15f}. †

שִׁגָּעוֹן: **madness** Dt 28_{28} 2K 9_{20} Zc 12_4. †

שֶׁגֶר: cs. שְׁגַר & Ex 13_{12} † שֶׁגֶר: **offspring** (of cattle) Ex 13_{12} Dt 7_{13} $28_{4.18.51}$. †

***שַׁד**: שָׁד; du. שָׁדַיִם, שָׁדָיִם, cs. שְׁדֵי, sf. שָׁדַי, שְׁדֵיהֶן, שָׁדֶיהָ: **breast**: sg. (of jackal) La 4_3, du. Gn 49_{25} (presumably of women & female animals), otherw. of women Is 28_9.

***שֵׁד**: pl. שֵׁדִים: **evil spirit, demon** Dt 32_{17} Ps 106_{37}. †

I **שֹׁד**: **breast** Is 60_{16} 66_{11} Jb 24_9. †

II **שֹׁד**: **violence, destruction** Is 22_4.

שׁדד: **qal**: pf. שָׁדְדוּ, sf. שַׁדּוּנִי; impf. יָשׁוּד, sf. יְשָׁדֵּם, יְשָׁדְדֵם Pr 11_3 Qr; impv. שָׁדְדוּ; inf. שָׁדוֹד, לִשְׁדוֹד; pt. שׁ(וֹ)דֵד, pl. שֹׁדְדִים, cs. שׁוֹדְדֵי, pass. שָׁדוּד, שְׁדוּדָה: **devastate, lay waste, overpower** Je 5_6; subj. Y. Je 25_{36}; abs. Is 21_2; pt. devastator Is 16_4.

nif.: pf. נְשַׁדֻּנוּ: **be devastated** Mi 2_4. †

piel: impf. תְּשַׁדֵּד; pt. מְשַׁדֶּד־: **maltreat** (do violence to?) Ps 19_{26}; **assault, destroy** Pr 24_{15}. †

pual (**qal** pass.?): pf. שֻׁדַּד, שֻׁדַּד, שֻׁדְּדָה, שֻׁדָּדָה Na 3_7, שֻׁדְּדָה, שֻׁדְּדוּ, שֻׁדַּדְנוּ: **be devastated**: city Is 15_1, field Jl 1_{10}.

polel: impf. יְשֹׁדֵד: **devastate** Ho 10_2. †

hof. (**qal** pass.?): impf. יוּשַּׁד, תּוּשַּׁד: **be devastated** Is 33_1 Ho 10_{14}. †

שִׁדָּה: שִׁדָּה וְשִׁדּוֹת Ec 2_8: **lady** (concubine) (?). †

שַׁדּוּן Jb 19_{29} Qr: ↗ שַׁדִּין. †

שַׁדַּי, **שַׁדָּי**: n. of deity, identified w. Y., Gn 17_1.

שְׁדֵיאוּר: n. pers.

שַׁדִּין Jb 19_{29}, txt. corr., prp. rd. תֵּדְעוּ יֵשׁ דַּיָּן. †

שְׁדֵמָה: pl. שְׁדֵמוֹת, cs. שַׁדְמ(וֹ)ת: **terrace** 2K 23_4.

שׁדף: **qal**: pt. pass. f. pl. שְׁדוּפוֹת, שְׁדֻפוֹת: **scorch** (by wind) Gn $41_{6.23.27}$. †

שְׁדֵפָה: **scorching** (of standing grain by desert wind) 2K 19_{26}. †

שִׁדָּפוֹן: **scorching** Dt 28_{22} 1K 8_{37} Am 4_9 Hg 2_{17} 2C 6_{28}. †

שַׁדְרַךְ: n. pers.

I **שֹׁהַם**: a precious stone, trad. onyx; sugg. carnelian or lapis lazuli Gn 2_{12}.

II **שֹׁהַם**: n. pers. 1C 24_{27}. †

שָׁו Jb 15_{31} Kt: rd. שָׁוְא ?. †

שׁוא: **hif.**: impf. יַשִּׁי < *יַשִּׁיא Ps 55_{16} Qr, יַשִּׁא Ps 89_{23} w. *ʿal*: **treat badly**. †

שָׁוְא: — 1. **worthless** Is 1_{13}; *laššāwʾ* **in vain, without result** Je 2_{30}; *dibbēr šāwʾ* speak empty words, falsely Is 59_4; *nāšāʾ šēm* *laššāwʾ* use a name unnecessarily, idly; misuse a name Ex 20$_7$; *šēmaʿ/ʿēd šawʾ* empty = false report, witness Ex 23$_1$ Dt 5$_{20}$; *(hablê) šāwʾ* what is empty = **idols** Je 18$_{15}$ Ps 31$_7$; — 2. **deceit, fraud** Ps 24$_4$; — 3. adv. **(in) vain**: adv. Ps 89$_{48}$; w. inf. it is vain to ... Ma 3$_{14}$.

שְׁוָא: n. pers.

***שׁוֹא**: pl. sf. שֹׁאֵיהֶם Ps 35$_{17}$: sugg. = ꟻ שׁוֹאָה; oth.: txt. corr., ꟻ comm. †

שׁוֹאָה, שֹׁאָה: cs. שֹׁאַת: trad. **ruin, storm**; but recent sugg. **pit** Is 10$_3$ Ps 35$_8$.

I **שׁוּב**: **qal** (670×): pf. שָׁב, שָׁבָה, שַׁבְתָּ, שַׁבְתְּ, שָׁבוּ, שַׁבְתֶּם; impf. יָשׁוּב, יָשָׁב, יָשֹׁב, וַיָּשָׁב, תָּשׁוּבִי, אָשׁוּבָה, יָשׁוּבוּ, יָשָׁבוּ, יְשָׁבוּן, יְשׁוּבוּן, תָּשֹׁבְןָ, וַתָּשֹׁבְנָה, תְּשֻׁבֶינָה, נָשׁוּבָה; impv. שׁוּב, שֹׁב, שׁוּבָה, שׁוּבִי, שֻׁבוּ, שֹׁבְנָה; inf. שׁוּב, שֹׁב, שׁוּבְךָ, שׁוּבְכֶם, abs. שׁוֹב; pt. שָׁב, שָׁבָה, שָׁבִים, שָׁבֵי, sf. שָׁבֶיהָ, pass. שׁוּבֵי txt. corr.: — 1. **return, go back, come back**: a) physical motion to point of departure: subj. person Gn 15$_{16}$, God Gn 18$_{10}$, animal Gn 8$_9$, waters Jos 4$_{18}$; b) motion back in direction of point of departure Gn 14$_7$; c) retrograde motion, oft. under pressure of battle: w. *mēʾaḥ^arê* 1K 22$_{33}$, *ʾāḥôr* Ps 6$_{11}$; d) less spec. motion in opposite direction: i) inf. or pt. of vb. of motion + *w^e* + inf. or pt. of *šwb*: **back & forth**: raven went to & fro Gn 8$_7$; ii) in genl. Gn 14$_{17}$; e) recurrent motion Gn 43$_{10}$; — 2. w. another verb: a) do **again** Gn 26$_{18}$; b) w. *lāqaḥ* take **back** 2K 13$_{25}$; c) w. vb. of sustaining: he shall return (= reverse his anger) and have compassion Mi 7$_{19}$; d) w. *ʿôd* & adj., **still (great)er** Ez 8$_6$; e) **more and more** Ez 8$_{17}$; — 3. **return** (to relationship): a) to a person: marriage Je 3$_1$, kingship 1K 12$_{27}$, religious support Je 15$_{19}$; b) to harlotry Is 23$_{17}$; c) from priestly service Nu 8$_{25}$; — 4. **revert** (in ownership) 1K 12$_{26}$; — 4. life & death: subj. pers.: **return** (to ground &c.) Gn 3$_{19}$; (from death to life) 2S 12$_{23}$; subj. *rû^aḥ*, *ʿāfār*; to dust Ec 12$_7$; subj. *nefeš*, to life, 1K 17$_{21f}$; subj. parts of body: **return** (to health = be restored) 1K 13$_6$; — 6. **turn** into (= change into), w. *l^e* Is 29$_{17}$; — 7. context of emotions, attitudes, plans, etc.: a) God subj., **turn back** (fm. anger) 2K 23$_{26}$; b) man subj. **change one's mind** (?) Jb 6$_{29}$; c) **go back** (on a vow, oath) Ju 11$_{35}$; d) God subj., **turn back** (fm. one's purpose) Je 4$_{28}$; e) God subj., impv., no immediate ctxt., **return** (= change total orientation) Is 63$_{17}$; — 8. subj. other nouns as expression of pers.: a) *dābār* (of God) Is 45$_{23}$; b) anger Gn 27$_{44f}$; c) blood, punishment, plot: return (on one's head = to his hurt) 1K 2$_{33}$; — 9. ctxt. of psychic defeat: **turn back** La 1$_8$; — 10. ctxt. of covenant relation: a) **turn** = change loyalty, subj. Isr. Je 4$_1$; b) **return** (to God) 1K 8$_{33}$; c) **turn back** (fm. evil) 1K 8$_{35}$; d) **withdraw** (fm. following God), w. *mēʾaḥ^arê* 1K 9$_6$; e) **turn back** (fm. good to evil) Jos 23$_{12}$; f) **turn** = change loyalty, subj. God Jos 24$_{20}$; g) **return** (to Isr.), subj. God Zc 1$_3$; h) **withdraw** (fm. Isr.), subj. God Dt 23$_{15}$.

polel: pf. שׁוֹבַבְתִּי, שׁוֹבְבָתֶךָ, שׁוֹבַבְתִּיךָ; impf. יְשׁוֹבֵב; inf. שׁוֹבֵב, sf. שׁוֹבְבִי; pt. מְשׁוֹבֵב, מְשׁוֹבֶבֶת, Je 50$_6$ שׁוֹבְבִים = Kt שׁוֹבָבִים & Qr שׁוֹבְבוּם: — 1. **bring back** (spatial) Is 49$_5$; — 2. **restore** (to ideal condition) Is 58$_{12}$; — 3. **lead astray** Is 47$_{10}$.

polal: pt. מְשׁוֹבֶבֶת: **be brought back** Ez 38$_8$. †

hif. (350×): pf. הֵשִׁיב, הֵשִׁיבָה, הֱשִׁיבוֹתָ & Dt 4$_{39}$ 30$_1$ וַהֲשֵׁבֹתָ, הֲשִׁבֹתִי, הֲשִׁיבוֹתִי, הֵשִׁ(י)בוּ, (וַ)הֲשֵׁ(י)בֹתֶם, הֱשִׁיבֹנוּ, sf. הֱשִׁיבְךָ & הֲשִׁבְךָ, הֲשִׁבוֹתִים, וַהֲשִׁ(י)בֹתִיךָ, הֲשֵׁבֹתוֹ, הֱשִׁבַנִי, הֲשֵׁ(י)בוֹתָם; וְהֱשִׁ(י)בוּם; impf. יָשִׁיב, יָשֵׁב, וָאָשִׁיב, אָשִׁיבָה, אָשִׁיב, תָּשִׁבִי, תָּשֶׁב, וַיָּשֶׁב, Ne 2$_{20}$ 6$_4$ & וָאָשֵׁב, יָשִׁיבוּ, תָּשֵׁבְנָה, sf. יְשִׁיבֶנּוּ, אֲשִׁיבֶךָ, אֲשִׁבְךָ, תְּשִׁיבֵם, יְשִׁיבֵנִי, יְשִׁיבֶנָּה,

וַיְּשִׁבוּם; impv. הָשֵׁב, הָשִׁיב 2K 8_{6}, הָשַׁב, הָשִׁיב, הָשִׁבוּ, הָשִׁבָה, sf. הֲשִׁיבֵנוּ, הֲשִׁבֵנִי; inf. הָשִׁיב, הֲשִׁיבוֹ, הֲשִׁיבֵנִי, abs. הָשֵׁב; pt. מֵשִׁיב, f. cs. מְשִׁיבַת, pl. מְשִׁיבִים: — 1. physical motion: a) **bring back, lead back, carry back** (to point of departure): God subj., persons obj. Gn 28_{15}, obj. waters Ex 15_{19}; human subj., human obj. **cause** s.one **to go/come back, see that s.one gets back** 1S 29_{4}; **bring, lead, take, guide** s.one **back** Gn 24_{5}; take back, reaccept (slaves) Je 34_{11}; obj. person & thgs. as booty Gn 14_{16}; obj. animals, **lead, take back** 1S 6_{7}; obj. inanimate, **transport, carry, bring back** Gn 43_{12}; obj. diseases Dt 28_{60}; **turn back** (s.one or s.thg) (in defeat): obj. pers. Is 44_{25}, obj. thg. Ps 89_{44}; — 2. obj. thg., **put back** (in position), **replace**: movable obj. Gn 29_{3}; obj. borders 2K 14_{25}; — 3. **restore** (s.one to an office) Gn 40_{13}; — 4. **give back** (a moveable obj.) 1S 12_{3}; **pay back**: God subj. Zc 9_{12}, human subj. Ex 21_{34}; **bring back** (wares in trade) Ez 27_{15}; **give up** (wealth at death &c.) Jb 20_{10}; **give back** (a person as property) Gn 20_{7}; **restore** (ownership of territory &c.) 1K 20_{34}; **restore** (an office to s.one) 2S 16_{3}; **restore** (to onesf. the ownership of property), **get back** Lv 25_{28}; **make** (property) **revert, see that** (property) **is restored** (to s.one) 2K 8_{6}; **give back**, God subj., obj. joy Ps 51_{14}; **give** (in return for payment) Lv 26_{26}; **give** (tribute to king, offering to God in return for security &c.) 2K 3_{4} 1S 6_{3}; **give back** (punishment, revenge) Gn 50_{15}, abs. = **recompense** 2S 22_{21}; — 5. ctxt. of life & death: **bring** s.one **back** (to death) Ps 90_{3}, (fm. death) 2S 12_{23}, **restore** (Isr. to former estate) Is 49_{6}; obj. *nefeš* = life, **rescue** Ps 35_{17}, = spirit, courage, **revive, restore** Ps 19_{8}; obj. *rûaḥ* draw (breath) Jb 9_{18}; — 6. obj. part of the body: a) obj. *pānîm*, subj. & possessor of 'face' different, **repulse** (s.one in humiliation &c.) 1K 2_{16}; subj. & possessor of 'face' same, = **return, turn back** (intrans.) Ez 14_{6}; b) obj. hand: **bring back** Gn 38_{29}, **put back** Ex 4_{7}; hand = power: **withdraw** (one's own hand fm. a threat) Ez 20_{22}; **turn, push back** (s.one else's hand) Is 14_{27}; **restore** (one's own power) 2S 8_{3}; w. *'al* + pers. or place, **put back** (one's own hand against) Is 1_{25}; **bring back** (one's hand fm. evil) Ez 18_{8}; c) obj. foot = habit Is 58_{13}; d) obj. *lēb* (of s.one else): **bring back** (s.one's loyalty) Ma 3_{24}; — 7. obj. *dābār* or the like, bring, send back (word) = **answer** Gn 37_{14}; — 8. obj. anger: subj. & possessor of anger the same, **abate** (one's anger) Ps 78_{38}; subj. & possessor of anger different, **bring back, abate** (s.one's anger) Nu 25_{11} (God's), Pr 15_{1} (fellow's); — 9. w. *'el/'al lēb(āb)*, bring back ([on] to one's heart ...) = **bring back** (an idea into operation), **recall** 1K 8_{47}; — 10. emotions, plans, blessings, punishment as expression of pers.: **make** (God) **change** (his mind) Jb 9_{12}; **revoke** (one's own will) Am 1_{3}; subj. God, **annul, hinder** (s.one's will) Is 43_{13}; — 11. ctxt. of covenant relation: a) 'to God' implied: God subj., **accept** (Isr.) **back** Je 15_{19}; human subj., **bring, lead** (Isr.) **back** Ne 9_{26}; b) human subj., **bring** (Isr.) **back** (fm. evil) Ma 2_{6}; c) subj. Isr., impv. vb., no obj. **let onesf. be turned back** Ez 14_{6}.

hof.: pf. הוּשַׁב; impf. וַיּוּשַׁב; pt. מוּשָׁב, מוּשָׁבִים: — 1. **be brought back** Ex 10_{8} Je 27_{16}; — 2. **be replaced** Gn 42_{28} 43_{12}; — 3. **be paid back** Nu 5_{8}. †

II **שׁוּב**: only in ↗ שְׁבוּת (שָׁב); = I שׁוּב?

שׁוּבָאֵל: ↗ שְׁבוּאֵל.

I **שׁוֹבָב**: pl. שׁוֹבָבִים: **faithless, rebellious** Is 57_{17} Je $3_{14 \cdot 22}$. †

II **שׁוֹבָב**: n. pers.

*שׁוֹבֵב: f. שׁוֹבֵבָה: **backturning, faithless** Je 31_{22} 49_4. †

שׁוּבָה: **returning** Is 30_{15} (oth.: rd. *šēbâ 'settling'). †

שׁוֹבָךְ: n. pers.

שׁוֹבָל: n. pers.

שׁוֹבֵק: n. pers.

I שָׁוָה: **qal**: pf. שׁ׳; impf. יִשְׁווּ, אֶשְׁוֶה, תִּשְׁוֶה; pt. שֹׁוֶה: — 1. **be(come) like, equal**: w. *'el* Is 40_{25}, w. *le* Pr 26_4, w. *be* 3_{15} 8_{11}; — 2. *šōweh le* **suitable, satisfying for** Est 3_8 7_4. †

nif.: pf. נִשְׁתָּוָה rd נִשְׁוְתָה: **be equivalent to, be like** Pr 27_{15}. †

piel: pf. שִׁוִּיתִי, שִׁוָּה; pt. מְשַׁוֶּה: — 1. **make** (ground) **level** Is 28_{25}; — 2. **soothe** Ps 131_2; — 3. **make** (s.thg.) **like** (s.thg. else) 2S 22_{34} Ps 18_{34}. †

hif.: impf. תַּשְׁווּ, אַשְׁוֶה; w. *le* **equate, compare** Is 46_5 La 2_{13}. †

II שׁוה: **piel**: pf. שִׁוִּיתִי; impf. תְּשַׁוֶּה: **place, put** Ps 16_8.

[**pual**: impf. תְּשֻׁוֶּה Jb 30_{22} Kt rd תְּשֻׁאָה. †]

*שָׁוֶה: cs. שָׁוֵה: **plain** (trad. part of n. loc.) Gn 14_5. †

שָׁוֵה: n. loc. = *שָׁוֶה Gn 14_{17}. †

שׁוח: **qal**: pf. שָׁחָה: **sink down** Pr 2_{18}. †

שׁוּחַ: n. terr.

I שׁוּחָה: **pit** (for trapping animals &c.) Je 2_6.

II שׁוּחָה: n. pers. 1C 4_{11}. †

שׁוּחִי, שֻׁחִי: gent. of שׁוּחַ.

שׁוּחָם: n. pers.

שׁוּחָמִי: gent. of שׁוּחָם.

I שׁוט: **qal**: pf. שָׁטוּ; impf. וַיָּשֻׁטוּ; impv. שׁוּט; inf. שֻׁט; pt. שָׁטִים: — 1. **roam around, rove around** 2S 24_2; — 2. pass over (the water), **row** Ez 27_8.

polel: impf. יְשׁוֹטְטוּ; impv. שׁוֹטְטוּ; pt. מְשׁוֹטְטִים, מְשׁוֹטְטוֹת: **roam around** Je 5_1.

hitpolel: impv. הִתְשׁוֹטַטְנָה: **turn this way and that** (?) Je 49_3. †

II שׁוט: **qal**: pt. שָׁאטִים, שָׁאטוֹת: **slight, despise** Ez 16_{57} $28_{24 \cdot 26}$. †

I שׁוֹט: pl. שׁוֹטִים: **whip** 1K $12_{11 \cdot 14}$.

II שׁוֹט: **(sudden) flood** Is 28_{15} Qr $_{18}$ Jb 9_{23}. †

*שׁוּל: pl. cs. שׁוּלֵי, sf. שׁוּלָיו, שׁוּלַיִךְ: **flowing skirt, hem of skirt** Is 6_1.

שׁוֹלָל: **barefoot** Mi 1_8 Qr Jb 12_{19}. †

שׁוּלַמִּית SS 7_1, f. noun of unknown derivation: woman of Shûnēm? f. of Solomon? F comm. †

שׁוּמִים: **garlic**, *Allium sativum* Nu 11_5. †

שׁוֹמֵם: F שׁמם polel.

שׁוֹמֵר: n. pers.

I שׁוּנִי: n. pers. Gn 46_{16} Nu 26_{15}. †

II שׁוּנִי: gent. of I, Nu 26_{15}. †

שׁוּנֵם: n. loc.

*שׁוּנַמִּי: gent. of שׁוּנֵם: f. שׁוּנַמִּית, שֻׁנַמִּית.

שׁוע: **piel**: pf. שִׁוַּעְתִּי; impf. תְּשַׁוַּע, תְּשַׁוֵּעַ, יְשַׁוְּעוּ, יְשַׁוֵּעוּ, וָאֲשַׁוֵּעָה; inf. sf. שַׁוְּעוֹ; pt. מְשַׁוֵּעַ: **cry for help** Is 58_9.

*שֶׁוַע: sf. שַׁוְעִי: **cry for help** Ps 5_3. †

I שׁוֹעַ: **noble** Is 32_5 Jb 34_{19}. †

II שׁוֹעַ: n. peop. Ez 23_{23}. †

I שׁוּעַ: sf. שׁוּעֵךְ: unexpl., Jb 30_{24} 36_{19}; perh. 'cry for help,' but F comm. †

II שׁוּעַ: n. pers. Gn $38_{2 \cdot 12}$ 1C 2_3. †

שׁוּעָא: n. pers. f.

שַׁוְעָה: cs. שַׁוְעַת, sf. שַׁוְעָתָם: **cry for help** 1S 5_{12}.

I שׁוּעָל: **fox**, *Vulpus niloticus & flavescens* Ju 15_4.

II שׁוּעָל: n. pers. 1C 7_{36}. †

III שׁוּעָל: n. loc. 1S 13_{17}. †

שׁוֹעֵר, שֹׁעֵר: pl. שֹׁעֲרִים, cs. שֹׁעֲרֵי: **gatekeeper** 2K 7_{10f}.

I שׁוּף: **qal**: impf. sf. יְשׁוּפְךָ: w. acc. & *rō'š*: **crush** Gn 3_{15}. †

II שׁוּף: **qal**: impf. sf. יְשׁוּפֵנִי, תְּשׁוּפֶנּוּ: w. acc. **snap at, snatch at** Gn 3_{15} Jb 9_{17}. †

שׁוּפָךְ: n. pers.

שׁוּפָמִי: gent. of a presumed *שׁוּפָם n. pers.

שׁוּפָן: n. loc. F עֲטָרוֹת.

שׁוֹפָר, שֹׁפָר: cs. שׁוֹפַר; pl. שׁוֹפָרוֹת, cs. שׁוֹפְרוֹת, sf. שׁוֹפְרֹתֵיהֶם: **ram's horn** (for blowing a signal) 1K 1_{34}; *qôl šôfār* 1K 1_{41}; *bešôfārôt* w. the sounding of horns 2C 15_{14}, *bedê šôfār* as soon as the horn blows Jb 39_{25}.

שׂוק: **hif.**: pf. הֵשִׂיקוּ: prove (too) narrow, **overflow** Jl 2_{24} 4_{13}. †

polel: impf. sf. וַתְּשֹׁקְקֶהָ: make (too) narrow, **bestow abundantly** Ps 65_{10}. †

שׁוֹק: du. שֹׁקַיִם, cs. שׁוֹקֵי, sf. שׁוֹקָיו: the **thigh**, esp. the lower part, and then, by extension, the **leg** in genl.: of man Is 47_2; of sacrificial animal 1S 9_{24}; idiom in Ju 15_8 obscure.

שׁוּק: pl. שְׁוָקִים: **street** (within a town) Pr 7_8 SS 3_2 Ec 12_{4f}. †

***שֹׁקֵק, שׁוֹקֵק**: f. שׁ(ו)קֵקָה: of *nefeš*: **narrow, dried out** Is 29_8 Ps 107_9 (oth.: pt. of *šqq* 'rushing' [for water]). †

I **שׁוּר**: **qal**: impf. יָשׁוּר, תָּשׁוּר, אָשׁוּר, יְשׁוּרֶנּוּ, יְשׁוּרֶנָּה, תְּשׁוּרֵנִי, אֲשׁוּרֶנּוּ; impv. שׁוּר: **gaze on, regard, see** Nu 23_9.

II **שׁוּר**: **qal**: impf. תָּשׁוּרִי, וַתָּשֻׁרִי; pt. pl. f. sf. שָׁרוֹתַיִךְ: **journey**, perh. **descend** Is 57_9 SS 4_8; pt. f. **caravan** Ez 27_{25}. †

שׁוֹר: sf. שׁוֹרְךָ, שֹׁרְךָ, שׁוֹרוֹ; pl. שְׁוָרִים: fully-grown male bovine, whether castrated or not: **bull, ox, steer**, oft. for cattle in genl., oft. coll. Gn 32_6.

I **שׁוּר**: **wall**: around well Gn 49_{22}, betw. fields 2S 22_{30} Ps 18_{30}. †

II **שׁוּר**: n. loc.

***שׁוּרָה**: pl. sf. שׁוּרֹתָם: **retaining wall** (of terrace) Jb 24_{11}. †

***שׁוֹרֵר**: pl. sf. שׁוֹרְרַי, שׁוֹרְרָי: **enemy** Ps 5_9.

שַׁוְשָׁא: n. pers.

I **שׁוּשַׁן**: שׁוּשָׁן m., שׁוֹשַׁנָּה f., cs. שׁוֹשַׁנַּת; pl. שׁוֹשַׁנִּים: — 1. **lily**, *Lilius candidum* 1K 7_{26}; — 2. **lotus**(-flower, as ornament) 1K 7_{19}; — 3. for superscription Ps 45_1 &c. ℱ comm.

II **שׁוּשַׁן**: n. loc. **Susa** Ne 1_1 Est $1_{2.5}$ 3_{15} Dn 8_2. †

שׁוּשַׁק: ℱ שִׁישַׁק.

שׁוּת: ℱ שִׁית.

שׁוּתֶלַח: n. pers.

שׁזף: **qal**: pf. sf. שְׁזָפַתּוּ, שְׁזָפַתְנִי: — 1. subj. eye, **catch sight of** Jb 20_9 28_7; — 2. subj. sun, **tan, scorch** SS 1_6. †

שׁזר: **hof.**: pt. מָשְׁזָר: **twisted** Ex 26_1.

שַׁח: *šaḥ ʿênayim*, **w. downcast eyes** Jb 22_{29}. †

שׁחד: **qal**: impf. וַתִּשְׁחֳדִי; impv. שִׁחֲדוּ: **give a gift** Ez 16_{33}, w. *baʿad* in favor of Jb 6_{22}. †

שֹׁחַד: — 1. **gift, present** 1K 15_{19}; — 2. **bribe** Is 1_{23}; w. *lāqaḥ* 1S 8_3.

שׁחה: **qal**: impv. שְׁחִי: **bow down** (intrans.) Is 51_{23}. †

hif.: impf. sf. יַשְׁחֶנָּה: **bow** (s.one) **down** Pr 12_{25}. †

hitp. (170×): pf. הִשְׁתַּחֲוָה, הִשְׁתַּחֲוִיתָ, הִשְׁתַּחֲווּ; impf. יִשְׁתַּחֲוֶה, אֶשְׁתַּחֲוֶה, יִשְׁתַּחֲווּ, וַתִּשְׁתַּחֲוֶיןָ, וַיִּשְׁתַּחֲווּ, וַיִּשְׁתַּחוּ > וַיִּשְׁתַּחֲוֶה; impv. הִשְׁתַּחֲוִי, הִשְׁתַּחֲווּ; inf. הִשְׁתַּחֲוֹת; pt. מִשְׁתַּחֲוֶה, מִשְׁתַּחֲוִים: — 1. **bow down** (deeply), **do homage** Gn 18_2 47_{31}; — 2. **prostrate onesf.** before, **worship** Gn 24_{26}.

שְׁחוֹר Je 2_{18}: ℱ שִׁיחוֹר.

שְׁחוֹר: **soot** La 4_8; **blackness** cj. Jl 2_2. †

[***שְׁחוּת**: בִּשְׁחוּתוֹ Pr 28_{10}, rd. בְּשַׁחְתּוֹ. †]

שׁחח: **qal**: pf. שַׁח, שַׁח(ו)תִי, שַׁחוּ, שָׁחֲחוּ; impf. יָשֹׁחַ, וַיָּשֹׁחוּ, La 3_{20} rd תָּשׁוֹחַ Qr; inf. שְׁחוֹחַ: **stoop** Ps 10_{10}, **crouch** (of lion) Jb 38_{40}; **have to stoop** (in humility) Is $2_{11.17}$; *hālak šeḥôaḥ* **come stooping** Is 60_{14}.

nif. (**qal**?): impf. וַיִּשַּׁח, תִּשַּׁח, יִשַּׁחוּ: **have to stoop** Is 2_9 5_{15}; **sound muffled, low** Is 29_4 Ec 12_4. †

hif.: pf. הֵשַׁח: **bring down, lay low** Is 25_{12} 26_5. †

I **שָׁחַט**: **qal** (81×): pf. שָׁחֲטוּ, שְׁחַטְתֶּם, שׁ׳, sf. שְׁחָטוֹ; impf. יִשְׁחַט, יִשְׁחָט, וַתִּשְׁחֲטִי, וַיִּשְׁחָטֵהוּ, וַיִּשְׁחָטוּם; impv. שַׁחֲטוּ; inf. שַׁחֲטָם, שְׁחֹט, שָׁחֹט; pt. שֹׁחֵט, pl. cs. שֹׁחֲטֵי, pass. שָׁחוּט, שְׁחוּטָה, שְׁחֻטָה: — 1. **slaughter** (animals) Gn 37_{31}, esp. for sacrifice 1S 1_{25}; *šāḥaṭ ʾarṣâ* slaughter on the bare ground 1S 14_{32}; — 2. **slaughter** (obj. person) Gn 22_{10} 1K 18_{40}.

nif.: impf. יִשָּׁחֵט: **be slaughtered** Lv 6_{18} Nu 11_{22}. †

II שׁחט: **qal**: pt. pass. שָׁחוּט: **alloyed** 1K 10_{16f} 2C 9_{15f} (oth. rd. *šāṭûᵃḥ* 'beaten'). †

cj. שַׁחַט: cj. שַׁחַט הַשֵּׂטִים **corruption** = fornication of Ho 5_2; oth. rd. שַׁחַת pit. †

שְׁחִי: ℱ שׁוּחִי.

*שְׁחִיטָה: cs. שְׁחִיטַת: **slaughter** 2C 30_{17}. †

שְׁחִין: **boil, inflamed spot** Ex 9_{9ff}; Dt $28_{27.28}$ Jb 2_7 perh. **smallpox**.

שָׁחִיס Is 37_{30}: < ℱ סָחִישׁ. †

*שְׁחִית: pl. sf. שְׁחִיתוֹתָם: trad. **pit** Ps 107_{20} La 4_{20}, but perh. txt. corr., ℱ comm. †

שַׁחַל: שָׁחַל: **lion-cub** Ho 5_{14}.

שְׁחֵלֶת: **onycha**, ingredient of incense, prob. the closing-flap of a strombus (a certain mollusk) Ex 30_{34}. †

שַׁחַף: שָׁחַף: unclean bird, trad. **seagull**; but sugg. **bat** Lv 11_{16} Dt 14_{15}. †

שַׁחֶפֶת: undetermined illness, trad. **consumption** Lv 26_{16} Dt 28_{22}. †

*שַׁחַץ: שָׁחַץ: *bᵉnê šāḥaṣ*, **proud beasts** (w. mythological overtones) Jb 28_8 41_{26}. †

שַׁחֲצוּמָה Jos 19_{22}: Kt ־צוּ־, Qr ־צִי־, sugg. rd. שַׁחֲצִימָה, loc. of *שַׁחֲצַיִם: n. loc. †

שׁחק: **qal**: pf. שָׁחַקְתָּ, שָׁחֲקוּ; impf. sf. אֶשְׁחָקֵם: **grind down, rub away**, obj. stones Jb 14_{19}, incense Ex 30_{36}, foes like dust 2S 22_{43} Ps 18_{43}. †

שַׁחַק: pl. שְׁחָקִים: — 1. sg. coll. **(layer of) dust** Is 40_{15} †; — 2. sg. coll. trad. **clouds**, but sugg. 'clouds of dust' Ps $89_{7.38}$ †; — 3. pl. **clouds** 2S 22_{12}.

I שָׁחַר: **qal**: pf. שׁ׳: **become black** Jb 30_{30}. †

II שׁחר: **qal**: pt. שֹׁחֵר: **be intent on** (s.thg.) Pr 11_{27}. †

piel: pf. שִׁחֲרוּ, sf. שִׁחֲרוֹ, שִׁחֲרֻתַּנִי; impf. תְּשַׁחֵר, sf. יְשַׁחֲרֻנְנִי, אֲשַׁחֲרֶךָּ; inf. שַׁחֵר, שַׁחֲרָה; pt. pl. cs. מְשַׁחֲרֵי, sf. מְשַׁחֲרַי: — 1. w. acc. **be intent on, inquire for, seek** Jb 7_{21}, obj. God Is 26_9; — 2. w. 2 accs. *šiḥᵃrô mûsār* is intent on disciplining him Pr 13_{24}; — 3. *šaḥrāh* **magic (spell)** against it Is 47_{11}.

שָׁחֹר: f. שְׁחוֹרָה; pl. שְׁחֹרִים, שְׁחֹרוֹת: **black**: hair Lv $13_{31.37}$, raven SS 5_{11}, horses Zc $6_{2.6}$, complexion SS 1_5. †

שַׁחַר: שַׁחַר (reddish) **(light before) dawn** Gn 19_{15}.

שְׁחֹר: ℱ שְׁחוֹר.

שִׁחֹר: ℱ שִׁיחוֹר.

שַׁחֲרוּת: dark hair? **prime of youth**? Ec 11_{10}. †

*שְׁחַרְחֹר: f. שְׁחַרְחֹרֶת: **swarthy** (in complexion) SS 1_6. †

שְׁחַרְיָה: n. pers.

שַׁחֲרַיִם: n. pers.

שׁחת: **nif.**: pf. נִשְׁחֲתָה, נִשְׁחַת; impf. תִּשָּׁחֵת; pt. pl. f. נִשְׁחָתוֹת: **become corrupt, spoiled** Gn 6_{11f} Ex 8_{20}.

piel: pf. שִׁחֵת, שִׁחַתָּ, שִׁחֲתוּ, שִׁחֵתוּ, sf. שִׁחֶתְךָ, שִׁחֲתָהּ; impv. שַׁחֲתוּ; inf. שַׁחֵת, שַׁחֲתָהּ, שַׁחֶתְכֶם: — 1. **wipe out, spoil, ruin** Gn 6_{17}; obj. vineyard Je 12_{10}, man 2S 1_{14}, eye Ex 21_{26}; suppress (one's compassion) Am 1_{11}; corrupt, misuse (one's wisdom) Ez 28_{17}; — 2. w. *lᵉ*, **bring ruin on** Nu 32_{15}; — 3. abs. **act ruinously, cause trouble** 2S 14_{11}.

hif.: pf. הִשְׁחִית, הִשְׁחַתִּי, הִשְׁחִיתוּ; impf. יַשְׁחִית, תַּשְׁחֵת, תַּשְׁחִיתוּן, נַשְׁחִיתָה, sf. וַתַּשְׁחִיתֵם, וָאַשְׁחִיתֵךְ; inf. הַשְׁחִית, הַשְׁחִיתֶךָ, abs. הַשְׁחֵת; pt. מַשְׁחִית, sf. מַשְׁחִיתָם: — 1. **spoil, ruin** Gn 18_{28}, bring ruin on Ps 78_{45}; abs. **act ruinously** Dt 4_{16}; — 2. **wipe out** 1S 26_{15}; subj. God Gn 6_{13}; abs. 2S 20_{20}; spec.: *hišḥît darkô* one's ways have become corrupt Gn 6_{12}; spoil (= clip) (edge of beard) Lv 19_{27}; fell (to the ground) Ju 20_{21}; undermine (wall) 2S 20_{15}; impair (inheritance) Ru 4_6; let (houses) fall in 2C 34_{11}; *wattašḥēt ʿagbātāh min*, she became more dreadfully lustful than Ez 23_{11}; *hašḥît nafšô* destroy onesf. Pr 6_{32}; N.B. *ʾal-tašḥēt* unexplained term Ps 57_1 &c.; — 4. pt. ℱ *mašḥît*!: (*'aryēh*) *mašḥît* slaughtering Je 2_{30}; *hammal'āk hammašḥît* destroying angel 2S 24_{16}, > *hammašḥît* Ex 12_{13}; *mašḥît* = spec. group of soldiers 1S 13_{17}.

hof.: pt. מָשְׁחָת: **polluted** Pr 25_{26}; **damaged, blemished** (animal) Ma 1_{14} (castrated?). †

שַׁחַת: שָׁחַת, sf. שַׁחְתָּם: — 1. **pit** (to trap animals) Ez 19_4; — 2. **pit, grave**: abode of the dead (= Sheol) Is 38_{17}.

שִׁטָּה: pl. שִׁטִּים: **acacia**, *Acacia nilotica* (tree & wood) Ex 25_5.

שׁטח: **qal**: pf. שְׁטָחוּם; impf. וַיִּשְׁטְחוּ, וַתִּשְׁטַח; pt. שֹׁטֵחַ: **spread out** (trans.) Nu 11_{32} Je 8_2 Jb 12_{23}; pour out (grain) 2S 17_{19}. †

piel: pf. שִׁטַּחְתִּי: **spread out** (hands) Ps 88_{10}. †

שֹׁטֵט Jos 23_{13}: rd. שֹׁטִים (√שׁוט). †

שִׁטִּים: n. loc.: — 1. Nu 33_{49} > *haššiṭṭîm* 25_1 Jos 2_1 3_1 Mi 6_5; — 2. *naḥal haššiṭṭîm* Jl 4_{18}. †

שָׁטַף: **qal**: pf. 'שׁ, sf. שְׁטָפוּנוּ, שְׁטָפָתְנִי; impf. יִשְׁטְפוּךָ, תִּשְׁטְפֵנִי, sf. יִשְׁטְפוּ, וְאֶשְׁטֹף, יִשְׁטוֹף; pt. שׁ(ו)טֵף: — 1. w. acc. (subj. floods &c.): **wash away** Is 28_{17}; **wash off** (obj. chariot) 1K 22_{38}; — 2. abs.: **flood, overflow** Is 8_8; subj. horse, **storm in** Je 8_6; subj. *ḥayil*, **flood out** Dn 11_{10}.

nif.: impf. יִשָּׁטֵף, יִשָּׁטְפוּ; cj. inf. הִשָּׁטֵף Dn 11_{22}: **be washed off** Lv 15_{12} Dn 11_{22}. †

pual (or **qal** pass): שֻׁטַּף: **be washed off** Lv 6_{21}. †

שֶׁטֶף, שֵׁטֶף **flood** Na 1_8 Ps 32_6 Jb 38_{25} Dn 9_{26}; metaph. of anger Pr 27_4. †

שׁטר: **qal**: pt. שׁ(ו)טֵר, שֹׁטְרִים, שֹׁטְרֵי, sf. שֹׁטְרָיו: **record-keeper, officer**: of Egypt Ex 5_6, of Isr. Jos 1_{10}.

שִׁטְרַי: n. pers.

שַׁי: שָׁי: **gift, present** Is 18_7 Ps 68_{30} 76_{12}. †

שְׁיָא: n. pers., ꟳ (Qr) שְׁוָא 2S 20_{25}. †

שִׁיאֹן: n. loc.

[***שִׁיבָה**: cs. שִׁיבַת rd. שְׁבִית Ps 126_1; sf. שִׁיבָתוֹ rd. שִׁבְתּוֹ 2S 19_{33}. †]

[**שׁיה**: **qal**: pf. תֶּשִׁי Dt 32_{18}: rd. תַּשִּׁי (√נשה). †]

שִׁיזָא: n. pers.

שׁיח: **qal**: pf. שָׁחָה: w. *le'āfār*, **melt away** (into dust) Ps 44_{26}. †

hitpolel: impf. תִּשְׁתּוֹחֲחִי, תִּשְׁתּוֹחָח: subj. *nefeš*, turn out to be dissolved, **melt away** Ps $42_{6f.12}$ 43_5. †

N.B.: These may be referred to ꟳ *šḥḥ* & forms of the latter root be referred here.

שִׁיחָה: pl. שִׁיחוֹת: **pit** (to trap animals) Je 18_{22} Kt, Ps 57_7 119_{85}. †

שִׁחוֹר, שִׁיחוֹר Je 2_{18}, שִׁחֹר Is 23_3: **river, canal** (in Egypt) Jos 13_3 Is 23_3 Je 2_{18} 1C 13_5. †

שִׁיחוֹר לִבְנָת: name of canal Jos 19_{26}. †

שַׁיִט Is 28_{15}: ꟳ II שׁוֹט. †

שַׁיִט: **oar** Is 33_{21}.

שִׁילֹה, Qr שִׁילוֹ Gn 49_{10}: unexpl., ꟳ comm. †

שִׁילוֹ: n. loc. **Shiloh**, ꟳ שִׁלֹה.

שֵׁילָל Mi 1_8 Kt: rd שׁוֹלָל.

שִׁילֹנִי: gent. of שִׁילוֹ.

שִׁימוֹן: n. pers.

שׁין: **'hiftil'** (or the like): pt. מַשְׁתִּין: **pass water, urinate** 1S $25_{22\cdot34}$ 1K 14_{10} 16_{11} 21_{21} 2K 9_8. †

***שַׁיִן**: pl. sf. שֵׁינֵיהֶם: **urine** Is 36_{12} 2K 18_{27} (both) Kt, Qr euphem. †

שׁיר: **qal**: pf. שָׁר; impf. אָשִׁירָה, וַתָּשַׁר, יָשִׁיר, נָשִׁיר, יָשִׁירוּ; impv. שִׁירוּ; inf. 1S 18_6 Kt שׁוּר, Qr שִׁיר; pt. שָׁר, שָׁרִים, שָׁרוֹת: — 1. **sing** 1S 18_6, w. cogn. acc. Ex 15_1; w. obj. of topic: recount in song, **sing of** Ps 21_{14}; w. *leyhwh* to the honor of Y. Ex 15_1; — 2. pt. **singer** 2S 19_{36}.

polel: pf. שֹׁרְרוּ; impf. יְשׁוֹרֵר; pt. מְשׁוֹרֵר, מְשֹׁרְרִים, מְשֹׁרְרוֹת: **continually sing (of)** † Zp 2_{14} Jb 36_{24}; subj. *šîr* (song), **resound** 2C 29_{28}; otherw. pt. **singer** (m. or f.) (in temple) 1C 6_{18}.

hof. (or **qal** pass.) impf. יוּשַׁר: **be sung** Is 26_1. †

***שֵׁיר** Is 3_{19}, ꟳ I *שֵׁר.

שִׁיר: sf. שִׁירוֹ, שִׁירֹה Ps 42_9; pl. שׁ(י)רִים, sf.

שִׁירֵיכֶם: **song** (of any sort): drinking-song Is 24_{9}, of prostitute 23_{16}; *šîr haššîrîm* the loveliest song SS 1_{1}; at departure Gn 31_{27}; at festivals Is 30_{29}; w. instruments Am 6_{5}; *benôt haššîr* (voices?) Ec 12_{4}; but largely of cultic songs, e.g. Ps 30_{1}.

שִׁירָה: cs. שִׁירַת: **song** 2S 22_{1}, usage = *šîr*.

שַׁיִשׁ: **alabaster** 1C 29_{2}. †

שִׁישָׁא: n. pers.

שִׁישַׁק: שִׁישָׁק: ‎⁊ שׁוּשַׁק 1K 14_{25} Kt: n. of pers. (Egyp. king).

שִׁית: **qal**: pf. שָׁת, שָׁתָה, שַׁתָּה & שַׁתָּ Ps 90_{8}, וְשַׁתִּי, שָׁתוּ, שַׁתּוּ Ps 73_{9}, sf. שָׁתָם, שַׁתַּנִי, שַׁתִּהָ; impf. יָשִׁית, יָשֵׁת, וַיָּשֶׁת, תָּשִׁיתִי, אָשִׁית, יָשִׁיתוּ, sf. יְשִׁיתֵהוּ, אֲשִׁיתֶנּוּ, אֲשִׁיתֵךְ, תְּשִׁיתֵמוֹ; Je 13_{16} יְשִׁית (Kt יָשִׁית, Qr וְשִׁית) rd וְשָׁת; impv. שִׁית, שִׁיתָה, שִׁיתִי, שִׁיתוּ, sf. שִׁיתֵמוֹ; inf. שִׁית, sf. שִׁתִי, abs. שֹׁת: — 1. **put, set, lay**: obj. hand (on s.one) Gn 46_{4}; of bird, obj. young Ps 84_{4}; of God, obj. world (on pillars) 2S 2_{8}; *šāt ʿal*: load up s.one, put (a load) on s.one Ru 3_{15}, impose (a fine) on Ex 21_{22}, set (s.one) over (a country) Gn 41_{33}, join with 30_{40}; *šāt lebāddô* set apart 30_{40}; *šāt yādô le* make common cause w. Ex 23_{1}; *šāt ḥaṭṭāʾt ʿal* put the blame on Nu 12_{11}; — 2. **order, appoint, send for**: a sign Ex 10_{1}, feast Je 51_{39}; w. *lekissēʾ* appoint for the throne = set on the thr. Ps 132_{11}; — 3. **direct, fix**: fix (one's refuge in Y.) Ps 73_{28}; (boundary) Ex 23_{31}; *šāt libbô le* take s.thg to heart 2S 13_{20}, observe Je 31_{21}, w/o *le* 1S 4_{20}, w. *ʾel* Jb 7_{17}; *šāt pānāyw ʾel* turn one's face toward Nu 24_{1}; *šāt ʿênāyw le* & inf. set one's eyes to Ps 17_{11}; *šāt pîw be* gape toward Ps 73_{9}; — 4. w. 2 acc., **make** s.thg or s.one (into) s.thg: make (darkness his canopy) 2S 22_{12}, make (him ruler) 1K 11_{34}; = w. acc. & *le* Je 2_{15}; w. acc. & *ke* make s.thg or s.one like Ho 2_{5}; w. acc. & *šekem* make (him) show his shoulder (in submission) Ps 21_{13}; — 5. var.: *šātû haššāʿrâ* took up their position at the gate Is 22_{7}; *šāt be* treat (as heir) like Je 3_{19}.

hof. (or **qal** pass.): impf. יוּשַׁת: **be imposed** (of ransom) Ex 21_{30}. †

שִׁית: **garment** Ps 73_{6} Pr 7_{10}. †

שַׁיִת: שָׁיִת, sf. שִׁיתוֹ: **weeds** Is 5_{6} 7_{23ff} 9_{17} 10_{17} 27_{4}. †

שָׁכַב: **qal**: pf. ש׳, שָׁכֵב, שָׁכְבָה, שָׁכַבְתָּ, שָׁכַבְתִּי, שָׁכְבוּ, שְׁכַבְתֶּם; impf. יִשְׁכַּב, יִשְׁכָּב, אֶשְׁכְּבָה, יִשְׁכְּבוּ, יִשְׁכְּבֻן, יִשְׁכָּבוּן, נִשְׁכְּבָה; impv. שְׁכַב, שְׁכָב, שִׁכְבָה, שִׁכְבִי; inf. שְׁכַב, לִשְׁכַּב־, שִׁכְבָהּ, שָׁכְבְּךָ, abs. שָׁכֹב; pt. שֹׁכֵב, שֹׁכֶבֶת, שֹׁכְבִים, שֹׁכְבֵי: — 1. **lie down**: to sleep Gn 19_{4}, when ill 2K 9_{16}; *šākab libbô* one's mind rests Ec 2_{23}; — 2. *šākab ʾet-ʾabōtāyw* lie w. one's fathers (i.e. after death) Gn 47_{30}; — 3. = sexual intercourse, w. *ʿim* Gn 19_{32}, w. *ʾēt* 19_{33}; for sexual perversion Ex 22_{18}; w. acc., lie w. a woman 2S 13_{14} (txt.?).

nif.: impf. תִּשָּׁכַבְנָה (Qr euphem. for שׁגל nif.): **be lain with** Is 13_{16} Zc 14_{2}. †

pual: pf. שֻׁכַּבְתְּ (Qr euphem. for שׁגל pual): **be lain with** Je 3_{2}. †

hif.: pf. הִשְׁכִּיבָה, sf. הִשְׁכַּבְתִּים; impf. יַשְׁכִּיב, sf. וַיַּשְׁכִּבֵהוּ, וַיַּשְׁכִּיבֵהוּ; inf. הַשְׁכֵּב: — 1. **lay** (s.one somewhere) 1K 3_{20} 17_{19} 2K 4_{21} 2C 16_{14}; **let** (s.one) **lie down** Ho 2_{20}, **make** (s.one) **lie down** 2S 8_{2}; **tilt** (a vessel for pouring) Jb 38_{37}. †

hof.: pf. הָשְׁכַּב; impv. הָשְׁכְּבָה; pt. מֻשְׁכָּב: **be laid (down)** 2K 4_{32} Ez $32_{19 \cdot 32}$. †

***שְׁכָבָה** (or *שְׁכָבָה): cs. שִׁכְבַת: — 1. **layer** (of dew) Ex 16_{13f}; — 2. *šikbat zeraʿ* **emission of semen** Lv $15_{16f \cdot 32}$ 22_{4}; *šākab šikbat zeraʿ* lie (w. a woman and there is) an emission of semen Lv 15_{18} 19_{20} Nu 5_{13}. †

***שְׁכֹבֶת**: sf. שְׁכָבְתּוֹ, שְׁכָבְתְּךָ: **sexual intercourse**: *nātan šekobtô ʾel*, consummate intercourse with Lv 18_{20}; w. *be* with Lv 18_{23} 20_{15} Nu 5_{20}. †

שׂכה: **hif.**: pt. מַשְׁכִּים (but to be analysed as *מַאֲשִׁיכִים, denom. fm. אֶשֶׁךְ): **exhibiting (strong) testicles** Je 5_{8}. †

שְׁכוֹל: **bereavement** (by loss of children) Is $47_{8f.}$ †

שַׁכּוּל: f. שַׁכֻּלָה; pl. f. שַׁכֻּלוֹת: **bereaved** of children Je 18_{21}, (of bear) who has lost her cubs (& is therefore fierce) 2S 17_8 Ho 13_8 Pr 17_{12}; so of ewe who has lost her lambs SS 4_2 6_6. †

שְׁכוּלָה: adj. f. **bereaved** of children Is 49_{21}. †

שִׁכּוֹר, שִׁכֹּר: f. שִׁכֹּרָה; pl. שִׁכּוֹרִים, cs. שִׁכֹּרֵי: **drunk(en)** 1S 1_{13}; *šōteh šikkôr* drinking to drunkenness 1K 16_9 20_{16}.

שָׁכַח: **qal** (102×): pf. שׁ׳, שָׁכֵחָה Pr 2_{17}, שָׁכַחַתְּ (= שָׁכַחַתְּ or שָׁכַ֫חַת) Is 17_{10}, שְׁכַחְתֶּם, שָׁכָחְתִּי, sf. שְׁכֵחוּךְ, שְׁכֵחֻנִי, שְׁכֵחָנִי, שְׁכֵחֲנוּךָ, שְׁכַחְתָּנִי; impf. תִּשְׁכָּחֵנִי, תִּשְׁכָּחוּ, תִּשְׁכָּחִי, יִשְׁכַּח, sf. תִּשְׁכָּחֵנִי, אֶשְׁכָּחֵךְ; impv. שִׁכְחִי; inf. שָׁכוֹחַ; pt. שֹׁכְחֵי: **forget** Gn 40_{23} (obj. person), Je 2_{32} (obj. a thing); w. *ʼēt ʼašer-* that which, what Gn 27_{45}; w. *kî* Jb 39_{15}; oft. obj. Y. Dt 8_{14}, God's law Ho 4_6 &c.; w. *min* & inf. forget to Ps 102_5.

nif.: pf. נִשְׁכַּחְתִּי, נִשְׁכַּ֫חַת, נִשְׁכַּח, נִשְׁכָּח; impf. תִּשָּׁכַח, יִשָּׁכַח; pt. נִשְׁכָּחָה, נִשְׁכָּחִים: **fall into oblivion, be forgotten** Gn 41_{30}.

piel: pf. שִׁכַּח: **wipe out the memory of,** cause s.thg to be lost to memory La 2_6. †

hitp.: impf. יִשְׁתַּכְּחוּ: **be forgotten** Ec 8_{10}. †

*שָׁכֵחַ: pl. שְׁכֵחִים, cs. שְׁכֵחֵי: **one who forgets** Is 65_{11} Ps 9_{18}. †

שׁכך: **qal**: pf. שָׁכָכָה; impf. וַיָּשֹׁכּוּ; inf. שֹׁךְ: **go down, abate**: of water Gn 8_1, anger Est 2_1 7_{10}. †

hif.: pf. הֲשִׁכֹּתִי: w. *mēʻal*, **drain off** (complaints) from Nu 17_{20}. †

שׁכל: **qal**: pf. שָׁכֹלְתִּי, שָׁכָלְתִּי; impf. תְּשַׁכֵּל, אֶשְׁכָּל: w. acc. **be bereft of (one's child[ren])** Gn 27_{45} 43_{14} 1S 15_{33}. †

piel: pf. שִׁכְּלָה, שִׁכֵּלוּ, שִׁכַּלְתִּים, שִׁכַּלְתְּ; impf. תְּשַׁכֵּל, תְּשַׁכֶּל־, תְּשַׁכְּלִי; inf. sf. שַׁכְּלָם; pt. f. מְשַׁכֵּלָה, מְשַׁכֶּלֶת, מְשַׁכֶּלֶת: — 1. **deprive & bereave of children, make** s.one **childless** Gn 42_{36}; — 2. **cause miscarriage** 2K $2_{19.21}$; — 3. **have a miscarriage, miscarry** Gn 31_{38}; — 4. of vine, **fail to bear** Ma 3_{11}.

hif.: pt. מַשְׁכִּיל: **miscarrying** Ho 9_{14}. †

*שִׁכֻּלִים: sf. שִׁכֻּלָיִךְ: **bereavement**, i.e. situation of mother who has lost her children Is 49_{20}. †

שׁכם (denom. of I שְׁכֶם): **hif.** (66×): pf. הִשְׁכִּים, הִשְׁכִּימוּ, הִשְׁכַּמְתֶּם; impf. וַיַּשְׁכֵּם, נַשְׁכִּימָה, וַיַּשְׁכִּ(י)מוּ, תַּשְׁכִּים; impv. הַשְׁכֵּם; inf. הַשְׁכֵּ(י)ם; pt. מַשְׁכִּים, pl. cs. מַשְׁכִּימֵי: load up early on one's shoulder or back of animals > do s.thg early > do s.thg eagerly: — 1. **get up, rise early** 1S 15_{12}; *hiškîm lᵉdarkô* get on one's way early Ju 19_9; inf. *haškîm* early Pr 27_{14}; *maškîmê qûm* those who rise early Ps 127_2; *haškēm wᵉhaʻarēb* early & late 1S 17_{16}; — 2. **do** (s.thg) **early**: *wayyaškēm ... wayyiqrāʼ* in the early morning he called Gn 20_8; so oft., even. w. *babbōqer* added Gn 19_{27}; *maškîm hōlēk* (dew) which goes away early Ho 6_4; — 3. **do** (s.thg) **eagerly, repeatedly**: *hiškîmû hišḥîtû* they were eager to do evil Zp 3_7, *haškēm wᵉšālōaḥ* sending over & over again Je 7_{25}.

I שְׁכֶם: sf. שִׁכְמוֹ, שִׁכְמֶךָ: — 1. **both shoulders,** neck & upper part of back Gn 9_{23} 21_{14}; *hifnâ šikmô lᵉ* = turn to leave 1S 10_9; *šᵉkem ʼeḥād* = shoulder to shoulder Zp 3_9; *šît šᵉkem* turn s.one to flight Gn 21_{13}; — 2. metaph. **mountain-ridge** † Gn 48_{22}.

II שְׁכֶם: n. loc. **Shechem.**

III שְׁכֶם: n. pers. Gn $34_{2\text{-}26}$ (11×) Jos 24_{32} Ju 9_{28}. †

שֶׁכֶם: n. pers.

שִׁכְמִי: gent. of שֶׁכֶם Nu 26_{31}. †

שָׁכַן: **qal** (111×): pf. שׁ׳, שָׁכֵן, שָׁכְנָה, שָׁכַנְתְּ; impf. יִשְׁכֹּ(ו)ן, יִשְׁכָּן־, אֶשְׁכְּנָה, אֶשְׁכֹּנָה, יִשְׁכְּנוּ, תִּשְׁכֹּנָּה (!נּ) Ez 17_{23}; impv. שְׁכֹן, שְׁכָן־, שִׁכְנוּ; inf. לִשְׁכֹּן, sf. לְשָׁכְנִי Ex 29_{46}, לְשִׁכְנוֹ Dt 12_5; pt. שֹׁכֵן, cs. שֹׁכְנִי, f. cs. שֹׁכַנְתִּי Je 51_{13}, pl. שֹׁכְנִים, sf. שֹׁכְנֵיהֶם: — 1. **submit** (onesf.) †

Ps 68_{19}; — 2. **settle** (temporarily) (intrans.): of Y.'s *kābôd* Ex 24_{16}, of lion Dt 33_{20}; camp by tribes Nu 24_2; — 3. **stay, stop** (at a place) † Ju 5_{17} Pr 7_{11}; — 4. **settle (to live)** (i.e. dwell), 'settle down' Gn 14_{13}; w. acc. **live in, inhabit**, obj. *'ereṣ* Ps 37_3; *šākan taḥtāyw* live at one's place = undisturbed 2S 7_{10}, w. *(le)betaḥ* Dt $33_{12\cdot 28}$; subj. the dead Ps 94_{17}; — 5. subj. God, w. *behar ṣiyyôn* Is 8_{18} &c.; — 6. subj. things: of tent of meeting, **sojourn, be found** Lv 16_{16}; of Jerus. (personified?) **dwell** Je 33_{16}; abstract, of *mišpāṭ* Is 32_{16}.

piel: pf. שִׁכַּנְתִּי, שִׁכֵּן; impf. אֲשַׁכְּנָה; inf. שַׁכֵּן: **let, make** s.one **live** (=**dwell**) Nu 14_{30}; obj. *šemô šām* make one's name dwell Dt 12_{11}.

hif.: pf. הִשְׁכַּנְתִּי; impf. יַשְׁכֵּן, וַיַּשְׁכִּינוּ: **settle** s.one; **let, make** s.one/s.thg **dwell** Gn 3_{24}.

שָׁכֵן: cs. שְׁכַן (txt.? Ho 10_5), sf. שְׁכֵנוֹ; f. sg. sf. שְׁכֶנְתָּהּ; pl. sf. שְׁכֵנָיו, שְׁכֵנְכִי 2K 4_3, שְׁכֵנֵינוּ; f. pl. שְׁכֵנוֹת: — 1. **inhabitant** † Is 33_{24}; — 2. **neighbor** 2K 4_3; designating neighboring town Je 49_{18}, neighboring people Dt 1_7.

שְׁכַנְיָה: n. pers.

שְׁכַנְיָהוּ: n. pers.

שׁכר: **qal**: pf. שָׁכְרוּ; impf. יִשְׁכָּר, וַיִּשְׁכְּרוּ, יִשְׁכָּרוּן; impv. שִׁכְרוּ; inf. לְשָׁכְרָה: **be(come) drunk(en)** Gn 9_{21}; w. *dām* be drunk w. blood Is 49_{26}.

piel: impf. וַיְשַׁכְּרֵהוּ; inf. שַׁכֵּר; pt. מְשַׁכֶּרֶת: **make** s.one **drunk(en)** 2S 11_{13} Je 51_7 Hb 2_{15}. †

hif.: pf. הִשְׁכַּרְתִּי, הִשְׁכַּרְתִּים; impf. אַשְׁכִּיר; impv. הַשְׁכִּירֻהוּ: **make** s.one (s.thg) **drunk(en)** Dt 32_{42} Je 48_{26} $51_{39\cdot 57}$. †

hitp.: impf. תִּשְׁתַּכָּרִין: **act drunk(en)** 1S 1_{14}. †

שֵׁכָר: intoxicating drink, evid. a kind of **beer** 1S 1_{15}.

*שָׁכֵר: f. cs. שְׁכֻרַת: **drunk(en)** Is 51_{21}. †

I שִׁכָּרוֹן: **drunken fit, drunkenness** Je 13_{13} Ez 23_{33} 39_{19}. †

II *שִׁכְּרוֹן: n. loc., loc. שִׁכְּרוֹנָה.

שַׁל 2S 6_7: disdain, irreverence ?? txt. corr. ? ↗ comm. †

שֶׁל: ↗ שֶׁ.

[שַׁלְאֲנָן Jb 21_{23}: rd. שַׁאֲנָן. †]

שׁלב: **pual**: pt. pl. f. מְשֻׁלָּבֹת: **dovetailed, joined** (w. tenons) Ex 26_{17} 36_{22}. †

*שָׁלָב: pl. שְׁלַבִּים: **cross-piece, cross-bar** 1K 7_{28f}. †

שׁלג: **hif.**: impf. תַּשְׁלֵג: **snow** Ps 68_{15}. †

I שֶׁלֶג: שֶׁלֶג: **snow** 2K 5_{27}.

II שֶׁלֶג: **soapwort**, *Saponaria* Jb 9_{30}. †

שׁלה: **qal**: pf. שָׁלוּ, שָׁלַוְתִּי; impf. יִשְׁלָיוּ: **have peace and quiet** Je 12_1 Ps 122_6 Jb 3_{26} 12_6 La 1_5. †

nif.: impf. תִּשָּׁלוּ: **relax** (and thus be negligent) 2C 29_{11}. †

hif.: impf. תַשְׁלֶה: **lull** (w. false hopes) 2K 4_{28}. †

I *שֵׁלָה: sf. שֵׁלָתֵךְ: 1S 1_{17}: ↗ שְׁאֵלָה. †

II שֵׁלָה: n. pers.

שִׁלֹה (21×), שִׁלוֹ (8×), שִׁילוֹ (2×): n. loc. **Shiloh**.

שַׁלְהֶבֶת: שַׁלְהֶבֶת: **flame** Ez 21_3 Jb 15_{30}. †

[שַׁלְהֶבֶתְיָה SS 8_6: rd שַׁלְהָבֹתֶיהָ שַׁלְהֶבֶת יָהּ (but oth. accept txt. mng. 'a mighty flame').]

שָׁלֵו, שָׁלֵיו Jb 21_{23}, שְׁלֵיו Je 49_{31}: f. שְׁלֵוָה; pl. cs. שַׁלְוֵי: **undisturbed, at ease, unconcerned, heedless** Je 49_{31} Zc 7_7 Ps 73_{12} Jb 16_{12} 21_{23} 1C 4_{40}. †

*שֶׁלֶו: cs. שַׁלְוִי: **ease, unconcern** Ps 30_7. †

שִׁלוֹ: ↗ שִׁלֹה & שִׁילוֹ.

שַׁלְוָה: cs. שַׁלְוַת; pl. sf. שַׁלְוֹתַיִךְ: — 1. sg. **ease, unconcern** Ps 122_7 Pr 1_{32} 17_1, *bešalwâ* while they are relaxed Dn 8_{25} $11_{21\cdot 24}$; *šalwat hašqēṭ* careless ease Ez 16_{49}; — 2. pl. sf. the time of your success Je 22_{21}. †

*שִׁלּוּחִים: sf. שִׁלּוּחֶיהָ: — 1. **dismissal** (of wife to her father's house), **divorce** Ex 18_2; — 2. **farewell-gift, dismissal-gift** (of father of bride to the bride), dowry 1K 9_{16} Mi 1_{14}. †

שָׁלוֹם, שָׁלֹם (236×): cs. שְׁלוֹם; sf. שְׁלֹמָהּ, שְׁלוֹמֶךָ, שְׁלוֹמִי, שְׁלֹמָם, שְׁלוֹמֵנוּ; pl. שְׁלוֹמִים: **being whole**, **intact**; **prosperity**, **peace**: — 1. **ease**, **unaffectedness**: *lᵉšālôm* calmly, unaffectedly Gn 37_4; *šālôm lākem*, do not be worried Gn 43_{24}; *ʾîš šᵉlômî* my confidant Ps 41_{10}, so pl. *ʾanšê šᵉlōmî* Je 38_{22} & *ʾᵉnôš šᵉlômî* Je 20_{10}; — 2. **prosperity**, **success** Is 48_{18}; *šᵉlôm parʿōh* what is advantageous to Ph. Gn 41_{16}; — 3. **intactness**, **wholeness**: *lᵉšālôm* unmolested Gn 44_{17}; *bᵉšālôm* unhurt 26_{29}; *hāyâ šālôm* be safe 2S 17_3; *šālôm lāk* (as formula of greeting) Ju 19_{20}; *šālôm* all is well 2K 4_{23}; — 4. (personal wholeness:) **well-being**, **state of health** &c.: *šᵉlôm ʾaḥeykā* how your brothers are Gn 37_{14}; *šālôm lô*, he is fine 43_{28}; *hᵃšālôm ʾattâ* how are you? 2S 20_9; *mâ haššālôm* how can everything be all right? 2K 9_{22}; *šᵉlôm hammilḥāmâ* how the battle is going 2S 11_7; *(lišʾōl) lišlôm* ask how s.one is Gn 43_{27} 2K 10_{13}; — 5. prosperous relationship = **peace**: *bên … ûbên* 1S 7_{14}; *qārāʾ lᵉšālôm lᵉ/ʾel* offer peace to Dt 20_{10} Ju 21_{13}; *ʿānâ šālôm ʾēt* accept peace w. Dt 20_{11}; *ʿāśâ šālôm lᵉ* make peace w. Jos 9_{15}; *bāʾ ʾel-ʾᵃbōtāyw bᵉšālôm* = die Gn 15_{15}; *lᵉšālôm* w. peaceful intentions 1K 20_{18}; *bāʾ šālôm* enter into peace Is 57_2; — 6. (weakened >) **kindness**: *ʾāsaf šᵉlōmô mēʾēt* withdraw one's friendship from Je 16_5; *dibber šālôm* speak in a friendly fashion to Ps 28_3; — 7. (strengthened >) total prosperity, **salvation**: *(hāyâ) šālôm mēʿim yhwh lᵉ* prosperity, salvation from Y. to 1K 2_{33}; *yhwh šālôm* as name of altar Ju 6_{24}; *bᵉrît šᵉlōmî* my covenant of salvation Is 54_{10}.

שַׁלּוּם, שַׁלֻּם: n. pers.

שִׁלּוּם & Ho 9_7 שִׁלֻּם: pl. שִׁלּוּמִים: **repayment**, **retribution** Is 34_8 Ho 9_7 Mi 7_3. †

שַׁלּוּן: n. pers.

שְׁלוֹנִי: F שִׁילֹנִי.

שָׁלוֹשׁ: F שָׁלֹשׁ.

שָׁלַח: **qal** (562×): pf. שׁ׳, שָׁלַח־ La 1_{13}, שָׁלְחָה, שְׁלַחְתֶּם, sf. שְׁלָחוֹ, שְׁלַחְתִּיו; impf. יִשְׁלַח, תִּשְׁלַח, אֶשְׁלְחָה, יִשְׁלְחוּ, תִּשְׁלַחְנָה, sf. יִשְׁלָחֲךָ, תִּשְׁלָחֵם; impv. שְׁלַח, וּשְׁלַח 2K 9_{17}, שִׁלְחָה, שִׁלְחוּ, sf. שְׁלָחֵנִי; inf. שְׁלֹחַ & שְׁלַח Is 58_9, שָׁלְחִי, abs. שָׁלוֹחַ; pt. שֹׁלֵחַ, sf. שֹׁלְחִי, שֹׁלַחֲךָ, pl. sf. שֹׁלְחָיו, pass. שָׁלוּחַ, שְׁלוּחָה, שְׁלֻחָה, F שְׁלֻחוֹת noun: — 1. **give free play to**, **let go**: *šālaḥ pîw bᵉ* give free rein to one's mouth for Ps 50_{19}; *šᵉluḥâ* let loose Gn 49_{21}; — 2. **stretch out** (trans.): obj. one's hand Gn 3_{22}, w. *bᵉ* lay one's hand on Jb 28_9, lay hands on Gn 37_{22}; obj. finger Is 58_9, obj. staff 1S 14_{27}; — 3. **let** s.one **go**: w. *lᵉfānāyw* ahead Gn 45_5; — 4. **send** Gn 37_{13}; subj. God, obj. prophets 2K 2_2; *šōlᵉḥî* (God) who sends me 2S 24_{13}; *šālaḥ dābār lᵉ* send a message to Gn 45_{23}, w. *dᵉbārîm* news Pr 26_6; subj. God, obj. things Ex 9_{14}; send s.thg. *bᵉyad* by s.one 1S 16_{20}; *šālûᵃḥ qāšâ* sent w. bad news 1K 14_6; direct (by messengers) 1K 5_{23}.

nif.: inf. נִשְׁלוֹחַ: **be sent** Est 3_{13}. †

piel (265×): pf. שִׁלַּח, שִׁלְּחָה > שִׁלְּחָה Ez 17_7 31_4 like שִׁלְּחוּ Ps 74_7, שִׁלֵּחוּ, sf. שִׁלְּחוֹ, שִׁלַּחְתָּנִי, שִׁלַּחְתִּיךָ, שִׁלְּחוּךָ; impf. יְשַׁלַּח, אֲשַׁלַּח, וַיְשַׁלְּחוּ, יְשַׁלֵּחוּ, תְּשַׁלַּחְנָה, sf. וַיְשַׁלְּחֵם, תְּשַׁלְּחֶנּוּ, אֲשַׁלֵּחֲךָ, וָאֲשַׁלֵּחֲךָ; impv. שַׁלַּח, שַׁלְּחוּ, sf. שַׁלְּחֵנִי, שַׁלְּחֵנִי; inf. שַׁלַּח, שַׁלְּחָם, שִׁלְּחוֹ 1C 8_8, שַׁלְּחוֹ Ex 4_{23}, abs. שַׁלֵּחַ; pt. מְשַׁלֵּחַ, pl. cs. מְשַׁלְּחֵי: — 1. **give free play to, let loose**, **let go** (away): obj. pers. Gn 30_{25}, cattle Ex 22_4, water Ez 31_4, hair 44_{20}; set (discord) free Pr 6_{14}, get free of (labor-pains) Jb 39_3; **stretch out** (one's hand) Pr 31_{20}, spread out (roots) Je 17_8; — 2. **let go**, **let free**: Gn 31_{42}, obj. one's opponent Gn 32_{27}; *haḥûṣâ* let (daughters) go outside the clan (to marry) Ju 12_9; — 3. **escort**, accompany Gn 12_{20}; — 4. **send away, out, off**: obj. pers. Gn 28_{6}, arrow 1S 20_{20}; w. *bᵉ* hand over to Ps 81_{13}; turn away, drive out Gn 3_{23}; dismiss (a wife) Dt 21_{14} (*lᵉnafšāh* wherever she wants to go); — 5. **send**, obj. pers. Gn 19_{13}, thing Ne 8_{12}; esp. of God who sends afflictions &c. 2K 17_{25}; idiom: *šillaḥ bāʾēš* set on fire 2K 8_{12}.

pual: pf. שֻׁלַּח, שֻׁלָּח, שֻׁלַּחְתִּי; impf. יְשֻׁלַּח; pt. מְשֻׁלָּח: — 1. **be sent off** (on a journey) Gn 44_{3}; w. *bᵉ* fall into (a net) Jb 18_{8}; pt. left to onesf. Pr 29_{15}; — 2. **be sent** (subj. messenger) Ob $_{1}$ Pr 17_{11} Dn 10_{11}; **be dismissed, sent away** (by divorce) Is 50_{1}; pt. chased away Is 16_{2}, deserted Is 27_{10}; be carried away? Ju 5_{15}. †

hif.: pf. הִשְׁלַחְתִּי; inf. הַשְׁלִיחַ; pt. מַשְׁלִיחַ: w. acc. & *bᵉ*, **let loose** upon, obj. insect pests Ex 8_{17}, beasts of field Lv 26_{22}, enemy 2K 15_{37}, famine Ez 14_{13} Am 8_{11}. †

I שֶׁלַח: שֶׁלַח; sf. שִׁלְחוֹ: **javelin, dart** Jl 2_{8}.

II שֶׁלַח: **canal, water-channel** Ne 3_{15}. †

III שֶׁלַח: n. pers. Gn 10_{24} $11_{12\text{-}15}$ 1C $1_{18\cdot24}$. †

שִׁלֹחַ: *mê haššilōᵃḥ* water of Shiloah = Siloam Is 8_{6}. †

*שְׁלֻחוֹת: sf. שְׁלֻחוֹתֶיהָ: **tendrils, shoots** Is 16_{8}. †

שִׁלְחִי: n. pers.

*שְׁלָחִים: sf. שְׁלָחַיִךְ: **skin** (oth.: 'womb'; 'shoots') SS 4_{13}. †

שִׁלְחִים: n. loc. Jos 15_{32}. †

שֻׁלְחָן: cs. שֻׁלְחַן, sf. שֻׁלְחָנִי; pl. שֻׁלְחָנוֹת, cs. שֻׁלְחֲנוֹת: — 1. secular use: perh. animal skin laid on the ground for a meal, Is 21_{5}; > **table** (w. dishes), esp. for king 1K 5_{7}; — 2. cultic use: **(sacrificial) table**: for the *leḥem pānîm* Ex 25_{23}, for sacrificial meat Ez 40_{39ff}.

שָׁלַט: **qal**: pf. שׁ׳, שָׁלְטוּ; impf. יִשְׁלַט, יִשְׁלְטוּ; inf. שְׁלוֹט: — 1. **gain power** over (*bᵉ*) Est 9_{1}; — 2. **have power** over (*bᵉ*) Ec 2_{19} 8_{9}; — 3. **lord it over, tyrannize** (*ʿal*) Ne 5_{15}. †

hif.: pf. sf. הִשְׁלִיטוֹ; impf. ־תַּשְׁלֶט, sf. יַשְׁלִיטֶנּוּ: — 1. **let** s.thg **gain power** Ps 119_{133}; — 2. w. acc., of God, **grant, permit** Ec 5_{18} 6_{2}. †

*שֶׁלֶט: pl. שְׁלָטִים, cs. שִׁלְטֵי, sf. שִׁלְטֵיהֶם: (small round) **shield** 2K 11_{10}.

שִׁלְטוֹן: noun as adj., (that) **which has power**, i.e. '(his word) is law' Ec $8_{4\cdot8}$. †

שַׁלֶּטֶת: **domineering** Ez 16_{30}. †

*שְׁלִי: שֶׁלִי: **uninterruptedness**: *bᵉšeli* (speak) quietly, privately 2S 3_{27}. †

*שִׁלְיָה: sf. שִׁלְיָתָהּ: **afterbirth** Dt 28_{57}. †

שָׁלֵיו, שְׁלֵיו: F שָׁלֵו.

שַׁלִּיט: pl. שַׁלִּיטִים: **ruler** Gn 42_{6} Ec 7_{19}, tyrant Ec 8_{8} 10_{5}. †

I שָׁלִישׁ: **third** (of a given measure now unknown) Is 40_{12} Ps 80_{6}. †

II *שָׁלִישׁ: pl. שָׁלִשִׁים: musical instrument (w. 3 strings? in 3 sections? w. 3 corners?), sugg. lute, triangle, sistrum 1S 18_{6}. †

III שָׁלִישׁ: sf. שָׁלִישׁוֹ, שָׁלִישׁה; pl. שָׁלִ(י)שִׁ(י)ם, sf. שָׁלִשָׁיו: the 3rd man in a war-chariot, who is the shield- & armor-bearer of the warrior, thus **adjutant** 1K 9_{22}.

שְׁלִישִׁי (105×): f. שְׁלִישִׁיָּה & שְׁלִ(י)שִׁ(י)ת; pl. m. שְׁלִשִׁים: — 1. ord. number, **third** Gn 1_{13}; pl. a 3rd group 1S 19_{21}; *baššᵉlišît* for the 3rd time 1S 3_{8}; *haššᵉlîšît* day after tomorrow 1S 20_{5}; — 2. fraction, **one-third** 2S 18_{2}; — 3. *ʿeglat-šᵉlîšiyyâ*, n. loc.

שלך: **hif.** (111×): pf. הִשְׁלִיךְ, הִשְׁלִיכָה, הִשְׁלַכְתִּי, הִשְׁלַכְתִּיךָ, sf. הִשְׁלִיכוֹ, הִשְׁלַכְתּוֹ; impf. וַיַּשְׁלֵךְ, וַיַּשְׁלֶךְ־, אַשְׁלִיךְ, וָאַשְׁלִיכָה, וַתַּשְׁלִיכֵנִי, וַיַּשְׁלִכֵהוּ, sf. תַּשְׁלִכוּן, וַיַּשְׁלִכוּ, וַיַּשְׁלִיכוּם; impv. הַשְׁלֵךְ, הַשְׁלִיכוּ, sf. הַשְׁלִיכֵהוּ; inf. הַשְׁלִיךְ, sf. הַשְׁלִכוֹ 2K 24_{20} Je 52_{3}; pt. מַשְׁלִיךְ, pl. cs. מַשְׁלִיכֵי: — 1. **throw down** (Aaron's rod) Ex 7_{9}; **throw away** 2K 7_{15}; throw (salt into water) 2K 2_{21}, (Joseph into pit) Gn 37_{20}, toss (child under bush) Gn 21_{15}; — 2. spec.: *hišlîk gôrāl* cast lots Jos $18_{8\cdot10}$; *hišlîk ʾaḥᵃrê* *gawwô* throw behind one's back = reject, turn one's back on 1K 14_{9}; subj. God, *hišlîk mē'al-pānāyw* dismiss fm. one's presence 2K 13_{23}, = *mippānāyw* 2K 17_{20}, *mill^efānāyw* Ps 51_{13}; God throws sins behind his back Is 38_{17}.

hof.: הָשְׁלַךְ, הָשְׁלְכָה, הָשְׁלַכְתָּ, הָשְׁלְכוּ; impf. וַתָּשְׁלְכִי, יָשְׁלְכוּ; pt. מֻשְׁלָךְ, מֻשְׁלֶכֶת, מֻשְׁלָכִים: — 1. **be thrown** 2S 20_{21}; — 2. **be thrown down**, of dead body 1K 13_{24f}; w. *'al* be thrown onto (God for protection) Ps 22_{11}; — 3. **be overturned, tumbled down** (place of sanctuary) Dn 8_{11}.

שָׁלָךְ: unclean bird: **cormorant**?; oth.: a fish-catching owl, *Ketupa zeylonensis* (?) Lv 11_{17} Dt 14_{17}. †

I שַׁלֶּכֶת: **felling** (of tree) Is 6_{13}. †

II שַׁלֶּכֶת: name of a temple-gate 1C 26_{16}. †

I שׁלל: **qal**: impf. תָּשֹׁלּוּ; inf. שֹׁל: **pull out** (stalks of grain fm. bundle) Ru 2_{16}. †

II שָׁלַל: **qal**: pf. שׁ׳, שַׁלּוֹתָ, שָׁלְלוּ; impf. sf. יָשֹׁלּוּךָ; inf. שָׁלֹל; pt. שֹׁלְלִים, sf. שֹׁלְלֶיהָ: **plunder** Je 50_{10}; *šālal šālāl* take plunder Is 10_{6}.

hitp.: pf. (not impf.) אֶשְׁתּוֹלְלוּ; pt. מִשְׁתּוֹלֵל: **stand plundered** Is 59_{15} Ps 76_{6}. †

שָׁלָל (75×): cs. שְׁלַל, sf. שְׁלָלָהּ, שְׁלַלְכֶם: — 1. **booty, plunder** 2K 3_{23}; *š^elal dāwid* plunder taken by D. 1S 30_{20}, *š^elal h^adad 'ezer* plunder taken from H. 2S 8_{12}; includes prisoners of war 1S 30_{19}; *hāy^etâ lô nafšô l^ešālāl* = escape w. his life Je 21_{9}; in n. pers. Is $8_{1\cdot 3}$; — 2. (weakened >) **profit** Pr 1_{13}.

שׁלם: **qal**: pf. שָׁלְמוּ; impf. וַיִּשְׁלַם, וַתִּשְׁלַם; impv. שְׁלָם; pt. pass. pl. cs. שְׁלֻמֵי: — 1. **be finished, completed**: work 1K 7_{51}, wall Ne 6_{15}; **come to an end** (period of time) Is 60_{20}; — 2. **stay sound, healthy, uninjured** Jb 9_{4}; — 3. **keep peace, keep quiet** Jb 22_{21}.

piel: pf. שִׁלֵּם, שִׁלְּמוּ, שִׁלַּמְתֶּם; impf. יְשַׁלֵּם, יְשַׁלֶּם־, אֲשַׁלֵּם, אֲשַׁלְּמָה, נְשַׁלְּמָה, sf. יְשַׁלְּמֶךָּ, יְשַׁלְּמֶנָּה, יְשַׁלְּמוּנִי; impv. שַׁלֵּם, שַׁלְּמוּ; inf. שַׁלֵּם, sf. שַׁלְּמִי; pt. מְשַׁלֵּם, מְשַׁלְּמִים, cs. מְשַׁלְּמֵי: — 1. make intact, complete, **make amends** Ex 21_{34}, w. *taḥat* for 21_{36f}; w. *n^esî* pay a debt 2K 4_{7}; — 2. **repay, reward, requite**: good Ru 2_{12}, evil Is 65_{6}; w. acc. of thing Pr 20_{22}; w. *l^e* & pers. 2K 9_{26}; w. acc. pers. 1S 24_{20}, w. *taḥat* for Gn 44_{4}; — 3. *šillam nēder* pay, **fulfill a vow** 2S 15_{7}; — 4. **restore** Jb 8_{6}; — 5. **finish, complete**: house 1K 9_{25}.

pual: impf. יְשֻׁלַּם, יְשֻׁלָּם; pt. מְשֻׁלָּם: — 1. **be a repayment, recompense** Je 18_{20}; — 2. **be rewarded, requited** Pr 11_{31} 13_{31}; — 3. (of vow) **be paid, fulfilled** Ps 65_{2}. †

hif.: pf. הִשְׁלִימָה, הִשְׁלִימוּ; impf. יַשְׁלִ(י)ם, וַיַּשְׁלֵם, sf. תַּשְׁלִימֵנִי: — 1. **bring to completion, consummate** Is 44_{26}; — 2. **surrender completely** Is 38_{12f}; — 3. denom. of *šālôm*, w. *'ēt* **make peace** w. 2S 10_{19}; w. *'im*, **come to peaceful terms** w. Dt 20_{12}; **live in peace** w. 1K 22_{45}; w. acc., **make** s.one **be at peace** Pr 16_{7}.

hof.: pf. הָשְׁלְמָה: **be brought into peace** w. Jb 5_{23}. †

*שְׁלָם: cs. שְׁלָם: *bišlām* by **agreement** Ezr 4_{7}. †

שֶׁלֶם: sg. in Am 5_{22} doubtful; pl. (coll.) שְׁלָמִים, cs. שַׁלְמֵי, sf. שְׁלָמָיו, שַׁלְמֵיהֶם: 49× out of 86× **w.** *zebaḥ*, but always in connection w. other terms for sacrifice: **settlement-sacrifice** (oth. sugg. a sim. term **communion-sacrifice**) 1K 8_{64}.

I שָׁלֵם: f. שְׁלֵמָה; pl. שְׁלֵמִים, f. שְׁלֵמוֹת: — 1. **uninjured, safe** Gn 33_{18}; — 2. **complete** Gn 15_{16}; — 3. **peaceable, in relation of peace** Gn 34_{21}; *lēb(āb) šālēm* undivided, peaceable heart or mind 1K 8_{61} Is 38_{3}.

II שָׁלֵם: n. loc., presumably = Jerusalem Gn 14_{18} Ps 76_{3}. †

[שִׁלֵּם Dt 32_{35}: rd. אֲשַׁלֵּם.]

שִׁלֵּם: n. pers. Gn 46_{24} Nu 26_{49}. †

שִׁלֻּם: ↗ שַׁלּוּם.

שִׁלֵּם: ↗ שִׁלּוּם.
***שִׁלְמָה**: cs. שִׁלְמַת: **retribution** (on) Ps 91_8. †
שַׁלָּמָה SS 1_7, ↗ מָה D. 3. b).
שְׁלֹמֹה: n. pers. **Solomon**.
שְׁלֹמוֹת: n. pers.
שְׁלֹמִי: n. pers. Nu 34_{27}. †
שִׁלֵּמִי: gent. of שִׁלֵּם.
שְׁלֻמִיאֵל: n. pers.
שֶׁלֶמְיָה: n. pers.
שֶׁלֶמְיָהוּ: n. pers.
שְׁלֹמִית: n. pers. m. & f.
שַׁלְמַן: n. pers.
שַׁלְמַנְאֶסֶר: n. pers., Assyrian king.
שַׁלְמֹנִים: **gifts** Is 1_{23}. †
שֵׁלָנִי: gent. of שֵׁלָה.
שָׁלַף: **qal**: pf. ׳שׁ; impf. וַיִּשְׁלֹף, sf. וַיִּשְׁלְפָהּ; impv. שְׁלֹף; pt. שֹׁלֵף, pass. שְׁלוּפָה: **draw** (sword) 1S 17_{51}; *šōlēf ḥereb* swordsman 2K 3_{26}; *šālaf naʿal* **take off** (sandal) Ru 4_{7f}.
שֶׁלֶף: n. loc.
שִׁלֵּשׁ: **piel**: pf. שִׁלַּשְׁתָּ; impf. וַיְשַׁלֵּשׁוּ; impv. שַׁלֵּשׁוּ: — 1. **divide into three parts** (districts) Dt 19_3; — 2. **do** s.thg **or be** (in a condition) **on the third day** 1S 20_{19}; — 3. **do** s.thg **for the third time** 1K 18_{34}. †
pual: pt. מְשֻׁלָּשׁ, מְשֻׁלֶּשֶׁת, pl. f. מְשֻׁלָּשׁוֹת: — 1. **three years old** (oth.: 'of the third litter' = best) Gn 15_9; — 2. **threefold**: cord Ec 4_{12}; in three stories (priests' chambers) Ez 42_6. †
שָׁלשׁ, שָׁלוֹשׁ: cs. שְׁלשׁ, ־שְׁלָשׁ, f. שְׁלֹשָׁה, cs. שְׁלֹשֶׁת, sf. שְׁלָשְׁתְּכֶם: **three**: *šālōš* 3 things 2S 24_{12}, *šālōš ʿārîm* 3 cities Am 4_8; *šᵉlōš-ʾēlleh* these 3 Ex 21_{11}; *lišlōšet hayyāmîm* within 3 days Ezr 10_{8f}, by the 3rd day Ex 19_{15}, *hayyôm šᵉlōšet hayyāmîm* 3 days ago 1S 9_{20}; *šᵉlōš ʿeśrēh* 1K 7_1 (& sim. forms) = **thirteen**; pl. שְׁלֹשִׁים **thirty** Jos 7_5; for details of use of these forms, ↗ gramm.
שֵׁלֶשׁ: n. pers.
שָׁלִשׁ: ↗ שָׁלִישׁ.
שָׁלִשָׁה: n. loc.
שִׁלְשָׁה: n. pers.
שִׁלְשׁוֹם, שִׁלְשֹׁם: alw. w. ↗ אֶתְמוֹל, אִתְמוֹל, תְּמוֹל: 3 days ago = **day before yesterday**, but alw. in comb. as idiom = up to now Gn 31_2.
שִׁלֵּשִׁים: descendants of 3rd generation: spec., **grandchildren** Gn 50_{23} Ex 20_5 Nu 14_{18} Dt 5_9, & evid. **great-grandchildren** Ex 34_7. †
שְׁלַתִּיאֵל: n. pers., ↗ שְׁאַלְתִּיאֵל.
שָׁם: loc. שָׁמָּה: — 1. spatial: *šām* **there** Gn 2_{12}, (to) there 1S 2_{14}; *ʾašer* … *šām* where 2S 15_{21}, (to) where Je 19_{14}; *šām* … *šām* here … there Is 28_{10}; — 2. temporal: **then** Ps 36_{13}; — 3. *miššām* from there Gn 2_{10}; out of it, from it 1K 17_{13}, from these Ez 5_3; *ʾašer* … *miššām* from where Dt 9_{28}; — 4. *šāmmâ* (to) there Gn 19_{20}, there Ez 48_{35}; *ʾašer* … *šāmmâ* (to) where Gn 20_{13}, where 2K 23_8.
I **שֵׁם** (860×): cs. שֵׁם, ־שֵׁם, ־שֶׁם, sf. שְׁמוֹ, שִׁמְךָ, שִׁמְכָה Je 29_{25}, שְׁמֶךָ, שְׁמֵךְ; pl. שֵׁמ(וֹ)ת, cs. שְׁמוֹת, sf. שְׁמוֹתָם, שְׁמוֹתָן: — 1. **name**: of animals Gn 2_{19}, of persons 3_{20}, of town 1K 16_{24}; *mî šᵉmô* what is his name? Ju 13_{17}; *śām šᵉmô dān* named him D. Ju 8_{31}; *wayyassēb šᵉmô dān* he changed his name to D. 2K 23_{34}; — 2. name > **standing, reputation** Ec 7_1; *ṭᵉmēʾat haššēm* w. a stained reputation Ez 22_5; > **renown**: *ʿāśâ lô šēm* make a name for onesf. Gn 11_4, *šēm gādôl* 2S 7_9, *giddēl šēm* Gn 12_2; *śām lᵉšēm* make famous Zp 3_{19} = *śām lô šēm* 2S 7_{23}; *wayyēṣēʾ lāk šēm* your fame spread abroad Ez 16_{14}; — 3. > **posthumous renown, memory** Jb 18_{17}; *šēm ûšᵉʾērît* 2S 14_7; — 4. name, posthumous renown > existence after death (in those carrying one's name) Dt 25_7; — 5. spec., the name of God: *niqrāʾ šēm yhwh ʿal* 2S 6_2; oft. *šēm yhwh* = the name 'Yahweh,' Ps 5_{12}, > Y.'s being & power Jb 1_{21}; *haššēm* Lv 24_{11} evid. = 'Yahweh.'

II שֵׁם: n. pers. Gn 5_{32}.
שַׁמָּא: n. pers.
שֶׁמְאֵבֶר: n. pers.
שִׁמְאָה: n. pers.
שַׁמְגַּר: n. pers.
שׁמד: **nif.**: pf. נִשְׁמַדְתִּי, נִשְׁמְדָה, נִשְׁמַד; impf. יִשָּׁמֵד, תִּשָּׁמֵדוּן; inf. הִשָּׁמֵד, sf. הִשָּׁמֶדְךָ, הִשָּׁמְדָךְ: **be exterminated**, of persons Gn 34_{30}, of name Is 48_{19}; > **be made useless**: of a plain Je 48_8, high places Ho 10_8.
hif.: pf. הִשְׁמַדְתִּי, הִשְׁמִיד, sf. הִשְׁמִידוֹ, הִשְׁמִידְךָ, הִשְׁמַדְתִּיו, הִשְׁמִידָם; impf. יַשְׁמִיד, וַיַּשְׁמֵד, sf. יַשְׁמִידֵם, אַשְׁמִידְךָ, וַיַּשְׁמִידוּם; impv. הַשְׁמֵד; inf. לְהַשְׁמִיד > Is 23_{11} לַשְׁמִיד, הַשְׁמִידוֹ, הַשְׁמִידָם, הִשְׁמִדְךָ Dt 7_{24} & הִשְׁמִידוֹ 28_{48}, abs. הַשְׁמֵ(י)ד: **exterminate**: obj. family 1K 13_{34}, name 1S 24_{22}, high places Nu 33_{52}; inf. = noun, extermination Is 14_{23}.
*שֶׁמֶד: שֶׁמֶד: n. pers.
שָׁמָּה: ↗ שָׁם.
I שַׁמָּה: pl. שַׁמּוֹת † Ps 46_9: — 1. **what is horrible, frightful** (alw. devastation in judgment): *hāyâ lᵉšammâ* 2K 22_{19}, *nātan lᵉšammâ* Je 25_{18} &c.; — 2. **horror** Is 24_{12}; — 3. pl. **what causes astonishment, horror** Ps 46_9.
II שַׁמָּה: n. pers.
שַׁמְהוּת: n. pers.
שְׁמוּאֵל: n. pers. **Samuel**.
שַׁמּוּעַ: n. pers.
שְׁמוּעָה, שְׁמֻעָה: cs. שְׁמֻעַת, sf. שְׁמֻעָתֵנוּ; pl. שְׁמֻעוֹת: what is heard: — 1. **news, report** 1K 2_{28}; *šᵉmûʿâ ṭôbâ* good news 1S 2_{24}; *hāyâ lišmûʿâ bᵉfî* be on the tongue of = be 'bad news,' a bad example Ez 16_{56}; — 2. pl. rumors Dn 11_{44}; — 3. (what is heard by prophets) **revelation** Is 28_9; *šᵉmuʿātēnû* what we have heard (& must reveal) Is 53_1.
שָׁמוּר: n. pers.
שַׁמּוֹת: n. pers.
cj. שׁמח: **qal**: cj. impf. יִשְׁמַח (for שׂ): **be magnanimous** to Is 9_{16}. †

שׁמט: **qal**: pf. וְשָׁמַטְתָּה, שָׁמְטוּ; impf. sf. וַיִּשְׁמְטוּהָ, תִּשְׁמְטֶנָּה; inf. שָׁמוֹט: — 1. **let fall, drop** 2K 9_{33}; **let** (one's hand [txt. emended]) **drop** Je 17_4; drop (the land) = **leave it untilled, fallow** Ex 23_{11}; **let** (a cart) **go off** (by itself), almost overturn 2S 6_6 1C 13_9, but dub.; — 2. w. *maššēh yādô* **remit** (a loan) Dt 15_7. †
nif.: pf. נִשְׁמְטוּ: (presumably) **be thrown down** Ps 141_6, but txt. dub. †
hif.: impf. תַּשְׁמֵט: **release** Dt 15_3 (but rd qal ?). †
שְׁמִטָּה: **remission** (of a debt) Dt $15_{1f.9}$ 31_{10}. †
שַׁמַּי: n. pers.
שְׁמִידָע: n. pers.
שְׁמִידָעִי: gent. of שְׁמִידָע.
שָׁמַיִם (420×): שָׁמָיִם, cs. שְׁמֵי, sf. שָׁמֶיךָ, שָׁמָיו, שְׁמֵיכֶם; loc. הַשָּׁמַיְמָה, (oft. w. pl. adj. or vb.): **heaven(s), sky**: — 1. = firmament Gn 1_8; windows of heaven 7_{11}; rain fm. heaven 8_2, fire fm. heaven 19_{24}; stars in heaven 22_{17}; — 2. = upper atmosphere (below the 'firmament'), **air, sky**: birds of, Gn 1_{26}; — 3. associated w. God as his dwelling 1K 8_{23}, but heavens cannot contain God 8_{27}.
שְׁמִינִי: f. שְׁמִינִית: ord. **eighth** 1K 6_{38}; *ʿal-haššᵉmînît* on the eight-stringed (instrument) ? (oth.: on the octave) Ps 6_1.
I שָׁמִיר: sf. שְׁמִירוֹ: sugg. Christ's thorn, *Paliurus spina-Christi* (= *P. aculeatus*), or wild carrot, *Daucus aureus*, but perh. genl. term for **thorn-bush** Is 5_6.
II שָׁמִיר: **emery** (oth.: diamond) Je 17_1 Ez 3_9 Zc 7_{12}. †
III שָׁמִיר: n. pers. 1C 24_{24} Qr. †
IV שָׁמִיר: n. loc. Jos 15_{48} Ju $10_{1f.}$ †
שְׁמִירָמוֹת: n. pers.
שַׁמְלַי Ezr 2_{46}: rd. שַׂלְמַי. †
שׁמם: **qal**: pf. שָׁמֵמָה, שָׁמְמוּ, שָׁמֵמָה Ez 35_{12} = Kt שָׁמֵמָה, Qr שָׁמֵמוּ; impf. יֵשַׁם, יָשֹׁמּוּ, תֵּשַׁם, תִּישַׁמְנָה, וַתֵּשַׁם, תֵּשָׁם (as if fm. ישׁם) Ez 6_6; impv. שֹׁמּוּ; pt. שׁוֹמֵם, שֹׁמֵמָה, שׁוֹמְמִים, שׁוֹמֵמִין

La 1_4, שְׁמֵמוֹת, sf. שֹׁמְמֹתֵינוּ: — 1. subj. settled areas: **be deserted, desolated** Gn 47_{19}; — 2. subj. pers.: **be removed fm. contact w. people** (because of having been seduced or having an affliction) 2S 13_{20} Is 54_1; — 3. **shudder, be horrified** (at desolation or judgment of God) 1K 9_8.

nif.: pf. נָשַׁמּוּ; pt. נְשַׁמָּה, נְשַׁמּוֹת: — 1. **be made deserted, desolate** (by violence): road Lv 26_{22}, city Is 54_3, land Je 12_{11}; — 2. **be made to shudder, to be horrified** (subj. pers.) Je 4_9.

polel: pt. מְשֹׁ(וֹ)מֵם > שׁוֹמֵם: — 1. reduced to shuddering, **appalled, stupefied** Ezr 9_{3f}; — 2. desolating = **destroyer, devastator** Dn 8_{13} 9_{27}; *šiqqûṣ šōmêm* Dn 12_{11} evid. word-play on *ba'al šāmêm*. †

hif.: pf. הֵשַׁמּוּ, הֲשִׁמֹּתִי, הֲשִׁמּוֹתָ; impf. יַשִּׁים, sf. וַיְשִׁמֵּם; impv. הָשַׁמּוּ (rd. הִשַּׁמּוּ nif.) Jb 21_5; inf. הַשְׁמֵם: — 1. **make deserted, desolate**: obj. city Ez 30_{14}, sanctuary Lv 26_{31}; — 2. **make** s.one **disconcerted, awestruck** 1S 5_6.

hof.: inf. הָשַּׁמָּה & בָּהָשַׁמָּה (< בְּהָשַּׁמָּה*) as noun: **desolation** Lv $26_{34f.43}$ 2C 36_{21}. †

hitp.: impf. יִשְׁתּוֹמֵם, וָאֶשְׁתּוֹמֵם, < תִּשּׁוֹמֵם Ec 7_{16}: — 1. **prove** (onesf.) **driven to astonishment** Is 59_{16} 63_5, **consternation** Dn 8_{27}, **numbness** Ps 143_4; — 2. **ruin onesf.** Ec 7_{16}. †

שָׁמֵם: f. שְׁמֵמָה: **desolate, deserted** Je 12_{11} La 5_{18} Dn 9_{17}. †

שְׁמָמָה: pl. cs. שִׁמְמוֹת: an area deserted and thus arousing awe or terror, **sinister desolation** Ex 23_{29}.

שִׁמְמָה Ez 35_7: rd. שְׁמָמָה וּמְשַׁמָּה. †

שִׁמָּמוֹן: **horror, shuddering** Ez 4_{16} 12_{19}. †

שְׁמָמִית: ↗ שְׂמָמִית.

שׁמן: **qal**: pf. שָׁמְנוּ; impf. וַיִּשְׁמַן: **grow, be fat** Dt 32_{15} Je 5_{28}. †

hif.: impf. וַיַּשְׁמִינוּ; impv. הַשְׁמֵן: — 1. **make fat, unreceptive** (obj. heart) Is 6_{10}; — 2. **put on fat** Ne 9_{25}. †

שֶׁמֶן (190×): שֶׁמֶן, sf. שַׁמְנָהּ; pl. שְׁמָנִים, sf. שְׁמָנֶיךָ: — 1. (olive) **oil**: *šemen zayit* Ex 27_{20}, *zêt šemen* Dt 8_8; in genl. Gn 28_{18}; — 2. olives? Je 40_{10}; *ben-šemen* fertile in olives? Is 5_1; — 3. pl. dishes w. much oil Is 25_6; kinds of oil mixed w. perfumes Am 6_6; — 4. *'ēṣ šemen*, pl. *'^{a}ṣê šemen*: **oleaster,** *Eleagnus hortensis* (oth.: Aleppo pine, *Pinus halepensis*) 1K 6_{23}, distinguished fm. olive-tree Ne 8_{15}.

***שָׁמָן**: pl. שְׁמָנִים, cs. שְׁמַנֵּי: **fat** (i.e. fertile) **field** Gn $27_{28.39}$ Is $28_{1.4}$. †

שָׁמֵן: f. שְׁמֵנָה: **fat**: animal Ez 34_{16}, pasture 34_{14}, food Gn 49_{20}; = well-fed (people) Ju 3_{29}.

שְׁמֹנֶה, שְׁמוֹנֶה: f. שְׁמֹ(וֹ)נָה, cs. שְׁמֹנַת; pl. שְׁמֹ(וֹ)נִים: **eight** Gn 17_{12}; pl. **eighty** 2K 10_{24}; for forms & usages ↗ gramm.

שְׁמַנֵּי: ↗ *שָׁמָן.

שׁמע: **qal** (1050×): pf. שָׁמַע, ש׳, שָׁמְעָה, שָׁמַעְתָּ, שָׁמַעַתְּ = *שָׁמַעְתְּ or שָׁמַעַת 1K 1_{11}, שָׁמַעְתִּי = *שָׁמַעְתִּי or שָׁמַעַת Je 4_{19}, שָׁמְעוּ, שְׁמַעְתֶּם, sf. שְׁמַעְתָּם, שְׁמַעְתִּיו, שְׁמֵעוּהָ, שְׁמַעְנוּהָ; impf. יִשְׁמָעוּ, יִשְׁמְעוּ, יִשְׁמַע, אֶשְׁמַע, וְאֶשְׁמְעָה, נִשְׁמַע, תִּשְׁמַעְנָה, תִּשְׁמָעוּן, תִּשְׁמְעוּן; impv. שְׁמַע, וּשְׁמַע, שְׁמָעָה & שִׁמְעָה, שִׁמְעִי, שִׁמְעוּ, שְׁמַעְנָה, שְׁמַעַן, sf. שְׁמָעֵנִי, שְׁמָעֶנָּה, שְׁמָעוּנִי; inf. שְׁמֹעַ, sf. שָׁמְעִי, שָׁמְעוֹ, שָׁמְעָתוֹ Is 30_{19}, abs. שָׁמוֹעַ; pt. שֹׁמֵעַ, שֹׁמַעַת, שֹׁמַעַת, שֹׁמְעִים: — 1. **hear**: abs. Is 1_2; w. acc.: s.one speak Gn 27_6, voice 3_{10}, trumpet Je 4_{19} &c. w. *'al* Gn 41_{15} & *'el* 2K 19_9 of, about; w. *'el* **listen to** s.one Ez 3_7; w. acc. of thing (content of message) Ps 132_6; w. *kî* 2S 11_{26}; w. indir. qn. Ju 7_{11}; w. dir. qn. w/o introduction Dt 9_2; — 2. **listen to** s.thg Am 5_{23}, abs. Gn 27_5; listen (& agree) 23_8; w. *'el* Is 46_3, w. *l^e* Pr 8_{34}; w. *b^e* gladly hear 2S 19_{36}; — 3. **heed** (a request) Gn 17_{20}; w. *b^eqôl* 30_6, w. *'el* 16_{11}; — 4. hear > **obey** Ex 24_7; w. *b^eqôl* Gn 22_{18}, w. *'el* 28_7; abs. be obedient 2K 14_{11}; — 5. hear = **understand**: obj. *šāfâ* Gn 11_7; *lēb šōmē^a'*

understanding mind 1K 3_{6}; — 6. *šāmaʿ bên* **try, examine** (as a judge) Dt 1_{16}; *šāmaʿ haṭṭôb wᵉhāraʿ* distinguish 2S 14_{17}.

nif. (42×): pf. נִשְׁמַע, נִשְׁמָע, נִשְׁמְעוּ; impf. יִשָּׁמַע, יִשָּׁמֵעַ, יִשָּׁמְעוּ; inf. הִשָּׁמַע; pt. נִשְׁמָע, נִשְׁמַעַת, נִשְׁמָעִים: — 1. **be heard**: news Gn 45_{16}, tool 1K 6_{7}, indef. anything like this Dt 4_{32}; impers.: *nišmaʿ lô* it is heard by him = he is told Ne 6_{1}; — 2. **be granted** 2C 30_{27}; — 3. **be(come) obedient** 2S 22_{45}.

piel: impf. וַיְשַׁמַּע: (cause to hear =) **summon** 1S 15_{4} 23_{8}. †

hif. (63×): pf. הִשְׁמִיעַ, הִשְׁמַעְתִּי, הִשְׁמִיעוּ, הִשְׁמִיעֲךָ, הִשְׁמִיעָנוּ; impf. יַשְׁמִיעַ, תַּשְׁמַע, יַשְׁמִעוּ, אַשְׁמִיעֵם, יַשְׁמִיעֻנוּ; impv. הַשְׁמִיעוּ, הַשְׁמִיעֵנִי, הַשְׁמִיעֻנוּ; inf. הַשְׁמִיעַ, לַשְׁמִיעַ (< לְהַשְׁמִיעַ) Ps 26_{7}; pt. מַשְׁמִיעַ, מַשְׁמִיעִים: — 1. **let** s.one **hear, make** s.one **hear** s.thg Dt 4_{10}; w/o. acc. pers. **let** sthg. **be heard** Jos 6_{10}; — 2. **proclaim, announce** (peace &c.) Is 52_{7}; — 3. w/o. acc. of thing (i.e. *qôl* &c.), **summon** 1K 15_{22}, w. *ʿal* against Je 51_{27}; — 4. *hišmîᵃʿ bᵉqôl* **let onesf. be heard loudly**: in wailing Ez 27_{30}, proclamation Ps 26_{7}; — 5. w/o *qôlô*: **make onesf. heard**: as singer Ne 12_{42}, musician 1C 15_{19}.

I *שֶׁמַע: שֶׁמַע: **(pleasing, musical) sound** Ps 150_{5}. †

II שֶׁמַע: n. pers.

שֵׁמַע: sf. שִׁמְעִי, שִׁמְעֲךָ: — 1. *šēmaʿ ʾōzen* **hearsay** Ps 18_{45}; — 2. **report** Gn 29_{13}; *šēmaʿ šāwʾ* slander Ex 23_{1}.

שָׁמָע: n. pers.

*שֹׁמַע: sf. שָׁמְעוֹ: **rumor** Jos 6_{27} 9_{9} Je 6_{24} Est 9_{9}. †

שְׁמַע: n. loc.

שִׁמְעָא: n. pers.

שִׁמְעָה: n. pers.

שְׁמָעָה: הַשְּׁמָעָה: n. pers.

שְׁמֻעָה: ← שְׁמוּעָה.

שִׁמְעוֹן: n. peop. (tribe), n. pers.: **Simeon**.

I שִׁמְעִי: n. pers.

II שִׁמְעִי: gent. of I: Nu 3_{21} Zc 12_{13}. †

שְׁמַעְיָה: n. pers.

שְׁמַעְיָהוּ: n. pers.

שִׁמְעֹנִי: gent. of שִׁמְעוֹן.

שִׁמְעָת: n. pers. (f. ?).

*שִׁמְעָתִי: gent. of יִשְׁמְעָה? שִׁמְעָת?: pl. שִׁמְעָתִים: 1C 2_{55}. †

שֶׁמֶץ: unexpl.: a whisper? a little? Jb 4_{12} 26_{14}. †

שִׁמְצָה: unexpl.: usu. derisive whisper, or trifle (i.e. idolatry) Ex 32_{25}. †

שָׁמַר: **qal** (420×): pf. ׳שׁ, שָׁמָר, שָׁמָרוּ, sf. שְׁמָרוֹ, שְׁמָרָה (< *שְׁמָרָהּ), שְׁמַרְתִּיךָ, שְׁמָרַנִי; impf. יִשְׁמֹר, יִשְׁמָר־, אֶשְׁמְרָה, אֶשְׁמֹרָה Ps 59_{10}, sf. יִשְׁמָרְךָ, תִּשְׁמְרֵם; impv. שְׁמֹר, שְׁמָר־, שָׁמְרָה, שִׁמְרוּ, sf. שָׁמְרֵנִי; inf. שְׁמֹ(ו)ר, שָׁמְרוֹ, שָׁמְרְךָ, abs. שָׁמֹ(ו)ר; pt. שֹׁמֵר, שֹׁמְרִים, שֹׁמְרֵי, sf. שֹׁמְרֶיךָ, pass. שָׁמוּר, שְׁמֻרָה: — 1. **watch, guard**: obj. garden Gn 2_{15}, sheep 1S 17_{20}; *šōmēr habbᵉgādîm* the priest who looks after the cultic cleanness of priestly garb 2K 22_{14}; *šōmēr hannāšîm* custodian of harem Est 2_{3}; *šᵉmōr nafšô* spare his life Jb 2_{6}; — 2. *šāmar* w. *bᵉ* 2S 18_{12}, w. *ʾel* 1S 26_{15}, w. *ʿal* 1S 26_{16} **be careful about, protect**; *šāmar min* keep, protect fm. Ps 121_{7}; — 3. **save, retain**: obj. food Gn 41_{35}, silver or goods Ex 22_{6}; obj. *dābār* keep in mind Gn 37_{11}; obj. anger Am 1_{11}, ellipt. Je 3_{5}; — 4. protect > **observe, watch** 1S 1_{12} Is 42_{20}; *šāmar ʾel* keep patiently observing 2S 11_{16}; *šāmar lᵉ* consider 2C 5_{11}; — 5. w. a 2nd vb. = do s.thg **carefully, attentively**: *šāmar wᵉʿāśâ* Dt 4_{6} = *šāmar laʿᵃśôt* 5_{1}; *šāmar lᵉdabbēr* speak accurately, faithfully Nu 23_{12}; — 6. **keep watch, stand guard**: *šōmᵉrîm* guards Ju 1_{24}, *šōmᵉrîm mišmār* Ne 12_{25}; w. acc. **keep in custody** Jb 10_{14}; — 7. w. acc. of thg. **observe, keep** (an order, agreement, obligation): *derek yhwh* Gn 18_{19}, *bᵉrît* 17_{9}; — 8. **revere** Ps 31_{7}.

nif.: pf. נִשְׁמַר, נִשְׁמָר, נִשְׁמָרוּ; impf. יִשָּׁמֵר,

יִשָּׁמֵרוּ; impv. הִשָּׁמֵר, הִשָּׁמֶר, הִשָּׁמְרִי, הִשָּׁמְרוּ: — 1. **be protected** Ho 12_{14}; — 2. be on one's guard, **be careful**, oft. w. 'ethical dative' *lô* &c., w. *min* = of, not to Gn 31_{29}, w. *b^e* 2S 20_{10}, w. *pen* that … not Gn 24_6, w. *'al* not to Ex 10_{28}; abs. be on one's guard, be careful 2K 6_{10}; *nišmar l^{e}nafšô* (or *b^e*-) Dt 4_{15} Je 17_{21} be on one's guard, be careful.

piel: pt. pl. מְשַׁמְּרִים: **revere** Jon 2_9. †

hitp.: impf. וָאֶשְׁתַּמֵּר, וָאֶשְׁתַּמְּרָה: **be on one's guard, be careful** 2S 22_{24} Ps 18_{24}. †

I שֶׁמֶר: pl. שְׁמָרִים, sf. שְׁמָרָיו, שִׁמְרֵיהֶם: **dregs** (of wine) Is 25_6 Je 48_{11} Zp 1_{12} Ps 75_9. †

II שֶׁמֶר: שָׁמֶר: n. pers.

שֹׁמֵר: n. pers. f. 2K 12_{22}. †

שָׁמְרָה: **guard, watch** Ps 141_3. †

*שְׁמֻרָה: pl. שְׁמֻרוֹת: **eyelid** Ps 77_5. †

I שִׁמְרוֹן: n. loc. Jos 11_1 12_{20} 19_{15}. †

II שִׁמְרוֹן: n. pers. Gn 46_{13} Nu 26_{24} 1C 7_1. †

שֹׁמְרוֹן: loc. שֹׁמְר֫וֹנָה: n. loc. **Samaria**.

שִׁמְרִי: n. pers.

*שַׁמְרַי: ↗ שַׁמְשְׁרַי.

שְׁמַרְיָה: n. pers.

שְׁמַרְיָהוּ: n. pers.

שִׁמֻּרִים: coll. pl.: **night-watch, vigil** Ex 12_{42}. †

שְׁמִרֵימוֹת: ↗ שְׁמִירָמוֹת.

שֹׁמְרֹנִי: gent. of שֹׁמְרוֹן.

שִׁמְרַת: n. pers.

שֶׁמֶשׁ (133×): sf. שִׁמְשֵׁךְ, שִׁמְשָׁהּ: pl. sf. שִׁמְשֹׁתַיִךְ: 23× m., 17× f.: — 1. **sun**: w. *bô'* sets Gn 15_{12}, *yāṣā'* rises 19_{23}; *m^{e}bô' haššemeš* sunset = **west** Dt 11_{30}, *mizraḥ šemeš* sunrise = **east** Ju 11_{18}; — 2. *neged haššemeš* before the sun = publicly 2S 12_{12}; — 3. metaph. Is 60_{20}; — 4. **sun-dial** Is 38_8; — 5. **(sun-shaped) shield**: *šemeš ûmāgēn* Ps 84_{12}; — 6. *šemeš* as deity 2K 23_5.

שִׁמְשׁוֹן: n. pers.

שִׁמְשַׁי: n. pers.

שַׁמְשְׁרַי: n. pers.

שֻׁמָתִי: gent. of *שֻׁמָה.

שֵׁן, שַׁן: ↗ בֵּית שְׁאָן.

שֵׁן: cs. שֵׁן, שֶׁן־, sf. שִׁנּוֹ; du. שִׁנַּיִם, cs. שִׁנֵּי, sf. שִׁנָּיו, שִׁנֵּיהֶם, שִׁנֵּימוֹ: f.: — 1. **tooth**: of man Ex 21_{27}, *l^{e}ben-šinnayim* w. white teeth Gn 49_{12}; of animal Jl 1_6; — 2. **ivory** 1K 10_{18}; — 3. **prong, tine** (of fork) 1S 2_{13}; — 4. tooth, **crag** (of rock) 1S 14_{4f}.

שׁנא (evid. orthographic distinction fm. שׁנה, thus = *II שׁנה):

qal: impf. יִשְׁנָא: **shine** La 4_1. †

[**piel, pual**: שִׁנָּא 2K 25_{29}, יְשֻׁנֶּא Ec 8_1, ↗ שָׁנָה vb.]

שֵׁנָא: **sleep** Ps 127_2. †

שִׁנְאָב: n. pers.

שִׁנְאָן: **sublimity** (oth.: **archers**) Ps 68_{18}. †

שֶׁנְאַצַּר: n. pers.

שָׁנָה: **qal**: pf. שָׁנִיתִי, שׁ׳; impf. אֶשְׁנֶה, וַיִּשְׁנוּ, תִּשְׁנוּ; impv. שְׁנוּ; pt. שֹׁנ(ו)ֶה, שׁוֹנִים, שֹׁנוֹת: — 1. **change** (intrans.), subj. God Ma 3_6; — 2. **be different** (from) Est 1_7 3_8; — 3. **repeat, do s.thg again**, for the second time 1K 18_{34}; w. *b^e* & noun, repeat Pr 17_9; w. *lô* repeat it for him = need one more 1S 26_8.

nif.: inf. הִשָּׁנוֹת: **be repeated** Gn 41_{32}. †

piel: pf. שִׁנָּה > שִׁנָּא 2K 25_{29}; impf. וַיְשַׁנֶּה, אֲשַׁנֶּה, sf. וַיְשַׁנֶּהָ, וַיְשַׁנּוֹ; inf. שַׁנּוֹת, sf. שַׁנּוֹתוֹ; pt. מְשַׁנֶּה: — 1. **change** (trans.) Je 2_{36}; > **pervert** Pr 31_5; — 2. w. *beged*, **take off** (clothes) 2K 25_{29}; w. acc. pers. & *l^{e}ṭôb*, **move** s.one to a better room Est 2_9; w. *ṭa'mô*, **pretend to be insane** 1S 21_{14}.

[**pual**: impf. יְשֻׁנֶּא: rd. יְשַׁנֶּנּוּ piel sf. Ec 8_{1f}.]

hitp.: pf. הִשְׁתַּנֵּית: **disguise onesf.** 1K 14_2. †

שָׁנָה (877×): cs. שְׁנַת, sf. שְׁנָתוֹ; pl. שָׁנִים, cs. שְׁנֵי & (9×) שְׁנוֹת, sf. שָׁנָיו, שָׁנֵינוּ, שְׁנֵיהֶם, Jb 36_{11} & שְׁנוֹתַי, שְׁנוֹתֶיךָ, שְׁנוֹתָם; du. שְׁנָתַיִם, שְׁנָתָיִם: **year** Gn 1_{14}; *baššānâ* yearly Ex 23_{14}, *šānâ (b^e)šānâ* year by year Dt 14_{22} 15_{20}; *ben-šānâ* one year old Ex 12_5, = *ben-š^{e}nātô* Lv 12_6 (oth.: in his 1st year); *š^{e}nat molkô* his accession year 2K 25_{27} :: *haššānâ hāri'šônâ* 1st full year 2C 29_3; *š^{e}nātayim* _yāmîm 2 full years Gn 41_1; for forms w. numbers ↗ gramm.

שֵׁנָה (cf. שֵׁנָא Ps 127_2): cs. שְׁנַת, sf. שְׁנָתוֹ; pl. שֵׁנוֹת: **sleep** Gn 28_{16}.

שֶׁנְהַבִּים: **ivory** 1K 10_{22} 2C 9_{21}. †

I **שָׁנִי**: cs. שְׁנִי; pl. שָׁנִים: **crimson, scarlet,** a vivid dye obtained fm. eggs of the shield-louse, collected on leaves of oak-tree: thread Jos 2_{18}; *šānî* = crimson thread Gn 38_{28}; = garment 2S 1_{24}; *tôlaʿat šānî* crimson material Ex 25_4, *šᵉnî tôlaʿat* crimson dye Lv 14_4.

cj. II **שָׁנִי**: **full-grown** (bull) Ju $6_{25\cdot26\cdot28}$ (for הַשֵּׁנִי rd. הַשָּׁנִי). †

שֵׁנִי (157×): f. שֵׁנִית; pl. שְׁנִיִּם: **second**: *baššānâ haššēnît* Gn 47_{18}; *šēnît* a 2nd time Gn 22_{15}; *wᵉhaššēnît* and in the 2nd place [I must say] 2S 16_{19}; pl. *šᵉniyyim* = 2nd story (deck-level) Gn 6_{16}.

שְׁנַיִם (768×): שְׁנַיִם, cs. שְׁנֵי, sf. שְׁנֵיהֶם; f. שְׁתַּיִם (mixed-form of שְׁתַּיִם and שְׁתַּיִם?), שְׁתַּיִם, שְׁתַּיִם Jon 4_{11}, cs. שְׁתֵּי; w. *bᵉ*, *kᵉ* > בִּשְׁתֵּי, כִּשְׁתֵּי, but מִשְּׁתֵּי Ju 16_{28}, sf. שְׁתֵּיהֶם: — 1. **two** Am 3_3, *šᵉnênû* the two of us Gn 31_{27}, *šᵉnê ʾeḥāyw* his 2 brothers 9_{22}; *šᵉtê leḥem* 2 pieces of bread 1S 10_4; — 2. phr.: *šᵉnayim šᵉnayim* 2 by 2 Gn 7_9; *šᵉnayim* double Ex 22_3; *pî šᵉnayim* 2 portions Dt 21_{17}; *šᵉtayim* 2 things Pr 30_7; *paʿam ûšᵉtayim* once or twice Ne 13_{20}; — 3. *šᵉnêm ʿāśār*, *šᵉtêm ʿāśār* **twelve** Gn 17_{20} 14_4; for details of use of numbers, esp. in reckoning time, ↗ gramm.

שְׁנִינָה: **(sharp) taunt** Dt 28_{37} 1K 9_7 Je 24_9 2C 7_{20}. †

שְׁנִיר: ↗ שְׂנִיר.

I **שנן**: **qal**: pf. שַׁנּוֹתִי, שָׁנְנוּ; pt. pass. שָׁנוּן, שְׁנוּנִים: **sharpen**: obj. sword Dt 32_{41}, arrow Is 5_{28}, tongue Ps 64_4.

hitpolel: אֶשְׁתּוֹנָן: **feel sharply stabbed** Ps 73_{21}. †

II **שנן**: **piel**: pf. sf. וְשִׁנַּנְתָּם: **repeat, say again & again** Dt 6_7. †

שנס: **piel**: impf. וַיְשַׁנֵּס: **gird up** (one's loins) = tuck up one's cloak 1K 18_{46}. †

שִׁנְעָר: n. terr.

שְׁנָת: ↗ שֵׁנָה.

שסה: **qal**: pf. שָׁסוּ; impf. יִשְׁסֶה; pt. sg. sf. שֹׁסֵהוּ 1S 14_{48}, pl. שֹׁסִים, sf. שׁוֹסֵינוּ, שֹׁסֵיהֶם, pass. שָׁסוּי: **plunder** 2K 17_{20}.

poel: pf. שׁוֹשֵׂתִי: **plunder bare** Is 10_{13}. †

שסס: **qal**: pf. sf. שַׁסֻּהוּ; impf. וַיָּשֹׁסּוּ: **plunder** Ju 2_{14} 1S 17_{53} Ps 89_{42}. †

nif.: pf. נָשַׁסּוּ; impf. יִשַּׁסּוּ: **be plundered**: subj. houses Is 13_{16} Zc 14_2. †

שסע: **qal**: pt. cs. שֹׁסַע, f. שֹׁסַעַת, pass. שְׁסוּעָה: *šāsaʿ šesaʿ* exhibit a cleft = **have a cloven (split) hoof** Lv $11_{3\cdot7\cdot26}$ Dt 14_6; pt. pass. **cloven (split)** Dt 14_7. †

piel: pf. שִׁסַּע; impf. וַיְשַׁסַּע, sf. וַיְשַׁסְּעֵהוּ; inf. שַׁסַּע: — 1. w. acc. & *bᵉ*, **tear** s.thg (but not separate) Lv 1_{17}; — 2. w. acc. **tear in pieces** Ju 14_6; 1S 24_8, sugg. 'scold,' but prob.: **disperse**.

שֶׁסַע: **cleft** (split) (of hoof) Lv $11_{3\cdot7\cdot26}$ Dt 14_6. †

שסף: **piel**: impf. וַיְשַׁסֵּף: **cut to pieces**? 1S 15_{33}. †

שָׁעָה: **qal**: pf. 'שׁ', שָׁעוּ; impf. יִשְׁעֶה, וַיִּשַׁע, יִשְׁעוּ; impv. שְׁעֵה, שְׁעוּ: **look** (w. favor) at: w. *ʾel* Gn 4_4, w. *ʿal* Is 17_7; w. *bᵉ* **care** about Ex 5_9; w. *min* **look** away fm. Is 22_4.

[**hif.**: impv. הָשַׁע Ps 39_{14}: sugg. rd. qal impv.]

hitp.: impf. תִּשְׁתָּע, נִשְׁתָּעָה: trad. **look around** (in anxiety) Is $41_{10\cdot23}$, but better ↗ cj. שׁתע. †

***שְׁעָטָה** or ***שַׁעֲטָה**: cs. שַׁעֲטַת: **stamping** (of horses' hoofs) Je 47_3. †

שַׁעַטְנֵז: **material of wide mesh** Lv 19_{19} Dt 22_{11}. †

שֵׁעִיר: ↗ שֵׂעִיר.

***שֹׁעַל**: sf. שָׁעֳלוֹ; pl. שְׁעָלִים, cs. שַׁעֲלֵי: **hollow hand, handful** 1K 20_{10} Is 40_{12} Ez 13_{19}. †

שַׁעַלְבִים (w/o *dagheš*): n. loc.

שַׁעַלְבִין: n. loc.
שַׁעַלְבֹנִי: gent. of *שַׁעַלְבֹן.
שַׁעֲלִים: n. loc.
שׁען: **nif.**: pf. נִשְׁעַנּוּ, נִשְׁעֲנוּ, נִשְׁעַן; impf. יִשָּׁעֵן, אֶשָּׁעֵן, יִשָּׁעֲנוּ, וַתִּשָּׁעֲנוּ; impv. הִשָּׁעֲנוּ; inf. הִשָּׁעֵן, sf. הִשָּׁעֶנְךָ; pt. נִשְׁעָן: — 1. w. *'al*, **lean** on s.thg 2S 1_6 2K 5_{18}, lean against s.thg Ju 16_{26}; abs. Jb 24_{23}; — 2. **(stretch out and) rest** Gn 18_4; — 3. metaph. **lean** on (of slope of valley) Nu 21_{15}; — 4. metaph. lean on = **depend** on (obj. e.g. God) Is 10_{20}.
I **שׁעע**: **qal**: impv. שֹׁעוּ Is 29_9, but sugg. rd. שְׁעוּ (שׁעה√); cj. impf. תְּשֹׁעֶינָה Is 32_3 (for שׁעה√): of eyes, **be smeared, stuck shut.** †
hif.: impv. הָשַׁע: **stick** (eyes) **shut** Is 6_{10}. †
[**hitpalpel**: impv. הִשְׁתַּעַשְׁעוּ: **turn out to be stuck shut** Is 29_9, but prob. rd. הִשְׁתָּעוּ (hitp. שׁעה).]
II **שׁעע**: **pilpel**: pf. שִׁעֲשַׁע; impf. יְשַׁעַשְׁעוּ: **pat** on, **play** at Is 11_8; **treat fondly, caress** Ps 94_{19}. †
pulpal (**pilpel** pass.): impf. תְּשָׁעֳשָׁעוּ: **be dandled** Is 66_{12}. †
hitpalpel: impf. אֶשְׁתַּעֲשַׁע, שָׁע־: **find onesf. delighted** Ps $119_{16\cdot47}$. †
שַׁעַף: n. pers.
שָׁעַר: **qal**: pf. 'שׁ: **estimate** Pr 23_7 (but txt. corr. ?). †
I **שַׁעַר** (370×): שָׁעַר, loc. שַׁעְרָה; pl. שְׁעָרִים, cs. שַׁעֲרֵי, sf. שַׁעֲרֵיכֶם: **gate**: of city Gn 34_{20}, court Ex 27_{16}, camp 32_{26}, of river (= canal) Na 2_7, of heavens Gn 28_{17}, of Sheol Is 38_{10}.
II ***שַׁעַר**: pl. שְׁעָרִים: a **measure** (of grain) Gn 26_{12}. †
***שֹׁעָר**: pl. שֹׁעָרִים: **burst open** (of figs) Je 29_{17} (oth.: putrid). †
שֹׁעֵר: F שׁוֹעֵר.
***שַׁעֲרוּר**: f. שַׁעֲרוּרָה: **s.thg horrible** Je 5_{30} 23_{14}. †
***שַׁעֲרוּרִי**: f. שַׁעֲרוּרִיָּה Ho 6_{10} Qr, שַׁעֲרִרִת Je 18_{13}: **s.thg horrible.** †
שְׁעַרְיָה: n. pers.
שַׁעֲרַיִם: n. loc.
שַׁעַשְׁגַז: n. pers.
שַׁעֲשׁוּעִים: sf. שַׁעֲשֻׁעָיו: **delight, rapture** Is 5_7.
שׁפה: **nif.**: pt. נִשְׁפֶּה: **swept bare** (by wind), **w. bare rocks** Is 13_2. †
pual: pf. שֻׁפּוּ Jb 33_{21} Qr, rd impf. יְשֻׁפּוּ (Kt שְׁפִי noun): **grow bare, without flesh.** †
***שָׁפָה**: F שְׁפוֹת.
שְׁפוֹ: n. pers.
שְׁפוֹט: **judgment** 2C 20_9. †
שְׁפוּפָם: n. pers.
שְׁפוּפָן: n. pers.
שְׁפוֹת (sg. *שָׁפָה?): **curds** 2S 17_{29}. †
שִׁפְחָה: cs. שִׁפְחַת, sf. שִׁפְחָתִי; pl. שְׁפָח(וֹ)ת, sf. שִׁפְחוֹתֵיכֶם, שִׁפְחֹתָיו: **female slave, maid-servant** (not clearly distinguished fm. *'āmâ*) Gn 16_1; humble self-designation 1S 1_{18}.
שָׁפַט: **qal** (180×): pf. 'שׁ, שָׁפַט, שָׁפַטְתִּי, שָׁפְטוּ, sf. שְׁפָטוֹ, שְׁפָטְךָ, שְׁפָטָנוּ; impf. יִשְׁפֹּט, יִשְׁפָּט־, יִשְׁפּוּטוּ, יִשְׁפְּטוּ, יִשְׁפֹּטוּ Ex 18_{26}, sf. אֶשְׁפְּטֵם, יִשְׁפְּטֵהוּ, אֶשְׁפָּטֶךָ Ez 44_{24} Qr; impv. שָׁפְטָה Ps 82_8, שִׁפְטוּ, שְׁפֹטוּ, sf. שָׁפְטֵנִי; inf. לִשְׁפֹּט, שָׁפְטֵנוּ, שָׁפְטֶךָ, abs. שָׁפוֹט; pt. שֹׁפֵט, f. שֹׁפְטָה Ju 4_4, pl. שֹׁפְטִים, cs. שֹׁפְטֵי, sf. שֹׁפְטַיִךְ, שֹׁפְטֵיהֶם: — 1. *šāfaṭ bên … ûbên* **decide, settle** (a dispute) betw. Gn 16_5, = *bên … l^e* Ez 34_{17}; — 2. *šāfaṭ dābār* **settle** a case Ex 18_{26}; — 3. *šāfaṭ 'et(-yātôm)* **help** (the orphan) **get justice**, give legal aid to Is 1_{17}; abs. **make decisions, act as judge** Gn 19_9; — 4. pt. *šôfēṭ* **judge** (in sense of arbitrator, legal counselor): *šôf^eṭîm wayyôšî'ûm* Ju 2_{16}; — 5. God is *šôfēṭ* Ps 7_{12}; — 6. **judge** (= administer justice) Lv 19_{15}; — 7. **judge** = **punish** 1S 3_{13}; w. *b^e* execute judgment on 2C 20_{12}; *šāfaṭ mišpāṭ* + acc. set the punishment on Ez 16_{38}; — 8. *šôfēṭ* > **ruler** Mi 4_{14}.
nif.: pf. נִשְׁפַּטְתִּי; impf. אִשָּׁפֵט, אִשָּׁפְטָה, יִשָּׁפְטוּ, נִשָּׁפְטָה; inf. הִשָּׁפֵט, sf. הִשָּׁפְטוֹ; pt. נִשְׁפָּט: — 1. **go to court, plead** Is 43_{26}, *lifnê*

yhwh 1S 12_7; — 2. **seek one's claim** Is 66_{16}.
[**poel**: pt. sf. לְמְשֹׁפְטִי Jb 9_{15}, rd. לְמִשְׁפָּטִי.]
***שֶׁפֶט**: pl. שְׁפָטִים, sf. שְׁפָטַי: **act of judgment** (i.e. punishment) Ex 6_6; w. *ʿāśâ bᵉ* execute judgment on Ex 12_{12}.
שָׁפָט: n. pers.
שְׁפַטְיָה: n. pers.
שְׁפַטְיָהוּ: n. pers.
שִׁפְטָן: n. pers.
I **שְׁפִי**: שֶׁפִי; pl. שְׁפָיִ(י)ם: **(bare caravan-)track** (worn bare by traffic) Nu 23_3.
II **שְׁפִי**: n. pers. 1C 1_{40}. †
שְׁפִיפֹן: a kind of snake, sugg. **horned snake**, *Zamenis diadema* Gn 49_{17}. †
שָׁפִיר: n. loc.
שָׁפַךְ: **qal** (113×): pf. שׁ׳, שָׁפַךְ, שָׁפַכְתְּ, שָׁפְכוּ, שָׁפְכָה Dt 21_7, sf. שְׁפָכְתִהוּ; impf. יִשְׁפֹּךְ, תִּשְׁפְּכוּ, אֶשְׁפְּכָה, sf. תִּשְׁפְּכֻנּוּ; impv. שְׁפֹךְ, שִׁפְכוּ, שְׁפָךְ־; inf. שְׁפוֹךְ, לִשְׁפָּךְ־, sf. שָׁפְכְּךָ; pt. שׁוֹפֵךְ, שֹׁפֶכֶת, שֹׁפְכִים, שֹׁפְכוֹת, sg. sf. שֹׁפְכוֹ, pass. שָׁפוּךְ: — 1. **pour out, spill**: obj. blood, **shed** Gn 9_6, water Ex 4_9, dust Lv 14_{41}, bowels 2S 20_{10}, pour out = heap up (siege-mound) 2S 20_{15}; — 2. cultic: pour out water *lifnê yhwh* 1S 7_6, drink offering Is 57_6; — 3. metaph. pour out, obj. anger Je 6_{11} (oft., w. variety of synonyms), obj. *rûᵃḥ* Ez 39_{29}, s.one's evil Je 16_{14}; obj. *libbô* pour out one's heart Ps 62_9, *nafšô* = speak one's mind 1S 1_{15}.

nif.: pf. נִשְׁפַּךְ, נִשְׁפַּכְתִּי; impf. יִשָּׁפֵךְ: **be poured out, spilled**: subj. blood, be shed Gn 9_6; ashes 1K 13_3.

pual: pf. שֻׁפַּךְ, שֻׁפְּכָה Ps 73_2: **be poured out** Nu 35_{33} Zp 1_{17}; subj. steps, be poured out = stumble Ps 73_2. †

hitp.: impf. תִּשְׁתַּפֵּךְ; inf. הִשְׁתַּפֵּךְ: **lie piled around** (stones) La 4_1; **be poured out** (*nefeš*) Jb 30_{16} (= emotions are drained), **flow out** (*nefeš*) = **expire** La 2_{12}. †
שֶׁפֶךְ: **dumping-ground** (for ashes) Lv 4_{12}. †
שָׁפְכָה: (urinary organ =) **penis** Dt 23_2. †
שָׁפֵל: **qal**: pf. שׁ׳, שָׁפַלְתְּ, שָׁפֵלוּ; impf. יִשְׁפַּל, יִשְׁפְּלוּ; inf. שְׁפַל: **be low, sink** Is 10_{33}, sink down 32_{19}; **be humble, abased** Is 2_9; *šāfēl dibber* **speak from below** Is 29_4; subj. *qôl* **become quiet** Ec 12_4.

hif.: pf. הִשְׁפִּיל, הִשְׁפַּלְתִּי; impf. תַּשְׁפִּיל, sf. יַשְׁפִּילֶהָ, יַשְׁפִּילֶנָּה; impv. הַשְׁפִּילוּ, sf. הַשְׁפִּילֵהוּ; inf. הַשְׁפִּיל, sf. הַשְׁפִּילְךָ; pt. מַשְׁפִּיל, הַמַּשְׁפִּילִי Ps 113_6: — 1. **bring down, lay low**: obj. fortifications Is 25_{12}, tree Ez 17_{24}; **put** s.one **at a lower place** (at table) Pr 25_7; — 2. **humiliate, abase** 1S 2_7; — 3. *hašpîlû šēbû* **sit at a lower place** Je 13_{18}; *hišpîl lirʾôt* **looks down** Ps 113_6; *šālaḥ hišpîl* **sends down** Is 57_9.
שֵׁפֶל: sf. שִׁפְלֵנוּ: **low, humble situation** Ps 136_{23} Ec 10_6. †
שָׁפָל: cs. שְׁפַל, f. שְׁפָלָה, cs. שִׁפְלַת; pl. שְׁפָלִים: — 1. **deep** (below the surface) Lv 13_{20}; — 2. **low**: tree Ez 17_{24}; in social respect 2S 6_{22}; *šiflat qômâ* low in height Ez 17_6; — 3. **humble** Is 57_{15}.
שָׁפֵל: **low** Is 2_{12}, but evid. textual error. †
שִׁפְלָה: **lowliness** Is 32_{19}. †
שְׁפֵלָה: n. loc.; = 'the lowland' 1K 10_{27}.
שִׁפְלוּת: *bišfᵉlût yādayim*, at the lowering of hand = through **inactivity** Ec 10_{18}. †
שָׁפָם: n. pers.
שְׁפָם: n. loc., loc. שְׁפָמָה.
שֻׁפִּם: n. pers. 1C $7_{12\cdot15}$, > שֻׁפִּים 26_{16} (if txt. correct). †
שִׁפְמִי: gent., of שְׁפָם?
I **שָׁפָן**: pl. שְׁפַנִּים: (Syrian) **coney** (= **daman**), *Procavia syriaca* (= *Hyrax syriacus*) Lv 11_5 Dt 14_7 Ps 104_{18} Pr 30_{26}. †
II **שָׁפָן**: n. pers.
cj. **שׁפע**: **qal**: cj. impf. יִשְׁפַּע: **overflow** cj. Jb 40_{23}. †
שֶׁפַע: **superabundance** Dt 33_{19}. †
שִׁפְעָה: cs. שִׁפְעַת: **mass, flood**: of water Jb 22_{11} 38_{34}, of horses Ez 26_{10}, camels Is 60_6. †

שִׁפְעִי: n. pers.

שׁפר: **qal**: pf. שָׁפְרָה: **be pleasing** Ps 16_{6}. †
cj. **piel**: pf. שִׁפְּרָה: **polish** cj. Jb 26_{13}; for oth. sugg. Ƒ comm. †

I *שֶׁפֶר: שֶׁפֶר: **antlers** Gn 49_{21} (oth.: trad. 'loveliness'). †

II *שֶׁפֶר: שֶׁפֶר: name of mountain Nu 33_{23f}. †

שְׁפַר: Ƒ שׁוֹפָר.

שִׁפְרָה: Jb 26_{23} Ƒ שׁפר cj. piel. †

שִׁפְרָה: n. pers. f. Ex 1_{15}. †

*שַׁפְרִיר: sf. שַׁפְרִירוֹ: **pavilion, canopy** ? Je 43_{10}. †

שׁפת: **qal**: impf. תִּשְׁפֹּת, sf. תִּשְׁפְּתֵנִי; impv. (or inf.) שְׁפֹת: — 1. *šāfat sîr*, **put a pot on** (the fire) 2K 4_{38} Ez 24_{3}; — 2. w. acc. & *lᵉ* **put** (s.one) **onto** (dust) Ps 22_{16}; — 3. w. acc. & *lᵉ* + pers. **prepare** (peace) **for** Is 26_{12}. †

שְׁפַתַּיִם: (rim or) **slab** ? Ez 40_{43}; (panniers or) **saddle-bags** Ps 68_{14} (oth.: sheepfolds). †

*שֶׁצֶף: cs. שֶׁצֶף: **flooding** (of anger) Is 54_{8}. †

I שָׁקַד: **qal**: pf. ׳שׁ, שָׁקַדְתִּי; impf. יִשְׁקוֹד, אֶשְׁקֹד; impv. שִׁקְדוּ; inf. שְׁקֹד; pt. שֹׁקֵד, pl. cs. שֹׁקְדֵי: **be vigilant, watchful** Ps 127_{1} Je 1_{12}; w. acc. **lie in wait for** Is 29_{20}.
nif.: pf. נִשְׁקַד La 1_{14} (so rd. w. mss.): **keep vigilant.** †
pual: pt. מְשֻׁקָּדִים: Ƒ מְשֻׁקָּד.

II שׁקד: **qal**: pf. שָׁקַדְתִּי: **be emaciated** Ps 102_{8} (oth.: I). †

שָׁקֵד: pl. שְׁקֵדִים: **almond-tree**, pl. **almonds** (*Amygdalus communis*) Je 1_{11} Ec 12_{5}, pl. Gn 43_{11} Nu 17_{23}. †

שׁקה: [**nif.**: pf. וְנִשְׁקְהָ Am 8_{8}, rd. w. Qr & mss. וְנִשְׁקְעָה.]
hif.: pf. הִשְׁקָה, הִשְׁקְתָה, הִשְׁקִיתָ, הִשְׁקֵיתִי, הִשְׁקוּ, הִשְׁקִינוּ, sf. הִשְׁקָהּ, הִשְׁקִיתָנוּ, הִשְׁקִיתִים; impf. יַשְׁקֶה, וַיַּשְׁק, (וָ)אַשְׁקֶה, יַשְׁקוּ, וַתַּשְׁקֶיןָ, אַשְׁקְךָ, sf. וַתַּשְׁקֵמוֹ, וַיַּשְׁקֵנוּ, יַשְׁקֵנִי, נַשְׁקֶה, אַשְׁקֶנָּה, וַיַּשְׁקֵהוּ, נַשְׁקֶנּוּ; impv. הַשְׁקוּ, sf. הַשְׁקֵהוּ, הַשְׁקִינִי; inf. הַשְׁקוֹת, sf. הַשְׁקוֹתוֹ; pt. מַשְׁקֶה, cs. מַשְׁקֵה, sf. מַשְׁקֵהוּ, pl. מַשְׁקִים, sf. מַשְׁקָיו: — 1. **give a drink to**: w. acc. pers. Gn 21_{19}; w. 2 acc. (pers. & liquid) Gn 19_{32}; subj. Y. Is 27_{3}; — 2. **water** (obj. land, ground, garden, plants) Gn 2_{6}; — 3. **supply a drink for** 2S 23_{15}; — 4. **pass a drink** (around table) Est 1_{7}; — 5. pt. *mašqeh* **cup-bearer** Gn 40_{1}; — 6. *mašqāyw* his **drinking-service** or **wine-vaults** † 1K 10_{5} 2C 9_{4}.
pual: impf. יְשֻׁקֶּה: **be moistened** Jb 21_{24}. †

שִׁקּוּי: pl. sf. שִׁקּוּיָי, שִׁקֻּוָי: **drink** Ho 2_{7} Ps 102_{10}, **refreshment** Pr 3_{8}. †

שִׁקּוּץ, שִׁקֻּץ: pl. שִׁקּוּצִים, cs. שִׁקּוּצֵי, sf. שִׁקּוּצֶיךָ, שִׁקּוּצֵיהֶם: — 1. (pagan) **abominable idol** 2K 23_{24}, of Milcom 1K 11_{5} &c.; — 2. **s.thg abominable** (related to pagan cult) Na 3_{6}.

שָׁקַט: **qal**: pf. ׳שׁ, שָׁקְטָה; impf. יִשְׁקֹט, תִּשְׁקְטִי, אֶשְׁקוֹט, אֶשְׁקֳוטָה = Qr אֶשְׁקֳטָה, Kt אֶשְׁקוֹטָה Is 18_{4}; pt. שֹׁקֵט, f. שֹׁקֶטֶת: — 1. **have peace, quiet, be at peace**: subj. land Jos 11_{23}, city 2K 11_{20}; — 2. **keep quiet** Is 62_{1}, subj. Y. Is 18_{4}; **undertake nothing, be idle** Ru 3_{18}.
hif.: impf. יַשְׁקִ(י)ט; impv. הַשְׁקֵט; inf. cs. הַשְׁקֵט, הַשְׁקִ(י)ט, abs. הַשְׁקֵט: — 1. **provide peace, quiet** Ps 94_{13}; *hišqîṭ rîb* **allay contention** Pr 15_{18}; — 2. **have peace, quiet** Is 32_{17}; **keep quiet** Is 7_{4}; *šalwat hašqēṭ* **unworried ease** Ez 16_{49}.

שֶׁקֶט: (political) **tranquillity** 1C 22_{9}. †

שָׁקַל: **qal**: pf. ׳שׁ; impf. יִשְׁקֹל, תִּשְׁקוֹל, וָאֶשְׁקֳלָה Je 32_{9} & וָאֶשְׁקוֹלָה (= ־קֳ־ Qr, ־קוֹ־ Kt) Ezr 8_{25}, יִשְׁקְלוּ, sf. יִשְׁקְלֵנִי; inf. שָׁקוֹל, לִשְׁקוֹל; pt. שֹׁקֵל: — 1. **weigh** (w. acc. of obj. weighed, and acc. of [amount of] weight) 2S 14_{26}; **weigh out**, obj. silver Gn 23_{16}, tribute Is 33_{18}, mountains in scales Is 40_{12}; — 2. weigh out = **pay** (acc. of amount paid) 1K 20_{39}; — 3. metaph. **weigh** (obj. sorrows) Jb 6_{2}.
nif.: pf. נִשְׁקַל; impf. יִשָּׁקֵל: **be weighed (out)**: silver &c. Jb 28_{15} Ezr 8_{33}; metaph. sorrows Jb 6_{2}. †

שֶׁקֶל: שָׁקֶל; pl. שְׁקָלִים, cs. שִׁקְלֵי: a spec.

weight, **shekel**, varying in amount, roughly 12 grams or 1/2 oz.; *šeqel kesef* Gn 23_{15}; *šeqel haqqōdeš* = shekel valid at sanctuary Ex 30_{13}; *šeqel beʾeben hammelek*, guaranteed by king 2S 14_{26}.

*שִׁקְמָה: pt. שִׁקְמִים, sf. שִׁקְמוֹתָם: **sycamore-(-fig) tree**, *Ficus sycomorus* L. 1K 10_{27}.

שׁקע: **qal**: pf. שָׁקְעָה; impf. תִּשְׁקַע: **sink down, collapse**: fire Nu 11_2, Babylon Je 51_{64}, Egypt Am 9_5. †

nif.: pf. נִשְׁקְעָה: **sink down, collapse**: Egypt Am 8_8 Qr. †

hif.: impf. תַּשְׁקִיעַ: — 1. **hold down** (tongue of crocodile) Jb 40_{25}; — 2. **let** (waters) **settle, become clear** Ez 32_{14}. †

*שְׁקַעֲרוּרָה: pl. שְׁקַעֲרוּרֹת: **depression** (in wall) Lv 14_{37}. †

שׁקף: **nif.**: pf. נִשְׁקָף, נִשְׁקְפָה, נִשְׁקַפְתִּי; pt. נִשְׁקָף, נִשְׁקָפָה: **look down**, w. *ʿal* on (sugg.: fm. point of view of one standing above, i.e. 'look down there'): 1S 13_{18} 2S 6_{16}.

hif.: pf. הִשְׁקִיף; impf. וַיַּשְׁקֵף, יַשְׁקִיף; impv. הַשְׁקִיפָה: **look down** (sugg.: fm. point of view of one standing below, i.e. 'look down here') Gn 18_{16}.

שֶׁקֶף 1K 7_5: sugg. rd. רִבְעֵי מַשְׁקֹף; oth. sugg. noun **lintel**. †

שְׁקֻפִים: s.thg to do w. windows: sugg. slatted or latticed, or embrasured, slabbed 1K 6_4 7_4. †

שׁקץ: **piel**: pf. שִׁקַּץ; impf. תְּשַׁקְּצוּ, תְשַׁקְּצוּ, sf. תְּשַׁקְּצֶנּוּ; inf. שַׁקֵּץ: — 1. **detest** (as cultically unclean) Lv $11_{11\cdot 13}$ Dt 7_{26} Ps 22_{25}; — 2. w. *nafšô* **make onesf. detestable** (as cultically unclean) Lv 11_{43} 20_{25}. †

שֶׁקֶץ: **s.thg** (cultically) **detestable** Lv 7_{21} $11_{10\text{-}42}$ Is 66_{17} Ez 8_{10}. †

שׁקק: **qal**: impf. יָשֹׁקּוּ; pt. שׁ(וֹ)קֵק; w. *be*, **rush, leap** on s.thg Is 33_4 Jl 2_9, **rush forth, charge** Pr 28_{15}. †

hitpalpel: impf. יִשְׁתַּקְשְׁקוּן: **rush to & fro** Na 2_5. †

*שֹׁקֵק: → *שׁוֹקֵק.

שׁקר: **qal**: impf. תִּשְׁקֹר: **trick, deal falsely w.** Gn 21_{23}. †

piel: pf. שִׁקַּרְנוּ; impf. יְשַׁקֵּר, יְשַׁקְּרוּ: **trick, deceive** 1S 15_{29}, w. *be* **treat** s.one **falsely** Lv 19_{11}.

שֶׁקֶר (109×): שָׁקֶר; pl. שְׁקָרִים, sf. שִׁקְרֵיהֶם: — 1. **lie, falsehood, deception** (in words): *debar-šeqer* Ex 23_7, *ʿēd šeqer* Ex 20_{16}; *nibbāʾ baššeqer* Je 5_{31}, *nišbaʿ laššeqer* Lv 5_{24}; *rûᵃḥ šeqer* lying spirit 1K 22_{22}; *leḥem šeqer* bread gained by deception Pr 20_{17}; — 2. **lie, falsehood, deception** (in act): *ʿāśâ šeqer be* treat s.one falsely 2S 8_{13} = *pāʿal šeqer* Ho 7_1; *hālak baššeqer* Je 23_{14}; — 3. more genl., **what is wrong, false, pretended, unreal**: teach s.thg false Is 9_{14}, idols are false Je 10_{14}; *baššeqer* in pretense (opp. sincerely) Je 3_{10}; — 4. *laššeqer* **in vain** 1S 25_{21}; *šeqer* **a lie!** = you are evading the qn. 2K 9_{12}; *šeqer* **without reason** Ps 35_{19}; — 5. *ṭāfal šeqer* → *ṭpl*.

cj. שַׁקָּר: **liar** cj. Pr 17_4 (or rd. מְשַׁקֵּר). †

שֶׁקֶת: pl. cs. שִׁקְתוֹת: **watering-trough** (for cattle) Gn 24_{20} 30_{38}. †

I *שֵׁר: pl. שֵׁירוֹת: **bracelet** or **bangle** Is 3_{19}. †

II *שֵׁר: sf. שָׁרֶּךָ (w. *dagheš*) Pr 3_8: rd. בְּשָׂרֶךָ or שְׁאֵרֶךָ. †

*שֹׁר: sf. שָׁרֵּךְ (w. *dagheš*) & שָׁרְרֵךְ: — 1. **navel** SS 7_3; — 2. **navel-cord** Ez 16_4. †

שָׁרָב: **parching heat**: ref. to **hot sand** Is 35_7, to **desert-wind** 49_{10}. †

שֵׁרֵבְיָה: n. pers.

שַׁרְבִיט, שַׁרְבֵט: **staff, scepter** Est 4_{11} 5_2 8_4. †

שׁרה: **qal**: impf. sf. יִשְׁרֵהוּ: **let loose**, subj. God, obj. thunder Jb 37_3. †

[**piel**: pf. sf. שֵׁרִיתִךָ Je 15_{11} Qr (Kt √שׁרר 'be firm,' Aram.), rd. שֵׁרַתִּיךָ √שׁרת. †]

*שָׂרָה: pl. sf. שָׁרוֹתֶיהָ Je 5_{10} **vine-terrace**, or rd. שׁוּרֹתֶיהָ → שׁוּרָה w. same mng.; שָׁרוּתַיִךְ Ez 27_{25} rd. שָׁרוֹתַיִךְ → cj. שָׁיָרָה. †

*שֵׁרָה pl. שֵׁירוֹת Is 3_{19}; → I *שֵׁר.

שָׁרוּחֶן: n. loc.

שָׁרוֹן: n. terr.
שָׁרוֹנִי: gent. of שָׁרוֹן.
*שְׁרוּקָה Je 18_{16}: ↗ שְׁרֵקָה.
שִׁרְטַי: ↗ שִׁטְרַי.
שָׁרַי: n. pers.
שִׁרְיָה: **arrowhead** Jb 41_{18}. †
שִׁרְיוֹן 1S $17_{5\cdot38}$, otherw. שִׁרְיָן: **coat of mail, scale-armor**.
*שָׁרִיר: pl. cs. שְׁרִירֵי: **muscle** Jb 40_{16}. †
שְׁרִירוּת: ↗ שְׁרִרוּת.
שֵׁרִית: ↗ שְׁאֵרִית.
שְׁרֵמוֹת Je 31_{40} Kt: rd Qr שְׁדֵמוֹת. †
שָׁרַץ: **qal**: pf. 'שׁ; impf. יִשְׁרֹץ; impv. שִׁרְצוּ; pt. שֹׁרֵץ, שֹׁרֶצֶת: — 1. **swarm, teem, be innumerable**: subj. creatures Gn 7_{21}; — 2. w. acc. of creatures, subj. water or land, **swarm, teem with** Gn 1_{20f}.
שֶׁרֶץ: **swarming things**: tiny animals occurring in large numbers, in water Gn 1_{20}, in air Lv 11_{20}, on ground Gn 7_{21}.
שָׁרַק: **qal**: pf. 'שׁ, שָׁרֵק; impf. יִשְׁרֹק, אֶשְׁרְקָה: — 1. **whistle** (when passing ruins & deserted areas, perh. to ward off demons or the like) 1K 9_8; — 2. w. *le* **whistle for** s.one (to call him) Is 5_{26}.
שְׁרֵקָה: **whistling** (perh. to ward off demons) Je 19_8.
*שְׁרִקָה: pl. שְׁרִקוֹת: **piping, flute-playing** Ju 5_{16}; Je 18_{16} Qr rd שְׁרֵקוֹת. †
שָׁרָר: n. pers.
*שֹׁרֵר: ↗ *שׁוֹרֵר.
שְׁרִרוּת, Je 11_8 Ps 81_{13} שְׁרִירוּת: alw. cs. (=) w. *lēb*: **hardness, stubbornness** Dt 29_{18}.
שרשׁ: **piel**: pf. sf. שֵׁרֶשְׁךָ: **uproot** Ps 52_7. †
pual: impf. יְשֹׁרָשׁוּ: **be uprooted** Jb 31_8. †
poel: pf. שֹׁרֵשׁ: **put out roots** Is 40_{24}. †
poal: pf. שֹׁרָשׁוּ: **take root** Je 12_2. †
hif.: impf. יַשְׁרֵשׁ, וַתַּשְׁרֵשׁ; pt. מַשְׁרִישׁ: **put out roots** Is 27_6 Ps 80_{10} Jb 5_3. †
*שֶׁרֶשׁ: שָׁרֶשׁ: n. pers.
שֹׁרֶשׁ: sf. שָׁרְשִׁי, שָׁרְשָׁם; pl. cs. שָׁרְשֵׁי, sf. שָׁרָשָׁיו (*šorāšāyw*), שָׁרָשֶׁיהָ: — 1. **root** (of plant) 2K 19_{30}, **rootstock** Is 11_1, **sucker** Is 53_2; w. vbs. *sillaḥ* or *hikkâ*, take root Je 17_8 Ho 14_6; — 2. metaph.: *šōreš yišay* Is 11_{10}; root = **foundation** Pr 12_3; *šōreš dābār* root (= basis) of the matter Jb 19_{28}; her roots = her **family** Dn 11_7.
[*שַׁרְשָׁה: pl. שַׁרְשֹׁת Ex 28_{22}: ↗ *שַׁרְשְׁרָה.]
*שַׁרְשְׁרָה: pl. שַׁרְשְׁר(וֹ)ת: **chain** Ex 28_{14} 1K 7_{17} 2C $3_{5\cdot16}$; Ex 28_{22} rd. שַׁרְשְׁרֹת. †
שרת: **piel**: pf. שֵׁרֵת, שֵׁרְתוֹ; impf. וַיְשָׁרֶת, יְשָׁרְתֻהוּ, וַתְּשָׁרְתֵהוּ, יְשָׁרְתֵנִי, sf. יְשָׁרְתוּ, יְשָׁרְתוּנֶךָ; inf. שָׁרֵת, לְשָׁרֶת, sf. שָׁרְתוֹ, שָׁרְתֵנִי; pt. מְשָׁרֵת, מְשָׁרְתוֹ, f. מְשָׁרַת (!) 1K 1_{15}, pl. מְשָׁרְתִים, cs. מְשָׁרְתֵי, sf. מְשָׁרְתַי, מְשָׁרְתָו 1K 10_5 Kt: — 1. serve, i.e. **be an attendant to, wait on**, w. acc. Gn 39_4 40_4, w. *le* 2C 22_8; — 2. in cult at sanctuary, **serve, minister** 1K 8_{11}; — 3. **be in service of God** 1S 2_{11}.
שָׁרֵת = שרת piel inf., **cultic service** Nu 4_{12} 2C 24_{14}. †
ששׂה: ↗ שסה.
I שֵׁשׁ: -שֵׁשׁ, f. שִׁשָּׁה, cs. שֵׁשֶׁת; pl. שִׁשִּׁים: sg. **six** Gn 7_6; pl. **sixty** Gn 46_{26}; for details of use of numbers, ↗ gramm.
II שֵׁשׁ: **alabaster** (calcium carbonate) SS 5_{15} Est 1_6. †
III שֵׁשׁ: (Egyptian) **linen** Gn 41_{42}.
ששׂא: **piel**: pf. sf. שִׁשֵּׁאתִיךָ: **lead** (a child learning to walk) Ez 39_2. †
שֵׁשְׁבַּצַּר: n. pers.
[ששׂה: **piel**: pf. שִׁשִּׁיתֶם: rd. שִׁשִּׁית, ↗ שִׁשִּׁי Ez 45_{13}. †]
שָׁשַׁי: n. pers.
שֵׁשַׁי: n. pers.
[שֵׁשִׁי Ez 16_{13}: rd. Qr שֵׁשׁ. †]
שִׁשִּׁי: f. שִׁשִּׁית: — 1. **sixth** Gn 1_{31}; — 2. **one-sixth** Ez 4_{11}.
שֵׁשַׁךְ: name of Babylon, evid. by 'athbash' cipher = בָּבֶל Je 25_{26} 51_{41}. †
שֵׁשָׁן: n. pers.
שֹׁשַׁנִּים: ↗ שׁוֹשָׁן.
שָׁשָׁק: n. pers.

שָׁשַׁר: red pigment used for paint: **minium** (lead oxide) or **vermilion** (= red ocher, hematite, an iron oxide) Je 22_{14} Ez 23_{14}. †

I **שֵׁת**: pl. שָׁתוֹת, sf. שְׁתוֹתֵיהֶם: **buttocks** 2S 10_4 Is 20_4; pl. sugg. **foundations** Ps 11_3 or emend txt.; Is 19_{10} ↗ I *שתה. †

II **שֵׁת**: n. pers. Gn 4_{25f} 5_{3-8} 1C 1_1. †

[III **שֵׁת** Nu 24_{17}: sugg. rd. שֵׁת < שְׂאֵת **defiance**; or rd II.]

cj. I **שתה**: **qal**: pt. pl. cj. שׁוֹתֶיהָ for שָׁתֹתֶיהָ: **weave** cj. Is 19_{10}. †

II **שָׁתָה**: **qal**: pf. שְׁתִיתֶם, שָׁתוּ, שָׁתִית, שׁ׳; impf. יִשְׁתָּיוּן, יִשְׁתּוּ, וָאֵשְׁתְּ, תִּשְׁתִּי, יֵשְׁתְּ, יִשְׁתֶּה, תִּשְׁתֶּינָה, sf. יִשְׁתָּהוּ; impv. שְׁתוּ, שְׁתֵה; inf. שָׁתֹה, שָׁתוֹ, abs. שְׁתוֹתוֹ, sf. Pr 31_4 שְׁתוֹ־, לִשְׁתֹּת שָׁתוֹת Is 22_{13}; pt. שֹׁתֶה, f. שֹׁתָה, pl. שֹׁתִים, cs. שׁוֹתֵי: **drink**: subj. man Gn 9_{21}, animal 24_{19}, God Ps 50_{13}; obj. water Nu 20_{11}, wine Gn 9_{21}, blood Ez 39_{17} &c.; metaph. obj. violence Pr 26_6; *šātâ bᵉ* drink from Gn 44_5, also *min* 2S 12_3; obj. cup Is 51_{17}; SS 5_1 evid. obj. enjoyment of love.

nif.: impf. יִשָּׁתֶה: **be drunk** (subj. a drink) Lv 11_{34}. †

(**hif.**: ↗ שקה hif.).

[**שָׁתוֹת**: Is 19_{10} ↗ cj. I שתה; Is 22_{13} ↗ II שָׁתָה; Ps 11_3 ↗ I שֵׁת.]

I **שְׁתִי**: a particular kind of **woven material**; or sugg. **warp** Lv 13_{48-59}. †

II **שְׁתִי**: **drinking** Ec 10_{17}. †

שְׁתִיָּה: (manner or time of) **drinking** Est 1_8. †

***שָׁתִיל**: pl. cs. שְׁתִלֵי: **slip**, **cutting** (of tree) Ps 128_3. †

שְׁתַּיִם: ↗ שְׁנַיִם.

שתל: **qal**: pf. שְׁתַלְתִּי; impf. אֶשְׁתֳּלֶנּוּ; pt. pass. שָׁתוּל, שְׁתוּלָה: **plant, transplant** Ez 17_8 Ps 1_3.

***שָׁתִל**: ↗ *שָׁתִיל.

שֻׁתַלְחִי: gent. of שׁוּתֶלַח.

שְׁתֻם Nu $24_{3\cdot15}$: rd. שְׁתֻם. †

שתן: מַשְׁתִּין: ↗ שין.

cj. **שתע**: **qal**: impf. תִּשְׁתָּע, נִשְׁתָּעָה: **be afraid** Is $41_{10\cdot23}$ (rather than שעה hitp.). †

שתק: **qal**: impf. יִשְׁתֹּק, יִשְׁתְּקוּ: **become calm**, waves of sea Jon 1_{11f} Ps 107_{30}, quarrel Pr 26_{20}. †

שֵׁתָר: n. pers.

שְׁתַר בּוֹזְנַי: n. pers.

[**שתת**: **qal**: pf. שַׁתּוּ Ps 49_{15} 73_9, prob. rd. שָׁתוּ (√ שית). †]

***שָׁתֹת** Is 19_{10}: ↗ cj. I שתה.

ת

תָּא: pl. תָּאִים, תָּאוֹת Ez 40_{12}, cs. תָּאֵי, sf. תָּאָו (Qr תָּאָיו): **guardroom**, of palace 1K 14_{28}, of temple Ez 40_{7-36}. †

I **תאב**: **qal**: pf. תָּאַבְתִּי: w. *lᵉ* **long for** Ps $119_{40\cdot174}$. †

II **תאב**: **piel**: pt. מְתָאֵב = מְתָעֵב: **abhor** Am 6_8. †

תַּאֲבָה: **longing** Ps 119_{20}. †

תאה: **piel**: cj. pf. תֵּאִיתֶם Nu 34_{10}; impf. תְּתָאוּ: **draw a line, mark out** Nu 34_{7f}.cj.$_{10}$. †

תְּאוֹ Dt 14_5, cs. תּוֹא Is 51_{20}: unidentified clean animal: **wild sheep**? (oth.: antelope). †

תַּאֲוָה: cs. תַּאֲוַת, sf. תַּאֲוָתָם: **longing, (eager) desire, appetite** Is 26_8; *hitʾawwâ taʾᵃwâ* show a craving, a strong appetite for Nu 11_4; *hēbîʾ taʾᵃwâ lᵉ* satisfy s.one's craving Ps 78_{29}, *taʾᵃwâ bāʾâ, t. nihyâ* desire fulfilled Pr $13_{12\cdot19}$; *taʾᵃwâ lᵉʿênayim* delight to the eyes Gn 3_6; *taʾᵃwat gibʿōt* desirable things on the hills 49_{26}.

תְּאוֹמִים: ↗ תּוֹאֲמִים.

***תַּאֲלָה**: sf. תַּאֲלָתְךָ: **curse** La 3_{65}. †

תאם: **hif.**: pt. מַתְאִימוֹת: **bear twins** SS 4_2 6_6. †

***תַּאֲנָה**: sf. תַּאֲנָתָהּ: (time of) **heat, rut** Je 2_{24}. †

תְּאֵנָה: sf. תְּאֵנָתוֹ; pl. תְּאֵנִים, cs. תְּאֵנֵי: **fig**, *Ficus Carica L.*: — 1. the tree 2K 18_{31}, *ʿalēh teʾēnâ* fig-leaves Gn 3_7; — 2. the fruit Nu 13_{23}.

תֹּאֲנָה: *biqqēš tōʾanâ*, seek an **excuse**, **occasion** (for a quarrel) Ju 14_4. †

תַּאֲנִיָּה: **grief** Is 29_2 La 2_5. †

תְּאֵנִים Ez 24_{12}: dittgr. †

תַּאֲנַת שִׁלֹה: n. loc.

תָּאַר: **qal**: pf. ׳תּ: (of border), **turn**, **bend** Jos $15_{9\cdot 11}$ $18_{14\cdot 17}$. †

piel: impf. sf. יְתָאֲרֵהוּ: **outline**, **sketch** (statue of idol) Is 44_{13}. †

[**pual**: pt. מְתֹאָר Jos 19_{13}: rd. וְתָאַר qal.]

תֹּאַר: sf. תָּאֳרוֹ, תֹּאֲרוֹ: **form**, **shape**: of woman Gn 29_{17}, of cow 41_{19}, of olive-tree Je 11_{16}; of man, **dignity**, fine, impressive **appearance** 1S 16_{18}.

תַּאְרֵעַ: ↗ תַּחְרֵעַ.

תְּאַשּׁוּר: a tree, almost surely **cypress**, *Cupressus sempervirens var. horizontalis* Is 41_{19} 60_{13}. †

תֵּבָה: cs. תֵּבַת: — 1. **ark** Gn 6_{14}-9_{18}; — 2. **chest** Ex $2_{3\cdot 5}$. †

תְּבוּאָה: cs. תְּבוּאַת, sf. תְּבוּאָתוֹ; pl. תְּבוּאֹת: — 1. **produce**, **yield** (of land &c.) sg. Ex 23_{10}, pl. (same mng.) 2K 8_6; *battebûʾōt* every time there is a harvest Gn 47_{24}; — 2. metaph. *tebûʾat ḥokmâ* **yield**, **gain** of wisdom Pr 3_{14}.

תְּבוּנָה: sf. תְּבוּנָתִי; pl. תְּבוּנוֹת, sf. תְּבוּנוֹתֵיכֶם: **intelligence**, **aptitude**, **skill** (of artisan) 1K 7_{14}; of God in creating Is 40_{14}; more genl. 1K 5_9; *ʾîš tebûnâ/-nôt* man of insight Pr 10_{23} 11_{12}; *ḥasar tebûnôt* man w/o insight 28_{16}.

***תְּבוּסָה**: cs. תְּבוּסַת: lit. **crushing** (under foot), i.e. collapse 2C 22_7. †

תָּבוֹר: n. loc.

תֵּבֵל: f., never w. art., oft. // *ʾereṣ* e.g. Ps 90_2, so transl. **world**, but evid. more spec. **continent(s)**: situated on 'pillars of the earth' 1S 2_8; foundations of *tēbēl* 2S 22_{16}.

תֶּבֶל: **abominable confusion**, **contamination** (ref. to sexual sins) Lv 18_{23} 20_{12}. †

תֻּבַל, **תּוּבַל**: n. pers. = peop.; cf. ↗ תּוּבַל קַיִן.

***תַּבְלִית**: sf. תַּבְלִיתָם: **annihilation** Is 10_{25}. †

תְּבַלֻּל: *teballul beʿênô*: **having a** (white) **spot** in the eye Lv 21_{20} (oth.: w. obscurity or defect [in vision]). †

תֶּבֶן: chopped stalks, **straw**, as fodder Gn 24_{25}, mixed w. clay for bricks Ex 5_7.

תִּבְנִי: n. pers.

תַּבְנִית: sf. תַּבְנִיתוֹ: **shape**, **form**: — 1. **pattern** (given by God, for making tabernacle &c.) Ex 25_9; — 2. **image**, **form** (graven image in the **form** of any figure) Dt 4_{16}; — 3. **model** 2K 16_{10}; — 4. **image** (i.e. wall-paintings) Ez 8_{10}; — 5. *tabnît yād* form of a hand = **s.thg like** a hand (i.e. hand of God) Ez 8_3; — 6. (architect's) **plan** 1C 28_{19}.

תַּבְעֵרָה: n. loc.

תֵּבֵץ: n. loc.

תבר: ↗ I ברר hitp.

תִּגְלַת פִּלְאֶסֶר 2K 15_{29} 16_{10}, ׳תּ פְּלֶסֶר 2K 16_7, תִּלְּגַת פִּלְנְאֶסֶר 1C 5_6 2C 28_{20}, תִּלְּגַת פִּלְנֶסֶר 1C 5_{26}: n. of Assyrian king.

***תַּגְמוּל**: sf. תַּגְמוּלוֹהִי (Aram.): **gracious act**, **benefit** Ps 116_{12}. †

***תִּגְרָה**: cs. תִּגְרַת: **agitation** Ps 39_{11}, but txt. corr.?. †

תֹּגַרְמָה & תּוֹגַרְמָה: n. terr.

תִּדְהָר: unidentified tree in Lebanon, evid. a conifer, sugg. **fir-tree** Is 41_{19} 60_{13}. †

תַּדְמֹר: n. loc.

תִּדְעָל: n. pers.

תֹּהוּ: w. art. only 1S 12_{21} Is 29_{21} 40_{23} Jb 6_{18}: **wasteland** Dt 32_{10}, solitude or emptiness Gn 1_2; *qiryat-tōhû* deserted city Is 24_{10}; emptiness = **nothingness**, **nonentity** 1S 12_{21}; empty plea (in court) Is 29_{21}; adv. **in vain** 45_{19}.

תְּהוֹם: pl. תְּהֹ(וֹ)מ(וֹ)ת: w. art. only Is 63_{13} Ps 106_9: — 1. sg. **primeval ocean**, **deep** Gn 1_2; — 2. pl. Ps 77_{17}; **deeps of sea** Ex 15_5

(quasi-mythological?); — 3. **subterranean water** Dt 8_7.

תָּהֳלָה: **error**; *śîm toh^olâ b^e* charge w. error Jb 4_{18}. †

תְּהִלָּה: cs. תְּהִלַּת, sf. תְּהִלָּתִי; pl. תְּהִלּוֹת: — 1. **renown, praise, glory**: of Isr. Dt 10_{21}; *ʿîr t^ehillâ* glorious city Je 49_{25}; **praise, glory** of (i.e. ascribed to) God Is 42_8; **praise** (wh. is sung) Ps 22_{26}; — 2. so, as a tech. musical term, **song of praise** Ps 145_1, pl. Is 63_7; — 3. pl. **praiseworthy deeds** Is 60_6.

[תַּהֲלֻכֹת Ne 12_{31}: trad. **festal procession**, but sugg. rd. וְהָאַחַת הֹלֶכֶת. †]

תָּו: sf. תָּוִי: name of last letter of Heb. alphabet, orig. in shape of X: **mark** Ez $9_{4.6}$, (one's own) **mark** or **signature** (confirming a document) Jb 31_{35}. †

תוא: ₣ תְּאוֹ.

תּוֹאֲמִים: 2 forms: 1) *תָּאוֹם, pl. תְּאוֹמִים Gn 38_{27} > תּוֹמִים 25_{24}, cs. תְּאוֹמֵי SS 4_5; 2) *תּוֹאָם, pl. תוֹאֲמִם Ex 36_{29}, תְּאֲמִים 26_{24}, cs. תָּאֳמֵי SS 7_4: — 1. **twins**, of man Gn 25_{24} 38_{27}, of animals SS 4_5 7_4; — 2. **double**, of pieces of wood Ex 26_{24}. †

תּוּבַל קַיִן: n. pers.

תּוּבָנֶת Jb 26_{12}: ₣ תְּבוּנָה.

תּוּגָה: cs. תּוּגַת: **sorrow, trouble**: in genl. Ps 119_{28} Pr 14_{13}; (son is) a trouble (to father) Pr 10_1 17_{21}. †

תּוֹגַרְמָה: ₣ תֹּגַרְמָה.

תּוֹדָה: cs. תּוֹדַת; pl. תּוֹד(ו)ת: **song of thanksgiving** Is 51_3, > (song of) **confession** † Jos 7_{19} Ezr 10_{11}; *zebaḥ/zibḥê tôdâ* **sacrifice (s) of thanksgiving** Lv 22_{29} Ps 107_{22}, > *tôdâ* **sacrifice of thanksgiving** Am 4_5; *tôdâ* **choir** (singing songs of thanksgiving) Ne 12_{31}.

I תוה: **piel**: impf. וַיְתָו 1S 21_{14} Kt (Qr sim.): if true txt., **scribble**; but prob. rd. וַיָּתָף. †

hif.: pf. הִתְוִיתָ: w. cogn. acc., **make a mark** Ez 9_4. †

II תוה: **hif.**: pf. הִתְווּ: **trouble** Ps 78_{41}. †

תּוֹחַ: n. pers.

תּוֹחֶלֶת: sf. תּוֹחַלְתִּי: **expectation, hope** Ps 39_8 Pr 10_{28} 11_7 13_{12} Jb 41_1 La 3_{18}. †

תָּוֶךְ: cs. תּוֹךְ, sf. תּוֹכוֹ, תּוֹכֹה, תּוֹכֵךְ, תּוֹכֵכִי Ps 116_{19} 135_9, תּוֹכִי, תֹּכָם Jb 2_1, תּוֹכֶהְנָה (3. pl. f.), תּוֹכְכֶם: **midst, middle**: — 1. abs.: *battāwek* (cut pieces up) through the **middle** Gn 15_{10}, in the middle Ju 15_4; *hāyâ b^etāwek l^e* find onesf. in the **midst** of Jos 8_{22}; *ʿammûdê hattāwek* the middle pillars Ju 16_{29}; — 2. cs. w/o prep.: *tôk hannaḥal* the **middle** of the ravine Dt 3_{16}, *tôk heḥāṣēr* the middle of the court; & sf. w/o prep.: *tôkô* the middle of it Ez 15_4; — 3. cs. w. prep.: a) *b^etôk* in the middle of, midst of Gn 1_6; *ʿāśâ b^etôk* (gold leaf to) work into (the material) Ex 39_3; *ʿābar b^etôk* go through (the city) Ez 9_4; b) *ʾel-tôk* to the middle of Dt 13_{17}; c) *mittôk* out of [the middle of] (the bush) Ex 3_4; d) *mēʿal-tôk* above [the midst of] Ez 11_{23}; N.B. thus *tôk* often loses full mng., & *b^etôk* = *b^e* &c.

תּוֹךְ: ₣ תֹּךְ.

תּוֹכֵחָה: pl. תּוֹכֵחוֹת: **punishment, chastisement** 2K 19_3 Is 37_3 Ho 5_9 Ps 149_7. †

תּוֹכַחַת: cs. =, sf. תּוֹכַחְתִּי; pl. תּוֹכָחוֹת, cs. תּ(ו)כְחוֹת: — 1. (in lawsuit or public argument) **reprimand** Ez 5_{15}; **protest, objection** Hb 2_1; **contradiction, recrimination** Ps 38_{15}; — 2. (in education, instruction) **reproach, reprimand** Pr 1_{23}.

תּוּכִּיִּים: ₣ תֻּכִּיִּים.

תּוֹלָד: n. pers.

*תּוֹלֵדוֹת: cs. תּוֹלְדוֹת, sf. תּוֹלְדֹתָיו, תּוֹלְדֹתָם: coll. pl.: — 1. **(line) of descendants** (i.e. genealogical list fm. ancestor) Gn 5_1 & oft.; — 2. (one's) **generation, contemporaries** Gn 6_9; — 3. story of development of generations > **history** Gn 37_2; > **origin** Gn 2_4; > **order of birth** Ex 28_{10}.

*תּוֹלָל: pl. sf. תּוֹלָלֵינוּ Ps 137_3: presumably **oppressor**, but perh. rd. מוֹלִיכֵינוּ (הלך√). †

I תּוֹלָע: **material dyed red** (w. *šānî*) Is 1_{18} La 4_5. †

II **תּוֹלָע**: n. pers.

תּוֹלֵעָה, תּוֹלַעַת: sf. תּוֹלַעְתָּם; pl. תּוֹלָעִים: genl. term for insect larvae & worms: — 1. **maggot** (in manna) Ex 16_{20}; — 2. **worm** (in plant) Jon 4_7; — 3. evid. **vine-weevil**, *Cochylis ambiguella* Dt 28_{39}; — 4. *tôla'at šānî*, shield-louse wh. attacks oak-leaves, eggs used for crimson, scarlet dye, > **crimson material** Ex 25_4, *šānî tôla'at* **crimson dye** Lv 14_4.

תּוֹלָעִי: gent. of תּוֹלָע.

תּוֹמִיךְ Ps 16_5: F תמך.

תּוֹעֵבָה (112×): cs. תּוֹעֲבַת; pl. תּ(וֹ)עֵבוֹת, cs. תּוֹעֲבוֹת, sf. תּוֹעֲבֹתָם, תּוֹעֲבוֹתַיִךְ: **s.thg abominable, detestable** (in cultic, then in moral & more genl. sense): — 1. for Egyptians to eat w. Hebrews Gn 43_{32}; homosexual relations Lv 18_{22}; unclean animals for food Dt 14_3; — 2. spec., *tô'ēbôt* = foreign gods Dt 32_{16}, sg. Is 44_{19}; *tô'ēbôt* = detestable customs of foreign nations 1K 14_{24}; *'ammê tô'ēbôt* Ezr 9_{14}; — 3. set usage of Ez., e.g. *tô'ᵃbôt bêt yiśrā'ēl* Ez 6_{11}; — 4. **s.thg offensive, an offense** Pr 24_9.

תּוֹעָה: **confusion, chaos, perversion** Is 32_6 Ne 4_2. †

תּוֹעָפוֹת: cs. תּוֹעֲפֹת: — 1. **horns** (of wild ox) Nu 23_{22} 24_8; — 2. **tops** (of mountains) Ps 95_4; — 3. **best, choice** Jb 22_{25} (oth.: pile.)†

תּוֹצָאוֹת: cs. תּוֹצְאוֹת, sf. תּוֹצְאֹתָם: — 1. **exits** (fm. city) Ez 48_{30}; — 2. **starting-point** (of life) Pr 4_{23}; — 3. **limits, end** (of territory) 1C 5_{16}; *tôṣᵉ'ōt haggᵉbûl hāyû* the boundary ends Jos 15_4; — 4. **escape** Ps 68_{21}.

תָּוֹקְהַת: n. pers.

תּוֹקְעִים: **striking or shaking hands** (in a bargain, pledge) Pr 11_{15}. †

תּוּר: **qal**: pf. תַּרְתִּי, תָּרוּ, תַּרְתֶּם; impf. יָתֻרוּ, תָּתוּרוּ; inf. תּוּר; pt. pl. תָּרִים: — 1. **go about** (after one's desire) Nu 15_{39}; — 2. **reconnoiter, spy out** Nu 13_2; — 3. abs. **investigate** Ec 1_{13}; *tartî bᵉlibbî* I thought out 2_3. **hif.**: impf. וַיָּתִירוּ: **have a reconnaissance made** Ju 1_{23}. †

I **תּוֹר, תֹּר**: pl. תּוֹרִים, cs. תּוֹרֵי: — 1. (one's) **turn**: *higgî*ᵃ*' tōr 'et-* (one's) turn came (to) Est $2_{12.15}$; — 2. pl. **strings, pendants** (of ornaments) SS 1_{10f}. †

II **תּוֹר, תֹּר**: pl. תֹּרִים: **turtle-dove**, *Streptopelia turtur* (& oth. species of *Columba*) Gn 15_9.

תּוֹרָה: cs. תּוֹרַת, sf. תּוֹרָתִי; pl. תּוֹרוֹת, sf. תֹּרֹתָיו, תּוֹרֹתַי: — 1. (orig.) **direction, instruction** (asked of God in a given situation) Dt 17_{11}, administered by priests Je 18_{18}; — 2. **instruction** (given by men) Pr 1_8; — 3. sg. (an established instruction > single) **law**: *tôrat hā'ôlâ* Lv 6_2; *mᵉnā'ôt hattôrâ* portions required by the law Ne 12_{44}; — 4. *tôrâ*, **the law** (= summation, contents of the laws): *tôrat yhwh* 2K 10_{31}; *tôrat mōšeh* 1K 2_3; oft. w. sf. = God's 2K 22_8.

תּוֹשָׁב: cs. תּוֹשַׁב, sf. תּוֹשָׁבְךָ; pl. תּוֹשָׁבִים: **alien**, sometimes identical w. *gēr*, Gn 23_4, sometimes distinguished fm. him Nu 35_{15}; if distinction, evid. *tôšāb* was less assimilated than *gēr* (cf. Ex 12_{45}), & seems to be attached to s.one else's household (Lv 22_{10}).

תּוּשִׁיָּה, תֻּשִׁיָּה Pr 3_{21} †: — 1. **success, (good) results** Is 28_{29}; *'āśâ tûšiyyâ* achieve success Jb 5_{12}; sugg. effective counsel 26_3; — 2. **circumspection, prudence**? Pr 3_{21}.

תּוֹתָח: **cudgel** Jb 41_{21}. †

תזז: **hif.**: pf. הֵתַז: **break off** (spreading tendrils) Is 18_5. †

תַּזְנוּת: sf. תַּזְנוּתֵךְ, תַּזְנוּתָם: **obscene manner** Ez $16_{15\text{-}36}$ $23_{7\text{-}35}$. †

תַּחְבֻּלוֹת: sf. תַּחְבּוּלֹתָו (rd. Qr ־תָיו): **steering, shrewd guidance** Pr 1_5 11_{14} 12_5 20_{18} 24_6 Jb 37_{12}. †

תֹּחוּ: F תֹּחַ.

תַּחְכְּמֹנִי 2S 23_8: rd. הַחַכְמֹנִי.

תַּחֲלֻאִים: cs. תַּחֲלוּאֵי, sf. תַּחֲלֻאֶיהָ, תַּחֲלוּאָיְכִי: **diseases** Dt 29_{21} Je 14_{18} 16_4 Ps 103_3 2C 21_{19}. †

תְּחִלָּה: cs. תְּחִלַּת: **beginning** 2K 17_{25}; *batt^{e}ḥillâ* in, at the beginning, the first time Gn 41_{21} 43_{18}, right at the beginning 2S 17_{9}; at first Gn 13_{3}.

תְּחֶלֶת: ↗ תּוֹחֶלֶת.

תַּחְמָס: an unclean bird, perh. a kind of owl (sugg.: *Otus brucei*; oth.: **nighthawk**, *Caprimulgus*) Lv 11_{16} Dt 14_{15}. †

תַּחַן: n. pers.

I **תְּחִנָּה**: cs. תְּחִנַּת, sf. תְּחִנָּתוֹ; pl. תְּחִנּוֹת, sf. תְּחִנּוֹתֵיהֶם: — 1. **supplication** (for favor) 1K 8_{28} & oft.; — 2. (opportunity for supplication >) **pardon, mercy** † Jos 11_{20}.

II **תְּחִנָּה**: n. pers. 1C 4_{12}. †

***תַּחֲנוּן**: pl. תַּחֲנוּנִים, תַּחֲנוּנוֹת Ps 86_{6} †, cs. תַּחֲנוּנֵי, sf. תַּחֲנוּנָיו: **supplication** (for favor) Je 3_{21}.

תַּחֲנִי: gent. of תַּחַן.

תַּחֲנֹתִי 2K 6_{8}: sugg. rd. תַּחֲנוּ אִתִּי, or תִּנְחָתוּ, or תֵּחָבְאוּ.

תַּחְפַּנְחֵס, תְּחַפְנְחֵס Je 2_{16} Kt & Ez 30_{18}: n. loc.

תַּחְפְּנֵיס: n. pers. f.

תַּחְרָא: **leather cuirass** Ex 28_{32} 39_{23}. †

***תחרה**: impf. תְּתַחֲרֶה Je 12_{5}, pt מְתַחֲרֶה Je 22_{15}; ↗ I חרה tifel. †

תַּחְרֵעַ: n. pers.

I **תַּחַשׁ, תָּחַשׁ**: pl. תְּחָשִׁים: sugg. **porpoise**, *Tursiops tursis Fabr.*, or kind of **dolphin**, thus *ʿôr taḥaš* Nu 4_{6} &c. would be dolphin-skin, so pl. Ex 25_{5}, and *ʿôr taḥaš* > *taḥaš* for such skin Nu 4_{25}; in any event, a leather (perh. imported) of fine quality.

II **תַּחַשׁ**: n. pers. Gn 22_{24}. †

I **תַּחַת** (490×): תָּחַת, sf. תַּחְתָּיו, תַּחְתֶּיהָ, תַּחְתֵּיכֶם, also תַּחְתָּם, תַּחְתֵּנִי 2S $22_{37.40.48}$, תַּחְתֶּנָּה: — 1. (as noun) **what is underneath, below**: *taḥtennâ* Gn 2_{21}, sugg. (closed) what was underneath ([with] flesh); *taḥtāyw* 2S 2_{23} Qr (and he died) where he stood; — 2. prep. **under, beneath**: *taḥat hāʿēṣ* Gn 18_{4}; — 3. in his place > **instead of, for (the sake of)**: Gn 4_{25}; *taḥat ʿênô* (he shall let him go free) for (the sake of) his eye Ex 21_{26}; *taḥat meh* why? Je 5_{19} (but ironic reversal of *ʿal-meh?*); — 4. *ʾel-taḥat* (to) under Je 3_{6}; — 5. *taḥat-ʾ^{a}šer* inasmuch as Dt 28_{47}; — 6. *taḥat kî* inasmuch as Pr 1_{29}; — 7. *taḥat l^{e}* underneath (in relation to) Ez 10_{2}; — 8. *mittaḥat* (out) from under(neath): *hôṣîʾ mittaḥat* Ex 6_{7}; — 9. *mittaḥat* adv. beneath Ex 20_{4}; — 10. *mittaḥat l^{e}* underneath (in relation to) Gn 1_{7}; — 11. = *l^{e}mittaḥat l^{e}* 1K 7_{32}; — 12. *ʿad-mittaḥat l^{e}* as far as below 1S 7_{11}.

II **תַּחַת**: n. pers. 1C $6_{9.22}$ 7_{20}. †

III **תַּחַת**: n. loc. Nu 33_{26f}. †

תַּחְתּוֹן: f. תַּחְתֹּנָה; pl. תַּחְתֹּנוֹת: **the lower, lowest** 1K 6_{6}.

תַּחְתִּי: f. תַּחְתִּית, תַּחְתִּיָּה; pl. תַּחְתִּיּוֹת: **the lower, lowest**: storey Gn 6_{16}, millstone Jb 41_{16}; *taḥtiyyôt hāʾāreṣ* the depths of the earth Is 44_{23}, = *ʾereṣ taḥtît* Ez 31_{14} & *ʾereṣ taḥtiyyôt* 26_{20}; *taḥtiyyôt l^{e}* lowest parts of Ne 4_{7}.

תַּחְתִּים חָדְשִׁי: n. loc.

תִּיכוֹן, תִּיכֹן: f. תִּיכוֹנָה; pl. תִּיכוֹנוֹת: **the middle** (i.e. not lower or upper) 1K 6_{6}.

תִּילוֹן: n. pers. 1C 4_{20} Qr. †

תֵּימָא, תֵּמָא: n. loc., peop., pers.

I **תֵּימָן, תֵּמָן**: loc. תֵּימָנָה: — 1. **south, southern area** Jos 15_{1}; *têmānâ* southwards Ex 26_{18}; — 2. **south wind** Ps 78_{26}.

II **תֵּימָן**: n. terr., pers., Gn 36_{11} & oft.

תֵּימָנִי, תֵּמָנִי: gent. of II תֵּימָן & תֵּימָא.

***תִּימָרָה**: pl. cs. תִּימְרוֹת: **column** (of smoke) Jl 3_{3} SS 3_{6}. †

תִּיצִי: gent. (of *תֵּיץ?).

תִּירוֹשׁ, תִּירֹשׁ: sf. תִּירוֹשְׁךָ: (archaic word for) **wine** (in ritual & poetic ctxts.) Gn 27_{28}.

תִּירְיָא: n. pers.

תִּירָס: n. pers., peop.

תִּירֹשׁ: ↗ תִּירוֹשׁ.

תַּיִשׁ: תָּ֫יִשׁ: pl. תְּיָשִׁים: **he-goat** Gn 30_{35} 32_{15} Pr 30_{31} 2C 17_{11}. †

תֹּךְ, תּוֹךְ: pl. תְּכָכִים: **oppression** Ps 10_{7}; **oppressor, extortioner** † Pr 29_{13}.

תכה: **pual**: impf. תֻּכּוּ Dt 33_{3}, unexpl.; sugg. crowd together. †

תְּכוּנָה: sf. תְּכוּנָתוֹ: — 1. **(fixed) place, abode** Jb 23_{3}; — 2. **arrangement, furnishing** (of a house) Ez 43_{11} Na 2_{10}. †

תֹּכַחַת: ↗ תּוֹכַחַת.

תֻּכִּיִּים, תּוּכִּיִּים: sugg. **poultry**, but prob. **baboons** 1K 10_{22} 2C 9_{21}. †

תְּכָכִים: ↗ תֹּךְ.

תִּכְלָה: **perfection** (?) Ps 119_{96}. †

תַּכְלִית: **consummation, extremity**: *taklît śin'â* extremity of hatred Ps 139_{22}; *lᵉkol-taklît* to the uttermost depths Jb 28_{3}; *'ad-taklît* to the end of Jb 11_{7} 26_{10} Ne 3_{21}. †

תְּכֵלֶת: **purple wool** (for thread, material) Ex 25_{4}.

תכן: **qal**: pt. תֹּכֵן; **examine**: subj. God, obj. heart, spirit (= consider s.one's motives) Pr 16_{2} 21_{2} 24_{12}. †

nif.: pf. נִתְכְּנוּ; impf. יִתָּכֵן, יִתָּכְנוּ, יִתָּכֵנוּ: — 1. **be examined** (actions, by God) 1S 2_{3}; — 2. **be in order, be fair** (of God's way w. man) Ez $18_{25.29}$ $33_{17.20}$. †

piel: pf. תִּכֵּן, תִּכַּנְתִּי: — 1. **steady** (obj. pillars of earth) Ps 75_{4}; — 2. **determine the measure of** (obj. waters) Is 40_{12} Jb 28_{25}, **put in order** (obj. *rûᵃḥ yhwh*) Is 40_{13}. †

pual: pt. מְתֻכָּן: **set in order, counted out** (silver) 2K 12_{12}. †

I **תֹּכֶן**: — 1. **specific amount** Ex 5_{18}; — 2. **standard of measurement** Ez 45_{11}. †

II **תֹּכֶן**: n. loc.

תָּכְנִית: **(perfect) example** Ez 28_{12} 43_{10}. †

תַּכְרִיךְ: **mantle** Est 8_{15}. †

תֵּל: sf. תִּלָּהּ: — 1. **mound of ruins** Dt 13_{17} Jos 8_{28} 11_{13} Je 30_{18} 49_{2} †; — 2. in n. loc.: a) תֵּל אָבִיב; b) תֵּל חַרְשָׁא; c) תֵּל מֶלַח.

תלא (= ↗ תָּלָה): **qal**: pf. sf. תְּלָוּם 2S 21_{12} = תְּלָאוּם Qr, תְּלוּם Kt; pt. pass. pl. תְּלוּאִים, תְּלֻאִים: **hang (up)**, obj. bodies 2S 21_{12}; subj. of pt. pass. 'life' Dt 28_{66}; Ho 11_{7} be hung up = cling, hold fast to?. †

תַּלְאֻבוֹת: *'ereṣ tal'ubôt*; sugg. **land of fever-bouts**, but prob. **land of drought** Ho 13_{5}. †

תְּלָאָה: **hardship, trouble** Ex 18_{8} Nu 20_{14} La 3_{5}; Ma 1_{13} מַתְּלָאָה = מַה־תְּלָאָה. †

תְּלַאשָּׂר 2K 19_{12}, תְּלַשָּׂר Is 37_{12}: n. loc.

תִּלְבֹּשֶׁת: **clothing** Is 59_{17}. †

תַּלְגַּת: ↗ תִּגְלַת.

תָּלָה: **qal**: pf. תָּלוּ, תְּלִינוּ, ת׳, sf. תְּלוּם 2S 21_{12} Kt; impf. יִתְלוּ, sf. וַיִּתְלֵם; impv. sf. תְּלֻהוּ; inf. תְּלוֹת; pt. pass. תָּלוּי, pl. תְּלוּיִם: **hang** (obj. pers.) Gn 40_{19}.

nif.: pf. נִתְלוּ; impf. וַיִּתָּלוּ: **be hanged** La 5_{12} Est 2_{23}. †

piel: pf. תִּלּוּ: **hang** (obj. shields) Ez 27_{10f}. †

תָּלוּל: **towering** Ez 17_{22}. †

תְּלוּנֹּת: ↗ תְּלֻנּוֹת.

תֶּלַח: n. pers.

***תְּלִי**: sf. תֶּלְיְךָ: lit. hanger (for weapons), but in ctxt. no doubt **quiver** Gn 27_{3}. †

תלל: **hif.**: pf. הֵתֵל, הֵתַלְתָּ; impf. יְהָתֶּל, תְּהָתֵּלוּ; inf. הָתֵל: **cheat, deceive** Gn 31_{7}.

hof.: pf. הוּתַל: **be deceived** Is 44_{20}. †

תֶּלֶם: pl. cs. תַּלְמֵי, sf. תְּלָמֶיהָ: **furrow** Ho 10_{4} 12_{12} Ps 65_{11} Jb 31_{38} 39_{10}. †

תַּלְמַי: n. pers.

תַּלְמִיד: **pupil** 1C 25_{8}. †

תְּלֻנּוֹת, תְּלוּנֹּת: sf. תְּלוּנֹּתָם, תְּלֻנֹּתֵיכֶם: **complaining, grumbling** Ex $16_{7.9.12}$ Nu 14_{27} $17_{20.25}$. †

תלע: **pual**: pt. מְתֻלָּעִים: **enveloped in scarlet** (material) Na 2_{4}. †

תַּלְפִּיּוֹת: (in) **courses of stones** SS 4_{4}. †

תְּלַשָּׂר: ↗ תְּלַאשָּׂר.

***תַּלְתַּל**: pl. תַּלְתַּלִּים: **date-cluster** (more spec., cluster of flower or fruit of date-palm) SS 5_{11}. †

תָּם: f. sf. תַּמָּתִי; pl. תַּמִּים: — 1. **complete,**

right, sound, orderly, normal; thus peaceful, quiet Gn 25_{27}, pure, blameless Jb 8_{20}; — 2. *tammātî* † SS 5_2 6_9: my all?; my perfect one?.

תֹּם: cs. תָּם־, sf. תֻּמּוֹ; pl. תֻּמִּים, sf. תֻּמֶּיךָ: **perfection, completeness**, &c. see תָּם above: — 1. *beʿeṣem-tummô* in full vigor Jb 21_{23}; — 2. *tom-lēbāb* integrity of heart = guilelessness, good faith Gn 20_{5f}, blamelessness, purity of heart 1K 9_4; > *tōm* Ps 7_9 & oft.; *letummām* unsuspectingly 2S 15_{11}, *letummô* unwittingly 1K 22_{34}; *hālak tōm* walk in integrity Pr 2_7 = *hālak battōm* 10_9 = *hithallēk betummô* 20_7; *tom-derek* integrity of way (= conduct) Pr 13_6 = *tōm derākîm* Jb 4_6.

תֵּמָא: ↗ תֵּימָא.

תמה: **qal**: pf. תָּמָהוּ; impf. תִּתְמַהּ, וַיִּתְמְהוּ, יִתְמָהוּ; impv. תְּמָהוּ: **be benumbed, transfixed** (w. astonishment): — 1. **be stunned, astounded** Is 29_9 Je 4_9 Hb 1_5 Ps 48_6 Jb 26_{11}; — 2. **look in astonishment** Gn 43_{33}, **look aghast** Is 13_8; — 3. **be surprised, shocked** Ec 5_7. †

hitp.: impv. הִתַּמְּהוּ Hb 1_5 = hifalal (?) הִתְמַהְמְהוּ Is 29_9 (if txt. correct; note, not √ *mhh*!): **gaze at each other**. †

תֻּמָּה: cs. תֻּמַּת, sf. תֻּמָּתוֹ: **integrity, uprightness** Pr 11_3 Jb $2_{3.9}$ 27_5 31_6. †

תִּמָּהוֹן: cs. תִּמְהוֹן: **confusion** (of mind) Dt 28_{28}, panic Zc 12_4. †

תַּמּוּז: (the god) **Tammuz** Ez 8_{14}. †

תְּמוֹל, תְּמֹל: **yesterday** 2S 15_{20}; *temôl šilšōm* yesterday three days ago = **heretofore, before** Ex 5_8, so *kitmôl šilšōm* as before Gn 31_2; *mittemōl šilšōm* in the past Ex 21_{29}.

תְּמוּנָה: cs. תְּמוּנַת: — 1. **form, shape** (of Y.) Nu 12_8; — 2. artistic form, **image, representation** Ex 20_4.

תְּמוּרָה: sf. תְּמוּרָתוֹ: — 1. *temûrātô, -tāh*: what is exchanged for s.thg else, **its substitute** Lv 27_{10}; — 2. **exchange, exchanging** † Ru 4_7.

תְּמוּתָה: **death**; *benê temûtâ* those condemned to die Ps 79_{11} 102_{21}. †

***תֶּמַח**: תֶּמַח: n. pers.

תָּמִיד (103×): **continuance, unceasingness**: — 1. adv. **continually** 1K 10_8 (62×); — 2. after cs.: *ʾanšê tāmîd* men w. the standing responsibility to Ez 39_{14}; *ʾēš tāmîd* fire continually burning Lv 6_6; *ʾaruḥat tāmîd* permanent maintenance 2K 25_{30}; esp. w. type of sacrifice: *ʿôlat tāmîd* regular burnt-offering Ex 29_{42}, *minḥat tāmîd* Nu 4_{16}; *hattāmîd* the regular sacrifice Dn 8_{11ff}.

תָּמִים: cs. תְּמִים, f. תְּמִימָה; pl. תְּמִימִים, f. תְּמִימֹת: — 1. **whole, entire**: day Jos 10_{13}, year Lv 25_{30}; — 2. **intact**: tree Ez 15_5; — 3. **unobjectionable**: way 2S 22_{31}, **free of blemish**: sacrificial animals Ex 12_5; *betāmîm* unobjectionably Jos 24_{14}; — 4. **blameless** Gn 6_9; *temîmê derek* Ps 119_1; — 5. w. *dōbēr* Am 5_{10}, *hōlēk* Ps 15_2 **sincerely, honestly**; — 6. *temîm dēʿîm, -ʿôt* one **perfect** in knowledge Jb 36_4 37_{16}.

תֻּמִּים: **Thummim**, ↗ אוּרִים, apparatus or routine for gaining oracle by lot Ex 28_{30} Lv 8_8 Dt 33_8 Ezr 2_{63} Ne 7_{65}, cj. 1S 14_{41}, but exact nature & mng. uncert., ↗ comms. †

תמך: **qal**: pf. תָּמְכָה, תָּמַכְתָּ, sf. תְּמַכְתִּיךָ; impf. יִתְמְכוּ, אֶתְמָךְ־, וַיִּתְמֹךְ; inf. תְּמוֹךְ, תָּמֹךְ; pt. תּוֹמֵךְ, pl. sf. תֹּמְכֶיהָ: — 1. **take hold of**: obj. s.one's hand Gn 48_{17}, pers. Is 41_{10}; — 2. **hold, grasp (firmly)**: obj. scepter Am 1_5.

nif.: impf. יִתָּמֵךְ: **be held fast** Pr 5_{22}. †

תְּמֹל: ↗ תְּמוֹל.

תמם: **qal**: pf. תַּם, תַּמּוּ, תָּמּוּ, תַּמְנוּ, תָּמְנוּ; impf. יִתֹּם, תִּתֹּם, וַתִּתֹּם, אֵיתָם Ps 19_{14} rd אֶתָּם, יִתַּמּוּ, יִתָּמּוּ, וַיִּתְּמוּ; inf. תֹּם, תָּם־, sf. תֻּמּוֹ: — 1. **be complete** Dt 31_{24}; *tammû nikrātû* were completely cut off Jos 3_{16}; *tōm laʿabōr* had completely passed by 2S 15_{24}; *tammû lāmût* = they all die Dt 2_{16}; *hatammû* are they all (here)? 1S 16_{11}; — 2. **be finished, completed**:

year Gn 47_{18}, words Jb 31_{40}; — 3. **be used up, spent, gone** Gn 47_{15} & oft.; perish Je 14_{15}, so *'ad-tummām* until they were annihilated Dt 2_{15}; — 4. **be blameless** Ps 19_{14}.

hif.: pf. הֲתִמֹּתִי; impf. תַּתֵּם; inf. הָתֵם, sf. הֲתִמְּךָ: — 1. **get, make** s.thg **ready** (meat, by boiling) Ez 24_{10}; — 2. **finish** (doing s.thg) Is 33_{1} Dn 8_{23} 9_{24} Qr; — 3. **remove, get rid of** Ez 22_{15}; — 4. **make** (ways) **blameless** Jb 22_{3}. †

hitp.: impf. תִּתַּמָּם: **show onesf. blameless** 2S 22_{26} Ps 18_{26}. †

תֵּמָן: ↗ תֵּימָן.

תִּמְנָה: n. loc.

תֵּמָנִי: ↗ תֵּימָנִי.

תִּמְנִי: gent. of תִּמְנָה.

תִּמְנָע, תִּמְנַע: n. pers. f., n. of tribe.

תֶּמֶס: **dissolving, wasting away** Ps 58_{9}. †

I **תָּמָר**: pl. תְּמָרִים: **date-palm**, *Phoenix dactylifera* Ex 15_{27} Nu 33_{9} Lv 23_{40} Jl 1_{12} Ps 92_{13} SS 7_{8f} Ne 8_{15}. †

II **תָּמָר**: n. pers. f.

III **תָּמָר**: n. loc. 1K 9_{18} Kt, Ez 47_{19} (cj. $_{18}$) 48_{28}. †

I **תֹּמֶר**: n. loc.

II **תֹּמֶר**: **scarecrow** Je 10_{5}. †

תִּמֹרָה: pl. תִּמֹרִים, sf. תִּמֹּרָו (Qr ־רָיו) Ez 40_{22} & תִּמֹּר(ו)ת: **ornament of palm-tree** 1K 6_{29}.

תַּמְרוּק: pl. cs. תַּמְרוּקֵי, sf. תַּמְרוּקֵיהֶן: pl. **(application of) massage & ointments** Est $2_{3\cdot9\cdot12}$; sg. **massage** Pr 20_{30} Qr, but txt. corr.?. †

I **תַּמְרוּרִים**: **bitterness** Je 6_{26} 31_{15}, Ho 12_{15} but txt. corr.?. †

II **תַּמְרוּרִים**: **road-markers, signposts** Je 31_{21} †

***תַּן**: pl. תַּנִּים, תַּנִּין La 4_{3} Kt (Qr תַּנִּים): **jackal**, *Canis aureus* Is 13_{22}.

תנה: [**qal**: impf. יִתְנוּ Ho 8_{10} ↗ comm.; impv. תְּנָה Ps 8_{2} ↗ comm. †]

hif.: pf. הִתְנוּ Ho 8_{9}: sugg. **receive prostitute's pay**, but txt. corr.? ↗ comm. †

piel: impf. יְתַנּוּ Ju 5_{11}, but txt. dub.; inf. תַּנּוֹת Ju 11_{40}; usu. for both passages **sing, celebrate in song**, but sugg. for Ju 11_{40} **lament** (so Verss.). †

***תְּנוּאָה**: sf. תְּנוּאָתִי; pl. תְּנוּאוֹת: — 1. sg. **displeasure, surprise** Nu 14_{34}; — 2. pl. **occasions, causes for displeasure, surprise** Jb 33_{10}. †

תְּנוּבָה: cs. תְּנוּבַת, sf. תְּנוּבָתִי; pl. תְּנוּבוֹת: **produce**: of field Dt 32_{13} Ez 36_{30} La 4_{9}, of earth Is 27_{6}, of fig-tree Ju 9_{11}. †

תְּנוּךְ: **earlobe** Ex 29_{20} Lv 8_{23f} $14_{14\cdot17\cdot25\cdot28}$. †

תְּנוּמָה: pl. תְּנוּמוֹת: **sleep, slumber** Ps 132_{4} Pr 6_{4}, pl. Pr 6_{10} 24_{33} Jb 33_{15}. †

תְּנוּפָה: cs. תְּנוּפַת; pl. תְּנוּפֹת: — 1. *tenûfat yad-yhwh* **waving, shaking** (of Y.'s hand, in menace) † Is 19_{16}; — 2. 'wave-offering,' an offering waved toward the altar & away fm. it in consecration Ex 29_{24}; *leḥem tenûfâ* bread for consecration (in wave-offering) Lv 23_{17}; *zehab tenûfâ* Ex 38_{24}.

תַּנּוּר: pl. תַּנּוּרִים, sf. תַּנּוּרֶיךָ: — 1. **fire-pot** Gn 15_{17}; — 2. usu. **oven** (for baking) Ex 7_{28}, **furnace** Ps 21_{10}.

***תַּנְחוּמוֹת, ־חֻמ־**: sf. תַּנְחוּמֹתֵיכֶם: **consolation** Jb 15_{11} 21_{2}. †

תַּנְחוּמִים: sf. תַּנְחֻמֶיהָ: **consolation** Is 66_{11} Je 16_{7} Ps 94_{19}. †

תַּנְחֻמֶת: n. pers.

תַּנִּים: ↗ *תַּן; ↗ תַּנִּין.

תַּנִּין, תַּנִּים Ez 29_{3} 32_{2}; pl. תַּנִּינ(י)ם: — 1. **sea monster** † Gn 1_{21} Ps 148_{7}, **sea-dragon** Is 27_{1} + 6×; — 2. **serpent** † Ex $7_{9\cdot12}$ Dt 32_{33} Ps 91_{13}.

I ***תִּנְשֶׁמֶת**: תִּנְשֶׁמֶת: evid. a kind of lizard, sugg. **chameleon**, *Chamaeleo chamaeleo* Lv 11_{30}. †

II **תִּנְשֶׁמֶת**: תִּנְשֶׁמֶת: evid. a kind of owl, sugg. **barn owl**, *Tyto alba* Lv 11_{18} Dt 14_{16}. †

תעב: **nif.**: pf. נִתְעַב; pt. נִתְעָב: **be loathed, abhorrent** Is 14_{19} Jb 15_{19} 1C 21_{6}. †

piel: pf. sf. תִּעֲבוּנִי; impf. יְתָעֵב, יְתָעֲבוּ,

תִּתְעֵב (!תַ), וְאֶתְעֲבָה, וַתְּתַעֲבִי, sf. תְּתַעֲבֻנוּ; inf. תַּעֵב; pt. מְתַעֲבִים: **loathe, abhor**, treat as ↗ *tô'ēbâ* Dt 23_{8}; subj. Y. Ps 5_{7}; **make** (one's beauty) **an abomination** † Ez 16_{25}.

cj. **pual**: pt. cs. מְתֹעַב: **abhorred, loathed** cj. Is 49_{7}. †

hif.: pf. הִתְעַבְתָּ, הִתְעִיבוּ; impf. וַיַּתְעֵב: **act abominably** 1K 21_{26} Ez 16_{52} Ps 14_{1} 53_{2}. †

תָּעָה: **qal**: pf. תָּעוּ, תָּעִיתִי, תָּ׳ Is 16_{8}; impf. יִתְעוּ, תֵּתַע; inf. תְּעוֹת; pt. תֹּעֶה, pl. cs. תֹּעֵי: **wander off, around** Gn 21_{14} & oft.; of animal, **go astray** Ex 23_{4}; **stagger** Is 28_{7}; subj. *lēbāb*, **be confused** (of mind) Is 21_{4}; *tô'ê rûaḥ* those w. confused or disordered disposition Is 29_{24}.

nif.: pf. נִתְעָה; inf. הִתָּעוֹת: — 1. **fall into staggering** Is 19_{14}; — 2. **be led astray** Jb 15_{31}. †

hif.: pf. הִתְעָה, הִתְעוּ, הִתְעֵיתֶם, sf. הִתְעוּם; impf. וַיֵּתַע, וַיַּתְעוּ, sf. וַיַּתְעוּם, תַּתְעֵנוּ; pt. מַתְעֶה, מַתְעִים: — 1. **lead astray** Is 3_{12}, **let** s.one **wander off** (from) Is 63_{17}, **make** s.one **wander off** Gn 20_{13}; w. *le* & inf. **seduce** ... to 2K 21_{9}; — 2. **let** (flock) **go astray** Je 50_{6}; — 3. **make** s.one **stagger** Is 19_{13f}; — 4. *hit'â benafšô* Je 42_{20}: sugg. **deceive onesf.**, oth. make a fatal mistake, play w. one's own life.

תֹּעוּ, תֹּעִי: n. pers.

תְּעוּדָה: — 1. **attestation, confirmation** Ru 4_{7}; — 2. **testimony** Is $8_{16 \cdot 20}$. †

I **תְּעָלָה**: — 1. **trench** 1K 18_{32}; — 2. **conduit** (for water-supply) 2K 18_{17}; — 3. **channel** Ez 31_{4}.

II **תְּעָלָה**: **healing** (spec. the coating of new, healthy tissue over a wound) Je 30_{13} 46_{11}. †

תַּעֲלוּלִים: sf. תַּעֲלוּלֵיהֶם: coll. pl.: — 1. **wantonness** Is 3_{4}; — 2. **ill-treatment** Is 66_{4}. †

[**תַּעֲלֻם***: sf. תַּעֲלֻמָהּ Jb 28_{11}: rd. תַּעֲלֻמָה.]

תַּעֲלֻמָה: pl. תַּעֲלֻמוֹת: **s.thg hidden, secret** Ps 44_{22} Jb 11_{6} 28_{11} (rd. ־מָה). †

תַּעֲנוּג: pl. תַּעֲנוּגִים, sf. תַּעֲנוּגֶיךָ, ־גֶיהָ, & תַּעֲנֻגוֹת: **comfort, enjoyment** Pr 19_{10}; *bêt ta'anugéhā* comfortable houses Mi 2_{9}; pl. **pleasures** Ec 2_{8}, **pampering** Mi 1_{16} SS 7_{7}. †

תַּעֲנִית: **mortification, penitential exercise** (fasting) Ezr 9_{5}. †

תַּעְנַךְ, תַּעֲנָךְ: n. loc.

תעע: **pilpel**: pt. מְתַעְתֵּעַ: **act up** (in this case, profaning s.thg solemn) Gn 27_{12}. †

hitpalpel: pt. מִתַּעְתְּעִים: **make fun of** 2C 36_{16}. †

cj. **תְּעָפָה**: **darkness** cj. Jb 11_{17}. †

תַּעֲצֻמוֹת: **vigor** Ps 68_{36}. †

תַּעַר: sf. תַּעְרָהּ, תַּעְרְךָ, תַּעְרָהּ: f. — 1. **razor, knife** for shaving Nu 8_{7}, for cutting the hair 6_{5}; (presumably) **penknife** (of scribe) Je 36_{23}; — 2. **sheath** (of sword) 1S 17_{51}.

תַּעֲרוּבוֹת: coll. pl. **pledge**; *bene ta'arûbôt* **hostages** 2K 14_{14} 2C 25_{24}. †

תַּעְתֻּעִים: **derision** Je 10_{15} 51_{18}. †

תֹּף: pl. תֻּפִּים, sf. תֻּפֶּיךָ: **timbrel, tambourine** Gn 31_{27}.

תִּפְאֶרֶת: sf. תִּפְאַרְתּוֹ, תִּפְאַרְתְּכֶם: — 1. **ornament, decoration, beauty** Ex 28_{2}; — 2. **glory, splendor** Is 3_{18}; *bêt tif'artî* my splendid house Is 60_{7} = Temple; — 3. **glory, distinction, honor, respect** Ju 4_{9}; — 4. **pride, arrogance** Is 10_{13}.

I **תַּפּוּחַ**: pl. תַּפּוּחִים, cs. תַּפּוּחֵי: — 1. **apple** (fruit) SS 2_{5} 7_{9}; *tappûḥê zāhāb* Pr 25_{11}; — 2. **apple-tree** Jl 1_{12} SS 2_{3} 8_{5}. †

(II **תַּפּוּחַ**,) תַּפֻּחַ: n. pers. 1C 2_{43}. †

III **תַּפּוּחַ**: n. loc.

תְּפוֹצָה*: pl. sf. תְּפוֹצוֹתֵיכֶם **dispersion** Je 25_{34} (but txt. prob. corr.). †

תַּפֻּחַ: ↗ II תַּפּוּחַ.

[**תֻּפִינִים***: pl. cs. תֻּפִינֵי Lv 6_{14}: trad. baked goods, but dub.; rd. תְּפַתֶּנָּה (√פתת). †]

תפל: cj. **qal**: pf. תָּפַלְתִּי: **talk nonsense, in silly fashion** cj. Ps 141_{5}. †

hitp.: impf. תִּתַּפָּל: **behave in a silly fashion** 2S 22_{27}, but cf. Ps 18_{27} √פתל.

I תָּפֵל: **mud-plaster, whitewash** Ez 13$_{10f.14f}$22$_{28}$. †

II תָּפֵל: **what is insipid, worthless**: food Jb 6$_{6}$, prophetic vision La 2$_{14}$. †

תֹּפֶל: n. loc.

תִּפְלָה: **what is insipid, empty, unsteady** Jb 1$_{22}$, **unseemly** Je 23$_{13}$. †

תְּפִלָּה: cs. תְּפִלַּת, sf. תְּפִלָּתִי; pl. תְּפִלּוֹת: **prayer**: w. *hitpallēl* 1K 8$_{28}$, many oth. vbs.; *bêt tᵉfillâ* Is 56$_{7}$.

*תִּפְלֶצֶת: sf. תִּפְלַצְתְּךָ: Je 49$_{16}$; uncert.; sugg.: the horror wh. you caused; oth.: your 'horror' (implying pagan god); or, that you escaped. †

תִּפְסַח: n. loc.

תפף: **qal**: cj. impf. וַיָּתָף; pt. תּוֹפֵפוֹת: **drum** Ps 68$_{26}$, cj. 1S 21$_{14}$. †

polel: pt. מְתוֹפְפוֹת: **keep beating** Na 2$_{8}$. †

תפר: **qal**: pf. תָּפַרְתִּי; impf. וַיִּתְפְּרוּ; inf. לִתְפּוֹר: **sew (together)** Gn 3$_{7}$ Jb 16$_{15}$ Ec 3$_{7}$. †

piel: pt. מְתַפְּרוֹת: **sew (together)** Ez 13$_{18}$. †

תָּפַשׂ: **qal**: pf. תְּ׳, תָּפְשׂוּ, תְּפַשְׂתֶּם, sf. תְּפָשָׂהּ; impf. וַיִּתְפֹּשׂ, וָאֶתְפֹּשׂ, sf. וַיִּתְפְּשֵׂהוּ, נִתְפְּשֵׂם; impv. תִּפְשׂוּ, sf. תִּפְשׂוּם; inf. לְתָפְשׂ, תָּפְשָׂם, abs. תָּפֹשׂ; pt. תֹּפֵשׂ, תֹּפְשֵׂי, pass. תָּפוּשׂ: — 1. w. *bᵉ*: **take hold of**, obj. garment 1K 11$_{30}$, obj. pers. Is 3$_{6}$; — 2. w. acc.: **take hold of, seize, capture**, obj. pers. 1K 13$_{4}$; *tāfaś ḥay* seize, capture s.one alive 1K 20$_{18}$; w. acc. of pers. & *bᵉ* + garment, seize s.one by his ... Gn 39$_{12}$; — 3. w. acc.: **have to do w., deal w., handle**: lyre & pipe Gn 4$_{21}$, sword Ez 38$_{4}$, *tôrâ* Je 2$_{8}$; — 4. obj. *ʿîr*: **seize, capture, occupy** a city 2K 14$_{7}$; *tᵉfōś yiśrāʾēl bᵉlibbām* touch the heart of Isr. Ez 14$_{5}$; — 5. *tāfûś zāhāb*, **overlaid** w. gold Hb 2$_{19}$; — 6. *tāfaś šēm ʾᵉlōhîm* **profane** the name of God (?) Pr 30$_{9}$.

nif.: pf. נִתְפַּשׂ, נִתְפָּשׂ, נִתְפְּשָׂה, נִתְפָּשָׂה, נִתְפַּשְׂתְּ, נִתְפָּשׂוּ; impf. תִּתָּפֵשׂ, תִּתָּפְשׂוּ; inf. הִתָּפֵשׂ: — 1. **be seized, caught**: wife in adultery Nu 5$_{13}$; **be captured**, king by enemy Je 34$_{3}$; — 2. **be caught** (in a trap) Je 50$_{24}$; — 3. **be conquered, captured**: city Je 48$_{41}$; **be occupied, seized**: ford Je 51$_{32}$.

piel: impf. תְּתַפֵּשׂ: **catch** (obj. lizard) Pr 30$_{28}$. †

I תֹּפֶת: **spitting** (i.e. an object of spitting) Jb 17$_{6}$. †

II תֹּפֶת: n. loc.

[תָּפְתֶּה Is 30$_{33}$: sugg rd. תָּפְתּוֹ (i.e. his Tophet); ↗ comm.]

תָּקְהַת 2C 34$_{22}$ Qr: ↗ תּוֹקְהַת (n. pers.). †

I *תִּקְוָה: cs. תִּקְוַת: **cord** Jos 2$_{18.21}$. †

II תִּקְוָה: cs. תִּקְוַת, sf. תִּקְוָתִי: **expectation, hope** Je 31$_{17}$; *ʾᵃsîrê hattiqwâ* prisoners who still have hope Zc 9$_{12}$.

III תִּקְוָה: n. pers. 2K 22$_{14}$ Ezr 10$_{15}$. †

תְּקוּמָה: **power to stand** (before one's enemies) Lv 26$_{37}$. †

[*תְּקוֹמֵם: pl. sf. תְּקוֹמְמֶיךָ Ps 139$_{21}$: rd. מִתְקוֹמְמֶיךָ (√קום hitpolel). †]

תְּקוֹעַ: n. loc.

תְּקֹעִי, תְּקוֹעִי: f. תְּקֹעִית; pl. תְּקֹעִים: gent. of תְּקוֹעַ.

תְּקוּפָה: cs. תְּקוּפַת, sf. תְּקוּפָתוֹ; pl. תְּקֻפוֹת: **turning** (of sun at solstice) Ps 19$_{7}$; (of the year, i.e. end of year, at autumnal equinox) Ex 34$_{22}$; (of the days [i.e. of the year] = end of year) 1S 1$_{20}$.

תַּקִּיף: **strong** Ec 6$_{10}$. †

תקן: **qal**: inf. לִתְקֹן: **be straight** Ec 1$_{15}$, but perh. rd. nif., ↗ below. †

cj. **nif.**: inf. לְהִתָּקֵן: **be straightened** cj. Ec 1$_{15}$. †

piel: pf. תִּקֵּן; inf. תַּקֵּן: **make straight** Ec 7$_{13}$, **get** (proverbs) **into good order** 12$_{9}$. †

תָּקַע: **qal**: pf. תְּ׳, תָּקַעְתִּי, תָּקְעוּ, sf. תְּקַעְתִּיו; impf. וַיִּתְקַע, יִתְקַע, יִתְקְעוּ, יִתָּקְעוּ, sf. וַיִּתְקָעֵהוּ; pt. תֹּקֵעַ, pass. תְּקוּעָה: — 1. **drive, thrust** (weapon into s.one) 2S 18$_{14}$; *tāqaʿ ʾōhel* (drive in tent-pegs =) **pitch a** tent Gn 31_{25}; — 2. *tāqa' kaf*, **clap one's hands** Ps 47_2, **strike hands** (w. s.one) = conclude a bargain, confirm a contract Pr 6_1; — 3. *tāqa' b^e* **blow** (a wind-instrument, e.g. *šôfār*) 1K 1_{34}; *b^e'aḥat* blow only a single instrument Nu 10_4; — 4. w. acc. *šôfār(ôt)* **blow** Jos 6_9; *t^erû'â* sound an alarm Nu 10_{5f}; abs. 10_7.

nif.: impf. יִתָּקַע: **be blown** (of *šôfār*) Is 27_{13} Am 3_6; Jb 17_3 **strike** onesf. (into s.one's hand), but perh. rd. ↗ qal 2. †

תֵּקַע: cs. =: *tēqa' šôfār* **blast** of (ram's) horn Ps 150_3. †

תְּקֹעִי: gent. of תְּקוֹעַ, ↗ תְּקוֹעִי.

תקף: **qal**: impf. sf. תִּתְקְפֵהוּ: **overcome, overpower** Jb 14_{20} 15_{24} Ec 4_{12}. †

[**hif.**: impf. הַתְקִיף Ec 6_{10} Kt: rd Qr ↗ תַּקִּיף. †]

תֹּקֶף: תָּקְפּוֹ: **strength, power, authority** Est 9_{29} 10_2 Dn 11_{17}. †

תֹּר: ↗ I & II תּוֹר.

תַּרְאֲלָה: n. loc.

תַּרְבּוּת: **breed, brood** (of sinful men) Nu 32_{14}. †

תַּרְבִּית: **increase** (of money when loaned, so =) **extra charge, interest** (distinction fm. *nešek* not completely clear) Lv 25_{36} Ez $18_{8\cdot13\cdot17}$ 22_{12} Pr 28_8. †

תִּרְגַּלְתִּי: ↗ רגל tifil.

תרגם: pt. pass. מְתֻרְגָּם: **translated** Ezr 4_7. †

תַּרְדֵּמָה: **deep sleep** (oft. w. implication of supernatural stupor) Gn 2_{21} 15_{12}.

תִּרְהָקָה: n. pers.

תְּרוּמָה: cs. תְּרוּמַת, sf. תְּרוּמָתִי; pl. תְּרוּמוֹת, sf. תְּרוּמוֹתֵיכֶם: (what is lifted, dedicated =) **tribute, contribution** (at the cult) Ex 25_2; gen. can be either subjective or objective: *t^erûmat yadkem* = what your hand contributes (voluntarily) Dt 12_6, & *t^erûmat yhwh* = contribution offered to Y. Ex 35_5, = *t^erûmâ l^eyhwh* Lv 7_{14}; consists of gold, meat, grain &c.

תְּרוּמִיָּה: **tribute, contribution** Ez 48_{12}. †

תְּרוּעָה: cs. תְּרוּעַת: — 1. **(signal of) alarm**: *hêrî^a' t^erû'â* Jos 6_5; — 2. **shout (of joy)** 1S 4_{5f}; — 3. (any) **signal** (given w. wind-instrument) Lv 25_9.

תְּרוּפָה: **healing** Ez 47_{12}. †

תִּרְזָה: unknown tree Is 44_{14}, ctxt. sugg. a conifer or an oak. †

תֶּרַח: n. pers.

תֶּרַח: n. loc.

תִּרְחֲנָה: n. pers.

[תָּרְמָה: *b^etormâ* Ju 9_{31}, trad. treachery, but rd. בָּארוּמָה (אֲרוּמָה n. loc.). †]

[תַּרְמוּת Je 14_{14} Kt: rd. תַּרְמִית Qr. †]

תַּרְמִית: **deceit(fulness)** Je 8_5 14_{14} Qr 23_{26} Zp 3_{13}. †

תֹּרֶן: sf. תָּרְנָם: **flagstaff** Is 30_{17}, **mast** Is 33_{23} Ez 27_5. †

cj. *תַּרְעִית: cj. sf. תַּרְעִיתָם: **thoughts, speculation** cj. Ps 119_{118}. †

תַּרְעֵלָה: **staggering** Is $51_{17\cdot22}$ Ps 60_2. †

תִּרְעָתִים: n. peop.

תְּרָפִים: both. w. & w/o art.: **idols**, evid. figurines or household gods Gn $31_{19\cdot34f}$ &c.; but for 1S $19_{13\cdot16}$ sugg. **rags**.

I תִּרְצָה: n. pers. f. Nu 26_{33} 27_1 36_{11} Jos 17_3. †

II תִּרְצָה: n. loc.

תרר: ↗ נתר qal 1.

תֶּרֶשׁ: n. pers.

I תַּרְשִׁישׁ: n. loc.

II תַּרְשִׁישׁ: a precious stone, sugg. **chrysolite** Ex 28_{20} 39_{13} Ez 1_{16} 10_9 28_{13} SS 5_{14} Dn 10_6. †

III תַּרְשִׁישׁ: n. pers. Est 1_{14} 1C 7_{10}. †

תִּרְשָׁתָא: alw. w. art., Persian title, **governor** Ne 8_9 10_2. †

תַּרְתָּן: Assyrian title, **commander of the army** 2K 18_{17} Is 20_1. †

תַּרְתָּק: n. of god.

*תְּשׂוּמָה: cs. תְּשׂוּמֶת: *t^esûmet-yād*: deposit? **joint property**? Lv 5_{21}. †

*תְּשֻׁאָה: pl. תְּשֻׁאוֹת: **noise** Is 22_2 Jb 39_7, **shouts** Zc 4_7, **crashing** Jb 36_{29} (& ↗ 30_{22}). †

תְּשָׁב: ☞ תּוֹשָׁב.

תִּשְׁבִּי: gent. of cj. *תִּשְׁבֵּי.

cj. *תִּשְׁבֵּי: n. loc. cj. 1K 17_1.

תִּשְׁבִּי 1K 17_1: ☞ cj. *תִּשְׁבֵּי.

תַּשְׁבֵּץ: **checkered work** (?) Ex 28_4. †

תְּשׁוּבָה: cs. תְּשׁוּבַת, sf. תְּשׁוּבָתוֹ; pl. תְּשֻׁבֹת, sf. תְּשׁוּבֹתֵיכֶם: — 1. **return** (to a place) 1S 7_{17}; *litšûbat haššānâ* in the return of the year = spring 2S 11_1 1K $20_{22\cdot26}$ 1C 20_1 2C 36_{10}; — 2. pl. **answers, responses** Jb 21_{34} 34_{36}. †

תְּשֻׁוָּה Jb 30_{22}: Qr תְּשִׁיָּה, rd. Kt תְּשֻׁוָּה = ☞ *תְּשָׁאָה. †

תְּשׁוּעָה, תְּשֻׁעָה: cs. תְּשׁוּעַת, sf. תְּשׁוּעָתִי, תְּשׁוּעָתֶךָ: **rescue, deliverance** 1S 11_9 2K 13_{17}, > **salvation** Is 45_{17}.

*תְּשׁוּקָה: sf. תְּשׁוּקָתוֹ, תְּשׁוּקָתֵךְ: **urge, craving, impulse** Gn 3_{16} 4_7 SS 7_{11}. †

תְּשׁוּרָה: **gift** ?; sugg. anything left over 1S 9_7. †

תְּשִׁיָּה Jb 30_{22} Qr, rd Kt תְּשֻׁוָּה = ☞ *תְּשָׁאָה. †

תְּשִׁיעִי, תְּשִׁעִי: f. תְּשִׁיעִ(י)ת: ord. **ninth** 2K 17_6.

תֵּשַׁע: cs. תְּשַׁע, f. תִּשְׁעָה, cs. תִּשְׁעַת; pl. תִּשְׁעִים: sg. **nine** Gn 5_5; pl. **ninety** Gn 5_{17}; for use of numbers, ☞ gramm.

תְּשֻׁעָה: ☞ תְּשׁוּעָה.

תְּשִׁעִי: ☞ תְּשִׁיעִי.

LEXICON OF THE ARAMAIC PORTIONS

א

*אַב: Heb. אָב: sf. אֲבִי Dn 5_{13}, אֲבוּךְ, אֲבוּהִי; pl. sf. אֲבָהָתִי, אֲבָהָתָךְ, אֲבָהָתַנָא: **father** Dn 5_2; pl. **forefathers** 2_{23} Ezr 4_{15}.

*אֵב: Heb. =: sf. אִנְבֵּהּ: **fruit** Dn $4_{9\cdot11\cdot18}$. †

אבד: Heb. =: **peal**: impf. pl. juss. יֵאבַדוּ: **go to ruin, perish** Je 10_{11}. †

hafel: impf. תְּהוֹבֵד, יְהֹבְדוּן; inf. הוֹבָדָה: **slay, kill** Dn $2_{12\cdot18\cdot24}$, abs. **destroy** 7_{26}. †

hofal: pf. הוּבַד: **be destroyed** Dn 7_{11}. †

אֶבֶן: Heb. =: det. אַבְנָא, f.: **stone**: — 1. a single stone Dn $2_{34f\cdot45}$ 6_{18}; — 2. as material Dn $5_{4\cdot23}$ Ezr 5_8 6_4.

אִגְּרָה/א: Heb. אִגֶּרֶת: det. אִגַּרְתָּא, f.: **letter** Ezr $4_{8\cdot11}$ 5_6. †

אֱדַיִן: Heb. אָז, אֱזַי: **then** Dn 2_{15}, *bē'dayin* **then** Dn 2_{14} Ezr 4_{24}; *min-'edayin* from that time on Ezr 5_{16}.

אֲדָר: Heb. =: **Adar**, name of the 12th month Ezr 6_{15}. †

*אִדַּר: pl. cs. אִדְּרֵי: **threshing-floor** Dn 2_{35}. †

*אֲדַרְגָּזַר: pl. אֲדַרְגָּזְרַיָּא: **counselor** Dn 3_{2f}. †

אַדְרַזְדָּא: adv. **diligently, zealously** Ezr 7_{23}. †

אֶדְרָע: Heb. אֶזְרוֹעַ & זְרוֹעַ: **arm**, metaph. **force** Ezr 4_{23}. †

*אזד: אַזְדָּא, noun det. or adj. f.: (the word = command is) **promulgated** (by me) Dn $2_{5\cdot8}$. †

אזה: **peal**: inf. מֵזֵא, sf. מֵזְיֵהּ; pt. pass. אֲזֵה: light (a fire), **heat** Dn $3_{19\cdot22}$. †

אֲזַל: Heb. =: **peal**: pf. 'אֲזַל, א, אֲזַלוּ, אֲזַלְנָא; [impf. fm. ☞ הלך]; impv. אֱזֶל־ Ezr 5_{15}: **go** Dn 2_{17} Ezr 4_{23}.

*אַח: Heb. II אָח: pl. sf. rd. Kt. אַחַיִךְ (Qr. אֶחָךְ): **brother** Ezr 7_{18}. †

אַחֲוָיַת: Dn 5_{12}, ☞ חוה hafel.

*אֲחִידָה: Heb. חִידָה: pl. אֲחִידָן: **riddle** Dn 5_{12}. †

אַחְמְתָא: n. loc.

*אַחַר: Heb. =, אַחֲרֵי: pl. cs. אַחֲרֵי, sf.

אַחֲרֵיהֹן: **after** Dn 7_{24}, *'aḥᵃrê dᵉnâ* hereafter $2_{29\cdot45}$. †

*__אַחֲרִי__: Heb. אַחֲרִית: cs. אַחֲרִית: **end**, *'aḥᵃrît yômayyā'* Dn 2_{28}. †

אָחֳרִי: f. of אָחֳרָן: **another** (f.) Dn 2_{39} $7_{5f\cdot8\cdot20}$. †

אחרין: Qr אָחֳרָן, Kt אַחֲרֵן, אַחֲרֵין, or אַחֲרִין: adv. *'ad-'ḥryn* **at last** Dn 4_5. †

אָחֳרָן: **another** (m.) Dn 2_{11}.

*__אֲחַשְׁדַּרְפַּן__: pl. det. אֲחַשְׁדַּרְפְּנַיָּא: **satrap** Dn $3_{2f\cdot27}$ $6_{2-5\cdot7f}$. †

אִילָן: Heb. אֵלוֹן: det. אִילָנָא: **tree** Dn $4_{7f\cdot11\cdot17\cdot20\cdot23}$. †

*__אֵימְתָן__: f. אֵימְתָנִי: **frightful** Dn 7_7. †

אִיתַי: Heb. אִשׁ, יֵשׁ: sf. Qr אִיתָךְ Kt אִיתַיךְ, אִיתֵיכוֹן, Qr אִיתָנָא & אִיתָנָא Kt אִיתַנָא: **existence; there is, are** (French *il y a*) Dn 2_{28}; *hēn 'îtay dî* whether it is true that Ezr 5_{17}; as accented verb 'be' before pt. or adj.: *hēn 'îtay ... yākil* Dn 3_{17} if he **is** able; w. sf. 2_{26}, w. pleon. sf. 2_{11}.

אכל: Heb. =: **peal**: pf. אֲכַלוּ; impf. יֵאכֻל, תֵּאכֻל; impv. f. אֲכֻלִי; pt. f. אָכְלָה: **eat**, live on Dn 4_{30}, abs. 7_7, metaph., obj. *'ar'ā'* devastate 7_{23}; w. *qarṣîn*, F **qᵉraṣ*.

אַל: Heb. =: **not** (for prohibition) Dn 2_{24} 4_{16} 5_{10}. †

*__אֵל__: Heb. VI אֵל: pron. demonstr. pl. (sg. F *dᵉnâ*): **these** Ezr 5_{15} Qr (Kt F *'ēlleh*). †

אֱלָהּ: Heb. אֱלוֹהַּ: cs. =, det. אֱלָהָא, sf. אֱלָהִי, אֱלָהָךְ, אֱלָהֵהּ, אֱלָהָנָא (Dn 3_{17} ־הָנָא), אֱלָהֲכוֹן & אֱלָהֲכֹם, אֱלָהֲהוֹן & אֱלָהֲהֹם; w. pref. לֶאֱלָהּ, but det. or sf. לֵאלָהָא, וֵאלָהָא &c.; pl. אֱלָהִין, det. אֱלָהַיָּא, cs. אֱלָהֵי, לֵאלָהֵי, sf. לֵאלָהָיִךְ, לֵאלָהַי $3_{12\cdot18}$ (Kt ־הַיִךְ, Qr ־הָךְ): **God/god**: — 1. sg.: **god** Dn 3_{15}; in descriptive phr., **God** = Yahweh: *'ᵉlāh rab* Dn 2_{20}, *'ᵉlāhā' rabbā'* Ezr 5_8 &c., & w. gen. *'ᵉlāh šᵉmayyā'* Dn 2_{18f} &c.; — 2. pl. **gods** Dn 2_{11}; *bar 'ᵉlāhîn* = divine being, angel Dn 3_{25}; pl. w. mng. of sg. = Yahweh Dn 6_{17}.

אֵלֶּה: Heb. =: pron. demonst. pl.: **these** Je 10_{11} Ezr 5_{15} Kt (Qr *'ēl*); sg. F *dᵉnâ*. †

אֲלוּ: interj. **behold!**, *wa'ᵃlû* Dn $4_{7\cdot10}$ 7_8. †

אִלֵּין, Dn 6_7 אִלֵּן: pron. demonstr. pl. **these** Dn $2_{40\cdot44}$ $6_{3\cdot7}$ 7_{17}; sg. F *dᵉnâ*. †

אִלֵּךְ: pron. demonstr. pl. **these** Dn 3_{12f}; sg. F *dᵉnâ*.

אִלֵּן: F אִלֵּין.

אֲלַף: Heb. II אֶלֶף: cs. אֲלַף, det. אַלְפָּא; pl. אַלְפִּין Dn 7_{10} Qr (Kt אַלְפִים): **thousand** Dn 5_1; *'elef 'alpîn* 7_{10} = many thousands. †

*__אַמָּה__: Heb. =: pl. אַמִּין: **cubit** Dn 3_1 Ezr 6_3. †

אֻמָּה: Heb. =: pl. det. אֻמַּיָּא Dn $3_{7\cdot31}$, אֻמַיָּא 3_4 5_{19} 6_{26} 7_{14}: **nation** Dn 3_{29} Ezr 4_{10}, pl. (as previous listing). †

אמן: Heb. =: **hafel**: pf. הֵימִן; pt. pass. מְהֵימַן: **trust in** (w. *bᵉ*) Dn 6_{24}; pt. pass. **trustworthy** 2_{45} 6_5. †

אמר: Heb. =: **peal**: pf. א׳, 3. f. אֲמַרַת, 1. אַמְרֵת, pl. אֲמַרוּ; impf. יֵאמַר, pl. תֵּאמְרוּן; impv. אֱמַר, אֱמַר; inf. מֵאמַר Dn 2_9 & מֵמַר Ezr 5_{11}; pt. אָמַר, pl. אָמְרִין: — 1. **say**, w. dir. discourse Dn 2_7; *lᵉmēmar* (= Heb. לֵאמֹר) † Ezr 5_{11}; *'āmᵉrîn* it is said † Dn 4_{28} Ezr 5_3; — 2. **say** s.thg Dn 3_{29}, tell (dream) 2_4; — 3. **command**, w. dir. discourse, *'āmᵉrîn* it is commanded Dn 3_4; w. *lᵉ* & inf. 2_{12}; w. pf. of execution of command 5_{29}.

אִמַּר: pl. אִמְּרִין: **lamb** (as sacrificial animal) Ezr $6_{9\cdot17}$ 7_{17}. †

אִנְבֵּהּ: F אֵב.

אֲנָה: Heb. אֲנִי: **I** Dn 2_8, reinforcing Dn 7_{15}; *minnî 'ᵃnâ* Ezr 7_{21}.

אִנּוּן: f. אִנִּין Dn 7_{17} Qr (Kt אִנּוּן): pron. pers. pl. (sg. F הוּא, הִיא) **they**; as copula Dn 7_{17} Ezr 5_4, as acc. Dn 6_{25}; pron. dem. **those** Dn 2_{44}; F *himmô(n)*. †

*__אֱנוֹשׁ__: F אֱנָשׁ.

אֲנַחְנָא, **אֲנַחְנָה** Ezr 4_{16}: Heb. (אֲ)נַחְנוּ: pron. pers. pl. **we** Dn 3_{16f} Ezr 4_{16} 5_{11}. †

אנס: Heb. =: **peal**: pt. אָנֵס: oppress, **distress** Dn 4_{6}. †

*אֲנַף: Heb. אנף, אַף: du. sf. אַנְפּוֹהִי: **face** Dn 2_{46} 3_{19}. †

אֱנָשׁ, *אֱנוֹשׁ: cs. =, det. אֲנָשָׁא, אֱנוֹשָׁא Dn 4_{13f} Kt; pl. אֲנָשִׁים 4_{14}: — 1. sg. det. coll. **mankind** Dn 4_{13f}; people of a particular country Ezr 4_{11}; *malkût ʾanāšāʾ* Dn 4_{14}, *zeraʿ ʾanāšāʾ* 2_{43}; *benê ʾanāšāʾ* 2_{38} men (as individuals), *bar ʾenāš* (a single) man 7_{13}; — 2. (a single) **man** (i.e. person) Dn 2_{10}; *kol-ʾenāš* everyone 3_{10}.

אַנְתָּה Kt, אַנְתְּ Qr (Ezr 7_{25} Kt also אַנְתְּ): Heb. אַתָּה: pron. pers. sg. m. **thou, you** Dn 2_{29}.

אַנְתּוּן: Heb. אַתֶּם: pron. pers. pl. **you** Dn 2_{8}. †

אֱסוּר: Heb. אֵסוּר: pl. אֱסוּרִין: **bonds, fetters** Dn $4_{12.20}$, pl. imprisonment Ezr 7_{26}. †

אָסְנַפַּר: n. of Assyrian king, prob. = **Assurbanipal** Ezr 4_{10}. †

אָסְפַּרְנָא: adv. **exactly, eagerly** Ezr 5_{8} $6_{8.12f}$ $7_{17.21.26}$. †

אֱסָר: Heb. אִסָּר: cs. =, det. אֱסָרָא: (legal) prohibition, **interdict** Dn 6_{8-16}. †

אָע: Heb. עֵץ: det. אָעָא: **wood** Dn $5_{4.23}$, beam Ezr 5_{8} $6_{4.11}$. †

אַף: Heb. I אַף: **also**, *weʾaf* Dn 6_{23} Ezr $5_{10.14}$ 6_{5}. †

*אֲפָרְסָי: pl. det. אֲפָרְסָיֵא Ezr 4_{9}, uncert.; n. peop., or else a title of officials. †

*אֲפַרְסְכָי: pl. det. אֲפַרְסְכָיֵא Ezr 5_{6} 6_{6}, uncert.; perh. n. peop., but prob. a title of officials. †

*אֲפַרְסַתְכָי: pl. det. אֲפַרְסַתְכָיֵא Ezr 4_{9}, **title of officials**. †

אַפְּתֹם: Ezr 4_{13}, uncert.; sugg. cs. **treasury**; oth.: adv. eventually, or positively. †

*אֶצְבַּע: Heb. =: pl. אֶצְבְּעָן, cs. אֶצְבְּעָת: — 1. **finger** Dn 5_{5}; — 2. **toe** Dn 2_{41f}. †

*אַרְבַּע: Heb. =: f. אַרְבְּעָה: **four** Dn 3_{25} $7_{2f.6.17}$ Ezr 6_{17}. †

*אַרְגְּוָן: Heb. אַרְגָּמָן: det. אַרְגְּוָנָא: **purple (garment)** Dn $5_{7.16.29}$. †

אֲרוּ: interj., **behold**: *waʾarû* Dn $7_{2.5.7.13}$. †

*אֲרַח: Heb. אֹרַח: pl. sf. אֹרְחָתָךְ, אֹרְחָתֵהּ: **way**; pl. (God's) ways of dealing, acting Dn 4_{34}; experiences (of men) 5_{23}. †

אַרְיֵה: Heb. =: pl. det. אַרְיָוָתָא: **lion** Dn 6_{8}.

אַרְיוֹךְ: Heb. =: n. pers.

אֲרִיךְ: **fitting**, w. *le* Ezr 4_{14}. †

*אַרְכֻבָּה: pl. sf. אַרְכֻבָּתֵהּ: f.: **knee** Dn 5_{6}. †

אַרְכָה: Heb. אֹרֶךְ: f.: **length(ening), prolongation** Dn 4_{24} 7_{12}. †

*אַרְכְּוָי: pl. det. אַרְכְּוָיֵא Qr, אַרְכְּוָיֵ Kt: n. people (↗ Heb. אֶרֶךְ).

אֲרַע: Heb. אֶרֶץ: det. אַרְעָא: — 1. **the earth** Dn 2_{35} Ezr 5_{11}; — 2. *ʾárʿāʾ* Kt, *ʾaraʿ* Qr to the earth, **downwards**; *ʾaraʿ minnāk* under you, inferior to you † Dn 2_{39}.

*אַרְעִי: cs. אַרְעִית: **bottom** (of pit &c.) Dn 6_{25}. †

*אֲרַק: = ↗ אֲרַע, Heb. אֶרֶץ: det. אַרְקָא: **the earth** Je 10_{11}. †

אַרְתַּחְשַׁשְׂתְּא & אַרְתַּחְשַׁסְתְּא: n. pers.

*אשׁ: Heb. I שֵׁת: pl. det. אֻשַּׁיָּא: **foundation** Ezr 4_{12} 5_{16}; 6_{13} rd. אֱשׁוֹהִי or אֻשַּׁיָּא, ↗ אֶשָּׁא, or else מְשְׁחוֹהִי, ↗ *מְשַׁח. †

אֶשָּׁא: Heb. אֵשׁ & אִשֶּׁה: f. — 1. **fire** Dn 7_{11}; — 2. **offering by fire**, pl. abs. or sf. cj. Ezr 6_{3}, ↗ אשׁ. †

אָשַׁף: Heb. אַשָּׁף: pl. אָשְׁפִין, det. אָשְׁפַיָּא: **conjurer** Dn $2_{10.27}$ 4_{4} $5_{7.11.15}$. †

*אשׁרן: det. אֻשַּׁרְנָא Ezr $5_{3.9}$: uncert., some kind of wooden structure; sugg. outfit; timber or panelling; roof scaffolding. †

אֶשְׁתַּדּוּר: **revolt** Ezr $4_{15.19}$. †

אִשְׁתְּיו Dn 5_{3f}, ↗ שׁתה.

*אָת: Heb. אוֹת: pl. אָתִין, det. אָתַיָּא, sf. אָתוֹהִי: **sign** Dn 3_{32f} 6_{28}. †

אֲתָה: Heb. =: **peal**: pf. 'א, Ezr $5_{3.16}$ אֲתָא, 3. pl. אֲתוֹ; impv. pl. אֱתוֹ; inf. מֵתֵא (< *מֶאתֵא); pt. אָתֵה: **come** Dn 3_{2} Ezr 4_{12}.

hafel: pf. הַיְתִי, 3. pl. הַיְתִיו; inf. הַיְתָיָה: **bring**, obj. persons Dn 3_{13}, things 5_{2f}; pass.

3. sg. f. הֵיתָיִת, 3. pl. הֵיתָיו be brought † Dn 3_{13} 6_{18}.

***אַתּוּן**: cs. =, det. אַתּוּנָא: **furnace** Dn 3_6.

אָתֵי: ↗ אִיתַי.

אֲתַר: Heb. אֲשֶׁר: sf. אַתְרֵהּ: — 1. **trace** Dn 2_{35} (oth.: 2); — 2. **place**: *'al-'atrēh* Ezr 5_{15} 6_7 & *le'atrēh* at, on its place; *'atar dî* 6_3 the place where (oth.: as a place where); — 3. ↗ בָּאתַר. †

ב

בְּ: Heb. =: sf. בִּי, בָּךְ, בֵּהּ, בַּהּ, בְּהוֹן: prep.: — 1. **in**: place where Dn 2_{28}; *ḥalāq be* a share in Ezr 4_{16}; time when Dn 2_{28}; — 2. **into** &c.: place to which Dn 2_{38}, *'adâ be* come to = touch Dn 3_{27}; — 3. **through, by (means of)** Dn 2_{30}; *be* of price, **for** (the price of) Ezr 7_{17}; — 4. of accompanying condition: *beḥedwâ* with joy Ezr 6_{16}; — 5. oth. connections: *šātâ be* drink from (= Heb.) Dn 5_2; *hêmîn be* believe in 6_{24}; *šelēṭ be* rule over 2_{38}; *'abad be* = treat 4_{32}; *yôm beyôm* day by day Ezr 6_9; — 6. comb., ↗ בָּאתַר & גַּו.

***בְּאִישׁ**: f. det. בְּאִישְׁתָּא: **evil** Ezr 4_{12}. †

בְּאֵשׁ: Heb. =: **peal**: pf. ב׳: be bad, w. *'al* is **displeasing** to = he is displeased Dn 6_{15}. †

בָּאתַר: sf. בָּתְרָךְ: **after** Dn 2_{39} 7_{6f}. †

בָּבֶל: Heb. =: n. loc. **Babylon**.

***בָּבְלָי**: gent. of בָּבֶל: pl. det. בָּבְלָיֵא: **Babylonian** Ezr 4_9. †

בדר: Heb. פזר & בזר: **pael**: impv. pl. בַּדַּרוּ: **scatter** Dn 4_{11}. †

בְּהִילוּ: **haste** Ezr 4_{23}. †

בהל: Heb. =: **pael**: impf. pl. sf. יְבַהֲלֻנַּנִי, יְבַהֲלוּנֵּהּ יְבַהֲלֻנֵּהּ, juss. יְבַהֲלָךְ & יְבַהֲלוּךְ: **frighten** Dn $4_{2\cdot16}$ $5_{6\cdot10}$ $7_{15\cdot28}$. †

hitpeel: inf. ↗ הִתְבְּהָלָה as noun: **haste, hurry** Dn 2_{25} 3_{24} 6_{20}. †

hitpaal: pt. מִתְבְּהַל: **be frightened** Dn 5_9. †

בטל: Heb. =: **peal**: pf. 3. f. בְּטֵלַת; pt. f. בָּטְלָא: **stop** (intrans.), **be discontinued** Ezr 4_{24}. †

pael: pf. pl. בַּטִּלוּ; inf. בַּטָּלָא: **(order to) stop** s.thg Ezr $4_{21\cdot23}$ 5_5; *dî-lā' lebaṭṭālā'* Ezr 6_8 without interruption, or without time-limit. †

בֵּין: Heb. =: sf. Kt בֵּינֵיהוֹן, Qr ־הֵין: **between** Dn $7_{5\cdot8}$. †

בִּינָה: Heb. =: **insight** Dn 2_{21}. †

***בִּירָה**: Heb. =: det. בִּירְתָא: **citadel, fortress** Ezr 6_2. †

בית: **peal**: pf. בָּת: **pass the night** Dn 6_{19}. †

***בַּיִת**: Heb. =: det. בַּיְתָא & בַּיְתָה, cs. בֵּית, sf. בַּיְתֵהּ, בַּיְתִי; pl. sf. בָּתֵּיכוֹן: — 1. **house** Dn 2_{17}; = palace 4_1; in comb.: *bêt malkā'* royal treasury Ezr 6_4, *bêt malkû* residence Dn 4_{27}; *bêt mišteyā'* banquet-hall 5_{10}; *bêt ginzayyā'* treasure-house(s) Ezr 5_{17}; *bêt sifrayyā'* archives 6_1; — 2. temple Ezr 5_3; *bêt 'elāhâ* 4_{24}, *bêt 'elāh šemayyā'* 7_{23}.

בָּל: **heart**: *śām bāl*, w. *le* & inf., set one's mind on Dn 6_{15}. †

בלא: ↗ בלה.

בֵּלְאשַׁצַּר: n. pers., = בֵּלְשַׁאצַּר.

בלה: Heb. =: **pael**: impf. יְבַלֵּא: **wear (s.one) down, out** Dn 7_{25}. †

בְּלוֹ: **tax** (paid in kind) Ezr $4_{13\cdot20}$ 7_{24}. †

בֵּלְטְשַׁאצַּר: n. pers.

בֵּלְשַׁאצַּר: n. pers.

בנה: Heb. =: **peal**: pf. 3 sg. sf. בְּנָהִי, 1 sg. sf.

בֱּנַיְתַהּ, 3 pl. בְּנוֹ; impf. pl. יִבְנוֹן; inf. מִבְנֵא Ezr 5_2 6_8, מִבְנְיָה 5_9, לְבְּנֵא $5_{3\cdot13}$; pt. pl. בָּנַיִן, pass. בְּנֵה: **build** Dn 4_{27} Ezr 4_{12}.

hitpeel: impf. יִתְבְּנֵא, תִּתְבְּנֵא; pt. מִתְבְּנֵה: **be built** Ezr 4_{13}, w. acc. of material 5_8.

*בִּנְיָן: Heb. = (< Aram.): det. בִּנְיָנָא: **building** Ezr 5_4. †

בְּנַיִן: ☞ II בַּר.

בְּנַס: **peal**: pf. ב׳: **become angry** Dn 2_{12}. †

בְּעָה: Heb. =: **peal**: pf. בְּעָה/א, pl. בְּעוֹ, בְּעֵינָא; impf. יִבְעֵא, אֶבְעֵא; inf. מִבְעֵא; pt. בָּעֵה/א, pl. בָּעַיִן: — 1. **seek** (to do s.thg) Dn 6_5; — 2. **request**: w. *min* + pers. Dn 2_{13}, w. *min-qᵒdām* 2_{18}; w. cogn. acc. *bāʿû*, offer prayer Dn 6_8; abs. pray 6_{12}; — 3. w. inf. † Dn 2_{13} **be on the point of, run the risk of** (oth.: they sought to, or [pt. pass.] were sought).

pael: impf. pl. יְבַעוֹן: **seek out** s.one **(eagerly)** Dn 4_{33} (oth.: seek for). †

בָּעוּ: sf. בָּעוּתֵהּ: **petition, prayer** Dn $6_{8\cdot14}$. †

*בְּעֵל: Heb. בַּעַל: cs. =: **owner, master, lord**, in phr. *beʿēl-ṭeʿēm* (☞ *ṭeʿēm*) commander Ezr $4_{8f\cdot17}$. †

*בִּקְעָה: Heb. =: cs. בִּקְעַת: **plain** Dn 3_1. †

בקר: Heb. = (< Aram.): **pael**: pf. pl. בַּקַּרוּ; impf. יְבַקַּר; inf. בַּקָּרָא/ה: **search**, **investigate** Ezr 4_{15} (but rd. pl. or **hitpaal**) $._{19}$ 6_1 7_{14}. †

hitpaal: impf. יִתְבַּקַּר: **be investigated** (i.e. let a search be made) Ezr 5_{17}. †

I בַּר: Heb. IV בַּר: det. בָּרָא: **field**: *ḥêwat bārāʾ* Dn 2_{38}, *ditʾāʾ dî bārāʾ* 4_{12}.

II בַּר: Heb. I בַּר (< Aram.) & בֵּן: cs. =, sf. בְּרֵהּ; pl. cs. בְּנֵי, sf. בְּנוֹהִי, בְּנֵיהוֹן: — 1. **son** Dn 5_{22} Ezr 5_2, pl. children Dn 6_{25}; (king &) his sons = princes Ezr 6_{10}, = his descendants 7_{23}, grandson 5_1; *bᵉnê tôrîn* young bulls Ezr 6_9; — 2. of remoter & metaph. relationships: *bᵉnê yiśrāʾēl* Ezr 6_{16}, *bᵉnê gālûtāʾ* Dn 2_{25}; *bar ʾᵉnāš* a man Dn 7_{13}, *bᵉnê ʾᵃnāšāʾ* men 2_{38}; *bar ʾᵉlāhîn*, an angel 3_{25}; *bar šᵉnîn*, (so many) years old 6_1.

I ברך: Heb. I ברך: **peal**: pt. בָּרֵךְ: **kneel down** Dn 6_{11} (but oth.: II). †

II ברך: Heb. II ברך: **peal**: pt. pass. בְּרִיךְ: **blessed** Dn 3_{28}. †

pael: pf. בָּרֵךְ Dn 2_{19}, (בָּרֵךְ 6_{11} if not I), בָּרְכֵת; pt. pass. מְבָרַךְ: **bless** (obj. God) Dn 2_{19f} 4_{31} (oth.: + 6_{11}). †

*בְּרַךְ or *בְּרֵךְ: Heb. בֶּרֶךְ: pl. sf. בִּרְכוֹהִי: **knee** Dn 6_{11}. †

בְּרַם: **but, yet** Dn 2_{28} $4_{12\cdot20}$ 5_{17} Ezr 5_{13}. †

בְּשַׂר: Heb. בָּשָׂר: det. בִּשְׂרָא: — 1. **flesh** (devoured by beast) Dn 7_5; — 2. metaph. coll. *(kol-)biśrāʾ* flesh = mankind Dn 2_{11}, animals 4_9. †

*בַּת: Heb. II בַּת: pl. בַּתִּין: **bath** = a liquid measure Ezr 7_{22}. †

בָּתַר: ☞ בָּאתַר.

ג

*גַּב: pl. sf. Kt גַּבַּיַהּ, Qr sg. sf. גַּבַּהּ: *gappîn ʾarbaʿ … ʿal-gabbayah/-gabbah* Dn 7_6: either **back** (Heb. =), or **side** (√*gnb*). †

*גֹּב: Heb. גֵּב & I גּוֹב (n. loc.): cs. גֹּב Dn $6_{8\cdot25}$, גּוֹב 6_{13}, det. גֻּבָּא: **pit** (for lions) Dn $6_{8\cdot13\cdot17f\cdot20f\cdot24f}$. †

*גְּבוּרָה: Heb. =: det. גְּבוּרְתָא: **strength** Dn $2_{20\cdot23}$. †

גְּבַר: Heb. גֶּבֶר: pl. גֻּבְרִין, det. גֻּבְרַיָּא: **man** (adult male) Dn 2_{25} Ezr 4_{21}; *gubrîn gibbārê ḥayil* Dn 3_{20}; *gubrîn kaśdāʾîn, g. yᵉhûdāʾîn* $3_{8\cdot12}$.

*גְּבַר: Heb. גִּבּוֹר: pl. cs. גִּבָּרֵי: **strong man** Dn 3_{20}. †

*גְּדָבַר: pl. det. גְּדָבְרַיָּא: **treasurer** Dn 3_{2f} (if txt. good; ↗ comm.). †

גדד: Heb. =: **peal**: impv. גֹּדּוּ: **cut down** (a tree) Dn $4_{11 \cdot 20}$. †

*גַּו or *גֹּו: Heb. II גֵּו: cs. גּוֹא, sf. גַּוַּהּ, גַּוַּהּ: **interior**, alw. w. prep.: a) *begô'*, *begaww-* **in (the midst of)** Dn 3_{25} Ezr 5_7; b) *legô'* **into** Dn 3_6; c) *min-gô'* **out from** Dn 3_{26}.

גּוֹא: ↗ *גַּו.

גּוֹב: ↗ גֹּב.

גֵּוָה: Heb. = (> Aram. ?): **pride** Dn 4_{34}. †

גוח: Heb. גִּיחַ: **hafel**: pt. pl. f. מְגִיחָן: **stir up** (the sea) Dn 7_2. †

cj. גּוֹן or גִּין: ↗ נִדְנֶה.

*גִּזְבַּר: Heb. גִּזְבָּר: pl. det. גִּזַּבְרַיָּא: **treasurer** Ezr 7_{21}. †

גזר: Heb. =: **peal**: pt. pl. גָּזְרִין, det. גָּזְרַיָּא: Dn 2_{27} 4_4 $5_{7 \cdot 11}$: **astrologers**, or those who consult livers (Latin *haruspices*); oth.: **exorcists**. †

hitpeel, **itpeel**: pf. 3. sg. f. הִתְגְּזֶרֶת Dn 2_{34}, אִתְגְּזֶרֶת 2_{45}: **be cut out, quarried** (of stone). †

*גְּזֵרָה: Heb. =: cs. גְּזֵרַת, f.: **decree** Dn $4_{14 \cdot 21}$. †

cj. גִּין: ↗ נִדְנֶה.

*גִּיר: Heb. גִּר (< Aram.): det. גִּירָא: **plaster** Dn 5_5. †

*גַּלְגַּל: Heb. = & גִּלְגַּל: pl. sf. גַּלְגִּלּוֹהִי: **wheel** Dn 7_9. †

גלה: Heb. =: **peal**: pt. גָּלֵא/ה; inf. מִגְלֵא; **peil** (pass.) pf. גֲּלִי Dn 2_{19}, גֱּלִי 2_{30}: **reveal, disclose** Dn $2_{22 \cdot 28f \cdot 47}$; pass. $2_{19 \cdot 30}$. †

hafel: pf. הַגְלִי: **deport** Ezr 4_{10} 5_{12}. †

*גָּלוּ: Heb. גָּלוּת: det. גָּלוּתָא, f.: **exile**, *benê gālûtā'* the exiles Dn 2_{25} 5_{13} 6_{14} Ezr 6_{16}. †

גְּלָל: *'eben gelāl* Ezr 5_8 6_4, coll. **blocks of stone** Ezr 5_8 6_4. †

גמר: Heb. =: **peal**: pt. pass. גְּמִיר: **finished** Ezr 7_{12}, but uncert. in ctxt.; abbreviated formula? or word(s) fallen out?. †

*גְּנַז: Heb. II *גֶּנֶז (< Aram.): pl. det. גִּנְזַיָּא, cs. גִּנְזֵי: **treasure**, *bêt ginzayyā'* treasure-houses Ezr 5_{17} 7_{20}, & so rd. 6_1. †

*גַּף: pl. גַּפִּין, sf. גַּפַּיהּ or גַּפֵּיהּ Kt, גַּפַּהּ Qr, f.: **wing** Dn $7_{4 \cdot 6}$. †

*גְּרַם or *גְּרֵם: Heb. גֶּרֶם: pl. sf. גַּרְמֵיהוֹן: **bone** Dn 6_{25}. †

*גְּשֵׁם: sf. גִּשְׁמַהּ, גִּשְׁמֵהּ, גֶּשְׁמְהוֹן; pl. sf. Kt of mss. גֶּשְׁמֵיהוֹן Dn 3_{27f}: **body** Dn 3_{27f} 4_{30} 5_{21} 7_{11}. †

ד

דָּא: Heb. זֹאת, זוֹ, זֹה: pron. demonstr. f., ↗ m. דְּנָה: **this** (f.) Dn 4_{27} 7_8; *dā' ledā'* one against the other 5_6, *dā' min-dā'* from each other 7_3. †

דֹּב: Heb. =: **bear** Dn 7_5. †

דבח: Heb. זָבַח: **peal**: pt. pl. דָּבְחִין: **sacrifice** (w. cogn. acc.) Ezr 6_3. †

*דְּבַח: Heb. זֶבַח: pl. דִּבְחִין: **sacrifice** (of animals) Ezr 6_3. †

דבק: Heb. =: **peal**: pt. pl. דָּבְקִין: **stick, hold together** Dn 2_{43}. †

*דִּבְרָה: Heb. =: cs. דִּבְרַת: **affair, matter**: *'al-dibrat dî* = *'ad-dibrat dî*, to the end that = in order that Dn 2_{30} 4_{14}. †

דְּהַב: Heb. זָהָב: דְּהַב Ezr 7_{15}, det. דַּהֲבָא Dn, דַּהֲבָה Ezr: **gold** Dn 2_{32} Ezr 7_{15f}.

דהוא Kt, דֶּהָיֵא Qr Ezr 4_9: trad. n. peop., but rd. דִּי־הוּא **that is**. †

דור: Heb. =: **peal**: impf. תְּדוּר, pl. יְדוּרוּן Dn 4_9 Kt, יְדֻרָן Qr; pt. pl. דָּאֲרִין Kt, דָּיְרִין Qr, cs. דָּאֲרֵי Kt, דָּיְרֵי Qr: **live** (= dwell) Dn 2_{38} 3_{31} $4_{9 \cdot 18 \cdot 32}$ 6_{26}. †

דּוּרָא: n. terr. Dn 3_{1}. †

דּוּשׁ: Heb. = : **peal**: impf. sf. תְּדוּשִׁנַּהּ: **trample down** Dn 7_{23}. †

*דחוה: pl. דַּחֲוָן Dn 6_{19}: uncert.; sugg. concubines; oth. food, musical instruments, tables, or perfumes. †

דחל: **peal**: pt. pl. דָּחֲלִין, pass. דְּחִיל, f. דְּחִילָה: **fear**, w. *min-qᵒdām* Dn 5_{19} 6_{27}; pt. pass. **frightening, frightful** 2_{31} $7_{7\cdot19}$. †

pael: impf. sf. וִידַחֲלִנַּנִי: **frighten, make** s.one **afraid** Dn 4_{2}. †

דִּי, דְּ in ☞ דהוא: = Heb. זוּ, זֶה: orig. demonstr., then particle of relation: — 1. mark of gen. after det. noun: *šallîṭāʾ dî malkāʾ* Dn 2_{15}; after indeterminate noun, *nᵉhar dî nûrāʾ* 7_{10}; if both nouns are det., oft. w. proleptic sf., *šᵉmēh dî ʾᵉlāhāʾ* his name, i.e. God's 3_{8}; material, *rēʾšâ dî dahᵃbāʾ* the head of gold 2_{38}, *rēʾšēh dî dᵃhab* his head was of gold 2_{33}; — 2. introducing a rel. clause (Heb. *ʾᵃšer*): a) after a noun, *hêkᵉlāʾ dî bîrûšᵉlem* the temple in Jerus. Dn 5_{2}; *dî* as subj. 4_{19}, as obj. 2_{26}; = what, that which 2_{23}; *kol-dî* everything that Ezr 7_{23}; followed by noun w. sf., *dî šᵉmēh* whose name Dn 4_{5}; phr.: *bᵉʿiddānāʾ dî* as soon as Dn 3_{5}, *ʾᵃtar dî* Ezr 6_{3} ☞ *ʾᵃtar*; followed by pers. pron.: *dî hîʾ* that is Ezr 6_{15}, *dî ʾinnîn* who are Dn 7_{17}; b) after interr. pron.: *man-dî* Dn 3_{6}, *mâ/māʾ dî* 2_{28} (= Heb. *mî ʾᵃšer, mah-šše*); c) in other comb.: *dî … tammâ* where Ezr 6_{1}; *dî lēh* are his Dn 2_{20}; *dî lāʾ titḥabbal* indestructible Dn 6_{27}; w. inf., *dî lāʾ lᵉhašnāyâ* irrevocable 6_{9}; *dî-lāʾ* without Ezr 6_{9}, *dî lāʾ bîdayin* without human assistance; — 3. conj., not alw. distinguishable fm. 2 (cf. Heb. *ʾᵃšer* & *kî*): a) **that** after vb. of knowing Dn 2_{8}, hearing Ezr 5_{14} &c.; w. *ʿᵃtîd*, ready to Dn 3_{15}; *min-qᵉšoṭ dî*, it pertains to the truth that = truly 2_{47}; *wᵉdî* whereas 2_{41}; *kol-qᵒbēl dî*, just as 2_{41}; b) introduces dir. discourse (Heb. *kî* 7.) Dn 2_{25}; c) purpose, so that, in order that Dn 4_{3}, = inf. Ezr 6_{10}; *dî lāʾ* so that … not, lest Dn 2_{18}, = *dî-lᵉmâ* Ezr 7_{23}; d) result, so that Ezr 5_{10}; e) causal, for, because Dn 2_{20}; f) w. prep: α) *kᵉdî* (Heb. *kaʾᵃšer*) as Dn 2_{43}, when 3_{7}; β) *min-dî* after Ezr 4_{23}; as soon as, to the extent that Dn 4_{23}; because 3_{22}; γ) *ʿal/ʿad-dibrat dî*, ☞ **dibrâ*; *ʿad-dî* ☞ *ʿad*; *loqᵒbēl dî* & *kol-qᵒbēl dî*, ☞ *qᵒbēl*.

דִּין: Heb. = : **peal**: pt. pl. דָּאֲנִין Kt, דָּיְנִין Qr: **judge** Ezr 7_{25}. †

דִּין: Heb. = : det. דִּינָא: — 1. **judgment**, w. *ʿbd* hitp. & *min*, is being given on Ezr 7_{26}, w. *yᵉhîb* & *lᵉ* (favorable) judgment is being given in favor of Dn 7_{22}; justice 4_{34}; — 2. **council of judges** Dn $7_{10\cdot26}$. †

*דַּיָּן: Heb. = : pl. דַּיָּנִין: **judge** Ezr 7_{25}. †

דִּינָיֵא: m. pl. Ezr 4_{9}, trad. n. peop.; but better rd. דַּיָּנַיָּא judges. †

דֵּךְ: f. דָּךְ: demonstr. adj., **that**: *šēšbaṣṣar dēk* Ezr 5_{16}, *qiryᵉtāʾ dāk* 4_{13}.

דִּכֵּן: demonstr. pron., m. & f. **that**: m. Dn 2_{31}, f. $7_{20\cdot21}$. †

*דְּכַר: Heb. זָכָר: pl. דִּכְרִין: **ram** Ezr $6_{9\cdot17}$ 7_{17}. †

*דִּכְרוֹן: Heb. זִכָּרוֹן: det. דִּכְרוֹנָה: **minutes, memorandum** Ezr 6_{2}. †

*דָּכְרָן: pl. det. דָּכְרָנַיָּא: **minutes, memorandum**, *sᵉfar-dokrānayyāʾ* Ezr 4_{15}. †

דלק: Heb. = : **peal**: pt. דָּלִק: **burn** Dn 7_{9}. †

דמה: Heb. = : **peal**: pt. דָּמֵה, f. דָּמְיָה: **resemble** Dn 3_{25} 7_{5}. †

דְּנָה: demonstr. pron. & adj. m. (f. ☞ דָּא), **this**: — 1. adj.: *dāniyyēʾl dᵉnâ* Dn 6_{4}; before the noun Ezr 5_{4}; — 2. pron.: this is Dn 2_{28}; — 3. otherw.: *kidnâ*, so Je 10_{11} Dn 3_{29} Ezr 5_{7}; *millâ kidnâ* such a thing Dn 2_{10}; *dᵉnâ ʿim-dᵉnâ* one with another 2_{43}; *kol-dᵉnâ* all this 5_{22}; *ʿal-dᵉnâ* therefore Ezr 4_{14}, in regard to this Dn 3_{16}; *ʾaḥᵃrê-dᵉnâ* Dn 2_{29} = *bāʾtar dᵉnâ* 7_{6} after this/him.

דָּנִיֵּאל: n. pers. **Daniel** (= Heb.).

דקק: Heb. =: **peal**: pf. pl. דָּקוּ: **break into pieces** 3 pl. Dn 2_{35}: people broke them = they were broken (oth.: intrans.). †

hafel: pf. 3 f. הַדֶּקֶת, pl. הַדִּקוּ; impf. תַּדִּק, sf. תַּדִּקִנַּהּ; pt. מְהַדִּק, f. מַדֱּקָה & מַדֲּקָה: **pulverize, crush** Dn $2_{34\cdot40\cdot44f}$ 6_{25} $7_{7\cdot19\cdot23}$. †

דָּר: Heb. דּוֹר: **generation**: *ʿim-dār wedār* from generation to generation Dn 3_{33} 4_{31}. †

דָּרְיָוֶשׁ: n. pers. **Darius** (= Heb.).

*דְּרָע: Heb. זְרוֹעַ: pl. sf. דְּרָעוֹהִי: **arm** Dn 2_{32}. †

דָּת: Heb. =: cs. =, det. דָּתָא, sf. דָּתְכוֹן; pl. cs. דָּתֵי Ezr 7_{25}, f.: — 1. (royal) **decree** Dn $2_{13\cdot15}$, *dātekôn* the judgment on you 2_9; — 2. **state law** Dn $6_{9\cdot13\cdot16}$, *dî malkā'* Ezr 7_{26}; — 3. **law** (of God) (= *tôrâ*) Ezr $7_{12\cdot14\cdot21\cdot25f}$, abs. Dn 7_{25}; w. sf. = religion 6_6. †

*דֶּתֶא: Heb. דֶּשֶׁא: det. דִּתְאָא: **grass** Dn $4_{12\cdot20}$. †

*דְּתָבַר: pl. det. דְּתָבְרַיָּא: **judge** Dn 3_{2f}. †

ה

הֲ, הַ: Heb. =: interr. particle, functions as in Heb.: Dn 2_{26} 3_{14} 6_{21}; *halā'* 3_{24} 4_{27} 6_{13}. †

הָא: Heb. הֵא: **behold**! Dn 3_{25}. †

הֵא: Heb. =: *hē'-kedî* Dn 2_{43} **just as**, but prob. rd. *hē'k* (= *hêk*) *dî* (ƒ Heb. *'êk, hêk*). †

*הַדָּבַר: pl. det. הַדָּבְרַיָּא, cs. הַדָּבְרֵי, sf. הַדָּבְרוֹהִי, הַדָּבְרַי: (high) **royal official** Dn $3_{24f\cdot27}$ 4_{33} 6_8. †

*הַדָּם: pl. הַדָּמִין: **member, limb** (of body), *haddāmîn hitʿabēd* **be dismembered** Dn 2_5 3_{29}. †

הדר: Heb. =: **pael**: pf. 2. sg. הַדַּרְתָּ, 1. הַדְּרֵת; pt. מְהַדַּר: **glorify** Dn $4_{31\cdot34}$ 5_{23}. †

*הֲדַר: Heb. הֶדֶר, הָדָר: det. הַדְרָה/א, sf. הַדְרִי: **splendor, majesty** Dn $4_{27\cdot33}$ 5_{18}. †

הוּא: Heb. =: pers. pron., **he** Dn 2_{22}; demonstr. adj., **that** 2_{32}; stressing the subj., 6_{17}, as pseudo-copula (= 'is') 2_{28}; ƒ f. הִיא, pl. אִנּוּן, אִנִּין & הִמּוֹן.

הֲוָה: Heb. הָיָה, II הוה: **peal**: pf. הֲוָא, ה׳, f. הֲוָת, הֲוַת, 2. m. הֲוַיְתָ, 1. הֲוֵית, 3. pl. הֲווֹ; impf. לֶהֱוֵא, לֶהֱוֵה, 3. f. תֶּהֱוֵא, תֶּהֱוֵה, pl. לֶהֱוֹן, f. לֶהֶוְיָן; impv. pl. הֱווֹ, הֲווֹ: **be**: — 1. **happen** Dn 2_{28}; — 2. **exist** Dn 7_{23}; subj. anger, arise, come over s.one Ezr 7_{23}; w. *le* become Dn 2_{35}, fall to (s.one's share) 4_{24}, belong to 5_{17}; — 3. **be**: w. prep. Dn 4_{22}, as copula 2_{40}; — 4. w. pt. pass. to express passive Dn 2_{20}; w. pt. act. to express future 2_{43}, to express perfect 5_{19}.

הִיא: Heb. =; pers. pron., **she** Dn 2_{44}; as pseudo-copula (= 'is') 2_9 Ezr 6_{15}.

*הֵיכַל: Heb. הֵיכָל: cs. =, det. הֵיכְלָא, sf. הֵיכְלִי, הֵיכְלֵהּ: — 1. **palace** Dn 4_1 Ezr 4_{14}; — 2. **temple**, in Jerus. Dn 5_2 Ezr 5_{14}, pagan in Babylon Ezr 5_{14}.

הלך: Heb. =: **peal**: impf. יְהָךְ; inf. מְהָךְ; usu. derived fm. *הוך; pf. & impv. supplied fm. ƒ אֲזַל: **go** Ezr 7_{13}; subj. thg., reach, w. *le* 5_5 6_5. †

pael: pt. מְהַלֵּךְ: **walk around** Dn 4_{26}. †

[**hafel**: pt. pl. מַהְלְכִין: rd. pael pt. pl. מְהַלְּכִין Dn 3_{25} 4_{34}. †]

הֲלָךְ: a kind of **tax** Ezr $4_{13\cdot20}$ 7_{24}. †

הִמּוֹ Ezr & הִמּוֹן Dn: Heb. הֵם, הֵמָּה: pers. pron. pl. m. **they, them**: nominative (as pseudo-copula, 'are') Ezr 5_{11}, acc. Dn 2_{34} Ezr 4_{10}.

*הַמּוֹנֵךְ: det. Kt המונכא, Qr. הַמְנִיכָא: **necklace** Dn $5_{7\cdot16\cdot29}$. †

הֵן: Heb. =, **אִם**: conj.: — 1. **if** Dn 2_6 Ezr 4_{13}; *hēn lā'*, if not Dn 2_5; w/o finite vb. 3_{18}; w/o main clause 3_{15a}; *hēn ... hēn ... hēn*, whether ... or ... or Ezr 7_{26}; — 2. in indir. qn., **whether** Dn 4_{24} Ezr 5_{17}.

***הַנְזָקָה**: cs. **הַנְזָקַת**: **injury, disadvantage** Ezr 4_{22}. †

הַצְדָּא Dn 3_{14}: ↱ **צְדָא**.

***הַרְהֹר**: pl. **הַרְהֹרִין**: **dream-fantasies** Dn 4_2. †

הִתְבְּהָלָה: orig. hitpeel inf. **בהל**: **hurry**, w. *bᵉ* in a hurry Dn 2_{25} 3_{24} 6_{20}. †

***הִתְנַדָּבוּ**: orig. hitpaal inf. **נדב**: cs. **הִתְנַדָּבוּת**: **contribution, offering** Ezr 7_{16}. †

ו

וְ, וּ: Heb. =: treated like Heb. in vocalization & usage, conj., **and**; betw. 3 or more words it is either betw. all, Dn 2_6; before the last 2, Dn 2_{37}; or is distributed irregularly, Dn 3_2; or absent Dn 2_{27}; spec. uses: a) and specifically Ezr 6_8; b) intensifying, and also Dn 6_{29}; c) adversatively, but Dn 2_6; d) or Ezr 7_{26}; e) explanatory, for Dn 4_{22}; f) continuing, then; oft. to be omitted in transl., after impv. Dn 2_4, impf. 2_7; after narrative pf. (= Heb. impf. consec.) Dn 5_{29}, w. impf. 4_2, w. pt. 2_7; g) expressing purpose w. impf. 5_2, w. pt. 2_{13}, w. inf. 2_{16}.

ז

זבן: **peal**: pt. pl. **זָבְנִין**: **buy**, metaph., obj. time Dn 2_8. †

***זְהִיר**: pl. **זְהִירִין**: **cautious, careful**; w. *hᵃwâ* & inf. be careful to Ezr 4_{22}. †

זוד or **זיד**: Heb. =: **hafel**: inf. **הֲזָדָה**: **act insolently, haughtily** Dn 5_{20}. †

זון: Heb. =: **hitpeel**: impf. **יִתְּזִין**: **feed on, live on**, w. *min* Dn 4_9. †

זוע: Heb. =: **peal**: pt. pl. Kt **זָאֲעִין**, Qr **זָיְעִין**: **tremble**, w. *min-qᵒdām* before Dn 5_{19} 6_{27}. †

זיד: ↱ **זוד**.

***זִיו**: Heb. **זִו**: sf. **זִיוֵהּ, זִוַי**; pl. sf. **זִיוַי**, **זִיוָ֫יִךְ** Kt **זִיוָךְ** Qr, **זִיוֹ֫הִי**: **brightness** Dn 2_{31} 4_{33}; pl. (fresh) **complexion** $5_{6\cdot9f}$ 7_{28}. †

זָכוּ: Heb. √**זכה**: **innocence** Dn 6_{23}. †

זְכַרְיָה: n. pers. Ezr 5_1 6_{14} (= Heb.). †

זמן: (Heb. =, as denom. of noun): **hitpeel**: pf. Qr **הִזְדְּמִנְתּוּן** **agree**; Kt **hitpaal** **הִזְּמִנְתּוּן** or **hafel** **הַזְמִנְתּוּן** **come to a decision**, w. inf. Dn 2_9. †

זְמָן Dn 2_{16} & **זְמַן** 7_{12} (= Heb. < Aram.): det. **זִמְנָא**; pl. **זִמְנִין**, det. **זִמְנַיָּא**, m.: — 1. (spec., fixed) **time** Dn 7_{12}, pl. 2_{21}; postponement 2_{16}; moment: *bēh zimnā'* at that time Dn 3_8 Ezr 5_3, at the same time Dn 4_{33}, *bēh zimnā' kᵉdî* as soon as 3_7; holy time, feast 7_{25}; — 2. **time** = occurrence: *zimnîn tᵉlātâ* 3 times Dn 6_{11}.

***זְמָר**: det. **זְמָרָא**: **string-music**, musical instruments Dn $3_{5\cdot7\cdot10\cdot15}$. †

***זַמָּר**: pl. det. **זַמָּרַיָּא**: musician, **singer** Ezr 7_{24}. †

***זַן**: Heb. =: pl. cs. **זְנֵי**: **kind, sort** Dn $3_{5\cdot7\cdot10\cdot15}$. †

***זְעֵיר**: Heb. =: f. **זְעֵירָה**: **small** Dn 7_8. †

זעק: Heb. = & **צעק**: **peal**: pf. **זְעִק**: **cry out, shout** Dn 6_{21}. †

זקף: Heb. =: **peal**: pt. pass. **זְקִיף**: **(as one) impaled** Ezr 6_{11}. †

זְרֻבָּבֶל: n. pers. Ezr 5_2 (Heb. =).

***זְרַע**: Heb. **זֶרַע**: cs. =: **seed, descendants**, *zᵉraʿ ʾᵃnāšā'* Dn 2_{43}. †

ח

חֲבוּלָה: hurtful action, **crime** Dn 6_{23}. †

חבל: Heb. II חבל: **pael**: pf. pl. sf. חַבְּלוּנִי; impv. pl. sf. חַבְּלוּהִי; inf. חַבָּלָה: — 1. **hurt, injure** Dn 6_{23}; — 2. **destroy** Dn 4_{20} Ezr 6_{12}. †
hitpaal: impf. תִּתְחַבַּל, חִתְחַבַּל: be destroyed, **perish** Dn 2_{44} 6_{27} 7_{14}. †

חֲבָל: det. חֲבָלָא: **hurt, injury** Dn 3_{25} 6_{24}, **damage** Ezr 4_{22}. †

*חֲבַר: Heb. חָבֵר: pl. sf. חַבְרוֹהִי: **companion** Dn $2_{13.17f}$. †

*חַבְרָה: pl. sf. חַבְרָתַהּ: companion Dn 7_{20}: its companions = **the other** (horns). †

חַגַּי: n. pers. Ezr 5_1 6_{14} (= Heb.). †

חַד: Heb. אֶחָד: f. חֲדָה: **one**: a) numeral Dn 4_{16}; b) only one 2_9; c) as indef. art. Dn 2_{31} Ezr 4_8; d) in reckoning of years, *bišnat ḥadâ* in the 1st year Dn 7_1 Ezr 5_{13}; e) *ḥad šibʿâ* 7 times Dn 3_{19}; f) *kaḥadâ* together Dn 2_{35}.

*חֲדֵה: Heb. חָזֶה: pl. sf. חֲדוֹהִי: **breast** Dn 2_{32}. †

חֶדְוָה: Heb. =: **joy** Ezr 6_{16}. †

חֲדַת: Heb. חָדָשׁ: **new** Ezr 6_4, but rd. חַד. †

חוה: Heb. I חוה: **pael**: impf. נְחַוֵּא, אֲחַוֵּא/ה, sf. יְחַוִּנַּהּ, יְחַוִּנַּנִי: show, **make known** Dn $2_{4.24}$ 5_7; w. *qodām* 2_{11}. †
(h)afel: impf. נְהַחֲוֵה, יְהַחֲוֵה, pl. תְּהַחֲוֹן, sf. תְּהַחֲוֻנַּנִי; impv. pl. sf. הַחֲוֹנִי; inf. הַחֲוָיָא/ה, cs. אַחֲוָיַת: **make known** Dn $2_{6f.9f.16.27}$ 3_{32} $5_{12b.15}$; **interpret** 5_{12a}. †

חוט or חיט: **peal** or **hafel**: impf. יַחִיטוּ Ezr 4_{12}: form, etymology & mng. uncert.; sugg. 'repair,' or 'lay,' or 'inspect'; or rd. יְהִיבוּ (cf. 5_{16}). †

חִוָּר: **white** Dn 7_9. †

חֲזָה: Heb. =: **peal**: pf. חֲזָא/ה, 2. m. חֲזַיְתָ, חֲזַיְתָה Dn 2_{41}, 1. חֲזֵית, pl. חֲזַיתוּן; inf. מֶחֱזֵא; pt. חָזֵה, pl. חָזַיִן, pass. חֲזֵה: **see**: — 1. acc. of thg. Dn 3_{25} Ezr 4_{14}, w. *dî* Dn 2_{45}, abs. 5_{23}; in vision & dream Dn 4_{17}, w. 2 acc. (thg. & material) 2_{41}, abs. 2_{31}, w. *ʿad dî* 2_{34}; — 2. **perceive** Dn 2_8; — 3. pt. pass. proper, **customary** Dn 3_{19}.

*חֵזוּ or *חֱזוּ: det. חֶזְוָא, sf. חֶזְוֵהּ, חֶזְוִי; pl. cs. חֶזְוֵי: — 1. **vision** (i.e. apparition) Dn 7_2; *ḥezwê rēʾš* 2_{28}, night vision 2_{19}; — 2. **appearance** Dn 7_{20}. †

*חֲזוֹת: sf. חֲזוֹתֵהּ: **sight** = it was to be seen Dn $4_{8.17}$. †

*חֲטָי: sf. Kt חֲטָיָךְ, Qr חֲטָאָךְ: **sin** Dn 4_{24}. †

חֲטָיָא Kt, חַטָּאָה Qr: Heb. חַטָּאת: **sin-offering** Ezr 6_{17}. †

חַי: Heb. =: cs. =, det. חַיָּא; pl. חַיִּין, cs. חַיֵּי, det. חַיַּיָּא: — 1. **living, alive**, of God Dn 6_{21}; pl. w/o noun = (all) men Dn 2_{30}; — 2. חַיִּין **life** † Dn 7_{12} Ezr 6_{10}.

חיה: Heb. =: **peal**: impv. חֱיִי: **live** Dn 2_4 3_9 5_{10} $6_{7.22}$. †
hafel: pt. מַחֵא: **keep** (s.one) **alive, restore to life** Dn 5_{19}. †

חֵיוָה: Heb. חַיָּה: cs. חֵיוַת, det. חֵיוְתָא; pl. חֵיוָן & חֵיוָתָא: **beast, animal** Dn 4_{13}; sg. coll. 4_{11f}.

חיט: ↗ חוט.

חַיִל: Heb. =: cs. חֵיל, sf. חֵילֵהּ: — 1. **strength**: *beʾedrāʿ weḥayil* w. strong arm Ezr 4_{23} (oth.: by force of arms, 2); *gibbārê ḥayil* Dn 3_{20}; *qerāʾ beḥayil* shout 3_4; — 2. **army** † Dn 3_{20}, *ḥêl šemayyāʾ* 4_{32}.

חַכִּים: Heb. חָכָם: pl. חַכִּימִין, cs. חַכִּימֵי, det. חַכִּימַיָּא: **wise (man)** Dn 2_{21}, pl. (group of) wise men (of Babylon) 2_{12ff}.

חָכְמָה: Heb. =: cs. חָכְמַת, det. חָכְמְתָא: **wisdom** Dn $2_{20f.23.30}$ $5_{11.14}$ Ezr 7_{25}. †

חֵלֶם: Heb. חֲלוֹם: det. חֶלְמָא, sf. חֶלְמִי, חֶלְמָךְ; pl. חֶלְמִין: **dream** Dn 2_4.

חלף: Heb. I חלף: **peal**: impf. pl. יַחְלְפוּן: **pass by, over**, w. *ʿal* & pers. Dn $4_{13.20.22.29}$. †

חֲלָק: **portion, lot** (*be* in) Dn $4_{12.20}$ Ezr 4_{16}.

חֱמָה Dn 3_{13}, חֶמָא 3_{19}: Heb. חֵמָה: f.: **rage, fury** Dn $3_{13.19}$. †

חֲמַר: Heb. חֶמֶר: det. חַמְרָא: **wine** Dn $5_{1f\cdot4\cdot23}$ Ezr 6_9 7_{22}. †

***חִנְטָה**: Heb. חִטָּה: pl. חִנְטִין: **(grains of) wheat** Ezr 6_9 7_{22}. †

***חֲנֻכָּה**: (< Heb.): cs. חֲנֻכַּת: **dedication** Dn 3_{2f} Ezr 6_{16f}. †

חנן: Heb. I חנן: **peal**: inf. מִחַן: **show mercy** Dn 4_{24}. †

hitpaal: pt. מִתְחַנַּן: **implore** Dn 6_{12}. †

חֲנַנְיָה: n. pers. Dn 2_{17} ₣ 1_{6f} (= Heb.). †

חַסִּיר: Heb. חָסֵר: defective, **of poor quality** Dn 5_{27}. †

חסן: Heb. =: **hafel**: pf. pl. הֶחֱסִנוּ; impf. יַחְסְנוּן: **take possession of, possess** Dn $7_{18\cdot22}$.†

***חֱסֵן**: Heb. חֹסֶן: det. חִסְנָא, sf. חִסְנִי: **might** Dn 2_{37}, 4_{27} (but oth.: wealth). †

חֲסַף: חֲסַף, cs. =, det. חַסְפָּא: **formed clay** (i.e. some object of pottery, whether potsherd or tile) Dn $2_{33ff\cdot42\cdot45}$, *ḥ^a^saf dî peḥār* potter's work 2_{41}, *ḥ^a^saf ṭînā'* earthenware $2_{41\cdot43}$. †

חצף: **hafel**: pt. f. מְהַחְצְפָה Dn 2_{15}, מְהַחְצְפָא 3_{22}: **harsh, severe** Dn 2_{15} 3_{22}. †

חרב: **hofal**: pf. 3. f. הָחָרְבַת: **be devastated, destroyed** Ezr 4_{15}. †

חַרְטֹם: Heb. =: pl. חַרְטֻמִּין, det. חַרְטֻמַיָּא (w/o dageš): **magician** (i.e. Magus, pl. Magi) Dn $2_{10\cdot27}$ 4_4; *rab ḥarṭummîn* chief magician 4_6 5_{11}. †

חרך: **hitpaal**: pf. הִתְחָרַךְ: **be singed** Dn 3_{27}. †

***חֲרַץ**: Heb. חֲלָצַיִם: sf. חַרְצֵהּ **hip**, *qiṭrê ḥarṣēh* his hip-joint Dn 5_6. †

חשב: Heb. =: **peal**: pt. pass. pl. חֲשִׁיבִין: reckon, **regard**, pass. regarded Dn 4_{32}. †

***חֲשׁוֹךְ**: Heb. חֹשֶׁךְ: det. חֲשׁוֹכָא: **darkness** Dn 2_{22}. †

חשח: **peal**: pt. pl. חָשְׁחִין: **need**, w. *l^e^* & inf. Dn 3_{16}. †

***חַשְׁחָה**: pl. חַשְׁחָן: **need**, *mâ ḥašḥān* what is needed Ezr 6_9. †

***חַשְׁחוּ**: cs. חַשְׁחוּת: **need** Ezr 7_{20}. †

חשל: **peal**: pt. חָשֵׁל: **crush, pulverize** Dn 2_{40}. †

חתם: Heb. =: **peal**: pf. sf. חַתְמַהּ: **seal** Dn 6_{18}. †

ט

טאב: Heb. טוב & יטב: **peal**: pf. טְאֵב: **be good**, w. *'al* it is good for him = he is glad Dn 6_{24}. †

טָב: Heb. טוֹב: **good**: *d^e^hab ṭāb* pure gold Dn 2_{32}; *hēn 'al malkā' ṭāb* if it pleases the king Ezr 5_{17}. †

***טַבָּח**: Heb. =: pl. det. טַבָּחַיָּא: **executioner, body-guard**, *rab-ṭabbāḥayyā'* Dn 2_{14}. †

טוּר: Heb. צוּר: det. טוּרָא: **mountain** Dn $2_{35\cdot45}$. †

טְוָת: f.: **fasting**, adv. **in fasting, in hunger** Dn 6_{19}. †

***טִין**: Heb. טִיט: det. טִינָא: **(wet) clay**: *ḥ^a^saf ṭînā'* earthenware Dn $2_{41\cdot43}$. †

***טַל**: Heb. =: cs =: **dew**, *ṭal š^e^mayyā'* Dn $4_{12\cdot20\cdot22\cdot30}$ 5_{21}. †

טלל: Heb. III צלל & טלל (< Aram.): **hafel**: impf. תַּטְלֵל: trad.: seek shade, but better, **make a nest** Dn 4_9. †

טעם: Heb. =: **pael**: impf. pl. יְטַעֲמוּן, sf. יְטַעֲמוּנֵּהּ: **feed, make** s.one **eat** Dn $4_{22\cdot29}$ 5_{21}. †

טְעֵם: Heb. טַעַם: cs. =, but cs. טַעַם of God Ezr 6_{14} 7_{23}, det. טַעְמָא: — 1. **understanding, good sense**, *h^a^tîb 'ēṭâ ûṭ^e^'ēm* Dn 2_{14}; *śîm ṭ^e^'ēm 'al* take into consideration 3_{12}; — 2. **command**: *min-ṭa'am ᵓ^e^lāh* Ezr 6_{14}; *śîm ṭ^e^'ēm* give a command Dn 3_{10} Ezr 4_{21}, pass. Dn 3_{29} Ezr 4_{19}; *b^e^'ēl-ṭ^e^'ēm* ₣ 4; *biṭ'ēm ḥamrā'* under the influence of wine (oth.: when he tasted the wine) Dn 5_2; — 3. advice, **report** Ezr 5_5, *y^e^hab ṭ^e^'ēm* give account Dn 6_3;

beʿēl-ṭeʿēm government official Ezr $4_{8f.17}$.

***טְפַר**: Heb. צִפֹּרֶן: pl. sf. טִפְרוֹהִי Dn 4_{30}, טִפְרַיִהּ 7_{19} Kt (so rd.), Qr sg. טִפְרַהּ: — 1. **nail** (of finger) Dn 4_{39}; — 2. **claw** 7_{19}. †

טרד: Heb. =: **peal**: pt. pl. טָרְדִין: pass. pf. טְרִיד: **drive away**, w. *min* Dn $4_{22.29}$, pass. 4_{30} 5_{21}. †

***טַרְפְּלָי**: pl. det. טַרְפְּלָיֵא Ezr 4_{9}: uncert.: class of officials, or n. peop. †

י

יבל: Heb. =: **hafel**: pf. הֵיבֵל; inf. הֵיבָלָה: **bring** Ezr 5_{14} 6_{5} 7_{15}. †

safel (trad. סבל polel, or emend to cj. כּיל itpeel): pt. pl. מְסוֹבְלִין: **offer** Ezr 6_{3}. †

***יַבֶּשָׁה**: Heb. יַבָּשָׁה: det. יַבֶּשְׁתָּא: dry land, det. **the earth** Dn 2_{10}. †

***יְגַר**: cs. =: **heap of stones**, *yegar śāhᵃdûtā'* Gn 31_{47} = Heb. גַּלְעֵד. †

***יַד**: Heb. יָד: cs =, det. יְדָא, Dn 5_{5} יְדָה, sf. יְדָךְ, יְדֵהּ, יְדְהֹם; du. יְדַיִן; pl. sf. יְדַי, f.: — 1. **hand**, of man Dn 2_{34} Ezr 5_{8}, of God Dn 4_{32}; paw (of lion) 6_{28} (oth.: 2); *šelaḥ yad* (= Heb.) Ezr 6_{12}; — 2. **power**, w. *be* Dn 2_{38} Ezr 5_{12}, of God Dn 5_{23}, w. *min* Dn 3_{15}.

ידה: Heb. =: **hafel**: pt. מְהוֹדֵא Dn 2_{23} > מוֹדֵא 6_{11}: **praise** Dn 2_{23}, *qodām* 6_{11}. †

יְדַע: Heb. =: **peal**: pf. יְדַעַת, יִדְעֵת, יְדַעְתְּ ,י׳; impf. תִּנְדַּע, אִנְדַּע, pl. יִנְדְּעוּן; impv. דַּע; pt. יָדַע, pl. יָדְעִין, cs. יָדְעֵי, pass. יְדִיעַ: **know**, w. *dî* Dn 2_{8f}, w. acc. 2_{22} Ezr 7_{25}; = learn, w. *dî* Dn 6_{11} Ezr 4_{15}; = understand, w. *dî* Dn 4_{14}, w. acc. 2_{30}, abs. 5_{23}; *yedîaʿ lehewē'* let it be known Dn 3_{23} Ezr 4_{12f}.

hafel: pf. הוֹדַע, הוֹדַעְנָא, sf. הוֹדְעָךְ, הוֹדַעְתֶּנִי, הוֹדַעְתֶּנָא Dn 2_{23}; impf. יְהוֹדַע, pl. תְּהוֹדְעוּן, יְהוֹדְעוּן, sf. תְּהוֹדְעֻנַּנִי, יְהוֹדְעֻנַּנִי, תְּהוֹדְעֻנַּנִי, יְהוֹדְעֻנַּנִי, אֲהוֹדְעִנֵּהּ; inf. הוֹדָעָה, sf. הוֹדָעוּתַנִי, הוֹדָעֻתַנִי, הוֹדָעוּתָךְ; pt. pl. מְהוֹדְעִין: **let** s.one **know**, **communicate to** Dn 2_{5} Ezr 5_{10}, w. *dî* Ezr 4_{16}, instruct Ezr 7_{25}.

יְהַב: Heb. =: **peal**: pf. יְהַבְתְּ ,י׳, pl. וִיהַבוּ; impf. ꟳ *ntn*; impv. הַב; pt. pl. יָהֲבִין; pass. pf. יְהִ(י)ב 3. f. יְהִיבַת, Dn 7_{12} יְהִיבַת, pl. יְהִיבוּ: **give** Dn 2_{21}, pass. 5_{28} Ezr 5_{14}; w. *beyad* Dn 2_{38} Ezr 5_{12}; surrender (obj. one's body) Dn 3_{28}, pass. be given over 7_{11}; obj. *ṭaʿmā'* give a report 6_{3}, obj. *'uššayyā'* lay foundations Ezr 5_{16}.

hitpeel: impf. תִּתְיְהֵב, תִּתְיְהִב, יִתְיְהִב, pl. יִתְיַהֲבוּן; pt. מִתְיְהֵב, f. מִתְיַהֲבָה, pl. מִתְיַהֲבִין: **be given** Dn 4_{13} Ezr 4_{20} 7_{19}, w. *beyad* Dn 7_{25}; subj. costs, be borne, defrayed Ezr $6_{4.8f}$. †

יְהוּד: Heb. יְהוּדָה: **Judah**, **Judea** Dn 2_{25} 5_{13} 6_{14} Ezr $5_{1.8}$ 7_{14}. †

***יְהוּדַי**: Heb. יְהוּדִי: pl. Kt יְהוּדָאִין Qr יְהוּדָיִן, det. יְהוּדָיֵא: **Jew** Dn $3_{8.12}$ Ezr $4_{12.23}$ $5_{1.5}$ $6_{7f.14}$. †

יוֹם: Heb. =: det. יוֹמָא; pl. יוֹמִין, cs. יוֹמֵי, det. יוֹמַיָּא, sf. יוֹמֵיהוֹן, & pl. cs. יוֹמָת: **day** Dn 6_{8} Ezr 6_{15}; *beyômā'* (3 times) a day Dn 6_{11}, *yôm beyôm* day by day Ezr 6_{9}; pl. = time of reign Dn 2_{44}; = age (of life), *ʿattîq yômîn* very old Dn 7_{9}; *liqṣat yômayyā'* at the end of this time 4_{31}; *min yômāt ʿālemā'* from ancient times Ezr 4_{15}; eschatological: *be'aḥᵃrît yômayyā'* at the end of days Dn 2_{28}; *yôm telātā lîraḥ* on the 3rd day of the month Ezr 6_{15}.

יוֹצָדָק: n. pers. Ezr 5_{2}, ꟳ Heb. יְהוֹצָדָק. †

יזב: ꟳ שֵׁיזִב.

יטב: Heb. =: **peal**: impf. יֵיטַב: **it suits, pleases** s.one (w. *ʿal*) Ezr 7_{18}; pf. supplied by ꟳ טאב. †

יְכִל: Heb. =: **peal**: pf. יְכִלְתָּ ,י׳; impf. יִכֻּל,

תְּכֻל Dn 5_{16} Qr (5_{16} Kt תּוּכַל & 2_{10} יוּכַל are erroneous Heb. forms); pt. יָכִל, f. יָכְלָה, pl. יָכְלִין: — 1. **be able**, w. l^e & inf. Dn 2_{10}; — 2. **overpower**, w. l^e † Dn 7_{21}.

*יַם: Heb. יָם: det. יַמָּא: **sea** Dn 7_{2f}. †

יסף: Heb. =: **hofal**: pf. 3. f. הוּסְפַת: **be added** Dn 4_{33}. †

יעט: Heb. יָעַץ: **peal**: pt. pl. sf. יָעֲטֹ(ו)הִי: **advise**, pt. **counsellor** Ezr 7_{14f}. †

itpaal: pf. אִתְיָעַטוּ: **take counsel together, deliberate** Dn 6_8. †

יצב: Heb. =: **pael**: inf. יַצָּבָא: **make certain** of, w. *ʿal* Dn 7_{19}. †

יַצִּיב: det. & f. יַצִּיבָא: well-established, **reliable**, word Dn 6_{13}, dream 2_{45}; f. as noun, reliable information 7_{16}; adv. *min-yaṣṣîb* **surely** 2_8, *yaṣṣîbāʾ* yes, certainly 3_{24}. †

יקד: Heb. =: **peal**: pt. f. det. יָקִדְתָּא: **burn** Dn $3_{6\cdot11\cdot15\cdot17\cdot20f\cdot23\cdot26}$. †

*יְקֵדָה: cs. w. l^e לִיקֵדַת: **burning**, **y^eqēdat ʾeššâ* fire, conflagration Dn 7_{11}. †

*יַקִּיר: Heb. =: det. יַקִּירָא, f. יַקִּרָה: — 1. **difficult** Dn 2_{11}; — 2. **noble** Ezr 4_{10}. †

*יְקָר: Heb. = (< Aram.): w. w^e, וִיקָר Dn 7_{14}, cs. w. l^e, לִיקָר $4_{27\cdot33}$, det. w. w^e וִיקָרָא 2_{37} 5_{18}, וִיקָרָה 5_{20}: **honor, majesty** Dn $2_{6\cdot37}$ $4_{27\cdot33}$ $5_{18\cdot20}$ 7_{14}. †

יְרוּשְׁלֶם: Heb. יְרוּשָׁלַםִ &c.: n. loc. **Jerusalem** Dn 5_{2f} Ezr 4_8.

*יְרַח: Heb. יֶרַח: cs. w. l^e, לִירַח; pl. יַרְחִין: **month** Dn 4_{26} Ezr 6_{15}. †

*יַרְכָה: in mng. = Heb. יָרֵךְ, in form = *יְרֵכָה: pl. sf. יַרְכָתֵהּ: **upper thigh** Dn 2_{32}. †

יִשְׂרָאֵל: n. peop., **Israel** Ezr 5_1 (= Heb.). †

יֵשׁוּעַ: n. pers. Ezr 5_2 (= Heb.). †

יָת: Heb. I אֵת: sf. יָתְהוֹן: mark of acc. Dn 3_{12}. †

יתב: Heb. יָשַׁב: **peal**: pf. ״, יְתִב; impf. יִתִּב; pt. pl. יָתְבִין: — 1. take one's seat, **sit down** Dn $7_{9f\cdot26}$; — 2. **dwell, live** (somewhere) Ezr 4_{17}. †

hafel: pf. הוֹתֵב: let s.one dwell, **settle** Ezr 4_{10}. †

יַתִּיר: f. יַתִּירָה & Dn 3_{22} 6_4 7_7 יַתִּירָא: — 1. **extraordinary** Dn 2_{31} 4_{33} 5_{12} 6_4; — 2. f. adv. **extremely** 3_{22} $7_{7\cdot19}$. †

כ

כְּ: Heb. =: treated like Heb. k^e: **like** Dn 2_{35}; **corresponding to** 4_5 Ezr 6_9; indicating number & time, **about**, *k^ešāʿār ḥ^adâ* Dn 4_{16}, *k^ebar š^enîn* … 6_1; w. inf. **as soon as** 6_{21}; in compounds like *k^edî* ₣ other member.

כִּדְבָה: Heb. כָּזָב: **lie**, *millâ kidbâ* Dn 2_9 (appos.). †

כָּה: Heb. כֹּה: adv. **here**, *ʿad-kâ* **hitherto**, up to this point Dn 7_{28}. †

כהל: **peal**: pt. כָּהֵל, pl. כָּהֲלִין: **be able**, w. l^e & inf. Dn 2_{26} 4_{15} $5_{8\cdot15}$. †

*כָּהֵן: Heb. כֹּהֵן: det. כָּהֲנָא; pl. det. כָּהֲנַיָּא, sf. כָּהֲנוֹהִי: **priest** Ezr $6_{9\cdot16\cdot18}$ $7_{12f\cdot16\cdot21\cdot24}$. †

*כַּוָּה: pl. כַּוִּין, f.: **window** Dn 6_{11}. †

כּוֹרֶשׁ: n. pers. **Cyrus** Dn 6_{28} Ezr $5_{13f\cdot17}$ $6_{3\cdot14}$ (= Heb.). †

cj. כיל: Heb. כּוּל: **itpeel**: pt. pl. cj. מִתְּכִילִין **be fixed** cj. Ezr 6_3, ₣ cj. II מְשַׁח, but questionable, ₣ יבל safel. †

*כַּכַּר: Heb. כִּכָּר: pl. כַּכְּרִין: **talent** Ezr 7_{22}. †

*כֹּל: Heb. =: cs. =, or כָּל־, det. (or fossilized acc.) כֹּלָּא, כֹּלָּא, sf. כָּלְּהוֹן Dn 2_{38} & Kt 7_{19} (Qr ־הֵין): **totality**: usu. placed before the accompanying noun, in cs.; but after the noun, *š^elāmāʾ kōllāʾ* all peace Ezr 5_7: — 1. before det. sg., (the) **whole** (earth), *kol-ʾarʿāʾ* Dn 2_{35}, so Ezr 4_{20}; — 2. before det. pl., **all** (the wise men) Dn 2_{12}, so Ezr 7_{21}; w. sf., *koll^ehôn* all of them Dn 2_{38}, *kol-ʾillên* all these 2_{40}; before coll. noun, all (flesh) *kol-biśrā'* Dn 4_9; before abs. (!) *kol-kᵉsaf* Ezr 7_{16}, *kōllā'* everything Dn 2_{40}, *lᵉkōllā'* for all (pers. & thg.) 4_9; *kol-dᵉnâ* all this 5_{22}; *kol-dî* everything which Ezr 7_{21}; — 3. w. indeterminate sg., **every** (people), *kol-ʿam* Dn 3_{29}, so Ezr 6_{11}; *kol-dî* everyone who Dn 6_8 Ezr 7_{26}, *kol-'ᵉnāš dî* Dn 6_{13}, anyone who Dn 2_{10}; *kol-melek lā'* no king Dn 2_{35}; *lā'* ... *kol-* 6_6, *lā'* ... *lᵉkol-* 3_{28}; *kol-qᵒbēl* ⸗ *qᵒbēl*.

כלל: Heb. =: **šafel**: pf. pl. שַׁכְלִ֫לוּ Ezr 6_{14} & Qr 4_{12} (Kt corr., ⸗ comm.), sf. שַׁכְלְלֵהּ; inf. שַׁכְלָלָה: **finish** Ezr 4_{12} $5_{3\cdot 9}$, *bᵉnâ wᵉšaklil* finish building 5_{11} 6_{14}. †

hištafal: impf. pl. יִשְׁתַּכְלְלוּן: **be finished** Ezr $4_{13\cdot 16}$. †

כְּמָה: ⸗ מָה.

כֵּן: Heb. =: כֵּן־ Ezr 6_2: **thus, so,** w. *'mr* & (Ezr 6_2) *ktb*, alw. w. ref. to what follows, Dn 2_{24f} 4_{11} 6_7 $7_{5\cdot 23}$ Ezr 5_3 6_2. †

כְּנֵ֫מָא & כְּנֵמָא: perh. *kēn* + *mâ*: adv. **thus, so,** w. ref. to what follows, w. *'mr* Ezr 4_8 $5_{4\cdot 9\cdot 11}$; w. ref. to what precedes, w. *ʿbd* Ezr 6_{13}. †

כנשׁ: Heb. כנס: **peal**: inf. מִכְנַשׁ: **assemble** (trans.) Dn 3_2. †

hitpaal: pt. pl. מִתְכַּנְּשִׁין: **assemble** (intrans.) Dn $3_{3\cdot 27}$. †

***כְּנָת**: Heb. = (< Aram.): pl. sf. כְּנָוָתֵהּ, כְּנָוָתְהוֹן: **colleague** Ezr $4_{9\cdot 17\cdot 23}$ $5_{3\cdot 6}$ $6_{6\cdot 13}$. †

כַּסְדַּי: ⸗ כַּשְׂדַּי.

כְּסַף: Heb. כֶּסֶף: כְּסַף, det. כַּסְפָּא: **silver**: — 1. as material Dn 2_{32} Ezr 7_{15f}; — 2. as money † Ezr $7_{17\cdot 22}$.

כְּעַן: (related to Heb. עַתָּ): **now**, alw. at beginning of clause Dn 2_{23} Ezr 4_{13}; *ʿad-kᵉʿan* until now Ezr 5_{16}.

כְּעֶנֶת Ezr 4_{10f} 7_{12} & **כְּעֶת** 4_{17}: like *kᵉʿan*, connected w. what follows: **(and) now.** †

כְּעֶת: ⸗ כְּעֶנֶת.

כפת: **peal**: pf. pass. pl. כְּפִתוּ: **be bound, tied up** Dn 3_{21}. †

pael: inf. כַּפָּתָה; pt. pass. pl. מְכַפְּתִין: **bind, tie up** Dn 3_{20}, pass. 3_{23f}. †

***כֹּר**: Heb. =: pl. כֹּרִין: **kor**, dry measure (ca. 350-400 liters) Ezr 7_{22}. †

***כַּרְבְּלָה**: pl. sf. כַּרְבְּלָתְהוֹן: **cap** Dn 3_{21}. †

כרה: **itpeel**: pf. 3. f. אֶתְכְּרִיַּת: **be anxious, distressed** Dn 7_{15}. †

***כָּרוֹז**: det. כָּרוֹזָא: **herald** Dn 3_4. †

כרז: **hafel**: pf. pl. הַכְרִ֫זוּ: **proclaim** Dn 5_{29}. †

***כָּרְסֵא**: Heb. כִּסֵּא: cs. =, sf. כָּרְסְיֵהּ; pl. כָּרְסָוָן: — 1. **seat** Dn 7_9; — 2. **throne**, for king 5_{20}, for God 7_9. †

כַּשְׂדַּי: Heb. כַּשְׂדִּים: det. כַּשְׂדָּיָא Dn 5_{30} = Kt ־דָּיָא, Qr ־דָּאָה, so also כַּסְדָּיָא Ezr 5_{12}; pl. כַּשְׂדָּאִין, det. כַּשְׂדָּיֵא Dn 2_5 = Kt ־דָּיֵא, Qr ־דָּאֵי: — 1. n. peop. **Chaldean(s)** Dn 3_8 5_{30} Ezr 5_{12}; — 2. Chaldeans as astrologers Dn $2_{5\cdot 10}$ 4_4 $5_{7\cdot 11}$. †

כתב: Heb. =: **peal**: pf. כ׳, pl. כְּתַ֫בוּ; impf. נִכְתֻּב; pt. f. כָּתְבָה/א, pl. f. כָּתְבָן, pass. (or pf. pass.?) כְּתִיב: **write** Dn 5_5 6_{26} 7_1 Ezr 4_8 5_{10}, pass. Ezr 5_7 6_2. †

כְּתָב: Heb. = (< Aram.): cs. =, det. כְּתָבָא, Dn $5_{7\cdot 15}$ כְּתָבָה: — 1. **writing, inscription** Dn $5_{7f\cdot 15\cdot 17\cdot 24f}$; — 2. **document** (& its contents) Dn $6_{9\cdot 11}$, **prescription, rule** Ezr 6_{18}, *dî-lā' kᵉtāb* without prescription = without limit 7_{22}. †

***כְּתַל**: Heb. כּוֹתֶל: cs. =; pl. det. כָּתְלַיָּא: **wall** Dn 5_5 Ezr 5_8. †

ל

לְ: Heb. =: sf. לִי, לָךְ, לֵהּ, לַהּ, לַ֫נָא, לְכֹם & Dn 3_4 לְכוֹן; לְהוֹם Je 10_{11} & לְהֹם & לְהוֹן & Dn 7_{21} לְהֵן: prep., in genl. equivalent to Heb. *lᵉ*, but also to Heb. *'el* & *ʿal*: — 1. indicating direction or aim of movement Dn 2_{17}; — 2. temporal, *liqṣāt* at the end of Dn $4_{26\cdot31}$, *lᵉʿālᵉmîn* for ever 2_4; — 3. indicating purpose, (which I have built) **as, for** (a royal residence) Dn 4_{27} Ezr 6_9, w. *hᵃwâ* become Dn 2_{35}; — 4. w. inf. after vbs. of going, sending, saying, being able &c., **to** Dn 2_9 Ezr 4_{22}; — 5. w. inf. after *lā'* to express prohibition: *lā' lᵉhašnāyâ* not to be changed Dn 6_9; — 6. w. pers. obj., (tell) **(to)** (s.one) Dn 2_4; at beginning of letters, w/o vb. Dn 3_{31} Ezr 5_7; — 7. 'dat. of ref.' Dn 4_9 Ezr 6_{10}; — 8. dat of. possession, belong to = possess Dn 6_{16} Ezr 4_{16}; — 9. oth. relationships: w. resemble Dn 7_5, corresponding to Ezr 6_{17}; — 10. as periphrasis for gen. Ezr 5_5; — 11. in dates: *yôm ... lîraḥ* Ezr 6_{15}; *šᵉnat ... lᵉ* Dn 7_1 Ezr 4_{24}; — 12. replaces pers. obj. (acc.) Dn 2_{12} Ezr 5_2; neuter obj. Dn 2_{34} Ezr 4_{12}, indeterminate † Dn 2_{10}; — 13. introduces emphatic appos., 'to wit' Ezr 7_{25}; — 14. compounds, ↗ *gô', mâ, ʿad, qᵒbēl*.

לָא, Dn 4_{32} לָה: Heb. לֹא: **not**: — 1. negating a clause Je 10_{11} Dn 2_5 Ezr 4_{13}; w. *dî* & impf. = lest, ↗ *dî* 3c; in prohibition, only Ezr 4_{21}, ↗ *'al*; w. pt. Dn 2_{27}, w. adj. Ezr 4_{14}; ↗ *'îtay*: *lā' 'îtay* (= Heb. *'ayin*) Dn 2_{10} Ezr 4_{16}; ellipt., *wᵉhēn lā'* and if not Dn 3_{18}; — 2. negating a word: not because of Dn 2_{30}; *kᵉlâ ḥᵃšîbîn* like persons of no account 4_{32}; *kol-melek ... lā'* no king Dn 2_{10}; *lā' ... kol* 6_6; *dî lā'* without ↗ *dî* 2c.; w. *lᵉ* & inf.: *dî lā' lᵉhašnāyâ* irrevocable 6_9, *dî-lā' lᵉbaṭṭālā'* unlimited Ezr 6_8; *hᵃlā'* ↗ *hᵃ*.

***לֵב**: Heb. =: sf. לִבִּי: **heart** Dn 7_{28}. †

***לְבַב**: Heb. לֵבָב: cs. =, sf. לִבְבָךְ, לִבְבֵהּ: **heart** Dn 2_{30} 4_{13} $5_{20\cdot22}$ 7_4. †

***לְבוּשׁ**: Heb. =: sf. לְבוּשֵׁהּ; pl. sf. לְבוּשֵׁיהוֹן: **garment** Dn 3_{21} 7_9. †

לבשׁ: Heb. =: **peal**: impf. יִלְבַּשׁ, תִּלְבַּשׁ: **be clothed with** Dn $5_{7\cdot16}$. †

hafel: pf. pl. הַלְבִּשׁוּ: **clothe** (s.one) Dn 5_{29}. †

לָה: ↗ לָא.

I **לָהֵן**: Heb. =: **therefore** Dn $2_{6\cdot9}$ 4_{24}. †

II **לָהֵן**: — 1. conj. **unless** Dn 6_6; before noun or phrase, **except** 2_{11} 3_{28} $6_{8\cdot13}$; — 2. adversative particle, **but, but rather** Dn 2_{30} Ezr 5_{12}. †

***לֵוִי**: Heb. לֵוִי: pl. det. Kt לֵוָיֵא, Qr לֵוָאֵי: n. gent. **Levite** Ezr $6_{16\cdot18}$ $7_{13\cdot24}$. †

***לְוָת**: prep., **near, beside**, w. *min* (Heb. מֵעִם) & sf. *min-lᵉwātāk* from you Ezr 4_{12}. †

לְחֶם: Heb. לֶחֶם: bread > meal, **feast** Dn 5_1. †

***לְחֵנָה**: pl. sf. לְחֵנָתֵהּ, לְחֵנָתָךְ: **concubine** Dn $5_{2f\cdot23}$. †

***לֵילֵי**: Heb. לַיִל: det. לֵילְיָא: **night**, as time of vision Dn 2_{19} $7_{2\cdot7\cdot13}$; *bēh bᵉlêlᵉyā'* in the same night 5_{40}. †

לִשָּׁן: Heb. לָשׁוֹן: pl. det. לִשָּׁנַיָּא: tongue > **language**, sg. Dn 3_{29}, pl. $3_{4\cdot7\cdot31}$ 5_{19} 6_{26} 7_{14}, = people.

מ

מָא Ezr 6_8: ↗ מָה.

מְאָה: Heb. מֵאָה: du. מָאתַיִן: **hundred** Dn 6_2 Ezr 6_{17} 7_{22}; du. 200 Ezr 6_{17}. †

***מֹאזְנֵא**: Heb. מֹאזְנַיִם: det. מֹאזַנְיָא: **balance** (i.e. scales) Dn 5_{27}. †

***מֵאמַר**: Heb. מַאֲמָר: cs. =: **word, order** Dn 4_{14} Ezr 6_9. †

***מָאן**: Heb. אֳנִיָּה, אֳנִי: pl. cs. מָאנֵי, det. מָאנַיָּא: **vessel** (i.e. receptacle) Dn $5_{2f\cdot23}$ Ezr 5_{14f} 6_5 7_{19}. †

מְגִלָּה: Heb. =: **scroll** Ezr 6_2. †

מגר: Heb. =: **pael**: impf. יְמַגַּר: **overthrow** Ezr 6_{12}. †

***מַדְבַּח**: Heb. מִזְבֵּחַ: det. מַדְבְּחָא: **altar** Ezr 7_{17}. †

מִדָּה Ezr 4_{20} & מִנְדָּה 4_{13} 7_{24}: Heb. II *מִדָּה: cs. מִדַּת: **tax, tribute** Ezr $4_{13\cdot20}$ 6_8 7_{24}. †

***מְדוֹר** & Dn 2_{11} ***מְדָר**: sf. מְדוֹרֵהּ, מְדָרָךְ, מְדֹרְהוֹן: **dwelling** Dn 2_{11} $4_{22\cdot29}$ 5_{21}. †

מָדַי: Heb. =: det. Kt מָדָיָא, Qr מָדָאָה: n. terr. & peop., **Media** Ezr 6_2, the **Medes** Dn 5_{28} $6_{9\cdot13\cdot16}$; det. the Mede Dn 6_1. †

***מְדִינָה**: Heb. =: cs. מְדִינַת, det. מְדִינְתָּא; pl. מְדִינָן, det. מְדִינָתָא: — 1. administrative district, **province**, spec. the satrapies of the Pers. empire Dn 3_{2f} Ezr 4_{15}, *yᵉhûd mᵉdîntā'* 5_8, *māday mᵉdîntā'* 6_2; — 2. **city** (oth.: 1), *mᵉdînat bābel* Dn 2_{48f} $3_{1\cdot12\cdot30}$ Ezr 7_{16}. †

***מְדָר**: ↗ מְדוֹר.

מָה, Ezr 6_8 מָא: Heb. מָה: — 1. interr. pron. **what?** Dn 4_{32}; — 2. rel. pron. **what** (= that which) Dn 2_{22} Ezr 6_9, = *mâ dî* Dn 2_{28}, ↗ *dî* 2; — 3. w. prep.: a) *kᵉmâ* **how!** Dn 3_{33}; b) *lᵉmâ* Ezr 4_{22} & *dî-lᵉmâ* 7_{23} for what purpose > **lest**; *lᵉmā' dî* on how Ezr 6_8; c) *'al-mâ* **why?** Dn 2_{15}.

מוֹת: Heb. מָוֶת: **death** Ezr 7_{26}. †

מָזוֹן: **food** Dn $4_{9\cdot18}$. †

מחא: Heb. מָחַץ & (< Aram.) I מחא & II מחה: **peal**: pf. 3. f. מְחָת: **strike** Dn 2_{34f}. †

pael: impf. יְמַחֵא: w. *bᵉyad*, strike w. the hand = **prevent** Dn 4_{32}. †

hitpeel: impf. יִתְמְחֵא: w. *'al 'ā'*, **be impaled** (on the stake) Ezr 6_{11}. †

מַחֵא Dn 5_{19}: ↗ חיה hafel.

***מַחְלְקָה**: Heb. מַחֲלֹקֶת: pl. sf. מַחְלְקָתְהוֹן: **division** (of the Levites) Ezr 6_{18}. †

מִחַן: ↗ חנן.

מְטָא: Heb. [*מטה &] מָצָא (?): **peal**: pf. מ׳ Dn 4_{25} & מְטָה $7_{13\cdot22}$, 3. f. מְטָת, pl. מְטוֹ; impf. יִמְטֵא: — 1. **extend, reach** (to) (w. *lᵉ*) Dn $4_{8\cdot17\cdot19}$; **reach** (= arrive at) 6_{25}; arrive, come, w. *'ad* 7_{13}; — 2. abs., subj. time, **come** Dn 7_{22}, w. *'al* happen to $4_{21\cdot25}$. †

מִישָׁאֵל: n. pers. Dn 2_{17} (= Heb.). †

מֵישַׁךְ: n. pers. Dn 2_{49} $3_{12\text{-}30}$ (= Heb.). †

מלא: Heb. מָלֵא: **peal**: pf. 3. f. מְלָת: **fill** Dn 2_{35}. †

hitpeel: pf. הִתְמְלִי: **be filled with**, w. acc. Dn 3_{19}. †

***מַלְאַךְ**: Heb. מַלְאָךְ: sf. מַלְאֲכֵהּ: **angel** Dn 3_{28} 6_{23}. †

מִלָּה: Heb. =: cs. מִלַּת, det. מִלְּתָא; pl. מִלִּין, cs. מִלֵּי, det. מִלַּיָּא: — 1. **word**: the spoken word Dn 2_5, God's word of judgment 4_{30}, written word 5_{15}, pl. account, report (oth.: 2) Dn 7_1; — 2. matter, **affair** † Dn $2_{10f\cdot15\cdot17\cdot23}$ 6_{15}, vision 7_{28}, pl. 7_{16}.

מלח: **peal**: pf. 1. pl. מְלַחְנָא: w. *mᵉlaḥ hêkᵉlā'*, **eat** (the) **salt** (of the palace), i.e. be bound in loyalty to the king Ezr 4_{14}. †

מְלַח: Heb. מֶלַח: cs. =: **salt** Ezr 4_{14} 6_9 7_{22}. †

מֶלֶךְ: Heb. =: cs. =, det. מַלְכָּא (Dn 2_4 &c. voc.) & Dn 2_{11} מַלְכָּה; pl. מַלְכִין, wrongly מַלְכִים Ezr 4_{13}, det. מַלְכַיָּא: **king** Dn 2_4 Ezr 4_8, *melek malkayyā'* (= king of Babylon) Dn 2_{37}, (= king of Persia) Ezr 7_{12}, in comb. = God Dn 2_{47} 4_{34}; *bêt malkā'* Ezr 6_4; *malkîn* = kingdoms Dn 7_{17}.

***מְלַךְ**: Heb. II מלך: sf. מִלְכִּי: **counsel** Dn 4_{24}. †

***מַלְכָּה**: Heb. =: det. מַלְכְּתָא: **queen** (i.e. queen-mother) Dn 5_{10}. †

מַלְכוּ: Heb. מַלְכוּת: cs. מַלְכוּת, det. מַלְכוּתָא & Dn 2_{44} 4_{28} $7_{24\cdot27}$ ־תָה, sf. מַלְכוּתִי, מַלְכוּתָךְ, מַלְכוּתֵהּ; pl. cs. מַלְכְוָת, det. מַלְכְוָתָא: — 1. **kingship**, sovereignty Dn 2_{37}, *bêt malkû* royal residence 4_{27}, *hêkal malkûtā'* royal palace 4_{26}, *korsē' malkûtēh* his royal throne 5_{20}; — 2. (period of) **reign** † Dn 6_{29} Ezr 4_{24} 6_{15}; — 3. (not easily distinguished fm. 1.) **kingdom, realm** Dn 2_{39} Ezr 7_{13}; *malkût 'ᵃnāšā'* Dn 4_{14}, of God 3_{33}.

מלל: Heb. III מלל: **pael**: pf. מַלִּל; impf.

יְמַלִּל; pt. מְמַלִּל, מְמַלְּלָה: **speak** s.thg Dn $7_{8\cdot11\cdot20\cdot25}$, abs. w. *ʿim* 6_{22}. †

מַן: Heb. II מָן 'what': — 1. interr. pron., **who?** Ezr 5_3; *man-hûʾ ʾelāh dî* who is a god who = what god? Dn 3_{15}; *man-ʾinnûn šemāhāt* who (= what) are the names? Ezr 5_4; — 2. rel. pron. **whoever** Dn $3_{6\cdot11}$, *leman-dî* (to) whomever 4_{14} 5_{21}.

מִן: Heb. =: sf. מִנִּי, מִנָּךְ, מִנֵּהּ, Kt מִנְּהוֹן & Qr מִנְּהֹ(י)ן Dn $2_{33\cdot41f}$; *n* is rarely assimilated, *miṭṭûrāʾ* Dn 2_{45}, *mēʾarʿāʾ* Je 10_{11}: prep.: — 1. spatial: a) **from, out of** Dn 2_{35} 5_2; w. compounds (*gôʾ* &c.), ↗ other element; b) abstract, (deliver) *min-yad* from the hand of Dn 3_{15}; (judgment is executed) *min* = upon (him) Ezr 7_{26} &c.; — 2. in comparisons: (different) **from** Dn 7_3, (more) **than** 2_{30}, so for comparative degree † Dn 2_{39} 6_3; — 3. partitive: **from, of** Dn 5_{13}; *min-niṣbetāʾ* something of (the hardness) 2_{41}; *minnehôn ... ûminnehôn* some of them ... others of them 2_{33}, & *minnah ... ûminnah* partly ... partly 2_{42}; — 4. temporal: since Ezr 4_{15}; *min ... weʿad* Dn 2_{20} Ezr 5_{16}; *miqqadmat denâ* formerly 5_{11}; *min-dî* conj. after, because ↗ *dî* 3. f. β; — 5. indicating reason, cause, originator: *minnî* Dn 2_5, *miṭṭal* 4_{22}; (feed) on 4_9; on account of 5_{19}; — 6. **according to** (the command of God) Ezr 6_{14}; adv. *min-yaṣṣîb* certainly Dn 2_8, *min-qešōṭ dî* it corresponds to the truth that = in fact 2_{47}.

מְנֵא Dn 5_{25f}: as noun, **mina**, unit of weight of gold & silver, ↗ Heb. מָנֶה; as pt. pass. of ↗ מְנָה, **numbered**, ↗ comm. †

מִנְדָּה: ↗ מִדָּה.

מַנְדַּע: Heb. מַדָּע: det. מַנְדְּעָא sf. מַנְדְּעִי understanding Dn 2_{21} $4_{31\cdot33}$ 5_{12}. †

מְנָה: Heb. =: **peal**: pf. מ׳; pt. pass. (↗) מְנֵא: **count, number** Dn 5_{25f}. †

pael: pf. מַנִּיתָ, מַנִּי; impv. מַנִּי: **appoint** Ezr 7_{25}, *ʿal* over Dn 2_{49} 3_{12}, w. *le* & inf. 2_{24}. †

מִנְחָה: (< Heb.): pl. sf. מִנְחָתְהוֹן: **offering** Dn 2_{46}, spec. grain-offering Ezr 7_{17}. †

***מִנְיָן**: cs. =: **number** Ezr 6_{17}. †

***מַעֲבָד**: Heb. =: pl. sf. מַעֲבָדוֹהִי: **work** Dn 4_{34}. †

***מְעֵה**: Heb. *מֵעִים: pl. sf. מְעוֹהִי: **belly** Dn 2_{32}. †

***מֶעָל**: pl. cs. מֶעָלֵי: **sunset** Dn 6_{15}. †

***מָרֵא**: cs. =, sf. Kt מָרְאִי Qr מָרִי: **lord**, = king Dn $4_{16\cdot21}$, = God 2_{47} 5_{23}. †

מְרַד: Heb. מֶרֶד: **rebellion** Ezr 4_{19}. †

***מָרָד**: f. מָרָדָא, det. מָרָדְתָּא: **rebellious** Ezr $4_{12\cdot15}$. †

מרט: Heb. =: **peal**: pf. pass. pl. מְרִיטוּ: **pluck out**, pass. Dn 7_4. †

מֹשֶׁה: n. pers. Ezr 6_{18} (= Heb.). †

I **מְשַׁח**: **oil** (for anointing) Ezr 6_9 7_{22}. †

cj. II ***מְשַׁח**: cj. pl. sf. מִשְׁחוֹהִי: **measure** cj. Ezr 6_3, ↗ cj כֵּיל; but questionable. †

***מִשְׁכַּב**: Heb. מִשְׁכָּב: sf. מִשְׁכְּבִי, מִשְׁכְּבָךְ, מִשְׁכְּבֵהּ: place for lying, **bed** Dn 2_{28f} $4_{2\cdot7\cdot10}$ 7_1. †

***מִשְׁכַּן**: Heb. מִשְׁכָּן: sf. מִשְׁכְּנֵהּ: **dwelling** (of God in Jerus.) Ezr 7_{15}. †

***מַשְׁרוֹקִי**: det. מַשְׁרוֹקִיתָא, Dn 3_{10} ־רֹ־: **pipe** (musical instrument) Dn $3_{5\cdot7\cdot10\cdot15}$. †

***מִשְׁתֵּא**: Heb. מִשְׁתֶּה: det. מִשְׁתְּיָא: drinking-(-bout), **feast**, *bêt mištᵉyāʾ* banquet-hall Dn 5_{10}. †

***מַתְּנָה**: Heb. מַתָּן, מַתָּנָה: pl. מַתְּנָן, sf. מַתְּנָתָךְ: **gift** Dn $2_{6\cdot48}$ 5_{17}. †

נ

נבא: < Heb.?: **hitpaal**: pf. Kt הִתְנַבִּי, Qr הִתְנַבִּיא: appear as a prophet, **prophesy** Ezr 5_1. †

***נְבוּאָה**: < Heb.: cs. נְבוּאַת: **prophesying** Ezr 6_{14}. †

נְבוּכַדְנֶצַּר Dn 2_{28}-5_2 Ezr $5_{12\cdot14}$ 6_5, נְבֻכַ׳ Dn 3_{14} $5_{11\cdot18}$: n. pers. **Nebuchadnezzar**, ↗ Heb. †

נְבִזְבָּה: pl. sf. נְבִזְבְּיָתָךְ (txt.?): **present, gift** Dn 2_6 5_{17}. †

נְבִיא: < Heb. נָבִיא: det. Kt נְבִיאָה Qr נְבִיָּא; det. Kt נְבִיאַיָּא Qr נְבִיַּיָּא: **prophet** Ezr 5_{1f} 6_{14}. †

נֶבְרְשָׁה: det. נֶבְרַשְׁתָּא: **lampstand** Dn 5_5. †

נגד: Heb. =: **peal**: pt. נָגֵד: **flow** Dn 7_{10}. †

נֶגֶד: Heb. =: in the direction of, **toward** Dn 6_{11}. †

***נֹגַהּ**: det. נָגְהָא: **brightness**, *b^{e}noghā'* at dawn Dn 6_{20}. †

נְגוֹ(א): ↗ עֲבֵד נְגוֹ(א).

נדב: Heb. =: **hitpaal**: pf. pl. הִתְנַדַּבוּ; pt. מִתְנַדַּב, pl. מִתְנַדְּבִין; inf. cs. הִתְנַדָּבוּת: — 1. pt. **disposed, willing**, w. *l^e* & inf. Ezr 7_{13}; — 2. **bestow** Ezr 7_{15f}; inf. as noun, **contribution** 7_{16}. †

נִדְבָּךְ: pl. נִדְבָּכִין: **course** (of stones or timber) Ezr 6_4. †

נדד: Heb. =: **peal**: pf. 3. f. נַדַּת: **flee**, subj. sleep, fm. s.one Dn 6_{19}. †

נִדְנֶה: Dn 7_{15} *rûḥî ... b^{e}gô' nidneh*: trad. rd. *n^{e}dānah*, 'in its sheath,' i.e. 'in its body,' but prob. rd. בְּגוֹן דְּנָה or בְּגִין דְּנָה, **on account of this**. †

***נְהוֹר**: det. Qr נְהוֹרָא (Kt נְהִירָא ↗ *נְהִיר): **light** Dn 2_{22}. †

***נְהִיר**: det. Kt נְהִירָא (Qr נְהוֹרָא ↗ *נְהוֹר): **light** Dn 2_{22}. †

נַהִירוּ: **illumination** (of mind) Dn $5_{11\cdot14}$. †

נְהַר: Heb. נָהָר: det. נַהֲרָה, Ezr 4_{16} נַהֲרָא: **stream, river,** of fire Dn 7_{10}; spec. of Euphrates, *'^{a}bad-nah^{a}râ* Ezr 4_{10}-7_{25} (14×). †

נוד: Heb. =: **peal**: impf. תְּנֻד: **flee** Dn 4_{11}. †

נְוָלוּ Ezr 6_{11} & נְוָלִי Dn 2_5 3_{29}: garbage-heap, & heap of ruins & debris Dn 2_5 3_{29} Ezr 6_{11}: either (houses) shall be turned into public privy, or pulled down as punishment. †

נוּר: Heb. =: det. נוּרָא, f. Dn 3_{6ff}, m. 7_9: **fire** Dn $3_{6\cdot11\cdot15\cdot17\cdot20\text{-}27}$ 7_{9f}. †

נזק: Heb. נֵזֶק (< Aram.): **peal**: pt. נָזִק: **suffer loss** Dn 6_3. †

hafel: impf. תְּהַנְזִק; inf. cs. הַנְזָקַת; pt. f. cs. מְהַנְזְקַת: **wrong, injure** Ezr $4_{13\cdot15\cdot22}$. †

נְחָשׁ: Heb. נְחוּשָׁה & I נְחֹשֶׁת: det. נְחָשָׁא: **copper, bronze** Dn $2_{32\cdot45}$ $4_{12\cdot20}$ $5_{4\cdot23}$ 7_{19}. †

נחת: Heb. = (< Aram.): **peal**: pt. נָחִת: **come down** (fm. heaven) Dn $4_{10\cdot20}$. †

(h)afel: impf. תַּחֵת; impv. m. sg. אֲחֵת; pt. pl. מְהַחֲתִין: **deposit, store** Ezr 5_{15} 6_1; 6_5 rd. hofal. †

hofal: pf. הָנְחַת; cj. impf. יָנְחַת Ezr 6_5: **be deposed** (fm. throne) Dn 5_{20}, **be deposited** cj. Ezr 6_5. †

נטל: Heb. =: **peal**: pf. 1. sg. נִטְלֵת; pf. pass. 3. f. נְטִילַת: **lift up**, subj. eyes Dn 4_{31}; pass. **be lifted up** 7_4. †

נטר: Heb. נצר & (< Aram.) I נטר: **peal**: pf. 1. sg. נִטְרֵת: **keep** (in one's heart) Dn 7_{28}. †

***נִיחוֹחַ**: < Heb. רֵיחַ נִיחוֹחַ: pl. נִיחֹ(וֹ)חִין: **incense** Dn 2_{46} Ezr 6_{10}. †

***נְכַס**: Heb. נְכָסִים: pl. נִכְסִין, cs. נִכְסֵי: **treasures**: *niksê malkā'* royal **treasury** Ezr 6_8, *'^{a}nāš niksîn* **fine** 7_{26}. †

נְמַר: Heb. נָמֵר: **panther** Dn 7_6. †

נסח: Heb. =: **hitpeel**: impf. יִתְנְסַח: **be pulled out** Ezr 6_{11}. †

נסך: Heb. I נָסַךְ: **pael**: inf. נַסָּכָה: **offer** (in sacrifice) Dn 2_{46}. †

***נְסַךְ** or ***נְסֵךְ**: Heb. נֶסֶךְ/נֵסֶךְ: pl. sf. נִסְכֵּיהוֹן: **drink-offering, libation** Ezr 7_{17}. †

נְפַל: Heb. =: **peal**: pf. נ׳, pl. נְפַלוּ Dn 7_{20} Kt, Qr נְפַ֫לָה; impf. יִפֶּל, יִפֵּל־, pl. תִּפְּלוּן; pt. pl. נָפְלִין: — 1. **fall**: into furnace Dn 3_{23}; fall off (subj. horns) 7_{20}; = come down (a voice, fm. heaven) 4_{28}; — 2. **fall** (on one's face) Dn $3_{5\cdot7\cdot10f\cdot15}$; — 3. fall to s.one, **be incumbent** on s.one, w. l^e + pers. & l^e + inf. Ezr 7_{20}. †

נְפַק: **peal**: pf. נ׳, 3. f. נֶפְקַת, pl. נְפַ֫קוּ Kt, Qr נְפַ֫קָה; impv. pl. פֻּ֫קוּ; pt. נָפֵק, pl. נָפְקִין: **go out** Dn 2_{14} 3_{26} 7_{10}; come forth, appear 5_{5}; = be issued 2_{13}. †

hafel: pf. הַנְפֵּק, pl. הַנְפִּ֫קוּ: **take out** Dn 5_{2f} Ezr 5_{14} 6_{5}. †

***נִפְקָה**: det. נִפְקְתָא: **cost** Ezr $6_{4\cdot8}$. †

***נִצְבָּה**: Heb. נצב: det. נִצְבְּתָא: **firmness, hardness** Dn 2_{41}. †

נצח: Heb. =: **hitpaal**: pt. מִתְנַצַּח: **distinguish onesf.**, w. *'al* Dn 6_{4}. †

נצל: Heb. =: **hafel**: inf. הַצָּלָה, sf. לְהַצָּלוּתֵהּ; pt. מַצִּל: **deliver, rescue**, subj. God Dn 3_{29} 6_{28}, man 6_{15}. †

נְקֵא: Heb. נָקִי: **pure** Dn 7_{9}. †

נקשׁ: Heb. =: **peal**: pt. pl. f. נָֽקְשָׁן: **knock together** Dn 5_{6}. †

נְשָׂא: Heb. =: **peal**: pf. נ׳; impv. שָׂא: — 1. carry = **take** Ezr 5_{15}; — 2. **carry away** Dn 2_{35}. †

hitpaal (< Heb.?): pt. f. מִתְנַשְּׂאָה: **rise up**, w. *'al* against Ezr 4_{19}. †

***נְשִׁין**: Heb. נָשִׁים: sg. *אִנְתָּה (= Heb. אִשָּׁה): (pl.) sf. נְשֵׁיהוֹן: **wives** Dn 6_{25}. †

***נִשְׁמָה**: Heb. נְשָׁמָה: sf. נִשְׁמְתָךְ: **breath** (of life) Dn 5_{23}. †

נְשַׁר: Heb. נֶשֶׁר: pl. נִשְׁרִין: **eagle** Dn 4_{30} 7_{4}. †

***נִשְׁתְּוָן**: Heb. =: det. נִשְׁתְּוָנָא: official document, **decree** Ezr $4_{18\cdot23}$ 5_{5}. †

***נְתִין**: Heb. נָתִין: pl. det. נְתִינַיָּא: one who is presented, **temple-slave** Ezr 7_{24}. †

נתן: Heb. =: **peal**: (pf., impv. & pt. supplied by יְהַב); impf. יִנְתֶּן־, יִנְתֵּן, תִּנְתֵּן, pl. יִנְתְּנוּן, sf. יִתְּנִנַּהּ; inf. מִנְתַּן: **give** Dn 2_{16} $4_{14\cdot22\cdot29}$, defray Ezr 7_{20}, pay off (taxes) 4_{13}. †

נתר: **afel**: impv. pl. אַתַּ֫רוּ: **shake off** (leaves) Dn 4_{11}. †

ס

סַבְּכָא Dn 3_{5}: ↗ שַׂבְּכָא.

סבל: Heb. =: **poel**: pt. pass. pl. מְסוֹבְלִין Ezr 6_{3}, but dub.; presumably 'were to be preserved,' but oth. sugg. 'offer' (יבל safel), or 'its measurements are to be fixed' (↗ cj. כיל).†

סבר: Heb. שׂבר: **peal**: impf. יִסְבַּר: **strive, seek**, w. l^e & inf. Dn 7_{25}. †

סְגִד: Heb. = (< Aram.): **peal**: pf. ס׳; impf. יִסְגֻּד, תִּסְגֻּד, pl. יִסְגְּדוּן, תִּסְגְּדוּן, נִסְגֻּד; pt. pl. סָגְדִין: **pay homage** to, w. l^e: God & idols Dn $3_{5\cdot7\cdot10\cdot12\cdot14f\cdot18\cdot28}$, pers. 2_{46}. †

***סְגַן**: Heb. *סָגָן: pl. סִגְנִין, det. סִגְנַיָּא: **prefect, governor** Dn $3_{2f\cdot27}$ 6_{8}; *rab signîn* chief prefect 2_{48}. †

סְגַר: Heb. =: **peal**: pf. וּס׳: **shut** Dn 6_{23}. †

סוּמְפֹּנְיָה/א Dn $3_{5\cdot15}$, 3_{10} Kt סִיפֹּ־, Qr סוּפֹּ־: last in list of musical instruments, most say **bagpipe**, but oth. say 'concord, harmony.' †

סוּף: Heb. =: **peal**: pf. 3. f. סָ֫פַת: **be fulfilled** (subj. a word) Dn 4_{30}. †

hafel: impf. 3. f. תָּסֵיף: put an end to, **annihilate** Dn 2_{44}. †

***סוֹף**: Heb. =: cs. =, det. סוֹפָא: **end** Dn $4_{8\cdot19}$ 7_{28}; *'ad-sôfā'* for ever 6_{27}, totally 7_{26}. †

סוּפֹּנְיָא: ↗ סוּמְפֹּנְיָה.

סְטַר: ↗ שְׂטַר.

סִיפֹּנְיָא: ↗ סוּמְפֹּנְיָה.

סלק: Heb. =: **peal**: pf. 3. f. סְלִקַת Dn 7_{20}, סִלְקַת 7_8 rd. סְלִקַת, pl. סְלִקוּ; pt. pl. f. סָלְקָן: **go up, come up**: Dn 2_{29} $7_{3\cdot8\cdot20}$ Ezr 4_{12}. †

hafel: pf. 3. pl. הַסִּקוּ; inf. הַנְסָקָה: **take up** Dn 3_{22}, haul up 6_{24}. †

hofal: pf. הֻסַּק: **be taken up, hauled up** Dn 6_{24}. †

סעד: Heb. =: **pael**: pt. pl. מְסָעֲדִין: **support** Ezr 5_2. †

***סְפַר**: Heb. סֵפֶר: cs. =; pl. סִפְרִין, det. סִפְרַיָּא: **book** Dn 7_{10}, *sefar mōšeh* Ezr 6_{18}, *sefar dokrānayyā'* record books 4_{15}; *bêt sifrayyā'* archives 6_1. †

***סָפַר**: Heb. סוֹפֵר: cs. =, det. סָפְרָא: **clerk, secretary** (of governor) Ezr $4_{8f\cdot17\cdot23}$; Ezra is *sāfar dātā' dî 'elāh šemayyā'* $7_{12\cdot21}$ indicating scope of office. †

סַרְבָּל: pl. sf. סַרְבָּלֵיהוֹן: a kind of **garment** Dn $3_{21\cdot27}$, trousers or cloak; for discussion F comm. †

***סָרַךְ**: pl. סָרְכִין, cs. סָרְכֵי, det. סָרְכַיָּא: (high) **official** Dn $6_{3\cdot5\cdot7f\cdot16}$. †

I **סתר**: Heb. סתר: **pael**: pt. pass. pl. f. det. מְסַתְּרָתָא: **hidden things** Dn 2_{22}. †

II **סתר**: Heb. שׂתר: **peal**: pf. sf. סַתְרֵהּ: **destroy, demolish** Ezr 5_{12}. †

ע

עֲבַד: Heb. =: **peal**: pf. 'ע, 2. m. עֲבַדְתְּ, 1. sg. עַבְדֵת, pl. עֲבַדוּ; impf. pl. תַּעַבְדוּן; inf. מֶעְבַּד; pt. עָבֵד, f. עָבְדָה/א, pl. עָבְדִין: — 1. **do**, abs. Dn 4_{32b} Ezr 6_{13}; treat, w. *be* Dn 4_{32a}, w. *'im* Ezr 6_8; — 2. **make**, subj. God, obj. heaven & earth Je 10_{11}, signs & wonders Dn 3_{32}; subj. man, obj. image Dn 3_1, revolt Ezr 4_{15} &c.; comply with (law of God) Dn 7_{26}; commit (negligence, wrong) Dn 6_{23} Ezr 4_{22}; arrange (bread) Dn 5_1, wage (war) 7_{21}.

hitpeel: impf. יִתְעֲבֵד & Dn 6_{12} 7_{21} יִתְעֲבִד, pl. תִּתְעַבְדוּן; pt. מִתְעֲבֵד־ ,מִתְעֲבֵד, f. מִתְעַבְדָא: — 1. **be made, performed**: work Ezr 5_8, decree 6_{12}, judgment 7_{26}; — 2. **be turned into** † Dn 2_5 3_{29} Ezr 6_{11}. †

***עֲבֵד**: Heb. עֶבֶד: cs. =, pl. sf. Kt עבדיך Qr עַבְדוֹהִי ,עַבְדָךְ: **servant**: of king Dn $2_{4\cdot7}$ Ezr 4_{11}, of God Dn $3_{26\cdot28}$ 6_{21} Ezr 5_{11}. †

עֲבֵד נְגוֹ, Dn 3_{29} עֲבֵד נְגוֹא: n. pers. Dn 2_{49} $3_{12\cdot30}$, = Heb. †

***עֲבִידָה**: Heb. עֲבֹדָה: cs. עֲבִידַת, det. עֲבִידְתָּא: — 1. **work** Ezr 4_{24} 5_8 6_7, service 6_{18}; — 2. **administration** Dn 2_{49} 3_{12}. †

***עֲבַר**: Heb. I עֵבֶר: cs. =: **the opposite bank**, *'abar-naharā'* Ezr $4_{10f\cdot16f\cdot20}$ $5_{3\cdot6}$ $6_{6\cdot8\cdot13}$ $7_{21\cdot25}$, i.e. west of the Euphrates. †

עַד: Heb. II עַד: — 1. prep. **up to, until**: a) spatial, up to Dn 7_{13}, *'ad-kā'* thus far 7_{28}; quantitative Ezr 7_{22}; b) temporal, until Dn 6_{15} Ezr 4_{24}, *'ad-ke'an* until now Ezr 5_{16}; up to (thirty days) = during Dn 6_8; *'ad-'oḥorên* at last Dn 4_5; — 2. conj. **until**: w. impf. Ezr 4_{21}; *'ad dî* w. impf. Dn 2_9; w. pf. Dn 2_{34}; *lā' ... 'ad dî* not ... until = hardly, scarcely 6_{25}.

עדה: Heb. I עָדָה (prob. < Aram.): **peal**: pf. 3. f. עֲדָת; impf. יֶעְדֵּה ,תֶּעְדֵּא: **go**: — 1. w. *be*, = touch Dn 3_{27}; — 2. go away = be taken away Dn 4_{28}, abs. vanish 7_{14}; = be annulled $6_{9\cdot13}$. †

hafel: pf. pl. הֶעְדִּיו Dn 7_{12} & הֶעְדִּיו 5_{20}; impf. יְהַעְדּוֹן; pt. מְהַעְדֵּה: **take away** Dn 5_{20} $7_{12\cdot26}$, remove 2_{21}. †

עִדּוֹא: n. pers. Ezr 5_1 6_{14}, = Heb. עִדּוֹ ,עִדֹּא. †

***עִדָּן**: det. עִדָּנָא; pl. עִדָּנִין, det. עִדָּנַיָּא: — 1. **time**: duration Dn 2_8 7_{12}; (changing) times $2_{9\cdot21}$; *be'iddānā' dî* (at the time) when = as soon as $3_{5\cdot15}$; — 2. = **year** Dn $4_{13\cdot20\cdot22\cdot29}$ 7_{25}. †

עוֹד: Heb. =: **still** (= yet) Dn 4_{28}. †

*עֲוָיָה: pl. sf. עֲוָיָתָךְ: **offense** Dn 4_{24}. †

עוֹף: Heb. =: cs. =: **bird** Dn 7_6, coll. birds *ʿôf-šᵉmayyāʾ* 2_{38}. †

עוּר: **chaff** Dn 2_{35}. †

*עֵז: Heb. =: pl. עִזִּין: **goat**, *ṣᵉfîrê ʿizzîn* he-goats (pl. duplicated) Ezr 6_{17}. †

*עִזְקָה: sf. עִזְקְתֵהּ; pl. cs. עִזְקָת: **signet-ring** Dn 6_{18}. †

עֶזְרָא: n. pers. **Ezra** Ezr $7_{12\cdot21\cdot25}$, F Heb. †

עֲזַרְיָה: n. pers. Dn 2_{17}, F Heb. †

עֵטָה: Heb. עֵצָה: **counsel** Dn 2_{14}. †

*עַיִן: Heb. =: cs. עֵין; pl. (for du.) עַיְנִין, cs. עַיְנֵי, sf. עַיְנַי, f.: **eye** Dn 4_{31} $7_{8\cdot20}$, of God Ezr 5_5. †

עִיר: Heb. עֵר n. pers.: pl. עִירִין: awake > watcher > **angel** Dn $4_{10\cdot14\cdot20}$. †

עַל: Heb. =: sf. עֲלַי, עֲלַיִךְ Kt עֲלָךְ Qr, עֲלַיִהּ Kt עֲלַהּ Qr, עֲלֵינָא, עֲלֵיהֹם & עֲלֵיהוֹן: prep., = Heb. *ʿal* & *ʾel*: — 1. **(up)on**: a) at rest Dn 2_{10} Ezr 5_{15}; on (one's neck) = around Dn 5_7; b) motion, on(to) Dn 2_{34} Ezr 5_5; — 2. **over**, e.g. (appointed) over (the administration) Dn 2_{49}, so (kings were) over (Jerusalem) Ezr 4_{20} &c. w. var. vbs.; *mᵉṭāʾ ʿal* fall to (s.one) Dn 4_{21}; — 3. **against** Dn 3_{19} Ezr 4_{19}; — 4. **toward** (= Heb. *ʾel*, w. vb. of motion) Dn 2_{24} Ezr 4_{12}; in epistolary style, to Ezr 4_{11}; — 5. relating to the mind, w. *śîm ṭᵉʿēm* Dn 3_{12} & *śîm bāl* 6_{15}; (be pleasing) to 4_{24} Ezr 5_{17}; — 6. **concerning** Dn 2_{18} Ezr 4_8, for = on behalf of Ezr 6_{17}; *ʿal-mâ* why? Dn 2_{15}, *ʿal-dᵉnâ* therefore Ezr 4_{15}, in this matter Dn 3_{16} Ezr 4_{22}; — 7. in comparison, **above** Dn 6_4, *ʿal dî* more than 3_{19}.

עֵלָּא: **above**, *ʿēllāʾ min*, over Dn 6_3. †

עִלָּה Dn 6_5, עִלָּא 6_6: ground for complaint, **pretext** Dn 6_{5f}. †

*עלוה (*עֲלָוָה, *עֲלְוָה or better *עֲלָה, *עֲלָת?): Heb. עֹלָה: pl. עֲלָוָן: **burnt-offering** Ezr 6_9. †

*עִלָּי: det. Qr עִלָּאָה Kt עִלָּיָא: superior, **highest**: phr. *ʾᵉlāhāʾ ʿillāʾâ* the most high God Dn $3_{26\cdot32}$ $5_{18\cdot21}$, *ʿillāʾâ* alone in this mng. $4_{14\cdot21f\cdot29\cdot31}$ 7_{25}, cf. F Heb. עֶלְיוֹן. †

*עִלִּי: Heb. =: sf. עִלִּיתֵהּ: **roof-chamber** Dn 6_{11}. †

*עֶלְיוֹן: < Heb.: pl. עֶלְיוֹנִין: **the Most High**, *qaddîšê ʿelyônîn* Dn $7_{18\cdot22\cdot25\cdot27}$ (double pl. or imitating Heb. *ʾᵉlōhîm*) the saints of the Most High. †

עלל: Heb. II עלל: **peal**: pf. עַל, f. עַלַּת Qr (Kt עֲלַלַת or עֲלַלַת); pt. pl. עַלִּין Qr (Kt עָלְלִין): **go in**, esp. to audience w. king &c. $2_{16\cdot24}$ 4_{4f} $5_{8\cdot10}$, otherw. 6_{11}. †

hafel: pf. הַנְעֵל Dn 2_{25} 6_{19}, sf. הַעֵלְנִי 2_{24}; inf. הַעָלָה 5_7 & הַנְעָלָה 4_3: **bring in**, introduce 2_{24f} 4_3 5_7 6_{19}. †

hofal: pf. הֻעַל, pl. הֻעַלּוּ: **be brought in, introduced** Dn $5_{13\cdot15}$. †

עָלַם: Heb. עוֹלָם: cs. =, det. עָלְמָא; pl. עָלְמִין, det. עָלְמַיָּא: **remote time,** 'eternity' (F Heb.): of the past, *min-yômāt ʿālᵉmāʾ* Ezr 4_{15}; of the future, oft. pl.: when greeting the king, *lᵉʿālᵉmîn ḥᵉyî* Dn 2_4; of God, *ḥay ʿālᵉmāʾ* 4_{31} &c.; *min ʿālᵉmāʾ wᵉʿad ʿālᵉmāʾ* 2_{20}, *lᵉʿālᵉmîn/-mayyāʾ* 6_{27} for ever, *lᵉʿālᵉmîn lāʾ* never 2_{44}, *ʿad-ʿālᵉmāʾ wᵉʿad ʿālam ʿālᵉmayyāʾ* 7_{18} to all eternity.

*עֵלְמָי: n. gent., cf. Heb. עֵילָם: pl. עֵלְמָיֵא: **Elamite** Ezr 4_9. †

*עֲלַע: Heb. צֵלָע: pl. עִלְעִין, f.: **rib** Dn 7_5. †

עַם: Heb. II עַם: cs. =, det. עַמָּא Ezr 7_{16} & עַמָּה 5_{12} $7_{13\cdot25}$; pl. det. עַמְמַיָּא: **people** (i.e. ethnic group): Isr. Dn 7_{27} Ezr 5_{12} $7_{13\cdot16\cdot25}$, Gentiles Dn 2_{44} Ezr 6_{12}, in series, sg. Dn 3_{29}, pl. $3_{4\cdot7\cdot31}$ 5_{19} 6_{26} 7_{14}. †

עִם: Heb. =: sf. עִמִּי, עִמָּךְ, עִמֵּהּ, עִמְּהוֹן: **(along) with**: — 1. spatial, with Dn 2_{18} Ezr 5_2, near Dn 2_{11}; w. spec. vbs., e.g. speak with = to Dn 6_{22}, (wonders he has done) with = toward 3_{32}; (what you shall do) with (s.one) = treat s.one Ezr 6_{8}; — 2. temporal, *ʿim-lêl^{e}yāʾ* by night Dn 7_{2}, *ʿim-dār w^{e}dār* 3_{33} 4_{31}.

***עֲמִיק**: Heb. עָמֹק: pl. f. עַמִּיקָתָא: **deep**, pl. f. deep (= impenetrable) things Dn 2_{22}. †

עֲמַר: Heb. צֶמֶר: **wool**, *kaʿ^{a}mar n^{e}qēʾ* Dn 7_{9}. †

***עַן**: F כְּעַן.

ענה: Heb. I עָנָה: **peal**: pf. 3. f. עֲנָת Dn 5_{10}, pl. עֲנוֹ; pt. עָנֵה, pl. עָנַיִן: alw. w. *ʾmr*, e.g. *ʿānēh w^{e}ʾāmar* Dn 2_{5}: — 1. **answer** Dn 2_{5}; — 2. **begin (to speak)** Dn 2_{15}.

***עֲנֵה**: Heb. עָנִי, עָנָו: pl. עֲנַיִן: **miserable** Dn 4_{24}. †

עֲנָיִן: F עֲנֵה*.

***עֲנָן**: Heb. עָנָן: pl. cs. עֲנָנֵי: **cloud** Dn 7_{13}. †

***עֲנַף**: Heb. עָנָף: pl. sf. עַנְפוֹהִי: **branch** (of tree) Dn $4_{9\cdot11\cdot18}$. †

***עֲנָשׁ**: Heb. עֹנֶשׁ: cs. =: **fine** (imposed) Ezr 7_{26}. †

***עֶנֶת**: F כְּעֶנֶת.

***עֳפִי**: Heb. = (< Aram.): sf. עָפְיֵהּ: **foliage, leaves** Dn $4_{9\cdot11\cdot18}$. †

עֲצִיב: **sorrowful, afflicted** Dn 6_{21}. †

עקר: Heb. =: **itpeel**: pf. pl. Kt אֶתְעֲקַרוּ, Qr אֶתְעֲקַרָה: **be plucked out** Dn 7_{8}. †

***עִקַּר**: cf. Heb. עֵקֶר: cs. =: **root**, *ʿiqqar šoršôhî* taproot, rootstock Dn $4_{12\cdot20\cdot23}$. †

***עָר**: Heb. צַר: sf. Qr עָרָךְ, Kt עָרַיִךְ: **adversary** Dn 4_{16}. †

ערב: Heb. II ערב: **pael**: pt. pass. מְעָרַב: **mix**, pt. pass. mixed Dn $2_{41\cdot43}$. †
hitpaal: pt. מִתְעָרַב, pl. מִתְעָרְבִין: **mix, join** (intrans.) Dn 2_{43}. †

***עֲרָד**: Heb. עָרוֹד: pl. det. עֲרָדַיָּא: **wild ass** Dn 5_{21}. †

***עַרְוָה**: Heb. עֶרְוָה: cs. עַרְוַת: nakedness, metaph. **dishonor** Ezr 4_{14}. †

***עֲשַׂב**: Heb. עֵשֶׂב: cs. =, det. עִשְׂבָּא: coll. greens, **grass** Dn $4_{22\cdot29f}$ 5_{21}; *ʿ^{a}śab ʾarʿāʾ* 4_{12}. †

עֲשַׂר & עַשְׂרָה: Heb. עֶשֶׂר, עֲשָׂרָה: **ten**, *ʿ^{a}śar* w. f. Dn $7_{7\cdot20\cdot24}$, *ʿaśrâ* w. m. 7_{24}; *t^{e}rê-ʿ^{a}śar* **twelve** 4_{26} Ezr 6_{17}. †

עֶשְׂרִין: Heb. עֶשְׂרִים: **twenty** Dn 6_{2}. †

עשת: Heb. II עשת: **peal**: עֲשִׁית, not pf. intrans. but pt. pass. m. w. active mng., or adj.: **think, plan**, w. inf. Dn 6_{4}. †

***עֵת**: F כְּעֵת.

***עֲתִיד**: Heb. עָתִיד: pl. עֲתִידִין: **ready to**, w. F *dî* (3 c) & impf. Dn 3_{15}. †

***עַתִּיק**: Heb. =: cs. =: **old**, *ʿattîq yômîn* aged Dn $7_{9\cdot13\cdot22}$. †

פ

***פֶּחָה**: Heb. =: cs. פַּחַת; pl. פַּחֲוָתָא: **governor**: of Babylonian & Pers. empires Dn $3_{2f\cdot27}$ 6_{8} Ezr $5_{3\cdot6}$ $6_{6\cdot13}$, of Judea 5_{14} 6_{7}. †

פֶּחָר: **potter** Dn 2_{41}. †

***פטישׁ**: pl. sf. Qr פַּטִּישֵׁיהוֹן, Kt פַּטְשֵׁיהוֹן or פַּטְ׳: a **garment**, coat or trousers Dn 3_{21}. †

פלג: Heb. =: **peal**: pt. pass. f. פְּלִיגָה: **divide**, pass. divided, not united Dn 2_{41}. †

***פְּלַג**: Heb. I פֶּלֶג 'canal': **cs. =: half** Dn 7_{25}. †

***פְּלֻגָּה**: Heb. =: pl. sf. פְּלֻגָּתְהוֹן: **division** (of priests) Ezr 6_{18}. †

פלח: Heb. = (w. distinct mng.): **peal**: impf. pl. יִפְלְחוּן; pt. פָּלַח, pl. פָּלְחִין, פָּלְחֵי: **serve** (God), w. acc. Dn 3_{17}, w. *l^{e}* $3_{12\cdot14\cdot18\cdot28}$ $6_{17\cdot21}$ $7_{14\cdot27}$; pt. servant Ezr 7_{24}. †

***פָּלְחָן**: cs. =: (cultic) **service** Ezr 7_{19}. †

פֻּם: Heb. פֶּה: cs. =, sf. פֻּמַּהּ: — 1. **mouth** Dn 4_{28} 6_{23} 7_{5} 8_{20}; — 2. **mouth, entrance** (of lion's den) Dn 6_{18}. †

פַּס: Heb. =: cs. =, det. פַּסָּא: Dn $5_{5\cdot24}$, trad. palm (of hand), but more prob. back of hand, or whole hand proper below the wrist. †

פְּסַנְטֵרִין Dn 3_7 & **פְּסַנְתֵּרִין** $3_{5 \cdot 10 \cdot 15}$: **harp**, a three-cornered stringed instrument w. sounding board. †

פַּרְזֶל: Heb. בַּרְזֶל: פַּרְזֶל, det. פַּרְזְלָא, m.: **iron** Dn $2_{33 \cdot 35 \cdot 40 \cdot 43 \cdot 45}$ $4_{12 \cdot 20}$ $5_{4 \cdot 23}$ $7_{7 \cdot 19}$. †

פרס: Heb. =: **peal**: pf. pass. 3. f. פְּרִיסַת: **divide**, pass. Dn 5_{28}. †

פְּרֵס: pl. פַּרְסִין Dn 5_{25}: unit of measure & weight, trad. half-mina, but prob. **half-shekel** Dn $5_{25 \cdot 28}$, w. word-play v. $_{28}$. †

פָּרַס, פָּרָס: Heb. =: **Persia, the Persians** Dn 5_{28} $6_{9 \cdot 13 \cdot 16}$ Ezr 4_{24} 6_{14}. †

***פַּרְסַי**: Heb. פָּרְסִי: gent. of פָּרַס: det. Kt פַּרְסָיָא Qr פַּרְסָאָה: adj. & noun **Persian** Dn 6_{29}. †

פרק: Heb. =: **peal**: impv. פְּרֻק: **unloose, abolish** (one's own sins) Dn 4_{24} (oth.: break off). †

פרשׁ: Heb. =: **pael**: pt. pass. מְפָרַשׁ: separate, pt. pass. Ezr 4_{18} trad. read separately, i.e. distinctly, but oth.: translate in sections. †

***פַּרְשֶׁגֶן**: Heb. פַּתְשֶׁגֶן: cs. =: **copy** Ezr $4_{11 \cdot 23}$ 5_6. †

פשׁר: cf. Heb. פֵּשֶׁר & פָּתַר: **peal**: inf. מִפְשַׁר: **interpret** Dn 5_{16}, w. cogn. acc. †

pael: pt. מְפַשַּׁר: **interpreter** Dn 5_{12}, but sugg. rd. peal inf. †

***פְּשַׁר**: Heb. פֵּשֶׁר: cs. =, det. פִּשְׁרָא & Dn 2_7 5_{12} פְּשְׁרָה, sf. פִּשְׁרֵהּ 4_{15f}, 5_8 Qr פִּשְׁרֵהּ (Kt det.); pl. פִּשְׁרִין: **interpretation** Dn 2_4 & oft.

פִּתְגָם: Heb. =: det. פִּתְגָמָא: — 1. **word**: *hatib pitgām*, reply Dn 3_{16}, give an account of Ezr 5_{11}; *šelaḥ pitgām*, report Ezr 4_{17} 5_7; — 2. **decree** Dn 4_{14} Ezr 6_{11}. †

פתח: Heb. =: **peal**: pf. pass. pl. פְּתִ֫יחוּ; pt. pass. pl. f. פְּתִיחָן: **open** Dn 6_{11} 7_{10}. †

***פְּתָי**: sf. פְּתָיֵהּ: **width** Dn 3_1 Ezr 6_3. †

צ

צבה: **peal**: pf. 1. sg. צְבִית; impf. יִצְבֵּא, Dn 5_{21} יִצְבֵּה; inf. sf. מִצְבְּיֵהּ; pt. צָבֵא: — 1. **long to, desire to**, w. *le* & inf. Dn 7_{19}; — 2. **wish, like** Dn $4_{14 \cdot 22 \cdot 29}$ $5_{19 \cdot 21}$, *kemiṣbeyēh* according to his will 4_{32}. †

צְבוּ: affair, **thing**, *lā'...ṣebû* nothing Dn 6_{18}. †

צבע: Heb. cj. *צבע: **pael**: pt. pl. מְצַבְּעִין: **wet**, w. *min* Dn 4_{22}. †

hitpaal: impf. יִצְטַבַּע: **be wet**, w. *min* or *be* Dn $4_{12 \cdot 20 \cdot 30}$ 5_{21}. †

***צַד**: Heb. =: cs. =: **side**, w. prep. *leṣad*, against Dn 7_{25}; *miṣṣad* from the side of = regarding 6_5. †

צְדָא: w. *ha* interr., **is it true?** Dn 3_{14}. †

צִדְקָה: Heb. צְדָקָה: right action, **beneficence** Dn 4_{24}. †

***צַוַּאר**: Heb. צַוָּאר: sf. צַוְּארֵהּ, צַוְּארָךְ: **neck** Dn $5_{7 \cdot 16 \cdot 29}$. †

צלה: **pael**: pt. מְצַלֵּא, pl. מְצַלַּ֫יִן: **pray** Dn 6_{11} w. *qodām*, Ezr 6_{10} w. *le*. †

צלח: Heb. =: **hafel**: pf. הַצְלַח; pt. מַצְלַח, pl. מַצְלְחִין: — 1. **cause** s.one **to prosper** Dn 3_{30}; — 2. **make progress** (w. work) Ezr 6_{14}; go well, **prove a success, prosper**, subj. pers. Dn 6_{29}, thg. Ezr 5_8. †

צְלֵם: Heb. צֶלֶם: cs. = 3_{19}, otherw. צֶלֶם (< Heb.) as artificial differentiation, det. צַלְמָא: image: **statue** Dn $2_{31f \cdot 34f}$ $3_{1 \cdot 18}$, *ṣelēm 'anpôhî* Dn 3_{19} his features. †

***צְפִיר**: Heb. צָפִיר: pl. cs. צְפִירֵי: **he-goat**, *ṣefîrê ʿizzîn* he-goats Ezr 6_{17}. †

***צִפַּר**: Heb. צִפּוֹר: pl. צִפְּרִין, cs. צִפְּרֵי, det. צִפְּרַיָּא, f. Dn 4_9 Qr $_{18}$, m. 4_9 Kt: **bird** Dn $4_{9 \cdot 11 \cdot 18 \cdot 30}$. †

ק

קבל: Heb. =: **pael**: pf. קַבֵּל; impf. pl. תְּקַבְּלוּן, וִיקַבְּלוּן: **receive** Dn 2_6; obj. *malkûtā'* = take over the rule 6_1 7_{18}. †

קֳבֵל: w. *l^e*, לָקֳבֵל, sf. לָקָבְלָךְ: prep.: — 1. **before** (spatial), **in front of** Dn 2_{31} 3_3 5_1, = opposite 5_5; because of 5_{10}; *hēn ... loq^{o}bēl d^{e}nâ*, if ... then Ezr 4_{16}, *loq^{o}bēl dî* just as 6_{13}; — 2. w. *kol-* (not *kōl* 'all' but *k^e* + *l^e*): *kol-q^{o}bēl d^{e}nâ*, accordingly Ezr 7_{11}; thereupon, then Dn $2_{12\cdot24}$ 3_7 6_{10}, *kol-q^{o}bēl dî* because Dn 2_8 & oft., although Dn 5_{22}, *kol-q^{o}bēl d^{e}nâ min-dî* just because 3_{22}.

קַדִּישׁ: Heb. קָדוֹשׁ: pl. קַדִּישִׁין, cs. קַדִּישֵׁי: **holy**: gods Dn $4_{5f\cdot15}$ 5_{11}; noun = angels 4_{14}, *'îr w^{e}qaddîš* $4_{10\cdot20}$; pl. = Isr. 7_{21}, *qaddîšê 'elyônîn* $7_{18\cdot22\cdot25}$ & *'am qaddîšê 'elyônîn* 7_{27}. †

קֳדָם, קֳדָם־ Dn $2_{10\cdot36}$: cf. Heb. קֶדֶם: sf. קָדָמַי, קֳדָמַי, קֳדָמָךְ Qr קֳדָמַיִךְ Kt, קֳדָמוֹהִי, 7_{13} וּקְדָמוֹהִי, f. Qr קֳדָמַהּ Kt קדמיה, w. prep. מִן־קֳדָמַי/־מוֹהִי/־מיה, pl. קֳדָמֵיהוֹן: prep. **before**: — 1. temporal Dn 7_7; — 2. spatial: before, in front of the king Dn 2_9, king before those present Dn 4_4 Ezr 4_{23}, before God Dn 6_{11f} Ezr 7_{19}; = in s.one's eyes Dn 6_{23}, *š^{e}far q^{o}dām* Dn 3_{32}; — 3. *min-q^{o}dām* = **before** Dn 7_8; be afraid of (cf. Heb. *millifnê*) 5_{19}; from (cf. Heb. *mipp^{e}nê*) Dn 2_6 Ezr 7_{14}.

***קַדְמָה**: Heb. *קַדְמָה, *קִדְמָה: cs. קַדְמַת: **former times**, w. *min* > prep., *min-qadmat-d^{e}nâ* Dn 6_{11} & *miqq-* Ezr 5_{11} adv. formerly. †

***קַדְמַי**: f. det. קַדְמָיְתָא; pl. det. קַדְמָיֵא, f. det. קַדְמָיָתָא: **first** Dn 7_4, former $7_{8\cdot24}$. †

קוּם: Heb. =: **peal**: pf. קָם, pl. קָמוּ; impf. יְקוּם, pl. יְקוּמוּן & Dn 7_{24} יְקֻמוּן; impv. f. קוּמִי; pt. קָאֵם, pl. Kt קָאֲמִין Qr קָיְמִין, det. קָאֲמַיָּא: — 1. **stand up, rise up** Dn 3_{24} 6_{20} 7_5, arise 2_{39} $7_{17\cdot24}$; set about, begin Ezr 5_2; — 2. **stand** (i.e. be standing) Dn 2_{31} 3_3 $7_{10\cdot16}$; — 3. **endure, continue** Dn 2_{44}. †

pael: inf. קַיָּמָה: **set up**, metaph. establish (a statute) Dn 6_8. †

(h)afel: pf. הֲקִים & Dn 6_2 וַהֲקִים, 2. הֲקֵימְתָּ, 1. הֲקֵימֶת, pl. הֲקִימוּ, sf. הֲקִימֵהּ & Dn 3_1 (afel) אֲקִימֵהּ; impf. יְקִים & Dn 5_{21} 6_{16} יְהָקֵים, תְּקִים; inf. sf. הֲקָמוּתֵהּ; pt. מְהָקֵים: — 1. **set up** (a statue) Dn $3_{1\cdot3\cdot5\cdot7\cdot12\cdot14\cdot18}$; — 2. **establish** (a kingship) Dn 2_{44}; — 3. **appoint** (kings, officials) Dn 2_{21}, w. 2 acc. 5_{11}, w. acc. & *b^e* Ezr 6_{18}, w. acc. & *'al* Dn 4_{14} 5_{21} $6_{2\cdot4}$; — 4. **establish** (a statute) Dn $6_{9\cdot16}$. †

hofal: pf. 3. f. הֳקִ(י)מַת: **be set up** Dn 7_{4f}. †

קטל: Heb. =: **peal**: pt. קָטֵל; pf. pass. קְטִיל, 3. f. קְטִילַת: **kill** Dn 5_{19}, pass. 5_{30} 7_{11}. †

pael: pf. קַטִּל; inf. קַטָּלָה: **kill** Dn 2_{14} 3_{22}. †

hitpeel: inf. הִתְקְטָלָה: **be killed** Dn 2_{13}. †

hitpaal: pt. pl.: מִתְקַטְּלִין: **be killed**, pt. were to be killed Dn 2_{13}. †

***קְטַר**: pl. קִטְרִין, cs. קִטְרֵי: **knot**: — 1. **joint**, *qiṭrê ḥarṣēh* Dn 5_6 joints of the hips; — 2. difficult task (orig. magic knot?) Dn $5_{12\cdot16}$. †

קַיִט: Heb. קַיִץ: **summer** Dn 2_{35}. †

קְיָם: cs. =: **statute, decree** Dn $6_{8\cdot16}$. †

קַיָּם: f. קַיָּמָה: **enduring**: *malkûtāk lāk qayyāmâ* Dn 4_{23} = remains secure for you; *'elāhā' qayyām l^e'āl^{e}mîn* 6_{27}. †

קיתרס: Kt קִיתְרֹס or קִיתָרֹס, Qr קַתְרֹ(ו)ס: a variety of Greek **kithara**, i.e. a kind of lyre or lute Dn $3_{5\cdot7\cdot10\cdot15}$. †

קָל: Heb. קוֹל: cs. =: **voice** Dn 4_{28} 6_{21}; **sound**, of words 7_{11}, of music $3_{5\cdot7\cdot10\cdot15}$. †

קנה: Heb. I קָנָה: **peal**: impf. תִּקְנֵא: **buy** Ezr 7_{17}. †

קְצַף (vb.): Heb. =: **peal**: pf. ׳ק: **become furious** Dn 2_{12}. †

קְצַף (noun): < Heb. קֶצֶף: **wrath** (of God) Ezr 7_{23}. †

קצץ: Heb. =: **pael**: impv. pl. קַצִּצוּ: **cut off** Dn 4_{11}. †

***קְצָת**: Heb. = (< Aram.): cs. =, f.: — 1. **end**, *liqṣāt yômîn/yarḥîn* Dn $4_{26\cdot31}$; — 2. w. *min*, **part**, w. gen., *min-qᵉṣāt malkûtāʾ*, part of the kingdom, &c. Dn 2_{42}. †

קרא: Heb. =: **peal**: pf. pass. קְרִי; impf. יִקְרֵה, אֶקְרֵא, pl. יִקְרוֹן; inf. מִקְרָא; pt. קָרֵא: — 1. **shout** Dn 3_4 4_{11} 5_7; — 2. **read** Dn $5_{7f\cdot15\cdot17}$; pass. Ezr $4_{18\cdot23}$. †
  hitpeel: impf. יִתְקְרֵי: **be called, summoned** Dn 5_{12}. †

קרב: Heb. =: **peal**: pf. ׳ק, 1. sg. קִרְבֵת, pl. קְרִיבוּ; inf. sf. מִקְרְבֵהּ: **approach, step up to** Dn 3_8 6_{13}, w. *lᵉ* of place 3_{26} 6_{21}, w. *ʿal* & pers. 7_{16}. †
  pael: impf. תְּקָרֵב: **offer** Ezr 7_{17}. †
  hafel: pf. pl. הַקְרִבוּ, sf. הַקְרְבוּהִי; pt. pl. מְהַקְרְבִין: — 1. **bring** (s.one) **near, present** Dn 7_{13}; — 2. **offer** Ezr $6_{10\cdot17}$. †

קְרָב: Heb. = (< Aram.): **war** Dn 7_{21}. †

קִרְיָה Ezr 4_{10} & **קִרְיָא** 4_{15}: Heb. קִרְיָה: det. קִרְיְתָא, f.: inhabited place, town, **city**: = Jerus. Ezr $4_{12f\cdot15f\cdot19\cdot21}$, as coll. pl. 4_{10}. †

קֶרֶן: Heb. =: det. קַרְנָא; du. קַרְנַיִן (pl. mng.); pl. det. קַרְנַיָּא, f.: **horn**: — 1. of animal Dn $7_{7f\cdot11\cdot20\cdot21\cdot24}$; — 2. musical instrument Dn $3_{5\cdot7\cdot10\cdot15}$. †

***קְרַץ**: pl. sf. קַרְצוֹהִי, קַרְצֵיהוֹן: **piece**: idiom, 'eat pieces of' = **slander** Dn 3_8 6_{25}, cf. Eng. 'backbite.' †

קשׁט: Heb. קֹשֶׁט: **truth** Dn 4_{34}, *min-qᵉšōṭ dî* truly 2_{47}. †

ר

ראשׁ: Heb. ראשׁ: cs. =, det. רֵאשָׁא, sf. רֵאשִׁי, רֵאשָׁךְ, רֵאשֵׁהּ, רֵאשַׁהּ, רֵאשְׁהוֹן; pl. רֵאשִׁין, sf. רָאשֵׁיהֹם (< Heb.): — 1. **head** Dn $2_{32\cdot38}$ 3_{27} $7_{6\cdot9\cdot20}$, *ḥezwê rēʾš* 2_{28} $4_{2\cdot7\cdot10}$ $7_{1\cdot15}$; metaph. Ezr 5_{10} (at their) head; — 2. **beginning**, *rēʾš millîn* Dn 7_1 (oth.: essential contents, or complete account). †

רַב: Heb. =: det. רַבָּא, f. det. רַבְּתָא; reduplicated pl. רַבְרְבִין, f. רַבְרְבָן, det. רַבְרְבָתָא: — 1. **great** Dn 2_{31} & oft.; w. *millayyāʾ* or vb. *mallēl*, insolent (words) † Dn $7_{8\cdot11\cdot20}$; — 2. w. gen. pl. as a title, **chief** … † Dn $2_{14\cdot48}$ 4_6 5_{11}.

רְבָה: Heb. I רבה: **peal**: pf. ׳ר, 3. f. רְבָת, 2. m. Kt רְבַיְתָ Qr רְבַת Dn 4_{19}: become great, **grow up** Dn $4_{8\cdot17\cdot19\cdot30}$. †
  pael: pf. רַבִּי: make great, **exalt** Dn 2_{48}. †

***רִבּוֹ**: Heb. = (< Aram.): cs. =; pl. Qr רִבְבָן Kt רִבְּוָן: great number, **ten thousand**, *ribbô ribbᵉwān* Dn 7_{10}. †

רְבוּ: det. רְבוּתָא, sf. רְבוּתָךְ: **greatness** Dn $4_{19\cdot33}$ 5_{18f} 7_{27}. †

***רְבִיעָי**: Heb. רְבִיעִי: det. Kt רְבִיעָיָא Qr רְבִיעָאָה, f. Kt רְבִיעָיָה Qr רְבִיעָאָה, det. רְבִיעָיְתָא: **fourth** Dn 2_{40} 3_{25} $7_{7\cdot19\cdot23}$. †

***רַבְרְבָנִין**: sf. רַבְרְבָנַי, Kt רַבְרְבָנַיִךְ Qr ־נָךְ, רַבְרְבָנוֹהִי: **lords, nobles** Dn 4_{33} $5_{1\cdot3\cdot9f\cdot23}$ 6_{18}. †

רגז: Heb. =: **hafel**: pf. pl. הַרְגִּזוּ: **anger** Ezr 5_{12}. †

רְגַז: Heb. רֹגֶז: **rage** Dn 3_{13}. †

***רְגַל** or ***רְגַל**: Heb. רֶגֶל: du. רַגְלַיִן, det. רַגְלַיָּא, sf. רַגְלוֹהִי, Qr רַגְלַהּ Kt רַגְלַיַהּ or רַגְלֵיהּ, f.: **foot** Dn $2_{33f\cdot41f}$ $7_{4\cdot7\cdot19}$. †

רגשׁ: Heb. =: **hafel**: pf. pl. הַרְגִּשׁוּ: **storm in** Dn $6_{7\cdot12\cdot16}$ (oth.: come by prior agreement, or try to influence). †

***רֵו**: sf. רֵוֵהּ: **appearance** Dn 2_{31} 3_{25}. †

רוּחַ: Heb. =: cs. =, det. רוּחָא, sf. רוּחִי, רוּחֵהּ; pl. cs. רוּחֵי, f.: — 1. **wind** Dn 2_{35} 7_2;

— 2. **spirit** (of man), mind Dn 5_{20} 7_{15}, *rûaḥ yattîrâ* 5_{12} 6_4; — 3. **divine spirit**, *rûaḥ ʾelāhîn* $4_{5f\cdot15}$ $5_{11\cdot14}$. †

רום: Heb. =: **peal**: pf. רָם: **raise onesf.**, subj. *lēb*, be haughty Dn 5_{20}. †

polel: pf. מְרוֹמֵם: **praise** Dn 4_{34}. †

hafel: pt. מָרִים: **raise up, exalt** Dn 5_{19}. †

hitpolel: pf. הִתְרוֹמַמְתָּ: **rise up** against (*ʿal*) Dn 5_{23}. †

*__רוּם__: sf. רוּמֵהּ: **height** Dn 3_1 $4_{7f\cdot17}$ Ezr 6_3. †

רָז: det. רָזָה Dn $2_{18f\cdot27}$ רָזָא 2_{30}; pl. רָזִין, det. רָזַיָּא: **secret** Dn $2_{18f\cdot27\cdot30}$. †

רְחוּם: n. pers. Ezr $4_{1f\cdot17\cdot23}$, = Heb. †

*__רַחִיק__: Heb. רָחוֹק: pl. רַחִיקִין: **far**, *hawâ raḥîq*, keep (onesf.) away Ezr 6_6. †

רַחֲמִין Heb. רַחֲמִים: **compassion** Dn 2_{18}. †

רחץ: **hitpeel**: pf. pl. הִתְרְחִצוּ: **rely** on, **put one's trust** in, w. *ʿal* Dn 3_{28}. †

*__רֵיחַ__: Heb. =: cs. =, f.: **smell**, of fire Dn 3_{27}. †

רמה: Heb. I רָמָה: **peal**: pf. pl. רְמִינָה ,רְמוֹ; inf. מִרְמֵא; pf. pass. pl. רְמִיו Dn 3_{21}: — 1. **throw** Dn 3_{20} $6_{17\cdot25}$, w. *legôʾ* 3_{24}, pass. 3_{21}; — 2. **place** (thrones), pass. Dn 7_9; — 3. **impose** (a tax) on, *ʿal* Ezr 7_{24}. †

hitpeel: impf. יִתְרְמֵא, pl. תִּתְרְמוֹן: **be thrown** Dn $3_{6\cdot11\cdot15}$ $6_{8\cdot13}$. †

*__רְעוּ__: Heb. II רְעוּת: cs. רְעוּת: **will, decision**, of the king Ezr 5_{17}, of God 7_{18}. †

*__רַעְיוֹן__: Heb. =: pl. cs. רַעְיוֹנֵי, sf. רַעְיוֹנַי, Qr רַעְיוֹנָךְ Kt ־נַיִךְ, רַעְיֹנֹהִי: **thought** Dn 2_{29f} 4_{16} $5_{6\cdot10}$ 7_{28}. †

רַעֲנַן: Heb. רַעֲנָן: **prosperous, flourishing** Dn 4_1. †

רעע: Heb. רצץ & (< Aram.) רעע: **peal**: impf. 3. f. תֵּרֹעַ: **shatter** Dn 2_{40}. †

pael: pt. מְרָעַע: **shatter** Dn 2_{40}. †

רפס: Heb. רפס ,רפשׂ: **peal**: pt. f. רָפְסָה: **trample down** Dn $7_{7\cdot19}$. †

רְשַׁם: Heb. = (< Aram.): **peal**: pf. ר׳, רְשַׁמְתָּ; impf. תִּרְשֻׁם; pf. pass. רְשִׁים: **write** Dn $6_{9f\cdot13f}$, pass. 5_{24f} 6_{11}. †

שׂ

*__שָׂב__: pl. cs. שָׂבֵי, det. שָׂבַיָּא: one w. gray hair, pl. **elders** Ezr $5_{5\cdot9}$ $6_{7f\cdot14}$. †

שַׂבְּכָא Dn $3_{7\cdot10\cdot15}$ & סַבְּכָא 3_5, a type of lyre, evid. triangular, w. 4 strings & a bright tone. †

שׂגא: Heb. שׂגה (< Aram.): **peal**: impf. יִשְׂגֵּא: **grow, become great** Ezr 4_{22}; in salutation Dn 3_{31} 6_{26}. †

שַׂגִּיא: Heb. = (< Aram.): pl. f. שַׂגִּיאָן: — 1. **great** Dn $2_{6\cdot31\cdot48}$ 4_7; — 2. **much, many**, w. sg. coll. Dn $4_{9\cdot18}$ 7_5, w. pl. Ezr 5_{11}; — 3. adv. **very** Dn 2_{12} 5_9 $6_{15\cdot24}$ 7_{28}. †

*__שָׂהֲדוּ__: det. שָׂהֲדוּתָא: **testimony** Gn 31_{47}. †

שְׂטַר: **side**, *liśṭar ḥad* Dn 7_5. †

שׂיב: Heb. =: **peal**: pt. ⸢ *שָׂב.

שׂים: Heb. =: **peal**: pf. ־שָׂם, 2. m. שָׂמְתָּ, 1. sg. שָׂמֶת, sf. שָׂמֵהּ; impv. pl. שִׂימוּ; pf. pass. שִׂים, 3. f. שָׂמַת Dn 6_{18}: **set, lay, put**: pass. Dn 6_{18}; spec.: appoint (as, to be), w. 2 acc. Ezr 5_{14}; *śîm ṭeʿēm* give an order Dn 3_{10} Ezr 4_{21} & oft., pass. Dn 3_{29} Ezr 4_{19} & oft.; *śîm ṭeʿēm ʿal* care about Dn 3_{12}; *śîm bāl le* set one's mind on Dn 6_{15}; *śîm šum* w. gen., give a name to Dn 5_{12}.

hitpeel: impf. יִתְּשָׂם, pl. יִתְּשָׂמוּן; pt. מִתְּשָׂם: **be put, laid** Ezr 5_8; be turned into (w. *le*) Dn 2_5; subj. *ṭeʿēm*, be given Ezr 4_{21}. †

שׂכל: Heb. I שָׂכַל: **hitpaal**: pt. מִשְׂתַּכַּל: **consider**, w. *be* Dn 7_8. †

שָׂכְלְתָנוּ, f.: **insight** Dn $5_{11f\cdot14}$. †

cj. *__שָׁלָה__, Dn 3_{29} for ⸢ שָׁלָה: **insolence, rebellion**, w. *ʾmr* speak insolently Dn 3_{29}. †

שׂנא: Heb. =: **peal**: pt. pl. sf. Qr שָׂנְאָךְ Kt שָׂנְאַיִךְ: **hate**, pt. enemy Dn 4_{16}. †

*__שְׂעַר__: Heb. שֵׂעָר: cs. =, sf. שַׂעֲרֵהּ: **hair**, coll. Dn 3_{27} 4_{30} 7_9. †

שׁ

שְׁאֵל: Heb. =: **peal**: pf. 'שׁ, 1. pl. שְׁאֵלְנָא; impf. sf. יִשְׁאֲלֻנְכוֹן; pt. שָׁאֵל: — 1. **ask, desire, require**, w. acc. thg. Dn 2_{11}, w. *le* (of) & pers. 2_{10}, w. 2 acc. Ezr 7_{21}; — 2. **ask** (a question, for information), w. acc. thg. Dn 2_{27} Ezr 5_{10}, w. *le* & pers. Ezr 5_9. †

*שְׁאֵלָה: Heb. =: det. שְׁאֵלְתָא: request, **question** Dn 4_{14} (oth.: matter, affair). †

שְׁאַלְתִּיאֵל: n. pers. Ezr 5_2 (= Heb.). †

*שְׁאָר: Heb. =: cs. =, det. שְׁאָרָא: **remainder, rest** (coll.) Dn $7_{7.19}$, w. gen. Dn 2_{18} 7_{12} Ezr $4_{9f.17}$ 6_{16} $7_{18.20}$. †

שׁבח: Heb. I שׁבח: **pael**: pf. שַׁבַּחְתְּ, 1. sg. שַׁבְּחֵת, pl. שַׁבַּחוּ; pt. מְשַׁבַּח: **praise** Dn 2_{23} $4_{31.34}$ $5_{4.23}$. †

*שְׁבַט or *שְׁבֵט: Heb. שֵׁבֶט: pl. cs. שִׁבְטֵי: **tribe** (of Isr.) Ezr 6_{17}. †

*שְׁבִיב: Heb. שָׁבִיב: det. שְׁבִיבָא; pl. שְׁבִיבִין: **flame** Dn 3_{22} 7_9. †

*שְׁבַע: Heb. שֶׁבַע: f. שִׁבְעָה, cs. שִׁבְעַת: **seven** Dn $4_{13.20.22.29}$ Ezr 7_{14}, *ḥad-šibʿâ* 7 times Dn 3_{10}. †

שׁבק: **peal**: impv. pl. שְׁבֻקוּ; inf. מִשְׁבַּק: **leave** (s.thg somewhere) Dn $4_{12.20.23}$; Ezr 6_7 leave undisturbed, or give a free hand to. †

hitpeel: impf. תִּשְׁתְּבִק: **be left** to, **pass on** to (of sovereignty) Dn 2_{44}. †

שׁבשׁ: **hitpaal**: pt. pl. מִשְׁתַּבְּשִׁין: **be perplexed** Dn 5_9. †

*שֵׁגַל: (< Heb.): pl. sf. שֵׁגְלָתֵהּ, שֵׁגְלָתָךְ: **concubine** (of king) Dn $5_{2f.23}$. †

שׁדר: **hitpaal**: pt. מִשְׁתַּדַּר: **strive**, w. *le* & inf. Dn 6_{15}. †

שַׁדְרַךְ: n. pers. Dn 2_{49} 3_{12-30}. †

שׁוה: Heb. I & II שׁוה: **peal**: pf. pass. Kt שְׁוִי or שֻׁוִּי: **be like**, pass. be made like, w. *ʿim* Dn 5_{21}. †

pael: pf. pl. Qr שַׁוִּיו: **make like**, w. acc. & *ʿim* Dn 5_{21}. †

hitpaal: impf. יִשְׁתַּוֵּה: **be made** (into), w. acc. Dn 3_{29}. †

*שׁוּר: Heb. =: pl. det. Ezr 4_{12} Qr שׁוּרַיָּא (Kt שׁורי, → כלל šafel & שׁרה pael), $_{13.16}$ שׁוּרַיָּה (but sugg. sf. שׁוּרַיה): **wall** Ezr $4_{12f.16}$. †

*שׁוּשַׁנְכָי: pl. det. שׁוּשַׁנְכָיֵא: **inhabitant of Susa** Ezr 4_9. †

שׁחת: Heb. =: **peal**: pt. pass. f. שְׁחִיתָה: **spoil**, pt. pass. corrupt Dn 2_9, f. as noun, s.thg bad, **mischief** Dn 6_5 (also 2_9 ?). †

שֵׁיזִב: loanword, but understood as šafel: pf. שֵׁיזִב Dn 3_{28} & שֵׁיזִיב 6_{28}; impf. יְשֵׁיזִב, sf. יְשֵׁיזְבִנְכוֹן, יְשֵׁיזְבִנָּךְ; inf. sf. שֵׁיזָבוּתָךְ, ־תֵהּ, ־תַּנָא; pt. מְשֵׁיזִב: **rescue, save** Dn $3_{17.28}$ $6_{15.17}$, w. *min* 3_{17} 6_{21}, w. *min-yad* $3_{15.17}$ 6_{28b}, abs. 6_{28a}. †

שֵׁיצִיא: loanword, but understood as šafel: pf. Kt שֵׁיצִיא Qr שֵׁיצִי: **finish** Ezr 6_{15}. †

שׁכח: Heb. שָׁכַח 'forget': **hafel**: pf. 1. sg. הַשְׁכַּחַת, pl. הַשְׁכַּחוּ, הַשְׁכַּחְנָה/א; impf. נְהַשְׁכַּח, תְּהַשְׁכַּח; inf. הַשְׁכָּחָה: **find** (s.one or s.thg) Dn 2_{25} $6_{5f.12}$, w. *dî* that Ezr $4_{15.19}$, = get 7_{16}. †

hitpeel: pf. הִשְׁתְּכַח, 3. f. הִשְׁתְּכַחַת, 2. m. הִשְׁתְּכַחַתְּ: **be found**, find onesf., w. *be* Dn $5_{11f.14}$ 6_{24} Ezr 6_2, w. *ʿal* Dn 6_5, w. *le* 2_{35} 6_{23}; be found (to be) 5_{27}. †

שַׁכְלֵל: → כלל.

שׁכן: Heb. =: **peal**: impf. 3. pl. f. יִשְׁכְּנָן: **live** (i.e. dwell) Dn 4_{18}. †

pael: pf. שַׁכִּן: **make** (one's name) **dwell** Ez 6_{12}. †

שְׁלֵה: Heb. שָׁלֵו: (being) **at ease** Dn 4_1. †

שָׁלָה Dn 3_{29}: trad. w. Qr = → שָׁלוּ, or rd. *שְׁלָה < שְׁאֵלָה; but prob. rd. → *שָׁלָה. †

שָׁלוּ: Heb. שָׁלֵו & שַׁלְוָה: שָׁלוּ Ezr 6_9; pl. sf. שָׁלְוָתָךְ, f.: **negligence** Dn 6_5 Ezr 4_{22} 6_9; for Dn 3_{29} Qr → *שָׁלָה. †

*שְׁלֵוָה: Heb. שַׁלְוָה: sf. שְׁלֵוְתָךְ: **prosperity, fortune** Dn 4_{24}. †

שְׁלַח: Heb. =: **peal**: pf. שׁ׳, pl. שְׁלַחוּ, שְׁלַחְתּוּן, שְׁלַחְנָא; impf. יִשְׁלַח; pf. pass. שְׁלִיחַ: — 1. **send**: subj. God, obj. *malʾāk* Dn 3_{28}; subj. person, obj. letter, report &c. Ezr 4_{11}; abs. send an order Ezr 6_{13}, followed by fin. vb. 4_{14}, by *lᵉ* & inf. Dn 3_2; pass. Ezr 7_{14}; — 2. metaph., *šᵉlaḥ yad*, w. *lᵉ* & inf. stretch out the hand = **dare** Ezr 6_{12}.

שְׁלֵט: Heb. =: **peal**: pf. שׁ׳, pl. שְׁלִטוּ; impf. תִּשְׁלַט, יִשְׁלַט: — 1. **rule**, w. *bᵉ* Dn 2_{39}, have power over, w. *bᵉ* 3_{27}, abs. $5_{7\cdot16}$; — 2. **overpower**, w. *bᵉ* Dn 6_{25}. †

hafel: pf. sf. הַשְׁלְטָךְ, הַשְׁלְטֵהּ: **make** (s.one) **ruler** over, w. *bᵉ* or *ʿal* Dn $2_{38\cdot41}$. †

*שִׁלְטֹן: Heb. =: pl. cs. שִׁלְטֹנֵי: **high official**, *šilṭōnê mᵉdînātāʾ* the provincial administrators Dn 3_{2f}. †

שָׁלְטָן: cs. =, det. שָׁלְטָנָא, sf. שָׁלְטָנָךְ, שָׁלְטָנְהוֹן; pl. det. שָׁלְטָנַיָּא: **dominion, lordship** Dn 3_{33} $4_{19\cdot31}$ 6_{27b} $7_{6\cdot12\cdot14\cdot26f}$, *šolṭān malkûtî* 6_{27a}; pl. dominions, powers 7_{27}. †

שַׁלִּיט: Heb. =: det. שַׁלִּיטָא; pl. שַׁלִּיט(י)ן: — 1. **mighty, powerful** Dn 2_{10}; w. *bᵉ*, governing Ezr 4_{20}; lord, master over Dn $4_{14\cdot22\cdot29}$ 5_{21}; abs. 4_{23}; noun: officer 2_{15}, ruler 5_{29}; — 2. w. *lᵉ* & inf., it is **authorized, permitted** Ezr 7_{24}. †

שְׁלִם: Heb. =: **peal**: pf. שְׁלִם: **be finished** Ezr 5_{16}. †

hafel: pf. sf. הַשְׁלְמַהּ; impv. הַשְׁלֵם: **complete**: deliver (completely) Ezr 7_{17}, pay over, settle accounts Dn 5_{26} (oth.: finish, or abandon). †

שְׁלָם: Heb. שָׁלוֹם: det. שְׁלָמָא, sf. שְׁלָמְכוֹן: **well-being, good health, welfare**; hail (as greeting) Ezr 4_{17} 5_7, *šᵉlāmᵉkôn yiśgēʾ* Dn 3_{31} 6_{26}. †

*שֻׁם: Heb. I שֵׁם: cs. =, sf. שְׁמֵהּ; pl. cs. שְׁמָהָת, sf. שְׁמָהָתְהֹם: **name** Dn 2_{26} $4_{5\cdot16}$ 5_{12} Ezr $5_{4\cdot10}$, of God Dn 2_{20} Ezr 5_1 6_{12}; after n. pers., someone called Ezr 5_{14}. †

שמד: Heb. =: **hafel**: inf. הַשְׁמָדָה: **destroy, exterminate** Dn 7_{26}. †

*שְׁמַיִן: Heb. שָׁמַיִם: det. שְׁמַיָּא: **heaven, sky** (as in Heb.) Je 10_{11} Dn 4_8; as dwelling-place of God Dn 2_{28}; *ʾᵉlāh šᵉmayyāʾ* Dn 2_{18} Ezr 5_{11} & oth. phr.; *šᵉmayyāʾ* = God Dn 4_{23}.

שמם: Heb. =: **itpoal**: pf. אֶשְׁתּוֹמַם: **stiffen w. fright** Dn 4_{16}. †

שְׁמַע: Heb. =: **peal**: pf. שׁ׳, 1. sg. שִׁמְעֵת; impf. יִשְׁמַע, pl. תִּשְׁמְעוּן; pt. pl. שָׁמְעִין: **hear**, abs. Dn 5_{23}, obj. thg. $3_{5\cdot7\cdot10\cdot15}$ 6_{15}, w. *ʿal* & pers., & *dî* $5_{14\cdot16}$. †

hitpaal: impf. pl. יִשְׁתַּמְּעוּן: **obey**, w. *lᵉ* Dn 7_{27}. †

שָׁמְרַיִן: (town & province of) **Samaria** Ezr $4_{10\cdot17}$, ꟻ Heb. שֹׁמְרוֹן. †

שמש: **pael**: impf. pl. sf. יְשַׁמְּשׁוּנֵּהּ: **serve** Dn 7_{10}. †

*שְׁמַשׁ or *שֶׁמֶשׁ: Heb. שֶׁמֶשׁ: det. שִׁמְשָׁא: **sun** Dn 6_{15}. †

שִׁמְשַׁי: n. pers. Ezr $4_{8f\cdot17\cdot23}$. †

*שֵׁן: Heb. =: du. שִׁנַּיִן, sf. Qr שִׁנַּהּ, Kt שִׁנַּיהּ or שִׁנַּיִה, f.: **tooth**, du. orig. rows of teeth Dn $7_{5\cdot7\cdot19}$. †

שנה: Heb. =: **peal**: pf. pl. שְׁנוֹ, sf. שְׁנוֹהִי; impf. תִּשְׁנֵא, יִשְׁנֵא; pt. f. שָׁנְיָה/א, pl. שָׁנַיִן, f. שָׁנְיָן: — 1. **be different, diverse** Dn $7_{3\cdot19\cdot23f}$; — 2. **be changed** 3_{27} $5_{6\cdot9}$ 6_{18}. †

pael: pf. pl. שַׁנִּיו; impf. pl. יְשַׁנּוֹן; pt. pass. f. מְשַׁנְּיָה: — 1. **transform**, obj. *lᵉbab* Dn 4_{13}; pt. pass. **different** (from) 7_7; — 2. **violate** (an order) Dn 3_{28}. †

hafel: impf. יְהַשְׁנֵא; inf. הַשְׁנָיָה; pt. מְהַשְׁנֵא: — 1. **alter** (a decree &c.) Dn $6_{9\cdot16}$; subj. God, obj. times, seasons 2_{21} 7_{25}; — 2. **violate** (an order) Ezr 6_{11}, abs. 6_{12}. †

itpaal: pf. Dn 3_{19} Qr sg. אֶשְׁתַּנִּי, Kt pl. אֶשְׁתַּנּוֹ or אֶשְׁתַּנִּיו; impf. יִשְׁתַּנֵּא, pl. יִשְׁתַּנּוֹן, juss. יִשְׁתַּנּוֹ: **change** (intrans.) Dn 2_9 3_{19} 5_{10} 7_{28}. †

I *שְׁנָה: Heb. שָׁנָה: cs. שְׁנַת; pl. שְׁנִין: **year** Dn 6_1 Ezr 5_{11}; in dating, *bišnat* … Dn 7_1 Ezr 5_{13} $6_{3\cdot15}$. †

II *שְׁנָה: Heb. שֵׁנָה: sf. שִׁנְתֵּהּ: **sleep** Dn 6_{19}. †

שָׁעָה: det. שַׁעֲתָא Dn 3_6 4_{30} & שַׁעֲתָה 3_{15} 5_5: short space of time, **moment**, *bah šaʿatāʾ* at the same moment, at once Dn $3_{6\cdot15}$ 4_{30} 5_5; *kešāʿâ ḥadâ* for a moment 4_{16}. †

שפט: Heb. =: **peal**: pt. pl. שָׁפְטִין: **judge**, pt. **judge** Ezr 7_{25}. †

שַׁפִּיר: **fair, lovely** Dn $4_{9\cdot18}$. †

שפל: Heb. =: **hafel**: pf. 2. m. הַשְׁפֵּלְתְּ; impf. יְהַשְׁפִּל; inf. הַשְׁפָּלָה; pt. מַשְׁפִּיל: **bring low, humble** Dn 4_{34} 5_{19} 7_{24}; w. *lebab* humble onesf. 5_{22}. †

*שְׁפַל: Heb. שָׁפָל: cs. =: **low(ly)**, *šefal ʾanāšîm* the lowliest of men Dn 4_{14}. †

שְׁפַר: Heb. =: **peal**: pf. 'שׁ; impf. יִשְׁפַּר: **please, seem good**, w. *ʿal* Dn 4_{24}, w. *qodām* = I am pleased to, w. *le* & inf. 3_{32}, w. *we* & pf. 6_2. †

*שְׁפַרְפַּר: det. שְׁפַרְפָּרָא: **dawn** Dn 6_{20}. †

*שָׁק: Heb. שׁוֹק: du. sf. שָׁקוֹהִי: **(lower) leg** Dn 2_{33}. †

שרה: Heb. =: **peal**: inf. מִשְׁרֵא; pt. pass. שְׁרֵא, pl. שְׁרַיִן: — 1. **loosen**: pass. loosed (from fetters), free Dn 3_{25}; metaph. loosen knots = solve problems $5_{12\cdot16}$; — 2. pass. **dwell** Dn 5_6. †

pael: pf. 3. pl. שָׁרִיו; pt. מְשָׁרֵא (but rd. מִשְׁרֵא peal inf.): **begin**, w. *le* & inf. Ezr 5_2; Dn 5_{12} rd. peal inf. †

hitpaal: pt. pl. מִשְׁתָּרַיִן: be loosed, **shake**, knock together (of joints) Dn 5_6. †

*שְׁרֹשׁ or *שְׁרֶשׁ or *שֹׁרֶשׁ: Heb. שֹׁרֶשׁ: pl. sf. שָׁרְשׁוֹהִי: **root** Dn $4_{20\cdot23}$. †

שרשו Ezr 7_{26}, Kt שְׁרֹשׁוּ Qr שְׁרֹשִׁי: **banishment** or **exclusion** (fm. the community) Ezr 7_{26}. †

שֵׁשְׁבַּצַּר: n. pers. Ezr $5_{14\cdot16}$ (= Heb.). †

שֵׁת: Heb. שֵׁשׁ: שֵׁת: **six** Dn 3_1 Ezr 6_{15}. †

שתה: Heb. =: **peal**: pf. pl. (w. pref. א) אִשְׁתִּיו; impf. pl. יִשְׁתּוֹן; pt. שָׁתֵה, pl. שָׁתַיִן: **drink** Dn $5_{1\cdot4\cdot23}$, w. *be* (as Heb.) from. †

שִׁתִּין: Heb. שִׁשִּׁים: **sixty** Dn 3_1 6_1 Ezr 6_3. †

שְׁתַר בּוֹזְנַי: n. pers. Ezr $5_{3\cdot6}$ $6_{6\cdot13}$. †

ת

תבר: Heb. I שָׁבַר: **peal**: pt. pass. f. תְּבִירָה: **break**, pt. pass. **fragile** Dn 2_{42}. †

*תְּדִיר: det. תְּדִירָא: circling, **duration**, *bitdîrāʾ* continually Dn $6_{17\cdot21}$. †

תוב: Heb. I שׁוּב: **peal**: impf. יְתוּב: **return, come back**, w. *ʿal* Dn $4_{31\cdot33}$. †

hafel: pf. הֲתִיב, pl. sf. הֲתִיבוּנָא; impf. pl. יַהֲתִיבוּן Ezr 6_5 & יְתִיבוּן 5_5; inf. sf. הֲתָבוּתָךְ: **give back, return** (obj. an answer) Ezr 5_5 6_5; *hatîb pitgām* **answer**, w. acc. pers. Dn 3_{16} Ezr 5_{11}; *ḥatîb ʿētâ ûṭeʿēm*, w. *le* & pers., address onesf. w. wise & prudent words to Dn 2_{14}. †

תְּוַהּ: Heb. תמה: **peal**: pf. 'תּ: **be** amazed, **alarmed** Dn 3_{24}. †

*תּוֹר: Heb. שׁוֹר: pl. תּוֹרִין: **bull, ox, steer** Dn $4_{22\cdot29f}$ 5_{21}, for sacrifice Ezr 6_{17} 7_{17}, *benê tôrîn* 6_9. †

תְּחוֹת, but Dn 4_{11} *תְּחֵת (< Heb.), ⸗ sf.: Heb. תַּחַת: sf. תְּחֹתֹהִי Dn 4_9, & תַּחְתוֹהִי: prep., **under** Dn $4_{9\cdot18}$ 7_{27}; w. *min-*, from under Je 10_{11} Dn 4_{11}. †

תְּלַג: Heb. שֶׁלֶג: **snow** Dn 7_9. †

*תְּלִיתָי: Heb. שְׁלִישִׁי: f. Kt תְּלִיתָיָא Qr תְּלִיתָאָה: **third** Dn 2_{39}. †

תְּלָת: Heb. שָׁלוֹשׁ: f. (w. m. noun) תְּלָתָה/א, sf. תְּלָתֵהוֹן Dn 3_{23}: **three** Dn $7_{8\cdot20}$, before the numbered noun $7_{5\cdot24}$, after it 3_{24} $6_{3\cdot11\cdot14}$ Ezr 6_4; *yôm telātâ* the 3rd day; *telātēhôn* the 3 of them Dn 3_{23}. †

תַּלְתָּא Dn $5_{16\cdot29}$ & תַּלְתִּי 5_7: trad. triumvir, third in rank, or ruler over the third part of the empire, prob. orig. an Assyrian title of an official, mng. 'third'. †

תְּלָתִין: Heb. שְׁלֹשִׁים: **thirty** Dn $6_{8\cdot13}$. †

***תְּמַהּ**: pl. תִּמְהִין, det. תִּמְהַיָּא, sf. תִּמְהוֹהִי: **wonder, miracle** Dn 3_{32f} 6_{28}. †

תַּמָּה: Heb. שָׁם, שָׁמָּה: adv. **there** Ezr 5_{17} $6_{1\cdot12}$, *min-tammâ* from there 6_6, *dî* … *tammâ* where 6_1. †

***תִּנְיָן**: f. תִּנְיָנָה: **second** Dn 7_5. †

תִּנְיָנוּת: adv. **a second time** Dn 2_7. †

***תִּפְתָּי**: pl. Kt תִּפְתָּיֵא Qr תִּפְתָּאֵי: **police officer** or magistrate Dn 3_{2f}. †

***תַּקִּיף**: Heb. = (< Aram.): f. תַּקִּיפָה/א; pl. תַּקִּיפִין: — 1. **strong** Dn $2_{40\cdot42}$ 7_7 Ezr 4_{20}; — 2. **mighty** (i.e. prodigious) (wonders) Dn 3_{33}. †

תקל: Heb. שָׁקַל: **peal**: pf. pass. 2. m. תְּקִילְתָּה: **weigh**, pass. Dn 5_{27}. †

תְּקֵל: Heb. שֶׁקֶל: **shekel**, unit of measure & weight Dn $5_{25\cdot27}$, w. word-play on pass. vb. *t*^{e}*qîl* understood as pt. pass. †

תקן: Heb. תקן & תכן: **hofal**: 3. f. הָתְקְנַת (but rd. 1. sg. הָתְקְנֵת): **be reestablished** Dn 4_{33}. †

תקף: Heb. = (< Aram.): **peal**: pf. תְּקֵף, 3. f. תִּקְפַת, 2. m. תְּקֵפְתְּ: **be(come) strong** Dn $4_{8\cdot17\cdot19}$, grow hard (subj. spirit), w. *l*^{e} & inf. 5_{20}. †
pael: inf. תַּקָּפָה: make hard, **enforce** Dn 6_8. †

***תְּקֹף**: Heb. תֹּקֶף: det. תָּקְפָּא: **strength** Dn 2_{37}. †

***תְּקָף**: cs. =: **strength** Dn 4_{27}. †

תְּרֵין: Heb. שְׁנַיִם: f. תַּרְתֵּין: **two** Dn 6_1 Ezr 4_{24}, *t*^{e}*rê-*^{ʿa}*śar* twelve Dn 4_{26} Ezr 6_{17}. †

***תְּרַע**: Heb. שַׁעַר: cs. =: — 1. **door, opening** (of furnace) Dn 3_{26}; — 2. gate, *t*^{e}*raʿ malkāʾ* royal palace, **court** Dn 2_{49}. †

***תָּרָע**: Heb. שׁוֹעֵר: pl. det. תָּרָעַיָּא: **door-keeper** Ezr 7_{24}. †

תַּרְתֵּין: ↗ תְּרֵין.

תַּתְּנַי: n. pers. Ezr $5_{3\cdot6}$ $6_{6\cdot13}$. †

ADDENDA

(from page XVII)

p. 46b: entry בִּקֹּרֶת should read: **compensation for damage**

p. 135a: delete entry ילה (see entry להה, p. 173b)

p. 236a: hof.: line 2 should read:

outspread Is 8_8.† (delete entry 2)

p. 241a: after entry נַעַר, insert:

נֹעַר: (time of) **youth**, adolescence Ps 88_{16} Pr 29_{21} Job 33_{25} 36_{14}.†

p. 254a: after entry סוֹד: insert:

סוֹדִי: n. pers.

p. 271b: after entry עֵילָם, insert:

*עְיָם: Is 11_{15}: mng. uncert.; perh. read בְּעֹצֶם **with the power of.**

p. 352a: entry שׁכך: delete polel entry

p. 374a: after entry שְׁלֹמוֹת, insert:

שַׁלְמָי: n. pers.

p. 376a:delete entry שְׁמָמִית

p. 378a: after entry שְׁמַר יְמוֹת: insert:

שִׁמְרִית: n. pers. f.